The Cherry Red Non-League Newsdesk Annual 2008

by
James Wright

CONTENTS

PUBLISHED BY
James Wright
Non-League Newsdesk
6 Harp Chase
Taunton
Somerset TA1 3RY
(Tel: 07786 636659 Fax: 0871 994 3274)
Email: james@nlnewsdesk.co.uk

DESIGNED AND SET BY
Nigel Davis
Broomhouse Farmhouse
George Nympton
South Molton
Devon EX36 4JF
(Tel: 01769 572257/ 07768 204784)
Email: NigelDavis@aol.com or NLNAnnual@aol.com

PRINTED BY
CPI Antony Rowe
Bumpers Farm
Chippenham
Wiltshire SN14 6LH
(Tel: 01249 659 705 Fax: 01249 443 103)

ISBN 978-0-9539198-8-8

FRONT COVER

Robbie King of Heybridge Swifts (right) holds off AFC Hornchurch's Andy Tomlinson
Photo: Gavin Ellis / TGSPHOTO

EDITORIAL

Thank you for buying the ninth edition of the Cherry Red Non-League Newsdesk Annual. I apologise for the necessity to increase the cover price by a pound. This is our first price rise in three years though, and I've recently had a browse at some other football books and realise we are still offering, in my belief, exceptionally good value.

Happily the price increase does come with 32 extra pages. The main reason for taking this extra space is to include round-by-round details for some major county, and other, knock-out cups. While Richard Rundle and Tony Kempster have been giving these competitions good coverage online, I have been made aware that they have been lacking exposure in paper form since the Bureau of Non-League Football ceased publishing. Hopefully this new section will partly address the issue. I hope you agree with the initial selection of competitions – the section will, as the rest of this book has done over the years, evolve.

We have at last moved into the 21st century in that we can now take orders online – many of you will have bought the book by this method. Please take a look at the website at www.nlnewsdesk.co.uk. I hope to develop it further during the course of the season with items such as important amendments to this book and perhaps even news stories or a blog. However, I say this every year and events then get the better of me. At the very least you will be able to pick up from the site back issues and the earliest notification of the next edition.

For the ninth consecutive year I extend grateful thanks to Cherry Red Records for sponsoring this title. Thanks also to Michael Heatley, football and music author of note, for penning a lively introduction piece which you can find overleaf (slightly disappointed to see no mention of Taunton's famous win over Farnborough in January, though Michael!). And a huge thank-you to our army of contributors, as many of whom as possible I have attempted to list below.

As I pen these notes, it appears our economy is crashing headlong into its worst recession in years. Non-League football is not unaccustomed to hard times, and has indeed been bowled a succession of financial googlies over these recent years of widespread content. The National Lottery, live televised matches virtually every day of the week and an ill-advised league re-organisation had already hit a very large number of clubs very hard long before this recent general down-turn. A lot of clubs are already in desperate trouble, and the outlook is bleak.

But negatives can be turned into positives. The installation of big screens in most clubhouses allows televised 12.45pm games to bring punters into grounds early, and 5.20 kick-offs can keep them there longer. And as the pro game disappears further up its own corporate backside, priced-out fans seek a more affordable alternative. This trend is likely to be accentuated by a recession, and it is critical that non-League football markets itself appropriately to attract any possible new customers.

Everyone who knows me or has read my previous editorials knows I have long advocated the re-regionalisation of the pyramid. Surely now, with increased green awareness and spiralling fuel costs, there has never been a better opportunity.

JAMES WRIGHT

WWW.NLNEWSDESK.CO.UK

CONTRIBUTORS

Roy Ainge, Roger Allen, Martin Bayliss, Jim Bean, Gary Berwick, Mike Bidmead, Jeremy Biggs, Paul Birkitt, Ron Bridges, Martin Bryant, Ann Bullock, Ann Camm, Steve Clark, Ken Clarke, Alan Constable, Ian Craig, Philip Coulthard, Greg Cunningham, Peter Danzey, William Davies, John Does, Richard Durrant, Rolant Ellis, Denis Emery, Margaret Errington, Robert Errington, Tony Ford, Peter Francis, Bill Gardner, Peter Godfrey, Mark Goldsmith, Robin Goodwin-Davey, Arthur Green, Tony Griffiths, Rob Grillo, Michael Heatley, Phil Hiscox, Ron Holpin, Stephen Hosmer, Frank Hunt, David Jarrett, Geoff Jenkins, Dennis Johnson, Neil Johnson, Glynn Jones, Neil Juggins, Brian King, Phil Lewis, Len Llewellyn, David Lumley, David Marsay, Danny McConnell, Chris McCullough, Mark McIntyre, Mervyn Miles, Jim Milner, Phil Mitcham, Fiona Mitchell, Andrew Moffat, Andy Molden, Sylvia Moore, John Mugridge, David Munday, John Nisbet, Graham Phillips, Jane Phillips, Michael Piatek, Phil Platt, Stephen Poole, Malcolm Pratt, Brian Redmond, Hilary Redmond, Philip Rhodes, Paul Rivers, John Roberts, William Robson, Mark Rozzier, Richard Rundle, Keith Sales, Mike Sampson, Trevor Scorah, John Shenton, Nigel Spurling, Brenda Sprules, Mike Stokes, Rob Sutherland, Trevor Syms, John Thomas, Mel Thomas, Jim Thorn, Graham Thornton, Peter Toft, John Walker, Peter Wallis, David Ward, Alan Watkins, Elaine Waumsley, Nigel West, Jim Wicks, Chris Wight, David Wilcox, Mike Williams, Mike Wilson, Nigel Wood, Phil Woosnam

COTTAGE TO CONFERENCE

W hen clubs like AFC Wimbledon start at the bottom of the non-League pyramid and work their way up it's a shot in the arm for many clubs. And that's what happened when Frimley Green hosted them in their first season (2002-03) in the Combined Counties League – they expected a 1000-plus crowd, so hired Farnborough Town's Cherrywood Road ground to play the match. It was my first experience of non-League, and I wanted more. Little did I realise when I returned to Cherrywood the following week that attendances at Boro, then in the lofty Conference National, rarely reached four figures!

Annoyingly, too, someone had changed the kick-off time from 1 to 3 (international day), so I had to waste two hours downtown before 'enjoying' a defeat to basement club Kettering. But the bug had bitten – so I went back the following week to see Farnborough lose again, this time to second-bottom Nuneaton!

I'd been used to supporting lost causes – Fulham, where I'd been a season ticket holder, and brought my two sons up in the 'faith'. But the lure of the Premiership had been tainted by a move to Loftus Road – and, though we eventually returned to Craven Cottage, once you've seen Beckham/Owen/Ronaldo in the flesh (and lost to them) the attraction of 'the World's Greatest League' palls a little. Besides, it's not so much fun when you can't watch with your pals or bring a few extra to pay 'on the gate'.

So I joined the Boro faithful – my elder son sent me to Coventry (not literally) for a season, but has since forgiven me. In my first season I experienced the high of the FA Cup fourth round game at Highbury, the lows of our owner/manager taking his money and half the squad to another club a fortnight later, our eventual relegation from the Conference after several reprieves, and finally in 2007 the liquidation of Farnborough Town and the rebirth as Farnborough in the Southern League Division One South and West.

Even Mohamed Al Fayed's mind would boggle at the conspiracies (not to mention cock-ups) that have gone on in the past half-dozen years, and it's amazing there's a club to support at all. It puts Fulham's fall from grace into a little bit of perspective, though I do get up to the Cottage a couple of times a season when Boro have a blank Saturday.

In my five years at Cherrywood Road I've met heroes and villains, made friends (hopefully not too many enemies) and can reckon to pass the time of day with at least two dozen people each Saturday. Yes, we do play on Saturdays at 3pm! I try to bring friends along to swell the numbers – and, though we no longer serve real tea from teapots, there are plenty of grounds that do. You don't even have to queue at some of them.

The 18 Yarders, a hardy group with 'Yarder 18' on their replica shirts (guess where they stand?), have taken me on real ale pub crawls, the current chairman always stops for a chat and Farney Rubble, our mascot, occasionally offers me a pre-match lollipop. Incidentally, the club borrowed the Flintstone-esque name from a fan who in my early days showed me a real and unexpected kindness. Knowing my car had broken down on Christmas Eve, he did a 25-mile detour to pick me up, take me to the Boxing Day game and bring me back again. It was our former owner/manager's first return with his new team, whom we well and truly walloped. Fulham wins, or pre-match lollipops, had rarely tasted as sweet – thanks, Farney!

Last season saw us 'do an AFC' and bring a sizeable away crowd to grounds unused to breaking the three-figure barrier. And guess what? Our star player, Rob 'Soggy' Saunders, turned Wimbledon (now one step our superior) down when they put in a seven-day approach. You see he used to stand on the PRE – the Prospect Road End, from where I now watch my football – and wanted to finish the job with his hometown club. Who said loyalty is dead?

Non-League offers a communal experience which I hope will never fade. And there's always something around the corner, from quiz nights through fundraising entertainment to sponsored walks, that you can get yourself involved with. It's good to feel you can make a difference in some way or another, and very hard to walk away on Saturday at ten to five and forget about things for a week. If you hang around in the bar, you can even tell the players where you think they're going wrong (or right).

Many fans also support a 'proper' team, but when it comes to meeting friends, relishing a bit of banter with opposing fans or simply enjoying 90 minutes of good honest football you know where you'll find them. And me.

From FFC to F(T)FC...it's been a journey of discovery and it isn't over yet.

MICHAEL HEATLEY

WWW.CHERRYRED.CO.UK

SOME CONVENTIONS USED WITHIN THIS BOOK

Results grids
W-L: Points awarded to home side
L-W: Points awarded to away side
n/a: Game not scheduled, or not played due to one side having withdrawn
M: Scoreline awarded by management committee
(e.g. 0M0 denotes a goalless draw awarded for an unplayed game)

Some standard abbreviations
aet: after extra time
Corries: Corinthians
INT: Intermediate
INV: Invitation
OB: Old Boys
PF: Playing Field or Playing Fields
Res.: Reserves
Rgrs: Rangers
scr.: Scratched (in cup competitions)
Utd: United
w/o: Walkover (in cup competitions)
Wdrs: Wanderers

Inter-league movement
Promoted/relegated clubs are listed in alphabetical preference with abbreviations showing the origin of the move:-
(E) – Expelled; (F) – Folded; (P) – Promoted; (R) – Relegated; (S) – Switched;
(W) – Withdrew after season ended;
(WN) – Withdrew playing no games;
(WS) – Withdrew during the course of the season

League tables
All tables are final.
Points adjustments are italicised after the team names in league tables. They are an aggregate over the season, thus if a team benefits from a three point award but also incurs a one point penalty, its adjustment is shown as +2.
Total points and goal adjustments (eg -2g) are shown before the playing record.

Order of entries
The leagues in this book appear alphabetically.

Cup competitions
Penalty shoot-out scores are indicated in parentheses,
the first listed side's score preceding the second listed side.
So (3-4p) means the second listed side won 4-3 on penalties.
Some Welsh cup results are only recorded after penalties and are denoted as such.

Sponsors
For alphabetical ease of reference and historical continuity, sponsors names have been dropped from league titles.
Non-League football is indebted to its many sponsors.
The generosity of the 2007-08 sponsors is recognised in the strap line at the top of each page for major leagues and in parentheses under the title for minor leagues.
The constitution titles include the sponsors for the 2008-09 season.

CAPITAL COUNTIES FEEDER LEAGUES TROPHY

For Isthmian feeder clubs not entered in the FA Vase
Sponsored by Anagram Records – part of Cherry Red

2006-07 OUTSTANDING THIRD ROUND
Whitewebbs 1 **White Ensign** 4
2006-07 OUTSTANDING QUARTER-FINAL
Hertford Heath 3 **White Ensign** 6
2006-07 SEMI-FINALS
Stony Stratford Town 0 **Hatfield Town** 5, **White Ensign** 7 The 61 FC 0
2006-07 FINAL
(September 30th at Brache Sparta): **White Ensign** 4 Hatfield Town 1

FIRST ROUND
Standon & Puckeridge 1 **Sutton Common Rovers** 3
Tring Corinthians 2 Whitewebbs 1
SECOND ROUND
Amersham Town 2 Wormley Rovers 0
Bedmond Sports & Social 1 **Frenford Senior** 3
Buntingford Town 7 Hinton 0
Bushey Rangers 2 Park Street Village 1
Codicote 0 **Epping** 2
Evergreen 0 **Bovingdon** 1
Hertford Heath (w/o) v Kings Meadow (scr.)
Knebworth 1 Brache Sparta 0
London Lions 0 **Canning Town** 3
Manford Way 2 Aston Clinton 1 *aet*
Metropolitan Police Bushey 3 White Ensign 2
Sandridge Rovers 3 **Pitstone & Ivinghoe** 4
Sheerwater (w/o) v Kent Athletic (scr.)
Sutton Common Rovers 2 The 61 FC 0
Tring Corinthians 3 Takeley 4
Winslow United 9 Barnston 2
THIRD ROUND
Amersham Town 1 **Frenford Senior** 2
Bovingdon 3 Epping 2
Canning Town (w/o) v Sheerwater (scr.)
Hertford Heath 2 Knebworth 2 *aet* (3-0p)
Pitstone & Ivinghoe 3 Buntingford Town 0
Sutton Common Rovers 2 Metropolitan Police Bushey 1
Takeley 2 Bushey Rangers 1
Winslow United 1 **Manford Way** 4
QUARTER-FINALS
Canning Town 2 Pitstone & Ivinghoe 0 *aet*
Hertford Heath 0 **Frenford Senior** 1
Manford Way 0 **Takeley** 3
Sutton Common Rovers 2 Bovingdon 0
SEMI-FINALS
Sutton Common Rovers 2 **Canning Town** 2 *aet* (0-3p)
Takeley 1 **Frenford Senior** 1 *aet* (4-5p)
FINAL
(May 4th at Ilford)
Canning Town 0 **Frenford Senior** 1

AMATEUR FOOTBALL ALLIANCE

AMATEUR COMBINATION

	Albanian	Bealonians	Enfield Old Grammarians	Hale End Athletic	Honourable Artillery Company	Old Aloysians	Old Hamptonians	Old Meadonians	Old Parmiterians	UCL Academicals
Albanian		2-1	2-1	2-1	2-1	2-1	1-1	5-3	0-2	4-1
Bealonians	2-1	P	3-1	4-0	1-1	1-1	1-2	2-0	5-1	2-0
Enfield Old Grammarians	2-6	1-1	R	0-1	1-4	0-4	2-1	3-1	0-3	1-2
Hale End Athletic	1-3	2-1	3-1	E	2-1	1-3	1-5	0-2	1-4	3-3
Honourable Artillery Company	1-1	2-2	4-1	2-2	M	5-4	3-4	0-2	3-0	2-2
Old Aloysians	0-0	4-1	2-0	1-1	5-1		2-1	3-3	3-0	2-0
Old Hamptonians	1-4	0-1	3-1	2-2	1-1	1-3	D	1-2	1-1	3-3
Old Meadonians	1-1	1-1	2-2	6-1	3-1	2-5	4-0	I	4-1	1-2
Old Parmiterians	1-1	4-1	1-0	2-0	1-1	1-4	3-0	2-1	V	3-1
UCL Academicals	1-4	3-1	2-1	2-0	1-1	0-3	2-2	5-3	1-3	

Premier Division	P	W	D	L	F	A	Pts
Old Aloysians	18	12	4	2	50	20	40
Albanian	18	11	5	2	41	22	38
Old Parmiterians	18	10	3	5	33	27	33
Bealonians	18	7	5	6	31	26	26
Old Meadonians	18	7	4	7	41	35	25
UCL Academicals	18	6	5	7	31	39	23
Honourable Artillery Company	18	4	8	6	34	35	20
Old Hamptonians	18	4	6	8	29	37	18
Hale End Athletic	18	4	4	10	22	44	16
Enfield Old Grammarians	18	2	2	14	18	45	8

Senior Division One	P	W	D	L	F	A	Pts
Parkfield	20	12	5	3	56	31	41
Old Meadonians Res.	20	13	2	5	56	36	41
Old Salvatorians	20	9	5	6	37	26	32
Old Challoners	20	9	4	7	41	36	31
Old Suttonians	20	9	3	8	37	33	30
Old Ignatians	20	8	4	8	38	38	28
Glyn Old Boys	20	8	4	8	36	39	28
Clapham Old Xaverians	20	7	4	9	38	48	25
Sinjuns Grammarians	20	7	3	10	38	56	24
Southgate County	20	5	3	12	40	49	18
Old Tiffinians	20	3	3	14	27	52	12

Senior Division Two	P	W	D	L	F	A	Pts
Old Minchendenians	20	17	3	0	84	24	54
Old Belgravians	20	14	3	3	70	27	45
Hon. Artillery Company Res.	20	13	0	7	62	35	39
Old Danes	20	12	1	7	67	45	37
Wood Green Old Boys	20	10	4	6	65	51	34
Shene Old Grammarians	20	7	3	10	50	56	24
Old Dorkinians	20	7	2	11	45	43	23
Old Vaughanians	20	6	2	12	43	72	20
Old Pauline	20	4	7	9	47	52	19
Kings Old Boys	20	5	2	13	32	68	17
Mill Hill Village	20	1	1	18	11	103	4

Senior Division Three North	P	W	D	L	F	A	Pts
UCL Academicals Res.	20	11	5	4	49	23	38
Old Edmontonians	20	10	7	3	46	28	37
Old Kolsassians	20	10	5	5	55	36	35
Old Aloysians Res.	20	10	3	7	50	45	33
Old Salvatorians Res.	20	10	2	8	50	36	32
Enfield Old Gramms Res.	20	9	5	6	42	41	32
Latymer Old Boys	20	7	4	9	44	57	25
Old Manorians	20	6	6	8	36	34	24
Albanian Res.	20	6	5	9	32	45	23
Old Isleworthians	20	4	6	10	38	58	18
Brent	20	2	2	16	26	65	8

Senior Division Three South	P	W	D	L	F	A	Pts
Centymca	20	16	2	2	90	30	50
Old Hamptonians Res.	20	14	2	4	54	26	44
Economicals	20	11	5	4	49	29	38
Fulham Compton Old Boys	20	9	4	7	40	34	31
Hampstead Heathens	20	7	6	7	31	38	27
Old Guildfordians	20	7	6	7	33	41	27
Fitzwilliam Old Boys	20	7	6	7	28	40	27
Old Meadonians 'A'	20	7	2	11	38	48	23
John Fisher Old Boys	20	5	1	14	30	65	16
Wandsworth Borough	20	4	2	14	32	59	14
Kings Old Boys Res.	20	2	6	12	30	45	12

(Lower divisions in "Other Leagues" section – page 249)

ARTHURIAN LEAGUE

	Lancing Old Boys	Old Bradfieldians	Old Brentwoods	Old Carthusians	Old Cholmeleians	Old Etonians	Old Foresters	Old Harrovians	Old Tonbridgians	Old Westminsters
Lancing Old Boys		8-0	1-2	1-1	1-1	2-0	2-2	1-1	3-1	1-0
Old Bradfieldians	0-3	P	3-5	0-6	1-2	1-0	0-6	1-7	2-1	2-3
Old Brentwoods	3-1	6-1	R	0-2	2-1	2-0	5-0	5-1	0-0	5-2
Old Carthusians	3-0	4-0	1-4	E	7-0	2-0	4-0	5-2	4-0	2-1
Old Cholmeleians	0-5	2-3	1-2	0-1	M	3-2	1-2	2-2	0-3	1-1
Old Etonians	4-2	7-0	1-2	0-2	0-1		3-2	0-0	4-1	0-1
Old Foresters	4-1	3-1	1-4	1-7	1-1	2-4	D	3-2	3-1	1-3
Old Harrovians	1-1	5-2	2-2	0-2	1-0	0-2	3-4	I	4-2	2-4
Old Tonbridgians	1-2	1-1	0-4	2-3	1-2	1-6	0-0	2-3	V	3-6
Old Westminsters	2-0	2-2	2-1	0-5	1-2	6-1	3-1	3-2	1-2	

Premier Division		P	W	D	L	F	A	Pts
Old Carthusians		18	16	1	1	61	11	49
Old Brentwoods		18	14	2	2	54	20	44
Old Westminsters	-3	18	10	2	6	41	33	29
Lancing Old Boys		18	7	5	6	35	26	26
Old Etonians		18	7	1	10	34	30	22
Old Foresters		18	6	4	8	35	45	22
Old Harrovians		18	5	5	8	38	41	20
Old Cholmeleians		18	5	5	8	20	35	20
Old Bradfieldians		18	3	2	13	20	71	11
Old Tonbridgians		18	2	3	13	22	48	9

Division One	P	W	D	L	F	A	Pts
Old Malvernians	16	12	0	4	44	29	36
KCS Wimbledon	16	8	4	4	39	24	28
Old Aldenhamians	16	8	3	5	40	33	27
Old Haileyburians	16	5	7	4	28	30	22
Old Reptonians	16	6	2	8	45	42	20
Old Radleians	16	6	2	8	29	34	20
Old Wykehamists	16	5	3	8	26	37	18
Old Salopians	16	5	2	9	39	38	17
Old Chigwellians	16	5	1	10	21	44	16

Division Two		P	W	D	L	F	A	Pts
Old Carthusians Res.		16	11	2	3	43	18	35
Kings Scholars (Cant)		16	10	2	4	33	14	32
Old Haberdashers		16	7	2	7	41	32	23
Etonians Res.		16	7	2	7	37	36	23
Old Aldenhamians Res.		16	7	2	7	35	35	23
Old Brentwoods Res.	-3	16	7	1	8	36	31	19
Old Chigwellians Res.		16	5	4	7	19	29	19
Old Foresters Res.		16	6	1	9	30	46	19
Old Westminsters Res.	-3	16	3	2	11	19	52	8

Division Three	P	W	D	L	F	A	Pts
Old Harrovians Res.	14	8	3	3	43	28	27
Old Bradfieldians Res.	14	8	1	5	34	28	25
Old Foresters 'A'	14	7	3	4	38	30	24
Old Oundelians	14	7	2	5	34	29	23
Old Wellingtonians	14	5	4	5	37	31	19
Old Etonians Res.	14	5	2	7	41	39	17
Old Salopians Res.	14	3	4	7	27	41	13
Old Chigwellians 'A'	14	3	1	10	17	45	10

Division Four		P	W	D	L	F	A	Pts
Old Carthusians 'A'		12	8	2	2	37	13	26
Lancing Old Boys Res.		12	6	4	2	26	16	22
Old Cholmeleians Res.		12	5	1	6	23	29	16
Old Westminsters 'A'		12	3	5	4	31	35	14
Old Foresters 'B'	-3	12	5	2	5	28	33	14
Old Malvernians Res.		12	4	1	7	27	44	13
Old Brentwoods 'A'		12	2	3	7	32	34	9

Division Five		P	W	D	L	F	A	Pts
Old Harrovians 'A'		12	10	0	2	36	12	30
Old Eastbournians		12	10	0	2	37	16	30
Old Amplefordians		12	5	2	5	28	23	17
Old Wykehamists Res.	-3	12	5	4	3	22	16	16
Old Cholmeleians 'A'		12	3	1	8	18	19	10
Old Brentwoods 'B'		12	2	2	8	15	33	8
Old Cholmeleians 'B'	-3	12	2	1	9	7	44	4

ARTHUR DUNN CUP

FINAL
(April 19th at Imperial College Sports Ground, Teddington)
Old Carthusians 1 Old Brentwoods 0

WWW.CHERRYRED.CO.UK

SOUTHERN AMATEUR LEAGUE

	Alleyn Old Boys	Broomfield	Civil Service	Nottsborough	Old Actonians Association	Old Owens	Old Salesians	Old Wilsonians	Polytechnic	West Wickham	Winchmore Hill
Alleyn Old Boys	S	6-2	2-2	0-4	1-1	6-2	1-1	1-2	0-0	1-2	1-1
Broomfield	2-0	E	1-1	1-3	4-1	2-4	3-3	2-0	3-4	1-6	0-0
Civil Service	0-2	1-0	N	0-1	0-1	1-0	0-1	2-5	2-3	1-1	0-2
Nottsborough	0-3	3-5	2-2	I	2-2	4-1	1-1	2-2	2-1	1-2	1-0
Old Actonians Association	1-1	6-1	1-1	1-4	O	1-2	1-0	0-1	2-2	3-2	0-0
Old Owens	3-0	5-1	2-0	1-1	1-1	R	1-0	3-0	2-1	0-0	2-2
Old Salesians	0-0	3-3	0-1	3-4	2-1	3-1		2-2	2-0	1-2	2-1
Old Wilsonians	1-2	1-2	3-2	1-2	2-1	2-2	2-3		2-3	2-2	2-1
Polytechnic	4-2	3-5	3-1	2-1	2-3	0-4	2-5	1-1	O	0-1	1-2
West Wickham	1-0	1-0	3-1	3-1	0-0	W-L	1-1	3-2	1-1	N	1-0
Winchmore Hill	2-2	0-0	3-2	2-2	4-0	2-0	0-0	2-2	0-0	0-2	E

Senior Division One

		P	W	D	L	F	A	Pts
West Wickham		20	13	6	1	33	16	45
Nottsborough		20	9	6	5	41	33	33
Old Owens	-3	20	9	5	6	36	27	29
Old Salesians		20	7	8	5	33	27	29
Winchmore Hill		20	6	8	6	24	19	26
Polytechnic		20	7	4	9	35	41	25
Alleyn Old Boys		20	5	8	7	31	31	23
Old Wilsonians		20	6	5	9	33	38	23
Old Actonians Association		20	5	8	7	27	32	23
Broomfield		20	6	5	9	38	51	23
Civil Service		20	3	5	12	20	36	14

Senior Division Two

		P	W	D	L	F	A	Pts
Old Esthameians		20	14	3	3	50	20	45
Weirside Rangers		20	13	1	6	47	22	40
Merton		20	11	3	6	49	28	36
Norsemen		20	11	3	6	43	23	36
Carshalton		20	10	3	7	41	36	33
East Barnet Old Grammarians		20	9	2	9	43	36	29
HSBC		20	7	5	8	33	37	26
Kew Association		20	6	5	9	34	42	23
BB Eagles		20	7	2	11	28	46	23
Old Lyonians		20	4	4	12	27	58	16
South Bank Cuaco	-5	20	1	3	16	17	64	1

Senior Division Three

		P	W	D	L	F	A	Pts
Old Parkonians		20	15	4	1	78	28	49
Crouch End Vampires		20	12	5	3	48	22	41
Bank of England		20	11	4	5	36	26	37
Old Finchleians	-1	20	11	4	5	60	29	36
Lloyds TSB Bank		20	11	1	8	37	41	34
Ibis		20	8	6	6	46	37	30
Old Latymerians	-1	20	7	4	9	35	31	24
Old Westminster Citizens		20	7	3	10	35	43	24
Alexandra Park		20	5	2	13	40	54	17
Old Stationers		20	3	2	15	21	72	11
Southgate Olympic		20	2	1	17	15	68	7

Intermediate Division One

	P	W	D	L	F	A	Pts
Carshalton Res.	20	12	4	4	48	31	40
Nottsborough Res.	20	11	6	3	42	19	39
West Wickham Res.	20	10	3	7	40	22	33
Civil Service Res.	20	9	4	7	30	31	31
Winchmore Hill Res.	20	9	3	8	36	31	30
Old Owens Res.	20	8	5	7	45	37	29
HSBC Res.	20	7	2	11	33	38	23
East Barnet Old Gram. Res.	20	6	4	10	32	43	22
Old Esthameians Res.	20	6	4	10	32	55	22
Old Actonians Assoc. Res.	20	6	3	11	37	49	21
Old Wilsonians Res.	20	5	4	11	26	45	19

Intermediate Division Two

		P	W	D	L	F	A	Pts
Old Salesians Res.		20	13	2	5	48	29	41
Polytechnic Res.		20	12	4	4	65	39	40
Weirside Rangers Res.		20	11	3	6	48	30	36
Alleyn Old Boys Res.		20	11	2	7	47	32	35
Crouch End Vampires Res.		20	10	1	9	53	41	31
Norsemen Res.		20	9	2	9	39	47	29
Merton Res.		20	7	5	8	34	40	26
Old Finchleians Res.	-1	20	7	3	10	33	52	23
BB Eagles Res.		20	6	2	12	40	51	20
Bank of England Res.		20	4	5	11	32	45	17
Old Latymerians Res.	-1	20	5	1	14	29	62	15

Intermediate Division Three

		P	W	D	L	F	A	Pts
Old Parkonians Res.		20	14	2	4	57	27	44
Ibis Res.		20	11	4	5	47	34	37
Southgate Olympic Res.		20	10	3	7	52	44	33
Old Lyonians Res.		20	10	2	8	46	43	32
Alexandra Park Res.		20	9	3	8	36	40	30
South Bank Cuaco Res.		20	9	3	8	34	38	30
Broomfield Res.		20	8	3	9	39	37	27
Old Westminster Citizens Res.		20	7	4	9	49	62	25
Kew Association Res.	-6	20	7	7	6	49	42	22
Old Stationers Res.		20	6	1	13	38	32	19
Lloyds TSB Bank Res.		20	2	2	16	33	81	8

(Lower divisions in "Other Leagues" section – page 276)

ANGLIAN COMBINATION

	Acle United	Beccles Town	Blofield United	Brandon Town	Cromer Town	Dersingham Rovers	Halvergate United	Hempnall	Hindringham	Lowestoft Town Res.	Mattishall	North Walsham Town	Norwich Union	Sheringham	Sprowston Athletic	Wroxham Res.
Acle United	P	4-1	1-2	1-1	1-2	4-4	1-2	2-4	0-3	5-0	1-3	2-1	0-3	3-1	2-0	0-3
Beccles Town	4-2	R	5-3	3-1	0-3	2-6	1-2	1-2	4-0	2-3	1-0	2-2	0-2	0-4	2-1	1-1
Blofield United	0-0	1-1	E	1-1	2-3	5-0	10-1	2-2	3-0	4-1	6-0	3-1	4-1	1-3	3-2	1-3
Brandon Town	2-0	2-1	4-3	M	2-1	1-2	4-3	0-4	0-0	1-0	1-0	1-2	1-2	2-3	3-2	3-2
Cromer Town	0-6	2-1	1-1	1-1	I	2-1	1-5	1-1	2-1	2-1	3-1	3-1	1-1	3-0	4-2	1-2
Dersingham Rovers	2-2	1-3	1-0	4-0	0-2	E	2-2	5-1	4-1	6-2	1-2	1-2	1-3	1-3	3-1	0-6
Halvergate United	1-3	4-1	3-1	2-1	1-2	1-7	R	0-0	0-1	3-4	3-3	5-0	2-3	2-2	0-3	1-4
Hempnall	5-1	2-0	3-4	3-1	1-3	5-1	3-0		1-0	3-3	2-1	4-1	2-2	2-1	4-0	3-5
Hindringham	1-1	2-3	0-2	3-1	2-7	4-0	1-1	3-1	D	0-1	3-1	2-2	1-0	1-2	0-2	2-2
Lowestoft Town Res.	1-1	4-3	1-0	2-1	1-2	5-2	0-1	1-2	2-3	I	2-2	3-1	0-0	1-2	0-0	3-3
Mattishall	0-5	2-1	1-1	1-3	1-1	2-3	1-5	1-2	0-0	1-2	V	2-4	0-1	1-2	1-1	0-2
North Walsham Town	3-2	5-3	1-1	2-1	0-1	1-2	1-1	2-0	3-1	1-1	3-1	I	2-0	1-0	0-2	1-5
Norwich Union	2-3	1-2	2-2	3-2	3-1	4-2	2-0	2-2	4-3	1-1	2-0	1-3	S	0-1	2-0	1-2
Sheringham	1-3	0-5	1-3	2-0	1-1	0-0	2-0	3-2	0-0	1-0	1-1	2-0	1-2	I	1-1	1-2
Sprowston Athletic	2-2	1-2	1-2	2-1	1-2	1-0	2-3	3-1	2-3	3-2	2-0	4-1	0-1	0-3	O	1-1
Wroxham Res.	3-1	2-0	2-1	3-2	2-2	3-2	6-0	4-1	4-2	2-0	1-2	0-2	3-1	2-1	2-3	N

Premier Division	P	W	D	L	F	A	Pts
Wroxham Res.	30	21	5	4	82	38	68
Cromer Town	30	18	8	4	61	43	62
Hempnall	30	15	6	9	68	53	51
Norwich Union	30	14	7	9	50	42	49
Sheringham	30	14	6	10	45	40	48
Blofield United	30	13	8	9	72	46	47
North Walsham Town	30	13	5	12	49	56	44
Sprowston Athletic	30	11	5	14	45	49	38
Acle United	30	10	7	13	59	57	37
Dersingham Rovers	30	11	4	15	64	70	37
Beccles Town	30	11	3	16	55	65	36
Halvergate United	30	10	6	14	54	72	36
Lowestoft Town Res.	30	9	8	13	47	58	35
Brandon Town	30	9	5	16	44	59	32
Hindringham	30	8	7	15	41	55	31
Mattishall	30	4	8	18	31	64	20

MUMMERY CUP
(Premier and Division One teams)

FIRST ROUND

Acle United 1 Brandon Town 0

Blofield United 1 **Dersingham Rovers** 1 *aet* (4-5p)

Hempnall 3 Attleborough Town 2

Hindringham 3 **Beccles Town** 4

Holt United 8 Sprowston Wanderers 0

Long Stratton 1 **Watton United** 2

Lowestoft Town Res. 1 Stalham Town 0

Mattishall 1 **Cromer Town** 3

North Walsham Town 8 Scole United 1

Norwich Union 5 Sole Bay 0

Sheringham 1 Loddon United 0

Sprowston Athletic 0 **Kirkley & Pakefield Res.** 3

St Andrews (w/o) v Fakenham Town Res. (scr.)

Wells Town 2 Dereham Town Res. 1

Wroxham Res. 0 **Halvergate United** 3

Wymondham Town 2 Gayton United 1

DOLPHIN AUTOS ANGLIAN COMBINATION PREMIER DIVISION CONSTITUTION 2008-09

AFC NORWICH .... Dussindale Park, Pound Lane, Thorpe NR7 0SR .... None
ACLE UNITED .... Bridewell Lane, Acle, Norwich NR13 3RA 01493 751379
BECCLES TOWN .... College Meadow, Beccles NR34 7FA 07729 782817
BLOFIELD UNITED................... Old Yarmouth Road, Blofield, Norwich NR13 4LE........................ 01603 712576
BRANDON TOWN .... Remembrance Playing Field, Church Road, Brandon IP27 0JB................... 01842 813177
CROMER TOWN....................... Cabbell Park, Mill Road, Cromer NR27 0AD 01263 512185
DERSINGHAM ROVERS ...... Behind Feathers Hotel, Manor Road, Dersingham, King's Lynn PE31 6LN.... 01485 542707
HEMPNALL........................... Bungay Road, Hempnall, Norwich NR15 2NG 01508 498086
HINDRINGHAM........................ Wells Road, Hindringham, Fakenham NR21 0PL .... None
HOLT UNITED .... Sports Centre, Kelling Road, Holt NR25 7DU 01263 711217
LODDON UNITED .... George Lane Playing Fields, Loddon, Norwich NR14 6NB...................... 01508 528497
NORTH WALSHAM TOWN.......... Sports Centre, Greens Road, North Walsham NR28 0HW...................... 01692 406888
SHERINGHAM .... Weybourne Road, Sheringham NR26 8WD 01263 824804
SPROWSTON ATHLETIC... Sprowston Sports & Social Club, Blue Boar Lane, Sprowston, Norwich NR7 8RJ 01603 427688
WATTON UNITED .... Watton Playing Field, Dereham Road, Watton, Thetford IP25 6EZ 01953 881281
WROXHAM RESERVES .... Trafford Park, Skinners Lane, Wroxham NR12 8SJ 01603 783538

IN: Holt United (P), Loddon United (P), Watton United (P)
OUT: Halvergate United (W), Lowestoft Town Reserves (S – Eastern Counties League Reserve Division North), Mattishall (R)
Norwich Union become AFC Norwich

	Attleborough Town	Dereham Town Res.	Fakenham Town Res.	Gayton United	Holt United	Kirkley & Pakefield Res.	Loddon United	Long Stratton	Scole United	Sole Bay	Sprowston Wanderers	St Andrews	Stalham Town	Watton United	Wells Town	Wymondham Town
Attleborough Town		1-2	3-0	2-4	2-7	4-0	2-0	2-4	1-2	2-3	3-2	1-2	1-1	0-4	0-2	3-3
Dereham Town Res.	3-1		7-0	3-1	0-0	0-1	1-4	0-1	5-1	0-0	6-1	0-3	5-2	1-3	3-0	1-1
Fakenham Town Res.	0-6	2-7	D	1-4	1-3	1-8	1-7	0-1	0-1	0-4	1-6	0-11	0-2	1-5	0-3	1-6
Gayton United	2-2	1-3	9-1	I	4-2	2-5	2-5	3-0	3-1	1-1	2-0	1-3	6-4	0-2	2-1	0-1
Holt United	2-1	3-0	4-0	2-2	V	4-2	2-1	2-0	2-1	2-0	7-0	0-1	3-3	2-2	1-0	2-0
Kirkley & Pakefield Res.	3-1	1-2	11-0	3-1	0-1	I	0-2	2-1	3-0	2-1	13-0	3-1	4-1	0-1	3-1	1-1
Loddon United	2-0	2-2	7-0	10-1	3-0	2-1	S	4-0	2-1	2-1	2-0	5-2	3-0	3-4	1-0	2-1
Long Stratton	2-2	0-4	2-2	3-1	5-2	0-3	2-0	I	3-1	1-1	2-0	3-3	2-2	0-3	1-2	0-1
Scole United	1-0	1-4	7-2	1-3	2-2	1-3	2-0	0-2	O	3-0	2-3	1-1	1-3	1-2	2-1	2-1
Sole Bay	1-1	1-0	14-0	2-3	3-1	2-1	0-5	0-0	3-1	N	4-1	1-3	4-3	1-6	4-1	2-4
Sprowston Wanderers	1-1	0-2	3-2	0-6	1-4	0-1	0-5	0-4	0-3	0-6		1-3	3-3	2-2	1-4	0-11
St Andrews	5-1	1-0	12-0	3-2	1-2	1-3	1-1	0-1	2-0	2-0	8-1	O	2-2	1-0	3-0	2-3
Stalham Town	1-4	0-2	2-1	2-1	1-3	2-4	0-1	1-0	1-3	6-0	4-1	1-0	N	2-3	1-1	4-0
Watton United	4-1	0-0	3-0	8-3	1-4	0-1	3-2	3-2	1-0	3-0	7-1	3-3	1-1	E	5-2	2-1
Wells Town	1-0	2-1	10-1	3-5	3-0	4-0	1-4	0-1	4-0	0-1	2-2	1-1	1-0	3-0		1-0
Wymondham Town	1-2	1-5	9-1	3-0	1-3	2-1	1-2	1-2	4-0	1-0	3-1	1-0	2-0	0-3	0-0	

SECOND ROUND
Beccles Town 3 Sheringham 1
Cromer Town 3 Wymondham Town 0
Dersingham Rovers 3 Kirkley & Pakefield Res. 2
Hempnall 1 Acle United 0
Holt United 3 Norwich Union 2
Lowestoft Town Res. 2 **Watton United** 4 *aet*
North Walsham Town 3 Halvergate United 1
Wells Town 0 St Andrews 0 *aet* (3-1p)

QUARTER-FINALS
Beccles Town 0 **Watton United** 5
Cromer Town 3 Wells Town 0
Holt United 0 **Hempnall** 2
North Walsham Town 0 **Dersingham Rovers** 2

SEMI-FINALS
Dersingham Rovers 0 **Hempnall** 1
Watton United 2 Cromer Town 1

FINAL
(May 7th at Wroxham)
Hempnall 1 Watton United 0

Division One		P	W	D	L	F	A	Pts
Loddon United		30	22	2	6	89	31	68
Watton United		30	21	5	4	84	38	68
Holt United		30	19	5	6	72	41	62
Kirkley & Pakefield Res.		30	19	1	10	83	39	58
St Andrews		30	16	6	8	81	38	54
Dereham Town Res.		30	16	5	9	69	35	53
Wymondham Town		30	14	4	12	64	43	46
Long Stratton		30	13	6	11	45	45	45
Wells Town		30	13	4	13	54	43	43
Gayton United		30	13	3	14	75	77	42
Sole Bay	-3	30	12	5	13	60	55	38
Stalham Town		30	9	7	14	55	62	34
Scole United		30	10	2	18	42	61	32
Attleborough Town		30	7	6	17	50	65	27
Sprowston Wanderers		30	3	4	23	31	123	13
Fakenham Town Res.	-3	30	0	1	29	19	177	-2

DON FROST MEMORIAL CUP
(Premier Division champions v Mummery Cup holders)

(August 24th at Holt United)
Blofield United 2 **Gayton United** 3

DOLPHIN AUTOS ANGLIAN COMBINATION DIVISION ONE CONSTITUTION 2008-09

ATTLEBOROUGH TOWN . . . . Recreation Ground, Station Road, Attleborough NR17 2AS 01953 455365
BUNGAY TOWN . . . . Maltings Meadow, Ditchingham, Bungay 01986 894028
CAISTER . . . . Caister Playing Fields, off Allendale Road, Caister-on-Sea NR30 5ES . . . . None
CORTON . . . . Village Playing Field, Corton Long Lane, Corton, Lowestoft NR32 5HE . . . . None
GAYTON UNITED . . . . Lime Kiln Road, Gayton, King's Lynn PE32 1QB . . . . None
HORSFORD UNITED . . . . Holt Road, Horsford NR10 3DN . . . . None
KIRKLEY & PAKEFIELD RESERVES . . . Kirkley & Pakefield Community Centre, Walmer Road, Lowestoft NR33 7LE 01502 513549
LONG STRATTON . . . . Manor Road Playing Fields, Long Stratton, Norwich NR15 2XR . . . . None
MATTISHALL . . . . Mattishall Playing Fields, South Green, Mattishall, Norwich NR20 3JY 01362 850246
SCOLE UNITED . . . . Ransome Avenue Playing Field, Scole, Diss IP21 4EA 01379 741204
SOLE BAY . . . . Southwold Common, Southwold. . . . . None
ST ANDREWS . . . . Thorpe Recreation Ground, Laundry Lane, Thorpe St Andrew, Norwich NR7 0XQ 01603 300316
STALHAM TOWN . . . . Rivers Park, Stepping Stone Lane, Stalham, Norwich NR12 9EP . . . . None
WELLS TOWN . . . . Beach Road, Wells-next-the-Sea NR23 1DR 01328 710907
WYMONDHAM TOWN . . . . Kings Head Meadow, Wymondham NR18 0LB 01953 607326

IN: *Bungay Town (P), Caister (P), Corton (P), Horsford United (P), Mattishall (R)*
OUT: *Dereham Town Reserves (S – Eastern Counties League Reserve Division North), Fakenham Town Reserves (R), Holt United (P), Loddon United (P), Sprowston Wanderers (R), Watton United (P)*

	Anglian Windows	Aylsham Wanderers	Beccles Caxton	Bungay Town	Caister	Corton	Downham Town Res.	Great Yarmouth Town Res.	Horsford United	Mundford	Norwich St Johns	Norwich United Res.	Poringland Wanderers	Reepham Town	West Lynn SSC	Wortwell
Anglian Windows		2-1	3-1	2-1	0-5	0-7	2-2	2-4	2-2	1-1	1-1	1-4	2-1	0-4	3-2	1-0
Aylsham Wanderers	1-1		0-2	1-3	3-3	0-2	2-0	2-3	4-1	2-2	0-0	1-1	0-2	2-4	0-2	0-3
Beccles Caxton	5-1	4-3	D	3-0	4-2	0-2	5-2	8-1	1-2	2-0	1-1	2-0	2-1	1-1	5-1	4-0
Bungay Town	4-1	1-1	0-2	I	2-0	3-0	4-3	6-0	1-4	7-1	1-0	0-3	1-1	1-1	1-2	1-0
Caister	4-1	3-2	6-1	2-1	V	0-3	8-1	3-0	3-0	4-2	2-4	2-0	4-1	1-2	6-2	1-1
Corton	2-0	5-0	3-0	1-2	2-0	I	3-0	1-0	2-1	11-0	1-2	1-1	5-0	1-0	2-1	3-2
Downham Town Res.	3-2	4-2	1-1	1-3	2-3	0-4	S	1-1	0-2	1-0	2-2	2-0	1-3	1-0	2-3	0-5
Great Yarmouth Town Res.	2-2	4-0	2-3	0-2	2-2	1-5	1-2	I	3-1	1-2	0-0	1-5	1-2	3-1	1-4	2-0
Horsford United	1-1	1-0	4-0	2-1	3-0	1-3	11-0		O	5-1	1-1	3-3	4-1	4-1	3-1	6-0
Mundford	0-2	3-1	2-7	1-2	3-1	2-2	0-5	2-0	2-4	N	1-5	3-0	1-2	2-1	0-3	3-1
Norwich St Johns	1-1	8-1	1-1	2-0	0-2	0-2	3-1	4-1	1-2	6-2		0-1	2-1	3-2	2-2	2-2
Norwich United Res.	6-2	0-0	1-2	2-1	3-4	1-3	2-2	4-2	0-2	2-1	2-2	T	2-2	0-3	2-2	0-3
Poringland Wanderers	2-0	6-0	2-1	1-2	0-0	1-3	2-2	6-0	1-4	4-2	2-3	2-2	W	1-1	4-2	1-2
Reepham Town	1-3	3-1	2-0	0-1	3-0	4-1	3-1	1-2	1-3	3-1	1-3	2-0	1-1	O	2-1	0-0
West Lynn SSC	3-1	3-2	2-2	0-2	4-3	2-4	4-2	1-4	3-3	1-0	3-0	3-4	6-1	3-1		3-2
Wortwell	1-1	3-1	2-2	0-2	0-3	0-1	6-0	1-2	2-1	0-0	3-2	0-0	3-2	3-3	2-0	

Division Two		P	W	D	L	F	A	Pts
Corton		30	23	2	5	82	26	71
Horsford United		30	18	5	7	82	41	59
Caister		30	17	4	9	79	50	55
Beccles Caxton		30	16	6	8	72	48	54
Bungay Town		30	17	3	10	56	37	54
Norwich St Johns		30	12	11	7	61	42	47
Reepham Town		30	12	6	12	52	44	42
Wortwell		30	10	8	12	47	47	38
West Lynn SSC	-9	30	14	4	12	69	66	37
Poringland Wanderers		30	10	7	13	56	59	37
Norwich United Res.		30	9	10	11	51	54	37
Great Yarmouth Town Res.		30	9	4	17	44	84	31
Anglian Windows	-3	30	8	9	13	41	72	30
Downham Town Res.	-3	30	8	6	16	47	77	27
Mundford		30	7	4	19	40	86	25
Aylsham Wanderers		30	2	7	21	33	79	13

CYRIL BALLYN CUP

(Division Two, Three, Four, Five and Six first teams and external league reserve sides)

FIRST ROUND

Corton 4 Wortwell 3
Foulsham 4 Norwich CEYMS 3
Morley Village 9 Necton 3
Oulton Broad & Notleys 6 UEA 1
Poringland Wanderers 0 **Aylsham Wanderers** 1
South Walsham 2 **Marlingford** 6 *aet*
West Lynn SSC 1 Anglian Windows 1 *aet* (5-4p)

SECOND ROUND

Beccles Caxton 2 **Horsford United** 3
Bradenham Wanderers 2 **Oulton Broad & Notleys** 3
City of Norwich SOBU 3 **Aylsham Wanderers** 6
Corton 1 Newton Flotman 0
East Harling 3 **Martham** 4
Freethorpe 3 Thetford Rovers 2
Gorleston Res. 4 Foulsham 2
Great Yarmouth Town Res. 1 **Bungay Town** 2
Harleston Town 1 **Caister** 8
Marlingford 3 Mundford 2 *aet*
Norwich United Res. 4 Dereham Town Res. 2

DOLPHIN AUTOS ANGLIAN COMBINATION DIVISION TWO CONSTITUTION 2008-09

ACLE UNITED RESERVES . . . . Bridewell Lane, Acle, Norwich NR13 3RA 01493 751379
ANGLIAN WINDOWS . . . . Horsford Manor, Cromer Road, Norwich NR5 8AP 01603 404723
BECCLES CAXTON . . . . Caxton Meadow, Adjacent to Beccles Station, Beccles NR34 9QH 01502 712829
DOWNHAM TOWN RESERVES . . . Memorial Playing Field, Lynn Road, Downham Market PE38 9QG 01366 388424
FAKENHAM TOWN RESERVES . . . . Clipbush Park, Clipbush Lane, Fakenham NR21 8SW 01328 855445/855859
GREAT YARMOUTH TOWN RESERVES . . . Wellesley Road Rec Ground, Sandown Road, Great Yarmouth NR30 1EY. 01493 843373
HELLESDON . . . . Hellesdon Community Centre, Wood View Road, Hellesdon, Norwich NR6 5QB 01603 427675
NORWICH CEYMS . . . . Hilltops Sports Centre, Main Road, Swardeston, Norwich NR14 8DU 01508 578826
NORWICH ST JOHNS . . . . Cringleford Recreation Ground, Oakfields Road, Cringleford NR4 6XE 01508 578826
NORWICH UNITED RESERVES . . . . . Plantation Park, off Plantation Road, Blofield, Norwich NR13 4PL 01603 716963
OULTON BROAD & NOTLEYS . . . . Kirkley Recreation Ground, Walmer Road, Lowestoft NR33 8HZ. . . . . None
PORINGLAND WANDERERS . . . . . . Poringland Memorial Field, The Footpath, Poringland, Norwich NR14 7RF 01508 495198
REEPHAM TOWN . . . . Stimpsons Piece Rec Ground, Reepham, Norwich . . . . None
SPROWSTON WANDERERS . . . . Sprowston Cricket Club, Barkers Lane, Sprowston, Norwich NR7 8QZ 01603 404042
WEST LYNN SSC . . . . West Lynn Sports & Social Club, St Peters Road, West Lynn PE34 3LB 01553 761646
WORTWELL . . . . Wortwell Playing Field, opposite Bell PH, High Road, Wortwell, Harleston IP20 0HH . . . . None
IN: *Acle United Reserves (P), Fakenham Town Reserves (R), Hellesdon (P), Norwich CEYMS (P), Oulton Broad & Notleys (P), Sprowston Wanderers (R)*
OUT: *Aylsham (formerly Aylsham Wanderers) (R), Bungay Town (P), Caister (P), Corton (P), Horsford United (P), Mundford (R)*

	Acle United Res.	Beccles Town Res.	Caister Res.	Hellesdon	Hempnall Res.	Martham	Mattishall Res.	Morley Village	Norwich CEYMS	Oulton Broad & Notleys	South Walsham	Sprowston Athletic Res.	Swaffham Town Res.	Thetford Rovers	Thorpe Rovers	Thorpe Village
Acle United Res.		4-1	1-3	2-1	2-1	1-1	6-0	9-1	2-2	0-2	1-0	0-0	5-1	3-2	1-0	3-0
Beccles Town Res.	1-2	*D*	2-5	1-3	3-2	3-2	2-1	2-0	0-2	2-1	2-1	2-4	1-5	0-1	3-1	4-0
Caister Res.	1-3	5-1	*I*	0-2	5-2	7-0	5-4	5-1	0-4	1-1	1-1	9-0	1-2	1-3	1-3	5-2
Hellesdon	3-4	6-1	1-6	*V*	5-2	2-3	1-1	2-2	2-3	3-1	5-1	0-3	3-2	3-0	5-2	2-4
Hempnall Res.	3-1	3-3	3-1	0-4	*I*	0-2	0-1	0-3	3-1	2-2	2-2	0-1	4-3	2-1	1-1	1-3
Martham	1-2	5-2	3-3	2-2	1-0	*S*	8-0	6-2	1-5	2-3	1-1	3-1	2-6	4-0	4-2	5-0
Mattishall Res.	0-1	0-1	1-1	1-5	2-1	5-5	*I*	0-2	2-3	0-4	1-2	1-1	2-0	1-2	3-2	2-5
Morley Village	0-5	3-1	1-4	1-6	0-2	3-1	0-4	*O*	0-0	3-4	3-1	5-2	0-5	1-5	1-0	4-1
Norwich CEYMS	6-1	3-1	2-1	2-0	2-0	6-1	4-1	3-1	*N*	4-2	2-0	1-1	2-1	2-1	6-1	3-1
Oulton Broad & Notleys	2-1	3-2	3-1	2-2	2-0	4-1	4-0	4-1	1-0		1-2	3-0	5-0	4-1	1-0	2-3
South Walsham	0-2	1-6	0-1	0-3	0-5	0-1	4-2	4-1	0-2	0-2	*T*	4-0	1-2	0-4	2-2	2-2
Sprowston Athletic Res.	0-5	2-0	1-2	1-5	2-4	7-1	10-0	2-7	0-4	1-2	4-2	*R*	4-2	2-3	5-2	
Swaffham Town Res.	0-2	6-1	5-5	1-2	8-1	2-2	1-0	3-2	2-2	3-7	6-3	0-1	*R*	1-0	4-0	7-4
Thetford Rovers	3-2	2-3	4-2	2-2	3-1	9-1	2-0	4-2	2-4	1-3	7-0	3-0	2-0	*E*	2-3	3-1
Thorpe Rovers	1-5	1-1	4-2	4-4	3-5	1-3	3-3	5-2	0-4	2-1	0-2	2-0	2-2	0-1	*E*	1-3
Thorpe Village	1-2	1-0	3-1	1-2	0-2	1-0	3-3	3-0	0-3	0-2	2-1	2-1	2-1	5-0	1-0	

Reepham Town 8 Morley Village 1
Swaffham Town Res. 2 **Norwich St Johns** 5
Thorpe Rovers 1 **Easton** 2
Thorpe Village 0 **Hoveton Wherrymen** 2
West Lynn SSC 5 Hellesdon 2
THIRD ROUND
Bungay Town 0 **Freethorpe** 3 *(at Freethorpe)*
Caister 4 West Lynn SSC 2 *aet*
Easton 2 Aylsham Wanderers 0
Horsford United 6 Hoveton Wherrymen 1
Marlingford 1 **Gorleston Res.** 2
Norwich United Res. 0 **Corton** 3
Oulton Broad & Notleys 2 **Norwich St Johns** 4 *aet*
Reepham Town 9 Martham 0
QUARTER-FINALS
Caister 1 Norwich St Johns 0
Gorleston Res. 0 **Corton** 3
Horsford United 4 Freethorpe 2
Reepham Town 10 Easton 3
SEMI-FINALS
Horsford United 0 **Corton** 4
Reepham Town 2 **Caister** 3 *aet*
FINAL
(May 4th at Wroxham)
Corton 2 Caister 1

Division Three		P	W	D	L	F	A	Pts
Norwich CEYMS		30	24	4	2	87	28	76
Acle United Res.		30	21	3	6	78	37	66
Oulton Broad & Notleys		30	21	3	6	78	38	66
Hellesdon		30	16	6	8	86	55	54
Thetford Rovers		30	16	1	13	72	55	49
Caister Res.		30	13	5	12	85	63	44
Thorpe Village		30	14	2	14	56	67	44
Swaffham Town Res.		30	13	4	13	80	66	43
Martham		30	12	6	12	72	80	42
Beccles Town Res.		30	11	2	17	52	75	35
Hempnall Res.		30	10	4	16	52	67	34
Sprowston Athletic Res.	*-6*	30	11	3	16	58	75	30
Morley Village		30	9	2	19	52	93	29
Thorpe Rovers		30	7	6	17	49	75	27
South Walsham		30	6	5	19	37	73	23
Mattishall Res.		30	5	6	19	41	88	21

WWW.NLNEWSDESK.CO.UK

DOLPHIN AUTOS ANGLIAN COMBINATION DIVISION THREE CONSTITUTION 2008-09

AYLSHAM.................................Sir Williams Lane, Aylsham, Norwich NR11 6AN...................................None
BECCLES TOWN RESERVES.................College Meadow, Beccles NR34 7FA...07729 782817
BRADENHAM WANDERERS...............Hale Road, Bradenham, Thetford IP25 7RA...None
CAISTER RESERVES...........Caister Playing Fields, off Allendale Road, Caister-on-Sea NR30 5ES.........................None
CROMER TOWN RESERVES..............Cabbell Park, Mill Road, Cromer NR27 0AD 01263 512185
EAST HARLING......Memorial Fields, Church Street, East Harling, Norwich, NR16 2NB.....01953 718251
HEMPNALL RESERVES...................Bungay Road, Hempnall, Norwich NR15 2NG..01508 498086
LODDON UNITED RESERVES........George Lane Playing Fields, Loddon, Norwich NR14 6NB............................01508 528497
MARTHAM............Coronation Recreation Ground, Rollesby Road, Martham, Great Yarmouth NR29 4SP............01493 740252
MORLEY VILLAGE.................Golf Links Road, Morley St Peter, Wymondham NR18 9SU...............................None
MUNDFORD........................The Glebe, Mundford, Thetford IP26 5EJ...None
SPROWSTON ATHLETIC RESERVES..Sprowston Sports & Social Club, Blue Boar Lane, Sprowston, Norwich NR7 8RJ....01603 427688
SWAFFHAM TOWN RESERVES........Shoemakers Lane, off Cley Road, Swaffham PE37 7NT.............................01760 722700
THETFORD ROVERS......................Euston Park, Euston, near Thetford IP24 2QP.....................................None
THORPE ROVERS.....................Dussindale Park, Pound Lane, Thorpe NR7 0SR......................................None
THORPE VILLAGE.......Thorpe Recreation Ground, Laundry Lane, Thorpe St Andrew, Norwich NR7 0XQ.............01603 300316
IN: Aylsham (formerly Aylsham Wanderers) (R), Bradenham Wanderers (P), Cromer Town Reserves (P), East Harling (P), Loddon United Reserves (P), Mundford (R)
OUT: Acle United Reserves (P), Hellesdon (P), Mattishall Reserves (R), Norwich CEYMS (P), Oulton Broad & Notleys (R), South Walsham (R)

	Blofield United Res.	Bradenham Wanderers	Brandon Town Res.	Bungay Town Res.	City of Norwich SOBU	Cromer Town Res.	East Harling	Easton	Harleston Town	Hindringham Res.	Loddon United Res.	Norwich St Johns Res.	Norwich Union Res.	St Andrews Res.	Wells Town Res.	Wymondham Town Res.
Blofield United Res.		4-4	2-1	0-2	7-1	1-2	2-3	5-0	4-1	2-0	3-2	3-4	3-3	1-3	2-1	1-0
Bradenham Wanderers	8-1	D	2-2	3-1	5-1	3-2	5-1	2-0	2-0	3-0	0-2	4-2	6-1	9-2	4-0	2-3
Brandon Town Res.	0-1	3-3	I	6-1	8-0	0-3	2-5	1-4	1-2	4-1	2-2	1-0	1-2	3-2	2-0	2-3
Bungay Town Res.	0-2	1-7	5-1	V	2-1	0-2	2-8	1-2	1-1	1-3	0-1	1-5	2-3	3-2	2-2	1-3
City of Norwich SOBU	1-1	0-5	1-6	6-2	I	0-5	3-9	0-1	1-1	2-2	0-3	0-4	0-8	0-6	2-2	1-3
Cromer Town Res.	6-3	7-1	4-1	4-1	1-1	S	4-1	3-0	2-0	0-1	4-0	1-1	1-3	3-0	3-0	5-2
East Harling	2-1	2-5	1-1	3-3	4-0	0-1	I	3-1	3-1	3-0	1-4	3-0	4-0	3-0	8-0	2-1
Easton	1-2	1-2	4-1	7-0	3-3	1-3	0-5	O	5-2	4-1	1-3	6-2	1-3	2-1	2-2	4-2
Harleston Town	0-3	1-0	2-1	5-1	2-2	3-4	2-6	0-2	N	2-0	2-5	2-8	2-3	3-2	3-0	2-2
Hindringham Res.	2-1	2-2	2-2	4-2	5-0	3-3	3-2	1-2	6-3		0-1	3-5	1-5	1-3	1-1	1-3
Loddon United Res.	2-1	1-4	5-4	5-2	6-1	0-5	3-0	1-1	2-3	2-2		4-3	7-1	2-1	4-0	1-5
Norwich St Johns Res.	4-1	0-3	6-2	2-1	1-0	1-3	2-5	0-0	6-1	4-1	2-1	F	1-4	1-0	1-3	0-1
Norwich Union Res.	0-3	1-3	2-0	1-5	1-0	1-2	2-2	1-1	1-1	2-2	1-2	4-0	O	3-1	0-4	1-4
St Andrews Res.	2-2	1-1	2-0	2-1	4-0	0-2	2-3	2-1	3-4	5-0	2-0	5-0	2-2	U	0-0	1-1
Wells Town Res.	1-0	0-4	0-2	2-0	1-3	1-1	0-0	0-3	1-2	2-3	3-0	3-2	0-2	2-3	R	2-1
Wymondham Town Res.	1-0	2-4	3-5	3-1	3-0	2-3	2-2	4-1	1-2	0-4	3-1	5-1	4-3	0-0	0-1	

Division Four

	P	W	D	L	F	A	Pts
Bradenham Wanderers	30	21	5	4	106	44	68
Cromer Town Res. -6	30	23	3	4	89	33	66
East Harling	30	18	5	7	94	52	59
Loddon United Res.	30	17	3	10	72	57	54
Wymondham Town Res.	30	15	4	11	67	54	49
Norwich Union Res.	30	13	6	11	64	65	45
Easton	30	13	5	12	61	56	44
Blofield United Res.	30	13	4	13	62	57	43
Norwich St Johns Res.	30	13	2	15	68	71	41
St Andrews Res.	30	11	6	13	59	53	39
Wells Town Res.	30	10	6	14	36	57	36
Harleston Town	30	10	6	14	55	79	36
Hindringham Res.	30	9	7	14	55	71	34
Brandon Town Res. -3	30	9	6	15	66	70	30
Bungay Town Res. -3	30	5	3	22	45	96	15
City of Norwich SOBU	30	1	7	22	27	111	10

Division Five

	P	W	D	L	F	A	Pts
North Walsham Town Res.	26	21	5	0	111	24	68
Freethorpe	26	21	1	4	115	26	64
Marlingford	26	18	5	3	103	26	59
Foulsham	26	17	4	5	98	45	55
Newton Flotman	26	15	3	8	53	36	48
Sheringham Res.	26	10	5	11	68	72	35
Norwich CEYMS Res.	26	11	1	14	62	64	34
Watton United Res.	26	9	5	12	66	64	32
Attleborough Town Res.	26	8	7	11	60	79	31
Stalham Town Res.	26	8	6	12	60	61	30
Necton SSC	26	8	4	14	55	80	28
Aylsham Wanderers Res.	26	5	7	14	27	73	22
Sprowston Wanderers Res. -3	26	1	3	22	24	145	3
Mundford Res. -3	26	0	4	22	25	132	1

Division Six

	P	W	D	L	F	A	Pts
Gorleston Res.	28	24	2	2	127	32	74
Hoveton Wherrymen	28	23	2	3	125	37	71
UEA -12	28	22	2	4	95	16	56
Long Stratton Res.	28	17	2	9	74	49	53
Poringland Wanderers Res. -3	28	13	7	8	58	50	43
Scole United Res.	28	12	4	12	51	57	40
Hellesdon Res.	28	10	6	12	58	62	36
Holt United Res.	28	10	4	14	48	74	34
Horsford United Res. -3	28	11	0	17	46	51	30
Easton Res. -3	28	9	6	13	49	79	30
Thorpe Village Res.	28	9	2	17	45	85	29
Martham Res.	28	7	3	18	45	81	24
Wortwell Res.	28	6	4	18	34	83	22
Reepham Town Res. -6	28	6	2	20	37	94	14
Gayton United Res. -9	28	4	8	16	39	81	11

WWW.CHERRYRED.CO.UK

C S MORLEY CUP

(Anglian Combination club reserve teams)

FINAL

(May 9th at Wroxham)

Acle United Res. 1 North Walsham Town Res. 0

DOLPHIN AUTOS ANGLIAN COMBINATION DIVISION FOUR CONSTITUTION 2008-09

AFC NORWICH RESERVES .... Thorpe School, Pound Lane, Thorpe, NR7 0SR .... None
BLOFIELD UNITED RESERVES .... Old Yarmouth Road, Blofield, Norwich NR13 4LE 01603 712576
BRANDON TOWN RESERVES ...... Remembrance Playing Field, Church Road, Brandon IP27 0JB 01842 813177
EASTON .... Easton College, Bawburgh Road, Norwich NR9 5DX 01603 731208
FOULSHAM .... Playing Field, Guist Road, Foulsham, Dereham NR20 5RZ .... None
FREETHORPE .... School Road, Freethorpe, Norwich NR13 3NZ 01493 701533
HARLESTON TOWN .... Rec & Memorial Leisure Centre, Wilderness Lane, Harleston IP20 9DD 01379 854519
HINDRINGHAM RESERVES .... Wells Road, Hindringham, Fakenham NR21 0PL .... None
MARLINGFORD .... Bayer Social Club, Marlpit Lane, Norwich NR5 8YT 01603 787661
MATTISHALL RESERVES ...... Mattishall Playing Fields, South Green, Mattishall, Norwich NR20 3JY 01362 850246
NEWTON FLOTMAN .... Newton Flotman Village Centre, Grove Way, Newton Flotman, Norwich .... None
NORTH WALSHAM TOWN RESERVES .... Sports Centre, Greens Road, North Walsham NR28 0HW 01692 406888
SOUTH WALSHAM .... The Playing Field, South Walsham .... None
ST ANDREWS RESERVES .... Thorpe Recreation Ground, Laundry Lane, Thorpe St Andrew, Thorpe NR7 0XQ 01603 300316
WELLS TOWN RESERVES .... Beach Road, Wells-next-the-Sea NR23 1DR 01328 710907
WYMONDHAM TOWN RESERVES .... Kings Head Meadow, Wymondham NR18 0LB 01953 607326
IN: Foulsham (P), Freethorpe (P), Marlingford (P), Mattishall (P), Newton Flotman (P), North Walsham Town Reserves (P), South Walsham (R)
OUT: Bradenham Wanderers (P), Bungay Town Reserves (R), City of Norwich SOBU (R), Cromer Town Reserves (P), East Harling (P), Loddon United Reserves (P), Norwich St Johns Reserves (W)
Norwich Union Reserves become AFC Norwich Reserves

BEDFORDSHIRE LEAGUE

	AFC Kempston Town	Blunham	Caldecote	Campton	Ickwell & Old Warden	Luton Borough	Meltis Corinthians	Oakley Sports	Renhold United	Riseley Sports	Sandy	Sharnbrook	Westoning Recreation Club	Wilshamstead	Woburn
AFC Kempston Town		1-0	2-0	4-1	1-4	1-2	0-4	1-2	3-1	2-0	3-1	3-0	3-0	4-3	10-1
Blunham	3-1		3-2	1-5	0-3	3-1	2-0	1-1	6-1	2-0	3-0	2-2	2-4	4-2	3-2
Caldecote	0-0	1-1	P	5-3	2-3	2-2	1-3	4-0	8-1	6-1	3-1	3-0	4-2	1-1	1-0
Campton	1-3	5-3	4-0	R	3-5	4-0	2-0	5-2	6-1	6-1	1-0	2-0	5-0	2-0	10-1
Ickwell & Old Warden	2-2	1-3	1-1	1-5	E	3-1	2-4	1-3	2-1	1-1	4-1	2-1	W-L	2-1	2-2
Luton Borough	8-5	1-4	1-4	1-9	2-2	M	4-0	1-2	2-2	3-2	2-2	1-4	2-0	L-W	0-2
Meltis Corinthians	4-0	2-4	4-3	1-2	3-1	4-0	I	1-1	2-1	n/a	3-2	3-0	5-6	8-2	2-1
Oakley Sports	2-0	2-1	2-1	0-4	0-2	13-0	2-4	E	1-0	8-0	3-0	7-2	5-0	3-2	3-0
Renhold United	2-1	1-0	0-2	2-3	2-2	W-L	2-1	3-5	R	5-0	0-5	4-1	5-1	2-2	
Riseley Sports	5-4	L-W	2-1	2-2	0-5	1-3	0-2	2-3	1-4	—	1-2	0-1	3-4	2-0	4-3
Sandy	1-0	1-4	1-1	3-2	2-0	2-1	2-1	1-2	1-1	7-0	D	1-1	1-0	4-1	1-0
Sharnbrook	2-0	0-0	0-7	3-3	0-0	2-3	2-2	0-0	1-1	2-1	2-3	I	1-1	0-0	6-0
Westoning Recreation Club	2-3	1-1	L-W	0-3	4-3	1-7	3-2	2-1	6-1	1-2	0-3	0-4	V	4-1	6-4
Wilshamstead	2-3	1-1	2-4	1-4	1-10	3-1	1-4	0-4	1-6	3-0	0-2	0-1	1-2		3-1
Woburn	2-4	0-0	1-5	1-11	1-2	1-4	3-4	0-5	3-1	1-5	0-3	0-5	0-3	4-3	

Premier Division		P	W	D	L	F	A	Pts
Campton		28	21	2	5	113	41	65
Oakley Sports		28	19	3	6	82	38	60
Meltis Corinthians	-1	27	16	2	9	73	49	49
Ickwell & Old Warden		28	14	7	7	66	47	49
Blunham		28	14	7	7	57	41	49
Sandy		28	15	4	9	53	39	49
Caldecote		28	14	6	8	72	41	48
AFC Kempston Town		28	14	2	12	64	55	44
Renhold United		28	10	5	13	54	67	35
Sharnbrook		28	8	10	10	43	49	34
Westoning Recreation Club	-2	28	11	2	15	53	71	33
Luton Borough	-6	28	9	4	15	53	78	25
Riseley Sports	-3	27	6	2	19	36	81	17
Wilshamstead		28	4	3	21	36	86	15
Woburn		28	3	3	22	36	108	12

Meltis Corinthians v Riseley Sports not played

BEDFORDSHIRE LEAGUE SPORTSFORM PREMIER DIVISION CONSTITUTION 2008-09

AFC KEMPSTON TOWN .... Hillgrounds Road, Kempston, Bedford MK42 8QU 01234 852346
BEDFORD SPORTS ATHLETIC .... Cople Playing Fields, Cople, Bedford MK44 3TP .... None
BLUNHAM .... The Playing Fields, Blunham Road, Moggerhanger, Sandy MK44 3RG .... None
CALDECOTE .... Harvey Close, Upper Caldecote, Biggleswade SG18 9BQ .... None
CAMPTON .... The Recreation Ground, Church Road, Campton SG17 5BN .... None
DUNTON .... Horseshoe Close, Dunton SG18 8RY .... None
HENLOW .... Henlow Park, Groveside, Henlow Village SG16 6AW .... None
ICKWELL & OLD WARDEN .... Ickwell Green, Ickwell, Biggleswade SG18 9EF .... None
MELTIS CORINTHIANS .... Meltis Sports Club, Miller Road, Bedford MK42 9NY 01234 352872
OAKLEY SPORTS .... Oakley Village Sports Centre, Oakley, Bedford MK43 7RG .... None
RENHOLD UNITED .... Renhold Playing Fields, Renhold, Bedford. .... None
RISELEY SPORTS .... Gold Street, Riseley MK44 1EG .... None
SANDY .... Recreation Ground, Bedford Road, Sandy SG19 1BW .... None
SHARNBROOK .... Playing Fields, Lodge Road, Sharnbrook MK44 1JP .... None
WILSHAMSTEAD .... Jubilee Playing Fields, Bedford Road, Wilshamstead MK45 3HN .... None
IN: *Bedford Sports Athletic (formerly Bedford Salvation Army)(P), Dunton (P), Henlow (P)*
OUT: *Luton Borough (E), Westoning Recreation Club (R), Woburn (R)*

BRITANNIA CUP
(Bedfordshire League Premier Division teams)

FIRST ROUND

Campton 2 **Westoning Recreation Club** 5

Ickwell & Old Warden 1 **AFC Kempston Town** 2 *aet*

Luton Borough 3 Sandy 1

Meltis Corinthians 3 Woburn 1

Oakley Sports 1 **Blunham** 2

Sharnbrook 2 **Caldecote** 3

Wilshamstead 4 Riseley Sports 2

QUARTER-FINALS

AFC Kempston Town 2 **Sandy** 2 *aet* (3-5p)

Blunham 4 Wilshamstead 1 *aet*

Caldecote 2 Renhold United 1 *aet*

Meltis Corinthians 1 Westoning Recreation Club 0

SEMI-FINALS

Blunham 4 Caldecote 0

Meltis Corinthians 2 Sandy 1

FINAL

(May 7th at Biggleswade United)

Blunham 1 **Meltis Corinthians** 2

Division One		P	W	D	L	F	A	Pts
Bedford Salvation Army		26	20	3	3	96	34	63
Henlow		26	19	2	5	70	33	59
Dunton		26	17	2	7	78	42	53
Flitwick Town		26	15	3	8	49	40	48
Campton Res.	-3	26	14	3	9	60	40	42
Caldecote Res.		26	10	7	9	74	61	37
Stevington		26	12	1	13	75	73	37
Marston Social		26	12	1	13	63	83	37
Sandy Res.		26	9	5	12	56	59	32
Kempston		26	8	3	15	55	79	27
Reddings Wood	-3	26	9	2	15	64	82	26
Royal Oak Kempston	-3	26	8	2	16	41	74	23
AFC Kempston Town Res.		26	6	3	17	51	86	21
Elstow Abbey		26	3	3	20	40	86	12

Division Two		P	W	D	L	F	A	Pts
Bedford College		28	22	2	4	104	36	68
Meltis Albion		28	21	2	5	108	38	65
Ickwell & Old Warden Res.		27	17	3	7	65	51	54
Meppershall Jurassic		28	15	4	9	96	73	49
Mulberry Bush		28	13	6	9	40	45	45
Oakley Sports Res.		27	14	2	11	70	59	44
Newnham Athletic		28	13	5	10	77	70	44
Great Barford	-1	28	12	4	12	64	56	39
Marston Shelton Rovers		28	10	7	11	69	67	37
Clifton		28	10	5	13	70	78	35
Saffron		28	10	2	16	67	80	32
Blunham Res.	-3	28	10	4	14	62	102	31
Lidlington United Sports	-3	27	6	2	19	51	89	17
Woburn Res.	-6	27	5	5	17	40	86	14
Renhold Village	-7	28	3	1	24	43	96	3

*Ickwell & Old Warden Res. v Lidlington United Sports
and Woburn Res. v Oakley Sports Res. not played*

CENTENARY CUP
FINAL

(May 2nd at Biggleswade United)

Bedford Salvation Army 2 AFC Kempston Town Res. 1

JUBILEE CUP
FINAL

(May 5th at Biggleswade United)

Great Barford 3 Clifton 0

Division Three		P	W	D	L	F	A	Pts
Kings AFC		28	21	2	5	117	36	65
Blue Chip		28	19	4	5	109	43	61
Potton Wanderers	-3	28	20	4	4	108	59	61
Marabese Ceramics		28	16	7	5	89	36	55
Meltis Corinthians Res.		28	16	4	8	84	47	52
Riseley Sports Res.		28	13	6	9	82	44	45
Marsh Leys		28	13	5	10	79	70	44
Caldecote 'A'		27	12	5	10	84	77	41
Wilshamstead Res.	-6	28	14	3	11	78	62	39
Flitwick Town Res.		28	11	3	14	73	76	36
AFC Shillington		28	7	8	13	61	76	29
Sandy 'A'		28	8	2	18	51	71	26
Stewartby Village		28	6	2	20	56	119	20
Lidlington United Sports Res.		27	2	2	23	27	183	8
Exel United	-3	28	1	3	24	38	137	3

Lidlington United Sports Res. v Caldecote 'A' not played

WATSON SHIELD

FINAL *(May 3rd at Biggleswade United)*

Riseley Sports Res. 2 Kings AFC 1

CAMBRIDGESHIRE COUNTY LEAGUE

	Cambridge University Press	Cottenham United	Eaton Socon	Ely City Res.	Fordham	Great Paxton	Great Shelford	Histon 'A'	Hundon	Littleport Town	Needingworth United	Newmarket Town Res.	Over Sports	Waterbeach	Wickhambrook	Wisbech Town Res.
Cambridge University Press	P	1-0	8-1	1-1	5-0	4-1	1-3	2-2	2-2	3-0	1-0	5-1	1-1	1-1	5-1	3-1
Cottenham United	1-0	R	2-1	2-6	1-2	2-1	3-6	3-5	2-2	3-3	5-0	4-2	1-3	0-0	2-4	0-1
Eaton Socon	1-5	1-5	E	4-2	3-1	3-2	0-2	1-0	0-4	2-2	2-1	5-3	0-1	2-4	0-0	2-1
Ely City Res.	1-0	1-1	1-2	M	0-1	6-0	1-2	3-3	0-2	5-3	2-0	5-0	4-1	0-1	4-0	3-1
Fordham	2-4	2-3	3-5	2-6	I	5-2	1-3	0-2	2-2	0-1	0-5	4-1	4-3	1-4	0-1	2-0
Great Paxton	5-4	3-6	1-6	0-1	1-0	E	1-3	1-2	1-2	5-4	5-1	3-2	1-4	1-3	3-1	2-1
Great Shelford	1-1	2-1	6-2	3-0	2-3	9-0	R	2-1	3-0	2-2	1-1	6-0	3-1	2-3	0-0	4-0
Histon 'A'	2-3	4-0	3-1	3-2	2-1	5-0	0-2		2-0	3-2	1-1	11-0	1-2	2-3	3-1	4-0
Hundon	5-1	3-1	6-2	2-2	3-4	3-2	4-2	1-3	D	4-2	2-1	2-0	3-0	2-2	3-1	6-0
Littleport Town	2-4	3-0	1-3	2-1	2-1	5-2	3-1	0-2	1-3	I	6-2	0-2	0-2	0-2	2-1	1-0
Needingworth United	1-5	0-7	2-0	0-4	0-1	2-2	0-1	0-0	0-2	1-3	V	2-1	3-1	0-4	1-1	1-0
Newmarket Town Res.	0-6	0-1	0-5	0-1	2-4	4-0	1-0	1-3	0-7	1-1	1-0	I	2-0	2-5	1-0	3-0
Over Sports	0-1	4-1	7-1	1-2	2-1	3-2	0-2	1-0	4-0	2-1	1-1	2-1	S	1-0	3-2	3-0
Waterbeach	1-1	2-1	1-2	1-1	1-0	4-0	0-1	2-1	2-1	1-0	4-1	3-0	2-1	I	2-1	8-0
Wickhambrook	1-1	3-3	2-5	4-0	1-1	4-3	1-2	1-3	0-4	1-2	2-1	4-1	1-2	0-4	O	3-2
Wisbech Town Res.	0-4	0-3	1-2	0-3	0-3	3-2	1-2	0-1	1-3	4-3	0-1	2-3	0-5	1-1	2-2	N

Premier Division	P	W	D	L	F	A	Pts
Waterbeach	30	21	6	3	71	26	69
Great Shelford	30	21	4	5	78	32	67
Hundon	30	19	5	6	83	43	62
Cambridge University Press	30	17	8	5	83	38	59
Histon 'A'	30	18	4	8	74	36	58
Over Sports	30	18	2	10	61	41	56
Ely City Res.	30	15	5	10	68	42	50
Eaton Socon	30	15	2	13	64	77	47
Cottenham United	30	11	5	14	64	65	38
Littleport Town	30	11	4	15	57	63	37
Fordham	30	10	2	18	47	67	32
Wickhambrook	30	7	7	16	44	65	28
Newmarket Town Res.	30	9	1	20	35	87	28
Needingworth United	30	6	6	18	29	65	24
Great Paxton	30	7	1	22	52	102	22
Wisbech Town Res.	30	3	2	25	22	83	11

PREMIER DIVISION CUP

FIRST ROUND

Eaton Socon 3 Needingworth United 1

Ely City Res. 2 Over Sports 2 *aet* (6-5p)

Great Paxton 1 **Cottenham United** 2

Littleport Town 5 **Histon 'A'** 6

Newmarket Town Res. 1 **Great Shelford** 4

Waterbeach 5 Hundon 2

Wickhambrook 1 **Cambridge University Press** 6

Wisbech Town Res. 1 **Fordham** 2

QUARTER-FINALS

Cottenham United 4 Great Shelford 2

Ely City 1 **Cambridge University Press** 2

Fordham 0 **Eaton Socon** 2

Waterbeach 2 Histon 'A' 1

SEMI-FINALS

Cambridge University Press 7 Cottenham United 1

Eaton Socon 0 **Waterbeach** 2

FINAL

(May 5th at Histon)

Waterbeach 1 **Cambridge University Press** 2

CAMBRIDGESHIRE COUNTY LEAGUE KERSHAW PREMIER DIVISION CONSTITUTION 2008-09

CAMBRIDGE UNIVERSITY PRESS .... CUP Sports Ground, Shaftesbury Road, Cambridge CB2 2BS .... None
COTTENHAM UNITED....... King George V Playing Field, Lamb Lane, Cottenham, Cambridge CB4 8TB............... 01954 250873
EATON SOCON .... River Road, Eaton Ford, St Neots PE19 3AU .... None
ELY CITY RESERVES .... The Unwin Ground, Downham Road, Ely CB6 2SH 01353 662035
FORDHAM....................... Recreational Ground, Carter Street, Fordham, Ely CB7 5NJ............................ None
FULBOURN INSTITUTE............... Fulbourn Recreation, Home End, Fulbourn CB1 5BS.......................... None
GREAT SHELFORD .... Recreation Ground, Woollards Lane, Great Shelford CB2 5LZ...................... 01223 842590
HISTON 'A' ....The Glass World Stadium, Bridge Road, Impington, Cambridge CB4 9PH............... 01223 237373
HUNDON................................ Upper North Street, Hundon CO10 8EE .... None
LAKENHEATH.......................... The Nest, Wings Road, Lakenheath IP27 9HW............................ None
LITTLEPORT TOWN .... Sports Centre, Camel Road, Littleport, Ely CB6 1PU......................... 01353 860600
NEEDINGWORTH UNITED .... Mill Field, Holywell Road, Needingworth PE27 8TE .... None
NEWMARKET TOWN RESERVES. . .Sherbourn Stadium,Cricket Field Road, off New Cheveley Road, Newmarket CB8 8BT.. 01638 663637
OVER SPORTS .... Over Recreation Ground, The Dole, Over, Cambridge CB4 5NW...................... None
WATERBEACH .... Waterbeach Reacreation Ground, Cambridge Road, Waterbeach CB5 9NJ................... None
WICKHAMBROOK .... Recreation Ground, Cemetary Hill, Wickhambrook CB8 8XR .... None

IN: Fulbourn Institute (P), Lakenheath (P)
OUT: Great Paxton (R), Wisbech Town Reserves (R)

	Brampton	Comberton United	Debden	Foxton	Fulbourn Institute	Girton United	Hardwick	Hemingfords United	Lakenheath	Linton Granta	Mildenhall Town Res.	Soham Town Rangers Res.	Somersham Town	West Wratting	Whittlesford United
Brampton		2-3	1-2	1-4	1-2	1-5	2-2	1-4	3-0	1-3	2-1	4-4	3-0	3-2	1-2
Comberton United	2-2		0-0	3-2	0-2	2-2	1-4	1-1	2-3	6-0	2-2	3-2	4-1	0-2	1-3
Debden	3-3	1-1	S	2-2	0-1	1-2	1-0	1-1	0-3	2-1	1-6	2-2	3-1	3-0	1-0
Foxton	2-0	3-2	2-2	E	1-1	2-2	3-2	3-1	0-4	8-2	2-4	2-2	1-2	2-0	0-2
Fulbourn Institute	4-0	1-1	4-1	5-0	N	1-2	2-2	0-1	2-3	6-4	4-0	3-1	4-0	1-1	3-2
Girton United	1-0	2-2	1-2	0-4	0-1	I	6-1	0-2	2-4	2-1	7-0	2-0	2-2	2-3	3-2
Hardwick	4-5	3-5	1-1	3-0	1-1	2-2	O	1-0	0-3	7-3	1-4	2-3	4-2	1-0	1-3
Hemingfords United	1-1	2-2	1-1	1-4	2-2	1-1	2-2	R	2-1	2-0	1-1	1-2	2-0	1-3	2-1
Lakenheath	5-2	1-2	5-4	1-1	4-2	3-1	2-0	2-0		7-0	3-2	6-1	2-1	4-2	4-1
Linton Granta	2-3	1-4	1-1	3-3	1-2	0-1	4-0	1-2	0-6	D	0-6	0-6	4-1	3-1	0-3
Mildenhall Town Res.	2-3	2-3	1-0	3-2	1-2	2-0	4-0	6-1	1-2	5-0	I	0-1	1-1	0-3	1-1
Soham Town Rangers Res.	5-3	0-2	4-4	1-3	4-1	1-2	2-0	4-1	6-0	2-2	1-3	V	5-1	1-2	2-7
Somersham Town	1-2	4-2	0-2	1-1	0-3	3-1	2-1	1-0	0-4	8-2	4-1	2-5		5-0	2-2
West Wratting	4-2	3-1	0-3	2-0	5-1	3-1	5-3	1-1	1-5	2-1	4-1	5-1	3-3	A	2-2
Whittlesford United	6-1	3-0	3-2	1-2	1-2	4-1	3-1	3-1	2-2	5-1	2-0	4-2	2-2	4-2	

Senior Division A	P	W	D	L	F	A	Pts
Lakenheath	28	22	3	3	90	40	69
Fulbourn Institute	28	16	6	6	63	39	54
Whittlesford United	28	16	5	7	74	42	53
West Wratting	28	13	5	10	60	55	44
Foxton	28	11	8	9	59	53	41
Soham Town Rangers Res.	28	11	6	11	70	66	39
Girton United	28	11	6	11	53	50	39
Debden	28	9	11	8	46	47	38
Mildenhall Town Res.	28	11	4	13	60	53	37
Comberton United	28	9	10	9	57	55	37
Hemingfords United	28	8	10	10	37	46	34
Somersham Town	28	8	6	14	50	66	30
Brampton	28	8	5	15	53	76	29
Hardwick	28	6	6	16	49	71	24
Linton Granta	28	4	3	21	40	102	15

WILLIAM COCKELL CUP

FIRST ROUND

Comberton United 6 Whittlesford United 4

Debden 2 Hemingfords United 1

Foxton 2 Hardwick 1

Girton United 4 Linton Granta 1

Lakenheath 6 Mildenhall Town Res. 5

Soham Town Rangers Res. 2 **Brampton** 3

West Wratting 1 **Fulbourn Institute** 2

QUARTER-FINALS

Debden 3 Comerton United 2

Fulbourn Institute 1 **Brampton** 3

Girton United 0 **Foxton** 0 *aet* (3-4p)

Somersham Town 1 **Lakenheath** 2

SEMI-FINALS

Brampton 0 **Debden** 1

Foxton 1 **Lakenheath** 5

FINAL

(May 5th at Histon)

Lakenheath 2 Debden 1

	Bluntisham Rangers	Castle Camps	Cherry Hinton	Grampian	Great Chesterford	Haddenham Rovers	Helions Bumpstead	Huntingdon United RGE	Littleport Town Res.	Milton	Outwell Swifts	Saffron Crocus	Soham United	Swavesey Institute	West Row Gunners	Willingham
Bluntisham Rangers		0-3	2-4	2-1	1-1	3-1	0-5	3-1	0-0	1-1	0-3	0-5	2-2	0-0	5-0	3-2
Castle Camps	4-0		1-1	6-0	4-2	3-1	2-5	2-3	7-1	2-1	6-2	2-0	3-1	7-1	0-0	5-0
Cherry Hinton	1-0	3-0	S	6-0	2-1	7-1	1-0	2-1	6-1	2-2	0-1	3-3	7-0	3-0	2-0	4-1
Grampian	0-1	0-3	0-2	E	1-2	2-4	1-2	0-1	3-3	3-3	3-3	1-5	4-2	0-0	3-6	3-3
Great Chesterford	4-1	1-2	1-1	4-6	N	2-4	1-3	3-1	3-1	0-0	3-2	0-4	3-3	1-0	3-1	9-0
Haddenham Rovers	0-2	1-3	1-2	3-0	1-1	I	1-5	n/a	4-1	4-1	3-2	0-2	1-4	8-3	4-1	2-2
Helions Bumpstead	3-1	3-1	1-2	3-1	1-1	5-0	O	n/a	1-0	8-5	1-2	1-1	1-1	2-1	4-3	4-0
Huntingdon United RGE	2-2	0-3	n/a	n/a	n/a	n/a	n/a	R	1-4	2-1	3-4	4-2	2-3	3-6	1-3	4-1
Littleport Town Res.	1-0	1-5	0-1	2-2	3-7	2-3	3-4	1-5		3-4	1-2	1-2	2-8	0-3	0-0	6-0
Milton	2-0	3-0	1-2	2-2	3-2	0-1	3-5	1-0	7-2	D	0-3	4-0	0-5	7-3	2-2	4-0
Outwell Swifts	4-0	1-0	0-0	12-0	5-2	2-1	2-0	n/a	1-3	5-2	I	0-0	3-2	3-3	0-0	2-0
Saffron Crocus	3-1	1-2	1-3	5-1	2-2	5-3	2-1	n/a	7-0	3-2	3-5	V	1-0	5-0	0-1	3-0
Soham United	1-0	0-5	1-3	2-1	3-2	2-0	4-2	1-4	2-2	0-3	0-1	1-3		3-0	0-4	3-0
Swavesey Institute	2-0	1-1	0-6	4-2	0-5	3-3	1-8	7-1	1-3	1-1	0-1	2-3	5-0	B	2-3	4-2
West Row Gunners	0-1	0-1	3-1	4-2	4-0	3-1	2-2	n/a	5-2	3-6	1-0	0-1	3-5	2-1		6-0
Willingham	1-4	1-4	0-7	1-4	0-3	1-3	1-4	n/a	0-3	0-2	2-2	1-10	1-4	1-4	0-5	

Note – Huntingdon United RGE withdrew during the course of the season
Their results are shown above but are expunged from the league table

Senior Division B		P	W	D	L	F	A	Pts
Cherry Hinton		28	21	5	2	82	22	68
Castle Camps		28	20	3	5	82	31	63
Saffron Crocus		28	18	4	6	81	37	58
Helions Bumpstead		28	18	4	6	84	43	58
Outwell Swifts		28	17	6	5	69	36	57
West Row Gunners		28	13	5	10	62	44	44
Milton		28	11	7	10	71	62	40
Soham United		28	12	4	12	59	62	40
Great Chesterford		28	10	7	11	66	58	37
Haddenham Rovers		28	11	3	14	59	69	36
Bluntisham Rangers		28	8	5	15	30	54	29
Swavesey Institute		28	5	6	17	41	81	21
Littleport Town Res.		28	5	5	18	47	88	20
Grampian	-3	28	3	7	18	46	95	13
Willingham		28	1	3	24	21	114	6

Huntingdon United RGE – record expunged

PERCY OLDHAM CUP

FIRST ROUND

Cherry Hinton 6 Castle Camps 4 *aet*
Grampian 0 **West Row Gunners** 5
Great Chesterford 1 Saffron Crocus 0
Haddenham Rovers 3 Littleport Town Res. 2
Milton (w/o) v Swavesey Institute (scr.)
Outwell Swifts 3 Bluntisham Rangers 1
Soham United 5 Huntingdon United RGE 3
Willingham 2 **Helions Bumpstead** 7

QUARTER-FINALS

Helions Bumpstead 3 Haddenham Rovers 2
Outwell Swifts 2 Cherry Hinton 1
Soham United 2 **Great Chesterford** 5
West Row Gunners 3 Milton 0

SEMI-FINALS

Great Chesterford 1 **West Row Gunners** 2
Outwell Swifts 0 **Helions Bumpstead** 3

FINAL

(May 7th at Newmarket Town)
Helions Bumpstead 1 **West Row Gunners** 3

CAMBRIDGESHIRE COUNTY LEAGUE KERSHAW SENIOR DIVISION B CONSTITUTION 2008-09

BLUNTISHAM RANGERS . . . . Mill Lane, Bluntisham, Huntingdon PE28 3LR . . . . None
CHATTERIS TOWN . . . . West Street, Chatteris PE16 6HW 01354 692139
COTTENHAM UNITED RESERVES . . . . King George V Playing Field, Lamb Lane, Cottenham, Cambridge CB4 8TB 01954 250873
GREAT CHESTERFORD . . . . Great Chesterford Rec Ground, Newmarket Road, Great Chesterford CB10 1NS . . . . None
HADDENHAM ROVERS . . . . Hop Row, Haddenham, Ely CB6 3SR . . . . None
HELIONS BUMPSTEAD . . . The New Shed Recreation Ground, Church Hill Road, Helions Bumpstead CB9 7AJ . . . . None
LINTON GRANTA . . . . Recreation Ground, Meadow Lane, Linton, Cambridge CB1 6HX . . . . None
LITTLEPORT TOWN RESERVES . . . . . . Sports Centre, Camel Road, Littleport, Ely CB6 1PU 01353 860600
MARCH TOWN UNITED RESERVES . . . . GER Sports Ground, Robin Goodfellow Lane, March PE15 8HS 01354 653073
MILTON . . . . Milton Recreation Ground, The Sycamores, Milton, Cambridge CB4 6ZN . . . . None
OUTWELL SWIFTS . . . . The Nest, Wisbech Road, Outwell PE14 8PE . . . . None
RHS UNITED . . . . Royston Heath Sports Field, Baldock Road, Royston SG8 5BG . . . . None
SAFFRON CROCUS . . . . Ickleton Recreation Ground, Frogge Street, Ickleton CB10 1NS . . . . None
SAWSTON UNITED . . . . Spicers Sports Ground, New Road, Sawston CB2 4BW . . . . None
SOHAM UNITED . . . . Qua Fen Common, Soham, Ely CB7 5DH . . . . None
SWAVESEY INSTITUTE . . . . The Green, High Street, Swavesey CB4 5QU . . . . None
WEST ROW GUNNERS . . . . Chapel Row, West Row, Bury St Edmunds IP28 8PA . . . . None
IN: *Chatteris Town (P – Peterborough & District League Division One), Cottenham United Reserves (P – Division One B), Linton Granta (R),*
March Town United Reserves (P – Division One B), RHS United (formerly JM Sports) (P – Division One A), Sawston United (P – Division One A)
OUT: *Castle Camps (P), Cherry Hinton (P), Grampian (R – Division One A), Huntingdon United RGE (WS), Willingham (R – Division One B)*

WWW.CHERRYRED.CO.UK

Division One A

Team	P	W	D	L	F	A	Pts
Sawston United	28	19	6	3	93	38	63
J M Sports	28	19	3	6	76	35	60
Duxford United	28	17	6	5	62	36	57
West Wratting Res.	28	13	3	12	58	47	42
Litlington Athletic	28	13	3	12	57	50	42
Steeple Bumpstead	28	13	3	12	63	64	42
Fulbourn Institute Res.	28	13	1	14	48	63	40
Fowlmere	28	11	6	11	58	56	39
Cambourne Rovers	28	10	8	10	58	44	38
Girton United Res.	28	12	2	14	47	59	38
Barrington	28	11	2	15	57	66	35
Camden United	28	10	4	14	65	80	34
Sawston Rovers	28	9	4	15	54	77	31
Comberton United Res.	28	7	3	18	51	77	24
Great Shelford Res.	28	6	0	22	43	98	18

Division One B

Team	P	W	D	L	F	A	Pts
March Town United Res.	26	21	2	3	76	28	65
Cottenham United Res.	26	18	5	3	91	27	59
Ely City 'A'	26	18	4	4	93	40	58
Eaton Socon Res.	26	12	5	9	57	52	41
Fenstanton	26	11	3	12	66	62	36
Longstanton	26	10	5	11	53	51	35
Wisbech St Mary	26	9	6	11	44	46	33
Buckden	26	9	5	12	57	63	32
Barton Mills	26	9	4	13	41	67	31
Bottisham Sports	26	8	5	13	44	61	29
Gransden Chequers	26	8	4	14	39	63	28
St Ives Rangers	26	7	4	15	43	75	25
Waterbeach Res.	26	6	5	15	49	65	23
Great Paxton Res.	26	7	1	18	40	93	22

DIVISION ONE CHAMPIONSHIP PLAY-OFF *(May 14th at Sawston United)* Sawston United 1 **March Town United Res. 5**

Division Two A

Team	P	W	D	L	F	A	Pts
Cambridge Univ. Press Res.	26	23	3	0	94	12	72
Gamlingay United	26	20	2	4	108	28	62
Thaxted Rangers	26	18	0	8	85	58	54
Elsworth Sports	26	15	5	6	85	44	50
Balsham	26	11	6	9	79	58	39
Melbourn	26	12	3	11	66	54	39
Papworth	26	10	5	11	50	67	35
Wilbraham	26	10	4	12	66	56	34
Whittlesford United Res.	26	10	4	12	54	52	34
Great Chishill	26	8	3	15	38	63	27
Hardwick Res.	26	7	5	14	38	64	26
Linton Granta Res.	26	8	2	16	50	82	26
Mott MacDonald	26	6	3	17	42	92	21
Camden United Res. -6	26	1	1	24	20	145	-2

Division Two B

Team	P	W	D	L	F	A	Pts
Wisbech St Mary Res.	28	21	2	5	123	41	65
Newmarket White Lion	28	20	1	7	99	37	61
Hemingfords United Res.	28	19	2	7	71	42	59
Sutton United	28	19	1	8	108	44	58
Witchford	28	18	0	10	81	69	54
Somersham Town Res.	28	14	3	11	63	57	45
Pymoor	28	14	1	13	78	92	43
Over Sports Res.	28	12	4	12	59	51	40
Needingworth United Res.	28	11	2	15	57	74	35
Stretham Hotspurs	28	11	2	15	62	82	35
Godmanchester Rvrs Res.	28	9	4	15	54	74	31
Milton Res.	28	9	2	17	44	87	29
The Vine	28	8	3	17	55	69	27
Isleham United	28	5	4	19	37	88	19
Lode	28	3	3	22	35	119	12

DIVISION TWO CHAMPIONSHIP PLAY-OFF *(May 15th at CUP)* Cambridge University Press Res 3 Wisbech St Mary Res. 6
CREAKE CHARITY SHIELD FINAL *(May 6th at Histon)* Cottenham United Res. 3 Newmarket White Lion 5

Division Three A

Team	P	W	D	L	F	A	Pts
Cambridge Univ. Press 'A'	26	19	2	5	86	36	59
Fulbourn Sports & Social Club	26	18	2	6	91	38	56
Bassingbourn	26	16	3	7	62	32	51
J M Sports Res.	26	16	3	7	78	59	51
Dullingham	26	15	5	6	121	61	50
Steeple Morden	26	13	3	10	73	56	42
Great Chesterford Res.	26	12	5	9	76	68	41
Foxton Res.	26	11	2	13	51	76	35
Abington United	26	10	3	13	72	72	33
Ashdon Villa	26	9	3	14	60	73	30
Harston	26	7	3	16	35	79	24
Eaton Socon 'A'	26	7	2	17	61	98	23
Litlington Athletic Res.	26	6	2	18	44	78	20
Hempstead United	26	4	0	22	48	132	12

Division Three B

Team	P	W	D	L	F	A	Pts
March Rangers	28	24	2	2	109	36	74
Lakenheath Res.	28	21	2	5	95	44	65
Newmarket Town 'A'	28	17	2	9	82	43	53
Mepal Sports	28	15	6	7	68	37	51
Little Downham Swifts	28	14	6	8	74	55	48
Ely Crusaders	28	15	2	11	61	59	47
Wisbech St Mary 'A'	28	13	5	10	51	54	44
Brampton Res.	28	12	3	13	55	62	39
St Ives Town 'A'	28	10	3	15	58	62	33
Cottenham United 'A'	28	9	5	14	57	86	32
Huntingdon Utd RGE Res.	28	7	4	15	60	75	31
Fordham Res.	28	7	5	16	48	81	26
Soham United Res.	28	8	2	18	51	86	26
Bluntisham Rangers Res.	28	4	7	17	61	82	25
Haddenham Rvrs Res. -6	28	3	1	24	32	100	4

DIVISION THREE CHAMPIONSHIP PLAY-OFF *(May 13th at CUP)* Cambridge University Press 'A' 0 **March Rangers 3**
JOHN ABLETT CUP *(May 8th at Histon)* **Lakenheath Res. 2** Burwell Swifts 0

Division Four A

Team	P	W	D	L	F	A	Pts
Hundon Res.	28	23	2	3	110	52	71
Great Shelford 'A'	28	21	3	4	92	49	66
Sawston United Res.	28	20	2	6	91	50	62
Duxford United Res.	28	19	3	6	76	48	60
City Life	28	16	4	8	73	35	52
Barton	28	13	5	10	94	83	44
Steeple Bumpstead Res.	28	13	4	11	61	48	43
Dalehead United	28	11	7	10	53	44	40
Orwell	28	9	4	15	60	83	31
Saffron Crocus Res.	28	9	3	16	53	67	30
Saffron Rangers	28	8	5	15	49	77	29
Sawston Rovers Res.	28	9	1	18	52	73	28
Figleaves	28	8	4	16	55	79	28
Hardwick 'A'	28	3	2	23	41	111	11
Linton Granta 'A' -3	28	3	1	24	40	101	7

Division Four B

Team	P	W	D	L	F	A	Pts
Burwell Swifts	22	17	2	3	81	32	53
Hemingfords United 'A'	22	14	5	3	71	49	47
Milton 'A'	22	14	3	5	47	28	45
Fenstanton Res.	22	12	6	4	49	36	42
Wicken Amateurs	22	11	6	5	55	34	39
Exning Athletic	22	11	4	7	52	47	37
West Row Gunners Res. -3	22	10	0	12	42	44	27
Outwell Swifts Res.	22	5	5	12	38	56	20
The Vine Res.	22	5	4	13	36	61	19
Cottenham United 'B'	22	5	1	16	29	68	16
Barton Mills Res.	22	4	2	16	26	52	14
Swavesey Institute Res. -6	22	4	2	16	24	43	8

DIVISION FOUR CHAMPIONSHIP PLAY-OFF *(May 13th at Hundon)* **Hundon Res. 3** Burwell Swifts 2

Division Five A

Team	P	W	D	L	F	A	Pts
Fulbourn Institute 'A'	28	25	2	1	138	37	77
Cambridge Community Church	28	22	4	2	100	44	70
Hundon 'A'	28	16	5	7	82	49	53
Fowlmere Res.	28	13	7	8	95	69	46
Gransden Chequers Res.	28	14	3	11	76	67	45
Ambassadors	28	12	8	8	80	62	44
Melbourn Res.	28	12	4	12	70	105	40
Haslingfield	28	11	6	11	61	59	39
Barrington Res.	28	12	3	13	62	63	39
Great Chishill Res.	28	9	5	14	59	76	32
Comberton United 'A'	28	10	2	16	49	74	32
Steeple Morden Res.	28	9	4	15	61	67	31
Bottisham Sports Res.	28	7	5	16	51	79	26
Newport Veterans	28	5	2	21	44	116	17
Lode Res. -9	28	2	2	24	39	100	-1

Division Five B

Team	P	W	D	L	F	A	Pts
Estover Park	26	22	2	2	79	18	68
Earith United	26	20	4	2	144	43	64
Tydd United	26	16	6	4	110	56	54
Wisbech Fen Stars	26	16	2	8	103	51	50
Burwell Swifts Res.	26	14	3	9	74	65	45
Longstanton Res.	26	14	2	10	83	67	44
Supercue	26	12	6	8	81	76	42
Little Downham Swifts Res.	26	12	3	11	79	77	39
Walsoken United	26	8	5	13	72	97	29
Coldham United	26	8	3	15	52	103	21
Dataracks Elite -6	26	6	4	16	56	79	16
March Rangers Res.	26	4	4	18	37	98	16
Upwell Athletic	26	5	1	20	59	121	16
Wisbech St Mary 'B'	26	3	3	20	46	124	12

DIVISION FIVE CHAMPIONSHIP PLAY-OFF *(May 13th at Fulbourn)* Fulbourn Institute 'A' 0 **Estover Park 2**
REG HAIGH/ALEX PECK CUP *(May 9th at Histon)* Earith United 0 **Longstanton Res. 1**

CENTRAL MIDLANDS LEAGUE

	Appleby Frodingham	Askern Welfare	Bentley Colliery	Blackwell Miners Welfare	Clipstone Welfare	Dunkirk	Forest Town	Gedling Miners Welfare	Graham Street Prims	Greenwood Meadows	Grimsby Borough	Hatfield Main	Heanor Town	Holbrook Miners Welfare	Nettleham	Pinxton	Radcliffe Olympic	Radford	Rolls Royce Leisure	Southwell City
Appleby Frodingham		2-1	2-3	2-1	0-1	2-2	1-6	0-4	1-2	5-0	1-0	3-1	1-5	0-3	4-1	1-3	1-2	1-2	5-0	0-3
Askern Welfare	4-0		2-0	3-0	7-0	2-1	3-4	1-1	2-0	2-0	4-1	1-0	1-0	0-0	2-0	2-0	1-0	1-0	2-0	3-0
Bentley Colliery	1-1	0-5	S	3-2	10-1	2-1	2-1	1-2	4-2	2-2	2-1	2-0	4-3	1-4	6-0	6-1	1-4	2-1	1-1	1-0
Blackwell Miners Welfare	2-2	1-5	3-3	U	2-2	0-2	1-1	0-1	5-1	3-1	0-2	1-1	4-2	3-2	1-3	0-0	1-2	4-4	2-5	0-2
Clipstone Welfare	5-1	1-3	5-0	2-2	P	0-4	0-1	0-2	2-4	2-2	2-4	1-3	1-5	2-2	2-4	0-0	1-2	1-5	3-1	0-3
Dunkirk	4-1	2-3	5-0	2-1	2-1	R	0-3	2-2	1-0	4-0	2-1	2-1	2-2	3-1	7-2	6-3	0-3	4-2	3-0	3-1
Forest Town	5-1	4-0	2-0	7-0	5-0	0-1	E	1-1	7-2	2-1	0-1	4-0	0-1	0-2	3-0	1-0	1-0	4-1	5-1	0-0
Gedling Miners Welfare	4-0	0-2	1-3	4-2	4-0	0-5	3-4	M	4-1	5-0	2-2	1-2	2-2	3-1	1-3	0-0	0-1	0-0	4-0	1-1
Graham Street Prims	2-4	0-8	0-5	2-0	3-2	3-2	2-6	1-1	E	3-2	0-4	4-0	1-2	3-4	2-1	0-2	4-2	4-6	1-3	
Greenwood Meadows	2-2	3-6	1-1	2-5	0-3	2-0	2-4	2-4	2-2		2-1	2-2	2-2	3-6	3-3	3-1	0-0	1-2	4-3	0-1
Grimsby Borough	1-1	0-3	7-0	3-3	6-4	3-0	0-0	1-0	1-2	6-0	D	0-3	1-1	4-4	3-1	1-5	1-2	0-0	4-1	0-2
Hatfield Main	3-0	0-3	2-2	0-0	6-1	2-1	0-0	1-2	4-0	0-0	2-1	I	0-0	1-2	2-0	5-0	0-1	1-4	3-2	3-3
Heanor Town	4-3	1-2	5-1	0-2	2-1	1-0	1-2	1-2	1-3	3-0	6-4	1-0	V	1-3	1-2	2-0	0-2	2-0	2-0	3-3
Holbrook Miners Welfare	3-1	1-2	2-1	6-2	2-2	1-0	1-2	0-0	3-0	3-3	3-2	2-4	2-0	I	1-0	2-0	1-1	1-2	1-1	3-2
Nettleham	3-5	1-2	2-6	2-1	2-3	0-2	1-5	3-3	3-1	4-0	3-2	0-3	0-0	2-3	S	1-1	1-4	1-3	0-1	0-3
Pinxton	8-1	0-3	3-3	4-2	5-0	1-3	0-7	1-3	6-3	0-2	3-5	1-1	1-1	1-1	3-1	I	2-0	1-2	1-2	0-1
Radcliffe Olympic	3-0	0-0	1-0	6-2	6-0	2-3	2-0	1-3	4-1	6-1	0-0	1-0	2-1	3-1	6-3	5-2	O	5-0	3-2	5-0
Radford	3-1	1-2	4-0	4-0	1-0	0-1	0-1	0-1	1-2	5-3	3-1	0-1	1-1	0-3	0-0	4-3	1-0	N	4-0	1-0
Rolls Royce Leisure	2-3	0-4	3-3	0-3	5-4	0-5	0-2	1-0	1-0	0-0	3-1	1-5	2-0	1-3	2-4	4-0	1-3	0-1		1-2
Southwell City	4-2	1-3	2-1	0-2	0-4	3-1	1-5	2-4	4-2	1-1	1-3	3-1	0-0	3-2	5-1	2-2	4-1	1-2		

WWW.NLNEWSDESK.CO.UK

Supreme Division		P	W	D	L	F	A	Pts
Askern Welfare	-3	38	32	3	3	100	25	96
Forest Town		38	27	5	6	105	32	86
Radcliffe Olympic		38	27	5	6	92	33	86
Dunkirk		38	23	3	12	88	51	72
Holbrook Miners Welfare		38	20	10	8	81	54	70
Gedling Miners Welfare		38	19	10	9	75	46	67
Southwell City		38	18	7	13	69	63	61
Radford		38	18	5	15	65	57	59
Bentley Colliery		38	16	8	14	83	84	56
Hatfield Main	-3	38	15	9	14	63	52	51
Heanor Town		38	14	9	15	66	59	51
Grimsby Borough		38	13	7	18	76	71	46
Graham Street Prims		38	12	3	23	65	112	39
Pinxton		38	10	7	21	64	90	37
Blackwell Miners Welfare		38	9	9	20	66	92	36
Nettleham		38	10	5	23	62	101	35
Appleby Frodingham		38	10	5	23	61	103	35
Rolls Royce Leisure		38	9	5	24	54	97	32
Greenwood Meadows		38	5	13	20	54	104	28
Clipstone Welfare		38	7	4	27	57	120	25

Reserve Premier Division		P	W	D	L	F	A	Pts
Arnold Town Res.		26	20	3	3	103	27	63
Forest Town Res.		26	17	2	7	81	39	53
Holbrook Miners Welfare Res.		26	14	6	6	50	33	48
Radcliffe Olympic Res.		26	14	5	7	56	45	47
Dunkirk Res.		26	12	6	8	61	47	42
Calverton Miners Welfare Res.	-6	26	14	6	6	45	35	42
Rainworth Miners Welfare Res.		26	10	5	11	54	44	35
Southwell City Res.		26	11	2	13	51	64	35
Blidworth Welfare Res.		26	10	3	13	48	61	33
Radford Res.		26	8	4	14	40	54	28
Welbeck Welfare Res.	-3	26	8	6	12	45	59	27
Heanor Town Res.		26	6	5	15	48	93	23
Clipstone Welfare Res.		26	6	3	17	30	67	21
Blackwell Miners Welfare Res.		26	2	4	20	37	81	10

ABACUS LIGHTING CENTRAL MIDLANDS LEAGUE SUPREME DIVISION CONSTITUTION 2008-09

BLIDWORTH WELFARE ... Blidworth Recreation Centre, Mansfield Road, Blidworth, Mansfield NG21 0LR 01623 793361
CALVERTON MINERS WELFARE ... Calverton Miners Welfare, Hollinwood Lane, Calverton NG14 6NR 0115 965 4390
CLIPSTONE WELFARE.......... Lido Ground, Clipstone Road East, Clipstone, Mansfield NG21 9AZ 01623 477978
FOREST TOWN .... Forest Town Academy, Clipstone Rd West, Forest Town, Mansfield NG19 0EE............... 01623 624678
HARROWBY UNITED .... Dickens Road, Grantham NG31 9QY 01476 590822
HARWORTH COLLIERY INSTITUTE ... Recreation Ground, Scrooby Road, Bircotes, Doncaster DN11 8JT ... 01302 750614
HATFIELD MAIN............... Dunscroft Welfare Ground, Broadway, Dunscroft, Doncaster DN7 4HD 01302 841326
KIMBERLEY TOWN .... The Stag Ground, Nottingham Road, Kimberley NG16 2ND 0115 938 2788
KINSLEY BOYS .... Kinsley Playing Fields, Wakefield Road, Kinsley WF9 5EH 07883 373232
NETTLEHAM .... Mulsanne Park, Field Close, Nettleham, Lincoln LN2 2RX.......................... 01522 750007
NEWARK TOWN................... Collingham FC, Station Road, Collingham NG23 7RA 01636 892303
OLLERTON TOWN.................... The Lane, Walesby Lane, New Ollerton, Newark NG22 9UX....................... None
PINXTON.................... Welfare Ground, Wharf Road, Pinxton NG16 6NY............................... 07989 324249
RADCLIFFE OLYMPIC ..... Recreational Ground,Wharf Lane, Radcliffe-on-Trent, Nottingham NG12 2AN.......... 0115 963 2380
ROLLS ROYCE LEISURE .... Rolls Royce Sports & Social, Watnall Road, Hucknall NG15 6EU 0115 963 2380
SOUTHWELL CITY........... War Memorial Recreation Ground, Bishops Drive, Southwell NG25 0JP.................. 01636 814386
SUTTON TOWN .... The Fieldings, Huthwaite Road, Sutton-in-Ashfield NG17 2HB.......................... 01623 552376
YORKSHIRE MAIN................. Edlington Lane, Edlington, Doncaster DN12 1DA 07775 714558

IN: *Blidworth Welfare (P), Calverton Miners Welfare (P), Harrowby United (P – Lincolnshire League), Harworth Colliery Institute (P), Kimberley Town (P), Kinsley Boys (P), Newark Town (P), Ollerton Town (P), Sutton Town (P), Yorkshire Main (P)*
OUT: *Appleby Frodingham (P – Northern Counties East League Division One), Askern Welfare (P – Northern Counties East League Division One), Bentley Colliery (P – East Midlands Counties League), Blackwell Miners Welfare (P – East Midlands Counties League), Dunkirk (P – East Midlands Counties League), Gedling Miners Welfare (P – East Midlands Counties League), Graham Street Prims (P – East Midlands Counties League), Greenwood Meadows (P – East Midlands Counties League), Grimsby Borough (P – Northern Counties East League Division One), Heanor Town (P – East Midlands Counties League), Holbrook Miners Welfare (P – East Midlands Counties League), Radford (P – East Midlands Counties League)*

	Armthorpe	Blidworth Welfare	Bolsover Town	Calverton Miners Welfare	Harworth Colliery Institute	Kimberley Town	Kinsley Boys	Kiveton Park	Louth Town	Newark Flowserve	Newark Town	Ollerton Town	Parkhouse	Phoenix Sports & Social	Stanton Ilkeston	Sutton Town	Thoresby Colliery Welfare	Thorne Colliery	Welbeck Welfare	Yorkshire Main
Armthorpe		2-1	2-3	1-6	0-2	0-0	0-1	1-5	0-0	1-2	2-2	0-2	3-3	2-1	1-5	0-3	2-0	2-3	1-4	0-3
Blidworth Welfare	4-2		0-1	1-5	3-4	3-1	1-3	0-2	4-0	1-0	2-0	0-1	4-3	5-1	4-0	1-3	1-3	3-0	5-2	2-0
Bolsover Town	3-1	3-0	*P*	1-3	0-0	8-0	2-0	2-0	2-0	2-0	1-2	0-1	3-2	3-2	4-1	0-3	5-2	3-2	2-3	
Calverton Miners Welfare	5-2	4-0	4-0	*R*	4-0	4-0	3-0	1-0	4-1	0-0	1-0	3-3	3-0	1-2	4-3	2-1	4-0	9-0	2-0	1-2
Harworth Colliery Institute	0-1	1-3	1-2	2-0	*E*	0-1	1-0	0-4	0-1	1-0	2-2	2-3	0-0	3-3	3-0	1-4	1-2	2-1	1-0	1-1
Kimberley Town	2-0	3-1	2-2	0-1	4-0	*M*	2-1	0-2	5-3	4-1	0-1	0-1	1-1	1-0	0-2	5-2	0-3	7-0	1-2	3-1
Kinsley Boys	6-4	1-1	0-1	2-1	6-1	4-3	*I*	0-2	1-1	3-2	3-2	0-0	1-2	2-1	1-1	2-2	1-1	5-2	2-2	4-0
Kiveton Park	1-1	1-3	2-0	0-1	1-1	1-1	2-1	*E*	3-5	0-2	2-2	2-3	0-1	1-0	0-0	2-0	1-1	4-0	4-2	1-1
Louth Town	6-0	2-2	2-0	2-2	2-1	1-2	0-1	2-2	*R*	1-0	3-1	0-3	1-1	7-2	4-1	3-2	1-0	5-1	1-3	3-1
Newark Flowserve	1-0	2-3	1-1	0-4	2-0	5-0	1-3	4-2	2-1		1-3	1-1	0-1	3-1	3-1	1-4	3-3	0-1	1-2	2-0
Newark Town	5-2	1-1	0-0	1-1	1-0	1-3	1-0	2-4	2-1	0-1	*D*	0-2	1-1	5-0	3-0	0-3	0-2	3-0	6-2	0-2
Ollerton Town	4-0	1-0	2-2	0-0	0-1	2-0	1-0	2-0	2-0	2-0	1-0	*I*	4-2	3-2	0-3	3-2	1-2	6-0	4-0	1-5
Parkhouse	1-0	2-0	1-1	1-2	2-0	5-5	1-1	1-3	4-1	5-0	0-2	1-3	*V*	1-3	3-5	2-2	0-1	2-2	2-3	2-0
Phoenix Sports & Social	2-1	4-2	0-5	1-2	2-0	4-1	1-0	0-6	0-3	1-0	2-0	0-6	0-3	*I*	3-1	1-3	0-3	4-0	2-4	0-3
Stanton Ilkeston	1-3	2-3	0-4	0-8	3-1	6-0	0-4	3-1	4-0	2-4	2-0	0-3	0-6	2-3	*S*	1-3	0-3	1-2	2-3	1-3
Sutton Town	6-0	1-0	3-1	5-4	2-1	1-0	4-2	1-2	6-2	7-0	1-1	0-2	1-3	0-2	W-L	*I*	7-0	5-0	3-2	2-4
Thoresby Colliery Welfare	4-2	2-0	1-0	2-0	1-2	1-4	2-1	1-4	3-0	0-1	2-1	0-1	1-2	2-2	2-3	2-2	*O*	1-1	3-2	1-3
Thorne Colliery	1-2	1-6	3-2	1-0	1-1	1-3	1-2	0-4	1-3	1-1	2-0	2-5	0-2	0-1	4-1	0-8	0-1	*N*	3-1	1-6
Welbeck Welfare	3-2	1-1	2-3	1-4	3-2	3-4	2-4	1-2	3-1	1-1	4-7	0-2	5-5	7-2	5-1	0-2	4-4	4-2		8-2
Yorkshire Main	2-1	6-2	0-0	5-4	1-1	3-0	3-0	1-0	2-2	2-0	5-1	2-1	1-1	3-3	1-0	2-2	1-3	3-1	4-0	

Premier Division

	P	W	D	L	F	A	Pts
Ollerton Town	38	26	7	5	82	36	85
Calverton Miners Welfare	38	24	5	9	107	42	77
Yorkshire Main	38	23	8	7	88	55	77
Sutton Town	38	22	5	11	102	57	71
Kiveton Park	38	20	7	11	83	46	67
Bolsover Town	38	20	7	11	75	50	67
Kinsley Boys	38	17	9	12	70	56	60
Thoresby Colliery Welfare -1	38	18	7	13	66	60	60
Parkhouse	38	14	12	12	75	63	54
Louth Town	38	15	8	15	74	74	53
Kimberley Town	38	16	5	17	68	77	53
Blidworth Welfare	38	16	4	18	73	71	52
Newark Town	38	13	9	16	61	62	48
Newark Flowserve	38	13	6	19	64	45	45
Welbeck Welfare	38	12	7	19	93	104	43
Phoenix Sports & Social	38	12	4	22	58	104	40
Harworth Colliery Institute	38	10	8	20	40	66	38
Stanton Ilkeston	38	10	3	25	59	97	33
Thorne Colliery -3	38	8	4	26	40	119	25
Armthorpe	38	6	5	27	44	103	23

Reserve Division One

		P	W	D	L	F	A	Pts
Carlton Town Res.	-1	16	15	0	1	100	13	44
Pinxton Res.		16	13	1	2	80	27	40
Teversal Res.		16	12	1	3	69	27	37
Nettleham Res.		16	6	2	8	56	52	20
Thoresby Colliery Welfare Res.		16	5	3	8	30	52	18
Ollerton Town Res.		16	6	0	10	25	52	18
Graham Street Prims Res.		16	5	2	9	26	45	17
Greenwood Meadows Res.		16	3	2	11	36	53	11
Kimberley Town Res.		16	1	1	14	14	115	4

RESERVES CUP FINAL

FINAL

(April 16th at Blidworth Welfare)

Pinxton Res. 1 **Carlton Town Res. 3**

ABACUS LIGHTING CENTRAL MIDLANDS LEAGUE PREMIER DIVISION CONSTITUTION 2008-09

BENTLEY COLLIERY............Bentley Miners Welfare, The Avenue, Bentley, Doncaster DN5 0NP....................01302 874420
BOLSOVER TOWN.......Bolsover Town Sports & Social Club, Moor Lane, Bolsover, Chesterfield S44 6EW.............01246 822449
BULWELL TOWN......Goosedale Sports Ground, Goosedale Lane, Bestwood Village, Nottingham NG15 8FG...........0115 963 0180
CHURCH WARSOP WELFARE...Church Warsop Miner Welfare, Wood Lane, Church Warsop, Mansfield NG20 0SR.......01623 842020
HUTTON CRANSWICK UNITED...Rotsea Lane, Hutton Cranswick, Driffield YO25 9QG.................................None
KIRKBY TOWN.................Summit Centre, Lowmoor Road, Kirkby-in-Ashfield NG17 7LL....................01623 751822
KIVETON PARK.................Kiveton Park MW, Hard Lane, Kiveton Park, Sheffield S26 6NB....................07763 467979
LOUTH TOWN.....................Park Avenue, Louth LN11 8BY...07712 653791
MABLETHORPE ATHLETIC.........Sherwood Field, Sherwood Road, Mablethorpe LN12 1HU..........................None
NEWARK FLOWSERVE........Lowfields Works, Hawton Lane, New Balderton, Newark NG24 3EH....................01636 494780
PARKHOUSE.......................Mill Lane Ground, Mill Lane, Clay Cross, Chesterfield.....................07816 758778
PARRAMORE SPORTS..........Davy Sports & Social Club, Prince of Wales Road, Sheffield S9 4ER...................None
PHOENIX SPORTS & SOCIAL.....Phoenix Sports Complex, Bawtry Road, Brinsworth, Rotherham S60 5PA.............01709 363864
THORESBY COLLIERY WELFARE.....Thoresby Colliery Sports Ground, Fourth Avenue, Edwinstowe NG21 9NS.........07802 417987
THORNE COLLIERY.........Moorends Welfare, Grange Road, Moorends, Thorne, Doncaster DN8 4LU.............07855 545221
WELBECK WELFARE............Colliery Ground, Elkesley Road, Meden Vale, Warsop, Mansfield NG20 9PS.......01623 842267
WESTELLA & WILLERBY.....Hill Top Club, Willerby Low Road, Cottingham HU16 5JD.......................01482 671306

IN: *Bentley Colliery (R), Bulwell Town (P – Notts Amateur Alliance Division Two), Church Warsop Welfare (P – youth football), Hutton Cranswick United Reserves (P – East Riding County League Division One), Kirkby Town (P – Sunday football), Mablethorpe Athletic (P – East Lincolnshire Combination League Division One), Parramore Sports (P – Sheffield & Hallamshire County Senior League Division One), Westella & Willerby Reserves (P – East Riding County League Division One)*
OUT: *Armthorpe (W), Blidworth Welfare (P), Calverton Miners Welfare (P), Harworth Colliery Institute (P), Kimberley Town (P), Kinsley Boys (P), Newark Town (P), Ollerton Town (P), Stanton Ilkeston (W), Sutton Town (P), Yorkshire Main (P)*

LEAGUE CUP

FIRST ROUND
Armthorpe 0 **Pinxton 2**
Calverton Miners Welfare 0 **Forest Town 2**
Dunkirk 3 Thoresby Colliery Welfare 0
Gedling Miners Welfare 5 Louth Town 1
Heanor Town 1 **Blidworth Welfare 2**
Nettleham 3 Bentley Colliery 2
Newark Town 0 **Radcliffe Olympic 3**
Stanton Ilkeston 2 **Thorne Colliery 3** *(at Radford)*

SECOND ROUND
Appleby Frodingham 2 Yorkshire Main 2
Replay: **Yorkshire Main 6** Appleby Frodingham 2
Blidworth Welfare 3 Newark Flowserve 0
Bolsover Town 0 **Ollerton Town 3**
Clipstone Welfare 1 **Grimsby Borough 9**
Greenwood Meadows 0 **Askern Welfare 3**
Holbrook Miners Welfare 1 Hatfield Main 0
Kinsley Boys 1 Kiveton Park 0
Nettleham 1 **Gedling Miners Welfare 2**
Parkhouse 1 **Sutton Town 5**
Phoenix Sports & Social 7 Kimberley Town 2
Pinxton 3 Graham Street Prims 2
Radcliffe Olympic 4 Rolls Royce Leisure 3
Radford 1 **Dunkirk 2**
Southwell City 6 Harworth Colliery Institute 0
Thorne Colliery 2 Forest Town 2
Replay: **Forest Town 8** Thorne Colliery 1
Welbeck Welfare 1 Blackwell Miners Welfare 1
Replay: **Blackwell Miners Welfare 1** Welbeck
Welfare 0

THIRD ROUND
Askern Welfare 4 Forest Town 0
Blackwell Miners Welfare 1 Dunkirk 1
Replay: **Dunkirk 2** Blackwell Miners Welfare 0
Gedling Miners Welfare 7 Phoenix Sports & Social 4
Grimsby Borough 2 Southwell City 0
Holbrook Miners Welfare 0 Ollerton Town 0
Replay: Ollerton Town 1 **Holbrook Miners Welfare 2**
Kinsley Boys 0 **Pinxton 1**
Sutton Town 1 Radcliffe Olympic 1
Replay: **Radcliffe Olympic 2** Sutton Town 1
Yorkshire Main 1 **Blidworth Welfare 3**

QUARTER-FINALS
Askern Welfare 0 **Blidworth Welfare 1**
Dunkirk 5 Grimsby Borough 1
Holbrook Miners Welfare 1 Pinxton 1
Replay: Pinxton 0 **Holbrook Miners Welfare 1**
Radcliffe Olympic 0 Gedling Miners Welfare 0
Replay: **Gedling Miners Welfare 1** Radcliffe Olympic 1
aet (5-4p)

SEMI-FINALS
Blidworth Welfare 2 Holbrook Miners Welfare 1
(at Heanor Town)
Dunkirk 1 Gedling Miners Welfare 0
(at Greenwood Meadows)

FINAL
(May 4th at Alfreton Town)
Blidworth Welfare 0 **Dunkirk 1**

FLOODLIGHT TROPHY

FIRST ROUND
Blackwell Miners Welfare 1 **Grimsby Borough 4**
Clipstone Welfare 1 **Gedling Miners Welfare 8**
Graham Street Prims 0 **Calverton Miners Welfare 2**
Greenwood Meadows 3 Radford 1
Harworth Colliery Institute 0 **Askern Welfare 4**
Holbrook Miners Welfare 1 Heanor Town 0
Nettleham 2 Armthorpe 1
Ollerton Town 2 Blidworth Welfare 1
Pinxton 4 Stanton Ilkeston 1
Southwell City 2 Hatfield Main 1
Sutton Town 5 Kimberley Town 1

SECOND ROUND
Appleby Frodingham 0 **Ollerton Town 5**
Calverton Miners Welfare 1 **Gedling Miners Welfare 2**
Dunkirk 3 **Radcliffe Olympic 5**
Grimsby Borough 3 Newark Town 0
Holbrook Miners Welfare 3 Greenwood Meadows 2
Nettleham 2 **Pinxton 3**
Rolls Royce Leisure 1 **Sutton Town 3**
Southwell City 2 Askern Welfare 1

QUARTER-FINALS
Grimsby Borough 2 **Ollerton Town 2** *aet* (4-5p)
Holbrook Miners Welfare 3 Radcliffe Olympic 2
Pinxton 2 **Southwell City 3** *aet*
Sutton Town 2 Gedling Miners Welfare 1

SEMI-FINALS
Ollerton Town 1 **Southwell City 2**
Sutton Town 2 **Holbrook Miners Welfare 3**

FINAL
(April 2nd at Radford)
Holbrook Miners Welfare 1 Southwell City 1 *aet* (3-1p)

CHESHIRE LEAGUE

	Barnton	Crosfields	Curzon Ashton Res.	Gamesley	Garswood United	Greenalls Padgate St Oswalds	Knutsford	Linotype & Cheadle HN	Middlewich Town	Pilkington	Poynton	Rylands	Stalybridge Celtic Res.	Styal	Trafford Res.	Witton Albion Res.	Woodley Sports Res.
Barnton		2-5	1-2	1-1	2-4	1-3	2-2	1-0	2-0	1-2	4-2	4-2	1-0	0-1	2-1	1-1	0-3
Crosfields	0-1		1-3	1-3	0-1	3-2	4-1	4-3	0-1	1-0	5-0	3-1	0-0	3-2	3-0	4-3	0-0
Curzon Ashton Res.	4-0	3-1	D	0-2	1-2	0-2	4-0	3-0	1-4	1-1	3-0	2-1	3-1	1-3	1-1	6-0	2-2
Gamesley	1-2	0-5	0-4	I	4-2	0-5	0-2	5-3	0-3	4-2	2-2	2-3	1-1	1-2	0-2	3-0	2-1
Garswood United	3-0	2-1	2-3	3-0	V	2-1	3-0	3-1	2-2	4-3	0-0	1-1	1-2	0-5	4-2	4-2	2-1
Greenalls Padgate St Oswalds	3-2	3-2	2-2	2-0	3-0	I	0-0	2-2	4-3	0-4	3-1	4-0	5-2	3-3	4-1	2-0	2-1
Knutsford	3-1	1-2	2-4	4-3	4-3	5-2	S	1-3	2-1	0-3	4-1	0-1	3-4	1-2	0-1	2-0	1-0
Linotype & Cheadle HN	1-1	2-2	3-3	0-1	1-4	0-2	2-1	I	2-2	1-2	9-2	2-1	0-3	0-2	4-3	0-3	2-0
Middlewich Town	1-2	3-2	1-1	6-2	6-2	0-0	4-0	2-0	O	5-0	3-0	7-0	5-1	1-1	3-1	8-1	2-1
Pilkington	3-2	2-2	3-3	4-3	3-1	6-0	1-1	1-0	0-2	N	3-1	3-1	2-3	4-1	2-1	3-1	3-2
Poynton	2-1	0-1	2-3	1-2	0-3	1-6	0-2	1-3	0-1	1-3		4-1	2-2	3-3	4-3	0-4	2-3
Rylands	2-2	0-5	0-3	0-4	1-2	0-3	1-4	2-3	1-3	0-4	3-1		0-3	0-6	2-2	3-4	1-1
Stalybridge Celtic Res.	4-0	1-3	0-4	3-0	3-6	3-2	3-1	4-2	3-3	1-2	1-0	4-0	O	3-1	6-2	1-1	4-0
Styal	4-1	1-1	2-1	4-1	2-1	1-0	2-1	1-0	1-0	4-3	6-3	2-1	1-1	N	4-0	0-1	4-1
Trafford Res.	0-3	2-3	3-6	3-1	0-1	1-2	1-2	2-1	1-3	0-3	0-2	5-0	2-2	3-3	E	2-2	0-1
Witton Albion Res.	3-2	1-2	2-0	3-1	1-3	0-2	1-2	2-4	2-3	4-0	2-2	1-0	2-2	1-2	7-3		2-0
Woodley Sports Res.	1-1	1-2	2-3	1-2	3-1	2-1	2-2	4-1	0-3	1-2	2-2	5-0	0-4	1-7	4-1	1-3	

Division One	P	W	D	L	F	A	Pts
Styal	32	22	6	4	83	41	72
Middlewich Town	32	21	6	5	91	35	69
Pilkington	32	20	4	8	77	52	64
Greenalls Padgate St Oswalds	32	19	5	8	75	48	62
Curzon Ashton Res.	32	18	7	7	80	46	61
Garswood United	32	19	3	10	72	58	60
Crosfields	32	18	5	9	71	45	59
Stalybridge Celtic Res.	32	16	8	8	75	55	56
Knutsford	32	13	4	15	54	61	43
Witton Albion Res.	32	12	5	15	60	68	41
Barnton	32	10	6	16	46	64	36
Gamesley	32	11	3	18	51	75	36
Linotype & Cheadle HN	32	9	6	17	56	70	33
Woodley Sports Res.	32	8	6	18	47	64	30
Trafford Res.	32	4	6	22	49	86	18
Poynton	32	4	6	22	42	91	18
Rylands	32	3	4	25	29	99	13

COOPER SMITH ANNUAL CHALLENGE MATCH

(November 7th at Trafford)
Cheshire League 2 **West Cheshire League** 4

CHESHIRE BUILDING SOCIETY CHESHIRE LEAGUE DIVISION ONE CONSTITUTION 2008-09

BARNTON......................Townfield, Townfield Lane, Barnton, Northwich CW8 4LH...............................None
BILLINGE....................John Eddleston Sports Ground, Rainford Road, Billinge WN5 7PF....................07742 418591
CLUB AZ.....................Mulberries Sports Centre, Astra Zeneca (off 34), Macclesfield SK10 4TF................01625 514040
CROSFIELDS-RYLANDS..........Rylands Recreation Club, Gorsey Lane, Warrington WA2 7RZ................01925 625700
CURZON ASHTON RESERVES...The Tameside Stadium, Richmond Street, Ashton-under-Lyne OL7 9HG...............0161 330 6033
GAMESLEY....................Melandra Park, Melandra Castle Road, Gamesley, Glossop SK13 6UQ....................None
GARSWOOD UNITED....The Wooders, Simms Lane End, Garswood Road, Garswood, Ashton-in-Makerfield WN4 0XF.....01744 892258
GREENALLS PADGATE ST OSWALDS...Carlsberg Tetley Club, Long Lane, Warrington WA2 8PU.................01925 634971
KNUTSFORD......................Manchester Road, Knutsford WA16 0NU...............................None
LINOTYPE & CHEADLE HN........The Heath, Norbreck Avenue, Cheadle, Stockport SK8 2ET 0161 282 6574
MIDDLEWICH TOWN ....Seddon Street, Middlewich CW10 9DT.....................01606 835842
PILKINGTON....................Ruskin Drive, Dentons Green, St Helens WA10 6RP 01744 22893
STALYBRIDGE CELTIC RESERVES.....Bower Fold, Mottram Road, Stalybridge SK15 2RT 0161 338 2828/8443
STYAL ....Altrincham Road, Styal, Wilmslow SK9 4JE 01625 529303
TRAFFORD RESERVES ....Shawe View, Pennybridge Lane, Flixton, Urmston M41 5DL...............0161 747 1727749 8217
WOODLEY SPORTS RESERVES........Ridgeway Road, Timperley, Altrincham WA15 7EY.....................0161 283 1376

IN: Billinge (P), Club AZ (P)
OUT: Poynton (R), Witton Albion Reserves (E)
Crosfields and Rylands have merged to form Crosfields-Rylands

	Billinge	Broadheath Central	Club AZ	Congleton Town Res.	Crewe	Daten	Eagle Sports	FC United of Manchester Res.	Golborne Sports	Grappenhall Sports	Lostock Gralam	Maine Road Res.	Malpas	Monk Sports	Tarporley Victoria	Warrington Town Res.	Whitchurch Alport
Billinge		1-0	2-1	2-0	2-2	1-1	1-0	1-1	2-0	0-0	4-0	0-2	3-5	2-0	2-1	0-1	0-0
Broadheath Central	5-3		1-7	3-2	3-3	4-2	2-1	0-3	0-3	1-2	0-2	3-1	7-1	6-2	3-3	4-1	1-6
Club AZ	3-1	1-2	D	2-1	6-5	4-0	3-2	1-2	2-2	6-1	4-0	2-1	0-2	4-0	2-2	3-0	3-1
Congleton Town Res.	0-2	1-3	1-2	I	1-1	0-2	4-1	1-3	3-2	1-1	4-0	0-6	0-1	0-1	2-3	1-0	0-2
Crewe	1-1	1-2	2-1	4-1	V	4-2	4-2	0-2	4-5	2-1	1-0	2-1	1-0	4-1	3-1	0-4	1-1
Daten	3-1	1-1	1-5	0-1	4-1	I	0-1	1-1	1-2	3-1	1-2	1-7	2-1	4-1	2-0	3-3	1-0
Eagle Sports	3-1	1-1	2-1	1-1	2-2	0-4	S	0-4	0-1	2-1	2-1	2-1	0-3	5-1	2-4	1-3	0-0
FC United of Manchester Res.	1-3	0-1	3-1	5-2	2-0	8-1	1-3	I	2-1	1-1	2-0	1-0	3-0	6-0	0-1	3-1	1-1
Golborne Sports	0-1	1-2	3-3	2-0	1-3	3-0	2-0	2-0	O	2-2	3-1	4-0	4-3	2-2	1-2	1-1	1-1
Grappenhall Sports	1-2	2-9	0-3	2-1	3-0	3-2	3-2	2-2	2-1	N	3-3	5-6	1-2	1-2	4-2	3-1	2-2
Lostock Gralam	1-1	4-1	0-2	0-4	1-1	2-1	3-3	1-3	4-8	3-2		2-2	3-0	4-2	1-3	0-2	1-3
Maine Road Res.	1-4	0-1	1-2	6-2	4-0	0-5	2-0	0-4	4-2	2-5	1-1		4-2	4-2	2-3	2-4	2-2
Malpas	3-5	0-1	0-2	1-5	1-2	2-2	4-2	0-8	1-2	1-3	3-0	3-1	T	4-2	1-2	1-0	0-0
Monk Sports	1-3	0-1	1-4	3-0	3-1	5-2	4-2	0-3	7-0	3-2	6-2	0-2	1-0	W	0-3	0-4	0-2
Tarporley Victoria	2-3	1-1	3-1	2-1	3-0	3-1	2-1	1-3	3-4	1-0	6-0	0-0	4-0	2-4	O	2-3	3-1
Warrington Town Res.	1-3	2-0	0-0	3-2	3-0	6-1	2-1	1-2	4-1	4-0	0-1	2-3	3-3	3-2	2-1		0-0
Whitchurch Alport	2-1	1-0	0-0	2-4	0-1	1-0	3-0	2-2	2-1	0-3	1-0	2-2	1-1	3-2	2-0	0-1	

Division Two		P	W	D	L	F	A	Pts
FC United of Manchester Res.		32	21	6	5	82	29	69
Club AZ		32	19	5	8	81	42	62
Billinge		32	17	7	8	58	42	58
Warrington Town Res.		32	17	5	10	65	44	56
Broadheath Central		32	17	5	10	69	59	56
Tarporley Victoria		32	17	4	11	69	52	55
Whitchurch Alport		32	12	13	7	44	34	49
Golborne Sports		32	14	6	12	67	62	48
Crewe		32	13	7	12	56	64	46
Maine Road Res.		32	12	5	15	70	68	41
Grappenhall Sports		32	11	7	14	62	72	40
Daten		32	10	5	17	54	74	35
Malpas		32	10	4	18	49	74	34
Lostock Gralam		32	8	6	18	43	79	30
Eagle Sports		32	8	5	19	44	69	29
Monk Sports	-6	32	11	1	20	58	85	28
Congleton Town Res.		32	8	3	21	46	68	27

CHESHIRE BUILDING SOCIETY CHESHIRE LEAGUE DIVISION TWO CONSTITUTION 2008-09

BROADHEATH CENTRAL... Broadheath Central Club, Viaduct Road, Broadheath, Altrincham WA14 5DX .... Tel: 0161 928 5849
CONGLETON TOWN RESERVES... Booth Street Ground, off Crescent Road, Congleton CW12 4DG 01260 274460
CREWE .... Cumberland Arena, Thomas Street, Crewe CW1 2BD 01270 537913
DATEN..................... Culcheth Sports Club, Charnock Road, Culcheth, Warrington WA3 5SH 01925 763096
DENTON TOWN .... Whittles Park, Heather Lea, Denton M34 6EJ .... None
EAGLE SPORTS .... Eagle Sports Club, Thornton Road, Great Sankey, Warrington WA5 1RB 01925 632926
GOLBORNE SPORTS............. Simpson Playing Fields, Stone Cross Road, Lowton WA3 2FL 01942 510161
GRAPPENHALL SPORTS ... Grappenhall Sports Club, Stockton Lane, Grappenhall, Warrington WA4 3HQ....................... None
LOSTOCK GRALAM.............. The Park Stadium, Manchester Road, Lostock Gralam CW9 7PJ...................... 01606 42148
MAINE ROAD RESERVES .... Manchester County FA Ground, Branthingham Road, Chorlton-cum-Hardy M21 0TT........ 0161 881 2000
MALPAS .... Malpas & District Sports Club, Oxheys, Wrexham Road, Malpas SY14 7EJ 01948 860662
MONK SPORTS.......................... Hillock Lane, Woolston, Warrington WA1 4QL 01925 812320
MOORE UNITED .... Carlsberg Tetley Club, Long Lane, Warrington WA2 8PU...................... 01925 634971
POYNTON............................. London Road North, Poynton, Stockport SK12 1AG 01625 875765
TARPORLEY VICTORIA .... Tattenhall Recreation Club, Field Lane, Tattenhall CH3 9QF 01829 770710
WARRINGTON TOWN RESERVES..... Cantilever Park, Common Lane, Warrington WA4 2RS........................ 01925 631932
WHITCHURCH ALPORT .... Yockings Park, Blackpark Road, Whitchurch SY13 1PG 01948 667415

IN: Denton Town (P – Lancashire & Cheshire Amateur League Premier Division), Moore United (P – Warrington & District League Premier Division), Poynton (R)
OUT: Billinge (P), Club AZ (P), FC United of Manchester Reserves (W)

J B PARKER DIVISION ONE CUP

PRELIMINARY ROUND
Styal 4 Garswood United 0
FIRST ROUND
Greenalls Padgate St Oswalds 0 **Stalybridge Celtic Res.** 3
Knutsford 2 **Woodley Sports Res.** 3
Linotype & Cheadle HN 1 **Gamesley** 3
Middlewich Town Res. 5 Witton Albion Res. 3
Pilkington 2 **Crosfields** 3
Rylands 6 **Poynton** 7
Styal 0 **Curzon Ashton Res.** 1
Trafford Res. 5 Barnton 4

QUARTER-FINALS
Curzon Ashton Res. 3 Trafford Res. 2
Poynton 2 **Middlewich Town** 3
Stalybridge Celtic Res. 3 Gamesley 1
Woodley Sports Res. 1 **Crosfields** 3
SEMI-FINALS
Curzon Ashton Res. 2 Crosfields 0
Stalybridge Celtic Res. 0 **Middlewich Town** 1
FINAL
(April 2nd at Trafford)
Curzon Ashton Res. 3 Middlewich Town 2

DIVISION TWO CUP

PRELIMINARY ROUND
Billinge 2 Warrington Town Res. 1
FIRST ROUND
Billinge 2 Warrington Town Res. 1
Congleton Town Res. 2 Eagle Sports 1
Daten 3 **Golborne Sports** 4
Grappenhall Sports 3 FC United of Manchester Res. 2
Lostock Gralam 0 **Billinge** 2
Maine Road Res. 7 Malpas 3
Monk Sports 1 **Broadheath Central** 2
Tarporley Victoria 3 Crewe 1

QUARTER-FINALS
Club AZ 1 Grappenhall Sports 0
Golborne Sports 1 Billinge 0
Maine Road Res. 2 **Broadheath Central** 3
Tarporley Victoria 2 Congleton Town Res. 0
SEMI-FINALS
Broadheath Central 0 **Club AZ** 1
Tarporley Victoria 2 **Golborne Sports** 4
FINAL
(March 26th at Trafford)
Golborne Sports 3 Club AZ 1

PRESIDENT'S CUP

(First Round losers from Division One, Two and Reserve Cups)

PRELIMINARY ROUND
Daten Res. 3 Lostock Gralam 2
Eagle Sports 1 **Monk Sports** 5
FC United of Manchester Res. 1 **Broadheath Central Res.** 3
Garswood United 4 Gamesley Res. 0
Knutsford 2 Pilkington Res. 0
Linotype & Cheadle HN 0 **Pilkington** 1
Styal 4 Rylands 1
Warrington Town Res. 2 Whitchurch Alport 0
FIRST ROUND
Barnton 4 Daten 2
Crewe (w/o) v Rylands Res. (scr.)
Garswood Utd 2 Golborne Sports Res. 0
Greenalls Padgate St Oswalds 2 Malpas 1
Monk Sports 0 **Knutsford** 3

Pilkington 4 Styal 2
Warrington Town Res. 2 Daten Res. 0
Witton Albion Res. 5 Broadheath Central Res. 0
QUARTER-FINALS
Barnton 0 **Witton Albion Res.** 2
Garswood United 1 **Pilkington** 2
Greenalls Padgate St Oswalds 2 Knutsford 1
Warrington Town Res. 4 Crewe 2
(at Crewe)
SEMI-FINALS
Greenalls Padgate St Oswalds 2 **Witton Albion Res.** 5
Pilkington 3 **Warrington Town Res.** 4
FINAL
(May 10th at Trafford)
Witton Albion Res. 2 **Warrington Town Res.** 3

Reserve Division	P	W	D	L	F	A	Pts
Styal Res.	26	17	4	5	66	26	55
Poynton Res.	26	17	4	5	66	31	55
Pilkington Res.	26	15	4	7	48	30	49
Middlewich Town Res.	26	13	9	4	61	31	48
Garswood United Res.	26	14	5	7	57	40	47
Linotype & Cheadle HN Res.	26	14	3	9	64	36	45
Billinge Res.	26	10	6	10	51	50	36
Daten Res.	26	10	4	12	48	41	34
Golborne Sports Res.	26	8	9	9	33	44	33
Gamesley Res.	26	10	3	13	38	50	33
Greenalls Padgate St Oswalds Res.	26	9	4	13	41	51	31
Eagle Sports Res.	26	7	2	17	30	69	23
Broadheath Central Res.	26	4	4	18	40	69	16
Rylands Res.	26	1	5	20	20	95	8

MEMORIAL CUP

(Division One champions v J B Parker Cup holders)

(August 4th at Middlewich Town)
Middlewich Town 0 Knutsford 0 (3-1p)
*(Knutsford qualified as Division One Runners-up,
Middlewich having completed the double)*

RESERVES CUP

FINAL
(March 19th at Trafford)
Poynton Res. 2 Billinge Res. 2 aet (4-3p)

CLWYD LEAGUE

	Abergele Rovers	Aston Park Rangers	Denbigh Town Res.	Flint Town United Res.	Halkyn United Res.	Llandyrnog United Res.	Llansannan	Mochdre Sports	Penmaenmawr Phoenix	Prestatyn Town Res.	Rhuddlan Town	Rhyl Nomads	Trefnant Village
Abergele Rovers		2-2	6-3	2-4	3-1	5-3	1-1	1-0	2-2	1-3	3-0	1-1	5-0
Aston Park Rangers	1-2	P	5-2	2-4	5-3	3-3	6-2	9-2	1-5	4-5	4-2	3-2	2-1
Denbigh Town Res.	2-5	1-5	R	0-2	2-3	1-2	5-0	0-3	2-2	0-5	6-0	5-2	0-6
Flint Town United Res.	2-1	1-2	2-0	E	2-3	3-0	5-1	2-2	3-1	2-2	6-2	2-1	3-2
Halkyn United Res.	0-5	0-3	1-1	0-5	M	1-6	1-1	4-1	1-4	0-9	5-2	2-3	2-0
Llandyrnog United Res.	2-5	2-1	2-3	0-2	2-1	I	2-2	1-3	1-1	2-3	0-1	2-2	2-0
Llansannan	1-3	1-3	1-1	3-3	1-3	0-3	E	2-2	0-3	1-3	1-2	0-1	0-3
Mochdre Sports	0-1	1-1	4-5	1-0	3-1	2-1	3-0	R	1-1	1-4	2-1	1-2	2-1
Penmaenmawr Phoenix	4-3	5-1	7-3	3-3	6-1	4-0	3-1	1-1		3-1	3-0	4-3	4-2
Prestatyn Town Res.	0-2	1-1	2-4	2-1	2-0	2-2	6-0	3-0	4-0	D	9-1	2-1	5-1
Rhuddlan Town	2-3	1-5	2-0	4-2	3-5	2-2	2-1	2-3	3-6		I	2-2	3-1
Rhyl Nomads	2-4	7-1	3-2	1-2	2-3	7-2	3-0	4-1	1-1	0-9	2-1	V	4-1
Trefnant Village	0-4	1-6	1-1	2-3	3-1	2-1	6-0	3-2	1-2	4-6	0-2	0-1	

Premier Division	P	W	D	L	F	A	Pts
Prestatyn Town Res.	24	18	3	3	94	34	57
Flint Town United Res.	24	17	4	3	66	31	55
Penmaenmawr Phoenix	24	15	7	2	72	38	52
Abergele Rovers	24	16	4	4	70	36	52
Aston Park Rangers	24	13	4	7	76	56	43
Rhyl Nomads	24	11	4	9	57	51	37
Mochdre Sports	24	8	5	11	39	50	29
Llandyrnog United Res.	24	7	5	12	46	57	26
Rhuddlan Town	24	7	2	15	40	75	23
Denbigh Town Res.	24	6	4	14	49	71	22
Halkyn United Res.	24	6	2	16	37	75	20
Trefnant Village	24	6	1	17	41	61	19
Llansannan	24	0	7	17	21	73	7

PREMIER CUP

FIRST ROUND

Flint Town United Res. 2 **Aston Park Rangers** 4 *aet*

SECOND ROUND

Mochdre Sports 2 **Aston Park Rangers** 2 *aet* (2-4p)

Prestatyn Town Res. 1 **Abergele Rovers** 3

Rhyl Nomads 3 Halkyn United Res. 2

Trefnant Village 1 Denbigh Town Res. 0

QUARTER-FINALS

Aston Park Rangers 2 Llandyrnog United Res. 1

Llansannan 2 Rhyl Nomads 1

Penmaenmawr Phoenix 0 **Abergele Rovers** 1

Trefnant Village 2 **Rhuddlan Town** 2 *aet* (3-4p)

SEMI-FINALS

Abergele Rovers 3 Rhuddlan Town 0

Llansannan 2 **Aston Park Rangers** 3

FINAL

(May 29th at Halkyn United)

Aston Park Rangers 3 **Abergele Rovers** 3
aet (3-4p)

MACKENZIE JONES CLWYD LEAGUE PREMIER DIVISION CONSTITUTION 2008-09

ABERGELE ROVERS	Parc Pentre Mawr, Abergele LL22 7RE	None
ASTON PARK RANGERS	33 Club, Shotton Lane, Shotton, Deeside	None
BRYNFORD UNITED	Hafod-y-Bryn, Brynford, Holywell CH8 8AL	None
DENBIGH TOWN RESERVES	Central Park, Park Street, Denbigh LL16 3DD	01745 812505
FLINT TOWN UNITED RESERVES	Cae Y Castell, March Lane, Flint CH6 5PJ	01352 730982
GREENFIELD	Holywell High School, Strand Walk, Holywell CH8 7AW	01352 710011
HALKYN UNITED RESERVES	Pant Newydd, Halkyn	01352 780576
LLANDYRNOG UNITED RESERVES	Swyn Y Nant, Llandyrnog, Denbigh LL16 4HB	None
LLANSANNAN	Cae Chwareuon, Maeg Gogor, Llansannan, Conwy	None
MOCHDRE SPORTS	Mochdre Sports Club, Swan Road, Mochdre, Colwyn Bay LL28 5HA	01492 546661
PENMAENMAWR PHOENIX	Cae Sling, Conwy Road, Penmaenmawr, Conwy LL34 6BL	None
PRESTATYN TOWN RESERVES	Bastion Road, Prestatyn LL17 7ET	01745 856905
RHUDDLAN TOWN	Pengwern College, Bodelwyddan Road, Rhuddlan, Rhyl LL18 5UH	None
TREFNANT VILLAGE	Village Hall, Denbigh Road, Trefnant	None

IN: Brynford United (P), Greenfield (P)
OUT: Rhyl Nomads (W)

Division One	P	W	D	L	F	A	Pts
Greenfield	24	24	0	0	107	18	72
Brynford United	24	17	2	5	73	46	53
Sychdyn	24	14	1	9	69	42	43
Glan Conwy Res.	23	12	3	8	70	45	39
Caerwys	24	10	4	10	52	61	34
Aztec Sports	22	10	2	10	46	46	32
Betws-yn-Rhos	24	9	4	11	51	63	31
Aston Park Rangers Res.	24	8	5	11	47	63	29
Y Glannau	24	6	8	10	42	61	26
Abergele Rovers Res.	24	7	4	13	34	55	25
Point of Ayr	24	7	2	15	42	58	23
Cerrigydrudion	23	5	6	12	35	54	21
Rhuddlan Town Res.	24	4	1	19	47	103	13

Cerrigdrudion v Aztec Sports and
Glan Conwy Res. v Aztec Sports not played

Division Two		P	W	D	L	F	A	Pts
Connahs Quay Nomads Res.		26	19	4	3	103	41	61
Llandudno Town Res.		26	19	3	4	83	24	60
Llandudno Junction Res.		26	18	1	7	86	39	55
Prestatyn Town 'A'		26	15	6	5	87	48	51
Shotton Steel		26	15	4	7	77	54	49
St Asaph		26	11	5	10	61	57	38
Llannefydd		26	11	4	11	66	59	37
Rhos United		26	8	8	10	61	51	32
Aston Park Rangers 'A'	-1	26	9	4	13	73	79	30
Caerwys Res.		26	7	7	12	62	103	28
Mostyn Dragons		26	7	4	15	60	65	25
Penrhyn United		26	6	3	17	52	101	21
Wepre Rangers		26	5	5	16	42	93	20
Bro Cernyw		26	3	0	23	27	126	9

R.E.M. JONES CUP *(Div One teams)*

FINAL *(May 12th at Denbigh Town)*
Glan Conwy Res. 4 Greenfield 1

HALKYN CUP *(Div Two teams)*

FINAL *(May 10th at Hawarden Rangers)*
Aston Park Rangers 'A' 5 Mostyn Dragons 1

FINAL *(May 24th at Halkyn United)*
Abergele Rovers 2 Penmaenmawr Phoenix 0

PRESIDENT'S CUP *(All teams)*

COMBINED COUNTIES LEAGUE

	Ash United	Banstead Athletic	Bedfont	Bedfont Green	Bookham	Camberley Town	Chertsey Town	Chessington & Hook United	Cobham	Colliers Wood United	Cove	Dorking	Egham Town	Epsom & Ewell	Guildford City	Horley Town	Merstham	North Greenford United	Raynes Park Vale	Reading Town	Sandhurst Town	Wembley
Ash United		2-3	2-3	3-1	4-2	1-2	2-4	1-1	3-2	2-2	0-3	3-2	3-2	1-3	1-3	3-1	0-2	2-3	1-1	0-2	2-2	1-2
Banstead Athletic	1-2		3-1	2-3	3-1	0-1	5-1	3-0	6-4	4-2	2-2	1-0	2-8	1-3	3-2	4-2	0-2	0-3	1-1	5-4	1-1	1-0
Bedfont	1-2	1-1		2-2	0-3	1-1	4-1	1-2	1-0	3-3	2-1	1-4	2-2	0-1	1-0	0-2	1-2	4-2	2-2	0-4	2-1	0-1
Bedfont Green	2-0	4-1	0-4	P	6-1	1-5	3-3	4-3	0-1	3-3	2-3	3-1	1-1	0-2	0-1	0-1	0-1	4-1	2-0	2-2	2-1	1-1
Bookham	1-5	3-1	0-3	3-2	R	2-4	4-2	3-2	1-3	3-2	2-3	2-2	3-0	1-1	1-2	2-1	1-4	1-1	1-1	1-0	0-3	5-0
Camberley Town	3-2	7-1	3-0	0-4	3-1	E	4-2	1-2	0-1	1-0	0-1	2-1	1-1	3-5	0-1	1-1	0-2	2-1	3-0	1-1	3-3	3-2
Chertsey Town	4-2	1-2	3-2	0-5	3-1	2-3	M	5-1	2-1	2-3	0-5	5-2	2-2	2-1	1-3	0-0	1-4	1-0	3-0	3-2	0-1	1-0
Chessington & Hook United	2-1	1-1	6-0	2-0	1-0	5-1	3-1	I	2-2	3-4	1-0	3-0	1-3	1-1	1-3	0-2	1-1	3-2	2-2	1-0	2-1	2-1
Cobham	0-2	5-4	2-2	1-2	1-1	0-2	1-5	0-4	E	4-2	2-4	5-2	1-0	3-2	1-1	0-2	1-2	3-3	4-1	0-1	1-2	0-1
Colliers Wood United	4-3	3-2	9-1	0-1	3-1	0-3	2-3	2-1	3-0	R	2-2	2-1	3-2	1-1	2-1	3-1	2-3	2-1	1-1	1-1	4-0	2-2
Cove	0-1	1-0	2-0	4-3	4-2	2-2	3-1	3-2	2-1	1-0		0-1	0-3	3-3	3-0	0-1	1-0	0-1	2-3	3-3	4-2	1-2
Dorking	2-3	0-0	3-5	0-3	1-2	0-5	2-4	0-1	3-1	1-3	1-2	D	3-0	0-1	2-3	3-0	0-6	1-2	1-2	2-3	0-0	0-0
Egham Town	4-0	4-4	3-0	2-2	3-1	1-2	2-2	1-1	2-0	2-0	0-1	4-0	I	1-1	0-5	2-2	1-1	0-4	3-2	4-1	2-0	2-0
Epsom & Ewell	1-1	2-0	5-1	1-2	2-2	1-0	0-1	1-1	2-1	1-2	2-1	0-1	2-2	V	1-0	2-1	1-4	3-0	4-1	0-5	0-2	1-1
Guildford City	3-0	4-3	6-0	2-2	4-0	1-2	2-0	4-3	2-2	3-1	1-0	6-0	2-2	1-0	I	1-1	0-1	0-1	1-1	4-0	2-0	1-2
Horley Town	1-0	4-1	1-1	0-3	5-1	2-1	3-2	1-0	3-0	2-2	3-1	3-2	2-0	0-3	0-2	S	1-4	0-2	2-2	3-2	0-1	1-0
Merstham	3-1	4-0	4-0	2-0	2-0	1-0	2-1	3-2	5-0	2-0	3-2	4-0	6-0	1-1	1-1	3-0	I	1-1	4-0	4-2	2-0	1-0
North Greenford United	0-5	4-2	3-1	2-2	1-0	0-1	0-1	2-1	1-2	3-0	0-0	2-0	4-1	1-1	1-0	2-3	0-1	O	1-0	1-2	2-1	1-1
Raynes Park Vale	1-2	0-3	3-1	1-0	1-1	2-2	1-0	0-0	4-1	1-1	1-2	2-0	3-2	2-2	1-2	0-3	1-5	1-7	N	1-3	5-0	1-2
Reading Town	2-2	3-0	0-1	1-1	2-0	0-2	0-2	4-1	2-0	1-3	0-2	1-1	1-2	1-0	1-3	1-1	n/a	1-2	3-0		3-0	3-0
Sandhurst Town	1-3	1-1	2-0	2-1	2-2	0-2	1-3	2-5	4-3	3-2	3-0	1-0	2-4	3-2	2-3	2-2	0-7	3-5	4-3	0-2		1-0
Wembley	5-4	2-1	4-0	1-3	1-2	0-1	1-1	1-0	0-0	0-0	0-1	4-0	2-0	3-0	1-2	0-2	0-4	0-2	0-4	0-2	1-1	

Premier Division	P	W	D	L	F	A	Pts
Merstham	41	35	5	1	114	21	110
Guildford City	42	25	7	10	88	45	82
Camberley Town	42	24	7	11	83	54	79
Cove	42	22	6	14	75	58	72
Horley Town	42	20	9	13	66	59	69
North Greenford United	42	20	8	14	75	58	68
Colliers Wood United	42	18	10	14	86	75	64
Chertsey Town	42	19	5	18	81	85	62
Bedfont Green	42	17	10	15	82	67	61
Epsom & Ewell	42	16	13	13	66	58	61
Chessington & Hook Utd	42	17	9	16	76	68	60
Egham Town	42	15	13	14	80	75	58
Reading Town	41	16	7	18	67	62	55
Wembley	42	14	10	18	49	55	52
Ash United	42	15	6	21	78	87	51
Sandhurst Town	42	14	9	19	63	89	51
Banstead Athletic	42	14	8	20	79	99	50
Bookham	42	12	8	22	64	94	44
Raynes Park Vale	42	9	14	19	56	85	41
Bedfont	42	11	8	23	55	101	41
Cobham	42	10	7	25	60	93	37
Dorking	42	6	5	31	45	100	23

Reading Town v Merstham not played

Reserve Division		P	W	D	L	F	A	Pts
Staines Lammas Res.		40	32	2	6	146	54	98
Bedfont Green Res.		40	26	9	5	116	46	87
Farnham Town Res.		40	24	9	7	106	61	81
Warlingham Res.		40	24	8	8	111	65	80
CB Hounslow United Res.		40	23	7	10	85	54	76
Chessington & Hook Utd Res.		40	23	5	12	101	66	74
Guildford City Res.		40	21	8	11	124	83	71
Hanworth Villa Res.		40	21	7	12	113	71	70
Westfield Res.		40	20	8	12	97	76	68
Frimley Green Res.		40	17	8	15	63	59	59
Worcester Park Res.		40	15	6	19	77	90	51
Knaphill Res.		40	14	7	19	81	80	49
South Park Res.	-2	40	11	13	16	77	76	44
Farleigh Rovers Res.		40	12	7	21	54	84	43
Bookham Res.		40	11	9	20	65	107	42
Hartley Wintney Res.		40	11	8	21	81	101	41
Crescent Rovers Res.		40	11	6	23	67	113	39
Cove Res.		40	8	9	23	46	91	33
Merrow Res.		40	6	7	27	64	117	25
Sheerwater Res.		40	7	4	29	81	159	25
Tongham Res.	-4	40	7	5	28	62	164	22

PREMIER RESERVE CUP

FINAL

(May 3rd at Ashford Town (Middx))

Staines Lammas Res. 3 Frimley Green Res. 2

CHERRY RED COMBINED COUNTIES LEAGUE PREMIER DIVISION CONSTITUTION 2008-09

ASH UNITED .... Youngs Drive, Shawfield Road, Ash, near Aldershot GU12 6RE 01252 345757
BADSHOT LEA................... Farnborough FC, Cherrywood Road, Farnborough GU14 8UD................... 01252 541469
BANSTEAD ATHLETIC...................... Merland Rise, Tadworth KT20 5JG 01737 350982
BEDFONT............................. The Orchard, Hatton Road, Bedfont TW14 9QT 020 8890 7264
BEDFONT GREEN .... Windsor & Eton FC, Stag Meadow, St Leonards Road, Windsor SL4 3DR............... 01753 860656
BOOKHAM .... Dorking FC, Meadowbank, Mill Lane, Dorking RH4 1DX.................... 01306 884112
CAMBERLEY TOWN .... Krooner Park, Wilton Road, off Frimley Road, Camberley GU15 2QP 01276 65392
CHERTSEY TOWN .... Alwyns Lane, Chertsey KT16 9DW........................... 01932 561774/571792
CHESSINGTON & HOOK UNITED .... Chalky Lane, Chessington KT9 2PW............... 01372 745777
COBHAM .... Leg O'Mutton Field, Anvil Lane, Downsbridge Road, Cobham KT11 3BD............... 01932 865959
COLLIERS WOOD UNITED...... Wibbandune Sports Ground, Robin Hood Way, Kingston SW20 0AA 020 8942 8062
COVE........................... Oak Farm, 7 Squirrel Lane, Cove, Farnborough GU14 8PB 01252 543615
EGHAM TOWN..................... Runnymede Stadium, Tempest Road, Egham TW20 8HX 01784 435226/436466
EPSOM & EWELL................. Banstead Athletic FC, Merland Rise, Tadworth KT20 5JG 01737 350982
GUILDFORD CITY .... Spectrum Leisure Centre, Parkway, Guildford GU1 1UP 01483 443322
HARTLEY WINTNEY .... Memorial Playing Fields, Green Lane, Hartley Wintney RG27 8HD............... 01252 843586
HORLEY TOWN.................. The New Defence, Court Lodge Road, Horley RH6 8RS....................... 01293 822000
MOLESEY...................................... 412 Walton Road, West Molesey KT8 2JG.................... 020 8979 4823/8941 7989
NORTH GREENFORD UNITED .... Berkeley Fields, Berkeley Avenue, Greenford UB6 0NZ 020 8422 8923
RAYNES PARK VALE.......... Princes Georges Playing Field, Grand Drive, Raynes Park SW20 9LN 020 8540 8843
SANDHURST TOWN.......... Bottom Meadow, Memorial Park, Yorktown Road, Sandhurst GU47 9BJ 01252 878768
WEMBLEY............................. Vale Farm, Watford Road, Sudbury, Wembley HA0 4UR 020 8904 8169/8908 5461

IN: Badshot Lea (S – Hellenic League Premier Division), Hartley Wintney (P), Molesey (R – Isthmian League Division One South)
OUT: Dorking (R), Merstham (P – Isthmian League Division One South), Reading Town (S – Hellenic League Premier Division)

LEAGUE CUP

FIRST ROUND

Coulsdon United 0 **Neasden Foundation** 2
Cove 2 Sheerwater 0
Farnham Town 2 Reading Town 1
Feltham 2 **Westfield** 3
Hartley Wintney 1 **Sheerwater** 3
North Greenford United 2 **Epsom & Ewell** 3
Raynes Park Vale 3 Hanworth Villa 0
Tongham 0 **Staines Lammas** 5
Wembley 3 Horley Town 0
Worcester Park 1 **Guildford City** 3

SECOND ROUND

Banstead Athletic 5 Farleigh Rovers 0
Bookham 0 **Guildford City** 3
CB Hounslow United 1 **Ash United** 4
Chessington & Hook United 4 Bedfont 1
Chobham 4 Merrow 0
Cobham 5 South Park 1
Colliers Wood United 0 **Bedfont Green** 2
Cove 4 Sandhurst Town 1
Crescent Rovers 2 Frimley Green 0
Dorking 4 Knaphill 2
Egham Town 2 Westfield 1
Epsom & Ewell 2 Camberley Town 0
Neasden Foundation 0 **Chertsey Town** 2
Raynes Park Vale 3 **Farnham Town** 4 *aet*
Staines Lammas 3 Warlingham 2
Wembley 0 **Merstham** 3

THIRD ROUND

Banstead Athletic 4 **Bedfont Green** 9
Chertsey Town 2 **Farnham Town** 3
Chessington & Hook United 1 **Epsom & Ewell** 2
Chobham 0 **Crescent Rovers** 3
Cove 0 **Merstham** 1
Dorking 0 **Ash United** 2
Egham Town 5 Guildford City 2
Staines Lammas 1 **Cobham** 2
(at Cobham)

QUARTER-FINALS

Ash United 1 **Egham Town** 3
Cobham 0 **Farnham Town** 2
Epsom & Ewell 0 **Bedfont Green** 1
Merstham 4 Crescent Rovers 0

SEMI-FINALS

Egham Town 1 **Bedfont Green** 2
Farnham Town 3 **Merstham** 4

FINAL

(April 17th at Woking)
Merstham 4 Bedfont Green 2 *aet*

	CB Hounslow United	Chobham	Coulsdon United	Crescent Rovers	Farleigh Rovers	Farnham Town	Feltham	Frimley Green	Hanworth Villa	Hartley Wintney	Knaphill	Merrow	Neasden Foundation	Sheerwater	South Park	Staines Lammas	Tongham	Warlingham	Westfield	Worcester Park
CB Hounslow United		4-1	3-3	2-0	2-0	2-2	1-0	2-2	0-2	0-1	3-2	9-0	2-0	3-6	1-1	3-2	2-1	2-3	0-1	1-3
Chobham	0-5		4-0	3-4	2-0	1-4	2-0	0-2	1-4	0-1	2-0	7-2	n/a	3-4	1-1	0-3	2-2	1-3	3-2	1-3
Coulsdon United	2-2	1-2		3-2	4-3	1-3	1-1	0-0	0-3	2-2	1-3	3-0	0-1	2-0	0-3	1-5	0-3	1-6	1-2	2-3
Crescent Rovers	0-3	0-7	2-0		0-2	3-2	0-1	1-2	1-2	3-2	1-3	4-0	0-2	1-4	0-4	0-2	1-0	3-3	0-2	2-1
Farleigh Rovers	2-1	1-2	0-2	0-2	D	1-0	2-2	0-0	0-5	0-3	0-1	2-1	1-2	1-2	1-4	0-2	3-2	0-4	1-1	1-0
Farnham Town	4-2	6-1	4-2	4-0	2-1	I	2-0	4-1	2-8	0-1	3-1	6-2	8-0	3-1	3-3	0-4	1-1	1-1	0-0	2-2
Feltham	1-0	0-3	3-1	3-1	2-2	2-1	V	0-4	1-6	1-2	1-0	4-2	2-4	1-1	2-1	0-1	6-1	0-4	2-5	3-4
Frimley Green	1-3	1-2	5-0	2-3	3-1	0-0	4-1	I	0-0	0-1	1-4	8-1	0-3	3-0	0-2	1-0	2-0	5-3	2-1	2-2
Hanworth Villa	1-0	3-0	7-2	5-1	2-2	3-1	0-1	0-2	S	0-0	7-1	5-0	1-0	8-0	1-0	0-2	5-2	2-2	1-1	0-2
Hartley Wintney	3-2	0-0	5-1	2-0	3-0	1-1	2-2	2-4	0-2	I	5-0	5-0	3-2	2-2	2-1	0-0	4-0	4-0	2-0	2-0
Knaphill	6-0	2-1	5-0	3-3	4-1	0-0	1-1	4-2	3-3	0-4	O	4-2	6-1	4-4	2-1	1-3	1-1	2-1	0-3	1-0
Merrow	0-2	1-4	0-2	0-5	2-2	0-2	0-3	1-2	0-12	0-4	0-3	N	n/a	2-5	2-8	1-1	0-4	1-8	0-7	2-1
Neasden Foundation	n/a	1-2	n/a	n/a	2-1	2-3	3-0	2-0	1-2	0-1	n/a	n/a	n/a	0-1	3-4	8-1	n/a	3-2	2-1	2-1
Sheerwater	2-3	0-2	0-3	2-2	1-2	3-4	0-6	3-1	2-12	2-5	1-2	1-0	1-2		2-0	0-1	1-7	2-5	0-3	2-1
South Park	4-2	2-3	3-5	0-0	4-5	1-4	5-0	1-2	1-1	2-0	5-0	n/a	2-2		O	0-3	7-2	0-5	1-6	2-3
Staines Lammas	5-1	8-1	2-1	8-0	1-0	2-0	2-0	1-2	0-1	5-2	5-1	11-0	n/a	4-1	1-2	N	4-2	5-0	2-0	5-0
Tongham	2-4	2-2	3-2	0-1	0-0	1-3	4-3	0-1	2-3	0-6	1-3	2-1	1-2	4-0	2-0	0-4	E	0-1	2-4	0-3
Warlingham	1-3	2-4	2-1	1-2	3-1	2-1	1-1	1-2	2-2	3-1	1-1	9-0	0-3	2-2	3-3	1-1	6-1		2-2	3-2
Westfield	1-0	2-2	3-0	3-2	1-0	0-1	2-1	2-0	1-3	2-0	5-0	6-1	2-0	1-3	3-1	3-0	1-0	1-0		2-2
Worcester Park	0-1	1-0	2-1	1-0	2-0	2-1	1-1	2-0	2-1	1-1	2-3	2-3	4-0	n/a	6-1	5-1	0-2	2-3	2-1	

Division One	P	W	D	L	F	A	Pts
Staines Lammas	37	28	3	6	111	28	87
Hanworth Villa	38	25	9	4	124	38	84
Hartley Wintney	38	24	8	6	87	38	80
Westfield	38	24	6	8	86	40	78
Farnham Town	38	19	10	9	88	57	67
Frimley Green	38	19	6	13	71	53	63
Knaphill	37	18	7	12	77	72	61
Warlingham	37	16	10	11	95	65	58
Worcester Park	37	17	5	15	70	57	56
CB Hounslow United	37	17	5	15	76	65	56
Chobham	37	16	5	16	72	77	53
South Park	37	12	9	16	79	75	45
Feltham	38	12	7	19	57	77	43
Neasden Foundation	26	14	0	12	49	45	42
Crescent Rovers	37	12	4	21	50	84	40
Sheerwater	37	10	6	21	63	113	36
Tongham	38	9	5	24	59	99	32
Farleigh Rovers	38	8	7	23	39	76	31
Coulsdon United	37	8	4	25	51	99	28
Merrow	36	1	2	33	24	170	5

DIVISION ONE CUP

FIRST ROUND

Crescent Rovers 2 Farnham Town 2
aet (3-1p)
Frimley Green 1 **Chobham** 0
Warlingham 4 Sheerwater 0
Westfield 3 Farleigh Rovers 2

SECOND ROUND

Crescent Rovers 2 **Frimley Green** 3 *aet*
Feltham 1 **Neasden Foundation** 6
Knaphill 4 Hartley Wintney 1
Merrow 4 Coulsdon United 1
South Park 1 **Westfield** 3 *aet*
Staines Lammas 7 CB Hounslow United 1

Tongham 1 **Warlingham** 7
Worcester Park 1 **Hanworth Villa** 2

QUARTER-FINALS

Frimley Green 1 **Neasden Foundation** 3
Knaphill 1 **Staines Lammas** 4
Merrow 1 **Hanworth Villa** 6
Westfield 3 Warlingham 1 *aet*

SEMI-FINALS

Staines Lammas 5 Neasden Foundation 0
Westfield 1 **Hanworth Villa** 2 *aet*

FINAL

(May 5th at Ashford Town (Middx))
Hanworth Villa 2 Staines Lammas 1
aet

CHERRY RED COMBINED COUNTIES LEAGUE DIVISION ONE CONSTITUTION 2008-09

CB HOUNSLOW UNITED......... Osterley Sports Club, Tentelow Lane, Osterley, Southall UB2 4LW 020 8574 3774
CHOBHAM..................... Chobham Recreation Ground, Station Road, Chobham GU24 8AZ 01276 857876
COULSDON UNITED .... Woodplace Lane, Coulsdon CR5 1NB 01737 557509
CRESCENT ROVERS.......... Wallington Sports & Social Club, Mollison Drive, Wallington SM6 9BY 020 8647 2558
DORKING .... Meadowbank, Mill Lane, Dorking RH4 1DX 01306 884112
FARLEIGH ROVERS............. Parsonage Field, Harrow Road, Farleigh, Warlingham CR6 9EY 01884 626483
FARNHAM TOWN .... Memorial Ground, West Street, Farnham GU9 7DY 01252 715305
FELTHAM....................... Bedfont FC, The Orchard, Hatton Road, Bedfont TW14 9QT 020 8890 72648
FRIMLEY GREEN...... Frimley Green Rec. Ground, Frimley Green Road, Frimley Green, Camberley GU16 6LL 01252 835089
HANWORTH VILLA .... Rectory Meadow, Park Road, Hounslow Road, Hanworth 020 8831 9391
KNAPHILL................ Brookwood Country Park, Lower Guildford Road, Knaphill, Woking GU21 2AY .... None
MOLE VALLEY SCR........ Mole Valley Predators, River Lane, off Randalls Road, Leatherhead KT22 0AU................. None
SHEERWATER .... Blackmore Crescent, Sheerwater Estate, Woking GU21 5NW .... None
SOUTH PARK....................... Whitehall Lane, South Park, Reigate RH2 8LG .... None
STAINES LAMMAS............ Laleham Recreation Ground, The Broadway, Laleham, Staines TW18 1RX 01784 465204
WARLINGHAM.................. Verdayne Playing Fields, Verdayne Gardens, Warlingham CR6 9RP 01883 625718
WESTFIELD .... Woking Park, off Elmbridge Lane, Kingfield, Woking GU22 7AA 01483 771106
WORCESTER PARK.................. Skinners Field, Green Lane, Worcester Park KT4 8AJ....................... 020 8337 4995

IN: Dorking (R), Mole Valley SCR (formerly Sutton Common Rovers) (P – Middlesex County League Premier Division)
OUT: Hartley Wintney (P), Merrow (R – Surrey Intermediate League (Western) Premier Division), Neasden Foundation (WS), Tongham (R – Surrey Elite Intermediate League Intermediate Division)

CORNWALL COMBINATION

	Falmouth Tn Res.	Hayle Res.	Helston Athletic	Holmans Spts Club	Illogan RBL	Ludgvan	Mullion	Newquay Res.	Penryn Ath. Res.	Penzance Res.	Perranporth	Perranwell	Porthleven Res.	RNAS Culdrose	St Agnes	St Day	St Ives Town	St Just	Truro City Res.	Wendron Utd Res.
Falmouth Town Res.		2-1	0-4	1-2	0-2	2-0	5-1	0-3	1-0	3-0	1-1	2-1	3-0	1-2	3-2	6-1	2-1	2-3	3-7	6-3
Hayle Res.	2-1		0-3	0-6	0-8	3-2	1-0	3-1	1-2	5-0	1-2	1-2	1-3	1-1	1-7	3-1	0-0	2-2	0-3	4-0
Helston Athletic	2-1	4-0		4-1	3-0	3-1	3-2	4-0	2-3	6-1	2-1	6-0	1-4	3-0	0-1	1-0	2-2	4-1	1-2	4-1
Holmans Sports Club	4-2	10-0	0-3		1-0	3-1	4-1	1-0	3-1	7-2	2-1	1-3	4-0	6-3	5-4	2-1	1-1	0-1	0-5	7-0
Illogan RBL	3-0	5-1	0-1	0-0		3-0	1-2	2-2	1-3	6-1	1-0	1-0	1-0	1-0	1-2	2-0	1-1	0-0	1-4	5-1
Ludgvan	0-4	2-2	0-4	1-6	0-6		1-2	0-0	0-1	0-2	0-3	1-6	0-1	0-5	0-3	1-4	6-3	0-2	6-2	
Mullion	0-3	0-2	1-1	2-1	1-2	1-2		1-1	0-3	4-0	2-2	0-3	1-3	2-4	1-3	3-4	2-0	1-2	0-6	0-2
Newquay Res.	3-2	1-3	2-2	5-0	1-2	4-0	3-0		1-4	2-0	1-3	3-1	2-2	2-1	4-2	1-0	3-0	3-1	0-5	4-0
Penryn Athletic Res.	3-4	6-0	3-4	1-0	2-0	2-1	2-2			9-0	0-2	0-0	1-2	1-0	1-0	1-0	0-2	1-5	3-0	
Penzance Res.	1-5	1-3	1-7	1-3	2-1	1-2	1-1	0-2	2-0		0-1	0-4	0-2	1-3	1-6	3-3	0-2	0-3	0-1	2-1
Perranporth	1-3	2-2	1-5	5-2	1-1	5-0	1-0	1-2	1-0	3-0		1-4	1-6	1-1	1-2	0-4	3-1	4-1	0-2	3-1
Perranwell	9-0	7-0	2-0	3-1	2-3	7-0	8-3	2-1	4-2	7-0	8-0		6-2	4-1	3-1	4-0	0-2	1-0	1-3	2-1
Porthleven Res.	1-1	0-1	1-2	1-0	10-0	6-2	5-2	2-1	3-3	5-1	0-3	1-0		2-2	1-3	0-0			2-6	6-1
RNAS Culdrose	3-2	1-2	1-2	4-6	0-2	6-0	1-3	3-6	1-3	4-2	9-4	1-2	0-1		1-1	1-3	0-3	4-3	1-5	3-2
St Agnes	3-1	1-0	2-7	0-2	1-0	4-0	1-2	1-3	5-2	6-1	1-2	2-3	0-3	2-1		1-0	1-2	0-2	1-6	2-0
St Day	0-3	4-0	1-7	1-2	0-5	1-4	4-0	2-1	1-1	2-0	1-3	0-3	1-1	2-1	1-0		0-2	1-2	0-3	3-0
St Ives Town	0-3	5-0	2-4	5-1	1-0	1-3	2-2	0-0	7-0	3-1	1-1	0-7	1-0	6-2	0-2			5-3	1-4	4-4
St Just	2-0	4-0	1-3	1-3	0-2	2-1	2-1	1-2	1-2	6-2	1-2	2-2	2-5	0-1	1-0	3-1			0-3	3-0
Truro City Res.	6-1	1-0	4-1	7-3	4-0	6-0	7-1	8-1	7-0	5-0	2-0	2-2	6-0	3-1	1-2	5-1	3-0	1-1		9-0
Wendron United Res.	3-8	0-2	2-5	3-4	1-4	2-3	4-2	1-3	0-4	0-2	1-1	1-2	3-1	1-3	2-4	2-2	0-4			

	P	W	D	L	F	A	Pts
Truro City Res. -6	38	35	3	0	172	25	102
Perranwell	38	28	3	7	121	42	87
Helston Athletic	38	28	3	7	121	46	87
Holmans Sports Club	38	24	2	12	107	75	74
Porthleven Res.	38	21	7	10	95	61	70
Illogan RBL	38	20	5	13	73	38	65
Newquay Res.	38	19	7	12	79	67	64
St Agnes	38	20	2	16	84	71	62
Penryn Athletic Res.	38	19	5	14	70	57	62
St Ives Town -3	38	17	10	11	77	60	58
Falmouth Tn Res. -3	38	19	2	17	87	80	56
Perranporth	38	13	8	17	61	83	47
St Just -3	38	14	6	18	63	72	45
Hayle Res.	38	13	5	20	48	109	44
RNAS Culdrose	38	11	4	23	70	88	37
St Day	38	11	3	24	48	78	36
Mullion	38	7	4	27	46	102	25
Ludgvan	38	6	4	28	35	122	22
Wendron United Res.	38	5	4	29	50	131	19
Penzance Res.	38	5	3	30	32	132	18

LEAGUE CUP

PRELIMINARY ROUND
Penryn Athletic Res. 3 Ludgvan 1
Penzance Res. 1 **Perranporth** 3
Porthleven Res. 1 St Day 1
Rep: St Day 1 **Porthleven Res.** 5
RNAS Culdrose 2 **Perranwell** 4
FIRST ROUND
Hayle Res. 3 Mullion 1
Holmans Sports Club 1 Truro City Res. 1
Rep: **Truro City Res.** 4 Holmans Sports Club 1
Newquay Res. 1 Falmouth Tn Res. 1
Rep: Falmouth Town Res. 0 **Newquay Res.** 2
Penryn Athletic Res. 1 **Helston Athletic** 2

Perranporth 0 **Illogan RBL** 1
St Agnes 3 Perranwell 0
St Ives Town 0 **Porthleven Res.** 1
Wendron United Res. 2 **St Just** 4
QUARTER-FINALS
Hayle Res. 0 **Truro City Res.** 1
Illogan RBL 7 Newquay Res. 0
Porthleven Res. 5 St Just 3
St Agnes 2 **Helston Athletic** 4
SEMI-FINALS
Helston Athletic 4 Illogan RBL 0
(at Falmouth Town)
Truro City Res. 1 Porthleven Res. 1
(at Penryn Athletic)
FINAL
(March 23rd at Porthleven)
Truro City Res. 4 Helston Ath. 1

SUPPLEMENTARY CUP

(Teams eliminated in the Preliminary and First Round of the League Cup)

PRELIMINARY ROUND
Perranporth 5 Penzance Res. 1
RNAS Culdrose 0 **Penryn Athletic Res.** 1
St Ives Town 1 **Perranwell** 2
Wendron United Res. 2
Falmouth Town Res. 6

QUARTER-FINALS
Falmouth Tn Res. 2 Ludgvan 0
Mullion 0 **Penryn Ath. Res.** 1
Perranporth 1 **St Day** 4
Perranwell 2 **Holmans S Club** 4
SEMI-FINALS
Perranwell 1 Holmans Sports Club 0 *(at Penzance)*
St Day 1 **Penryn Athletic Res.** 4
(at Wendron United)
FINAL
(May 18th at Helston Athletic)
Falmouth Tn Res. 2 **Penryn Athletic Res.** 3

JOLLY'S CORNWALL COMBINATION CONSTITUTION 2008-09

FALMOUTH TOWN RESERVES . . . . Bickland Park, Bickland Water Road, Falmouth TR11 4PB 01326 375156
HAYLE RESERVES . . . . Trevassack Park, Viaduct Hill, Hayle TR27 5HT 01736 757157
HELSTON ATHLETIC . . . . Kellaway Parc, Clodgy Lane, Helston TR13 8BN 01326 573742
HOLMANS SPORTS CLUB . . . . . . Blaythorne Mem. Sports Ground, Pendarves, Camborne TR14 7QG 01209 713631
ILLOGAN RBL . . . . Oxland Park, Richards Lane, Illogan, Redruth TR16 4HA 01209 216488
LUDGVAN . . . . Ludgvan Community Centre, Fairfield, Ludgvan TR20 8ES 01736 740774
MULLION . . . . Clifden Parc, Clifden Close, Mullion, Helston TR12 7EQ 01326 240676
NEWQUAY RESERVES . . . . Mount Wise, Clevedon Road, Newquay TR7 2BU 01637 872935
PENRYN ATHLETIC RESERVES . . . . Kernick, Kernick Road, Penryn TR10 8QF 01326 375182
PENZANCE RESERVES . . . . Penlee Park, Alexandra Place, Penzance TR18 4NE 01736 361964
PERRANPORTH . . . . Budnick Estate, Perranporth TR6 0DB 01872 575000
PERRANWELL . . . . King George V Playing Field, School Hill, Perranwell Station TR3 7LA 01872 870202
PORTHLEVEN RESERVES . . . . Gala Parc, Mill Lane, Porthleven TR13 9LQ 01326 574754
PORTREATH . . . . Clijah Croft, Wheal Trefusis, Redruth TR15 2NQ 01209 216586
RNAS CULDROSE . . . . Sports Field, RNAS Culdrose, Helston TR12 7RH 01326 574121x7167
ST AGNES . . . . Enys Park, West Polperro, St Agnes TR5 0SS 01872 553673
ST DAY . . . . Vogue, St Day, Redruth TR16 5NP . . . . None
ST IVES TOWN . . . . The Saltings, Lelant TR6 3DL . . . . None
ST JUST . . . . Lafrowda Park, St Just, Penzance TR19 7RY 01736 788503
WENDRON UNITED RESERVES . . . . Underlane, Carnkie, Wendron, Helston TR13 0EH 01209 860946

IN: Portreath (P – Mining League Division One)
OUT: Truro City Reserves (P – South West Peninsula League Division One West)

CYMRU ALLIANCE

Note – Bodedern withdrew during the course of the season

Their results are shown herein but are expunged from the league table

	Bala Town	Bodedern	Buckley Town	Denbigh Town	Flint Town United	Gap Queens Park	Glantraeth	Gresford Athletic	Guilsfield	Holyhead Hotspur	Lex XI	Llandudno Town	Llandyrnog United	Llanfairpwll	Mynydd Isa	Penrhyncoch	Prestatyn Town	Ruthin Town
Bala Town		n/a	4-1	2-0	1-2	4-3	2-1	2-1	4-2	1-1	2-1	3-1	1-2	6-0	4-1	1-0	5-2	5-0
Bodedern	n/a		n/a	1-1	n/a	n/a	n/a	n/a	n/a	n/a	0-1	0-4	n/a	1-3	n/a	n/a	n/a	n/a
Buckley Town	1-4	n/a		0-2	0-3	1-7	2-2	1-1	2-0	2-2	2-2	3-0	2-2	1-4	3-2	1-0	0-5	3-0
Denbigh Town	1-0	n/a	3-2		0-2	0-3	0-2	1-1	3-1	3-1	4-2	2-3	4-0	0-1	3-2	0-0	0-2	1-1
Flint Town United	1-0	6-0	2-2	1-1		1-1	1-2	1-0	2-0	2-2	0-2	1-2	1-1	2-4	4-2	4-0	0-3	5-1
Gap Queens Park	4-2	n/a	7-0	2-1	0-5		5-1	3-0	2-2	3-2	3-3	0-1	5-0	6-1	1-2	2-2	0-3	3-1
Glantraeth	0-1	0-0	0-1	0-1	3-2	2-0		4-0	4-2	3-2	5-1	1-2	1-1	2-2	1-3	4-0	2-4	4-2
Gresford Athletic	2-1	n/a	3-1	1-1	2-3	0-1	0-2		2-2	1-4	1-3	0-4	1-1	2-1	1-3	1-3	1-5	2-1
Guilsfield	2-1	n/a	3-1	1-3	1-2	1-2	4-1	4-0		1-1	3-1	2-1	3-1	4-1	1-0	1-4	0-4	0-3
Holyhead Hotspur	2-1	2-2	4-2	4-2	1-1	4-4	2-2	1-0	5-0		6-0	1-0	4-0	2-1	3-1	6-0	0-1	1-0
Lex XI	3-1	n/a	1-1	3-4	1-1	0-4	2-2	4-2	0-6	2-2		0-1	0-1	1-4	3-2	3-0	0-3	0-1
Llandudno Town	1-0	n/a	1-1	2-0	1-2	2-2	3-1	2-0	4-0	1-3	6-0		2-1	1-1	1-1	0-0	1-3	0-0
Llandyrnog United	1-1	n/a	4-0	0-3	6-2	1-0	1-3	2-2	0-4	6-2	5-5	1-4		3-1	3-2	3-1	0-2	2-3
Llanfairpwll	2-2	n/a	3-2	2-3	0-0	4-4	0-2	1-0	3-5	1-0	1-3	3-3	3-3		2-2	3-3	2-3	2-2
Mynydd Isa	2-2	n/a	0-0	1-1	1-3	1-1	0-1	1-0	1-1	4-0	3-1	3-2	3-1	0-2		1-1	2-1	1-0
Penrhyncoch	1-3	n/a	2-3	1-1	1-1	2-2	0-1	3-1	3-2	2-2	0-0	3-0	2-0	2-4	0-2		0-2	1-2
Prestatyn Town	0-1	n/a	7-1	6-1	1-1	2-2	4-1	4-2	0-1	3-1	5-0	1-2	2-1	3-1	0-0	2-1		5-1
Ruthin Town	2-3	3-0	0-3	2-2	0-1	1-4	1-2	2-1	3-3	1-0	1-0	2-2	0-1	2-0	3-0	3-0	0-6	

		P	W	D	L	F	A	Pts
Prestatyn Town		32	24	4	4	93	29	76
Bala Town		32	19	4	9	71	42	61
Flint Town United		32	16	10	6	62	42	58
Llandudno Town		32	16	8	8	58	36	56
Holyhead Hotspur		32	15	9	8	76	53	54
Gap Queens Park	-3	32	15	10	7	82	47	52
Glantraeth		32	15	6	11	64	55	51
Denbigh Town		32	13	7	12	52	50	46
Guilsfield		32	12	5	15	57	62	41
Llanfairpwll		32	10	10	12	59	71	40
Mynydd Isa		32	10	9	13	45	51	39
Llandyrnog United		32	10	8	14	54	69	38
Ruthin Town		32	10	6	16	41	63	36
Buckley Town	-3	32	8	9	15	45	80	30
Penrhyncoch		32	6	8	18	38	66	26
Lex XI	-3	32	6	7	19	44	85	22
Gresford Athletic		32	4	6	22	32	72	18

Bodedern – record expunged

LEAGUE CUP

PRELIMINARY ROUND
Bala Town (w/o) v Bodedern (scr.)
Guilsfield 2 Gresford Athletic 0
FIRST ROUND
Buckley Town 3 Prestatyn Town 3 *aet* (6-5p)
Denbigh Town 2 Llanfairpwll 1
Flint Town United 0 **Mynydd Isa** 1
Lex XI 2 **Bala Town** 3
Llandudno Town 0 **Holyhead Hotspur** 2
Llandyrnog United 4 Glantraeth 1
Penrhyncoch 2 **Gap Queens Park** 4
Ruthin Town 3 Guilsfield 0
QUARTER-FINALS
Denbigh Town 6 Buckley Town 0
Holyhead Hotspur 0 **Mynydd Isa** 1
Llandyrnog United 0 **Bala Town** 6
Ruthin Town 0 **Gap Queens Park** 0 *aet* (3-4p)
SEMI-FINALS
Bala Town 2 Denbigh Town 1 *(at Llandudno Town)*
Gap Queens Park 2 Mynydd Isa 1 *(at Buckley Town)*
FINAL
(May 10th at Prestatyn Town)
Gap Queens Park 1 **Bala Town** 2 *aet*

WWW.NLNEWSDESK.CO.UK

HUWS GRAY CYMRU ALLIANCE CONSTITUTION 2008-09

BALA TOWN .... Maes Tegid, Castle Street, Bala LL23 7YB .... None
BUCKLEY TOWN .... Globe Way, Liverpool Way, Buckley CH7 3LL .... None
DENBIGH TOWN .... Central Park, Park Street, Denbigh LL16 3DD 01745 812505
FLINT TOWN UNITED .... Cae Y Castell, March Lane, Flint CH6 5PJ 01352 730982
GLANTRAETH .... Trefdraeth, Bodorgan, LL62 5EU 01407 840401
GRESFORD ATHLETIC.................... Clapper Lane, Gresford, Wrexham LL12 8RW .... None
GUILSFIELD .... Community Centre, Guilsfield, Welshpool SY21 9ND .... None
HOLYHEAD HOTSPUR............. New Oval, Leisure Centre, Kingsland, Holyhead LL65 2YE 01407 764111
LEX XI .... Stansty Park, Summerhill, Wrexham LL11 4YG............................ 01978 261148
LLANDUDNO TOWN....................... Maesdu Park, Builder Street, Llandudno LL30 1HH 01492 860945
LLANDYRNOG UNITED .... Swyn Y Nant, Llandyrnog, Denbigh LL16 4HB .... None
LLANFAIRPWLL .... Rear of Post Office, Ffordd Caergybi, Llanfairpwllgwyngyll LL61 5YG .... None
LLANGEFNI TOWN .... Cae Bob Parry, Talwrn Road, Llangefni LL77 7LP............................ 01248 724999
MOLD ALEXANDRA .... Alyn Park, Denbigh Road, Mold CH7 1SW .... None
MYNYDD ISA .... Agoed Sports Field, Snowden Avenue, Bryn-y-Baal, Mold CH7 6SZ............................ None
PENRHYNCOCH .... Cae Baker, Penrhynchoch, Aberystwyth SY23 3XH 01970 828992
RUTHIN TOWN .... Memorial Playing Fields, Park Road, Ruthin LL15 1NB............................ None

IN: Llangefni Town (R – Welsh Premier League), Mold Alexandra (P – Welsh National League (Wrexham Area) Premier Division)
OUT: Bodedern (WS), Gap Queens Park (F), Prestatyn Town (P – Welsh Premier League)

DEVON & EXETER LEAGUE

Note – Pinhoe withdrew during the course of the season

Their results are shown herein but are expunged from the league table

	Beer Albion	Bickleigh	Clyst Valley	Cullompton Rangers Res.	Exeter Civil Service	Feniton	Hatherleigh Town	Heavitree Harriers	Heavitree Social United	Pinhoe	Sidmouth Town	St Martins	Thorverton	Topsham Town	University of Exeter Res.	Wellington Town Res.
Beer Albion	P	1-2	3-2	3-3	2-3	3-1	0-2	0-1	1-1	3-1	1-3	3-1	1-0	1-0	2-2	3-3
Bickleigh	3-2	R	1-3	4-0	5-2	3-1	3-4	1-3	4-3	5-5	1-3	0-2	1-3	3-2	3-1	0-2
Clyst Valley	0-0	5-2	E	7-3	0-1	2-2	3-3	3-2	1-3	3-0	2-2	3-1	2-0	1-3	2-4	2-1
Cullompton Rangers Res.	0-2	0-2	2-5	M	0-1	1-6	1-3	3-1	1-2	n/a	0-6	0-7	1-5	3-8	1-4	2-1
Exeter Civil Service	2-2	1-3	3-1	12-0	I	7-1	0-2	0-0	2-1	n/a	4-2	4-0	2-4	1-2	3-1	1-4
Feniton	2-1	2-3	2-2	4-0	6-3	E	5-2	2-4	2-0	7-2	4-1	0-2	2-2	0-0	2-1	0-3
Hatherleigh Town	2-1	0-3	1-0	1-2	0-4	1-0	R	3-0	4-1	1-4	2-1	2-1	0-2	1-1	0-2	0-2
Heavitree Harriers	3-0	1-2	0-2	1-1	1-2	2-1	2-0		1-2	4-2	2-3	0-2	1-1	4-2	3-5	0-4
Heavitree Social United	1-4	1-0	0-3	2-1	1-1	0-1	3-2	1-1	D	3-2	4-2	1-5	1-0	4-4	1-2	0-8
Pinhoe	4-0	4-2	4-1	n/a	0-2	1-2	n/a	0-2	n/a	I	n/a	n/a	2-1	n/a	n/a	n/a
Sidmouth Town	1-1	1-2	2-4	2-0	0-0	0-2	2-4	0-1	3-5	n/a	V	3-3	0-0	2-4	0-1	2-0
St Martins	1-0	4-1	0-2	7-0	1-1	5-1	2-0	3-2	3-0	n/a	2-1	I	0-3	4-0	0-3	2-0
Thorverton	2-1	2-2	1-1	4-0	2-4	4-0	3-0	2-3	0-1	3-2	1-0	0-2	S	3-1	0-0	1-3
Topsham Town	0-1	3-3	2-0	5-2	1-6	1-2	0-3	2-1	1-4	6-1	2-5	2-1	1-2	I	0-1	1-3
University of Exeter Res.	0-1	3-2	4-0	9-0	2-4	6-2	3-0	5-0	6-1	1-3	2-2	1-1	2-1	6-0	O	2-2
Wellington Town Res.	4-0	3-1	2-1	5-1	1-1	0-1	1-2	1-4	3-0	2-3	3-1	2-4	1-1	2-1	0-1	N

Premier Division		P	W	D	L	F	A	Pts
University of Exeter Res.		28	17	5	6	78	34	56
St Martins	-1	28	17	3	8	66	35	53
Exeter Civil Service		28	15	6	7	75	45	51
Thorverton		28	13	7	8	50	31	46
Wellington Town Res.	-2	28	14	4	10	62	36	44
Bickleigh		28	14	2	12	60	58	44
Hatherleigh Town		28	14	2	12	44	48	44
Clyst Valley		28	12	6	10	59	50	42
Feniton		28	12	4	12	54	59	40
Heavitree Social United		28	12	4	12	45	65	40
Beer Albion		28	9	7	12	40	45	34
Heavitree Harriers	-1	28	10	4	14	44	53	33
Topsham Town		28	8	4	16	49	69	28
Sidmouth Town		28	7	6	15	50	57	27
Cullompton Rangers Res.		28	3	2	23	28	119	11

Pinhoe – record expunged

EAST DEVON SENIOR CUP

FIRST ROUND
Broadclyst Social Club 4
Culm United 3
Exeter St Thomas 1
Thorverton 3
Feniton 2 East Budleigh 1
Hatherleigh Town 4
Cullompton Rangers Res. 0
Heavitree Harriers 7
Wellington Town Res. 2
Heavitree Social United 1
Bickleigh 3
Otterton 1 **Sidmouth Town** 4
Pinhoe 2 Newtown 1
St Martins 5 Exmouth
Amateurs 3
Topsham Town 1 Beer Albion 2
(Beer Albion expelled)
Westexe Rovers 2 **Seaton
Town** 3

SECOND ROUND
Bickleigh 2 **Pinhoe** 4
Broadclyst Social Club 3
Alphington Res. 3 *aet* (1-4p)

Clyst Valley 4 Willand Rovers
Res. 1
Exeter Civil Service 0
Budleigh Salterton Res. 1
Feniton 0 **Heavitree Harriers** 2
Seaton Town 0 **St Martins** 4
Sidmouth Town *(bye)*
Topsham Town 3 **Hatherleigh
Town** 5

QUARTER-FINALS
Clyst Valley 4 Broadclyst
Social Club 0
Hatherleigh Town 4 Budleigh
Salterton Res. 2
Heavitree Harriers 2 **Sidmouth
Town** 4
Pinhoe 0 **St Martins** 4

SEMI-FINALS
Clyst Valley 5 Sidmouth Tn 5
aet (9-8p)
Hatherleigh 0 **St Martins** 1 *aet*

FINAL
(May 5th at Topsham Town)
St Martins 1 **Clyst Valley** 2

DEVON & EXETER LEAGUE PREMIER DIVISION CONSTITUTION 2008-09

BEER ALBION	Furzebrake, Stovar Long Lane, Beer EX12 3DY	None
BICKLEIGH	Happy Meadow, Bickleigh, Tiverton	None
BUDLEIGH SALTERTON RESERVES	Greenway Lane, Budleigh Salterton EX9 6SG	01395 443850
CLYST VALLEY	Winslade Park, Exmouth Road, Clyst St Mary	None
EXMOUTH AMATEURS	Warren View, Halsdon Avenue, Exmouth EX8 3DH	01395 222619
FENITON	Station Road, Feniton, Honiton EX14 3DF	01404 850835
HATHERLEIGH TOWN	The Sportsfield, Okehampton Road, Hatherleigh, Okehampton	01837 810346
HEAVITREE SOCIAL UNITED	Wingfield Park, East Wonford Hill, Exeter EX1 3BS	01392 273020
NEWTOWN	Grace Road, Marsh Barton, Exeter	None
OTTERTON	Stantaway Playing Fields, Otterton	None
SIDMOUTH TOWN	Manstone Recreation Ground, Manstone Lane, Sidmouth EX10 9TF	01395 577087
ST MARTINS	Minster Park, Exminster Hospital, Exminster	01392 823909
THORVERTON	Recreation Playing Field, Riaddon Road, Thorverton, Exeter	None
TOPSHAM TOWN	Coronation Field, Exeter Road, Topsham	01392 873678
UNIVERSITY OF EXETER RESERVES	University Sports Ground, Topsham Road, Topsham EX3 0LY	01392 879542
WELLINGTON TOWN RESERVES	Wellington Playing Field, North Street, Wellington TA1 8NA	01823 664810

IN: Budleigh Salterton Reserves (P), Exmouth Amateurs (now amalgamated with Heavitree Harriers) (P), Newtown (P), Otterton (P)
OUT: Cullompton Rangers Reserves (R), Exeter Civil Service (P – South West Peninsula League Division One East), Heavitree Harriers (W), Pinhoe (WS)

WWW.CHERRYRED.CO.UK

Senior Division One	P	W	D	L	F	A	Pts
Budleigh Salterton Res.	26	17	7	2	67	25	58
Newtown	26	18	3	5	69	31	57
Otterton	26	16	3	7	71	41	51
Seaton Town	26	15	5	6	52	32	50
Willand Rovers Res.	26	14	6	6	67	30	48
East Budleigh	26	14	3	9	43	36	45
Culm United	26	12	4	10	54	59	40
Westexe Rovers	26	10	3	13	46	61	33
Broadclyst Social Club	26	9	5	12	58	65	32
Alphington Res.	26	8	6	12	32	49	30
University of Exeter 'A'	26	8	3	15	44	48	27
Elmore Res.	26	8	3	15	45	68	27
Exeter St Thomas	26	2	4	20	31	83	10
Exmouth Amateurs	26	2	3	21	28	79	9

Senior Division Two	P	W	D	L	F	A	Pts
Bow AAC	26	19	3	4	72	23	60
Halwill	26	16	5	5	64	32	53
Upottery	26	16	5	5	60	40	53
Sidbury United	26	14	8	4	70	32	50
Barnstaple Town Res.	26	12	1	13	63	56	37
Honiton Town	26	11	1	14	53	64	34
Newtown Res.	26	9	6	11	53	51	33
University of Exeter 'B'	26	10	3	13	47	66	33
St Loyes Tap & Barrel	26	9	4	13	48	67	31
North Tawton	26	8	6	12	56	67	30
Exeter Civil Service Res.	26	7	7	12	46	56	28
Dawlish Town Res. -5	26	11	0	15	49	68	28
Lympstone	26	7	4	15	55	78	25
Sidmouth Town Res.	26	5	3	18	36	72	18

Senior Division Three	P	W	D	L	F	A	Pts
Morchard Bishop	26	22	2	2	102	24	68
Heavitree Social Utd Res.	26	17	2	7	92	53	53
Beacon Knights	26	16	4	6	81	47	52
Sandford	26	14	5	7	76	63	47
Colyton	26	14	5	7	64	54	47
Kentisbeare	26	12	7	7	54	45	43
Uplowman Athletic	26	12	4	10	60	60	40
Seaton Town Res. -1	26	10	3	13	46	63	32
Tipton St John	26	9	4	13	55	65	31
Winkleigh	26	8	4	14	60	73	28
Lapford	26	7	3	16	53	76	24
South Zeal United	26	6	5	15	44	71	23
Pinhoe Res. -1	26	7	1	18	49	96	21
Motel Rangers & Offwell	26	3	1	22	43	89	10

Senior Division Four	P	W	D	L	F	A	Pts
Witheridge Res.	26	20	3	3	89	34	63
Axminster Town Res.	26	20	2	4	92	39	62
Clyst Valley Res.	26	15	4	7	70	50	49
Bampton	26	11	7	8	44	39	40
Chard Town Res. -1	26	11	5	10	41	45	37
Newton St Cyres	26	11	4	11	63	75	37
Topsham Town Res.	26	10	5	11	58	64	35
Woodbury	26	9	7	10	59	54	34
Westexe Rovers Res.	26	10	2	14	44	66	32
Crescent	26	9	3	14	65	75	30
Dunkeswell Rovers	26	9	2	15	57	72	29
Newtown 'A'	26	7	4	15	47	67	25
Crediton United Res. -2	26	7	4	15	34	54	23
Tedburn St Mary -1	26	5	4	17	51	80	18

Senior Division Five	P	W	D	L	F	A	Pts
Phoenix Club	26	24	2	0	114	22	74
Oakwood	26	18	2	6	86	53	56
St Martins Res.	26	16	5	5	63	52	53
Dawlish United	26	13	7	6	84	49	46
Lord's XI	26	14	4	8	66	62	46
Thorverton Res.	26	15	0	11	68	48	45
Colaton Raleigh	26	14	1	11	80	58	43
Sidbury United Res.	26	12	3	11	64	45	39
Ottery St Mary Res. -4	26	11	8	7	72	48	37
Sampford Peverell	26	8	5	13	50	72	29
Broadclyst Social Club Res.	26	4	3	19	46	109	15
Legends -3	26	5	2	19	42	75	14
Kentisbeare Res.	26	4	2	20	47	122	14
Exmouth Amateurs Res. -1	26	2	0	24	29	96	5

Intermediate Division One	P	W	D	L	F	A	Pts
Okehampton Argyle Res.	26	16	5	5	70	30	53
Countess Wear Dynamoes	26	16	5	5	70	34	53
Axmouth United	26	16	5	5	75	53	53
Heavitree Harriers Res.	26	15	6	5	73	33	51
Bickleigh Res.	26	14	3	9	84	59	45
Cullompton Rangers 'A' -2	26	12	6	8	68	56	40
Culm United Res.	26	8	10	8	58	60	34
Exmouth Town Res. -4	26	11	4	11	63	46	33
Feniton Res.	26	9	6	11	53	64	33
Dawlish Town 'A' -4	26	10	6	10	58	65	32
Alphington 'A' -6	26	10	4	12	57	66	28
UAU Exeter -3	26	8	3	15	58	85	24
Newton Town	26	2	3	21	37	99	9
Culmstock -2	26	1	2	23	32	106	3

Intermediate Division Two	P	W	D	L	F	A	Pts
Hemyock	28	21	1	6	126	39	64
Beer Albion Res. -4	28	20	2	6	84	37	58
Honiton Town Res.	28	17	7	4	64	29	58
Uplowman Athletic Res.	28	17	6	5	94	54	57
Awliscombe United	28	17	4	7	83	49	55
Cheriton Fitzpaine	28	15	6	7	83	49	51
Lympstone Res.	28	11	6	11	71	71	39
Northlew -1	28	12	2	14	60	72	37
Oak -1	28	11	4	13	71	72	36
AFC Sidford	28	9	7	12	58	61	34
Axminster Town 'A'	28	9	7	12	58	68	34
Hatherleigh Town Res.	28	8	7	13	51	65	31
Rockbeare Rangers	28	7	3	18	39	80	24
Exmouth Amateurs 'A' -1	28	1	4	23	26	125	6
North Tawton Res. -2	28	1	2	25	25	122	3

Intermediate Division Three	P	W	D	L	F	A	Pts
Bow AAC Res.	26	18	3	5	70	39	57
Priory	26	18	1	7	115	49	55
Silverton -4	26	17	3	6	94	62	50
Heavitree Social United 'A'	26	14	3	9	88	55	45
Langdon Res.	26	12	8	6	80	59	44
East Budleigh Res. -4	26	12	9	5	64	42	41
Clyst Valley 'A'	26	12	5	9	54	43	41
Follygate & Inwardleigh	26	11	2	13	82	94	35
Halwill Res.	26	9	4	13	53	55	31
Newton St Cyres Res.	26	9	4	13	63	73	31
Colyton Res.	26	8	4	14	44	90	28
Met Office	26	7	6	13	36	64	27
Crediton Youth -1	26	4	3	19	33	92	14
Tedburn St Mary Res. -5	26	3	1	22	37	98	5

Sporting Club NA – record expunged

Intermediate Division Four	P	W	D	L	F	A	Pts
Bampton Res.	26	22	2	2	83	24	68
Okehampton Argyle 'A'	26	21	3	2	108	29	66
Amory Argyle	26	17	5	4	97	44	56
Beacon Knights Res.	26	17	2	7	84	48	53
Winkleigh Res.	26	12	7	7	82	65	43
Langdon 'A'	26	11	5	10	76	63	38
Bradninch	26	9	3	14	63	81	30
Otterton Res. -1	26	9	3	14	53	76	29
Sandford Res.	26	6	10	10	61	63	28
Lapford Res.	26	5	14	12	62	85	26
Seaton Town 'A' -1	26	7	3	16	60	99	23
Feniton 'A' -6	26	8	4	14	45	67	22
Awliscombe Utd Res. -1	26	5	2	19	40	106	16
Motel Rgs & Off. Res. -2	26	2	4	20	38	102	8

DORSET COUNTY LEAGUE

	AC Matravers	Allendale	Bournemouth University	Broadmayne	Chickerell United	Easton United	Kangaroos	Moreton	Okeford United	Stalbridge	Tintinhull	Wareham Rangers	Weymouth Sports	Witchampton United
AC Matravers		2-2	0-3	3-6	0-2	2-4	4-0	2-1	4-4	5-1	2-3	0-2	4-2	5-1
Allendale	3-0		1-2	2-0	0-4	1-1	1-0	3-2	0-1	4-1	0-0	0-2	0-3	0-0
Bournemouth University	2-1	0-1	S	2-1	1-1	3-0	2-2	3-0	0-2	3-1	6-2	3-3	6-1	4-2
Broadmayne	2-3	1-3	1-10	E	0-9	2-2	1-0	5-2	1-3	6-2	2-2	0-6	0-8	2-4
Chickerell United	4-0	5-0	3-0	3-1	N	1-1	5-1	2-0	4-0	12-0	0-0	3-0	2-1	7-1
Easton United	4-3	4-0	1-0	5-1	1-3	I	1-1	1-0	4-1	7-0	6-4	2-0	2-2	3-0
Kangaroos	3-0	6-1	0-5	1-0	0-6	0-3	O	2-2	0-1	2-0	0-1	0-3	2-2	1-1
Moreton	0-0	1-1	1-3	0-0	1-4	2-6	1-2	R	2-3	5-1	1-1	0-2	3-2	3-3
Okeford United	3-3	1-4	3-2	4-5	0-2	4-0	0-0	0-0		5-3	2-2	2-0	1-1	3-3
Stalbridge	1-2	0-1	1-2	2-5	0-9	2-9	0-2	1-4	0-3	D	1-3	0-4	0-3	0-3
Tintinhull	3-3	1-1	0-6	6-0	1-8	1-4	5-0	1-2	3-4	6-0	I	0-2	2-5	0-7
Wareham Rangers	1-0	3-0	0-3	4-0	1-1	3-1	3-1	1-1	2-3	4-1	4-1	V	1-1	6-2
Weymouth Sports	3-0	3-2	2-3	1-0	0-1	1-4	1-1	3-1	3-0	1-1	3-0	4-1		1-3
Witchampton United	0-3	3-2	4-2	0-1	1-4	2-0	1-2	2-0	0-1	2-2	3-4	0-5	1-0	

Senior Division		P	W	D	L	F	A	Pts
Chickerell United		26	22	4	0	105	11	70
Bournemouth University		26	17	3	6	76	34	54
Easton United		26	16	5	5	76	39	53
Wareham Rangers	-1	26	16	4	6	63	29	51
Okeford United		26	13	7	6	54	48	46
Weymouth Sports		26	11	6	9	57	41	39
Allendale		26	9	6	11	33	46	33
Witchampton United		26	9	5	12	49	61	32
AC Matravers		26	8	5	13	51	60	29
Kangaroos		26	7	7	12	29	50	28
Tintinhull	-1	26	7	7	12	52	72	27
Broadmayne	-1	26	7	3	16	43	87	23
Moreton		26	4	8	14	35	54	20
Stalbridge		26	0	2	24	21	112	2

DORSET COUNTY LEAGUE SENIOR DIVISION CONSTITUTION 2008-09

AC MATRAVERS.................Lytchett Matravers Recreation Ground, Lytchett Matravers.........................None
ALLENDALE...................Redcotts Recreation Ground, School Lane, Wimborne BH21 1HQ..........................None
BISHOP'S CAUNDLE................Bishop's Caundle Recreation Ground, Bishop's Caundle.......................None
BROADMAYNE................Thomas Hardye Leisure Centre, Coburg Road, Dorchester DT1 2HR........01305 266772
EASTON UNITED.........................Grove Road Playing Field, Easton, Portland..............................None
FC POLONIA.........................Branksome Recreation Ground..................................None
KANGAROOS................Thomas Hardye Leisure Centre, Coburg Road, Dorchester DT1 2HR........01305 266772
MORETON......................Recreation Field, Dick o'the Banks Road, Crossways DT2 8BJ...................None
OKEFORD UNITED.................Recreation Ground, Okeford Fitzpaine, Blandford Forum......................None
PARLEY SPORTS..................Parley Sports Club, Christchurch Road, West Parley..........................None
STOURPAINE....................Dick Draper Memorial Fields, Stourpaine, Blandford Forum....................None
TINTINHULL...................Montacute Road, Tintinhull, Yeovil BA22 8QD..........................None
WAREHAM RANGERS.............Purbeck Sports Centre, Worgret Road, Wareham BH20 4PH..........01929 556454
WEYMOUTH SPORTS.............Weymouth College, Cranford Avenue, Weymouth DT4 7LQ.............01305 208892
WITCHAMPTON UNITED....................Crichel Park, Witchampton..............................01258 840986
IN: *Bishop's Caundle (P), FC Polonia (P), Parley Sports (P), Stourpaine (P)*
OUT: *Bournemouth University (P – Hampshire Premier League), Chickerell United (P – Dorset Premier League), Stalbridge (R)*

Football Club History Database

The website that contains the most comprehensive record of statistical club histories, with over 6000 clubs covered. Also includes an ever-expanding section on cup results and final league tables.

www.fchd.info

Reserve Division

		P	W	D	L	F	A	Pts
Chickerell United Res.		22	17	3	2	79	22	54
Portland United Res.		22	13	4	5	72	24	43
Shaftesbury Res.		22	12	5	5	53	39	41
Poole Borough Res.	-1	22	12	5	5	41	24	40
Sherborne Town Res.		22	11	5	6	62	44	38
Cobham Sports Res.	-3	22	9	5	8	54	42	29
Wareham Rangers Res.		22	6	8	8	50	57	26
Sturminster Newton United Res.		22	7	4	11	25	37	25
Gillingham Town Res.	-1	22	6	5	11	37	65	22
Wincanton Town Res.		22	6	3	13	37	70	21
Blandford United Res.		22	5	4	13	29	52	19
Holt United Res.	-2	22	2	1	19	21	84	5

Division One

		P	W	D	L	F	A	Pts
Parley Sports	-3	26	19	4	3	89	26	58
Stourpaine		26	17	6	3	67	29	57
FC Polonia		26	15	4	7	55	25	49
Bishop's Caundle		26	14	5	7	49	32	47
Ferndown Sports	-1	26	13	4	9	76	42	42
AFC Bluebridge		26	12	5	9	42	35	41
Wool RBL		26	12	3	11	48	44	39
Swanage Town & Herston Res.	-4	26	10	6	10	41	49	32
Piddletrenthide United		26	9	3	14	49	61	30
Bere Regis		26	9	3	14	54	68	30
Cranborne Res.	-3	26	8	6	12	32	41	27
Corfe Castle		26	5	4	17	30	83	19
Lytchett Red Triangle		25	4	4	17	32	78	16
Bradford Sports	-1	25	4	3	18	30	81	14

Lytchett Red Triangle v Bradford Sports not played

Division Two

		P	W	D	L	F	A	Pts
Crossways		22	17	0	5	77	33	51
Upwey & Broadway		22	16	1	5	80	24	49
Chickerell United 'A'		22	14	3	5	64	31	45
The Balti House		22	13	4	5	51	31	43
Child Okeford		22	13	3	6	60	40	42
Poundbury		22	11	2	9	54	57	35
Horse & Groom		22	9	6	7	52	39	33
Sturminster Marshall Res.		22	6	2	14	37	62	20
Wyke Regis Social Club		22	5	3	14	33	64	18
Witchampton United Res.	-3	22	5	3	14	32	65	15
Puddletown		22	2	7	13	29	54	13
Handley Sports		22	3	2	17	19	88	11

Division Three

		P	W	D	L	F	A	Pts
Kingston Lacy	-3	22	20	1	1	104	15	58
FC Windowman		22	17	2	3	80	24	53
Piddlehinton United		22	12	2	8	87	55	38
Maiden Newton & Cattistock		22	11	2	9	48	53	35
Harbour View Developments		22	10	4	8	53	48	34
AC Matravers Res.		22	10	3	9	70	46	33
Swanage Town & Herston 'A'	-1	22	10	1	11	45	57	30
Catterick		22	8	5	9	64	66	29
Shaftesbury 'A'		22	5	2	15	31	87	17
Stickland United	-1	22	5	3	14	38	96	17
Donhead United		22	4	3	15	49	74	15
Sturminster Newton United 'A'		22	3	6	13	34	82	15

Division Four

		P	W	D	L	F	A	Pts
Dorchester Sports		20	15	4	1	75	18	49
Granby Rovers		20	15	3	2	66	19	48
Stourpaine Res.		20	13	2	5	65	34	41
Westover Spartans	-3	20	12	2	6	80	41	35
Piddletrenthide United Res.		20	10	5	5	57	37	35
Milborne Sports		20	8	3	9	59	50	27
Okeford United Res.		20	7	3	10	39	45	24
Wool RBL Res.		20	7	2	11	40	65	23
Winterborne Kingston		20	4	1	15	28	68	13
Owermoigne		20	3	2	15	29	77	11
Handley Sports Res.		20	1	3	16	14	98	6

DORSET PREMIER LEAGUE

	Blandford United	Bridport Res.	Cobham Sports	Cranborne	Gillingham Town	Hamworthy Recreation	Hamworthy United Res.	Holt United	Poole Borough	Portland United	Sturminster Marshall	Sturminster Newton United	Swanage Town & Herston	Westland Sports	Wincanton Town
Blandford United		1-0	3-0	1-1	1-1	1-2	1-4	3-1	3-1	0-1	3-2	2-0	3-3	2-3	0-5
Bridport Res.	2-0		0-1	5-3	0-4	2-1	3-4	0-2	1-4	0-1	2-2	1-0	2-2	0-4	4-1
Cobham Sports	2-3	6-0		1-3	0-4	2-4	0-3	2-2	2-0	1-4	1-0	2-0	1-1	1-2	2-3
Cranborne	3-1	2-1	3-2		0-2	0-5	0-0	4-2	1-2	1-7	5-0	1-1	1-2	1-1	1-2
Gillingham Town	6-0	2-0	2-2	4-3		2-1	3-0	1-2	4-4	2-3	3-2	2-0	5-0	2-1	2-0
Hamworthy Recreation	5-0	4-0	1-0	8-0	2-1		3-1	0-1	5-0	2-2	3-0	4-2	2-1	5-0	0-1
Hamworthy United Res.	2-4	1-1	1-3	1-1	1-2	2-4		0-1	1-1	3-1	6-3	1-0	4-1	0-0	3-3
Holt United	4-0	3-0	4-1	0-0	0-3	1-1	6-2		2-1	1-1	0-4	2-1	7-0	1-1	1-1
Poole Borough	3-2	3-2	3-2	0-1	0-2	1-1	5-0	0-2		2-2	4-0	1-1	4-1	2-3	2-0
Portland United	3-0	6-1	2-1	1-0	5-0	3-0	4-3	2-0	2-0		9-0	6-0	3-0	2-1	1-0
Sturminster Marshall	5-1	2-3	3-4	1-5	0-3	1-3	3-2	1-1	4-1	0-2		1-0	4-4	0-0	3-2
Sturminster Newton United	2-1	2-0	1-0	1-0	0-4	2-1	0-1	1-0	2-3	1-5	0-0		1-3	0-3	2-0
Swanage Town & Herston	7-0	1-1	5-2	0-2	0-1	0-6	0-6	1-2	1-4	1-1	2-1	3-4		1-4	1-3
Westland Sports	3-0	2-1	4-0	1-0	0-5	0-1	5-1	4-2	2-2	2-5	4-0	0-0	3-1		2-3
Wincanton Town	4-3	6-0	2-2	3-1	1-2	1-4	5-2	4-0	4-1	0-4	1-0	2-0	3-2	0-2	

		P	W	D	L	F	A	Pts
Portland United		28	23	4	1	88	22	73
Gillingham Town		28	21	3	4	74	28	66
Hamworthy Recreation		28	19	3	6	78	27	60
Westland Sports		28	15	6	7	57	38	51
Wincanton Town		28	15	3	10	60	47	48
Holt United		28	13	7	8	50	39	46
Poole Borough		28	11	6	11	54	53	39
Cranborne		28	9	6	13	43	55	33
Hamworthy United Res.	-3	28	9	6	13	55	63	30
Blandford United		28	8	3	17	39	75	27
Cobham Sports		28	7	4	17	43	63	25
Sturminster Newton United	-3	28	8	4	16	24	49	25
Sturminster Marshall		28	6	5	17	42	74	23
Bridport Res.		28	6	4	18	32	70	22
Swanage Town & Herston		28	5	6	17	44	80	21

EDGAR MAIDMENT CHARITY SHIELD

(League Champions v League Cup holders)

(October 13th at Hamworthy Recreation)
Westland Sports 3 **Hamworthy Recreation** 4

DORSET PREMIER LEAGUE CONSTITUTION 2008-09

BLANDFORD UNITED.............Recreation Ground, Park Road, Blandford Forum DT11 7BX.............................None
BRIDPORT RESERVES...............St Marys Field, Skilling Hill Road, Bridport DT6 5LN.......................01308 423834
CHICKERELL UNITED.............Weymouth College, Cranford Avenue, Weymouth DT4 7LQ.......................01305 208892
COBHAM SPORTS.........................Merley Park, Merley Lane, Wimborne BH21.................................01202 885773
CRANBORNE..................Recreation Ground, Penny's Lane, Cranborne, Wimborne BH21 5QE...................None
HAMWORTHY RECREATION...Hamworthy Recreation Club, Magna Road, Canford Magna, Wimborne BH21 3AP........01202 881922
HAMWORTHY UNITED RESERVES...The County Ground, Blandford Close, Hamworthy, Poole BH15 4BF..............01202 674974
HOLT UNITED..................................Gaunts Common, Holt, Wimborne BH21 4JR...........................01258 840379
POOLE BOROUGH...........Turlin Moor Rec Ground, Blandford Moor, Hamworthy, Poole BH21 5XX.....None (Office: 01202 674973)
PORTLAND UNITED...........................New Grove Corner, Grove Road, Portland DT5 1DP.........................01305 861489
STURMINSTER MARSHALL.............Churchill Close, Sturminster Marshall BH21 4BQ.......................None
STURMINSTER NEWTON UNITED...Barnetts Field, Honeymead Lane, Sturminster Newton DT10 7EW.................01258 471406
SWANAGE TOWN & HERSTON.......Day's Park, off De Moulham Road, Swanage BH19 2JW...........01929 424673
WESTLAND SPORTS.........................Alvington Lane, Yeovil BA22 8UX..................................None
WINCANTON TOWN...............Wincanton Sports Ground, Moor Lane, Wincanton BA9 9EJ.................01963 31815

IN: Chickerell United (P – Dorset County League Senior Division)
OUT: Gillingham Town (P – Western League Division One)

LEAGUE CUP

GROUP A

	P	W	D	L	F	A	Pts
Portland United	4	4	0	0	14	4	12
Wincanton Town	3	2	0	1	5	3	6
Poole Borough	3	0	1	2	1	5	1
Sturminster Marshall	4	0	1	3	5	13	1

Poole Borough 0 Portland United 3
Poole Borough 1 Sturminster Marshall 1
Poole Borough v Wincanton Town *(not played)*
Portland United v Poole Borough *(not played)*
Portland United 4 Sturminster Marshall 2
Portland United 2 Wincanton Town 1
Sturminster Marshall v Poole Borough *(not played)*
Sturminster Marshall 1 Portland United 5
Sturminster Marshall 1 Wincanton Town 3
Wincanton Town 1 Poole Borough 0
Wincanton Town v Portland United *(not played)*
Wincanton Town v Sturminster Marshall *(not played)*

GROUP B

	P	W	D	L	F	A	Pts
Hamworthy Rec.	6	5	0	1	18	10	15
Swantage Town & H.	6	3	2	1	20	9	11
Holt United	6	2	2	2	13	15	8
Blandford United	6	0	0	6	4	21	0

Blandford United 2 Hamworthy Recreation 3
Blandford United 1 Holt United 2
Blandford United 0 Swanage Town & Herston 2
Hamworthy Recreation 2 Blandford United 1
Hamworthy Recreation 4 Holt United 2
Hamworthy Recreation 4 Swanage Town & Herston 2
Holt United 4 Blandford United 0
Holt United 0 Hamworthy Recreation 5
Holt United 2 Swanage Town & Herston 2
Swanage Town & Herston 8 Blandford United 0
Swanage Town & Herston 3 Hamworthy Recreation 0
Swanage Town & Herston 3 Holt United 3

GROUP C

	P	W	D	L	F	A	Pts
Gillingham Town	4	3	0	1	13	3	9
Sturminster Newton Utd	4	3	0	1	6	2	9
Hamworthy Utd Res.	4	0	0	4	2	16	0

Gillingham Town 4 Hamworthy United Res. 1
Gillingham Town 1 Sturminster Newton Utd 0
Hamworthy United Res. 0 Gillingham Town 8
Hamworthy United Res. 1 Sturminster Newton Utd 2
Sturminster Newton Utd 2 Hamworthy United Res. 0
Sturminster Newton Utd 2 Gillingham Town 0

SEMI-FINALS
Gillingham Town 1 **Westland Sports** 2 *aet*
Portland United 1 **Hamworthy Recreation** 2 *aet*
FINAL
(April 29th at Dorchester Town)
Westland Sports 0 **Hamworthy Recreation** 3

GROUP D

	P	W	D	L	F	A	Pts
Westland Sports	6	4	2	0	26	8	14
Cobham Sports	6	2	3	1	11	11	9
Cranborne	6	2	0	4	13	14	6
Bridport Res.	6	0	3	3	4	21	3

Bridport Res. 1 Cobham Sports 1
Bridport Res. 0 Cranborne 5
Bridport Res. 2 Westland Sports 2
Cobham Sports 1 Bridport Res. 1
Cobham Sports 4 Cranborne 2
Cranborne 4 Bridport Res. 0
Cranborne 0 Cobham Sports 1
Cranborne 1 Westland Sports 3
Westland Sports 8 Bridport Res. 0
Westland Sports 3 Cobham Sports 0
Westland Sports 6 Cranborne 1

WWW.NLNEWSDESK.CO.UK

DURHAM ALLIANCE

Note – Blackhall Hardwick withdrew during the course of the season

Their results are shown herein but are expunged from the league table

	Birtley Town Res.	Blackhall Hardwick	Brandon British Legion	Cornforth United	Ebchester Consett	Hartlepool Town	Herrington Colliery Welfare	Newton Aycliffe	Ryton Res.	Seaham Kitchen Magic	Shildon Railway	Simonside Social Club	Thornley	Washington Res.	Wheatley Hill WMC	Whitehill
Birtley Town Res.		n/a	2-2	3-6	3-1	1-1	2-0	1-4	3-3	0-2	4-2	2-2	2-1	1-3	6-0	0-3
Blackhall Hardwick	n/a		1-5	n/a	n/a	1-3	5-2	n/a	n/a	0-3	n/a	n/a	4-3	1-1	2-1	n/a
Brandon British Legion	2-2	n/a		1-1	5-3	0-2	3-1	1-4	5-0	2-6	5-3	2-2	3-3	5-2	6-4	0-1
Cornforth United	2-2	n/a	7-4		1-1	5-2	6-1	2-2	4-1	0-4	6-3	4-1	2-0	1-4	3-4	2-4
Ebchester Consett	3-2	n/a	2-3	2-2		3-4	2-1	1-3	5-0	1-3	2-5	2-2	3-1	0-2	0-2	1-2
Hartlepool Town	4-1	1-1	5-2	2-2	1-2		1-4	0-1	5-1	0-2	1-4	0-3	4-2	3-2	3-2	2-0
Herrington Colliery Welfare	4-4	n/a	2-1	2-3	2-3	0-1		0-3	4-2	1-1	2-3	3-7	6-1	2-3	6-1	1-3
Newton Aycliffe	0-2	6-0	11-1	3-1	0-2	3-0	9-0		8-1	0-0	6-3	3-1	3-0	4-0	3-0	3-1
Ryton Res.	4-2	4-7	0-3	1-3	0-4	4-3	1-2	0-7		1-4	0-10	2-3	1-3	2-2	0-1	0-4
Seaham Kitchen Magic	5-3	n/a	1-1	2-3	6-0	3-1	0-0	3-5	2-0		5-2	1-1	4-4	6-0	4-1	0-1
Shildon Railway	2-3	n/a	2-1	7-2	0-1	0-2	1-2	1-2	3-1	0-2		1-5	3-1	0-3	2-1	1-2
Simonside Social Club	1-1	4-1	4-2	3-3	2-2	2-1	2-1	1-6	3-2	2-0	3-1		6-0	3-3	4-1	1-2
Thornley	2-3	n/a	0-1	2-1	7-2	2-5	2-2	1-4	5-2	1-2	4-0	1-2		3-4	0-4	1-2
Washington Res.	0-4	n/a	1-2	0-2	3-1	3-1	2-1	0-7	4-0	3-4	2-5	1-2	2-3		6-0	1-3
Wheatley Hill WMC	1-0	n/a	2-1	2-8	4-4	2-1	5-2	0-4	3-0	1-2	1-2	3-2	1-1	3-5		0-4
Whitehill	1-1	3-1	7-0	7-0	1-1	4-0	6-0	2-4	10-0	2-4	4-0	10-3	7-1	1-1	11-1	

		P	W	D	L	F	A	Pts
Newton Aycliffe		28	24	2	2	112	25	74
Whitehill		28	21	3	4	105	29	66
Seaham Kitchen Magic	-1	28	18	6	4	78	36	59
Simonside Social Club		28	14	8	6	73	60	50
Cornforth United		28	13	7	8	82	70	46
Washington Res.		28	12	3	13	62	69	39
Hartlepool Town		28	12	2	14	55	60	38
Birtley Town Res.		28	9	9	10	60	61	36
Brandon British Legion		28	10	6	12	64	80	36
Shildon Railway		28	11	0	17	66	73	33
Ebchester Consett		28	9	6	13	54	67	33
Wheatley Hill WMC		28	10	2	16	50	90	32
Herrington Colliery Welfare		28	7	4	17	52	78	25
Thornley		28	6	4	18	52	81	22
Ryton Res.		28	2	2	24	29	115	8

Blackhall Hardwick – record expunged

CARCRAFT DURHAM ALLIANCE CONSTITUTION 2008-09

BIRTLEY TOWN RESERVES . . . . Birtley Sports Complex, Durham Road, Birtley, Chester-le-Street DH3 2TB . . . . None
BRANDON BRTISH LEGION . . . . Community Centre, Brandon Lane, Brandon DH7 8PU . . . . None
BRANDON UNITED RESERVES . . . . Welfare Ground, Commercial Street, Brandon DH7 8PL 0191 378 1730
CONSETT U-21S . . . . Belle Vue Park, Ashdale Road, Consett DH8 5SR 01207 503788
CORNFORTH UNITED . . . . . . West Cornforth Community Centre, Station Road, West Cornforth DL17 9JQ 01740 654628
DURHAM GARDEN HOUSE . . . . Garden House Park, Durham . . . . None
EBCHESTER CONSETT . . . . Crookhall, Delves Lane, Consett DH8 7LR . . . . None
HARTLEPOOL ST FRANCIS . . . Hartlepool Sixth Form College, Blakelock Road, Brinkburn, Hartlepool TS25 5PF 01429 294444
HARTLEPOOL TOWN . . . . Grayfields Enclosure, Jesmond Road, Hartlepool TS26 0HN . . . . None
RYTON RESERVES . . . . Kingsley Park, Stannerford Road, Crawcrook, Ryton NE40 3SN 0191 413 4448
SEAHAM KITCHEN MAGIC . . . . . . Dawdon Welfare Park, Green Drive, Dawdon, Seaham SR7 7XL . . . . None
SHILDON RAILWAY . . . . Shildon Railway Sports/Social, Hackworth Street, Shildon DL4 1XL . . . . None
SIMONSIDE SOCIAL CLUB . . . . . Boldon Community Association, New Road, Boldon Colliery NE35 9DS . . . . . . 0191 536 4180 (Cricket Club)
SUNDERLAND SOUTH . . . . Houghton Sports Complex, Leyburn Road, Houghton-le-Spring . . . . None
THORNLEY . . . . Thornley Colliery Welfare, Ashfield Grove, Thornley . . . . None
WHEATLEY HILL WMC . . . . Old Fire Station, Quetlaw Road, Wheatley Hill DH6 3SB . . . . None
WHITEHILL . . . . Riverside Ground, Chester-le-Street . . . . None

IN: Brandon United Reserves (N), Consett u-21s (N), Durham Garden House (N), Hartlepool St Francis (P – Sunday football), Sunderland South (N)
OUT: Blackhall Hardwick (WS), Ferryhill Athletic (WN), Herrington Colliery Welfare (W), Jarrow Town (WN), Newton Aycliffe (P – Wearside League), Washington Reserves (W)

EAST MIDLANDS COUNTIES LEAGUE
(new for 2008-09)

EAST MIDLANDS COUNTIES LEAGUE CONSTITUTION 2008-09

BARDON HILL SPORTS	Bardon Close, Coalville LE67 4BS	01530 815569
BARROW TOWN	Riverside Park, Meynell, Barrow Road, Quorn, Loughborough LE12 8PJ	01509 620650
BLACKWELL MINERS WELFARE	The Welfare Ground, Primrose Hill, Blackwell, Alfreton DE55 5JF	01773 811295
BORROWASH VICTORIA	Robinson Construction Bowl, Borrowash Road, Spondon, Derby DE21 7PH	01332 669688
DUNKIRK	Ron Steel Sports Ground, Lenton Lane, Clifton Bridge, Nottingham NG7 2SA	0115 985 0803
ELLISTOWN	1 Terrace Road, Ellistown, Coalville LE67 1GD	01530 230159
GEDLING MINERS WELFARE	Plains Social Club, Plains Road, Mapperley, Nottingham NG3 5RH	0115 926 6300
GEDLING TOWN	Ferryboat Ground, Stoke Lane, Stoke Bardolph, Gedling NG14 5HX	0115 940 2145
GRAHAM STREET PRIMS	Asterdale Sports Centre, Borrowash Road, Spondon, Derby DE21 7PH	01332 668656
GREENWOOD MEADOWS	Lenton Lane, Clifton Bridge, Nottingham NG7 2AX	0115 986 5913
HEANOR TOWN	The Town Ground, Mayfield Avenue, Heanor DE75 7EN	01773 713742
HINCKLEY DOWNES	Hinckley United FC, Marstons Stadium, Leicester Road, Hinckley LE10 3DR	01455 840088
HOLBROOK MINERS WELFARE	Welfare Ground, Shaw Lane, Holbrook DE56 0TG	01332 880259
HOLWELL SPORTS	Welby Road, Asfordby Hill, Melton Mowbray LE14 3RD	01664 812715
IBSTOCK UNITED	The Welfare, Leicester Road, Ibstock LE67 6HN	01530 260656
KIRBY MUXLOE SC	Ratby Lane, Kirby Muxloe, Leicester LE9 9AQ	0116 239 3201
RADFORD	Selhurst Street, off Radford Road, Radford, Nottingham NG7 5EH	0115 942 3250
ST ANDREWS SC	Canal Street, Aylestone, Leicester LE2 8LX	0116 283 9298

IN: Bardon Hill Sports (P – Leicestershire Senior League Premier Division), Barrow Town (P – Leicestershire Senior League Premier Division), Blackwell Miners Welfare (P – Central Midlands League Supreme Division), Borrowash Victoria (S – Northern Counties East League Division One), Dunkirk (P – Central Midlands League Supreme Division), Ellistown (P – Leicestershire Senior League Premier Division), Gedling Miners Welfare (P – Central Midlands League Supreme Division), Gedling Town (S – Northern Counties East League Division One), Graham Street Prims (P – Central Midlands League Supreme Division), Greenwood Meadows (P – Central Midlands League Supreme Division), Heanor Town (P – Central Midlands League Supreme Division), Hinckley Downes (P – Leicestershire Senior League Premier Division), Holbrook Miners Welfare (P – Central Midlands League Supreme Division), Holwell Sports (P – Leicestershire Senior League Premier Division), Ibstock United (P – Leicestershire Senior League Premier Division), Kirby Muxloe SC (P – Leicestershire Senior League Premier Division), Radford (P – Central Midlands League Supreme Division), St Andrews SC (P – Leicestershire Senior League Premier Division)

EASTERN COUNTIES LEAGUE

	CRC	Dereham Town	Felixstowe & W.	Harwich & P.	Haverhill Rovers	Histon Res.	Ipswich Wdrs	King's Lynn Res.	Kirkley & P.	Leiston	Lowestoft Town	Mildenhall Tn	Needham Mkt	Newmarket Tn	Norwich United	Soham Tn Rgrs	Stanway Rovers	Swaffham Town	Walsham-le-W.	Wisbech Town	Woodbridge	Wroxham
CRC		0-0	1-1	2-4	2-1	1-1	3-0	1-2	0-2	3-3	1-2	0-0	1-3	3-2	4-0	2-0	0-1	2-0	2-3	4-2	4-0	2-2
Dereham Town	2-3		3-0	3-3	2-1	3-0	10-1	1-0	1-3	0-0	5-0	2-1	2-2	2-0	1-2	2-0	1-5	3-2	7-0	6-0	3-2	3-0
Felixstowe & Walton United	3-2	3-0		7-1	4-2	2-1	2-0	2-2	2-1	4-1	0-1	1-4	2-1	3-2	4-1	0-2	1-1	1-1	2-2	2-0	4-1	0-1
Harwich & Parkeston	1-3	4-0	3-3	P	0-1	2-1	4-1	0-2	2-1	1-0	1-3	0-1	1-2	1-1	2-0	0-6	0-3	2-2	0-2	1-2	3-0	0-1
Haverhill Rovers	0-0	2-1	1-2	4-1	R	7-0	0-0	4-3	3-1	2-1	3-1	3-1	0-2	0-1	0-5	1-3	0-1	3-0	4-0	3-1	4-2	1-2
Histon Res.	2-1	1-0	2-3	2-0	1-3	E	7-1	0-0	2-0	0-1	4-1	1-2	3-4	5-4	3-2	2-3	2-3	2-3	4-0	0-1	4-2	0-2
Ipswich Wanderers	2-3	1-3	0-2	0-3	2-2	2-1	M	0-1	0-6	1-3	3-1	1-3	0-4	4-3	0-2	2-3	4-3	1-0	1-2	1-3	2-3	0-1
King's Lynn Res.	2-6	3-2	0-2	0-1	2-2	3-0	6-1	I	1-4	6-1	2-1	0-2	0-1	0-3	6-1	0-3	1-1	2-0	3-0	1-0	0-0	0-3
Kirkley & Pakefield	1-0	2-1	3-3	1-2	0-1	2-2	2-1	1-1	E	2-2	4-2	2-1	3-3	1-1	1-1	2-1	2-1	2-1	6-1	2-1		0-2
Leiston	1-0	3-1	4-2	5-2	6-1	1-1	1-0	2-0	1-1	R	2-0	0-0	2-2	2-0	0-1	0-1	0-1	1-1	3-0	1-0	1-3	1-0
Lowestoft Town	3-2	1-2	5-2	3-1	1-2	2-1	6-0	2-2	0-4	2-2		0-1	1-1	7-0	1-0	1-3	2-5	5-0	4-0	1-0	5-3	1-4
Mildenhall Town	1-1	2-2	5-1	2-0	1-0	1-0	3-1	1-0	2-0	1-0	7-0	D	1-4	1-1	2-2	0-3	1-1	1-3	1-1	3-1	3-0	3-3
Needham Market	3-2	2-1	2-1	2-1	2-1	3-0	8-1	2-1	1-1	3-0	3-1	1-0	I	4-3	5-0	3-2	2-2	2-5	7-1	4-0	1-2	1-2
Newmarket Town	3-1	2-3	0-2	4-0	0-1	1-7	0-1	2-3	2-0	0-0	2-4	0-4	1-3	V	2-3	1-6	2-6	4-3	2-3	2-4	1-4	0-2
Norwich United	3-0	1-1	2-0	2-1	0-1	0-2	0-5	1-3	1-0	0-3	1-1	1-1	1-1	2-0	I	1-0	2-1	3-2	2-0	1-0	0-2	0-3
Soham Town Rangers	1-0	0-0	2-1	4-0	2-0	1-0	1-1	2-1	2-3	2-0	5-1	3-1	4-0	2-0	2-1	S	1-0	4-0	1-0	9-0	9-1	4-0
Stanway Rovers	1-1	1-4	2-3	3-0	1-4	6-1	2-2	4-2	0-1	5-1	4-1	2-0	1-3	0-1	2-2	1-1	I	1-1	1-3	0-1	2-0	0-3
Swaffham Town	2-1	1-2	3-2	3-8	1-0	2-0	2-0	1-2	0-3	2-6	0-5	1-1	1-3	2-2	0-2	0-1	2-2	O	2-2	1-3	3-0	0-6
Walsham-le-Willows	0-2	0-1	0-1	4-2	2-0	1-0	2-1	1-0	1-3	3-2	2-2	1-2	2-4	2-1	3-1	2-5	1-2	2-2	N	1-2	1-6	1-5
Wisbech Town	1-5	0-1	3-0	3-1	5-1	2-0	2-1	1-1	2-2	1-3	2-1	2-5	2-6	1-0	3-0	0-1	1-2	2-1	0-2		2-1	1-1
Woodbridge Town	1-2	0-3	3-2	2-3	1-1	2-1	2-1	3-0	0-2	2-2	0-5	3-1	0-4	0-2	2-2	1-1	0-1	1-2	3-0	1-1		2-1
Wroxham	1-4	5-0	3-0	7-0	1-2	4-1	4-2	0-0	0-2	0-0	6-0	0-2	1-2	3-1	2-1	3-0	5-0	4-1	3-0	0-2	5-5	

Premier Division

	P	W	D	L	F	A	Pts
Soham Town Rangers	42	31	6	5	108	34	99
Needham Market	42	29	7	6	114	56	94
Wroxham	42	27	6	9	103	44	87
Dereham Town	42	23	7	12	92	59	76
Mildenhall Town	42	22	10	10	75	47	76
Kirkley & Pakefield	42	21	10	11	82	54	73
Stanway Rovers	42	20	10	12	82	62	70
Felixstowe & Walton United	42	20	7	15	82	74	67
Leiston	42	17	11	14	65	57	62
Haverhill Rovers	42	19	5	18	72	66	62
Lowestoft Town	42	18	4	20	88	91	58
Wisbech Town	42	18	4	20	60	83	58
CRC	42	16	9	17	77	63	57
King's Lynn Res.	42	15	9	18	66	64	54
Norwich United	42	13	8	21	49	75	47
Walsham-le-Willows	42	14	5	23	54	98	47
Woodbridge Town	42	13	7	22	67	96	46
Harwich & Parkeston	42	13	4	25	62	98	43
Histon Res.	42	12	4	26	67	84	40
Swaffham Town *-1*	42	10	9	23	59	99	38
Newmarket Town	42	8	6	28	62	107	30
Ipswich Wanderers	42	7	4	31	44	119	25

RIDGEONS EASTERN COUNTIES LEAGUE PREMIER DIVISION CONSTITUTION 2008-09

CRC . . . . Cambridge United FC, The Trade Recruitment Stadium, Newmarket Road, Cambridge CB5 8LN 01223 566500
DEREHAM TOWN . . . . Aldiss Park, Norwich Road, Dereham NR20 3AL 01362 690460/693677
ELY CITY . . . . The Unwin Ground, Downham Road, Ely CB6 2SH 01353 662035
FELIXSTOWE & WALTON UNITED . . . . Town Ground, Dellwood Avenue, Felixstowe IP11 9HT 01394 282917
HARWICH & PARKESTON . . . . Royal Oak, Main Road, Dovercourt, Harwich CO12 4AA 01255 503643
HAVERHILL ROVERS . . . . Hamlet Croft, Haverhill CB9 8EH 01440 702137
HISTON RESERVES . . . . The Glass World Stadium, Bridge Road, Impington, Cambridge CB4 9PH 01223 237373
KING'S LYNN RESERVES . . . . The Walks Stadium, Tennyson Road, King's Lynn PE30 5PB 01553 760060
KIRKLEY & PAKEFIELD . . . . Kirkley & Pakefield Community Centre, Walmer Road, Lowestoft NR33 7LE 01502 513549
LEISTON . . . . LTAA, Victory Road, Leiston IP16 4DQ 01728 830308
LOWESTOFT TOWN . . . . Crown Meadow, Love Road, Lowestoft NR32 2PA 01502 573818
MILDENHALL TOWN . . . . Recreation Way, Mildenhall, Bury St Edmunds IP28 7HG 01638 713449
NEEDHAM MARKET . . . . Bloomfields, Quinton Road, Needham Market IP6 8DA 01449 721000
NORWICH UNITED . . . . Plantation Park, off Plantation Road, Blofield, Norwich NR13 4PL 01603 716963
STANWAY ROVERS . . . . Hawthorns, New Farm Road, Stanway, Colchester CO3 0PG 01206 578187
TIPTREE UNITED . . . . Chapel Road, Tiptree, near Colchester CO5 0RA 01621 815213
WALSHAM-LE-WILLOWS . . . . . . Walsham Sports Club, Summer Road, Walsham-le-Willows IP31 3AH 01359 259298
WHITTON UNITED . . . . King George V Playing Fields, Old Norwich Road, Ipswich IP6 6LE 01473 464030
WISBECH TOWN . . . . Fenland Park, Lerowe Road, Wisbech PE13 3QH 01945 584176
WIVENHOE TOWN . . . . Broad Lane Sports Ground, Elmstead Road, Wivenhoe CO7 7HA 01206 825380
WOODBRIDGE TOWN . . . . Notcutts Park, Fynn Road, off Seckford Hall Lane, Woodbridge IP12 4DA 01394 385308
WROXHAM . . . . Trafford Park, Skinners Lane, Wroxham NR12 8SJ 01603 783538

IN: Ely City (P), Tiptree United (P), Whitton United (P), Wivenhoe Town (R – Isthmian League Division One North)
OUT: Ipswich Wanderers (R), Newmarket Town (R), Soham Town Rangers (P – Southern League Division One Midlands), Swaffham Town (R)

	Cornard United	Debenham Leisure Centre	Diss Town	Downham Town	Ely City	FC Clacton	Fakenham Town	Godmanchester Rovers	Gorleston	Great Yarmouth Town	Hadleigh United	Halstead Town	Long Melford	March Town United	Saffron Walden Town	Stowmarket Town	Thetford Town	Tiptree United	Whitton United
Cornard United		1-4	3-2	0-1	1-4	2-3	2-2	0-0	0-7	1-1	0-0	1-2	2-0	1-1	2-2	1-2	1-2	1-3	1-2
Debenham Leisure Centre	3-0		2-0	6-0	0-1	2-2	2-2	2-1	3-0	3-2	1-0	3-3	2-0	2-0	0-2	4-1	1-1	3-1	1-2
Diss Town	6-0	1-1		0-0	2-1	0-1	3-1	1-2	2-3	5-1	1-2	1-2	1-4	3-3	1-0	1-0	2-0	0-1	0-0
Downham Town	1-0	0-1	0-4	D	2-5	1-1	1-0	4-1	4-1	2-2	1-1	0-0	1-0	0-0	0-2	2-2	3-3	1-5	1-0
Ely City	4-4	1-1	1-1	4-0	I	4-2	4-3	2-0	3-1	1-0	0-1	2-1	3-0	2-1	3-1	2-0	2-1	3-3	
FC Clacton	3-1	1-0	1-4	1-1	0-1	V	2-2	3-0	1-1	4-0	2-2	1-2	2-1	1-1	2-1	4-1	4-1	1-3	0-1
Fakenham Town	5-2	0-0	0-2	1-3	0-6	1-5	I	3-2	1-5	2-1	0-6	0-3	0-4	0-2	1-0	3-2	2-3	0-3	1-7
Godmanchester Rovers	0-2	2-0	1-5	2-3	1-3	0-3	1-0	S	3-4	3-2	1-1	0-6	3-1	2-1	0-1	0-2	1-3	1-4	1-1
Gorleston	4-0	2-0	2-4	2-2	2-3	1-3	8-0	1-0	I	3-3	1-3	2-1	3-0	3-2	2-2	3-3	1-1	1-3	3-5
Great Yarmouth Town	5-0	2-1	4-0	2-1	0-0	3-2	0-0	2-1	2-4	O	0-2	2-2	0-1	5-0	2-1	1-5	0-5	0-3	1-1
Hadleigh United	3-1	2-1	1-2	4-1	0-1	3-3	2-0	3-0	0-1	2-1	N	2-3	3-1	6-1	0-0	1-3	1-1	0-1	2-4
Halstead Town	0-0	1-1	0-4	2-0	3-2	2-3	3-0	0-1	0-0	2-4	1-4		5-0	3-3	0-1	2-2	3-1	2-1	1-1
Long Melford	4-0	0-6	1-4	0-2	0-4	1-3	3-0	0-1	0-3	2-2	1-3	0-5		2-2	1-2	1-4	0-4	2-3	0-0
March Town United	2-2	4-1	1-4	1-0	4-3	1-2	3-3	1-1	2-2	2-3	2-2	0-1	3-2	O	0-3	1-1	1-2	2-3	4-2
Saffron Walden Town	2-0	0-0	1-1	2-1	1-1	1-1	2-1	2-2	3-0	2-1	1-0	1-1	1-0	3-1	N	1-1	4-2	0-3	0-2
Stowmarket Town	1-2	1-3	2-9	1-2	1-1	3-2	7-1	2-0	1-5	2-3	0-2	0-4	1-0	1-1	1-2	E	2-2	2-0	0-4
Thetford Town	6-1	1-3	2-6	2-1	0-1	3-3	1-3	2-2	1-1	0-1	1-1	1-2	0-2	2-2	1-1	1-0		0-4	0-0
Tiptree United	3-1	0-2	2-1	6-0	2-2	4-0	5-1	1-0	2-1	2-0	2-2	2-1	2-0	1-0	1-0	5-4	4-2		2-1
Whitton United	4-0	2-2	1-3	3-0	1-1	4-1	7-1	5-0	1-2	4-0	1-2	2-3	6-0	8-1	3-1	0-0	5-2	1-2	

Division One		P	W	D	L	F	A	Pts
Tiptree United		36	28	2	6	88	39	86
Ely City		36	22	8	6	81	42	74
Whitton United		36	18	10	8	94	42	64
Diss Town		36	19	6	11	86	46	63
Hadleigh United		36	18	9	9	71	42	63
Halstead Town	-1	36	18	10	8	72	45	63
Saffron Walden Town		36	17	10	9	49	36	61
Gorleston		36	17	9	10	87	62	60
Debenham Leisure Centre	-3	36	17	10	9	66	38	58
FC Clacton		36	16	10	10	73	59	58
Great Yarmouth Town		36	12	8	16	58	71	44
Downham Town		36	11	10	15	42	67	43
Thetford Town		36	9	12	15	59	71	39
Stowmarket Town		36	10	9	17	61	76	39
March Town United		36	6	14	16	54	82	32
Godmanchester Rovers		36	8	6	22	36	76	30
Fakenham Town		36	6	6	24	40	112	24
Cornard United		36	4	9	23	36	94	21
Long Melford		36	5	4	27	35	87	19

RIDGEONS EASTERN COUNTIES LEAGUE DIVISION ONE CONSTITUTION 2008-09

BRANTHAM ATHLETIC..... Athletic & Social Club, New Village, Brantham, near Manningtree CO11 1RZ 01206 392506
CORNARD UNITED............ Blackhouse Lane Sport Ground, Great Cornard, Sudbury CO10 0NL.................... 07811 096832
DEBENHAM LEISURE CENTRE .... Gracechurch Street, Debenham, Stowmarket IP14 6BY.......................... 01728 861101
DISS TOWN .... Brewers Green Lane, Diss IP22 4QP..................... 01379 651223
DOWNHAM TOWN .... Memorial Playing Field, Lynn Road, Downham Market PE38 9QE..................... 01366 388424
FC CLACTON .... Rush Green Bowl, Rush Green Road, Clacton-on-Sea CO16 7BQ..................... 01255 432590
FAKENHAM TOWN ... Clipbush Park, Clipbush Lane, Fakenham NR21 8SW.................. 01328 855445/855859
GODMANCHESTER ROVERS........ Bearscroft Lane, Godmanchester, Huntingdon PE29 2LQ..................... 07950 367417
GORLESTON......................... Emerald Park, Woodfarm Lane, Gorleston NR31 9AQ..................... 01493 602802
GREAT YARMOUTH TOWN... Wellesley Road Rec Ground, Sandown Road, Great Yarmouth NR30 1EY..................... 01493 843373
HADLEIGH UNITED .... Millfield, Tinkers Lane, off Duke Street, Hadleigh IP7 5NG..................... 01473 822165
HALSTEAD TOWN.................. Rosemary Lane, Broton Industrial Estate, Halstead CO9 1HR..................... 01787 472082
IPSWICH WANDERERS .... SEH Sports Centre, Humber Doucy Lane, Ipswich IP4 3PB..................... 01473 728581
LONG MELFORD .... Stoneylands Stadium, New Road, Long Melford CO10 9JY..................... 01787 312187
MARCH TOWN UNITED.......... GER Sports Ground, Robin Goodfellow Lane, March PE15 8HS..................... 01354 653073
NEWMARKET TOWN ... Sherbourn Stadium,Cricket Field Road, off New Cheveley Road, Newmarket CB8 8BT..................... 01638 663637
SAFFRON WALDEN TOWN.......... Catons Lane, Saffron Walden CB10 2DU..................... 01799 522789
STOWMARKET TOWN................ Greens Meadow, Bury Road, Stowmarket IP14 1JQ..................... 01449 612533
SWAFFHAM TOWN.................. Shoemakers Lane, off Cley Road, Swaffham PE37 7NT..................... 01760 722700
THETFORD TOWN .... Recreation Ground, Mundford Road, Thetford IP24 1NB..................... 01842 766120

IN: Brantham Athletic (P – Suffolk & Ipswich League Senior Division), Ipswich Wanderers (R), Newmarket Town (R), Swaffham Town (R)
OUT: Ely City (P), Tiptree United (P), Whitton United (P)

LEAGUE CUP

PRELIMINARY ROUND
FC Clacton 2 Halstead Town 1
Great Yarmouth Town 0 **Gorleston** 3
Hadleigh United 3 Tiptree United 0
Haverhill Rovers 2 Saffron Walden Town 0
Histon Res. 0 **CRC** 1
Long Melford 2 Whitton United 0
Norwich United 3 March Town United 2
Woodbridge Town 1 **Diss Town** 2
Wroxham 2 Wisbech Town 0

FIRST ROUND
Debenham Leisure Centre 0 **Gorleston** 2
Dereham Town 3 King's Lynn Res. 0
Diss Town 2 Kirkley & Pakefield 1
Downham Town 2 **Wroxham** 2 *aet* (3-4p)
Ely City 1 Walsham-le-Willows 0
FC Clacton 2 Hadleigh United 0
Felixstowe & Walton Utd 4 Harwich & Parkeston 3 *aet*
Haverhill Rovers 2 Godmanchester Rovers 0
Ipswich Wanderers 3 Long Melford 1
Lowestoft Town 3 Leiston 1
Mildenhall Town 3 Soham Town Rangers 0
Newmarket Town 6 CRC 4 *aet*
Norwich United 1 **Thetford Town** 2
Stanway Rovers 2 **Cornard United** 0
(Stanway Rovers expelled)

Stowmarket Town 0 **Needham Market** 1
Swaffham Town 8 Fakenham Town 1

SECOND ROUND
Cornard United 0 **FC Clacton** 3
Dereham Town 2 Swaffham Town 1
Ely City 2 Newmarket Town 1
Gorleston 2 Lowestoft Town 2 *aet* (5-4p)
Ipswich Wanderers 2 **Felixstowe & Walton United** 6
Mildenhall Town 1 **Haverhill Rovers** 5
Needham Market 4 Diss Town 2 *aet*
Thetford Town 2 Wroxham 1 *aet*

QUARTER-FINALS
Felixstowe & Walton United 3 Dereham Town 1
Gorleston 4 Ely City 2
Haverhill Rovers 2 FC Clacton 0
Needham Market 5 Thetford Town 2

SEMI-FINALS
Felixstowe & Walton United 1 **Needham Market** 4
Haverhill Rovers 1 **Gorleston** 2

FINAL
(5th May at Diss Town)
Needham Market 2 Gorleston 1

DIVISION ONE CUP

PRELIMINARY ROUND
Long Melford 0 **Halstead Town** 6
March Town United 1 **Ely City** 2
Thetford Town 1 Diss Town 0

FIRST ROUND
Cornard United 2 Tiptree United 1
Downham Town 1 **Ely City** 4
Fakenham Town 1 **Gorleston** 4
Godmanchester Rovers 1 **Saffron Walden Town** 2
Great Yarmouth Town 3 **Thetford Town** 4
Hadleigh United 2 **Whitton United** 3 *aet*
Halstead Town 3 FC Clacton 2
Stowmarket Town 2 Debenham Leisure Centre 0

QUARTER-FINALS
Cornard United 2 **Ely City** 4
Gorleston 0 **Whitton United** 0 *aet* (2-4p)
Saffron Walden Town 0 **Halstead Town** 1
Stowmarket Town 2 Thetford Town 1

SEMI-FINALS
Ely City 2 Whitton United 1 *aet*
Halstead Town 4 Stowmarket Town 2

FINAL
(April 23rd at Mildenhall Town)
Halstead Town 1 Ely City 1 *aet* (5-6p)

Reserve Division (North)	P	W	D	L	F	A	Pts
Walsham-le-Willows Res.	22	13	4	5	51	31	43
Ipswich Wanderers Res.	22	13	3	6	56	34	42
Thetford Town Res.	22	10	8	4	43	30	38
Woodbridge Town Res.	22	11	4	7	54	36	37
Whitton United Res.	22	10	2	10	40	41	32
Felixstowe & Walton Utd Res.	22	9	2	11	41	42	29
Stowmarket Town Res.	22	9	2	11	39	51	29
Hadleigh United Res.	22	8	4	10	51	49	28
Debenham Leisure Centre Res.	22	7	7	8	30	28	28
Needham Market Res.	22	7	3	12	41	63	24
Diss Town Res.	22	4	8	10	32	44	20
Leiston Res.	22	5	5	12	31	60	20

Reserve Division (South)	P	W	D	L	F	A	Pts
Haverhill Rovers Res.	20	16	2	2	44	16	50
AFC Sudbury Res.	20	12	3	5	41	25	39
Tiptree United Res.	20	12	2	6	54	30	38
Stanway Rovers Res.	20	11	3	6	52	31	36
Harwich & Parkeston Res.	20	10	3	7	39	34	33
Witham Town Res.	20	9	3	8	40	41	30
Braintree Town Res.	20	7	3	10	22	29	24
Wivenhoe Town Res.	20	7	1	12	33	39	22
Long Melford Res.	20	5	5	10	22	36	20
Halstead Town Res.	20	4	2	14	15	49	14
FC Clacton Res.	20	3	1	16	27	59	10

RESERVES CHAMPIONSHIP
(Reserve Division (North) champions
v Reserve Division (South) champions)

(April 29th at Hadleigh United)
Walsham-le-Willows Res. 1 **Haverhill Rovers Res.** 1 *aet* (5-6p)

RESERVES TROPHY
FINAL
(April 16th at Diss Town)
Ipswich Wanderers Res. 2 Wroxham Res. 1

WWW.CHERRYRED.CO.UK

ESSEX OLYMPIAN LEAGUE

	Benfleet	Bishop's Stortford Swifts	Canning Town	Epping	Frenford Senior	Galleywood	Harold Wood Athletic	Kelvedon Hatch	Manford Way	Mountnessing	Shell Club Corringham	Takeley	White Ensign
Benfleet		2-1	2-2	4-0	0-2	W-L	0-2	3-0	2-2	W-L	3-0	1-2	1-0
Bishop's Stortford Swifts	2-3	P	1-5	1-2	0-2	4-0	3-2	0-3	1-2	2-1	5-1	0-2	0-1
Canning Town	1-2	4-0	R	0-0	2-0	5-1	4-0	3-3	3-0	1-4	1-1	0-1	3-4
Epping	2-3	1-1	1-1	E	3-0	1-4	1-2	0-1	3-0	1-1	5-0	1-1	1-3
Frenford Senior	2-3	3-0	1-1	3-1	M	2-2	3-0	2-1	2-0	4-1	W-L	1-2	3-0
Galleywood	3-1	1-1	2-3	2-0	0-3	I	0-0	0-0	0-2	3-3	1-0	1-1	1-4
Harold Wood Athletic	1-3	1-1	1-3	0-0	2-1	3-0	E	1-0	2-2	3-4	3-0	L-W	2-3
Kelvedon Hatch	4-0	1-4	4-3	3-2	1-0	0-2	1-2	R	4-2	2-2	6-0	4-1	4-0
Manford Way	1-3	3-1	3-3	1-3	0-1	2-0	2-0	0-1		1-5	4-1	1-3	1-2
Mountnessing	8-0	2-4	1-1	3-2	2-5	4-1	1-2	3-3	3-2	D	1-2	1-4	1-2
Shell Club Corringham	1-2	2-1	2-0	0-1	0-4	1-3	4-4	0-4	2-2	1-2	I	1-11	0-1
Takeley	2-2	2-0	W-L	5-0	2-0	2-1	0-0	3-1	1-1	1-3	4-0	V	0-2
White Ensign	3-1	W-L	4-0	2-0	1-3	2-0	3-2	1-2	3-2	1-3	3-0	4-2	

Premier Division	P	W	D	L	F	A	Pts
White Ensign	24	18	0	6	49	32	54
Takeley	24	15	5	4	52	25	50
Frenford Senior	24	15	2	7	47	24	47
Benfleet	24	14	3	7	41	41	45
Kelvedon Hatch	24	13	4	7	53	34	43
Mountnessing	24	10	5	9	58	48	35
Canning Town	24	8	8	8	49	38	32
Harold Wood Athletic	24	8	6	10	35	39	30
Epping	24	6	6	12	31	41	24
Galleywood	24	6	6	12	28	44	24
Manford Way	24	6	5	13	36	49	23
Bishop's Stortford Swifts	24	6	3	15	33	46	21
Shell Club Corringham	24	3	3	18	19	70	12

SENIOR CHALLENGE CUP

(Division One champions v Senior Cup holders)

(August 28th at White Ensign)
White Ensign 1 Kelvedon Hatch 0

SENIOR CUP

(All teams from Premier Division, Division One and Division Two)

FIRST ROUND
Basildon Town 1 **Frenford Senior** 4
Bishop's Stortford Swifts 5 Hannakins Farm 5 *aet* (6-5p)
Broomfield 2 Linford Wanderers 1
Galleywood 2 Benfleet 1
Kelvedon Hatch 2 Roydon 1 *aet*
M & B Club 2 Newham United 1
Metpol Chigwell NE 0 **Writtle** 1
Shell Club Corringham 3 Mountnessing 1
Shenfield Association 0 **Ongar Town** 4
Westhamians 2 Springfield 1

SECOND ROUND
Canning Town 4 Faces 2
Epping 3 Runwell Hospital 2
Frenford Senior 3 Broomfield 0
Galleywood 4 Barnston 0

Harold Wood Athletic 2 **White Ensign** 3
Herongate Athletic 2 Old Chelmsfordians 0
Kelvedon Hatch 5 Bishop's Stortford Swifts 3
Leytonstone United 1 **Takeley** 5
M & B Club 5 Hutton 3
Ongar Town 5 Stambridge United 3 *aet*
Ramsden 0 **Manford Way** 2
Rayleigh Town 3 Leigh Ramblers 2
Ryan 0 **Westhamians** 0 *aet* (4-5p)
Sandon Royals 6 Great Baddow 0
Shell Club Corringham 4 Potter Street 1
Writtle 3 Upminster 2

THIRD ROUND
Canning Town 1 **Ongar Town** 1
Epping 0 **Writtle** 1

Frenford Senior 2 Sandon Royals 0
Galleywood 0 **Takeley** 2
M & B Club 1 White Ensign 0
Manford Way 3 Herongate Athletic 0
Rayleigh Town 1 **Kelvedon Hatch** 4
Shell Club Corringham 0 **Westhamians** 1

QUARTER-FINALS
Kelvedon Hatch 2 Ongar Town 0
Manford Way 0 **Frenford Senior** 1
Takeley 0 **Westhamians** 0 *aet* (2-4p)
Writtle 2 **M & B Club** 5

SEMI-FINALS
Kelvedon Hatch 5 Frenford Senior 2
M & B Club 3 Westhamians 2

FINAL
(May 13th at Billericay Town)
Kelvedon Hatch 1 M & B Club 1 *aet* (3-2p)

LFC INSURANCE ESSEX OLYMPIAN LEAGUE PREMIER DIVISION CONSTITUTION 2008-09

BEAUMONT ATHLETIC .... Mile End Stadium, Rhodeswell Road, Burdett Road, Poplar E14 7TW 020 8980 1885
BENFLEET .... The Club House, Woodside Extension, Manor Road, Benfleet, Rayleigh SS7 4BG 01268 743957
CANNING TOWN .... Gooseleys Playing Fields, St Albans Avenue, East Ham E6 6HQ .... None
EPPING .... Stonards Hill Rec Ground, Tidy's Lane, Epping CM16 6SP .... None
FACES .... Ford Sports & Social Club, Aldbrough Road South, Newbury Park, Ilford IG3 8HG 020 8590 3797
FRENFORD SENIOR .... Oakfields Sports Ground, Forest Road, Barkingside IG6 3HD 020 8500 1998
GALLEYWOOD .... Clarkes Field, Slades Lane, Galleywood, Chelmsford CM2 8RW 01245 352975
HAROLD WOOD ATHLETIC .... Harold Wood Recreation Park, Harold View, Harold Wood RM3 0LX 01708 348827
KELVEDON HATCH .... New Hall, School Road, Kelvedon Hatch, Brentwood CM15 0DH 01277 372153
M & B CLUB .... M & B Sports & Social Club, Dagenham Road, Dagenham RM10 .... 020 8919 2427
MANFORD WAY................. London Marathon Sports Ground, Forest Road, Hainault IG6 3HJ 020 8500 3486
MOUNTNESSING .... The Football Academy, Sports Pavilion, Langston Road, Loughton IG10 3TQ 0870 084 2111
ONGAR TOWN .... Love Lane, High Street, Ongar CM5 9BL 01277 363838
POTTER STREET .... Minton Lane, Church Langley Country Park, Harlow CM17 9TG .... None
WHITE ENSIGN .... Borough Football Comb. HQ, Eastwoodbury Lane, Southend-on-Sea SS2 6XG .... None
IN: Beaumont Athletic (R – Essex Senior League), Faces (P), M & B Club (P), Ongar Town (P), Potter Street (P)
OUT: Bishop's Stortford Swfts (R), Shell Club Corringham (R), Takeley (P – Essex Senior League)

WWW.NLNEWSDESK.CO.UK

	Faces	Herongate Athletic	Leigh Ramblers	Leytonstone United	M & B Club	Old Chelmsfordians	Ongar Town	Potter Street	Rayleigh Town	Roydon	Ryan	Sandon Royals	Springfield	Stambridge United
Faces		3-2	3-2	1-1	1-4	4-1	2-4	0-2	1-2	W-L	W-L	2-0	5-1	7-3
Herongate Athletic	3-3	*D*	4-3	1-0	1-2	1-0	0-1	2-2	1-1	W-L	3-0	0-0	0-1	5-2
Leigh Ramblers	3-6	1-4	*I*	1-2	0-1	0-4	1-2	1-2	1-3	W-L	2-1	3-0	0-0	1-0
Leytonstone United	2-5	1-1	2-4	*V*	3-7	2-2	1-3	0-5	0-0	1-2	3-6	2-4	0-3	W-L
M & B Club	3-1	2-1	2-1	8-0	*I*	2-2	4-1	1-3	2-3	W-L	1-1	3-1	5-0	W-L
Old Chelmsfordians	1-0	1-1	3-2	3-5	0-2	*S*	1-2	0-2	2-2	3-0	0-3	2-2	7-0	3-1
Ongar Town	3-3	1-0	2-1	3-1	4-2	4-1	*I*	2-5	2-1	3-2	5-1	2-2	4-1	2-2
Potter Street	0-2	2-1	1-0	6-1	0-2	3-1	2-1	*O*	2-0	2-0	3-1	5-0	5-2	2-1
Rayleigh Town	4-4	3-0	2-2	4-1	4-2	0-2	4-1	0-1	*N*	1-2	4-2	2-2	4-0	8-1
Roydon	4-5	0-2	4-2	1-3	1-3	3-0	3-2	1-4	0-2		5-1	1-6	2-4	W-L
Ryan	2-1	1-1	2-1	4-2	2-5	3-5	2-2	1-2	1-1	5-3	*O*	2-3	1-1	6-1
Sandon Royals	2-3	0-1	2-3	3-2	1-2	1-0	1-6	0-2	2-1	2-0	1-2	*N*	1-1	W-L
Springfield	3-1	5-1	1-2	2-4	1-2	0-4	1-1	1-5	1-2	1-2	1-1	2-3	*E*	4-3
Stambridge United	1-7	0-2	2-2	3-2	L-W	0-3	L-W	1-5	0-3	1-4	0-2	1-2	4-1	

Division One		P	W	D	L	F	A	Pts
Potter Street	-3	26	23	1	2	73	22	67
M & B Club	-3	26	21	2	3	67	29	62
Ongar Town		26	16	5	5	63	44	53
Faces		26	15	3	8	72	53	48
Rayleigh Town		26	12	7	7	58	35	43
Old Chelmsfordians	+3	26	10	5	11	51	45	38
Herongate Athletic		26	10	7	9	38	35	37
Sandon Royals		26	10	5	11	41	50	35
Ryan		26	9	6	11	53	56	33
Roydon		26	9	0	17	40	53	27
Leigh Ramblers		26	7	3	16	39	55	24
Leytonstone United	+3	26	5	3	18	41	84	21
Springfield	-3	26	6	5	15	38	69	20
Stambridge United	+3	26	2	2	22	27	71	11

LFC INSURANCE ESSEX OLYMPIAN LEAGUE DIVISION ONE CONSTITUTION 2008-09

BISHOP'S STORTFORD SWIFTS ... Silver Leys, Hadham Road (A1250), Bishop's Stortford CM23 2QE 01279 658941
BUCKHURST HILL.............................. Roding Lane, Buckhurst Hill IG9 5BJ.................................. 020 8504 1189
BURNHAM RAMBLERS RESERVES ... Leslie Field, Springfield Road, Burnham-on-Crouch CM0 8TE 01621 784383
HANNAKINS FARM.................... Hannakins Farm, Rosebay Avenue, Billicay CM12 0SY 01277 630851
HERONGATE ATHLETIC........ Adjacent to 77 Billericay Road, Herongate, Brentwood CM13 3PU 01277 811260
HUTTON.......................... Polo Fields, Hall Green Lane, Hutton, Brentwood CM13 2QT 01277 262257
LEIGH RAMBLERS................. Belfairs Park, Eastwood Road North, Leigh-on-Sea SS9 4LR............... 01702 421077
LEYTONSTONE UNITED.............. Ilford Wanderers RFC, Forest Road, Hainault IG6 3HJ 020 8500 4622
LINFORD WANDERERS .... Lakeside Pitches, Thurrock RM20 2ZL.............................. None
OLD CHELMSFORDIANS .... Lawford Lane, Roxwell Road, Chelmsford CM1 2NS.................... 01245 420442
RAYLEIGH TOWN............. Rayleigh Town Sports/Soc. Club, London Road, Rayleigh SS6 9HR 01268 784001
ROYDON .... Roydon Playing Fields, Harlow Road, Roydon, Harlow CM19 5HE 01268 784001
RYAN .... Old Parmiters Sports Ground, 102a Nelson Road, Chingford E4 9AS .... None
SANDON ROYALS .... Sandon Sports Club, Rectory Chase, Sandon, Chelmsford CM2 7SQ 01245 476626
SHELL CLUB CORRINGHAM .... Shell Club, Springhouse Road, Corringham SS17 7QT 01375 673100
WESTHAMIANS .... Fairlop Oak Playing Fields, Forest Road, Hainault IG6 3HT.......................... None

IN: Bishop's Stortford Swfts (R), Buckhurst Hill (S – Herts Senior County League Division One), Burnham Ramblers Reserves (S – Essex & Herts Border Combination), Hannakins Farm (P), Hutton (P), Linford Wanderers (P), Shell Club Corringham (R), Westhamians (P)
OUT: Faces (P), M & B Club (P), Ongar Town (P), Potter Street (P), Springfield (R), Stambridge United (R)

DENNY KING MEMORIAL CUP
(All teams eliminated from Rounds One and Two of the Senior Cup)

FIRST ROUND
Barnston 3 **Ryan** 4
Hannakins Farm 1 **Mountnessing** 2
Leigh Ramblers 1 **Bishop's Stortford Swifts** 2
Metpol Chigwell NE 4 Great Baddow 3
Old Chelmsfordians 0 **Harold Wood Athletic** 3
Potter Street 2 Hutton 0
Ramsden 2 **Faces** 4
Runwell Hospital 0 **Broomfield** 1
Springfield 1 **Benfleet** 4
Stambridge United 1 Newham United 0 *aet*
SECOND ROUND
Basildon Town 3 **Ryan** 5
Bishop's Stortford Swifts (w/o) v Metpol Chigwell NE (scr.)
Broomfield 0 **Benfleet** 2
Faces 3 Leytonstone United 3 *aet (6-5p)*

Harold Wood Athletic 2 Roydon 1
Mountnessing 4 Stambridge United 0
Shenfield Association 1 **Linford Wanderers** 3
Upminster 1 **Potter Steet** 3
QUARTER-FINALS
Benfleet 2 **Faces** 6
Linford Wanderers 0 **Harold Wood Athletic** 5
Potter Street 2 Mountnessing 2 *aet (6-5p)*
Ryan 3 Bishop's Stortford Swifts 0
SEMI-FINALS
Faces 4 Ryan 1
Potter Street 3 Harold Wood Athletic 1 *aet*
FINAL
(May 24th at White Notley)
Potter Street 2 Faces 1 *aet*

	Barnston	Basildon Town	Broomfield	Great Baddow	Hannakins Farm	Hutton	Linford Wanderers	Metpol Chigwell NE	Newham United	Ramsden	Runwell Hospital	Shenfield Association	Upminster	Westhamians	Writtle
Barnston		1-2	0-7	1-1	1-6	0-4	1-4	0-3	2-1	2-4	2-1	5-0	1-2	1-4	3-4
Basildon Town	1-1	D	1-0	2-0	1-3	2-0	0-3	3-1	1-2	2-1	0-2	5-2	1-0	1-2	3-1
Broomfield	3-0	2-1	I	3-1	1-1	3-4	1-2	3-1	1-2	1-4	4-1	4-1	2-1	2-5	2-1
Great Baddow	3-1	1-3	3-0	V	1-2	0-7	W-L	2-4	0-2	1-1	6-0	3-1	0-1	1-2	
Hannakins Farm	7-1	1-0	2-3	0-0	I	4-1	0-1	4-1	2-1	2-1	2-2	3-2	1-3	3-2	2-1
Hutton	9-1	3-4	5-1	7-0	3-3	S	4-1	5-4	0-2	1-4	4-2	7-1	7-2	0-3	2-4
Linford Wanderers	4-0	6-1	2-0	1-0	2-1	1-1	I	0-3	0-2	3-0	4-2	6-1	3-1	0-0	0-2
Metpol Chigwell NE	3-1	0-1	W-L	3-2	1-3	1-6	0-3	O	2-4	2-4	5-3	1-1	5-3	1-2	0-3
Newham United	W-L	3-3	4-0	8-1	3-6	1-1	7-3	2-6	N	2-3	6-0	W-L	3-0	3-1	1-2
Ramsden	6-4	5-1	1-2	5-0	1-3	2-4	0-1	3-1	1-3		2-1	3-2	2-2	1-4	2-6
Runwell Hospital	3-0	4-2	1-3	2-1	2-4	1-5	1-4	2-0	4-1	1-2		3-1	W-L	3-2	3-2
Shenfield Association	0-8	1-4	0-3	2-3	0-8	2-3	0-3	0-5	L-W	2-5	0-7	T	2-2	0-2	0-9
Upminster	2-2	L-W	0-1	0-2	0-2	1-7	3-1	0-3	1-1	3-1	0-3	6-3	W	0-3	6-2
Westhamians	2-1	3-1	3-0	10-0	2-2	1-5	2-3	4-2	0-1	2-2	5-2	6-1	4-1	O	0-1
Writtle	W-L	1-0	2-4	1-0	5-2	3-6	0-3	2-0	2-2	1-0	3-2	5-1	4-2	1-2	

Division Two		P	W	D	L	F	A	Pts
Linford Wanderers		28	21	2	5	73	31	65
Hannakins Farm		28	19	5	4	79	39	62
Hutton		28	18	3	7	106	55	57
Westhamians		28	18	3	7	77	38	57
Newham United		28	17	4	7	70	45	55
Writtle		28	18	1	9	70	49	55
Ramsden		28	15	1	12	67	56	46
Broomfield		28	15	1	12	56	49	46
Basildon Town		28	14	2	12	46	49	44
Runwell Hospital		28	12	2	14	59	65	38
Metpol Chigwell NE		28	9	1	18	51	65	28
Great Baddow		28	7	3	18	32	70	24
Upminster	-1	28	5	3	20	38	70	17
Barnston		28	4	3	21	40	86	17
Shenfield Association		28	0	2	26	25	122	2

RESERVE DIVISIONS CHALLENGE CUP

(Reserve Div One champions v Reserve Div Cup holders)

(August 25th at Harold Wood Athletic)

Harold Wood Athletic Res. 2 Shell Club Corringham Res. 1

WWW.NLNEWSDESK.CO.UK

LFC INSURANCE ESSEX OLYMPIAN LEAGUE DIVISION TWO CONSTITUTION 2008-09

BARNSTON .... High Easter Road, Barnston, Dunmow CM6 1LZ 01371 876364
BASILDON TOWN ..... GEC Avionics Sports Ground, Gardiners Lane South, Gardiners Way, Basildon SS14 3AP 01268 883128
BROOMFIELD .... The Angel Meadow, Main Road, Broomfield, Chelmsford CM1 7AH 01245 443819
DEBDEN SPORTS RESERVES .... Chigwell Lane, Loughton, Ilford IG10 3TP 020 8508 9392
MALDON ST MARYS .... King George IV Playing Field, Colchester Road, Heybridge CM9 4AL .... None
METPOL CHIGWELL NE .... Met Police Sports Club, High Road, Chigwell IG7 6BD ...... 020 8500 1017. Office: 020 8500 2735
NEWHAM UNITED .... Southern Road Playing Fields, Cave Road, Plaistow E13 0HZ .... None
RAMSDEN .... Nursery Sports Ground, Downham Road, Ramsden Heath, Billericay CM11 1PU 01268 711502
RUNWELL HOSPITAL .... Runwell Hospital, Runwell Chase, Wickford SS11 7QE 01268 562967
SHENFIELD ASSOCIATION .... The Drive, Warley, Brentwood CM13 3BH .... None
SOUTHMINSTER ST LEONARDS ... King George IV Playing Fields, Station Road, Southminster CM0 7EW .... None
SPRINGFIELD .... Springfield Hall Park, Arun Close, Springfield, Chelmsford CM1 7QE .... None
STAMBRIDGE UNITED ..... Stambridge Recreation Ground, Rochford Road, Great Stambridge, Rochford SS4 2AX 01702 258988
SUNGATE .... Ford Sports & Social Club, Aldborough Road South, Newbury Park, Ilford IG3 8HG 01708 722766
TAKELEY RESERVES ...... Station Road (adjacent to rail bridge), Takeley, Bishop's Stortford CM22 6SG 01279 870404
UPMINSTER .... Hall Lane Playing Fields, Hall Lane, Upminster, Romford RM14 1AU 01708 220320
WRITTLE .... Paradise Road Playing Fields, Writtle, Chelmsford CM1 3HW 01245 420332

IN: Debden Sports Reserves (P – Romford & District League Senior Division), Maldon St Marys (P – Mid-Essex League Premier Division), Southminster St Leonards (P – Mid-Essex League Premier Division), Springfield (R), Stambridge United (R), Sungate (P – Essex Business Houses Premier Division), Takeley Reserves (P – Reserve Division Two)
OUT: Great Baddow (R – Mid-Essex League Division Two), Hannakins Farm (P), Hutton (P), Linford Wanderers (P), Westhamians (P)

Reserve Division One		P	W	D	L	F	A	Pts
Harold Wood Ath. Res.		24	19	3	2	74	24	60
Shell Club Corringham Res.		24	16	3	5	57	23	51
Canning Town Res.		24	16	1	7	49	26	49
Frenford Senior Res.		24	14	2	8	57	41	44
Manford Way Res.		24	12	4	8	49	41	40
Rayleigh Town Res.	-3	24	13	3	8	39	42	39
Bishop's S'ford Swifts Res.		24	9	3	12	40	49	30
White Ensign Res.		24	8	3	13	43	59	27
Epping Res.	-3	24	9	2	13	36	45	26
Galleywood Res.	+3	24	6	4	14	32	62	25
O Chelmsfordians Res.	+3	24	6	3	15	38	59	24
Runwell Hospital Res.		24	5	3	16	38	59	18
Ryan Res.		24	4	4	16	20	42	16

Reserve Division Two		P	W	D	L	F	A	Pts
M & B Club Res.		20	15	3	2	74	22	48
Mountnessing Res.		20	12	5	3	59	36	41
Kelvedon Hatch Res.		20	12	4	4	34	18	40
Hutton Res.		20	12	3	5	46	35	39
Takeley Res.	-4	20	10	6	4	59	25	32
Ramsden Res.		20	8	5	7	35	30	29
Faces Res.	+2	20	6	3	11	28	59	23
Hannakins Farm Res.	+3	20	5	1	14	26	47	19
Basildon Town Res.		20	4	2	14	22	47	14
Herongate Athletic Res.		20	2	7	11	21	45	13
Metpol Chigwell NE Res.		20	3	3	14	23	52	12

Reserve Division Three		P	W	D	L	F	A	Pts
Leigh Ramblers Res.		20	13	6	1	47	23	45
Benfleet Res.		20	14	2	4	47	19	44
Newham United Res.	+2	20	10	3	7	45	33	35
Barnston Res.		20	7	6	7	30	28	27
Sandon Royals Res.	+1	20	7	5	8	32	33	27
Broomfield Res.		20	6	8	6	38	34	26
Writtle Res.		20	8	2	10	36	40	26
Linford Wanderers Res.		20	7	4	9	44	53	25
Westhamians Res.		20	5	6	9	26	37	21
Springfield Res.	-1	20	5	6	9	35	42	20
Leytonstone United Res.		20	3	2	15	21	59	11

LEN CHITTY TROPHY

(March 5th at Aveley)

Romford & District Leagues XI 0 **Essex Olympian League XI** 1

RESERVE DIVISIONS CUP

(May 6th at Billericay Town)

Takeley Res. 1 **Shell Club Corringham Res.** 2

ESSEX SENIOR LEAGUE

	Barking	Barkingside	Basildon United	Beaumont Athletic	Bowers & Pitsea	Burnham Ramblers	Clapton	Concord Rangers	Enfield	Eton Manor	Hullbridge Sports	London APSA	Mauritius Sports & Pennant	Romford	Sawbridgeworth Town	Southend Manor	Stansted
Barking		0-3	3-0	2-2	4-1	2-1	3-1	0-1	0-2	1-3	1-1	1-0	4-1	2-0	4-0	1-2	1-3
Barkingside	0-0		3-1	5-0	0-1	0-0	2-0	0-1	1-3	3-1	3-1	3-0	2-0	0-3	2-0	1-0	2-0
Basildon United	1-1	0-4		1-2	1-2	1-2	3-0	1-5	0-0	0-3	2-2	2-0	4-2	1-5	1-2	0-5	0-2
Beaumont Athletic	0-2	1-4	1-1		1-5	1-4	0-3	0-2	1-8	3-1	1-2	3-2	2-2	0-5	2-3	1-2	0-3
Bowers & Pitsea	3-2	0-3	2-1	2-0		2-2	0-1	4-0	0-3	0-1	0-0	5-1	2-1	4-1	0-2	1-0	5-1
Burnham Ramblers	3-2	2-1	5-0	10-1	0-1		2-2	1-2	0-1	2-2	2-0	3-1	6-2	2-3	2-3	1-1	2-1
Clapton	0-0	0-3	2-1	2-3	2-2	0-0		1-5	2-2	1-3	5-1	2-1	3-1	1-2	0-3	0-1	2-2
Concord Rangers	2-1	0-1	8-0	13-0	2-1	1-0	4-0		2-1	3-1	5-0	12-0	3-1	3-2	6-1	0-1	2-1
Enfield	2-0	3-2	4-1	5-1	3-1	4-0	4-1	1-0		2-2	3-0	2-2	2-2	1-4	3-0	4-0	2-1
Eton Manor	4-2	1-2	4-0	6-0	3-2	3-2	2-2	4-2	0-2		2-0	1-0	3-1	2-2	6-1	1-0	1-2
Hullbridge Sports	1-1	2-4	2-2	3-1	1-2	2-3	0-0	1-1	1-3	3-3		2-2	1-2	1-3	2-1	0-1	1-5
London APSA	0-3	0-4	6-0	3-4	0-2	0-5	1-0	0-1	0-4	0-4	1-1		2-3	0-4	1-1	1-4	1-5
Mauritius Sports & Pennant	0-2	1-3	0-0	0-3	1-2	1-2	2-1	0-2	2-4	2-3	1-2	5-0		1-1	2-1	1-3	0-0
Romford	4-0	2-5	4-1	3-1	2-1	0-0	1-2	1-1	2-1	1-4	1-1	4-0	3-1		2-1	3-1	1-1
Sawbridgeworth Town	1-4	0-5	0-0	5-0	1-3	1-2	0-1	0-1	0-4	0-2	1-1	1-1	1-2	0-3		0-1	2-1
Southend Manor	0-1	1-4	1-0	2-1	1-2	2-0	0-1	1-1	0-3	3-0	3-0	3-0	1-2	4-0	1-1		2-2
Stansted	1-4	1-4	0-0	2-0	0-0	2-3	1-1	1-3	2-3	3-2	1-0	4-0	0-1	1-1	1-2	0-2	

	P	W	D	L	F	A	Pts
Concord Rangers	32	25	2	5	94	26	77
Enfield	32	24	5	3	88	29	77
Barkingside	32	24	2	6	79	25	74
Eton Manor	32	20	5	7	81	44	65
Romford	32	19	7	6	75	41	64
Southend Manor	32	18	4	10	50	31	58
Bowers & Pitsea	32	17	5	10	57	41	56
Burnham Ramblers	32	15	7	10	69	45	52
Barking	32	14	6	12	54	43	48
Stansted	32	10	8	14	50	50	38
Clapton	32	8	9	15	38	57	33
Sawbridgeworth Town	32	8	4	20	34	69	28
Mauritius Sports & Pennant	32	7	5	20	41	70	26
Hullbridge Sports	32	4	12	16	35	66	24
Beaumont Athletic	32	6	3	23	36	113	21
Basildon United	32	3	8	21	26	82	17
London APSA	32	2	4	26	24	99	10

GORDON BRASTED MEMORIAL TROPHY

PRELIMINARY ROUND
Barkingside 1 Basildon United 0
FIRST ROUND
Barking 3 Beaumont Athletic 0
Burnham Ramblers 2 **Romford** 3
Concord Rangers 2 Barkingside 1
Enfield 4 Clapton 2 *aet*
Eton Manor 2 Stansted 1
Hullbridge Sports 1 **Mauritius Sports & Pennant** 3
Sawbridgeworth Town 4 Bowers & Pitsea 1
Southend Manor 2 London APSA 0
QUARTER-FINALS
Concord Rangers 6 Barking 0
Enfield 3 Romford 1
Mauritius Sports & Pennant 2 **Eton Manor** 7
Sawbridgeworth Town 2 **Southend Manor** 3 *aet*
SEMI-FINALS
Concord Rangers 2 Enfield 1
Eton Manor 2 Southend Manor 0
FINAL
(March 22nd at Burnham Ramblers)
Concord Rangers 3 Eton Manor 2

ESSEX SENIOR LEAGUE CONSTITUTION 2008-09

BARKING.............................Mayesbrook Park, Lodge Avenue, Dagenham RM8 2JY.........................020 8595 6511
BARKINGSIDE.............Redbridge FC, Oakside Stadium, Station Road, Barkingside, Ilford IG6 1NB...............020 8550 3611
BASILDON UNITED.............The Stadium, Gardiners Close, Gardiners Lane, Basildon SS14 3AN...................01268 520268
BOWERS & PITSEA......Len Salmon Stadium, Crown Avenue, off Kenneth Road, Pitsea, Basildon SS14 2BE.............01268 452068
BURNHAM RAMBLERS...........Leslie Field, Springfield Road, Burnham-on-Crouch CM0 8TE....................01621 784383
CLAPTON.........................Old Spotted Dog Ground, Upton Lane, Forest Gate E7 9NP........................020 8472 0822
ENFIELD......................Ware FC, Wodson Park, Wadesmill Road, Ware SG12 0HZ.........................01920 463247
ETON MANOR.........Waltham Abbey FC, Capershotts, Sewardstone Road, Waltham Abbey, Essex EN9 1LU..........01992 711287
HULLBRIDGE SPORTS.....................Lower Road, Hullbridge, Hockley SS5 6BJ............................01702 230420
LONDON APSA.................Terence McMillan Stadium, Maybury Road, Plaistow E13 8RZ......................020 7511 4477
MAURITIUS SPORTS & PENNANT...Wadham Lodge Sports Ground, Kitchener Road, Walthamstow E17 4JP............020 8527 2444
ROMFORD.....................Aveley FC, Mill Field, Mill Road, Aveley RM15 4SJ.........................01708 865940
SAWBRIDGEWORTH TOWN.........Crofters End, West Road, Sawbridgeworth CM21 0DE.......................01279 722039
SOUTHEND MANOR.............Southchurch Park Arena, Lifstan Way, Southend-on-Sea SS1 2TH....................01702 615577
STANSTED........................Hargrave Park, Cambridge Road, Stansted CM24 8DL.........................01279 812897
TAKELEY.............Station Road (adjacent to rail bridge), Takeley, Bishop's Stortford CM22 6SG...............01279 870404
IN: Takeley (P – Essex Olympian League Premier Division)
OUT: Beaumont Athletic (R – Essex Olympian League Premier Division), Concord Rangers (P – Isthmian League Division One North)

LEAGUE CUP

GROUP A

	P	W	D	L	F	A	Pts
Enfield	6	4	2	0	16	2	14
Southend Manor	6	2	2	2	7	5	8
Clapton	6	2	1	3	8	13	7
Basildon United	6	1	1	4	8	19	4

Basildon United 0 Clapton 3
Basildon United 0 Enfield 4
Basildon United 1 Southend Manor 2
Clapton 2 Basildon United 5
Clapton 1 Enfield 1
Clapton 2 Southend Manor 1
Enfield 7 Basildon United 1
Enfield 3 Clapton 0
Enfield 1 Southend Manor 0
Southend Manor 1 Basildon United 1
Southend Manor 3 Clapton 0
Southend Manor 0 Enfield 0

GROUP B

	P	W	D	L	F	A	Pts
Concord Rangers	8	6	0	2	34	10	18
Burnham Ramblers	8	6	0	2	21	8	18
Hullbridge Sports	8	3	1	4	9	17	10
Mauritius Sports & Pennant	8	2	1	5	9	20	7
Beaumont Athletic	8	2	0	6	13	31	6

Beaumont Athletic 1 Burnham Ramblers 3
Beaumont Athletic 2 Concord Rangers 5
Beaumont Athletic 2 Hullbridge Sports 3
Beaumont Athletic 0 Mauritius Sports & Pennant 2
Burnham Ramblers 8 Beaumont Athletic 2
Burnham Ramblers 0 Concord Rangers 2
Burnham Ramblers 4 Hullbridge Sports 0
Burnham Ramblers 2 Mauritius Sports & Pennant 1
Concord Rangers 8 Beaumont Athletic 0
Concord Rangers 1 Burnham Ramblers 3
Concord Rangers 4 Hullbridge Sports 0
Concord Rangers 7 Mauritius Sports & Pennant 1
Hullbridge Sports 0 Beaumont Athletic 2
Hullbridge Sports 1 Burnham Ramblers 0
Hullbridge Sports 4 Concord Rangers 3
Hullbridge Sports 0 Mauritius Sports & Pennant 1
Mauritius Sports & Pennant 2 Beaumont Athletic 4
Mauritius Sports & Pennant 0 Burnham Ramblers 2
Mauritius Sports & Pennant 1 Concord Rangers 4
Mauritius Sports & Pennant 1 Hullbridge Sports 1

GROUP C

	P	W	D	L	F	A	Pts
Sawbridgeworth Town	6	4	2	0	12	3	14
Romford	6	3	1	2	9	10	10
Bowers & Pitsea	6	2	2	2	14	10	8
London APSA	6	0	1	5	6	18	1

Bowers & Pitsea 5 London APSA 1
Bowers & Pitsea 4 Romford 1
Bowers & Pitsea 1 Sawbridgeworth Town 1
London APSA 2 Bowers & Pitsea 2
London APSA 1 Romford 2
London APSA 1 Sawbridgeworth Town 4
Romford 3 Bowers & Pitsea 2
Romford 2 London APSA 1
Romford 0 Sawbridgeworth Town 1
Sawbridgeworth Town 2 Bowers & Pitsea 0
Sawbridgeworth Town 3 London APSA 0
Sawbridgeworth Town 1 Romford 1

GROUP D

	P	W	D	L	F	A	Pts
Eton Manor	6	5	0	1	16	8	15
Barking	6	3	1	2	9	3	10
Stansted	6	1	2	3	8	14	5
Barkingside	6	0	3	3	3	11	3

Barking 4 Barkingside 0
Barking 3 Eton Manor 0
Barking 0 Stansted 2
Barkingside 0 Barking 0
Barkingside 0 Eton Manor 3
Barkingside 1 Stansted 1
Eton Manor 1 Barking 0
Eton Manor 2 Barkingside 1
Eton Manor 5 Stansted 1
Stansted 0 Barking 2
Stansted 1 Barkingside 1
Stansted 3 Eton Manor 5

Top two teams from each group qualify for knockout stage

QUARTER-FINALS
(played over two legs)
Concord Rangers 4 Southend Manor 1, Southend Manor 2 **Concord Rangers** 3
Enfield 3 Romford 3 *(at Romford)*, Romford 0 **Enfield** 1 *aet*
Eton Manor 1 Burnham Ramblers 2, Burnham Ramblers 2 **Eton Manor** 3 *aet* (6-7p)
Sawbridgeworth Town 1 Barking 0, **Barking** 5 Sawbridgeworth Town 1

SEMI-FINALS
(played over two legs)
Barking 0 Eton Manor 1, **Eton Manor** 2 Barking 1
Concord Rangers 1 Enfield 0, Enfield 1 **Concord Rangers** 3

FINAL
(May 5th at Bowers & Pitsea)
Concord Rangers 2 **Eton Manor** 3

ESSEX & SUFFOLK BORDER LEAGUE

Note – Walton Town withdrew during the course of the season

Their results are shown herein but are expunged from the league table

	Alresford Colne Rangers	Brightlingsea Regent	Coggeshall Town	Dedham Old Boys	Earls Colne	Gas Recreation	Great Bentley	Hatfield Peverel	Lawford Lads	Little Oakley	Team Bury	Tiptree Heath	University of Essex	Walton Town	Weeley Athletic	West Bergholt
Alresford Colne Rangers	P	2-0	0-0	0-1	0-1	1-1	2-0	0-4	3-1	1-1	3-2	1-2	4-3	1-1	3-1	1-1
Brightlingsea Regent	1-0	R	1-1	0-1	6-3	1-3	1-1	1-3	5-2	3-1	4-1	1-2	2-1	n/a	1-1	4-2
Coggeshall Town	1-1	1-5	E	2-1	1-2	3-3	1-3	0-1	1-0	1-3	0-1	3-1	0-2	n/a	2-3	3-4
Dedham Old Boys	7-0	0-2	2-2	M	2-1	0-3	1-0	3-1	6-1	3-1	4-0	2-2	2-5	5-1	0-1	4-3
Earls Colne	2-2	1-0	0-2	5-2	I	2-4	2-2	0-2	2-1	2-2	4-0	1-2	1-1	9-1	4-4	1-4
Gas Recreation	2-2	6-1	1-0	3-0	2-3	E	6-1	W-L	3-0	2-1	4-3	1-0	1-1	9-0	1-0	5-2
Great Bentley	3-1	1-1	1-7	0-2	1-2	0-1	R	2-3	3-3	3-3	1-5	3-0	1-2	n/a	1-2	0-3
Hatfield Peverel	1-0	1-2	3-2	0-0	2-0	3-4	1-1		1-0	2-3	0-1	4-1	3-3	1-3	1-0	2-3
Lawford Lads	1-2	1-2	0-5	1-2	0-3	0-4	1-1	1-2	D	0-3	1-4	0-4	1-3	n/a	4-1	2-3
Little Oakley	4-2	3-4	4-3	0-1	0-1	0-6	3-1	4-3	3-1	I	2-1	6-1	1-2	2-2	0-1	1-3
Team Bury	0-3	1-2	1-0	0-1	3-2	4-4	2-4	0-1	4-0	5-1	V	0-1	3-2	n/a	1-0	0-6
Tiptree Heath	2-2	2-3	1-4	0-1	2-2	0-4	4-3	1-1	2-2	2-2	2-2	I	3-2	n/a	2-2	2-5
University of Essex	3-0	1-1	3-0	0-1	1-1	2-1	2-3	3-1	4-1	1-1	1-1	0-1	S	6-0	0-3	1-1
Walton Town	0-3	1-1	n/a	n/a	0-11	1-7	0-2	n/a	2-4	n/a	0-5	n/a	n/a	I	1-3	n/a
Weeley Athletic	2-1	1-2	2-1	0-1	0-0	1-1	0-2	0-1	1-3	1-2	0-1	1-1	2-4	2-0	I	0-1
West Bergholt	0-2	1-2	4-0	4-1	2-2	2-2	2-0	1-2	3-2	2-1	0-1	1-0	1-0	n/a	4-1	N

WWW.CHERRYRED.CO.UK

Premier Division		P	W	D	L	F	A	Pts
Gas Recreation		28	19	7	2	78	33	64
West Bergholt		28	17	4	7	70	33	55
Dedham Old Boys		28	17	3	8	51	37	54
Brightlingsea Regent		28	16	5	7	58	44	53
Hatfield Peverel	-3	28	15	4	9	50	37	46
University of Essex		28	11	8	9	53	41	41
Earls Colne		28	10	9	9	50	50	39
Team Bury		28	12	3	13	47	53	39
Little Oakley		28	11	5	12	56	58	38
Alresford Colne Rangers		28	9	8	11	39	47	35
Tiptree Heath		28	8	9	11	43	59	33
Weeley Athletic		28	7	6	15	33	48	27
Coggeshall Town		28	7	5	16	46	53	26
Great Bentley		28	6	7	15	42	63	25
Lawford Lads	+3	28	2	3	23	30	80	12

Walton Town – record expunged

Reserve Premier Division	P	W	D	L	F	A	Pts
University of Essex Res.	24	16	5	3	68	26	53
Gas Recreation Res.	24	16	2	6	68	28	50
West Bergholt Res.	24	14	4	6	53	26	46
Little Oakley Res.	24	14	3	7	65	44	45
Earls Colne Res.	24	12	3	9	39	42	39
Coggeshall Town Res.	24	11	4	9	40	31	37
Alresford Colne Rangers Res.	24	10	3	11	38	52	33
Weeley Athletic Res.	24	10	1	13	44	41	31
Great Bentley Res.	24	9	4	11	46	57	31
Mistley United Res.	24	7	4	13	37	52	25
Brightlingsea Regent Res.	24	7	1	16	47	61	22
Lawford Lads Res.	24	6	3	15	32	73	21
Dedham Old Boys Res.	24	4	3	17	31	75	15

Reserve Division One	P	W	D	L	F	A	Pts
Clacton United Res.	20	14	5	1	88	33	47
White Notley Res.	20	15	2	3	73	25	47
Clare Town Res.	20	12	3	5	53	39	39
Bures United Res.	20	10	2	8	41	37	32
Tiptree Heath Res.	20	8	5	7	46	35	29
Hatfield Peverel Res.	20	7	3	10	36	44	24
Gosfield United Res.	20	6	3	11	42	59	21
Great Bradfords Res.	20	5	5	10	26	46	20
Boxted Lodgers Res.	20	6	2	12	36	57	20
Mersea Island Res.	20	5	3	12	31	58	18
Foxash Social Res.	20	5	1	14	30	69	16

A V LEE MEMORIAL TROPHY

(Premier Division champions v League Cup holders)

(August 28th at Gas Recreation)
Gas Recreation 1 **University of Essex 2**

KENT BLAXILL ESSEX & SUFFOLK BORDER LEAGUE PREMIER DIVISION CONSTITUTION 2008-09

ALRESFORD COLNE RANGERS . . . . Ford Lane, Alresford, Colchester CO7 8AY 07796 036467
BRIGHTLINGSEA REGENT . . . . North Road, Brightlingsea, Colchester CO7 0PL 01206 304199
COGGESHALL TOWN . . . . The Crops, West Street, Coggeshall CO6 1NS 01376 562843
DEDHAM OLD BOYS . . . . The Old Grammar School, Royal Square, Dedham, Colchester CO7 6AA 01206 322302
EARLS COLNE. . . . . Green Farm Meadow, Halstead Road, Earls Colne, Colchester CO6 2NG 01787 223584
GAS RECREATION . . . . Bromley Road, Colchester CO4 3JF 01206 860383
GREAT BENTLEY . . . . The Green, Great Bentley, Colchester CO7 8LX 01206 251532
HATFIELD PEVEREL . . . . Strutt Memorial Field, Maldon Road, Hatfield Peverel CM3 2JP . . . . None
LITTLE OAKLEY . . . . War Memorial Club Ground, Harwich Road, Little Oakley, Harwich CO12 5EB 01255 880370
MERSEA ISLAND . . . . The Glebe, Colchester Road, West Mersea CO5 8JZ 01206 385216
TEAM BURY . . . . Out Risbygate, Bury St Edmunds IP33 3RL 01284 701301
TIPTREE HEATH . . . . Colchester Road, Tiptree CO5 0EX 07889 463004
UNIVERSITY OF ESSEX . . . . Wivenhoe Town FC, Broad Lane Sports Ground, Wivenhoe CO7 7HA 01206 825380
WEELEY ATHLETIC. . . . . Weeley Playing Fields, Clacton Road, Weeley, Clacton-on-Sea CO16 9DH . . . . None
WEST BERGHOLT . . . . Lorkin Daniel Field, Lexden Road, West Bergholt, Colchester CO6 3BW 01206 241525
WHITE NOTLEY . . . . Oak Farm, Faulkbourne, Witham CM8 1ST 01376 519864
IN: Mersea Island (P), White Notley (P)
OUT: Lawfords Lads (R), Walton Town (WS)

	Boxted Lodgers	Bradfield Rovers	Bures United	Foxash Social	Glemsford & Cavendish Utd	Gosfield United	Great Bradfords	Hedinghams United	Holland	Kelvedon Social	Mersea Island	Mistley United	Rowhedge	St Osyth	Sudbury Athletic	White Notley
Boxted Lodgers		4-1	2-1	2-2	0-2	4-0	3-4	4-3	1-0	2-1	1-1	2-6	6-0	2-1	3-5	1-1
Bradfield Rovers	1-0		2-2	4-1	4-0	4-6	2-1	1-3	2-3	7-1	0-5	3-2	4-5	2-1	1-1	0-3
Bures United	1-4	3-2	D	2-0	4-1	2-1	1-1	3-2	1-0	1-0	1-1	1-1	2-1	7-0	0-1	1-1
Foxash Social	0-0	0-0	1-4	I	1-1	0-1	2-0	3-5	1-3	3-2	1-2	1-2	1-3	1-0	1-0	2-3
Glemsford & Cavendish United	4-4	2-2	1-0	W-L	V	2-0	2-2	4-1	2-1	4-2	2-3	6-1	4-0	4-1	0-1	0-4
Gosfield United	2-4	7-2	1-2	2-3	3-6	I	5-2	1-3	2-5	3-2	0-4	1-3	7-1	8-1	1-1	1-10
Great Bradfords	0-3	5-2	0-1	1-3	4-5	7-0	S	1-3	2-3	5-2	0-0	5-4	3-3	5-3	3-2	1-6
Hedinghams United	2-1	5-0	5-4	5-1	2-1	0-1	4-0	I	2-3	3-0	4-7	3-2	2-2	5-0	7-0	0-1
Holland	2-2	8-0	3-2	3-2	3-3	0-1	4-1	1-2	O	7-2	5-2	4-1	2-3	2-3	1-1	1-1
Kelvedon Social	3-3	3-2	0-1	2-3	3-1	0-2	3-3	2-5	0-3	N	3-5	L-W	4-4	2-3	1-3	0-7
Mersea Island	2-1	3-0	1-0	2-1	4-2	6-0	5-2	3-1	2-0	6-0		0-0	4-2	3-1	3-2	4-3
Mistley United	5-2	2-3	1-6	9-0	4-0	1-2	1-3	2-3	1-1	3-2	2-2	O	0-6	1-0	2-2	1-7
Rowhedge	0-6	1-1	1-1	3-2	0-3	3-0	3-1	2-2	1-1	3-2	2-2	0-6	N	2-2	4-0	2-3
St Osyth	3-1	2-1	0-5	2-0	3-1	2-3	2-4	2-3	2-1	5-1	0-4	3-0	1-0	E	3-3	1-6
Sudbury Athletic	2-4	2-0	2-0	1-2	1-1	2-1	3-3	3-0	1-2	1-0	1-2	W-L	2-2	3-0		1-5
White Notley	11-1	5-1	2-3	5-1	6-1	6-0	4-1	2-1	1-1	6-1	4-0	2-3	8-0	5-0	2-1	

LEAGUE CUP

FIRST ROUND

Boxted Lodgers 1 **Mersea Island 3**

Bradfield Rovers 3 **Little Oakley** 3 *aet* (3-5p)
(at Little Oakley)

Brightlingsea Regent 1 **Alresford Colne Rangers 2**

Coggeshall Town 6 Holland 1

Foxash Social 2 **Hatfield Peverel** 2 *aet* (2-4p)

Gas Recreation 9 St Osyth 0

Gosfield United 1 **Mistley United 5**

Great Bentley 3 **Tiptree Heath 5**

Great Bradfords 0 **Hedinghams United 1**

Kelvedon Social 0 **Earls Colne 8**

Lawford Lads 2 Rowhedge 0

Sudbury Athletic 1 **Glemsford & Cavendish United 5**

University Of Essex 1 Team Bury 0

Weeley Athletic 0 **Dedham Old Boys** 0 *aet* (2-3p)

West Bergholt 3 Bures United 1

White Notley 3 Walton Town 0

SECOND ROUND

Alresford Colne Rangers 2 Gas Recreation 2 *aet* (4-2p)

Dedham Old Boys 6 Hedinghams United 2

Glemsford & Cavendish United 0 **Hatfield Peverel 3**

Lawford Lads 1 **Mistley United 4**

Little Oakley 4 University of Essex 1 *aet*

Mersea Island 3 Earls Colne 1

Tiptree Heath 4 Coggeshall Town 2 *aet*

West Bergholt 2 **White Notley 2** *aet* (6-7p)

QUARTER-FINALS

Alresford Colne Rangers 1 **Dedham Old Boys 2**

Hatfield Pev. 2 Little Oakley 0

Mersea Island 2 Mistley United 2

Tiptree Heath 1 **White Notley 3**

SEMI-FINALS

Mistley Utd 0 **Hatfield Peverel 3**

White Notley 2 Dedham O B 0

FINAL
(April 16th at AFC Sudbury)
Hatfield Peverel 4 White Notley 0

Division One	P	W	D	L	F	A	Pts
White Notley	30	23	4	3	130	30	73
Mersea Island	30	22	5	3	88	43	71
Hedinghams United	30	18	2	10	86	57	56
Bures United	30	16	6	8	62	38	54
Holland	30	15	7	8	77	46	52
Boxted Lodgers	30	13	7	10	73	66	46
Glemsford/Cavendish Utd	30	13	6	11	65	64	45
Sudbury Athletic +2	30	12	7	11	49	54	45
Mistley United	30	11	5	14	70	66	38
Gosfield United	30	12	1	17	62	88	37
Rowhedge +3	30	7	11	12	52	86	35
Great Bradfords	30	9	6	15	70	84	33
St Osyth -1	30	9	4	17	48	89	30
Bradfield Rovers	30	7	6	17	54	87	27
Foxash Social -6	30	8	4	18	39	69	22
Kelvedon Social +3	30	3	3	24	45	103	15

WWW.NLNEWSDESK.CO.UK

RESERVES CUP

FINAL
(May 5th at Little Oakley)
University of Essex Res. 4 White Notley Res. 3

TOMMY THOMPSON CUP

FINAL
(April 23rd at Wivenhoe Town)
Weeley Athletic Res. 0 **West Bergholt Res. 1**

KENT BLAXILL ESSEX & SUFFOLK BORDER LEAGUE DIVISION ONE CONSTITUTION 2008-09

BOXTED LODGERS................The Playing Field, Cage Lane, Boxted, Colchester CO4 5RE........................01206 271969
BRADFIELD ROVERS............The Playing Field, The Street, Bradfield, Manningtree CO11 2UU............................None
BURES UNITED........................Recreation Ground, Nayland Road, Bures CO8 5BX...None
FOXASH SOCIAL............Foxash Playing Field, Harwich Road, Lawford, Manningtree CO11 2LP....................01206 231309
GLEMSFORD & CAVENDISH UTD......Memorial Hall, Melford Road, Cavendish CO10 8AA............................None
GOSFIELD UNITED ....The Playing Field, Gosfield, Halstead..None
GREAT BRADFORDS................Notley Sports Centre, Notley Road, Braintree CM7 1WX............................01376 323873
HEDINGHAMS UNITED........Lawn Meadow, Yeldham Road, Sible Hedingham, Halstead CO9 3QJ.........................None
HOLLAND......................Eastcliff Sports Ground, Dulwich Road, Holland-on-Sea CO15 5HR.........................01255 814874
KELVEDON SOCIAL.................The Chase, High Street, Kelvedon, Colchester CO5 9JD............................01376 572240
LAWFORD LADS ....School Lane, Lawford, Manningtree CO11 2JA............................01206 397211
MISTLEY UNITED....................Furze Hill, Shrubland Road, Mistley CO11 1HS....................01206 392714
ROWHEDGE ....Rectory Road, Rowhedge CO5 7HP..................................None
ST OSYTH........................Cowley Park, Mill Street, St Osyth, Clacton-on-Sea CO16 8EJ........................None
SUDBURY ATHLETIC.............Lucas Social Club, Alexandra Road, Sudbury CO10 2XH........................01787 881143
IN: Lawfords Lads (R)
OUT: Mersea Island (P), White Notley (P)

FOOTBALL CONFERENCE

	Aldershot Town	Altrincham	Burton Albion	Cambridge United	Crawley Town	Droylsden	Ebbsfleet United	Exeter City	Farsley Celtic	Forest Green Rovers	Grays Athletic	Halifax Town	Histon	Kidderminster Harriers	Northwich Victoria	Oxford United	Rushden & Diamonds	Salisbury City	Stafford Rangers	Stevenage Borough	Torquay United	Weymouth	Woking	York City
Aldershot Town		2-1	1-0	0-0	0-1	3-1	2-0	2-0	4-3	0-1	3-2	1-0	3-1	2-1	5-0	1-0	2-1	2-1	4-3	3-1	0-3	0-0	2-1	2-0
Altrincham	1-2		0-0	0-3	2-3	3-2	1-3	1-4	0-0	1-0	0-1	3-3	1-2	2-1	1-2	1-3	1-2	3-1	2-0	1-5	1-1	3-2	2-2	2-2
Burton Albion	2-0	2-1		1-2	1-0	3-0	1-1	4-4	1-0	1-1	2-3	2-1	1-1	2-1	0-2	4-1	1-2	2-1	4-3	2-1	3-0	3-1	2-1	2-0
Cambridge United	1-1	2-1	0-0		2-1	5-0	1-1	0-1	5-1	2-0	1-0	2-2	1-0	0-3	2-1	2-1	1-0	1-1	1-2	2-1	2-0	0-0	1-0	2-0
Crawley Town	0-1	0-1	1-1	2-1	P	5-0	1-2	2-2	4-1	3-0	2-1	0-4	1-0	0-4	2-1	2-0	4-1	1-1	1-1	2-1	2-3	1-1	5-3	6-1
Droylsden	2-2	0-2	0-2	1-2	R	1-1	2-3	0-3	5-3	1-2	2-0	0-1	1-0	1-3	3-1	1-4	0-0	1-1	0-3	1-2	1-3	1-1	3-4
Ebbsfleet United	2-2	2-0	2-1	2-1	1-0	2-0	E	1-1	3-1	0-2	4-1	1-0	5-4	2-1	1-3	0-3	2-1	2-1	0-1	2-1	4-1	1-1	1-1	1-2
Exeter City	1-1	2-1	1-4	1-1	2-0	1-1	1-1	M	2-1	3-3	1-0	1-0	2-1	1-0	2-1	2-0	2-2	4-2	4-1	4-0	4-3	0-0	2-2	1-1
Farsley Celtic	1-3	1-1	0-1	2-1	1-5	1-2	1-1	0-2	I	0-2	1-3	3-0	1-3	1-1	2-1	0-1	0-1	2-1	1-0	0-0	1-2	4-2	3-0	1-4
Forest Green Rovers	2-3	3-1	3-1	3-1	1-0	3-2	2-2	1-1	2-2	E	1-2	2-0	3-1	2-2	4-1	0-0	0-1	0-3	1-2	4-2	2-2	3-2	2-1	1-2
Grays Athletic	2-1	1-0	0-0	2-1	2-1	3-1	1-1	0-2	1-0	0-1	R	3-3	0-1	5-1	3-1	0-0	3-0	1-1	5-1	0-2	2-0	0-2	1-1	0-2
Halifax Town	0-0	2-2	2-2	1-2	3-0	3-0	1-0	0-3	2-0	1-1	0-0		0-0	1-6	3-1	0-3	1-1	1-1	0-0	1-2	3-2	2-1	1-0	2-2
Histon	1-2	1-0	2-2	1-0	3-0	2-0	3-2	2-2	1-2	2-2	2-2	1-3	D	2-1	1-1	1-0	2-1	2-0	3-3	1-4	4-5	2-2	0-1	3-1
Kidderminster H.	1-2	1-1	4-1	1-0	1-1	3-1	2-1	4-0	2-1	1-0	1-0	1-0	1-1	I	0-0	2-0	1-2	6-0	0-2	1-5	2-5	0-2	1-1	3-0
Northwich Victoria	1-2	1-2	0-2	0-2	2-0	3-3	3-3	0-0	4-0	1-1	1-0	2-2	1-3	1-1	V	1-0	1-0	0-1	4-3	0-1	3-2	1-3	0-1
Oxford United	2-3	4-0	0-3	1-2	1-0	1-0	0-0	2-2	5-1	1-0	0-0	1-3	3-0	0-0	0-1	I	1-0	2-1	2-1	2-1	3-3	0-1	0-0	1-1
Rushden/Diamonds	1-1	1-0	0-1	1-1	1-1	0-0	0-1	0-0	1-1	1-2	1-1	2-2	2-3	0-1	1-0	5-0	S	0-0	1-1	0-0	2-1	3-2	2-1	1-1
Salisbury City	0-4	3-3	2-0	0-2	4-1	3-1	2-1	2-0	1-1	0-0	0-1	1-0	3-3	0-1	2-0	3-1	1-1	I	1-0	1-0	0-0	1-1	2-1	3-0
Stafford Rangers	1-2	1-1	0-3	1-1	1-1	1-3	2-1	1-1	1-5	0-2	1-3	0-2	2-3	1-1	1-3	0-0	0-1	0-1	O	1-2	0-2	2-1	0-1	3-2
Stevenage Borough	3-1	2-1	3-1	1-2	3-1	5-0	3-1	0-1	4-0	0-0	0-0	2-3	2-1	2-1	1-2	0-0	2-1	3-1	3-0	N	1-3	3-0	1-1	3-2
Torquay United	1-2	1-1	1-2	1-2	1-2	2-1	3-1	1-0	1-0	1-0	3-1	1-0	1-0	3-2	3-2	4-0	2-0	4-2	3-1	3-0		3-2	2-0	0-0
Weymouth	0-2	2-2	1-2	2-2	1-2	2-1	2-0	3-1	0-0	0-6	1-1	2-1	0-1	2-1	2-0	0-1	1-2	0-3	1-3	1-0	0-0		0-1	1-2
Woking	0-1	2-0	2-1	0-0	1-1	1-1	1-0	1-1	0-1	1-1	0-1	1-0	3-3	3-0	2-3	1-2	1-1	3-2	2-2	0-2	0-1	1-1		0-3
York City	2-0	1-2	0-1	1-2	1-2	0-1	3-2	4-1	0-2	2-0	3-2	1-1	0-1	2-3	1-3	2-0	0-2	0-1	2-0	2-3		

Premier Division

		P	HOME					AWAY					TOTAL					
			W	D	L	F	A	W	D	L	F	A	W	D	L	F	A	Pts
Aldershot Town		46	18	2	3	44	21	13	6	4	38	27	31	8	7	82	48	101
Cambridge United		46	14	6	3	36	17	11	5	7	32	24	25	11	10	68	41	86
Torquay United		46	15	3	5	39	21	11	5	7	44	36	26	8	12	83	57	86
Exeter City		46	13	9	1	44	26	9	8	6	39	32	22	17	7	83	58	83
Burton Albion		46	15	3	5	48	31	8	9	6	31	25	23	12	11	79	56	81
Stevenage Borough		46	13	5	5	47	25	11	2	10	35	30	24	7	15	82	55	79
Histon		46	10	7	6	42	36	10	5	8	34	31	20	12	14	76	67	72
Forest Green Rovers		46	11	6	6	45	34	8	8	7	31	25	19	14	13	76	59	71
Oxford United		46	10	8	5	32	21	10	3	10	24	27	20	11	15	56	48	71
Grays Athletic		46	11	6	6	35	23	8	7	8	23	24	19	13	14	58	47	70
Ebbsfleet United		46	14	3	6	40	29	5	9	9	25	32	19	12	15	65	61	69
Salisbury City		46	12	7	4	35	22	6	7	10	35	38	18	14	14	70	60	68
Kidderminster Harriers		46	12	5	6	38	23	7	5	11	36	34	19	10	17	74	57	67
York City		46	8	5	10	33	34	9	6	8	38	40	17	11	18	71	74	62
Crawley Town	-6	46	12	5	6	47	31	7	4	12	26	36	19	9	18	73	67	60
Rushden & Diamonds		46	7	10	6	26	22	8	4	11	29	33	15	14	17	55	55	59
Woking		46	7	9	7	28	27	5	8	10	25	34	12	17	17	53	61	53
Weymouth		46	7	5	11	24	34	4	8	11	29	39	11	13	22	53	73	46
Northwich Victoria		46	6	7	10	30	36	4	4	14	22	42	11	11	24	52	78	44
Halifax Town	-10	46	8	10	5	30	29	4	6	13	31	41	12	16	18	61	70	42
Altrincham		46	6	6	11	32	44	3	8	12	24	38	9	14	23	56	82	41
Farsley Celtic		46	6	5	12	27	38	4	4	15	21	48	10	9	27	48	86	39
Stafford Rangers		46	2	4	17	16	48	3	6	14	26	51	5	10	31	42	99	25
Droylsden		46	4	5	14	27	45	1	4	18	19	58	5	9	32	46	103	24

PLAY-OFFS

SEMI-FINALS *(1st leg)* **SEMI-FINALS** *(2nd leg)*

(May 1st) Exeter City 1 Torquay United 2 *Att* 8,276 *(May 5th)* Torquay United 1 **Exeter City** 4 *Att* 6,015

(May 2nd) Burton Albion 2 Cambridge United 2 *Att* 5,757 *(May 6th)* **Cambridge United** 2 Burton Albion 1 *Att* 7,276

FINAL *(May 18th at Wembley Stadium)*
Cambridge United 0 **Exeter City** 1 *Att* 43,511

DATES & GATES

The following table records the date and attendance (gate) for each fixture. Each row is the listed team; each column is the opponent. Cells read "date / gate". The diagonal cells carry the team name.

	Aldershot Town	Altrincham	Burton Albion	Cambridge United	Crawley Town	Droylsden	Ebbsfleet United	Exeter City	Farsley Celtic	Forest Green Rovers	Grays Athletic	Halifax Town	Histon	Kidderminster Harriers	Northwich Victoria	Oxford United	Rushden & Diamonds	Salisbury City	Stafford Rangers	Stevenage Borough	Torquay United	Weymouth	Woking	York City
Aldershot Town	—	30 Sep / 2,991	2 Mar / 1,971	9 Dec / 1,295	3 Oct / 3,595	22 Sep / 3,610	3 Mar / 1,940	7 Apr / 733	9 Sep / 1,439	23 Jan / 5,005	17 Apr / 1,545	20 Mar / 1,614	19 Sep / 662	20 Jan / 1,976	4 Nov / 877	25 Nov / 5,811	17 Feb / 2,197	19 Aug / 1,786	28 Aug / 981	1 Jan / 3,070	6 Mar / 4,510	15 Aug / 1,782	6 Oct / 4,356	6 Oct / 3,092
Altrincham	28 Apr / 2,079	—	2 Dec / 1,012	2 Mar / 1,295	30 Dec /	9 Sep / 3,950	16 Feb / 1,257	3 Feb / 996	15 Aug /	25 Nov / 738	28 Apr / 814	9 Dec / 1,401	14 Apr / 1,178	20 Feb / 1,535	14 Oct / 1,761	9 Sep /	3 Feb / 1,364	20 Jan / 2,310	26 Dec /	6 Mar / 1,662	21 Apr / 4,533	3 Feb / 1,391	20 Jan / 4,336	5 Nov / 2,079
Burton Albion	9 Dec / 1,882	2 Mar / 5,791	—	19 Sep / 982	18 Nov / 715	30 Dec / 3,382	6 Mar /	17 Mar / 906	18 Nov / 665	1 Sep / 943	9 Dec / 1,265	27 Nov / 1,206	21 Apr / 1,179	25 Mar / 1,314	3 Feb /	30 Sep / 4,392	9 Apr / 1,807	31 Jan / 2,359	30 Dec / 3,121	27 Jan / 4,533	31 Mar / 3,321	13 Mar / 1,404	12 Sep / 1,493	25 Aug / 1,882
Cambridge United	22 Sep / 3,136	6 Mar / 3,259	30 Dec / 2,263	—	3 Oct / 1,559	17 Feb / 906	3 Sep / 1,024	14 Oct / 2,975	24 Nov / 634	4 Nov / 1,179	25 Mar / 3,721	1 Jan / 1,402	30 Sep / 1,197	14 Apr / 1,314	3 Mar / 1,512	23 Jan / 4,422	16 Nov / 2,358	15 Aug / 1,710	27 Jan / 3,368	19 Aug / 4,533	30 Dec / 2,727	12 Sep / 1,805	10 Oct / 1,502	6 Jan / 3,136
Crawley Town	3 Mar / 3,610	21 Apr / 2,457	19 Sep / 1,187	18 Nov / 2,457	—	1 Jan / 825	27 Jan / 423	21 Oct / 3,726	14 Apr / 932	12 Aug / 471	11 Apr / 1,305	20 Feb / 1,063	17 Feb / 1,302	7 Apr / 585	26 Nov / 821	4 Nov / 4,655	16 Nov / 1,534	10 Feb / 1,317	6 Jan / 1,186	20 Apr / 4,331	7 Apr / 470	13 Mar / 1,333	13 Mar / 1,102	15 Aug / 2,212
Droylsden	7 Apr / 1,940	14 Apr / 1,104	17 Mar /	26 Mar / 1,773	9 Sep / 788	—	27 Jan / 986	23 Jan / 803	23 Apr / 969	21 Jan / 1,226	20 Mar / 1,177	20 Feb / 552	19 Sep / 813	10 Mar / 1,045	12 Sep / 1,450	30 Sep / 5,521	27 Jan / 1,345	21 Oct / 1,310	13 Mar / 1,456	24 Mar / 2,037	15 Aug / 1,572	28 Apr / 1,255	4 Nov / 1,140	25 Nov / 3,042
Ebbsfleet United	3 Mar / 733	17 Feb / 1,178	14 Apr / 1,385	28 Aug / 932	1 Jan / 825	27 Jan / 986	—	14 Apr / 1,521	11 Nov / 2,845	17 Feb / 1,538	17 Mar / 714	16 Sep / 582	9 Dec /	6 Mar /	12 Sep / 641	14 Apr / 4,851	27 Jan / 1,351	24 Mar / 1,472	6 Mar /	26 Dec /	20 Jan /	17 Mar / 1,448	3 Mar /	16 Sep / 2,256
Exeter City	9 Sep / 5,005	19 Sep / 3,501	10 Oct / 3,823	14 Oct / 2,000	12 Aug / 3,071	27 Dec / 2,923	14 Apr / 1,489	—	20 Jan / 624	9 Sep /	23 Sep / 724	23 Sep /	6 Mar / 931	18 Nov / 812	21 Mar / 590	28 Feb / 2,165	1 Sep /	31 Jan / 2,903	20 Jan /	26 Dec / 2,465	30 Mar /	7 Apr / 2,995	13 Mar /	3 Mar / 2,134
Farsley Celtic	23 Jan / 1,439	9 Dec / 911	18 Nov / 861	3 Oct / 1,501	21 Oct / 3,071	10 Mar / 813	20 Apr / 2,753	23 Apr / 803	—	26 Apr / 450	4 Nov / 1,094	17 Feb / 973	24 Feb / 400	17 Mar / 866	10 Oct / 812	23 Aug / 3,812	20 Feb / 492	21 Apr / 2,783	9 Apr / 4,079	23 Sep / 719	14 Oct / 952	4 Oct / 951	19 Aug / 1,205	23 Jan / 1,886
Forest Green Rovers	19 Sep / 1,103	25 Nov / 738	1 Sep / 496	7 Apr / 853	12 Aug / 471	21 Jan / 1,044	3 Sep / 1,396	6 Mar / 930	26 Apr / 628	—	19 Sep / 746	12 Feb /	18 Nov / 546	10 Oct /	21 Apr / 859	28 Aug / 1,177	18 Apr / 475	12 Dec / 507	19 Sep /	28 Apr / 1,460	7 Apr / 779	19 Sep / 1,004	2 Dec / 550	12 Sep / 2,294
Grays Athletic	17 Apr / 1,545	28 Apr / 645	9 Dec / 696	30 Sep / 1,197	24 Apr / 853	27 Jan / 1,302	17 Mar / 1,063	3 Jan /	4 Nov / 1,094	19 Aug / 746	—	16 Sep /	9 Dec / 400	21 Apr / 497	21 Mar /	10 Feb / 2,106	4 Nov / 502	26 Dec /	21 Apr /	9 Apr / 763	14 Oct / 1,018	9 Apr / 1,335	26 Dec / 779	21 Oct / 2,531
Halifax Town	20 Mar / 1,614	14 Apr / 1,401	27 Feb / 1,206	1 Jan / 1,402	20 Feb / 1,063	20 Feb / 552	16 Sep / 582	23 Sep / 1,617	17 Feb / 973	12 Feb / 628	16 Sep / 975	—	12 Feb / 1,204	14 Apr / 1,290	18 Nov / 1,201	14 Apr / 1,624	6 Mar / 1,369	20 Jan / 2,783	31 Jan / 512	25 Nov / 2,229	20 Jan / 763	17 Mar / 1,133	1 Sep / 891	23 Jan / 2,199
Histon	19 Sep / 662	9 Dec / 480	21 Apr / 1,177	17 Feb / 1,197	17 Feb / 1,302	19 Sep / 813	10 Mar / 1,045	4 Nov / 1,160	24 Feb / 1,538	18 Nov /	9 Dec /	12 Feb /	—	9 Dec / 1,097	31 Mar /	1 Sep / 1,369	9 Sep / 502	23 Jan / 1,237	23 Jan / 825	9 Apr / 916	9 Sep / 894	9 Apr / 971	28 Aug / 1,018	9 Apr / 1,021
Kidderminster Harriers	20 Jan / 1,976	12 Feb / 814	25 Mar / 1,265	14 Apr / 1,314	11 Apr / 1,462	10 Mar / 1,307	6 Mar /	18 Nov / 812	17 Mar / 866	10 Oct / 552	21 Apr /	12 Feb / 1,280	9 Dec / 1,097	—	31 Mar / 1,097	27 Mar / 2,025	31 Jan / 1,624	12 Dec / 475	18 Nov / 1,093	23 Jan / 2,229	14 Oct / 2,382	1 Sep / 719	18 Nov / 779	9 Apr / 1,603
Northwich Victoria	4 Nov / 877	14 Oct / 1,761	3 Feb /	3 Mar / 1,512	26 Mar / 821	12 Sep / 1,450	12 Sep / 641	21 Mar /	10 Oct / 812	21 Apr / 651	21 Mar /	18 Nov / 1,201	31 Mar /	31 Mar / 1,097	—	21 Aug / 859	21 Sep / 590	18 Nov / 542	17 Mar /	9 Apr / 1,460	7 Apr / 1,018	9 Apr /	9 Nov /	9 Apr / 1,014
Oxford United	25 Nov / 5,811	9 Sep / 3,950	30 Sep / 4,392	23 Jan / 4,422	4 Nov / 4,655	30 Sep / 5,521	14 Apr / 4,851	28 Feb / 4,560	23 Aug / 4,266	28 Aug / 1,852	10 Feb / 2,106	14 Apr / 1,365	1 Sep /	27 Mar / 2,025	21 Aug / 4,673	—	14 Apr / 5,380	18 Nov / 1,177	21 Apr / 1,240	25 Nov / 2,382	4 Nov / 4,633	9 Apr / 3,996	9 Apr /	14 Oct / 4,944
Rushden & Diamonds	17 Feb / 2,197	3 Feb / 1,257	9 Apr / 1,807	16 Nov / 2,358	16 Nov / 1,534	27 Jan / 1,345	27 Jan / 1,351	1 Sep /	20 Feb / 492	18 Apr / 475	4 Nov / 502	6 Mar / 1,369	9 Sep / 502	31 Jan / 1,624	21 Sep / 590	14 Apr / 5,380	—	1 Sep / 1,384	9 Dec / 542	28 Aug / 1,460	20 Jan / 1,276	4 Nov / 1,448	21 Apr / 1,018	28 Apr / 2,044
Salisbury City	19 Aug / 1,786	3 Feb / 1,364	31 Jan / 1,433	15 Aug / 1,710	10 Feb / 1,317	21 Oct / 1,307	24 Mar / 1,472	31 Jan / 2,903	21 Apr / 2,783	12 Dec / 507	26 Dec /	20 Jan / 2,783	23 Jan / 1,237	12 Dec / 475	18 Nov / 542	18 Nov / 1,177	1 Sep / 1,384	—	9 Dec / 1,226	11 Nov / 3,436	25 Nov / 894	2 Dec /	31 Mar / 1,304	24 Jan / 2,303
Stafford Rangers	28 Aug / 981	26 Dec /	30 Dec / 3,121	27 Jan / 3,368	6 Jan / 1,186	13 Mar / 1,456	6 Mar /	20 Jan /	9 Apr / 4,079	19 Sep /	21 Apr /	31 Jan / 512	23 Jan / 825	18 Nov / 1,093	17 Mar /	21 Apr / 1,240	9 Dec / 542	9 Dec / 1,226	—	26 Dec / 2,229	6 Mar / 612	9 Apr / 1,055	21 Oct / 825	10 Feb / 1,784
Stevenage Borough	1 Jan / 3,070	6 Mar / 1,662	27 Jan / 4,533	19 Aug / 4,533	20 Apr / 1,717	24 Mar / 2,320	26 Dec /	26 Dec / 2,146	23 Sep / 2,186	28 Apr / 1,630	9 Apr / 763	25 Nov / 2,229	9 Apr / 916	23 Jan / 2,229	9 Apr / 1,460	25 Nov / 2,382	28 Aug / 1,460	11 Nov / 3,436	26 Dec / 2,229	—	20 Feb / 2,633	3 Nov / 3,261	12 Sep / 2,052	3 Oct / 3,139
Torquay United	6 Mar / 4,510	26 Dec / 2,310	31 Mar / 3,321	30 Dec / 2,704	7 Apr / 470	15 Aug /	20 Jan /	30 Mar /	14 Oct / 952	7 Apr / 779	14 Oct / 1,018	20 Jan / 763	9 Sep / 894	14 Oct / 2,382	7 Apr /	4 Nov / 4,633	20 Jan / 1,276	25 Nov / 894	6 Mar / 612	20 Feb / 2,633	—	6 Mar /	9 Nov / 763	14 Oct / 2,483
Weymouth	15 Aug / 1,782	3 Feb / 1,391	13 Mar / 1,404	12 Sep / 1,805	13 Mar / 1,333	28 Apr / 1,255	17 Mar / 1,448	7 Apr / 2,995	4 Oct / 951	19 Sep / 1,004	9 Apr / 1,335	17 Mar / 1,133	9 Apr / 971	1 Sep / 719	9 Apr /	9 Apr / 3,996	4 Nov / 1,448	2 Dec /	9 Apr / 1,055	3 Nov / 3,261	6 Mar /	—	17 Feb / 2,181	3 Feb / 2,483
Woking	6 Oct / 4,356	20 Jan / 1,728	12 Sep / 1,493	10 Oct / 1,502	13 Mar / 1,102	4 Nov / 1,140	3 Mar /	13 Mar /	19 Aug / 1,205	2 Dec / 550	26 Dec / 779	1 Sep / 891	28 Aug / 1,018	18 Nov / 779	9 Nov /	9 Apr /	21 Apr / 1,018	31 Mar / 1,304	21 Oct / 825	12 Sep / 2,052	9 Nov / 763	17 Feb / 2,181	—	29 Dec / 2,246
York City	6 Oct / 3,092	5 Nov / 2,079	25 Aug / 1,882	6 Jan / 3,136	15 Aug / 2,212	25 Nov / 3,042	16 Sep / 2,256	3 Mar / 2,134	23 Jan / 1,886	12 Sep / 2,294	21 Oct / 2,531	23 Jan / 2,199	9 Apr / 1,021	9 Apr / 1,603	9 Apr / 1,014	14 Oct / 4,944	28 Apr / 2,044	24 Jan / 2,303	10 Feb / 1,784	3 Oct / 3,139	14 Oct / 2,483	3 Feb / 2,483	29 Dec / 2,246	—

BLUE SQUARE FOOTBALL CONFERENCE
PREMIER DIVISION CONSTITUTION 2008-09

ALTRINCHAM
Moss Lane, Altrincham, Cheshire WA15 8AP
Tel: 0161 928 1045   Fax: 0161 926 9934
Manager: Graham Heathcote   www.altrinchamfc.com   Colours: Red, white & black

BARROW
Holker Street Stadium, Wilkie Road, Barrow-in-Furness, Cumbria LA14 5UW
Tel: 01229 820346   www.barrowafc.com   Fax: 01229 820346
Manager: Darren Sheridan/David Bayliss   Colours: Blue & white

BURTON ALBION
Pirelli Stadium, Princess Way, Burton-on-Trent, Staffordshire DE13 0AR
Tel: 0870 190 0060   Fax: 01283 523199
Manager: Nigel Clough   www.burtonalbionfc.co.uk   Colours: Yellow & black

CAMBRIDGE UNITED
The Trade Recruitment Stadium, Newmarket Road, Cambridge, Cambridgeshire CB5 8LN
Tel: 01223 566500   Fax: 01223 566502
Manager: Gary Brabin   www.cambridge-united.co.uk   Colours: Amber & black

CRAWLEY TOWN
Broadfield Stadium, Brighton Road, Crawley, West Sussex RH11 9RX
Tel: 01293 410000   Club: 01293 410001   Fax: 01293 410002
Manager: Steve Evans   www.crawleytownfc.net   Colours: Red

EASTBOURNE BOROUGH
Langney Sports Club, Priory Lane, Eastbourne, East Sussex BN23 7QH
Tel: 01323 766265   Fax: 01323 741627
Manager: Garry Wilson   www.eastbourneboroughfc.co.uk   Colours: Red & black

EBBSFLEET UNITED
Stonebridge Road, Northfleet, Gravesend, Kent DA11 9BA
Tel: 01474 533796   Fax: 01474 324754
Manager: Liam Daish   www.ebbsfleetunited.co.uk   Colours: Red & white

FOREST GREEN ROVERS
Nympsfield Road, Forest Green, Nailsworth, Gloucestershire GL6 0ET
Tel: 01453 834860   Fax: 01453 835291
Manager: Jim Harvey   www.fgrfc.co.uk   Colours: Black & white

GRAYS ATHLETIC
Recreation Ground, Bridge Road, Grays, Essex RM17 6BZ
Tel: 01375 377753   Fax: 01375 391649
Manager: Mick Woodward   www.graysathletic.co.uk   Colours: Sky blue

HISTON
The Glass World Stadium, Bridge Road, Impington, Cambridge, Cambridgeshire CB4 9PH
Tel: 01223 237373   Fax: 0845 345 9235
Manager: Steve Fallon   www.histonfc.co.uk   Colours: Red & black

KETTERING TOWN
Rockingham Road, Kettering, Northants NN16 9AW
Tel: 01536 483028   Clubhouse: 01536 410815   Fax: 01536 412273
Manager: Mark Cooper   www.ketteringtownfc.co.uk   Colours: Red & black

KIDDERMINSTER HARRIERS
Aggborough Stadium, Hoo Road, Kidderminster, Worcestershire DY10 1NB
Tel: 01562 823931   Fax: 01562 827329
Manager: Mark Yates   www.harriers.co.uk   Colours: Red & white

LEWES
The Dripping Pan, Mountfield Road, Lewes, East Sussex BN7 1XN
Tel: 01273 472100   Fax: 01273 472100
Manager: Kevin Keehan   www.lewesfc.com   Colours: Red & black

MANSFIELD TOWN
Field Mill, Quarry Lane, Mansfield, Notts NG18 5DA
Tel: 0870 756 3160   01623 482495
Manager: Billy McEwan   www.mansfieldtown.net   Colours: Yellow & blue

NORTHWICH VICTORIA
Victoria Stadium, Wincham Avenue, Wincham, Northwich, Cheshire CW9 6GB
Tel: 01606 41450   Fax: 01606 330577
Manager: Dino Maamria   www.northwichvics.co.uk   Colours: Green & white

OXFORD UNITED
The Kassam Stadium, Grenoble Road, Oxford, Oxfordshire OX4 4XP
Tel: 01865 337500   Fax: 01865 337501
Manager: Darren Patterson   www.oufc.co.uk   Colours: Yellow & navy blue

RUSHDEN & DIAMONDS
Nene Park, Diamond Way, Irthlingborough, Northants NN9 5QF
Tel: 01933 652000   Fax: 01933 652606
Manager: Garry Hill   www.thediamondsfc.com   Colours: Red

SALISBURY CITY
The Raymond McEnhill Stadium, Partidge Way, Old Sarum, Salisbury, Wiltshire SP4 6PU
Tel: 01722 326454   Fax: 01722 323100
Manager: Nick Holmes   www.salisburyjournal.co.uk   Colours: White & black

STEVENAGE BOROUGH
Broadhall Way Stadium, Broadhall Way, Stevenage, Herts SG2 8RH
Tel: 01438 223223   Fax: 01438 743666
Manager: Graham Westley   www.stevenageborofc.com   Colours: White & red

TORQUAY UNITED
Plainmoor Ground, Torquay, Devon TQ1 3PS
Tel: 01803 328666   Fax: 01803 323976
Manager: Paul Buckle   www.torquayunited.com   Colours: Yellow & blue

WEYMOUTH
Wessex Stadium, Radipole Lane, Weymouth, Dorset DT4 9XJ
Tel: 01305 785558   Fax: 01305 766658
Manager: John Hollins   www.theterras.co.uk   Colours: Claret, blue & white

WOKING
Kingfield, Kingfield Road, Woking, Surrey GU22 9AA
Tel: 01483 772470   Fax: 01483 729230
Manager: Kim Grant   www.wokingfc.co.uk   Colours: Red, white & black

WREXHAM
The Racecourse Ground, Mold Road, Wrexham, Denbighshire LL11 2AH
Tel: 01978 262129   01978 357821
Manager: Brian Little   www.wrexhamafc.co.uk   Colours: Red & white

YORK CITY
Kit Kat Crescent, Grosvenor Road, York, North Yorkshire YO30 7AQ
Tel: 01904 624447   Fax: 01904 631457
Manager: Colin Walker   www.ycfc.net   Colours: Red & white

IN: Barrow (P – Football Conference North), Eastbourne Borough (P – Football Conference South), Kettering Town (P – Football Conference North), Lewes (P – Football Conference South), Mansfield Town (R – Football League Division Two), Wrexham (R – Football League Division Two)
OUT: Aldershot Town (P – Football League Division Two), Droylsden (R – Football Conference North), Exeter City (P – Football League Division Two), Farsley Celtic (R – Football Conference North), FC Halifax Town (formerly Halifax Town) (R – Northern Premier League Division One North), Stafford Rangers (R – Football Conference North)

WWW.NLNEWSDESK.CO.UK

	AFC Telford United	Alfreton Town	Barrow	Blyth Spartans	Boston United	Burscough	Gainsborough Trinity	Harrogate Town	Hinckley United	Hucknall Town	Hyde United	Kettering Town	Leigh RMI	Nuneaton Borough	Redditch United	Solihull Moors	Southport	Stalybridge Celtic	Tamworth	Vauxhall Motors	Worcester City	Workington
AFC Telford United		3-0	0-2	3-1	1-1	1-0	2-1	3-1	3-0	1-0	2-1	0-1	6-1	0-0	1-0	4-0	1-5	3-0	4-1	3-2	1-1	3-3
Alfreton Town	0-1		0-0	1-1	2-1	1-2	3-1	1-2	0-0	2-1	0-3	1-2	1-0	1-3	0-0	0-0	1-2	3-4	1-2	4-0	3-1	2-0
Barrow	4-0	2-1		1-1	1-0	4-1	4-1	2-2	0-1	2-1	1-0	1-1	1-2	0-1	2-0	5-1	1-0	1-3	2-0	4-1	1-0	1-1
Blyth Spartans	1-2	2-0	2-3	C	2-1	1-4	1-1	0-1	1-3	1-2	0-2	2-0	2-0	2-0	1-0	2-4	1-2	1-0	0-1	1-1	0-2	6-0
Boston United	2-1	2-1	2-1	3-2	O	0-1	0-1	0-1	1-1	1-2	2-3	2-1	0-1	5-1	1-1	3-0	2-0	1-2	3-1	1-0	5-1	2-2
Burscough	1-3	1-1	2-1	2-2	2-1	N	2-2	2-1	1-1	2-1	3-2	1-1	5-2	2-0	2-2	1-1	0-2	2-3	0-0	2-1		0-1
Gainsborough Trinity	1-1	2-2	1-1	4-0	1-3	0-1	F	0-1	2-2	4-1	3-3	3-1	1-1	3-0	0-2	0-3	2-1	1-0	3-0	1-1	1-1	1-1
Harrogate Town	1-0	0-1	2-2	0-1	3-2	0-1	3-1	E	1-1	0-0	2-1	0-0	0-0	1-2	2-0	1-0	1-0	2-0	3-2	2-0	0-1	1-1
Hinckley United	1-1	1-0	1-1	0-1	1-0	1-0	1-2	2-3	R	2-1	3-1	0-0	3-1	0-0	1-2	0-1	2-3	0-3	2-0	0-1	2-4	2-1
Hucknall Town	0-2	2-2	0-1	0-3	1-2	0-2	0-1	0-1	1-1	E	1-4	0-2	3-0	2-2	1-2	2-0	1-2	0-3	3-1	2-0	5-0	1-3
Hyde United	1-0	0-2	2-1	2-4	2-1	1-0	3-0	2-2	5-2	4-2	N	0-3	1-1	2-0	4-0	3-0	1-3	1-3	1-2	6-3	3-1	1-2
Kettering Town	3-0	1-1	3-1	1-0	3-0	0-1	2-1	3-1	5-2	3-2	0-2	C	3-0	3-2	2-0	6-1	5-2	0-1	2-1	6-0	3-0	3-1
Leigh RMI	0-3	1-0	1-2	0-2	2-2	1-3	0-2	2-2	2-0	1-5	1-4	1-3	E	1-3	0-1	1-0	1-1	0-1	1-3	0-0	3-1	0-1
Nuneaton Borough	2-0	1-0	0-0	1-1	2-2	2-3	2-2	1-2	4-0	2-1	1-0	1-1	1-0		2-1	0-2	2-1	1-0	2-0	1-1	1-1	3-0
Redditch United	0-1	1-1	0-5	1-0	3-1	3-1	1-0	1-3	3-2	0-1	3-1	0-2	1-1	0-0	N	0-1	1-1	0-2	3-1	2-0	3-0	2-0
Solihull Moors	2-0	0-3	1-1	1-1	0-1	3-1	3-1	3-1	0-2	2-2	1-4	1-3	1-0	3-1	0-0	O	4-1	0-4	1-0	1-1	2-3	2-2
Southport	1-1	1-0	1-1	2-1	2-2	1-0	3-0	0-0	4-0	5-0	2-1	0-1	2-0	2-2	1-1	3-2	R	2-3	2-2	3-2	0-1	1-1
Stalybridge Celtic	1-2	3-1	2-2	0-0	3-0	2-4	5-1	3-2	2-1	0-3	3-1	0-1	3-1	0-2	6-0	4-0	2-2	T	0-0	4-1	1-0	3-0
Tamworth	0-0	0-1	0-0	3-0	1-1	4-2	2-2	1-1	3-0	4-0	2-1	1-2	2-0	1-2	1-0	0-2	1-3	2-0	H	1-1	0-2	2-0
Vauxhall Motors	1-3	3-2	1-0	2-0	0-0	0-3	0-1	0-1	0-3	3-4	0-6	2-2	0-0	2-0	3-2	1-2	2-5	1-3	1-3		1-1	2-5
Worcester City	0-3	1-1	1-1	2-2	2-1	2-0	1-0	1-1	1-1	2-0	2-3	3-1	0-4	1-0	0-0	2-1	2-1	3-3	1-0			2-2
Workington	0-1	1-2	0-1	2-0	0-1	0-1	1-2	0-1	1-1	1-3	2-0	1-1	2-1	2-0	1-1	1-1	2-3	1-0	5-0	1-0	1-0	

Conference North

	P		HOME					AWAY					TOTAL					
		W	D	L	F	A	W	D	L	F	A	W	D	L	F	A	Pts
Kettering Town	42	17	1	3	57	19	13	6	2	36	15	30	7	5	93	34	97
AFC Telford United	42	14	4	3	45	21	10	4	7	25	22	24	8	10	70	43	80
Stalybridge Celtic	42	12	4	5	47	24	13	0	8	41	27	25	4	13	88	51	79
Southport	42	10	8	3	38	21	12	3	6	39	29	22	11	9	77	50	77
Barrow	42	13	4	4	40	18	8	9	4	30	21	21	13	8	70	39	76
Harrogate Town	42	10	6	5	25	16	11	5	5	30	25	21	11	10	55	41	74
Nuneaton Borough	42	12	6	3	32	17	7	8	6	26	23	19	14	9	58	40	71
Burscough	42	8	5	8	33	30	11	0	10	29	28	19	8	15	62	58	65
Hyde United	42	12	2	7	45	32	8	1	12	39	34	20	3	19	84	66	63
Boston United	42	12	3	6	39	22	5	5	11	26	35	17	8	17	65	57	59
Gainsborough Trinity	42	8	8	5	35	26	7	4	10	27	39	15	12	15	62	65	57
Worcester City	42	8	7	6	27	30	6	5	10	21	38	14	12	16	48	68	54
Redditch United	42	10	4	7	28	24	5	4	12	13	34	15	8	19	41	58	53
Workington	42	8	4	9	25	20	5	7	9	27	36	13	11	18	52	56	50
Tamworth	42	9	6	6	31	20	4	5	12	22	39	13	11	18	53	59	50
Alfreton Town	42	7	5	9	27	26	5	6	10	22	28	12	11	19	49	54	47
Solihull Moors	42	7	5	9	29	36	5	6	10	21	40	12	11	19	50	76	47
Blyth Spartans	42	7	2	12	27	31	5	8	8	25	31	12	10	20	52	62	46
Hinckley United	42	7	4	10	24	28	4	8	9	24	41	11	12	19	48	69	45
Hucknall Town	42	4	4	13	25	36	7	2	12	28	39	11	6	25	53	75	39
Vauxhall Motors	42	5	4	12	26	47	2	3	16	16	53	7	7	28	42	100	28
Leigh RMI	42	5	4	12	21	38	1	4	16	15	49	6	8	28	36	87	26

PLAY-OFFS

SEMI-FINALS *(April 30th, 1st leg)*
Barrow 2 AFC Telford United 0 *Att* 2,701
Southport 1 Stalybridge Celtic 0 *Att* 1,361

SEMI-FINALS *(May 4th, 2nd leg)*
AFC Telford United 0 **Barrow** 2 *Att* 4,123
Stalybridge Celtic 2 Southport 1 *aet* (5-3p) *Att* 1,735

FINAL
(May 9th at Burton Albion)
Barrow 1 Stalybridge Celtic 0 *Att* 2,530

DATES & GATES

The following cross-reference grid lists, for each fixture, the date and attendance (gate). Row = home club; column = opponent.

	AFC Telford United	Alfreton Town	Barrow	Blyth Spartans	Boston United	Burscough	Gainsborough Trinity	Harrogate Town	Hinckley United	Hucknall Town	Hyde United	Kettering Town	Leigh RMI	Nuneaton Borough	Redditch United	Solihull Moors	Southport	Stalybridge Celtic	Tamworth	Vauxhall Motors	Worcester City	Workington
AFC Telford United	—	18 Sep 1,852	29 Feb 1,893	1 Dec 1,919	18 Jan 2,203	6 Oct 1,957	1 Sep 1,895	23 Feb 3,226	1 Mar 2,161	26 Jan 1,984	16 Feb 2,107	1 Nov 2,818	19 Jan 1,780	11 Mar 1,788	15 Mar 2,101	14 Aug 2,072	22 Mar 2,351	27 Oct 2,010	11 Dec 2,527	22 Dec 2,361	5 Jan 1,798	20 Oct 1,798
Alfreton Town	23 Feb 635	—	9 Feb 343	23 Feb 563	27 Aug 299																	
Barrow	17 Nov 943	5 Apr 1,062	—	4 Mar 870	26 Feb 338																	
Blyth Spartans	15 Sep 619	11 Aug 597	1 Sep 320	—	22 Sep 278																	
Boston United	9 Feb 1,572	29 Dec 1,303	1 Sep 1,475	19 Apr 1,118	—																	
Burscough	26 Apr 723	2 Feb 293	2 Feb 474	22 Mar 392	22 Sep 417	—																
Gainsborough Trinity	2 Feb 418	6 Oct 396	6 Oct 303	22 Mar 417			—															
Harrogate Town	8 Sep 781	17 Nov 549	19 Jan 582	19 Apr 419	1 Jan 1,294			—														
Hinckley United	8 Sep 844	11 Feb 405	16 Feb 465	18 Aug 514	26 Jan 662				—													
Hucknall Town	11 Aug 812	26 Dec 801	24 Mar 352	20 Oct 408	13 Oct 184					—												
Hyde United	22 Nov 567	19 Jan 509	20 Oct 461	5 Jan 380	3 Feb 477						—											
Kettering Town	5 Apr 2,520	17 Nov 1,540	1 Mar 1,410	12 Apr 1,110	26 Apr 1,332							—										
Leigh RMI	5 Feb 345	15 Mar 225	26 Apr 295	8 Apr 238	23 Oct 175								—									
Nuneaton Borough	24 Mar 1,273	1 Mar 797	26 Mar 850	5 May 852	22 Mar 712									—								
Redditch United	3 Nov 888	15 Apr 321	8 Sep 421	22 Mar 294	29 Mar 377										—							
Solihull Moors	12 Jan 615	23 Oct 182	11 Aug 320	20 Oct 203	1 Sep 283											—						
Southport	25 Jan 1,338	15 Apr 757	29 Dec 912	17 Nov 864	26 Mar 1,707												—					
Stalybridge Celtic	19 Apr 943	11 Mar 403	25 Aug 471	8 Sep 440	17 Nov 481													—				
Tamworth	26 Dec 1,509	25 Aug 1,011	15 Sep 805	19 Jan 1,238	26 Dec 885														—			
Vauxhall Motors	23 Oct 354	1 Sep 231	1 Dec 266	16 Feb 165	29 Dec 121															—		
Worcester City	29 Dec 1,636	24 Mar 669	1 Dec 802	26 Dec 753	11 Mar 719																—	
Workington	2 Feb 375	1 Apr 259	8 Apr 498	27 Aug 505	23 Feb 386																	—

BLUE SQUARE FOOTBALL CONFERENCE NORTH
CONSTITUTION 2008-09

AFC TELFORD UNITED
New Bucks Head Stadium, Watling Street, Wellington, Telford, Shropshire TF1 2TU
Tel: 01952 640064   Fax: 01952 640021
Manager: Rob Smith   www.telfordunited.com   Colours: White & black

ALFRETON TOWN
Impact Arena, North Street, Alfreton, Derbyshire DE55 7FZ
Tel: 01773 830277   Club: 01773 832819   Fax: 01773 836164
Manager: Nicky Law   www.alfretontownfc.com   Colours: Red

BLYTH SPARTANS
Croft Park, Plessey Road, Blyth, Northumberland NE24 3JE
Tel: 01670 352373   Club: 01670 354818   Fax: 01670 545592
Manager: Harry Dunn   www.blythspartansafc.co.uk   Colours: Green & white

BURSCOUGH
Victoria Park, Mart Lane, Burscough, Ormskirk, Lancashire L40 0SD
Tel: 01704 893237   Fax: 01704 893237
Manager: Joey Dunn   www.burscoughfc.co.uk   Colours: Green & white

DROYLSDEN
Butchers Arms, Market Street, Droylsden, Manchester M43 7AY
Tel: 0161 370 1426   Club: 0161 301 1352   Fax: 0161 370 8341
Manager: David Pace   www.droylsdenfc.co.uk   Colours: Red & black

FARSLEY CELTIC
Throstle Nest, Newlands, Farsley, Pudsey, Leeds, West Yorkshire LS28 5BE
Tel: 0113 255 7292   Fax: 0113 257 1058
Manager: John Deacy   www.farsleyceltic.net   Colours: Blue

FLEETWOOD TOWN
Highbury Stadium, Park Avenue, Fleetwood, Lancashire FY7 6TX
Tel: 01253 770702   Fax: 01253 777607
Manager: Tony Greenwood   www.fleetwoodtownfc.com   Colours: Red & black

GAINSBOROUGH TRINITY
The Northolme, North Street, Gainsborough, Lincolnshire DN21 2QN
Tel: 01427 613295   Club: 01427 615625   Fax: 01427 613295
Manager: Steve Charles   www.gainsboroughtrinity.com   Colours: Blue & white

GATESHEAD
The International Stadium, Neilson Road, Gateshead, Tyne & Wear NE10 0EF
Tel: 0191 478 3883   Fax: 0191 478 3883
Manager: Ian Bogie   www.gateshead-fc.com   Colours: Black & white

HARROGATE TOWN
Wetherby Road, Harrogate, North Yorkshire HG2 7SA
Tel: 01423 880675   Fax: 01423 880675
Manager: Neil Aspin   www.harrogatetown.com   Colours: Yellow & black

HINCKLEY UNITED
The Marstons Stadium, Leicester Road, Hinckley, Leicestershire LE10 3DR
Tel: 01455 840088   Fax: 01455 840088
Manager: Dean Thomas   www.hinckleyunitedfc.org   Colours: Red & blue

HUCKNALL TOWN
Watnall Road, Hucknall, Nottinghamshire NG15 6EY
Tel: 0115 963 0206   Club: 0115 956 1253   Fax: 0115 963 0716
Manager: Mick Galloway   www.hucknalltownfc.com   Colours: Yellow & black

HYDE UNITED
Ewen Fields, Grange Road, Hyde, Cheshire SK14 2SB

Tel: 0871 200 2116   Club: 0161 368 1621   Fax: 0871 200 2118
Manager: Steve Waywell   www.hydeunited.co.uk   Colours: Red & white

KING'S LYNN
The Walks Stadium, Tennyson Road, King's Lynn, Norfolk PE30 5PB

Tel: 01553 760060
Manager: Keith Webb   www.thelinnets.co.uk   Colours: Blue & gold

REDDITCH UNITED
Valley Stadium, Bromsgrove Road, Redditch, Worcestershire B97 4RN

Tel: 01527 67450   Fax: 01527 60611
Manager: Gary Whild   www.redditchunitedfc.co.uk   Colours: Red

SOLIHULL MOORS
Damson Park, Damson Parkway, Solihull, West Midlands B91 2PP

Tel: 0121 705 6770   Fax: 0121 711 4045
Manager: Bob Faulkner   www.solihullmoorsfc.co.uk   Colours: Amber & black

SOUTHPORT
Haig Avenue, Southport, Merseyside PR8 6JZ

Tel: 01704 533422   Club: 01704 530182   Fax: 01704 533455
Manager: Liam Watson   www.southportfc.net   Colours: Yellow & black

STAFFORD RANGERS
Marston Road, Stafford, Staffordshire ST16 3BX

Tel: 01785 602430   Fax: 01785 602431
Manager: Steve Bull   www.staffordrangers.co.uk   Colours: Black & white

STALYBRIDGE CELTIC
Bower Fold, Mottram Road, Stalybridge, Cheshire SK15 2RT

Tel: 0161 338 2828   Club: 0161 338 8443   Fax: 0161 338 8256
Manager: Steve Burr   www.stalybridgeceltic.co.uk   Colours: Blue & white

TAMWORTH
The Lamb Ground, Kettlebrook, Tamworth, Staffordshire B77 1AA

Tel: 01827 65798   Fax: 01827 62236
Manager: Gary Mills   www.thelambs.co.uk   Colours: Red

VAUXHALL MOTORS
Vauxhall Sports Ground, Rivacre Road, Hooton, Ellesmere Port, South Wirral CH66 1NJ

Tel: 0151 328 1114   Club: 0151 327 2294   Fax: 0151 328 1114
Manager: Carl Macauley   www.vmfc.com   Colours: White & navy blue

WORKINGTON
Borough Park, Workington, Cumbria CA14 2DT

Tel: 01900 602871   Fax: 01900 67432
Manager: Darren Edmondson   www.workingtonafc.com   Colours: Red

IN: Droylsden (R), Farsley Celtic (R), Fleetwood Town (P – Northern Premier League Premier Division), Gateshead (P – Northern Premier League Premier Division), King's Lynn (P – Southern League Premier Division), Stafford Rangers (R)
OUT: Barrow (P), Boston United (R – Northern Premier League Premier Division), Kettering Town (P), Leigh Genesis (formerly Leigh RMI) (R – Northern Premier League Premier Division), Nuneaton Town (formerly Nuneaton Borough) (R – Southern League Division One Midlands), Worcester City (S – Football Conference South)

	Basingstoke Town	Bath City	Bishop's Stortford	Bognor Regis Town	Braintree Town	Bromley	Cambridge City	Dorchester Town	Eastbourne Borough	Eastleigh	Fisher Athletic	Hampton & Richmond	Havant & Waterlooville	Hayes & Yeading United	Lewes	Maidenhead United	Newport County	St Albans City	Sutton United	Thurrock	Welling United	Weston-super-Mare
Basingstoke Town		0-0	2-1	3-0	1-0	3-1	3-1	0-0	1-1	1-1	2-3	1-2	1-5	3-4	2-3	1-0	2-1	1-1	2-2	3-2	1-2	0-4
Bath City	1-0		2-0	3-1	2-3	3-0	1-1	2-0	1-1	2-2	1-1	2-0	0-1	2-0	0-0	1-0	2-0	1-1	0-0	0-0	4-0	0-1
Bishop's Stortford	2-2	1-2		1-0	3-1	3-4	0-0	2-1	1-5	0-1	4-1	6-2	1-2	2-2	2-1	0-0	4-0	2-0	3-4	5-3	1-1	0-0
Bognor Regis Town	2-0	0-0	3-1	*C*	1-1	1-0	0-2	1-2	0-5	3-0	1-1	2-4	0-1	0-3	0-2	0-0	2-0	1-2	2-1	0-2	1-3	1-1
Braintree Town	4-0	2-1	0-0	1-0	*O*	0-0	0-0	1-1	3-0	0-1	1-0	3-0	2-3	0-2	1-0	1-0	0-1	2-1	3-2	2-1	2-0	2-1
Bromley	3-1	2-0	8-1	1-0	3-4	*N*	2-2	1-1	1-2	2-1	2-1	0-2	1-2	1-3	0-1	3-1	4-0	2-1	3-1	1-1	3-2	
Cambridge City	5-1	3-1	2-2	4-1	4-0	0-2	*F*	3-0	1-3	1-4	2-0	1-2	3-2	1-1	1-1	2-2	1-2	0-0	2-2	2-4	2-2	3-0
Dorchester Town	1-2	0-0	0-1	0-0	0-3	2-3	2-1	*E*	1-3	1-0	0-1	2-1	0-1	0-4	3-2	2-3	0-1	1-1	0-1	1-1	0-4	1-1
Eastbourne Borough	2-2	1-0	1-0	3-0	4-0	0-0	2-1	0-2	*R*	3-1	2-2	0-0	4-0	3-2	4-1	0-1	1-2	2-0	3-0	1-1	0-0	6-0
Eastleigh	3-2	3-1	0-0	1-2	1-1	3-2	3-0	3-0	1-4	*E*	1-1	3-0	1-2	3-1	1-0	1-4	2-1	1-0	0-0	4-4		1-1
Fisher Athletic	3-1	3-2	6-4	2-0	0-0	1-3	0-1	0-3	4-2	4-2	*N*	0-3	1-4	0-4	1-1	1-1	0-3	2-0	3-1	0-1	2-1	4-1
Hampton & Richmond	5-1	4-0	2-3	2-2	4-1	1-0	1-1	6-0	4-1	1-1	0-2	*C*	3-1	0-2	4-0	2-2	3-2	3-0	1-1	1-1	0-0	2-2
Havant & Waterlooville	1-1	1-0	3-0	2-0	3-1	2-0	0-3	1-2	4-1	0-3	1-0	1-0	*E*	2-1	4-0	2-1	1-0	0-0	2-0	1-2	1-0	1-1
Hayes & Yeading United	2-2	0-1	1-1	3-3	2-1	1-3	1-4	2-1	3-1	0-0	2-1	2-4	1-1		2-2	3-1	6-1	3-3	0-2	2-2	3-0	1-1
Lewes	3-0	2-0	1-0	4-0	0-2	1-0	0-0	2-1	4-0	1-2	1-0	3-2	2-2	2-0	*S*	3-1	2-0	0-0	0-1	1-0	1-0	4-0
Maidenhead United	0-0	0-1	1-2	1-1	0-0	2-3	0-0	0-1	3-3	1-2	2-3	0-5	1-2	3-1	1-1	*O*	2-3	0-1	1-2	5-0	0-1	1-2
Newport County	5-0	0-1	1-4	2-0	2-0	1-1	1-3	1-3	0-1	2-2	1-2	1-1	3-2	4-1	1-1	2-0	*U*	2-0	2-2	1-0	2-3	2-0
St Albans City	0-3	1-2	0-5	1-2	0-0	0-3	1-1	2-0	1-0	1-1	0-1	3-2	0-3	0-2	1-0	1-1		*T*	1-1	1-2	1-2	4-1
Sutton United	0-3	1-2	1-0	0-0	0-1	2-3	0-3	1-2	1-3	2-1	0-2	0-0	1-5	1-3	0-3	2-2	0-3	0-2	*H*	0-1	0-4	1-2
Thurrock	3-2	2-0	2-1	1-1	3-0	2-3	2-3	2-0	0-2	0-5	0-0	4-1	3-2	3-1	5-2	2-1	1-1	1-0	1-0		1-0	1-1
Welling United	2-1	2-2	0-0	0-0	1-2	0-2	0-4	1-2	1-1	1-3	0-1	3-1	1-0	1-1	2-6	3-1	0-2	2-3	2-1	1-0		0-1
Weston-super-Mare	0-3	3-1	3-0	0-3	2-2	1-2	1-2	3-1	3-1	2-2	1-1	0-3	1-0	0-1	0-1	1-2	3-2	0-4	0-2	3-3		

Conference South

	P	HOME					AWAY					TOTAL					
		W	D	L	F	A	W	D	L	F	A	W	D	L	F	A	Pts
Lewes	42	14	4	3	37	13	13	4	4	44	26	27	8	7	81	39	89
Eastbourne Borough	42	12	6	3	42	15	11	5	5	41	23	23	11	8	83	38	80
Hampton & Richmond	42	10	8	3	49	23	11	6	4	38	26	21	14	7	87	49	77
Fisher Athletic	42	10	3	8	35	36	12	2	7	30	25	22	5	15	65	61	71
Braintree Town	42	13	4	4	30	14	6	8	7	22	28	19	12	11	52	42	69
Eastleigh	42	9	7	5	34	29	10	3	8	42	33	19	10	13	76	62	67
Havant & Waterlooville	42	14	3	4	33	16	5	7	9	26	37	19	10	13	59	53	67
Bath City	42	10	8	3	30	12	7	7	7	29	24	17	15	10	59	36	66
Newport County	42	9	5	7	37	27	9	7	5	27	22	18	12	12	64	49	66
Bishop's Stortford	42	9	6	6	43	32	9	4	8	29	28	18	10	14	72	60	64
Bromley	42	11	3	7	44	29	8	4	9	33	37	19	7	16	77	66	64
Thurrock	42	13	4	4	39	26	5	5	11	24	38	18	9	15	63	64	63
Hayes & Yeading United	42	7	9	5	40	35	7	3	11	27	38	14	12	16	67	73	54
Cambridge City	42	8	7	6	43	32	6	3	12	28	40	14	10	18	71	72	52
Basingstoke Town	42	8	6	7	33	34	4	8	9	21	41	12	14	16	54	75	50
Welling United	42	6	5	10	23	34	7	2	12	18	30	13	7	22	41	64	46
Maidenhead United	42	2	6	13	24	34	9	6	6	32	25	11	12	19	56	59	45
Bognor Regis Town	42	6	5	10	21	31	5	6	10	28	36	11	11	20	49	67	44
St Albans City	42	5	5	11	21	35	5	7	9	22	34	10	12	20	43	69	42
Weston-super-Mare	42	6	4	11	28	38	3	6	12	24	47	9	10	23	52	85	37
Dorchester Town	42	5	4	12	17	33	3	6	12	19	37	8	10	24	36	70	34
Sutton United	42	2	3	16	13	45	3	6	12	19	41	5	9	28	32	86	24

WWW.CHERRYRED.CO.UK

PLAY-OFFS

SEMI-FINALS *(April 29th, 1st leg)*
Braintree Town 0 Eastbourne Borough 2 *Att* 1,017
Fisher Athletic 1 Hampton & Richmond Borough 1
Att 450

SEMI-FINALS *(May 3rd, 2nd leg)*
Eastbourne Borough 3 Braintree Town 0 *Att* 1,802
Hampton & Richmond Borough 0 Fisher Athletic 0
aet (4-2p) *Att* 1,489

FINAL
(May 8th at Stevenage Borough)
Eastbourne Borough 2 Hampton & Richmond Borough 0 *Att* 1,077

DATES & GATES

WWW.NLNEWSDESK.CO.UK

The following grid lists, for each fixture, the date played (upper figure) and the attendance (lower figure). Rows are the home clubs; columns are the visiting clubs.

Home \ Away	Basingstoke Town	Bath City	Bishop's Stortford	Bognor Regis Town	Braintree Town	Bromley	Cambridge City	Dorchester Town	Eastbourne Borough	Eastleigh	Fisher Athletic	Hampton & Richmond	Havant & Waterlooville	Hayes & Yeading Utd	Lewes	Maidenhead United	Newport County	St Albans City	Sutton United	Thurrock	Welling United	Weston-super-Mare
Basingstoke Town	—	22 Dec / 354	27 Oct / 509	15 Sep / 442	1 Dec / 302	8 Dec / 570	10 Nov / 761	18 Sep / 453	18 Sep / 621	23 Feb / 705	1 Jan / 261	5 Jan / 516	26 Apr / 745	18 Aug / 270	7 Sep / 620	19 Mar / 912	21 Apr / 1,144	3 Nov / 853	12 Apr / 380	27 Aug / 310	29 Dec / 464	11 Aug / 244
Bath City	27 Aug / 1,080	—	19 Jan / 295	16 Feb / 574	24 Mar / 747	8 Mar / 431	14 Apr / 322	10 Nov / 361	18 Sep / 958	11 Dec / 712	23 Sep / 182	12 Jan / 808	1 Sep / 452	18 Aug / 240	1 Mar / 752	24 Mar / 258	21 Apr / 912	3 Nov / 394	9 Feb / 436	23 Oct / 255	8 Dec / 437	25 Apr / 298
Bishop's Stortford	23 Feb / 442	16 Feb / 621	—	3 Nov / 364	1 Dec / 471	7 Sep / 798	3 Nov / 386	23 Sep / 439	19 Jan / 640	11 Dec / 958	1 Sep / 235	1 Sep / 585	5 Apr / 652	17 Nov / 223	3 Nov / 640	29 Jan / 322	24 Feb / 853	22 Mar / 444	14 Aug / 443	22 Mar / 326	5 Apr / 494	1 Mar / 237
Bognor Regis Town	22 Mar / 353	—	19 Jan / —	—	22 Mar / 471	12 Apr / 651	1 Aug / 516	1 Dec / —	1 Sep / 769	19 Jan / 609	1 Sep / 640	29 Jan / —	5 Apr / 652	17 Nov / 223	29 Jan / 717	15 Mar / 369	3 Nov / 640	26 Apr / 496	27 Aug / 609	16 Feb / 326	22 Dec / 605	26 Dec / 788
Braintree Town	4 Mar / 316	1 Dec / 302	24 Mar / 471	—	8 Mar / 494	22 Sep / 486	29 Mar / 521	26 Jan / 501	19 Jan / 804	1 Mar / 609	29 Jan / 241	12 Jan / 407	24 Mar / 577	29 Jan / 362	15 Mar / 717	6 Oct / 343	24 Oct / 500	24 Mar / 527	12 Feb / 370	23 Feb / 242	27 Feb / 168	—
Bromley	16 Feb / 514	8 Mar / 431	8 Mar / 431	8 Mar / —	—	12 Apr / 651	29 Mar / 615	26 Jan / —	1 Sep / 603	18 Sep / 683	27 Oct / 284	24 Mar / 493	24 Mar / 877	8 Mar / 362	2 Sep / 496	6 Oct / 638	22 Mar / 638	18 Aug / 580	4 Mar / 434	26 Dec / 245	22 Dec / 479	17 Apr / 326
Cambridge City	10 Nov / 488	14 Apr / 322	19 Jan / 361	1 Aug / 516	29 Mar / 521	15 Apr / 535	—	1 Apr / —	29 Dec / 615	19 Jan / 609	27 Oct / 284	25 Aug / 410	19 Apr / 715	1 Jan / 284	2 Sep / —	9 Feb / —	22 Mar / —	14 Aug / 500	27 Jan / 479	14 Aug / 310	26 Jan / 605	17 Nov / 264
Dorchester Town	22 Sep / 458	10 Nov / 361	19 Jan / 439	19 Jan / —	26 Jan / —	29 Dec / —	1 Apr / —	—	22 Mar / 677	1 Mar / 652	20 Oct / 215	22 Sep / 538	24 Apr / —	8 Dec / 207	27 Oct / 531	9 Feb / 436	24 Oct / 531	18 Sep / 370	23 Feb / 434	23 Feb / —	26 Jan / —	17 Nov / 278
Eastbourne Borough	29 Mar / 813	18 Sep / 621	11 Dec / 640	1 Sep / 769	10 Nov / 804	27 Nov / 603	29 Dec / 144	22 Mar / 263	—	18 Aug / 603	22 Mar / 215	24 Apr / 215	3 Nov / 566	2 Feb / 332	15 Sep / 609	26 Dec / 368	19 Apr / —	12 Feb / 580	8 Dec / 527	14 Aug / —	12 Dec / 242	12 Jan / —
Eastleigh	8 Sep / 454	23 Feb / 705	11 Dec / 958	19 Jan / 609	19 Jan / 804	27 Nov / 603	18 Aug / —	8 Sep / 580	18 Aug / 911	—	18 Mar / 482	18 Aug / 541	25 Aug / 574	27 Apr / 350	19 Jan / 850	15 Sep / 351	22 Mar / 455	18 Sep / 616	7 Sep / 434	4 Mar / 138	4 Mar / 286	8 Mar / 274
Fisher Athletic	18 Aug / 210	1 Jan / 261	23 Sep / 182	1 Sep / 640	10 Nov / 609	18 Sep / 683	1 Mar / 652	20 Oct / 545	15 Mar / 581	23 Feb / —	—	1 Apr / 911	2 Feb / 645	23 Oct / 202	11 Jan / 609	15 Sep / 406	8 Mar / 353	11 Aug / 601	1 Jan / 420	3 Nov / 245	26 Dec / 603	4 Feb / 261
Hampton & Richmond	1 Dec / 448	12 Jan / 516	12 Jan / 585	29 Jan / —	20 Oct / 407	24 Mar / 493	22 Sep / 410	22 Apr / 538	24 Apr / 215	18 Aug / 541	1 Apr / 1,255	—	1 Apr / 874	27 Nov / 527	18 Aug / 656	26 Apr / 372	22 Mar / 1,003	15 Dec / 414	18 Aug / 455	26 Apr / 372	11 Aug / 245	22 Oct / 277
Havant & Waterlooville	14 Apr / 926	1 Sep / 452	5 Apr / 652	5 Apr / 652	12 Jan / 577	24 Mar / 877	19 Apr / 715	25 Aug / 566	3 Nov / —	25 Aug / 574	2 Feb / 645	1 Apr / 874	—	3 Nov / 539	17 Nov / 609	22 Mar / 330	9 Feb / 657	17 Nov / 414	18 Sep / 457	25 Aug / 718	9 Feb / 504	4 Mar / 354
Hayes & Yeading United	14 Aug / 228	18 Aug / 240	17 Nov / 223	17 Nov / 223	29 Jan / 241	8 Mar / 362	1 Jan / 282	8 Dec / 207	2 Feb / 332	27 Apr / 350	23 Oct / 202	3 Nov / 203	3 Nov / 539	—	27 Jan / —	22 Mar / 353	8 Mar / 725	22 Mar / 353	8 Sep / 434	6 Oct / 228	5 Apr / 228	24 Apr / 273
Lewes	26 Apr / 1,017	7 Sep / 620	1 Mar / 717	29 Jan / 717	15 Mar / 717	2 Sep / 496	2 Sep / —	27 Oct / 531	15 Sep / 609	19 Jan / 850	11 Jan / 1,064	18 Aug / 725	27 Jan / 725	23 Oct / —	—	16 Feb / 850	8 Mar / 691	11 Aug / —	1 Jan / —	26 Dec / —	1 Dec / 745	8 Sep / —
Maidenhead United	8 Jan / 214	19 Mar / 912	24 Mar / 322	15 Mar / 369	6 Oct / 343	6 Oct / 638	9 Feb / 436	9 Feb / 436	26 Dec / 368	15 Sep / 351	15 Sep / 406	11 Aug / 850	22 Mar / 353	16 Feb / 850	22 Mar / —	—	22 Mar / 725	26 Jan / 479	7 Sep / 622	26 Apr / 372	26 Dec / 245	4 Feb / 261
Newport County	1 Jan / 1,030	21 Apr / 1,144	29 Jan / 640	3 Nov / 640	24 Oct / 500	22 Mar / 638	22 Sep / 410	24 Oct / 531	19 Apr / —	22 Mar / 455	8 Mar / 353	22 Mar / 1,003	9 Feb / 657	8 Mar / 725	8 Mar / 691	22 Mar / 725	—	22 Mar / 926	2 Feb / 2,299	18 Aug / 2,007	1 Dec / 799	23 Oct / —
St Albans City	27 Oct / 395	3 Nov / 853	24 Feb / 444	26 Apr / 496	24 Mar / 527	18 Aug / 580	14 Aug / 500	18 Sep / 370	12 Feb / 580	18 Sep / 616	11 Aug / 601	15 Dec / 414	17 Nov / 414	22 Mar / 353	11 Aug / 1,064	26 Jan / 479	22 Mar / 926	—	12 Apr / 455	6 Oct / 372	16 Feb / 455	22 Mar / —
Sutton United	6 Oct / 397	9 Feb / 436	14 Aug / 443	27 Aug / 609	26 Jan / 609	27 Oct / 479	27 Jan / 479	23 Feb / 434	4 Mar / 527	7 Sep / 434	1 Jan / 420	18 Aug / 455	18 Sep / 457	8 Sep / 434	1 Jan / —	7 Sep / 622	2 Feb / 2,299	12 Apr / 455	—	6 Oct / 322	5 Jan / 323	22 Dec / —
Thurrock	5 Jan / 180	23 Oct / 255	22 Mar / 326	16 Feb / 326	4 Mar / 242	4 Mar / 168	14 Aug / 310	23 Feb / 242	8 Sep / 245	4 Mar / 138	26 Dec / 245	26 Apr / 372	5 Apr / 279	6 Oct / 228	2 Feb / 253	1 Jan / 346	18 Aug / 372	6 Oct / 372	1 Sep / 322	—	2 Feb / 253	28 Aug / —
Welling United	15 Mar / 450	8 Dec / 464	5 Apr / 494	22 Dec / 605	27 Feb / 506	17 Nov / 494	26 Jan / 605	15 Sep / 500	1 Dec / —	1 Sep / 439	26 Dec / 603	11 Aug / 245	9 Feb / 504	5 Apr / 228	1 Dec / 745	26 Dec / 245	1 Dec / 799	16 Feb / 455	5 Jan / 323	2 Feb / 253	—	24 Apr / —
Weston-super-Mare	9 Feb / 297	11 Aug / 244	25 Apr / 298	1 Mar / 237	26 Dec / 788	17 Apr / 326	17 Nov / 264	17 Nov / 278	12 Jan / —	8 Mar / 274	4 Feb / 261	22 Oct / 277	4 Mar / 354	24 Apr / 273	8 Sep / —	4 Feb / 261	23 Oct / —	22 Mar / —	22 Dec / —	28 Aug / —	24 Apr / —	—

BLUE SQUARE FOOTBALL CONFERENCE SOUTH CONSTITUTION 2008-09

AFC WIMBLEDON
Cherry Red Records Fans Stadium, Kingsmeadow, Jack Goodchild Way,
Kingston-upon-Thames, Surrey KT1 3PB
Tel: 020 8547 3528
Manager: Terry Brown   www.afcwimbledon.co.uk   Colours: Blue

BASINGSTOKE TOWN
The Camrose, Western Way, Basingstoke, Hampshire RG22 6EZ
Tel: 01256 327575   Club: 01256 464353   Fax: 01256 869997
Manager: Frank Gray   www.btfc.co.uk   Colours: Blue & yellow

BATH CITY
Twerton Park, Twerton, Bath, North Somerset BA2 1DB
Tel: 01225 423087   Club: 01225 313247   Fax: 01225 481391
Manager: John Relish   www.bathcityfc.com   Colours: Black & white

BISHOP'S STORTFORD
Woodside Park, Dunmow Road, Bishop's Stortford, Hertfordshire CM23 5RG
Tel: 08700 339930   www.bsfc.co.uk   Fax: 08700 339931
Manager: Martin Hayes   Colours: Blue & white

BOGNOR REGIS TOWN
Nyewood Lane, Bognor Regis, West Sussex PO21 2TY
Tel: 01243 822325   Club: 01243 862045   Fax: 01243 866151
Manager: Mick Jenkins   www.therocks.co.uk   Colours: White & green

BRAINTREE TOWN
Cressing Road Stadium, Clockhouse Way, Braintree, Essex CM7 6RD
Tel: 01376 345617   Fax: 01376 323369
Manager: Lee Patterson   www.braintreetownfc.org.uk   Colours: Yellow

BROMLEY
The Stadium, Hayes Lane, Bromley, Kent BR2 9EF
Tel: 020 8460 5291
Manager: Mark Goldberg   www.bromleyfc.net   Colours: White & black

CHELMSFORD CITY
Chelmsford Sport & Athletics Centre, Salerno Way, Chelmsford, Essex CM1 2EH
Tel: 01245 290959
Manager: Jeff King   www.chelmsfordcityfc.com   Colours: Claret

DORCHESTER TOWN
The Avenue Stadium, Weymouth Avenue, Dorchester, Dorset DT1 2RY
Tel: 01305 262451   Fax: 01305 267623
Manager: Shaun Brooks   www.dorchestertownfc.co.uk   Colours: Black & white

EASTLEIGH
Silverlake Stadium, Ten Acres, Stoneham Lane,
North Stoneham, Eastleigh, Hampshire SO50 9HT
Tel: 023 8061 3361   Fax: 023 8061 2379
Manager: Ian Baird   www.eastleigh-fc.co.uk   Colours: White & navy blue

FISHER ATHLETIC
Champion Hill Stadium, Edgar Kail Way, Dog Kennel Hill,
East Dulwich, London SE22 8BD
Tel: 020 7326 1360
Manager: Wayne Burnett   www.fisherathletic.co.uk   Colours: Black & white

HAMPTON & RICHMOND BOROUGH
Beveree Stadium, Beaver Close, Station Road, Hampton, Middlesex TW12 2BT
Tel: 020 8941 2838   Club: 020 8979 2456   Fax: 020 8941 7048
Manager: Alan Devonshire   www.hamptonfc.net   Colours: Red & blue

HAVANT & WATERLOOVILLE
Westleigh Park, Martin Road, Havant, Hampshire PO9 5TH
Tel: 023 9278 7822   Club: 023 9278 7855   Fax: 023 9226 2367
Manager: Shaun Gale   www.havantandwaterlooville.net   Colours: White

HAYES & YEADING UNITED
Townfield House, Church Road, Hayes, Middlesex UB3 2LE
Tel: 020 8573 2075   Fax: 020 8573 0933
Manager: Garry Haylock   www.hyufc.net   Colours: Red, white & black

MAIDENHEAD UNITED
York Road, Maidenhead, Berkshire SL6 1SQ
Tel: 01628 636314   www.maidenheadunitedfc.co.uk   Club: 01628 624739
Manager: Johnson Hippolyte   Colours: Black & white

NEWPORT COUNTY
Newport Stadium, Stadium Way, Newport International Sports Village,
Newport, Gwent NP19 4PT
Tel: 01633 662262   Stadium: 01633 671815   Fax: 01633 666107
Manager: Dean Holdsworth   www.newport-county.co.uk   Colours: Amber & black

ST ALBANS CITY
Clarence Park, York Road, St Albans, Hertfordshire AL1 4PL
Tel: 01727 864296   Club: 01727 866819   Fax: 01727 866235
Manager: Steve Castle   www.sacfc.co.uk   Colours: Yellow & blue

TEAM BATH
Bath City FC, Twerton Park, Twerton, Bath, North Somerset BA2 1DB
Tel: 01225 423087   Club: 01225 313247   Fax: 01225 481391
Manager: Ged Roddy   www.teambath.com/?page_id=77   Colours: Yellow & blue

THURROCK
Ship Lane, Grays, Essex RM19 1YN
Tel: 01708 865492   Club: 01708 865492   Fax: 01708 868863
Manager: Hakan Hayrettin   www.thurrock-fc.com   Colours: Yellow & green

WELLING UNITED
Park View Road, Welling, Kent DA16 1SY
Tel: 020 8301 1196   Fax: 020 8301 5676
Manager: Andy Ford   www.wellingunited.com   Colours: Red & white

WESTON-SUPER-MARE
Woodspring Stadium, Winterstoke Road, Weston-super-Mare, North Somerset BS24 9AA
Tel: 01934 621618   Fax: 01934 622704
Manager: Tony Ricketts   www.westonsupermareafc.co.uk   Colours: White & blue

WORCESTER CITY
St George's Lane, Barbourne, Worcester, Worcestershire WR1 1QT
Tel: 01905 23003   Fax: 01905 26668
Manager: Richard Dryden   www.worcestercityfc.co.uk   Colours: Blue & white

IN: AFC Wimbledon (P – Isthmian League Premier Division), Chelmsford City (P – Isthmian League Premier Division), Team Bath (P – Southern League Premier Division), Worcester City (S – Football Conference North)
OUT: Cambridge City (R – Southern League Premier Division), Eastbourne Borough (P), Lewes (P), Sutton United (R – Isthmian League Premier Division)

SETANTA SHIELD

NORTHERN SECTION	SOUTHERN SECTION

FIRST ROUND

AFC Telford United 3 Solihull Moors 2 *aet (Oct 2)*	Att: 828	Basingstoke Tn 1 **Hampton & Richmond Boro'** 3 *(Oct 2)* Att: 223
Alfreton Town 3 Hucknall Town 0 *(Oct 9)*	Att: 187	**Bath City** 3 Weston-super-Mare 2 *aet (Oct 16)* Att: 168
Barrow 4 Leigh RMI 0 *(Oct 2)*	Att: 346	**Bromley** 2 Sutton United 1 *(Oct 9)* Att: 309
Burscough 2 Vauxhall Motors 0 *(Oct 2)*	Att: 147	Cambridge City 1 **Thurrock** 3 *(Oct 13)* Att: 195
Gainsborough Trinity 1 **Boston United** 2 *(Oct 2)*	Att: 490	**Dorchester Town** 3 Eastleigh 2 *(Oct 9)* Att: 201
Stalybridge Celtic 0 **Blyth Spartans** 0 *aet (3-4p) (Oct 25)*	Att: 840	**Maidenhead United** 3 Hayes & Yeading Utd 0 *(Oct 9)* Att: 224

SECOND ROUND

AFC Telford United 2 Redditch United 0 *(Nov 13)*	Att: 970	Bishop's Stortford 0 **Thurrock** 1 *(Oct 27)* Att: 303
Alfreton Town 1 **Hinckley United** 2 *(Nov 13)*	Att: 170	**Eastbourne Borough** 3 Bognor Regis Town 0 *(Nov 13)* Att: 257
Harrogate Town 3 Blyth Spartans 2 *aet (Nov 13)*	Att: 259	**Hampton & Richmond Boro'** 5 Dorchester Tn 2 *(Nov 13)* Att: 178
Kettering Town 2 Boston United 0 *(Oct 29)*	Att: 884	Havant & Waterlooville 2 **Lewes** 3 *(Nov 12)* Att: 181
Southport 3 Burscough 2 *(Nov 13)*	Att: 577	Maidenhead United 1 **Bromley** 2 *(Nov 13)* Att: 249
Tamworth 3 Hyde United 2 *aet (Nov 13)*	Att: 187	Newport County 3 Bath City 2 *(Nov 19)* Att: 419
Worcester City 1 **Nuneaton Borough** 2 *(Nov 12)*	Att: 568	**St Albans City** 1 Braintree Town 1 *aet (5-4p) (Nov 20)* Att: 127
Workington 2 **Barrow** 2 *aet (6-7p) (Nov 13)*	Att: 425	**Welling United** 2 Fisher Athletic 1 *(Nov 13)* Att: 164

THIRD ROUND

Kettering Town 2 **Hinckley United** 4 *aet (Dec 3)*	Att: 402	Bromley 1 **Welling United** 2 *aet (Dec 4)* Att: 419
Nuneaton Borough 4 AFC Telford United 2 *aet (Dec 4)*	Att: 440	**Eastbourne Borough** 7 Lewes 2 *(Dec 4)* Att: 595
Southport 2 **Barrow** 3 *aet (Dec 4)*	Att: 355	**Hampton & Richmond Boro'** 2 Newport County 1 *(Dec 4)* Att: 213
Tamworth 3 Harrogate Town 1 *(Dec 4)*	Att: 204	**St Albans City** 2 Thurrock 1 *(Dec 15)* Att: 203

FOURTH ROUND

Barrow 0 **Northwich Victoria** 2 *(Jan 22)*	Att: 708	**Aldershot Town** 1 Oxford United 0 *(Dec 22)* Att: 1,573
Burton Albion 2 Tamworth 1 *(Dec 22)*	Att: 1,152	Eastbourne Borough 1 **Crawley Town** 2 *(Dec 22)* Att: 552
Cambridge United 0 **Rushden & Diamonds** 1 *(Dec 21)*	Att: 1,309	Exeter City 2 **Ebbsfleet United** 3 *aet (Dec 21)* Att: 1,009
Droylsden 2 Farsley Celtic 1 *(Feb 5)*	Att: 224	Hampton & Richmond 0 **Forest Green Rvrs** 1 *(Dec 22)* Att: 344
Hinckley United 1 **Kidderminster Harriers** 2 *(Dec 22)*	Att: 474	Salisbury City 1 **Weymouth** 2 *(Dec 22)* Att: 667
Histon 1 **Halifax Town** 2 *(Dec 22)*	Att: 231	**St Albans City** 2 Torquay United 0 *(Dec 22)* Att: 454
Nuneaton Borough 2 Altrincham 1 *(Dec 22)*	Att: 533	Welling United 1 **Grays Athletic** 3 *(Jan 29)* Att: 261
Stafford Rangers 0 **York City** 2 *aet (Dec 22)*	Att: 515	**Woking** 2 Stevenage Borough 1 *(Dec 22)* Att: 830

FIFTH ROUND

Droylsden 0 **Burton Albion** 2 *(Mar 6)*	Att: 172	**Crawley Town** 4 Grays Athletic 0 *(Feb 5)* Att: 564
Kidderminster Harriers 1 **Rushden & Diamonds** 3 *(Feb 26)*	Att: 739	St Albans City 0 **Aldershot Town** 4 *(Feb 5)* Att: 375
Nuneaton Borough 0 **Halifax Town** 1 *(Feb 26)*	Att: 469	**Weymouth** 4 Ebbsfleet United 0 *(Feb 5)* Att: 508
York City 3 **Northwich Victoria** 3 *aet (2-3p) (Feb 6)*	Att: 763	**Woking** 1 Forest Green Rovers 0 *(Feb 4)* Att: 725

QUARTER-FINALS

Halifax Town 3 Burton Albion 1 *(Feb 18)*	Att: 632	Crawley Town 2 **Aldershot Town** 6 *(Feb 26)* Att: 827
Northwich Vic. 0 **Rushden & Diamonds** 4 *(Mar 8)*	Att: 440	**Woking** 3 Weymouth 0 *(Feb 26)* Att: 690

SEMI-FINAL

Rushden & Diamonds 1 Halifax Tn 0 *(Mar 18)*	Att: 880	**Aldershot Tn** 2 Woking 2 *aet (4-3p) (Mar 27)* Att: 1,629

FINAL

(April 3rd at Aldershot Town)

Aldershot Town 3 Rushden & Diamonds 3 *aet* (4-3p) *Att:* 3,714

GLOUCESTERSHIRE COUNTY LEAGUE

	AXA	Berkeley Town	DRG Stapleton	Ellwood	Hanham Athletic	Hardwicke	Henbury	Highridge United	Kings Stanley	Patchway Town	Pucklechurch Sports	Taverners	Thornbury Town	Tuffley Rovers	Wotton Rovers	Yate Town Res.
AXA		1-1	1-0	2-3	3-3	1-2	3-2	2-0	2-0	2-1	4-0	0-1	2-1	1-0	4-1	1-2
Berkeley Town	1-5		2-1	2-5	0-3	2-3	2-3	1-2	3-4	3-2	0-0	1-4	2-0	4-4	1-0	2-6
DRG Stapleton	0-3	3-1		5-2	0-4	1-1	2-2	2-2	0-3	2-2	4-1	0-2	0-2	2-2	2-0	0-2
Ellwood	2-2	4-1	2-0		1-0	1-1	4-0	2-2	1-4	5-4	1-0	1-1	4-2	1-0	6-1	1-2
Hanham Athletic	6-1	2-0	4-2	4-2		1-2	0-1	0-1	4-1	3-0	4-1	4-1	0-0	1-0	4-1	1-2
Hardwicke	3-1	4-0	2-1	0-0	3-0		3-1	1-0	3-1	2-0	6-1	1-0	7-0	0-1	3-1	1-1
Henbury	2-4	2-3	2-2	3-1	0-3	0-1		0-4	0-1	2-2	1-1	0-1	0-0	2-3	5-1	1-1
Highridge United	2-3	1-1	2-2	4-2	3-2	0-2	4-1		1-1	2-0	0-0	0-2	3-1	3-1	9-2	3-1
Kings Stanley	3-3	4-2	5-0	3-1	0-5	2-2	2-0	1-4		1-3	5-1	1-0	1-0	3-0	0-2	1-2
Patchway Town	2-2	1-1	3-1	3-1	2-2	1-0	4-3	0-1	2-1		4-0	2-2	2-1	1-3	6-1	1-1
Pucklechurch Sports	1-1	1-2	2-2	2-1	1-5	1-2	0-0	0-1	1-2	0-2		1-2	2-2	0-1	4-0	0-1
Taverners	1-0	3-2	0-1	1-2	0-1	0-3	1-2	1-1	1-1	1-4	2-0		0-1	0-1	6-0	0-0
Thornbury Town	2-0	1-3	0-0	1-2	0-5	0-3	1-1	0-1	4-1	1-1	1-1	0-4		1-2	4-1	0-4
Tuffley Rovers	0-3	1-1	5-0	3-1	2-2	0-3	2-1	3-2	0-1	1-1	0-1	2-1	1-0		3-0	1-0
Wotton Rovers	0-3	5-1	1-1	0-5	0-3	0-7	2-1	4-0	0-7	0-3	1-3	1-5	1-3	2-4		1-1
Yate Town Res.	1-1	1-1	1-0	0-1	3-1	0-3	2-0	1-2	4-0	1-2	1-1	2-0	1-2	1-3	2-0	

		P	W	D	L	F	A	Pts
Hardwicke		30	23	5	2	74	18	74
Highridge United	-1	30	17	7	6	64	35	57
Hanham Athletic	-3	30	18	5	7	78	33	56
Tuffley Rovers		30	16	5	9	49	39	53
AXA		30	15	7	8	61	43	52
Ellwood		30	15	5	10	65	53	50
Patchway Town		30	13	9	8	61	46	48
Yate Town Res.		30	13	9	8	47	32	48
Kings Stanley	-3	30	15	4	11	60	51	46
Taverners		30	12	5	13	43	35	41
Thornbury Town		30	7	7	16	31	55	28
Berkeley Town		30	7	7	16	46	76	28
DRG Stapleton		30	5	10	15	36	61	25
Henbury		30	5	8	17	38	60	23
Pucklechurch Sports		30	4	9	17	27	58	21
Wotton Rovers		30	3	2	25	25	110	11

LES JAMES MEMORI AL CUP

FIRST ROUND
Berkeley Town 1 **Hardwicke** 3
Ellwood 2 Yate Town Res. 1
Highridge United 0 **AXA** 2
Kings Stanley 1 **DRG Stapleton** 5
Pucklechurch Sports 0 **Patchway Town** 1
Taverners 3 Thornbury Town 0
Tuffley Rovers 1 Hanham Athletic 0
Wotton Rovers 0 **Henbury** 1

QUARTER-FINALS
AXA 1 DRG Stapleton 0
Hardwicke 1 Patchway Town 0
Henbury 3 Tuffley Rovers 2
Taverners 1 **Ellwood** 2

SEMI-FINALS
AXA 0 **Hardwicke** 1 *(at Yate Town)*
Ellwood 2 Henbury 2 (5-3p) *(at Yate Town)*

FINAL
(April 10th at Yate Town)
Hardwicke 0 Ellwood 0 (4-3p)

GLOUCESTERSHIRE COUNTY LEAGUE CONSTITUTION 2008-09

AXA .... AXA Sports Ground, Station Road, Henbury, Bristol BS10 7TB. 0117 950 2303
B & W AVONSIDE .... Coombe Dingle Sport Complex, Coombe Dingle, Bristol BS9 2BJ 0117 962 6718
BERKELEY TOWN .... Station Road, Berkeley GL13 9AJ. 07831 232100
BISHOPS CLEEVE RESERVES .... Kayte Lane, Bishops Cleeve, Cheltenham GL52 3PD. 01242 676166
CHIPPING SODBURY TOWN ..... The Ridings, Wickwar Road, Chipping Sodbury, Bristol BS37 6BQ. 07787 522100
DRG STAPLETON .... Frenchay Park Road, Frenchay, Bristol BS16 1LG. 07810 544151
ELLWOOD .... Bromley Road, Ellwood, Coleford GL16 7LY. 01594 832927
HANHAM ATHLETIC .... The Playing Fields Pavilion, 16 Vicarage Road, Hanham, Bristol BS15 3AH 07900 262902
* HARTPURY COLLEGE .... Hartpury College, Hartpury House, Hartpury, Gloucester GL19 3BE. 01452 700283
(subject to completing ground improvements)
HENBURY .... Arnell Drive Playing Field, Henbury, Bristol BS10 7AS 0117 959 0475
HIGHRIDGE UNITED .... Bristol Manor Farm FC, The Creek, The Portway, Sea Mills, Bristol BS9 2HY. 0117 968 3571
KINGS STANLEY .... Marling Close, Broad Street, Kings Stanley, Stonehouse GL10 3PN. 01453 828975
PATCHWAY TOWN .... Scott Park, Coniston Road, Patchway, Bristol BS34 5JR. 0117 949 3952
SLIMBRIDGE. .... Wisloe Road, Cambridge GL2 7AS 01453 890361
TAVERNERS. .... Nailsworth Primary School, Forest Green, Nailsworth, Stroud GL6 0ET. 01453 834860
THORNBURY TOWN .... Mundy Playing Fields, Kington Lane, Thornbury BS35 1NA. 01454 413645
TUFFLEY ROVERS. .... Glevum Park, Lower Tuffley Lane, Gloucester GL2 5DT. 01452 423402
YATE TOWN RESERVES .... Lodge Road, Yate, Bristol BS37 7LE .... Club: 01454 228103
IN: B & W Avonside (P – Bristol & Suburban League Premier Division One), Bishops Cleeve Reserves (P – Gloucestershire Northern Senior League Division One), Chipping Sodbury Town (P – Bristol Premier Combination Premier Division), Hartpury College (P – colleges football), Slimbridge (P – Gloucestershire Northern Senior League Division One),
OUT: Hardwicke (P – Hellenic League Division One West), Pucklechurch Sports (R – Bristol Premier Combination Premier Division), Wotton Rovers (R – Gloucestershire Northern Senior League Division One)

GLOUCESTERSHIRE NORTHERN SENIOR LEAGUE

	Bishops Cleeve Res.	Bourton Rovers	Brimscombe & Thrupp	Broadwell Amateurs	Brockworth Albion	Cam Bulldogs	Cheltenham Civil Service	Kingswood	Longlevens	Lydbrook Athletic	Newton Heath	Sharpness	Shortwood United Res.	Slimbridge	Star	Tetbury Town
Bishops Cleeve Res.		8-0	2-1	1-1	5-1	1-4	6-1	2-3	2-1	1-0	6-2	2-1	1-2	1-1	7-0	4-1
Bourton Rovers	2-3		1-3	1-1	0-3	1-2	1-0	1-2	1-2	1-5	1-7	0-4	2-7	0-3	0-4	1-0
Brimscombe & Thrupp	1-2	2-0	D	1-0	4-0	3-2	2-1	2-5	1-3	3-3	1-1	3-0	0-1	1-3	5-1	2-0
Broadwell Amateurs	1-2	1-0	3-2	I	4-0	4-1	2-3	0-4	2-4	0-1	0-1	3-0	1-3	0-4	2-2	1-4
Brockworth Albion	2-4	2-1	1-1	1-1	V	5-1	0-2	4-2	2-2	0-3	2-2	2-5	1-0	0-2	3-3	2-3
Cam Bulldogs	1-2	0-1	1-2	1-1	2-2	I	2-1	1-1	3-2	1-4	4-1	1-1	2-2	2-3	3-3	2-1
Cheltenham Civil Service	2-3	0-1	2-1	2-2	3-2	2-3	S	1-2	1-5	0-3	2-1	1-0	1-3	0-0	2-3	3-2
Kingswood	1-2	2-0	0-0	2-2	1-0	4-1	6-0	I	1-1	1-0	7-0	2-2	3-4	1-2	3-2	2-3
Longlevens	2-2	4-1	1-1	4-1	2-2	4-1	5-0	1-0	O	1-4	2-1	1-0	4-1	1-3	2-0	3-2
Lydbrook Athletic	1-1	2-2	2-2	3-0	1-2	3-1	2-2	2-2	1-1	N	9-2	1-0	3-0	0-5	2-0	1-2
Newton Heath	0-2	2-1	1-4	0-2	1-3	2-2	4-1	0-2	1-3	0-0		3-1	0-2	0-6	0-2	3-4
Sharpness	0-1	4-0	5-2	0-0	2-0	1-2	6-1	2-1	4-3	1-2	2-1	O	1-0	1-3	2-1	2-2
Shortwood United Res.	0-1	2-2	0-0	1-4	1-1	2-1	1-3	3-2	4-0	0-1	2-1	0-0	N	0-1	1-5	0-2
Slimbridge	3-2	7-1	1-0	3-3	2-0	2-1	5-1	2-1	1-0	3-1	3-1	2-2	8-1	E	3-1	8-1
Star	0-0	3-2	1-1	0-1	2-1	2-4	2-1	0-0	4-2	1-2	0-1	1-3	1-1	0-3		2-1
Tetbury Town	0-3	6-1	0-0	2-2	0-0	0-1	1-3	3-3	4-2	0-2	3-0	3-2	3-1	0-3	2-1	

Division One		P	W	D	L	F	A	Pts
Slimbridge		30	26	4	0	95	23	82
Bishops Cleeve Res.		30	21	5	4	79	35	68
Lydbrook Athletic		30	16	8	6	64	35	56
Longlevens		30	15	6	9	68	51	51
Kingswood		30	13	8	9	66	43	47
Sharpness		30	12	6	12	54	44	42
Brimscombe & Thrupp		30	11	9	10	51	43	42
Tetbury Town		30	12	5	13	55	60	41
Shortwood Utd Res.	-1, -2g	30	11	6	13	43	55	38
Cam Bulldogs		30	10	7	13	53	63	37
Broadwell Amateurs		30	8	10	12	45	53	34
Star		30	9	7	14	47	60	34
Brockworth Albion		30	7	9	14	44	62	30
Cheltenham Civil Service	-1g	30	9	3	18	41	76	30
Newton Heath		30	6	4	20	39	79	22
Bourton Rovers		30	4	3	23	26	91	15

REG DAVIS MEMORIAL CUP

FIRST ROUND

Ashton Keynes 0 **Kingswood** 1
Bishops Cleeve Res. 4 Bredon 0
Bourton Rovers 1 **Newton Heath** 2
Dursley Town 7 Charfield 0
Gala Wilton 7 Huntley 2
Harrow Hill Res. 1 **Lydbrook Athletic** 1 (3-4p)
Hatherley Rangers 1 **Brockworth Albion** 1 (4-5p)
Longford 1 **Cam Bulldogs** 7
Longlevens 1 Brimscombe & Thrupp 0
Mitcheldean 1 **Viney St Swithins** 3
Ramblers 5 Chalford 0 *(at Chalford)*
Sharpness 2 **Cheltenham Civil Service** 3
Slimbridge 6 Stonehouse Town 2
Star 4 Smiths Athletic 1

GLOUCESTERSHIRE NORTHERN SENIOR LEAGUE DIVISION ONE CONSTITUTION 2008-09
BRIMSCOMBE & THRUPP . . . . The Meadow, London Road, Brimscombe, Stroud GL5 2QE 01453 885039
BROADWELL AMATEURS . . . . The Hawthornes, Poolway Road, Broadwell, Coleford GL16 7BE 01594 837347
BROCKWORTH ALBION . . . . Parton Road, Churchdown GL3 2JH. 01452 713528
CAM BULLDOGS . . . . Recreation Ground, Everlands, Cam, Dursley GL11 5NL 01453 546736
CHELTENHAM CIVIL SERVICE . . . Civil Service Sports Ground, Tewkesbury Road, Uckington, Cheltenham GL51 9SL. 01242 680424
DURSLEY TOWN . . . . Memorial Ground, Kingshill Road, Dursley GL11 4BJ 01453 546122
GALA WILTON. Gala Club, Fairmile Gardens, Longford, Gloucester GL2 9EB 01452 524447
KINGSWOOD . . . . Wickwar Road, Kingswood, Wotton-under-Edge GL12 8RF. 07836 734020
LONGLEVENS . . . . Longford Lane, Longlevens, Gloucester GL2 9EU 01452 530388
LYDBROOK ATHLETIC . . . . Reeds Sports Ground, Lower Lydbrook 01594 860870
RAMBLERS . . . . Wagon Works Sports & Social, Tuffley Park, Tuffley Avenue, Gloucester GL1 5NS 01452 524621
SHARPNESS. . . . . Berkeley Vale Community School, Sharpness 01453 511617
SHORTWOOD UNITED RESERVES . . . . Meadowbank, Shortwood, Nailsworth, Stroud GL6 0SJ. 01453 833936
STAR . . . . Kayte Lane, Bishops Cleeve, Cheltenham GL52 3PD 01242 674440
TETBURY TOWN. . . . . Preston Park, Cirencester Road, Tetbury GL8 8EZ. . . . . None
WOTTON ROVERS . . . . Synwell Playing Fields, Synwell Lane, Wotton-under-Edge GL12 7HQ 01453 842929
IN: Dursley Town (P), Gala Wilton (P), Ramblers (P), Wotton Rovers (R – Gloucestershire County League)
OUT: Bishops Cleeve Reserves (P – Gloucestershire County League), Bourton Rovers (R), Newton Heath (R), Slimbridge (P – Gloucestershire County League)

Note – Ashton Keynes and Huntley withdrew during the course of the season. Their results are shown herein but expunged from the league table	Ashton Keynes	Bredon	Chalford	Charfield	Dursley Town	Gala Wilton	Harrow Hill Res.	Hatherley Rangers	Huntley	Longford	Mitcheldean	Ramblers	Smiths Athletic	Stonehouse Town	Tidenham	Viney St Swithins
Ashton Keynes		n/a	n/a	n/a	n/a	n/a	n/a	1-5	n/a	1-2	n/a	n/a	n/a	n/a	n/a	2-2
Bredon	2-1		5-0	1-1	1-1	0-3	1-0	7-1	4-0	2-0	1-1	1-2	4-0	2-1	2-1	2-0
Chalford	n/a	1-1	D	5-1	0-1	1-2	1-2	2-3	2-5	3-0	2-0	0-0	1-5	0-1	2-3	5-3
Charfield	n/a	0-3	2-1	I	2-4	0-2	1-1	0-4	0-2	0-4	0-3	0-3	2-2	0-7	2-0	3-0
Dursley Town	n/a	3-2	3-1	3-1	V	1-0	5-2	0-0	n/a	3-0	2-0	2-1	1-1	1-1	2-2	1-3
Gala Wilton	n/a	1-1	4-1	2-0	1-0	I	3-0	1-1	n/a	4-1	5-2	2-0	3-0	1-0	2-2	1-1
Harrow Hill Res.	n/a	0-2	1-0	3-0	4-2	3-1	S	0-1	4-2	2-1	2-1	0-1	1-3	2-3	2-0	4-1
Hatherley Rangers	n/a	1-0	1-4	0-2	3-2	1-3	0-1	I	n/a	4-1	0-0	2-0	1-2	2-2	3-0	2-1
Huntley	n/a	n/a	n/a	n/a	2-4	0-5	n/a	n/a	O	2-1	n/a	n/a	n/a	0-0	n/a	0-3
Longford	n/a	1-2	4-2	2-3	0-2	0-2	1-0	2-1	n/a	N	1-4	1-2	3-0	0-1	1-1	1-2
Mitcheldean	n/a	2-1	2-1	4-1	1-2	0-3	2-0	0-2	n/a	1-4		1-3	4-1	1-6	2-1	3-1
Ramblers	n/a	2-2	3-0	3-0	1-1	0-4	2-2	3-2	n/a	1-1	0-0	T	3-3	1-0	4-1	8-1
Smiths Athletic	n/a	1-1	3-3	13-0	0-3	0-1	2-1	0-3	n/a	1-2	3-2	0-3	W	2-5	3-1	1-1
Stonehouse Town	n/a	1-4	2-1	3-1	4-0	2-3	1-1	1-3	n/a	1-0	4-1	1-1	0-1	O	4-0	2-0
Tidenham	4-1	0-2	4-1	2-1	1-4	2-1	5-3	2-2	4-1	1-2	1-0	1-1	1-2	2-2		5-2
Viney St Swithins	n/a	5-1	2-2	3-2	0-1	1-4	3-0	0-4	n/a	0-3	5-1	0-1	4-2	4-0	2-0	

Tetbury Town 5 Shortwood United Res. 3
Tidenham 0 Broadwell Amateurs 1

SECOND ROUND
Bishops Cleeve Res. 1 Slimbridge 3
Broadwell Amateurs 0 Viney St Swithins 1
Dursley Town 2 Cam Bulldogs 2 (4-5p)
Gala Wilton 5 Lydbrook Athletic 3
Kingswood 3 Brockworth Albion 3 (5-4p)
Newton Heath 6 Ramblers 2
Star 2 Cheltenham Civil Service 2 (1-3p)
Tetbury Town 0 Longlevens 1

QUARTER-FINALS
Gala Wilton 2 Longlevens 3
Kingswood 2 Cam Bulldogs 0
Newton Heath 0 Viney St Swithins 3
Slimbridge 12 Cheltenham Civil Service 1

SEMI-FINALS
Kingswood 7 Viney St Swithins 0
Slimbridge 2 Longlevens 3

FINAL
(October 3rd at Tuffley Rovers)
Kingswood 5 Longlevens 0

Division Two		P	W	D	L	F	A	Pts
Gala Wilton		26	19	4	3	59	20	61
Dursley Town		26	15	6	5	50	32	51
Ramblers		26	13	9	4	49	28	48
Bredon		26	13	7	6	51	29	46
Stonehouse Town		26	13	5	8	55	34	44
Hatherley Rangers		26	13	5	8	47	36	44
Smiths Athletic		26	9	6	11	51	54	33
Harrow Hill Res.		26	10	3	13	37	43	33
Viney St Swithins		26	10	3	13	46	57	33
Tidenham		26	7	7	12	40	54	28
Longford	-3, -2g	26	9	2	15	34	45	26
Mitcheldean		26	7	4	15	36	54	25
Chalford		26	5	4	17	40	58	19
Charfield		26	5	3	18	25	78	18

Ashton Keynes and Huntley – records expunged

GLOUCESTERSHIRE NORTHERN SENIOR SENIOR LEAGUE DIVISION TWO CONSTITUTION 2008-09

BARNWOOD UNITED .. Birds Eye Walls Sports & Social Club, Hammond Way, Barnwood, Gloucester GL4 3HG 01452 610277
BOURTON ROVERS .... Rissington Road, Bourton-on-the-Water, Cheltenham GL54 2AY..................... 01451 821977
BREDON .... Main Road, Bredon, Tewkesbury GL20 7EG 01684 773152
CHALFORD............... Chalford Sports & Social Club, Highfield Way, Chalford Hill, Stroud GL6 8BD 01453 884214
CHARFIELD.................................. Charfield Memorial Hall, Charfield 01454 260204
HARROW HILL RESERVES .... Larksfield Road, Harrow Hill, Drybrook GL17 9JP 01594 543873
HATHERLEY RANGERS........ King George V Playing Fields, Brooklyn Road, Cheltenham GL51 8DT .... None
LONGFORD .... Playing Field, Longford Lane, Gloucester GL2 9EU .... None
MITCHELDEAN .... Townsend Playing Fields, Mitcheldean GL17 0BA .... None
NEWTON HEATH .... The Newlands, Bishops Cleeve .... None
SMITHS ATHLETIC........ Dowty Rotol Sports Ground, Hatherley Lane, Staverton, Cheltenham GL51 4NF 01242 525515
SOUDLEY........................... Soudley Playing Field, Soudley, Cinderford .... None
STONEHOUSE TOWN .... Oldends Lane, Stonehouse GL10 2DG .... None
TIDENHAM .... Tidenham Recreation Ground, Coleford Road, Tutshill............................. None
VINEY ST SWITHINS................. Viney Sports & Social Club, Viney Hill, Lydney GL15 4NF 01594 510658
WINCHCOMBE TOWN .... Mill Lane, Winchcombe, Cheltenham GL54 5LT.............................. None

IN: Barnwood United (P – Stroud & District League Division One), Bourton Rovers (R), Newton Heath (R), Soudley (P – North Gloucestershire League Division One), Winchcombe Town (P – Cheltenham Association League Division One)
OUT: Ashton Keynes (WS), Dursley Town (P), Gala Wilton (P), Huntley (WS), Ramblers (P)

GWENT COUNTY LEAGUE

	Abercarn United	Abertillery Bluebirds	Albion Rovers	Blaenavon Blues	Cefn Fforest	Chepstow Town	Clydach Wasps	Coed Eva Athletic	Cwmffrwdoer Sports	Mardy	Newport Civil Service	Panteg	Spencer Youth & Boys	Treowen Stars	Undy Athletic
Abercarn United		2-0	5-0	0-0	0-1	4-4	1-2	1-0	2-4	2-2	1-3	3-6	7-3	1-1	0-1
Abertillery Bluebirds	5-1	D	2-1	0-3	1-0	3-0	5-1	3-0	2-1	7-0	1-1	4-0	1-0	4-3	2-1
Albion Rovers	1-2	1-1	I	1-2	3-1	1-6	5-0	3-1	3-3	1-1	0-2	3-1	5-3	2-1	4-3
Blaenavon Blues	1-3	1-2	0-2	V	4-1	3-5	1-5	0-0	0-4	2-0	3-7	3-1	1-3	1-3	1-3
Cefn Fforest	2-1	0-3	1-3	1-3	I	1-5	2-6	3-0	1-3	2-0	0-4	1-0	3-3	0-1	3-4
Chepstow Town	3-3	3-2	2-1	3-1	3-0	S	3-2	4-2	9-1	1-5	2-0	3-2	4-1		5-2
Clydach Wasps	2-3	2-0	2-1	1-1	1-1	2-4	I	5-2	3-1	3-2	1-3	1-1	4-2	1-2	4-4
Coed Eva Athletic	2-1	1-2	2-1	1-2	2-1	4-3	1-0	O	2-5	3-0	1-2	2-0	4-2	1-2	0-4
Cwmffrwdoer Sports	5-0	2-2	3-2	4-2	1-2	5-1	2-0	1-1	N	1-2	1-5	7-2	7-2	10-0	1-1
Mardy	3-2	2-2	0-3	3-1	3-0	1-4	5-3	1-1	2-7		1-2	1-4	5-5	3-5	0-3
Newport Civil Service	5-0	4-1	0-2	2-2	5-1	1-1	4-0	4-0	1-2	4-0		3-3	2-1	3-1	5-2
Panteg	1-2	1-2	0-2	0-2	1-2	1-6	4-1	0-1	0-1	2-3	2-5	O	1-3	1-1	2-1
Spencer Youth & Boys	2-5	1-6	0-2	1-0	2-2	2-3	1-4	2-3	2-3	5-3	2-4	1-3	N	4-2	2-2
Treowen Stars	3-3	0-2	2-2	2-1	0-3	2-2	2-1	2-1	3-0	5-0	0-2	4-1	6-1	E	0-1
Undy Athletic	2-0	0-2	0-0	3-1	4-0	2-5	1-1	4-2	4-4	5-0	2-2	3-1	3-2	2-0	

Division One	P	W	D	L	F	A	Pts
Newport Civil Service	28	21	5	2	90	32	68
Chepstow Town	28	20	4	4	101	57	64
Abertillery Bluebirds	28	19	4	5	67	32	61
Cwmffrwdoer Sports	28	16	5	7	90	51	53
Undy Athletic	28	14	7	7	67	49	49
Albion Rovers	28	13	5	10	55	46	44
Treowen Stars	28	12	5	11	54	57	41
Clydach Wasps	28	10	5	13	59	68	35
Abercarn United	28	9	6	13	55	64	33
Coed Eva Athletic	28	10	3	15	40	57	33
Blaenavon Blues	28	8	4	16	42	61	28
Cefn Fforest	28	8	3	17	35	66	27
Mardy	28	6	5	17	44	93	23
Spencer Youth & Boys	28	5	4	19	59	94	19
Panteg	28	5	3	20	39	70	18

LEAGUE CUP

FIRST ROUND

Abergavenny Thursdays 1 **Rogerstone Welfare** 2
Crickhowell 2 **Panteg** 4
Crusaders 0 **Fairfield United** 5
Govilon 8 Underwood Social Club 3
Lliswerry 5 Villa Dino Christchurch 0
Malpas Gladiators 6 West Pontnewydd 2
New Inn 2 **Trinant** 4
Newport Civil Service 2 Chepstow Town 1
Sebastopol 0 **Llanhilleth Athletic** 4
Trethomas Bluebirds 3 **Newport Corinthians** 4
Whiteheads 1 **Cromwell Youth** 2

SECOND ROUND

AC Pontymister 1 **Treowen Stars** 3
Caldicot Castle 1 **Clydach Wasps** 8
Coed Eva Athletic 0 **Abertillery Bluebirds** 3
Cwmffrwdoer Sports 3 Lliswerry 1
Fairfield United 0 **Albion Rovers** 4
Govilon 4 Abercarn United 2
Lucas Cwmbran 1 **Tranch** 3
Mardy 1 **Newport Civil Service** 5
Newport Corinthians 1 Llanhilleth Athletic 0
Panteg 0 **Cromwell Youth** 1
Pentwynmawr Athletic 4 Blaenavon Blues 1

WELSH AUTOPARTS GWENT COUNTY LEAGUE DIVISION ONE CONSTITUTION 2008-09

ABERCARN UNITED . . . . Welfare Ground, Abercarn, Blackwood NP12 3XX 01495 243047
ABERTILLERY BLUEBIRDS . . . . Cwmnantygroes Field, Six Bells, Abertillery NP13 2PR 01495 213999
ABERTILLERY EXCELSIOR . . . . Woodland Field, Cwmtillery, Abertillery NP13 1LA 01495 217839
ALBION ROVERS . . . . Kimberley Park, Malpas Road, Newport NP20 6WE . . . . None
BLAENAVON BLUES . . . . . . Co-op Field, Recreation Ground, Coed Cae Road, Blaenavon, Pontypool NP4 9PP. . . . . None
CEFN FFOREST . . . . Welfare Ground, Ty Isha Terrace, Cefn Fforest, Blackwood NP12 1ER . . . . None
CHEPSTOW TOWN . . . . Larkfield Ground, Newport Road, Chepstow NP16 5PR 01291 629220
CLYDACH WASPS . . . . Recreation Ground, Clydach . . . . None
COED EVA ATHLETIC . . . . Cwmbran Park, Wesley Street, Cwmbran NP44 3LX 01633 485491
CWMFFRWDOER SPORTS . . . . Cwmffrwdoer Sports Ground, Gwenhallt Industrial Estate, Cwmffrwdoer . . . . None
MARDY . . . . Mardy Playing Field, Mardy . . . . None
PENTWYNMAWR ATHLETIC . . . . Welfare Ground, Pentwynmawr, Newbridge, Newport 01495 243046
RTB EBBW VALE . . . . Eugene Cross Park, Pontygof, Ebbw Vale NP23 5AZ 01495 302995
SPENCER YOUTH & BOYS . . . . Ringland Park, Newport NP18 2TA . . . . None
TREOWEN STARS . . . . Bush Park, Newbridge 01495 248249
UNDY ATHLETIC . . . . Undy Playing Fields, The Causeway, Undy, Caldicot NP26 3EN 01633 881352

IN: Abertillery Excelsior (R – Welsh League Division Three), Pentwynmawr Athletic (P), RTB Ebbw Vale (P)
OUT: Newport Civil Service (P – Welsh League Division Three), Panteg (R)

	Cromwell Youth	Fairfield United	Llanhilleth Athletic	Lliswerry	Lucas Cwmbran	Malpas Gladiator	Newport Corinthians	Pentwynmawr Athletic	RTB Ebbw Vale	Rogerstone Welfare	Tranch	Trethomas Bluebirds	Trinant	West Pontnewydd
Cromwell Youth		0-1	3-4	3-2	2-2	4-1	1-1	2-2	2-3	1-3	1-3	2-2	2-2	4-2
Fairfield United	6-1	D	4-0	2-3	2-1	3-1	5-0	0-3	1-1	3-1	1-1	2-1	1-2	2-2
Llanhilleth Athletic	1-1	1-1	I	2-2	0-0	1-2	2-1	0-1	0-3	1-3	1-1	2-3	4-0	1-0
Lliswerry	1-3	1-1	2-3	V	7-1	3-1	2-0	3-1	2-2	4-0	1-0	1-4	4-0	2-1
Lucas Cwmbran	0-4	0-1	1-3	2-1	I	1-2	3-3	1-2	0-3	0-2	1-4	0-8	3-6	0-2
Malpas Gladiator	1-2	0-2	4-1	0-3	2-2	S	0-4	1-1	1-1	2-1	1-7	1-1		7-0
Newport Corinthians	1-2	1-0	1-1	4-0	1-1	0-0	I	0-1	0-0	1-1	1-1	2-4	1-0	0-2
Pentwynmawr Athletic	2-3	4-1	0-2	3-2	6-0	5-4	2-6	O	2-2	1-0	2-2	1-3	4-1	3-1
RTB Ebbw Vale	2-1	1-1	0-1	2-3	6-3	4-2	4-2	2-1	N	1-0	1-1	1-0	3-1	1-3
Rogerstone Welfare	1-5	2-1	0-0	3-4	2-4	3-1	2-0	0-3	1-0		1-1	4-1	1-1	3-2
Tranch	0-2	2-2	4-0	5-2	6-2	1-2	3-1	2-1	4-2	4-2	T	2-2	2-1	6-1
Trethomas Bluebirds	4-4	2-2	2-0	2-3	3-4	3-2	3-0	0-3	2-3	3-4	4-1	W	2-2	6-1
Trinant	4-1	2-4	2-3	2-2	0-1	1-2	2-5	1-5	3-2	1-2	2-1	1-3	O	8-0
West Pontnewydd	2-0	0-4	2-3	3-1	1-4	3-6	2-3	2-3	1-4	1-3	4-8	2-2	2-4	

Rogerstone Welfare 1 **Cefn Fforest** 3
Spencer Youth & Boys 6 **Malpas Gladiator** 8
Sudbrook Cricket Club 6 RTB Ebbw Vale 2
Trinant 1 **PILCS** 3
Undy Athletic 3 Race 0

THIRD ROUND
Cefn Fforest 0 **Clydach Wasps** 5 (at Clydach Wasps)
Cromwell Youth 0 **Albion Rovers** 2
Cwmffrwdoer Sports 4 Sudbrook Cricket Club 0
Malpas Gladiator 1 **Govilon** 4
Newport Civil Service 1 **Pentwynmawr Athletic** 2
PILCS (w/o) v Newport Corinthians (scr.)
Tranch 0 **Treowen Stars** 3
Undy Athletic 3 Abertillery Bluebirds 3 *aet* (4-3p)

QUARTER-FINALS
Clydach Wasps 2 **Albion Rovers** 3
Cwmffrwdoer Sports 4 Treowen Stars 2
Govilon 2 **PILCS** 3
Undy Athletic 4 Pentwynmawr Athletic 2

SEMI-FINALS
Albion Rovers 5 Cwmffrwdoer Sports 2 (at Undy Athletic)
Undy Athletic 3 PILCS 2 (at Mardy)

FINAL
(May 2nd at Abergavenny Thursdays)
Albion Rovers 5 Undy Athletic 1

Division Two	P	W	D	L	F	A	Pts
Pentwynmawr Athletic	26	15	4	7	62	41	49
RTB Ebbw Vale	26	14	6	6	59	38	48
Tranch	26	12	8	6	66	42	44
Fairfield United	26	12	8	6	53	33	44
Lliswerry	26	13	4	9	61	50	43
Trethomas Bluebirds	26	12	6	8	76	50	42
Rogerstone Welfare	26	12	5	9	45	45	41
Cromwell Youth	26	10	7	9	56	53	37
Llanhilleth Athletic	26	10	7	9	37	43	37
Newport Corinthians	26	7	8	11	39	44	29
Malpas Gladiator	26	8	5	13	47	63	29
Trinant	26	7	5	14	50	61	26
Lucas Cwmbran	26	5	5	16	37	79	20
West Pontnewydd	26	5	2	19	42	88	17

WELSH AUTOPARTS GWENT COUNTY LEAGUE DIVISION TWO CONSTITUTION 2008-09

CROMWELL YOUTH .... Hartridge Comprehensive School, Ringland Way, Newport NP18 2TA .... None
FAIRFIELD UNITED .... Garndiffaith Ravine, Pontypool 01495 773745
GOVILON .... King George V Playing Fields, Govilon, Abergavenny NP7 9NU .... None
LLANHILLETH ATHLETIC .... Llanhilleth Park, Llanhilleth 01495 217840
LLISWERRY .... Spytty Park, Newport NP9 0RH 01633 281087
LUCAS CWMBRAN .... Lucas Sports Ground, Cwmbran 01633 861624
MALPAS GLADIATOR .... Westfield, Darwin Drive, Malpas, Newport .... None
NEWPORT CORINTHIANS .... Coronation Park, Stephenson Street, Newport NP19 0RB 01633 274717
PANTEG .... Panteg House Sports Ground, Greenhill Road, Griffithstown NP4 5BE 01495 763605
ROGERSTONE WELFARE .... Welfare Ground, Rogerstone, Newport .... None
SUDBROOK CRICKET CLUB .... Mill Lane, Caldicot NP26 4BN .... None
TRANCH .... Tranch Recreation Ground, Tranch .... None
TRETHOMAS BLUEBIRDS .... Llanfabon Drive, Trethomas, Caerphilly CF83 8GJ .... None
TRINANT .... Trinant Recreation, Trinant, Caerphilly .... None

IN: Govilon (P), Panteg (R), Sudbrook Cricket Club (P)
OUT: Pentwynmawr Athletic (P), RTB Ebbw Vale (P), West Pontnewydd (R)

	AC Pontymister	Abergavenny Thursdays	Caldicot Castle	Crickhowell	Crusaders	Govilon	New Inn	PILCS	Race	Sebastopol	Sudbrook Cricket Club	Underwood Social Club	Villa Dino Christchurch	Whiteheads
AC Pontymister	D	3-2	3-0	5-1	2-4	3-1	1-2	1-0	4-2	5-4	1-2	4-0	1-1	5-0
Abergavenny Thursdays	1-2	I	5-0	2-2	2-0	4-4	2-0	3-2	2-0	3-0	1-3	0-2	2-0	1-1
Caldicot Castle	1-1	1-4	V	1-0	6-1	2-7	3-2	1-0	1-2	1-1	3-2	3-0	1-1	2-3
Crickhowell	1-2	1-0	4-2	I	3-1	3-5	2-2	0-5	0-0	5-2	1-3	4-4	3-2	3-1
Crusaders	0-6	2-8	0-2	5-1	S	1-7	3-5	1-6	1-3	4-3	2-4	2-1	1-2	1-0
Govilon	4-0	3-1	4-2	5-3	6-2	I	4-0	5-2	4-1	4-1	1-0	4-3	3-1	11-0
New Inn	7-4	1-2	4-2	3-0	3-0	2-3	O	2-5	4-1	2-1	1-1	0-0	2-1	1-4
PILCS	1-4	10-1	7-1	4-0	9-0	1-1	3-2	N	1-1	3-1	2-4	2-0	3-2	6-2
Race	2-1	5-3	2-1	3-0	5-0	1-5	2-4	2-2		2-0	1-5	3-4	2-0	4-0
Sebastopol	1-3	1-5	1-4	1-3	2-1	0-6	2-1	1-1	2-0	T	1-3	4-2	4-1	3-2
Sudbrook Cricket Club	3-2	2-2	6-0	8-2	6-0	1-5	7-1	3-2	2-1	3-1	H	4-2	3-2	8-1
Underwood Social Club	2-1	3-5	2-1	3-3	5-1	3-7	2-5	2-6	6-1	0-5	3-2	R	0-0	2-2
Villa Dino Christchurch	1-5	2-1	5-0	4-2	2-2	1-9	1-2	1-4	2-3	2-3	2-4	9-3	E	1-2
Whiteheads	1-0	1-5	3-1	7-2	2-3	1-4	4-5	2-2	1-2	3-0	2-4	4-1	1-3	E

Division Three	P	W	D	L	F	A	Pts
Govilon	26	23	2	1	122	39	71
Sudbrook Cricket Club	26	20	2	4	93	42	62
PILCS	26	14	5	7	89	43	47
AC Pontymister	26	15	2	9	69	44	47
Abergavenny Thursdays	26	13	4	9	67	51	43
New Inn	26	13	3	10	63	60	42
Race	26	12	3	11	51	55	39
Caldicot Castle	26	8	3	15	42	70	27
Whiteheads	26	8	3	15	50	80	27
Sebastopol	26	8	2	16	45	69	26
Underwood Social Club	26	7	5	14	55	82	26
Crickhowell	26	7	5	14	49	80	26
Villa Dino Christchurch	26	6	4	16	49	66	22
Crusaders	26	6	1	19	38	101	19

WELSH AUTOPARTS GWENT COUNTY LEAGUE DIVISION THREE CONSTITUTION 2008-09

ABERGAVENNY THURSDAYS . . . . Penypound Stadium, Pen-Y-Pound, Abergavenny 01873 854405

AC PONTYMISTER . . . . Pontymister Recreation Ground, Pontymister, Caerphilly NP11 6LT . . . . None

CALDICOT CASTLE . . . . Caldicot Castle Grounds, Caldicot NP26 4HU 01291 431584

CRICKHOWELL . . . . Elvicta Estate, Brecon Road, Crickhowell NP8 1DG . . . . None

* LLANWERN RTB . . . . Spencer Sports Ground, Llanwern . . . . None

NEW INN. . . . . Woodfield Road Rec Ground, New Inn, Pontypool NP4 0PS 01495 755169

PILCS. . . . . PILCS Sports & Social Club, New Road, Griffithstown, Pontypool NP4 0TL 01495 762039

RACE . . . . Coleg Gwent, Blaendare Road, Pontypool NP4 5YE 01495 333100

ROCKFIELD ROVERS . . . . Rockfield Community Centre, Cornwallis Close, Monmouth. . . . . None

SEBASTOPOL. . . . . Cwmbran Park, Wesley Street, Cwmbran NP44 3LX . . . . None

UNDERWOOD SOCIAL CLUB . . . . Larch Grove Playing Fields, Newport NP20 6JB . . . . None

VILLA DINO CHRISTCHURCH . . . . Black Ash Park, Lliswerry, Newport . . . . None

WEST PONTNEWYDD . . . . The Birches, West Pontynewydd, Pontypool. . . . . None

WHITEHEADS . . . . Whiteheads Sports Ground, Park View, Bassaleg NP10 8LA. 01633 893227

*IN: * Llanwern RTB (P – Newport & District Premier Division X), Rockfield Rovers (P – East Gwent League Division One), West Pontnewydd (R)*

OUT: Crusaders (W), Govilon (P), Sudbrook Cricket Club (P)

* *Llanwern RTB's inclusion is subject to appeal*

GWYNEDD LEAGUE

	Barmouth & Dyffryn	Beaumaris Town	Bethel	Blaenau Ffestiniog	Bodedern Res.	Bontnewydd	Cemaes	Gaerwen	Holyhead H. Res.	Llanfairfechan Town	Llangefni Town Res.	Llanllyfni	Llanystumdwy	Porthmadog Res.	Real Llandudno	University of Bangor
Barmouth/Dyffryn Utd		4-2	4-1	2-1	0-1	1-0	6-1	4-2	5-0	5-0	6-0	1-3	2-1	6-2	7-0	n/a
Beaumaris Town	5-4		3-3	1-3	2-1	3-3	7-0	1-1	6-1	5-1	4-0	1-3	4-2	2-1	0-0	3-0
Bethel	1-5	2-0		3-2	2-2	3-2	13-0	3-2	6-1	8-2	1-3	1-0	4-2	3-2	2-1	2-1
Blaenau Ffestiniog Am.	2-0	3-0	1-2		1-2	3-2	6-1	2-0	4-3	2-3	3-1	5-2	2-0	2-3	3-1	6-3
Bodedern Res.	1-2	1-1	1-5	2-0		1-0	6-0	0-1	2-0	5-0	1-1	0-1	1-4	1-3	2-0	2-1
Bontnewydd	0-1	1-3	1-3	0-3	1-3		2-1	2-3	3-1	3-1	7-5	0-2	1-1	2-3	2-6	0-1
Cemaes	0-5	1-5	0-5	1-6	0-2	1-1		0-3	0-3	3-5	1-6	1-4	0-1	0-3	1-1	0-2
Gaerwen	0-1	0-2	4-1	0-2	4-1	1-1	6-0		3-2	4-1	1-1	1-3	1-6	1-4	5-0	1-2
Holyhead Hotspur Res.	1-3	3-2	0-2	7-1	4-1	2-2	5-2	3-1		6-2	1-3	0-2	4-1	3-4	4-0	3-3
Llanfairfechan Town	0-3	3-3	4-2	0-2	2-7	3-0	4-2	2-3	5-2		2-3	1-2	0-3	3-5	5-3	2-1
Llangefni Town Res.	2-3	1-2	2-6	1-1	4-1	0-1	8-0	3-2	4-1	3-4		2-4	4-3	2-1	5-2	1-1
Llanllyfni	1-0	2-3	3-2	5-2	5-1	4-0	5-0	4-1	2-1	3-2	1-0		2-1	3-3	4-0	1-1
Llanystumdwy	2-1	5-1	1-6	2-1	2-0	3-2	5-0	3-3	2-2	3-1	3-1	0-2		0-1	9-2	4-3
Porthmadog Res.	1-3	2-3	5-2	1-4	1-1	5-0	15-0	3-0	0-3	3-1	5-4	5-1	3-3		1-3	3-1
Real Llandudno	2-3	2-4	0-3	4-1	1-3	4-0	2-3	0-7	2-3	0-1	4-2	1-2	2-6			1-1
University of Bangor	n/a	1-3	1-2	1-2	3-1	5-2	2-1	2-3	0-4	2-0	0-2	0-2	5-1	0-5	5-1	

	P	W	D	L	F	A	Pts
Llanllyfni	30	24	1	5	78	38	73
Barmouth & Dyffryn United	28	22	0	6	87	32	66
Bethel	30	21	2	7	99	55	65
Porthmadog Res.	30	18	3	9	99	59	57
Beaumaris Town	30	17	6	7	81	54	57
Blaenau Ffestiniog Amateurs	30	18	1	11	78	53	55
Llanystumdwy	30	15	4	11	75	60	49
Llangefni Town Res.	30	13	4	13	73	68	43
Bodedern Res.	30	12	5	13	51	51	41
Gaerwen	30	12	4	14	60	61	40
Holyhead Hotspur Res.	30	12	3	15	77	73	39
Llanfairfechan Town	30	10	1	19	62	98	31
University of Bangor	28	9	3	16	47	58	30
Bontnewydd	30	6	5	19	44	73	23
Real Llandudno	30	5	4	21	48	97	19
Cemaes	30	0	2	28	17	146	2

Barmouth v University of Bangor and University of Bangor v Barmouth not played

PRESIDENT'S CUP
(Previous season's top eight teams)

FIRST ROUND
Barmouth & Dyffryn United 1 Bethel 0
Beaumaris Town 0 Bontnewydd 1
Holyhead Hotspur Res. 1 Llangefni Town Res. 1
Porthmadog Res. 3 Blaenau Ffestiniog Amateurs 1

SEMI-FINALS
Bontnewydd 0 Barmouth & Dyffryn United 0 *aet* (6-5p)
Holyhead Hotspur Res. 0 Porthmadog Res. 2

FINAL
(May 22nd at Porthmadog)
Porthmadog Res. 3 Bontnewydd 1

GWYNEDD CUP

FIRST ROUND
Bethel 4 **Bodedern Res.** 4 *aet* (1-3p)
Bontnewydd 4 Llanfairfechan Town 3 *aet*
Cemaes 1 **Blaenau Ffestiniog Amateurs** 9
Gaerwen 3 Llanllyfni 1
Holyhead Hotspur Res. 4 **Beaumaris Town** 6
Porthmadog Res. 5 Llanystumdwy 1
Real Llandudno 1 **Llangefni Town Res.** 3
University of Bangor 3 Barmouth & Dyffryn United 0

QUARTER-FINALS
Bontnewydd 4 University of Bangor 2
Gaerwen 1 Blaenau Ffestiniog Amateurs 1 *aet* (3-1p)
Llangefni Town Res. 1 **Beaumaris Town** 2
Porthmadog Res. 0 **Bodedern Res.** 1

SEMI-FINALS
Boderdern Res. 3 Beaumaris Town 0
Bontnewydd 1 **Gaerwen** 3

FINAL
(April 24th at Llangefni Town)
Gaerwen 2 Bodedern Res. 1

ERYRI SHIELD

FIRST ROUND
Barmouth & Dyffryn United 3 Blaenau Ffestiniog Amateurs 1
Bethel 5 Llangefni Town Res. 3
Bodedern Res. 2 Bontnewydd 0
Gaerwen 0 **Holyhead Hotspur Res.** 4
Llanllyfni 2 **Beaumaris Town** 4
Llanystumdwy 2 Porthmadog Res. 1 *aet*
Real Llandudno 8 Llanfairfechan Town 0
University of Bangor 5 Cemaes 0

QUARTER-FINALS
Bethel 6 Real Llandudno 1
Bodedern Res. 2 **Beaumaris Town** 3
Holyhead Hotspur Res. 1 **Llanystumdwy** 3
University of Bangor 0 **Barmouth & Dyffryn United** 1

SEMI-FINALS
Beaumaris Town 0 **Bethel** 2
Llanystumdwy 1 **Barmouth & Dyffryn United** 2

FINAL *(May 14th at Porthmadog)*
Barmouth & Dyffryn Utd 4 Bethel 3 *aet*

TEEJAC .COM GWYNEDD LEAGUE CONSTITUTION 2008-09

BARMOUTH & DYFFRYN UNITED .... Wern Mynach, Park Road, Barmouth LL42 1PL .... None
BEAUMARIS TOWN .... The Green, Beaumaris .... None
BETHEL .... Coed Boelyn, Bethel, Caernarfon .... None
BLAENAU FFESTINIOG AMATEURS ...... Cae Clyd, Manod, Blaenau Ffestiniog LL41 4BA .... None
BODEDERN ATHLETIC .... Cae Ty Cristion, Bodedern, Anglesey LL65 3UB .... None
BONTNEWYDD .... Cae Stanley, Bontnewydd .... None
GAERWEN .... Lon Groes, Gaerwen, Anglesey LL60 6DD .... None
GWALCHMAI .... Maes Meurig, Gwalchmai, Holyhead LL65 4SA .... None
HOLYHEAD HOTSPUR RESERVES ... New Oval, Leisure Centre, Kingsland, Holyhead LL65 2YE 01407 764111
LLANFAIRFECHAN TOWN .... Recreation Ground, Station Road, Llanfairfechan LL33 0BD .... None
LLANGEFNI TOWN RESERVES .... Cae Bob Parry, Talwrn Road, Llangefni LL77 7LP 01248 724999
LLANYSTUMDWY .... Parc Dwyfor, Llanystumdwy, Cricieth .... None
PORTHMADOG RESERVES.............. Y Traeth, Porthmadog LL49 9PP 01766 514687
REAL LLANDUDNO............................. The Oval, Llandudno .... None
RHIWLAS .... Beach Road, Bangor LL57 1DG .... None
UNIVERSITY OF BANGOR .... Maesglas Sports Field, Ffriddoedd Road, Bangor LL57 2EH 01248 382571

IN: Gwalchmai (P – Anglesey League), Rhiwlas (P – Caernarfon & District League Division One)
OUT: Cemaes (R – Anglesey League), Llanllyfni (P – Welsh Alliance)
Bodedern Reserves become Bodedern Athletic

WWW.NLNEWSDESK.CO.UK

HAMPSHIRE LEAGUE 2004

Note – AFC Wolversdene withdrew during the course of the season

Their results are shown herein but are expunged from the league table

	AFC Wolversdene	Academicals	Broughton	Crusaders	Denmead & Purbrook	Durley	East Lodge	Fair Oak	Four Marks	Ludgershall Sports	Michelmersh & Timsbury	Mottisfont	Netley Central Sports	Twyford	Wellow
AFC Wolversdene		n/a	n/a	n/a	1-6	3-4	n/a	4-1	n/a	n/a	n/a	n/a	n/a	n/a	n/a
Academicals	n/a		5-0	1-1	2-9	1-3	2-2	2-3	2-2	5-4	2-3	2-4	0-3	1-4	3-0
Broughton	n/a	0-1		1-1	1-2	2-3	4-1	2-2	4-3	1-0	3-3	2-4	1-2	3-5	3-0
Crusaders	3-2	2-0	2-2		1-5	1-3	0-5	2-1	1-2	3-2	0-0	1-6	2-1	5-1	4-2
Denmead & Purbrook	3-4	1-3	4-1			5-0	3-1	4-3	4-2	4-2	3-3	1-3	0-3	5-2	10-0
Durley	n/a	5-2	7-1	3-1	1-1		4-2	5-0	1-2	4-1	4-1	0-1	0-5	4-0	4-0
East Lodge	n/a	4-2	2-2	5-2	1-3	4-0		1-2	3-1	3-0	4-1	2-2	1-1	1-1	5-0
Fair Oak	n/a	1-4	2-1	3-2	2-2	4-4	4-1		4-6	4-1	1-1	2-3	1-1	2-1	3-2
Four Marks	n/a	2-1	2-1	2-0	0-2	1-2	5-1	3-1		W-L	0-1	1-3	1-3	2-2	4-2
Ludgershall Sports	1-1	0-0	2-2	2-3	0-5	2-5	1-2	1-1	2-3		0-0	1-4	W-L	0-3	6-0
Michelmersh & Timsbury	n/a	1-3	1-3	1-1	2-0	1-1	1-2	5-3	3-1	4-1		1-3	1-3	3-1	6-1
Mottisfont	n/a	5-4	4-1	3-0	1-2	1-0	5-0	4-0	0-0	2-1	4-1		0-0	W-L	5-0
Netley Central Sports	n/a	4-0	3-2	1-0	1-0	6-1	3-0	1-1	3-1	4-0	1-1	2-1		4-0	4-1
Twyford	n/a	2-2	2-0	1-1	3-2	0-0	W-L	4-3	1-3	3-1	0-3	0-6	1-3		5-0
Wellow	n/a	0-5	3-1	1-6	2-4	0-4	0-7	2-1	0-1	0-3	0-7	0-4	2-2	0-3	

	P	W	D	L	F	A	Pts
Mottisfont	26	22	2	2	78	22	68
Netley Central Sports	26	18	5	3	64	19	59
Denmead & Purbrook	26	16	3	7	84	44	51
Durley	26	15	4	7	68	45	49
Four Marks	26	13	3	10	50	47	42
East Lodge	26	12	3	11	59	49	39
Michelmersh & Timsbury	26	10	8	8	55	45	38
Twyford	26	10	5	11	45	54	35
Fair Oak	26	8	7	11	54	65	31
Crusaders	26	8	6	12	43	58	30
Academicals	26	8	5	13	56	67	29
Broughton	26	6	6	14	46	63	24
Ludgershall Sports	26	3	4	19	33	65	13
Wellow	26	2	1	23	18	110	7

AFC Wolversdene – record expunged

LEAGUE CUP

FIRST ROUND (*played over two legs*)
Academicals 1 Twyford 0, Twyford 0 **Academicals** 1
Crusaders 2 Michelmersh & Timsbury 1, Michelmersh & Timsbury 2 **Crusaders** 1 (1-4p)
Durley 2 Fair Oak 0, Fair Oak 2 **Durley** 5
East Lodge 0 Mottisfont 2, **Mottisfont** 4 East Lodge 2
Four Marks 3 Broughton 0, **Broughton** 3 Four Marks 1 *aet*
Ludgershall Sports 2 Wellow 0, Wellow 1 **Ludgershall Sports** 5
Netley Central Sports 0 Denmead & Purbrook 1, **Denmead & Purbrook** 4 Netley Central Sports 3
QUARTER-FINALS (*played over two legs*)
Academicals 2 Mottisfont 4, **Mottisfont** 2 Academicals 0
AFC Wolversdene (scr.) v **Denmead & Purbrook** (w/o)
Four Marks 2 Crusaders 2, **Crusaders** 5 Four Marks 4 *aet*
Ludgershall Sports 1 Durley 2, **Durley** 2 Ludgershall Sports 1
SEMI-FINALS (*played over two legs*)
Denmead & Purbrook 4 Crusaders 1, Crusaders 0 **Denmead & Purbrook** 2
Mottisfont 0 Durley 0, Durley 0 **Mottisfont** 1 *aet* (4-5p)
FINAL (*Apr 30th at Hamble ASSC*)
Mottisfont 1 **Denmead & Purbrook** 3

ZENITH COACH TRAVEL HAMPSHIRE LEAGUE 2004 CONSTITUTION 2008-09
ANDOVER RESERVES . . . . The Portway Stadium, West Portway Industrial Estate, Andover SP10 3LF 01264 351302
BOTLEY VILLAGE . . . . Botley Recreation Ground, High Street, Botley, Southampton SO30 2EA 01489 780440
BROUGHTON . . . . The Sportsfield, Buckholt Road, Broughton, Stockbridge SO20 8DA 01794 301150
CRUSADERS . . . . Worthies Sports & Social Club, Eversley Park, Kings Worthy, Winchester SO23 7NJ 01962 880457
DENMEAD & PURBROOK . . . . King George V Playing Field, Southwick Road, Denmead, Waterlooville PO7 6XT . . . . None
DURLEY . . . . Kytes Lane, Durley, Southampton SO32 2AE . . . . None
EAST LODGE . . . . Langstone Harbour Sports Ground, Eastern Road, Portsmouth 023 9282 4798
FAIR OAK . . . . Lapstone Park, Pavilion Close, Botley Road, Fair Oak, Eastleigh SO50 7AN . . . . None
FOUR MARKS . . . . The Recreation Ground, Upland Lane, Four Marks, Alton GU34 5AF . . . . None
HEDGE END RANGERS . . . . Norman Rodaway Rec Ground, Heathouse Lane, Hedge End, Southampton SO30 0LE . . . . None
LUDGERSHALL SPORTS . . . . Astor Crescent, Ludgershall, Andover SP11 9RG 01264 398200
MICHELMERSH & TIMSBURY . . . Timsbury Recreational Trust, Mannyngham Way, Timsbury, Romsey SO51 0NJ 01794 368955
MOTTISFONT . . . . Bengers Lane, Mottisfont, Romsey SO51 0LR . . . . None
NETLEY CENTRAL SPORTS . . . Netley Recreation Ground, Station Road, Netley Abbey, Southampton SO21 5AF 023 8045 2267
SOUTH WONSTON SWIFTS . . . AGC Worthy Down Military Base, Winchester SO21 2RG . . . . None
TWYFORD . . . . Hunters Park, Park Lane, Twyford, Winchester SO21 1QT . . . . None
IN: Andover Reserves (N), Botley Village (S – Southampton League Premier Division), Hedge End Rangers (S – Southampton League Premier Division), South Wonston Swifts (P – Winchester & District League)
OUT: AFC Wolversdene (WS), Academicals (R – Southampton League Junior Division Three), Wellow (R – Southampton League Senior Division One)

HAMPSHIRE PREMIER LEAGUE

	AFC Stoneham	Bishops Waltham Town	Clanfield	Colden Common	Fleetlands	Hamble Club	Headley United	Locks Heath	Ludwig Leisure B'stoke	Lyndhurst STJs	Otterbourne	Overton United	Paulsgrove	QK Southampton	Sporting BTC	Team Solent	Winchester Castle
AFC Stoneham		3-0	1-0	3-2	4-0	3-0	3-2	6-2	8-1	3-2	0-0	1-0	2-5	1-0	3-0	4-0	2-2
Bishops Waltham Town	2-4		1-3	2-0	1-5	3-2	7-0	3-0	1-2	3-0	0-6	1-3	0-1	0-2	0-2	0-3	3-2
Clanfield	2-4	2-0		6-2	7-0	2-2	1-4	2-0	3-0	4-1	2-0	5-2	1-0	3-2	2-3	2-1	4-2
Colden Common	2-3	1-1	3-1		3-3	3-1	3-3	0-4	3-2	1-4	2-1	4-3	2-1	2-0	0-4		1-2
Fleetlands	0-4	W-L	2-2	3-3		6-0	1-3	1-1	1-1	1-1	1-2	1-0	0-1	4-0	2-1	8-0	4-0
Hamble Club	0-4	0-1	4-2	2-0	2-0		0-3	1-5	3-2	3-0	0-4	3-1	3-2	1-1	0-1	0-2	1-3
Headley United	4-3	2-0	3-2	1-3	3-1			1-1	1-0	0-5	3-3	3-0	2-2	1-1	1-1	4-3	4-1
Locks Heath	2-2	4-1	0-2	4-0	0-2	3-1	7-0		1-1	2-0	1-0	5-3	2-2	3-0	3-1	1-3	3-0
Ludwig Leisure Basingstoke	0-6	1-0	1-7	3-3	0-2	3-3	2-3	1-3		0-2	0-2	2-1	1-4	0-2	1-2	1-2	1-4
Lyndhurst STJs	5-4	2-1	1-2	2-4	0-1	1-2	0-5	0-3	3-2		2-2	2-2	1-2	2-0	2-1	5-1	1-3
Otterbourne	3-2	4-1	3-2	4-1	0-2	0-0	4-0	3-0	2-1	2-1		3-0	4-2	1-0	3-1	2-0	2-1
Overton United	2-3	0-1	2-6	2-1	0x0	0-0	2-1	2-2	2-4	3-0	0-3		4-1	0-4	2-2	2-1	1-4
Paulsgrove	0-2	2-0	0-2	1-2	3-0	9-0	5-2	1-0	6-1	2-0	1-1	6-3		6-0	2-2	3-0	5-1
QK Southampton	1-4	1-0	0-2	1-0	2-6	1-1	4-1	1-3	5-2	2-0	2-7	2-0	0-7		1-1	2-1	1-0
Sporting BTC	1-5	0-0	0-1	0-2	3-4	2-0	5-1	0-3	1-0	2-1	0-2	3-0	1-0	0-2		1-0	1-0
Team Solent	0-1	3-0	1-5	3-0	W-L	3-1	2-0	2-1	0-1	0-0	0-4	2-1	1-5	3-0	3-1		4-0
Winchester Castle	2-4	5-0	1-6	5-2	2-2	1-1	5-3	3-4	0-1	0-1	1-7	4-5	1-3	1-3	1-0	2-3	

	P	W	D	L	F	A	Pts
AFC Stoneham	32	25	3	4	102	42	78
Otterbourne	32	24	5	3	87	28	77
Clanfield	32	22	2	8	93	43	68
Paulsgrove	32	19	5	8	93	43	62
Locks Heath	32	17	6	9	73	45	57
Fleetlands	32	15	8	9	65	47	53
Team Solent	32	16	2	14	52	57	50
Headley United	32	14	6	12	67	79	48
Sporting BTC	32	11	6	15	39	50	39
QK Southampton	32	11	6	15	40	64	39
Colden Common	32	10	5	17	56	80	35
Lyndhurst STJs	32	10	4	18	46	64	34
Winchester Castle	32	9	4	19	58	81	31
Hamble Club	32	8	7	17	38	74	31
Overton United	32	7	5	20	46	78	26
Bishops Waltham Town	32	8	2	22	33	65	26
Ludwig Leisure Basingstoke	32	6	4	22	38	86	22

Combination	P	W	D	L	F	A	Pts
Locks Heath Res.	22	15	5	2	59	19	50
Clanfield Res.	22	14	5	3	67	17	47
Paulsgrove Res.	22	13	2	7	56	34	41
Otterbourne Res.	22	11	4	7	42	33	37
AFC Stoneham Res.	22	10	5	7	44	44	35
Team Solent Res.	22	9	6	7	58	41	33
Winchester Castle Res.	22	10	3	9	46	33	33
Overton United Res.	22	10	2	10	46	33	32
Ludwig Leisure B'stoke Res.	22	8	3	11	37	52	27
Fleetlands Res.	22	4	3	15	28	80	15
QK Southampton Res.	22	4	2	16	21	74	14
Hamble Club Res.	22	3	2	17	34	78	11

WWW.NLNEWSDESK.CO.UK

COMBINATION CUP

FINAL *(May 5th at Winchester City)*
Paulsgrove Res. 0 **Locks Heath Res.** 1

LEAGUE CUP

PRELIMINARY ROUND
Clanfield 1 **Sporting BTC** 1 *aet* (1-4p)
Lyndhurst STJs 1 **Bishops Waltham Tn** 2
Paulsgrove 2 QK Southampton 0
Paulsgrove 4 Headley United 0
FIRST ROUND
AFC Stoneham 7 Ludwig Leisure B'stoke 0
Sporting BTC 1 **Team Solent** 2 *aet*
Team Solent 1 Locks Heath 1 *aet* (22-21p)
Fleetlands 4 Overton United 1
Winchester Castle 1 **Otterbourne** 3
SEMI-FINALS *(both at Locks Heath)*
Hamble Club 3 **Locks Heath** 3 *aet* (1-4p)
QUARTER-FINALS
AFC Stoneham 2 Paulsgrove 2 *aet* (4-3p)
Headley United 1 Colden Common 0
AFC Stoneham 1 Bishops Waltham Tn 0
Team Solent 2 Otterbourne 0
Fleetlands 2 **Otterbourne** 6
FINAL *(May 5th at Winchester City)*
AFC Stoneham 2 **Team Solent** 2 *aet* (4-5p)

HAMPSHIRE PREMIER LEAGUE CONSTITUTION 2008-09

AFC STONEHAM . . . . Stoneham Park, Stoneham Lane, Eastleigh, Southampton SO50 9HT. 02380 618812/613334
BOURNEMOUTH UNIVERSITY . . . . . Bournemouth Sports, Chapel Gate, East Parley, Christchurch BH23 6BD 01202 581933
CLANFIELD . . . . Peel Park, Chalton Lane, Clanfield, Waterlooville PO8 0RJ 07765 238231
COLDEN COMMON . . . Colden Common Recreation Ground, Main Road, Colden Common, Winchester SO21 1RP. 01962 712365
FLEETLANDS . . . . DARA Fleetlands, Lederle Lane, Gosport PO13 0AA 01329 239723
* HAMBLE CLUB . . . . Shell Mex Ground, Hamble Lane, Hamble-le-Rice, Southampton SO31 4QJ 07881 766085
(Hamble Club may temporarily play part of season at Mount Pleasant Recreation Ground, Hamble Lane, Hamble-le-Rice, Southampton)
HEADLEY UNITED . . . . Headley Pavilion, Mill Lane, Headley GU35 0PD. . . . . None
LISS ATHLETIC . . . . Newman Collard Ground, Hill Brow Road, Liss GU33 7LH 01730 894022
LOCKS HEATH . . . . Locksheath Rec, 419 Warsash Road, Titchfield Common, Fareham PO14 4JX 01489 600932
LUDWIG LEISURE BASINGSTOKE. . . . . Lord Rank Pitch, Micheldever. . . . . None
LYNDHURST STJS . . . . Wellands Road, Lyndhurst SO43 7AB . . . . None
OTTERBOURNE . . . . Oakwood Park, Oakwood Avenue, Otterbourne SO21 2ED 01962 714681
OVERTON UNITED . . . . Overton Recreation Centre, Bridge Street, Overton RG25 3LZ. 01256 770561
PAULSGROVE. . . . . . . Paulsgrove Social Club, Marsden Road, off Allaway Avenue, Paulsgrove, Portsmouth PO6 4JB 02392 324102
QK SOUTHAMPTON . . . . Lordshill Recreation Centre, Redbridge Lane, Lordshill, Southampton SO16 9BP 023 8073 2531
SPORTING BTC . . . . Priory Park, Elizabeth Way, Bishops Waltham, Southampton SO32 1SQ . . . . None
TEAM SOLENT . . . . Hardmoor Sports Ground, Stoneham Lane, Eastleigh, Southampton SO50 9HY 023 8061 7574
WINCHESTER CASTLE . . . . Hants County Council Sports Ground, Petersfield Rd (A31), Chilcomb, Winchester SO23 8ZB . . . . . . None
IN: Bournemouth University (P – Dorset County League Senior Division), Liss Athletic (P – Wessex League Division One)
OUT: Bishops Waltham Town (F)

HELLENIC LEAGUE

	AFC Wall'ford	Abingdon Town	Almondsb'y Tn	Ardley United	Badshot Lea	Bicester Town	Carterton	Fairford Town	Flackwell Hth	Harrow Hill	Highworth Tn	Hook Norton	Hungerford Tn	Kidlington	Lydney Town	Milton United	North Leigh	Pegasus Juniors	Shortwood Utd	Shrivenham	Wantage Town	Witney United
AFC Wallingford		1-4	1-6	0-11	0-2	3-4	0-3	1-5	1-4	1-0	0-5	1-3	1-6	1-3	0-2	1-1	0-8	2-3	0-2	1-3	1-8	2-3
Abingdon Town	1-2		1-0	2-2	3-0	1-1	5-0	4-0	2-0	4-1	3-1	0-3	1-4	1-4	0-2	2-1	1-6	1-2	3-3	0-1	1-2	2-2
Almondsbury Town	3-0	3-1		1-1	1-0	3-0	6-0	1-1	2-2	9-2	1-1	4-1	0-1	2-1	0-0	1-0	0-1	6-0	2-1	4-1	3-2	2-0
Ardley United	3-0	1-1	0-1	P	3-2	1-1	4-0	1-0	9-1	3-1	1-3	1-3	0-4	3-2	2-3	2-4	0-1	1-1	2-3	1-3	3-2	1-4
Badshot Lea	5-1	5-1	0-0	2-0	R	3-2	3-3	3-3	3-3	4-2	3-1	2-1	0-5	3-1	1-3	1-2	3-3	4-3	1-2	2-4	5-1	3-3
Bicester Town	3-1	1-2	0-1	1-1	0-2	E	2-1	3-0	4-2	2-0	2-2	1-2	0-0	2-0	0-4	0-2	0-5	2-2	1-1	1-2	4-1	2-2
Carterton	1-0	2-4	0-4	1-1	1-1	2-3	M	4-0	3-1	7-1	0-2	0-0	3-3	0-4	0-3	1-3	0-4	1-1	2-4	1-2	2-1	1-3
Fairford Town	2-0	2-2	0-4	0-1	2-2	0-1	1-4	I	1-2	1-1	2-1	2-3	0-3	1-2	2-0	0-4	1-3	0-2	2-1	4-4	2-3	2-4
Flackwell Heath	6-0	3-1	1-2	3-2	4-4	4-0	6-0	1-3	E	2-0	0-5	4-2	1-4	3-2	2-4	5-1	3-3	1-3	1-1	2-0	3-4	1-3
Harrow Hill	3-1	1-0	0-3	1-2	2-5	0-0	5-7	1-1	0-3	R	0-2	1-2	0-1	0-4	1-1	1-1	0-2	2-2	1-3	2-0	0-4	0-4
Highworth Town	2-1	2-0	2-3	3-3	4-2	2-2	0-0	3-0	1-0	0-0		0-2	1-0	0-1	1-0	0-4	0-0	1-2	2-0	4-2	0-2	
Hook Norton	2-1	3-3	0-1	0-5	1-2	0-1	1-0	3-1	0-5	2-2	2-0	D	2-2	5-3	1-1	2-3	0-0	1-1	0-2	0-0	0-0	1-3
Hungerford Town	9-0	5-2	1-2	1-1	2-1	2-0	1-2	2-1	2-1	3-0	4-1	6-0	I	1-1	5-1	2-1	2-3	2-0	0-0	4-1	6-3	4-3
Kidlington	11-0	3-1	0-2	1-0	0-4	1-1	1-1	0-0	3-0	4-1	1-3	1-2	0-1	V	4-2	2-2	2-2	6-2	1-0	4-2	0-1	2-2
Lydney Town	3-1	2-1	0-2	3-2	4-1	3-3	1-0	1-2	1-5	5-1	0-3	2-0	5-3	3-0	I	1-1	1-2	1-0	1-2	3-1	0-2	0-3
Milton United	1-1	1-1	1-3	3-2	0-2	2-1	2-0	3-2	1-0	1-0	2-2	0-1	3-3	1-0		S	5-1	5-2	2-1	1-5	3-1	4-1
North Leigh	6-0	4-2	1-1	5-2	2-1	3-1	1-0	2-0	2-3	3-1	3-4	4-0	3-3	4-2	2-1	3-0	I	4-4	2-1	0-0	4-4	0-0
Pegasus Juniors	4-3	2-0	2-2	1-3	1-2	0-1	2-4	4-1	1-2	1-1	0-1	2-0	1-1	1-1	1-1	1-3	0-3	O	2-1	2-0	2-1	0-1
Shortwood United	4-0	2-0	0-1	3-1	7-1	2-1	4-0	7-1	4-1	3-1	1-1	1-1	2-5	5-2	2-1	1-1	2-4	1-1	N	0-1	3-0	1-1
Shrivenham	2-0	1-0	2-2	2-2	5-2	2-0	1-2	1-0	0-2	2-0	2-2	4-1	3-1	1-5	3-2	0-4					3-1	2-2
Wantage Town	2-0	2-1	1-4	2-0	1-0	1-1	0-0	3-2	2-0	4-1	1-2	0-4	0-0	6-0	4-0	1-1	2-3	0-2	1-1			3-2
Witney United	5-0	4-0	1-0	1-5	4-0	3-2	2-0	5-0	1-1	3-0	2-4	3-1	0-0	2-1	2-0	2-2	1-2	1-0	2-0	2-0	3-0	

Premier Division

		P	W	D	L	F	A	Pts
North Leigh		42	29	9	4	123	53	96
Almondsbury Town		42	29	9	4	98	30	96
Hungerford Town		42	28	8	6	118	47	92
Witney United		42	25	10	7	97	51	85
Shortwood United		42	23	8	11	93	50	77
Highworth Town		42	22	8	12	75	52	74
Milton United		42	19	10	13	75	67	67
Shrivenham		42	19	7	16	72	72	64
Flackwell Heath		42	19	6	17	95	86	63
Lydney Town		42	19	6	17	71	71	63
Badshot Lea		42	17	9	16	92	91	60
Wantage Town		42	17	7	18	80	78	58
Ardley United		42	15	9	18	90	76	54
Hook Norton		42	14	12	16	55	74	54
Kidlington		42	14	11	17	86	73	53
Bicester Town		42	13	12	17	57	70	51
Pegasus Juniors	-3	42	12	12	18	61	78	45
Carterton		42	11	9	22	59	93	42
Abingdon Town		42	11	8	23	65	87	41
Fairford Town		42	8	8	26	52	100	32
Harrow Hill		42	2	8	32	36	117	14
AFC Wallingford	-1	42	2	2	38	30	164	7

Reserve Division One

		P	W	D	L	F	A	Pts
Kidlington Res.		32	25	3	4	121	44	78
Abingdon United Res.		32	25	5	4	92	37	74
Headington Amateurs Res.	-3	32	24	5	4	94	38	73
Didcot Town Res.		32	22	4	6	91	44	70
North Leigh Res.		32	19	5	8	76	44	62
Henley Town Res.		32	19	3	10	105	49	60
Wantage Town Res.		32	14	3	15	68	76	45
Cheltenham Saracens Res.		32	13	5	14	63	60	44
Hungerford Town Res.		32	10	10	12	52	53	40
Finchampstead Res.		32	12	3	17	59	84	39
Binfield Res.		32	9	7	16	52	63	34
Milton United Res.	-1	32	9	6	17	61	87	32
Abingdon Town Res.		32	9	2	21	34	83	29
Fairford Town Res.		32	8	3	21	42	100	27
Carterton Res.		32	6	6	20	46	88	24
Wootton Bassett Town Res.		32	7	3	22	47	94	24
Badshot Lea Res.		32	5	4	23	47	106	19

FTL FUTBOL HELLENIC LEAGUE PREMIER DIVISION CONSTITUTION 2008-09

ABINGDON TOWN . . . . Culham Road, Abingdon OX14 3HP 01235 521684
ALMONDSBURY TOWN . . . . Oakland Park, Gloucester Road, Almondsbury, Bristol BS32 4AG 01454 612220
ARDLEY UNITED . . . . The Playing Field, Oxford Road, Ardley, Bicester OX27 7NZ 07711 009198
BICESTER TOWN . . . . Sports Ground, Oxford Road, Bicester OX26 2AD 01869 241036
CARTERTON . . . . Kilkenny Lane, Swinbrook Road, Carterton OX18 1DY 01993 842410
CHALFONT WASPS . . . . Chalfont St Peter FC, Mill Meadow FC, Gravel Hill, Amersham Road, Chalfont St Peter SL9 9QX 01753 885797
FAIRFORD TOWN . . . . Cinder Lane, London Road, Fairford GL7 4AX 01285 712071
FLACKWELL HEATH . . . . Wilks Park, Magpie Lane, Flackwell Heath, High Wycombe HP10 9EA 01628 523892
HARROW HILL . . . . Larksfield Road, Harrow Hill, Drybrook GL17 9JP 01594 543873
HIGHWORTH TOWN . . . . The Elm Recreation Ground, Highworth, Swindon SN6 7DD. 01793 766263
HOOK NORTON . . . . The Playfields, The Bourne, Hook Norton OX15 5PB 01608 737132
HUNGERFORD TOWN . . . . War Memorial Ground, Bulpit Lane, Hungerford RG17 0AY 01488 682539
KIDLINGTON . . . . Yarnton Road, Kidlington OX5 1AT 01865 841526
MARLOW UNITED . . . . Flackwell Heath FC, Wilks Park, Magpie Lane, Flackwell Heath, High Wycombe HP10 9EA 01628 523892
MILTON UNITED . . . . The Sports Field, Potash Lane, Milton Heights, Abingdon OX13 6AG 01235 832999
OLD WOODSTOCK TOWN . . . . Abingdon United FC, Northcourt Road, Abingdon OX14 1PL 01235 203203
PEGASUS JUNIORS . . . . Old School Lane, Hereford HR1 11EX 07980 456995/07931 971765
READING TOWN . . . . Scours Lane, Tilehurst, Reading RG30 4AJ 0118 945 3555
SHORTWOOD UNITED . . . . Meadowbank, Shortwood, Nailsworth, Stroud GL6 0SJ. 01453 833936
SHRIVENHAM . . . . Recreation Ground, Highworth Road, Shrivenham, Swindon SN6 8BJ. 07767 371414
WANTAGE TOWN. . . . . Alfredian Park, Manor Road, Wantage OX12 8DW 01235 764781
WITNEY UNITED . . . . Polythene UK Stadium, Downs Road, Culbridge, Witney OX29 7WT 01993 848558

IN: Chalfont Wasps (P – Division One East), Marlow United (P – Division One East), Old Woodstock Town (P – Division One West), Reading Town (S – Combined Counties League Premier Division)
OUT: AFC Wallingford (R – North Berks League Division One), Badshot Lea (S – Combined Counties League Premier Division), Lydney Town (R – Division One West), North Leigh (P – Southern League Division One South & West)

	Ascot United	Binfield	Bisley Sports	Chalfont Wasps	Chinnor	Englefield Green Rovers	Eton Wick	Finchampstead	Henley Town	Holyport	Kintbury Rangers	Marlow United	Penn & Tylers Green	Prestwood	Rayners Lane	Thame United	Wokingham & Emmbrook
Ascot United	D	0-2	1-1	0-4	7-0	3-2	5-0	1-1	1-1	5-1	0-1	0-1	3-0	4-3	2-4	0-1	2-1
Binfield	0-1	I	1-2	1-1	1-2	2-2	3-0	5-0	1-1	3-1	1-1	2-3	0-0	2-0	3-0	2-2	0-1
Bisley Sports	1-2	1-0	V	0-2	5-2	2-0	5-2	4-2	1-3	3-2	4-3	0-1	2-0	10-0	0-2	0-2	1-0
Chalfont Wasps	5-2	2-1	2-3	I	3-1	3-1	10-0	5-1	2-0	2-0	5-0	3-2	4-0	3-0	3-0	1-0	8-0
Chinnor	1-2	0-2	1-1	0-4	S	0-3	2-1	0-1	1-3	1-1	0-7	1-2	1-3	2-1	0-0	1-3	1-2
Englefield Green Rovers	4-3	1-3	4-0	3-0	1-0	I	5-0	1-1	1-3	0-1	1-3	0-3	1-0	0-1	0-0	3-1	2-0
Eton Wick	1-7	0-4	1-5	0-6	0-1	1-5	O	1-1	0-4	2-6	1-6	2-2	0-3	0-2	3-5	1-5	0-2
Finchampstead	1-2	0-2	1-2	2-4	2-1	2-3	3-1	N	0-1	1-6	2-2	0-1	1-1	4-1	1-3	0-4	2-1
Henley Town	2-1	2-2	6-2	0-1	1-0	1-2	3-1	0-1		0-3	1-2	2-2	0-2	4-1	2-0	2-1	1-0
Holyport	1-3	2-2	4-7	2-2	1-1	4-1	1-0	2-1	2-3	O	4-1	1-3	2-0	5-2	7-0	1-0	3-0
Kintbury Rangers	3-6	0-2	1-5	2-2	3-1	1-2	7-2	3-0	0-1	3-0	N	0-1	2-0	4-0	4-1	2-1	4-1
Marlow United	0-0	2-1	1-0	2-0	2-1	1-4	5-0	2-0	1-1	6-0	2-0	E	2-0	6-1	2-2	0-0	3-2
Penn & Tylers Green	2-0	0-0	1-0	1-1	0-2	1-2	1-1	3-2	0-1	2-3	1-0	0-2		1-1	2-1	3-2	5-0
Prestwood	0-1	2-7	0-0	2-4	0-3	2-2	4-1	3-3	1-3	0-4	1-2	2-2	1-5	(E	1-1	1-8	0-3
Rayners Lane	1-3	2-2	4-5	1-4	4-1	0-3	1-0	1-1	2-1	1-2	1-4	0-3	2-1	0-0	A	1-3	0-3
Thame United	1-3	2-3	2-2	1-4	1-0	0-1	1-0	0-0	2-1	3-2	0-1	2-0	0-1	4-0	3-0	S	2-2
Wokingham & Emmbrook	0-3	4-0	2-1	2-2	2-1	0-1	4-0	1-0	3-5	0-4	0-1	2-0	1-1	1-0	2-2	1-2	T

Division One (East)		P	W	D	L	F	A	Pts
Chalfont Wasps		32	24	5	3	102	30	77
Marlow United		32	21	7	4	65	29	70
Englefield Green Rovers		32	19	4	9	61	39	61
Ascot United		32	18	4	10	73	46	58
Kintbury Rangers		32	18	3	11	71	48	57
Henley Town		32	17	6	9	57	39	57
Holyport		32	17	4	11	80	59	55
Bisley Sports		32	17	4	11	75	55	55
Binfield	-1	32	13	10	9	60	37	48
Thame United		32	14	5	13	57	41	47
Penn & Tylers Green		32	12	7	13	40	40	43
Wokingham & Emmbrook		32	12	4	16	43	58	40
Rayners Lane		32	9	8	15	45	69	35
Finchampstead		32	6	7	19	36	67	25
Chinnor		32	6	4	22	29	69	22
Prestwood		32	3	7	22	33	99	16
Eton Wick		32	0	3	29	22	124	3

Reserve Division Two (East)	P	W	D	L	F	A	Pts
Chalfont Wasps Res.	24	16	3	5	73	29	51
Kintbury Rangers Res.	24	14	4	6	64	38	46
Englefield Green Rovers Res.	24	15	1	8	58	34	46
Ascot United Res.	24	14	4	6	50	35	46
Thame United Res.	24	12	5	7	71	36	41
Penn & Tylers Green Res.	24	12	4	8	48	26	40
Wokingham & Emmbrook Res.	24	11	2	11	53	35	35
Aylesbury United Res.	24	10	5	9	56	48	35
Holyport Res.	24	9	5	10	57	53	32
Chinnor Res.	24	9	3	12	38	53	30
Rayners Lane Res.	24	8	4	12	45	60	28
Eton Wick Res.	24	4	0	20	22	105	12
Prestwood Res.	24	1	2	21	24	107	5

ANNUAL CHALLENGE MATCH

(Not contested in 2007-08)

FTL FUTBOL HELLENIC LEAGUE DIVISION ONE EAST CONSTITUTION 2008-09

ASCOT UNITED . . . . Ascot Race Course Car Park 10, Winkfield Road, Ascot SL5 7LJ . . . . None
BINFIELD . . . . Stubbs Hill, Binfield, Bracknell RG42 5NR 01344 860822
BISLEY SPORTS . . . . Lion Park, Church Lane, Bisley GU24 9ER 07795 322031
CHINNOR . . . . Station Road, Chinnor OX39 4PV 01844 352579
ENGLEFIELD GREEN ROVERS . . . Coopers Hill Sports Ground, Coopers Hill Lane, Englefield Green TW20 0JZ 01784 435666
ETON WICK . . . . Haywards Mead, Eton Wick, Windsor SL4 6JN 01753 852749
FINCHAMPSTEAD . . . . Memorial Park, The Village, Finchampstead RG40 4JR 0118 973 2890
HENLEY TOWN . . . . The Invesco Perpetual Triangle Ground, Mill Lane, Henley-on-Thames RG9 4HB 01491 411083
HOLYPORT . . . . Blackamoor Lane, Summerleaze Village, Maidenhead SL6 8SP 07768 746594
KINTBURY RANGERS . . . . Inkpen Road, Kintbury, Hungerford RG17 9TY 01488 657001
LAUNTON SPORTS . . . . The Playing Field, Bicester Road, Bicester OX26 5DP 01869 242007
NEWBURY . . . . Faraday Road, Newbury RG14 1AD 01635 35864
PENN & TYLERS GREEN . . . . French School Meadows, Elm Road, Penn HP10 8LF 01494 815346
PRESTWOOD . . . . Sprinters Leisure Centre, Honor End Lane, Prestwood, Great Missenden HP16 9HG 01494 865946
RAYNERS LANE . . . . Tithe Farm Social Club, 151 Rayners Lane, South Harrow HA2 0XH 020 8868 8724
SOUTH KILBURN . . . . Broadfields Country Club Headstone Lane North Harrow Middlesex HA2 6NN. 020 8421 4739/5260
THAME UNITED . . . . Wallingford Sports Park, Hithercroft Road, Wallingford OX10 9RB 01491 835044
WOKINGHAM & EMMBROOK . . . . Emmbrook Sports Ground, Lowther Road, Emmbrook, Wokingham RG41 1JB 01189 780209

IN: *Launton Sports (S – Division One West), Newbury (P – Reading League Senior Division), South Kilburn (P – Middlesex County League Premier Division)*
OUT: *Chalfont Wasps (P), Marlow United (P)*

	Banbury United Res.	Cheltenham Saracens	Cirencester United	Clanfield	Cricklade Town	Easington Sports	Headington Amateurs	Launton Sports	Letcombe	Malmesbury Victoria	Old Woodstock Town	Oxford City Nomads	Pewsey Vale	Purton	Trowbridge Town	Tytherington Rocks	Winterbourne United	Wootton Bassett Town
Banbury United Res.	D	0-7	6-1	1-4	1-3	1-7	2-1	1-2	0-1	2-3	1-2	0-2	0-2	0-6	2-6	0-3	0-3	0-5
Cheltenham Saracens	3-1	I	5-0	1-1	4-1	3-0	1-1	6-0	1-1	2-2	1-2	3-1	3-2	2-0	0-1	1-0	1-2	4-0
Cirencester United	0-1	0-8	V	3-2	2-5	0-5	0-3	0-2	0-13	0-3	1-4	0-1	0-2	1-3	0-1	0-4		0-2
Clanfield	2-2	3-2	2-0	I	2-0	1-0	2-1	1-3	1-2	2-1	3-2	5-1	3-6	3-2	2-4	2-1	1-2	4-0
Cricklade Town	2-1	0-3	5-1	3-1	S	0-3	4-2	3-1	1-1	3-0	2-2	0-0	2-0	4-0	4-0	2-2	0-0	2-0
Easington Sports	2-2	1-2	4-1	3-0	3-0	I	4-3	5-1	4-0	6-0	0-0	3-2	0-0	2-2	3-2	1-1	1-0	4-1
Headington Amateurs	1-1	1-1	1-1	3-2	2-2	1-2	O	6-5	0-2	1-3	0-3	0-2	2-1	1-3	5-0	5-2	0-5	0-2
Launton Sports	3-0	2-6	2-0	2-0	1-2	2-1	3-1	N	0-3	0-0	0-1	0-5	0-0	4-1	2-7	0-1	4-0	1-0
Letcombe	3-0	2-2	5-0	2-1	5-1	4-1	2-0	5-3		2-0	0-4	4-1	2-3	2-2	4-0	1-2		2-1
Malmesbury Victoria	0-1	2-2	1-2	2-2	0-2	1-4	1-1	4-1	2-0	O	0-3	1-0	0-4	1-2	1-1	0-0	0-4	2-1
Old Woodstock Town	8-0	1-0	7-1	2-2	2-0	2-0	1-2	3-1	1-2	2-0	N	2-0	2-1	5-0	0-3	2-3	1-2	2-0
Oxford City Nomads	4-1	0-0	5-1	3-3	4-2	1-0	0-1	4-0	3-5	4-1	3-1	E	2-2	2-1	2-0	0-3	1-1	6-2
Pewsey Vale	3-0	1-0	3-2	2-1	0-0	0-2	0-1	2-1	1-0	0-1	2-0			2-0	1-0	1-0	1-2	3-1
Purton	6-3	0-7	4-0	3-1	1-4	1-0	0-2	1-0	0-3	5-0	0-5	3-1	1-1	(W	0-1	0-2	1-7	1-0
Trowbridge Town	3-1	2-1	6-1	5-0	3-1	1-0	2-0	1-1	0-2	0-0	3-2	0-2	1-3	3-1	E	2-2	2-1	5-1
Tytherington Rocks	9-0	2-2	8-0	5-2	2-1	2-2	1-1	1-1	1-1	1-2	2-1	3-0	0-0	6-1	0-1	S	1-1	2-0
Winterbourne United	9-1	0-1	3-0	6-3	5-0	1-2	2-1	7-0	2-1	0-1	2-2	1-1	4-2	3-2	2-1	1-0	T)	
Wootton Bassett Town	3-0	1-4	2-0	3-1	0-1	2-1	1-1	3-1	1-0	1-1	1-2	1-0	1-1	1-2	2-4	1-3	3-2	

Division One (West)	P	W	D	L	F	A	Pts
Winterbourne United	34	22	5	7	90	36	71
Old Woodstock Town	34	21	4	9	77	36	67
Letcombe	34	20	5	9	83	41	65
Trowbridge Town	34	20	5	9	76	46	65
Cheltenham Saracens	34	18	9	7	89	53	63
Easington Sports	34	17	7	10	74	40	58
Pewsey Vale	34	17	7	10	51	36	58
Tytherington Rocks	34	15	11	8	70	38	56
Oxford City Nomads	34	16	6	12	66	49	54
Cricklade Town	34	16	6	12	63	56	54
Purton	34	14	2	18	55	78	44
Clanfield	34	12	5	17	66	79	41
Launton Sports	34	12	4	18	49	79	40
Headington Amateurs	34	10	8	16	50	63	38
Wootton Bassett Town	34	11	3	20	43	66	36
Malmesbury Victoria	34	9	9	16	35	62	36
Banbury United Res.	34	4	3	27	32	119	15
Cirencester United	34	2	1	31	16	128	7

Reserve Division Two (West)		P	W	D	L	F	A	Pts
Highworth Town Res.		22	19	1	2	108	28	58
Witney United Res.	-3	22	14	5	3	69	29	44
Shrivenham Res.		22	13	2	7	60	25	41
Ardley United Res.		22	12	2	8	63	37	38
Old Woodstock Town Res.	-3	22	12	2	8	52	39	35
Cricklade Town Res.		22	10	5	7	49	47	35
Letcombe Res.		22	9	4	9	40	43	31
Easington Sports Res.		22	9	3	10	36	37	30
Hook Norton Res.		22	7	1	14	33	52	22
Clanfield Res.		22	5	4	13	30	80	19
Launton Sports Res.		22	3	2	17	23	89	11
Cirencester United Res.		22	3	1	18	34	91	10

CHAIRMAN'S CUP

FINAL

(May 5th at Abingdon Town)

Shrivenham Res. 2 Headington Amateurs Res. 0

FTL FUTBOL HELLENIC LEAGUE DIVISION ONE WEST CONSTITUTION 2008-09

CHELTENHAM SARACENS .... Petersfield Park, Tewkesbury Road, Gloucester GL51 9DY 01242 584134
CIRENCESTER UNITED .... 29 Regt Army Base, South Cerney GL7 5RD 07969 637810
CLANFIELD .... Radcot Road, Clanfield, Faringdon OX18 2ST 01367 810314
CRICKLADE TOWN .... Cricklade Leisure Centre, Stones Lane, Cricklade SN6 6JW 01793 750011
EASINGTON SPORTS .... Addison Road, Easington Estate, Banbury OX16 9DH 01295 257006
HARDWICKE .... Hardwicke Playing Field, Green Lane, Hardwicke, Gloucester GL2 4QA 07815 869510
HEADINGTON AMATEURS .... Recreation Ground, Barton, Oxford OX3 9LA 01865 760489
LETCOMBE .... Bassett Road, Letcombe Regis, Wantage OX12 9JU 07765 144985
LYDNEY TOWN .... Lydney Recreation Ground, Swan Road, Lydney GL15 5RU 01594 844523
MALMESBURY VICTORIA .... Flying Monk Ground, Gloucester Road, Malmesbury SN16 0AJ 01666 822141
OXFORD CITY NOMADS .... Oxford City FC, Court Place Farm, Marsh Lane, Marston OX3 0NQ 01865 744493/742492
PEWSEY VALE .... Recreation Ground, Kings Corner, Ball Road, Pewsey SN9 5BS 01672 562990
PURTON .... The Red House, Church Street, Purton SN5 4DY 01793 770262
TROWBRIDGE TOWN .... Woodmarsh, North Bradley, Trowbridge BA14 0SB .... None
TYTHERINGTON ROCKS .... Hardwicke Playing Fields, Woodlands Road, Tytherington, Wotton-under-Edge GL12 8UJ 07837 555776
WINTERBOURNE UNITED .... The Rec, Parkside Avenue, Winterbourne, Bristol BS36 1LX 01454 850059
WOOTTON BASSETT TOWN .... Gerard Buxton Sports Ground, Rylands Way, Wootton Bassett SN4 8AW 01793 853880

IN: Hardwicke (P – Gloucestershire County League), Lydney Town (R)
OUT: Banbury United Reserves (W), Launton Sports (S – Division One East), Old Woodstock Town (P)

LEAGUE CUP
(All teams in league)

PRELIMINARY ROUND
Ardley United 1 **Chalfont Wasps** 3
Ascot United 3 Abingdon Town 2
Banbury United Res. 1 **Almondsbury Town** 8
Bicester Town 1 **Binfield** 3
Bisley Sports 2 **Kidlington** 3
Cheltenham Saracens 4 Pegasus Juniors 1
Chinnor 2 Penn & Tylers Green 0
Clanfield 1 Carterton 0
Cricklade Town 0 **Pewsey Vale** 2
Fairford Town 5 Cirencester United 0
Finchampstead 2 **Badshot Lea** 3
Flackwell Heath 3 Holyport 2
Henley Town 2 AFC Wallingford 0
Highworth Town 4 Oxford City Nomads 0
Hungerford Town 10 Wokingham & Emmbrook 0
Launton Sports 3 Harrow Hill 2 *aet*
Malmesbury Victoria 0 **Old Woodstock Town** 2
Marlow United 1 **Kintbury Rangers** 4
Rayners Lane 2 Prestwood 1
Thame United 1 **Milton United** 2
Trowbridge Town 3 Purton 0
Wantage Town 0 **Tytherington Rocks** 1
Winterbourne United 3 **Shrivenham** 5 *aet*
Witney United 0 **Letcombe** 1
Wootton Bassett Town 1 Shortwood United 0

FIRST ROUND
Almondsbury Town 5 Clanfield 2
Ascot United 1 Henley Town 0
Badshot Lea 1 Binfield 0 *aet*
Chalfont Wasps 3 Flackwell Heath 2
Chinnor 0 **Rayners Lane** 1
Easington Sports 1 **Cheltenham Saracens** 1 *aet* (3-5p)
Englefield Green Rovers 0 **Kidlington** 3
Eton Wick 0 **Milton United** 2
Fairford Town 0 **Letcombe** 2
Headington Amateurs 1 **Wootton Bassett Town** 2 *(at Wootton Bassett Town)*
Hook Norton 0 **Hungerford Town** 3
Kintbury Rangers 2 **North Leigh** 5
Launton Sports 2 **Highworth Town** 5
Lydney Town 0 **Tytherington Rocks** 1
Old Woodstock Town 1 Shrivenham 0
Pewsey Vale 0 **Trowbridge Town** 2

SECOND ROUND
Almondsbury Town 2 Chalfont Wasps 0
Ascot United 0 **Hungerford Town** 8
Highworth Town 2 North Leigh 1
Letcombe 1 **Wootton Bassett Town** 3
Milton United 2 Kidlington 1
Old Woodstock Town 3 Rayners Lane 1
Trowbridge Town 1 **Cheltenham Saracens** 2
Tytherington Rocks 3 **Badshot Lea** 5

QUARTER-FINALS
Almondsbury Town 1 Badshot Lea 0
Hungerford Town 3 Old Woodstock Town 2
Milton United 2 Highworth Town 2 *aet* (4-2p)
Wootton Bassett Town 1 **Cheltenham Saracens** 4

SEMI-FINALS
(played over two legs)
Almondsbury Town 1 Cheltenham Saracens 0
Cheltenham Saracens 2 **Almondsbury Town** 2,
Hungerford Town 4 Milton United 0
Milton United 0 **Hungerford Town** 3

FINAL
(May 3rd at Fairford Town)
Almondsbury Town 1 **Hungerford Town** 2

SUPPLEMENTARY CUP
(League Cup Preliminary and First Round losers)

PRELIMINARY ROUND
Binfield 1 **Flackwell Heath** 2
Henley Town 2 **Bicester Town** 3
Launton Sports 0 **Englefield Green Rovers** 2
Lydney Town 3 **Winterbourne United** 5 *aet*
Malmesbury Victoria 0 **Cricklade Town** 2
Oxford City Nomads 5 Prestwood 1
Penn & Tylers Green 0 **Abingdon Town** 5
Pewsey Vale 2 Purton 0
Thame United 4 Banbury United Res. 1

FIRST ROUND
Ardley United 4 Bisley Sports 2
Carterton 3 Headington Amateurs 0
Clanfield 4 Pegasus Juniors 3 *aet*
Cricklade Town 0 **Shortwood United** 2
Easington Sports 3 AFC Wallingford 1
Eton Wick 0 **Bicester Town** 2
Fairford Town 1 **Witney United** 2
Finchampstead 1 **Abingdon Town** 3
Harrow Hill 2 **Winterbourne United** 3
Holyport 2 Chinnor 1
Kintbury Rangers 1 **Marlow United** 3
Oxford City Nomads 3 Cirencester United 1
Shrivenham 3 Pewsey Vale 0
Thame United 3 Flackwell Heath 1
Wantage Town 4 Hook Norton 1
Wokingham & Emmbrook 1 **Englefield
Green Rovers** 2

SECOND ROUND
Abingdon Town 2 Shrivenham 1
Bicester Town 0 **Oxford City Nomads** 2
Carterton 5 Holyport 0
Clanfield 1 Witney United 1 *aet* (5-4p)
Marlow United 2 Easington Sports 1
Shortwood United 2 Englefield Green Rovers 1
Wantage Town 4 Thame United 1
Winterbourne United 0 **Ardley United** 0 *aet* (4-3p)

QUARTER-FINALS
Ardley United 4 Marlow United 2
Clanfield 0 **Abingdon Town** 2
Shortwood United 5 Oxford City Nomads 1
Wantage Town 1 Carterton 0

SEMI-FINALS
(played over two legs)
Ardley United 2 Wantage Town 0,
Wantage Town 2 **Ardley United** 1
Shortwood United 5 Abingdon Town 0,
Abingdon Town 2 **Shortwood United** 6

FINAL
(May 3rd at Fairford Town)
Shortwood United 4 Ardley United 2

NORMAN MATTHEWS FLOODLIGHT CUP

PRELIMINARY ROUND
Hungerford Town 8 Penn & Tylers Green 0
North Leigh 4 Hook Norton 0
Shrivenham 1 Lydney Town 0
Wantage Town 3 Pewsey Vale 1
FIRST ROUND
Abingdon Town 2 Thame United 1
AFC Wallingford 1 **Hungerford Town** 5
Almondsbury Town 3 **Wootton Bassett Town** 6 *aet*
Badshot Lea 0 **Ardley United** 3
Bicester Town 3 Abingdon United 3 *aet* (6-5p)
Carterton 2 Wantage Town 0
Flackwell Heath 4 Milton United 4 *aet* (4-2p)
Harrow Hill 3 Fairford Town 1
Highworth Town 10 Banbury United Res. 0
Kidlington 4 Bisley Sports 1
Malmesbury Victoria 6 Clanfield 3 *aet*
Marlow United 1 **Henley Town** 3
North Leigh 3 Didcot Town 2
Pegasus Juniors 2 Cheltenham Saracens 1
Shrivenham 1 **Oxford City Nomads** 3
Witney United 4 Shortwood United 1
SECOND ROUND
Carterton 1 **Kidlington** 5
Harrow Hill 1 **Witney United** 4

Henley Town 1 Pegasus Juniors 0
Highworth Town 0 **Ardley United** 4
Hungerford Town 1 **North Leigh** 2
Malmesbury Victoria 0 **Bicester Town** 2
Oxford City Nomads 1 **Abingdon Town** 2
Wootton Bassett Town 2 **Flackwell Heath** 5

QUARTER-FINALS
Ardley United 3 Abingdon Town 0
Flackwell Heath 2 Bicester Town 1
North Leigh 1 **Kidlington** 2
Witney United 3 Henley Town 0

SEMI-FINALS
(played over two legs)
Flackwell Heath 0 Ardley United 4
Ardley United 1 Flackwell Heath 0,
Kidlington 2 Witney United 1
Witney United 0 **Kidlington** 1

FINAL
(played over two legs)
(March 27th)
Kidlington 4 Ardley United 1
(April 10th)
Ardley United 2 **Kidlington** 3

HERTS SENIOR COUNTY LEAGUE

	Bedmond Sports & Social	Bovingdon	Buntingford Town	Bushey Rangers	Codicote	Evergreen	Hatfield Town	Hertford Heath	Knebworth	London Lions	Metropolitan Police Bushey	Park Street Village	Sandridge Rovers	Standon & Puckeridge	Whitewebbs	Wormley Rovers
Bedmond Sports & Social	P	2-5	4-3	0-1	1-2	1-0	0-6	2-3	1-2	5-3	1-5	1-2	0-5	1-4	1-3	2-1
Bovingdon	5-1	R	1-4	8-2	2-1	0-0	3-1	1-2	4-3	2-2	0-4	1-1	1-1	2-3	2-0	4-2
Buntingford Town	7-0	1-0	E	2-3	2-3	1-3	4-1	1-2	5-2	3-2	0-2	1-2	2-0	6-0	2-2	1-2
Bushey Rangers	3-1	2-3	1-3	M	2-3	0-5	1-6	0-3	2-7	2-4	0-1	1-4	0-1	3-2	2-4	0-0
Codicote	5-1	2-2	2-0	3-3	I	2-1	3-5	3-1	3-0	2-0	1-0	1-2	2-1	2-3	2-2	3-2
Evergreen	2-1	2-1	4-0	1-1	3-3	E	1-1	1-1	3-3	1-2	0-1	1-1	4-1	1-2	3-2	0-3
Hatfield Town	10-0	1-0	2-1	6-1	5-0	3-1	R	3-3	2-0	3-0	1-0	4-0	3-1	3-2	2-0	4-1
Hertford Heath	1-1	3-2	0-1	W-L	4-1	4-0	0-0		1-2	1-5	0-2	2-0	2-1	1-2	2-1	2-3
Knebworth	4-0	5-1	4-1	4-1	1-1	3-3	2-4	1-3	D	1-0	0-3	0-1	1-1	3-4	3-2	2-6
London Lions	2-0	1-1	0-1	2-0	2-1	2-0	0-6	2-3	4-2	I	1-1	1-0	3-1	4-4	5-1	2-0
Metropolitan Police Bushey	2-1	0-2	4-0	3-1	2-2	4-2	2-2	1-4	2-1	0-2	V	2-1	3-1	7-5	5-0	3-1
Park Street Village	7-2	1-1	2-1	1-1	1-0	3-0	3-1	1-1	3-0	1-0	0-1	I	1-1	1-2	1-1	W-L
Sandridge Rovers	0-0	3-1	4-2	2-2	4-3	1-1	0-2	1-4	3-0	2-1	0-0	0-3	S	6-3	2-1	1-3
Standon & Puckeridge	1-0	6-2	2-3	2-2	2-0	3-1	0-4	1-4	3-0	2-2	3-4	1-0	3-0	I	0-2	0-6
Whitewebbs	2-1	1-0	1-2	2-3	2-1	2-1	2-1	2-1	4-0	4-1	0-3	2-2	1-1	5-0	O	2-0
Wormley Rovers	13-2	3-0	0-2	W-L	4-1	4-0	2-4	4-0	0-1	2-1	1-2	1-1	4-0	1-2	2-0	N

Premier Division

		P	W	D	L	F	A	Pts
Hatfield Town		30	23	4	3	98	31	73
Metropolitan Police Bushey		30	21	4	5	72	34	67
Park Street Village	-3	30	16	8	6	48	27	53
Hertford Heath		30	15	7	8	56	43	52
Standon & Puckeridge	+2	30	15	4	11	74	72	51
Buntingford Town		30	14	1	15	62	55	43
London Lions	-1	30	13	5	12	53	52	43
Whitewebbs	+3	30	12	4	14	46	56	43
Codicote		30	12	6	12	58	60	42
Wormley Rovers	-4	30	14	2	14	69	46	40
Bovingdon		30	10	7	13	57	60	37
Sandridge Rovers		30	9	7	14	44	57	34
Knebworth		30	10	4	16	56	70	34
Evergreen	+3	30	7	9	14	45	56	33
Bedmond Sports & Social	+3	30	4	2	24	33	109	17
Bushey Rangers	-5	30	5	6	19	40	83	16

Reserve Division One

		P	W	D	L	F	A	Pts
Hatfield Town Res.		24	19	3	2	87	26	60
Metropolitan Police Bushey Res.		24	18	2	4	94	34	56
Bovingdon Res.		24	14	4	6	61	48	46
Evergreen Res.		24	12	5	7	47	36	41
Codicote Res.		24	11	5	8	58	51	38
Knebworth Res.		24	11	2	11	46	72	35
Hinton Res.		24	9	4	11	53	56	31
Sarratt Res.		24	9	3	12	56	68	30
London Lions Res.		24	8	5	11	41	49	29
Lemsford Res.		24	7	1	16	41	56	22
Buntingford Town Res.		24	6	4	14	35	54	22
Bedmond Sports & Social Res.		24	5	4	15	36	65	19
Standon & Puckeridge Res.	-2	24	5	2	17	43	83	15

(Whitewebbs Res. – record expunged)

Reserve Division Two

		P	W	D	L	F	A	Pts
Park Street Village Res.		22	18	2	2	81	24	56
Baldock Town Res.		22	16	2	4	82	35	50
Sandridge Rovers Res.		22	15	2	5	63	22	47
Buckhurst Hill Res.		22	15	2	5	66	26	47
Wormley Rovers Res.		22	12	3	7	55	29	39
Wodson Park Res.		22	11	4	7	61	47	37
Cuffley Res.		22	8	2	12	41	54	26
Old Parmiterians Res.		22	7	1	14	41	80	22
Chipperfield Corinthians Res.		22	5	1	16	23	78	16
Mill End Sports Res.		22	4	3	15	27	69	15
Croxley Guild Res.		22	2	7	13	23	62	13
Bushey Rangers Res.	-1	22	4	1	17	27	64	12

(Bedwell Rangers Res. – record expunged)

RESERVES CUP

FINAL

(April 26th at Welwyn Playing Fields)

Baldock Town Res. 3 Evergreen Res. 0

HERTS SENIOR COUNTY LEAGUE PREMIER DIVISION CONSTITUTION 2008-09

BALDOCK TOWN . . . . Knights Templar School, Weston Way, Baldock SG7 6EY 01462 631300
BEDMOND SPORTS & SOCIAL . . . Toms Lane Recreation Ground, Toms Lane, Bedmond, Abbots Langley WD5 0RA 01923 267991
BOVINGDON . . . . Green Lane, Bovingdon, Hemel Hempstead HP3 0LB 01442 832628
BUNTINGFORD TOWN . . . . Sainsburys Depot Sports Ground, London Road, Buntingford SG9 9JR . . . . None
CODICOTE . . . . John Clements Memorial Ground, Bury Lane, Codicote SG4 8XX 01438 821072
EVERGREEN . . . . South Way, Kings Langley, Abbots Langley WD5 0JL 01923 267812
HERTFORD HEATH . . . . The Playing Field, Trinity Road, Hertford Heath SG13 7QR . . . . None
KNEBWORTH . . . . The Recreation Ground, Watton Road, Knebworth, Stevenage SG3 6AH. . . . . None
LEMSFORD . . . . Gosling Sports Park, Stanborough Road, Welwyn Garden City AL8 6XE 01707 331056
LONDON LIONS . . . . Laing Sports, Rowley Lane, Barnet EN5 3HW 020 8441 6051
METROPOLITAN POLICE BUSHEY . . . Met. Police Sports Club, Aldenham Road, Bushey, Watford WD2 3TR. 01923 243947
MILL END SPORTS . . . . . . King George V Playing Fields, Shepherds Lane, Mill End, Rickmansworth WD3 8JN 01923 776392
PARK STREET VILLAGE . . Park Street Recreation Ground, Park Street Lane, Park Street, St Albans AL2 2JB . . . . None
SANDRIDGE ROVERS . . . . Spencer Recreation Ground, Sandridge, St Albans AL4 9BZ 01727 835506
STANDON & PUCKERIDGE . . . . Station Road, Standon, near Ware SG11 1QW 01920 823460
WORMLEY ROVERS . . . . Wormley Sports Club, Church Lane, Wormley EN10 7QF 01992 460650

IN: Baldock Town (P), Lemsford (P), Mill End Sports (P)
OUT: Bushey Rangers (R), Hatfield Town (P – Spartan South Midlands League Division One), Whitewebbs (W)

	Allenburys Sports	Baldock Town	Bedwell Rangers	Buckhurst Hill	Chipperfield Cor.	Croxley Guild	Cuffley	Debden Sports	Hinton	Lemsford	Mill End Sports	North Mymms	Old Parmiterians	Sarratt	St Peters	Wodson Park
Allenburys Sports		3-6	3-4	1-5	2-1	2-2	0-4	3-4	0-2	1-4	0-3	0-1	1-1	1-1	1-4	2-1
Baldock Town	7-1		2-0	1-1	3-1	1-0	3-0	6-1	5-1	2-0	3-0	1-0	2-0	2-0	6-1	2-0
Bedwell Rangers	0-5	0-6	D	2-3	1-4	1-3	1-2	2-3	0-3	0-6	1-7	2-5	1-3	0-0	1-3	1-9
Buckhurst Hill	4-1	1-2	5-0	I	2-0	0-2	4-2	3-4	2-2	4-2	2-4	0-2	10-3	1-2	2-0	0-1
Chipperfield Corinthians	2-1	0-4	3-1	3-1	V	4-3	11-0	4-2	1-2	0-3	3-1	1-2	3-0	3-3	6-0	2-1
Croxley Guild	3-2	2-3	5-2	0-4	0-2	I	4-0	4-4	2-1	2-2	0-3	4-1	0-1	0-2	0-3	0-3
Cuffley	0-1	2-6	2-1	0-7	1-2	0-2	S	5-0	3-2	1-1	2-4	2-0	3-4	0-0	3-1	1-6
Debden Sports	1-1	3-3	3-0	3-2	3-2	2-0	3-0	I	2-1	1-2	1-4	3-3	2-0	1-1	5-1	1-3
Hinton	0-2	1-3	3-0	2-4	1-0	3-2	3-1	1-2	O	1-3	2-1	5-3	3-0	0-3	3-2	2-3
Lemsford	7-2	3-3	4-0	3-2	3-2	0-2	0-0	2-2	3-1	N	4-4	4-1	4-1	2-1	3-2	0-5
Mill End Sports	4-3	0-1	5-0	4-1	1-2	3-0	0-0	1-3	2-2	2-0		4-1	1-1	4-1	1-3	0-2
North Mymms	0-0	1-2	1-2	2-0	3-4	1-2	0-0	2-2	2-2	4-2	2-6	O	3-0	2-2	2-0	L-W
Old Parmiterians	1-2	1-5	7-1	2-3	4-4	1-2	2-0	2-5	3-2	1-2	1-2	0-1	N	0-0	2-4	1-4
Sarratt	2-2	1-3	4-1	0-2	2-5	1-1	6-2	1-1	1-3	3-1	3-4	1-1	1-3	E	0-4	0-1
St Peters	4-2	1-0	1-0	1-3	1-2	1-2	3-1	3-3	3-0	0-2	0-3	2-0	3-0	2-0		0-6
Wodson Park	3-1	2-1	6-2	3-0	5-2	4-4	4-0	1-2	2-1	4-2	2-1	3-3	2-1	5-1	2-1	

Division One	P	W	D	L	F	A	Pts
Baldock Town	30	25	3	2	94	27	78
Wodson Park	30	24	2	4	93	34	74
Mill End Sports	30	17	4	9	79	44	55
Lemsford	30	16	7	7	76	54	55
Debden Sports	30	15	9	6	72	63	54
Chipperfield Corinthians	30	17	2	11	79	56	53
Buckhurst Hill	30	15	2	13	78	54	47
St Peters	30	14	1	15	54	61	43
Croxley Guild	30	12	5	13	53	57	41
Hinton	30	12	3	15	55	60	39
North Mymms	30	9	8	13	49	56	35
Sarratt	30	6	12	12	43	56	30
Cuffley	30	7	5	18	37	81	26
Allenburys Sports	30	6	6	18	46	81	24
Old Parmiterians	30	6	4	20	43	78	22
Bedwell Rangers	30	2	1	27	27	116	7

AUBREY CUP

FIRST ROUND

Bovingdon 4 Bushey Rangers 3 *aet*
Chipperfield Corinthians 4 Cuffley 3
Codicote 3 Buntingford Town 3 *aet (3-1p)*
Evergreen 2 Allenburys Sports 1
Hatfield Town 2 Metropolitan Police Bushey 0
Hertford Heath 5 Croxley Guild 2
Lemsford 2 Bedmond Sports & Social 1
London Lions 2 **Wormley Rovers** 4
North Mymms 3 Hinton 1
Old Parmiterians 6 Sarratt 0
Park Street Village 7 Bedwell Rangers 0
Sandridge Rovers 0 **Debden Sports** 2
St Peters 1 **Baldock Town** 3
Standon & Puckeridge 6 Knebworth 1
Whitewebbs 8 Buckhurst Hill 2
Wodson Park 2 Mill End Sports 2 *aet (4-2p)*

SECOND ROUND

Baldock Town 2 **North Mymms** 5 *(at North Mymms)*
Bovingdon 2 Whitewebbs 0
Codicote 5 O Parmiterians 3 *aet*
Evergreen 6 Chipperfield Corinthians 2 *aet*
Hatfield Town 3 Wormley Rovers 1
Hertford Heath 1 **Standon & Puckeridge** 4
Lemsford 1 **Debden Sports** 2 *aet*
Park Street 3 Wodson Park 1

QUARTER-FINALS

Bovingdon 4 Codicote 3
Debden Sports 0 **Evergreen** 3
Hatfield Town 1 Standon & Puckeridge 0
Park Street Village 5 North Mymms 1

SEMI-FINALS

Evergreen 0 **Park Street Village** 2
Hatfield Town 2 **Bovingdon** 3

FINAL

(May 5th at HCFA, Letchworth)
Bovingdon 1 **Park Street Village** 3 *aet*

HERTS SENIOR COUNTY LEAGUE DIVISION ONE CONSTITUTION 2008-09

AFC HATFIELD TOWN . . . . Birchwood Leisure Centre, Birchwood, Longmead, Hatfield AL10 0AS 01707 270772
ALLENBURYS SPORTS . . . . Glaxo Smith Kline, Westfield, Park Road, Ware SG12 0DP . . . . None
BEDWELL RANGERS . . . . Meadway Park, Gunnelswood Road, Stevenage SG1 2EF . . . . None
BUSHEY RANGERS . . . . Moatfield, Bournehall Lane, Bushey WD23 3JU 020 8386 1875
CHIPPERFIELD CORINTHIANS . . . . Queens Street, Chipperfield, Kings Langley WD4 9BT 01923 269554
CROXLEY GUILD . . . . Croxley Guild of Sport, The Green, Croxley Green, Rickmansworth WD3 3HT 01923 770534
CUFFLEY . . . . King George's Playing Fields, Northaw Road East, Cuffley EN6 4LL 07815 174434
DEBDEN SPORTS . . . . Chigwell Lane, Loughton, Ilford IG10 3TP. 020 8508 9392
HARPENDEN ROVERS . . . . Cravells Road, Acres Corner, Harpenden Common AL5 1DH . . . . None
HINTON . . . . Holtwhites Sports & Social, Kirkland Drive, Enfield EN2 0RU 020 8363 4449
HITCHIN TOWN ARENA. . . . . The Arena, Norton Road, Baldock SG7 5AU 01462 720088
KIMPTON ROVERS . . . . Kimpton Recreation Ground, High Street, Kimpton, Hitchin SG4 8QP . . . . None
LETCHWORTH GARDEN CITY EAGLES . . . Pixmore Pitches, Baldock Road, Letchworth SG6 2ER. . . . . None
NORTH MYMMS . . . . Welham Green Recreation, Dellsome Lane, North Mymms, Hatfield AL9 7DY 01707 266972/260338
OLD PARMITERIANS . . . . Parmiters School, High Elms Lane, Garston, Watford WD25 0JU. 01923 682805
SARRATT . . . . King George V Playing Fields, King Georges Avenue, Sarratt . . . . None
ST PETERS . . . . William Bird Playing Fields, Toulmin Drive, St Albans AL3 6DX. 01727 852401
IN: AFC Hatfield Town (N), Bushey Rangers (R), Harpenden Rovers (P – West Herts League Premier Division), Hitchin Town Arena (N), Kimpton Rovers (P – North & Mid Herts League Division One Mid), Letchworth Garden City Eagles (P – youth football)
OUT: Baldock Town (P), Buckhurst Hill (S – Essex Olympian League Division One), Lemsford (P), Mill End Sports (P), Wodson Park (P – Spartan South Midlands League Division Two)

HUMBER PREMIER LEAGUE

	Barton Town Old Boys Res.	Beverley Town	Easington United	Hedon Rangers	Hessle Rangers	Hornsea Town	Hutton Cranswick United	LSS Lucarly's	Malet Lambert YC	North Ferriby United Res.	Pocklington Town	Reckitts	Sculcoates Amateurs	Smith & Nephew	Westella & Willerby	Withernsea
Barton Town Old Boys Res.	P	0-5	2-1	2-5	1-2	2-0	3-3	0-1	2-3	5-2	0-0	1-2	0-4	1-2	2-1	7-0
Beverley Town	3-1	R	1-1	1-2	6-1	3-0	0-1	4-3	1-1	1-4	2-0	2-2	1-2	0-0	2-1	5-0
Easington United	4-2	0-2	E	2-1	8-0	0-0	2-2	0-2	2-0	2-3	2-2	2-2	1-3	2-1	3-2	1-0
Hedon Rangers	5-2	2-2	1-2	M	3-4	3-1	4-3	4-3	4-4	1-1	4-3	0-2	0-1	3-4	2-2	4-0
Hessle Rangers	4-1	1-2	0-3	0-5	I	1-3	0-2	1-2	1-5	0-3	1-5	0-4	1-4	1-6	0-3	6-1
Hornsea Town	3-1	1-1	3-2	1-4	2-3	E	3-4	1-3	0-0	1-1	4-2	0-2	2-0	0-2	1-1	6-0
Hutton Cranswick United	5-2	2-0	1-1	1-1	3-0	1-1	R	3-2	6-1	3-2	3-0	0-4	2-0	1-2	2-3	2-4
LSS Lucarly's	1-1	0-2	3-1	2-3	2-0	1-5	1-6		4-0	1-0	1-3	3-4	3-2	0-6	1-3	4-1
Malet Lambert YC	3-2	1-0	1-0	2-1	0-0	1-1	2-5	0-2	D	2-2	1-1	1-1	0-2	2-1	3-1	2-1
North Ferriby United Res.	3-1	1-4	2-2	5-0	2-1	3-0	1-1	1-2	2-1	I	2-2	0-0	4-1	3-1	3-2	4-1
Pocklington Town	1-1	0-2	2-1	2-2	4-1	1-0	3-2	3-2	1-0	2-1	V	2-1	0-2	1-1	0-1	5-0
Reckitts	1-1	1-1	4-0	1-1	5-2	2-0	1-0	4-0	2-1	3-0	1-0	I	1-4	0-1	1-0	9-2
Sculcoates Amateurs	2-0	2-1	3-1	5-0	2-0	3-1	1-1	3-1	2-0	5-4	1-0	0-0	S	0-0	2-1	7-0
Smith & Nephew	4-1	1-2	0-1	4-1	3-1	1-1	4-1	0-1	5-2	1-0	4-1	6-3	4-1	I	4-1	7-0
Westella & Willerby	2-1	1-2	2-1	5-1	0-0	0-0	4-1	3-2	6-1	0-0	1-2	0-1	1-1	1-0	O	5-0
Withernsea	2-1	0-3	0-4	0-6	2-2	0-2	0-7	1-3	4-3	2-3	0-4	2-1	0-6	1-7	1-3	N

Premier Division	P	W	D	L	F	A	Pts
Sculcoates Amateurs	30	21	4	5	71	30	67
Smith & Nephew	30	19	4	7	82	33	61
Reckitts	30	17	8	5	65	32	59
Beverley Town	30	16	7	7	61	32	55
Hutton Cranswick United	30	14	7	9	74	52	49
North Ferriby United Res.	30	13	8	9	62	48	47
Pocklington Town	30	13	7	10	52	44	46
Westella & Willerby	30	13	6	11	56	40	45
Hedon Rangers	30	12	7	11	73	67	43
LSS Lucarly's	30	14	1	15	56	65	43
Easington United	30	11	7	12	52	47	40
Malet Lambert YC	30	9	8	13	43	62	35
Hornsea Town	30	8	9	13	43	48	33
Barton Town Old Boys Res.	30	5	5	20	46	74	20
Hessle Rangers	30	5	3	22	34	92	18
Withernsea	30	4	1	25	25	129	13

HUMBER PREMIER LEAGUE PREMIER DIVISION CONSTITUTION 2008-09

BARTON TOWN OLD BOYS RESERVES ... The Euronics Ground, Marsh Lane, Barton-on-Humber DN15 5HB 07900 105204
BEVERLEY TOWN .... Recreation Ground, Norwood, Beverley HU17 9HW 01482 862520
CHALK LANE .... Hull University, Inglemire Lane, Hull HU17 7TE .... None
CLEETHORPES TOWN .... Wilton Road, Humberston, Grimsby DN36 4AW 01472 812936
EASINGTON UNITED .... Low Farm, Beck Street, Easington, Hull HU12 0TT .... None
HEDON RANGERS .... Destiny Fitness, Staithes Road, Hedon, Hull HU12 8DX 01482 896113
HESSLE RANGERS .... Blackburn Leisure, Prescott Avenue, Brough HU15 1BB .... None
HORNSEA TOWN .... Hollis Recreation Ground, Atwick Road, Hornsea HU18 1EL .... None
HUTTON CRANSWICK UNITED .... Rotsea Lane, Hutton Cranswick, Driffield YO25 9QG .... None
MALET LAMBERT YC .... Malet Lambert School, James Reckitt Avenue, Hull HU8 0JD 01482 374211
NORTH FERRIBY UNITED RESERVES ... Humberside Police Sports Ground, Inglemire Lane, Hull HU6 8JG 01482 856954
POCKLINGTON TOWN .... The Balk, Pocklington, York YO25 2NZ 01759 303638
RECKITTS .... Humberside Police Sports Ground, Inglemire Lane, Hull HU6 8JG 01482 326111x2317
SCULCOATES AMATEURS .... Hull & East Riding Sports Club, Chanterlands Avenue, Hull HU5 4ED 01482 342156
ST ANDREWS POLICE CLUB ...... East Mount Recreation Ground, Waverley Road, Hull HU6 8JG 01482 326111x2317
WESTELLA & WILLERBY .... Hill Top Club, Willerby Low Road, Cottingham HU16 5JD 01482 671306

IN: St Andrews Police Club (P)
OUT: Withernsea (R)
LSS Lucarly's become Cleethorpes Town, Smith & Nephew become Chalk Lane

Note – Discount Carpets and Mill Lane United withdrew during the course of the season Their results are shown herein but are expunged from the league table	Brandesburton	Bransholme Athletic	Discount Carpets	Hall Road Rangers Res.	Hessle Sporting Club	Kinnersley	Long Riston	Mill Lane United	North Cave	Pinefleet Wolfreton	Selby Town Res.	St Andrews Police Club
Brandesburton	D	4-3	n/a	2-5	0-2	5-4	1-2	n/a	1-2	2-1	2-4	0-3
Bransholme Athletic	2-2	I	0-2	0-0	7-3	2-2	4-2	n/a	3-2	2-5	4-1	3-1
Discount Carpets	1-1	n/a	V	0-5	1-1	0-6	1-2	n/a	0-3	3-0	2-6	n/a
Hall Road Rangers Res.	3-6	3-1	n/a	I	5-0	0-0	3-0	n/a	0-4	1-0	3-2	1-2
Hessle Sporting Club	4-1	4-2	n/a	2-4	S	1-3	6-1	5-2	3-4	2-0	2-5	2-3
Kinnersley	2-1	4-0	3-0	1-1	4-1	I	3-4	n/a	1-0	2-3	1-4	3-2
Long Riston	2-2	0-1	n/a	2-2	2-4	0-6	O	1-3	0-3	4-2	0-3	1-2
Mill Lane United	2-4	n/a	n/a	n/a	n/a	n/a	n/a	N	1-1	n/a	n/a	3-1
North Cave	2-0	4-0	1-2	1-2	1-1	3-3	2-0	n/a		3-1	3-4	3-3
Pinefleet Wolfreton	2-1	3-1	n/a	3-3	5-1	1-3	8-1	3-3	0-3	O	6-3	3-2
Selby Town Res.	3-2	2-0	n/a	3-4	3-4	2-4	3-2	n/a	2-0	1-1	N	1-2
St Andrews Police Club	2-3	1-1	3-1	8-0	5-3	2-1	4-1	n/a	2-1	2-1	3-0	E

Division One

		P	W	D	L	F	A	Pts
St Andrews Police Club		18	12	2	4	49	28	38
Kinnersley		18	9	4	5	47	32	31
North Cave		18	9	3	6	41	26	30
Hall Road Rangers Res.	-3	18	9	5	4	40	37	29
Selby Town Res.		18	9	1	8	46	43	28
Pinefleet Wolfreton		18	8	2	8	45	37	26
Bransholme Athletic		18	6	4	8	36	43	22
Hessle Sporting Club		18	7	1	10	45	55	22
Brandesburton		18	5	2	11	35	48	17
Long Riston		18	3	2	13	24	59	11

Discount Carpets and Mill Lane United – records expunged

HUMBER PREMIER LEAGUE DIVISION ONE CONSTITUTION 2008-09

BRANDESBURTON........Brandesburton Playing Fields, Catwick Lane, Brandesburton, Driffield YO25 8SB....................None
BRANSHOLME ATHLETIC...............Hull University, Inglemire Lane, Hull HU6 7TE.......................01482 466000
BRIDLINGTON SPORTS CLUB....Bridlington Sports Club, Dukes Park, Moorfield Road, Bridlington YO16 4LE..........01262 606016
HALL ROAD RANGERS RESERVES...Dene Park, Dene Close, Beverley Road, Dunswell, Hull HU6 0AB.................01482 850101
HESSLE SPORTING CLUB..........South Hunsley School, Melton, North Ferriby HU14 3HS......................01482 631208
INTER CHARTER..............................East Mount, Hull....................................None
KINGBURN ATHLETIC.....................................Springhead, Hull..............................None
KINNERSLEY............................Hull YPI, Chanterlands Avenue, Hull HU5 4EF........................None
LONG RISTON.........................Long Riston Playing Fields, Long Riston.............................None
NORTH CAVE...................North Cave Playing Fields, Church Street, North Cave, Brough...................None
NORTH FERRIBY ATHLETIC..........South Hunsley School, Melton, North Ferriby HU14 3HS....................01482 631208
PINEFLEET WOLFRETON.....Marist RU Club, Cranbrook Avenue, Cottingham Road, Hull HU6 7TT...................01482 859216
SCARBOROUGH ATHLETIC RESERVES...Hutton Cranswick FC, Rotsea Lane, Hutton Cranswick, Driffield YO25 9QG..........None
WITHERNSEA.......................Hull Road, Withernsea HU19 2EG.................................None

IN: Bridlington Sports Club (P – Driffield & District League), Inter Charter (P – East Riding Amateur League Premier Division), Kingburn Athletic (P – East Riding Amateur League Premier Division), North Ferriby Athletic (P – East Riding County League Premier Division), Scarborough Athletic Reserves (N), Withernsea (R)
OUT: Discount Carpets (WS), Mill Lane United (WS), Selby Town Reserves (W), St Andrews Police Club (P)

LEAGUE CUP

FIRST ROUND
Beverley Town 0 **Westella & Willerby** 1
Bransholme Athletic 0 **North Cave** 3
Discount Carpets 0 **LSS Lucarly's** 7
Hedon Rangers 3 Hessle Sporting Club 2
Kinnersley 3 Barton Town Old Boys Res. 0
Long Riston 0 **Hornsea Town** 1
Mill Lane United 1 **Malet Lambert YC** 3
North Ferriby United Res. 1 Selby Town Res. 0
Reckitts 4 Brandesburton 1
Smith & Nephew 3 Easington United 0
St Andrews Police Club 2 Pinefleet Wolfreton 1
Withernsea 1 **Pocklington Town** 3
SECOND ROUND
Hedon Rangers 4 Hutton Cranswick United 2
LSS Lucarly's 3 **Westella & Willerby** 3 *aet (3-5p)*
Malet Lambert YC 4 Hall Road Rangers Res. 1

North Cave 0 **Reckitts** 1
North Ferriby United Res. 5 St Andrews Police Club 0
Pocklington Town 2 Hornsea Town 0
Sculcoates Amateurs 1 **Kinnersley** 1 *aet (3-4p)*
Smith & Nephew 4 Hessle Sporting Club 1
QUARTER-FINALS
Pocklington Town 3 Hedon Rangers 2
Reckitts 1 **Malet Lambert YC** 2
Smith & Nephew 2 Kinnersley 1
Westella & Willerby 2 **North Ferriby United Res.** 4
SEMI-FINALS
(both at Hutton Cranswick United)
North Ferriby United Res. 0 **Smith & Nephew** 2
Pocklington Town 6 Malet Lambert YC 0
FINAL
(May 2nd at Hall Road Rangers)
Smith & Nephew 1 Pocklington Town 0

ISTHMIAN LEAGUE

	AFC Hornchurch	AFC Wimbledon	Ashford Town (Middx)	Billericay Town	Boreham Wood	Carshalton Athletic	Chelmsford City	East Thurrock United	Folkestone Invicta	Harlow Town	Harrow Borough	Hastings United	Hendon	Heybridge Swifts	Horsham	Leyton	Maidstone United	Margate	Ramsgate	Staines Town	Tonbridge Angels	Wealdstone
AFC Hornchurch		1-0	2-1	0-0	3-1	2-0	2-0	9-0	1-2	1-0	1-0	3-2	3-1	0-1	2-1	0-1	1-0	3-2	2-3	0-2	1-2	1-1
AFC Wimbledon	6-1		2-2	1-1	2-0	2-1	2-0	5-0	2-4	1-0	3-2	4-0	1-2	1-2	0-0	1-2	0-1	2-0	0-1	2-1	2-1	1-0
Ashford Town (Middx)	4-1	2-1		4-2	3-0	0-0	1-2	0-2	3-0	3-2	4-4	3-1	3-2	1-0	1-1	1-0	4-0	3-0	2-1	4-1	1-4	4-5
Billericay Town	1-0	2-2	0-1	*P*	2-0	0-1	4-0	4-0	1-0	3-2	1-1	6-0	1-1	2-1	4-1	2-5	1-1	4-2	0-4	0-0	2-2	0-2
Boreham Wood	0-2	0-4	1-2	1-1	*R*	0-1	1-2	3-0	0-2	1-2	1-2	3-0	1-1	2-1	2-1	2-2	4-2	0-0	2-0	3-1	1-0	2-1
Carshalton Athletic	1-0	2-0	3-3	2-1	3-0	*E*	2-1	2-1	0-1	1-0	0-2	1-2	1-1	1-2	1-1	1-2	1-0	0-0	0-0	0-2	0-2	0-2
Chelmsford City	3-1	2-2	3-0	1-1	5-1	7-0	*M*	2-1	0-0	0-0	5-1	1-1	3-0	2-1	2-0	2-0	3-0	4-1	1-0	4-0	3-2	0-4
East Thurrock United	1-0	0-2	1-3	1-1	2-0	2-4	1-0	*I*	0-1	0-0	3-2	2-1	0-0	1-3	2-1	0-3	0-1	1-0	2-4	3-1	1-0	1-2
Folkestone Invicta	1-4	3-2	1-3	0-3	1-1	0-1	2-0	4-1	*E*	2-2	0-4	1-0	1-1	1-0	1-1	0-0	0-3	0-1	3-2	0-0	3-2	0-0
Harlow Town	1-1	1-1	0-1	3-0	1-1	1-2	6-1	1-1	2-2	*R*	3-1	0-0	3-2	0-3	0-3	2-0	2-0	2-2	1-2	1-2	1-3	0-0
Harrow Borough	1-5	2-1	1-3	3-1	0-1	0-1	5-2	4-0	5-0	1-2		1-0	2-6	2-1	1-0	0-4	1-3	3-1	3-1	3-1	0-2	0-2
Hastings United	1-3	0-2	2-0	2-3	2-1	4-0	0-1	1-0	1-0	3-4	1-0	*D*	2-1	6-1	2-2	0-3	3-0	2-1	0-1	2-0	1-3	0-0
Hendon	1-2	3-2	2-1	0-0	1-1	2-1	1-2	2-0	1-1	3-3	0-0	1-1	*I*	2-2	4-2	2-1	0-5	0-1	0-0	3-1	0-2	3-1
Heybridge Swifts	3-1	4-1	2-2	0-2	3-3	2-1	0-0	3-2	0-0	0-1	4-0	1-0	0-1	*V*	3-0	1-2	3-0	4-1	2-2	0-6	2-1	3-1
Horsham	4-0	0-3	2-4	1-1	1-0	1-2	5-1	1-2	1-2	2-1	1-0	0-1	1-0	3-0	*I*	2-1	4-1	3-2	0-1	2-1	0-2	3-1
Leyton	0-1	0-4	2-2	0-3	2-4	0-1	4-3	0-3	1-11	0-3	0-3	0-0	0-1	1-3	1-2	*S*	1-4	4-0	0-2	0-3	2-2	2-5
Maidstone United	2-2	2-1	0-1	2-3	1-2	2-1	0-2	1-2	3-2	1-1	2-1	1-1	2-0	3-1	1-2	2-0	*I*	1-0	1-4	1-2	0-2	0-2
Margate	3-3	3-1	1-1	1-3	3-4	2-1	2-0	5-4	0-2	1-2	2-1	1-1	4-5	4-1	1-1	4-2	1-2	*O*	1-0	2-1	1-1	1-1
Ramsgate	2-2	1-1	0-1	1-0	4-0	3-2	3-2	2-1	2-1	4-1	1-3	0-0	2-1	4-0	2-0	0-2	5-0	2-1	*N*	3-1	1-1	1-1
Staines Town	0-1	1-1	2-0	1-1	4-2	5-1	4-0	2-0	0-2	2-2	5-1	3-0	2-0	1-1	2-2	4-0	3-2	1-2	2-0		2-5	1-1
Tonbridge Angels	2-1	2-2	2-0	3-2	2-1	3-0	1-5	3-0	4-0	1-0	3-0	1-2	1-2	0-0	0-1	2-1	2-2	2-2	3-0	2-2		1-1
Wealdstone	1-3	1-2	1-2	2-4	2-1	2-0	1-1	2-2	3-2	3-3	1-1	2-1	3-1	1-0	1-2	2-5	3-0	2-2	1-3	1-2	2-0	

WWW.CHERRYRED.CO.UK

Premier Division

		P	HOME					AWAY					TOTAL					Pts
			W	D	L	F	A	W	D	L	F	A	W	D	L	F	A	
Chelmsford City		42	15	5	1	53	16	11	4	6	31	23	26	9	7	84	39	87
Staines Town		42	12	6	3	50	23	10	6	5	35	31	22	12	8	85	54	78
AFC Wimbledon		42	12	3	6	40	21	10	6	5	41	26	22	9	11	81	47	75
AFC Hornchurch		42	13	2	6	38	20	7	8	6	30	24	20	10	12	68	44	70
Ramsgate		42	13	5	3	43	21	6	6	9	24	32	19	11	12	67	53	68
Ashford Town (Middx)		42	14	3	4	51	29	6	3	12	28	36	20	6	16	79	65	66
Hendon		42	9	4	8	32	28	9	3	9	47	39	18	11	13	79	67	65
Tonbridge Angels		42	11	6	4	40	24	6	6	9	37	33	17	12	13	77	57	63
Margate		42	11	5	5	46	35	6	6	9	25	33	17	11	14	71	68	62
Billericay Town		42	10	6	5	40	26	6	6	9	26	31	16	12	14	66	57	60
Horsham		42	12	1	8	37	26	6	4	11	26	37	18	5	19	63	63	59
Heybridge Swifts		42	10	5	6	38	27	4	7	10	26	37	14	13	15	64	64	55
Wealdstone		42	8	5	8	37	37	7	4	10	31	38	15	9	18	68	75	54
Hastings United		42	11	2	8	35	26	4	6	11	23	41	15	8	19	58	67	53
Harlow Town		42	6	8	7	31	28	7	5	9	25	24	13	13	16	56	52	52
Harrow Borough		42	11	0	10	38	37	4	7	10	23	37	15	7	20	61	74	52
Maidstone United		42	7	4	10	30	33	9	0	12	26	46	16	4	22	56	79	52
East Thurrock United	-1	42	9	3	9	24	29	5	6	10	24	38	14	9	19	48	67	51
Carshalton Athletic		42	7	7	7	21	21	7	1	13	31	44	14	8	20	52	65	50
Boreham Wood		42	9	4	8	30	27	6	1	14	26	46	15	5	22	56	73	50
Folkestone Invicta		42	7	7	7	24	31	6	3	12	25	39	13	10	19	49	70	49
Leyton		42	2	3	16	20	60	2	1	18	15	63	4	4	34	35	123	16

PLAY-OFFS

SEMI-FINALS (April 29th)
AFC Wimbledon 3 AFC Hornchurch 1 *Att* 2,987
Staines Town 2 Ramsgate 1 *Att* 502

FINAL
(May 3rd at Staines Town)
Staines Town 1 **AFC Wimbledon** 2 *Att* 2,460

DATES & GATES

Each cell shows the fixture date (top) and the attendance (bottom). Rows are the home team; columns are the away team.

Home \ Away	AFC Hornchurch	AFC Wimbledon	Ashford Town (Middx)	Billericay Town	Boreham Wood	Carshalton Athletic	Chelmsford City	East Thurrock United	Folkestone Invicta	Harlow Town	Harrow Borough	Hastings United	Hendon	Heybridge Swifts	Horsham	Leyton	Maidstone United	Margate	Ramsgate	Staines Town	Tonbridge Angels	Wealdstone
AFC Hornchurch	—	22 Dec / 441	27 Oct / 349	15 Sep / 389	11 Aug / 322	17 Nov / 424	8 Dec / 471	26 Apr / 318	12 Apr / 355	29 Mar / 339	16 Feb / 331	6 Oct / 330	2 Feb / 385	1 Jan / 364	1 Sep / 264	18 Sep / 266	25 Aug / 806	23 Feb / 385	15 Mar / 335	12 Jan / 1,030	10 Nov / 302	24 Mar / 1,362
AFC Wimbledon	27 Aug / 2,254	—	3 Mar / 2,733	15 Apr / 2,723	1 Dec / 2,829	8 Mar / 2,227	14 Aug / 2,648	10 Nov / 2,508	18 Sep / 2,689	23 Feb / 2,406	29 Mar / 2,770	5 Jan / 2,711	12 Jan / 2,601	18 Aug / 2,942	7 Sep / 2,284	29 Dec / 2,875	5 Apr / 3,124	19 Jan / 2,903	3 Nov / 2,092	19 Jan / 2,429	17 Nov / 2,341	20 Oct / 2,575
Ashford Town (Middx)	23 Feb / 275	16 Feb / 2,733	—	19 Sep / 310	9 Feb / 165	22 Mar / 183	11 Aug / 235	3 Nov / 135	27 Nov / 216	1 Dec / 135	8 Jan / 182	18 Sep / 153	6 Oct / 184	26 Jan / 143	1 Mar / 291	27 Oct / 357	19 Jan / 210	15 Mar / 233	16 Feb / 157	9 Feb / 221	18 Aug / 705	29 Dec / 215
Billericay Town	22 Mar / 593	15 Apr / 2,723	19 Sep / 310	—	14 Aug / 165	12 Apr / 183	22 Sep / 403	22 Apr / 165	29 Mar / 366	19 Jan / 456	19 Apr / 532	8 Sep / 604	14 Aug / 492	26 Jan / 484	29 Jan / 298	9 Feb / 174	1 Sep / 450	22 Mar / 532	14 Aug / 500	18 Aug / 885	26 Dec / 705	29 Dec / 239
Boreham Wood	4 Mar / 231	1 Dec / 2,829	8 Mar / 159	14 Aug / 165	—	26 Dec / 268	23 Oct / 219	23 Feb / 135	10 Nov / 216	27 Aug / 456	26 Jan / 532	16 Feb / 383	14 Aug / 371	26 Jan / 484	27 Aug / 209	3 Nov / 318	26 Apr / 371	4 Mar / 353	3 Nov / 209	8 Mar / 717	26 Dec / 437	4 Feb / 375
Carshalton Athletic	16 Feb / 211	8 Mar / 2,227	2 Feb / 268	12 Apr / 183	26 Dec / 268	—	1 Jan / 173	12 Apr / 183	18 Sep / 159	27 Oct / 230	24 Jan / 103	27 Nov / 142	11 Mar / 266	1 Sep / 159	6 Oct / 208	26 Apr / 96	24 Mar / 252	16 Apr / 208	26 Apr / 289	6 Oct / 215	2 Feb / 352	17 Apr / 242
Chelmsford City	12 Apr / 1,446	14 Aug / 2,648	11 Aug / 219	22 Sep / 403	23 Oct / 219	1 Jan / 173	—	23 Feb / 135	27 Aug / 216	10 Nov / 456	6 Dec / 235	14 Aug / 604	26 Jan / 492	6 Oct / 484	15 Mar / 298	11 Jan / 174	8 Dec / 351	15 Dec / 445	14 Apr / 235	23 Feb / 445	17 Nov / 352	12 Jan / 281
East Thurrock United	22 Sep / 134	10 Nov / 2,508	26 Jan / 135	22 Apr / 165	23 Feb / 135	27 Oct / 157	20 Oct / 147	—	1 Apr / 110	22 Sep / 157	1 Sep / 142	1 Mar / 105	8 Aug / 161	1 Dec / 134	29 Dec / 278	23 Oct / 173	20 Nov / 61	19 Jan / 201	6 Oct / 467	19 Jan / 186	22 Sep / 94	18 Sep / 201
Folkestone Invicta	29 Mar / 414	18 Sep / 2,689	19 Jan / 364	24 Jan / 326	12 Jan / 446	8 Mar / 326	2 Sep / 130	24 Oct / 140	—	2 Feb / 259	26 Apr / 177	11 Mar / 235	9 Feb / 251	11 Dec / 278	25 Feb / 298	3 Nov / 250	8 Sep / 219	23 Oct / 328	24 Jan / 465	8 Sep / 431	11 Aug / 407	18 Sep / 278
Harlow Town	8 Sep / 190	23 Feb / 2,406	19 Jan / 425	19 Jan / 425	10 Nov / 142	27 Oct / 270	27 Oct / 157	20 Oct / 157	1 Mar / 172	—	14 Dec / 202	12 Apr / 105	15 Dec / 159	1 Dec / 298	27 Nov / 199	23 Oct / 247	10 Nov / 245	2 Feb / 169	23 Oct / 169	27 Aug / 214	16 Oct / 218	19 Jan / 316
Harrow Borough	18 Aug / 540	29 Mar / 2,770	19 Jan / 323	19 Apr / 323	24 Mar / 326	24 Jan / 103	27 Oct / 270	22 Dec / 280	18 Aug / 146	14 Apr / 88	—	14 Apr / 235	1 Sep / 159	18 Sep / 170	17 Nov / 158	11 Aug / 134	17 Nov / 155	24 Mar / 166	29 Mar / 195	14 Aug / 166	5 Jan / 316	5 Jan / 387
Hastings United	1 Dec / 523	5 Jan / 2,711	5 Apr / 576	8 Sep / 595	12 Jan / 595	27 Oct / 142	18 Sep / 243	22 Mar / 157	1 Mar / 280	1 Sep / 88	1 Apr / 277	—	22 Mar / 282	9 Feb / 208	29 Dec / 208	22 Dec / 132	11 Aug / 210	22 Sep / 203	1 Jan / 174	8 Sep / 218	22 Apr / 155	18 Aug / 331
Hendon	14 Apr / 446	12 Jan / 2,601	19 Jan / 253	14 Aug / 253	14 Aug / 253	8 Mar / 326	26 Jan / 253	22 Dec / 147	15 Mar / 146	6 Apr / 235	12 Apr / 235	12 Apr / 235	—	1 Dec / 278	4 Mar / 212	22 Sep / 282	10 Nov / 153	14 Aug / 266	8 Mar / 307	5 Apr / 247	9 Feb / 118	18 Sep / 170
Heybridge Swifts	14 Aug / 252	18 Aug / 2,942	26 Jan / 143	26 Jan / 425	26 Jan / 484	1 Sep / 159	6 Oct / 110	1 Dec / 157	11 Dec / 177	1 Dec / 463	8 Dec / 235	18 Sep / 118	26 Jan / 492	—	17 Nov / 199	8 Sep / 91	14 Dec / 245	1 Dec / 203	24 Mar / 465	18 Aug / 164	1 Dec / 540	14 Aug / 162
Horsham	26 Apr / 414	7 Sep / 2,284	1 Mar / 291	12 Jan / 220	27 Aug / 209	6 Oct / 208	15 Apr / 177	22 Sep / 157	2 Feb / 239	27 Aug / 143	3 Nov / 250	17 Nov / 208	22 Sep / 212	1 Mar / 186	—	22 Sep / 186	9 Feb / 122	1 Mar / 427	9 Feb / 134	9 Feb / 301	26 Jan / 736	26 Dec / 316
Leyton	8 Jan / 84	29 Mar / 2,875	27 Oct / 155	22 Sep / 96	22 Sep / 96	2 Sep / 154	22 Sep / 157	15 Jan / 78	15 Sep / 219	16 Feb / 195	11 Feb / 54	8 Mar / 96	5 Jan / 351	1 Dec / 94	18 Sep / 201	—	20 Nov / 404	9 Feb / 194	9 Feb / 218	1 Mar / 116	1 Mar / 675	1 Mar / 271
Maidstone United	1 Dec / 436	21 Apr / 3,124	29 Dec / 63	29 Dec / 96	22 Apr / 499	6 Oct / 490	24 Oct / 140	24 Oct / 408	2 Feb / 177	26 Apr / 417	26 Apr / 250	8 Mar / 526	19 Apr / 411	18 Sep / 505	23 Jan / 201	6 Oct / 467	—	22 Sep / 62	9 Feb / 155	9 Feb / 166	25 Aug / 473	1 Mar / 238
Margate	27 Oct / 310	12 Apr / 2,903	22 Mar / 371	22 Mar / 181	27 Apr / 384	27 Apr / 384	18 Sep / 358	22 Mar / 268	25 Mar / 222	1 Sep / 284	26 Apr / 318	16 Feb / 317	26 Dec / 432	14 Aug / 426	23 Feb / 417	19 Apr / 252	19 Sep / 194	—	3 Oct / 174	22 Sep / 247	24 Apr / 165	8 Mar / 238
Ramsgate	6 Oct / 285	27 Aug / 304	22 Mar / 198	22 Mar / 198	26 Jan / 383	27 Apr / 181	16 Feb / 279	14 Dec / 187	27 Apr / 272	1 Jan / 209	26 Apr / 208	16 Feb / 208	26 Dec / 289	6 Oct / 215	8 Mar / 717	1 Jan / 252	19 Aug / 496	22 Sep / 231	—	26 Jan / 203	12 Jan / 149	18 Aug / 211
Staines Town	5 Jan / 297	22 Mar / 191	22 Mar / 191	14 Aug / 383	14 Aug / 279	17 Nov / 198	22 Dec / 187	14 Aug / 279	4 Mar / 353	3 Nov / 318	3 Nov / 317	9 Feb / 317	5 Apr / 432	25 Aug / 289	26 Apr / 426	6 Oct / 174	27 Oct / 357	16 Feb / 328	1 Jan / 308	—	16 Feb / 500	9 Feb / 221
Tonbridge Angels	15 Mar / 506	29 Dec / 482	30 Oct / 565	22 Mar / 565	27 Feb / 926	17 Nov / 410	26 Jan / 685	12 Jan / 281	20 Oct / 389	1 Mar / 636	26 Dec / 437	22 Sep / 352	3 Apr / 432	25 Aug / 426	2 Feb / 855	3 Nov / 455	19 Apr / 393	22 Sep / 294	3 Oct / 287	22 Apr / 281	—	21 Apr / 233
Wealdstone	9 Feb / 293	11 Aug / 225	25 Aug / 230	1 Mar / 265	26 Dec / 239	17 Apr / 242	17 Nov / 244	12 Jan / 205	17 Sep / 308	8 Mar / 245	4 Feb / 375	22 Oct / 215	7 Apr / 250	24 Mar / 194	3 Nov / 410	19 Apr / 268	1 Sep / 268	15 Dec / 230	20 Oct / 259	29 Dec / 874	15 Dec / 752	—

RYMAN ISTHMIAN LEAGUE
PREMIER DIVISION CONSTITUTION 2008-09

AFC HORNCHURCH
The Stadium, Bridge Avenue, Upminster, Essex RM14 2LX
Tel: 01708 220080   Fax: 01708 227931
Manager: Colin McBride   www.hornchurchfc.com   Colours: Red, white & black

ASHFORD TOWN (MIDDX)
Short Lane Stadium, Short Lane, Stanwell, Staines, Middlesex TW19 7BH
Tel: 01784 245908   www.ashfordtownmiddlesexfc.co.uk
Manager: Mark Butler   Colours: Tangerine, white & black

BILLERICAY TOWN
New Lodge, Blunts Wall Road, Billericay, Essex CM12 9SA
Tel: 01277 652188   www.billericaytownfc.net   Fax: 01277 655177
Managers: Jason Broom / Grant Gordon   Colours: Blue & white

BOREHAM WOOD
Meadow Park, Broughinge Road, Boreham Wood, Hertfordshire WD6 5AL
Tel: 020 8953 5097   Club: 020 8207 7982   Fax: 020 8207 7982
Manager: Ian Allinson   Colours: White & black
www.web-teams.co.uk/Home.asp?team=borehamwoodfc

CANVEY ISLAND
Park Lane, Canvey Island, Essex SS8 7PX
Tel: 01268 682991   Fax: 01268 698586
Manager: John Batch   www.canveyislandfc.com   Colours: Yellow, blue & white

CARSHALTON ATHLETIC
War Memorial Sports Ground, Colston Avenue, Carshalton, Surrey SM5 2PW
Tel: 020 8642 8658   Fax: 020 8643 0999
Manager: Hayden Bird   www.carshaltonathletic.org   Colours: White & maroon

DARTFORD
Princes Park, Grassbanks, Darenth Road, Dartford, Kent DA1 1RT
Tel: 01322 299990   Fax: 01322 299996
Manager: Tony Burman   www.dartfordfc.co.uk   Colours: White & black

DOVER ATHLETIC
Crabble Athletic Ground, Lewisham Road, River, Dover, Kent CT17 0JB
Tel: 01304 822373   Fax: 01304 821383
Manager: Andy Hessenthaler   www.dover-athletic.co.uk   Colours: White & Black

HARLOW TOWN
Barrows Farm Stadium, Elizabeth Way, The Pinnacles, Harlow, Essex CM19 5BL
Tel: 01279 445319
Manager: Ryan Kirby   Colours: Red & white

HARROW BOROUGH
Earlsmead Stadium, Carlyon Avenue, South Harrow, Middlesex HA2 8SS
Tel: 0844 561 1347   Fax: 020 8423 0159
Manager: David Howell   www.harrowboro.com   Colours: Red

HASTINGS UNITED
The Pilot Field, Elphinstone Road, Hastings, East Sussex TN34 2AX
Tel: 01424 444635   Club: 01424 430517   Fax: 01424 729068
Manager: Tony Dolby   www.hastingsunitedfc.co.uk   Colours: Claret & blue

HENDON
Claremont Road, Brent Cross, London NW2 1AE
Tel: 020 8201 9494   Club: 020 8455 9185   Fax: 020 8905 5966
Manager: Gary McCann   www.hendonfc.net   Colours: White & green

HEYBRIDGE SWIFTS
Scraley Road, Heybridge, Maldon, Essex CM9 8JA
Tel: 01621 852978   Club: 01621 852978
Manager: Brian Statham   www.heybridgeswifts.com   Colours: Black & white

HORSHAM
Worthing FC, Woodside Road, Worthing, West Sussex BN14 7HQ
Tel: 01903 239575   Fax: 01903 23957
Manager: John Maggs   www.hornetsreview.co.uk   Colours: Amber & green

MAIDSTONE UNITED
Sittingbourne FC, Bourne Park, Eurolink Industrial Estate, Church Road, Sittingbourne, Kent ME10 3SB
Tel: 01795 435077   www.maidstoneunited.co.uk
Managers: Lloyd Hume / Alan Walker   Colours: Amber & black

MARGATE
Hartsdown Park, Hartsdown Road, Margate, Kent CT9 5QZ
Tel: 01843 221769   Club: 07972 321789   Fax: 01843 221769
Manager: Brian Ashby   www.margate-fc.com   Colours: Royal blue & white

RAMSGATE
Southwood Stadium, Prices Avenue, Ramsgate, Kent CT11 0AN
Tel: 01843 591662
Manager: Jim Ward   www.ramsgate-fc.co.uk   Colours: Red

STAINES TOWN
Wheatsheaf Park, Wheatsheaf Lane, Staines, Middlesex TW18 2PD
Tel: 07825 067232
Manager: Steve Cordery   www.stainesmassive.co.uk   Colours: Old gold & blue

SUTTON UNITED
The Borough Sports Ground, Gander Green Lane, Sutton, Surrey SM1 2EY
Tel: 020 8644 4440   Fax: 020 8644 5120
Manager: Paul Doswell   www.suttonunited.net   Colours: Chocolate & amber

TONBRIDGE ANGELS
The Betterview Longmead Stadium, Darenth Avenue, Tonbridge, Kent TN10 3JW
Tel: 01732 352477   Club: 01732 352417
Manager: Tommy Warrilow   www.tonbridgeangels.co.uk   Colours: Black & white

TOOTING & MITCHAM UNITED
Imperial Fields, Bishopsford Road, Morden, Surrey SM4 6BF
Tel: 020 8648 3248   Boardroom: 020 8685 9229
Manager: Billy Smith   wwwtmufc.co.uk   Colours: White & black

WEALDSTONE
The Manor, Ruislip Manor Sports & Social, Grosvenor Vale, Ruislip, Middlesex HA4 6JQ
Tel: 01895 637487
Manager: Gordon Bartlett   www.come-to-wealdstonefc.co.uk   Colours: Blue & white

IN: Canvey Island (P – Isthmian League Division One North), Dartford (P – Isthmian League Division One North), Dover Athletic (P – Isthmian League Division One South), Sutton United (R – Football Conference South), Tooting & Mitcham United (P – Isthmian League Division One South)
OUT: AFC Wimbledon (P – Football Conference South), Chelmsford City (P – Football Conference South), East Thurrock United (R – Isthmian League Division One North), Folkestone Invicta (R – Isthmian League Division One South), Leyton (R – Isthmian League Division One North)

	AFC Sudbury	Arlesey Town	Aveley	Brentwood Town	Bury Town	Canvey Island	Dartford	Edgware Town	Enfield Town	Great Wakering Rovers	Ilford	Maldon Town	Northwood	Potters Bar Town	Redbridge	Tilbury	Waltham Abbey	Waltham Forest	Ware	Wingate & Finchley	Witham Town	Wivenhoe Town
AFC Sudbury		2-2	3-0	1-0	0-2	2-2	1-0	1-2	1-1	8-1	5-1	1-3	0-1	3-0	3-0	5-0	1-0	1-1	3-0	5-1	3-0	6-0
Arlesey Town	0-2		0-3	1-3	4-1	1-4	0-4	4-1	0-1	4-4	2-1	3-1	1-0	6-0	0-1	2-4	3-2	2-2	1-3	0-2	4-2	2-1
Aveley	3-1	0-0	D	0-6	4-1	1-6	2-2	0-3	3-1	1-0	2-1	0-0	0-0	2-0	3-0	4-0	2-0	1-0	1-1	1-1	1-2	2-0
Brentwood Town	2-2	2-0	1-1	I	1-1	0-2	2-2	2-0	1-1	0-2	4-1	2-1	4-1	0-1	2-0	3-1	4-0	4-0	2-1	0-0	0-4	2-1
Bury Town	3-1	4-1	4-1	2-3	V	1-0	1-1	0-0	3-0	3-0	2-2	1-1	3-0	3-0	0-2	2-1	1-0	3-0	5-1	0-3	1-0	1-0
Canvey Island	0-1	2-2	3-0	0-1	1-2	I	0-1	1-1	2-0	1-0	4-0	1-0	1-1	3-0	1-1	5-0	1-2	2-1	4-4	3-0	1-1	1-0
Dartford	1-0	1-0	4-0	0-1	1-2	6-1	S	0-0	6-1	3-0	5-0	2-2	4-2	4-0	2-0	5-0	2-3	1-0	2-1	1-0	7-2	4-2
Edgware Town	1-0	1-0	3-2	1-1	2-2	3-0	2-1	I	1-1	5-0	1-0	1-0	1-0	1-1	1-1	2-0	0-0	0-0	2-1	2-0	2-0	3-1
Enfield Town	0-1	2-2	3-1	0-0	2-2	0-2	0-3	0-1	O	1-0	2-0	1-0	2-2	1-1	1-4	1-2	1-2	0-3	0-0	0-1	1-0	2-0
Great Wakering Rovers	2-3	6-2	2-2	1-1	1-2	2-2	0-2	1-1	1-2	N	1-2	1-2	2-3	0-0	3-0	2-0	1-2	2-3	1-4	3-0	5-0	1-2
Ilford	0-1	2-3	1-1	0-1	0-1	1-3	0-1	4-1	0-2	1-4		0-3	2-2	2-1	0-1	1-2	2-1	2-4	1-1	3-1	5-2	1-0
Maldon Town	1-0	2-1	3-2	3-1	2-1	0-3	2-2	0-0	2-2	2-2	3-0	O	1-1	2-1	1-2	2-0	3-0	2-1	2-3	6-2	2-3	4-2
Northwood	0-1	3-3	0-2	5-0	4-3	0-2	3-2	0-0	1-3	1-0	3-1	2-1	N	1-1	2-1	2-2	1-1	6-0	2-1	1-0	2-0	2-0
Potters Bar Town	2-4	0-1	4-2	0-2	0-2	0-3	2-2	1-2	2-3	0-1	1-1	1-2	1-2	E	0-2	4-3	1-2	3-0	2-2	1-0	2-2	2-2
Redbridge	1-0	1-1	1-1	1-1	2-0	0-0	2-1	5-0	2-3	4-0	3-1	1-0	1-0	3-0		2-0	0-0	1-0	1-0	2-1	2-0	1-0
Tilbury	1-1	3-3	0-2	2-2	2-2	3-2	1-2	0-0	2-3	0-2	1-1	1-1	0-2	3-0	1-1	N	3-4	1-0	2-5	2-1	1-2	0-0
Waltham Abbey	0-2	2-0	0-3	1-2	0-2	0-0	0-5	1-0	2-8	0-0	0-0	2-0	2-2	1-2	0-3	2-0	O	1-1	0-5	1-1	1-0	2-0
Waltham Forest	0-3	2-1	0-0	3-4	0-2	0-0	2-4	1-1	0-0	0-1	0-1	3-5	1-1	0-0	0-1	1-1	1-1	R	0-2	1-1	5-1	1-3
Ware	1-2	4-0	2-3	2-0	3-0	4-0	5-2	1-1	3-1	5-2	4-2	4-1	2-3	1-1	7-0	2-0	4-2	2-0	T	3-1	4-1	1-0
Wingate & Finchley	2-2	2-0	1-3	0-1	1-1	2-3	0-2	0-1	3-0	0-1	3-2	1-5	0-1	0-0	3-4	3-2	1-1	0-0	2-2	H	3-2	0-2
Witham Town	2-3	0-2	3-3	0-2	4-1	1-5	0-4	1-2	2-4	2-4	5-2	1-1	5-3	2-3	3-4	1-0	2-1	4-1	1-3	4-2		2-1
Wivenhoe Town	1-1	1-0	2-2	2-0	1-3	0-2	0-3	0-2	2-0	1-2	0-0	1-2	0-3	1-2	2-6	6-1	2-2	0-3	1-5	1-1	4-3	

Division One North

		P	W	D	L	F	A	W	D	L	F	A	W	D	L	F	A	Pts
			HOME					AWAY					TOTAL					
Dartford		42	16	2	3	61	17	11	6	4	46	25	27	8	7	107	42	89
Redbridge	-1	42	13	5	5	35	14	11	4	6	35	29	24	9	9	70	43	81
AFC Sudbury		42	13	4	4	55	17	11	4	6	31	23	24	8	10	86	40	80
Ware		42	15	2	4	65	27	8	8	5	45	31	23	10	9	110	58	79
Canvey Island		42	10	6	5	37	18	13	4	4	45	21	23	10	9	82	39	79
Brentwood Town		42	11	6	4	38	22	11	5	5	32	27	22	11	9	70	49	77
Bury Town		42	14	4	3	43	17	8	5	8	33	36	22	9	11	76	53	75
Edgware Town		42	14	6	1	35	12	6	8	7	18	27	20	14	8	53	39	74
Maldon Town		42	12	5	4	45	29	7	5	9	33	34	19	10	13	78	63	67
Northwood		42	12	5	4	41	25	6	7	8	30	36	18	12	12	71	61	66
Aveley		42	11	6	4	33	25	7	6	8	35	40	18	12	12	68	65	66
Enfield Town		42	6	6	9	20	27	12	3	6	40	36	18	9	15	60	63	63
Great Wakering Rovers		42	5	5	11	38	35	8	4	9	26	31	13	9	20	64	66	48
Waltham Abbey		42	6	6	9	18	36	6	4	11	24	42	12	10	20	42	78	46
Arlesey Town		42	9	2	10	40	42	3	7	11	24	42	12	9	21	64	84	45
Witham Town		42	8	2	11	45	51	4	3	14	30	58	12	5	25	75	109	41
Potters Bar Town		42	4	5	12	29	40	6	4	11	16	37	10	9	23	45	77	39
Wingate & Finchley		42	5	6	10	27	35	3	5	13	18	37	8	11	23	45	72	35
Waltham Forest		42	3	7	11	23	35	4	5	12	21	39	7	12	23	44	74	33
Tilbury		42	4	9	8	29	36	3	3	15	20	60	7	12	23	49	96	33
Ilford		42	6	3	12	28	36	2	5	14	19	59	8	8	26	47	95	32
Wivenhoe Town		42	5	5	11	28	43	3	2	16	18	43	8	7	27	46	86	31

www.CHERRYRED.CO.UK

PLAY-OFFS

SEMI-FINALS *(April 29th)*
AFC Sudbury 2 **Canvey Island** 3 *aet Att* 437
Redbridge 4 Ware 2 *Att* 261

FINAL
(May 3rd at Redbridge)
Redbridge 1 **Canvey Island** 1 *aet* (4-5p) *Att* 905

DATES & GATES

WWW.NLNEWSDESK.CO.UK

Each cell shows the fixture date (top) and the attendance / gate (bottom, italic). Rows are the home team; columns are the away team.

Home \ Away	AFC Sudbury	Arlesey Town	Aveley	Brentwood Town	Bury Town	Canvey Island	Dartford	Edgware Town	Enfield Town	Gt Wakering Rovers	Ilford	Maldon Town	Northwood	Potters Bar Town	Redbridge	Tilbury	Waltham Abbey	Waltham Forest	Ware	Wingate & Finchley	Witham Town	Wivenhoe Town
AFC Sudbury	—	29 Sep / 277	18 Sep / 279	1 Mar / 273	26 Dec / 441	8 Apr / 253	9 Feb / 738	12 Apr / 295	15 Apr / 233	12 Jan / 309	8 Sep / 261	15 Dec / 281	10 Nov / 257	26 Apr / 333	15 Sep / 255	26 Jan / 286	16 Feb / 238	29 Mar / 270	1 Dec / 254	27 Oct / 234	4 Dec / 210	27 Aug / 312
Arlesey Town	5 Jan / 156	—	22 Sep / 78	9 Feb / 106	27 Apr / 163	24 Apr / 182	29 Mar / 1,159	27 Aug / 73	24 Nov / 209	27 Aug / 114	10 Nov / 59	29 Sep / 88	17 Nov / 121	1 Dec / 42	8 Sep / 87	15 Dec / 71	8 Sep / 67	26 Dec / 70	24 Mar / 230	16 Oct / 65	8 Jan / 80	5 Apr / 143
Aveley	22 Dec / 101	22 Sep / 78	—	3 Nov / 108	26 Apr / 183	11 Mar / 176	29 Mar / 824	5 Apr / 105	27 Aug / 234	22 Sep / 92	29 Nov / 57	10 Nov / 135	22 Mar / 82	26 Dec / 121	1 Mar / 72	1 Dec / 82	26 Jan / 84	8 Dec / 75	8 Feb / 135	16 Feb / 99	5 Jan / 75	19 Apr / 143
Brentwood Town	27 Nov / 128	1 Mar / 85	27 Apr / 163	—	4 Mar / 119	29 Mar / 176	24 Nov / 270	5 Apr / 86	18 Sep / 215	22 Sep / 136	10 Nov / 61	18 Mar / 135	22 Mar / 107	21 Apr / 198	1 Mar / 72	1 Dec / 121	26 Jan / 172	8 Dec / 75	8 Feb / 184	16 Oct / 99	15 Dec / 135	5 Jan / 99
Bury Town	25 Mar / 508	22 Dec / 130	3 Nov / 108	4 Mar / 119	—	11 Mar / 824	24 Nov / 320	8 Mar / 90	5 Jan / 215	26 Jan / 101	9 Feb / 95	18 Mar / 224	8 Mar / 138	26 Apr / 183	1 Mar / 212	24 Apr / 102	24 Nov / 120	26 Dec / 85	17 Nov / 108	18 Nov / 106	15 Mar / 165	8 Feb / 184
Canvey Island	8 Mar / 456	26 Jan / 203	11 Mar / 278	29 Mar / 176	19 Jan / 1,291	—	26 Dec / —	26 Feb / 212	26 Apr / 174	29 Sep / 152	29 Jan / 72	18 Sep / 263	27 Aug / 198	26 Jan / 172	27 Aug / 232	30 Oct / 221	19 Apr / 312	1 Apr / 294	1 Dec / 244	8 Apr / 273	15 Dec / 292	15 Apr / 124
Dartford	22 Sep / 926	26 Jan / 278	19 Apr / 969	24 Nov / 270	24 Nov / 824	26 Dec / 1,291	—	19 Apr / 819	24 Mar / 511	19 Jan / 305	15 Mar / 516	24 Dec / 203	22 Sep / 244	20 Nov / 112	23 Feb / 378	30 Oct / 232	21 Aug / 378	30 Oct / 221	29 Mar / 303	16 Feb / 231	27 Mar / 280	15 Aug / 216
Edgware Town	6 Oct / 148	5 Apr / 73	24 Nov / 85	5 Apr / 86	8 Mar / 90	26 Feb / 212	19 Apr / 819	—	5 Jan / 272	16 Oct / 137	13 Nov / 195	5 Apr / 205	18 Sep / 139	17 Nov / 66	27 Aug / 84	18 Aug / 198	27 Aug / 141	9 Feb / 84	29 Mar / 85	15 Dec / 124	27 Mar / 85	8 Sep / 106
Enfield Town	25 Aug / 303	30 Oct / 209	27 Aug / 225	18 Sep / 225	5 Jan / 215	26 Apr / 174	24 Mar / 511	5 Jan / 272	—	13 Nov / 253	19 Jan / 195	22 Mar / 109	26 Jan / 151	8 Jan / 138	17 Nov / 114	18 Aug / 84	1 Mar / 335	3 Nov / 151	18 Apr / 211	24 Mar / 267	20 Oct / 150	30 Mar / 150
Gt Wakering Rovers	25 Sep / 132	19 Apr / 85	22 Sep / 92	22 Sep / 114	26 Jan / 136	29 Sep / 137	13 Nov / 253	16 Oct / 137	13 Nov / 253	—	10 Nov / 57	22 Sep / 136	5 Apr / 137	8 Sep / 64	22 Dec / 84	29 Sep / 74	24 Apr / 63	22 Jan / 62	17 Nov / 60	17 Nov / 86	17 Nov / 60	26 Dec / 113
Ilford	2 Feb / 88	10 Nov / 59	29 Nov / 57	10 Nov / 61	9 Feb / 95	13 Nov / 195	15 Mar / 516	13 Nov / 195	1 Dec / 255	10 Nov / 57	—	2 Apr / 74	10 Nov / 56	18 Aug / 151	26 Jan / 41	27 Nov / 61	18 Dec / 51	16 Oct / 56	4 Mar / 56	8 Sep / 58	23 Feb / 63	16 Oct / 110
Maldon Town	21 Aug / 189	25 Aug / 84	10 Nov / 135	18 Mar / 135	8 Jan / 224	18 Sep / 203	24 Dec / 203	5 Apr / 205	19 Jan / 109	26 Jan / 136	27 Oct / 74	—	8 Jan / 182	20 Nov / 138	26 Jan / 94	8 Mar / 85	26 Apr / 61	8 Sep / 61	12 Apr / 65	16 Jan / 72	29 Jan / 92	26 Dec / 110
Northwood	23 Feb / 139	12 Jan / 121	17 Nov / 82	22 Mar / 107	8 Mar / 138	27 Aug / 152	22 Sep / 244	18 Sep / 139	26 Jan / 102	5 Apr / 137	10 Nov / 56	8 Jan / 182	—	25 Sep / 112	8 Jan / 61	5 Jan / 105	13 Oct / 85	24 Mar / 51	27 Aug / 57	16 Oct / 58	18 Aug / 92	1 Mar / 91
Potters Bar Town	3 Nov / 110	16 Feb / 42	26 Dec / 121	21 Apr / 198	26 Apr / 183	26 Jan / 172	20 Nov / 112	17 Nov / 66	8 Jan / 138	8 Sep / 64	18 Aug / 151	20 Nov / 138	25 Sep / 112	—	30 Oct / 47	29 Mar / 56	3 Nov / 90	10 Nov / 49	27 Aug / 81	8 Jan / 64	8 Dec / 49	17 Nov / 66
Redbridge	19 Apr / 145	8 Sep / 87	1 Mar / 72	1 Mar / 72	1 Mar / 212	27 Aug / 232	23 Feb / 378	27 Aug / 84	17 Nov / 114	22 Dec / 84	26 Jan / 41	26 Jan / 94	8 Jan / 61	30 Oct / 47	—	19 Jan / 62	8 Apr / 92	8 Mar / 61	16 Jan / 85	27 Oct / 41	29 Mar / 60	29 Mar / 110
Tilbury	13 Oct / 115	3 Nov / 52	1 Dec / 82	1 Dec / 121	24 Apr / 102	30 Oct / 221	30 Oct / 232	18 Aug / 198	18 Aug / 84	29 Sep / 74	27 Nov / 61	8 Mar / 85	5 Jan / 105	29 Mar / 56	19 Jan / 62	—	29 Dec / 59	15 Dec / 53	4 Mar / 72	27 Nov / 56	29 Sep / 50	27 Nov / 56
Waltham Abbey	17 Nov / 115	1 Feb / 67	8 Sep / 84	26 Jan / 172	24 Nov / 120	19 Apr / 312	21 Aug / 378	27 Aug / 141	1 Mar / 335	24 Apr / 63	18 Dec / 51	26 Apr / 61	13 Oct / 85	3 Nov / 90	8 Apr / 92	29 Dec / 59	—	5 Jan / 49	24 Nov / 90	18 Jan / 65	19 Mar / 55	16 Feb / 81
Waltham Forest	8 Dec / 156	3 Nov / 52	8 Dec / 75	8 Dec / 75	26 Dec / 85	1 Apr / 294	30 Oct / 221	9 Feb / 84	3 Nov / 151	22 Jan / 62	16 Oct / 56	8 Sep / 61	24 Mar / 51	10 Nov / 49	8 Mar / 61	15 Dec / 53	5 Jan / 49	—	27 Apr / 102	24 Nov / 71	8 Apr / 71	29 Mar / 94
Ware	15 Mar / 92	24 Mar / 230	8 Feb / 135	8 Feb / 184	17 Nov / 108	1 Dec / 244	29 Mar / 303	29 Mar / 85	18 Apr / 211	17 Nov / 60	4 Mar / 56	12 Apr / 65	27 Aug / 57	27 Aug / 81	16 Jan / 85	4 Mar / 72	24 Nov / 90	27 Apr / 102	—	9 Feb / 82	23 Feb / 92	16 Oct / 101
Wingate & Finchley	5 Apr / 90	8 Jan / 65	16 Feb / 99	16 Oct / 99	18 Nov / 106	8 Apr / 273	16 Feb / 231	15 Dec / 124	24 Mar / 267	17 Nov / 86	8 Sep / 58	16 Jan / 72	16 Oct / 58	8 Jan / 64	27 Oct / 41	27 Nov / 56	18 Jan / 65	24 Nov / 72	9 Feb / 83	—	8 Apr / 59	29 Sep / 175
Witham Town	26 Feb / 215	5 Apr / 80	27 Mar / 75	15 Dec / 135	15 Mar / 165	15 Dec / 292	27 Mar / 504	27 Mar / 85	20 Oct / 150	17 Nov / 85	23 Feb / 63	29 Jan / 92	18 Aug / 76	8 Dec / 92	29 Mar / 71	29 Sep / 71	19 Mar / 85	8 Apr / 71	23 Feb / 98	8 Apr / 92	—	24 Mar / 160
Wivenhoe Town	29 Dec / 264	5 Apr / 143	19 Apr / 143	5 Jan / 99	8 Feb / 184	15 Apr / 124	21 Aug / 216	8 Sep / 106	30 Mar / 150	17 Nov / 113	8 Mar / 110	26 Dec / 110	1 Mar / 108	20 Nov / 66	26 Dec / 102	19 Feb / 104	22 Feb / 85	3 Nov / 70	19 Jan / 153	13 Oct / 53	26 Dec / 101	—

	Ashford Town	Burgess Hill Town	Chatham Town	Chipstead	Corinthian Casuals	Cray Wanderers	Croydon Athletic	Dover Athletic	Dulwich Hamlet	Eastbourne Town	Horsham YMCA	Kingstonian	Leatherhead	Metropolitan Police	Molesey	Sittingbourne	Tooting & Mitcham United	Walton & Hersham	Walton Casuals	Whitstable Town	Whyteleafe	Worthing
Ashford Town		0-4	1-2	3-1	2-1	1-3	1-2	1-1	3-0	1-0	1-0	0-2	1-1	3-0	2-0	1-2	3-0	0-2	1-2	4-0	0-0	1-1
Burgess Hill Town	2-1		2-0	3-2	3-1	1-1	0-3	0-1	5-0	1-0	4-4	0-1	1-0	1-0	0-1	0-1	2-1	0-1	3-1	3-2	2-3	2-3
Chatham Town	2-1	0-2	D	1-2	1-0	0-1	2-2	1-3	3-2	2-0	0-0	3-1	3-2	1-2	1-4	3-1	0-0	0-1	0-0	1-2	2-3	0-1
Chipstead	1-2	3-1	3-1	I	1-2	1-3	0-1	0-1	5-0	1-3	2-1	2-2	3-1	2-3	1-0	1-3	3-3	0-2	2-2	1-4	2-3	2-1
Corinthian Casuals	1-2	0-3	3-3	1-1	V	3-0	2-5	3-1	2-1	1-1	4-1	0-1	1-0	1-2	1-4	0-2	2-2	0-5	1-0	0-0	1-2	0-2
Cray Wanderers	0-0	1-0	3-1	4-1	3-2	I	2-3	4-1	2-0	1-0	2-0	1-1	5-0	2-2	2-1	1-1	1-1	2-1	1-0	4-1	3-0	2-5
Croydon Athletic	2-2	2-0	1-2	0-0	2-1	3-1	S	0-1	1-3	2-1	1-1	1-2	1-2	0-1	1-2	1-3	2-1	3-1	3-0	6-2	1-1	2-1
Dover Athletic	3-0	3-0	1-1	2-0	2-0	3-1	0-2	I	2-0	5-2	1-0	3-0	1-0	0-0	2-2	3-0	3-2	3-0	2-1	0-1	1-0	1-1
Dulwich Hamlet	0-2	1-2	2-3	1-1	2-1	4-1	6-1	2-1	O	1-2	2-0	5-2	1-0	3-3	0-1	1-0	1-0	1-1	0-0	1-1	1-1	1-0
Eastbourne Town	2-2	0-1	3-2	1-0	0-0	1-3	2-1	3-3	2-5	N	0-1	0-0	1-2	1-1	0-4	2-3	1-2	3-2	2-4	3-3	2-2	4-1
Horsham YMCA	1-2	1-1	0-1	0-1	2-1	0-2	0-5	1-0	1-3	0-2		2-3	2-1	1-2	1-5	0-3	0-4	1-2	1-2	3-3	0-2	1-2
Kingstonian	3-2	1-0	3-0	3-1	2-2	0-3	5-1	1-0	1-0	1-0	2-0	O	1-2	3-0	2-2	1-0	1-1	2-1	4-0	0-1	2-3	1-2
Leatherhead	0-1	1-0	2-0	1-2	1-1	0-4	3-0	1-2	1-0	0-0	2-1	4-1	N	1-2	0-1	2-3	2-1	0-1	0-1	2-1	0-1	1-3
Metropolitan Police	0-2	2-0	2-1	2-1	2-1	2-1	2-1	2-0	2-3	2-1	2-0	3-1	0-2	E	0-1	3-2	0-1	4-0	2-0	1-0	2-1	1-1
Molesey	1-3	0-1	3-1	2-3	1-1	1-1	0-1	1-5	2-3	2-2	2-2	1-1	0-3	1-4		0-3	1-5	1-3	0-1	1-6	0-1	1-1
Sittingbourne	1-1	3-2	2-3	3-2	1-0	2-2	2-1	0-2	2-1	1-0	0-2	0-0	0-2	1-2	1-2	S	1-1	1-1	2-0	2-1	2-1	1-1
Tooting & Mitcham United	0-0	3-1	3-1	4-0	0-1	0-1	1-0	0-0	3-2	3-1	3-0	4-1	0-1	0-1	5-0	2-0	O	2-0	4-1	1-0	2-2	1-1
Walton & Hersham	2-2	5-2	2-1	2-2	0-1	1-1	0-1	2-1	2-1	3-3	1-1	4-1	1-0	0-3	4-1	0-2	2-2	U	2-1	2-1	3-1	1-2
Walton Casuals	1-2	0-1	1-2	2-2	1-1	1-0	1-1	2-3	3-1	1-1	2-2	3-1	2-2	0-3	2-2	2-0	0-0	0-0	T	4-3	1-0	2-1
Whitstable Town	3-1	2-3	2-3	2-1	0-4	0-2	1-1	0-3	2-1	2-3	2-0	2-2	2-2	4-2	1-1	4-2	1-2	3-0	2-1	H	1-1	2-2
Whyteleafe	0-2	4-2	2-2	1-4	0-2	2-0	5-0	1-0	2-2	3-2	3-0	3-1	1-0	0-1	2-0	3-4	0-2	1-2	0-0	0-0		0-1
Worthing	4-1	3-1	1-0	3-0	3-4	0-1	3-1	1-2	0-1	2-0	1-2	2-3	2-1	1-0	3-0	1-1	5-1	1-2	4-1	2-0	1-2	

Division One South

		P	HOME					AWAY					TOTAL					
			W	D	L	F	A	W	D	L	F	A	W	D	L	F	A	Pts
Dover Athletic		42	15	4	2	41	13	15	4	2	43	16	30	8	4	84	29	98
Tooting & Mitcham United		42	13	4	4	41	14	13	4	4	47	27	26	8	8	88	41	86
Cray Wanderers		42	14	5	2	47	21	11	6	4	40	21	25	11	6	87	42	86
Metropolitan Police		42	15	1	5	36	20	9	2	10	33	27	24	3	15	69	47	75
Worthing		42	12	1	8	43	24	10	6	5	34	25	22	7	13	77	49	73
Dulwich Hamlet		42	9	7	5	36	25	11	3	7	32	22	20	10	12	68	47	70
Kingstonian		42	13	3	5	39	21	7	7	7	27	31	20	10	12	66	52	70
Ashford Town		42	9	4	8	30	24	10	6	5	34	27	19	10	13	64	51	67
Sittingbourne		42	10	5	6	30	27	10	2	9	26	31	20	7	15	56	58	67
Burgess Hill Town	-8	42	11	2	8	35	27	7	6	8	26	30	18	8	16	61	57	62
Walton & Hersham		42	10	6	5	39	30	5	6	10	26	32	15	12	15	65	62	57
Whyteleafe		42	9	4	8	33	27	8	1	12	24	35	17	5	20	57	62	56
Croydon Athletic		42	9	4	8	35	28	5	5	11	30	48	14	9	19	65	76	51
Whitstable Town		42	7	6	8	36	38	7	2	12	33	46	14	8	20	69	84	50
Chipstead		42	7	3	11	36	39	8	2	11	22	37	15	5	22	58	76	50
Walton Casuals		42	6	10	5	31	30	5	5	11	24	38	11	15	16	55	68	48
Leatherhead		42	8	2	11	24	26	5	5	11	28	37	13	7	22	52	63	46
Chatham Town		42	7	4	10	26	30	5	6	10	32	40	12	10	20	58	70	46
Corinthian Casuals		42	6	5	10	27	38	5	6	10	24	39	11	11	20	51	77	44
Eastbourne Town		42	5	7	9	33	42	6	4	11	25	42	11	11	20	58	84	44
Horsham YMCA		42	3	2	16	18	47	4	4	13	18	38	7	6	29	36	85	27
Molesey		42	0	6	15	19	54	3	3	15	17	46	3	9	30	36	100	18

PLAY-OFFS

SEMI-FINALS
(April 29th) **Tooting & Mitcham United** 2 Worthing 0 *Att* 364
(May 1st) **Cray Wanderers** 2 Metropolitan Police 0 *Att* 286

FINAL
(May 3rd at Tooting & Mitcham United)
Tooting & Mitcham United 1 Cray Wanderers 0 *Att* 939

DATES & GATES

(Home →) (Away ↓)	Ashford Town	Burgess Hill Town	Chatham Town	Chipstead	Corinthian Casuals	Cray Wanderers	Croydon Athletic	Dover Athletic	Dulwich Hamlet	Eastbourne Town	Horsham YMCA	Kingstonian	Leatherhead	Metropolitan Police	Molesey	Sittingbourne	Tooting & Mitcham Utd	Walton & Hersham	Walton Casuals	Whitstable Town	Whyteleafe	Worthing
Ashford Town	—	13 Nov / 201	21 Apr / 259	30 Oct / 269	22 Apr / 159	12 Feb / 180	15 Sep / 267	27 Aug / 402	26 Jan / 226	8 Mar / 212	5 Apr / 411	18 Aug / 255	29 Sep / 204	15 Apr / 128	22 Sep / 168	8 Apr / 128	26 Dec / 855	23 Feb / 209	4 Mar / 137	8 Sep / 220	19 Apr / 189	17 Nov / 162
Burgess Hill Town	29 Dec / 364	—	1 Mar / 157	19 Feb / 137	13 Oct / 139	18 Aug / 148	2 Feb / 116	16 Oct / 851	16 Oct / 269	1 Dec / 125	10 Nov / 116	29 Mar / 247	29 Mar / 161	29 Sep / 93	5 Apr / 122	12 Jan / 168	23 Nov / 311	15 Dec / 122	15 Dec / 62	26 Apr / 221	3 Nov / 157	17 Nov / 285
Chatham Town	29 Jan / 117	16 Feb / 157	—	15 Mar / 219	12 Jan / 130	20 Nov / 131	19 Apr / 128	2 Feb / 1,116	22 Dec / 302	29 Sep / 155	8 Sep / 120	8 Mar / 234	26 Jan / 190	29 Sep / 121	5 Apr / 85	25 Mar / 324	9 Feb / 247	25 Aug / 125	29 Sep / 85	5 Jan / 193	21 Nov / 92	26 Feb / 220
Chipstead	1 Mar / 188	26 Dec / 130	19 Apr / 128	—	16 Oct / 112	8 Sep / 113	8 Sep / 112	12 Feb / 926	24 Nov / 303	24 Nov / 120	19 Jan / 116	15 Sep / 276	26 Apr / 171	29 Dec / 94	16 Feb / 97	25 Aug / 146	26 Oct / 288	24 Mar / 175	26 Apr / 182	30 Oct / 193	19 Feb / 124	19 Feb / 176
Corinthian Casuals	30 Oct / 131	22 Dec / 105	16 Oct / 107	12 Apr / 80	—	27 Nov / 193	1 Apr / 105	3 Dec / 757	5 Apr / 352	5 Nov / 198	20 Nov / 103	17 Nov / 103	27 Apr / 258	12 Jan / 94	23 Feb / 206	15 Dec / 157	23 Nov / 261	4 Apr / 206	22 Mar / 258	13 Oct / 132	26 Jan / 196	26 Jan / 424
Cray Wanderers	19 Jan / 180	18 Aug / 148	20 Nov / 131	8 Sep / 113	27 Nov / 193	—	24 Mar / 219	15 Mar / 1,215	19 Nov / 431	23 Feb / 320	16 Feb / 180	24 Mar / 449	12 Jan / 267	3 Nov / 231	17 Nov / 165	18 Dec / 231	26 Apr / 291	22 Mar / 126	22 Sep / 96	26 Dec / 311	25 Sep / 133	18 Aug / 301
Croydon Athletic	21 Aug / 138	2 Feb / 116	19 Apr / 128	8 Sep / 112	4 Apr / 350	24 Mar / 219	—	19 Apr / 1,237	14 Oct / 110	19 Jan / 350	29 Mar / 222	4 Apr / 110	15 Dec / 145	1 Mar / 105	18 Dec / 71	26 Apr / 229	20 Dec / 275	15 Apr / 229	3 Nov / 121	29 Dec / 235	29 Dec / 113	23 Nov / 223
Dover Athletic	8 Nov / 576	16 Jan / 757	24 Nov / 303	24 Nov / 116	3 Nov / 116	19 Nov / 352	24 Mar / 208	—	21 Apr / 350	24 Aug / 208	24 Mar / 289	11 Sep / 117	18 Sep / 152	20 Nov / 170	16 Feb / 313	13 Oct / 136	27 Oct / 138	15 Sep / 137	25 Aug / 184	8 Apr / 218	16 Oct / 305	10 Nov / 112
Dulwich Hamlet	25 Apr / 286	16 Oct / 269	22 Dec / 302	24 Nov / 303	17 Nov / 152	19 Nov / 431	14 Oct / 110	8 Mar / 864	—	22 Mar / 146	25 Aug / 340	21 Jan / 289	4 Dec / 183	18 Aug / 202	5 Jan / 439	18 Jan / 95	27 Sep / 475	25 Nov / 264	19 Jan / 275	8 Sep / 353	8 Apr / 244	8 Dec / 241
Eastbourne Town	25 Sep / 278	1 Dec / 125	29 Sep / 155	24 Nov / 120	24 Nov / 151	23 Feb / 320	29 Mar / 222	29 Oct / 774	22 Mar / 146	—	9 Feb / 278	3 Nov / 231	11 Aug / 170	1 Mar / 425	18 Apr / 313	27 Oct / 136	10 Nov / 152	8 Mar / 369	27 Oct / 120	15 Dec / 218	16 Oct / 305	24 Nov / 112
Horsham YMCA	25 Mar / 230	10 Nov / 116	8 Sep / 120	19 Jan / 116	20 Nov / 103	16 Feb / 180	19 Nov / 350	14 Mar / 983	25 Aug / 340	9 Feb / 278	—	6 Oct / 289	3 Nov / 475	30 Mar / 303	18 Nov / 311	10 Nov / 246	25 Aug / 278	25 Feb / 291	19 Jan / 182	8 Sep / 218	5 Apr / 150	10 Nov / 112
Kingstonian	15 Mar / 299	29 Mar / 247	8 Mar / 234	15 Sep / 276	17 Nov / 103	24 Mar / 449	4 Apr / 110	21 Jan / 907	21 Jan / 289	3 Nov / 231	6 Oct / 289	—	21 Jan / 273	30 Oct / 303	12 Apr / 376	13 Oct / 95	27 Oct / 236	29 Dec / 369	25 Aug / 120	15 Oct / 353	16 Oct / 180	24 Mar / 150
Leatherhead	2 Feb / 197	29 Mar / 161	26 Jan / 190	26 Apr / 171	27 Apr / 258	12 Jan / 267	15 Dec / 145	21 Aug / 914	4 Dec / 183	11 Aug / 170	3 Nov / 475	21 Jan / 273	—	26 Apr / 148	18 Jan / 239	12 Apr / 193	28 Aug / 273	14 Dec / 200	24 Nov / 103	5 Jan / 95	9 Feb / 72	26 Apr / 150
Metropolitan Police	22 Sep / 101	29 Sep / 93	29 Sep / 121	29 Dec / 94	12 Jan / 94	3 Nov / 231	1 Mar / 105	12 Jan / 824	18 Aug / 202	1 Mar / 425	30 Mar / 303	30 Oct / 303	26 Apr / 148	—	15 Dec / 185	26 Jan / 134	6 Nov / 272	25 Mar / 205	13 Oct / 117	16 Oct / 218	4 Dec / 180	16 Oct / 150
Molesey	10 Nov / 141	5 Apr / 122	5 Apr / 85	16 Feb / 97	23 Feb / 206	17 Nov / 165	18 Dec / 71	8 Sep / 921	5 Jan / 439	18 Apr / 313	18 Nov / 311	12 Apr / 376	18 Jan / 239	15 Dec / 185	—	10 Nov / 515	26 Apr / 317	1 Mar / 127	27 Oct / 75	27 Nov / 353	8 Dec / 88	24 Nov / 113
Sittingbourne	22 Dec / 145	12 Jan / 168	25 Mar / 324	25 Aug / 146	15 Dec / 157	18 Dec / 231	26 Apr / 229	9 Feb / 867	18 Jan / 95	27 Oct / 136	10 Nov / 246	13 Oct / 95	12 Apr / 193	26 Jan / 134	10 Nov / 515	—	24 Nov / 312	24 Nov / 190	26 Aug / 244	15 Mar / 137	23 Feb / 68	15 Dec / 217
Tooting & Mitcham United	8 Jan / 215	23 Nov / 311	9 Feb / 247	26 Oct / 288	23 Nov / 261	26 Apr / 291	20 Dec / 275	29 Dec / 1,021	27 Sep / 475	10 Nov / 152	25 Aug / 278	27 Oct / 236	28 Aug / 273	6 Nov / 272	26 Apr / 317	24 Nov / 312	—	23 Sep / 89	25 Sep / 137	8 Apr / 69	12 Apr / 72	13 Oct / 113
Walton & Hersham	5 Jan / 127	15 Dec / 122	25 Aug / 125	24 Mar / 175	4 Apr / 206	22 Mar / 126	15 Apr / 229	17 Nov / 906	25 Nov / 264	8 Mar / 369	25 Feb / 291	29 Dec / 369	14 Dec / 200	25 Mar / 205	1 Mar / 127	24 Nov / 190	23 Sep / 89	—	26 Jan / 112	26 Apr / 112	26 Jan / 101	1 Dec / 107
Walton Casuals	19 Apr / 150	15 Dec / 62	29 Sep / 85	26 Apr / 182	22 Mar / 258	22 Sep / 96	3 Nov / 121	23 Nov / 911	19 Jan / 275	27 Oct / 120	19 Jan / 182	25 Aug / 120	24 Nov / 103	13 Oct / 117	27 Oct / 75	26 Aug / 244	25 Sep / 137	26 Jan / 112	—	18 Aug / 101	5 Apr / 141	18 Aug / 112
Whitstable Town	16 Feb / 197	26 Apr / 221	5 Jan / 193	30 Oct / 193	13 Oct / 132	26 Dec / 311	29 Dec / 235	9 Feb / 754	8 Sep / 353	15 Dec / 218	8 Sep / 218	15 Oct / 353	5 Jan / 95	16 Oct / 218	27 Nov / 353	15 Mar / 137	8 Apr / 69	26 Apr / 112	18 Aug / 101	—	1 Apr / 155	5 Apr / 228
Whyteleafe	5 Apr / 177	3 Nov / 157	21 Nov / 92	19 Feb / 124	26 Jan / 196	25 Sep / 133	29 Dec / 113	1 Apr / 1,154	8 Apr / 244	16 Oct / 305	5 Apr / 150	16 Oct / 180	9 Feb / 72	4 Dec / 180	8 Dec / 88	23 Feb / 68	12 Apr / 72	26 Jan / 101	5 Apr / 141	1 Apr / 155	—	26 Apr / 457
Worthing	27 Oct / 326	17 Nov / 285	26 Feb / 220	19 Feb / 176	26 Jan / 424	18 Aug / 301	23 Nov / 223	24 Mar / 1,324	8 Dec / 241	24 Nov / 112	10 Nov / 112	24 Mar / 150	26 Apr / 150	16 Oct / 150	24 Nov / 113	15 Dec / 217	13 Oct / 113	1 Dec / 107	18 Aug / 112	5 Apr / 228	26 Apr / 457	—

RYMAN ISTHMIAN LEAGUE
DIVISION ONE NORTH CONSTITUTION 2008-09

AVELEY
Colours: Blue
The Mill Field, Mill Road, Aveley, Essex RM15 4SJ
Tel: 01708 865940 Fax: 01708 680995

BRENTWOOD TOWN
Colours: Sky & navy blue
The Arena, Brentwood Centre, Doddinghurst Road,
Brentwood, Essex CM15 9NN
Tel: 07505 242835

CHATHAM TOWN
Colours: Red & black
Sports Ground, Maidstone Road, Bourneville Avenue,
Chatham, Kent ME4 6EJ
Tel: 01634 812194 Fax: 01634 812194

CHESHUNT
Colours: Amber & black
The Stadium, Theobalds Lane, Cheshunt, Hertfordshire
EN8 8RU
Tel: 01992 633500 Fax: 01992 626752

CONCORD RANGERS
Colours: Yellow & blue
Thames Road Stadium, Thames Road, Canvey Island,
Essex SS8 0HH
Tel: 01268 691780 Fax: 01268 515750

EAST THURROCK UNITED
Colours: Amber & black
Rookery Hill, Corringham, Stanford-le-Hope, Essex
SS17 9LB
Tel: 01375 644166 Fax/Boardman: 01375 641009

ENFIELD TOWN
Colours: White & blue
Brimsdown Rovers FC, Goldsdown Road, Enfield,
Middlesex EN3 7RP
Tel: 020 8804 5491

GREAT WAKERING ROVERS
Colours: Green & white
Burroughs Park, Little Wakering Hall Lane,
Gt Wakering, Southend-on-Sea, Essex SS3 0HH
Tel: 01702 217812

HILLINGDON BOROUGH
Colours: White & royal blue
Middlesex Stadium, Breakspear Road, Ruislip,
Middlesex HA4 7SB
Tel: 01895 639544

ILFORD
Colours: Royal blue & white
Cricklefield Stadium, 486 High Road, Seven Kings,
Ilford, Essex IG1 1UE
Tel: 020 8514 8352

LEYTON
Colours: Blue & white
Leyton Stadium, 282 Lea Bridge Road, Leyton, London
E10 7LD
Tel: 020 8988 7642 Club: 020 8988 7642

MALDON TOWN
Colours: Blue & white
Wallace Binder Ground, Park Drive, Maldon, Essex
CM9 5XX
Tel: 01621 853762

NORTHWOOD
Colours: Red
Northwood Park, Chestnut Avenue, Northwood,
Middlesex HA6 1HR
Tel: 01923 827148 Fax: 020 8428 1533

POTTERS BAR TOWN
Colours: Red & royal blue
Parkfield, Watkins Rise, The Walk, Potters Bar,
Hertfordshire EN6 1QN
Tel: 01707 654833

REDBRIDGE
Colours: Blue
The Oakside Stadium, Station Road, Barkingside,
Ilford, Essex IG6 1NB
Tel: 020 8550 3611 Fax: 020 8550 3611

THAMESMEAD TOWN
Colours: Green & black
Bayliss Avenue, Thamesmead, London SE28 8NJ
Tel: 020 8311 4211

TILBURY
Colours: Black & white
Chadfields, St Chad's Road, Tilbury, Essex RM18 8NL
Tel: 01375 843093 Fax: 01375 859496

WALTHAM ABBEY
Colours: White & green
Capershotts, Sewardstone Road, Waltham Abbey, Essex
EN9 1LU
Tel: 01992 711287

WALTHAM FOREST
Colours: White & navy blue
Cricklefield Stadium, 486 High Road, Seven Kings,
Ilford, Essex IG1 1UE
Tel: 020 8514 8352

WARE
Colours: Blue & white
Wodson Park, Wadesmill Road, Ware, Hertfordshire
SG12 0UQ
Tel: 01920 463247

WINGATE & FINCHLEY
Colours: Blue & white
The Abrahams Stadium, Summers Lane, Finchley,
London N12 0PD
Tel: 020 8446 2217 Fax: 020 8343 8194

WITHAM TOWN
Colours: Red, black & white
Witham Town Football&Soc Club, Spa Road, Witham,
Essex CM8 1UN
Tel: 01376 511198Fax/Boardroom: 01376 520996

IN: Chatham Town (S – Isthmian League Division One South), Cheshunt (R – Southern League Premier Division), Concord Rangers (P – Essex Senior League), East Thurrock United (R), Hillingdon Borough (S – Southern League Division One South & West), Leyton (R), Thamesmead Town (P – Kent League Premier Division)
OUT: AFC Sudbury (S – Southern League Division One Midlands), Arlesey Town (S – Southern League Division One Midlands), Bury Town (S – Southern League Division One Midlands), Canvey Island (P), Dartford (P), Edgware Town (W), Wivenhoe Town (R – Eastern Counties League Premier Division)

WWW.CHERRYRED.CO.UK

RYMAN ISTHMIAN LEAGUE
DIVISION ONE SOUTH CONSTITUTION 2008-09

ASHFORD TOWN
Colours: Green & white
The Homelands Stadium, Ashford Road, Kingsnorth, Ashford, Kent TN26 1NJ
Tel: 01233 611838 Fax: 01233 662510

BURGESS HILL TOWN
Colours: Yellow & black
Leylands Park, Maple Drive, Burgess Hill, West Sussex RH15 8DL
Tel: 01444 242429 Fax: 01444 239102

CHIPSTEAD
Colours: Green, white & black
High Road, Chipstead, Surrey CR5 3SF
Tel: 01737 553250

CORINTHIAN CASUALS
Colours: Chocolate, pink & sky blue
King George's Field, Queen Mary Close, Tolworth, Surrey KT6 7NA
Tel: 020 8397 3368

CRAY WANDERERS
Colours: Amber & black
Bromley FC, Hayes Lane, Bromley, Kent BR2 9EF
Tel: 020 8460 5291

CROWBOROUGH ATHLETIC
Colours: White & blue
Alderbrook Recreation Ground, Fermor Road, Crowborough, East Sussex TN6 3BT
Tel: 01892 661893

CROYDON ATHLETIC
Colours: Maroon & white
The Keith Tuckey Stadium, Mayfield Road, Thornton Heath, Surrey CR7 6DN
Tel: 020 8664 8343 Fax: 020 8664 8343

DULWICH HAMLET
Colours: Navy blue & pink
Champion Hill Stadium, Edgar Kail Way, Dog Kennel Hill, East Dulwich, London SE22 8BD
Tel: 020 7274 8707/7501 9323 Fax: 020 7501 9255

EASTBOURNE TOWN
Colours: Yellow & blue
The Saffrons Sports Club, Compton Place Road, Eastbourne, East Sussex BN21 1EA
Tel: 01323 723734

FLEET TOWN
Colours: Navy & sky blue
Calthorpe Park, Crookham Road, Fleet, Hampshire GU51 5FA
Tel: 01252 623804 Fax: 01252 684749

FOLKESTONE INVICTA
Colours: Black & amber
The Buzzlines Stadium, Cheriton Road Sports Ground, Folkestone, Kent CT20 5JU
Tel: 01303 257461 Fax: 01303 255541

GODALMING TOWN
Colours: Yellow & green
Wey Court, Meadrow, Godalming, Surrey GU7 3JE
Tel: 01483 417520

KINGSTONIAN
Colours: Red & white
Cherry Red Records Fans Stadium, Kingsmeadow, Jack Goodchild Way, Kingston-upon-Thames, Surrey KT1 3PB
Tel: 020 8547 3528

LEATHERHEAD
Colours: Green & white
Fetcham Grove, Guildford Road, Leatherhead, Surrey KT22 9AS
Tel: 01372 360151 Fax/Boardroom: 01372 362705

MERSTHAM
Colours: Amber & black
Moatside, Weldon Way, Merstham, Surrey RH1 3PF
Tel: 01737 644046

METROPOLITAN POLICE
Colours: Blue
Imber Court Sports Club, Ember Lane, East Molesey, Surrey KT8 0BT
Tel: 020 8398 7358

SITTINGBOURNE
Colours: Red & black
Central Park Complex, Church Road, Eurolink, Sittingbourne, Kent ME10 3SB
Tel: 01795 435077

WALTON & HERSHAM
Colours: Red
Sports Ground, Stompond Lane, Walton-on-Thames, Surrey KT12 1HF
Tel: 01932 244967 Boardroom: 01932 245363

WALTON CASUALS
Colours: Tangerine & black
Waterside Stadium, Waterside Drive, Walton-on-Thames, Surrey KT12 2JG
Tel: 01932 787749

WHITSTABLE TOWN
Colours: Red & white
Belmont Road, Whitstable, Kent CT5 1QP
Tel: 01227 266012

WHYTELEAFE
Colours: Green & white
15 Church Road, Whyteleafe, Surrey CR3 0AR
Tel: 020 8660 5491 Fax/Boardroom: 020 8645 0422

WORTHING
Colours: Red
Woodside Road, Worthing, West Sussex BN14 7HQ
Tel: 01903 239575 Fax: 01903 239575

WWW.NLNEWSDESK.CO.UK

IN: Crowborough Athletic (P – Sussex County League Division One), Fleet Town (S – Southern League Division One South & West), Folkestone Invicta (R), Godalming Town (S – Southern League Division One South & West), Merstham (P – Combined Counties League Premier Division)
OUT: Chatham Town (S – Isthmian League Division One North), Dover Athletic (P), Horsham YMCA (R – Sussex County League Division One), Molesey (R – Combined Counties League Premier Division), Tooting & Mitcham United (P)

LEAGUE CUP

FIRST ROUND
Redbridge 2 Brentwood Town 0 *(Sep 11)*	Att: 81
Waltham Forest 2 **Arlesey Town** 3 *(Sep 11)*	Att: 53

SECOND ROUND
AFC Hornchurch 3 Tilbury 0 *(Nov 20)*	Att: 182
AFC Wimbledon 0 **Whyteleafe** 2 *(Oct 2)*	Att: 529
Arlesey Town 4 Enfield Town 0 *(Oct 23)*	Att: 75
Ashford Town 1 **Burgess Hill Town** 3 *(Oct 2)*	Att: 110
Ashford Town (Middx) 2 Walton & Hersham 1 *(Oct 2)*	Att: 93
Billericay Town 0 **AFC Sudbury** 3 *(Oct 2)*	Att: 202
Bury Town 2 **Chelmsford City** 3 *(Oct 2)*	Att: 206
Carshalton Athletic 4 Corinthian Casuals 0 *(Oct 2)*	Att: 75
Dartford 3 Aveley 0 *(Oct 2)*	Att: 318
Dover Athletic 2 **Eastbourne Town** 3 *(Oct 1)*	Att: 151
Dulwich Hamlet 0 **Tooting & Mitcham United** 0 *aet (3-5p) (Oct 2)*	Att: 149
Edgware Town 3 Staines Town 1 *(Oct 2)*	Att: 48
Great Wakering Rovers 4 Ilford 1 *(Oct 2)*	Att: 115
Harlow Town 1 **Ware** 3 *(Oct 2)*	Att: 131
Harrow Borough 0 **Metropolitan Police** 5 *(Oct 2)*	Att: 76
Hendon 2 **Boreham Wood** 3 *(Oct 23)*	Att: 101
Horsham 4 Hastings United 0 *(Oct 2)*	Att: 162
Horsham YMCA 4 Folkestone Invicta 3 *aet (Nov 6)*	Att: 50
Kingstonian 3 Cray Wanderers 1 *(Oct 1)*	Att: 179
Leatherhead 3 Croydon Athletic 2 *(Oct 2)*	Att: 67
Maidstone United 5 Canvey Island 2 *(Oct 3)*	Att: 131
Margate 2 **East Thurrock United** 3 *(Oct 2)*	Att: 174
Molesey 2 **Wealdstone** 3 *(Oct 2)*	Att: 106
Potters Bar Town 3 Leyton 1 *(Oct 2)*	Att: 41
Ramsgate 4 Chatham Town 2 *(Oct 2)*	Att: 87
Redbidge 2 Sittingbourne 1 *(Oct 2)*	Att: 41
Tonbridge Angels 4 Chipstead 1 *(Oct 23)*	Att: 159
Waltham Abbey 3 Wingate & Finchley 1 *(Oct 2)*	Att: 41
Walton Casuals 1 Northwood 0 *(Oct 2)*	Att: 34
Whitstable Town 4 Worthing 3 *(Oct 2)*	Att: 110
Witham Town 4 Maldon Town 0 *(Oct 23)*	Att: 87
Wivenhoe Town 0 **Heybridge Swifts** 2 *(Oct 24)*	Att: 44

THIRD ROUND
AFC Hornchurch 3 Maidstone United 0 *(Dec 18)*	Att: 225
AFC Sudbury 2 Chelmsford City 1 *(Nov 13)*	Att: 297
Arlesey Town 4 Witham Town 2 *(Nov 13)*	Att: 63
Ashford Town (Middx) 2 Metropolitan Police 0 *(Oct 23)*	Att: 88
Boreham Wood 2 **Wealdstone** 3 *(Dec 18)*	Att: 87
Burgess Hill Town 1 **Whyteleafe** 3 *(Nov 13)*	Att: 103
Carshalton Athletic 1 Leatherhead 0 *(Nov 13)*	Att: 160
Dartford 3 Whitstable Town 0 *(Dec 4)*	Att: 426
East Thurrock United 0 **Ramsgate** 1 *(Nov 13)*	Att: 63
Eastbourne Town 1 **Horsham** 5 *(Nov 14)*	Att: 137
Kingstonian 1 **Tooting & Mitcham United** 2 *aet (Nov 12)*	Att: 225
Potters Bar Town 1 **Edgware Town** 4 *(Oct 23)*	Att: 42
Redbridge 2 Great Wakering Rovers 1 *(Nov 13)*	Att: 56
Tonbridge Angels 4 Horsham YMCA 2 *aet (Jan 8)*	Att: 153
Waltham Abbey 0 **Heybridge Swifts** 4 *(at Heybridge Swifts) (Nov 13)*	Att: 62
Walton Casuals 2 Ware 1 *(Oct 23)*	Att: 39

FOURTH ROUND
AFC Hornchurch 1 **Ramsgate** 2 *(Jan 8)*	Att: 216
Arlesey Town 1 **Edgware Town** 4 *(Dec 4)*	Att: 79
Heybridge Swifts 3 Dartford 0 *(Jan 22)*	Att: 152
Horsham 1 **Walton Casuals** 2 *(Dec 18)*	Att: 187
Redbridge 0 **AFC Sudbury** 1 *aet (Dec 11)*	Att: 76
Tonbridge Angels 0 **Carshalton Athletic** 1 *(Feb 12)*	Att: 202
Tooting & Mitcham United 1 Whyteleafe 0 *(Dec 4)*	Att: 105
Wealdstone 1 Ashford Town (Middx) 0 *(Jan 29)*	Att: 88

QUARTER-FINALS
AFC Sudbury 1 Edgware Town 0 *(Feb 12)*	Att: 176
Carshalton Athletic 1 **Walton Casuals** 1 *aet (4-5p) (Feb 19)*	Att: 95
Ramsgate 1 Tooting & Mitcham United 1 *aet (4-3p) (Feb 12)*	Att: 182
Wealdstone 0 **Heybridge Swifts** 1 *aet (Feb 12)*	Att: 105

SEMI-FINALS
Heybridge Swifts 0 **AFC Sudbury** 6 *(Mar 4)*	Att: 189
Walton Casuals 0 **Ramsgate** 1 *(Mar 4)*	Att: 132

FINAL
(April 2nd at Dartford)
Ramsgate 0 AFC Sudbury 0 *aet (5-4p)* **Att:** 601

KENT COUNTY LEAGUE

	Bearsted	Bromley Green	Coney Hall	Cray Valley Paper Mills	Crockenhill	Fleet Leisure	Hollands & Blair	Lewisham Borough (Community)	Milton Athletic	Norton Sports	Orpington	Rusthall	Sheerness East	Snodland
Bearsted		1-2	1-0	0-4	2-2	2-4	0-2	1-2	1-2	2-0	4-1	1-0	1-1	0-1
Bromley Green	2-2	P	8-3	1-2	1-3	1-6	0-3	2-2	2-0	4-1	2-2	4-4	0-2	1-4
Coney Hall	0-3	2-2	R	1-6	4-0	3-4	1-5	0-2	1-6	0-4	1-0	1-0	2-6	1-0
Cray Valley Paper Mills	2-1	0-4	4-0	E	7-0	8-1	1-0	1-1	6-4	6-0	2-3	3-2	1-1	5-0
Crockenhill	1-3	1-2	2-1	1-7	M	2-0	0-3	0-3	1-1	1-1	2-7	4-4	1-1	2-1
Fleet Leisure	0-2	0-4	3-0	2-4	3-1	I	0-3	1-0	1-1	2-2	1-2	1-4	1-1	1-2
Hollands & Blair	2-1	2-0	6-1	1-5	3-1	2-1		4-1	1-0	3-0	3-1	7-0	3-0	1-1
Lewisham Borough (Community)	0-4	2-2	1-0	0-1	2-1	5-0	2-2	R	4-1	4-0	1-1	0-3	3-2	1-0
Milton Athletic	1-2	2-0	6-1	0-1	3-0	1-0	0-3	0-0		2-0	4-1	0-0	3-1	1-1
Norton Sports	1-2	1-2	4-1	1-10	2-2	2-2	3-5	6-5	1-2		1-3	4-1	1-1	2-0
Orpington	2-2	7-0	1-0	3-7	7-5	2-1	0-2	4-3	0-1	2-3	D	1-2	5-2	3-0
Rusthall	4-1	1-5	2-2	1-2	5-1	9-3	2-1	2-1	1-1	2-1	5-1	I	7-3	2-1
Sheerness East	1-1	3-1	5-2	0-5	4-1	2-0	0-2	0-2	1-2	2-0	0-1	3-1	V	4-1
Snodland	1-0	3-2	2-1	1-7	3-0	2-1	0-2	0-0	2-4	2-1	2-3	6-3	2-1	

Premier Division

		P	W	D	L	F	A	Pts
Norton Sports		26	23	2	1	100	23	71
Orpington		26	21	2	3	90	17	65
Fleet Leisure		26	15	5	6	49	34	50
Coney Hall		26	15	2	9	53	37	47
Hollands & Blair		26	14	1	11	51	44	43
Rusthall		26	10	7	9	39	38	37
Snodland		26	10	3	13	33	52	33
Bearsted		26	10	1	15	44	55	31
Cray Valley Paper Mills		26	8	5	13	45	47	29
Lewisham Borough (Community)		26	9	2	15	33	57	29
Sheerness East		26	7	7	12	37	63	28
Milton Athletic	-1	26	7	4	15	31	64	24
Bromley Green		26	6	2	18	38	75	20
Crockenhill		26	4	3	19	21	58	15

Reserve Division East

		P	W	D	L	F	A	Pts
University of Kent Res.		24	16	6	2	65	28	54
New Romney Res.		24	17	2	5	60	30	53
Bromley Green Res.		24	16	4	4	71	28	52
Bly Spartans Res.		24	13	5	6	66	53	44
Borden Village Res.		24	11	4	9	53	51	37
APM Mears Res.		24	8	6	10	43	44	30
Oakwood Res.		24	8	5	11	45	47	29
Bearsted Res.	-1	24	8	6	10	43	46	29
Kennington Res.		24	8	3	13	44	51	27
Otford United Res.		24	5	9	10	23	40	24
Platt United Res.		24	5	8	11	31	57	23
Lydd Town Res.		24	4	4	16	42	70	16
Larkfield/New Hythe Wdrs Res.		24	4	4	16	29	70	16

Reserve Division West

		P	W	D	L	F	A	Pts
Orpington Res.		24	18	4	2	80	33	58
Bromleians Sports Res.		24	15	5	4	65	34	50
Fleet Leisure Res.		24	15	5	4	52	31	50
Belvedere Res.		24	13	2	9	55	37	41
Westerham Res.		24	12	3	9	50	51	39
Crockenhill Res.		24	11	3	10	45	41	36
Greenways Res.		24	11	3	10	44	40	36
Coney Hall Res.	-3	24	11	4	9	54	42	34
Stansfeld O & B Club Res.		24	8	5	11	40	60	29
Chipstead Res.		24	8	4	12	50	60	28
Wickham Res.		24	3	6	15	34	65	15
Fleetdown United Res.		24	3	3	18	25	60	12
Borough United Res.		24	2	5	17	28	68	11

CHAMPIONS TROPHY

(Prem Div champions v Inter-Regional Challenge Cup holders)

(August 29th at Sevenoaks Town)

Holmesdale 1 Bly Spartans 0

VANDANEL / SHEPHERD NEAME KENT COUNTY LEAGUE PREMIER DIVISION CONSTITUTION 2008-09

BEARSTED . . . . Otham Sports Ground, Honey Lane, Otham, Maidstone ME15 8RG 07831 251657
BLY SPARTANS . . . . Bly Spartans Sports Ground, Rede Court Road, Strood ME2 3TU 01634 710577
BROMLEY GREEN . . . . The Swan Centre, Cudworth Road, South Willesborough, Ashford TN24 0BB 01233 645982
CONEY HALL . . . . Tie Pigs Lane, Coney Hall, West Wickham BR4 9BT 020 8462 4273
CRAY VALLEY PAPER MILLS . . . . . Badgers Sports Ground, Middle Park Avenue, Eltham SE9 5HT. 020 8850 4273
FLEET LEISURE . . . . Beauwater Leisure Sports Club, Nelson Road, Northfleet DA11 7EE 01474 359222
HOLLANDS & BLAIR . . . . . . Rochagas Sports & Social, Star Meadow, Dartford Avenue, Gillingham ME7 3AN 01634 573839
LEWISHAM BOROUGH (COMMUNITY) . . Ladywell Arena, Doggett Road, Catford SE6 4QX. 020 8314 1986
MILTON & FULSTON UNITED . . UK Paper Sports Ground, Gore Court Road, Sittingbourne ME10 1QN 01795 564213
ORPINGTON. . . . . Westcombe Park & Orpington SC, Goddington Lane, Orpington BR6 9SH 01689 834902
PHOENIX SPORTS . . . . Phoenix Sports Club, Mayplace Road East, Bexleyheath DA7 6JT 01322 526159
RUSTHALL . . . . Jockey Farm, Nellington Lane, Rusthall, Tunbridge Wells TN4 8SH 07940 277138
SHEERNESS EAST . . . . Sheerness East WMC, 47 Queensborough Road, Halfway, Sheerness ME12 3BZ 01795 662049
SNODLAND . . . . Potyn's Field, Paddlesworth Road, Snodland ME6 5DL 01634 243961
STANSFELD OXFORD & BERMONDSEY CLUB . . . . . Cray Wanderers FC, Oxford Road, Sidcup DA14 6LW 020 8300 2987

IN: Bly Spartans (P – Division One East), Phoenix Sports (P – Division One West), Stansfeld Oxford & Bermondsey Club (P – Division One West)
OUT: Crockenhill (R – Division One West), Norton Sports (P – Kent League Premier Division)
Milton Athletic have merged with Fulston Zebras to form Milton & Fulston United

WWW.CHERRYRED.CO.UK

Note – St Margarets and Uniflo withdrew during the course of the season. Their results are shown herein but are expunged from the league table

Division One East — results grid

	AFC Sheppey	Betteshanger Welfare	Bly Spartans	Guru Nanak	Kennington	Lydd Town	New Romney	Oakwood	St Margarets	Staplehurst & Monarchs	Uniflo	University of Kent
AFC Sheppey	D	4-0	1-2	5-2	1-0	2-0	1-0	3-2	n/a	5-1	3-1	4-2
Betteshanger Welfare	1-1	I	0-3	1-3	2-3	2-1	1-0	0-0	n/a	1-0	n/a	2-0
Bly Spartans	3-0	2-0	V	2-1	5-0	8-0	0-0	5-3	n/a	4-1	n/a	3-1
Guru Nanak	1-1	2-1	0-1		4-0	1-0	2-0	2-3	n/a	4-0	n/a	0-0
Kennington	3-1	0-2	2-4	0-1	O	3-0	0-2	0-2	n/a	5-1	n/a	1-3
Lydd Town	3-1	3-2	0-2	2-0	2-1	N	1-1	1-2	n/a	2-5	5-3	1-2
New Romney	1-4	5-1	0-2	3-0	4-1	4-1	E	0-2	n/a	4-3	n/a	3-2
Oakwood	4-0	1-0	2-3	0-1	2-0	6-3	1-2		n/a	5-1	n/a	1-0
St Margarets	n/a	n/a	0-5	n/a	n/a	n/a	0-3	n/a	E	n/a	2-2	n/a
Staplehurst & Monarchs United	0-4	2-3	3-7	3-2	1-1	4-1	1-3	1-1	n/a	A	n/a	1-3
Uniflo	n/a	n/a	0-6	n/a	n/a	n/a	n/a	n/a	0-0	n/a	S	n/a
University of Kent	0-1	1-1	2-0	3-2	2-2	2-2	2-0	0-0	n/a	1-3	n/a	T

Division One East — league table

	P	W	D	L	F	A	Pts
Bly Spartans	18	16	1	1	56	16	49
AFC Sheppey	18	11	2	5	39	25	35
New Romney	18	10	3	5	37	22	33
Guru Nanak	18	9	2	7	33	29	29
University of Kent	18	8	2	8	28	25	26
Betteshanger Welfare	18	8	2	8	27	25	26
Lydd Town	18	6	3	9	20	31	21
Kennington	18	4	3	11	26	48	15
Oakwood	18	3	3	12	19	42	12
Staplehurst & Monarchs Utd	18	3	2	13	18	54	11

St Margarets and Uniflo – records expunged

VANDANEL / SHEPHERD NEAME KENT COUNTY LEAGUE DIVISION ONE EAST CONSTITUTION 2008-09

AFC SHEPPEY . . . . Medway Ports Authority Ground, Holm Place, Halfway, Sheerness ME12 3AT 01795 668054
APM MEARS . . . . Cobdown Sports & Social Club, Ditton Corner, Station Road, Aylesford ME20 6AU 01622 716824
BETTESHANGER WELFARE . . . . Welfare Ground, Cavell Square, Mill Hill, Deal CT14 9HR 01304 372080
CANTERBURY CITY . . . . Bridge Recreation Ground, Patrixbourne Road, Bridge, Canterbury CT4 5BL . . . . None
GURU NANAK . . . . AEI Henley Sports Club, Dunkirk Close, Gravesend DA12 5NN . . . . None
KENNINGTON . . . . Kennington Cricket Club, Ulley Road, Kennington, Ashford TN24 9HY 07887 995219
LYDD TOWN . . . . The Lindsey Field, Dengemarsh Road, Lydd, Romney Marsh TN29 9JH 01797 321904
NEW ROMNEY . . . . The Maud Pavilion, Station Road, New Romney TN28 8SR 01797 364858
OAKWOOD . . . . Honey Lane, Otham, Maidstone ME15 8RG 07745 383328
OTFORD UNITED . . . . Otford Recreation Ground, High Street, Otford, Sevenoaks TN14 5PG 01959 524405
STAPLEHURST & MONARCHS UNITED . . . . The Old County Ground, Norman Road, West Malling ME19 6RL . . . . None
UNIVERSITY OF KENT . . . . The Oast House, Park Wood Road, Giles Lane, University of Kent, Canterbury CT2 7SY 01227 827430
IN: APM Mears (P – Division Two East), Canterbury City (P – Division Two East), Otford United (P – Division Two East)
OUT: Ashford Borough (WN), Bly Spartans (P), St Margarets (WS), Uniflo (WS)

Division One West — results grid

	Belvedere	Bridon Ropes	Bromleians Sports	Fleetdown United	Greenways	Metrogas	Phoenix Sports	Samuel Montagu Yth Club	Stansfeld O & B Club	Sutton Athletic	Tonbridge Invicta	Tudor Sports	Westerham
Belvedere	D	2-0	1-0	1-0	5-1	2-2	1-1	2-1	2-0	2-1	3-1	0-0	3-3
Bridon Ropes	3-1	I	2-2	3-0	2-2	3-4	0-3	1-1	1-4	1-1	2-4	2-1	2-3
Bromleians Sports	2-0	1-1	V	6-0	1-2	1-1	1-2	1-2	0-1	2-2	1-2	1-0	1-2
Fleetdown United	1-1	1-1	0-4		0-4	1-0	1-6	4-2	0-6	2-1	1-4	0-4	0-4
Greenways	1-0	4-2	1-3	2-0	O	1-2	1-2	W-L	1-3	2-0	5-3	2-2	1-1
Metrogas	5-1	0-0	2-1	2-1	4-2	N	1-4	3-0	1-0	2-1	5-1	2-2	2-1
Phoenix Sports	2-0	8-1	6-2	6-0	1-0	2-0	E	1-0	4-1	2-1	1-1	2-0	4-1
Samuel Montagu Youth Club	2-1	L-W	0-2	3-1	1-2	L-W	2-1		0-3	3-1	2-3	1-4	1-2
Stansfeld Oxford/Bermondsey Club	3-0	1-0	3-0	7-0	0-1	2-1	1-1	1-0	W	3-2	2-1	1-2	1-2
Sutton Athletic	2-2	1-3	0-1	2-1	4-3	1-5	4-1	1-5	1-3	E	2-1	2-1	2-1
Tonbridge Invicta	1-4	1-6	1-4	4-0	5-1	2-3	1-2	2-2	1-1	2-3	S	2-1	2-1
Tudor Sports	3-1	2-1	1-0	2-0	5-0	1-0	2-1	5-0	2-3	1-2	5-0	T	1-0
Westerham	2-2	3-1	0-4	2-0	2-2	1-1	1-0	0-3	3-1	0-1	1-3	1-4	

Division One West — league table

	P	W	D	L	F	A	Pts
Phoenix Sports	24	21	2	1	72	17	65
Stansfeld Oxford & Ber. Club	24	16	2	6	50	21	50
Metrogas	24	14	4	6	43	32	46
Tudor Sports	24	12	4	8	42	22	40
Belvedere	24	9	7	8	37	37	34
Westerham	24	9	5	10	39	48	32
Bromleians Sports	24	9	4	11	49	54	31
Sutton Athletic	24	9	4	11	38	55	31
Greenways	24	9	4	11	36	50	31
Tonbridge Invicta	24	9	3	12	45	45	30
Bridon Ropes	24	6	7	11	39	48	25
Samuel Montagu Youth Club	24	5	3	16	27	50	18
Fleetdown United	24	2	3	19	14	74	9

VANDANEL / SHEPHERD NEAME KENT COUNTY LEAGUE DIVISION ONE WEST CONSTITUTION 2008-09

BELVEDERE . . . . Memorial Ground, 101a Woolwich Road, Abbey Wood SE2 0DY 01322 436724
BRIDON ROPES . . . . Meridian Sports Club, Charlton Park Road, Charlton SE7 8QS 020 8856 1923
BROMLEIANS SPORTS . . . . Scrubbs Farm, Lower Gravel Road, Bromley BR2 8LL 020 8462 5068
CHIPSTEAD . . . . Chipstead Rec, Chevening Road, Chipstead, Sevenoaks TN13 2RZ 07753 603944
CROCKENHILL . . . . Wested, Eynsford Road, Crockenhill, Swanley BR8 8EH 01322 662067
FARNBOROUGH OLD BOYS GUILD . . . Farnborough (Kent) Sports Club, High Street, Farnborough BR6 7BA 01689 826949
GREENWAYS . . . . Fleet Leisure & Sports Club, Nelson Road, Northfleet DA11 7EE 01474 359222
HAWKHURST UNITED . . . . . . King George V Playing Field, Moor Hill, Hawkhurst, Cranbrook TN18 4QB . . . . None
METROGAS . . . . Marathon Playing Fields, Forty Foot Way, New Eltham SE9 2HL 020 8859 1579
SUTTON ATHLETIC . . . . The Roaches, Parsonage Lane, Sutton-at-Hone, Dartford DA4 9HD 01322 280507
TONBRIDGE INVICTA . . . . Swanmead Sports Ground, Swanwead Way, off Cannon Lane, Tonbridge TN9 1PP 01732 350473
TUDOR SPORTS . . . . 31 Eltham Road, Lee Green SE12 8ES . . . . None
WESTERHAM . . . . Westerham Sports Association, King George V PF, Costells Meadow, Westerham TN16 1BL 01959 561106
IN: Chipstead (P – Division Two West), Crockenhill (R), Farnborough Old Boys Guild (P – Division Two West), Hawkhurst United (P – Division Two West)
OUT: Fleetdown United (R – Division Two West), Phoenix Sports (P), Samuel Montagu Youth Club (F), Stansfeld Oxford & Bermondsey Club (P)

DIVISION ONE PLAY-OFF: *(at Phoenix Sports)* **Stansfeld Oxford & Bermondsey Club** 3 AFC Sheppey 2

	APM Mears	Atcost	Borden Village	Canterbury City	Lanes End	Larkfield & New Hythe Wanderers	Otford United	Pembury	Platt United	Saga Sports & Social	Tenterden Town	UK Paper	Woodstock Park	P	W	D	L	F	A	Pts
APM Mears	D	4-0	3-3	0-3	2-0	7-1	0-3	5-0	3-1	5-0	8-0	7-2	0-1	24	21	2	1	105	24	65
Atcost	3-6	I	3-2	2-2	4-1	2-3	0-5	5-2	1-1	3-1	2-0	2-3	1-3	24	15	6	3	73	26	51
Borden Village	5-1	8-1	V	2-8	4-0	2-3	2-5	4-2	0-1	4-1	3-2	4-1	3-3	24	14	3	7	81	38	45
Canterbury City	1-1	4-1	5-0		5-2	7-0	1-0	3-3	5-1	5-1	6-2	7-0	4-1	24	11	11	2	56	38	44
Lanes End	2-3	2-1	0-2	1-5	T	2-0	1-1	1-1	4-1	4-1	1-0	2-2	2-6	24	11	7	6	42	44	40
Larkfield & New Hythe Wanderers	1-5	3-2	2-2	0-1	2-1	W	2-4	2-1	1-1	2-2	6-0	3-3	2-3	24	11	5	8	70	34	38
Otford United	2-0	5-0	4-2	0-1	1-1	3-2	O	6-0	2-2	2-1	4-0	3-2	2-2	24	8	6	10	39	57	30
Pembury	6-2	0-3	3-7	2-5	0-3	1-5	1-4		0-3	2-0	2-1	4-1	2-2	24	8	3	13	48	49	27
Platt United	1-0	3-0	2-1	0-3	2-2	2-2	1-1	2-0	E	1-2	3-2	2-1	1-2	24	7	5	12	51	82	26
Saga Sports & Social	1-2	4-4	0-1	2-9	1-2	3-3	3-0	0-4	1-2	A	4-1	1-4	1-0	24	5	4	15	36	66	19
Tenterden Town	0-8	2-1	2-4	0-9	2-3	2-1	0-7	3-2	1-2	2-3	S	4-6	2-2	24	5	4	15	40	73	19
UK Paper	0-7	5-2	1-1	0-8	2-1	1-8	3-2	0-5	2-2	5-0	2-2	T	2-2	24	5	3	16	29	71	18
Woodstock Park	2-2	4-1	4-4	4-0	1-1	1-0	1-1	4-1	2-2	2-1	1-1	3-2		24	3	2	19	29	93	11

(Rotated side text: Division Two East — Canterbury City, Otford United, Woodstock Park, APM Mears, Platt United, Larkfield & New Hythe Wanderers, Lanes End, UK Paper, Saga Sports & Social, Atcost, Pembury, Tenterden Town; "Wdrs", "-3")

VANDANEL / SHEPHERD NEAME KENT COUNTY LEAGUE DIVISION TWO EAST CONSTITUTION 2008-09

AFC SEVENOAKS ...... Sevenoaks Town FC, Greatness Park, Seal Road (on main A25), Sevenoaks TN14 5BL 01732 741987
BORDEN VILLAGE .... Borden Playstool, Wises Lane, Borden, Sittingbourne ME9 8LP 07903 016794
BREDHURST JUNIORS .... 44 Two Sports Ground, Featherby Road, Gillingham ME8 6AN 01634 233350
LANES END .... Waller Park, Wood Lane, Darenth, Dartford DA2 7LR 01322 221006
LARKFIELD & NEW HYTHE WANDERERS ... Larkfield Sports Ground, New Hythe Lane, Larkfield, Aylesford ME20 6PU .. 01732 873310
MALGO .... The Old County Ground, Norman Road, West Malling ME19 6RL .... None
PEMBURY .... Woodside Recreation Ground, Henwoods Mount, Woodside Road, Pembury TN2 4BH 07970 026628
PLATT UNITED .... Stonehouse Field, Longmill Lane (off A25), Platt TN15 8QS 07702 634344
PREMIER .... Hersden Recreation Ground, Hersden, Canterbury CT3 4HY 07825 704504
SAGA SPORTS & SOCIAL .... Canteen Meadow, The Street, Bishopsbourne, Canterbury CT4 5HX .... None
TENTERDEN TOWN .... Recreation Ground Road, High Street, Tenterden TN30 6RA 07786 932151
UK PAPER .... UK Paper Sports Ground, Gore Court Road, Sittingbourne ME10 1QN 01795 477047
WOODSTOCK PARK .... Sittingbourne Research Centre, Broadoak Road, Sittingbourne ME9 8AG 07774 654912
IN: AFC Sevenoaks (formerly Cray W & NB) (S – Division Two West), Bredhurst Juniors (P – Rochester & District League Premier Division), Malgo (P – Maidstone & District League Premier Division), Premier (P – Canterbury & District League Premier Division)
OUT: APM Mears (P – Division One East), Atcost (W – Tonbridge & District League Premier Division), Canterbury City (P – Division One East), Otford United (P – Division One East)

Note – Old Addeyans withdrew during the course of the season. Their results are shown herein but are expunged from the league table

	Borough United	Chipstead	Chislehurst	Cray W & NB	Eltham Palace	Erith '147	Farnborough OB Guild	Halls	Hawkhurst United	Meridian Sports	Old Addeyans	Old Bexleians	Wickham Park	P	W	D	L	F	A	Pts
Borough United	D	2-4	3-5	3-1	1-1	1-3	4-1	2-1	1-7	2-2	n/a	1-3	3-0	22	19	0	3	70	19	57
Chipstead	2-2	I	3-0	12-3	9-1	2-2	0-3	3-2	6-2	3-1	n/a	4-2	6-2	22	18	1	3	76	33	55
Chislehurst	2-5	1-5	V	4-2	4-3	4-4	0-3	4-2	2-2	3-2	n/a	2-3	0-5	22	14	5	3	55	44	47
Cray W & NB	2-4	2-6	3-1		1-1	4-4	0-6	2-2	1-6	2-0	n/a	2-0	5-0	22	8	5	9	46	57	29
Eltham Palace	2-2	3-2	3-2	3-2	T	2-5	1-2	1-1	0-1	2-4	n/a	1-3	0-3	22	8	4	10	35	53	28
Erith '147	1-5	3-6	3-1	4-0	1-2	W	0-6	0-0	0-2	2-0	n/a	4-1	0-3	22	7	5	10	41	48	26
Farnborough Old Boys Guild	8-1	3-2	6-1	5-3	4-0	3-1	O	2-0	2-0	2-1	n/a	0-1	1-2	22	7	3	12	49	70	24
Halls	0-5	1-3	5-2	2-2	0-1	2-1	0-2		0-4	0-0	n/a	0-0	4-2	22	6	4	12	45	54	22
Hawkhurst United	4-3	3-1	W-L	2-0	4-1	7-1	2-3	5-3	W	4-0	n/a	5-3	4-2	22	6	4	12	72	71	22
Meridian Sports	1-0	3-2	1-2	1-2	0-1	1-0	0-1	1-0	1-2	E	n/a	2-1	1-1	22	6	2	14	29	44	20
Old Addeyans	n/a	n/a	n/a	n/a	n/a	0-3	n/a	n/a	n/a	n/a	S	n/a	n/a							
Old Bexleians	2-2	1-3	5-5	4-2	1-2	0-3	0-3	2-2	1-3	3-0	n/a	T	3-0	22	5	4	13	37	65	19
Wickham Park	3-2	2-5	2-4	1-1	2-2	1-4	0-4	0-2	2-7	0-3	n/a	2-1		22	4	6	12	37	37	18

(Rotated side text: Division Two West — Farnborough Old Boys Guild, Hawkhurst United, Chipstead, Borough United, Erith '147, Old Bexleians, Eltham Palace, Chislehurst, Meridian Sports, Cray W & NB, Halls, Wickham Park; "-1", "-3", Old Addeyans – record expunged)

VANDANEL / SHEPHERD NEAME KENT COUNTY LEAGUE DIVISION TWO WEST CONSTITUTION 2008-09

BLACKHEATH UNITED ... Bellingham Leisure & Lifestyle Centre, Randlesdown Road, Bellingham SE6 3BT 0208 697 0043
BOROUGH UNITED .... Princes Golf & Leisure Club, Darenth Road, Dartford DA1 1LZ 01322 276565
CHARLTON ATHLETIC COMMUNITY ... Samuel Montagu Youth Centre, 122 Broadwalk, Kidbrooke SE3 8ND 0208 856 1126/9680
CHISLEHURST .... Coldharbour Leisure Centre, Chaple Farm Road, New Eltham SE9 3LX 020 8851 8692
ELTHAM PALACE .... Beaverwood Lodge, Beaverwood Road, Chislehurst BR7 6HF 020 8300 1385
ERITH '147 .... STC Sports Ground, Ivor Grove, New Eltham SE9 2AJ .... None
FLEETDOWN UNITED .... Heath Lane Open Space, Heath Lane (Lower), Dartford BA1 2QD 01322 273848
FOREST HILL PARK .... Ladywell Arena, Doggetts Road, Catford SE6 4QX 0208 314 1986
HALLS .... Bexley Park Sports & Social Club, Calvert Drive, Bexley DA2 7GU .... None
MERIDIAN SPORTS .... Meridian Sports & Social, 110 Charlton Park Lane, Charlton SE7 8QS 020 8856 1923
OPK .... Meridian Sports & Social, 110 Charlton Park Lane, Charlton SE7 8QS 020 8856 1923
OLD BEXLEIANS .... Seven Acre Sports Club, Church Manor Avenue, Abbey Wood SE2 0HY .... None
WICKHAM PARK ...... Wickham Park Sports Club, 228-230 Pickhurst Rise, West Wickham, Bromley BR4 0AQ 020 8777 2550
IN: Blackheath United (P – Bromley & District League Premier Division), Charlton Athletic Community (P – South London Alliance Division Four), Fleetdown United (R – Division One West), Forest Hill Park (P – South London Alliance Premier Division), OPK (P – Bromley & District League Premier Division)
OUT: AFC Sevenoaks (formerly Cray W & NB) (S – Division Two East), Chipstead (P – Division One West), Farnborough Old Boys Guild (P – Division One West), Hawkhurst United (P – Division One West), Old Addeyans (WS)

WWW.NLNEWSDESK.CO.UK

BILL MANKELOW INTER-REGIONAL CHALLENGE CUP
(All clubs in Premier and First Divisions)

FIRST ROUND EAST
Bly Spartans 2 New Romney 1
Guru Nanak 2 Univ. of Kent 2 *aet* (4-2p)
Oakwood (w/o) v St Margarets (scr.)
Staplehurst & Monarchs United 2
Betteshanger Welfare 1
FIRST ROUND WEST
Bromleians Sports 2 Greenways 0
Fleetdown United 0 Tudor Sports 4
Samuel Montagu Youth Club 3
Metrogas 1
Stansfeld O & B Club 0 Westerham 1
Sutton Athletic 4 Tonbridge Invicta 1
SECOND ROUND EAST
Bearsted (w/o) v Ashford Borough (scr.)
Bly Spartans 4 Oakwood 0
Hollands & Blair 4 Bromley Green 1
Kennington 2 Guru Nanak 6
Milton Athletic 3 Lydd Town 0

Staplehurst & Monarchs United 5
Sheerness East 4
Tyler Hill (scr.) v AFC Sheppey (w/o)
Uniflo (scr.) v Norton Sports (w/o)
SECOND ROUND EAST
Belvedere 3 Lewisham Borough
(Community) 2
Bromleians Sports 0 Bridon Ropes 1
Crockenhill 2 Sutton Athletic 1
Fleet Leisure 4 Cray Valley Paper Mills 1
Phoenix Sports 3 Orpington 4 *aet*
Rusthall 3 Samuel Montagu Youth
Club 1 *aet*
Snodland 3 Coney Hall 4
Westerham (w/o) v Tudor Sports (scr.)
THIRD ROUND EAST
Bearsted 2 Hollands & Blair 6
Guru Nanak 0 Bly Spartans 1
Norton Sports 4 Milton Athletic 1

Staplehurst & Monarchs United 3 AFC
Sheppey 1
THIRD ROUND WEST
Belvedere 1 Coney Hall 0
Fleet Leisure 4 Rusthall 2 *aet*
Orpington 2 Crockenhill 0
Westerham 3 Bridon Ropes 4 *aet*
QUARTER-FINALS
Belvedere 0 Fleet Leisure 2
Bridon Ropes 2 Staplehurst & Monarchs
United 1
Norton Sports 2 Bly Spartans 3
Orpington 2 Hollands & Blair 1
SEMI-FINALS
Fleet Leisure 0 Bridon Ropes 0 *aet* (3-1p)
Orpington 1 Bly Spartans 2 *aet*
FINAL
(April 17th at Chatham Town)
Fleet Leisure 2 Bly Spartans 1

LES LECKIE CUP
(Eastern region clubs from outside the Premier Division)

FIRST ROUND
APM Mears 2 Woodstock Park 1
Atcost 0 Guru Nanak 4
Borden Village 2 Otford United 0
Canterbury City (w/o) v Ashford Borough (scr.)
Lanes End 0 Betteshanger Welfare 4
New Romney 2 University of Kent 3
Oakwood (w/o) Pembury (scr.)
Saga Sports & Social 0 AFC Sheppey 3
St Margarets (scr.) Larkfield & New Hythe Wanderers (w/o)
Staplehurst & Monarchs United 10 UK Paper 3
SECOND ROUND
Betteshanger Welfare 2 Kennington 4
Borden Village 0 Bly Spartans 5
Canterbury City 0 Tenterden Town 0 *aet* (3-2p)

Larkfield & New Hythe Wanderers 0 AFC Sheppey 3
Oakwood 1 APM Mears 0
Platt United 2 Lydd Town 0
Staplehurst & Monarchs United 1 University of Kent 2
Uniflo (scr.) v Guru Nanak (w/o)
QUARTER-FINALS
AFC Sheppey 4 Kennington 3
Bly Spartans 4 Platt United 0
Canterbury City 1 University of Kent 3
Oakwood 2 Guru Nanak 1
SEMI-FINALS
AFC Sheppey 3 Oakwood 2 *aet*
Bly Spartans 4 University of Kent 1
FINAL *(May 6th at Faversham Town)*
Bly Spartans 2 AFC Sheppey 0 *aet*

WEST KENT CHALLENGE SHIELD
(Western region clubs from outside the Premier Division)

FIRST ROUND
Bridon Ropes 1 Belvedere 3
Bromleians Sports 2 Farnborough Old Boys Guild 0
Cray W & NB 5 Chislehurst 0
Eltham Palace 1 Metrogas 5
Erith '147 2 Meridian Sports 1
Greenways 5 Chipstead 2
Halls 2 Borough United 2 *aet* (4-2p)
Old Addeyans (scr.) v Hawkhurst United (w/o)
Samuel Montagu Youth Club 1 Westerham 2
Wickham Park 5 Old Bexleians 0
SECOND ROUND
Erith '147 1 Belvedere 3
Greenways 3 Wickham Park 2
Phoenix Sports 8 Cray W & NB 1
Stansfeld O & B Club 2 Halls 0

Sutton Athletic 1 Fleetdown United 0
Tonbridge Invicta 2 Bromleians Sports 3
Tudor Sports 3 Metrogas 2
Westerham 0 Hawkhurst United 1
QUARTER-FINALS
Bromleians Sports 0 Belvedere 1
Greenways 1 Phoenix Sports 3
Hawkhurst United 3 Sutton Athletic 2 *aet*
Tudor Sports 4 Stansfeld O & B Club 1
SEMI-FINALS
Hawkhurst United 1 Tudor Sports 2
Phoenix Sports 5 Belvedere 1
FINAL
(April 24th at Sevenoaks Town)
Phoenix Sports 1 Tudor Sports 1 *aet* (4-2p)

FLOODLIGHT CUP
(All Eastern teams from Premier Division and selected teams from Div One East – all games played at Faversham Tn)

FIRST ROUND
Sheerness East 1 Norton Sports 2
SEMI-FINALS
Bearsted 0 New Romney 1
Norton Sports 2 Bly Spartans 3

FINAL
(March 4th at Faversham Town)
Bly Spartans 4 New Romney 1

(The 2006/07 competition was eventually abandoned after originally being held over to season 2007/08)

RESERVES CUP

FINAL *(May 13th at Lordswood)*
New Romney Res. 2 Borden Village Res. 3 *aet*

KENT LEAGUE

	Beckenham Town	Croydon	Deal Town	Erith Town	Erith & Belvedere	Faversham Town	Greenwich Borough	Herne Bay	Holmesdale	Hythe Town	Lordswood	Sevenoaks Town	Slade Green	Sporting Bengal United	Thamesmead Town	Tunbridge Wells	VCD Athletic
Beckenham Town	P	4-0	4-1	4-1	2-1	3-1	2-1	2-1	2-1	6-3	1-1	2-0	2-1	5-2	2-6	3-0	1-3
Croydon	1-2	R	1-0	1-2	1-1	3-4	0-3	0-7	0-0	0-2	0-2	1-0	3-0	1-0	0-1	6-0	0-3
Deal Town	0-0	0-1	E	1-1	1-4	3-1	1-2	3-2	1-1	2-1	5-1	5-1	2-3	3-2	5-5	4-0	1-2
Erith Town	2-2	4-2	2-0	M	1-1	1-1	2-0	2-4	1-2	2-3	3-0	1-1	0-1	5-0	1-1	2-0	1-1
Erith & Belvedere	0-5	1-3	1-3	0-0	I	1-2	1-1	0-0	1-0	4-1	1-1	3-2	6-1	4-0	4-2	8-1	0-3
Faversham Town	1-5	1-4	2-3	0-5	1-1	E	2-2	0-6	2-0	1-3	0-3	0-1	1-2	2-0	1-2	3-1	1-2
Greenwich Borough	1-1	2-2	2-0	1-1	1-0	0-2	R	1-0	0-3	1-1	1-0	0-2	1-0	5-1	1-2	1-0	1-2
Herne Bay	1-0	1-0	4-3	0-1	2-2	4-1	0-3		2-0	0-3	2-1	1-1	0-2	3-1	0-0	0-3	3-1
Holmesdale	3-3	0-0	0-2	0-2	2-4	4-0	1-1	1-3		1-2	1-1	4-2	1-1	2-4	1-2	1-5	1-4
Hythe Town	1-2	2-0	3-0	2-1	8-1	5-0	0-0	1-1	4-0	D	3-0	2-0	7-1	5-0	1-1	2-1	3-0
Lordswood	0-0	4-2	4-1	0-1	2-3	1-2	1-3	1-2	2-0	1-4	I	1-4	1-1	6-0	1-6	3-2	0-4
Sevenoaks Town	1-2	2-2	2-4	2-2	1-0	0-5	2-2	0-0	1-3	2-4	6-0	V	3-4	5-1	1-2	0-1	0-3
Slade Green	1-5	0-2	3-3	0-2	0-5	1-2	1-1	3-3	0-1	1-0	2-1	1-3	I	1-1	1-5	1-2	0-2
Sporting Bengal United	2-4	3-2	2-3	0-8	0-4	1-1	2-1	0-2	2-2	1-7	0-0	1-7	0-3	S	1-7	0-3	0-4
Thamesmead Town	1-0	2-0	3-0	2-1	2-2	2-1	1-0	4-2	2-1	1-1	4-0	2-4	5-0	5-1	I	2-0	4-2
Tunbridge Wells	1-1	7-0	3-1	2-2	0-4	5-2	1-5	2-2	2-0	4-0	2-0	2-0	0-1	0-1	0-1	O	1-1
VCD Athletic	2-3	1-0	3-1	1-1	0-0	5-0	2-0	4-2	1-1	2-1	1-0	3-1	3-2	5-2	1-2	2-0	N

Premier Division	P	W	D	L	F	A	Pts
Thamesmead Town	32	24	6	2	87	36	78
VCD Athletic	32	22	5	5	73	33	71
Beckenham Town	32	21	7	4	80	41	70
Hythe Town	32	20	5	7	85	35	65
Erith Town	32	13	12	7	61	35	51
Herne Bay	32	14	8	10	60	46	50
Erith & Belvedere	32	13	10	9	68	49	49
Greenwich Borough	32	12	10	10	44	36	46
Deal Town	32	12	5	15	62	66	41
Tunbridge Wells	32	12	5	15	53	60	41
Sevenoaks Town	32	9	6	17	57	64	33
Croydon	32	9	5	18	38	61	32
Faversham Town	32	9	4	19	43	79	31
Slade Green	32	8	6	18	38	75	30
Holmesdale	32	6	10	16	40	59	28
Lordswood	32	7	6	19	39	69	27
Sporting Bengal United	32	4	4	24	31	115	16

CHALLENGE SHIELD
(Premier Division champions v League Cup holders)
(August 4th at Whitstable Town)
Whitsable Town 3 Thamesmead Town 2

KENT LEAGUE LEAGUE CONSTITUTION 2008-09

BECKENHAM TOWN . . . . Eden Park Avenue, Beckenham BR3 3JJ 020 8650 1066
CROYDON . . . . Croydon Sports Arena, Albert Road, South Norwood SE25 4QL 020 8654 8555/3462
DEAL TOWN . . . . Charles Sports Ground, St Leonards Road, Deal CT14 9BB 01304 375623
ERITH TOWN . . . . Erith Sports Centre, Avenue Road, Erith DA8 3AJ 01322 350271
ERITH & BELVEDERE . . . . Welling United FC, Park View Road, Welling DA16 1SY 020 8304 0333
FAVERSHAM TOWN . . . . Salter Lane, Faversham ME13 8ND . . . . None
GREENWICH BOROUGH . . . . Harrow Meadow, Eltham Green Road, Eltham SE9 6BA 020 8859 5788
HERNE BAY . . . . Winchs Field, Stanley Gardens, Herne Bay CT6 5SG 01227 374156
HOLMESDALE . . . . Holmesdale Sports & Social, Oakley Road, Bromley Common BR9 8HG 020 8462 4440
HYTHE TOWN . . . . Reachfields Stadium, Fort Road, Hythe CT21 6JS 01303 264932
LORDSWOOD . . . . Martyn Grove, Northdane Way, Walderslade ME5 8YE 01634 669138
NORTON SPORTS . . . . Norton Park, Provender Lane, Norton, Faversham ME9 9JU 07989 581062
SEVENOAKS TOWN . . . . Greatness Park, Seal Road (on main A25), Sevenoaks TN14 5BL 01732 741987
SLADE GREEN . . . . The Small Glenn, 35 Moat Lane, Slade Green, Erith BA8 2ND 01322 351077
SPORTING BENGAL UNITED . . . Mile End Stadium, Rhodeswell Road, Burdett Road, Poplar E14 7TW 020 8980 1885
TUNBRIDGE WELLS . . . . Culverden Stadium, Culverden Down, Tunbridge Wells TN4 9SH 01892 520517
VCD ATHLETIC . . . . Oakwood, Old Road, Crayford DA1 4DN 01322 524262

IN: Norton Sports (P – Kent County League Premier Division)
OUT: Thamesmead Town (P – Isthmian League Division One North)

PREMIER DIVISION CUP

GROUP A

	P	W	D	L	F	A	Pts
VCD Athletic	8	4	2	2	12	8	14
Sevenoaks Town	8	3	2	3	8	9	11
Greenwich Borough	8	2	5	1	10	7	11
Sevenoaks Town	8	3	2	3	8	9	11
Tunbridge Wells	8	1	1	6	9	17	4

Greenwich Borough 1 Herne Bay 1
Greenwich Borough 2 Sevenoaks Town 0
Greenwich Borough 2 Tunbridge Wells 2
Greenwich Borough 1 VCD Athletic 1
Herne Bay 1 Greenwich Borough 1
Herne Bay 2 Sevenoaks Town 2
Herne Bay 1 Tunbridge Wells 0
Herne Bay 3 VCD Athletic 1
Sevenoaks Town 1 Greenwich Borough 0
Sevenoaks Town 1 Herne Bay 1
Sevenoaks Town 1 Tunbridge Wells 3
Sevenoaks Town 2 VCD Athletic 0
Tunbridge Wells 1 Greenwich Borough 3
Tunbridge Wells 1 Herne Bay 2
Tunbridge Wells 0 Sevenoaks Town 1
Tunbridge Wells 1 VCD Athletic 4
VCD Athletic 0 Greenwich Borough 0
VCD Athletic 2 Herne Bay 0
VCD Athletic 1 Sevenoaks Town 0
VCD Athletic 3 Tunbridge Wells 1

GROUP B

	P	W	D	L	F	A	Pts
Erith & Belvedere	6	4	2	0	23	7	14
Thamesmead Town	6	4	1	1	15	7	13
Deal Town	6	2	1	3	11	12	7
Faversham Town	6	0	0	6	5	28	0

Deal Town 1 Erith & Belvedere 1
Deal Town 5 Faversham Town 0
Deal Town 0 Thamesmead Town 2
Erith & Belvedere 5 Deal Town 2
Erith & Belvedere 9 Faversham Town 2
Erith & Belvedere 2 Thamesmead Town 1
Faversham Town 0 Deal Town 2
Faversham Town 0 Erith & Belvedere 5
Faversham Town 1 Thamesmead Town 2
Thamesmead Town 4 Deal Town 1
Thamesmead Town 1 Erith & Belvedere 1
Thamesmead Town 5 Faversham Town 2

GROUP C

	P	W	D	L	F	A	Pts
Croydon	6	4	1	1	15	6	13
Erith Town	6	3	0	3	9	6	9
Lordswood	6	2	2	2	5	6	8
Sporting Bengal United	6	1	1	4	6	17	4

Croydon 2 Erith Town 3
Croydon 2 Lordswood 0
Croydon 5 Sporting Bengal United 1
Erith Town 0 Croydon 1
Erith Town 0 Lordswood 1
Erith Town 1 Sporting Bengal United 2
Lordswood 1 Croydon 0
Lordswood 0 Erith Town 1
Lordswood 1 Sporting Bengal United 1
Sporting Bengal United 1 Croydon 4
Sporting Bengal United 0 Erith Town 4
Sporting Bengal United 1 Lordswood 2

GROUP D

	P	W	D	L	F	A	Pts
Hythe Town	6	5	0	1	16	5	15
Beckenham Town	6	4	0	2	13	6	12
Holmesdale	6	2	0	4	8	14	6
Slade Green	6	1	0	5	3	15	3

Beckenham Town 2 Holmesdale 1
Beckenham Town 4 Hythe Town 0
Beckenham Town 0 Slade Green 1
Holmesdale 1 Beckenham Town 5
Holmesdale 0 Hythe Town 3
Holmesdale 2 Slade Green 0
Hythe Town 3 Beckenham Town 0
Hythe Town 3 Holmesdale 0
Hythe Town 5 Slade Green 1
Slade Green 0 Beckenham Town 2
Slade Green 1 Holmesdale 4
Slade Green 0 Hythe Town 2

QUARTER-FINALS

Croydon 1 **Herne Bay** 2

Erith & Belvedere 1 **Beckenham Town** 2

Hythe Town 5 Thamesmead Town 0

VCD Athletic 1 **Erith Town** 2 *aet*

SEMI-FINALS *(played over two legs)*

Beckenham Tn 0 Erith Tn 0, **Erith Tn** 2 Beckenham Tn 1 *aet*

Hythe Town 4 Herne Bay 1, Herne Bay 0 **Hythe Town** 2

FINAL *(May 3rd at Folkestone Invicta)*

Hythe Town 0 **Erith Town** 1

Division One	P	W	D	L	F	A	Pts
Thamesmead Town Res.	22	14	5	3	44	23	47
Dartford Res.	22	12	4	6	42	28	40
Chatham Town Res.	22	13	1	8	48	38	40
Maidstone United Res.	22	11	5	6	50	26	38
Sevenoaks Town Res.	22	10	6	6	40	33	36
Cray Wanderers Res.	22	10	5	7	33	36	35
Erith & Belvedere Res.	22	10	3	9	46	48	33
Whitstable Town Res.	22	8	4	10	44	42	28
Margate Res.	22	6	6	10	49	56	24
Folkestone Invicta Res.	22	7	2	13	31	44	23
Ramsgate Res.	22	4	4	14	29	49	16
Erith Town Res.	22	2	5	15	22	55	11

Division Two		P	W	D	L	F	A	Pts
Dover Athletic Res.		24	18	3	3	67	28	57
Ashford Town Res.		24	14	5	5	68	36	47
Greenwich Borough Res.		24	14	5	5	56	30	47
VCD Athletic Res.		24	13	6	5	59	30	45
Deal Town Res.		24	13	4	7	43	29	43
Tunbridge Wells Res.		24	14	0	10	58	39	42
Holmesdale Res.		24	13	3	8	37	30	42
Faversham Town Res.		24	10	2	12	31	49	32
Hythe Town Res.		24	9	4	11	33	46	31
Sittingbourne Res.		24	5	4	15	31	55	19
Lordswood Res.		24	5	4	15	25	61	19
Herne Bay Res.		24	4	4	16	21	49	16
Croydon Res.	-1	24	1	2	21	19	66	4

DIVISION ONE/TWO CUP

FINAL *(April 19th at Whitstable Town)*

Ashford Town Res. 2 Dartford Res. 1

FLOODLIGHT CUP

FINAL *(April 29th at Faversham Town)*

Chatham Town Res. 0 **Deal Town Res.** 1

LEICESTERSHIRE SENIOR LEAGUE

	Anstey Nomads	Aylestone Park	Bardon Hill Sports	Barrow Town	Birstall United	Blaby & Whetstone Athletic	Ellistown	Highfield Rangers	Hinckley Downes	Holwell Sports	Ibstock United	Kirby Muxloe SC	Ratby Sports	Rothley Imperial	Saffron Dynamo	St Andrews SC	Thurmaston Town	Thurnby Rangers
Anstey Nomads		0-2	1-2	0-3	2-1	4-1	1-1	1-0	1-3	2-1	1-1	0-5	3-0	2-3	3-0	2-0	2-3	2-0
Aylestone Park	1-2	P	0-3	0-3	2-2	0-0	2-3	1-4	3-1	1-0	2-4	0-0	2-0	5-2	1-3	3-2	1-0	1-2
Bardon Hill Sports	1-2	0-2	R	4-5	2-4	3-5	3-0	4-1	2-2	3-5	2-1	2-3	3-1	3-2	0-2	2-2	1-1	5-1
Barrow Town	0-1	6-0	2-2	E	2-3	4-3	3-2	1-2	2-2	3-1	1-1	2-0	6-1	5-1	4-2	1-2	4-1	5-2
Birstall United	2-1	5-1	2-3	3-4	M	0-1	0-1	3-2	3-0	0-0	3-3	1-2	2-1	4-2	3-1	0-1	0-1	5-2
Blaby & Whetstone Athletic	3-0	4-0	1-2	1-2	2-2	I	5-1	6-1	3-1	0-3	0-1	0-7	3-1	0-1	1-3	2-1	3-2	2-0
Ellistown	2-2	3-0	0-2	3-3	4-0	3-2	E	2-0	1-2	2-4	3-3	1-1	3-0	4-0	1-2	0-3	3-1	5-0
Highfield Rangers	1-2	1-0	2-4	0-3	3-4	0-1	0-1	R	0-4	0-1	0-1	1-4	1-4	2-0	2-1	2-0	2-2	0-0
Hinckley Downes	3-1	2-1	2-3	1-1	2-1	4-3	3-2	5-0		2-2	6-1	0-2	6-0	3-1	1-3	1-0	1-1	2-1
Holwell Sports	1-1	6-1	3-1	3-3	1-0	2-0	5-1	6-1	1-3	D	2-0	1-0	2-3	4-1	1-0	2-4	4-0	4-1
Ibstock United	2-2	4-0	2-1	0-1	3-2	1-3	3-2	0-1	0-1	0-2	I	1-4	3-0	6-0	2-1	2-2	0-1	1-2
Kirby Muxloe SC	2-0	4-1	0-2	1-2	2-2	5-1	0-0	2-0	2-1	3-0	2-1	V	5-0	17-1	2-0	1-3	2-0	12-0
Ratby Sports	1-2	2-3	1-4	1-3	4-1	1-1	0-7	3-0	0-0	5-0	1-3	2-4	I	3-3	7-3	0-4	0-5	4-1
Rothley Imperial	1-2	3-2	2-4	2-1	1-1	4-3	3-2	2-0	0-1	1-1	1-3	1-2	5-1	S	4-1	0-2	1-2	2-0
Saffron Dynamo	3-1	0-2	3-2	2-2	1-2	2-1	3-1	3-0	2-1	2-2	3-3	1-2	2-0	2-0	I	3-2	1-1	2-1
St Andrews SC	3-0	4-1	4-0	1-0	1-2	3-3	0-1	3-1	2-4	2-1	3-2	1-0	1-2	0-3	0-2	O	3-2	7-0
Thurmaston Town	3-1	4-0	0-4	2-5	0-3	0-1	1-3	4-3	2-3	2-2	3-4	0-2	0-3	1-0	1-2	1-0	N	4-1
Thurnby Rangers	2-2	2-0	0-4	1-8	1-5	2-4	1-2	1-1	1-2	2-9	0-4	1-2	0-5	5-4	0-3	2-6	2-1	

Premier Division		P	W	D	L	F	A	Pts
Kirby Muxloe SC		34	24	4	6	105	28	76
Barrow Town	-3	34	22	7	5	102	51	70
Hinckley Downes		34	20	6	8	82	49	66
Holwell Sports		34	18	7	9	77	48	61
Bardon Hill Sports		34	18	4	12	83	64	58
Saffron Dynamo		34	18	4	12	67	58	58
St Andrews SC		34	17	3	14	67	48	54
Birstall United		34	15	6	13	71	59	51
Ellistown		34	15	6	13	70	58	51
Ibstock United		34	14	7	13	64	59	49
Blaby & Whetstone Athletic		34	15	4	15	69	66	49
Anstey Nomads		34	14	6	14	49	57	48
Thurmaston Town		34	12	5	17	52	64	41
Rothley Imperial		34	11	3	20	56	91	36
Aylestone Park		34	10	3	21	41	81	33
Ratby Sports		34	9	3	22	56	96	30
Highfield Rangers		34	8	1	25	34	79	25
Thurnby Rangers	-3	34	5	3	26	37	126	15

EVERARDS BREWERY LEICESTERSHIRE SENIOR LEAGUE PREMIER DIVISION CONSTITUTION 2008-09

ANSTEY NOMADS .... Cropston Road, Anstey LE7 7BY 0116 236 4868
ASFORDBY AMATEURS .... Hoby Road Sports Ground, Hoby Road, Asfordby, Melton Mowbray LE14 3TL 01664 434545
ASHBY IVANHOE .... Hood Park, North Street, Ashby-de-la-Zouch LE65 1HU 01530 412181
AYLESTONE PARK .... Dorset Avenue, Wigston, Leicester LE18 4WD 0116 277 5307
BIRSTALL UNITED .... Meadow Lane, Birstall LE4 4FN 0116 267 1230
BLABY & WHETSTONE ATHLETIC ... Blaby & Whetstone Boys Club, Warwick Road, Whetstone LE8 6LW 0116 286 4852
COTTESMORE AMATEURS .... Rogues Park, Main Street, Cottesmore, Oakham LE15 4DH 01572 813486
HIGHFIELD RANGERS .... 443 Gleneagles Avenue, Rushey Mead, Leicester LE4 7YJ 0116 266 0009
LEICS CONSTABULARY .... Police Headquarters, St Johns, Enderby. .... 0116 248 2198 (matchdays only)
RATBY SPORTS .... Desford Lane, Ratby, Leicester LE6 0LF 0116 239 2474
ROTHLEY IMPERIAL .... Loughborough Road, Mountsorrell, Leicester LE7 7NH 0116 292 0538
SAFFRON DYNAMO .... Cambridge Road, Whetstone LE8 3LG 0116 284 9695
THURMASTON TOWN .... Elizabeth Park, Checkland Road, Thurmaston, Leicester LE4 8FN 0116 260 2519
THURNBY RANGERS .... Dakyn Road, Thurnby Lodge Estate, Leicester LE5 2ED 0116 243 3698
IN: *Asfordby Amateurs (P), Ashby Ivanhoe (P), Cottesmore Amateurs (P), Leics Constabulary (P)*
OUT: *Bardon Hill Sports (P – East Midlands Counties League), Barrow Town (P – East Midlands Counties League), Ellistown (P – East Midlands Counties League), Hinckley Downes (P – East Midlands Counties League), Holwell Sports (P – East Midlands Counties League), Ibstock United (P – East Midlands Counties League), Kirby Muxloe SC (P – East Midlands Counties League), St Andrews SC (P – East Midlands Counties League)*

	Anstey Town	Asfordby Amateurs	Ashby Ivanhoe	Cottesmore Amateurs	Dunton & Broughton Rangers	Earl Shilton Albion	FC Braunstone Victoria	FC Khalsa	Hathern	Huncote Sports & Social	Leics Constabulary	Lutterworth Athletic	Lutterworth Town	Narborough & Littlethorpe	Ravenstone	Sileby Town
Anstey Town		0-2	2-5	3-7	1-3	1-2	2-1	3-0	2-2	1-1	5-0	0-3	3-0	1-3	1-0	2-5
Asfordby Amateurs	5-0		0-1	4-1	5-0	2-2	6-0	2-0	3-0	2-2	9-0	2-0	3-0	5-1	5-1	2-2
Ashby Ivanhoe	2-2	0-0	D	9-1	3-2	2-1	7-2	6-4	3-0	2-0	5-0	1-0	3-0	0-2	3-1	3-1
Cottesmore Amateurs	0-1	0-5	0-2	I	3-2	3-4	0-2	2-7	2-2	3-2	0-1	1-2	2-1	1-1	1-2	1-6
Dunton & Broughton Rangers	0-0	1-1	1-1	2-1	V	3-3	2-0	4-2	4-0	2-1	1-0	5-3	0-2	1-0	1-1	
Earl Shilton Albion	0-3	1-2	3-2	6-1	1-1	I	2-1	3-3	1-3	4-1	3-0	0-3	1-2	3-0	4-0	2-0
FC Braunstone Victoria	5-2	0-4	2-1	5-3	2-2	3-9	S	4-5	1-3	7-0	5-1	0-3	0-2	3-4	3-1	2-3
FC Khalsa	1-1	1-3	1-4	5-0	1-1	0-1	3-3	I	3-1	2-5	2-1	0-4	0-0	4-3	3-0	1-4
Hathern	3-1	0-2	1-3	4-0	1-1	1-1	2-1	1-3	O	2-0	3-1	1-3	1-3	2-5	5-1	1-3
Huncote Sports & Social	3-3	0-4	1-4	3-1	1-1	1-2	3-3	3-6	1-1	N	0-3	1-4	0-3	4-2	1-4	1-3
Leics Constabulary	1-2	0-5	2-3	1-4	1-1	1-1	1-4	2-3	0-0	1-3		1-3	0-3	4-1	2-1	2-3
Lutterworth Athletic	1-1	2-2	1-2	4-0	4-1	1-0	3-0	1-1	4-4	1-0	4-0	O	1-0	1-1	0-0	1-1
Lutterworth Town	3-1	1-1	0-4	5-0	2-2	0-1	4-0	4-3	5-3	0-0	1-1	1-2	N	2-0	4-1	0-0
Narborough & Littlethorpe	1-1	0-9	1-4	5-2	2-0	2-1	1-1	1-3	0-1	5-1	1-1	0-2	0-3	E	1-0	1-1
Ravenstone	0-2	0-1	1-1	0-0	2-2	3-2	1-3	1-2	0-0	0-1	3-0	1-3	2-4	1-0		0-1
Sileby Town	3-1	0-3	1-1	2-1	2-3	5-0	3-1	2-1	2-0	7-0	1-1	2-1	1-3	3-2	4-1	

Division One		P	W	D	L	F	A	Pts
Asfordby Amateurs		30	22	7	1	99	16	73
Ashby Ivanhoe		30	22	5	3	87	33	71
Lutterworth Athletic		30	18	7	5	62	25	61
Sileby Town		30	18	7	5	72	39	61
Lutterworth Town		30	15	6	9	59	41	51
Earl Shilton Albion		30	14	5	11	62	50	47
Dunton & Broughton Rangers		30	11	13	6	52	47	46
FC Khalsa		30	12	6	12	68	68	42
Narborough & Littlethorpe		30	10	6	14	48	64	36
Hathern		30	9	8	13	50	59	35
Anstey Town		30	9	8	13	48	62	35
FC Braunstone Victoria	-3	30	9	5	16	67	84	29
Huncote Sports & Social		30	5	7	18	39	85	22
Ravenstone		30	5	5	20	28	60	20
Leics Constabulary		30	4	6	20	30	81	18
Cottesmore Amateurs		30	5	3	22	41	98	18

EVERARDS BREWERY LEICESTERSHIRE SENIOR LEAGUE DIVISION ONE CONSTITUTION 2008-09

ANSTEY TOWN......................................Leicester Road, Thurcaston, Leicester LE7 7JH..........................0116 236 8231
BARLESTONE ST GILES.........................Barton, Leicester CV13 0EP.......................................01455 291392
DUNTON & BROUGHTON RANGERS........Station Road, Dunton Bassett LE17 5LF...............................07802 647846
EARL SHILTON ALBION..............Stoneycroft Park, New Street, Earl Shilton LE9 7FR.................01455 844277
EVINGTON......................Aylestone Park FC, Dorset Avenue, Wigston, Leicester LE18 4WB..........0116 277 5307
FC DYNAMO..................Nanpantan Sports Ground, Nanpantan Road, Loughborough LE11 3YD...........01509 237148
FC KHALSA.............Judgemeadow Community College, Marydene Drive, Evington, Leicester LE5 6HP.............0116 2417580
FRIAR LANE & EPWORTH RESERVES... Knighton Lane East, Aylestone Park, Leicester LE2 6FT.....................0116 283 3629
HATHERN.................................Pasture Lane, Hathern, Loughborough LE12 5LJ........................07952 113 090
LUTTERWORTH ATHLETIC.................Dunley Way, Lutterworth LE17 4NA................................01455 556650
LUTTERWORTH TOWN...............Hall Lane, Bitteswell, Lutterworth LE17 4LN............................01455 554046
NARBOROUGH & LITTLETHORPE..........Leicester Road, Narborough LE19 2DG.............................0116 275 1855
RAVENSTONE.......................Ravenslea, Ravenstone, Coalville LE67 2AW.........................07856 179485
SILEBY TOWN...........Memorial Park, Seagrave Road, Sileby, Loughborough LE12 7TP.........07708 231563 07860 842 046

IN: Barlestone St Giles (Leicester & District League Premier Division), Evington (P – Leicester City League Division One), FC Dynamo (P – North Leicestershire League Premier Division One), Friar Lane & Epworth Reserves (P – Midland Combination Reserve Division)
OUT: Asfordby Amateurs (P), Ashby Ivanhoe (P), Cottesmore Amateurs (P), FC Braunstone Victoria (W), Huncote Sports & Social (W), Leics Constabulary (P)

LEAGUE CUP

PREMIER DIVISION SECTION
FIRST ROUND
Ratby Sports 3 Rothley Imperial 1
St Andrews 2 Thurmaston Town 1
SECOND ROUND
Anstey Nomads 2 Barrow Town 1
Aylestone Park 1 **Saffron Dynamo** 2
Birstall United 1 Bardon Hill Sports 0
Ellistown 1 Ratby Sports 0
Highfield Rangers 1 Holwell Sports 1 (3-4p)
Ibstock United 2 **Blaby & Whetstone Athletic** 3
Kirby Muxloe SC 0 **Hinckley Downes** 2
Thurnby Rangers 1 **St Andrews SC** 1 (3-4p)
THIRD ROUND
Anstey Nomads 2 **St Andrews SC** 4
Bardon Hill Sports 3 Holwell Sports 1
Ellistown 3 **Hinckley Downes** 5
Saffron Dynamo 0 **Blaby & Whetstone Athletic** 1

DIVISION ONE SECTION
FIRST ROUND
Asfordby Amateurs 4 FC Braunstone Victoria 1
Ashby Ivanhoe 2 Lutterworth Athletic 1
Cottesmore Amateurs 4 Leics Constabulary 0
Hathern 3 **Dunton & Broughton Rangers** 4
Huncote Sports & Sports 5 FC Khalsa 2
(at FC Khalsa)
Lutterworth Town 2 **Ravenstone** 2 (9-10p)
Narborough & Littlethorpe 1 **Earl Shilton Albion** 1 (3-4p)
Sileby Town 3 Anstey Town 1
SECOND ROUND
Asfordby Amateurs 0 **Earl Shilton Albion** 0 (2-3p)
Cottesmore Amateurs 4 Dunton & Broughton Rangers 2
Huncote Sports & Social 2 Ashby Ivanhoe 1
Ravenstone 0 **Sileby Town** 2

QUARTER-FINALS
Blaby & Whetstone Athletic 3 Bardon Hill Sports 1
Cottesmore Amateurs 0 **St Andrews SC** 2
Earl Shilton Albion 1 Sileby Town 1 (5-4p)
Hinckley Downes 5 Huncote Sports & Social 1

SEMI-FINALS
Hinckley Downes 1 Earl Shilton Albion 1 (5-4p)
St Andrews SC 1 **Blaby & Whetstone Athletic** 5

FINAL
(May 13th at Barrow Town)
Hinckley Downes 1 **Blaby & Whetstone Athletic** 2

Combination One	P	W	D	L	F	A	Pts
Barrow Town Res.	28	21	5	2	98	37	68
Blaby & Whetstone Athletic Res.	28	18	6	4	79	43	60
Birstall United Res.	28	15	8	5	58	35	53
Thurmaston Town Res.	28	13	8	7	49	44	47
Anstey Town Res.	28	13	5	10	55	38	44
St Andrews SC Res.	28	13	4	11	67	56	43
Kirby Muxloe SC Res.	28	11	9	8	41	32	42
Leics Constabulary Res.	28	10	7	11	61	65	37
Earl Shilton Albion Res.	28	11	3	14	54	57	36
Rothley Imperial Res.	28	9	6	13	47	58	33
Sileby Town Res.	28	7	8	13	46	55	29
Ibstock United Res.	28	7	5	16	38	69	26
Ratby Sports Res.	28	8	2	18	39	79	26
Lutterworth Athletic Res.	28	6	6	16	31	53	24
Highfield Rangers Res.	28	3	8	17	39	81	17

Combination Two	P	W	D	L	F	A	Pts
Ellistown Res.	28	21	3	4	104	39	66
Holwell Sports Res.	28	18	3	7	75	34	57
Asfordby Amateurs Res.	28	17	4	7	83	45	55
Saffron Dynamo Res.	28	15	6	7	76	52	51
Ashby Ivanhoe Res.	28	13	8	7	75	51	47
Bardon Hill Sports Res.	28	14	5	9	53	34	47
Lutterworth Town Res.	28	13	4	11	71	54	43
Hathern Res.	28	11	5	12	53	53	38
Dunton & Broughton Rangers Res.	28	10	6	12	47	62	36
Narborough & Littlethorpe Res.	28	10	6	12	43	71	36
Anstey Nomads Res.	28	9	5	14	63	74	32
Huncote Sports & Social Res.	28	8	3	17	47	93	27
Ravenstone Res.	28	6	8	14	33	54	26
Cottesmore Amateurs Res.	28	6	4	18	36	74	22
FC Khalsa Res.	28	2	4	22	31	100	10

PRESIDENT'S CUP
FINAL
(May 8th at Kirby Muxloe SC)
St Andrews SC Res. 1 **Holwell Sports Res.** 4

WWW.NLNEWSDESK.CO.UK

LINCOLNSHIRE LEAGUE

Note – Keelby United withdrew during the course of the season

Their results are shown herein but are expunged from the league table

	Boston Town Res.	CGB Humbertherm	Caistor Rovers	Colsterworth United	Grantham Town Res.	Grimsby Soccer Club	Harrowby United	Horncastle Town	Hykeham Town	Keelby United	LSS Lucarly's Res.	Lincoln Moorlands Rail Res.	Lincoln United Res.	Louth United	Ruston Sports	Skegness Town	Sleaford Town Res.
Boston Town Res.		1-4	1-2	2-1	4-3	3-2	9-1	0-0	3-1	n/a	5-1	2-3	0-2	1-1	2-0	1-3	0-2
CGB Humbertherm	4-0		0-3	2-0	5-1	1-2	6-0	2-4	0-1	n/a	3-0	0-3	2-4	4-1	2-1	1-5	3-1
Caistor Rovers	1-1	1-4		5-1	4-3	4-0	4-3	0-1	2-1	n/a	1-0	2-1	0-3	1-3	4-5	2-3	3-1
Colsterworth United	2-2	1-3	1-7		7-0	4-3	3-2	3-3	2-3	n/a	2-0	3-4	4-2	1-4	1-5	0-2	1-3
Grantham Town Res.	4-2	W-L	2-0	6-0		4-1	3-0	0-1	3-3	n/a	6-1	0-1	2-1	0-4	5-1	0-3	2-3
Grimsby Soccer Club	3-3	1-0	3-0	3-1	8-1		W-L	1-1	1-6	2-1	2-0	4-3	0-0	1-5	3-5	1-7	2-3
Harrowby United	3-3	1-2	2-1	2-2	1-2	0-2		1-2	2-11	n/a	1-4	0-4	0-6	0-4	0-2	0-4	0-1
Horncastle Town	0-1	2-1	6-1	1-0	4-1	2-1	2-0		0-1	6-3	1-2	3-4	4-3	2-3	1-2	1-5	1-0
Hykeham Town	2-1	9-1	3-2	4-0	7-1	2-2	7-0	4-0		n/a	7-1	1-1	1-1	3-1	2-3	1-1	2-2
Keelby United	n/a	0-5	n/a	0-3	n/a	2-2	n/a	n/a	n/a		n/a	n/a	0-7	1-6	n/a	n/a	n/a
LSS Lucarly's Res.	2-1	1-2	2-1	0-5	W-L	W-L	5-1	0-2	0-4	n/a		0-2	0-6	2-5	1-1	0-2	3-1
Lincoln Moorlands Rail Res.	0-1	0-4	0-2	3-0	2-0	3-3	5-0	3-1	0-2	n/a	2-0		0-1	4-1	1-2	1-3	1-1
Lincoln United Res.	4-1	2-3	4-1	1-0	5-1	1-3	3-3	1-1	2-2	n/a	5-1	0-2		0-0	2-2	0-1	1-2
Louth United	2-3	1-2	2-2	6-1	3-4	2-0	6-1	1-2	L-W	n/a			3-2		1-0	1-6	1-2
Ruston Sports	5-0	2-1	3-1	3-2	0-3	9-0	8-0	3-1	1-1	n/a	2-0	4-0	5-2	5-1		2-0	2-2
Skegness Town	3-1	5-0	3-1	2-0	3-2	W-L	W-L	0-1	0-0	9-0	4-0	1-0	W-L	2-1	1-0		4-2
Sleaford Town Res.	4-0	2-2	3-2	1-0	5-1	6-0	2-1	0-5	1-2	n/a	4-0	1-0	1-2	1-1	1-4	0-1	

		P	W	D	L	F	A	Pts
Skegness Town	-3	30	26	2	2	74	19	77
Ruston Sports		30	20	4	6	87	41	64
Hykeham Town		30	18	9	3	93	34	63
Sleaford Town Res.		30	16	5	9	57	43	53
Horncastle Town		30	16	4	10	55	44	52
Lincoln M'lands Rail Res.	+3	30	15	3	12	56	43	51
CGB Humbertherm		30	16	1	13	64	55	49
Lincoln United Res.		30	12	7	11	66	45	43
Louth United		30	12	5	13	64	55	41
Grantham Town Res.		30	12	1	17	60	79	37
Boston Town Res.		30	10	6	14	54	65	36
Caistor Rovers		30	11	2	17	57	65	35
Grimsby Soccer Club		30	10	5	15	52	76	35
LSS Lucarly's Res.		30	8	2	20	24	78	26
Colsterworth United		30	6	3	21	48	84	21
Harrowby United		30	1	3	26	25	110	6

Keelby United – record expunged

WWW.CHERRYRED.CO.UK

LEAGUE CUP

FIRST ROUND
Horncastle Tn 0 **Ruston Sports** 3

SECOND ROUND
Caistor Rvrs 4 Boston Town Res. 2 *aet*
Colsterworth United 3 Grimsby Soccer Club 2
Grantham Town Res. 0 **CGB Humbertherm** 7
Hykeham Town 2 Sleaford Town Res. 1
Lincoln Moorlands Rail Res. 5 Keelby United 0
Lincoln United Res. 3 LSS Lucarly's Res. 1 *aet*
Ruston Sports 3 Harrowby United 1
Skegness Town 0 **Louth United** 3

QUARTER-FINALS
Caistor Rovers 3 Louth United 1
Colsterworth United 4 **Hykeham Town** 5
Lincoln Moorlands Rail Res. 1 Lincoln United Res. 1 *aet (3-2p)*
Ruston Sports 3 CGB Humbertherm 1

SEMI-FINALS
Hykeham Town 4 Caistor Rovers 0
Ruston Sports 1 **Lincoln Moorlands Railway Res.** 2

FINAL *(April 12th at Lincoln City)*
Hykeham Town 4 Lincoln Moorlands Railway Res. 1

SUPPLEMENTARY CUP

FIRST ROUND
Grantham Town Res. 4 Harrowby Utd Res. 0
Horncastle Town 2 Boston Town Res. 1
LSS Lucarly's Res. 2 Sleaford Town Res. 1
Skegness Town Res. 4 Grimsby Soccer Club 1

SEMI-FINALS
LSS Lucarly's Res. 4 Grantham Tn Res. 2 *aet*
Skegness Town 5 Horncastle Town 0

FINAL *(April 12th at Lincoln City)*
SkegnessTown 2 LSS Lucarly's Res. 1

SILLS & BETTERIDGE LINCOLNSHIRE LEAGUE CONSTITUTION 2008-09

BOSTON TOWN RESERVES . . . . The Stadium, Tattershall Road, Boston PE21 9LR 01205 365470
CGB HUMBERTHERM . . . . The Playing Fields, Fulstow, Louth . . . . None
CLEETHORPES TOWN RESERVES . . . . Wilton Road, Humberston, Grimsby DN36 4AW. 01472 812936
GRANTHAM TOWN RESERVES . . . South Kesteven Sports Stadium, Trent Road, Grantham NG31 7XQ 01476 402224/402225
GRIMSBY BOROUGH RESERVES . . . . St James School, 22 Bargate, Grimsby DN34 4SY 01472 503260
HORNCASTLE TOWN . . . . The Wong, Boston Road, Horncastle LE9 6EY. . . . . None
HYKEHAM TOWN. . . . . Memorial Hall Ground, Newark Road, North Hykeham, Lincoln LN6 9RJ. 01522 880035
LINCOLN MOORLANDS RAILWAY RESERVES . . . Moorlands Sports Ground, Newark Road, Lincoln LN6 8RT 01522 520184/874111
LINCOLN UNITED RESERVES . . . . Ashby Avenue, Hartsholme, Lincoln LN6 0DY 01522 696400/690674
LOUTH UNITED . . . . Main Road, Saltfleetby, Louth . . . . None
RUSTON SPORTS . . . . Ruston Marconi Sports Club, Newark Road, Lincoln 01522 882111
SKEGNESS TOWN . . . . Burgh Road, Skegness PE25 2RJ 01754 612654
SLEAFORD TOWN RESERVES. . . . . Eslaforde Park, Boston Road, Sleaford NG34 9GH. . . . . None

IN: Grimsby Borough Reserves (N)
OUT: Caistor Rovers (F), Colsterworth United (W – Grantham League), Grimsby Soccer Club (F), Harrowby United (P – Central Midlands League Supreme Division), Keelby United (WS)
LSS Lucarly's Reserves become Cleethorpes Town Reserves

LIVERPOOL COUNTY PREMIER LEAGUE

	BRNESC	Birchfield	Collegiate Old Boys	East Villa	Ford Motors	Lucas Sports	NELTC	Old Xaverians	Red Rum	Roma	South Liverpool	South Sefton Borough	Speke	St Aloysius	St Dominics	Waterloo Dock
BRNESC	P	1-3	2-0	0-5	2-0	0-4	1-3	1-4	1-5	0-2	1-6	2-4	2-2	4-1	3-2	0-1
Birchfield	1-0	R	1-0	1-2	0-0	5-0	4-0	0-3	2-3	1-0	2-1	2-1	2-2	2-3	2-2	1-0
Collegiate Old Boys	3-3	0-1	E	0-3	1-7	3-1	2-3	1-4	6-4	2-3	0-2	1-7	2-4	1-0	2-3	1-3
East Villa	1-1	3-1	6-0	M	0-1	4-3	3-0	0-2	2-0	2-2	2-1	7-1	2-1	3-3	4-1	3-0
Ford Motors	2-0	1-0	3-1	0-5	I	0-1	1-2	2-1	1-2	3-0	0-1	1-1	1-0	2-2	1-1	0-2
Lucas Sports	3-2	1-6	3-1	2-1	1-0	E	1-2	1-1	1-4	2-1	0-0	5-2	1-0	2-2	2-1	3-4
NELTC	4-3	1-0	3-1	3-3	1-2	1-0	R	3-2	3-1	3-0	1-0	1-0	1-1	1-3	1-1	2-3
Old Xaverians	3-0	0-0	6-2	1-3	0-1	3-0	1-1		2-0	2-2	1-1	2-0	1-0	4-0	3-2	0-1
Red Rum	3-1	2-1	W-L	1-2	1-0	2-0	1-3	3-1	D	5-1	2-2	3-1	6-2	5-1	3-2	0-6
Roma	3-1	3-3	2-4	0-5	2-5	1-2	2-4	0-3	1-5	I	0-5	3-2	1-0	0-2	1-4	0-5
South Liverpool	2-1	0-2	5-1	1-3	2-3	1-1	3-1	1-0	4-2	1-1	V	3-1	7-1	W-L	1-0	0-4
South Sefton Borough	3-3	0-2	2-1	0-1	2-2	0-0	3-1	0-1	3-2	2-1	0-4	I	1-3	1-3	2-2	2-4
Speke	7-0	0-2	3-2	3-3	4-1	2-1	2-4	1-4	1-0	12-2	1-2	1-0	S	5-2	3-0	3-3
St Aloysius	3-2	1-1	3-0	2-5	1-3	4-2	7-2	0-2	3-4	3-2	2-1	0-2	L-W	I	7-3	1-2
St Dominics	2-1	3-0	6-1	2-2	3-5	1-1	2-3	0-4	1-2	5-1	2-1	0-2	1-2	2-2	O	0-1
Waterloo Dock	W-L	2-0	2-0	1-3	4-3	0-0	1-2	2-1	5-0	4-0	0-2	2-0	3-0	2-0	3-2	N

LORD MAYOR'S CHARITY SHIELD

(August 11th at LCFA, Walton Hall Avenue)
Waterloo Dock 2 East Villa 2
(Charity Shield shared)

Premier Division		P	W	D	L	F	A	Pts
Waterloo Dock		30	23	2	5	70	29	71
East Villa		30	21	6	3	88	34	69
NELTC		30	18	4	8	60	54	58
Old Xaverians		30	17	5	8	62	28	56
Red Rum		30	18	1	11	67	56	55
South Liverpool		30	16	5	9	61	36	53
Birchfield		30	14	6	10	48	35	48
Speke		30	14	5	11	72	57	47
Ford Motors		30	14	5	11	51	43	47
Lucas Sports	-6	30	11	7	12	44	54	34
St Aloysius	-6	30	11	5	14	61	65	32
St Dominics		30	7	7	16	56	66	28
South Sefton Borough		30	7	5	18	44	65	26
Roma		30	5	4	21	39	101	19
BRNESC	-3	30	4	4	22	38	82	13
Collegiate Old Boys	-3	30	4	1	25	39	95	10

ZINGARI CHALLENGE CUP

FIRST ROUND
Birchfield 2 Old Xaverians 1
Ford Motors 0 **NELTC** 2
Lucas Sports 2 **BRNESC** 3 *aet*
Red Rum 2 Collegiate Old Boys 1
Roma 0 **South Liverpool** 5
Speke 3 East Villa 1
St Dominics 3 South Sefton Borough 0
Waterloo Dock 3 St Aloysius 1 *(at St Aloysius)*
QUARTER-FINALS
BRNESC 0 **South Liverpool** 2
NELTC 1 St Dominics 0
Red Rum 0 Birchfield 0 *aet* (7-6p)
Speke 0 **Waterloo Dock** 2
SEMI-FINALS
NELTC 0 **Red Rum** 3
South Liverpool 0 **Waterloo Dock** 1
FINAL
(May 7th at Litherland Sports Park)
Waterloo Dock 0 Red Rum 0 *aet* (3-1p)

FRANK ARMITT LIVERPOOL COUNTY PREMIER LEAGUE PREMIER DIVISION CONSTITUTION 2008-09

AIGBURTH PEOPLE'S HALL ..... Cheshire Lines FC, Southmead Road, Allerton, Liverpool L19 5NB 0151 427 7176
BIRCHFIELD .... Edge Hill College, St Helens Road, Ormskirk L39 4QP 01695 584745
CHESHIRE LINES .... Southmead Road, Allerton, Liverpool L19 5NB 0151 427 7176
EAST VILLA .... Litherland Sports Park, Boundary Road, Litherland Liverpool L21 7NW 0151 288 6338
FORD MOTORS .... Ford Sports & Social Club, Cronton Lane, Widnes WA8 5AJ 0151 424 7078
LUCAS SPORTS .... William Collins Memorial Ground, Commercial Road, Liverpool .... None
NELTC .... Edinburgh Park, Townsend Lane, Liverpool L13 9DY .... None
OLD XAVERIANS .... St Francis Xaviers College, Beaconsfield Road, Liverpool L25 6EG 0151 288 1000
PAGE CELTIC .... King George V Sports Complex, Long View Lane, Huyton L36 7UN 0151 443 5712
RED RUM .... Croxteth Community Comprehensive School, Parkstile Lane, Liverpool L11 0PB 0151 546 4168
SOUTH LIVERPOOL .... Jericho Lane, Aigburth, Liverpool L17 5AR .... None
SOUTH SEFTON BOROUGH .... Mill Dam Field, Bridges Lane, Sefton .... None
SPEKE .... Speke Hall Avenue, Speke, Liverpool L24 1YD 0151 486 1588
ST ALOYSIUS .... King George V Sports Complex, Long View Lane, Huyton, Liverpool L36 7UN 0151 443 5712
ST DOMINICS .... St Dominics School, Lordens Road, Huyton L14 8UD 0151 489 8279
WATERLOO DOCK .... Edinburgh Park, Townsend Lane, Liverpool L6 0BB 0151 263 5267
IN: Aigburth People's Hall (P), Cheshire Lines (P), Page Celtic (P)
OUT: BRNESC (R), Collegiate Old Boys (R), Roma (R)

WWW.NLNEWSDESK.CO.UK

Note – Northern Telecoms and Quarry Bank Old Boys withdrew during the course of the season. Their results are shown herein but are expunged from the league table.

	Aigburth People's Hall	Albany Athletic	Alder	Angus Village	Cheshire Lines	Copperas Hill	Edge Hill BCOB	Kingsley United	Mackets Grenadier	North Sefton	Northern Telecoms	Page Celtic	Quarry Bank Old Boys	REMYCA United	Stoneycroft	Warbreck
Aigburth People's Hall		2-1	4-2	6-0	6-3	1-1	3-2	4-0	4-0	5-1	n/a	1-2	n/a	4-3	6-2	2-0
Albany Athletic	0-1		2-0	4-2	2-3	1-2	4-4	1-2	2-4	4-2	1-2	1-1	n/a	1-2	1-4	1-1
Alder	1-3	3-0	D	5-2	0-5	1-3	1-2	4-1	2-1	6-2	8-2	0-2	n/a	3-0	4-2	6-3
Angus Village	2-2	1-2	5-1	I	4-2	3-2	1-2	1-1	5-2	1-4	0-1	n/a	n/a	3-3	2-3	1-3
Cheshire Lines	1-2	3-1	1-0	10-1	V	3-0	1-1	4-2	0-4	5-0	2-2	2-1	n/a	1-0	3-0	2-2
Copperas Hill	2-1	1-5	1-3	2-0	0-2	I	3-2	1-1	3-1	1-0	2-4	2-6	5-0	1-2	2-4	3-4
Edge Hill BCOB	2-3	1-0	4-1	2-1	2-1	1-2	S	2-3	4-2	3-2	2-2	4-2	n/a	3-4	0-9	5-3
Kingsley United	0-4	3-1	2-4	5-1	1-3	1-1	2-2	I	3-2	5-2	n/a	3-4	n/a	2-5	4-1	3-4
Mackets Grenadier	1-0	1-0	3-2	1-1	0-0	2-1	1-1	3-4	O	3-0	n/a	0-3	n/a	1-2	1-3	0-0
North Sefton	5-5	2-4	2-1	0-7	1-3	3-2	0-0	1-1	3-1	N	3-1	1-5	n/a	0-3	2-5	4-2
Northern Telecoms	2-5	1-3	3-1	3-6	3-4	1-5	n/a	n/a	2-4	5-2		0-7	n/a	2-1	1-1	2-3
Page Celtic	3-2	4-1	1-2	4-1	2-1	1-1	2-5	2-0	3-3	5-0	5-0	O	n/a	1-1	5-1	2-1
Quarry Bank Old Boys	n/a	n/a	1-7	n/a	n/a	n/a	n/a	n/a	n/a	n/a	n/a	6-3	N	n/a	n/a	n/a
REMYCA United	2-2	1-3	1-2	5-2	1-2	5-2	3-0	1-1	3-1	3-2	8-0	1-5	n/a	E	2-1	2-3
Stoneycroft	1-4	3-2	0-1	8-0	2-8	5-3	2-1	2-0	4-2	6-1	2-3	5-0	0-2			3-4
Warbreck	0-3	1-2	3-2	5-0	1-4	3-4	4-0	4-1	6-2	3-4	2-4	1-1	n/a	2-2	3-2	

WWW.CHERRYRED.CO.UK

Division One	P	W	D	L	F	A	Pts
Aigburth People's Hall	26	18	4	4	80	37	58
Page Celtic	26	17	5	4	71	37	56
Cheshire Lines	26	17	3	6	73	36	54
REMYCA United	26	13	5	8	59	48	44
Alder	26	13	0	13	57	55	39
Warbreck	26	11	5	10	66	61	38
Edge Hill BCOB	26	11	5	10	55	60	38
Stoneycroft -3	26	13	0	13	71	65	36
Copperas Hill	26	9	4	13	46	61	31
Mackets Grenadier	26	8	6	12	38	50	30
Kingsley United	26	8	5	13	49	64	29
Albany Athletic	26	8	3	15	46	54	27
North Sefton	26	5	3	18	43	89	18
Angus Village -6	26	4	4	17	48	85	13

Northern Telecoms and Quarry Bank Old Boys – records expunged

ROY WADE CUP

FIRST ROUND
Angus Village 0 **Stoneycroft** 2
Cheshire Lines 1 **Albany Athletic** 3
Copperas Hill 0 **Alder** 1
Kingsley United 3 Edge Hill BCOB 1
Mackets Grenadier 0 **Aigburth People's Hall** 3
North Sefton (w/o) v Quarry Bank Old Boys (scr.)
REMYCA United 1 **Northern Telecoms** 4
Warbreck 3 Page Celtic 2
QUARTER-FINALS
Albany Athletic 2 Stoneycroft 1
Alder 2 Aigburth People's Hall 1 *(at Aigburth People's Hall)*
North Sefton 1 **Warbreck** 3
Northern Telecoms 0 **Kingsley United** 3
SEMI-FINALS
Albany Athletic 0 **Warbreck** 2
Kingsley United 9 Alder 4
FINAL
(May 12th at Ford Motors)
Kingsley United 3 Warbreck 2 aet

PETER COYNE / GEORGE MAHON CUP
(All teams in league)

FIRST ROUND
North Sefton 2 Redgate Rovers 0
Northern Telecoms 3 Alder 1
Page Celtic (w/o) v Quarry Bank Old Boys (scr.)
REMYCA Utd 2 Kingsley Utd 1
Rockville Wallasey 1 **Stoneycroft** 7 *(at Stoneycroft)*
SECOND ROUND
Bankfield 2 BRNESC 0
Cheshire Lines 1 **Edge Hill BCOB** 6 aet
Collegiate Old Boys 3 REMYCA United 1
Copperas Hill 0 **Birchfield** 4
East Villa 2 South Sefton Borough 1
NELTC 4 Albany Ath. 3 aet
North Sefton 3 **Page Celtic** 5
Northern Telecoms 0 **Ford Motors** 1
Old Xaverians 3 Waterloo Dock 2 aet
Red Rum 3 **Aigburth People's Hall** 5
South Liverpool 6 Jubilee Triangle 0
Speke 0 **Sacre Coeur Former Pupils** 3
St Aloysius 3 Lucas Sports 1
St Dominics 10 Old Holts 2
Stoneycroft 5 Roma 2 *(at Roma)*
Warbreck 3 Blueline 2

THIRD ROUND
Birchfield 1 St Aloysius 0
Edge Hill BCOB 1 **Collegiate Old Boys** 3
NELTC 0 Sacre Coeur Former Pupils 0 aet (5-6p)
Page Celtic 0 **Old Xaverians** 1
South Liverpool 1 Bankfield 0
St Dominics 3 **Aigburth People's Hall** 4 aet
Stoneycroft 1 **Ford Motors** 4
Warbreck 1 **East Villa** 2 *(at East Villa)*
QUARTER-FINALS
Birchfield 3 Collegiate Old Boys 1
Old Xaverians 0 **Aigburth People's Hall** 2
Sacre Coeur Former Pupils 0 **Ford Motors** 2
South Liverpool 3 East Villa 3 aet (3-2p)
SEMI-FINALS
Birchfield 0 **Ford Motors** 1
South Liverpool 1 **Aigburth People's Hall** 2
FINAL
(May 15th at LCFA, Walton Hall Avenue)
Ford Motors 2 **Aigburth People's Hall** 3

FRANK ARMITT LIVERPOOL COUNTY PREMIER LEAGUE DIVISION ONE CONSTITUTION 2008-09

ALBANY ATHLETIC . . . . Millbank College, Bankfield Road, Liverpool L13 0BQ . . . . None
ALDER . . . . Alder Road Sports Club, Alder Road, West Derby, Liverpool L12 2BA . . . . None
ANGUS VILLAGE . . . . Joe Stone Memorial Ground, Lower Lane, Fazakerley, Liverpool L9 7AD . . . . None
BRNESC . . . . Melling Road, Aintree, Liverpool L9 0LQ . . . . None
BANKFIELD . . . . Lower Breck Road, Anfield, Liverpool L6 4BZ . . . . None
COLLEGIATE OLD BOYS . . . . Alder Road Sports Club, Alder Road, West Derby, Liverpool L12 2BA . . . . None
COPPERAS HILL . . . . Breckside Park, Liverpool . . . . None
EDGE HILL BCOB . . . . William Collins Memorial Ground, Commercial Road, Liverpool . . . . None
ESSEMMAY OLD BOYS . . . . Jericho Lane Playing Field, Jericho Lane, Liverpool L17 5AR . . . . None
KINGSLEY UNITED . . . . Quarry Bank School Playing Fields, Greenhill Road, Allerton Liverpool L18 6HF . . . . None
MACKETS GRENADIER . . . . Great Lakes, Lower Road, Halebank, Widnes WA8 8NT . . . . None
REMYCA UNITED . . . . Playfootball.com, Drummond Road, Thornton L20 6DX. . . . . None
ROMA . . . . Scargreen Playing Fields, Scargreen Avenue, Norris Green, Liverpool L11 3BE. . . . . None
SACRE COEUR FORMER PUPILS . . . . . Playfootball.com, Drummond Road, Thornton L20 6DX. . . . . None
STONEYCROFT . . . . Maiden Lane Playing Fields, Maiden Lane, Liverpool L13 9AN. . . . . None
WARBRECK . . . . Playfootball.com, Drummond Road, Thornton L20 6DX. . . . . None

IN: *BRNESC (R), Bankfield (P), Collegiate Old Boys (R), Essemmay Old Boys (P), Roma (R), Sacre Coeur Former Pupils (P)*
OUT: *Aigburth People's Hall (P), Cheshire Lines (P), North Sefton (W), Northern Telecoms (WS), Page Celtic (P), Quarry Bank Old Boys (WS)*

	Active Sefton	Bankfield	Blueline	Eli Lilly	Essemmay Old Boys	Jubilee Triangle	Leisure Sports Orchard	Leyfield	Liobians	Lydiate Weld	Old Holts	Redgate Rovers	Rockville Wallasey	Sacre Coeur Former Pupils
Active Sefton		0-7	n/a	n/a	2-3	0-2	n/a	n/a	n/a	1-8	0-3	n/a	n/a	1-8
Bankfield	8-0	D	2-2	3-1	2-0	5-0	11-0	1-1	3-0	4-1	4-4	1-0	5-1	1-0
Blueline	n/a	3-1	I	0-0	1-5	4-0	4-0	2-2	0-3	2-2	3-2	5-0	2-2	1-1
Eli Lilly	n/a	2-5	2-5	V	0-2	n/a	2-2	0-3	1-1	3-2	1-2	4-2	3-1	0-1
Essemmay Old Boys	n/a	2-1	1-1	6-1	I	2-0	6-0	2-0	4-0	5-0	2-1	4-1	3-1	2-2
Jubilee Triangle	n/a	n/a	n/a	1-2	1-4	S	n/a	2-7	2-1	3-2	3-4	4-4	n/a	n/a
Leisure Sports Orchard	4-4	1-2	5-2	0-1	1-4	2-2	I	1-4	2-6	3-3	2-4	1-1	2-3	0-3
Leyfield	n/a	2-3	3-4	2-1	2-1	n/a	5-1	O	2-3	3-2	0-1	3-2	3-0	1-5
Liobians	n/a	1-3	2-1	2-3	1-0	2-2	0-1	1-4	N	8-3	3-2	2-0	2-1	3-4
Lydiate Weld	n/a	3-4	L-W	2-3	1-2	n/a	5-2	3-3	2-2		3-4	1-0	4-1	0-10
Old Holts	n/a	2-4	2-2	1-5	0-2	3-2	5-1	2-3	2-5	W-L	T	1-0	8-1	2-3
Redgate Rovers	n/a	0-6	2-3	3-3	2-2	n/a	1-1	1-2	0-5	0-2	1-1	W	4-3	2-6
Rockville Wallasey	n/a	1-3	3-10	4-2	0-4	n/a	1-7	1-11	0-4	1-3	2-2	1-1	O	1-3
Sacre Coeur Former Pupils	n/a	2-0	2-0	6-1	2-1	n/a	6-0	4-0	1-0	7-0	1-1	2-1	4-1	

Note – Active Sefton and Jubilee Triangle withdrew during the course of the season
Their results are shown above but are expunged from the league table

Division Two		P	W	D	L	F	A	Pts
Sacre Coeur Former Pupils		22	18	3	1	75	18	57
Essemmay Old Boys		22	15	3	4	60	20	48
Bankfield	-6	22	16	3	3	69	29	45
Leyfield		22	12	3	7	62	40	39
Blueline		22	9	8	5	53	42	35
Liobians	-6	22	12	2	8	51	39	32
Old Holts		22	9	4	9	50	48	31
Eli Lilly		22	7	4	11	39	55	25
Leisure Sports Orchard		22	4	3	15	35	78	15
Lydiate Weld	-6	22	4	5	13	41	68	11
Rockville Wallasey		22	2	3	17	30	90	9
Redgate Rovers		22	1	5	16	23	61	8

Active Sefton and Jubilee Triangle – records expunged

LORD WAVERTREE CUP

FIRST ROUND
Active Sefton (scr.) v **Lydiate Weld** (w/o)
Blueline 3 Sacre Coeur Former Pupils 2 *aet*
Jubilee Triangle 0 **Eli Lilly** 1
Leyfield 5 Leisure Sports Orchard 1
Liobians 0 **Essemmay Old Boys** 2
Rockville Wallasey 0 **Bankfield** 3

QUARTER-FINALS
Eli Lilly 4 Bankfield 2
Leyfield 3 Blueline 2
Lydiate Weld 2 **Essemmay Old Boys** 3 *aet*
Old Holts 5 Redgate Rovers 1

SEMI-FINALS
Eli Lilly 0 **Old Holts** 3
Essemmay Old Boys 1 **Leyfield** 1 (4-5p)

FINAL
(April 30th at Litherland Sports Complex)
Old Holts 3 Leyfield 1 *aet*

WWW.NLNEWSDESK.CO.UK

FRANK ARMITT LIVERPOOL COUNTY PREMIER LEAGUE DIVISION TWO CONSTITUTION 2008-09

BLUELINE . . . . Buckley Hill Playing Fields, Buckley Hill Lane, Netherton, Bootle L29 1YB . . . . None
EAST VILLA RESERVES . . . . Scargreen Playing Fields, Scargreen Avenue, Norris Green, Liverpool L11 3BE . . . . None
ELI LILLY . . . . Thomas Lane Playing Fields, Thomas Lane, Liverpool L14 5NR . . . . None
FARMERS . . . . Clubmoor Rec Playing Fields, Townsend Avenue, Clubmoor, Liverpool L4 . . . . None
HALEWOOD TOWN . . . . Hollies Road Playing Fields, Hollies Road, Halewood, Liverpool L26 0TH . . . . None
LEISURE SPORTS ORCHARD . . . Clarence House School, West Lane, Freshfield, Formby, Liverpool L37 7AZ 01704 872151
LEYFIELD . . . . Thomas Lane Playing Fields, Thomas Lane, Liverpool . . . . None
LIOBIANS . . . . Mersey Road, Aigburth, Liverpool L17 6AG . . . . None
NELTC RESERVES . . . . Edinburgh Park, Townsend Lane, Liverpool L13 9DY . . . . None
OLD HOLTS . . . . Simpson Ground, Hillfoot Road, Liverpool L25 0ND 0151 486 3166
OLD XAVERIANS RESERVES . . . . . St Francis Xaviers College, Beconsfield Road, Liverpool L25 6EG 0151 288 1000
PINEWOODS . . . . Carr Lane Playing Fields, Carr Lane, Ainsdale, Southport . . . . None
REDGATE ROVERS . . . . Clarence House School, West Lane, Freshfield, Formby, Liverpool L37 7AZ . . . . 01704 872151.
ROCKVILLE WALLASEY . . . . Belvidere Recreation Ground, Belvidere Road, Liscard, Wallesey CH45 4RY . . . . None
SOUTH LIVERPOOL RESERVES . . . . Jericho Lane, Aigburth, Liverpool L17 5AR . . . . None
WARBRECK RESERVES . . . . Playfootball.com, Drummond Road, Thornton L20 6DX . . . . None

IN: East Villa Reserves (P – St Helens Combination Division One), Farmers (N), Halewood Town (N), NELTC Reserves (P – I Zingari Combination Division One), Old Xaverians Reserves (P – I Zingari Combination Division One), Pinewoods (P – Sunday football), South Liverpool Reserves (P – I Zingari Combination Division One), Warbreck Reserves (P – I Zingari Combination Division One)
OUT: Active Sefton (WS), Bankfield (P), Essemmay Old Boys (P), Jubilee Triangle (WS), Lydiate Weld (W), Sacre Coeur Former Pupils (P)

MANCHESTER LEAGUE

	AFC Blackley	Atherton Town	Breightmet United	East Manchester	Gregorians	Hindsford	Hollinwood	Irlam	Leigh Athletic	Pennington	Prestwich Heys	Rochdale Sacred Heart	Royton Town	Springhead	Stockport Georgians	Walshaw Sports Club	Whitworth Valley	Wigan Robin Park	Wythenshawe Amateur
AFC Blackley		3-3	2-1	4-2	3-2	1-3	0-1	4-2	2-1	3-3	2-3	2-1	1-3	L-W	4-1	1-4	1-3	0-3	3-5
Atherton Town	5-2	P	0-0	3-2	3-0	4-0	0-3	2-1	1-0	1-4	4-1	1-1	1-1	2-2	2-2	5-2	3-3		1-0
Breightmet United	3-4	0-4	R	1-1	1-1	1-6	2-4	1-2	2-1	1-9	0-3	3-5	1-2	0-0	1-3	1-1	2-2	1-4	0-2
East Manchester	3-2	2-0	4-2	E	2-1	2-3	0-0	1-4	1-1	2-1	3-0	2-3	3-2	0-0	2-0	3-0	4-1	3-2	4-1
Gregorians	3-1	1-0	2-1	4-0	M	2-1	3-1	2-0	0-3	1-1	0-0	5-1	3-2	2-0	1-0	3-2	2-0	0-3	2-2
Hindsford	1-1	0-1	1-2	0-2	0-1	I	0-4	0-2	0-6	1-3	0-1	2-0	1-2	2-1	2-2	0-2	10-1	4-2	2-3
Hollinwood	5-2	0-5	8-1	1-0	3-3	3-3	E	4-1	3-4	3-2	2-3	4-4	0-1	3-1	4-1	4-1	8-1	1-2	1-1
Irlam	2-3	1-3	8-0	1-0	5-1	0-1	1-0	R	2-1	3-2	4-2	1-2	0-2	7-2	0-1	3-0	6-1	1-1	1-1
Leigh Athletic	7-1	1-6	5-3	3-2	0-1	1-0	3-2	1-2		0-1	2-2	2-4	5-1	1-0	3-0	1-1	W-L	0-3	0-3
Pennington	1-2	2-0	5-2	1-3	2-2	3-1	2-3	1-3	1-3		1-0	0-1	1-1	2-0	2-2	0-4	6-3	2-1	2-1
Prestwich Heys	2-0	1-2	2-1	2-2	0-0	2-0	3-2	4-2	0-3	0-3	D	5-3	1-2	3-0	1-2	1-1	9-2	1-5	0-0
Rochdale Sacred Heart	2-1	3-1	3-2	3-2	1-1	2-2	1-2	2-0	2-2	6-0	1-1	I	4-4	2-1	2-0	1-0	3-2	5-6	2-0
Royton Town	4-1	0-2	2-1	1-1	0-4	4-0	4-1	1-1	3-1	4-1	0-1	1-0	V	2-1	1-3	0-4	3-1	0-3	2-0
Springhead	2-6	3-0	2-2	0-1	0-2	1-0	0-1	3-2	1-1	5-1	2-3	3-2	2-3	I	1-2	0-2	2-0	0-3	2-0
Stockport Georgians	9-1	0-0	1-2	2-0	0-1	3-0	2-1	0-1	0-2	2-3	0-1	0-2	1-4	1-0	S	1-0	3-1	1-2	1-3
Walshaw Sports Club	2-0	2-0	4-2	4-1	1-2	2-4	0-7	2-1	1-4	4-3	2-3	2-0	0-1	1-1	1-1	I	11-0	1-2	4-2
Whitworth Valley	1-4	0-4	1-6	0-3	2-3	0-1	0-4	0-5	1-2	2-2	1-6	5-3	0-6	0-2	1-5	0-1	O	1-4	1-2
Wigan Robin Park	2-2	3-0	6-0	2-1	1-3	2-1	1-0	3-1	2-1	2-0	3-0	6-2	1-2	1-2	2-0	1-1	8-0	N	1-1
Wythenshawe Amateur	5-1	0-4	5-3	0-0	3-3	2-1	1-1	1-1	1-3	1-1	3-4	0-0	1-0	0-1	0-1	2-1	5-1	2-1	

Premier Division

		P	W	D	L	F	A	Pts
Wigan Robin Park		36	23	5	8	95	46	74
Gregorians		36	21	9	6	69	45	72
Royton Town		36	19	9	8	76	49	66
Atherton Town		36	18	9	9	73	46	63
Leigh Athletic		36	18	6	12	76	56	60
Hollinwood		36	18	5	13	91	62	59
Prestwich Heys	-5	36	19	7	10	75	57	59
Irlam		36	18	4	14	79	53	58
East Manchester		36	16	8	12	62	52	56
Walshaw Sports Club		36	15	6	15	68	61	51
Rochdale Sacred Heart	-6	36	16	8	12	78	75	50
Wythenshawe Amateur		36	13	10	13	58	56	49
Pennington		36	13	7	16	70	73	46
Stockport Georgians		36	13	7	16	53	54	46
Springhead		36	12	7	17	47	59	43
Hindsford		36	10	4	22	53	70	34
Breightmet United		36	3	9	24	53	116	18
AFC Blackley	-25	36	12	4	20	70	100	15
Whitworth Valley		36	2	2	32	36	152	8

GILGRYST CUP

FIRST ROUND
East Manchester 1 **Wythenshawe Amateurs 4**
Gregorians 3 Hollinwood 1
Royton Town 5 Pennington 1
SECOND ROUND
Atherton Town 1 Irlam 0
Hindsford 1 Rochdale Sacred Heart 0
Prestwich Heys 0 **Leigh Athletic 2**
Royton 1 **Springhead** aet (4-5p)
Walshaw Sports Club 1 **AFC Blackley 2**
Whitworth Valley 1 **Gregorians 2**
Wigan Robin Park 2 Breightmet United 0
Wythenshawe Amateur 0 **Stockport Georgians 1**
QUARTER-FINALS
Atherton Town 5 Hindsford 4
Leigh Athletic 6 AFC Blackley 1
Stockport Georgians 1 **Gregorians 4**
Wigan Robin Park 2 Springhead 1
SEMI-FINALS
Leigh Athletic 4 Gregorians 2
Wigan Robin Park 1 Atherton Town 0
FINAL (*May 12th at Trafford*)
Leigh Athletic 3 **Wigan Robin Park 3** aet (2-4p)

BRIDGEWATER OFFICE SUPPLIES MANCHESTER LEAGUE PREMIER DIVISION CONSTITUTION 2008-09

AVRO . . . . Lancaster Club, Broadway, Failsworth, Oldham M35 0DX 0161 681 3083
ATHERTON TOWN . . . . Howe Bridge Sports Centre, Leigh Road, Atherton M46 0PJ 01942 884882
BREIGHTMET UNITED . . . . Moss Park, Bury Road, Breightmet, Bolton BL2 6QB 01204 533930
CHAPEL TOWN . . . . Rowton Ground, Willow Drive, Chapel-en-le-Frith, High Peak SK23 0ND . . . . None
EAST MANCHESTER . . . . GMB Social Club, Mount Road, Gorton M19 3ET 0161 224 1176
ELTON VALE . . . . Elton Sports Club, Elton Vale Road, Bury BL8 2RZ 0161 762 0666
GREGORIANS . . . . MCFC, Platt Lane Complex, Yew Tree Road, Fallowfield M14 7UU . . . . None
HINDSFORD . . . . Squires Lane, Tyldesley M29 8JH . . . . None
HOLLINWOOD . . . . Chapel Road Playing Fields, Grammer School Road, Hollinwood, Oldham OL8 4QY 0161 911 5017
LEIGH ATHLETIC . . . . Leigh Sports Village, Madley Park, Charles Street, Leigh WN7 1BG 01942 673500
PENNINGTON . . . . Jubilee Park, Leigh Road, Atherton M46 0RN . . . . None
PRESTWICH HEYS . . . . Sandgate Road, Whitefield M45 6WG 0161 773 8888
ROCHDALE SACRED HEART . . . . Fox Park, Belfield Mill Lane, Rochdale OL16 2UB . . . . None
ROYTON TOWN . . . . Crompton Cricket Club Complex, Christine Street, Shaw, Oldham OL2 7SF 01706 847421
SPRINGHEAD . . . . St John Street, Lees, Oldham OL4 4DB 0161 627 0260
STOCKPORT GEORGIANS . . . . Cromley Road, Woodsmoor, Stockport SK6 8BP 0161 483 6581
WALSHAW SPORTS CLUB . . . . Walshaw Sports Club, Sycamore Road, Tottington, Bury BL8 3EG 01204 882448
WYTHENSHAWE AMATEUR . . . . Longley Lane, Northenden, Wythenshawe M22 4LA 0161 998 7268
IN: AVRO (P), Chapel Town (P), Elton Vale (P)
OUT: AFC Blackley (R), Irlam (P – North West Counties League Division One), Wigan Robin Park (P – North West Counties League Division One), Whitworth Valley (R)

	Avro	Chapel Town	Dukinfield Town	Elton Vale	Fives Athletic	Heywood St James	Manchester Juniors	Milton	Monton Amateurs	Old Altrinchamians	Salford Victoria	Stand Athletic	West Didsbury & Chorlton	Wilmslow Albion	Wythenshawe Town
Avro		4-0	3-2	2-0	3-1	8-2	3-1	4-1	3-3	3-0	4-2	4-3	4-0	7-0	7-1
Chapel Town	2-1	*D*	3-0	2-0	3-1	5-0	6-1	4-1	2-1	5-1	3-2	2-1	3-0	4-1	1-0
Dukinfield Town	0-4	0-0	*I*	0-1	5-1	2-1	2-1	1-1	2-1	3-2	5-4	1-3	2-1	2-3	4-3
Elton Vale	4-2	5-1	2-1	*V*	4-3	5-0	2-1	3-0	6-2	1-2	2-2	1-0	4-1	1-0	5-0
Fives Athletic	1-3	2-2	0-2	2-2	*I*	1-1	2-0	3-2	0-1	2-2	3-3	2-0	2-0	1-3	5-4
Heywood St James	7-1	0-2	2-1	1-6	2-1	*S*	4-2	9-0	2-5	3-5	W-L	1-3	1-3	2-0	4-6
Manchester Juniors	2-4	1-1	2-4	1-2	4-2	2-1	*I*	6-0	2-0	1-5	4-2	1-1	1-1	4-2	1-6
Milton	1-5	0-6	0-2	1-12	2-2	1-1	4-5	*O*	0-7	1-6	2-3	0-4	1-6	2-2	1-6
Monton Amateurs	1-1	2-1	4-1	3-1	5-1	1-0	3-0	3-0	*N*	0-3	4-3	1-0	4-0	4-0	2-1
Old Altrinchamians	2-2	3-2	1-0	1-2	4-3	2-2	0-1	5-0	0-1		5-4	3-2	1-0	2-0	6-3
Salford Victoria	1-3	0-4	4-3	1-1	4-3	0-2	W-L	10-1	1-5	4-1		5-5	1-2	6-0	4-3
Stand Athletic	0-2	1-1	1-0	0-3	5-1	4-1	5-2	1-2	0-0	2-6	3-2	*O*	2-0	2-1	1-1
W Didsbury/Chorlton	2-1	1-5	3-2	0-5	1-4	4-0	1-1	3-0	2-2	1-7	3-3	3-0	*N*	2-3	1-4
Wilmslow Albion	1-5	1-2	1-3	3-0	1-1	5-2	2-1	4-1	0-1	1-2	0-2	3-6	2-3	*E*	4-4
Wythenshawe Town	3-0	3-5	4-1	1-2	4-3	1-2	1-2	4-2	1-4	2-2	2-1	4-2	2-1	3-3	

Division One

	P	W	D	L	F	A	Pts
Chapel Town	28	20	4	4	77	33	64
Avro	28	20	3	5	93	43	63
Elton Vale	28	20	3	5	82	33	63
Monton Amateurs	28	19	4	5	67	33	61
Old Altrinchamians	28	17	4	7	79	51	55
Wythenshawe Town	28	12	4	12	77	74	40
Stand Athletic	28	11	5	12	57	53	38
Dukinfield Town	28	12	2	14	51	56	38
Salford Victoria	28	9	5	14	74	73	32
Manchester Juniors	28	9	4	15	50	66	31
West Didsbury & Chorlton	28	9	4	15	45	64	31
Heywood St James	28	9	3	16	53	76	30
Wilmslow Albion	28	7	4	17	45	75	25
Fives Athletic	28	5	7	16	51	71	22
Milton	28	1	4	23	27	127	7

MURRAY SHIELD

FIRST ROUND
Chapel Town 5 Wilmslow Albion 0
Dukinfield Town 1 **Manchester Juniors** 3
Elton Vale 1 **Monton Amateurs** 1 *aet*
(1-3p)
Fives Athletic 3 Stand Athletic 2
Heywood St James 1 **Avro** 3
Milton 0 **Old Altrimchamians** 4
Salford Victoria 2 **Wythenshawe Town** 4

QUARTER-FINALS
Monton Amateurs 1 Avro 1 *aet* (3-0p)
Old Altrinchamians 4 **Chapel Town** 4
aet (2-4p)
West Didsbury & Chorlton 6 Fives Athletic 1
Wythenshawe Town 3 **Manchester Juniors** 3 *aet* (1-3p)

SEMI-FINALS
Chapel Town 2 **Monton Amateurs** 3 *aet*
Manchester Juniors 2 **West Didsbury & Chorlton** 3

FINAL
(May 23rd at MCFC, Platt Lane)
West Didsbury & Chorlton 3 Monton Amateurs 1

OPEN TROPHY

FINAL
(April 6th at Elton Vale)
Springhead Res. 3 Irlam Res. 1

LEAGUE CUP

FINAL
(May 5th at Irlam)
Pennington Res. (w/o) v Dukinfield Town 'A' (scr.)

WWW.NLNEWSDESK.CO.UK

BRIDGEWATER OFFICE SUPPLIES MANCHESTER LEAGUE DIVISION ONE CONSTITUTION 2008-09

AFC BLACKLEY	Albert Park, Grecian Street, Salford M7 1JF	None
BEECHFIELD UNITED	Salford Sports Village, Littleton Road, Salford M7 3NQ	0161 604 7600
BURY AMATEURS	Springfield Park, Bolton Road, Rochdale OL11 4RE	None
DUKINFIELD TOWN	Woodhams Park, Birch Lane, Dukinfield SK16 5AP	0161 343 4529
FIVES ATHLETIC	Harriet Street, Walkden, Worsley M28 3QA	None
HEYWOOD ST JAMES	Phoenix Ground, Shepherd Street, Heywood OL10 2JG	None
MANCHESTER JUNIORS	Ford Lane, Church Road, Northenden M20 2TJ	None
MONTON AMATEURS	Granary Lane, Worsley M28 2PH	None
OLD ALTRINCHAMIANS	Crossford Bridge Sports Ground, Danefield Road, Sale M33 7WR	0161 767 9233
SALFORD VICTORIA	Salford Sports Village, Lower Kersal, Littleton Road, Salford M7 3NQ	0161 604 7600
STAND ATHLETIC	Elms Park, George Street, Whitefield, Manchester M45 7FD	None
STANDIANS	Ringley Road, Whitefield M45 7LN	None
WEST DIDSBURY & CHORLTON	Brookburn Road, Chorlton-cum-Hardy M21 8EH	None
WHITWORTH VALLEY	Rawston Street Stadium, Whitworth, Rochdale OL12 8BA	None
WILMSLOW ALBION	Oakwood Farm, Styal Road, Wilmslow SK9 4HP	01625 535823
WYTHENSHAWE TOWN	Ericstan Park, Timpson Road, Baguley M23 9LL	0161 998 5076

IN: AFC Blackley (R), Beechfield United (P – Lancashire & Cheshire Amateur League Premier Division), Bury Amateurs (P – Lancashire Amateur League Premier Division), Standians (formerly Old Standians) (P – Lancashire & Cheshire Amateur League Premier Division), Whitworth Valley (R)
OUT: AVRO (P), Chapel Town (P), Elton Vale (P), Milton (R – Lancashire & Cheshire Amateur League Premier Division))

Division Two

	P	W	D	L	F	A	Pts
East Manchester Res.	28	20	4	4	63	25	64
Prestwich Heys Res.	-10 28	21	2	5	91	30	55
Stockport Georgians Res.	28	13	8	7	77	48	47
Gregorians Res.	28	13	8	7	60	46	47
Irlam Res.	-3 28	13	6	9	76	61	42
Walshaw Sports Club Res.	28	12	6	10	69	75	42
Leigh Athletic Res.	28	11	7	10	67	69	40
Monton Amateurs Res.	28	11	6	11	57	55	39
Wythenshawe Am Res.	28	10	8	10	48	49	38
Elton Vale Res.	28	9	10	9	46	42	37
Springhead Res.	28	10	5	13	60	66	35
Avro Res.	28	10	3	15	53	76	33
Dukinfield Town Res.	28	5	6	17	35	68	21
W Didsbury/Chorlton Res.	28	4	5	19	45	96	17
Breightmet United Res.	28	4	4	20	43	86	16

Division Three

	P	W	D	L	F	A	Pts
Hindsford Res.	24	18	2	4	99	35	56
Rochdale Sacred Heart Res.	24	17	1	6	92	40	52
Gregorians 'A'	24	16	2	6	63	46	50
Chapel Town Res.	24	13	2	9	48	49	41
Wythenshawe Town Res.	24	12	1	11	70	55	37
Stand Athletic Res.	24	10	7	7	61	49	37
Atherton Town Res.	24	10	4	10	42	50	34
Hollinwood Res.	24	9	3	12	70	70	29
Royton Town Res.	24	8	5	11	59	70	29
Walshaw Sports Club 'A'	24	7	3	14	46	63	24
WDidsbury/Chorlton 'A'	24	6	3	15	52	84	21
Milton Res.	24	5	4	15	56	97	19
Leigh Athletic 'A'	24	4	5	15	37	89	17

Division Four

	P	W	D	L	F	A	Pts
Stockport Georgians 'A'	22	15	4	3	66	35	49
Old Altrinchamians Res.	22	15	3	4	81	26	48
Hollinwood 'A'	22	14	1	7	70	40	43
Wigan Robin Park Res.	22	12	3	7	58	41	39
Wilmslow Albion 'A'	22	12	2	8	58	57	38
Salford Victoria Res.	-6 22	12	3	7	56	33	33
Fives Athletic Res.	-6 22	10	2	10	45	56	26
Gregorians 'B'	22	8	1	13	35	57	25
Wilmslow Albion Res.	22	5	6	11	38	59	21
Irlam 'A'	22	5	4	13	30	64	19
Pennington Res.	22	4	6	12	44	59	18
Dukinfield Town 'A'	22	2	1	19	25	79	7

MID-WALES LEAGUE

	Aberystwyth Town Res.	Berriew	Bow Street	Caersws Res.	Carno	Four Crosses	Kerry	Knighton Town	Llanfyllin Town	Llanidloes Town	Llanrhaeadr	Newbridge-on-Wye	Newtown Res.	Presteigne St Andrews	The New Saints Res.	Tywyn & Bryncrug	UW Aberystwyth	Waterloo Rovers
Aberystwyth Town Res.		3-1	0-2	2-0	3-1	2-0	2-0	8-0	4-2	5-0	2-0	2-2	4-2	4-1	5-1	3-0	3-1	2-3
Berriew	0-2		3-1	4-3	2-0	4-0	1-1	4-0	2-1	6-0	2-1	2-2	0-1	4-1	0-1	1-1	0-0	0-0
Bow Street	2-3	3-3		3-2	7-0	3-1	4-0	8-2	3-1	3-2	5-1	2-3	3-2	6-0	1-2	5-4	3-2	4-0
Caersws Res.	0-2	0-1	1-1		2-1	1-3	2-0	4-1	3-3	4-0	3-3	2-2	1-2	6-0	4-2	2-2	2-0	2-1
Carno	1-1	0-2	1-2	3-0		1-2	1-0	4-1	1-2	3-0	0-1	1-0	2-3	2-2	0-1	3-1	3-1	3-3
Four Crosses	0-1	0-0	1-3	0-1	0-8		3-1	3-0	1-5	0-2	2-0	2-3	3-3	0-4	0-1	0-2	6-0	1-1
Kerry	1-5	0-2	2-5	0-3	1-1	1-2		0-0	2-1	0-3	2-2	2-1	1-7	0-1	0-3	1-2	2-0	1-2
Knighton Town	1-4	0-4	2-4	1-1	2-0	3-2	3-2		2-3	1-2	3-1	2-2	3-2	2-5	3-4	2-4	0-4	2-3
Llanfyllin Town	1-5	1-2	0-0	3-2	1-4	2-1	1-1	0-7		1-0	3-3	0-3	2-2	1-1	1-1	1-3	5-2	1-3
Llanidloes Town	0-6	1-3	0-1	1-1	0-6	1-1	1-2	3-0	4-0		2-3	1-3	0-5	1-1	2-5	0-0	1-2	1-4
Llanrhaeadr	2-1	1-1	3-4	0-1	0-4	4-2	6-3	5-0	3-3	7-0		3-2	2-3	4-2	3-5	3-3	1-0	4-1
Newbridge-on-Wye	3-1	0-2	6-3	2-1	0-5	4-3	3-1	3-1	2-2	4-1	3-0		2-5	2-1	0-0	0-4	2-3	6-1
Newtown Res.	3-1	0-0	4-1	3-0	3-1	3-0	1-1	3-0	2-3	3-0	2-1	1-0		8-2	1-0	1-0	4-0	7-1
Presteigne St Andrews	1-3	2-2	5-0	1-1	1-1	1-0	2-1	2-2	3-0	7-0	5-1	1-2	1-2		0-3	1-6	3-0	3-0
The New Saints Res.	2-1	1-0	4-0	1-4	5-1	3-2	1-2	7-0	3-1	7-0	0-1	4-1	1-2	5-1		1-1	4-0	8-0
Tywyn & Bryncrug	0-2	2-0	3-2	7-1	3-0	1-0	0-0	6-1	4-2	4-2	3-1	2-2	2-0	1-5	0-3		4-3	4-2
UW Aberystwyth	0-2	2-1	3-2	1-0	0-2	2-1	0-1	8-0	3-1	2-2	0-0	0-2	4-0	3-1	1-3			3-3
Waterloo Rovers	2-3	2-0	2-6	1-1	2-2	2-0	2-0	4-0	2-1	5-3	3-0	1-7	1-1	3-5	0-4	0-10	2-2	

WWW.CHERRYRED.CO.UK

		P	W	D	L	F	A	Pts
Aberystwyth Town Res.		34	25	3	6	96	35	78
Newtown Res.		34	24	5	5	93	39	77
The New Saints Res.		34	23	3	8	94	40	72
Tywyn & Bryncrug		34	20	7	7	92	51	67
Bow Street		34	21	3	10	102	68	66
Berriew		34	17	10	7	61	31	61
Newbridge-on-Wye		34	16	8	10	77	62	56
Presteigne St Andrews		34	13	7	14	71	77	46
Carno		34	13	6	15	66	54	45
Caersws Res.		34	12	9	13	61	57	45
Llanrhaeadr		34	12	7	15	72	77	43
Waterloo Rovers		34	11	9	14	60	98	42
UW Aberystwyth		34	12	5	17	56	68	41
Llanfyllin Town		34	8	9	17	56	85	33
Four Crosses		34	7	4	23	42	73	25
Kerry		34	6	7	21	32	73	25
Llanidloes Town		34	5	4	25	35	106	19
Knighton Town	-3	34	6	4	24	47	119	19

LEAGUE CUP

PRELIMINARY ROUND
Bow Street 3 Carno 1
Waterloo Rovers 1 UW Aberystwyth 1 *aet* (4-2p)
FIRST ROUND
Aberystwyth Town Res. 1 **Bow Street** 2
Berriew 2 Caersws Res. 0
Kerry 2 Four Crosses 1
Llanidloes Town 2 Knighton Town 0
Llanrhaeadr 1 **Newbridge-on-Wye** 4
Newtown Res. 5 The New Saints Res. 4
Tywyn & Bryncrug 2 Llanfyllin 0
Waterloo Rovers 0 **Presteigne St Andrews** 7
QUARTER-FINALS
Bow Street 4 Presteigne St Andrews 3 *aet*
Llanidloes Town 3 Kerry 2
Newbridge-on-Wye 2 **Berriew** 6
Newtown Res. 1 Tywyn & Bryncrug 0
SEMI-FINALS
Llanidloes Town 0 **Bow Street** 5
Newtown Res. 2 Berriew 1
FINAL
(May 16th at Llanidloes Town)
Newtown Res. 4 Bow Street 1 *aet*

SPAR MID-WALES LEAGUE CONSTITUTION 2008-09

ABERYSTWYTH TOWN RESERVES .... Park Avenue Stadium, Maesgogerddan, Aberystwyth SY23 1PG 01970 617939/630380
BERRIEW .... Recreation Ground, Berriew .... None
BOW STREET .... Rhydpennau Playing Field, Bow Street .... None
CAERSWS RESERVES .... Recreation Ground, Bridge Street, Caersws SY17 5DT 01686 688753
CARNO .... Recreation Ground, Carno .... None
DYFFRYN BANW .... Llangadfan School, Llangadfan, Welshpool SY21 0NW 01938 820226
* FOUR CROSSES .... Foxen Manor, Four Crosses, Llanymynech .... None
* KERRY .... Dolforgan Park, Glanmule, Kerry 01686 670637
LLANFYLLIN TOWN .... High School, Llanfyllin .... None
LLANRHAEADR .... The Recreation Field, ... None
NEWBRIDGE-ON-WYE .... Penbont Field, Newbridge-on-Wye .... None
NEWTOWN RESERVES .... GF Grigg Latham Park, Park Lane, Newtown SY1 6XX 01686 623120/626159
PENPARCAU .... Minyddol, Penparcau, Aberystwyth .... None
PRESTEIGNE ST ANDREWS .... Llanandras Park, Clatterbrune, Presteigne 01544 267838
RHAYADER TOWN .... Y Weirglodd, Water Lane, Bridge Street, Rhayader LD6 5AN 01597 810067
THE NEW SAINTS RESERVES .... Park Hall, Burma Road, Oswestry SY11 4AS 01691 684840
TYWYN & BRYNCRUG .... Bryncrug Recreation Ground, Bryncrug .... None
UW ABERYSTWYTH .... Vicarage Fields, Llanbadarn, Aberystwyth 01970 623036
WATERLOO ROVERS .... Maesydre Extension, Welshpool SY21 7SU .... None
IN: Dyffryn Banw (P – Montgomeryshire League Premier Division), Penparcau (P – Aberystwyth & District League Division One), Rhayader Town (P – Mid-Wales (South) League)
OUT: Knighton Town (R – Mid-Wales (South) League), Llanidloes Town (R – Mid-Wales (South) League)
* Depending on appeal, either Four Crosses or Kerry will also be relegated

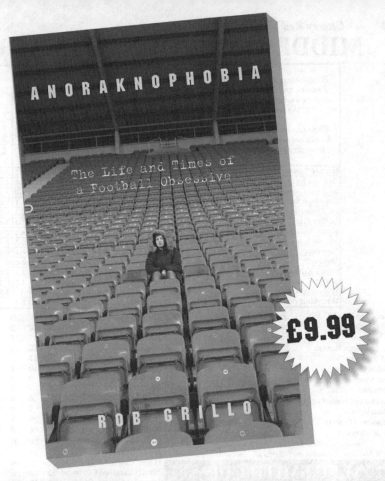

ANORAKNOPHOBIA

The Life and Times of
a Football Obsessive

£9.99

ROB GRILLO

EXPLORING THE WEIRD AND WONDERFUL WORLD OF THE FOOTBALL ANORAK...

Available directly from
The History Press on 01453 883300
or from all good bookshops

MIDDLESEX COUNTY LEAGUE

Note – Kings Meadow, Neasden and Signcraft withdrew during the course of the season

Their results are shown herein but are expunged from the league table

	Barnet Town	Bedfont Sports	Bethnal Green United	Brazilian Sports Club	FC Deportivo Galicia	Indian Gymkhana	Kings Meadow	Marsh Rangers	Neasden	Signcraft	South Kilburn	Sutton Common Rovers	Willesden Constantine	Wraysbury
Barnet Town		2-3	W-L	1-0	5-1	7-0	0-1	L-W	n/a	n/a	6-1	1-1	2-2	3-1
Bedfont Sports	0-2	P	2-2	1-2	4-0	2-5	2-2	2-0	6-0	3-2	1-3	1-4	2-0	4-0
Bethnal Green United	1-2	4-4	R	0-1	3-2	3-1	6-1	6-2	1-1	5-0	3-1	1-2	2-0	3-3
Brazilian Sports Club	L-W	0-4	1-2	E	L-W	2-0	5-1	4-2	n/a	3-2	0-2	0-6	3-1	2-0
FC Deportivo Galicia	0-3	0-2	3-3	0-4	M	3-1	4-2	4-1	n/a	2-2	0-5	1-7	2-3	5-2
Indian Gymkhana	3-0	2-1	3-2	5-2	3-1	I	n/a	2-1	n/a	1-1	1-1	3-3		1-4
Kings Meadow	n/a	0-2	n/a	3-1	1-2	1-6	E	2-2	3-4	n/a	n/a	1-2	n/a	n/a
Marsh Rangers	0-5	1-1	2-7	2-3	2-2	0-3	W-L	R	3-2	n/a	2-1	0-2	0-3	1-7
Neasden	n/a	2-1	0-4	3-4	2-1	1-3	2-1	n/a		n/a	0-6	n/a	1-1	0-5
Signcraft	n/a	L-W	n/a	n/a	2-3	2-4	3-0	2-1	n/a		n/a	0-5	2-6	0-2
South Kilburn	0-0	n/a	2-0	1-0	4-0	1-2	n/a	3-0	n/a	n/a	D	1-1	3-1	1-0
Sutton Common Rovers	1-2	1-3	2-1	1-0	5-4	0-1	2-1	5-2	4-4	n/a	2-3	I	4-3	5-1
Willesden Constantine	2-1	2-0	1-0	2-1	4-0	0-1	n/a	2-0	1-1	n/a	4-1	4-2	V	3-1
Wraysbury	3-1	4-0	3-3	1-4	3-2	2-3	5-2	7-2	n/a	3-1	2-2	4-2	3-3	

Premier Division

		P	W	D	L	F	A	Pts
Indian Gymkhana		20	13	3	4	43	33	42
South Kilburn		19	11	4	4	36	19	37
Sutton Common Rovers		20	11	3	6	54	34	36
Barnet Town	-3	20	11	3	6	37	19	33
Willesden Constantine	-3	20	11	3	6	43	31	33
Bedfont Sports		19	8	3	8	37	34	27
Wraysbury		20	7	4	9	51	50	25
Bethnal Green United	-3	20	7	5	8	46	37	23
Brazilian Sports Club	-6	20	9	0	11	29	31	21
FC Deportivo Galicia		20	3	2	15	27	66	11
Marsh Rangers		20	2	2	16	20	69	8

South Kilburn v Bedfont Sports not played
Kings Meadow, Neasden and Signcraft – records expunged

ALEC SMITH CUP

FIRST ROUND
Marsh Rangers 1 **Indian Gymkhana** 2
Sutton Common Rovers (w/o) v Signcraft (scr.)
Willesden Constantine 4 Brazilian Sports Club 1
Wrasbury 3 Barnet Town 2

QUARTER-FINALS
Indian Gymkhana 0 **South Kilburn** 2
Sutton Common Rovers 2 FC Deportivo Galicia 1 *aet*
Willesden Constantine 3 Kings Meadow 2
Wraysbury 0 **Bethnal Green United** 1

SEMI-FINALS
Bethnal Green United 3 Willesden Constantine 1
Sutton Common Rovers 4 South Kilburn 1

FINAL
(April 19th at Yeading)
Bethnal Green United 1 Sutton Common Rovers 1 *aet* (4-3p)

Division One Central & East

		P	W	D	L	F	A	Pts
Park View		20	14	3	3	72	20	45
Southall		20	13	3	4	57	38	42
South Acton		20	12	1	7	40	36	37
Sloane		20	11	2	7	39	28	35
FC Assyria		20	10	4	6	35	30	34
London Utd F'ball Academy		20	9	3	8	39	25	30
Stonewall		20	7	6	7	32	37	27
West End United	-3	20	6	8		30	40	21
Wilberforce Wanderers		20	3	6	11	40	46	15
Bridge Rovers	-3	20	4	1	15	26	63	10
St John's Athletic		20	1	5	14	24	71	8

Division One West

		P	W	D	L	F	A	Pts
Kodak Harrow		22	16	5	1	53	18	53
Hayes United	-6	22	17	0	5	93	35	45
North Greenford Utd Social		22	12	5	5	57	42	41
Imperial College Old Boys		22	10	3	9	60	49	33
Hounslow Wanderers		22	8	6	8	35	45	30
Brentham		22	8	4	10	34	36	28
Northfield Shamrocks		22	9	1	12	44	61	28
Hillingdon Abbots Seniors		22	7	5	10	60	52	26
CB Hounslow United Social		22	8	2	12	54	53	26
Broadfields United		22	7	2	13	42	56	23
Locomotive Dynamos	-3	22	8	2	12	25	41	23
Bedham	-6	22	4	1	17	20	89	7

JIM ROGERS DIVISION ONE PRESIDENT'S CUP
FINAL
(April 26th at Yeading)
Hayes United 4 FC Assyria 0

CHERRY RED MIDDLESEX COUNTY LEAGUE PREMIER DIVISION CONSTITUTION 2008-09

BEDFONT SPORTS .... Bedfont Sports Club, Hatton Road, Bedfont, Feltham TW14 9NP............................ None
BETHNAL GREEN UNITED ...Sporting Bengal United FC, Mile End Stadium, Rhodeswell Road, Burdett Road, Poplar E14 7TW .. 020 8980 1885
BRAZILIAN SPORTS CLUB .... Wadham Lodge, Kitchener Road, Walthamstow E17 4JP........................... 020 8527 2444
BROADFIELDS UNITED .... Broadfields Country Club, Broadfields, Headstone Lane, North Harrow HA2 6NN 020 8421 4739/5260
FC DEPORTIVO GALICIA........ Osterley Sports Club, Tentelow Lane, Osterley, Southall UB2 4LW 020 8574 3774
HAYES GATE.................... Springfield Road, Hayes UB4 0JS............................. 020 8573 1203
HAYES UNITED.................... Rosedale College, Wood End Green Road, Hayes UB3 2SE 020 8573 2097/7103
INDIAN GYMKHANA .... Indian Gymkhana Club, Thornbury Avenue, Osterley TW7 4NQ 020 8568 4009
KODAK HARROW .... Zoom Leisure Centre, Kodak Sports Ground, Harrow View, Harrow HA2 6QQ 020 8427 1957
MARSH RANGERS.......... Stockley Park, Chestnut Avenue, West Drayton UB7 8BT .... None
NEWHAM BOROUGH (SECP)....... Flanders Playing Fields, Melbourne/Napier Road, East Ham .... None
NORTH GREENFORD UNITED SOCIAL... Ealing Sports Centre, Horsenden Lane South, Perivale UB6 8AD 020 8998 7524
PARK VIEW .... New River Sports Stadium, White Hart Lane, Wood Green N22 5QW 020 8881 2323
SOUTHALL .... Osterley Sports Club, Tentlow Lane, Norwood Green UB2 4LW 020 8574 3774
WILLESDEN CONSTANTINE........ Alperton Sports Ground, Alperton Lane, Wembley HA0 1JH 020 8997 9909

IN: *Broadfields United (P – Division One West), Hayes Gate (P – London Commercial League Division One), Hayes United (P – Division One West), Kodak Harrow (P – Division One West), Newham Borough (SECP) (P – Essex Business Houses League Division One), North Greenford United Social (P – Division One West), Park View (P – Division One West)*
OUT: *Barnet Town (W), Kings Meadow (WS), Mole Valley SCR (formerly Sutton Common Rovers) (P – Combined Counties League Division One), Neasden (WS), Signcraft (WS), South Kilburn (P – Hellenic League Division One East), Wraysbury (S – Surrey Elite Intermediate League Intermediate Division)*

Division Two		P	W	D	L	F	A	Pts
Harrow St Mary's		20	16	0	4	57	25	48
Blue Marlin		20	14	4	2	61	30	46
FC Baresi		20	13	3	4	56	39	42
LPOSSA		20	10	3	7	41	38	33
North Kensington		20	9	4	7	51	34	31
Greens United		20	10	1	9	45	40	31
North Hayes Academicals		20	7	4	9	42	49	25
Junior All Stars	-9	20	6	4	10	26	31	13
Maiwand	-3	20	3	4	13	25	50	10
Haringey Town	-6	20	4	1	15	27	48	7
Park Place Sports Club	-6	20	2	4	14	31	78	4

SIR JOHN SALMOND DIVISION TWO CUP FINAL
(May 5th at Yeading)
FC Baresi 4 Junior All Stars 2

Division Three		P	W	D	L	F	A	Pts
Harrow Club		24	23	0	1	124	25	69
Hendon Res.		24	18	1	5	98	55	55
Uxbridge Town		24	17	1	6	86	33	52
FC Tilburg Regents		24	16	0	8	72	52	48
Hilltop		24	14	2	8	81	42	44
Barn Elms	-3	24	13	3	8	77	50	39
Warren	-3	24	11	4	9	56	55	34
Renegades	-3	24	10	3	11	48	54	30
AMU		24	5	3	16	34	77	18
Phoenix Rovers	-3	24	6	1	17	55	86	16
Sporting Hounslow		24	4	2	18	46	111	14
Acton Town		24	3	4	17	40	123	13
The Wanderers	-3	24	3	2	19	42	96	8

Senior Reserve Division	P	W	D	L	F	A	Pts
Bedfont Sports Res.	16	13	2	1	70	21	41
CB Hounslow Utd Social Res.	16	12	2	2	56	19	38
Hanworth Villa 'A'	16	9	0	7	26	28	27
Willesden Constantine Res.	16	8	2	6	74	23	26
Hounslow Wanderers Res.	16	7	3	6	44	40	24
Brentham Res.	16	7	1	8	42	35	22
Imperial College OB Res.	16	5	3	8	42	55	18
FC Tilburg Regents Res.	16	2	1	13	18	58	7
Park Place Spts Club Res. -6	16	2	0	14	23	116	0

JEFF NARDIN SENIOR RESERVE DIVISION TROPHY
(April 5th at Yeading)
CB Hounslow United Social Res. 11 Bedham Res. 0

Division Three		P	W	D	L	F	A	Pts
Hounslow & District								
Stedfast United		16	13	3	0	104	26	42
Feltham Town		16	11	2	3	35	20	35
Hillingdon		16	11	1	4	60	26	34
Bedfont Town		16	10	0	6	41	45	30
Eutectic		16	6	1	9	44	45	19
Osterley Royals	-12	16	8	1	7	42	23	13
Hanworth		16	4	0	12	31	64	12
Barnhill Explorers	-3	16	3	0	13	22	62	6
BAA Heathrow		16	2	0	14	20	88	6

P D MARDON DIVISION THREE CUP FINAL
(April 12th at Yeading)
Stedfast United 2 Barn Elms 0

SENIOR OPEN CUP

FIRST ROUND
Bedfont Sports 9 Maiwand 1
Bethnal Green United 3 Blue Marlin 2
Brazilian Sports Club 8 Park Place Sports Club 1
Harrow St Mary's 5 Bridge Rovers 4
Hayes United 6 Broadfields United 3
Hillingdon Abbots Seniors (w/o) v Brunswick (scr.)
Imperial College Old Boys 0 **Southall** 3
Kodak Harrow 5 Haringey Town 1
LPOSSA (w/o) v Junior All Stars (scr.)
Marsh Rangers 2 **Locomotive Dynamos** 3
North Hayes Academicals 4 St Lukes 1
Park View 6 The Wilberforce Wanderers 1
Signcraft 3 **Indian Gymkhana** 4
Sloane 2 Hounslow Wanderers 1 *aet*
South Acton 2 **Wraysbury** 5
South Kilburn 10 St John's Athletic 0
Sutton Common Rovers 2 **Neasden** 2 *aet* (2-4p)
Willesden Constantine 5 West End United 1
SECOND ROUND
Bedham (scr.) v **Greens United** (w/o)
Bethnal Green United 10 Sloane 1
Brentham 2 **Brazilian Sports Club** 3
C.B. Hounslow United Social 6 Locomotive Dynamos 5 *aet*
FC Deportivo Galicia 2 **London United Football Academy** 4
Harrow St Mary's (w/o) v North Hayes Academicals (scr.)
Hayes United 4 Willesden Constantine 2
Hillingdon Abbots Seniors 4 Kodak Harrow 3
Indian Gymkhana 0 **FC Baresi** 1

Kings Meadow 4 **Neasden** 7 *aet*
LPOSSA 2 **Bedfont Sports** 4
North Greenford United Social 2 FC Assyria 1
North Kensington 0 **Stonewall** 6
Northfield Shamrocks 3 **Barnet Town** 5
Southall 0 **Park View** 4
Wraysbury 2 **South Kilburn** 3
THIRD ROUND
Bedfont Sports 2 Hillingdon Abbots Seniors 0
C.B. Hounslow United Social 1 Bethnal Green United 0
FC Baresi 0 **Park View** 5
Greens United 0 **Barnet Town** 6
Harrow St Mary's 4 **Brazilian Sports Club** 3
London United Football Academy 3 Hayes United 2
Neasden 1 **North Greenford United Social** 3
Stonewall 0 **South Kilburn** 1 *aet*
QUARTER-FINALS
Barnet Town (scr.) v **C.B. Hounslow United Social** (w/o)
Bedfont Sports 1 Harrow St Mary's 0
London United Football Academy 0 **North Greenford United Social** 2
Park View 5 South Kilburn 1
SEMI-FINALS
C.B. Hounslow United Social 0 **Bedfont Sports** 2
Park View 7 North Greenford United Social 0
FINAL
(May 10th at Yeading)
Park View 1 **Bedfont Sports** 2

JUNIOR OPEN CUP

FINAL
(May 5th at Yeading)
Stedfast United 3 Bedfont Sports Res. 1

MIDLAND ALLIANCE

	Alvechurch	Atherstone	Barwell	Biddulph V.	Boldmere	Causeway	Coalville Tn	Coventry S.	Cradley Tn	Friar Lane	Loughboro'	Mkt Drayton	Oadby Tn	Oldbury U.	RC Warwick	Rocester	Shifnal Tn	Stapenhill	Stratford T.	Studley	Tipton Town	Westfields
Alvechurch		0-3	2-3	2-4	0-4	1-1	0-2	3-1	2-1	0-1	2-1	2-3	1-0	3-2	1-3	2-3	3-1	2-3	2-1	1-1	3-0	0-2
Atherstone Town	3-1		3-0	1-2	1-1	2-2	4-0	4-0	6-0	0-0	1-2	0-3	3-1	4-1	4-0	1-2	2-0	1-1	4-3	4-0	2-1	2-0
Barwell	2-1	1-1		3-0	1-2	0-2	0-2	2-0	2-2	2-1	0-2	3-1	1-1	1-0	0-0	0-1	3-2	3-2	2-2	0-1	1-3	2-1
Biddulph Victoria	2-1	1-3	1-4		2-2	0-1	2-0	1-3	4-0	4-1	0-0	0-5	2-1	2-2	4-1	0-1	0-1	5-1	1-3	1-1	2-0	1-2
Boldmere St Michaels	0-0	0-1	1-1	2-0		1-0	3-1	2-0	11-0	4-2	1-0	0-5	2-0	1-0	2-1	4-1	0-2	4-0	0-2	3-1	4-0	0-2
Causeway United	1-2	0-0	1-0	0-1	4-1		1-0	4-1	2-0	2-1	0-1	0-0	1-1	1-0	2-1	1-1	1-0	2-1	1-1	4-0	1-2	1-1
Coalville Town	4-1	2-4	4-2	1-1	2-0	1-1		3-1	1-1	1-1	0-3	0-1	1-2	1-4	3-2	0-0	1-2	7-0	3-2	3-1	0-2	2-0
Coventry Sphinx	0-1	2-3	1-3	1-1	2-0	1-0	1-0		2-3	3-2	0-3	5-4	5-2	1-4	4-1	1-1	2-3	5-1	3-5	0-1	2-3	0-6
Cradley Town	1-0	1-3	1-2	1-2	0-1	0-3	0-0	1-0		2-4	2-1	0-8	0-6	1-1	0-5	2-2	0-3	1-0	0-6	2-4	0-1	0-1
Friar Lane & Epworth	1-1	1-0	1-0	2-3	1-1	4-1	1-0	1-3	3-1		2-2	5-2	1-1	3-2	2-4	2-1	2-1	1-5	0-3	2-4		1-3
Loughborough Dynamo	1-1	0-0	4-2	1-0	2-1	1-4	5-0	8-0	2-1	3-1		3-1	2-2	1-0	3-2	2-1	2-1	2-1	3-0	2-1	3-3	
Market Drayton Town	0-2	1-1	1-1	2-1	0-0	3-1	2-0	1-2	1-0	2-1	1-0		4-2	2-2	1-2	1-2	2-2	3-1	4-0	5-3	4-0	0-4
Oadby Town	0-1	2-2	2-1	0-1	0-3	0-1	3-1	1-3	2-3	0-2	0-1		3-2	2-0	4-2	1-1	6-0	2-1	2-0	3-4	1-2	
Oldbury United	2-2	2-2	2-2	2-2	0-0	0-1	0-3	0-1	1-0	3-1	2-3	0-2	0-1		0-2	2-3	1-1	2-0	0-2	1-1	0-2	2-2
Racing Club Warwick	1-6	0-0	2-0	2-3	1-1	2-2	3-1	1-2	4-1	0-2	1-1	1-5	0-0	3-0		0-3	1-0	5-3	3-1	0-2	1-0	3-2
Rocester	1-3	0-3	1-1	2-3	4-3	2-1	3-1	1-2	4-0	3-3	1-1	2-2	4-3	1-1	4-4		0-3	3-1	1-1	0-1	1-3	1-0
Shifnal Town	2-3	0-2	1-1	1-1	0-2	2-1	0-1	4-0	4-1	3-3	4-3	0-4	2-1	0-2	1-1	0-3		4-1	1-1	2-0	1-1	0-0
Stapenhill	1-1	0-3	2-2	4-1	1-1	1-4	1-1	2-2	1-2	2-5	1-0	1-0	0-1	1-1	1-1		1-3	2-2	0-2	0-1		
Stratford Town	2-1	3-3	0-1	2-0	3-3	1-1	3-1	3-1	6-1	1-0	0-2	2-3	1-1	2-0	1-1	4-2	0-1		2-4	2-0	1-2	
Studley	1-2	0-6	1-1	1-0	3-1	1-1	0-1	2-0	2-1	2-4	1-0	3-4	0-1	3-1	3-5	0-2			2-0		1-0	
Tipton Town	2-0	0-2	1-2	2-1	2-2	1-2	0-3	3-2	0-2	2-1	1-4	1-0	3-4	0-1	3-1	3-5	0-2		2-0	1-0		1-0
Westfields	1-6	0-1	0-3	0-2	1-0	2-0	0-2	1-1	1-1	1-6	1-2	3-0	2-3	5-0	6-1	0-1	1-1	1-1	1-1	3-1		

	P	W	D	L	F	A	Pts
Atherstone Town	42	25	11	6	94	36	86
Loughborough Dynamo	42	25	10	7	90	47	85
Market Drayton Town	42	25	7	10	96	54	82
Boldmere St Michaels	42	20	11	11	75	49	71
Rocester	42	18	13	11	77	72	67
Causeway United	42	18	12	12	59	42	66
Stratford Town	42	17	12	13	88	63	63
Coalville Town	42	18	7	17	64	56	61
Tipton Town	42	19	4	19	58	63	61
Barwell	42	16	12	14	61	60	60
Westfields	42	17	8	17	66	56	59
Biddulph Victoria	42	17	8	17	65	65	59
Studley	42	17	8	17	58	73	59
Alvechurch	42	17	7	18	68	68	58
Shifnal Town	42	15	11	16	64	64	56
Friar Lane & Epworth	42	15	11	16	72	77	56
Oadby Town	42	14	9	19	71	68	51
Racing Club Warwick	42	14	8	20	65	82	50
Coventry Sphinx	42	14	3	25	62	97	45
Stapenhill	42	8	11	23	53	97	35
Oldbury United -1	42	7	12	23	48	71	32
Cradley Town	42	6	5	31	31	125	23

LEAGUE CUP

FIRST ROUND
Barwell 1 **Alvechurch** 2
Coalville Town 2 Atherstone Tn 1
Rocester 2 Biddulph Victoria 1 *aet*
Shifnal Tn 2 Causeway Utd 1 *aet*
Stapenhill 0 **R. Club Warwick** 4
Studley 0 Tipton Town 0 *aet (4-3p)*

SECOND ROUND
Alvechurch 3 Rocester 0
Coalville Town 4 Cradley Town 2
Friar Lane 2 **Coventry Sphinx** 3
Loughborough 0 **Stratford Town** 2
Market Drayton Tn 1 **Shifnal Tn** 2
Oldbury United 1 **Studley** 2
RC Warwick 1 **Boldmere St M.** 2
Westfields 4 **Oadby Town** 5

QUARTER-FINALS
Coventry Sphinx 5 Boldmere 2
Oadby Town 1 **Alvechurch** 2
Stratford Town 1 **Shifnal Town** 2
Studley 1 **Coalville Town** 2 *aet*

SEMI-FINALS
(played over two legs)
Alvechurch 0 Shifnal Town 1,
Shifnal Town 1 Alvechurch 0
Coventry Sphinx 2 Coalville
Town 2, **Coalville Town** 2
Coventry Sphinx 1

FINAL
(May 6th at Walsall)
Coalville Town 1 **Shifnal Town** 2

JOE McGORRIAN CUP

(League champions v League Cup holders)

(August 4th at Leamington)
Leamington 2 Romulus 1 *aet*
(Leamington did the double – Romulus were League Runners-up)

ASPIRE MIDLAND ALLIANCE CONSTITUTION 2008-09
ALVECHURCH .... Lye Meadow, Redditch Road, Alvechurch B48 7RS 0121 445 2929
BARWELL .... Kirkby Road, Barwell LE9 8FQ 01455 843067
BIDDULPH VICTORIA .... Tunstall Road, Knypersley, Stoke-On-Trent ST8 7AQ 01782 522737
BOLDMERE ST MICHAELS ... Trevor Brown Memorial Ground, Church Road, Boldmere, Sutton Coldfield B73 5RY ... 0121 384 7531/373 4435
BRIDGNORTH TOWN .... Crown Meadow, Innage Lane, Bridgnorth WV16 4HS 01746 762747
CAUSEWAY UNITED ... Stourbridge FC, War Memorial Athletic Ground, High Street, Amblecote, Stourbridge DY8 4HN ... 01384 394040
COALVILLE TOWN .... Owen Street Sports Ground, Owen Street, Coalville LE67 3DA 01530 833365
COVENTRY SPHINX ..... Sphinx Sports & Social Club, Siddeley Avenue, Stoke Aldermoor, Coventry CV3 1WA .. 024 7645 1361
CRADLEY TOWN .... Beeches View Avenue, Cradley, Halesowen B63 2HB 01384 569658
FRIAR LANE & EPWORTH .... Knighton Lane East, Aylestone Park, Leicester LE2 6FT 0116 283 3629
HIGHGATE UNITED .... The Coppice, Tythe Barn Lane, Shirley, Solihull B90 1PH 0121 744 4194
MARKET DRAYTON TOWN....... Greenfield Sports Club, Greenfield Lane, Market Drayton TF9 3SL 01630 655088
OADBY TOWN .... Topps Park, Wigston Road, Oadby LE2 5QG. 0116 271 5728
OLDBURY UNITED .... The Cricketts, York Road, Oldbury, Warley B65 0RT 0121 559 5564
RACING CLUB WARWICK .... Townsend Meadow, Hampton Road, Warwick CV34 6JP 01926 495786
ROCESTER. .... Hillsfield, Mill Street, Rocester, Uttoxeter ST14 5TX 01889 590463
SHIFNAL TOWN .... Phoenix Park, Coppice Green Lane, Shifal TF11 8PB. 01952 463667
STAPENHILL .... Maple Grove, Stapenhill, Burton-on-Trent DE15 9NN *(or Gresley Rovers FC)*. 01283 562471
STRATFORD TOWN. .... Masons Road, Stratford-on-Avon CV37 9NF 01789 297479
STUDLEY .... The Bee Hive, Abbeyfield Drive, off Birmingham Road, Studley B80 7BE 01527 853817
TIPTON TOWN .... Tipton Sports Academy, Wednesbury Oak Road, Tipton DY4 0BS. 0121 502 5534/556 5067
WESTFIELDS .... Allpay Park, Widemarsh Common, Hereford HR4 9NA. 07860 410548
IN: Bridgnorth Town (P – West Midlands (Regional) League Premier Division), Highgate United (P – Midland Combination Premier Division)
OUT: Atherstone Town (P – Southern League Division One Midlands), Loughborough Dynamo (P – Northern Premier League Division One South)

MIDLAND COMBINATION

	Barnt Green Spartak	Bartley Green	Bolehall Swifts	Brereton Social	Brocton	Cadbury Athletic	Castle Vale	Coleshill Town	Continental Star	Coventry Copsewood	Feckenham	Heath Hayes	Heather St John	Highgate United	Loughborough University	Massey-Ferguson	Meir KA	Nuneaton Griff	Pershore Town	Pilkington XXX	Southam United	Walsall Wood
Barnt Green Spartak		2-4	1-3	2-1	1-1	2-2	0-1	0-5	3-4	2-3	2-4	3-3	0-1	2-1	3-0	3-0	0-0	4-1	0-1	2-3	0-3	1-3
Bartley Green	0-2		3-2	3-1	3-1	0-1	1-1	1-2	1-4	0-4	2-0	4-0	0-0	0-3	0-3	1-2	3-2	6-1	1-4	1-5	1-2	1-0
Bolehall Swifts	1-4	0-2		1-0	2-3	2-2	1-4	0-5	2-1	1-1	2-1	0-1	2-2	2-3	1-1	0-2	1-0	2-2	3-1	1-2	1-2	2-3
Brereton Social	0-5	1-1	0-1	*P*	0-1	1-2	1-2	1-7	2-2	0-5	1-2	2-1	0-2	1-4	1-2	1-3	0-0	0-2	0-2	0-5	1-2	1-3
Brocton	2-1	3-2	1-1	2-0	*R*	1-0	4-4	2-2	5-2	1-1	0-0	1-5	1-2	0-1	1-1	2-1	2-1	2-4	4-0	2-2	1-1	1-1
Cadbury Athletic	2-3	2-2	0-0	8-0	1-1	*E*	1-7	1-3	2-3	2-0	3-1	2-3	1-0	1-4	3-1	8-2	1-1	3-0	1-2	3-1	3-1	0-1
Castle Vale	1-0	3-2	2-1	0-1	1-3	0-1	*M*	2-2	2-1	2-0	5-0	3-1	0-1	3-0	3-1	4-2	1-1	2-1	0-1	5-2	1-1	1-4
Coleshill Town	3-2	4-0	1-3	9-1	0-3	1-0	3-0	*I*	5-0	2-0	2-1	3-2	2-0	2-3	0-1	6-0	2-0	1-1	2-1	4-1	4-0	0-1
Continental Star	0-4	1-4	1-1	5-0	2-0	4-5	1-1	1-4	*E*	4-1	4-2	1-1	4-1	0-1	1-3	1-2	2-2	1-2	1-4	4-4	1-2	2-2
Coventry Copsewood	2-3	0-4	1-4	1-2	0-2	0-2	2-3	2-5	3-4	*R*	1-1	2-2	1-0	3-4	1-4	0-3	2-0	3-3	5-1	0-3	0-1	1-0
Feckenham	1-1	0-4	2-2	2-0	4-1	0-2	2-1	2-1	2-1	1-1		2-3	1-2	2-2	2-2	1-2	1-4	0-1	2-1	2-2	3-1	0-2
Heath Hayes	2-2	2-3	3-4	4-0	1-0	3-3	2-3	2-2	1-0	4-1	5-1	*D*	2-4	2-1	2-1	7-2	5-0	0-0	2-0	2-4	3-1	1-3
Heather St John	0-1	2-1	4-1	3-1	6-2	1-1	4-2	1-1	3-4	2-1	0-2	2-2	*I*	2-4	2-1	0-1	1-0	5-1	1-2	6-0	1-1	2-0
Highgate United	1-0	2-2	3-1	3-0	4-1	0-0	2-2	3-1	1-0	4-1	2-0	4-2	2-0	*V*	3-2	1-0	3-2	3-1	2-1	1-2	2-1	2-1
Loughborough University	1-1	3-1	2-1	3-0	2-1	5-0	3-1	2-3	3-2	1-1	2-0	4-2	2-3	1-1	*I*	0-0	2-0	1-2	1-3	2-0	0-3	2-0
Massey-Ferguson	1-2	0-0	0-0	3-0	3-2	2-1	3-1	1-4	3-4	0-2	9-0	0-4	1-3	1-6	3-3	*S*	0-0	1-3	0-1	1-5	2-4	2-0
Meir KA	3-1	2-0	2-1	5-0	0-4	3-2	1-2	1-6	1-1	0-0	0-1	2-3	3-3	1-3	1-0	3-0	*I*	1-0	0-2	1-2	2-1	2-0
Nuneaton Griff	3-1	3-2	0-1	5-1	0-2	3-2	0-0	1-2	1-0	0-0	4-0	2-2	2-2	0-1	2-3	2-0	4-0	*O*	2-1	2-2	3-1	0-0
Pershore Town	3-0	4-1	0-0	4-2	2-2	2-3	1-1	0-3	4-1	2-3	5-1	4-1	2-1	1-1	0-2	4-1	1-3	3-2	*N*	1-0	1-1	1-0
Pilkington XXX	3-1	2-1	2-1	1-1	0-2	1-1	1-1	1-3	3-1	2-0	2-2	2-2	2-2	0-3	0-1	2-2	2-1	1-0	1-0		2-1	3-1
Southam United	1-0	4-1	5-2	3-0	1-5	4-1	2-2	1-4	4-1	1-0	4-0	1-2	1-1	0-2	3-1	5-0	3-2	2-2	5-2			0-4
Walsall Wood	1-0	3-1	2-0	0-0	0-1	1-1	1-5	1-3	2-2	1-0	5-1	1-4	6-1	1-1	1-1	0-3	2-1	1-1	2-2	2-0	0-0	

Premier Division

		P	W	D	L	F	A	Pts
Coleshill Town		42	30	5	7	124	47	95
Highgate United		42	29	8	5	95	49	95
Southam United		42	22	9	11	83	63	75
Loughborough University		42	21	10	11	78	55	73
Castle Vale	-1	42	20	11	11	85	62	70
Pilkington XXX		42	19	11	12	83	75	68
Heather St John		42	19	10	13	80	64	67
Pershore Town	-3	42	21	7	14	77	61	67
Brocton		42	18	12	12	77	65	66
Heath Hayes		42	18	10	14	99	80	64
Walsall Wood		42	17	11	14	62	53	62
Cadbury Athletic		42	16	11	15	80	72	59
Nuneaton Griff		42	16	11	15	69	66	59
Bartley Green		42	14	6	22	70	83	48
Massey-Ferguson		42	14	6	22	65	94	48
Barnt Green Spartak		42	13	7	22	67	75	46
Bolehall Swifts		42	11	11	20	57	77	44
Continental Star		42	11	9	22	79	99	42
Feckenham		42	11	9	22	52	96	42
Meir KA	-3	42	11	9	22	51	73	39
Coventry Copsewood		42	9	11	22	57	84	38
Brereton Social		42	2	6	34	25	122	12

(see overleaf for the 2008-09 constitution)

TONY ALLDEN MEMORIAL CUP

(Premier Division champions v Challenge Cup holders)

(November 7th at Coventry Sphinx)

Coventry Sphinx 4 Coventry Copsewood 3

Reserve Division

	P	W	D	L	F	A	Pts
Chasetown Res.	26	20	2	4	89	38	62
Boldmere St Michaels Res.	26	17	3	6	78	29	54
Barwell Res.	26	16	3	7	60	40	51
Mickleover Sports Res.	26	13	7	6	51	34	46
Oadby Town Res.	26	10	8	8	49	42	38
Friar Lane & Epworth Res.	26	12	2	12	46	49	38
Coventry Sphinx Res.	26	11	4	11	57	55	37
Coleshill Town Res.	26	11	4	11	51	49	37
Rugby Town Res.	26	9	7	10	59	56	34
Quorn Res.	26	9	7	10	43	47	34
Rushall Olympic Res.	26	8	3	15	33	54	27
Gresley Rovers Res.	26	8	2	16	46	57	26
Walsall Wood Res.	26	5	3	18	25	82	18
Rothwell Town Res.	26	5	1	20	34	89	16

CHALLENGE TROPHY

FINAL

(April 26th at Boldmere St Michaels)

Boldmere St Michaels Res. 3 Coventry Sphinx Res. 0

CHALLENGE BOWL

FINAL

(May 7th at Coleshill Town)

Coleshill Town Res. 1 Chasetown Res. 0

MIDLAND COMBINATION PREMIER DIVISION CONSTITUTION 2008-09

BARTLEY GREEN .... Illey Lane, Halesowen B62 4LB .... None
BOLEHALL SWIFTS....................... Rene Road, Bolehall, Tamworth B77 3NN............................... 01827 62637
BROCTON.............................. Silkmore Lane, Queensville, Stafford ST17 4JN .... None
CADBURY ATHLETIC .... Triplex Sports, Eckersall Road, Kings Norton, Birmingham B38 8SR. 0121 458 4570
CASTLE VALE .... Vale Stadium, Farnborough Road, Castle Vale, Warwick, Birmingham B35 7DA 0121 747 6969
COLESHILL TOWN .... Pack Meadow, Packington Lane, Coleshill B46 3JQ 01675 463259
CONTINENTAL STAR .... Oldbury Leisure Centre, Newbury Road, Oldbury, Warley B69 1HE.............. 0121 552 4497
COTON GREEN .... Brereton Social FC, Red Lion Ground, Armitage Lane, Brereton, Rugeley WS15 1ED 01889 585526
COVENTRY COPSEWOOD.... Copsewood Sports & Social Club, Allard Way, Binley, Coventry CV3 1HQ 02476 635992
GSA....................... Alvechurch FC, Lye Meadow, Redditch Road, Alvechurch B48 7RS 0121 445 2929
HEATH HAYES .... Coppice Colliery Ground, Newlands Lane, Heath Hayes, Cannock WS12 3HH 07977 239193
HEATHER ST JOHN .... St John's Park, Ravenstone Road, Heather LE67 2QJ 01530 263986
KNOWLE ....Studley FC, The Bee Hive, Abbeyfield Drive, off Birmingham Road, Studley B80 7BE 01527 853817
LOUGHBOROUGH UNIVERSITY ... Loughborough Dynamo FC, Nanpantan Road, Loughborough LE11 3YD............. 01509 237148
MASSEY-FERGUSON .... Bannerbrook Park, off Banner Lane, Tile Hill, Coventry CV5 9GF 07985 000222
MEIR KA .... Kings Park, Hilderstone Road, Meir Heath, Stoke-on-Trent ST3 7NT 07888 750532
NUNEATON GRIFF .... The Pingles Stadium, Avenue Road, Nuneaton CV11 4LX ..... 024 7637 0688 Club: 024 7673 5344
OLDBURY ATHLETIC.......... Oldbury Leisure Centre, Newbury Lane, Oldbury, Warley B69 1HE.................... 0121 552 4497
PERSHORE TOWN .... King George V Playing Fields, King George's Way, Pershore WR10 1AA 01386 556902
PILKINGTON XXX .... Triplex Sports Ground, Eckersall Road, Kings Norton, Birmingham B38 8SR............... 0121 458 4570
SOUTHAM UNITED.................... Banbury Road, Southam, Leamington Spa CV47 2BJ........................ 01926 812091
WALSALL WOOD.................. Oak Park, Lichfield Road, Walsall Wood WS9 9NP 01543 361084

IN: Coton Green (P), Knowle (P), Oldbury Athletic (P)
OUT: Brereton Social (R), Feckenham (R – Division Two), Highgate United (P – Midland Alliance)
Barnt Green Spartak become GSA

CHALLENGE CUP
(All clubs)

PRELIMINARY ROUND
Austin Sports & Social 2 **Dosthill Colts** 3 *aet*
BNJS Mann & Co. (w/o) v Studley Athletic (scr.)
Castle Vale JKS (w/o) v Warwick Town (scr.)
Droitwich Spa 1 **Greenhill** 1 *aet* (1-3p)
Earlswood Town 4 Enville Athletic 0
GSA & Smethwick Town (scr.) v **Perrywood** (w/o)
Henley Forest 2 **Chelmsley Town** 3
Kenilworth Town KH 4 Shipston Excelsior 1

FIRST ROUND
Alveston 0 **Mile Oak Rovers** 1
BNJS Mann & Co 3 Newhall United 0
Burntwood Town 1 **Chelmsley Town** 2
Castle Vale JKS 6 Earlswood Town 0
Fairfield Villa 4 Bartley Green 2
Greenhill 0 **Loughborough University** 4
Kenilworth Town KH 0 **Stockingford AA** 3
Knowle 4 Leamington Hibernian 1
Littleton 2 **Dosthill Colts** 4
Northfield Town 0 **Archdale** 1
Perrywood 0 **Oldbury Athletic** 5
Thimblemill REC 2 Continental Star 1
West Midlands Police 2 Coton Green 1

SECOND ROUND
Archdale 2 **Pilkington XXX** 3 *aet*
Barnt Green Spartak 2 Brereton Social 1
BNJS Mann & Co. 2 **Massey Ferguson** 3
Cadbury Athletic 2 Dosthill Colts 0
Castle Vale 5 Brocton 2
Castle Vale JKS 2 Oldbury Athletic 1
Fairfield Villa 1 **Southam United** 2 *aet*
Feckenham 3 Coventry Copsewood 2

Highgate United 4 Heather St Johns 2
Loughborough University 2 Meir KA 0
Mile Oak Rovers 3 **Knowle** 6 *aet*
Nuneaton Griff 0 **Heath Hayes** 1
Pershore Town 3 Bolehall Swifts 2
Stockingford AA 1 **Coleshill Town** 4
Thimblemill REC 0 **Chelmsley Town** 4
West Midlands Police 2 Walsall Wood 0

THIRD ROUND
Castle Vale 1 **Knowle** 2
Chelmsley Town 1 **Barnt Green Spartak** 6
Coleshill Town 0 **Highgate United** 2
Heath Hayes 2 **Massey-Ferguson** 3
Loughborough University 7 Feckenham 1
Pershore Town 2 Castle Vale JKS 0
Southam United 3 Pilkington XXX 1
West Midlands Police 1 **Cadbury Athletic** 2 *aet*

QUARTER-FINALS
Highgate United 4 Pershore Town 0
Loughborough University 3 Barnt Green Spartak 0
Massey-Ferguson 0 **Knowle** 1
Southam United 3 Cadbury Athletic 1

SEMI-FINALS
(played over two legs)
Cadbury Athletic 1 Highgate United 0,
Highgate United 1 **Cadbury Athletic** 1 *aet*
Loughborough University 2 Knowle 1,
Knowle 1 **Loughborough University** 3

FINAL
(May 5th at Hednesford Town)
Cadbury Athletic 0 **Loughborough University** 2

	Alveston	Archdale	Burntwood Town	Coton Green	Droitwich Spa	Earlswood Town	Fairfield Villa	Knowle	Leamington Hibernian	Littleton	Mile Oak Rovers	Newhall United	Northfield Town	Oldbury Athletic	Stockingford AA	Thimblemill REC	West Midlands Police
Alveston		0-2	3-1	0-2	0-0	0-0	3-2	0-4	3-1	1-3	0-0	1-0	0-4	1-5	0-4	0-5	0-5
Archdale	3-0		2-3	2-4	2-3	2-2	1-2	3-3	4-2	2-5	1-5	1-2	3-5	0-3	3-3	2-3	1-1
Burntwood Town	3-1	1-1	D	2-3	1-1	2-1	0-3	0-4	0-1	1-1	1-2	1-1	1-1	4-2	0-3	1-5	1-0
Coton Green	2-0	3-1	3-0	I	2-0	1-3	4-2	0-2	5-0	2-3	3-1	2-1	1-1	2-1	0-1	3-0	0-0
Droitwich Spa	3-0	0-5	3-0	1-3	V	2-1	1-2	0-2	2-2	1-6	1-1	0-1	0-1	1-1	2-4	1-0	1-1
Earlswood Town	6-0	2-4	5-3	1-2	2-0	I	2-3	1-3	3-0	2-1	1-1	0-1	0-1	1-2	0-8	1-0	0-1
Fairfield Villa	4-0	1-3	5-3	0-4	5-3	3-4	S	1-1	2-2	5-1	1-3	5-2	1-2	1-4	1-2	2-3	2-1
Knowle	6-0	2-0	6-0	1-1	2-0	2-0	1-1	I	3-0	1-0	3-0	2-0	0-2	2-2	7-0	2-1	2-0
Leamington Hibernian	5-0	0-3	1-1	2-3	1-2	1-0	1-3	1-4	O	1-0	2-4	3-0	1-5	1-1	1-3	2-1	1-1
Littleton	1-3	2-1	5-1	1-4	4-1	1-5	0-2	2-3	2-1	N	0-2	2-2	0-1	1-2	2-0	6-1	2-1
Mile Oak Rovers	3-0	3-0	6-2	3-3	1-1	4-2	1-5	0-2	6-1	2-1		3-1	1-0	0-1	1-1	4-0	5-3
Newhall United	5-0	1-1	3-3	1-3	0-1	2-6	1-3	0-3	4-3	3-1	0-3		1-4	1-1	0-2	3-2	2-4
Northfield Town	1-1	1-1	6-1	2-2	5-1	2-0	0-1	1-1	3-0	1-1	2-1	4-2	O	2-0	1-0	7-0	2-4
Oldbury Athletic	2-4	2-1	7-3	4-3	6-1	5-2	6-2	1-1	9-0	3-0	3-1	1-3	2-0	N	2-0	6-2	1-3
Stockingford AA	5-0	2-0	4-1	1-2	2-2	0-2	2-1	2-1	5-1	2-1	4-3	2-1	2-0	2-4	E	4-0	1-1
Thimblemill REC	3-0	0-4	4-0	2-1	2-5	2-1	4-3	0-2	1-1	1-2	1-2	4-2	2-2	0-6	0-1		0-4
West Midlands Police	4-2	3-0	2-0	1-2	1-3	1-1	2-3	2-4	3-0	2-1	3-1	3-3	0-2	3-3	2-2	4-0	

Division One		P	W	D	L	F	A	Pts
Knowle		32	23	7	2	82	21	76
Coton Green		32	21	5	6	75	40	68
Oldbury Athletic		32	20	6	6	98	48	66
Northfield Town		32	19	8	5	71	31	65
Stockingford AA		32	20	5	7	74	42	65
Mile Oak Rovers		32	17	6	9	73	49	57
Fairfield Villa		32	16	3	13	77	67	51
West Midlands Police		32	13	9	10	66	48	48
Littleton		32	12	3	17	58	60	39
Earlswood Town		32	11	4	17	57	60	37
Droitwich Spa		32	9	8	15	43	66	35
Archdale		32	8	7	17	59	69	31
Newhall United		32	8	6	18	49	74	30
Thimblemill REC	-3	32	10	2	20	49	84	29
Leamington Hibernian		32	6	6	20	39	86	24
Burntwood Town		32	5	7	20	41	95	22
Alveston		32	6	4	22	23	94	22

PRESIDENT'S CUP

FIRST ROUND
Archdale 4 Fairfield Villa 1
SECOND ROUND
Alveston 1 **Stockingford AA** 4
Archdale 2 Newhall United 0
Burntwood Town 3 **West Midlands Police** 3 *aet* (5-6p)
Coton Green 2 Leamington Hibernian 1
Droitwich Spa 1 **Northfield Town** 4
Knowle 4 Mile Oak Rovers 3
Littleton 4 Earlswood Town 3
Oldbury Athletic 4 Thimblemill REC 0
QUARTER-FINALS
Archdale 3 Stockingford AA 2
Littleton 1 **Northfield Town** 3
Oldbury Athletic 4 Coton Green 3 *aet*
West Midlands Police 1 **Knowle** 2
SEMI-FINALS
(played over two legs)
Archdale 1 Northfield Town 1, **Northfield Town** 3 Archdale 1
Knowle 2 Oldbury Athletic 1, Oldbury Athletic 2 **Knowle** 3
FINAL
(May 10th at Studley)
Knowle 1 Northfield Town 0

MIDLAND COMBINATION DIVISION ONE CONSTITUTION 2008-09

ALVESTON................Home Guard Club, Main Street, Tiddington, Stratford-upon-Avon CV37 7AY................01789 297718
ARCHDALE.........................County Sports Ground, Claines Lane, Worcester WR3 7SS........................07736 309670
BRERETON SOCIAL.............Red Lion Ground, Armitage Lane, Brereton, Rugeley WS15 1ED...............01889 585526
BURNTWOOD TOWN...............Memorial Ground, Rugeley Road, Burntwood WS7 9BE..............07946 269153
CASTLE VALE JKS...........Vale Stadium, Farnborough Road, Castle Vale, Birmingham B35 7DA...................0121 747 6969
DOSTHILL COLTS.................Bolehall Swifts FC, Rene Road, Bolehall, Tamworth B77 3NN.................01827 62637
DROITWICH SPA................Droitwich Spa Leisure Centre, Briar Mill, Droitwich WR9 8UE................07860 591091
EARLSWOOD TOWN..............The Pavilions, Malthouse Lane, Earlswood, Solihull B94 5DX................07923 415501
FAIRFIELD VILLA..............Recreation Ground, Stourbridge Road, Fairfield, Bromsgrove B61 9LZ................01527 877049
LEAMINGTON HIBERNIAN...Racing Club Warwick FC, Townsend Meadow, Hampton Road, Warwick CV34 6JP...01926 495786
LITTLETON....................Five Acres, Pebworth Road, North Littleton, Evesham WR11 8QL................07966 297971
MILE OAK ROVERS.........Mile Oak Community Ground, Price Avenue, Mile Oak, Tamworth B78 3NL...........01827 289614
NEWHALL UNITED................The Hadfields, St Johns Drive, Newhall, Swadlincote DE11 0SU................01283 551029
NORTHFIELD TOWN.....Shenley Lane Community Centre, Shenley Lane, Selly Oak, Birmingham B29 4HZ.............0121 475 3870
STOCKINGFORD AA..............The Pavilion, Ansley Road, Stockingford, Nuneaton CV10 8LP................024 7638 7743
THIMBLEMILL REC.........Pavilion Sports Ground, Thimblemill Road, Smethwick, Warley B66 6NR................0121 429 2459
WEST MIDLANDS POLICE....Tally Ho! Traing Centre, Pershore Road, Edgbaston, Birmingham B5 7RD................0121 626 8228
IN: Brereton Social (R), Castle Vale JKS (P), Dosthill Colts (P)
OUT: Coton Green (P), Knowle (P), Oldbury Athletic (P)

Note – Warwick Town withdrew during the course of the season. Their results are shown herein but are expunged from the league table	BNJS Mann & Co	Burntwood Town Res.	Cadbury Athletic Res.	Castle Vale JKS	Chelmsley Town	Continental Star Res.	Dosthill Colts	Droitwich Spa Res.	Enville Athletic	Feckenham Res.	Greenhill	Northfield Town Res.	Perrywood	Warwick Town	Worcester City Academy
BNJS Mann & Co		0-0	3-1	0-2	2-3	3-2	1-1	1-1	2-1	0-2	1-1	1-2	3-2	n/a	1-5
Burntwood Town Res.	1-7	D	2-4	2-6	0-2	4-2	1-7	0-0	2-2	2-2	2-3	1-1	3-1	n/a	2-9
Cadbury Athletic Res.	6-1	6-2	I	1-7	5-0	3-0	0-4	2-0	1-2	3-1	0-1	4-1	2-0	n/a	0-3
Castle Vale JKS	3-0	2-0	1-1	V	4-0	1-1	2-2	4-1	5-0	3-0	2-0	3-0	2-0	n/a	3-0
Chelmsley Town	0-1	3-1	2-4	3-1	I	1-0	1-4	3-1	2-0	5-1	2-1	1-0	4-2	n/a	1-5
Continental Star Res.	3-0	2-0	1-3	0-5	2-2	S	1-1	2-1	1-1	3-2	4-0	1-1	0-1	n/a	0-1
Dosthill Colts	3-1	1-0	4-3	2-2	5-1	2-0	I	6-0	3-1	1-1	2-2	1-2	1-0	n/a	2-0
Droitwich Spa Res.	0-1	4-1	0-2	0-2	0-0	1-3	2-1	O	2-2	1-1	3-2	2-0	1-3	n/a	2-4
Enville Athletic	1-3	6-2	3-2	2-1	0-1	4-2	1-3	5-0	N	3-3	2-0	2-0	2-0	n/a	3-2
Feckenham Res.	2-0	1-0	1-2	1-6	3-3	4-3	0-4	2-2	4-1		1-2	1-2	2-1	n/a	1-4
Greenhill	1-3	8-0	1-3	1-2	1-0	0-0	0-1	0-2	1-1	0-1		0-1	2-2	n/a	2-2
Northfield Town Res.	0-1	3-2	2-2	0-3	0-2	0-2	0-3	1-0	0-1	0-3	1-2	T	0-5	n/a	1-5
Perrywood	2-3	12-0	1-1	1-4	3-0	0-2	1-2	0-1	1-3	0-3	1-7	3-0	W	n/a	0-1
Warwick Town	n/a	n/a	n/a	n/a	n/a	n/a	n/a	n/a	n/a	n/a	n/a	1-1	n/a	O	n/a
Worcester City Academy	4-2	16-0	3-1	1-2	2-1	1-2	0-2	4-1	1-1	2-1	1-1	3-0	2-2	n/a	

Division Two		P	W	D	L	F	A	Pts
Castle Vale JKS		26	20	4	2	78	19	64
Dosthill Colts		26	18	6	2	68	23	60
Worcester City Academy		26	16	4	6	81	34	52
Cadbury Athletic Res.	-3	26	14	3	9	62	46	42
Enville Athletic		26	12	6	8	50	44	42
Chelmsley Town		26	13	3	10	43	48	42
BNJS Mann & Co		26	11	4	11	41	49	37
Continental Star Res.		26	9	6	11	39	42	33
Feckenham Res.		26	9	6	11	44	53	33
Greenhill		26	7	7	12	39	40	28
Droitwich Spa Res.		26	6	6	14	28	52	24
Northfield Town Res.		26	6	3	17	18	54	21
Perrywood	-3	26	6	3	17	44	51	18
Burntwood Town Res.		26	2	5	19	30	110	11

Warwick Town – record expunged

CHALLENGE VASE

FIRST ROUND

BNJS Mann & Co. (w/o) v Warwick Town (scr.)
Burntwood Town Res. 0 **Chelmsley Town** 7
Cadbury Athletic Res. 3 Continental Star Res. 2 *aet*
Dosthill Colts 1 **Northfield Tn Res.** 2
Droitwich Spa Res. 2 **Feckenham Res.** 4
Greenhill 2 Enville Ath. 2 *aet* (4-3p)
Worcester City Academy 2 Perrywood 0

QUARTER-FINALS
Feckenham Res. 5 BNJS Mann & Co. 3 *aet*

Greenhill 1 Chelmsley Town 0
(at Chelmsley Town)
Northfield Town Res. 2 **Castle Vale JKS** 4
Worcester City Academy 3 **Cadbury Athletic Res.** 3 *aet* (3-4p)

SEMI-FINALS
(played over two legs)
Cadbury Athletic Res. 3 **Castle Vale JKS** 4, **Castle Vale JKS** 2 Cadbury Athletic Res. 0
Greenhill 2 Feckenham Res. 1, Feckenham Res. 1 **Greenhill** 1

FINAL
(May 10th at Stratford Town)
Castle Vale JKS 3 Greenhill 0

MIDLAND COMBINATION DIVISION TWO CONSTITUTION 2008-09

AFC PUMAS......................Knowle FC, Hampton Road, Knowle, Solihull B93 0NX.........................01564 779807
BNJS MANN & CO..............Warley Rugby Club, Tat Bank Road, Oldbury, Warley B69 4NH.................0121 552 1048
CADBURY ATHLETIC RESERVES.......Cadbury Rec Ground, Bournville Lane, Bournville.........0121 458 2000x3316 Club: 454 4264
CASTLE VALE RESERVES................The Glades, Lugtrout Lane, Solihull B91 2RX......................0121 711 1422
CHELMSLEY TOWN.............The Pavilions, Coleshill Road, Marston Green, Birmingham B37 7HW.............0121 779 5400
CONTINENTAL STAR RESERVES..Holly Lane S&S, Holly Lane, Erdington, Birmingham B24 9LH............0121 373 0979
DROITWICH SPA RESERVES......Droitwich Spa Leisure Centre, Briar Mill, Droitwich WR9 8UE.....................07860 591091
ENVILLE ATHLETIC.............Enville Athletic Club, Hall Drive, Enville, Stourbridge DY5 5HB...................01384 872368
FECKENHAM..................................Mill Lane, Feckenham, Redditch B96 6HZ...................................01527 892611
GREENHILL...................Cradley Town FC, Beeches View Avenue, Cradley, Halesowen B63 2HB.............01384 569658
PERRYWOOD..................Neel Park, Droitwich Road, Perdiswell, Worcester WR3 7SN......................01905 756617
RACING CLUB WARWICK RESERVES...Warks College, Stratford Road, Henley-in-Arden B95 6AB.................07745 786110
SHIRLEY TOWN................Tilehouse Lane, Whitlocks End, Solihull B90 1PN.................................None
WORCESTER CITY ACADEMY...Football Development Ground, Bilford Road, Worcester WR3 8QA................07778 216579
IN: *AFC Pumas (formerly GSA & Smethwick Town) (P), Castle Vale Reserves (P), Feckenham (R – Premier Division), Racing Club Warwick Reserves (P), Shirley Town (formerly Austin Sports & Social) (P)*
OUT: *Burntwood Town Reserves (W), Castle Vale JKS (P), Dosthill Colts (P), Feckenham Reserves (W), Northfield Town Reserves (W), Warwick Town (WS)*

JACK MOULD TROPHY *(Division Two and Three clubs)*

FIRST ROUND

Chelmsley Town Res. (w/o) v Studley Athletic (scr.)
Dosthill Colts 1 **Castle Vale Res.** 2
Enville Athletic 3 Littleton Res. 0
Evesham United 'A' 2 Shipston Excelsior 0
Greenhill 0 **Castle Vale JKS** 4
GSA & Smethwick Town 7 Feckenham Res. 2
Heather St Johns Res. 3 Cadbury Athletic Res. 3 *aet* (4-3p)

Henley Forest 5 Burntwood Town Res. 0
Knowle Res. 4 Droitwich Spa Res. 0
Northfield Town Res. 4 Earlswood Town Res. 2
Racing Club Warwick Res. 0 **Chelmsley Town** 4
(at Chelmsley Town)
Warwick Town 4 **Continental Star Res.** 5 *aet*
Worcester City Academy 0 **Austin Sports & Social** 3

	Austin Sports & Social	Castle Vale Res.	Chelmsley Town Res.	Earlswood Town Res.	Evesham United 'A'	GSA & Smethwick Town	Heather St John Res.	Henley Forest	Kenilworth Town KH	Knowle Res.	Littleton Res.	Racing Club Warwick Res.	Shipston Excelsior
Austin Sports & Social		3-4	4-2	4-0	2-0	0-4	4-0	2-1	4-3	6-5	5-2	4-0	9-2
Castle Vale Res.	5-2		2-1	4-0	11-0	1-2	5-0	2-0	3-2	5-1	9-1	4-2	3-0
Chelmsley Town Res.	1-4	0-5	D	2-4	0-1	1-3	2-2	4-4	2-5	4-0	1-1	2-1	4-2
Earlswood Town Res.	0-5	1-1	1-5	I	3-1	5-4	0-1	1-2	3-1	0-5	2-1	1-2	0-5
Evesham United 'A'	1-2	0-2	1-5	2-0	V	1-2	1-3	1-4	2-3	1-3	2-3	2-8	1-2
GSA & Smethwick Town	1-2	3-2	3-0	5-0	4-0		0-2	2-2	5-1	6-1	1-1	1-0	1-1
Heather St John Res.	2-0	1-1	1-1	2-1	4-0	0-1	T	2-1	0-4	2-0	0-1	1-3	
Henley Forest	1-3	0-0	2-2	2-1	5-0	0-2	1-1	H	2-1	1-0	8-0	2-0	3-0
Kenilworth Town KH	0-1	1-0	1-0	6-0	1-1	2-5	9-1	2-0	R	2-3	4-0	3-4	0-1
Knowle Res.	1-1	2-2	1-3	2-1	2-1	1-2	4-3	4-0	1-3	E	3-0	0-3	8-1
Littleton Res.	0-5	1-4	1-1	2-0	3-3	0-5	0-0	0-5	0-3	3-2	E	0-2	5-2
Racing Club Warwick Res.	3-0	0-0	3-1	2-0	5-0	1-3	1-0	0-2	3-1	2-1	5-1		3-0
Shipston Excelsior	2-4	2-2	3-1	3-0	2-1	2-2	0-2	4-1	2-0	5-0	3-1	2-1	

Division Three	P	W	D	L	F	A	Pts
GSA & Smethwick Town	24	17	4	3	67	26	55
Austin Sports & Social	24	18	1	5	76	40	55
Castle Vale Res.	24	15	6	3	77	25	51
Racing Club Warwick Res. *-3*	24	15	1	8	52	30	43
Henley Forest	24	12	5	7	50	32	41
Shipston Excelsior	24	12	3	9	49	53	39
Knowle Res.	24	10	2	12	54	55	32
Heather St John Res.	24	9	5	10	30	42	32
Kenilworth Town KH	24	10	1	13	55	45	31
Chelmsley Town Res.	24	6	6	12	45	55	24
Littleton Res.	24	4	5	15	26	77	17
Earlswood Town Res.	24	5	1	18	24	69	16
Evesham United 'A'	24	2	2	20	23	79	8

CHALLENGE URN

FIRST ROUND
Chelmsley Town Res. 1 **GSA & Smethwick Town** 2
Heather St Johns Res. 2
Knowle Res. 4
Henley Forest 4 Earlswood Town Res. 1
Littleton Res. 0 **Kenilworth Town KH** 3
Racing Club Warwick Res. 5 Evesham United 'A' 0
Shipston Excelsior (w/o) v Studley Athletic (scr.)

QUARTER-FINALS
Austin Sports & Social 4 Racing Club Warwick Res. 2
Kenilworth Town KH 1 **GSA & Smethwick Town** 3

Knowle Res. 0 **Henley Forest** 1
Shipston Excelsior 0 **Castle Vale Res.** 3

SEMI-FINALS
(played over two legs)
Castle Vale Res. 2 GSA & Smethwick Town 2, GSA & Smethwick Town 3 **Castle Vale Res.** 4 *aet*
Henley Forest 0 Austin Sports & Social 1, **Austin Sports & Social** 2 Henley Forest 0

FINAL
(May 13th at Pilkington XXX)
Austin Sports & Social 2
Castle Vale Res. 1

MIDLAND COMBINATION DIVISION THREE CONSTITUTION 2008-09

CHELMSLEY TOWN RESERVES . . . The Pavilions, Coleshill Road, Marston Green, Birmingham B37 7HW 0121 779 5400
CLEMENTS '83 . . . . Mackadown Sports & Social, Mackadown Lane, Kitts Green, Birmingham B33 0JG 0121 783 9929
COTON GREEN RESERVES . . . . New Mill Lane, Fazeley, Tamworth B78 3RX . . . . None
COVENTRY AMATEURS . . . David Sinclair Sports Ground, Westwood Heath Road, Westwood Heath, Coventry . . . . None
DOSTHILL COLTS RESERVES . . . The Sports Ground, Tamworth Road, Hermitage Hill, Polesworth, Tamworth B78 1HS 01827 892482
EVESHAM UNITED 'A' . . . . Evesham High School, Four Pools Road, Evesham WR11 1EA 07718 990555
HAMPTON . . . . Field Lane Sports Ground, Lugtrout Lane, Solihull B91 2SB . . . . None
HENLEY FOREST . . . . Henley-in-Arden Sports & Social, Stratford Road, Henley-in-Arden B95 6AD 01564 792022
KENILWORTH TOWN KH . . . . Gypsy Lane, off Rouncil Lane, Kenilworth CV8 1FQ 01926 850851
KNOWLE RESERVES . . . . Hampton Road, Knowle, Solihull B93 0NX 01564 779807
LICHFIELD CITY . . . . Brownsfield Park, Brownsfield Road, off Eastern Avenue, Lichfield WS13 6AY . . . . None
LITTLETON RESERVES . . . . Five Acres, Pebworth Road, North Littleton, Evesham WR11 8QL 07966 297971
NUNEATON TOWN RESERVES . . . . Liberty Way Stadium, Liberty Way, Nuneaton CV11 6RR 024 7638 3206
SHIPSTON EXCELSIOR . . . . Shipston Sports Club, London Road, Shipston-on-Stour CV36 4EP 01608 661139

IN: Clements '83 (N), Coton Green Reserves (P – Birmingham AFA Division Six), Coventry Amateurs (N), Dosthill Colts Reserves (N), Hampton (N), Lichfield City (P – Burton & District FA Premier Division), Nuneaton Town Reserves (N)
OUT: AFC Pumas (formerley GSA & Smethwick Town) (P), Castle Vale Reserves (P), Earlswood Town Reserves (W), Heather St John Reserves (S – Reserve Division), Racing Club Warwick Reserves (P), Shirley Town (formerley Austin Sports & Social) (P), Studley Athletic (WN)

SECOND ROUND
Austin Sports & Social 1 **Castle Vale JKS** 2
Cadbury Athletic Res. 2 **BNJS Mann & Co.** 4
Casle Vale Res. 1 **Knowle Res.** 1 *aet* (4-5p)
Evesham United 'A' 5 Chelmsley Town Res. 4
GSA & Smethwick Town 3 Kenilworth Town KH 2
Henley Forest 6 Chelmsley Town 4
Northfield Town Res. 1 **Enville Athletic** 3
Perrywood 4 **Continental Star Res.** 5 *aet*

QUARTER-FINALS
JS Mann & Co. 1 Evesham United 'A' 0

Castle Vale JKS 3 Enville Athletic 0
Continental Star Res. 1 **Henley Forest** 3
Knowle Res. 3 GSA & Smethwick Town 2 *aet*

SEMI-FINALS
(played over two legs)
Castle Vale JKS 5 BNJS Mann & Co. 0, BNJS Mann & Co. 0 **Castle Vale JKS** 1
Knowle Res. 1 Henley Forest 0, **Henley Forest** 3 Knowle Res. 0

FINAL
(April 26th at Highgate United)
Henley Forest 1 **Castle Vale JKS** 4

NORTH BERKS LEAGUE

	Ardington & Lockinge	Blewbury	Coleshill United	Drayton	Faringdon Town	Harwell International	Harwell Village	Lambourn Sports	Marcham	Saxton Rovers	Steventon	Wootton & Dry Sandford
Ardington & Lockinge	D	4-4	2-0	0-1	1-3	1-1	3-2	3-0	3-0	2-1	3-1	3-2
Blewbury	1-3	I	3-2	4-2	2-1	4-2	3-2	0-2	5-1	2-0	3-4	2-1
Coleshill United	2-3	1-2	V	0-2	2-3	1-3	0-0	2-2	6-1	0-3	1-2	2-0
Drayton	3-1	4-3	3-3	I	1-2	4-0	1-3	1-2	3-1	1-1	2-0	1-3
Faringdon Town	1-1	1-2	2-3	0-2	S	0-0	3-1	0-2	6-1	4-0	1-1	2-1
Harwell International	0-5	2-3	3-1	4-2	1-0	I	2-2	0-3	0-2	1-2	2-1	5-1
Harwell Village	3-1	1-2	3-1	4-2	4-2	2-0	O	0-4	7-2	1-5	2-3	0-0
Lambourn Sports	2-0	3-1	2-0	0-3	1-1	2-2	0-0	N	7-2	2-1	3-2	1-1
Marcham	0-3	1-3	3-5	0-1	1-5	2-4	0-2	2-7		1-3	1-0	0-5
Saxton Rovers	2-0	1-1	6-1	1-1	1-1	1-3	1-1	2-3	3-0	O	8-0	0-5
Steventon	3-5	1-0	2-5	1-3	3-1	1-4	2-4	0-4	5-1	2-2	N	4-2
Wootton & Dry Sandford	2-2	1-2	1-0	2-3	0-2	1-0	1-3	1-2	3-0	2-2	5-5	E

Division One	P	W	D	L	F	A	Pts
Lambourn Sports	22	15	5	2	54	24	50
Blewbury	22	14	2	6	52	40	44
Ardington & Lockinge	22	12	4	6	49	34	40
Drayton	22	12	3	7	46	35	39
Harwell Village	22	10	5	7	47	38	35
Faringdon Town	22	9	5	8	41	31	32
Saxton Rovers	22	8	7	7	46	34	31
Harwell International	22	9	4	9	39	41	31
Steventon	22	8	3	11	46	62	27
Wootton & Dry Sandford	22	6	5	11	40	41	23
Coleshill United	22	5	3	14	38	51	18
Marcham	22	1	0	21	22	89	3

NORTH BERKS LEAGUE DIVISION ONE CONSTITUTION 2008-09

AFC WALLINGFORD............Wallingford Sports Park, Hithercroft Road, Wallingford OX10 9RB 01491 835044
ARDINGTON & LOCKINGE ....White Road, Ardington, Wantage ....None
BLEWBURY ....Bohams Road, Blewbury, Didcot OX11 9QF..None
CROWMARSH GIFFORD........Crowmarsh Recreation Ground, Crowmarsh Gifford, Wallingford....................07951 959090
DRAYTON ....Recreation Ground, Lockway, Drayton, Abingdon OX14 4LG ....None
FARINGDON TOWN ....Tucker Park, Park Road, Faringdon SN7 7BP.........................01367 241759
HARWELL INTERNATIONAL ...Main Gate, Harwell International Business Centre, Didcot OX11 0RA.................01235 820220
HARWELL VILLAGE ....Westfields Recreation Ground, Harwell, Didcot ....None
LAMBOURN SPORTS.................Bockhampton Road, Lambourn, Hungerford RG17 8PS 01488 72214
SAXTON ROVERS.................Recreation Ground, Caldecott Road, Abingdon OX14 5ET ....None
STEVENTON ....Steventon Green, Milton Lane, Steventon, Abingdon OX13 6SA ....None
WOOTTON & DRY SANDFORD ....Wootton & Dry Sandford CC, Besseleigh Road, Wootton ....None

IN: AFC Wallingford (R – Hellenic League Premier Division), Crowmarsh Gifford (P)
OUT: Coleshill United (R), Marcham (R)

NORTH BERKS CUP

FIRST ROUND
Ardington & Lockinge 3 Coleshill United 0
Benson 3 Long Wittenham Athletic 1
Blewbury 5 Sutton Courtenay 0
Botley Utd (w/o) v Lambourn Sports (scr.)
Crowmarsh Gifford 1 Faringdon Town 5
Didcot Casuals 11 Hagbourne United 1
East Hendred 2 Steventon 1
Grove Rangers 1 Wootton & Dry Sandford 3
Harwell International 2 Drayton 0
Harwell Village 7 Challow United 2
Kingsclere 5 Hanney United 2
Saxton Rovers 1 Childrey United 0

Stanford-in-the-Vale 1 Warborough & Shillingford 3

SECOND ROUND
Botley United 4 Didcot Casuals 2
Faringdon Town 3 Blewbury 2
Harwell International 8 Uffington United 0
Kingsclere 5 East Hendred 1
Long Wittenham Athletic 1 Ardington & Lockinge 5
Saxton Rovers 2 Bensnon Lions 0
Warborough & Shillingford 0 Harwell Village 16
Wootton & Dry Sandford 2 Marcham 2 aet (4-5p)

QUARTER-FINALS
Ardington & Lockinge 3 Harwell International 0
Harwell Village 5 Botley United 2
Kingsclere 5 Saxton Rovers 1
Marcham 0 Faringdon Town 2

SEMI-FINALS
Ardington & Lockinge 2 Kingsclere 1 aet
(at Lambourn Sports)
Faringdon Town 2 Harwell Village 1
(at Ardington & Lockinge)

FINAL
(May 10th at Abingdon United)
Faringdon Town 0 Ardington & Lockinge 1

CHARITY SHIELD

FIRST ROUND	SECOND ROUND	QUARTER-FINALS

FIRST ROUND
Benson Lions 0 **Harwell International** 3
Challow United 1 **Botley United** 4
Coleshill United 5 Steventon 2
Crowmarsh Gifford 5 Grove Rangers 1
East Hendred 1 **Ardington & Lockinge** 10
Faringdon Town 2 Wootton & Dry Sandford 1
Hagbourne United 1 **Childrey United** 4
Hanney United 1 **Lambourn Sports** 10
Marcham 1 **Drayton** 2
Saxton Rovers 2 Harwell Village 0
Stanford-in-the-Vale 1 **Didcot Casuals** 3
Sutton Courtenay 3 **Kingsclere** 4
Uffington United 1 **Blewbury** 7

SECOND ROUND
Ardington & Lockinge 4 Childrey United 0
Blewbury 1 **Drayton** 3
Botley United 3 Kingsclere 2
Coleshill United 3 Long Wittenham Athletic 0
Faringdon Town 1 Saxton Rovers 0
Harwell International 2 Didcot Casuals 0
Lambourn Sports 3 Crowmarsh Gifford 0
Warborough & Shillingford 0 **Benson** 2

QUARTER-FINALS
Benson 2 **Ardington & Lockinge** 6
Coleshill United 3 **Harwell International** 4
Drayton 1 **Faringdon Town** 2
Lambourn Sports 2 **Botley United** 4

SEMI-FINALS
Botley United 0 Ardington & Lockinge 0
(3-1p) *(at Faringdon Town)*
Harwell International 0 **Faringdon Town** 2
(at Saxton Rovers)

FINAL
(May 3rd at Abingdon United)
Faringdon Town 4 Botley United 0

Division Two	P	W	D	L	F	A	Pts
Crowmarsh Gifford	20	16	2	2	68	24	50
Lambourn Sports Res.	20	12	2	6	47	21	38
Grove Rangers	20	12	1	7	50	37	37
AFC Benson	20	10	4	6	51	32	34
Kingsclere	19	7	4	8	30	25	25
East Hendred	20	7	3	10	34	44	24
Coleshill United Res.	20	7	3	10	37	48	24
Saxton Rovers Res.	19	8	0	11	38	55	24
Sutton Courtenay	20	7	3	10	35	54	24
Long Wittenham Athletic	20	7	1	12	40	58	22
Shrivenham 'A'	20	4	1	15	35	67	13

Kingsclere v Saxton Rovers Res. not played

Division Three	P	W	D	L	F	A	Pts
Didcot Casuals	22	16	3	3	61	27	51
Warborough & Shillingford	22	14	2	6	50	37	44
Faringdon Town Res.	22	13	3	6	52	29	42
Ardington & Lockinge Res.	22	13	2	7	63	36	41
Drayton Res.	22	11	1	10	42	28	34
Childrey	22	10	3	9	53	42	33
Benson Lions	22	10	3	9	41	39	33
Botley United	22	10	2	10	52	35	32
Blewbury Res.	22	6	3	13	36	52	21
Grove Rangers Res.	22	6	3	13	41	78	21
Stanford-in-the-Vale	22	4	5	13	53	86	17
Marcham Res.	22	4	0	18	23	78	12

Division Four	P	W	D	L	F	A	Pts
Harwell International Res.	20	16	3	1	61	15	51
Harwell Village Res.	20	11	5	4	48	32	38
Wootton & Dry Sandford Res.	20	12	1	7	66	45	37
Steventon Res.	20	9	1	10	51	46	28
East Hendred Res.	20	7	7	6	29	29	28
Didcot Casuals Res.	20	7	7	6	39	47	28
Hanney United	20	8	3	9	38	48	27
Challow United	20	7	5	8	37	42	26
Hagbourne United	20	5	5	10	24	44	20
Long Wittenham Athletic Res.	20	2	8	10	29	42	14
Uffington United	20	2	3	15	26	58	9

Division Five	P	W	D	L	F	A	Pts
Benson Lions Res.	22	19	2	1	105	21	59
Faringdon Town 'A'	22	17	1	4	67	31	52
Harwell International 'A'	22	16	2	4	110	24	50
Coleshill United 'A'	22	15	2	5	64	25	47
Kennington United Res.	22	12	3	7	52	38	39
Stanford-in-the-Vale Res.	22	10	4	8	63	47	34
Challow United Res.	22	7	2	13	38	70	23
Hanney United Res.	22	6	0	16	32	78	18
Hagbourne United Res.	22	4	5	13	33	56	17
Uffington United Res.	22	5	0	17	40	86	15
Grove Rangers 'A'	22	4	3	15	36	91	15
Sutton Courtenay Res.	22	5	0	17	41	114	15

WWW.NLNEWSDESK.CO.UK

WAR MEMORIAL CUP

FINAL
(April 25th at Wantage Town)
Childrey United 0 **Crowmarsh Gifford** 1

A G KINGHAM CUP

FINAL
(May 10th at Abingdon United)
Lambourn Sports Res. 1 Faringdon Town Res. 0

LEAGUE CUP

FINAL
(April 26th at AFC Wallingford)
Didcot Casuals Res. 2 Coleshill United Res. 0

NAIRNE PAUL CUP

FINAL
(May 3rd at Abingdon United)
Ardington & Lockinge Res. 4 East Hendred Res. 1

NORTH DEVON LEAGUE

	Appledore Res.	Barnstaple AAC	Boca Seniors	Bradworthy United	Braunton	Combe Martin	Dolton Rangers	Georgeham	Grosvenor & Lovacott	Hartland	Kilkhampton	Morwenstow Res.	North Molton	Northam Lions	Putford	Shamwickshire Rovers
Appledore Res.	P	0-2	2-3	2-2	1-2	2-3	10-0	4-0	3-2	2-2	4-0	4-0	1-1	1-0	2-1	2-1
Barnstaple AAC	3-0	R	1-3	2-1	2-3	2-1	3-2	1-1	3-0	4-1	4-1	3-0	0-4	4-0	2-2	1-1
Boca Seniors	2-4	7-3	E	3-1	4-2	3-1	5-0	6-1	6-0	3-1	6-0	8-4	5-4	4-4	8-2	1-2
Bradworthy United	4-1	1-1	1-3	M	0-4	6-0	0-1	3-1	1-2	3-1	3-2	2-1	2-1	5-1	0-1	2-5
Braunton	3-0	1-1	5-0	4-0	I	7-0	8-0	1-3	4-1	7-1	10-0	4-2	1-4	1-1	5-1	3-1
Combe Martin	6-0	6-2	3-4	2-0	3-3	E	6-1	3-2	4-1	4-0	3-2	7-0	5-2	5-0	2-0	1-1
Dolton Rangers	4-2	0-6	1-8	2-5	1-8	4-3	R	2-11	3-2	1-1	1-3	1-2	0-0	4-3	1-2	1-5
Georgeham	3-1	2-0	3-5	3-0	0-1	5-0	13-0		2-3	1-1	6-2	2-2	1-1	1-1	4-4	1-2
Grosvenor & Lovacott	4-4	3-3	1-4	2-2	1-2	1-2	2-1	0-4	D	2-1	4-0	1-2	2-5	3-0	2-3	1-4
Hartland	2-2	2-4	0-3	1-6	1-5	2-3	W-L	1-4	3-4	I	4-1	6-3	2-4	2-2	2-4	1-3
Kilkhampton	1-3	2-3	0-8	1-5	1-3	2-7	10-4	1-7	2-8	1-2	V	2-3	3-2	5-3	1-2	2-4
Morwenstow Res.	2-2	2-7	2-4	2-4	1-1	1-1	5-1	3-2	2-5	2-2	8-1	I	2-4	5-1	1-4	2-4
North Molton	3-0	1-0	2-3	1-1	1-2	1-1	2-4	2-1	2-1	0-1	3-0	1-3	S	6-1	1-3	0-1
Northam Lions	1-3	1-2	3-4	2-5	1-4	1-3	0-2	1-7	1-3	0-5	1-1	2-4	0-5	I	1-0	1-6
Putford	3-1	1-2	2-5	2-4	1-2	3-5	7-1	0-1	5-1	4-3	4-0	1-1	4-3	2-1	O	4-4
Shamwickshire Rovers	1-4	3-1	1-5	2-1	3-2	5-1	8-0	2-2	3-2	6-0	5-3	4-1	4-2	4-0	1-2	N

WWW.CHERRYRED.CO.UK

Premier Division		P	W	D	L	F	A	Pts
Boca Seniors		30	26	1	3	133	56	79
Braunton		30	22	4	4	108	36	70
Shamwickshire Rovers		30	21	4	5	96	49	67
Combe Martin		30	18	4	8	91	63	58
Barnstaple AAC		30	16	6	8	72	52	54
Putford		30	15	4	11	74	67	49
Georgeham		30	13	7	10	94	53	46
Bradworthy United		30	14	4	12	70	56	46
Appledore Res.		30	12	6	12	67	61	42
North Molton		30	12	5	13	68	54	41
Grosvenor & Lovacott		30	10	3	17	64	81	33
Morwenstow Res.		30	9	6	15	68	91	33
Hartland		30	6	6	18	51	88	24
Dolton Rangers	-3	30	7	2	21	43	140	20
Kilkhampton		30	4	1	25	50	130	13
Northam Lions		30	1	5	24	34	106	8

BRAYFORD CUP

FIRST ROUND
Boca Seniors 4 Hartland 1
Braunton 0 **Georgeham** 2
Combe Martin 1 **Barnstaple AAC** 3
Grosvenor & Lovacott 4 Kilkhampton 0
Morwenstow Res. 1 **Bradworthy United** 3
North Molton 8 Dolton Rangers 1
Northam Lions 3 **Appledore Res.** 5
Shamwickshire Rovers 2 Putford 0
QUARTER-FINALS
Appledore Res. 5 Grosvenor & Lovacott 4
Barnstaple AAC 2 Boca Seniors 1
Georgeham 2 North Molton 1
Shamwickshire Rovers 1 Bradworthy United 1 *aet* (4-3p)
SEMI-FINALS
Georgeham 2 **Appledore Res.** 4
Shamwickshire Rovers 3 Barnstaple AAC 2 *aet*
FINAL
(May 10th at Torrington)
Shamwickshire Rovers 4 **Appledore Res.** 5 *aet*

NORTH DEVON JOURNAL NORTH DEVON LEAGUE PREMIER DIVISION CONSTITUTION 2008-09

APPLEDORE RESERVES . . . . Marshford, Churchill Way, Appledore EX39 1PA 01237 477099
BARNSTAPLE AAC . . . . Pottington Road, Barnstaple EX31 1JQ . . . . None
BOCA SENIORS . . . . Tarka Tennis Centre, Seven Brethren Bank, Barnstaple EX31 2AS 01271 377701
BRADWORTHY UNITED . . . . North Road, Bradworthy, Holsworthy EX22 7TJ . . . . None
BRAUNTON . . . . Lobb Sports Field, Saunton Road, Braunton EX33 1EB . . . . None
COMBE MARTIN . . . . Hollands Park, Chapel Lane, Combe Martin . . . . None
DOLTON RANGERS . . . . The Playing Field, Cleave Hill, Dolton EX19 8QT . . . . None
GEORGEHAM . . . . The Recreation Ground, Newberry Road, Georgeham . . . . None
GROSVENOR & LOVACOTT . . . . . Tarka Tennis Centre, Seven Brethren Bank, Barnstaple EX31 2AS 01271 377701
HARTLAND . . . . Playing Field, Hartland . . . . None
ILFRACOMBE TOWN RESERVES . . . Marlborough Park, Marlborough Road, Ilfracombe EX34 8JB 01271 865939
MORWENSTOW RESERVES . . . . Playing Field, Shop, Morwenstow, Bude EX23 9SQ . . . . None
NORTH MOLTON . . . . Rocksfield, Old Road, North Molton . . . . None
PUTFORD . . . . Parkham Village Hall, Parkham, Bideford EX39 5PG 01237 472462
SHAMWICKSHIRE ROVERS . . . . . Pollyfield Community Centre, Avon Road, East-the-Water, Bideford EX39 4BL . . . . None
TORRIDGESIDE . . . . Donnacroft, Great Torrington EX38 7HT . . . . None
IN: *Ilfracombe Town Reserves (P), Torridgeside (P)*
OUT: *Kilkhampton (R), Northam Lions (R)*

Senior Division	P	W	D	L	F	A	Pts
Ilfracombe Town Res.	24	17	4	3	68	18	55
Torridgeside	24	17	2	5	93	33	53
Chittlehampton	24	14	4	6	58	39	46
Braunton Res.	24	14	3	7	60	28	45
Torrington	24	9	10	5	61	36	37
Shamwickshire Rovers Res.	24	11	2	11	58	55	35
South Molton	24	11	1	12	44	69	34
Pilton Academicals	24	10	2	12	55	51	32
Clovelly	24	8	4	12	55	65	28
Bratton Fleming	24	7	5	12	47	64	26
Barnstaple AAC Res.	24	6	6	12	46	68	24
Northam Lions Res.	24	5	5	14	39	72	20
High Bickington	24	2	2	20	23	109	8

COMBE MARTIN FINAL
(April 26th at Combe Martin)
Braunton Res. 0 **Torrington** 2

Intermediate Division One	P	W	D	L	F	A	Pts
Combe Martin Res.	26	24	0	2	104	35	72
Shebbear United	26	23	2	1	103	25	71
Georgeham Res.	26	15	5	6	103	57	50
Landkey	26	14	4	8	89	57	46
Torrington Admirals	26	13	2	11	65	67	41
North Molton Res.	26	12	1	13	68	69	37
Bude Town Res.	26	11	3	12	56	57	36
Sporting Barum	26	10	6	10	65	76	36
Equalizers	26	10	4	12	53	58	34
Woolsery	26	7	3	16	45	56	24
Braunton 'A'	26	6	5	15	50	66	23
Grosvenor & Lovacott Res.	26	7	1	18	46	124	22
Hartland Res.	26	5	2	19	48	91	17
Lynton & Lynmouth -3	26	5	2	19	47	104	14

ARLINGTON CUP FINAL
(April 19th at Ilfracombe Town)
Combe Martin Res. 2 **Equalizers** 3

Intermediate Division Two	P	W	D	L	F	A	Pts
Anchor	26	23	1	2	118	40	70
Torrington Res.	26	19	4	3	94	37	61
Park United	26	19	1	6	103	51	58
Buckland Brewer	26	14	2	10	97	65	44
Mortehoe	26	12	4	10	75	62	40
Ilfracombe Town 'A'	26	12	3	11	77	69	39
Northam Lions 'A'	26	12	1	13	60	68	37
Bratton Fleming Res.	26	11	2	13	66	74	35
Bradworthy United Res.	26	11	0	15	68	97	33
South Molton Res. -3	26	8	5	13	60	81	26
Putford Res.	26	7	1	18	53	106	22
Pilton Academicals Res. -3	26	7	2	17	47	73	20
Chittlehampton Res.	26	6	2	18	63	104	20
North Molton 'A'	26	6	2	18	60	114	20

INTERMEDIATE TWO CUP FINAL
(May 14th at North Molton)
Anchor 3 Mortehoe 0

NORTH WEST COUNTIES LEAGUE

	Abbey Hey	Atherton Collieries	Atherton LR	Bacup Borough	Colne	Congleton Town	Flixton	Formby	Glossop North End	Maine Road	Nelson	Newcastle Town	Ramsbottom United	Runcorn Linnets	Salford City	Silsden	Squires Gate	St Helens Town	Trafford	Winsford United
Abbey Hey		1-1	2-2	1-0	0-4	2-4	1-4	0-5	1-5	2-5	2-2	0-1	1-1	2-5	0-4	2-1	1-1	4-2	1-4	0-2
Atherton Collieries	3-0		0-1	0-1	2-3	0-3	2-2	1-3	1-0	1-4	2-0	0-3	0-1	2-2	1-0	1-1	1-0	3-1	3-1	0-3
Atherton LR	2-2	0-0		2-2	0-2	0-6	1-3	2-1	0-3	1-2	2-1	1-2	0-3	0-2	1-2	0-1	3-3	3-1	3-5	1-3
Bacup Borough	0-2	1-1	2-2		0-1	0-3	0-1	0-2	1-3	2-3	2-2	1-2	0-1	2-2	2-2	0-5	3-1	2-2	0-1	1-1
Colne	2-2	0-0	4-1	1-0	*D*	5-4	4-3	3-0	1-4	1-2	3-2	1-1	1-0	0-0	1-2	1-3	1-3	5-0	0-2	1-0
Congleton Town	3-1	5-2	1-0	0-1	1-3	*I*	1-0	1-0	2-3	3-0	5-2	3-3	1-5	3-1	1-0	5-2	2-2	2-1		
Flixton	3-1	1-2	2-1	1-0	0-4	3-2	*V*	1-0	4-2	0-3	4-1	2-3	2-0	4-3	1-1	3-2	0-2	1-3	0-3	1-3
Formby	4-0	1-3	0-0	3-1	0-2	1-0	0-4	*I*	1-3	0-0	3-0	3-1	4-0	1-0	1-3	2-2	2-0	3-1	0-6	0-2
Glossop North End	2-5	4-0	1-1	0-0	1-1	3-0	3-1	1-0	*S*	1-0	0-1	1-0	4-1	0-1	1-1	5-1	3-1	1-2	1-0	
Maine Road	6-0	3-0	3-0	4-1	0-0	1-2	3-0	0-1	0-2	*I*	3-1	2-1	2-1	0-1	2-2	2-0	4-1	1-1	0-2	2-3
Nelson	0-3	1-2	5-1	1-3	2-2	0-0	1-4	2-1	1-1	1-1	*O*	1-4	1-2	0-1	1-3	0-4	1-2	1-0	2-4	1-3
Newcastle Town	5-0	4-2	6-0	2-2	2-2	3-2	4-1	1-0	3-0	3-0	10-1	*N*	4-0	4-0	2-2	0-1	0-0	2-4	2-3	0-0
Ramsbottom United	0-0	1-1	1-0	2-0	0-3	1-1	2-1	2-3	0-1	2-2	1-1	2-3		4-0	1-2	0-2	1-2	2-1	2-4	1-2
Runcorn Linnets	2-1	1-5	1-0	5-1	4-0	0-1	0-0	3-2	2-0	0-2	1-2	2-4	1-0	*O*	0-1	1-0	0-3	2-4	0-3	1-0
Salford City	3-1	2-2	2-1	1-0	0-0	2-1	0-1	2-1	2-1	2-3	2-1	0-1	1-0	2-1	*N*	0-1	5-0	3-0	0-2	3-1
Silsden	2-2	3-0	4-3	2-0	2-1	1-1	0-1	1-0	0-3	3-3	0-1	3-1	1-1	2-1	1-2	*E*	2-3	5-0	0-6	2-1
Squires Gate	4-1	2-0	3-0	0-0	0-1	2-0	2-0	1-0	2-1	0-0	2-1	1-1	1-1	0-0	0-1	1-0		2-1	3-3	2-0
St Helens Town	5-1	5-0	2-1	1-3	0-4	2-0	2-2	4-2	0-5	2-1	4-1	1-1	1-1	1-3	1-5	4-4	0-0		1-6	2-2
Trafford	3-0	1-1	3-0	3-1	2-0	2-1	2-1	5-1	3-1	2-0	1-1	1-2	2-0	2-1	0-3	3-0	2-0	3-0		1-1
Winsford United	4-0	1-0	0-1	3-0	0-0	3-1	2-2	2-1	3-0	1-4	1-0	3-4	2-2	2-1	1-2	2-2	0-1	1-2	1-2	

Division One		P	W	D	L	F	A	Pts
Trafford		38	30	5	3	102	35	95
Salford City		38	26	6	6	75	35	84
Newcastle Town		38	24	7	7	95	45	79
Maine Road		38	20	8	10	75	45	68
Colne		38	19	11	8	69	45	68
Squires Gate		38	19	9	10	52	43	66
Glossop North End		38	20	5	13	72	46	65
Flixton		38	17	7	14	65	65	58
Congleton Town		38	17	6	15	73	60	57
Winsford United		38	16	8	14	60	47	56
Silsden		38	15	10	13	65	57	55
Runcorn Linnets		38	14	6	18	53	64	48
Formby	-3	38	14	3	21	52	60	42
St Helens Town		38	11	8	19	64	93	41
Atherton Collieries		38	10	10	18	44	67	40
Ramsbottom United		38	9	10	19	41	59	37
Abbey Hey		38	6	9	23	45	106	27
Bacup Borough		38	5	11	22	35	69	26
Atherton LR		38	5	9	24	38	86	24
Nelson		38	5	8	25	42	90	23

VODKAT NORTH WEST COUNTIES LEAGUE PREMIER DIVISION (FORMERLY DIVISION ONE) CONSTITUTION 2008-09

AFC FYLDE . . . . Kellamergh Park, Brynning Lane, Warton, Preston PR4 1TN . . . . 07784 319583 (matchdays only)
ABBEY HEY. . . . . Abbey Stadium, Goredale Avenue, Gorton M18 7HD 0161 231 7147
ALSAGER TOWN. . . . . The Town Ground, Woodland Court, Alsager ST7 2DP. 01270 882336
ATHERTON COLLIERIES. . . . . Alder House, Alder Street, Atherton M46 9EY. 07729 374641
ATHERTON LR. . . . . Crilly Park, Spa Road, Atherton M46 9XX 01942 883950
BACUP BOROUGH. . . . . West View, Cowfoot Lane, Blackthorn, Bacup OL13 8EE 01706 878655
COLNE. . . . . Holt House Stadium, Harrison Drive, Colne BB8 9SE. 01282 862545
CONGLETON TOWN. . . . . Booth Street Ground, off Crescent Road, Congleton CW12 4DG 01260 274460
FLIXTON . . . . Valley Road, Flixton, Manchester M41 8RQ 0161 747 7757/748 2903
FORMBY. . . . . Altcar Road, Formby L37 8DL 01704 833505
GLOSSOP NORTH END . . . . Arthur Goldthorpe Stadium, Surrey Street, Glossop SK13 7AJ. 01457 855469
MAINE ROAD. . . . . Manchester County FA Ground, Branthingham Road, Chorlton-cum-Hardy M21 0TT 0161 660 7620
NEW MILLS. . . . . Church Lane, Church Road, New Mills SK22 4NP 01663 747435
NEWCASTLE TOWN . . Lyme Valley Parkway Stadium, Buckmaster Avenue, Clayton, Newcastle-under-Lyne ST5 3BF. . . . 01782 662351/622350
RAMSBOTTOM UNITED . . . . Riverside Ground, Acre Bottom, Ramsbottom BL8 3JH. 01706 822799
RUNCORN LINNETS . . . . . . Witton Albion FC, Wincham Park, Chapel Street, Wincham, Northwich CW9 6DA 01606 43008
SILSDEN . . . . Keighley Cougars RFC, Cougar Park, Hard Ings, Keighley BD21 3RF. 01535 213111
SQUIRES GATE . . . . School Road, Marton, Blackpool FY4 3DS 01253 798584
ST HELENS TOWN. . . . . St Helens RLFC, Knowsley Road, Dunriding Lane, St Helens WA10 4AD 08707 565252
WINSFORD UNITED. . . . . Barton Stadium, Kingsway, Winsford CW7 3AE. 01606 558447

IN: AFC Fylde (formerly Kirkham & Wesham) (P), Alsager Town (R – Northern Premier League Division One South), New Mills (P)
OUT: Nelson (R), Salford City (P – Northern Premier League Division One North), Trafford (P – Northern Premier League Division One North)

	Ashton Athletic	Ashton Town	Blackpool Mechanics	Bootle	Castleton Gabriels	Chadderton	Cheadle Town	Daisy Hill	Darwen	Eccleshall	Holker Old Boys	Kirkham & Wesham	Leek CSOB	New Mills	Norton United	Oldham Town	Padiham	Stone Dominoes
Ashton Athletic		1-3	1-1	1-1	2-0	1-2	5-0	3-0	2-0	3-0	5-2	0-2	4-0	1-0	2-2	3-2	2-2	2-2
Ashton Town	1-0		0-0	2-4	2-1	2-5	0-1	3-0	2-0	1-2	2-3	0-6	1-2	0-4	2-2	4-2	1-0	3-2
Blackpool Mechanics	0-2	1-1		1-1	2-0	0-1	5-0	1-5	0-2	4-0	1-1	0-3	1-1	0-1	0-0	3-1	1-1	1-0
Bootle	2-3	1-2	1-3	D	3-0	7-0	6-2	5-3	5-2	2-2	2-1	1-2	1-0	2-0	5-3	1-2	0-2	4-2
Castleton Gabriels	1-3	2-3	1-4	1-2	I	2-2	2-4	1-1	2-5	1-2	5-1	1-3	1-0	0-4	0-0	0-5	0-3	2-1
Chadderton	2-0	4-1	1-1	1-2	2-1	V	3-0	4-0	1-0	2-0	3-1	2-1	2-1	1-3	1-6	1-0	0-1	2-0
Cheadle Town	1-3	2-0	1-2	0-2	3-3	2-1	I	2-0	3-3	5-3	2-1	3-3	1-2	1-3	1-0	0-3	2-0	2-2
Daisy Hill	0-5	1-4	0-1	2-3	0-6	0-1	1-2	S	1-3	0-3	1-2	1-3	1-2	0-3	0-1	1-0	1-1	1-2
Darwen	0-1	5-1	2-1	4-1	1-1	0-1	2-0	1-1	I	4-2	2-0	1-3	0-2	0-2	1-2	4-0	1-1	1-0
Eccleshall	0-2	2-1	1-3	3-1	3-3	2-3	2-1	1-1	2-3	O	3-1	0-2	1-1	1-2	1-2	1-2	0-1	1-3
Holker Old Boys	0-1	1-3	1-1	0-7	2-4	2-1	1-0	2-0	4-0	0-1	N	3-4	1-2	2-3	1-0	1-3	2-1	0-2
Kirkham & Wesham	2-0	3-1	1-0	1-1	8-0	3-0	8-0	3-2	5-0	4-0	2-0		1-1	0-4	0-0	2-1	2-0	4-1
Leek CSOB	4-0	3-1	3-2	2-4	3-0	2-0	0-0	3-3	1-1	2-0	5-3	1-0	T	0-4	4-1	1-2	2-0	2-1
New Mills	0-0	7-0	5-2	2-0	6-1	6-1	1-0	4-0	4-0	4-0	9-0	2-1	2-0	W	1-1	2-3	6-1	3-1
Norton United	0-4	4-2	0-0	0-6	1-2	1-0	2-1	2-0	2-3	1-0	1-0	0-0	2-1	1-2	O	0-5	1-0	2-0
Oldham Town	1-1	3-0	1-0	2-2	4-1	3-3	7-0	5-1	4-2	1-1	2-1	1-0	3-0	2-2	3-3		3-0	1-1
Padiham	1-3	4-2	1-1	2-1	9-0	1-2	2-0	1-0	5-0	0-0	1-0	1-2	2-2	1-3	2-2	1-2		1-2
Stone Dominoes	1-2	2-2	6-3	0-0	3-1	0-0	2-2	3-0	2-3	3-1	3-1	3-4	5-2	0-3	2-2	1-0	2-1	

Division Two		P	W	D	L	F	A	Pts
New Mills		34	28	3	3	107	23	87
Kirkham & Wesham		34	24	5	5	88	31	77
Ashton Athletic		34	20	7	7	68	35	67
Oldham Town		34	19	7	8	79	44	64
Chadderton		34	19	4	11	55	52	61
Bootle		34	18	6	10	86	53	60
Leek CSOB		34	16	7	11	57	51	55
Norton United		34	13	11	10	47	52	50
Blackpool Mechanics		34	11	12	11	47	45	45
Stone Dominoes		34	12	8	14	60	59	44
Darwen		34	13	5	16	55	65	44
Padiham		34	11	8	15	50	48	41
Ashton Town		34	12	4	18	53	80	40
Cheadle Town	-3	34	10	6	18	44	80	33
Eccleshall		34	8	6	20	41	69	30
Holker Old Boys		34	8	2	24	41	82	26
Castleton Gabriels		34	6	6	22	46	97	24
Daisy Hill		34	2	5	27	28	86	11

Reserve Division		P	W	D	L	F	A	Pts
Bootle Res.		30	23	4	3	104	25	73
Glossop North End Res.		30	20	6	4	80	34	66
New Mills Res.		30	17	8	5	84	36	59
Kirkham & Wesham Res.		30	17	8	5	72	33	59
Oldham Town Res.		30	15	7	8	69	54	52
Colne Res.	-6	30	16	6	8	79	56	48
Padiham Res.	-6	30	13	6	11	58	44	39
Ashton Town Res.		30	11	6	13	53	72	39
Nelson Res.	-7	30	12	4	14	67	78	33
Ashton Athletic Res.		30	7	8	15	52	71	29
Cheadle Town Res.	-3	30	8	8	14	52	86	29
Daisy Hill Res.		30	8	5	17	44	84	29
Flixton Res.	-7	30	8	7	15	50	72	24
Chadderton Res.	-6	30	8	6	16	48	72	24
Atherton LR Res.		30	5	1	24	34	89	16
Blackpool Mechanics Res.	-10	30	5	4	21	49	89	9

RESERVES CUP

FINAL *(May 14th at New Mills)*
New Mills Res. 2 Glossop North End Res. 0

VODKAT NORTH WEST COUNTIES LEAGUE DIVISION ONE (FORMERLY DIVISION TWO) CONSTITUTION 2008-09

AFC LIVERPOOL	Prescot Cables FC, Valerie Park, Hope Street, Prescot L35 6HD ... 0151 430 0507
ASHTON ATHLETIC	Brocstedes Park, Farm Road, Ashton-in-Makerfield WN4 0NQ ... 01942 716360
ASHTON TOWN	Edge Green Street, Ashton-in-Makerfield, Wigan WN4 8SL ... 01942 510677
BLACKPOOL MECHANICS	Jepson Way, Common Edge Road, Blackpool FY4 5DY ... 01253 761721
BOOTLE	New Bucks Park, Vestey Road, off Bridle Road, Bootle, Liverpool L30 4UN ... 07866 912625
CASTLETON GABRIELS	Butterworth Park, Heywood Road, Castleton, Rochdale OL11 3BY ... 01706 527103
CHADDERTON	Andrew Street, Chadderton, Oldham OL9 0JT ... 0161 624 9733
CHEADLE TOWN	Park Road Stadium, Park Road, Cheadle, Stockport SK8 2AN ... 0161 428 2510
DAISY HILL	New Sirs, St James Street, Westhoughton, Bolton BL5 2EB ... 01942 818544
DARWEN	Anchor Ground, Anchor Road, Darwen BB3 0BB ... 01254 705677
ECCLESHALL	Pershall Park, Chester Road, Eccleshall ST21 6NE ... 01785 851351
HOLKER OLD BOYS	Rakesmoor Lane, Hawcoat, Barrow-in-Furness LA14 4QB ... 01229 828176
IRLAM	Silver Street, Irlam M44 6JL ... None
LEEK CSOB	Leek Town FC, Harrison Park, Macclesfield Road, Leek ST13 8LD ... 01538 399278
NELSON	Victoria Park, Lomeshaye Way, Nelson BB9 7AF ... 01282 613820
NORTON UNITED	Norton CC & MW Institute, Community Drive, Smallthorne, Stoke-on-Trent ST6 1QF ... 01782 838290
OLDHAM TOWN	Whitebank Stadium, Whitebank Road, Hollins, Oldham OL8 3JH ... 0161 624 2689
PADIHAM	Arbories Memorial Sports Ground, Well Street, Padiham BB12 8LE ... 01282 773742
STONE DOMINOES	Yarnfield Lane, Yarnfield, Stone ST15 0NF ... 01782 761891
WIGAN ROBIN PARK	Robin Park Arena, Newton (adjacent to Wigan Athletic FC), Wigan WN5 0UZ ... None

IN: AFC Liverpool (N), Irlam (P – Manchester League Premier Division), Nelson (R), Wigan Robin Park (P – Manchester League Premier Division)
OUT: AFC Fylde (formerly Kirkham & Wesham) (P), New Mills (P)

LEAGUE CUP

FIRST ROUND
Ashton Athletic 2 Padiham 2 *aet*
Padiham 0 **Ashton Athletic** 3 *replay*
Blackpool Mechanics 1 **Norton United** 2
Bootle 7 Daisy Hill 0
Holker Old Boys 0 **New Mills** 4
Leek CSOB 2 **Kirkham & Wesham** 3
(at Kirkham & Wesham)
Stone Dominoes 3 **Oldham Town** 4
SECOND ROUND
Abbey Hey 0 **Squires Gate** 3
Ashton Athletic 1 **Bootle** 4
Ashton Town 1 **Colne** 2
Atherton LR 0 **Atherton Collieries** 1
Bacup Borough 0 **Salford City** 4
Congleton Town 0 **Maine Road** 1
Darwen 2 Nelson 0
Eccleshall 1 **Cheadle Town** 2
Glossop North End 5 Flixton 2
New Mills 2 **Chadderton** 3
Newcastle Town 1 **Trafford** 4
Norton United 1 Silsden 0 *aet*
Oldham Town 1 Formby 0
Ramsbottom United 2 Kirkham & Wesham 0
Runcorn Linnets 4 Castleton Gabriels 0
Winsford United 6 St Helens Town 1
THIRD ROUND
Chadderton 3 Ramsbottom United 2 *aet*
Cheadle Town 3 Runcorn Linnets 2
Darwen 0 **Bootle** 2 *(at Bootle)*
Maine Road 2 Glossop North End 1 *aet*
Oldham Town 6 Colne 4 *aet*
Salford City 5 Atherton Collieries 2
Squires Gate 1 Norton United 0
Trafford 0 **Winsford United** 3
QUARTER-FINALS
Cheadle Town 0 **Maine Road** 4
Oldham Town 0 **Chadderton** 3
Squires Gate 0 **Bootle** 2
Winsford United 2 Salford City 0

SEMI-FINALS
(played over two legs)
Bootle 2 Winsford United 2, Winsford United 1 **Bootle** 2
Maine Road 0 Chadderton 0, Chadderton 0 **Maine Road** 6

FINAL
(April 30th at Curzon Ashton)
Maine Road 2 Bootle 2 *aet* (5-3p)

DIVISION TWO TROPHY

FIRST ROUND
Chadderton 4 Blackpool Mechanics 1
New Mills 8 Castleton Gabriels 1
SECOND ROUND
Bootle 2 Leek CSOB 1
Chadderton 7 Daisy Hill 1
Cheadle Town 3 Holker Old Boys 1
Darwen 1 **Kirkham & Wesham** 2
Eccleshall 1 **Oldham Town** 5
New Mills 2 Norton United 1
Padiham 1 **Ashton Athletic** 2
Stone Dominoes 0 **Ashton Town** 1

QUARTER-FINALS
Bootle 2 New Mills 1
Cheadle Town 0 **Chadderton** 2
Kirkham & Wesham 1 Ashton Town 0
Oldham Town 2 **Ashton Athletic** 3 *aet*
SEMI-FINALS
(played over two legs)
Ashton Athletic 0 Kirkham & Wesham 0, **Kirkham & Wesham** 2 Ashton Athletic 1 *aet*
Chadderton 1 Bootle 0, **Bootle** 2 Chadderton 0
FINAL
(April 24th at Trafford)
Kirkham & Wesham 1 Bootle 0

NORTHAMPTONSHIRE COMBINATION

	Brixworth All Saints	Corby Madisons	Corby Pegasus	Harpole	Heyford Athletic	Kettering Nomads	Kislingbury	Milton	Moulton	Ravensthorpe LB	Roade	Stanion United	Whitefield Norpol
Brixworth All Saints		0-2	3-3	1-4	3-1	2-3	0-2	1-1	0-6	1-1	0-4	0-2	1-2
Corby Madisons	1-1	*P*	3-2	2-2	0-0	3-1	2-1	4-0	1-3	3-1	0-3	1-1	4-4
Corby Pegasus	0-2	1-3	*R*	1-3	3-3	7-1	2-2	3-2	4-2	5-4	5-1	4-1	3-2
Harpole	8-1	5-2	3-5	*E*	3-0	1-0	3-0	2-0	4-2	3-2	1-0	2-0	2-1
Heyford Athletic	3-3	0-3	1-2	1-0	*M*	2-1	1-2	1-0	2-1	1-1	4-4	4-0	2-4
Kettering Nomads	2-2	1-3	0-2	0-3	2-3	*I*	0-2	0-5	0-2	1-4	0-1	1-5	4-1
Kislingbury	2-1	1-3	1-0	0-3	1-1	6-0	*E*	2-0	1-0	2-2	1-0	4-0	3-0
Milton	1-0	1-2	1-1	0-0	3-2	3-0	0-1	*R*	1-0	2-6	1-4	1-1	1-0
Moulton	3-0	3-1	2-3	2-5	5-2	6-0	3-0	2-1		0-1	2-0	2-2	1-6
Ravensthorpe LB	3-1	3-7	2-4	1-2	1-0	3-0	0-2	0-1	5-5	*D*	3-2	1-1	3-2
Roade	4-2	0-0	1-1	0-1	4-1	0-2	1-2	1-3	2-3	6-3	*I*	6-0	1-1
Stanion United	0-5	0-5	2-2	0-9	1-3	2-2	0-6	2-4	9-1	2-2	1-4	*V*	1-4
Whitefield Norpol	3-0	1-4	1-2	0-3	1-0	3-2	6-2	0-1	2-3	5-1	1-2	5-1	

Premier Division		P	W	D	L	F	A	Pts
Harpole		24	20	2	2	72	21	62
Corby Madisons		24	14	6	4	59	35	48
Kislingbury		24	15	3	6	46	28	48
Corby Pegasus		24	13	6	5	65	46	45
Moulton		24	12	2	10	59	52	38
Roade		24	10	4	10	51	38	34
Milton		24	10	4	10	33	35	34
Whitefield Norpol		24	10	2	12	55	47	32
Ravensthorpe LB	-3	24	8	6	10	53	58	27
Heyford Athletic		24	7	6	11	38	48	27
Stanion United		24	3	7	14	34	78	16
Brixworth All Saints		24	3	6	15	30	61	15
Kettering Nomads		24	3	2	19	23	71	11

PREMIER DIVISION CUP

FIRST ROUND
Brixworth All Saints 0 **Roade** 3
Harpole 4 Kislingbury 3
Milton 2 Kettering Nomads 0
Ravensthorpe LB 0 **Heyford Athletic** 1
Whitefield Norpol 2 **Corby Pegasus** 3

QUARTER-FINALS
Corby Madsisons 1 **Milton** 1 *aet* (2-3p)
Corby Pegasus 0 **Harpole** 1
Moulton 1 Heyford Athletic 0
Stanion United 1 **Roade** 10

SEMI-FINALS
Harpole 3 Roade 0
Milton 1 **Moulton** 1 *aet* (1-3p)

FINAL
(May 6th at Northampton Town)
Moulton 1 **Harpole** 2

NORTHANTS COMBINATION/ NORTHAMPTON TOWN LEAGUE CHAMPIONS CUP

(14th May at Northampton Spencer)
Harpole 1 **Northampton Harlequins** 0
(Northampton Harlequins represented Town League as champions Duston United folded)

MDH TEAMWEAR NORTHANTS COMBINATION PREMIER DIVISION CONSTITUTION 2008-09

BRIXWORTH ALL SAINTS .... St Davids Close, off Froxhill Crescent, Brixworth NN6 9EA 01604 880073
CORBY MADISONS .... Corby Rugby Club, Rockingham Road, Corby NN17 1AE .... None
CORBY PEGASUS .... West Glebe South Pavilion, Cottingham Road, Corby NN17 1EL 01536 402041
HARBOROUGH TOWN .... Leisure Centre, Northampton Road, Market Harborough LE16 9HE 01858 465934
HARPOLE .... Playing Field, Larkhall Lane, Harpole NN7 4DP .... None
HEYFORD ATHLETIC................. Nether Heyford Playing Field, Nether Heyford NN7 3LL .... None
KISLINGBURY .... Beech Lane, Kislingbury, Northampton NN7 4AL 01604 831225
MEDBOURNE .... Medbourne Sports & Social Club, Hallaton Road, Medbourne LE16 8DR .... None
MILTON .... Collingtree Road, Milton Malsor NN7 3AF .... None
MOULTON............................ Brunting Road, Milton, Northampton NN3 7QX 01604 492675
ROADE................................ Connolly Way, Hyde Road, Roade NN7 2LU 01604 862814
STANION UNITED....................... Village Hall, Brigstock Road, Stanion NN14 1BX......................... None
WELDON UNITED .... Oundle Road, Weldon NN17 3JT .... None
WHITEFIELD NORPOL .... Sports Hall, Wootton Hall PHQ, Mereway, Northampton NN4 0JF .... None

IN: Harborough Town (P), Medbourne (P), Weldon United (P)
OUT: Kettering Nomads (R), Ravensthorpe LB (W)

Division One		P	W	D	L	F	A	Pts
Weldon United		26	22	2	2	92	29	68
Harborough Town		26	19	3	4	89	24	60
Medbourne		26	18	3	5	75	34	57
Corby Kingfisher Athletic		26	14	4	8	60	30	46
Wootton St George		26	12	6	8	42	41	42
Welford Victoria		26	11	5	10	41	40	38
Stanwick Rovers		26	11	3	12	52	54	36
Corby Phoenix		26	11	2	13	52	65	35
Earls Barton United		26	8	9	9	38	41	33
James King Blisworth	-6	26	7	6	13	34	52	21
Queen Eleanor Great Houghton		26	6	3	17	36	63	21
Spratton		26	6	2	18	43	69	20
Bective Wanderers	-9	26	8	4	14	48	69	19
Crick Athletic		26	3	0	23	26	117	9

Division Two		P	W	D	L	F	A	Pts
Cold Ashby Rovers	-3	24	17	1	6	72	32	49
Punjab United		24	15	4	5	76	39	49
Wollaston Victoria		24	13	9	2	66	37	48
Finedon Volta		24	15	2	7	68	42	47
Burton United		24	12	4	8	53	47	40
Gretton		24	11	4	9	73	56	37
Clipston		24	11	4	9	43	43	37
Wellingborough Ranelagh		24	8	5	11	46	55	29
Islip United		24	7	3	14	50	60	24
Weedon	-3	24	6	6	12	40	58	21
Ringstead Rangers	-3	24	5	8	11	42	67	20
Wilbarston		24	4	5	15	29	76	17
Kettering Orchard Park		24	4	1	19	29	75	13

DIVISION ONE CUP FINAL
(April 14th at Wellingborough Town)
Harborough Town 6 Welford Victoria 1

DIVISION TWO CUP FINAL
(April 22nd at Rounds Town)
Punjab United 2 Finedon Volta 1 *aet*

Division Three		P	W	D	L	F	A	Pts
Corby Danesholme Vikings		24	18	2	4	81	39	56
Ristee Towers		24	16	5	3	63	28	53
Daventry Drayton Grange		24	15	4	5	83	37	49
Great Doddington		24	11	9	4	49	34	42
Wellingborough Old Grammarians		24	13	3	8	68	58	42
Dainite Sports		24	11	7	6	74	62	40
Hillmorton	-3	24	8	5	11	56	66	26
Weavers Old Boys		24	7	4	13	41	47	25
Wilby		24	7	3	14	51	76	24
Corby Locomotives		24	6	5	13	42	65	23
Staverton Park Rangers		24	5	5	14	40	71	20
Wellingborough Raffertys	-3	24	6	4	14	57	76	19
West Haddon		24	4	2	18	32	78	14

Division Four	P	W	D	L	F	A	Pts
Corby Strip Mills	18	13	2	3	72	23	41
Corby Eagles	18	12	1	5	49	32	37
Corby Everards	18	11	3	4	66	33	36
Corby Leaf	18	10	3	5	51	38	33
Wellingborough Rising Sun	18	8	5	5	52	36	29
Wellingborough WMC	18	8	2	8	47	54	26
CSV United	18	6	2	10	36	53	20
Kettering Park Rovers	18	6	1	11	37	66	19
Yardley United	18	3	1	14	32	64	10
Thrapston	18	2	2	14	24	67	8

DIVISION THREE CUP FINAL
(April 8th at Cogenhoe United)
Great Doddington 1 Wellingborough Old Grammarians 0

DIVISION FOUR CUP FINAL
(April 1st at Wellingborough Town)
Corby Eagles 1 Corby Everards 0

Reserve Premier Division		P	W	D	L	F	A	Pts
Corby Madisons Res.		26	18	2	6	82	46	56
Weldon United Res.		26	16	4	6	68	34	52
Roade Res.		26	14	5	7	63	44	47
Bugbrooke St Michaels 'A'	-3	26	14	6	6	73	40	45
Moulton Res.		26	13	3	10	68	64	42
Kislingbury Res.		26	11	5	10	47	49	38
Kettering Nomads Res.	-3	26	13	2	11	50	54	38
James King Blisworth Res.		26	10	5	11	41	47	35
Corby Pegasus Res.	-3	26	10	6	10	55	54	33
Milton Res.		26	7	5	14	43	61	26
Northampton ON Chenecks 'A'		26	7	4	15	40	52	25
Heyford Athletic Res.		26	6	7	13	51	75	25
Gretton Res.		26	8	0	18	45	79	24
Harpole Res.		26	5	6	15	39	66	21

Reserve Division One		P	W	D	L	F	A	Pts
Whitefield Norpol Res.		26	22	2	2	122	34	68
Bugbrooke St Michaels 'B'		26	19	2	5	82	37	59
Wollaston Victoria Res.		26	13	6	7	80	55	45
Harborough Town Res.	-6	26	16	2	8	71	30	44
Medbourne Res.	-3	26	14	4	8	76	59	43
Stanion United Res.		26	12	2	12	66	74	38
Harpole 'A'		26	12	1	13	64	67	37
Ringstead Rangers Res.		26	11	2	13	70	81	35
Spratton Res.	-3	26	10	3	13	73	89	30
Queen Eleanor Great Houghton Res.		26	8	4	14	47	85	28
Wootton St George Res.		26	7	3	16	51	63	24
Finedon Volta Res.		26	7	2	17	36	71	23
Corby Locomotives Res.		26	6	3	17	46	91	21
Brixworth All Saints Res.	-3	26	6	2	18	48	96	17

RESERVE PREMIER DIVISION CUP FINAL
(April 17th at Cogenhoe United)
Corby Madisons Res. 4 Moulton Res. 1 *aet*

RESERVE DIVISION ONE CUP FINAL
(April 26th at Wellingborough Town)
Harborough Town Res. 1 **Whitefield Norpol Res.** 1 *aet* (1-3p)

Reserve Division Two		P	W	D	L	F	A	Pts
Weldon United 'A'		22	16	2	4	89	34	50
Kettering Orchard Park Res.		22	14	4	4	59	22	46
Stanwick Rovers Res.		22	14	3	5	47	24	45
Welford Victoria Res.		22	13	3	6	77	40	42
Islip United Res.		22	12	3	7	55	36	39
Wellingborough Old Grammarians Res.		22	10	3	9	51	52	33
Earls Barton United Res.	-6	22	9	2	11	51	50	23
Daventry Drayton Grange Res.	-3	22	7	3	12	46	43	21
Dainite Sports Res.	-6	22	7	2	12	32	72	20
Wilby Res.		22	5	0	17	31	99	15
Weedon Res.	-6	22	5	3	14	50	70	12
Crick Athletic Res.	-3	22	4	2	16	29	75	11

RESERVE DIVISION TWO CUP FINAL
(April 3rd at Rounds Town)
Welford Victoria Res. 1 **Weldon United 'A'** 2

NORTHERN ALLIANCE

	Alnwick Town	Ashington Colliers	Blyth Town	Carlisle City	Cramlington Town	Gateshead Leam Rangers	Gillford Park	Harraby Catholic Club	Heaton Stannington	Heddon	Newcastle University	Northbank Carlisle	Peterlee Town	Ponteland United	Seaton Delaval Amateurs	Shankhouse	Walker Central
Alnwick Town	P	3-2	5-1	2-4	0-1	n/a	0-4	1-3	3-0	0-1	9-0	5-0	0-1	2-2	6-2	3-1	1-1
Ashington Colliers	1-1	R	1-2	1-1	3-3	n/a	3-1	3-2	3-1	1-1	1-3	3-1	2-4	2-1	3-3	2-4	0-5
Blyth Town	0-2	2-3	E	2-1	2-1	n/a	3-2	1-0	1-1	1-1	0-1	1-1	0-4	3-2	1-0	3-2	2-2
Carlisle City	1-0	3-1	6-1	M	5-1	n/a	1-1	1-5	0-2	2-2	1-0	1-1	1-4	1-4	2-3	3-6	2-3
Cramlington Town	2-1	2-0	4-1	2-1	I	n/a	0-0	0-1	2-2	2-2	1-0	1-2	9-1	4-1	0-3	2-2	0-2
Gateshead Leam Rangers	0-1	n/a	n/a	1-0	4-2	E	2-1	n/a	n/a	n/a	n/a	n/a	n/a	n/a	n/a	n/a	n/a
Gillford Park	6-2	2-1	5-2	3-1	2-1	n/a	R	0-0	2-0	3-1	5-0	8-2	1-1	3-2	1-1	1-1	0-1
Harraby Catholic Club	2-0	6-1	4-0	0-2	4-1	3-2	1-1		3-1	1-2	3-0	6-1	2-1	2-2	4-0	4-1	1-1
Heaton Stannington	5-0	3-1	3-3	1-1	1-1	n/a	1-1	2-1		3-3	4-3	3-0	5-2	2-1	4-0	1-0	2-0
Heddon	3-1	0-0	1-0	3-1	1-0	0-2	0-1	1-1	2-2	D	2-1	4-1	1-4	3-0	1-4	0-4	1-1
Newcastle University	3-0	1-3	2-3	3-1	0-1	n/a	0-1	0-1	0-4	1-2	I	3-1	1-1	0-5	0-3	5-0	1-6
Northbank Carlisle	1-0	2-3	3-3	0-2	1-2	n/a	0-4	1-2	2-4	1-3	1-6	V	2-3	0-4	3-4	2-2	1-6
Peterlee Town	0-4	2-1	1-3	2-0	3-2	0-2	2-3	2-3	3-1	2-1	5-0	3-2	I	5-2	4-2	1-2	0-5
Ponteland United	3-0	0-4	5-2	2-2	3-1	n/a	0-2	0-3	6-2	1-2	2-3	5-0	1-3	S	2-0	3-2	0-3
Seaton Delaval Amateurs	2-3	0-1	1-2	3-3	2-1	n/a	0-0	1-4	0-3	0-2	2-1	5-0	7-0	3-2	I	3-4	1-3
Shankhouse	3-1	2-0	2-0	1-0	4-0	n/a	1-2	1-3	0-0	0-1	4-0	2-3	1-0	1-5	0-1	O	4-3
Walker Central	4-0	3-1	5-2	1-0	1-1	3-3	2-1	1-1	3-0	3-0	4-0	3-2	3-0	3-1	5-1		N

Note – Gateshead Leam Rangers withdrew during the course of the season

Their results are shown herein but are expunged from the league table

WWW.NLNEWSDESK.CO.UK

Premier Division		P	W	D	L	F	A	Pts
Walker Central		30	21	7	2	86	27	70
Harraby Catholic Club		30	19	6	5	73	29	63
Gillford Park		30	17	10	3	67	30	61
Heddon		30	14	9	7	47	42	51
Peterlee Town		30	16	2	12	66	67	50
Heaton Stannington	-4	30	14	9	7	63	47	47
Shankhouse		30	13	4	13	58	57	43
Blyth Town		30	11	6	13	47	71	39
Cramlington Town		30	10	7	13	48	51	37
Seaton Delaval Amateurs		30	11	4	15	57	63	37
Ponteland United		30	11	3	16	66	63	36
Ashington Colliers		30	10	6	14	51	64	36
Carlisle City		30	8	7	15	50	60	31
Alnwick Town	-3	30	10	3	17	55	59	30
Newcastle University	-6	30	8	1	21	38	75	19
Northbank Carlisle		30	3	4	23	35	102	13

Gateshead Leam Rangers – record expunged

CHALLENGE CUP

PRELIMINARY ROUND
Ponteland United 4 Blyth Town 1
FIRST ROUND
Alnwick Town 2 Gillford Park 1
Ashington Colliers 2 Northbank Carlisle 1
Carlisle City 5 Seaton Delaval Amateurs 3 *aet*
Cramlington Town 5 Newcastle University 0
Heaton Stannington 1 **Harraby Catholic Club** 3
Peterlee Town 2 Heddon 1
Shankhouse 4 Ponteland United 1
Walker Central 1 Gateshead Leam Rangers 0
QUARTER-FINALS
Alnwick Town 0 **Peterlee Town** 3
Ashington Colliers 3 Shankhouse 1
Harraby Catholic Club 2 Cramlington Town 0
Walker Central 0 **Carlisle City** 2
SEMI-FINALS
Harraby Catholic Club 2 Ashington Colliers 0
Peterlee Town 3 Carlisle City 1
FINAL
(May 6th at Prudhoe Town)
Harraby Catholic Club 1 Peterlee Newtown 1 *aet* (7-6p)

RE/MAX NORTHERN ALLIANCE PREMIER DIVISION CONSTITUTION 2008-09

ALNWICK TOWN . . . . St Jame's Park, Weavers Way, Alnwick NE66 1BG 01665 603162
ASHINGTON COLLIERS . . . . Hirst Welfare, Alexandra Road, Ashington NE63 9HF 01670 811991
BLYTH TOWN . . . . South Newsham Playing Fields, Blyth . . . . None
CARLISLE CITY . . . . Sheepmount Sports Complex, Sheepmount, Carlisle CA3 8XL 01228 625599
CRAMLINGTON TOWN . . . . Sporting Club of Cramlington, Highburn, Cramlington NE23 6YB 01670 591970
GILLFORD PARK . . . . Gillford Park Railway Club, Petteril Bank Road, Carlisle CA1 3AF 01228 526449
HARRABY CATHOLIC CLUB . . . . Harraby Community Centre, Edgehill Road, Carlisle CA1 3SL . . . . None
HEATON STANNINGTON . . . . Grounsell Park, Newton Road, High Heaton, Newcastle-upon-Tyne NE7 7HP . . . . None
HEDDON . . . . Bullockstead Sports Complex, Ponteland Road, Kenton Bank Foot, Newcastle-upon-Tyne NE13 8AH 0191 271 1153
MURTON . . . . Recreation Park, Church Lane, Murton, Seaham SR7 9RD . . . . None
NEWCASTLE UNIVERSITY . . . . . . Cochrane Park, Etherstone Avenue, Newcastle-upon-Tyne NE7 7JX . . . . None
PETERLEE TOWN . . . . Eden Lane Playing Fields, Peterlee SR8 5DS 0191 586 3004
PONTELAND UNITED . . The Leisure Centre Ground, Callerton Lane, Ponteland, Newcastle-upon-Tyne NE20 9EG 01661 825441
SEATON DELAVAL AMATEURS . . . . . Wheatridge Park, Seaton Delaval, Whitley Bay NE25 0QH . . . . None
SHANKHOUSE . . . . Northburn Sports Complex, Crawhall Lane, Cramlington NE23 3YP 01670 714154
WALKER CENTRAL . . . . Monkchester Green, Walker, Newcastle-upon-Tyne NE6 5LJ 0191 265 7270
WARK . . . . Wark Sports Club, Wark, Hexham NE48 3NP 01434 230259
IN: Murton (P), Wark (P)
OUT: Gateshead Leam Rangers (WS), Northbank Carlisle (R)

Note – Haydon Bridge United withdrew during the course of the season

Their results are shown herein but are expunged from the league table

	Berwick United	Chopwell Officials Club	Gosforth Bohemian Garnett	Haydon Bridge United	Hebburn Reyrolle	Murton	Newcastle East End Rail Club	Penrith United	Percy Main Amateurs	Red Row Welfare	Rutherford Newcastle	Seaton Burn	Stocksfield	Wallington	Wark	Westerhope JG	Whitley Bay 'A'
Berwick United		2-3	1-1	3-2	1-2	0-1	3-0	1-2	4-1	4-2	1-3	0-1	3-2	2-3	1-3	2-2	4-11
Chopwell Officials Club	1-2		2-3	6-0	1-1	0-2	3-1	0-1	0-1	3-1	3-3	3-3	3-0	3-1	1-4	3-1	1-7
Gosforth Bohemian Garnett	0-0	1-2	*D*	n/a	1-3	3-3	4-0	0-2	4-0	2-3	1-0	2-2	3-3	1-3	4-4	1-3	1-3
Haydon Bridge United	0-3	n/a	1-4	*I*	1-2	1-8	0-3	2-2	n/a	n/a	n/a	2-4	1-7	1-7	0-3	1-0	1-0
Hebburn Reyrolle	2-0	2-0	1-5	n/a	*V*	1-1	4-3	1-2	0-3	1-2	3-3	3-2	1-5	2-6	1-6	2-2	1-4
Murton	2-0	5-1	3-0	9-1	2-0	*I*	2-1	4-1	1-0	9-0	2-2	0-1	6-2	2-2	3-0	0-2	3-2
Newcastle East End Rail Club	0-4	0-0	4-3	4-2	4-0	1-3	*S*	1-0	2-2	2-0	0-6	3-3	1-4	2-5	0-5	0-3	4-4
Penrith United	1-4	10-2	6-2	4-0	7-1	5-6	4-0	*I*	1-0	6-1	2-4	3-2	1-2	1-1	2-3	5-1	4-2
Percy Main Amateurs	3-1	2-2	5-1	n/a	1-0	0-4	4-1	1-3	*O*	1-1	0-5	2-0	0-2	1-2	2-3	2-3	2-1
Red Row Welfare	2-4	0-2	5-1	2-0	4-3	1-2	5-0	3-0	2-1	*N*	1-1	1-0	2-2	0-0	4-6	1-1	4-0
Rutherford Newcastle	1-2	4-1	1-5	4-2	2-0	1-1	4-1	1-0	3-1	3-2		2-1	1-2	0-2	1-3	3-2	1-3
Seaton Burn	2-2	1-3	0-0	n/a	3-3	0-6	W-L	0-2	0-1	2-3	0-1		0-5	2-1	1-2	4-2	1-3
Stocksfield	6-1	2-0	6-3	n/a	4-0	4-0	1-6	1-2	2-2	6-0	2-1	3-2	*O*	1-3	0-5	3-2	1-5
Wallington	1-1	6-0	3-4	n/a	3-1	3-4	2-1	4-2	2-0	3-2	3-2	3-1	3-1	*N*	2-2	2-1	5-3
Wark	7-1	7-0	4-5	n/a	2-0	4-2	W-L	9-1	7-2	3-2	4-1	6-0	2-2	4-2	*E*	4-1	7-1
Westerhope JG	2-0	4-3	1-1	n/a	3-2	1-3	7-2	5-2	1-0	3-4	4-5	1-0	3-1	6-1	3-4		6-3
Whitley Bay 'A'	1-5	1-4	2-2	n/a	2-1	4-0	6-1	2-1	4-0	7-3	3-3	0-2	0-1	3-4	4-0	5-1	

Division One		P	W	D	L	F	A	Pts
Wark	-6	30	26	2	2	123	42	74
Murton		30	21	4	5	83	38	67
Rutherford Newcastle		30	16	6	8	70	53	54
Wallington		30	16	6	8	76	61	54
Stocksfield		30	15	4	11	74	63	49
Westerhope JG		30	14	5	11	83	69	47
Whitley Bay 'A'		30	13	3	14	95	82	42
Penrith United	-6	30	15	1	14	79	73	40
Red Row Welfare		30	11	5	14	57	73	38
Gosforth Bohemian Garnett		30	9	9	12	64	72	36
Berwick United		30	10	5	15	56	68	35
Percy Main Amateurs		30	10	5	15	43	57	35
Chopwell Officials Club		30	10	5	15	50	78	35
Seaton Burn		30	6	6	18	38	68	24
Hebburn Reyrolle		30	5	5	20	39	88	20
Newcastle East End Rail Club	-9	30	5	5	18	48	91	11

Haydon Bridge United – record expunged

LEAGUE CUP *(All teams in league)*

PRELIMINARY ROUND
Killingworth YPC 2 Shields United 1
Peterlee Tn (scr.) v Gateshead Leam Rangers (w/o)
Ponteland United 3 Heaton Stannington 0
Walker Central 3 Wallsend Town 1
Hexham 1 **Shankhouse** 3
Jesmond 0 **Ashington Colliers** 3
Killingworth YPC 4 Willington Quay Saints 3
Lowick (scr.) v **Amble United** (w/o)
Newcastle University 0 **Gillford Pk** 3
North Shields Athletic 1 **Heddon** 2

FIRST ROUND
Amble 2 **Ponteland United** 3
Blyth Town 3 Northbank Carlisle 1
Carlisle City 3 Alnwick Town 1
Cramlington Town 2 **Walker Central**
Cullercoats 2 Seaton Delaval Amateurs
Tynemouth United 2 **Newcastle Chemfica** 4
Wallsend BC (scr.) v **Gateshead Leam Rangers** (w/o)
Whitley Bay Tn 4 Newcastle British Telecom 3
Wideopen & District 0 **Harraby Catholic Club** 4

COMBINATION CUP

PRELIMINARY ROUND
Seaton Burn 0 **Rutherford Newcastle** 3

FIRST ROUND
Chopwell Officials Club 1 **Gosforth Bohemian Garnett** 2
Murton 2 Wallington 1
Newcastle East End Rail Club 4 Hebburn Reyrolle 0
Percy Main Amateurs 1 Stocksfield 0
Red Row Welfare 2 Whitley Bay 'A' 1
Rutherford Newcastle 2 **Penrith United** 4
Wark 5 Haydon Bridge United 2
Westerhope JG 3 Berwick United 1

QUARTER-FINALS
Newcastle East End Rail Club 1 **Gosforth Bohemian Garnett** 4
Penrith United 1 **Murton** 2 *aet*
Percy Main Amateurs 2 Westerhope JG 2 *aet* (7-6p)
Wark 5 Red Row Welfare 2

SEMI-FINALS
Gosforth Bohemian Garnett 2 Percy Main Amateurs 0
Wark 3 Murton 0

FINAL *(May 9th at Haydon Bridge United)*
Gosforth Bohemian Garnett 4 Wark 3

RE/MAX NORTHERN ALLIANCE DIVISION ONE CONSTITUTION 2008-09

BERWICK UNITED .... Swan Leisure Centre, Northumberland Road, Tweedmouth, Berwick-on-Tweed TD15 2AS 01289 330603
CHOPWELL OFFICIALS CLUB .... Welfare Park, Chopwell, Newcastle-upon-Tyne NE17 7BZ .... None
CULLERCOATS .... Links Avenue, Farringdon Road, Cullercoats NE30 3EY .... None
GATESHEAD RUTHERFORD ... Farnacres, Beggarswood Park, Coach Lane, Lobley Hill, Gateshead NE11 8HJ .... None
GOSFORTH BOHEMIAN GARNETT ...... Benson Park, Gosforth, Newcastle-upon-Tyne .... None
HEBBURN REYROLLE .... Hebburn Sports Ground, 16 South Drive, Hebburn NE31 1UN 0191 483 5101
KILLINGWORTH YPC .... Miller's Dene, Fossway, Walkerville, Newcastle-upon-Tyne NE6 4YA .... None
NEWCASTLE EAST END RAIL CLUB ... Swan Hunter Rec, Stotts Road, Walkergate, Newcastle-upon-Tyne NE6 4UD .... None
NORTHBANK CARLISLE .... Sheepmount Sports Complex, Sheepmount, Carlisle CA3 8XL 01228 625599
PENRITH 'A' .... Frenchfield Sports Centre, Brougham, Penrith CA11 8UA .... None
PERCY MAIN AMATEURS .... Purvis Park, St John's Green, Percy Main, North Shields NE29 6HE 0191 257 4831
RED ROW WELFARE .... Red Row Welfare Ground, Red Row, Amble NE61 5BG .... None
SEATON BURN .... Seaton Burn Welfare, Seaton Burn, Newcastle-upon-Tyne .... None
STOCKSFIELD .... Stocksfield Sports Field, Main Road, Stocksfield, Prudhoe NE42 5DH .... None
WALLINGTON .... Oakford Park, Scots Gap, Morpeth NE61 4EJ .... None
WESTERHOPE JG .... Westerhope Institute, Westerhope, Newcastle-upon-Tyne NE5 1NE 0191 267 3757
WHITLEY BAY 'A' .... Hillheads Park, Rink Way, Whitley Bay NE25 8HR 0191 291 3636

IN: Cullercoats (P), Killingworth YPC (P), Northbank Carlisle (R)
OUT: Haydon Bridge United (R), Murton (P), Wark (P)
Penrith United become Penrith 'A', Rutherford Newcastle become Gateshead Rutherford

	Amble	Amble United	Cullercoats	Hexham	Jesmond	Killingworth YPC	Newcastle British Telecom	Newcastle Chemfica	North Shields Athletic	Shields United	Tynemouth United	Wallsend BC	Wallsend Town	Whitley Bay Town	Wideopen & District	Willington Quay Saints
Amble		0-2	1-7	3-0	2-2	0-1	8-1	1-2	4-2	0-1	2-1	3-4	3-3	2-0	2-1	1-2
Amble United	6-0		2-1	7-1	3-3	1-3	7-1	5-1	4-1	7-1	5-0	2-3	2-1	4-3	3-0	3-2
Cullercoats	3-1	6-1	D	4-0	2-1	1-5	4-2	7-3	2-1	3-3	8-0	4-2	2-0	5-1	6-2	5-0
Hexham	0-2	0-8	2-1	I	1-3	0-1	4-2	1-2	2-2	2-2	3-1	1-3	2-3	1-4	1-2	1-0
Jesmond	2-0	2-1	3-3	2-1	V	2-3	8-2	5-1	1-0	2-1	3-0	2-4	2-0	3-5	3-0	2-2
Killingworth YPC	3-0	1-0	2-1	4-3	4-2	I	5-2	4-2	1-1	3-0	6-1	3-0	2-4	2-1	2-2	3-1
Newcastle British Telecom	4-5	0-5	1-7	1-0	1-4	1-3	S	3-4	2-3	0-4	2-2	1-8	2-3	3-4	1-5	3-0
Newcastle Chemfica	0-0	2-7	1-3	3-3	1-1	1-4	3-4	I	0-5	2-4	3-1	2-3	5-1	2-3	4-2	2-0
North Shields Athletic	4-3	0-3	3-3	1-1	1-3	1-2	0-4		O	2-3	6-1	1-3	1-4	3-5	0-1	0-2
Shields United	1-0	2-2	2-5	2-1	1-1	0-1	1-1	2-2	2-0	N	4-0	0-0	0-2	1-1	2-2	0-1
Tynemouth United	1-3	1-3	0-2	1-2	3-6	1-5	1-3	3-4	0-6	1-3		0-5	1-3	2-5	0-4	4-3
Wallsend BC	1-1	1-0	0-2	2-2	4-0	1-2	3-3	1-2	6-1	1-2	4-0	T	0-3	3-2	3-0	
Wallsend Town	1-0	1-3	4-2	5-2	4-0	4-6	4-1	4-0	5-0	2-3	3-2	2-1	W	3-1	8-2	2-2
Whitley Bay Town	3-6	0-5	1-3	2-0	0-4	0-6	0-9	4-2	3-1	3-0	4-1	4-3	1-3	O	1-3	5-3
Wideopen & District	1-2	2-3	0-1	0-1	4-1	3-3	4-2	7-1	2-2	4-1	3-1	4-3	2-0	2-4		4-1
Willington Quay Saints	1-3	2-5	1-3	1-5	1-2	1-1	5-3	1-2	4-2	0-1	4-2	3-0	1-2	2-4	1-2	

AMATEUR CUP

PRELIMINARY ROUND
North Shields Athletic(w/o) v Lowick (scr.)

FIRST ROUND
Amble United 2 Cullercoats 1
Jesmond 3 Shields United 0
Killingworth 3 Tynemouth Utd 1
Newcastle British Telecom 3 North Shields Athletic 4
Wallsend BC 2 Amble 1
Wallsend Town 3 Newcastle Chemfica 2 *aet*
Whitley Bay 3 Hexham 3 (2-4p)
Willington Quay Saints 1 Wideopen & District 2

QUARTER-FINALS
Killingworth YPC 0 Jesmond 4
North Shields Athletic 0 Wallsend BC 1 *aet*
Wallsend Town 5 Amble United 2
Wideopen & District 5 Hexham 1

SEMI-FINALS
Wallsend BC 2 Jesmond 3 *aet*
Wideopen & District 0 Wallsend 1

FINAL
(April 25th at Ponteland United)
Wallsend Town 1 Jesmond 0

SECOND ROUND
Ashington Colliers 4 Percy Main Ams 0
Berwick United 1 **Ponteland United** 5
Cullercoats 3 Chopwell Officials Club 1
Gosforth Bohemian Garnett 7 Newcastle Chemfica 0
Harraby Catholic Club 0 **Carlisle City** 1
Haydon Bridge United 1 **Seaton Burn** 5
Hebburn Reyrolle 2 **Rutherford Newcastle** 4
Newcastle EE Rail Club 1 **Gillford Pk** 3
Penrith United 3 Amble United 2
Red Row Welfare 0 **Shankhouse** 4
Stocksfield 0 **Wallington** 2
Wallsend BC 1 **Blyth Town** 3
Wark 0 **Heddon** 1
Westerhope JG 3 Murton 2
Whitley Bay 'A' 4 Killingworth 2 *aet*
Whitley Bay Town 0 **Walker Central** 4

THIRD ROUND
Carlisle City 1 **Ashington Colliers** 2
Cullercoats 0 **Rutherford Newcastle** 1
Gosforth Bohemian Garnett 0 **Blyth Tn** 3
Heddon 2 Gillford Park 0
Ponteland United 0 **Wallington** 1
Seaton Burn 2 **Penrith United** 3
Walker Central 4 Westerhope JG 2
Whitley Bay 'A' 4 Shankhouse 1

QUARTER-FINALS
Ashington Colliers 1 **Heddon** 1 *aet* (9-10p)
Penrith United 1 **Wallington** 4
Rutherford Newcastle 0 **Shankhouse** 4
Walker Central 4 Blyth Town 1

SEMI-FINALS
Heddon 0 **Wallington** 1
Walker Central 2 Shankhouse 1
FINAL *(May 14th at Heaton Stannington)*
Walker Central 3 Wallington 1

Division Two

		P	W	D	L	F	A	Pts
Killingworth YPC		30	25	4	1	92	37	79
Cullercoats		30	23	2	5	106	44	71
Amble United		30	22	2	6	109	41	68
Wallsend Town	-3	30	19	2	9	79	54	56
Jesmond		30	15	7	8	73	55	52
Whitley Bay Town		30	16	1	13	74	84	49
Wallsend BC		30	14	4	12	72	52	46
Shields United		30	12	9	9	49	51	45
Wideopen & District	-6	30	14	4	12	72	63	40
Amble		30	12	4	14	58	60	40
Newcastle Chemfica		30	11	4	15	63	89	37
Hexham		30	8	5	17	48	73	29
Willington Quay Saints		30	7	3	20	47	75	24
Newcastle British Telecom		30	6	3	21	63	115	21
North Shields Athletic	-3	30	5	5	20	52	79	17
Tynemouth United		30	1	1	28	32	117	4

WWW.NLNEWSDESK.CO.UK

RE/MAX NORTHERN ALLIANCE DIVISION TWO CONSTITUTION 2008-09

AMBLE .... Amble Welfare Ground, Acklington Road, Amble NE65 0NG .... None
AMBLE UNITED .... Running Track Pitch, Coquet High School, Acklington Road, Amble NE65 0NG 01665 710636
BENFIELD CHEMFICA .. Benfield School of Sporting Excellence, Benfield Road, Newcastle-upon-Tyne NE6 4NQ 0191 265 6091
FOREST HALL .... Palmersville Community Centre, Great Lime Road, Forest Hall NE12 9HW .... None
HAYDON BRIDGE UNITED .... Low Hall Park, Haydon Bridge, Hexham NE47 6AF .... None
HEXHAM........................ Wentworth Leisure Centre, Wentworth Park, Hexham NE46 3PD 01434 607080
NEWCASTLE BRITISH TELECOM.. Burradon Welfare Ground, Front Street, Burradon NE23 7NG................. None
NORTH SHIELDS ATHLETIC ..... Collingwood View PF, West Percy Road, North Shields NE29 7RQ .... None
SOUTH SHIELDS UNITED.... Chuter Ede Community Centre, Galsworthy Road, South Shields NE34 9UG 0191 536 0515
STOBSWOOD WELFARE .... Stobswood Welfare Ground, Stobswood, Morpeth NE61 3AZ .... None
TYNEMOUTH UNITED .... Western Community School, Rutland Road, Wallsend NE28 8QL 0191 260 5336
WALLSEND BOYS CLUB .... St Peter's Road, Wallsend NE28 7LQ .... None
WALLSEND TOWN..... Langdale School Ground, Mitford Gardens, Wallsend, Newcastle-upon-Tyne NE28 0HG .... None
WHITLEY BAY TOWN...... Churchill Playing Fields, Hartley Avenue, Monkseaton, Whitley Bay NE26 3NS .... None
WIDEOPEN & DISTRICT .... Lockey Park, Great North Road, Wideopen, Newcastle-upon-Tyne NE13 6LN .... None
WILLINGTON QUAY SAINTS ... Wallsend Rising Sun Ground, King's North Road, Wallsend NE28 9JQ .... None
IN: *Forest Hall (P – Tyneside Amateur League Division One), Haydon Bridge United (R), Stobswood Welfare (P – North Northumberland League Division One)*
OUT: *Cullercoats (P), Jesmond (W), Killingworth YPC (P), Lowick (WN)*
Newcastle Chemfica become Benfield Chemfica, Shields United become South Shields United

CHARITY CUP *(League Cup First Round losers)*

PRELIMINARY ROUND
Peterlee Town 11 Newcastle British Telecom 0
Wideopen & District 2 Tynemouth Utd 1
FIRST ROUND
Heaton Stannington 4 Alnwick Tn 2 *aet*
Hexham 1 **Newcastle University** 2 *aet*
North Shields Athletic 3 Shields United 2
Northbank Carlisle 4 **Wideopen & District** 5

Peterlee Town 3 Cramlington Town 1
Seaton Delaval Amateurs (w/o) v Gateshead Leam Rangers (scr.)
Wallsend Town 5 Amble 0
Willington Quay Saints 0 **Jesmond** 7
QUARTER-FINALS
Newcastle University 9 Wideopen & District 2
North Shields Athletic 0 **Heaton Stannington** 3

Seaton Delaval Amateurs 0 **Peterlee Town** 5
Wallsend Town 4 **Jesmond** 4 *aet* (1-2p)
SEMI-FINALS
Jesmond 2 Heaton Stannington 1
Peterlee Newtown 3 Newcastle University 0
FINAL
(May 20th at Heaton Stannington)
Jesmond 0 **Peterlee Newtown** 2 *aet*

NORTHERN COUNTIES EAST LEAGUE

	Armthorpe Welfare	Arnold Town	Brodsworth Miners Welfare	Eccleshill United	Glapwell	Glasshoughton Welfare	Hallam	Lincoln Moorlands Railway	Liversedge	Long Eaton United	Maltby Main	Mickleover Sports	Nostell Miners Welfare	Parkgate	Pickering Town	Selby Town	Shirebrook Town	South Normanton Athletic	Thackley	Winterton Rangers
Armthorpe Welfare		3-4	3-2	5-0	1-4	5-1	1-3	3-2	1-0	2-0	1-1	3-1	6-1	2-1	0-0	2-1	3-0	1-1	1-0	0-3
Arnold Town	3-0		2-0	0-2	0-1	3-1	0-2	3-1	1-6	1-1	3-1	1-1	1-4	1-0	3-0	1-1	1-0	0-0	0-0	1-2
Brodsworth Miners Welfare	3-3	1-3	P	0-3	0-4	2-0	0-3	4-2	1-2	3-1	2-0	1-0	2-1	1-4	1-1	0-7	2-1	0-3	4-0	1-4
Eccleshill United	4-3	2-3	1-1	R	2-3	0-0	4-1	3-1	0-2	0-2	2-1	0-2	3-1	1-3	1-0	2-2	2-0	1-0	1-0	0-3
Glapwell	5-2	1-0	6-3	2-0	E	1-1	3-1	1-0	1-1	5-2	0-2	1-0	1-2	1-1	0-0	1-1	3-2	3-0	5-0	1-1
Glasshoughton Welfare	1-2	1-0	2-3	0-4	0-5	M	0-2	2-0	0-4	1-1	0-3	1-5	0-4	1-0	0-4	1-3	0-2	2-2	1-4	0-3
Hallam	3-3	1-1	1-3	6-0	1-5	3-1	I	3-1	0-0	2-0	4-1	5-2	4-2	0-5	3-0	3-5	6-0	3-1	2-3	0-3
Lincoln Moorlands Railway	2-2	0-4	3-1	2-0	1-3	1-1	3-3	E	1-2	1-2	2-2	1-3	0-1	3-0	0-3	2-3	1-0	2-1	3-0	
Liversedge	0-1	1-2	2-0	3-3	2-2	3-0	0-1	3-1	R	3-0	2-1	4-1	4-0	4-1	3-0	1-1	1-1	1-1	1-0	2-5
Long Eaton United	2-0	1-0	0-3	0-1	0-6	3-1	0-1	0-2	1-0		3-1	1-1	0-3	5-0	0-2	0-1	2-1	1-1	3-2	2-0
Maltby Main	1-3	0-2	2-2	2-1	0-1	2-0	2-0	4-0	1-2	1-2	D	3-3	1-4	0-5	3-4	2-2	0-0	2-1	0-0	1-3
Mickleover Sports	4-1	0-0	5-3	1-1	4-1	2-3	4-2	1-3	0-2	1-1	1-2	I	2-1	1-5	0-0	1-3	0-3	2-0	3-1	1-4
Nostell Miners Welfare	1-1	4-3	5-1	4-1	1-0	3-3	3-1	2-3	3-1	1-4	2-0	4-0	V	0-0	1-1	2-1	2-2	0-2	7-3	2-1
Parkgate	3-0	2-1	6-0	2-0	2-3	1-2	1-4	3-1	0-1	2-2	1-2	6-1	3-0	I	2-3	0-2	5-1	4-1	4-1	0-3
Pickering Town	3-2	0-1	6-3	2-1	1-2	2-0	2-1	4-1	1-0	3-0	2-0	6-0	1-0	0-1	S	1-4	3-1	5-0	3-2	2-0
Selby Town	0-2	0-0	1-3	2-3	3-1	4-0	2-2	3-3	1-1	3-2	0-0	1-0	0-0	1-1	2-3	I	2-3	3-1	1-3	0-1
Shirebrook Town	0-3	0-1	1-2	1-1	1-0	0-3	0-2	2-1	2-1	0-0	0-0	1-1	1-0	1-1	1-4	0-1	O	0-1	4-0	2-1
South Normanton Athletic	4-2	2-1	1-2	0-2	0-2	0-2	2-1	1-1	2-4	0-0	3-2	2-1	0-4	2-2	0-1	1-2	2-0	N	2-1	1-5
Thackley	2-0	1-0	1-1	3-2	1-0	3-1	2-0	6-2	0-0	5-1	0-4	0-2	3-4	2-4	0-1	1-1	0-0	1-1		0-2
Winterton Rangers	3-0	6-3	4-2	7-1	2-2	7-0	6-0	2-0	3-2	4-2	6-1	3-1	3-0	3-0	0-0	2-2	5-0	1-0	5-2	

Premier Division	P	W	D	L	F	A	Pts
Winterton Rangers	38	29	4	5	116	37	91
Glapwell	38	23	9	6	86	38	78
Pickering Town	38	22	7	9	68	42	73
Liversedge	38	20	8	10	73	41	68
Nostell Miners Welfare	38	19	7	12	81	64	64
Hallam	38	19	5	14	82	69	62
Selby Town	38	16	12	10	76	52	60
Parkgate	38	18	4	16	80	54	58
Armthorpe Welfare	38	17	7	14	73	69	58
Arnold Town	38	16	8	14	54	49	56
Eccleshill United	38	15	5	18	57	74	50
Long Eaton United	38	14	7	17	48	63	49
Brodsworth Miners Welfare -2	38	14	5	19	61	91	47
Mickleover Sports	38	11	10	17	58	78	43
Shirebrook Town	38	11	9	18	38	63	42
Thackley	38	11	7	20	54	75	40
South Normanton Athletic -3	38	11	9	18	43	64	39
Maltby Main	38	9	9	20	52	72	36
Lincoln Moorlands Railway	38	9	6	23	53	83	33
Glasshoughton Welfare	38	4	6	28	26	101	18

KOOLSPORT NORTHERN COUNTIES EAST LEAGUE PREMIER DIVISION CONSTITUTION 2008-09

ARMTHORPE WELFARE......... Welfare Ground, Church Street, Armthorpe, Doncaster DN3 3AG.......... 07775 915503 (matchdays)
ARNOLD TOWN.................. King George V Playing Field, Gedling Road, Arnold NG5 6NQ................... 0115 926 3660
BRIDLINGTON TOWN........ The Lane Rental Queensgate Stadium, Queensgate, Bridlington YO16 7LN................. 01262 606879
BRODSWORTH MINERS WELFARE...... Welfare Ground, Woodlands, Doncaster DN6 7PP......................... 01302 728380
DINNINGTON TOWN .... Phoenix Park, Dinnington Resource Centre, 131 Laughton Road, Dinnington S25 2PP......... 01909 518555
ECCLESHILL UNITED .... Plumpton Park, Kingsway, Wrose, Bradford BD2 1PN 01274 615739
HALL ROAD RANGERS .... Dene Park, Dene Close, Beverley Road, Dunswell, Hull HU6 0AB.............. 01482 850101
HALLAM .... Sandygate, Sandygate Road, Crosspool, Sheffield S10 5SE 0114 230 9484
LINCOLN MOORLANDS RAILWAY.. Moorlands Sports Ground, Newark Road, Lincoln LN6 8RT 01522 520184/874111
LIVERSEDGE................ Clayborn Ground, Quaker Lane, Hightown Road, Cleckheaton WF15 8DA 01274 862108
LONG EATON UNITED .... Grange Park, Station Road, Long Eaton NG10 2EG............... 0115 973 0352
MALTBY MAIN .... Maltby Miners Welfare, Muglet Lane, Maltby, Rotherham S66 7JQ................... 07941 057883
MICKLEOVER SPORTS......... Mickleover Sports Club, Station Road, Mickleover, Derby DE3 9FB................. 01332 521167
NOSTELL MINERS WELFARE... Miners Welfare Ground, Middle Lane, New Crofton, Wakefield WF4 1LB.............. 01924 866010
PARKGATE .... Roundwood Sports Complex, Green Lane, Rawmarsh, Rotherham S62 6LA............... 01709 826600
PICKERING TOWN .... Recreation Ground, off Mill Lane, Malton Road, Pickering YO18 7DB 01751 473317
SELBY TOWN .... Flaxley Road Ground, Richard Street, Scott Road, Selby YO8 0BS 01757 210900
SHIREBROOK TOWN ...... BRSA Sports Ground, Langwith Road, Shirebrook, Mansfield NG20 8TF 01623 747638
THACKLEY .... Dennyfield, Ainsbury Avenue, Thackley, Bradford BD10 0TL 01274 615571
WINTERTON RANGERS................. 54 West Street, Winterton, Scunthorpe DN15 9QF................. 01724 732628

IN: Bridlington Town (R – Northern Premier League Division One North), Dinnington Town (P), Hall Road Rangers (P)
OUT: Glapwell (P – Northern Premier League Division One South), Glasshoughton Welfare (R), South Normanton Athletic (F)

	AFC Emley	Barton Town Old Boys	Borrowash Victoria	Bottesford Town	Dinnington Town	Gedling Town	Hall Road Rangers	Leeds Metropolitan Carnegie	Pontefract Collieries	Rainworth Miners Welfare	Rossington Main	Scarborough Athletic	Staveley Miners Welfare	Tadcaster Albion	Teversal	Worsbrough Bridge Miners Welfare	Yorkshire Amateur
AFC Emley		0-1	5-2	1-4	0-1	1-4	4-0	0-1	1-1	0-4	3-3	2-3	4-0	4-2	3-3	1-3	3-1
Barton Town Old Boys	2-1		3-3	2-0	4-4	3-4	1-1	4-2	6-0	1-1	7-3	3-3	0-1	1-2	2-0	4-1	4-4
Borrowash Victoria	0-2	2-1	D	0-1	2-4	1-2	1-2	0-3	4-1	1-1	2-3	2-2	2-3	2-1	1-1	2-0	2-2
Bottesford Town	5-1	2-0	3-0	I	0-2	2-2	2-0	3-2	4-1	1-2	2-3	2-1	2-0	2-0	5-2	3-1	1-0
Dinnington Town	2-2	3-2	4-1	3-0	V	3-1	2-0	1-0	2-0	5-2	4-2	4-2	2-2	2-0	5-1	1-1	7-0
Gedling Town	1-1	2-1	2-3	3-1	2-3	I	7-1	5-0	4-1	0-0	2-0	1-2	2-2	3-0	1-1	2-1	2-0
Hall Road Rangers	5-1	4-0	4-2	2-0	4-0	2-0	S	2-3	3-1	0-2	3-1	2-0	2-1	2-0	2-1	2-0	4-1
Leeds Metropolitan Carnegie	2-0	3-3	2-0	0-1	2-3	0-2	1-0	I	3-0	0-2	2-1	1-4	0-1	5-0	1-1	4-0	4-0
Pontefract Collieries	0-3	1-3	1-4	2-3	0-2	0-4	1-2	2-4	O	0-2	2-2	1-2	3-5	1-1	2-3	2-3	1-3
Rainworth Miners Welfare	5-2	3-1	2-0	1-2	1-3	1-1	1-2	3-3	0-1	N	2-0	1-3	2-0	1-1	2-1	3-0	3-1
Rossington Main	1-3	0-5	2-0	1-2	1-3	4-3	0-5	0-2	3-0	1-3		1-5	1-3	1-2	2-3	2-0	3-1
Scarborough Athletic	2-2	2-6	8-0	1-1	1-1	4-1	3-1	0-2	1-0	1-3	4-0		2-1	2-2	2-2	4-0	3-0
Staveley Miners Welfare	2-1	0-3	3-0	1-0	2-1	1-2	2-3	2-1	3-0	2-3	1-2	0-3	O	1-0	3-3	1-2	1-0
Tadcaster Albion	1-1	3-3	2-6	2-1	1-2	2-1	4-1	2-4	1-0	1-1	4-1	0-1	3-1	N	1-1	4-1	0-2
Teversal	3-3	4-2	3-0	4-4	3-3	1-2	0-2	0-5	1-1	1-1	2-0	2-1	2-3	3-2	E	0-3	2-0
Worsbrough Bridge Miners Welfare	1-2	3-4	2-3	0-1	0-2	2-2	0-1	2-2	2-2	1-1	4-2	0-3	1-0	4-2	1-2		1-1
Yorkshire Amateur	1-2	0-0	1-1	1-1	1-4	1-0	0-1	1-3	1-1	2-1	3-2	0-5	1-1	5-2	1-2	2-0	

Division One		P	W	D	L	F	A	Pts
Dinnington Town		32	24	6	2	88	40	78
Hall Road Rangers		32	22	1	9	65	42	67
Bottesford Town		32	19	5	8	62	40	62
Rainworth Miners Welfare		32	16	9	7	60	38	57
Scarborough Athletic	-6	32	18	7	7	80	45	55
Gedling Town		32	16	7	9	70	45	55
Leeds Metropolitan Carnegie		32	17	4	11	67	45	55
Staveley Miners Welfare		32	14	4	14	49	53	46
Barton Town Old Boys	-3	32	13	9	10	82	62	45
Teversal		32	10	12	10	58	66	42
AFC Emley		32	10	8	14	59	66	38
Tadcaster Albion		32	9	7	16	48	66	34
Borrowash Victoria		32	8	6	18	49	76	30
Yorkshire Amateur		32	7	8	17	37	67	29
Worsbrough Bridge MW		32	7	6	19	40	67	27
Rossington Main		32	7	3	22	47	87	24
Pontefract Collieries		32	1	6	25	29	85	9

KOOLSPORT NORTHERN COUNTIES EAST LEAGUE DIVISION ONE CONSTITUTION 2008-09

AFC EMLEY . . . . Emley Welfare Sports Ground, Emley, Huddersfield HD8 9RE. 01924 849329
APPLEBY FRODINGHAM . . . . Brumby Hall, Ashby Road, Scunthorpe DN16 1AA. 01724 843024
ASKERN WELFARE . . . . Welfare Sports Ground, Manor Way, Askern, Doncaster DN6 0AL. 01302 700957
BARTON TOWN OLD BOYS . . . . . . The Euronics Ground, Marsh Lane, Barton-on-Humber DN18 5HB. 07966 427565
BOTTESFORD TOWN . . . . Birch Park, Ontario Road, Bottesford, Scunthorpe DN17 2QT. 01724 871883
BRIGHOUSE TOWN . . . . St Giles Road, Hove Edge, Brighouse HD6 2PL 01484 380088
GLASSHOUGHTON WELFARE . . . . Leeds Road, Glasshoughton, Castleford WF10 4PF. 01977 511234
GRIMSBY BOROUGH . . . . Brigg Town FC, The Hawthorns, Hawthorn Avenue, Brigg DN20 8PG 01652 651605
HEMSWORTH MINERS WELFARE . . . . Fitzwilliam Stadium, Wakefield Road, Fitzwilliam, Pontefract WF9 5AJ. 01977 610444
LEEDS CARNEGIE . . . . Farsley Celtic FC, Throstle Nest, Newlands, Farsley, Pudsey, Leeds LS28 5BE. 0113 255 7292
PONTEFRACT COLLIERIES . . . . Skinner Lane, Pontefract WF8 4QE 01977 600818
RAINWORTH MINERS WELFARE . . . Welfare Ground, Kirklington Road, Rainworth, Mansfield NG21 0JY. 01623 792495
ROSSINGTON MAIN . . . . Welfare Ground, Oxford Street, Rossington, Doncaster DN11 0DU. 01302 865524
SCARBOROUGH ATHLETIC . . . Bridlington Town FC, The Lane Rental Queensgate Stadium, Queensgate, Bridlington YO16 7LN . . 01262 606879
STAVELEY MINERS WELFARE . . . . Inkersall Road, Staveley, Chesterfield S43 3JL. 01246 471441
TADCASTER ALBION. . . . . The Park, Ings Lane, off Centre Lane, Tadcaster LS24 9AY 01937 834119
TEVERSAL. . . . . Teversal Grange Sports & Social Centre, Carnarvon Street, Teversal, Sutton-in-Ashfield NG17 3HJ. 01623 555944
WORSBROUGH BRIDGE MINERS WELFARE . . . Park Road, Worsbrough Bridge, Barnsley S70 5LJ. 01226 284452
YORKSHIRE AMATEUR . . . . The Bracken Edge, Roxholme Road, Leeds LS8 4DZ 0113 262 4093

IN: Appleby Frodingham (P – Central Midlands League Supreme Division), Askern Welfare (P – Central Midlands League Supreme Division), Brighouse Town (P – West Riding County Amateur League Premier Division), Glasshoughton Welfare (R), Grimsby Borough (P – Central Midlands League Supreme Division), Hemsworth Miners Welfare (West Riding County Amateur League Premier Division)
OUT: Borrowash Victoria (S – East Midlands County League), Dinnington Town (P), Gedling Town (S – East Midlands County League), Hall Road Rangers (P)
Leeds Metropolitan Carnegie become Leeds Carnegie

LEAGUE CUP
(All sides in league)

FIRST ROUND
Barton Town Old Boys 6 Rossington Main 1
Borrowash Victoria 2 AFC Emley 1
Bottesford Town 4 Teversal 2
Scarborough Athletic 1 **Pontefract Collieries** 1 *aet* (1-3p)
Tadcaster Albion 3 Staveley Miners Welfare 1

SECOND ROUND
Arnold Town 0 **Hallam** 1
Barton Town Old Boys 1 Pickering Town 1 *aet* (4-2p)
Bottesford Town 2 Tadcaster Albion 1
Brodsworth Miners Welfare 1 **Borrowash Victoria** 2
Eccleshill United 2 Maltby Main 1
Hall Road Rangers 3 Worsbrough Bridge MW 1
Leeds Metropolitan Carnegie 0 **Armthorpe Welfare** 1
Liversedge 0 **Glapwell** 1
Long Eaton United 1 **Rainworth Miners Welfare** 3
Mickleover Sports 2 **Dinnington Town** 4
Parkgate 1 Gedling Town 0
Selby Town 3 Pontefract Collieries 1
Shirebrook Town 1 **Lincoln Moorlands Railway** 2 *aet*
South Normanton Athletic 4 Yorkshire Amateur 1
Thackley 0 **Glasshoughton Welfare** 1
Winterton Rangers 4 Nostell Miners Welfare 0

THIRD ROUND
Barton Town Old Boys 1 South Normanton Athletic 0
Dinnington Town 1 **Bottesford Town** 2
Hallam 2 Armthorpe Welfare 0
Lincoln Moorlands Railway 3 Eccleshill United 1
Parkgate 1 Glasshoughton Welfare 0
Rainworth Miners Welfare 1 **Glapwell** 1 (4-5p)
Selby Town 2 Borrowash Victoria 0
Winterton Rangers 5 Hall Road Rangers 1

QUARTER-FINALS
Barton Town Old Boys 3 Lincoln Moorlands Railway 2 *aet*
Glapwell 1 **Parkgate** 3
Hallam 2 Bottesford Town 0
Selby Town 0 **Winterton Rangers** 5

SEMI-FINALS
Barton Town Old Boys 0 **Parkgate** 1
Winterton Rangers 1 Hallam 1 *aet* (4-2p)

FINAL
(May 5th at Staveley Miners Welfare)
Winterton Rangers 3 Parkgate 1

PRESIDENT'S CUP
(Top eight finishers from Premier and Division One)

FIRST ROUND
Glapwell 2 Maltby Main 1
Long Eaton United 2 **South Normanton Athletic** 5
Mickleover Sports 1 **Armthorpe Welfare** 4
Pickering Town 0 **Nostell Miners Welfare** 1
Selby Town 2 Parkgate 1
Staveley Miners Welfare 2 Lincoln Moorlands Railway 2 *aet* (5-3p)
Tadcaster Albion 2 **Liversedge** 3
Winterton Rangers 3 Worsbrough Bridge MW 1

QUARTER-FINALS
Armthorpe Welfare 4 Staveley Miners Welfare 0
Glapwell 0 **Selby Town** 3
Nostell Miners Welfare 0 **Liversedge** 3
Winterton Rangers 4 South Normanton Athletic 0

SEMI-FINALS
Armthorpe Welfare 3 Selby Town 1
Winteron Rangers 0 **Liversedge** 1

FINAL
(played over two legs)
(April 1st)
Liversedge 1 Armthorpe Welfare 1
(April 8th)
Armthorpe Welfare 1 **Liversedge** 3 *aet*

WILKINSON SWORD SHIELD
(Division One sides)

FIRST ROUND
Hall Road Rangers 3 Worsbrough Bridge MW 2

SECOND ROUND
Barton Town Old Boys 4 AFC Emley 1
Gedling Town 10 Rossington Main 0
Hall Road Rangers 2 Borrowash Victoria 2 *aet* (4-2p)
Leeds Metropolitan Carnegie 2 **Dinnington Town** 5
Pontefract Collieries 1 Staveley Miners Welfare 0
Scarborough Athletic 0 **Rainworth Miners Welfare** 1
Teversal 3 Tadcaster Albion 2
Yorkshire Amateur 1 **Bottesford Town** 3

QUARTER-FINALS
Dinnington Town 0 **Bottesford Town** 2
Gedling Town 3 Barton Town Old Boys 2
Pontefract Collieries 0 **Teversal** 2
Rainworth Miners Welfare 0 **Hall Road Rangers** 3

SEMI-FINALS
Bottesford Town 1 **Teversal** 2
Hall Road Rangers 2 Gedling Town 1

FINAL
(played over two legs)
(March 18th)
Teversal 1 Hall Road Rangers 1
(April 2nd)
Hall Road Rangers 2 Teversal 1 *aet*

NORTHERN LEAGUE

Results grid — column codes: ASH = Ashington, BED = Bedlington Terriers, BSY = Billingham Synthonia, BTO = Billingham Town, BIS = Bishop Auckland, CLS = Chester-le-Street Town, CON = Consett, DUN = Dunston Federation, DUR = Durham City, JAR = Jarrow Roofing Boldon CA, MOR = Morpeth Town, NBE = Newcastle Benfield, NOR = Northallerton Town, SEA = Seaham Red Star, SHI = Shildon, SPE = Spennymoor Town, SUN = Sunderland Nissan, TOW = Tow Law Town, WAS = Washington, WAC = West Allotment Celtic, WAT = West Auckland Town, WHI = Whitley Bay

	ASH	BED	BSY	BTO	BIS	CLS	CON	DUN	DUR	JAR	MOR	NBE	NOR	SEA	SHI	SPE	SUN	TOW	WAS	WAC	WAT	WHI
Ashington		1-1	0-1	1-2	1-0	4-0	2-5	0-1	1-2	3-1	2-2	2-1	2-1	2-3	0-2	2-2	1-2	1-1	2-0	1-1	0-4	0-3
Bedlington Terriers	2-1		2-3	0-2	1-1	0-1	1-5	1-0	0-3	1-1	1-1	1-3	2-2	0-1	2-1	2-2	2-1	1-0	0-2	3-5	2-2	1-5
Billingham Synthonia	0-0	3-0		1-4	2-1	2-0	0-0	2-0	2-4	0-3	2-3	2-1	1-0	2-2	1-1	3-1	1-3	0-1	1-0	2-0	4-2	1-5
Billingham Town	0-2	3-3	3-2		3-3	3-0	4-2	2-3	1-2	3-1	1-2	4-2	5-0	3-0	1-3	2-0	2-1	0-2	1-3	1-2	2-3	3-1
Bishop Auckland	0-1	2-2	1-2	0-1		2-1	0-3	0-1	1-2	1-1	0-2	2-5	1-2	3-1	1-2	0-1	3-2	0-3	3-2	2-0	3-1	0-2
Chester-le-Street Town	1-3	0-3	3-3	1-1	4-3	*D*	0-3	0-2	0-1	2-1	2-1	0-2	2-2	1-1	2-1	1-1	2-1	1-3	2-2	2-3	1-1	0-6
Consett	7-0	0-1	2-1	2-2	8-1	2-0	*I*	1-1	2-4	3-0	1-0	2-0	1-2	5-1	3-0	1-0	3-3	2-0	3-0	3-3	1-1	2-0
Dunston Federation	1-0	4-0	2-3	3-0	1-1	2-0	1-0	*V*	1-1	1-0	1-1	2-1	2-4	3-1	0-4	3-2	2-1	1-2	2-1	2-1	1-4	3-3
Durham City	5-0	1-0	0-0	4-1	2-1	4-0	0-3	2-0	*I*	3-1	3-1	2-4	3-0	2-0	1-0	3-1	1-1	5-2	9-0	3-1	5-1	2-2
Jarrow Roofing Boldon CA	2-0	0-3	1-2	2-3	2-1	0-3	1-4	1-2	1-3	*S*	1-3	0-1	1-2	1-2	1-6	0-5	0-1	4-0	1-3	0-4	1-3	0-3
Morpeth Town	2-0	0-2	2-3	1-2	4-1	2-4	0-1	2-2	1-2	4-3	*I*	2-1	2-2	1-1	3-1	4-1	1-2	4-0	2-1	2-1	1-3	1-3
Newcastle Benfield	0-2	3-1	0-0	2-0	1-1	1-0	2-1	3-0	1-1	1-0	4-1	*O*	2-2	1-1	1-1	3-1	3-0	4-1	3-0	4-1	1-2	2-2
Northallerton Town	1-2	3-0	3-2	4-2	1-2	1-0	0-2	0-4	0-2	2-2	1-3	1-0	*N*	1-4	0-1	2-3	2-2	1-3	0-2	0-1	1-2	2-3
Seaham Red Star	1-0	2-3	2-1	2-5	1-2	1-2	3-2	3-1	2-1	1-2	1-1	2-2	0-1		5-2	2-2	1-1	1-2	3-2	1-1	3-2	0-1
Shildon	2-1	4-2	2-0	4-0	0-2	1-3	1-2	1-0	1-2	1-0	2-2	2-3	2-0	2-5	*O*	2-1	3-0	3-0	3-0	1-1	2-1	1-1
Spennymoor Town	2-3	1-1	0-1	0-0	3-0	5-0	0-0	1-1	1-3	6-0	0-1	2-0	3-1	2-1	0-1	*N*	2-1	5-1	1-1	2-1	0-0	1-2
Sunderland Nissan	2-2	4-2	1-0	2-0	1-3	1-1	1-2	1-1	1-3	4-1	1-1	0-3	3-1	0-1	0-1	2-1	*E*	1-4	1-0	4-2	0-2	2-1
Tow Law Town	5-3	1-0	1-2	3-2	2-1	2-1	1-2	3-2	1-2	0-0	1-2	1-2	3-1	2-0	0-1	2-0	1-2		1-5	4-1	5-1	1-0
Washington	0-0	0-5	0-2	1-4	0-1	4-2	0-1	1-7	1-0	1-0	2-2	0-1	1-0	4-2	0-2	1-2	0-4	1-1		2-3	2-1	1-2
West Allotment Celtic	1-1	0-2	2-0	0-1	1-4	6-1	2-4	2-3	1-2	0-0	0-5	2-1	1-3	1-6	3-2	2-1	3-1	2-2	3-1		4-0	1-1
West Auckland Town	4-0	2-1	3-2	0-0	2-1	0-3	0-1	3-2	2-4	0-0	0-1	0-1	2-1	1-3	1-1	1-1	1-2	2-4	3-4	0-0		1-1
Whitley Bay	4-1	4-3	2-1	3-1	4-0	1-2	3-3	2-3	2-1	5-0	0-1	4-0	3-5	2-1	1-1	0-2	1-0	5-2	3-1	3-2	3-1	

Division One

	P	W	D	L	F	A	Pts
Durham City	42	32	6	4	106	42	102
Consett	42	26	8	8	105	43	86
Whitley Bay	42	26	7	9	99	55	85
Newcastle Benfield	42	22	7	13	67	51	73
Shildon	42	22	6	14	80	53	72
Dunston Federation	42	19	11	12	67	59	68
Tow Law Town	42	21	5	16	70	63	68
Morpeth Town	42	18	10	14	78	64	64
Billingham Synthonia	42	19	7	16	63	63	64
Billingham Town	42	19	6	17	80	73	63
Sunderland Nissan	42	17	12	13	70	64	63
Spennymoor Town	42	14	14	14	68	52	56
West Allotment Celtic	42	16	8	18	75	80	56
Seaham Red Star	42	14	10	18	78	83	52
Bedlington Terriers	42	12	10	20	60	80	46
West Auckland Town	42	12	9	21	65	81	45
Ashington	42	12	9	21	50	77	45
Chester-le-Street Town	42	12	9	21	51	86	45
Northallerton Town	42	13	4	25	53	85	43
Bishop Auckland	42	12	6	24	55	82	42
Washington	42	12	5	25	53	97	41
Jarrow Roofing Boldon CA	42	4	7	31	36	96	19

J R CLEATOR CUP

(League champions v League Cup holders)

(4th August at Whitley Bay)
Whitley Bay 2 Newcastle Benfield 2 *aet* (5-4p)

WWW.NLNEWSDESK.CO.UK

NORTHERN LEAGUE DIVISION ONE CONSTITUTION 2008-09

ASHINGTON . . . . Hirst Welfare, Woodhorn Lane, Ashington NE63 9HF 07517 764653
BEDLINGTON TERRIERS . . . . Welfare Ground, Park Road, Bedlington NE22 5DA 01670 825485
BILLINGHAM SYNTHONIA . . . . PTS Stadium, Central Avenue, Billingham TS23 1LL 01642 532348
BILLINGHAM TOWN . . . . Ron Greig Stadium, Bedford Terrace, Billingham TS23 4AF 01642 560043
BISHOP AUCKLAND . . . . West Auckland Town FC, Darlington Road, West Auckland DL14 9HU 07974 286812
CHESTER-LE-STREET TOWN . . . . Moor Park, Chester Moor, Chester-le-Street DH2 3RW 07972 419275
CONSETT . . . . Belle Vue Park, Ashdale Road, Consett DH8 6LR 01207 503788
DUNSTON FEDERATION . . . . Federation Park, Wellington Road, Dunston, Gateshead NE11 9JL 0191 493 2935
MORPETH TOWN . . . . Craik Park, Morpeth Common, Morpeth NE61 2YX 01670 513785
NEWCASTLE BENFIELD . . . Sam Smith's Park, Chesterwood, Benfield Road, Newcastle-upon-Tyne NE6 4NU 0191 265 9357
NORTHALLERTON TOWN . . . . The Regency Stadium, Ainderby Road, Romanby, Northallerton DL7 8HA 01609 772418
PENRITH TOWN . . . . World Group Stadium, Southend Road, Penrith CA11 8JH 01768 859990
RYTON . . . . Kingsley Park, Stannerford Road, Crawcrook, Ryton NE40 3SN 0191 413 4448
SEAHAM RED STAR . . . . Seaham Town Park, Stockton Road, Seaham SR7 0JT 0191 581 1347
SHILDON . . . . Dean Street, Shildon DL4 1EZ 01388 773877
SOUTH SHIELDS . . . . Filtrona Park, Shaftsbury Avenue, Simonside Industrial Estate, Jarrow NE32 3UP 0191 427 9839
SPENNYMOOR TOWN . . . . Brewery Field, Wood View, Spennymoor DL16 6JN 07824 182471
SUNDERLAND NISSAN . . . . Nissan Sports Complex, Washington Road, Sunderland SR5 3NS 0191 415 2354
TOW LAW TOWN . . . . Ironworks Road, Tow Law, Bishop Auckland DL13 4EQ 01388 731443
WEST ALLOTMENT CELTIC . . . . Blue Flames, Whitley Road, Benton, Newcastle-upon-Tyne NE12 9FA 0191 270 0885
WEST AUCKLAND TOWN . . . . . . Darlington Road Ground, Darlington Road, West Auckland DL14 9HU 07800 796630
WHITLEY BAY . . . . Hillheads Park, Rink Way, off Hillheads Road, Whitley Bay NE25 8HR 0191 291 3637

IN: Penrith Town (P), Ryton (P), South Shields (P)
OUT: Durham City (P – Northern Premier League Division One North), Jarrow Roofing Boldon CA (R), Washington (R)

	Birtley Town	Brandon United	Crook Town	Darlington Railway Athletic	Esh Winning	Guisborough Town	Hebburn Town	Horden Colliery Welfare	Marske United	North Shields	Norton & Stockton Ancients	Penrith Town	Prudhoe Town	Ryton	South Shields	Stokesley Sports Club	Sunderland Ryhope CA	Team Northumbria	Thornaby	Whickham
Birtley Town		3-1	2-4	0-1	1-3	0-3	2-1	0-3	0-3	1-1	0-4	0-0	3-1	3-1	1-2	0-1	0-3	1-1	2-1	4-2
Brandon United	0-1		2-2	1-3	0-5	1-8	1-1	2-3	1-2	1-0	0-4	1-4	0-3	2-1	0-2	0-5	0-4	0-1	0-5	0-5
Crook Town	1-0	2-1		0-0	2-2	1-1	3-0	3-1	2-1	2-3	0-3	1-2	1-0	0-4	1-6	4-0	0-2	2-0	1-0	0-3
Darlington Railway Athletic	2-3	5-2	1-1		0-3	2-4	2-5	1-3	0-2	2-3	0-1	3-1	0-1	1-3	2-2	3-1	0-2	0-1	1-1	2-3
Esh Winning	1-1	6-0	5-1	1-4	D	4-2	2-2	1-2	0-1	2-1	1-1	0-1	1-5	4-1	1-1	0-0	1-2	3-0	1-2	1-4
Guisborough Town	1-1	3-0	2-1	1-2	2-1	I	0-1	5-2	1-3	2-3	2-0	0-1	1-1	0-3	0-4	1-2	1-2	2-1	4-2	4-0
Hebburn Town	3-1	2-2	7-3	1-0	0-1	0-4	V	0-1	0-2	3-1	1-0	1-1	2-1	1-1	1-6	3-2	1-0	2-2	0-1	0-1
Horden Colliery Welfare	1-3	5-1	1-2	3-0	2-1	3-0	0-1	I	1-0	2-0	1-2	2-1	3-1	1-3	4-2	2-1	2-1	1-1	3-3	0-3
Marske United	1-2	3-1	0-1	0-0	2-1	1-0	4-0	4-1	S	2-2	3-0	3-3	4-0	1-1	1-0	1-3	2-2	3-0	3-1	1-2
North Shields	0-4	3-0	2-1	4-1	1-4	3-2	2-4	0-1	2-0	I	1-4	1-6	1-1	0-2	0-3	1-2	3-7	1-4	0-3	2-1
Norton & Stockton Ancients	2-3	8-0	3-0	4-0	0-2	1-2	0-0	1-2	3-2	1-0	O	0-0	4-0	0-3	2-1	0-1	0-1	2-1	5-1	0-1
Penrith Town	2-4	4-1	3-1	2-0	0-3	0-1	3-0	4-1	0-0	2-0	3-2	N	1-0	0-1	1-2	1-3	3-2	3-1	1-0	3-1
Prudhoe Town	2-3	7-1	0-2	0-3	5-1	2-1	1-2	0-0	2-1	1-1	2-0	1-4		1-0	2-4	2-2	3-2	3-0	3-2	2-2
Ryton	0-1	2-0	4-1	7-1	2-1	4-0	3-1	0-2	2-0	2-0	2-1	1-3	4-2	T	2-1	1-2	5-0	2-0	0-3	5-1
South Shields	5-2	4-2	2-2	3-2	2-0	1-2	3-0	2-2	2-1	4-1	0-2	1-2	4-0	3-2	W	1-0	1-0	5-2	1-3	3-0
Stokesley Sports Club	2-1	3-1	2-4	2-3	1-4	2-1	2-0	1-1	1-1	1-2	2-1	0-2	1-1	1-2	4-5	O	5-2	4-0	0-3	4-2
Sunderland Ryhope CA	2-0	5-1	2-2	3-1	1-1	4-1	3-2	3-2	3-2	3-0	1-0	1-3	0-1	0-3	6-1			3-0	3-1	3-1
Team Northumbria	0-1	0-0	3-3	1-1	1-3	1-5	0-4	3-1	1-8	2-1	0-3	0-3	1-1	2-1	0-0	1-2	0-2		1-3	5-1
Thornaby	2-2	2-2	2-2	1-0	3-2	1-1	4-1	0-4	1-0	1-3	3-0	1-5	4-0	1-3	3-2	4-0	2-2	4-3		1-2
Whickham	3-1	5-0	2-1	2-0	2-0	3-3	7-2	1-2	1-1	4-3	4-1	2-2	1-0	3-1	3-5	4-2	2-1	4-3	3-3	

Division Two	P	W	D	L	F	A	Pts
Penrith Town	38	24	7	7	78	40	79
South Shields	38	24	5	9	98	52	77
Ryton	38	24	3	11	83	41	75
Sunderland Ryhope CA	38	22	4	12	83	54	70
Horden Colliery Welfare	38	21	5	12	71	57	68
Whickham	38	20	6	12	87	73	66
Thornaby	38	18	7	13	78	64	61
Marske United	38	17	8	13	69	43	59
Stokesley Sports Club	38	17	5	16	68	71	56
Norton & Stockton Ancients	38	17	3	18	66	46	54
Birtley Town	38	16	6	16	57	66	54
Guisborough Town	38	16	5	17	73	64	53
Esh Winning	38	15	7	16	73	58	52
Crook Town	38	14	9	15	60	74	51
Hebburn Town	38	14	7	17	55	72	49
Prudhoe Town	38	13	9	16	61	68	48
North Shields	38	11	4	23	50	87	37
Darlington Railway Athletic	38	10	6	22	51	78	36
Team Northumbria -3	38	6	8	24	43	90	23
Brandon United	38	2	4	32	26	132	10

NORTHERN LEAGUE DIVISION TWO CONSTITUTION 2008-09

BIRTLEY TOWN . . . . Birtley Sports Complex, Durham Road, Birtley, Chester-le-Street DH3 2TB 07958 540389
BRANDON UNITED . . . . Welfare Ground, Commercial Street, Brandon DH7 8PL 07717 673090
CROOK TOWN . . . . Millfield Ground, West Road, Crook DL15 9PW 01388 762959
DARLINGTON RAILWAY ATHLETIC . . . Darlington Rail Athletic Club, Brinkburn Road, Darlington DL3 9LF 01325 468125
ESH WINNING . . . . West Terrace, Waterhouses, Esh Winning DH7 9BQ 0191 373 3872
GUISBOROUGH TOWN . . . . King George V Playing Fields, Howlbeck Road, Guisborough TS14 6LA 01287 636925
HEBBURN TOWN . . . . Hebburn Sports & Social Club, North Drive, Victoria Road West, Hebburn NE31 1UN 0191 483 5101
HORDEN COLLIERY WELFARE . . . . Welfare Park Ground, Park Road, Horden, Peterlee SR8 4BE. 0191 587 3549
JARROW ROOFING BOLDON CA . . Boldon CA Sports Club, New Road, Boldon Colliery NE35 9DS 0191 519 1391
MARSKE UNITED . . . . Mount Pleasant, Mount Pleasant Avenue, Marske-by-Sea TS11 7BW 01642 471091
NORTH SHIELDS . . . . Ralph Gardner Park, West Percy Road, Chirton, North Shields NE29 7RG 07969 239476
NORTON & STOCKTON ANCIENTS . . . Norton Sports Complex, Station Road, Norton, Stockton-on-Tees TS20 1PE 01642 530203
PRUDHOE TOWN. . . . . Kimberley Park, Broomhouse Road, Prudhoe NE42 5EH 01661 835900
STOKESLEY SPORTS CLUB . . Stokesley Sports Club, Broughton Road, Stokesley, Middlesbrough TS9 5JQ 01642 710051
SUNDERLAND RYHOPE CA . . . Meadow Park, Beechbrooke, off Waterworks Road, Ryhope, Sunderland SR2 0NZ 0191 523 6555
TEAM NORTHUMBRIA . . . Coach Lane Sports Ground, Coach Lane, Benton, Newcastle-upon-Tyne NE7 7XA 0191 215 6575
THORNABY . . . . Teesdale Park, Acklam Road, Thornaby, Stockton-on-Tees TS17 7JU 07833 524659
WASHINGTON . . . . Albany Park, Spout Lane, Concord, Washington N37 2AB 0191 417 7779
WHICKHAM . . . . Glebe Sports Ground, Rectory Lane, Whickham, Newcastle-upon-Tyne NE16 4NA. 0191 420 0186
WHITEHAVEN AMATEURS . . . . Focus Scaffolding Sports Complex, Coach Road, Whitehaven CA22 9DB 01946 692211
IN: *Jarrow Roofing Boldon CA (R), Washington (R), Whitehaven Amateurs (P – Wearside League)*
OUT: *Penrith Town (P), Ryton (P), South Shields (P)*

LEAGUE CUP

FIRST ROUND
Ashington 1 **Norton & Stockton Ancients** 1 *aet* (5-3p)
Brandon United 2 **West Allotment Celtic** 4
Dunston Federation 0 **Seaham Red Star** 2
Durham City 1 **South Shields** 3
Esh Winning 1 **Ryton** 3
Horden Colliery Welfare 0 **Penrith Town** 3
Spennymoor Town 4 Bishop Auckland 1
Stokesley Sports Club 2 **Jarrow Roofing Boldon CA** 4
Team Northumbria 0 **Hebburn Town** 1
Thornaby 2 **Whickham** 3

SECOND ROUND
Bedlington Terriers 3 West Allotment Celtic 1
Billingham Synthonia 2 Seaham Red Star 1
Billingham Town 4 Northallerton Town 0
Birtley Town 1 Sunderland Ryhope CA 0
(at Sunderland Ryhope CA)
Chester-le-Street Town 1 Ashington 0
Consett 0 **West Auckland Town** 1
Crook Town 2 Hebburn Town 1
Darlington Railway Athletic 2 **Tow Law Town** 3
Guisborough Town 1 Sunderland Nissan 1 *aet* (5-4p)
Marske United 0 **Penrith Town** 2
Morpeth Town 2 Washington 1
Newcastle Benfield 3 South Shields 0
North Shields 0 **Whitley Bay** 4
Prudhoe Town 1 **Shildon** 6
Ryton 0 **Jarrow Roofing Boldon CA** 1
Spennymoor Town 4 Whickham 0

THIRD ROUND
Bedlington Terriers 2 **Billingham Town** 5
Billingham Synthonia 1 **Birtley Town** 2
Guisborough Town 0 **Newcastle Benfield** 2
Morpeth Town 3 **Whitley Bay** 4 *aet*
Penrith Town 3 Crook Town 0
Shildon 2 West Auckland Town 0
Spennymoor Town 2 **Chester-le-Street Town** 3 *aet*
Tow Law Town 0 **Jarrow Roofing Boldon CA** 1

QUARTER-FINALS
Billingham Town 7 Penrith Town 4
Chester-le-Street Town 2 Birtley Town 1
Jarrow Roofing Boldon CA 2 Whitley Bay 1
Shildon 2 Newcastle Benfield 1

SEMI-FINALS
Jarrow Roofing Boldon CA 0 **Billingham Town** 1
Shildon 1 Chester-le-Street Town 0 *aet*

FINAL
(May 7th at Seaham Red Star)
Billingham Town 2 Shildon 1

ERNEST ARMSTRONG MEMORIAL CUP
(Division Two clubs)

FIRST ROUND
Darlington Railway Athletic 0 **Thornaby** 4
Hebburn Town 1 **Penrith Town** 2
Stokesley Sports Club 1 **North Shields** 4
Sunderland Ryhope CA 2 Team Northumbria 0

SECOND ROUND
Birtley Town 1 **Brandon United** 3
Crook Town 0 **Esh Winning** 3
Horden Colliery Welfare 1 **Norton & Stockton Ancients**
Marske United 1 **Sunderland Ryhope CA** 2
North Shields 2 Ryton 2 *aet* (4-2p)
Penrith Town 2 Guisborough Town 1

South Shields 4 Prudhoe Town 0
Whickham 1 **Thornaby** 3

QUARTER-FINALS
Esh Winning 3 Brandon United 0
Norton & Stockton Ancients 3 North Shields 2
Penrith Town 3 **Sunderland Ryhope CA** 4
South Shields 3 Thornaby 2

SEMI-FINALS
Norton & Stockton Ancients 0 **Esh Winning** 1
Sunderland Ryhope CA 4 South Shields 1

FINAL
(May 5th at Ryton)
Esh Winning 3 Sunderland Ryhope CA 0

NORTHERN PREMIER LEAGUE

	Ashton United	Buxton	Eastwood Town	Fleetwood Town	Frickley Athletic	Gateshead	Guiseley	Hednesford Town	Ilkeston Town	Kendal Town	Leek Town	Lincoln United	Marine	Matlock Town	North Ferriby United	Ossett Town	Prescot Cables	Stamford	Whitby Town	Witton Albion	Worksop Town
Ashton United		2-2	1-0	3-5	7-2	0-1	0-0	2-1	0-0	2-2	1-5	1-2	1-3	2-1	3-1	1-1	2-2	1-1	0-0	1-2	1-0
Buxton	3-1		1-1	0-2	4-0	0-4	2-0	0-2	3-1	0-1	1-0	5-1	2-2	5-1	0-2	3-2	2-1	2-3	1-1	0-2	2-1
Eastwood Town	5-2	0-2	P	2-1	2-2	1-3	3-2	2-2	0-0	2-0	1-0	3-0	1-0	2-3	0-2	3-2	2-1	3-2	4-1	1-0	1-1
Fleetwood Town	3-0	2-1	1-1	R	1-1	2-3	2-2	2-1	2-1	3-2	6-3	1-0	2-3	3-0	2-1	3-1	2-0	3-2	1-0	0-0	2-1
Frickley Athletic	4-2	0-0	0-0	0-1	E	3-4	1-0	4-0	2-1	2-1	0-1	3-1	1-1	0-0	2-2	2-3	1-0	1-1	0-2	0-1	3-1
Gateshead	1-1	5-0	1-1	2-0	5-2	M	1-0	6-2	1-2	3-0	2-0	2-0	1-2	2-0	3-1	1-0	3-0	2-1	2-1	0-2	0-1
Guiseley	3-1	1-2	1-0	0-2	1-1	1-2	I	1-1	0-1	2-1	2-0	1-1	3-1	3-1	2-1	2-0	1-1	0-0	4-1	1-1	0-3
Hednesford Town	0-2	1-3	0-3	0-3	3-0	3-2	2-5	E	2-0	1-3	2-0	2-2	1-1	3-1	0-1	3-1	2-1	6-1	0-0	2-2	3-1
Ilkeston Town	3-3	1-2	4-0	3-3	3-1	2-0	2-0	0-0	R	2-3	0-1	4-5	2-4	3-2	2-4	0-2	1-1	2-1	3-0	0-2	3-3
Kendal Town	2-2	1-1	1-1	1-1	1-0	1-3	2-2	1-3	2-2		1-2	3-1	6-0	2-1	0-1	1-1	3-1	4-0	3-2	0-2	1-1
Leek Town	1-1	0-2	1-3	1-2	0-1	2-2	1-0	2-1	1-1	5-0		1-1	0-4	0-0	2-2	1-0	0-1	2-3	3-3	2-2	2-1
Lincoln United	2-4	1-1	1-2	0-3	0-0	3-3	0-2	0-2	0-2	2-0	3-4	D	0-2	2-3	0-2	2-3	0-1	2-1	0-2	1-0	1-1
Marine	1-2	0-1	2-0	0-1	2-3	1-5	0-2	2-1	5-3	4-1	3-0	3-1	I	3-1	3-0	0-1	1-0	3-2	3-2	0-2	1-2
Matlock Town	2-3	3-0	1-0	0-0	2-2	1-1	0-1	1-1	1-1	4-2	2-2	2-1	2-3	V	2-1	0-1	3-1	3-1	2-1	0-2	3-0
North Ferriby United	1-1	1-0	1-0	1-2	3-1	1-4	0-5	2-0	1-2	1-3	1-1	0-1	2-1	3-2	I	2-1	0-4	2-3	1-4	1-1	2-4
Ossett Town	0-0	0-1	0-2	0-1	0-1	0-3	1-5	0-1	1-1	2-1	1-3	3-2	2-3	3-1	0-0	S	3-1	0-0	4-2	0-0	1-0
Prescot Cables	1-0	0-1	1-0	1-3	1-1	0-2	0-1	2-5	1-1	2-1	3-1	1-2	1-1	1-2	1-1	1-1	I	2-1	1-0	1-0	0-1
Stamford	1-1	0-1	0-3	0-3	4-2	1-1	2-3	0-2	5-4	1-1	2-2	2-2	2-1	2-1	3-1	3-2	0-2	O	1-3	1-1	0-2
Whitby Town	2-3	1-1	1-2	0-1	3-0	2-1	1-2	1-0	4-0	1-2	2-1	0-3	2-0	3-0	2-3	2-5	3-3	6-3	N	1-6	4-1
Witton Albion	2-1	3-0	2-0	0-3	3-0	2-2	1-0	3-1	2-1	3-0	3-0	6-0	3-1	2-0	4-2	2-0	6-1	4-0	3-0		0-3
Worksop Town	5-2	1-3	1-2	2-1	1-1	0-4	1-2	2-0	0-0	1-1	2-1	3-0	1-0	2-2	1-1	2-2	1-4	2-0	2-2	1-2	

Premier Division

		HOME					AWAY					TOTAL					
	P	W	D	L	F	A	W	D	L	F	A	W	D	L	F	A	Pts
Fleetwood Town	40	14	4	2	43	23	14	3	3	38	16	28	7	5	81	39	91
Witton Albion	40	17	1	2	54	15	10	7	3	30	13	27	8	5	84	28	89
Gateshead	40	14	2	4	43	16	12	5	3	50	26	26	7	7	93	42	85
Eastwood Town	40	13	4	3	40	24	7	5	8	21	21	20	9	11	61	45	69
Buxton	40	10	3	7	36	27	10	5	5	24	23	20	8	12	60	50	68
Guiseley	40	9	6	5	29	21	10	4	6	36	22	19	10	11	65	43	67
Marine	40	11	0	9	37	30	8	4	8	33	35	19	4	17	70	65	61
Hednesford Town	40	9	4	7	36	32	6	4	10	26	33	15	8	17	62	65	53
Worksop Town	40	6	8	6	31	32	7	4	9	28	30	13	12	15	59	62	51
Ashton United	40	6	8	6	31	31	5	7	8	32	42	11	15	14	63	73	48
Kendal Town	40	7	8	5	36	27	5	3	12	25	43	12	11	17	61	70	47
Whitby Town	40	9	2	9	41	37	4	5	11	27	38	13	7	20	68	75	46
Prescot Cables *-1*	40	8	4	8	21	24	5	4	11	27	38	13	8	19	48	62	46
Frickley Athletic	40	8	6	6	29	22	3	7	10	21	46	11	13	16	50	68	46
North Ferriby United	40	7	3	10	26	40	6	4	10	27	36	13	7	20	53	76	46
Matlock Town	40	9	4	5	34	24	3	3	14	21	44	12	9	19	55	68	45
Ilkeston Town	40	6	6	8	40	39	4	8	8	24	33	10	14	16	64	72	44
Ossett Town	40	6	4	10	21	28	6	4	10	27	32	12	8	20	48	60	44
Leek Town	40	5	8	7	27	30	6	3	11	27	38	11	11	18	54	68	44
Stamford	40	6	6	8	30	38	5	4	11	29	48	11	10	19	59	86	43
Lincoln United	40	2	4	14	18	39	5	4	11	26	46	7	8	25	44	85	29

PLAY-OFFS

SEMI-FINALS
(April 29th)
Gateshead 4 Eastwood Town 0 *Att* 539
Witton Albion 1 **Buxton** 1 *aet* (5-6p) *Att* 586

FINAL
(May 3rd at Gateshead)
Gateshead 2 Buxton 0 *Att* 1,402

WWW.CHERRYRED.CO.UK

DATES & GATES

Home \ Away	Ashton United	Buxton	Eastwood Town	Fleetwood Town	Frickley Athletic	Gateshead	Guiseley	Hednesford Town	Ilkeston Town	Kendal Town	Leek Town	Lincoln United	Marine	Matlock Town	North Ferriby United	Ossett Town	Prescot Cables	Stamford	Whitby Town	Witton Albion	Worksop Town
Ashton United		27 Oct / 280	13 Oct / 143	27 Oct / 264	22 Sep / 132	18 Apr / 147	1 Mar / 145	3 Sep / 210	29 Mar / 132	17 Nov / 132	8 Sep / —	7 Apr / 142	31 Mar / —	8 Mar / 184	23 Feb / 115	1 Jan / 154	26 Jan / 143	8 Oct / 172	29 Oct / 163	15 Mar / 213	22 Mar / 163
Buxton	24 Mar / 367		5 Apr / 416	1 Apr / 364	22 Sep / 132	22 Apr / 414	15 Oct / 375	15 Oct / 367	13 Oct / 348	10 Feb / 266	25 Sep / 550	6 Oct / 182	22 Dec / 374	21 Apr / 711	27 Aug / 172	27 Aug / 202	26 Apr / 315	19 Apr / 306	18 Aug / 357	29 Dec / 557	19 Jan / 502
Eastwood Town	15 Mar / 220	29 Mar / —		12 Apr / 429	1 Apr / 364	22 Sep / 132	25 Aug / 301	1 Mar / 273	10 Sep / 392	29 Dec / 231	26 Apr / 469	3 Nov / 127	12 Jan / —	4 Mar / 238	24 Nov / 144	29 Jan / —	26 Jan / 166	18 Jan / 306	26 Jan / 254	29 Dec / 405	21 Aug / 409
Fleetwood Town	24 Nov / 543	12 Apr / 429	22 Sep / 177		1 Sep / —	26 Apr / 455	15 Dec / —	1 Mar / 301	8 Apr / 240	6 Oct / —	22 Apr / 392	11 Apr / 255	12 Jan / 190	15 Mar / 220	27 Nov / 180	18 Aug / 209	11 Sep / 255	1 Dec / 235	8 Mar / 326	15 Apr / 261	26 Feb / 251
Frickley Athletic	16 Feb / 309	11 Sep / 289	3 Feb / 365	22 Dec / 365		1 Sep / —	1 Sep / 360	1 Dec / 417	23 Feb / 261	22 Apr / 309	15 Mar / 276	1 Apr / —	12 Jan / 226	26 Jan / 258	29 Sep / 151	26 Dec / —	8 Apr / 153	6 Oct / 226	27 Aug / 304	15 Apr / 703	26 Feb / 324
Gateshead	22 Dec / 205	1 Mar / 345	17 Nov / 201	26 Apr / 2,666	19 Jan / 294		29 Mar / 232	29 Oct / 276	13 Oct / 331	2 Feb / 249	15 Apr / 309	24 Dec / 276	24 Mar / 229	27 Oct / 241	11 Sep / 156	24 Nov / 123	8 Apr / 214	1 Dec / 272	24 Mar / 311	15 Apr / 454	24 Mar / 324
Guiseley	19 Jan / 336	8 Mar / 375	1 Dec / 417	1 Sep / 365	26 Apr / 454	19 Jan / 550		1 Jan / 646	4 Sep / 361	26 Dec / 308	15 Apr / 249	13 Oct / 152	2 Feb / 150	23 Feb / 302	27 Oct / 216	6 Oct / 209	21 Apr / 226	29 Dec / 229	8 Apr / 311	1 Jan / 316	19 Apr / 310
Hednesford Town	12 Apr / 401	15 Oct / 367	18 Apr / 246	1 Dec / 322	4 Mar / 360	17 Nov / 353	10 Oct / 505		8 Sep / 385	1 Sep / 276	22 Mar / 294	17 Apr / 249	22 Sep / 273	9 Sep / 336	19 Apr / 179	1 Mar / 262	29 Mar / 229	21 Mar / 262	21 Dec / 252	10 Nov / 447	1 Sep / 337
Ilkeston Town	5 Apr / 257	13 Oct / 348	21 Mar / 392	27 Oct / 285	30 Oct / 267	17 Nov / 364	18 Aug / 276	1 Dec / 332		1 Apr / 261	8 Sep / 331	24 Sep / 245	17 Apr / 261	22 Sep / 336	1 Sep / 161	19 Apr / 177	26 Feb / 209	16 Oct / 195	21 Mar / 489	10 Nov / 252	11 Sep / 338
Kendal Town	1 Dec / 222	10 Feb / 266	29 Dec / 231	22 Apr / 467	23 Feb / 309	27 Oct / 276	1 Dec / 245	25 Aug / 642	12 Apr / 711		24 Nov / 198	5 Mar / 266	1 Mar / 398	24 Nov / 268	6 Oct / 177	21 Apr / 209	21 Apr / 210	10 Nov / 205	16 Oct / 271	12 Jan / 470	11 Sep / 248
Leek Town	21 Aug / 367	25 Sep / 550	22 Apr / 469	15 Mar / 276	15 Apr / 331	15 Apr / 246	24 Sep / 249	21 Aug / 547	24 Sep / 165	6 Oct / 398		5 Mar / 325	1 Sep / 346	27 Aug / 257	24 Dec / 229	10 Dec / —	16 Oct / 226	29 Dec / 231	6 Oct / 269	8 Mar / 464	12 Apr / 248
Lincoln United	29 Dec / 110	6 Oct / 182	26 Apr / 146	8 Apr / 110	15 Mar / 309	13 Oct / 276	15 Apr / 153	9 Feb / 261	26 Apr / 398	2 Feb / 108	1 Mar / 123		24 Nov / 359	11 Dec / 266	5 Mar / 177	21 Jan / 209	1 Apr / 210	21 Jan / 226	22 Feb / 140	25 Mar / 151	16 Oct / —
Marine	11 Sep / 267	22 Dec / 374	12 Jan / —	26 Jan / 158	15 Mar / 158	2 Feb / 152	9 Feb / 153	12 Feb / —	24 Mar / 229	8 Apr / 192	1 Mar / —	1 Dec / —		26 Feb / —	22 Sep / 182	23 Feb / 179	15 Apr / 257	22 Dec / —	24 Dec / —	18 Aug / 195	18 Aug / 255
Matlock Town	26 Apr / 382	21 Apr / 711	4 Mar / 238	15 Mar / 302	23 Feb / 150	12 Feb / 164	18 Aug / —	24 Sep / —	8 Sep / 316	5 Apr / 257	29 Dec / 352	21 Aug / 331	9 Oct / 301		8 Mar / 390	13 Oct / 289	12 Apr / 124	4 Sep / 278	26 Apr / 384	18 Apr / 314	13 Oct / 321
North Ferriby United	16 Oct / 131	27 Aug / 172	24 Nov / 144	27 Nov / 180	29 Sep / 151	11 Sep / 156	27 Oct / 216	22 Sep / 179	1 Sep / 161	6 Oct / 177	24 Dec / 243	15 Apr / 257	5 Apr / 182	9 Oct / 126		24 Nov / 251	24 Mar / 168	25 Sep / 246	5 Apr / 168	27 Aug / 308	22 Sep / 321
Ossett Town	10 Nov / 183	27 Aug / 202	29 Jan / 127	18 Aug / 209	26 Apr / 123	24 Nov / 123	11 Dec / 214	19 Apr / 177	15 Mar / 158	22 Dec / 216	23 Feb / 182	22 Sep / 301	21 Aug / 191	1 Mar / 133	4 Sep / 204		27 Oct / 302	9 Feb / 269	22 Aug / 211	25 Aug / 304	4 Sep / 418
Prescot Cables	25 Sep / 182	26 Apr / 315	26 Jan / 190	11 Sep / 255	8 Apr / 153	1 Apr / 156	27 Aug / 226	1 Apr / 209	16 Oct / 209	21 Apr / 210	1 Apr / 226	24 Jan / 161	5 Apr / 130	22 Sep / 185	4 Sep / 199	13 Oct / —		19 Jan / 323	24 Nov / —	27 Oct / —	15 Sep / 279
Stamford	1 Sep / 202	19 Apr / 306	1 Dec / 235	12 Jan / 190	24 Mar / 214	24 Nov / 177	26 Feb / 262	29 Feb / 195	16 Oct / —	10 Nov / 205	24 Mar / 140	25 Mar / 151	22 Sep / 295	15 Mar / —	27 Aug / —	6 Oct / —	8 Mar / —		23 Feb / 248	15 Dec / 220	2 Feb / 336
Whitby Town	12 Jan / 236	18 Aug / 357	26 Jan / 254	8 Mar / 261	27 Aug / 304	1 Jan / 311	21 Jan / 316	29 Mar / 252	26 Apr / 489	6 Oct / 271	3 Nov / 269	17 Nov / 247	26 Apr / 206	6 Nov / 193	26 Dec / 392	25 Sep / 226	17 Nov / 282	8 Sep / 293		8 Sep / 306	29 Mar / 298
Witton Albion	26 Apr / 495	29 Dec / 557	1 Sep / 261	27 Aug / 304	15 Apr / 454	21 Apr / 252	1 Mar / 316	12 Apr / 262	12 Jan / —	16 Oct / —	21 Apr / 339	12 Apr / 366	6 Nov / 377	25 Aug / 393	15 Mar / 373	21 Oct / 410	9 Nov / 362	25 Aug / 353	23 Feb / 442		8 Dec / 246
Worksop Town	6 Oct / 312	19 Jan / 502	21 Aug / 409	26 Feb / 251	24 Mar / 324	24 Mar / 310	19 Apr / 337	11 Sep / 337	11 Sep / 338	12 Apr / 248	12 Apr / 279	16 Oct / 304	1 Mar / 254	12 Jan / 427	25 Sep / 291	18 Mar / 239	27 Oct / 314	18 Mar / 389	24 Nov / 248	26 Apr / 662	

UNIBOND NORTHERN PREMIER LEAGUE
PREMIER DIVISION CONSTITUTION 2008-09

ASHTON UNITED
Hurst Cross, Surrey Street, Ashton-under-Lyne, Lancashire OL6 8DY
Tel: 0161 339 4158   Club: 0161 330 1511   Fax: 0161 339 4158
Manager: Danny Johnson   www.ashtonutd.com   Colours: Red, white & black

BOSTON UNITED
Staffsmart Stadium, York Street, Boston, Lincolnshire PE21 6JN
Tel: 01205 364406   Club: 01205 362967   Fax: 01205 354063
Manager: Tommy Taylor   www.bufc.co.uk   Colours: Amber & black

BRADFORD PARK AVENUE
Horsfall Stadium, Cemetary Road, Low Moor, Bradford, West Yorkshire BD6 2NG
Tel: 01274 691020   Fax: 01274 691020
Manager: Dave Cameron   www.bpafc.com   Colours: White & green

BUXTON
The Silverlands, Buxton, Derbyshire SK17 6QH
Tel: 01298 23197   Fax: 01298 24733
Manager: John Reed   www.buxtonfc.co.uk   Colours: Blue & white

CAMMELL LAIRD
Kirklands, St Peters Road, Rock Ferry, Birkenhead, Merseyside CH42 1PY
Tel: 0151 645 3121
Manager: Ken McKenna   www.cammelllairdfc.co.uk   Colours: Royal blue

EASTWOOD TOWN
Coronation Park, Chewton Street, Eastwood, Nottinghamshire NG16 3HB
Tel: 01773 712301   Club: 01773 715823
Manager: Paul Cox   www.eastwoodtownfc.co.uk   Colours: Black & white

FC UNITED OF MANCHESTER
Bury FC, Gigg Lane, Bury, Lancashire BL9 9HR
Tel: 0161 764 4881   Fax: 0161 764 5521
Manager: Karl Marginson   www.fc-utd.co.uk   Colours: Red & white

FRICKLEY ATHLETIC
Westfield Lane, South Elmsall, Pontefract, West Yorkshire WF9 2EQ
Tel: 01977 642460   Fax: 01977 642460
Manager: Billy Heath   www.frickleyafc.co.uk   Colours: Blue

GUISELEY
Nethermoor Park, Otley Road, Guiseley, Leeds, West Yorkshire LS20 8BT
Tel: 01943 873223   Club: 01943 872872
Manager: Steve Kittrick   www.guiseleyafc.co.uk   Colours: White & navy blue

HEDNESFORD TOWN
Keys Park, Keys Park Road, Hednesford, Staffs WS12 2DZ
Tel: 01543 422870   Fax: 01543 428180
Manager: Dean Edwards   www.hednesfordtown.com   Colours: White & black

ILKESTON TOWN
The New Manor Ground, Awsworth Road, Ilkeston, Derbyshire DE7 8JF
Tel: 0115 932 4094   Club: 0115 930 5622
Manager: Nigel Jemson   http://www.whiteballproject.co.uk/   Colours: Red

KENDAL TOWN
Lakeland Radio Stadium, Parkside Road, Kendal, Cumbria LA9 7BL
Tel: 01539 727472   Club: 01539 722469   Fax: 01539 727472
Manager: Lee Ashcroft   www.kendaltownfootballclub.co.uk   Colours: Black & white

LEIGH GENESIS
Leigh Sports Village Stadium, Sale Way, Leigh Sports Village, Leigh, Lancs WN7 4GY
(Leigh Genesis will start the season at Hilton Park, Kirkhall Lane, Leigh WN7 1RN
with the move to the Leigh Sports Village Stadium scheduled for September 2008)
Tel: 01942 487818
Manager: Steve Bleasdale   www.leighgenesis.com   Colours: White & black

MARINE
Arriva Stadium, College Road, Crosby, Liverpool, Merseyside L23 3AS
Tel: 0151 924 1743   Club: 0151 924 4046   Fax: 0151 924 1743
Manager: Alvin McDonald   www.marinefc.com   Colours: White & black

MATLOCK TOWN
The Geoquip Stadium, Causeway Lane, Matlock, Derbyshire DE4 3AR
Tel: 01629 583866   Club: 01629 553362   Fax: 01629 583866
Managers: Phil Brown / Gareth Williams www.matlocktownfc.co.uk Colours: Royal blue

NANTWICH TOWN
The Weaver Stadium, Waterloode, Nantwich, Cheshire CW5 5BS
Tel: 01270 621771
Manager: Steve Davis   www.nantwichtownfc.com   Colours: Black & white

NORTH FERRIBY UNITED
Grange Lane, Church Road, North Ferriby, East Yorkshire HU14 3AA
Tel: 01482 634601   Fax: 01482 634601
Manager: Neil Allison   www.northferribyunited.co.uk   Colours: White & green

OSSETT TOWN
Ingfield, Prospect Road, Ossett, Wakefield, West Yorkshire WF5 9HA
Tel: 01924 272960
Manager: Simon Collins   www.ossett-town.com   Colours: Red & white

PRESCOT CABLES
Valerie Park, Hope Street, Prescot, Merseyside L34 6HD
Tel: 0151 430 0507
Manager: Andy Gray   www.prescotcablesfc.co.uk   Colours: Gold & black

WHITBY TOWN
The Turnbull Ground, Upgang Lane, Whitby, North Yorkshire YO21 3HZ
Tel: 01947 604847   Club: 01947 603193   Fax: 01947 603779
Managers: Phil Brumwell / Graham Clarke   www.whitby-town.com   Colours: Royal blue

WITTON ALBION
Wincham Park, Chapel Street, Wincham, Northwich, Cheshire CW9 6DA
Tel: 01606 43008   Club: 01606 47117   Fax: 01606 43008
Manager: Jim Vince   www.wittonalbionfc.com   Colours: Red & white

WORKSOP TOWN
Hucknall Town FC, Watnall Road, Hucknall, Nottinghamshire NG15 6EY
Tel: 0115 963 0206
Manager: Peter Rinckavage   www.worksoptownfc.co.uk   Colours: Yellow & black

IN: Boston United (R – Football Conference North), Bradford Park Avenue (P – Northern Premier League Division One North), Cammell Laird (P – Northern Premier League Divsion One South), FC United of Manchester (P – Northern Premier League Division One North), Leigh Genesis (formerly Leigh RMI) (R – Football Conference North), Nantwich Town (P – Northern Premier League Division One South)
OUT: Fleetwood Town (P – Football Conference North), Gateshead (P – Football Conference North), Leek Town (R – Division One South), Lincoln United (R – Division One South), Stamford (R – Division One South)

STANDARD SEASON (see page 148 for the extra league matches)	Bamber Bridge	Bradford Park Avenue	Bridlington Town	Chorley	Clitheroe	Curzon Ashton	FC United of Manchester	Garforth Town	Harrogate Railway Athletic	Lancaster City	Mossley	Newcastle Blue Star	Ossett Albion	Radcliffe Borough	Rossendale United	Skelmersdale United	Wakefield	Woodley Sports
Bamber Bridge		2-1	2-1	4-1	2-2	1-1	3-0	1-0	0-2	3-1	4-2	1-1	1-2	2-0	2-4	0-0	0-1	1-0
Bradford Park Avenue	3-2		3-0	2-1	1-1	1-2	0-0	1-0	1-0	3-0	3-0	2-0	3-4	2-2	9-0	2-1	3-1	2-0
Bridlington Town	0-2	0-5	D	2-2	4-0	0-3	0-3	0-2	0-0	4-0	2-3	3-2	1-2	1-2	1-2	0-4	1-3	1-0
Chorley	0-1	0-2	2-1	I	1-1	1-1	0-3	1-1	0-0	4-0	3-1	1-3	2-2	1-2	1-1	0-0	2-1	5-0
Clitheroe	0-2	0-1	1-0	5-1	V	2-1	0-3	1-2	2-3	1-2	3-2	2-3	1-0	3-2	3-3	2-3	1-2	1-1
Curzon Ashton	2-0	0-1	6-0	1-2	2-2	I	0-2	4-2	1-0	2-1	4-1	2-0	2-0	1-1	2-0	1-2	1-0	6-1
FC United of Manchester	2-2	3-4	6-0	2-1	3-0	3-2	S	0-1	2-0	2-2	5-2	3-2	3-1	2-2	5-1	3-0	2-1	1-1
Garforth Town	0-2	1-4	0-1	1-2	1-1	1-0	1-2	I	0-1	1-2	2-1	0-0	5-3	2-1	5-2	0-3	2-1	0-4
Harrogate Railway Athletic	0-1	2-2	3-1	0-3	1-3	2-4	1-3	1-3	O	1-1	1-1	1-0	2-1	1-2	3-2	1-0	1-1	3-1
Lancaster City	0-2	4-3	2-2	1-0	2-0	1-2	2-1	1-1	2-0	N	0-2	1-2	1-3	0-0	1-1	2-5	1-0	1-0
Mossley	1-2	1-1	2-1	4-2	1-3	1-2	2-0	2-2	0-4	0-4		2-1	3-1	2-2	1-3	4-3	0-2	0-3
Newcastle Blue Star	3-0	0-0	2-1	5-3	3-1	0-0	0-4	1-1	3-0	2-2	5-1	O	3-1	1-1	1-0	0-1	2-2	3-1
Ossett Albion	0-5	2-1	1-1	2-0	5-1	1-3	3-1	0-2	0-0	5-1	4-2	1-0	N	2-3	0-0	1-1	1-1	4-3
Radcliffe Borough	2-3	0-2	0-1	2-2	3-1	2-3	1-1	0-1	2-2	0-4	0-1	3-4	2-3	E	1-2	0-1	0-1	0-1
Rossendale United	0-1	3-2	1-1	2-2	2-0	1-2	1-2	2-2	1-0	2-1	1-2	1-0	1-3	2-0		4-1	1-3	1-0
Skelmersdale United	4-0	0-1	5-0	5-0	3-5	4-1	3-1	3-2	1-0	3-1	5-0	2-1	1-1	3-1	3-3	N	3-0	0-0
Wakefield	2-0	3-1	0-1	0-0	2-1	0-0	3-2	0-0	4-1	0-1	2-1	2-0	0-1	4-2	0-3	1-4		2-0
Woodley Sports	2-2	1-0	1-1	2-0	1-0	0-0	1-2	0-3	1-1	1-0	1-2	1-4	0-2	1-1	0-1	1-3	1-2	

Division One North

		HOME					AWAY					TOTAL					
	P	W	D	L	F	A	W	D	L	F	A	W	D	L	F	A	Pts
Bradford Park Avenue	42	16	3	2	57	15	9	4	8	34	28	25	7	10	91	43	82
FC United of Manchester	42	14	5	2	58	26	10	4	7	33	23	24	9	9	91	49	81
Skelmersdale United	42	13	5	3	58	21	10	4	7	36	25	23	9	10	94	46	78
Curzon Ashton	42	14	2	5	46	22	9	7	5	32	26	23	9	10	78	48	78
Bamber Bridge	42	10	5	6	33	25	12	3	6	37	29	22	8	12	70	54	74
Ossett Albion	42	11	6	4	40	28	9	4	8	37	37	20	10	12	77	65	70
Wakefield	42	10	8	3	30	26	9	4	8	28	23	19	7	16	58	49	64
Newcastle Blue Star	42	10	9	2	40	24	7	3	11	31	34	17	12	13	71	58	63
Rossendale United	42	9	5	7	32	30	7	6	8	34	44	16	11	15	66	74	59
Garforth Town	42	9	2	10	32	34	7	6	8	28	29	16	8	18	60	63	56
Lancaster City	42	9	4	8	27	30	6	5	10	27	40	15	9	18	54	70	54
Harrogate Railway Athletic	42	8	6	7	29	31	5	6	10	22	27	13	12	17	51	58	51
Clitheroe	42	7	5	9	33	35	6	6	9	30	42	13	11	18	63	77	50
Chorley	42	5	8	8	28	28	5	4	12	28	52	10	12	20	56	80	42
Mossley	42	7	5	9	31	43	5	1	15	29	57	12	6	24	60	100	42
Radcliffe Borough	42	3	3	15	21	39	6	8	7	32	36	9	11	22	53	75	38
Woodley Sports -1	42	4	7	10	19	30	3	6	12	19	35	7	13	22	38	65	33
Bridlington Town	42	4	3	14	23	49	4	5	12	19	50	8	8	26	42	99	32

PLAY-OFFS

SEMI-FINALS

(April 29th) **Skelmersdale United** 4 Curzon Ashton 0 *Att* 245

(April 30th) **FC United of Manchester** 3 Bamber Bridge 2 *Att* 1,820

FINAL

(May 3rd at Bury)

FC United of Manchester 4 Skelmersdale United 1 *Att* 3,258

STANDARD SEASON
(see page 148 for the extra league matches)

WWW.NLNEWSDESK.CO.UK

DATES & GATES (home ↓ / away →)	Woodley Sports	Wakefield	Skelmersdale United	Rossendale United	Radcliffe Borough	Ossett Albion	Newcastle Blue Star	Mossley	Lancaster City	Harrogate Railway Athletic	Garforth Town	FC United of Manchester	Curzon Ashton	Clitheroe	Chorley	Bridlington Town	Bradford Park Avenue	Bamber Bridge
Bamber Bridge	19 Jan 170	22 Apr 85	1 Jan 330	12 Feb 146	15 Mar 168	24 Apr 162	9 Apr 148	5 Jan 202	20 Nov 209	25 Aug 95	8 Sep 132	1 Mar 3,348	1 Oct 267	21 Aug 265	24 Mar 457	22 Dec 235	10 Nov 466	
Bradford Park Avenue	19 Apr 210	11 Sep 171	15 Mar 383	26 Apr 453	12 Mar 162	22 Aug 212	13 Feb 284	25 Aug 285	15 Sep 234	26 Dec 244	24 Nov 310	25 Sep 2,283	12 Nov 447	24 Mar 304	3 Nov 279	26 Apr 244		16 Feb 296
Bridlington Town	12 Apr 102	29 Sep 85	29 Sep 301	24 Apr 101	27 Oct 179	24 Oct 152	3 Oct 236	22 Aug 161	25 Nov 173	8 Sep 112	25 Nov 144	25 Nov 2,253	12 Jan 247	12 Jan 204	27 Oct 226		25 Sep 369	17 Nov 663
Chorley	27 Aug 169	6 Oct 96	29 Jan 271	26 Dec 157	18 Dec 132	22 Sep 263	8 Sep 220	8 Mar 205	5 Jan 243	23 Feb 86	9 Feb 126	12 Jan 2,011	9 Feb 204	27 Feb 148		18 Aug 226	26 Apr 244	27 Oct 244
Clitheroe	18 Aug 113	29 Jan 84	5 Apr 258	26 Dec 170	29 Dec 143	12 Jan 153	22 Sep 205	17 Nov 216	19 Jan 281	12 Mar 86	9 Apr 204	17 Nov 1,624	27 Feb 268		23 Feb 175	5 Jan 113	24 Nov 447	21 Aug 265
Curzon Ashton	11 Sep 175	2 Feb 94	26 Apr 349	29 Dec 82	1 Apr 147	25 Aug 141	3 Nov 150	21 Aug 343	18 Aug 201	29 Mar 90	15 Aug 116	5 Mar 1,879		19 Apr 148	9 Feb 204	8 Mar 192	12 Nov 294	1 Oct 267
FC United of Manchester	24 Mar 1,066	5 Apr 1,378	2 Oct 617	27 Aug 2,023	26 Dec 456	19 Apr 647	27 Nov 889	21 Aug 2,257	18 Aug 1,290	9 Apr 365	29 Dec 2,216		26 Apr 1,215	17 Nov 1,215	3 Nov 1,006	7 Apr 1,264	25 Sep 1,435	17 Nov 1,736
Garforth Town	10 Nov 80	10 Nov 125	25 Mar 205	25 Aug 86	20 Oct 105	13 Oct 105	26 Jan 223	3 Nov 131	27 Nov 251	2 Feb 134		26 Apr 2,216	22 Sep 175	22 Aug 116	21 Mar 126	11 Sep 136	24 Nov 164	8 Sep 132
Harrogate Railway Ath	9 Feb 75	23 Jan 70	23 Jan 200	17 Nov 141	17 Nov 160	15 Mar 120	5 Apr 131	27 Nov 107	18 Aug 158		2 Feb 251	15 Mar 2,196	22 Sep 223	17 Nov 190	5 Jan 150	1 Jan 117	8 Mar 333	23 Oct 138
Lancaster City	17 Nov 105	12 Jan 102	12 Jan 290	27 Oct 137	29 Jan 191	22 Sep 142	15 Mar 120	13 Oct 174		7 Nov 107	3 Nov 134	29 Mar 1,859	17 Mar 174	24 Mar 325	26 Jan 134	21 Aug 117	19 Apr 464	9 Feb 237
Mossley	17 Nov 125	9 Feb 70	10 Nov 102	24 Nov 116	26 Feb 72	16 Feb 101	26 Apr 88		24 Nov 186	12 Sep 102	18 Aug 141	1 Jan 2,017	24 Mar 186	21 Aug 325	19 Apr 112	1 Jan 117	27 Aug 216	5 Feb 206
Newcastle Blue Star	3 Nov 49	10 Nov 76	10 Nov 116	25 Aug 285	1 Dec 119	18 Aug 206		5 Apr 159	1 Mar 207	15 Mar 120	5 Jan 137	15 Mar 2,048	12 Apr 207	26 Jan 334	19 Jan 169	11 Sep 316	8 Mar 316	12 Jan 180
Ossett Albion	29 Dec 75	24 Nov 107	10 Nov 139	22 Dec 212	29 Jan 191		22 Sep 205	1 Apr 142	10 Nov 245	27 Oct 162	22 Sep 180	22 Mar 2,160	15 Sep 220	19 Jan 245	5 Jan 115	1 Oct 309	1 Oct 179	19 Apr 197
Radcliffe Borough	23 Oct 92	12 Feb 204	18 Aug 102	17 Nov 109		16 Feb 107	26 Apr 107	1 Dec 72	24 Mar 137	3 Oct 109	28 Dec 119	22 Mar 2,163	28 Aug 203	1 Jan 302	22 Apr 142	22 Dec 618	22 Dec 170	11 Dec 170
Rossendale United	20 Oct 69	10 Oct 112	16 Feb 112		8 Sep 227	8 Sep 120	8 Sep 72	21 Aug 191	24 Nov 186	27 Oct 137	24 Mar 132	14 Nov 1,691	19 Apr 116	3 Oct 255	25 Aug 142	22 Sep 330	17 Nov 299	10 Nov 245
Skelmersdale United	26 Dec 87	11 Mar 79		8 Sep 118	16 Apr 102	3 Nov 102	19 Apr 176	16 Apr 109	3 Oct 116	6 Nov 87	28 Jan 238	16 Feb 2,168	17 Nov 319	1 Jan 255	8 Mar 146	19 Jan 311	23 Feb 316	18 Mar 185
Wakefield	23 Feb 75		27 Oct 225	24 Nov 125	12 Feb 204	10 Oct 118	6 Nov 87	15 Mar 101	16 Apr 98	6 Nov 87	25 Aug 139	10 Oct 1,955	25 Sep 241	8 Sep 139	5 Feb 103	12 Apr 574	5 Nov 278	1 Apr 151
Woodley Sports		8 Dec 65	21 Apr 216	12 Jan 146	26 Jan 119	21 Mar 179	1 Jan 223	15 Sep 101	15 Mar 101	5 Jan 241	27 Oct 241	15 Jan 2,283	27 Oct 177	8 Sep 241	11 Dec 123	8 Mar 108	1 Apr 151	

STANDARD SEASON
(based on first meetings)

EXTRA DIVISION ONE NORTH LEAGUE MATCHES

26 Dec	Bamber Bridge	1	Chorley	2	Att:	366
23 Feb	Bamber Bridge	0	FC United of Manchester	0	Att:	1,236
27 Nov	Bamber Bridge	3	Radcliffe Borough	0	Att:	173
21 Mar	Bamber Bridge	0	Skelmersdale United	4	Att:	327
14 Apr	Bradford Park Avenue	7	Bridlington Town	0	Att:	486
29 Mar	Bradford Park Avenue	3	Garforth Town	0	Att:	512
21 Mar	Bradford Park Avenue	4	Mossley	1	Att:	469
21 Apr	Bradford Park Avenue	2	Ossett Albion	0	Att:	1,061
13 Oct	Bridlington Town	3	Curzon Ashton	3	Att:	118
1 Apr	Bridlington Town	0	Harrogate Railway	3	Att:	96
1 Dec	Bridlington Town	0	Newcastle Blue Star	4	Att:	143
22 Mar	Bridlington Town	0	Wakefield	4	Att:	133
8 Apr	Chorley	2	Clitheroe	3	Att:	202
15 Mar	Chorley	0	Lancaster City	1	Att:	309
12 Apr	Chorley	2	Rossendale United	4	Att:	256
16 Feb	Chorley	0	Woodley Sports	0	Att:	334
26 Apr	Clitheroe	2	Bamber Bridge	2	Att:	320
10 Nov	Clitheroe	2	FC United of Manchester	1	Att:	1,245
29 Mar	Clitheroe	1	Radcliffe Borough	1	Att:	245
4 Mar	Clitheroe	0	Skelmersdale United	0	Att:	195
5 Apr	Curzon Ashton	2	Bradford Park Avenue	0	Att:	325
23 Feb	Curzon Ashton	2	Garforth Town	1	Att:	186
15 Dec	Curzon Ashton	4	Mossley	2	Att:	273
26 Dec	Curzon Ashton	1	Ossett Albion	4	Att:	134
26 Mar	FC United of Manchester	3	Chorley	0	Att:	1,645
12 Apr	FC United of Manchester	5	Lancaster City	2	Att:	2,704
1 Dec	FC United of Manchester	2	Rossendale United	1	Att:	1,744
23 Apr	FC United of Manchester	1	Woodley Sports	1	Att:	1,558
15 Dec	Garforth Town	3	Bridlington Town	0	Att:	131
21 Mar	Garforth Town	3	Harrogate Railway	2	Att:	156
16 Feb	Garforth Town	4	Newcastle Blue Star	0	Att:	128
22 Dec	Garforth Town	0	Wakefield	2	Att:	135
1 Mar	Harrogate Railway	2	Bradford Park Avenue	0	Att:	256
12 Apr	Harrogate Railway	0	Curzon Ashton	0	Att:	151
12 Jan	Harrogate Railway	2	Mossley	1	Att:	156
24 Mar	Harrogate Railway	1	Ossett Albion	1	Att:	107
29 Dec	Lancaster City	3	Bamber Bridge	0	Att:	214
21 Mar	Lancaster City	0	Clitheroe	1	Att:	328
23 Feb	Lancaster City	1	Radcliffe Borough	5	Att:	212
12 Feb	Lancaster City	1	Skelmersdale United	0	Att:	246
4 Mar	Mossley	2	Bridlington Town	5	Att:	87
22 Apr	Mossley	2	Garforth Town	1	Att:	114
9 Feb	Mossley	1	Newcastle Blue Star	1	Att:	156
26 Apr	Mossley	0	Wakefield	0	Att:	151
17 Apr	Newcastle Blue Star	0	Bradford Park Avenue	0	Att:	287
23 Apr	Newcastle Blue Star	2	Curzon Ashton	1	Att:	117
8 Mar	Newcastle Blue Star	2	Harrogate Railway	2	Att:	102
23 Feb	Newcastle Blue Star	2	Ossett Albion	2	Att:	63
1 Mar	Ossett Albion	1	Bridlington Town	1	Att:	105
8 Dec	Ossett Albion	4	Garforth Town	1	Att:	114
16 Apr	Ossett Albion	2	Mossley	1	Att:	100
1 Jan	Ossett Albion	1	Wakefield	0	Att:	208
19 Apr	Radcliffe Borough	1	Chorley	4	Att:	225
15 Apr	Radcliffe Borough	0	FC United of Manchester	2	Att:	743
1 Mar	Radcliffe Borough	1	Rossendale United	0	Att:	192
5 Apr	Radcliffe Borough	1	Woodley Sports	0	Att:	113
5 Apr	Rossendale United	1	Bamber Bridge	5	Att:	125
23 Feb	Rossendale United	2	Clitheroe	2	Att:	170
4 Mar	Rossendale United	1	Lancaster City	1	Att:	91
12 Jan	Rossendale United	2	Skelmersdale United	0	Att:	118
2 Feb	Skelmersdale United	7	Chorley	0	Att:	312
1 Apr	Skelmersdale United	0	FC United of Manchester	0	Att:	674
12 Apr	Skelmersdale United	1	Radcliffe Borough	2	Att:	281
24 Nov	Skelmersdale United	2	Woodley Sports	2	Att:	181
29 Dec	Wakefield	2	Bradford Park Avenue	3	Att:	141
26 Feb	Wakefield	0	Curzon Ashton	1	Att:	98
19 Apr	Wakefield	2	Harrogate Railway	1	Att:	107
15 Apr	Wakefield	1	Newcastle Blue Star	3	Att:	50
29 Mar	Woodley Sports	2	Bamber Bridge	3	Att:	90
2 Feb	Woodley Sports	1	Clitheroe	2	Att:	121
26 Apr	Woodley Sports	0	Lancaster City	0	Att:	87
15 Dec	Woodley Sports	1	Rossendale United	1	Att:	75

UNIBOND NORTHERN PREMIER LEAGUE
DIVISION ONE NORTH CONSTITUTION 2008-09

BAMBER BRIDGE
Colours: White & black
Irongate, Brownedge Road, Bamber Bridge, Preston,
Lancashire PR5 6UX
Tel: 01772 909690 Fax: 01772 909691 Club: 01772
909695

CHORLEY
Colours: Black & white
Chorley Nissan Victory Park Stadium, Duke Street,
Chorley, Lancashire PR7 3DU
Tel/Fax: 01257 263406 Club: 01257 241625

CLITHEROE
Colours: Blue
Shawbridge, off Pendle Road, Clitheroe, Lancashire
BB7 1LZ
Tel: 01200 423344

COLWYN BAY
Colours: Sky blue & claret
Llanelian Road, Old Colwyn, Colwyn Bay, Clwyd
LL29 8UN
Tel/Fax: 01492 514581 Club: 01492 513944

CURZON ASHTON
Colours: Royal blue
The Tameside Stadium, Richmond Street,
Ashton-under-Lyne, Lancashire OL7 9HG
Tel: 0161 330 6033

DURHAM CITY
Colours: Yellow & blue
Arnott Stadium, Belmont Industrial Estate, Durham,
County Durham DH1 1GG
Tel: 0191 386 9616

FC HALIFAX TOWN
Colours: Blue & white
The Shay Stadium, Shaw Hill, Halifax, West Yorkshire
HX1 2YS
Tel: 01422 341222 Fax: 01422 349487
Ticket Office: 01422 353423

GARFORTH TOWN
Colours: Yellow & blue
The Genix Healthcare Stadium, Cedar Ridge,
Garforth, Leeds, West Yorkshire LS25 2PF
Tel: 0113 287 7145

HARROGATE RAILWAY ATHLETIC
Colours: Red & green
Station View, Station View Road, Starbeck, Harrogate,
North Yorkshire HG2 7JA
Tel: 01423 883104

LANCASTER CITY
Colours: Sky blue
Giant Axe, West Road, Lancaster,
Lancashire LA1 5PE
Tel: 01524 382238 Fax: 01524 841710
Club: 01524 843500

MOSSLEY
Colours: White & black
Seel Park, Market Street, Mossley, Ashton-under-Lyne,
Lancashire OL5 0ES
Tel: 01457 835989 Club: 01457 836104

NEWCASTLE BLUE STAR
Colours: Blue & white
Kingston Park Stadium, Brunton Road, Kenton Bank
Foot, Newcastle-upon-Tyne, Tyne & Wear NE13 8AF
Tel: 0191 214 5588 Fax: 0191 214 2826

OSSETT ALBION
Colours: Gold & black
Queens Terrace, Dimple Wells, Ossett, Wakefield, West
Yorkshire WF5 8RN
Tel: 01924 280450 Club: 01924 273618

RADCLIFFE BOROUGH
Colours: Blue & white
The Inn2Gether Stadium, Pilkington Road, Radcliffe,
Manchester M26 3PE
Tel: 0161 724 8346 Fax: 0161 723 3178
Club: 0161 724 5937

ROSSENDALE UNITED
Colours: Blue & white
Dark Lane, Staghills Road, Newchurch, Rossendale,
Lancashire BB4 7UA
Tel: 01706 215119 Fax: 01706 230970
Club: 01706 213296

SALFORD CITY
Colours: Tangerine & black
Moor Lane, Kersal, Salford, Manchester M7 3PZ
Tel: 0161 792 6287 Fax: 0161 792 6287

SKELMERSDALE UNITED
Colours: Blue
Ashley Travel Stadium, Selby Place, Stanley Industrial
Estate, Skelmersdale, Lancashire WN8 8EF
Tel: 01695 722123 Fax: 01695 722123

TRAFFORD
Colours: White
Shawe View, Pennybridge Lane, Flixton, Urmston,
Manchester M41 5DL
Tel/Fax: 0161 747 1727 Club: 0161 749 8217

WAKEFIELD
Colours: Blue & yellow
College Grove, Eastmore Road, Wakefield, West
Yorkshire WF1 3RR
Tel: 01924 365007

WARRINGTON TOWN
Colours: Yellow & blue
Cantilever Park, Common Lane, Warrington, Cheshire
WA4 2RS
Tel: 01925 631932 Fax: 01925 653044

WOODLEY SPORTS
Colours: Blue, red & white
Lambeth Grove Stadium, Lambeth Grove, Woodley,
Stockport, Cheshire SK6 1QX
Tel: 0161 406 6896 Club: 0161 494 6429

WWW.NLNEWSDESK.CO.UK

IN: Colwyn Bay (S – Northern Premier League Division One South), Durham City (P – Northern League Division One), FC Halifax Town (formerly Halifax Town) (R – Football Conference Premier Division), Salford City (P – North West Counties League Division One), Trafford (P – North West Counties League Division One), Warrington Town (S – Northern Premier League Division One South)
OUT: Bradford Park Avenue (P), Bridlington Town (R – Northern Counties East League Premier Division), FC United of Manchester (P)

STANDARD SEASON
(see page 152 for the extra league matches)

	ALS	BEL	BRI	CAM	CAR	COL	GOO	GRA	GRE	KID	NAN	QUO	RET	SHE	SHD	SPA	STO	WAR
Alsager Town		1-4	1-4	0-2	1-1	1-2	2-0	2-1	0-1	1-1	1-2	0-0	1-5	3-3	0-1	5-1	2-1	3-2
Belper Town	2-1		4-1	2-1	3-2	2-2	1-1	1-1	2-1	1-1	3-0	1-4	0-2	1-4	2-2	1-1	0-2	2-1
Brigg Town	4-4	1-1	*D*	2-2	1-1	1-3	1-1	3-5	0-1	1-3	0-4	3-5	0-4	2-2	2-2	2-2	0-1	0-2
Cammell Laird	2-1	3-2	3-1	*I*	4-0	2-2	4-1	1-1	2-0	2-0	2-1	2-0	1-2	4-1	3-1	1-1	2-1	2-0
Carlton Town	0-1	4-1	3-3	2-2	*V*	1-0	2-1	1-1	1-1	3-0	1-5	3-1	4-4	4-1	3-2	1-2	0-2	3-6
Colwyn Bay	6-2	2-2	3-1	3-1	3-4	*I*	0-2	1-4	2-1	5-2	2-0	1-0	1-1	0-0	6-0	4-2	1-3	7-1
Goole	3-1	1-1	2-3	2-0	0-1	3-4	*S*	4-0	1-1	6-2	1-0	3-0	1-2	1-2	4-1	4-3	2-2	2-1
Grantham Town	0-3	3-2	1-2	6-0	1-2	2-1	1-0	*I*	1-2	2-1	2-0	2-0	0-1	3-2	1-0	1-0	3-1	1-0
Gresley Rovers	0-1	1-1	0-0	2-1	4-2	1-0	3-3	1-4	*O*	3-2	0-3	3-1	0-1	0-3	2-1	1-0	3-1	3-1
Kidsgrove Athletic	5-1	1-3	1-3	2-1	2-1	1-0	4-0	1-2	1-2	*N*	2-3	2-2	2-3	4-1	0-0	2-2	2-2	0-1
Nantwich Town	6-0	4-1	2-0	0-1	1-1	3-0	5-1	1-0	3-1	4-1		0-2	1-2	1-0	4-2	4-1	3-0	1-0
Quorn	3-2	1-1	1-0	1-2	2-6	0-2	6-2	6-3	4-0	2-0	1-4	*O*	2-2	0-3	2-0	1-1	4-2	0-2
Retford United	5-1	3-0	2-0	2-0	2-0	3-1	1-3	3-0	2-0	4-1	1-2	4-0	*N*	2-2	1-0	3-2	3-0	2-1
Sheffield	3-0	0-0	2-0	1-0	3-2	2-0	0-0	2-1	2-0	4-1	0-3	0-0	1-1	*E*	1-0	7-2	1-1	0-1
Shepshed Dynamo	1-0	2-1	3-0	2-3	2-0	1-1	1-1	2-0	1-2	2-0	0-3	2-1	1-2	0-2		0-1	2-3	0-1
Spalding United	1-4	0-2	0-2	1-2	1-3	2-6	2-3	0-1	1-2	2-4	1-4	3-3	0-1	0-3	0-0	*S*	0-2	0-2
Stocksbridge Park Steels	2-0	0-3	1-0	2-0	2-1	1-0	3-1	1-0	3-2	4-1	1-0	4-1	3-0	4-2				2-2
Warrington Town	0-1	0-2	2-2	0-1	0-5	2-3	3-3	1-0	1-0	2-2	2-2	1-1	0-0	2-1	1-2	3-1	3-0	

Division One South

		HOME					AWAY					TOTAL					
	P	W	D	L	F	A	W	D	L	F	A	W	D	L	F	A	Pts
Retford United	42	17	1	3	49	15	14	5	2	44	20	31	6	5	93	35	99
Cammell Laird	42	17	3	1	51	18	10	2	9	31	36	27	5	10	82	54	86
Nantwich Town	42	15	2	4	50	17	10	2	9	40	28	25	4	13	90	45	79
Sheffield	42	14	5	2	41	17	8	5	8	41	36	22	10	10	82	53	76
Stocksbridge Park Steels	42	15	4	2	40	19	6	5	10	32	42	21	9	12	72	61	72
Grantham Town	42	14	0	7	40	25	8	4	9	34	33	22	4	16	74	58	70
Colwyn Bay	42	12	3	6	54	31	7	5	9	32	34	19	8	15	86	65	65
Belper Town	42	9	6	6	39	34	8	7	6	34	30	17	13	12	73	64	64
Goole	42	12	4	5	48	27	6	6	9	29	42	18	10	14	77	69	64
Carlton Town	42	8	6	7	43	40	8	5	8	43	42	16	11	15	86	82	59
Gresley Rovers	42	11	3	7	33	32	7	2	12	20	37	18	5	19	53	69	59
Quorn	42	10	3	8	43	38	5	5	11	26	38	15	8	19	69	76	53
Warrington Town	42	6	7	8	27	36	7	1	13	24	42	13	8	21	51	78	47
Alsager Town	42	6	5	10	29	38	6	2	13	29	50	12	7	23	58	88	43
Shepshed Dynamo	42	7	4	10	27	32	3	4	14	17	43	10	8	24	44	75	38
Brigg Town	42	2	8	11	28	48	6	4	11	28	38	8	12	22	56	86	36
Kidsgrove Athletic	42	5	7	9	38	36	2	3	16	23	54	7	10	25	61	90	31
Spalding United	42	0	3	18	16	54	3	7	11	30	51	3	10	29	46	105	19

PLAY-OFFS

SEMI-FINALS (April 29th)
Nantwich Town 2 Grantham Town 1 *Att* 624
Sheffield 4 Stocksbridge Park Steels 1 *Att* 430
FINAL
(May 3rd at Nantwich Towm)
Nantwich Town 2 Sheffield 2 *aet* (4-1p) *Att* 1,354

CHAIRMAN'S CUP
(Division One North champions v Division One South champions)

(April 29th at Retford United)
Retford United 2 Bradford Park Avenue 0 *Att:* 131

STANDARD SEASON
(see page 152 for the extra league matches)

DATES & GATES

WWW.NLNEWSDESK.CO.UK

(home ↓ / away →)	Alsager Town	Belper Town	Brigg Town	Cammell Laird	Carlton Town	Colwyn Bay	Goole	Grantham Town	Gresley Rovers	Kidsgrove Athletic	Nantwich Town	Quorn	Retford United	Sheffield	Shepshed Dynamo	Spalding United	Stocksbridge Park Steels	Warrington Town
Alsager Town	—	29 Dec / 80	26 Jan / 92	26 Apr / 81	17 Nov / 70	4 Mar / 50	22 Sep / 90	8 Mar / 102	15 Dec / 259	26 Dec / 380	3 Nov / 79	13 Oct / 72	26 Apr / 92	12 Apr / 60	24 Nov / 76	25 Aug / 120	23 Feb / 40	29 Mar
Belper Town	19 Apr / 163	—	1 Mar / 127	27 Aug / 132	3 Nov / 193	2 Feb / 70	18 Aug / 124	2 Oct / 120	15 Jan / 235	9 Feb / 146	22 Sep / 204	24 Oct / 153	24 Mar / 189	13 Nov / 131	27 Nov / 117	29 Sep / 117	13 Oct / 125	4 Mar / 120
Brigg Town	22 Dec / 103	1 Apr / 111	—	6 Nov / 58	2 Feb / 58	8 Dec / 303	24 Mar / 303	27 Aug / 262	1 Jan / 365	10 Apr / 208	20 Nov / 238	23 Oct / 163	17 Nov / 301	15 Mar / 189	21 Mar / 195	25 Aug / 115	18 Aug / 112	8 Dec / 93
Cammell Laird	2 Apr / 84	12 Jan / 101	26 Apr / 121	—	24 Apr / 312	5 Apr / 178	12 Mar / 189	19 Apr / 142	21 Apr / 256	15 Mar / 208	25 Aug / 240	5 Apr / 184	15 Apr / 215	24 Apr / 122	18 Mar / 139	23 Apr / 115	13 Oct / 125	22 Aug / 83
Carlton Town	18 Aug / 88	26 Apr / 164	6 Nov / 48	22 Dec / 312	—	2 Feb / 72	24 Apr / 189	2 Feb / 120	27 Nov / 129	10 Apr / 146	8 Mar / 204	19 Apr / 114	17 Apr / 172	17 Apr / 192	26 Feb / 233	26 Apr / 509	5 Apr / 178	24 Mar / 70
Colwyn Bay	12 Feb / 181	24 Apr / 72	8 Dec / 303	5 Apr / 178	22 Dec / 229	—	22 Apr / 193	23 Feb / 281	26 Jan / 303	22 Mar / 184	29 Dec / 210	5 Jan / 53	1 Apr / 172	26 Feb / 215	26 Dec / 302	13 Oct / 147	18 Mar / 201	1 Jan / 275
Goole	1 Mar / 203	15 Mar / 161	26 Apr / 145	10 Nov / 118	26 Dec / 124	5 Apr / 193	—	19 Apr / 262	24 Nov / 256	27 Feb / 146	23 Apr / 288	19 Apr / 184	23 Feb / 145	1 Jan / 383	1 Dec / 247	5 Jan / 165	27 Oct / 178	15 Dec / 126
Grantham Town	5 Jan / 167	25 Aug / 212	21 Mar / 177	26 Apr / 142	23 Feb / 167	12 Mar / 303	19 Apr / 262	—	3 Nov / 143	10 Apr / 220	8 Sep / 262	5 Jan / 200	27 Nov / 172	26 Feb / 233	11 Mar / 268	23 Apr / 215	8 Mar / 178	15 Sep / 181
Gresley Rovers	10 Nov / 207	8 Sep / 223	1 Jan / 161	21 Apr / 256	26 Jan / 303	24 Nov / 256	24 Nov / 256	12 Jan / 143	—	27 Oct / 626	27 Oct / 143	26 Jan / 184	25 Aug / 219	15 Aug / 122	18 Mar / 139	26 Apr / 509	27 Dec / 202	2 Feb / 191
Kidsgrove Athletic	24 Mar / 207	28 Nov / 91	26 Apr / 219	4 Mar / 208	9 Feb / 114	10 Nov / 66	10 Nov / 222	22 Mar / 222	16 Feb / 626	—	22 Mar / 184	10 Nov / 203	12 Apr / 318	17 Apr / 215	27 Nov / 384	25 Aug / 509	13 Oct / 147	1 Jan / 95
Nantwich Town	1 Jan / 664	12 Apr / 564	10 Nov / 554	20 Nov / 238	1 Dec / 141	27 Feb / 210	8 Mar / 204	24 Nov / 200	22 Sep / 251	15 Dec / 127	—	8 Mar / 262	27 Feb / 219	26 Feb / 231	17 Nov / 139	27 Oct / 147	26 Jan / 145	24 Oct / 95
Quorn	2 Feb / 93	26 Jan / 153	27 Oct / 97	19 Apr / 184	24 Oct / 113	17 Nov / 113	13 Oct / 53	5 Jan / 114	16 Feb / 67	15 Dec / 127	23 Apr / 288	—	5 Jan / 234	24 Oct / 153	8 Mar / 203	13 Oct / 302	13 Oct / 147	15 Sep / 198
Retford United	5 Apr / 200	19 Apr / 248	23 Oct / 224	29 Mar / 128	17 Nov / 249	27 Nov / 219	1 Apr / 172	1 Apr / 251	20 Nov / 125	6 Oct / 239	15 Dec / 127	22 Dec / 184	—	12 Jan / 145	11 Mar / 251	1 Apr / 190	1 Mar / 172	24 Mar / 184
Sheffield	9 Feb / 256	21 Mar / 442	8 Mar / 274	1 Jan / 131	13 Oct / 131	26 Feb / 233	26 Feb / 192	2 Apr / 122	26 Apr / 526	10 Apr / 220	25 Apr / 239	26 Jan / 184	23 Feb	—	22 Dec / 128	1 Jan / 129	1 Mar / 453	15 Apr / 155
Shepshed Dynamo	27 Aug / 159	23 Oct / 149	24 Nov / 113	1 Dec / 124	29 Aug / 117	25 Aug / 384	26 Dec / 302	26 Feb / 204	15 Dec / 169	29 Aug / 384	24 Aug / 153	24 Oct / 153	27 Nov / 219	16 Feb / 231	—	26 Feb / 376	24 Mar / 133	29 Sep
Spalding United	8 Dec / 93	22 Sep / 98	13 Nov / 115	29 Sep / 191	23 Sep / 133	26 Apr / 509	9 Sep / 509	25 Aug / 509	26 Apr / 509	25 Aug / 509	23 Apr / 201	5 Apr / 201	26 Feb / 192	29 Apr / 511	11 Mar / 149	—	8 Sep / 112	8 Mar / 95
Stocksbridge Park Steels	15 Mar / 119	4 Mar / 181	18 Nov / 172	1 Mar / 142	1 Jan / 181	27 Feb / 172	15 Dec / 126	5 Apr / 104	15 Mar / 129	12 Apr / 140	26 Apr / 202	19 Jan / 220	22 Apr / 212	24 Apr / 104	9 Feb / 149	5 Jan / 165	—	19 Apr / 78
Warrington Town	16 Feb / 78	10 Nov / 120	18 Aug / 112	22 Aug / 83	22 Aug / 90	29 Jan / 121	15 Dec / 126	5 Apr / 104	15 Mar / 131	15 Mar / 122	26 Dec / 183	26 Jan / 146	29 Dec / 110	19 Apr / 155	9 Feb / 128	8 Sep / 86	22 Mar / 118	—

STANDARD SEASON
(based on first meetings)

EXTRA DIVISION ONE SOUTH LEAGUE MATCHES

Date	Home		Away			Att
1 Dec	Alsager Town	1	Belper Town	3	Att:	130
8 Sep	Alsager Town	2	Colwyn Bay	3	Att:	127
22 Aug	Alsager Town	1	Nantwich Town	0	Att:	285
3 Oct	Alsager Town	1	Stocksbridge Park Steels	1	Att:	70
22 Dec	Belper Town	1	Cammell Laird	3	Att:	141
20 Oct	Belper Town	3	Kidsgrove Athletic	0	Att:	134
11 Sep	Belper Town	1	Sheffield	4	Att:	136
8 Dec	Belper Town	6	Warrington Town	0	Att:	113
22 Aug	Brigg Town	3	Carlton Town	4	Att:	105
1 Jan	Brigg Town	1	Grantham Town	0	Att:	202
11 Sep	Brigg Town	1	Quorn	0	Att:	131
12 Jan	Brigg Town	0	Shepshed Dynamo	1	Att:	152
12 Sep	Cammell Laird	4	Alsager Town	2	Att:	112
24 Oct	Cammell Laird	2	Colwyn Bay	0	Att:	118
3 Nov	Cammell Laird	2	Nantwich Town	0	Att:	309
18 Aug	Cammell Laird	3	Stocksbridge Park Steels	1	Att:	169
20 Nov	Carlton Town	1	Goole	2	Att:	91
11 Sep	Carlton Town	3	Gresley Rovers	1	Att:	79
29 Sep	Carlton Town	2	Retford United	3	Att:	115
29 Dec	Carlton Town	1	Spalding United	1	Att:	60
27 Oct	Colwyn Bay	1	Belper Town	2	Att:	248
11 Sep	Colwyn Bay	2	Kidsgrove Athletic	0	Att:	362
6 Oct	Colwyn Bay	0	Sheffield	3	Att:	313
21 Aug	Colwyn Bay	4	Warrington Town	0	Att:	372
8 Sep	Goole	3	Brigg Town	2	Att:	231
3 Nov	Goole	1	Grantham Town	1	Att:	225
20 Oct	Goole	1	Quorn	0	Att:	165
2 Oct	Goole	3	Shepshed Dynamo	0	Att:	136
19 Jan	Grantham Town	1	Carlton Town	2	Att:	216
1 Dec	Grantham Town	5	Gresley Rovers	1	Att:	208
21 Aug	Grantham Town	2	Retford United	1	Att:	282
6 Nov	Grantham Town	2	Spalding United	4	Att:	176
29 Sep	Gresley Rovers	3	Brigg Town	2	Att:	218
6 Nov	Gresley Rovers	0	Goole	1	Att:	151
24 Nov	Gresley Rovers	0	Quorn	2	Att:	203
21 Aug	Gresley Rovers	3	Shepshed Dynamo	2	Att:	202
24 Nov	Kidsgrove Athletic	1	Alsager Town	1	Att:	277
22 Aug	Kidsgrove Athletic	1	Cammell Laird	2	Att:	94
23 Feb	Kidsgrove Athletic	2	Nantwich Town	2	Att:	306
8 Sep	Kidsgrove Athletic	3	Stocksbridge Park Steels	3	Att:	125
16 Feb	Nantwich Town	0	Belper Town	1	Att:	543
13 Oct	Nantwich Town	1	Colwyn Bay	1	Att:	613
20 Feb	Nantwich Town	3	Sheffield	2	Att:	328
11 Sep	Nantwich Town	3	Warrington Town	0	Att:	470
21 Mar	Quorn	4	Carlton Town	2	Att:	108
22 Sep	Quorn	0	Grantham Town	2	Att:	194
8 Sep	Quorn	0	Retford United	2	Att:	159
21 Aug	Quorn	3	Spalding United	0	Att:	131
19 Jan	Retford United	0	Brigg Town	1	Att:	245
11 Sep	Retford United	2	Goole	1	Att:	219
18 Aug	Retford United	2	Gresley Rovers	0	Att:	252
22 Aug	Retford United	2	Shepshed Dynamo	0	Att:	231
15 Sep	Sheffield	2	Alsager Town	1	Att:	195
8 Sep	Sheffield	4	Cammell Laird	0	Att:	286
13 Oct	Sheffield	2	Kidsgrove Athletic	1	Att:	232
26 Dec	Sheffield	4	Stocksbridge Park Steels	3	Att:	461
8 Sep	Shepshed Dynamo	2	Carlton Town	2	Att:	106
13 Oct	Shepshed Dynamo	0	Grantham Town	5	Att:	117
12 Feb	Shepshed Dynamo	2	Quorn	3	Att:	264
10 Nov	Shepshed Dynamo	1	Spalding United	1	Att:	108
3 Nov	Spalding United	1	Brigg Town	1	Att:	96
27 Aug	Spalding United	0	Goole	2	Att:	111
27 Oct	Spalding United	1	Gresley Rovers	2	Att:	114
2 Oct	Spalding United	0	Retford United	5	Att:	97
21 Aug	Stocksbridge Park Steels	1	Belper Town	1	Att:	169
27 Aug	Stocksbridge Park Steels	1	Colwyn Bay	1	Att:	210
17 Nov	Stocksbridge Park Steels	1	Nantwich Town	0	Att:	165
22 Dec	Stocksbridge Park Steels	1	Warrington Town	0	Att:	157
27 Oct	Warrington Town	0	Alsager Town	2	Att:	110
3 Oct	Warrington Town	1	Cammell Laird	6	Att:	125
18 Sep	Warrington Town	2	Kidsgrove Athletic	1	Att:	132
27 Aug	Warrington Town	1	Sheffield	1	Att:	160

UNIBOND NORTHERN PREMIER LEAGUE
DIVISION ONE SOUTH CONSTITUTION 2008-09

BELPER TOWN
Colours: Yellow & black
Christchurch Meadow, Bridge Street, Belper,
Derbyshire DE56 1BA
Tel: 01773 825549 Fax: 01773 825549

LOUGHBOROUGH DYNAMO
Colours: Gold & black
Nanpantan Sports Ground, Nanpantan Road,
Loughborough, Leicestershire LE11 3YD
Tel: 01509 237148

BRIGG TOWN
Colours: White & black
The Hawthorns, Hawthorn Avenue, Brigg, North Lincs
DN20 8PG
Tel/Fax: 01652 651605 Club: 01652 652767

QUORN
Colours: Red
Sutton Park, Farley Way, Quorn, Loughborough,
Leicestershire LE12 8RB
Tel: 01509 620232

CARLTON TOWN
Colours: Yellow & blue
Bill Stokeld Stadium, Stoke Lane, Gedling, Nottingham,
Nottinghamshire NG4 2QS
Tel: 0115 940 2531

RETFORD UNITED
Colours: Black & white
Canon Park, Leverton Road, Retford, Notts DN22 6QF
Tel/Fax: 01777 869468 Club: 01777 710300

GLAPWELL
Colours: Black & white
Hall Corner, Park Avenue, Glapwell, Chesterfield,
Derbyshire S44 5NJ
Tel: 01623 812213

RUSHALL OLYMPIC
Colours: Amber & black
Dales Lane, off Daw End Lane, Rushall, Walsall, West
Midlands WS4 1LJ
Tel: 01922 641021

GOOLE
Colours: Red & white
Victoria Pleasure Grounds, Marcus Street, Goole, East
Yorkshire DN14 6WW
Tel: 07792 962855 Club: 01405 762794

SHEFFIELD
Colours: Red & black
The Bright Finance Stadium, Stubley Hollow, Sheffield
Road, Dronfield, South Yorkshire S18 2GD
Tel: 01246 292622

GRANTHAM TOWN
Colours: Black & white
South Kesteven Sports Stadium, Trent Road, Grantham,
Lincolnshire NG31 7XQ
Tel: 01476 402224 Club: 01476 402225

SHEPSHED DYNAMO
Colours: Black, red & white
The Dovecote, Butt Hole Lane, Shepshed,
Loughborough, Leicestershire LE12 9BN
Tel: 01509 650992

GRESLEY ROVERS
Colours: Red & white
Moat Ground, Moat Street, Church Gresley,
Swadlincote, Derbyshire DE11 9RE
Tel: 01283 216315 Fax: 01283 221881

SPALDING UNITED
Colours: Blue & white
Sir Halley Stewart Field, Winfrey Avenue, Spalding,
Lincolnshire PE11 1DA
Tel: 01775 713328 Club: 01775 769771

KIDSGROVE ATHLETIC
Colours: Blue & white
The Stan Brown Stadium, Hollinwood Road,
Kidsgrove, Stoke-on-Trent, Staffordshire ST7 1DH
Tel: 01782 782412

STAMFORD
Colours: Red
The Vic Couzens Stadium, Kettering Road, Stamford,
Lincolnshire PE9 2JR
Tel: 01780 763079

LEEK TOWN
Colours: Blue & white
Harrison Park, Macclesfield Road, Leek, Staffordshire
ST13 8LD
Tel: 01538 399278 Fax: 01538 399826
Club: 01538 383734

STOCKSBRIDGE PARK STEELS
Colours: Yellow & royal blue
Look Local Stadium, Bracken Moor Lane,Stocksbridge,
Sheffield, South Yorkshire S36 5AN
Tel/Fax: 0114 288 8305 Fax: 0114 288 8305
Club: 0114 288 2045

LINCOLN UNITED
Colours: White
Sports Pavilion, Ashby Avenue, Hartsholme, Lincoln,
Lincolnshire LN6 0DY
Tel/Fax: 01522 696400 Club: 01522 690674

WILLENHALL TOWN
Colours: Red
Noose Lane, Willenhall, West Midlands WV13 3BB
Tel: 01902 636586

IN: Glapwell (P – Northern Counties East League Premier Division), Leek Town (R), Lincoln United (R), Loughborough Dynamo (P – Midland Alliance), Rushall Olympic (S – Southern League Division One Midlands), Stamford (R), Willenhall Town (S – Southern League Division One Midlands)
OUT: Alsager Town (R – North West Counties League Division One), Cammell Laird (P), Colwyn Bay (S – Northern Premier League Division One North), FC United of Manchester (P), Warrington Town (S – Northern Premier League Division One North)

LEAGUE CUP

FIRST ROUND

Bamber Bridge 2 Chorley 1 *(Sep 25)*   Att: 229
Cammell Laird 3 **Rossendale United** 4 *(Sep 26)*   Att: 116
Clitheroe 4 **Colwyn Bay** 4 *aet (2-4p) (Sep 25)*   Att: 155
FC United of Manchester 0 **Alsager Town** 1 *(Sep 5)*   Att: 867
Goole 2 Wakefield 0 *(Sep 15)*   Att: 130
Nantwich Town 1 Radcliffe Borough 1 *aet (7-6p) (Sep 4)* Att: 323
Ossett Albion 4 Harrogate Railway Athletic 2 *(Sep 26)* Att: 96
Quorn 2 Belper Town 1 *(Sep 25)*   Att: 60
Sheffield 6 Gresley Rovers 5 *aet (Sep 25)*   Att: 165
Shepshed Dynamo 3 **Grantham Town** 3 *aet (3-4p) (Oct 9)* Att: 77
Skelmersdale United 5 Lancaster City 0 *(Sep 25)*   Att: 141
Spalding United 2 Carlton Town 1 *(Sep 25)*   Att: 75
Stocksbridge Park Steels 2 Mossley 1 *(Sep 25)*   Att: 124
Woodley Sports 1 **Curzon Ashton** 2 *(Sep 18)*   Att: 110

SECOND ROUND

Alsager Town 1 **Curzon Ashton** 4 *(Oct 17)*   Att: 44
Bridlington Town 4 Brigg Town 2 *aet (Oct 16)*   Att: 106
Colwyn Bay 2 Bamber Bridge 1 *(Nov 13)*   Att: 102
Garforth Town 2 Ossett Albion 1 *aet (Oct 16)*   Att: 87
Goole 1 **Sheffield** 1 *aet (3-5p) (Oct 16)*   Att: 124
Kidsgrove Athletic 0 **Skelmersdale United** 3 *(Nov 14)*   Att: 98
Nantwich Town 5 Stocksbridge Park Steels 1 *(Oct 16)* Att: 306
Newcastle Blue Star 2 Bradford Park Avenue 1 *aet (Oct 17)* Att: 73
Retford United 1 **Quorn** 2 *(Oct 16)*   Att: 103
Spalding United 3 **Grantham Town** 6 *aet (Oct 16)*   Att: 70
Warrington Town 2 Rossendale United 0 *(Oct 16)*   Att: 85

THIRD ROUND

Bridlington Town 1 **Guiseley** 4 *(Nov 13)*   Att: 85
Colwyn Bay 2 **Witton Albion** 2 *aet (2-4p) (Nov 14)*   Att: 234
Curzon Ashton 1 Nantwich Town 1 *aet (5-4p) (Dec 3)* Att: 109
Eastwood Town 4 Matlock Town 3 *(Nov 13)*   Att: 191

Fleetwood Town 7 Warrington Town 3 *(Nov 14)*   Att: 224
Garforth Town 0 **Whitby Town** 6 *(Nov 13)*   Att: 113
Gateshead 2 Newcastle Blue Star 0 *(Nov 14)*   Att: 170
Hednesford Town 3 Ashton United 1 *aet (Nov 12)*   Att: 116
Ilkeston Town 2 Grantham Town 1 *(Nov 14)*   Att: 170
Kendal Town 3 **Skelmersdale United** 5 *aet (Nov 14)*   Att: 111
Leek Town 2 Buxton 1 *aet (Nov 13)*   Att: 320
Marine 3 Prescot Cables 1 *(Nov 13)*   Att: 120
North Ferriby United 2 Stamford 1 *(Nov 3)*   Att: 96
Ossett Town 0 **Frickley Athletic** 2 *(Nov 13)*   Att: 105
Sheffield 4 Lincoln United 2 *(Nov 13)*   Att: 150
Worksop Town 3 Quorn 0 *aet (Nov 13)*   Att: 190

FOURTH ROUND

Fleetwood Twn 2 **Marine** 3 *(Jan 5)*   Att: 421
Gateshead 3 Sheffield 2 *(Jan 5)*   Att: 217
Guiseley 3 **Eastwood Town** 4 *aet (Feb 9)*   Att: 242
Ilkeston Town 1 Hednesford Town 0 *(Jan 5)*   Att: 250
North Ferriby Utd 2 **Worksop Town** 2 *aet (4-5p) (Jan 5)* Att: 178
Skelmersdale United 3 Leek Town 1 *(Jan 5)*   Att: 176
Whitby Town 0 **Frickley Athletic** 1 *(Jan 5)*   Att: 119
Witton Albion 2 Curzon Ashton 1 *(Jan 5)*   Att: 231

QUARTER-FINALS

Ilkeston Town 1 **Eastwood Town** 1 *aet (3-4p) (Feb 9)* Att: 265
Skelmersdale United 2 Marine 0 *(Feb 9)*   Att: 314
Witton Albion 0 **Gateshead** 1 *(Feb 9)*   Att: 255
Worksop Town 0 **Frickley Athletic** 1 *aet (Feb 9)*   Att: 359

SEMI-FINALS

Eastwood Town 3 Frickley Athletic 1 *(Mar 8)*   Att: 279
Skelmersdale United 2 Gateshead 2 *aet (4-2p) (Mar 8)* Att: 259

FINAL

(Apr 21st at Curzon Ashton)
Eastwood Town 3 Skelmersdale United 0   Att: 372

PETER SWALES CHALLENGE CUP

(League champions v Chairman's Cup winners)

(May 3rd at Fleetwood Town)
Fleetwood Town 2 Bradford Park Avenue 1 *Att:* 388
(Chairman's Cup runners-up Bradford Park Avenue replaced winners Retford United
who had already arranged their presentation evening for May 3rd)

PRESIDENT'S CUP

(First Division teams)

FIRST ROUND

Garforth Town 3 **Wakefield** 3 *aet (2-3p) (Oct 2)*   Att: 60
Kidsgrove Athletic 1 **Radcliffe Borough** 3 *(Oct 31)*   Att: 84
Lancaster City 0 **Chorley** 2 *(Oct 2)*   Att: 115
Quorn 1 **Carlton Town** 4 *(Oct 2)*   Att: 59

SECOND ROUND

Belper Town 2 Gresley Rovers 1 *(Oct 30)*   Att: 115
Bridlington Town 2 **Ossett Albion** 3 *(Nov 6)*   Att: 77
Brigg Town 1 Carlton Town 1 *aet (4-2p) (Oct 20)*   Att: 97
Cammell Laird 3 Alsager Town 2 *(Oct 19)*   Att: 107
Chorley 1 **Nantwich Town** 2 *aet (Oct 30)*   Att: 136
Colwyn Bay 2 Woodley Sports 2 *aet (4-3p) (Oct 30)*   Att: 155
Curzon Ashton 1 **Stocksbridge Park Steels** 4 *(Oct 29)* Att: 119
FC United of Manchester 5 Bamber Bridge 0 *(Oct 30)* Att: 585
   (at Radcliffe Borough)
Goole 3 Spalding United 1 *(Oct 30)*   Att: 135
Harrogate Railway Ath 0 **Bradford Park Ave** 1 *(Nov 21)* Att: 65
Mossley 0 **Skelmersdale United** 0 *aet (5-6p) (Oct 30)* Att: 129
Newcastle Blue Star 1 **Wakefield** 2 *aet (Nov 28)*   Att: 68
Radcliffe Borough 4 Warrington Town 1 *(Dec 4)*   Att: 102
Rossendale United 3 Clitheroe 2 *(Oct 30)*   Att: 171
Sheffield 1 Grantham Town 0 *(Oct 30)*   Att: 218
Shepshed Dynamo 0 **Retford United** 2 *(Oct 30)*   Att: 122

THIRD ROUND

Brigg Town 3 Bradford Park Avenue 2 *(Jan 5)*   Att: 174
FC United of Manchester 2 Rossendale Utd 1 *(Jan 26)* Att: 1,554
Goole 2 Stocksbridge Park Steels 1 *(Jan 5)*   Att: 147
Nantwich Town 5 Cammell Laird 1 *(Jan 26)*   Att: 360
Ossett Albion 1 Colwyn Bay 0 *(Jan 5)*   Att: 115
Retford United 5 Sheffield 0 *(Jan 29)*   Att: 153
Skelmersdale United 1 **Radcliffe Borough** 2 *(Jan 8)*   Att: 153
Wakefield 2 Belper Town 1 *(Jan 5)*   Att: 79

QUARTER-FINALS

Goole 2 Wakefield 1 *(Feb 9)*   Att: 195
Nantwich Town 5 FC United of Manchester 1 *(Feb 25)* Att: 873
Radcliffe Borough 5 Brigg Town 1 *(Feb 9)*   Att: 142
Retford United 4 **Ossett Albion** 4 *aet (5-6p) (Feb 9)*   Att: 178

SEMI-FINALS

Goole 1 **FC United of Manchester** 3 *(Mar 8)*   Att: 967
Ossett Albion 0 **Radcliffe Borough** 1 *(Mar 8)*   Att: 125

FINAL

(Apr 17th at Curzon Ashton)
FC United of Manchester 2 Radcliffe Borough 0   Att: 1,753

NOTTS SENIOR LEAGUE

	Attenborough	Awsworth Villa	Basford United	Bilborough Peli.	Boots Athletic	Caribbean Cav.	Clifton	Cotgrave CW Utd	Gedling S'thbank	Keyworth United	Kimberley MW	Linby CW	Magdala Ams	Notts Police	Ruddington Utd	Sandhurst	Siemens EWS	Wollaton
Attenborough		3-4	2-1	0-0	0-2	2-1	2-2	3-2	4-2	1-2	1-2	3-2	0-5	1-3	2-0	2-2	5-3	4-3
Awsworth Villa	0-0	S	2-5	0-2	1-4	0-5	2-1	3-2	2-1	1-2	0-0	3-2	1-2	1-3	0-1	1-0	1-0	1-3
Basford United	1-0	5-3	E	W-L	0-1	3-0	3-5	1-3	2-0	1-2	4-1	1-2	4-1	2-0	2-0	1-1	3-2	4-0
Bilborough Pelican	2-0	2-0	2-4	N	4-1	2-3	3-2	3-0	2-1	3-2	3-1	9-0	1-1	4-0	4-3	2-1		1-2
Boots Athletic	3-1	0-0	1-1	2-2	I	3-3	2-0	4-0	2-3	4-1	2-2	0-0	2-1	2-0	1-2	1-1	3-2	0-1
Caribbean Cavaliers	2-2	7-0	2-0	5-1	1-1	O	1-0	3-0	5-1	0-0	4-3	3-1	5-1	3-2	3-1	2-1	2-1	4-3
Clifton	1-4	1-3	3-0	1-4	5-0	2-3	R	1-4	1-1	3-6	8-0	2-3	4-1	1-1	3-4	1-1	3-2	1-0
Cotgrave Colliery Welfare United	1-1	5-1	2-0	1-4	2-2	0-6	0-3		2-0	3-1	3-2	4-2	2-0	0-4	2-4	2-2	3-2	0-1
Gedling Southbank	3-2	4-1	1-3	1-3	0-1	0-1	2-1	2-0	D	2-2	1-1	1-3	2-2	0-2	1-1	3-2	2-0	2-3
Keyworth United	1-4	2-1	0-2	2-2	0-1	5-4	1-0	3-3	2-1	D	3-0	3-1	5-0	2-2	3-0	5-1	2-0	3-1
Kimberley Miners Welfare	3-2	4-1	3-1	2-2	4-0	1-3	4-1	4-2	0-1	1-2	I	1-2	3-1	2-1	0-0	6-0	0-0	
Linby Colliery Welfare	1-2	1-3	2-0	1-1	0-4	0-1	1-5	2-0	1-0	2-1	2-0	V	2-1	3-3	2-1	2-0	5-1	3-2
Magdala Amateurs	1-2	2-2	0-3	3-5	1-2	2-3	0-1	0-3	1-2	0-4	2-2	5-1	I	3-2	1-0	0-4	2-1	2-2
Notts Police	2-0	3-2	2-5	1-1	1-2	1-3	3-7	2-2	0-3	1-2	3-0	3-2	4-0	S	2-0	4-4	2-1	0-1
Ruddington United	0-3	1-4	2-0	0-5	1-0	0-0	1-1	1-2	1-4	1-3	1-2	0-0	1-1	1-2	I	4-2	5-1	2-3
Sandhurst	2-1	3-1	3-2	2-7	0-0	0-1	2-3	0-2	0-1	1-9	1-2	3-2	1-3	0-3	0-4	O	4-0	1-2
Siemens EWS	0-1	2-2	1-3	3-1	0-3	1-2	2-4	1-2	1-1	0-0	4-3	1-6	0-3	0-2	2-1	2-1	N	0-2
Wollaton	2-4	1-2	1-4	1-2	2-2	0-4	1-2	5-4	1-0	0-1	0-4	2-0	2-0	4-0	0-0	1-2	3-1	

Senior Division

	P	W	D	L	F	A	Pts
Caribbean Cavaliers	34	26	5	3	93	41	83
Keyworth United	34	21	6	7	85	47	69
Bilborough Pelican	34	20	8	6	92	49	68
Boots Athletic	34	17	10	7	60	40	61
Basford United	34	19	2	13	71	50	59
Wollaton	34	16	5	13	55	57	53
Notts Police	34	14	8	12	65	58	50
Attenborough	34	14	6	14	61	61	48
Cotgrave Colliery Welfare Utd	34	14	5	15	59	69	47
Kimberley Miners Welfare	34	13	7	14	61	64	46
Linby Colliery Welfare	34	14	4	16	58	61	46
Gedling Southbank	34	13	6	15	50	54	45
Clifton	34	13	5	16	79	70	44
Awsworth Villa	34	10	6	18	48	79	36
Ruddington United	34	10	5	19	43	64	35
Magdala Amateurs	34	9	5	20	49	87	32
Sandhurst	34	6	8	20	49	80	26
Siemens EWS	34	5	3	26	40	87	18

Division One

		P	W	D	L	F	A	Pts
Hucknall Rolls Leisure		34	31	3	0	115	28	96
Matrixgrade		34	23	4	7	85	34	73
Underwood Villa		34	23	4	7	91	49	73
Wollaton Res.		34	21	3	10	85	39	66
Bilborough Pelican Res.		34	21	3	10	62	45	66
Gedling Southbank Res.		34	18	3	13	85	60	57
Clifton Res.		34	17	3	14	77	62	54
Keyworth United Res.		34	15	6	13	63	53	51
Cotgrave Colliery Welfare Utd Res.	-3	34	15	5	14	62	68	47
Kimberley Miners Welfare Res.		34	12	6	16	68	89	42
Linby Colliery Welfare Res.		34	12	5	17	49	68	41
Boots Athletic Res.		34	12	4	18	60	69	40
Basford United Res.	-3	34	10	7	17	55	67	34
Caribbean Cavaliers Res.	-3	34	10	5	19	59	88	32
Magdala Amateurs Res.		34	10	2	22	58	89	29
Awsworth Villa Res.		34	6	6	22	54	102	24
Attenborough Res.		34	6	6	22	43	92	24
Sandhurst Res.		34	6	1	27	42	111	19

SENIOR CUP

PRELIMINARY ROUND
Awsworth Villa 1 **Siemens** 4
Bestwood Miners Welfare (scr.)
v **Clifton** (w/o)
Cotgrave Colliery Welfare
United 0 **Boots Athletic** 1
Notts Police 0 **Wollaton** 2
Sandhurst 1 **Matrixgrade** 2

FIRST ROUND
Basford United 1 **Boots Athletic** 4
Bilborough Pelican 1
Attenborough 2
Clifton 3 **Wollaton** 5
Hucknall Rolls Leisure 2
Matrixgrade 1
Magdala Amateurs 1 **Gedling
Southbank** 3
Ruddington United 0 Keyworth
United 0 *aet* (5-3p)
Siemens 0 **Caribbean Cavaliers** 5
Underwood Villa 1 **Linby C W** 4

QUARTER-FINALS
Attenborough 2 Basford United 1
Caribbean Cavaliers 2 Gedling
Southbank 0
Linby Colliery Welfare 3
Hucknall Rolls Leisure 2
Wollaton 0 **Ruddington United** 3

SEMI-FINALS
Attenborough 0 **Linby Colliery
Welfare** 2
(at Bilborough Pelican)
Caribbean Cavaliers 3
Ruddington United 3 *aet* (3-2p)
(at Cotgrave Colliery Welfare)

FINAL
(May 14th at Hucknall Town)
Caribbean Cavaliers 4 Linby
Colliery Welfare 0

JUNIOR CUP

FINAL
(May 12th at Hucknall Town)
Basford United Res. 2 **Wollaton** Res. 2 *aet* (2-3p)

WWW.NLNEWSDESK.CO.UK

PRECISION TRAINING NOTTS SENIOR LEAGUE SENIOR DIVISION CONSTITUTION 2008-09
ATTENBOROUGH . . . . Village Green, The Strand, Attenborough NG9 6AU 0115 925 7439
AWSWORTH VILLA . . . . Shilo Park, Attewell Road, Awsworth NG16 2SY 0115 849 8741
BASFORD UNITED . . . . Greenwich Avenue, Bagnall Road, Basford, Nottingham NG6 0LE 01949 839412
BILBOROUGH PELICAN . . Brian Wakefield Sports Ground, Trentside Lane, Old Lenton Lane, Nottingham NG7 2SA 0115 929 4728
BOOTS ATHLETIC . . . . . . Siemens Sports Ground, Trent Vale Road, Beeston Rylands, Nottingham NG9 1ND 07904 409689
CARIBBEAN CAVALIERS . . . . Carrington Sports Ground, Mansfield Road, Nottingham NG5 2EJ . . . . None
CLIFTON . . . . Green Lane, Clifton, Nottingham NG11 9AY 0115 921 5401
COTGRAVE COLLIERY WELFARE UNITED . . . The Woodview Ground, Woodview, Cotgrave, Nottingham NG12 3PJ 0115 989 2414
GEDLING SOUTHBANK . . . . Carlton Recreation Ground, Carlton Hill, Nottingham 0115 926 6375
HUCKNALL ROLLS LEISURE . . . Rolls Royce Sports & Social, Rolls Royce Number One Works, Watnall Road, Hucknall 0115 964 2380
KEYWORTH UNITED . . . . Platt Lane Sports Complex, Keyworth, Nottingham NG12 5GE 0115 974 5568
KIMBERLEY MINERS WELFARE . . . . Digby Street, Kimberley, Nottingham NG16 2HP 0115 938 4067
LINBY COLLIERY WELFARE . . . . Church Lane, Linby Village, Linby NG15 8AB 0115 953 8491
MAGDALA AMATEURS . . . . . . ROKO Health Club, Wilford Lane, West Bridgford, Nottingham NG2 7RN 0115 982 7799
MATRIXGRADE . . . . Bilsthorpe Miners Welfare, Eakring Road, Bilsthorpe, Newark NG22 8PY 07866 590693
NOTTS POLICE . . . . Bestwood Workshops, Park Road, Bestwood Village, Nottingham 0115 967 0999
RUDDINGTON UNITED . . . . The Elms Park, Loughborough Road, Ruddington NG11 6NX 0115 921 1204
SANDHURST . . . . Walesby Village Sports Club, Forest Lane, Walesby NG22 9PE 01623 860456
WOLLATON . . . . Wollaton Sports Association, Wollaton Road, Wollaton, Nottingham NG8 2AA 0115 928 3875
IN: Hucknall Rolls Leisure (P), Matrixgrade (P)
OUT: Siemens EWS (F)

OXFORDSHIRE SENIOR LEAGUE

	Adderbury Park	BCS Bardwell	Chadlington	Enstone Sports	Eynsham Association	Garsington	Horspath	Kennington United	Oxford University Press	Rover Cowley	Stonesfield Sports	Watlington Town	Worcester COB & Bletchington
Adderbury Park		8-0	1-1	2-1	3-1	1-4	0-4	2-2	3-0	3-4	1-2	5-1	1-3
BCS Bardwell	0-2	P	1-1	0-1	1-3	4-5	W-L	1-4	2-6	0-1	1-5	4-1	3-2
Chadlington	3-1	7-0	R	1-0	4-1	4-0	3-2	3-0	2-2	1-2	0-0	4-3	2-1
Enstone Sports	1-4	4-1	1-1	E	0-2	3-4	3-1	3-0	1-1	0-2	2-4	5-0	1-1
Eynsham Association	2-1	3-2	0-0	2-2	M	2-2	0-0	4-2	2-1	0-4	2-4	6-0	2-0
Garsington	4-2	6-2	4-4	5-4	2-1	I	2-5	2-5	4-3	3-0	1-3	4-3	3-5
Horspath	2-2	3-2	0-2	1-1	0-1	2-1	E	2-1	3-2	1-4	2-2	2-1	5-1
Kennington United	2-0	0-0	1-1	1-2	3-2	1-1	2-2	R	2-2	1-3	1-1	3-5	1-3
Oxford University Press	0-1	0-1	0-3	2-2	2-3	1-9	4-2	5-4		4-3	1-6	6-0	1-4
Rover Cowley	1-0	4-1	0-2	0-4	2-2	3-1	2-0	2-0	3-2	D	0-0	2-0	1-3
Stonesfield Sports	1-0	3-0	2-1	0-1	2-1	1-2	3-3	5-0	1-0	0-1	I	1-1	5-2
Watlington Town	1-1	5-1	0-3	2-4	1-4	2-0	0-5	1-5	1-1	2-10	0-2	V	0-6
Worcester COB & Bletchington	3-2	6-1	0-6	1-1	0-4	2-6	1-4	3-1	1-1	2-3	0-2	5-0	

Premier Division	P	W	D	L	F	A	Pts
Rover Cowley	24	17	2	5	57	32	53
Stonesfield Sports	24	15	6	3	55	23	51
Chadlington	24	14	8	2	59	22	50
Eynsham Association	24	13	5	6	51	37	44
Garsington	24	13	3	8	77	64	42
Horspath	24	10	6	8	51	40	36
Enstone Sports	24	9	7	8	47	38	34
Worcester COB & Bletchington	24	10	3	11	55	56	33
Adderbury Park	24	8	4	12	46	43	28
Kennington United	24	5	6	13	42	56	21
Oxford University Press	24	5	6	13	47	63	21
BCS Bardwell	24	4	2	18	28	80	14
Watlington Town	24	2	4	18	30	91	10

PRESIDENT'S CUP

FIRST ROUND
Enstone Sports 0 **Kidlington Old Boys** 2 *aet*
Garsington 4 Eynsham Association 2
Horspath 11 Yarnton 0
Kennington United 1 BCS Bardwell 0
Long Crendon 2 Wheatley '04 1
Middle Barton (scr.) v **Fritwell** (w/o)
Oakley United 2 **Adderbury Park** 6
Oxford University Press 5 Kings Sutton 1
Rover Cowley 2 Chadlington 1
Stonesfield Sports 4 Charlton United 0
Watlington Town 3 **North Oxford** 4
Worcester COB & Bletchington 1 Marston Saints 1 *aet*
(9-8p)

BEN TURNER CUP
(President's Cup First Round losers)

FIRST ROUND
Enstone Sports 2 Charlton United 0
Eynsham Association 1 Chadlington 0
Yarnton 2 **Wheatley '04** 6 *aet*
QUARTER-FINALS
Eynsham Association 1 Kings Sutton 0
Marston Saints 3 Watlington Town 2

Oakley United 4 BCS Bardwell 1 *aet*
Wheatley '04 1 **Enstone Sports** 2 *aet*
SEMI-FINALS
Enstone Sports 0 **Marston Saints** 2
Eynsham Association 2 **Oakley United** 3
FINAL *(May 10th at Charlton United)*
Oakley United 0 **Marston Saints** 2 *aet*

OXFORDSHIRE SENIOR LEAGUE PREMIER DIVISION CONSTITUTION 2008-09

ADDERBURY PARK........ Adderbury Park Playing Fields, Round Close Road, Adderbury, Banbury OX17 .... None
BLETCHINGTON .... Rover Cowley Sports Ground, Oxford 01865 775463
CHADLINGTON .... Chadlington Sports & Social, Chapel Road, Chadlington, Chipping Norton OX7 3NX 01608 676723
ENSTONE SPORTS .... Charlbury Road, Enstone, Oxford OX2 6UT 01608 677823
EYNSHAM ASSOCIATION .... Oxford Road, Eynsham, Witney OX29 4DA .... None
GARSINGTON .... Garsington Sports Club, Denton Lane, Garsington, Oxford OX44 9EL 01865 361720
HORSPATH .... Brookes University Campus, Wheatley, Oxford OX4 6LB .... None
KENNINGTON UNITED .... Playfield Road, Kennington, Oxford OX1 5RS.......................... None
MARSTON SAINTS........................ Boults Lane, Old Marston, Oxford OX3 0PW 01865 203970
OXFORD UNIVERSITY PRESS............. Jordan Hill, Banbury Road, Oxford OX2 8EF .... None
ROVER COWLEY .... Pressed Steel Sports Ground, Roman Way, Beckley, Oxford OX3 9UA .... None
STONESFIELD SPORTS................. Stonesfield Playing Field, off Longmore, Stonesfield .... None
IN: Marston Saints (P)
OUT: BCS Bardwell (R), Watlington Town (R)
Worcester COB & Bletchington become Bletchington

Note – Middle Barton withdrew during the course of the season

Their results are shown herein but are expunged from the league table

	Charlton United	Eynsham Association Res.	Fritwell	Garsington Res.	Kidlington Old Boys	Kings Sutton	Long Crendon	Marston Saints	Middle Barton	Middleton Cheney	North Oxford	Oakley United	Wheatley '04	Yarnton
Charlton United		2-4	2-2	1-4	1-3	4-0	3-0	3-0	3-1	0-1	2-1	0-4	3-2	1-1
Eynsham Association Res.	0-5	D	2-1	0-2	0-2	3-1	4-0	1-3	3-1	1-0	3-4	W-L	2-3	1-2
Fritwell	2-0	5-1	I	4-1	2-2	3-0	2-1	0-0	n/a	2-1	3-3	W-L	3-1	6-2
Garsington Res.	1-0	2-1	4-2	V	2-0	4-3	W-L	2-0	6-1	3-0	3-0	2-2	3-1	2-0
Kidlington Old Boys	4-2	8-1	2-2	2-2	I	5-1	12-0	2-0	n/a	0-3	0-9	4-3	4-2	2-1
Kings Sutton	5-2	2-3	1-3	0-7	0-5	S	2-2	0-3	n/a	2-4	1-3	L-W	1-1	2-0
Long Crendon	2-1	0-1	0-4	0-5	1-5	2-2	I	0-1	4-0	1-3	1-5	2-3	1-2	2-0
Marston Saints	3-2	3-3	3-0	3-0	2-2	5-1	2-0	O	4-0	1-2	5-0	2-1	6-0	3-1
Middle Barton	n/a	1-2	1-6	n/a	1-5	n/a	3-2	0-5	N	0-2	n/a	n/a	0-3	1-3
Middleton Cheney	3-1	5-1	2-2	1-2	0-1	7-2	2-0	1-3	1-0		2-0	2-0	4-0	3-1
North Oxford	3-1	5-2	1-2	1-1	2-2	3-2	3-0	0-2	5-2	1-0	O	1-3	3-0	0-0
Oakley United	1-3	2-3	1-3	1-6	1-2	4-0	5-1	1-4	n/a	3-1	1-0	N	2-5	2-2
Wheatley '04	2-2	0-1	1-4	0-4	0-3	5-3	4-0	1-3	n/a	1-6	3-1	1-3	E	0-1
Yarnton	0-5	3-2	0-1	3-3	1-4	3-3	2-5	0-2	n/a	0-4	0-2	1-1	1-2	

Division One	P	W	D	L	F	A	Pts
Garsington Res.	24	18	4	2	65	25	58
Marston Saints	24	17	3	4	59	23	54
Kidlington Old Boys	24	16	5	3	76	38	53
Fritwell	24	15	6	3	58	31	51
Middleton Cheney	24	15	1	8	57	28	46
North Oxford	24	10	5	9	51	41	35
Eynsham Association Res.	24	10	1	13	40	60	31
Oakley United	24	9	3	12	48	46	30
Wheatley '04	24	9	1	14	39	62	28
Charlton United	24	8	3	13	46	48	27
Yarnton	24	2	8	14	27	60	14
Long Crendon	24	3	1	20	21	74	10
Kings Sutton	24	2	3	19	34	85	9

Middle Barton – record expunged

Division Two	P	W	D	L	F	A	Pts
Worcester COB & Bletchington Res.	26	18	6	2	99	29	60
Oxford University Press Res.	26	18	5	3	71	36	59
Horspath Res.	26	17	4	5	92	36	55
Chadlington Res.	26	17	4	5	79	36	55
Kidlington Old Boys Res.	26	16	6	4	86	45	54
Yarnton Res.	26	14	2	10	84	39	44
Adderbury Park Res.	26	11	6	9	72	54	39
Stonesfield Sports Res.	26	10	6	10	37	41	36
Marston Saints Res.	26	10	3	13	58	69	33
Fritwell Res.	26	7	5	14	54	63	26
Oakley United Res.	26	7	3	16	51	79	24
Charlton United Res.	26	5	2	19	37	104	17
Enstone Sports Res.	26	3	4	19	35	104	13
Kings Sutton Res.	26	0	2	24	24	144	2

SECOND ROUND
Fritwell 1 **Kidlington Old Boys** 2

Garsington *(bye)*

Kennington United 5 Long Crendon 2

Middleton Cheney *(bye)*

North Oxford 2 **Horspath** 5 *aet*

Oxford University Press *(bye)*

Rover Cowley 1 **Adderbury Park** 4

Stonesfield Sports 3 Worcester COB & Bletchington 1

QUARTER-FINALS
Garsington 2 **Adderbury Park** 5

Horspath 0 **Stonesfield Sports** 1

Kennington United 2 Oxford University Press 1

Middleton Cheney 2 **Kidlington Old Boys** 5

SEMI-FINALS
Adderbury Park 3 Kennington United 0

Stonesfield Sports 2 Kidlington Old Boys 1 *aet*

FINAL
(March 24th at Oxford University Press)

Adderbury Park 1 **Stonesfield Sports** 2

CLARENDON CUP

FINAL
(March 24th at Oxford University Press)

Garsington Res. 3 Kidlington Old Boys Res. 1

IVOR GUBBINS CUP

FINAL
(April 26th at Garsington)

Yarnton 0 **Oxford University Press Res.** 4

OXFORDSHIRE SENIOR LEAGUE DIVISION ONE CONSTITUTION 2008-09

BCS BARDWELL...................Chaffinch Way, Mallards Way Estate, Bicester ....None
CHARLTON UNITED ....Charlton PF, Oddington Road, Charlton-on-Otmoor, Kidlington OX5 2TJ.......................None
EYNSHAM ASSOCIATION RESERVES ......Oxford Road, Eynsham, Witney OX29 4DA............................None
FRITWELL......................Playing Field, Fewcott Road, Fritwell OX27 7QA.....................None
GARSINGTON RESERVES ......Garsington Sports Club, Denton Lane, Garsington, Oxford OX44 9EL 01865 361720
KIDLINGTON OLD BOYS ....Exeter Close, Crown Road, Kidlington OX5 1AP.....................None
MIDDLETON CHENEY ....Astrop Road, Middleton Cheney, Banbury OX17 2PG ....None
NORTH OXFORD ....Lord Nuffield Club, Barracks Lane OR Rover Cowley, Romanway, Oxford ....None
OAKLEY UNITED ....Playfield Fields, Oxford Road, Oakley, Aylesbury HP18 9RE.....................None
WATLINGTON TOWN ....Shirburn Road, Watlington OX49 5BZ................................None
WHEATLEY '04............................Holton Playing Fields, Wheatley, Oxford ....None
YARNTON ....Green Lane, Yarnton 01865 842037
IN: BCS Bardwell (R), Watlington Town (R)
OUT: Kings Sutton (W), Long Crendon (R), Marston Saints (P), Middle Barton (WS)

PETERBOROUGH & DISTRICT LEAGUE

	AFC Fletton	Alconbury	Crowland Town	Deeping Sports	Hampton Athletic	Leverington Sports	Moulton Harrox	Oundle Town	Parson Drove	Perkins Sports	Peterborough Sports	Pinchbeck United	Stamford Belvedere	Uppingham Town	Whittlesey United	Wimblington
AFC Fletton	P	2-2	0-1	1-3	2-1	2-8	0-2	2-3	3-0	3-4	3-0	3-1	3-2	2-1	4-7	3-2
Alconbury	4-2	R	5-2	2-1	0-6	1-2	1-4	4-3	4-0	1-1	5-6	1-0	7-0	8-0	2-4	1-1
Crowland Town	1-2	0-2	E	2-4	3-5	2-3	0-0	1-1	0-5	4-5	1-7	2-1	4-1	1-3	1-5	4-2
Deeping Sports	1-3	5-4	3-1	M	1-1	0-3	1-2	4-1	0-2	1-1	0-0	1-0	5-1	3-2	2-2	0-1
Hampton Athletic	6-1	1-3	5-0	3-2	I	2-1	1-2	2-2	1-0	0-2	6-2	2-1	2-1	5-1	2-1	3-0
Leverington Sports	1-0	3-1	2-1	2-2	2-3	E	2-0	3-1	1-1	3-3	7-2	2-0	2-1	1-1	1-1	4-3
Moulton Harrox	3-0	1-1	3-0	1-0	1-1	1-2	R	0-1	3-1	1-2	1-2	2-0	1-1	7-0	1-0	0-1
Oundle Town	2-8	0-2	2-6	1-6	2-5	2-1	0-7		1-1	3-10	2-2	1-2	4-0	3-0	0-11	2-1
Parson Drove	0-1	1-0	1-1	1-0	0-2	2-0	3-2	2-1	D	0-0	2-0	2-0	3-0	4-0	1-0	1-0
Perkins Sports	1-0	7-4	5-2	1-1	4-3	2-0	1-0	7-1	1-0	I	0-4	6-3	6-0	5-0	0-1	5-1
Peterborough Sports	1-2	3-4	4-1	3-1	3-5	0-0	1-4	6-2	0-0	2-3	V	7-4	1-1	3-5	3-3	1-2
Pinchbeck United	1-2	6-3	1-4	2-2	4-2	3-0	1-0	4-0	0-0	1-2	4-2	I	2-2	4-2	3-1	0-2
Stamford Belvedere	1-2	0-4	3-0	1-2	0-1	0-1	0-4	1-5	2-0	1-3	2-0	2-2	S	3-1	1-3	1-2
Uppingham Town	2-6	1-8	3-2	1-4	1-4	3-3	1-3	2-0	1-1	4-1	1-2	2-4	1-2	I	0-4	2-1
Whittlesey United	2-5	3-1	3-0	1-2	5-2	2-0	2-0	6-0	2-3	1-2	6-0	0-1	2-3	4-1	O	3-4
Wimblington	0-3	5-1	6-2	2-1	2-3	1-2	0-3	2-1	3-0	1-5	4-1	3-1	1-3	3-5	1-1	N

WWW.CHERRYRED.CO.UK

Premier Division		P	W	D	L	F	A	Pts
Perkins Sports		30	22	6	2	95	43	72
Hampton Athletic		30	20	3	7	85	49	63
Moulton Harrox		30	17	4	9	61	24	55
AFC Fletton		30	17	1	12	70	63	52
Leverington Sports	-3	30	16	6	8	61	45	51
Whittlesey United		30	15	4	11	87	46	49
Parson Drove		30	14	6	10	36	29	48
Alconbury	-1	30	14	4	12	86	70	45
Deeping Sports	-1	30	12	7	11	58	48	42
Wimblington	-1	30	13	2	15	57	62	40
Pinchbeck United		30	11	4	15	54	59	37
Peterborough Sports	-1	30	8	6	16	67	84	29
Uppingham Town		30	8	3	19	49	100	27
Stamford Belvedere		30	6	5	19	38	78	23
Crowland Town		30	6	3	21	49	92	21
Oundle Town	-4	30	7	4	19	47	108	21

PETERBOROUGH SENIOR CUP

(Premier Division teams and
top eight Division One first teams)

FIRST ROUND
Ketton 1 **Deeping Sports** 4
Leverington Sports 2 Hampton Athletic 2 *aet* (5-4p)
Moulton Harrox 1 Long Sutton Athletic 0
Rutland Rangers 3 Stamford Belvedere 2
Thorney 3 Crowland Town 0
Wimblington 1 **Pinchbeck United** 3
SECOND ROUND
Moulton Harrox 2 **Chatteris Town** 3
Netherton United 2 Pinchbeck United 1
Oundle Town 2 Whittlesey United 0
Parson Drove 3 Thorney 2

Perkins Sports 2 Leverington Sports 1
Peterborough Sports 2 Deeping Sports 2 *aet* (5-4p)
Rutland Rangers 1 **AFC Fletton** 2
Uppingham Town 3 **Alconbury** 4
QUARTER-FINALS
AFC Fletton 6 Peterborough Sports 2
Chatteris Town 1 **Perkins Sports** 3
Netherton United 2 **Alconbury** 0
Parson Drove 1 Oundle Town 0
SEMI-FINALS
AFC Fletton 0 **Parson Drove** 1
Netherton United 1 **Perkins Sports** 2
FINAL
(May 5th at Peterborough United)
Perkins Sports 2 Parson Drove 0

JACK HOGG CHARITY SHIELD

(League champions v Peterborough Senior Cup holders)

(August 10th at PFA, Chestnut Avenue)
Peterborough Sports 10 Alconbury 1

MARSHALLS PETERBOROUGH & DISTRICT LEAGUE PREMIER DIVISION CONSTITUTION 2008-09

AFC FLETTON . . . . Celta Road, Peterborough PE2 9JD 01733 556104
ALCONBURY . . . . Great North Road, Alconbury, Huntingdon PE28 4EX 01480 891313
CROWLAND TOWN . . . . Snowden Field, Thorney Road, Crowland PE6 0AL 01733 211548
DEEPING SPORTS . . . . Deeping Rangers FC, Outgang Road, Towngate East, Market Deeping PE6 8LQ 01778 344701
LEVERINGTON SPORTS . . . . Church Road, Leverington, Wisbech PE13 5DE 01945 465082
MOULTON HARROX . . . . Broad Lane, Moulton, Spalding PE12 6PN 01406 371991
OUNDLE TOWN . . . . Station Road, Oundle, Peterborough PE8 4DE 01832 274188
PARSON DROVE . . . . Main Road, Parson Drove, Wisbech PE13 4LF . . . . None
PETERBOROUGH SPORTS . . . . . Peterborough Sports & Leisure, Lincoln Road, Peterborough PE1 3HA 01733 567835
PINCHBECK UNITED . . . . Glebe Playing Fields, Knight Street, Pinchbeck, Spalding PE11 3RB 01775 762057
RAMSEY TOWN . . . . Cricketfield Lane, Ramsey, Huntingdon PE26 1BG 01487 814218
RUTLAND RANGERS . . . . Greetham Community Centre, Great Lane, Greetham, Oakham LE15 7NG 01572 812544
STAMFORD BELVEDERE . . . . Queen Eleanor School, Green Lane, Stamford PE9 1HE 01780 751011
UPPINGHAM TOWN . . . . North Street East, Uppingham LE15 9QJ 01572 821446
WHITTLESEY UNITED . . . . Manor Leisure Centre, Station Road, Whittlesey, Peterborough PE7 1UE 01733 202298
WIMBLINGTON . . . . Parkfield Sports & Social Club, Chapel Lane, Wimblington, March PE15 0QX 01354 741555
IN: Ramsey Town (P), Rutland Rangers (P)
OUT: Chatteris Town (P – Cambridgeshire County League Senior Division B), Hampton Athletic (F), Perkins Sports (F)

Division One	P	W	D	L	F	A	Pts
Ramsey Town	24	21	3	0	93	16	66
Rutland Rangers	24	17	3	4	78	31	54
Netherton United	24	14	7	3	57	27	49
Coates Athletic	24	11	10	3	61	32	43
Long Sutton Athletic	24	10	6	8	56	48	36
Chatteris Town	24	7	8	9	48	50	29
Werrington Town	24	8	3	13	46	66	27
Guyhirn	24	7	4	13	52	69	25
Thorney	*-1*	24	7	5	12	36	63	25
Ketton	24	5	8	11	36	61	23
Kings Cliffe United	24	5	5	14	45	67	20
Sutton Bridge United	*-6*	24	6	3	15	34	82	15
Bretton Park Rangers	*-3*	24	2	7	15	29	59	10

Division Two	P	W	D	L	F	A	Pts
Stilton United	24	20	2	2	122	28	62
Eye Sports	24	20	1	3	87	32	61
Warboys Town	24	18	3	3	90	25	57
Manea United	24	18	0	6	92	35	54
Sawtry	*-1*	24	14	1	9	70	51	42
Langtoft United	*-3*	24	13	3	8	59	46	39
Castor & Ailsworth	*-7*	24	12	2	10	66	65	31
Doddington United	24	9	1	14	65	69	28
Real March	24	7	2	15	55	86	23
Peterborough Rovers	24	7	1	16	42	74	22
Benwick Athletic	24	3	3	18	32	101	12
March St Marys	*-1*	24	3	2	19	38	97	10
Chatteris Fen Tigers	24	1	1	22	27	136	4

Combination One	P	W	D	L	F	A	Pts
Whittlesey United Res.	28	22	3	3	124	32	69
Perkins Sports Res.	28	21	1	6	76	33	64
Ramsey Town Res.	*-1*	28	18	3	7	86	62	56
Moulton Harrox Res.	28	17	4	7	85	46	55
Holbeach United Res.	28	18	0	10	89	70	54
Deeping Sports Res.	28	13	2	13	67	58	41
Chatteris Town Res.	28	11	6	11	64	81	39
Parson Drove Res.	28	11	3	14	44	53	36
Oundle Town Res.	28	10	2	16	67	92	32
Alconbury Res.	28	9	3	16	43	72	30
Langtoft United Res.	*-1*	28	9	4	15	44	81	30
AFC Fletton Res.	*-4*	28	9	3	16	67	103	26
Leverington Sports Res.	*-4*	28	8	5	15	38	56	25
Hampton Athletic Res.	*-3*	28	8	1	19	50	70	22
Stamford Belvedere Res.	28	5	2	21	31	66	17

Combination Two	P	W	D	L	F	A	Pts
Wimblington Res.	26	19	5	2	76	35	62
Long Sutton Athletic Res.	26	18	2	6	82	42	56
Pinchbeck United Res.	*-4*	26	18	2	6	107	42	52
Netherton United Res.	26	11	7	8	53	44	40
Bretton Park Rangers Res.	*-1*	26	12	2	12	58	55	37
Ketton Res.	26	11	4	11	58	65	37
Eye Sports & Social Res.	26	11	3	12	62	72	36
Peterborough Sports Res.	*-1*	26	11	3	12	70	68	35
Stamford Belvedere 'A'	*-1*	26	9	5	12	41	63	31
Werrington Town Res.	26	8	4	14	52	62	28
Doddington United Res.	26	8	2	16	54	81	26
Uppingham Town Res.	26	8	2	16	40	71	26
Crowland Town Res.	26	8	1	17	54	82	25
Kings Cliffe United Res.	26	6	6	14	45	70	24

Combination Three		P	W	D	L	F	A	Pts
Ramsey Town 'A'		20	13	4	3	88	33	43
Coates Athletic Res.		20	12	6	2	52	27	42
Netherton United 'A'		20	11	7	2	68	35	40
Rutland Rangers Res.	*-3*	20	11	3	6	66	33	33
Wimblington 'A'		20	9	6	5	53	42	33
Leverington Sports 'A'		20	8	5	7	48	44	29
Chatteris Town 'A'		20	8	5	7	55	64	29
Thorney Res.		20	8	3	9	42	42	27
Manea United Res.	*-3*	20	4	4	12	39	68	13
Crowland Town 'A'		20	3	0	17	27	94	9
Sutton Bridge United Res.	*-3*	20	1	1	18	30	86	1

PETERBOROUGH CHALLENGE CUP

FINAL

(May 2nd at PFA, Chestnut Avenue)

Ramsey Town 2 Sawtry 1

PETERBOROUGH JUNIOR CUP

FINAL

(April 25th at PFA, Chestnut Avenue)

Deeping Sports Res. 0 **Whittlesey United Res.** 1

PETERBOROUGH MINOR CUP

FINAL

(April 9th at PFA, Chestnut Avenue)

Doddington United Res 0 **Peterborough Sports Res.** 2

READING LEAGUE

	Berks County Sports	Cookham Dean	Highmoor/IBIS	Mortimer	Newbury	Rabson Rovers	Reading YMCA	Royal Mail	Westwood United	Woodcote & Stoke Row	Woodley Town
Berks County Sports	S	0-2	0-1	2-1	0-3	2-2	0-1	3-2	2-1	2-1	3-2
Cookham Dean	4-0	E	1-1	3-1	0-2	3-0	2-0	0-2	1-2	1-0	2-3
Highmoor/IBIS	8-0	0-2	N	0-0	7-1	4-0	0-0	3-0	0-5	0-1	2-2
Mortimer	2-2	0-0	1-0	I	0-2	4-3	2-0	1-0	3-3	1-2	0-0
Newbury	2-3	0-0	3-1	4-0	O	1-1	4-0	2-1	1-1	5-2	1-3
Rabson Rovers	1-1	1-1	3-1	4-1	3-5	R	2-1	1-0	1-4	1-3	0-3
Reading YMCA	1-1	0-0	0-3	1-2	0-0	1-0		3-1	2-1	3-1	3-2
Royal Mail	0-0	0-6	1-0	3-1	1-1	3-3	3-4		2-3	3-1	1-0
Westwood United	3-0	0-0	4-0	2-4	4-2	3-1	2-2	3-2	D	2-1	2-0
Woodcote & Stoke Row	5-1	0-3	2-5	3-2	2-5	0-3	1-3	W-L	2-4	I	2-3
Woodley Town	0-0	1-3	0-5	7-1	0-2	5-2	0-1	3-0	2-1	4-1	V

WWW.CHERRYRED.CO.UK

SENIOR CUP
(Senior and Premier Division teams)

FIRST ROUND
AFC Corinthians 3 Marlow United Res. 2
Hurst 2 **Newbury** 8
Mortimer 8 Spencers Wood 0
Rabson Rovers 4 Frilsham & Yattendon 1
Royal Mail 2 Highmoor/IBIS 1
Shinfield 2 Wokingham & Emmbrook 'A' 1

SECOND ROUND
Berks County Sports 5 AFC Corinthians 3
Cookham Dean 4 Newbury 2 *aet*
Forest Old Boys (scr.) v **Mortimer** (w/o)
Royal Mail 3 Unity 1 *aet*
Taplow United 1 **Shinfield** 3
West Reading 1 **Reading YMCA** 6
Westwood United 4 **Rabson Rovers** 4 *aet* (4-5p)
Woodcote & Stoke Row 3 Woodley Town 2

QUARTER-FINALS
Berks County Sports 1 **Mortimer** 2
Rabson Rovers 1 **Cookham Dean** 2
Reading YMCA 5 Woodcote & Stoke Row 1
Royal Mail 1 **Shinfield** 4

SEMI-FINALS
Mortimer 0 **Cookham Dean** 2 *(at Highmoor/IBIS)*
Reading YMCA 3 **Shinfield** 5 *(at Mortimer)*

FINAL
(May 15th at Reading)
Cookham Dean 4 Shinfield 2

Senior Division	P	W	D	L	F	A	Pts
Westwood United	20	12	4	4	50	28	40
Newbury	20	11	5	4	46	29	38
Cookham Dean	20	10	6	4	34	13	36
Reading YMCA	20	9	5	6	26	27	32
Woodley Town	20	9	3	8	40	32	30
Highmoor/IBIS	20	8	4	8	41	26	28
Berks County Sports	20	6	6	8	22	42	24
Mortimer	20	6	5	9	27	41	23
Rabson Rovers	20	5	5	10	32	46	20
Royal Mail	20	5	3	12	25	38	18
Woodcote & Stoke Row	20	6	0	14	30	51	18

INTERMEDIATE CUP
FINAL
(May 10th at Reading Town)
South Reading 1 **REME Arborfield** 2

JUNIOR CUP
FINAL
(May 9th at Reading Town)
Barton Rovers 3
Wokingham & Emmbrook 'B' 2 *aet*

READING LEAGUE SENIOR DIVISION CONSTITUTION 2008-09
BERKS COUNTY SPORTS . . . Berks County Sports & Social Club, Sonning Lane, Sonning, Reading RG4 6ST . . . . None
COOKHAM DEAN . . . . Alfred Major Rec Ground, Hillcrest Avenue, Cookham Rise, Maidenhead SL6 9NB 01628 819423
HIGHMOOR/IBIS . . . . Prudential IBIS Sports Club, Scours Lane, Reading RG3 6AY 0118 942 4130
MORTIMER . . . . Alfred Palmer Memorial PF, West End Road, Mortimer, Reading RG7 3TJ . . . . None
RABSON ROVERS . . . . Lower Whitley Rec, Basingstoke Road, Reading RG2 0JA . . . . None
READING YMCA . . . . Reading Town FC, Scours Lane, Tilehurst, Reading RG30 6AY 0118 945 3555
ROYAL MAIL . . . . Prospect Park, Liebenwood Road, Reading RG30 2ND . . . . None
SANDHURST DEVELS . . . . Sandhurst Memorial Ground, York Town Road, Sandhurst GU47 9BJ . . . . None
TAPLOW UNITED . . . . Stanley Jones Field, Berry Hill, Taplow SL6 0DA 01628 621745
WESTWOOD UNITED . . . . Cotswold Sports Centre, Downs Way, Tilehurst, Reading RG31 6LX . . . . None
WOODCOTE & STOKE ROW . . . . Woodcote Recreation Ground, Woodcote, Reading RG8 0QY . . . . None
WOODLEY TOWN . . . . East Park Farm, Park Lane, Charvil, Reading RG10 9QP . . . . None
IN: Taplow United (P), Sandhurst Devels (P – Aldershot & District League Senior Division)
OUT: Forest Old Boys (WN), Newbury (P – Hellenic League Division One East)

	AFC Corinthians	Cookham Dean Res.	Frilsham & Yattendon	Highmoor/IBIS Res.	Hurst	Marlow United Res.	Shinfield	Spencers Wood	Taplow United	Unity	West Reading	Wokingham & Emmbrook 'A'
AFC Corinthians	P	0-4	1-0	3-0	1-3	1-4	3-4	2-1	1-1	1-1	1-0	3-3
Cookham Dean Res.	3-4	R	1-1	4-0	2-0	3-2	3-0	1-0	3-1	1-1	1-2	3-0
Frilsham & Yattendon	1-2	1-2	E	2-0	7-2	3-2	2-1	3-1	1-1	1-0	4-1	2-4
Highmoor/IBIS Res.	4-0	2-8	5-2	M	6-5	2-0	1-2	1-4	4-13	L-W	1-2	0-4
Hurst	3-2	3-5	2-0	4-1	I	2-6	2-2	3-3	1-5	0-3	2-1	3-3
Marlow United Res.	4-0	1-2	1-1	W-L	5-3	E	0-1	1-0	4-1	W-L	3-1	1-1
Shinfield	2-4	0-2	3-2	6-1	2-0	2-6	R	W-L	3-1	2-4	3-5	1-4
Spencers Wood	3-1	0-1	1-0	0-4	4-1	0-1	2-3		0-1	2-2	0-0	0-3
Taplow United	0-5	0-2	3-2	5-0	6-2	0-0	3-0	1-0		1-0	3-0	3-0
Unity	2-0	3-0	3-1	8-1	2-1	0-1	2-3	1-0	2-1	D	1-1	4-1
West Reading	0-1	1-4	0-1	1-2	0-2	1-2	3-1	2-2	0-2	0-2	I	0-3
Wokingham & Emmbrook 'A'	2-2	3-2	0-2	2-3	3-2	2-4	3-3	5-3	0-0	2-3	1-2	V

Premier Division

	P	W	D	L	F	A	Pts
Cookham Dean Res.	22	16	2	4	57	25	50
Marlow United Res.	22	14	3	5	48	26	45
Unity	22	13	4	5	44	20	43
Taplow United	22	12	4	6	52	30	40
Shinfield	22	10	2	10	44	53	32
AFC Corinthians	22	9	4	9	38	45	31
Wokingham & Emmbrook 'A'	22	8	6	8	49	46	30
Frilsham & Yattendon	22	9	3	10	39	36	30
Hurst	22	6	3	13	46	69	21
Highmoor/IBIS Res.	22	7	0	15	38	75	21
West Reading	22	5	3	14	23	42	18
Spencers Wood	22	4	4	14	26	37	16

READING LEAGUE PREMIER DIVISION CONSTITUTION 2008-09

AFC CORINTHIANS . . . . Civil Service Club, James Lane, Burghfield, Reading RG30 3RS 0118 983 3423
ASHRIDGE PARK . . . . Cantley Park, Twyford Road, Wokingham RG40 5QT . . . . None
COOKHAM DEAN RESERVES . . . . Alfred Major Rec Ground, Hillcrest Avenue, Cookham Rise, Maidenhead SL6 9NB 01628 819423
FRILSHAM & YATTENDON . . . . . Frilsham Playing Field, Frilsham Common, Frilsham, near Hermitage 01635 201847
HIGHMOOR/IBIS RESERVES . . . . . . Prudential IBIS Sports Club, Scours Lane, Reading RG3 6AY 0118 942 4130
HURST . . . . Cantley Park, Twyford Road, Wokingham RG40 5QT . . . . None
MARLOW UNITED RESERVES . . . . Gossmore Park, Gossmore Lane, Marlow SL7 1QF . . . . None
PARK UNITED . . . . Bishopswood Sports Ground, Horsepond Road, Sonning Common, Reading RG4 9BT . . . . None
SHINFIELD . . . . Millworth Lane, Shinfield, Reading RG2 9EN . . . . None
SOUTH READING . . . . Acadamy Sport Leisure Centre, Northumberland Avenue, Reading RG2 8DF 0118 9370 270
UNITY . . . . Cintra Park, Cintra Avenue, Reading RG2 7AU 0118 954 7275
WOKINGHAM & EMMBROOK 'A' . . . . . Cantley Park, Twyford Road, Wokingham RG40 5QT . . . . None
IN: Ashridge Park (P), Park United (P), South Reading (P)
OUT: Spencers Wood (R), Taplow United (P), West Reading (R)

Division One	P	W	D	L	F	A	Pts
South Reading	22	17	4	1	89	16	55
Ashridge Park	22	15	4	3	67	26	49
Park United	22	14	6	2	59	18	48
REME Arborfield	22	13	4	5	51	25	43
Westwood United Res.	22	11	2	9	49	42	35
SRCC	22	10	4	8	43	50	34
Sonning Common	22	9	5	8	40	32	32
Marlow United 'A'	22	6	4	12	26	62	22
Newtown Henley	22	5	6	11	22	43	21
Goring United	22	6	2	14	26	52	20
Radstock	22	5	1	16	32	62	16
Hurst Res.	22	0	0	22	16	92	0

Division Two	P	W	D	L	F	A	Pts
Berinsfield CA	20	14	4	2	58	16	46
Berks County Sports Res.	20	14	2	4	60	17	44
Theale	20	13	1	6	62	35	40
Woodley Town Res.	20	11	4	5	35	21	37
Finchampstead 'A'	20	9	4	7	57	37	31
Twyford & Ruscombe	20	10	1	9	48	41	31
Mortimer Res.	20	9	4	7	35	39	31
Sonning	20	6	2	12	32	59	20
Woodcote & Stoke Row Res.	20	5	3	12	30	64	18
Taplow United Res.	20	4	2	14	27	54	14
Wargrave	20	1	1	18	24	85	4

Division Three	P	W	D	L	F	A	Pts
Barton Rovers	18	15	2	1	102	24	47
Wokingham & Emmbrook 'B'	18	12	4	2	61	26	40
Linear United	18	11	4	3	49	33	37
Highmoor/IBIS 'A'	18	10	4	4	50	26	34
Woodley Town 'A'	18	9	3	6	34	31	30
Sonning Sports	18	8	3	7	37	39	27
Crowthorne Sports	18	6	1	11	49	74	19
Wokingham Wanderers	18	3	4	11	34	70	13
Compton	18	1	2	15	19	66	5
Englefield	18	0	3	15	13	59	3

Division Four	P	W	D	L	F	A	Pts
Bell & Bottle	20	17	0	3	102	20	51
Berinsfield CA Res.	20	16	0	4	92	44	48
Turnpike Sports	20	15	2	3	114	30	47
Reading YMCA Res.	20	14	2	4	72	27	44
Newbury Res.	20	14	1	5	76	30	43
The Hop Leaf	20	7	2	11	42	78	23
AFC Corinthians Res.	20	6	1	13	33	78	19
Goring United Res.	20	6	1	13	37	85	19
Winnershe Rangers	20	4	1	15	26	101	13
Sonning Res.	20	4	0	16	29	69	12
Taplow United 'A'	20	2	0	18	21	82	6

SHEFFIELD & HALLAMSHIRE COUNTY SENIOR LEAGUE

	Athersley Recreation	Dearne Colliery MW	Dinnington Town Res.	HSBC	Hollinsend Amateurs	Mexborough Main Street	Oughtibridge War Memorial SC	Outo Kumpu Sports & Social	Parkgate Res.	Sheffield Lane Top	Springwood Davy	Stocksbridge Park Steels Res.	Thorpe Hesley	Wombwell Main
Athersley Recreation		5-1	2-0	3-0	2-2	2-2	2-0	2-0	n/a	3-0	1-0	3-2	7-0	3-0
Dearne Colliery MW	0-1	*P*	1-6	2-2	2-3	1-1	3-2	4-2	2-1	1-1	2-0	3-1	3-1	1-1
Dinnington Town Res.	0-5	3-0	*R*	2-1	1-1	1-2	1-1	3-0	n/a	0-0	1-1	2-1	6-2	2-2
HSBC	4-4	2-1	0-2	*E*	0-6	0-3	0-0	6-3	0-1	1-4	1-2	4-0	3-3	1-3
Hollinsend Amateurs	2-1	3-3	4-2	3-1	*M*	4-2	1-2	2-0	3-2	3-1	1-2	1-2	2-0	2-3
Mexborough Main Street	2-1	2-0	0-6	1-3	1-1	*I*	4-2	2-0	n/a	3-1	4-0	0-0	1-2	3-4
Oughtibridge War Memorial SC	2-4	5-2	4-2	2-7	1-2	1-3	*E*	5-3	n/a	2-2	5-4	1-2	2-3	0-1
Outo Kumpu Sports & Social	0-2	2-1	3-1	4-3	1-2	1-3	5-2	*R*	n/a	1-3	2-3	1-3	4-2	3-7
Parkgate Res.	n/a	0-4	n/a	n/a	n/a	n/a	n/a	n/a		4-0	0-1	1-1	n/a	2-6
Sheffield Lane Top	1-2	1-4	0-5	2-4	4-1	2-1	2-4	1-5	5-2		1-2	0-2	2-2	1-2
Springwood Davy	2-3	5-2	2-1	1-5	4-2	0-0	2-5	1-2	3-0	2-4	*D*	0-2	2-0	2-0
Stocksbridge Park Steels Res.	1-6	2-4	1-2	2-0	1-2	1-4	2-3	2-1	n/a	4-3	2-0	*I*	4-2	0-2
Thorpe Hesley	1-3	2-0	3-2	2-5	3-1	5-1	2-0	1-3	5-2	2-1	3-5	1-1	*V*	0-4
Wombwell Main	1-0	2-0	3-0	3-2	1-1	3-2	3-0	2-2	n/a	3-0	7-1	5-1	2-1	

Note – Parkgate Res. withdrew during the course of the season
Their results are shown above but are expunged from the league table

Premier Division		P	W	D	L	F	A	Pts
Wombwell Main		24	18	4	2	64	28	58
Athersley Recreation		24	18	3	3	67	23	57
Hollinsend Amateurs		24	12	5	7	52	40	41
Dinnington Town Res.		24	10	5	9	51	39	35
Mexborough Main Street	-3	24	11	5	8	47	41	35
Stocksbridge Park Steels Res.		24	10	2	12	39	50	32
HSBC		24	8	4	12	55	58	28
Oughtibridge War Memorial SC		24	8	3	13	51	62	27
Thorpe Hesley		24	8	3	13	43	64	27
Springwood Davy	-6	24	10	2	12	43	56	26
Dearne Colliery MW		24	7	5	12	41	55	26
Outo Kumpu Sports & Social	-3	24	8	1	15	48	63	22
Sheffield Lane Top		24	5	4	15	37	59	19

Parkgate Res. – record expunged

WINDSOR FOOD SERVICE SHEFFIELD & HALLAMSHIRE COUNTY SENIOR LEAGUE PREMIER DIVISION CONSTITUTION 2008-09

ATHERSLEY RECREATION . . . . Carlton Park, Church Street, Carlton, Barnsley . . . . None
DEARNE COLLIERY MW . . . . Goldthorpe Road, Goldthorpe. . . . . None
DINNINGTON TOWN RESERVES . . . Resource Centre, 131 Laughton Road (The Stute), Dinnington S25 2HA 01909 518555
HSBC . . . . Limb Lane, Hathersage Road, Dore, Sheffield S17 3AA 0114 260 5681
HANDSWORTH . . . . Oliver's Mount, Oliver's Drive, Sheffield S9 4PA. . . . . None
HOLLINSEND AMATEURS . . . . Sheffield Transport Sports Club, Greenhill Main Road, Sheffield S8 7RH. 0114 237 3216
HOUGHTON MAIN . . . . Middlecliff Lane, Little Houghton, Barnsley S72 0HX. 01226 752978
MEXBOROUGH MAIN STREET. . . . . Hampden Road, Mexborough, Doncaster . . . . None
OUGHTIBRIDGE WAR MEMORIAL SC . . . . Station Lane, Oughtibridge, Sheffield . . . . None
PENISTONE CHURCH. . . . . Memorial Ground, Church View Road, Penistone S36 6AT 01226 370095
SPRINGWOOD DAVY . . . . Davy Sports & Social Club, Prince of Wales Road, Darnall, Sheffield . . . . None
STOCKSBRIDGE PARK STEELS RESERVES . . . Look Local Stadium, Bracken Moor,Stocksbridge, Sheffield S36 5AN . . 0114 288 8305/2045
THORPE HESLEY . . . . Civil Service Ground, Green Lane, Ecclesfield. . . . . None
WOMBWELL MAIN . . . . Wombwell Main Cricket Club, Windmill Lane, Wombwell, Barnsley S73 0LP 01226 211123

IN: Handsworth (P), Houghton Main (P), Penistone Church (P)
OUT: Outu Kumpu Sports & Social (R), Parkgate (WS), Sheffield Lane Top (R)

Division One		P	W	D	L	F	A	Pts
Handsworth		24	19	1	4	67	25	58
Penistone Church		24	16	1	7	49	35	49
Houghton Main		24	14	2	8	60	41	44
Everest		24	13	4	7	59	37	43
Parramore Sports	-3	24	12	6	6	48	41	39
Silkstone United		24	11	3	10	48	52	36
Worsbrough Common	-3	24	12	1	11	49	38	34
Worsbrough Bridge MW Res.		24	11	1	12	47	47	34
Frecheville Community Association		24	8	2	14	46	56	26
Ecclesfield Red Rose		24	7	4	13	34	52	25
Sheffield Athletic		24	7	2	15	62	76	23
South Kirkby Colliery		24	6	4	14	39	59	22
Wickersley Old Boys		24	2	5	17	20	69	11

Division Two		P	W	D	L	F	A	Pts
Millmoor Juniors		22	17	4	1	63	19	55
Sheffield Res.		22	15	4	3	62	22	49
Caribbean Sports		22	13	3	6	45	29	42
Shafton & District		22	13	1	8	46	32	40
Bramley Sunnyside Juniors		22	9	6	7	47	35	33
High Green Villa		22	9	6	7	47	36	33
Sheffield Bankers		22	6	5	11	35	51	23
Penistone Church Res.		22	6	5	11	35	55	23
Thorncliffe		22	3	10	9	33	57	19
Blackburn Railway	-1	22	3	8	11	32	48	16
De La Salle Old Boys		22	3	7	12	38	72	16
Phoenix Sports & Social Res.		22	3	5	14	30	57	14

LEAGUE CUP

FIRST ROUND

Ecclesfield Red Rose 2 Blackburn Railway 1
Mexborough Main Street 3 Athersley Recreation 1
Parkgate Res. 0 **Outo Kumpu S & SC** 1
Penistone Church Res. 1 **Parramore Sports** 7
Shafton & District 2 Silkstone United 1
Sheffield Athletic 0 **Hollinsend Amateurs** 12
Sheffield Res. 1 **Oughtibridge WMSC** 2
Worsbrough Bridge MW Res. 2 Houghton Main 1

SECOND ROUND

Bramley Sunnyside Juniors 5 Phoenix Sports & Social Res 1
Caribbean Sports 4 Sheffield Bankers 3
Dearne Colliery MW 1 Stocksbridge Park Steels Res. 0
Dinnington Town Res. 2 HSBC 2 *aet* (4-2p)
Ecclesfield Red Rose 3 De La Salle Old Boys 1
Everest 1 Hollinsend Amateurs 0
Frecheville CA 1 **Mexborough Main Street** 8
High Green Villa (w/o) v Thorncliffe (scr.)
Penistone Church 1 **Oughtibridge WMSC** 3
Penistone Church Res. 0 **Handsworth** 1
Shafton & District 3 South Kirkby Colliery 1
Sheffield Lane Top 6 Thorpe Hesley 2
Springwood Davy *(bye)*
Wombwell Main 5 Millmoor Juniors 0
Worsbrough Bridge MW Res. 0 **Parkgate Res.** 2
Worsbrough Common 1 **Wickersley Old Boys** 1 *aet* (3-4p)

THIRD ROUND

Bramley Sunnyside Juniors 1 **Oughtibridge WMSC** 2
Caribbean Sports 3 Ecclesfield Red Rose 3 *aet* (4-5p)
Everest 0 **Springwood Davy** 4
Handsworth 1 Dearne Colliery MW 0
Mexborough Main Street (w/o) v Parkgate Res. (scr.)
Shafton & District 2 **Wombwell Main** 3
Sheffield Lane Top 3 Dinnington Town Res. 0
Wickersley Old Boys 1 **High Green Villa** 3

QUARTER-FINALS

Caribbean Sports 2 Springwood Davy 1
Handsworth 1 **Wombwell Main** 4
High Green Villa 2 **Oughtibridge WMSC** 2 *aet* (4-5p)
Sheffield Lane Top 2 **Mexborough Main Street** 4

SEMI-FINALS

Caribbean Sports 3 Mexborough Main Street 2
(at South Kirkby Colliery)
Wombwell Main 1 High Green Villa 0
(at Penistone Church)

FINAL

(April 10th at Stocksbridge Park Steels)
Caribbean Sports 0 **Wombwell Main** 4

SHROPSHIRE COUNTY LEAGUE

	Broseley Juniors	Church Stretton Town	Clee Hill United	Hanwood United	Haughmond	Hopesgate United	Ludlow Town Res.	Market Drayton Town Res.	Morda United	Shifnal Town Res.	Shifnal United	Telford Juniors	Telford Town	Tibberton United	Wem Town
Broseley Juniors		0-0	0-1	0-3	3-0	2-0	0-1	0-1	2-2	0-0	2-1	3-5	2-1	3-1	0-0
Church Stretton Town	3-3		1-0	0-2	0-2	2-1	0-3	1-3	1-2	0-4	2-3	2-4	3-1	2-2	1-7
Clee Hill United	1-0	1-3	P	1-2	1-3	0-2	2-0	2-0	3-2	1-2	1-3	3-1	2-4	2-2	1-3
Hanwood United	2-0	3-1	2-0	R	1-1	1-0	3-1	4-0	3-1	2-4	3-1	1-1	3-0	4-3	0-1
Haughmond	0-2	2-2	1-0	1-0	E	5-0	2-0	2-0	1-1	1-2	2-0	4-0	3-1	3-0	2-0
Hopesgate United	3-1	3-1	2-1	0-1	1-2	M	1-1	1-0	2-0	0-2	1-2	2-5	0-0	0-2	0-4
Ludlow Town Res.	3-3	2-2	2-1	1-4	2-1	4-2	I	1-5	4-1	2-5	1-4	0-3	4-1	3-2	1-4
Market Drayton Town Res.	2-2	4-2	2-2	0-2	2-1	4-2	2-0	E	2-0	1-5	0-3	2-1	2-3	1-1	2-2
Morda United	0-3	4-2	3-0	0-2	0-2	4-1	2-1	1-1	R	1-1	1-4	1-2	1-2	4-2	1-1
Shifnal Town Res.	3-3	4-3	5-0	2-1	4-1	0-3	5-1	3-0	2-2		3-3	4-1	1-0	2-2	5-1
Shifnal United	5-1	4-2	6-1	1-2	2-2	4-1	4-2	1-2	4-0	1-2	D	4-0	2-0	5-1	2-1
Telford Juniors	5-1	0-0	3-1	0-1	1-2	2-0	4-0	5-0	4-1	3-1	3-3	I	7-0	4-2	5-1
Telford Town	1-2	3-2	2-3	1-3	0-2	4-0	3-1	4-1	1-2	3-3	1-4	4-2	V	2-4	2-3
Tibberton United	1-1	2-2	2-2	0-2	3-4	4-1	3-0	0-4	1-2	3-3	1-1	1-0	1-2		0-2
Wem Town	1-2	1-1	1-2	2-1	0-0	4-0	3-0	0-0	1-0	1-1	1-3	1-3	4-0	2-1	

Premier Division	P	W	D	L	F	A	Pts
Hanwood United	28	21	2	5	58	23	65
Shifnal Town Res.	28	17	9	2	78	40	60
Shifnal United	28	18	4	6	80	39	58
Haughmond	28	17	5	6	52	28	56
Telford Juniors	28	16	3	9	74	45	51
Wem Town	28	13	7	8	52	36	46
Market Drayton Town Res.	28	11	6	11	43	51	39
Broseley Juniors	28	9	9	10	41	46	36
Morda United	28	8	6	14	39	55	30
Telford Town	28	9	2	17	46	67	29
Clee Hill United	28	8	3	17	35	59	27
Ludlow Town Res.	28	8	3	17	41	72	27
Tibberton United	28	5	9	14	47	63	24
Hopesgate United	28	7	2	19	29	62	23
Church Stretton Town	28	4	8	16	41	70	20

PREMIER DIVISION CUP

FIRST ROUND
Broseley Juniors 2 **Tibberton United** 3
Clee Hill United 2 Haughmond 1
Hopesgate United 3 Shifnal Town Res. 1
Ludlow Town Res. 1 **Hanwood United** 4
Market Drayton Town Res. 1 **Telford Juniors** 4
Morda United 0 **Wem Town** 5

QUARTER-FINALS
Church Stretton Town 3 Clee Hill United 1
Shifnal United 8 Hopesgate United 2
Telford Juniors 2 Hanwood United 1
Wem Town 1 Tibberton United 1 *aet* (6-5p)

SEMI-FINALS
Church Stretton Town 0 **Shifnal United** 1
Telford Juniors 3 Wem Town 2

FINAL
(May 10th at Bridgnorth Town)
Shifnal United 2 Telford Juniors 1

SPORTSJAMKITS.COM SHROPSHIRE COUNTY LEAGUE PREMIER DIVISION CONSTITUTION 2008-09

BROSELEY JUNIORS .... Birchmeadow, Broseley TF12 5LP .... None
CLEE HILL UNITED .... Knowle Sports Ground, Tenbury Road, Clee Hill, Ludlow SY8 3NE .... None
DAWLEY BANK .... Doseley Road, Dawley, Telford TF4 3AY .... None
HAUGHMOND .... Mereside Recreation Centre, Springfield, Shrewsbury SY2 6LH 01743 357793
LUDLOW TOWN RESERVES .... SBS Stadium, Bromfield Road, Ludlow SY8 2BY 01584 876000
MARKET DRAYTON TOWN RESERVES .... Greenfield Sports Club, Greenfield Lane, Market Drayton TF9 3SL 01630 655088
MORDA UNITED .... Weston Road, Morda, Oswestry SY10 9NS 01691 659621
NEWPORT COUNTY BOROUGH .... Shukers Field, Avenue Road, Newport TF10 7EA 01952 825801
SHIFNAL TOWN RESERVES .... Phoenix Park, Coppice Green Lane, Shifal TF11 8PB........................ 01952 463667
SHIFNAL UNITED.................. Idsall Sports Centre, Coppice Green Lane, Shifnal TF11 8PD 01952 460499
ST MARTINS................. St Martins Playing Fields, Overton Road, St Martins, Oswestry SY11 3DG............................. None
TELFORD JUNIORS.............. Ironbridge Power Station, Buildwas Road, Ironbridge TF8 7BL .... None
TELFORD TOWN .... Grainger Road, Leegomery, Telford TF1 6UJ .... None
WEM TOWN .... Butler Sports Centre, Bowens Field, Wem SY4 5AW 01939 233287

IN: *Dawley Bank (P), St Martins (P)*
OUT: *Church Stretton Town (R), Hanwood United (P – West Midlands (Regional) League Division Two), Hopesgate United (R)*
Tibberton United become Newport County Borough

WWW.CHERRYRED.CO.UK

	Bobbington	Brown Clee	Craven Arms Town	Dawley Bank	Dawley Wanderers	Ellesmere Rangers Res.	Meole Brace	Morda United Res.	Oakengates Athletic	St Martins	Whitchurch Alport Res.	Wrockwardine Wood	Wroxeter Rovers
Bobbington	D	2-1	4-0	2-3	3-0	2-0	5-2	5-0	4-0	0-6	2-4	2-1	5-0
Brown Clee	1-2	I	5-2	3-3	0-1	2-2	5-1	3-0	2-0	4-0	1-4	4-1	0-1
Craven Arms Town	3-5	1-0	V	3-4	0-4	0-3	1-5	0-1	3-1	1-3	3-2	3-3	1-6
Dawley Bank	3-0	3-3	11-1	I	5-1	1-1	1-0	8-0	6-2	1-2	6-2	2-0	5-2
Dawley Wanderers	0-2	0-3	1-0	4-3	S	2-3	3-2	1-3	2-1	1-4	2-1	3-1	6-1
Ellesmere Rangers Res.	3-3	1-0	5-0	1-3	1-1	I	3-2	2-0	6-1	3-1	1-1	6-2	3-0
Meole Brace	2-2	1-1	2-1	0-1	7-2	3-1	O	5-0	5-2	1-6	2-0	3-1	2-4
Morda United Res.	0-1	0-5	2-1	1-3	1-2	0-4	1-1	N	3-4	2-1	1-8	3-1	0-5
Oakengates Athletic	0-4	2-2	5-1	2-4	4-5	2-5	1-6	1-0		0-3	5-4	2-1	2-3
St Martins	3-2	5-0	6-1	1-3	4-1	2-0	8-2	3-1	3-1		5-3	3-0	4-0
Whitchurch Alport Res.	1-0	2-4	6-0	1-1	3-2	0-5	6-0	6-1	2-1	0-4	O	4-3	0-1
Wrockwardine Wood	4-2	0-0	2-1	6-3	1-0	0-0	5-2	7-0	7-6	2-2	3-3	N	0-1
Wroxeter Rovers	2-2	1-0	7-2	1-1	2-3	0-2	1-0	4-0	4-3	4-2	1-0	2-1	E

DIVISION ONE CUP

FIRST ROUND
Bobbington 6 Dawley Bank 1
Dawley Wanderers 4 Craven Arms Town 1
St Martins 5 Meole Brace 2
Whitchurch Alport Res. 5 Morda United Res. 0
Wroxeter Rovers 6 Oakengates Athletic 0

QUARTER-FINALS
Bobbington 5 Whitchurch Alport Res. 1
Brown Clee 6 St Martins 3
Wrockwardine Wood 1 **Ellesmere Rangers Res.** 2
Wroxeter Rovers 4 Dawley Wanderers 0

SEMI-FINALS
Ellesmere Rangers Res. 3 Bobbington 1
Wroxeter Rovers 2 **Brown Clee** 3

FINAL
(May 8th at Bridgnorth Town)
Brown Clee 2 **Ellesmere Rangers Res.** 2
aet (4-5p)

RON JONES MEMORIAL CUP

FIRST ROUND
Bobbington 6 Wroxeter Rovers 0
Brown Clee 4 Church Stretton Town 1
Craven Arms Town 0 **Hanwood United** 1
Ellesmere Rangers Res. 4 Oakengates Athletic 0
Haughmond 5 Clee Hill United 0
Ludlow Town Res. 4 Dawley Bank 2
Meole Brace 2 **Dawley Wanderers** 3
Morda United 3 Market Drayton Town Res. 0
Telford Juniors 4 Whitchurch Alport Res. 1
Telford Town 2 **Shifnal Town Res.** 5
Wem Town 6 Morda United Res. 0
Wrockwardine Wood 1 Tibberton United 0

SECOND ROUND
Bobbington 0 Broseley Juniors *(Broseley Juniors expelled)*
Brown Clee 0 **St Martins** 3
Dawley Wanderers 2 Hopesgate United 1
Hanwood United 3 Shifnal Town Res. 0
Haughmond 2 **Ellesmere Rangers Res.** 3
Morda United 4 Ludlow Town Res. 3
Wem Town 3 **Telford Juniors** 4
Wrockwardine Wood 0 **Shifnal United** 5

QUARTER-FINALS
Bobbington 1 **Telford Juniors** 4 *(at Bridgnorth Town)*
Dawley Wanderers 2 St Martins 1
Ellesmere Rangers Res. 1 **Hanwood United** 2
Morda United 1 **Shifnal United** 2

SEMI-FINALS
Dawley Wanderers 2 Shifnal United 0
Telford Juniors 1 Hanwood United 1 *aet (8-7p)*

FINAL
(May 15th at Bridgnorth Town)
Shifnal United 2 Telford Juniors 1

Division One	P	W	D	L	F	A	Pts
St Martins	24	18	1	5	81	33	55
Dawley Bank	24	16	5	3	84	39	53
Ellesmere Rangers Res.	24	14	6	4	61	28	48
Wroxeter Rovers	24	15	2	7	53	44	47
Bobbington	24	14	3	7	61	39	45
Dawley Wanderers	24	12	1	11	47	55	37
Brown Clee	24	9	6	9	49	35	33
Whitchurch Alport Res.	24	10	3	11	63	54	33
Meole Brace	24	9	3	12	56	61	30
Wrockwardine Wood	24	7	5	12	52	57	26
Oakengates Athletic	24	5	1	18	48	85	16
Morda United Res.	24	5	1	18	20	81	16
Craven Arms Town	24	3	1	20	29	93	10

WWW.NLNEWSDESK.CO.UK

SPORTSJAMKITS.COM SHROPSHIRE COUNTY LEAGUE DIVISION ONE CONSTITUTION 2008-09

BROWN CLEE.........................Hall Meadow, Cleobury North, Bridgnorth WV16 6RP................................None
CHURCH STRETTON TOWN..............Russell's Meadow, Church Stretton SY6 6AT..................................None
CRAVEN ARMS TOWN.......Community Centre Playing Fields, Newington Way, Craven Arms SY7 9PS.................01588 672847
DAWLEY WANDERERS......................Doseley Road, Dawley, Telford TF4 3AY...................................None
ELLESMERE RANGERS RESERVES......Beech Grove Playing Fields, Ellesmere SY12 0BT..............................None
FC HODNET.........................Hodnet Sports Centre, Hodnet, Market Drayton..................................None
HOPESGATE UNITED....................................The Cotes, Snailbeach..................................None
IMPACT UNITED......................Grainger Road, Leegomery, Telford TF1 6UJ.................................None
MEOLE BRACE.........................Church Road, Meole Brace, Shrewsbury SY3 9HF................................None
MORDA UNITED RESERVES..........Weston Road, Morda, Oswestry SY10 9NS............................01691 659621
OAKENGATES ATHLETIC........................School Road, Oakengates.......................................None
WHITCHURCH ALPORT RESERVES....Yockings Park, Blackpark Road, Whitchurch SY13 1PG............01948 667415
WROCKWARDINE WOOD.................New Road, Wrockwardine Wood TF2 7AB........................01952 613086
WROXETER ROVERS.........................Springfield, Wroxeter..None

IN: Church Stretton Town (R), FC Hodnet (P – Shropshire Alliance), Hopesgate United (R), Impact United (P – Telford Combination)
OUT: Bobbington (F), Dawley Bank (P), St Martins (P)

SOMERSET COUNTY LEAGUE

	Bridgwater Town Res.	Burnham United	Castle Cary	Cheddar	Cleeve West Town	Cutters Friday	Frome Town Res.	Fry Club	Glastonbury Town	Ilminster Town	Mangotsfield United Res.	Nailsea United	Shirehampton	St George Easton-in-Gordano	Taunton Blackbrook	Timsbury Athletic	Wells City	Winscombe
Bridgwater Town Res.		3-2	3-4	5-3	6-0	3-2	6-3	2-4	3-0	6-1	1-0	1-1	5-2	0-0	1-1	5-2	0-1	1-2
Burnham United	1-2	P	2-3	3-1	1-3	3-0	1-0	4-1	2-0	1-1	2-0	3-2	1-2	2-0	2-3	3-2	0-1	1-4
Castle Cary	0-0	1-2	R	4-6	1-1	4-1	5-1	3-0	2-2	3-3	0-1	1-3	2-1	2-0	1-0	2-0	0-2	1-5
Cheddar	1-2	4-0	5-5	E	1-3	4-0	3-2	1-1	1-1	1-1	3-3	1-3	2-2	4-1	2-1	4-1	3-0	5-2
Cleeve West Town	2-7	2-2	0-2	2-1	M	2-4	3-0	2-2	1-1	4-2	3-2	0-1	3-1	4-1	0-2	2-2	2-1	2-1
Cutters Friday	1-2	0-1	2-2	2-2	0-3	I	3-2	3-0	1-1	4-1	2-1	1-3	1-3	2-2	4-2	3-0	1-4	2-4
Frome Town Res.	0-7	2-0	2-3	5-5	1-1	1-1	E	1-1	0-2	5-2	2-3	1-5	2-1	5-2	2-0	2-0	0-0	0-4
Fry Club	1-2	0-4	2-2	3-2	4-1	0-0	2-1	R	0-0	3-1	0-0	1-2	3-1	1-0	2-5	1-1	0-4	2-3
Glastonbury Town	0-0	0-0	2-1	1-1	0-1	1-3	1-0	1-0		3-1	0-1	1-3	2-2	0-0	0-0	2-2	1-2	1-1
Ilminster Town	1-1	0-3	1-1	1-2	0-3	2-2	2-4	5-2	2-1	D	2-3	1-0	1-2	2-0	1-2	2-2	1-1	3-1
Mangotsfield United Res.	2-2	0-2	1-1	0-2	1-3	3-0	2-3	0-2	3-0	3-2	I	2-3	1-2	2-2	0-1	1-1	2-2	3-1
Nailsea United	3-1	2-1	2-0	2-2	0-0	1-1	4-1	3-0	0-1	5-0	4-0	V	0-1	1-0	4-1	5-4	4-0	2-0
Shirehampton	2-1	1-1	1-0	3-2	1-4	1-1	5-1	1-1	2-0	1-3	1-3	1-2	I	3-1	1-3	1-3	0-2	2-1
St George Easton-in-Gordano	1-2	0-5	0-3	1-0	2-3	0-2	0-1	2-2	1-3	2-2	3-1	1-4	2-2	S	0-1	1-0	1-3	3-2
Taunton Blackbrook	3-1	1-7	0-1	1-3	2-2	0-0	1-2	1-0	3-0	0-1	1-1	0-6	2-0	1-3	I	0-3	0-2	0-3
Timsbury Athletic	0-4	3-2	0-1	3-2	1-3	2-3	2-4	2-0	4-3	2-4	3-2	1-4	5-2	3-2	1-3	O	1-1	1-3
Wells City	0-5	4-1	1-1	2-1	1-0	2-0	3-1	2-0	1-1	1-0	0-1	2-5	4-3	4-0	4-0	0-1	N	2-0
Winscombe	2-2	2-0	4-2	2-3	0-1	2-0	4-2	3-0	3-1	1-1	3-3	3-4	2-1	7-2	3-2	3-0	1-4	

Premier Division		P	W	D	L	F	A	Pts
Nailsea United		34	26	4	4	93	34	82
Wells City		34	22	6	6	64	35	72
Bridgwater Town Res.	-4	34	19	8	7	92	48	61
Winscombe		34	19	4	11	84	57	61
Cleeve West Town		34	17	8	9	66	56	59
Castle Cary		34	14	10	10	64	56	52
Burnham United	-1	34	16	4	14	65	50	51
Cheddar		34	13	10	11	82	67	49
Shirehampton		34	12	6	16	55	67	42
Glastonbury Town		34	9	14	11	36	43	41
Taunton Blackbrook		34	12	5	17	43	63	41
Mangotsfield Utd Res.	-2	34	10	9	15	53	59	37
Cutters Friday	-1	34	9	10	15	49	64	36
Timsbury Athletic		34	10	6	18	58	80	36
Frome Town Res.		34	10	5	19	56	88	35
Ilminster Town		34	8	10	16	53	75	34
Fry Club		34	7	10	17	42	70	31
St George Easton-in-Gordano		34	5	7	22	36	79	22

PREMIER/DIVISION ONE CUP

FIRST ROUND
Street Res. 2 Brislington Res. 1
Taunton Blackbrook 5 Backwell United Res. 2
Tunley Athletic Res. 4 Glastonbury Town 3

SECOND ROUND
Bishops Lydeard 1 **Cleeve West Town** 1 *aet* (5-6p)
Burnham United 3 Shirehampton 0
Castle Cary 4 Paulton Rovers Res. 2
Cheddar 4 Odd Down Res. 1
Churchill Club 0 **Bridgwater Town Res.** 4
Frome Town Res. 7 Street Res. 1
Ilminster Town 1 **Fry Club** 3
Keynsham Town Res. 0 **Taunton Blackbrook** 4
Peasedown Athletic 0 **Winscombe** 3
St George Easton-in-Gordano (scr.) v **Mangotsfield Utd Res.** (w/o)
Stockwood Green Robinsons 2 Wells City 0
Tunley Athletic 0 **Cutters Friday** 6
Watchet Town 3 Dundry Athletic 1
Welton Rovers 1 **Nailsea United** 3

SOMERSET COUNTY LEAGUE PREMIER DIVISION CONSTITUTION 2008-09

BACKWELL UNITED . . . . The Playing Fields, West Town Road, Backwell, Bristol BS48 3HG 01275 462612
BISHOPS LYDEARD . . . . Darby Way, Bishops Lydeard TA4 3BE. . . . . None
BRIDGWATER TOWN RESERVES . . . Fairfax Park, College Way, Bath Road, Bridgwater TA6 4TZ 01278 446899
BURNHAM UNITED . . . . Burnham Road Playing Fields, Cassis Close, Burnham-on-Sea TA8 1NN. 01278 794615
CASTLE CARY . . . . Donald Pither Memorial PF, Catherines Close, Castle Cary BA7 7HP 01963 351538
CHEDDAR . . . . Bowdens Park, Draycott Road, Cheddar BS27 3RL. 01934 743736
CLEEVE WEST TOWN. . . . . King George V Playing Fields, Meeting House Lane, Cleeve BS49 4PD 01934 832173
CUTTERS FRIDAY . . . . The Cutters Club, Stockwood Lane, Stockwood, Bristol BS14 8SJ 01275 839830
FROME TOWN RESERVES . . . . Badgers Hill, Berkley Road, Frome BA11 2EH. 01373 464087
GLASTONBURY TOWN . . . . Abbey Moor Stadium, Godney Road, Glastonbury BA6 9AF. 01458 831460
MANGOTSFIELD UNITED RESERVES . . . . Cossham Street, Mangotsfield, Bristol BS17 3EN 0117 956 0119
NAILSEA UNITED . . . . Grove Sports Ground, Old Church, Nailsea BS48 4ND 01275 856892
ODD DOWN RESERVES. . . . . . . Lew Hill Memorial Ground, Combe Hay Lane, Odd Down, Bath BA2 8PH. 01225 832491
SHIREHAMPTON . . . . Recreation Ground, Penpole Lane, Shirehampton, Bristol BS11 0EA. 0117 923 5461
TAUNTON BLACKBROOK. . . . . Taunton Town FC, Wordsworth Drive, Taunton TA1 2HG 01823 278191
TIMSBURY ATHLETIC. . . . . Recreation Ground, North Road, Timsbury, Bath BA2 0JH 01761 472523
WATCHET TOWN . . . . Memorial Ground, Doniford Road, Watchet TA23 0TG. 01984 631041
WINSCOMBE. . . . . Recreation Ground, The Lynch, Winscombe BS25 1AP . . . . 01934 842720 (cricket club)
IN: Backwell United (W – Western League Division One), Bishops Lydeard (P), Odd Down Reserves (P), Watchet Town (P)
OUT: Fry Club (R), Ilminster Town (R), St George Easton-in-Gordano (R), Wells City (P – Western League Division One)

	Backwell United Res.	Bishops Lydeard	Brislington Res.	Burnham United Res.	Churchill Club	Dundry Athletic	Keynsham Town Res.	Nailsea Town	Odd Down Res.	Paulton Rovers Res.	Peasedown Athletic	Stockwood Green Robinsons	Street Res.	Tunley Athletic	Watchet Town	Welton Rovers Res.	Westland United	Worle
Backwell United Res.		0-4	0-3	2-4	0-2	1-0	0-0	0-1	0-4	1-5	0-1	0-4	0-0	0-2	0-3	1-1	1-2	2-4
Bishops Lydeard	4-0		1-1	5-1	3-1	2-0	0-3	4-0	4-0	1-0	1-1	4-0	2-1	6-2	3-1	0-1	1-0	6-3
Brislington Res.	3-1	4-3		2-0	6-2	2-0	1-1	0-0	1-4	3-0	1-2	0-0	1-1	1-1	2-1	3-2	1-2	3-4
Burnham United Res.	1-2	0-1	2-1	D	2-2	3-0	2-2	0-5	1-1	1-1	1-3	2-2	0-2	2-0	1-0	4-0	1-0	1-3
Churchill Club	4-0	2-2	1-1	2-3	I	3-0	0-0	0-1	2-0	1-2	1-0	2-2	3-2	4-1	3-0	3-1	2-1	1-1
Dundry Athletic	2-1	4-3	2-1	3-2	2-0	V	1-1	1-2	1-5	0-1	0-1	1-0	1-0	2-1	0-1	4-2	0-0	2-5
Keynsham Town Res.	2-2	0-1	4-2	4-2	1-0	2-1	I	1-2	1-0	2-3	0-4	2-1	6-0	1-1	1-4	0-14		2-2
Nailsea Town	3-2	3-1	1-0	1-0	0-1	4-1	2-3	S	1-3	4-2	0-1	0-0	0-0	4-0	2-2	5-0	2-1	3-3
Odd Down Res.	10-2	1-0	1-0	3-1	2-1	3-1	2-1	0-0	I	4-1	1-2	3-1	2-2	2-1	0-0	2-0	3-0	1-1
Paulton Rovers Res.	8-2	1-3	1-0	1-2	4-2	1-2	2-1	1-4	1-2	O	0-2	0-1	3-1	6-2	1-1	2-3	3-0	5-2
Peasedown Athletic	4-2	1-1	2-1	1-2	3-2	1-1	1-2	2-2	0-1	2-2	N	1-4	1-0	0-1	1-0	2-0	1-4	3-0
Stockwood Green Robinsons	3-2	1-2	2-1	2-0	3-3	0-1	0-4	0-0	2-1	2-1	1-1		2-3	1-2	2-2	0-0	3-0	2-1
Street Res.	3-0	3-5	1-0	1-1	0-1	4-2	0-3	0-2	2-1	0-0	3-1	1-1	O	7-1	1-1	2-1	2-2	2-3
Tunley Athletic	1-2	1-1	1-5	1-1	3-1	2-0	2-1	3-1	2-2	0-3	2-3	0-4	2-3	N	0-2	1-0	1-1	0-3
Watchet Town	11-0	0-4	2-1	0-0	3-0	5-0	1-2	1-0	3-1	1-3	2-1	1-0	1-1	5-3	E	5-0	3-0	4-0
Welton Rovers Res.	4-1	2-3	1-3	1-1	2-1	5-0	3-4	1-1	0-0	0-3	0-0	1-1	0-1	0-1	1-2		4-1	1-1
Westland United	4-1	1-9	0-6	5-2	2-0	0-0	3-3	2-2	0-4	2-2	2-3	2-1	1-3	2-2	0-1	3-0		2-0
Worle	2-0	5-0	5-0	3-1	2-2	4-3	2-2	0-0	1-4	2-6	4-1	2-2	3-0	1-1	2-10	4-1	2-1	

Westland United 4 **Timsbury Athletic** 5 *aet*
Worle 1 **Nailsea Town** 5
THIRD ROUND
Burnham United 2 **Timsbury Athletic** 2 *aet* (4-5p)
Cleeve West Town 3 Taunton Blackbrook 0
Fry Club 1 **Cheddar** 1 *aet* (2-4p)
Mangotsfield United Res. 2 Winscombe 0
Nailsea Town 0 **Frome Town Res.** 1
Nailsea United 2 Bridgwater Town Res. 1
Tunley Athletic 1 **Stockwood Green Robinsons** 4
Watchet Town 0 **Castle Cary** 3
QUARTER-FINALS
Castle Cary 2 Cleeve West Town 1 *aet*
Nailsea United 5 Frome Town Res. 1
Stockwood Green Robinsons 3 Cheddar 2
Timsbury Athletic 1 **Mangotsfield United Res.** 2
SEMI-FINALS
Castle Cary 0 **Nailsea United** 1
Stockwood Green Robinsons 0 **Mangotsfield Utd Res.** 1
FINAL
(May 15th at Paulton Rovers)
Mangotsfield United Res. 0 **Nailsea United** 2

Division One		P	W	D	L	F	A	Pts
Bishops Lydeard	-1	34	22	5	7	90	44	70
Odd Down Res.		34	20	7	7	74	37	67
Watchet Town		34	19	8	7	77	35	65
Keynsham Town Res.		34	17	9	8	65	60	60
Peasedown Athletic		34	17	6	11	52	47	57
Nailsea Town		34	15	11	8	56	36	56
Worle	-4	34	15	10	9	81	75	51
Paulton Rovers Res.		34	15	5	14	72	55	50
Stockwood Green Robinsons	-2	34	12	12	10	53	44	46
Churchill Club		34	12	8	14	55	55	44
Brislington Res.		34	12	6	16	60	52	42
Street Res.	-5	34	12	10	12	53	49	41
Westland United		34	11	7	16	62	68	40
Burnham United Res.	-2	34	10	9	15	47	62	37
Dundry Athletic	-3	34	11	3	20	38	69	33
Tunley Athletic		34	8	7	19	43	86	31
Welton Rovers Res.		34	7	9	18	43	66	30
Backwell United Res.		34	3	4	27	28	109	13

SOMERSET COUNTY LEAGUE DIVISION ONE CONSTITUTION 2008-09

BRISLINGTON RESERVES . . . . Ironmould Lane, Brislington, Bristol BS4 5SA 0117 977 4030
BURNHAM UNITED RESERVES . . . . Burnham Road Playing Fields, Cassis Close, Burnham-on-Sea TA8 1NN 01278 794615
CHURCHILL CLUB . . . . Ladymead Lane, Churchill, Winscombe BS25 5NH. 01934 852739
FRY CLUB. . . . . Fry Club, Somerdale, Keynsham, Bristol BS31 2AU 0117 937 6500/6501
ILMINSTER TOWN . . . . Recreation Ground, Ilminster TA19 0EF . . . . None
KEYNSHAM TOWN RESERVES . . . . Crown Field, Bristol Road, Keynsham, Bristol BS31 2BE. 0117 986 5876
LANGFORD ROVERS . . . . Westland United FC, Winterstoke Road, Weston-super-Mare BS24 9AA. 01934 632037
LARKHALL ATHLETIC RESERVES. . . . Plain Ham, Charlcombe Lane, Larkhall, Bath BA1 8DJ. 01225 334952
NAILSEA TOWN. . . . . Fryth Way, Pound Lane, Nailsea BS48 2AS . . . . None
PAULTON ROVERS RESERVES . . . . Athletic Ground, Winterfield Road, Paulton BS39 7RF 01761 412907
PEASEDOWN ATHLETIC. . . . . Miners Welfare Park, Peasedown St John, Bath 01761 437319
PORTISHEAD RESERVES. . . . . Bristol Road Playing Fields, Portishead, Bristol BS20 6QB. 01275 847136
SALTFORD. . . . . Playing Fields, Norman Road, Saltford BS31 0BQ 01225 873725
ST GEORGE EASTON-IN-GORDANO . . . . Court Hay, Easton-in-Gordano, Bristol BS20 0PY 01275 374235
STOCKWOOD GREEN ROBINSONS . . . Hursley Lane, Woolard Lane, Whitchurch, Bristol BS14 0QY 01275 891300
STREET RESERVES . . . . The Tannery Ground, Middlebrooks, Street BA16 0TA. 01458 444987
WESTLAND UNITED. . . . . Westland Sports Club, Winterstoke Road, Weston-super-Mare BS24 9AA. 01934 632037
WORLE . . . . Worle Recreation Ground, Station Road, Worle, Weston-super-Mare BS22 6AU . . . . None
IN: Fry Club (R), Ilminster Town (R), Langford Rovers (P – Division Two West), Larkhall Athletic Reserves (P – Division Two East), Portishead Reserves (P – Division Two West), Saltford (P – Division Two East), St George Easton–in–Gordano (R)
OUT: Backwell United Reserves (R – Division Two West), Bishops Lydeard (P), Dundry Athletic (R – Division Two East), Odd Down Reserves (P), Tunley Athletic (R – Division Two East), Watchet Town (P), Welton Rovers Reserves (R – Division Two East)

	Bishop Sutton Res.	Cheddar Res.	Clutton	Frome Collegians	Fry Club Res.	Hengrove Athletic Res.	Imperial	Larkhall Athletic Res.	Saltford	Shepton Mallet Res.	Stockwood Green Robinsons Res.	Timsbury Athletic Res.	Wells City Res.
Bishop Sutton Res.	D	1-3	6-0	0-2	3-0	1-3	5-0	7-3	0-1	4-5	3-0	1-0	2-2
Cheddar Res.	3-2	I	3-0	4-0	3-1	3-3	2-0	2-1	0-3	3-2	4-0	1-1	0-0
Clutton	1-2	2-2	V	1-2	2-1	0-6	0-2	2-2	0-3	1-1	0-3	0-4	1-0
Frome Collegians	3-3	1-1	0-0		1-4	1-2	0-2	0-5	2-4	0-2	1-3	4-4	1-3
Fry Club Res.	0-3	2-4	1-1	1-1	T	3-3	0-2	1-7	1-3	2-5	3-1	0-4	2-0
Hengrove Athletic Res.	2-4	3-2	1-0	2-1	3-0	W	4-0	3-1	0-4	0-2	4-0	2-0	0-1
Imperial	2-3	2-4	1-1	1-3	0-1	3-1	O	3-3	4-3	1-4	1-0	1-3	0-6
Larkhall Athletic Res.	2-1	4-0	4-0	0-0	5-1	0-1	5-0		2-0	6-2	1-0	1-1	3-1
Saltford	5-0	2-0	1-2	2-0	3-0	1-1	6-0	1-3	E	3-3	3-1	4-1	0-1
Shepton Mallet Res.	0-2	2-1	1-2	4-3	2-1	1-3	3-0	0-3	1-3	A	1-0	2-1	2-0
Stockwood Green Robinsons Res.	0-1	2-0	1-2	0-3	1-1	1-2	2-2	0-5	1-2	0-4	S	2-2	1-1
Timsbury Athletic Res.	2-1	0-0	3-2	6-2	1-1	1-3	0-0	1-4	2-2	1-0	2-0	T	1-1
Wells City Res.	4-1	2-1	2-1	2-1	3-4	1-4	5-0	0-3	0-1	1-0	2-2	3-1	

Division Two East		P	W	D	L	F	A	Pts
Larkhall Athletic Res.	-1	24	16	4	4	73	27	51
Saltford		24	16	3	5	60	25	51
Hengrove Athletic Res.		24	16	3	5	56	31	51
Shepton Mallet Res.		24	13	2	9	49	41	41
Cheddar Res.		24	11	6	7	46	36	39
Bishop Sutton Res.		24	12	2	10	56	43	38
Wells City Res.		24	11	5	8	41	32	38
Timsbury Athletic Res.		24	8	9	7	42	37	33
Clutton		24	5	6	13	21	52	21
Fry Club Res.		24	5	5	14	31	61	20
Imperial	-3	24	6	4	14	27	64	19
Frome Collegians		24	4	6	14	32	56	18
Stockwood Green Robinsons Res.		24	3	5	16	21	50	14

DIVISION TWO CUP

FIRST ROUND

Berrow 2 Saltford 0

Bishop Sutton Res. 5 Wrington-Redhill 1

Combe St Nicholas (w/o) v Weston St Johns Res. (scr.)

Fry Club Res. 3 Clevedon United Res. 2

Imperial 1 **Langford Rovers** 3

Long Ashton 0 **Hengrove Athletic Res.** 2

Nailsea United Res. 4 Clutton 3

Shepton Mallet Res. 3 **Stockwood Green Robinsons Res.** 3 *aet* (3-5p)

Wells City Res. 2 Congresbury 1

Yatton Athletic 2 **Creech St Michael** 5

SECOND ROUND

Banwell 4 Frome Collegians 0

Bishop Sutton Res. 0 **Portishead Res.** 2

Cheddar Res. 4 Fry Club Res. 2

SOMERSET COUNTY LEAGUE DIVISION TWO EAST CONSTITUTION 2008-09

BISHOP SUTTON RESERVES . . . . Lake View, Wick Road, Bishop Sutton, Bristol BS39 5XP 01275 333097
CLUTTON. . . . . Warwick Fields, Upper Bristol Road, Clutton, Bristol BS39 5TA . . . . None
CUTTERS FRIDAY RESERVES . . . . The Cutters Club, Stockwood Lane, Stockwood, Bristol BS14 8SJ 01275 839830
DUNDRY ATHLETIC . . . . Dundry Playing Field, Crabtree Lane, Dundry, Bristol BS41 8LN 0117 964 5536
FROME COLLEGIANS. . . . . Selwood School, Berkley Road, Frome BA11 2EF . . . . None
FRY CLUB RESERVES. . . . . Fry Club, Somerdale, Keynsham, Bristol BS31 2AU 0117 937 6500/6501
HENGROVE ATHLETIC RESERVES . . . . Norton Lane, Whitchurch, Bristol BS14 0BT 01275 832894
IMPERIAL. . . . . Bristol Imperial Sports Club, West Town Lane, Whitchurch, Brislington BS4 5DT 01275 546000
RADSTOCK TOWN RESERVES. . . . . Southfield Recreation Ground, Frome Hill, Radstock BA3 3NZ. 01761 435004
SHEPTON MALLET RESERVES . . . West Shepton Playing Fields, Old Wells Road, Shepton Mallet BA4 5XN. 01749 344609
STOCKWOOD GREEN ROBINSONS RESERVES . . . Hursley Lane, Woolard Lane, Whitchurch, Bristol BS14 0QY. 01275 891300
TIMSBURY ATHLETIC RESERVES. . . Recreation Ground, North Road, Timsbury, Bath BA2 0JH 01761 472523
TUNLEY ATHLETIC . . . . The Recreation Centre, Bath Road, Tunley BA2 0EB . . . . None
WELTON ROVERS RESERVES . . . . West Clewes, North Road, Midsomer Norton BA3 2QD. 01761 412097
WESTFIELD . . . . Fosseway Playing Fields, Charlton Lane, Midsomer Norton BA3 4BD. . . . . None
IN: Cutters Friday Reserves (P – Bath & District League Premier Division), Dundry Athletic (R), Radstock Town Reserves (P – Mid-Somerset
League Premier Division), Tunley Athletic (R), Welton Rovers Reserves (R), Westfield (P – Mid-Somerset League Premier Division)
OUT: Cheddar Reserves (S – Division Two West), Larkhall Athletic Reserves (P), Saltford (P), Wells City Reserves (S – Division Two West)

	Banwell	Berrow	Clevedon United Res.	Combe St Nicholas	Congresbury	Creech St Michael	Langford Rovers	Long Ashton	Nailsea United Res.	Portishead Res.	Weston St Johns Res.	Wrington-Redhill	Yatton Athletic
Banwell	D	4-3	6-2	0-4	2-0	1-3	1-2	4-0	2-1	1-3	3-0	3-2	1-0
Berrow	1-1	I	1-1	0-4	2-1	0-6	3-1	3-2	2-1	0-1	5-1	1-0	1-1
Clevedon United Res.	1-4	2-2	V	1-1	2-1	2-0	1-5	1-1	2-2	3-1	6-1	1-2	4-1
Combe St Nicholas	1-1	2-2	4-1		1-1	3-1	0-1	0-1	1-0	2-5	6-0	4-1	1-1
Congresbury	0-2	4-0	1-0	1-1	T	2-4	1-5	3-0	0-2	0-0	6-1	4-2	2-2
Creech St Michael	1-3	2-0	0-1	1-1	6-2	W	1-3	4-0	4-1	2-4	10-1	4-0	3-2
Langford Rovers	4-3	3-0	3-1	3-0	3-2	2-4	O	4-1	5-1	0-4	9-0	4-0	1-2
Long Ashton	3-0	2-3	0-1	0-1	1-1	0-4	2-1		1-2	1-5	1-0	3-1	0-2
Nailsea United Res.	6-0	5-0	4-4	1-0	3-2	3-1	0-1	1-1	W	2-2	1-0	4-0	3-3
Portishead Res.	0-4	4-1	3-1	2-0	3-2	3-0	0-2	1-1	0-0	E	1-2	2-0	2-2
Weston St Johns Res.	0-7	0-2	1-6	2-3	1-3	3-2	0-3	5-3	1-3	1-3	S	2-5	3-1
Wrington-Redhill	0-5	1-4	3-2	1-5	1-5	0-3	1-4	4-2	2-4	1-5	5-1	T	1-2
Yatton Athletic	2-3	1-1	3-0	2-4	1-4	0-2	1-1	0-2	2-0	0-3	12-1	1-1	

Combe St Nicholas 1 **Nailsea United Res.** 3 *aet*

Creech St Michael 2 **Hengrove Athletic Res.** 3 *aet*

Langford Rovers 1 **Larkhall Athletic Res.** 4 *aet*

Stockwood Green Robinsons Res. 1 **Wells City Res.** 3 *aet*

Timsbury Athletic Res. 0 **Berrow** 1 *aet*

QUARTER-FINALS

Berrow 0 **Larkhall Athletic Res.** 2

Cheddar Res. 0 **Banwell** 2

Hengrove Athletic Res. 0 **Nailsea United Res.** 1

Portishead Res. 0 **Wells City Res.** 1

SEMI-FINALS

Banwell 2 Wells City Res. 1

Nailsea United Res. 1 **Larkhall Athletic Res.** 2

FINAL

(May 13th at Bishop Sutton)

Larkhall Athletic Res. 2 Banwell 0

Division Two West		P	W	D	L	F	A	Pts
Langford Rovers		24	18	1	5	70	29	55
Portishead Res.		24	15	5	4	57	28	50
Banwell		24	15	2	7	61	39	47
Creech St Michael		24	14	1	9	68	37	43
Combe St Nicholas		24	11	7	6	49	29	40
Nailsea United Res.		24	11	6	7	50	36	39
Berrow		24	9	6	9	37	50	33
Congresbury		24	8	5	11	48	45	29
Yatton Athletic		24	6	8	10	44	44	26
Long Ashton		24	6	4	14	28	51	22
Clevedon United Res.	-11	24	8	6	10	46	50	19
Wrington-Redhill		24	5	1	18	34	75	16
Weston St Johns Res.	-7	24	4	0	20	27	106	5

SOMERSET COUNTY LEAGUE DIVISION TWO WEST CONSTITUTION 2008-09

BACKWELL UNITED RESERVES .... The Playing Fields, West Town Road, Backwell, Bristol BS48 3HG 01275 462612

BANWELL .... Riverside Ground, Riverside, Banwell BS29 6EE............................. 01934 820773

BERROW .... Red Road Playing Fields, Berrow, Burnham-on-Sea TA8 2LY .... None

CHEDDAR RESERVES................. Bowdens Park, Draycott Road, Cheddar BS27 3RL.......................... 01934 743736

CLEVEDON UNITED RESERVES .. Coleridge Vale Playing Fields, Southley Road, Clevedon BS21 6PF 01275 871878

COMBE ST NICHOLAS .... Slades Cross, Combe St Nicholas TA20 3HQ 01460 234743

CONGRESBURY .... Broadstones Playing Fields, Stonewell Lane, Congresbury BS49 5DL 01934 832150

CREECH ST MICHAEL .... Creech St Michael Rec, Hyde Lane, Creech St Michael, Taunton TA3 5QJ .... None

LONG ASHTON...................... Long Ashton Rec., Keedwell Hill, Long Ashton BS41 9DP .... None

NAILSEA UNITED RESERVES .... Grove Sports Ground, Old Church, Nailsea BS48 4ND 01275 856892

WELLS CITY RESERVES .... The Athletic Ground, Rowdens Road, Wells BA5 1TU 01749 679971

WESTON ST JOHNS RESERVES... Coleridge Road, Bournville Estate, Weston-super-Mare BS23 3UP 01934 612862

WRINGTON-REDHILL .... Recreation Ground, Silver Street, Wrington BS40 5QE .... None

YATTON ATHLETIC................. Hangstones Playing Fields, Stowey Road, Yatton BS49 4HY .... None

IN: Backwell United Reserves (R), Cheddar Reserves (S – Division Two East), Wells City Reserves (S – Division Two East)

OUT: Langford Rovers (P), Portishead Reserves (P)

SOUTH DEVON LEAGUE

	Bishopsteignton United	Bovey Tracey	Brixham United	Brixham Villa	Chagford	East Allington United	Hele Rovers	Ipplepen Athletic	Kingskerswell & Chelston	Kingsteignton Athletic	Newton Abbot Spurs Res.	Torbay Gentlemen	Upton Athletic	Waldon Athletic
Bishopsteignton United		0-3	2-1	1-2	1-5	3-4	5-2	1-0	2-5	2-0	2-5	6-0	1-7	3-0
Bovey Tracey	3-1	P	5-1	5-2	5-1	5-0	4-1	1-0	1-1	1-0	13-0	20-0	0-0	5-2
Brixham United	1-4	4-5	R	4-2	0-0	2-1	3-1	0-0	1-1	1-1	4-3	5-1	1-3	0-4
Brixham Villa	3-2	7-3	2-1	E	1-3	0-0	1-1	3-2	2-2	1-1	2-2	3-2	1-2	0-4
Chagford	1-1	1-5	1-0	0-2	M	3-2	5-1	1-1	1-4	1-0	5-2	1-0	0-4	4-1
East Allington United	1-4	1-5	3-4	2-4	0-3	I	1-0	11-2	0-4	2-2	1-2	7-0	2-4	1-1
Hele Rovers	4-3	0-6	3-3	1-3	4-0	0-5	E	2-3	3-3	3-2	2-2	0-4	2-3	0-2
Ipplepen Athletic	1-3	1-5	1-2	1-7	0-4	2-3	0-6	R	2-0	0-2	0-9	1-1	0-7	0-2
Kingskerswell & Chelston	1-3	0-1	1-1	8-0	1-3	1-2	0-4	1-2		2-1	8-2	3-1	2-3	3-1
Kingsteignton Athletic	3-2	1-2	2-2	1-1	2-1	7-2	1-7	9-0	1-3		2-2	6-0	1-4	2-7
Newton Abbot Spurs Res.	0-3	3-5	0-0	3-3	5-1	3-4	3-3	0-5	4-6	3-1	D	2-3	0-5	4-0
Torbay Gentlemen	1-2	0-4	1-3	0-1	4-0	2-2	2-1	2-1	3-1	2-0	3-3	I	0-3	1-2
Upton Athletic	2-0	2-5	2-0	1-0	5-0	3-1	2-1	5-0	2-1	0-0	3-0	4-1	V	5-0
Waldon Athletic	2-4	2-3	2-3	1-3	3-4	1-2	3-1	7-4	1-2	1-2	2-3	5-1	1-7	

BELLI CUP

FIRST ROUND
East Allington United 4 Chagford 2
Hele Rovers 5 Bishopsteignton Utd 2
Newton Abbot Spurs Res. 3
Kingsteignton Athletic 2
Torbay Gentlemen 3 Brixham Utd 0
Upton Ath. 4 Brixham V. 4 *aet* (4-2p)
Walton Athletic 1 **Bovey Tracey** 3

QUARTER-FINALS
East Allington Utd 2 **Bovey Tracey** 3
Hele Rovers 4 Ipplepen Athletic 2
Kingskerswell & Chelston 5
Torbay Gentlemen 4 *aet*
Upton Athletic 4 Newton Abbot
Spurs Res. 0

SEMI-FINALS
Bovey Tracey 5 Hele Rovers 0
Upton Ath. 0 **Kingskerswell & C.** 3

FINAL
(May 12th at Buckland Athletic)
Bovey Tracey 5 Kingskerswell &
Chelston 3 *aet*

Premier Division

		P	W	D	L	F	A	Pts
Bovey Tracey		26	23	2	1	120	31	71
Upton Athletic		26	23	2	1	89	18	71
Brixham Villa		26	12	7	7	56	53	43
Bishopsteignton United		26	13	1	12	61	57	40
Chagford		26	12	3	11	49	58	39
Kingskerswell & Chelston		26	11	5	10	64	47	38
East Allington United		26	9	4	13	60	67	31
Brixham United	-6	26	9	8	9	47	51	29
Kingsteignton Athletic		26	7	7	12	50	52	28
Waldon Athletic		26	9	1	16	58	69	28
Torbay Gentlemen	+3	26	7	4	15	37	88	28
Newton Abbot Spurs Res.		26	7	6	13	65	87	27
Hele Rovers		26	7	5	14	56	69	26
Ipplepen Athletic	-9	26	4	3	19	29	94	6

Division One

		P	W	D	L	F	A	Pts
Newton Abbot Res.	-3	26	20	1	5	81	28	58
Totnes & Dartington SC Res.	-3	26	19	2	5	94	41	56
Riviera Spurs		26	17	4	5	77	36	55
Moretonhampstead		26	14	3	9	55	42	45
Dartmouth Res.	+5	26	11	5	10	53	42	43
Upton Athletic Res.		26	12	5	9	45	43	41
Paignton Saints		26	11	4	11	60	55	37
Loddiswell	-9	26	14	3	9	74	51	36
Watts Blake Bearne	-13	26	14	5	7	60	38	34
Ashburton		26	7	4	15	37	51	25
Newton '66	+3	26	6	2	18	42	83	23
Abbotskerswell	-6	26	9	1	16	47	69	22
Brixham Villa Res.	-3	26	7	6	13	33	58	21
Victoria Rangers	-6	26	0	0	26	21	142	-6

DARTMOUTH CUP FINAL
(May 9th at Dartmouth)
Brixham Villa Res. 0 **Totnes & Dartington SC Res.** 1 *aet*

WOOLLCOMBE BEER WATTS SOUTH DEVON LEAGUE PREMIER DIVISION CONSTITUTION 2008-09

BRIXHAM UNITED . . . . Wall Park, Wall Park Road, Brixham TQ5 9UF . . . . None
BRIXHAM VILLA . . . . St Marys Park, Brixham TQ5 9QY . . . . None
CHAGFORD . . . . War Memorial Playing Field, Manor Road, Chagford, Newton Abbot TQ13 8AS . . . . None
EAST ALLINGTON UNITED . . . . Poole Lane, East Allington, Totnes TQ9 7PZ . . . . None
GALMPTON UNITED & TORBAY GENTLEMEN RESERVES . . War Memorial Playing Field, Greenway Road, Galmpton, Brixham TQ5 0LP . . None
HELE ROVERS . . . . Barton Downs Plaing Fields, Lummaton Cross, Torquay TQ2 8ET . . . . None
KINGSKERSWELL & CHELSTON . . . . Armada Park, Nutbush Lane, Chelston, Torquay TQ2 6SQ . . . . None
KINGSTEIGNTON ATHLETIC . . . . . Broadpark, Broadway, Kingsteignton, Newton Abbot TQ12 3EH . . . . None
NEWTON ABBOT RESERVES . . . . Coach Road Stadium, Coach Road, Newton Abbot TQ12 1EJ 01626 335011
NEWTON ABBOT SPURS RESERVES . . . . Recreation Ground, Marsh Road, Newton Abbot TQ12 2AR 01626 365343
RIVIERA SPURS . . . . Quinta Playing Fields, Quinta Road, Torquay TQ1 3RN. . . . . None
TOTNES & DARTINGTON SC RESERVES . . . . . . Foxhole Sports Ground, Dartington TQ9 6EB. 01803 868032
UPTON ATHLETIC. . . . . Cricketfield Road, Torquay TQ2 7NP . . . . None
WALDON ATHLETIC. . . . . Windmill Hill Playing Fields, Higher Audley Avenue, Torquay TQ2 7PF. . . . . None

IN: Newton Abbot Reserves (P), Riviera Spurs (P), Totnes & Dartington SC Reserves (P)
OUT: Bishopsteignton United (W), Bovey Tracey (P – South West Peninsula League Division One East), Ipplepen Athletic (R)
Torbay Gentlemen become Galmpton United & Torbay Gentlemen Reserves

Division Two		P	W	D	L	F	A	Pts
Staverton & Landscove	+3	26	17	3	6	105	58	57
Galmpton United Res.		26	18	3	5	84	37	57
Paignton Villa	+2	26	12	7	7	66	50	45
Harbertonford		26	12	8	6	64	33	44
Langdon		26	14	2	10	58	50	44
Channings Wood	-9	26	16	2	8	111	70	41
Kingskerswell & Chelston Res.		26	10	9	7	61	49	39
South Brent	-4	26	10	7	9	60	55	33
East Allington United Res.		26	9	3	14	61	75	30
Stoke Gabriel Res.	-12	26	12	4	10	61	45	28
Kingsteignton Athletic Res.		26	7	6	13	50	86	27
Brixham United Res.		26	7	4	15	62	71	25
Chudleigh Athletic		26	3	3	20	28	103	12
Liverton United Res.		26	3	3	20	31	120	12

Division Three		P	W	D	L	F	A	Pts
Buckland Athletic Res.		24	19	3	2	89	20	60
Teign Village		24	18	3	3	100	35	57
Newton United		24	13	4	7	59	44	43
Meadowbrook Athletic	+3	24	10	3	11	36	46	36
Totnes & Dartington SC 'A'		24	10	6	8	51	62	36
Foxhole United	-3	24	11	3	10	60	54	33
Buckfastleigh Rangers Res.		24	9	5	10	57	54	32
Brixham Town		24	8	5	11	57	68	29
Nova	-3	24	8	5	11	54	63	26
Bovey Tracey Res.		24	7	1	16	48	72	22
Ilsington Villa		24	4	5	15	34	70	17
Hele Rovers Res.	-12	24	9	1	14	49	67	16
Newton Abbot 'A'	-9	24	6	4	14	41	80	13

LIDSTONE CUP FINAL
(May 5th at Kingsteignton Athletic)
Paignton Villa 4 Staverton & Landscove 3

RONALD CUP FINAL
(May 2nd at Liverton United)
Buckland Athletic Res. 5 Buckfastleigh Rangers Res. 0

Division Four		P	W	D	L	F	A	Pts
Dartmouth 'A'		20	15	3	2	80	35	48
Newton Abbot Spurs 'A'	-6	20	14	2	4	74	39	38
Broadhempston United	+3	20	11	1	8	51	45	37
Watts Blake Bearne Res.		20	11	3	6	59	42	36
Waldon Athletic Res.		20	10	2	8	45	43	32
Beesands Rovers		20	9	1	10	37	44	28
Babbacombe Corinthians		20	8	3	9	53	36	27
Bishopsteignton United Res.		20	8	2	10	58	55	26
Hookhills United		20	7	2	11	58	55	23
Kingskerswell & Chelston 'A'		20	6	2	12	41	48	20
Newton '66 Res.	-3	20	0	1	19	22	136	-2

Division Five		P	W	D	L	F	A	Pts
Staverton & Landscove Res.	+3	22	15	3	4	63	24	51
Stoke Fleming	-3	22	16	5	1	101	18	50
Stoke Gabriel 'A'		22	14	3	5	79	47	45
Malborough United		22	10	4	8	52	48	34
Torbay Christians		22	9	3	10	54	43	30
Teignmouth Res.	-3	22	10	2	10	76	66	29
Ashburton Res.	-3	22	9	4	9	64	65	28
Ipplepen Athletic Res.		22	7	6	9	43	67	27
Loddiswell Res.		22	7	5	10	44	73	26
Abbotskerswell Res.	-12	22	9	2	11	53	86	17
Broadhempston United Res.	+3	22	3	3	16	40	73	15
Chagford Res.	+3	22	2	2	18	21	80	11

LES BISHOP CUP FINAL
(April 25th at Totnes & Dartington SC)
Beesands Rovers 1 **Newton Abbot Spurs 'A'** 3

BILL TREEBY CUP FINAL
(May 8th at Buckfastleigh Rangers)
Ipplepen Athletic Res. 5 Stoke Fleming 3

Division Six		P	W	D	L	F	A	Pts
Buckland Athletic 'A'		22	20	1	1	85	12	61
Denbury Athletic	-1	22	16	2	4	73	26	49
Paignton Saints Res.		22	11	4	7	79	58	37
Dawlish United Res.	-4	22	10	5	7	57	55	31
Riviera Spurs Res.		22	8	5	9	46	47	29
Marldon		22	8	4	10	68	64	28
Babbacombe Corinthians Res.	-3	22	8	5	9	38	51	26
Moretonhampstead Res.		22	8	2	12	44	65	26
Harbertonford Res.	-3	22	8	4	10	55	67	25
Paignton Villa Res.		22	6	1	15	40	70	19
Chudleigh Athletic Res.	-6	22	7	3	12	40	63	18
Brixham Town Res.	-6	22	4	0	18	28	75	6

Division Seven		P	W	D	L	F	A	Pts
Watcombe Wanderers	-6	20	17	2	1	103	26	47
Torbay Rangers		20	14	3	3	81	35	45
Brixham Villa 'A'	+6	20	11	3	6	63	42	42
Newton United Res.		20	12	2	6	69	51	38
Foxhole United Res.		20	11	2	7	49	45	35
South Brent Res.	-3	20	9	2	9	76	42	26
Marldon Res.	+3	20	5	1	14	28	87	19
Kingsbridge & Kellaton	+3	20	3	4	13	22	63	16
Teign Village Res.		20	4	2	14	47	79	14
Dittisham United	-3	20	4	2	14	33	81	11
Stoke Fleming Res.	-33	20	8	1	11	46	66	-8

IVOR ANDREWS CUP FINAL
(May 16th at Stoke Gabriel)
Denbury Athletic 1 **Buckland Athletic 'A'** 2

CLIVE OLNEY CUP FINAL
(April 14th at Stoke Gabriel)
Foxhole United Res. 2 **Brixham Villa 'A'** 3

HERALD CUP

THIRD ROUND
Bishopsteignton United 4 Ashburton 0
Buckland Athletic Res. 2 Upton Athletic 1
Chagford 1 Harbertonford 1 *aet* (4-3p)
Ipplepen Athletic 1 **Hele Rovers** 7
Riviera Spurs 1 Torbay Gentlemen 0
Teign Village 1 **Newton Abbot Res.** 2
Teignmouth Res. 1 **Staverton & Landscove** 2
Waldon Athletic 3 Newton Abbot Spurs Res. 1 *aet*
QUARTER-FINALS
Buckland Athletic Res. 2 Bishopsteignton United 1

Chagford 7 Staverton & Landscove 3
Hele Rovers 3 Newton Abbot Res. 1
Riviera Spurs 2 Waldon Athletic 1
SEMI-FINALS
Buckland Athletic Res. 6 Chagford 2
(at Liverton United)
Hele Rovers 4 Riviera Spurs 2
(at Newton Abbot Spurs)
FINAL
(March 21st at Buckland Athletic)
Hele Rovers 2 Buckland Athletic Res. 0

SOUTH WALES AMATEUR LEAGUE

	AFC Porth	Aber Valley YMCA	Baglan Red Dragons	Caerau United	Carnetown	Corus Steel	Llangynwyd Rangers	Llanharry	Llantwit Major	Pantyscallog Village Juniors	Rhydyfelin	Taffs Well Res.	Trefelin BGC	Turberville Arms	Ynysddu Welfare Crusaders
AFC Porth		1-0	5-0	3-0	5-1	3-3	8-0	3-0	2-2	n/a	0-0	2-1	1-0	1-0	2-2
Aber Valley YMCA	0-0	D	0-1	6-1	5-5	2-0	3-0	7-1	5-2	5-2	3-1	1-2	3-2	1-2	4-0
Baglan Red Dragons	1-2	0-2	I	3-2	3-1	3-2	3-0	1-1	3-3	n/a	2-1	3-1	4-0	0-2	
Caerau United	0-1	0-4	0-5	V	3-2	2-4	1-1	1-1	2-1	n/a	2-3	1-2	2-8	2-0	1-2
Carnetown	1-4	2-5	3-1	4-0	I	3-0	5-1	2-1	1-0	n/a	2-1	1-1	1-2	3-1	1-0
Corus Steel	1-1	1-0	1-3	2-2	5-4	S	1-1	5-0	0-1	n/a	0-3	3-1	3-4	3-5	2-1
Llangynwyd Rangers	1-4	1-8	1-4	2-5	2-1	2-3	I	1-1	2-4	3-3	0-3	5-4	0-5	0-6	2-3
Llanharry	0-11	3-4	3-3	4-3	1-3	3-5	2-1	O	1-1	n/a	2-2	2-3	4-1	2-1	1-6
Llantwit Major	1-4	3-2	0-5	1-2	4-2	1-2	6-0	3-3	N	5-0	5-1	0-3	4-2	2-4	0-1
Pantyscallog Village Juniors	2-12	n/a	2-5	n/a	1-2	n/a	n/a	n/a	n/a		2-7	n/a	n/a	n/a	n/a
Rhydyfelin	2-4	1-1	1-2	4-2	1-1	2-2	3-2	1-2	2-1	n/a		0-0	0-3	1-3	0-0
Taffs Well Res.	0-6	1-1	0-2	4-0	1-2	0-0	6-0	2-1	3-1	4-3	0-2	O	1-6	2-1	0-2
Trefelin BGC	1-2	6-1	3-3	2-0	3-1	4-1	3-0	2-1	5-2	3-1	3-0	1-1	N	0-1	3-0
Turberville Arms	2-2	2-4	2-0	5-1	2-2	1-3	2-0	5-2	0-1	n/a	1-3	3-2	3-5	E	0-1
Ynysddu Welfare Crusaders	1-2	1-3	0-2	3-1	2-2	4-1	3-0	3-2	1-2	n/a	2-2	2-0	0-5	3-0	

Note – Pantyscallog Village Juniors withdrew during the course of the season
Their results are shown above but are expunged from the league table

Division One

		P	W	D	L	F	A	Pts
AFC Porth		26	19	7	0	79	20	64
Trefelin BGC		26	18	2	6	83	37	56
Baglan Red Dragons		26	15	5	6	57	36	50
Aber Valley YMCA		26	15	4	7	75	39	49
Ynysddu Welfare Crusaders		26	13	4	9	45	38	43
Carnetown		26	11	5	10	56	54	38
Corus Steel		26	10	6	10	53	56	36
Turberville Arms	-3	26	12	2	12	53	49	35
Rhydyfelin		26	8	8	10	40	45	32
Taffs Well Res.		26	8	7	11	39	45	31
Llantwit Major		26	9	4	13	51	58	31
Caerau United	-3	26	5	3	18	36	77	15
Llanharry	-3	26	3	8	15	42	83	14
Llangynwyd Rangers		26	2	3	21	25	97	9

Pantyscallog Village Juniors – record expunged

W JOHN OWEN CUP

FIRST ROUND

AFC Bargoed Redz 2 Graig 1
AFC Porth 2 Treforest 1
Baglan Red Dragons 3 Turberville Arms 1
Blaenrhondda 4 Brynna 0
Cardiff Draconians 4 Gilfach Goch Athletic 0
Carnetown 0 **Taffs Well Res.** 2
FC Abercwmboi 6 Llangynwyd Rangers 1
Ferndale Boys Club 2 **Aber Valley YMCA** 4
Hirwaun Welfare 6 Kenfig Hill 1
Llanharry 2 **Trelewis Welfare** 3
Llantwit Major 5 Caerau United 1
Pantyscallog Village Juniors 1 **Pencoed Athletic** 2
Rhydyfelin 4 Rhoose 0
Splott Albion (w/o) v Abercynon Athletic (scr.)
Ton & Gelli Boys Club (scr.) v **Ynysddu Welfare Crusaders** (w/o)
Trefelin BGC 2 **Corus Steel** 3

SOUTH WALES AMATEUR LEAGUE DIVISION ONE CONSTITUTION 2008-09

AFC BARGOED REDZ .... Bargoed Park, Bargoed .... None
ABER VALLEY YMCA .... Abertridwr Park, Tridwr Road, Abertridwr, Caerphilly CF83 4DN .... None
BAGLAN RED DRAGONS .... Evans Bevans, Baglan, Port Talbot .... None
CAERAU UNITED .... Athletic Ground, Humphries Terrace, Caerau, Bridgend CF34 0SG 01656 732471
CARNETOWN .... Cae Carnetown, Grovers Field, Grovers Lane, Carnetown, Abercynon .... None
CORUS STEEL .... Corus Playing Fields, Margam, Port Talbot 01639 882066
LLANGYNWYD RANGERS .... Llangynwyd Playing Fields, Llangynwyd, Maesteg .... None
LLANHARRY .... Recreation Ground, Llanharry .... None
LLANTWIT MAJOR .... Windmill Lane, Llantwit Major CF61 2SU .... None
RHOOSE .... Ceri Road, Rhoose, Barry CF62 3HF .... None
RHYDYFELIN .... Upper Boat Playing Field, Hawthorn, Rhondda .... None
SPLOTT ALBION .... University Playing Field, Llanrumney, Cardiff .... None
TAFFS WELL RESERVES .... Rhiw Dda'r, Parish Road, Taffs Well CF15 7QB 02920 811080
TREFELIN BGC .... Ynys Park, Cwmavon Road, Port Talbot SA12 8RD 01639 882609
TURBERVILLE ARMS .... Ely Playing Field, Penygraig, Cardiff .... None
YNYSDDU CRUSADERS .... Ynysddu Welfare Park, Graig View, Ynysddu, Newport NP11 7JG 01495 200377

IN: *AFC Bargoed Redz (P), Rhoose (P), Splott Albion (P)*
OUT: *AFC Porth (P – Welsh League Division Three), Abercynon Athletic (WN), Pantyscallog Village Juniors (WS)*
Ynysddu Welfare Crusaders become Ynysddu Crusaders

	AFC Bargoed Redz	Blaenrhondda	Brynna	Cardiff Draconians	FC Abercwmboi	Ferndale Boys Club	Gilfach Goch Athletic	Graig	Hirwaun Welfare	Kenfig Hill	Pencoed Athletic	Rhoose	Splott Albion	Ton & Gelli Boys Club	Treforest	Trelewis Welfare
AFC Bargoed Redz		2-5	3-2	2-2	2-1	2-2	8-1	8-0	3-1	1-3	3-1	3-2	1-4	2-2	2-2	2-1
Blaenrhondda	2-7		2-1	4-2	1-2	1-1	3-0	4-0	2-3	4-4	6-0	1-1	0-1	0-2	1-0	1-1
Brynna	6-1	0-1	D	5-1	3-0	4-1	3-2	5-1	4-1	2-0	2-3	3-4	3-2	4-2	1-4	2-0
Cardiff Draconians	1-3	3-2	4-1	I	2-2	2-3	5-1	5-2	0-3	2-5	7-2	1-2	1-1	3-4	0-1	1-1
FC Abercwmboi	1-3	1-3	0-8	1-0	V	3-0	2-1	1-0	2-1	1-3	5-3	1-3	2-1	5-2	3-2	1-3
Ferndale Boys Club	2-2	1-1	1-0	0-1	3-2	I	3-0	5-2	1-3	1-5	3-2	1-3	0-3	1-3	3-7	3-4
Gilfach Goch Athletic	0-3	2-3	1-7	4-4	2-3	1-4	S	3-1	2-2	3-2	2-5	0-4	1-7	2-3	0-8	2-1
Graig	0-2	1-3	2-5	0-3	0-0	0-5	4-1	I	0-4	3-3	5-1	1-2	0-1	3-3	1-3	0-2
Hirwaun Welfare	2-4	1-4	0-6	1-4	1-0	7-2	7-1	5-0	O	0-1	3-4	2-1	5-2	2-0	3-2	4-1
Kenfig Hill	1-4	1-0	4-2	0-0	2-0	5-2	0-3	1-0	1-2	N	2-1	1-0	1-2	2-1	4-1	2-4
Pencoed Athletic	1-3	1-3	1-4	1-0	2-2	3-0	4-1	4-2	2-1	1-1		1-4	2-4	3-3	2-1	3-0
Rhoose	3-1	2-1	3-0	7-1	1-2	3-1	1-0	2-2	5-3	2-0	1-0	T	1-4	3-0	5-2	3-0
Splott Albion	1-1	1-3	1-0	1-2	5-0	4-0	5-3	3-0	1-0	5-1	4-2	0-8	W	2-1	4-2	2-2
Ton & Gelli Boys Club	2-2	1-3	1-3	0-0	1-0	5-1	4-2	2-2	3-2	4-0	1-10	0-2	O		2-4	1-3
Treforest	0-1	2-4	0-2	3-3	4-2	6-1	2-1	2-4	0-2	3-0	7-3	1-2	6-2	4-0		1-2
Trelewis Welfare	2-0	1-4	1-3	1-0	1-2	1-0	5-0	1-1	5-1	1-3	2-2	0-1	3-3	1-1	2-1	

SECOND ROUND

Aber Valley YMCA 2 Cardiff Draconians 0
AFC Porth 2 AFC Bargoed Redz 0
Baglan Red Dragons 3 Hirwaun Welfare 2
Corus Steel 4 Blaenrhondda 0
FC Abercwmboi 1 **Rhydyfelin** 3
Pencoed Athletic 0 **Splott Albion** 8
Taffs Well Res. 0 **Ynysddu Welfare Crusaders** 4
Trelewis Welfare 3 Llantwit Major 3 *aet* (5-4p)

QUARTER-FINALS

AFC Porth 3 Rhydyfelin 0
Baglan Red Dragons 1 **Corus Steel** 2
Splott Albion 0 **Aber Valley YMCA** 3
Ynysddu Welfare Crusaders 3 Trelewis Welfare 0

SEMI-FINALS

AFC Porth 0 **Aber Valley YMCA** 1
Ynysddu Welfare Crusaders 0 Corus Steel 0 *aet* (4-2p)

FINAL

(May 10th at Pontypridd Town)
Aber Valley YMCA 1 Ynysddu Welfare Crusaders 0

Division Two		P	W	D	L	F	A	Pts
Rhoose		30	23	2	5	89	34	71
Splott Albion		30	19	4	7	78	51	61
AFC Bargoed Redz		30	17	7	6	81	53	58
Brynna		30	19	0	11	91	47	57
Blaenrhondda		30	17	5	8	72	45	56
Hirwaun Welfare		30	16	1	13	73	62	49
Kenfig Hill		30	15	4	11	60	54	49
Treforest		30	14	2	14	83	62	44
Trelewis Welfare		30	12	8	10	53	48	44
FC Abercwmboi		30	13	2	15	47	65	41
Ton & Gelli Boys Club		30	9	7	14	56	74	34
Cardiff Draconians	-3	30	9	8	13	60	63	32
Pencoed Athletic		30	8	5	17	58	88	29
Ferndale Boys Club	-3	30	8	4	18	51	85	25
Graig		30	4	5	21	39	89	17
Gilfach Goch Athletic	-3	30	4	2	24	42	113	11

SOUTH WALES AMATEUR LEAGUE DIVISION TWO CONSTITUTION 2008-09

AFC TALBOT GREEN . . . . Talbot Park, Talbot Green, Pontyclun, Llantrisant . . . . None
BLAENRHONDDA . . . . Blaenrhondda Park, Brook Street, Blaenrhondda CF42 5SF 01443 774772
BRYNNA . . . . Brynna Welfare Ground, Heol Dewi, Brynna, Pontyclun CF72 9SP 01443 226646
CARDIFF DRACONIANS . . . . Llanidloes Road, Gabalfa, Cardiff CF14 2ST . . . . None
FC ABERCWMBOI . . . . Recreation Ground, Abercwmboi, Rhondda . . . . None
FERNDALE BOYS CLUB . . . . Maerdy Park, Rowley Terrace, Maerdy, Ferndale CF43 4BH . . . . None
GILFACH GOCH ATHLETIC . . . . Abercerdin School Field, Kenry Street, Gilfach Goch, Porth CF39 8RS 01443 672262
GRAIG . . . . Pontypridd Town FC, Ynysangharad Park, Pontypridd 01443 486571
HIRWAUN WELFARE . . . . Manchester Place, Hirwaun, Aberdare CF44 9RB 01685 811900
KENFIG HILL . . . . Central Athletic Ground, Croft Goch, Kenfig Hill, Bridgend CF33 6HA . . . . None
PENCOED ATHLETIC . . . . Recreation Ground, Felindre Road, Pencoed, Bridgend CF35 5PB . . . . None
TON & GELLI BOYS CLUB . . . . Ton Pentre FC, Ynys Park, Sawmill Villas, Ton Pentre CF41 7AF 01443 432813
TREFOREST . . . . White Tips Stadium, Dan-Y-Bryn Road, Treforest, Pontypridd CF37 1RX 01443 485532
TRELEWIS WELFARE . . . . Parc Taff, Bargoed, Trelewis . . . . None
WYNDHAM . . . . Blaenrhondda FC, Blaenrhondda Park, Brook Street, Blaenrhondda CF42 5SF 01443 774772
IN: AFC Talbot Green (P – Taff Ely/Rhymney Valley League), Wyndham (P – Rhondda & District League Premier Division)
OUT: AFC Bargoed Redz (P), Rhoose (P), Splott Albion (P)
(Penarth Town will also be promoted from the Vale of Glamorgan League if a second appeal to the FAW against initial rejection is upheld)

SOUTH WALES SENIOR LEAGUE

	Bridgend Street	Butetown St Marys	Cogan Coronation	Cwm Welfare	Cwmbach Royal Stars	Fairwater	Fochriw	Grange Albion	Lewistown	Llanrumney United	Nelson Cavaliers	Penydarren Boys Club	St Athan	St Josephs	Sully Sports	Tonyrefail BGC
Bridgend Street		0-3	2-1	2-1	3-2	3-2	0-3	4-3	1-2	1-0	9-0	0-3	3-3	2-1	0-1	2-5
Butetown St Marys	1-4		1-3	4-4	5-4	2-3	4-2	3-3	1-1	2-1	5-0	2-4	2-4	5-0	0-5	0-1
Cogan Coronation	2-0	0-1	D	0-4	2-1	0-2	1-2	1-1	2-1	3-0	1-1	3-4	7-3	1-2	0-1	1-2
Cwm Welfare	4-3	7-0	1-3	I	4-0	1-5	0-3	2-1	1-2	2-0	1-3	1-2	5-2	1-1	1-2	3-4
Cwmbach Royal Stars	4-4	2-1	0-0	1-0	V	5-4	3-3	0-1	3-6	0-2	3-2	1-2	0-4	3-2	0-2	1-3
Fairwater	2-2	0-0	6-2	1-3	4-1	I	4-0	1-0	4-0	4-2	3-2	4-0	3-2	2-0	1-0	2-0
Fochriw	5-1	5-3	1-0	5-0	1-0		S	2-0	1-2	0-0	3-4	2-0	5-1	2-1	1-3	1-0
Grange Albion	2-3	8-2	3-2	4-5	6-2	2-3	5-1	I	2-5	5-1	4-2	2-0	4-3	2-3	1-0	2-4
Lewistown	3-4	1-0	3-1	1-1	4-0	0-3	0-0	2-1	O	3-3	5-1	1-1	4-2	4-3	1-3	1-1
Llanrumney United	5-4	4-2	2-4	1-3	4-1	1-1	3-5	2-0	1-3	N	2-2	2-3	1-5	3-0	1-2	4-2
Nelson Cavaliers	0-1	2-1	1-2	1-5	1-0	1-6	0-3	1-5	0-4	0-9		0-1	1-0	1-1	2-2	1-1
Penydarren Boys Club	7-3	2-2	2-1	1-1	1-1	2-1	0-2	0-1	2-3	3-3	2-0	O	2-1	3-1	4-2	2-0
St Athan	0-5	1-2	3-1	0-1	1-1	1-2	2-5	2-1	1-3	3-1	1-1	0-1	N	0-1	1-1	2-3
St Josephs	1-2	4-0	3-3	5-3	6-0	2-3	5-2	2-1	0-0	1-1	6-4	1-3	2-2	E	3-1	1-2
Sully Sports	6-0	4-1	0-0	2-3	5-0	3-6	2-3	2-3	2-2	1-2	3-0	2-0	3-1	4-1		2-1
Tonyrefail BGC	2-2	4-3	3-2	1-0	5-0	0-0	0-1	0-1	2-0	2-1	4-1	2-2	3-5	1-4	2-3	

Division One		P	W	D	L	F	A	Pts
Fairwater		30	21	4	5	82	38	67
Fochriw	-1	30	19	3	8	69	45	59
Lewistown	+2	30	16	8	6	67	47	58
Penydarren Boys Club		30	17	6	7	59	45	57
Sully Sports		30	17	4	9	69	41	55
Tonyrefail BGC	+3	30	15	5	10	60	50	53
Cwm Welfare		30	14	4	12	69	55	46
Bridgend Street		30	14	4	12	70	74	46
Grange Albion		30	14	2	14	74	60	44
St Josephs	-4, -4g	30	11	6	13	59	61	35
Llanrumney United		30	9	6	15	62	67	33
Cogan Coronation		30	9	5	16	49	56	32
Butetown St Marys		30	8	5	17	58	83	29
St Athan		30	7	5	18	56	74	26
Cwmbach Royal Stars		30	5	5	20	39	92	20
Nelson Cavaliers	-1	30	5	6	19	35	93	20

C W BRUTY CUP

FIRST ROUND

AFC Butetown 3 **AFC Llwynypia** 3
aet (5-6p)
AFC Caerphilly 0 **Butetown St Marys** 4
Brecon Corinthians 1 Bridgend St 0
Fairwater 5 Lisvane/Llanishen 0
Fochriw 5 Caerphilly Town 1
Hopkinstown 1 Cascade 0
Lewistown 2 **Tonyrefail BGC** 5
Llanbradach Social 2 Cogan Coronation 1 *aet*
Llanrumney United 2 Cwmbach Royal Stars 1
Nelson Cavaliers 2 Grange Albion 0
St Athan 1 **Penydarren Boys Club** 2
Stanleytown 1 **Penrhiwfer** 3 *aet* (8-9p)
Sully Sports 3 Cwm Welfare 0
Tongwynlais 0 **St Josephs** 1 *aet*
Tonypandy Albion 2 Cadoxton Cons 0
Ynyshir Albion 1 **AFC Whitchurch** 5

SECOND ROUND

AFC Caerphilly 1 **Tonypandy Albion** 4
AFC Llwynypia 4 Penrhiwfer 2
AFC Whitchurch 2 St Josephs 1
Fairwater 3 Brecon Corinthians 2
Fochriw 7 Hopkinstown 2
Penydarren Boys Club 4 Nelson Cavaliers 0
Sully Sports 4 Llanbradach Social 1
Tonyrefail BGC 7 Llanrumney Utd 2

QUARTER-FINALS

Fairwater 5 AFC Whitchurch 1
Llanbradach Social 2 AFC Llwynypia 2 *aet* (4-3p)
Penydarren Boys Club 4 Tonypandy Albion 0
Tonyrefail BGC 1 **Fochriw** 3

SEMI-FINALS

Fairwater 4 Penydarren Boys Club 1
Fochriw 1 **Llanbradach Social** 3

FINAL
(May 10th at Penydarren Boys Club)
Fairwater 3 Llanbradach Social 1

IN: Llandradach Social (P), Tonypandy Albion (P), Ynyshir Albion (P)
OUT: Cwmbach Royal Stars (R), Nelson Cavaliers (R), St Athan (R)
Butetown St Marys become St Marys Butetown

SOUTHAMPTON LEAGUE

Note – BTC Southampton withdrew during the course of the season. Their results are shown herein but are expunged from the league table

	AFC Solent	AFC Target	BTC Southampton	Botley Village	Burridge Sports	Bush Hill	Capital	Comrades	Hedge End Rangers	Malvern	Northend United	Nursling	Solent WTL	Spartans
AFC Solent		1-2	n/a	2-0	0-0	1-4	3-0	6-1	0-3	1-1	3-0	2-6	4-3	0-3
AFC Target	0-1	W-L	0-1	8-1	5-2	3-1	1-2	0-2	2-6	6-1	2-5	2-3		2-7
BTC Southampton	n/a	n/a	S	2-7	n/a	n/a	n/a	n/a	1-2	n/a	0-7	0-11	n/a	n/a
Botley Village	6-1	1-0	n/a	E	4-0	2-1	4-2	1-5	1-2	5-2	8-0	2-3	6-1	3-2
Burridge Sports	0-0	2-5	6-2	1-2	N	2-3	0-1	0-5	0-2	2-0	1-4	1-2	0-3	1-8
Bush Hill	0-3	4-0	n/a	4-1	6-1	I	6-1	4-2	3-1	2-1	4-1	2-1	6-1	5-2
Capital	5-5	2-1	n/a	5-3	1-0	3-13	O	3-3	3-2	4-3	3-0	1-2	2-4	0-4
Comrades	1-3	1-1	n/a	1-4	5-1	1-7	5-3	R	3-3	2-1	2-4	1-5	5-0	1-3
Hedge End Rangers	2-2	3-4	n/a	2-1	3-3	2-3	5-4	3-4		2-1	11-1	2-4	2-2	4-2
Malvern	5-0	3-4	8-3	2-4	2-1	1-5	4-0	1-3	2-1	D	4-1	0-10	2-0	2-2
Northend United	1-3	1-1	n/a	1-3	2-2	3-8	4-2	2-7	1-4	2-5	I	0-12	0-5	2-4
Nursling	4-2	1-1	n/a	0-2	4-1	1-2	7-0	5-1	5-1	5-0	3-2	V	4-1	2-0
Solent WTL	2-6	3-4	n/a	0-2	2-2	0-4	3-3	3-7	3-1	4-1	4-2	1-3		5-1
Spartans	2-2	1-3	n/a	1-1	1-1	2-2	6-1	0-3	2-1	1-2	11-0	1-4	6-2	

Premier Division

Team	P	W	D	L	F	A	Pts
Nursling	24	20	1	3	98	28	61
Bush Hill	24	20	1	3	100	38	61
Botley Village	24	16	3	5	71	55	51
Comrades	24	11	5	8	59	64	38
AFC Solent	24	11	3	10	51	51	36
AFC Target	24	11	2	11	72	55	35
Spartans	24	10	4	10	51	54	34
Hedge End Rangers	24	10	4	10	55	63	34
Malvern	24	9	2	13	51	75	29
Solent WTL	24	8	3	13	55	54	27
Capital	24	7	6	11	50	51	27
Northend United	24	7	3	14	35	90	24
Burridge Sports	24	3	1	20	23	118	10
BTC Southampton – record expunged							9

DREW SMITH HOMES SOUTHAMPTON LEAGUE PREMIER CONSTITUTION 2008-09

AFC SOLENT .... Green Park, Wimpson Lane, Millbrook, Southampton SO16 4QF 02380 790693
AFC TARGET .... Cutbush Lane, West End, Southampton SO18 2GF 023 8046 2371
BISHOPSTOKE WMC .... Lapstone Park, Pavilion Close, Botley Road, Fair Oak, Eastleigh SO50 7AN 023 8039 1530
BUSH HILL .... Green Park, Green Lane, Millbrook, Southampton SO16 4QF 02380 790693
CAPITAL .... Fryern Recreation Ground, Green Ways, Chandlers Ford 023 8057 5950
COMRADES .... BTC Sports Ground, Stoneham Lane, Eastleigh, Southampton SO16 2PA 023 8055 6613
FREEMANTLE .... BTC Sports Ground, Stoneham Lane, Eastleigh, Southampton SO16 2PA 023 8055 6613
MALVERN .... Cutbush Lane, West End, Southampton SO18 5RY 023 8046 2371
NURSLING .... Nursling Rec, Nursling Street, Romsey Road, Nursling, Southampton SO16 0XW .... None
SOLENT WTL .... Mount Pleasant Recreation Ground, Hamble Lane, Hamble-le-Rice .... None
SPARTANS .... Gang Warily, Newlands Road, Blackfield, Southampton SO45 1GA 023 8089 3603
SPORTING WESSEX .... Gang Warily, Newlands Road, Blackfield, Southampton SO45 1GA 023 8089 3603

IN: Freemantle (P), Bishopstoke WMC (P), Sporting Wessex (P)
OUT: BTC Southampton (WS), Botley Village (S – Hampshire League 2004), Burridge Sports (R), Hedge End Rangers (S – Hampshire League 2004), Northend United (R)

Senior Division

	P	W	D	L	F	A	Pts
Freemantle	24	20	1	3	86	31	61
Bishopstoke WMC	24	15	1	8	75	42	46
Sporting Wessex	24	14	2	8	55	45	44
Burridge	24	13	2	9	53	34	41
Netley Central Spts Res.	24	12	2	10	60	51	38
AFC Hop	24	12	2	10	46	50	38
Hythe Aztecs	24	11	1	12	50	47	34
Comrades Res.	24	10	3	11	48	65	33
Durley Res.	24	10	3	11	45	60	31
Michelmersh & T. Res.	24	6	6	12	38	52	24
Hythe & Dibden Res.	24	6	5	13	48	80	23
A P Sports	24	6	2	16	37	50	20
Inmar	24	6	2	16	53	87	20

Division One

	P	W	D	L	F	A	Pts
AFC Redbridge	18	18	0	0	77	14	54
Sholing Sports	18	11	2	5	63	38	35
Booker Sports	18	10	2	6	64	44	32
Langley Manor	18	10	1	7	39	31	31
Priory Rovers	18	9	1	8	45	44	28
Braishfield	18	8	1	9	45	47	25
Otterbourne 'A'	18	7	2	9	49	51	23
WEB	18	6	3	9	31	39	21
MMS (Southampton)	18	2	2	14	20	69	8
Test Park Rangers	18	2	0	16	30	106	6

Division Two

	P	W	D	L	F	A	Pts
AFC Hiltingbury	20	16	2	2	80	26	50
Beaney Park	20	13	6	1	69	36	45
London Airways	20	10	4	6	57	37	34
Allbrook	20	10	2	8	49	41	32
Cadnam United	20	9	3	8	36	45	30
East Boldre	20	9	2	9	50	32	29
Hythe Aztec Res.	20	7	3	10	29	44	24
BTC Southampton Res.	20	5	6	9	42	34	21
Rownhams	20	5	6	9	37	43	21
Lowford	20	5	2	13	22	65	17
Inter Northam	20	2	2	16	16	84	8

Division Three

	P	W	D	L	F	A	Pts
Warsash Wasps	18	17	1	0	68	15	52
Hedge End Town	18	14	1	3	72	26	43
Veracity Vipers	18	14	1	3	55	25	43
S & B Sports	18	10	1	7	53	37	31
Compton	18	9	1	8	53	34	28
Monks Brook	18	6	1	11	35	39	19
AFC Energy	18	6	1	11	27	64	19
DMH Gleneagles	18	5	0	13	26	68	15
Capital Res.	18	3	0	15	27	77	9
Spartans Res.	18	2	1	15	18	49	7

Division Four

	P	W	D	L	F	A	Pts
Nimbin United	18	17	0	1	82	32	51
Wheatshields Wanderers	18	15	2	1	91	26	47
Forest Town NFC	18	12	2	4	72	22	38
Academicals	18	10	2	6	51	31	32
AC Sholing	18	8	2	8	54	54	26
Southampton City	18	6	3	9	43	47	21
Flames	18	5	1	12	21	52	16
Gate	18	5	1	12	27	84	16
Priory Rovers Res.	18	4	2	12	24	73	14
Burridge Sports Res.	18	2	1	15	15	50	7

Division Five

	P	W	D	L	F	A	Pts
Rising Sun Colden Common	18	14	1	3	71	21	43
Swan	18	13	1	4	61	26	40
Netley Marsh	18	12	3	3	56	34	39
Redbridge Warriors	18	11	2	5	41	22	35
Sparky Albion	18	8	2	8	36	37	26
AFC Stoneham 'A'	18	7	2	9	41	48	23
MMS (Southampton) Res.	18	7	1	10	38	40	22
Michelmersh & T. 'A'	18	6	4	8	28	36	22
Lowford Res.	18	3	0	15	26	54	9
AFC Aldermoor	18	1	0	17	30	110	3

Division Six

	P	W	D	L	F	A	Pts
Wombles	14	12	2	0	42	9	38
SPI Lasers	14	7	4	3	34	18	25
Testwood	14	7	4	3	37	25	25
Real Way	14	7	0	7	32	37	21
Freemantle Res.	14	5	4	5	24	24	19
East Boldre Res.	14	5	1	8	37	44	16
AFC Millwool	14	3	1	10	12	33	10
London Airways Res.	14	2	0	12	19	47	6

Division Seven

	P	W	D	L	F	A	Pts
Warsash Wasps Res.	14	13	1	0	75	11	40
Lyndhurst STJs Res.	14	10	1	3	76	9	31
Hamble United	14	8	2	4	41	39	26
Eastleigh United	14	7	1	6	50	33	22
AFC Terminal	14	6	1	7	34	36	19
New Forest	14	4	2	8	31	41	14
Sholing Sharks	14	4	0	10	30	55	12
Southampton City Eagles	14	0	0	14	12	125	0

SENIOR CUP FINAL
(April 21st at Hamble ASSC)
Nursling 4 Comrades 1

ROY WIGHTMAN JUNIOR CUP FINAL
(May 5th at Blackfield & Langley)
Forest Town NFC 2 Allbrook 1

ROY VALLANCE JUNIOR PLATE FINAL
(May 5th at Blackfield & Langley)
Nimbin United 2 Hedge End Town 4

SOUTHERN LEAGUE

	Banbury United	Bashley	Bedford Town	Brackley Town	Bromsgrove Rovers	Cheshunt	Chippenham Town	Cirencester Town	Clevedon Town	Corby Town	Gloucester City	Halesowen Town	Hemel Hempstead	Hitchin Town	King's Lynn	Mangotsfield Utd	Merthyr Tydfil	Rugby Town	Swindon Su'marine	Team Bath	Tiverton Town	Yate Town
Banbury United		0-2	1-2	1-0	2-1	2-1	1-3	1-0	0-0	2-1	1-1	0-0	1-1	1-1	0-2	1-1	1-1	2-3	2-1	0-0	2-1	2-4
Bashley	2-1		1-1	0-0	4-0	2-1	2-0	3-1	0-0	0-0	0-0	2-1	2-3	2-3	1-1	1-0	3-0	1-1	1-0	4-3	2-1	3-1
Bedford Town	0-0	2-1		3-4	0-4	5-3	0-1	2-0	1-1	1-2	2-0	0-3	1-1	3-2	0-3	0-1	3-3	1-1	4-0	1-2	1-0	2-2
Brackley Town	2-1	1-0	2-1	*P*	3-0	6-0	2-4	2-1	1-1	2-2	1-3	1-2	0-3	3-1	1-1	1-2	1-0	1-1	2-0	0-1	0-2	2-2
Bromsgrove Rovers	0-2	0-0	0-2	1-1	*R*	3-3	0-0	1-1	1-0	0-2	1-4	1-0	0-3	3-1	1-1	3-1	1-1	4-0	0-0	2-3	1-1	1-2
Cheshunt	1-1	1-3	1-2	2-2	1-0	*E*	1-4	2-0	1-2	1-5	0-3	0-2	0-4	1-2	1-3	0-0	0-0	1-2	3-0	1-2	0-0	0-3
Chippenham Town	2-2	2-2	5-0	1-2	2-2	5-1	*M*	2-0	1-0	1-1	4-1	0-0	1-2	1-0	2-2	1-0	3-1	1-1	3-1	1-1	5-1	3-2
Cirencester Town	0-1	0-3	2-1	1-0	2-1	4-3	1-1	*I*	1-2	0-0	1-4	2-3	1-0	2-3	0-4	0-0	1-1	1-2	1-2	0-1	3-2	1-2
Clevedon Town	0-1	0-0	2-1	0-0	0-2	2-1	0-0	2-2	*E*	3-0	1-1	0-1	0-1	1-1	2-2	2-1	3-3	3-2	1-2	0-2	4-0	1-1
Corby Town	2-1	4-2	1-0	2-0	4-2	2-0	0-0	2-4	1-1	*R*	2-5	1-2	0-2	3-0	0-2	1-2	0-1	3-4	0-2	1-2	1-0	2-2
Gloucester City	0-0	0-2	1-2	1-3	5-0	4-0	3-0	0-0	2-1	2-1		1-1	0-0	2-0	1-1	0-1	3-1	2-3	5-0	2-1	4-1	2-3
Halesowen Town	2-2	0-0	1-1	1-1	3-0	3-2	2-2	4-0	0-2	3-1	0-2	*D*	1-1	4-1	6-0	1-1	1-0	4-1	2-2	2-3	4-0	5-1
Hemel Hempstead Town	1-1	1-0	1-2	2-0	0-0	1-0	2-1	4-0	1-1	1-0	1-0	0-3	*I*	4-1	1-2	0-3	2-0	3-1	2-0	3-0	1-0	1-1
Hitchin Town	1-1	3-0	2-2	0-2	3-3	6-1	3-1	2-2	1-1	2-4	2-1	0-0	3-1	*V*	2-1	1-4	1-3	2-1	3-3	1-1	0-1	2-2
King's Lynn	4-0	1-0	1-0	0-1	0-0	2-2	3-1	2-0	2-2	3-2	1-0	2-2	4-0	2-1	*I*	0-0	1-0	0-2	4-0	1-0	2-0	3-0
Mangotsfield United	1-2	0-1	5-0	1-2	0-1	2-3	1-1	3-1	1-2	0-5	2-3	1-2	3-0	0-1	0-0	*S*	2-3	0-0	1-1	1-2	0-1	0-0
Merthyr Tydfil	2-0	2-3	1-0	2-2	2-0	3-1	4-1	3-2	1-1	1-2	1-2	2-2	0-1	1-1	1-3	1-1	*I*	2-0	2-0	1-4	0-1	5-0
Rugby Town	4-1	1-2	1-2	1-1	1-1	1-0	0-2	0-3	2-3	3-2	0-1	1-1	1-0	2-0	1-1	0-0	0-1	*O*	1-2	0-5	1-2	0-3
Swindon Supermarine	1-2	0-4	0-1	0-2	3-2	2-2	0-3	1-3	1-5	0-0	0-2	2-1	1-3	1-2	0-3	2-3	0-1	0-0	*N*	1-0	1-2	0-3
Team Bath	1-1	1-0	1-0	1-0	1-1	2-1	5-2	3-1	3-2	4-1	0-0	0-5	0-2	2-0	2-3	2-3	3-0	1-1	2-1		2-0	3-2
Tiverton Town	0-1	1-0	2-1	2-3	0-2	3-1	2-6	1-1	1-0	3-1	0-1	1-3	1-1	1-2	0-4	0-2	1-2	0-0	0-0	2-2		2-1
Yate Town	3-3	0-2	0-4	3-2	1-2	0-1	0-1	1-0	1-2	0-3	1-1	2-2	1-1	2-2	1-1	1-2	2-2	0-3	3-0	3-1	0-3	

Premier Division

	P	HOME					AWAY					TOTAL					
		W	D	L	F	A	W	D	L	F	A	W	D	L	F	A	Pts
King's Lynn	42	14	6	1	52	14	10	7	4	39	22	24	13	5	91	36	85
Team Bath	42	12	4	5	38	22	13	4	4	33	19	25	8	9	71	41	83
Halesowen Town	42	13	4	4	46	25	9	9	3	34	21	22	13	7	80	46	79
Chippenham Town	42	11	8	2	46	22	9	5	7	27	22	20	13	9	73	44	73
Bashley	42	12	7	2	36	18	7	5	9	24	28	19	12	11	60	46	69
Gloucester City	42	10	5	6	40	21	9	6	6	41	29	19	11	12	81	50	68
Hemel Hempstead Town	42	8	6	7	33	29	11	5	5	34	21	19	11	12	67	50	68
Brackley Town	42	9	5	7	34	28	7	7	7	23	25	16	12	14	57	53	60
Banbury United	42	7	8	6	23	26	7	8	6	32	31	14	16	12	55	57	58
Yate Town	42	9	3	9	36	34	7	7	7	35	42	16	10	16	71	76	58
Clevedon Town	42	7	9	5	28	23	6	9	6	21	23	13	18	11	49	46	57
Swindon Supermarine	42	7	8	6	28	22	7	4	10	23	45	14	12	16	51	67	54
Merthyr Tydfil	42	10	5	6	40	30	3	9	9	25	40	13	14	15	65	70	53
Mangotsfield United	42	8	9	4	25	20	4	7	10	13	22	12	16	14	38	42	52
Rugby Town	42	7	5	9	30	31	6	7	8	25	35	13	12	17	55	66	51
Corby Town	42	8	3	10	32	34	6	5	10	28	33	14	8	20	60	67	50
Tiverton Town	42	10	6	5	26	19	3	5	13	19	41	13	11	18	45	60	50
Hitchin Town	42	8	5	8	28	25	4	6	11	18	36	12	11	19	46	61	47
Bedford Town	42	7	6	8	32	34	5	3	13	22	39	12	9	21	54	73	45
Bromsgrove Rovers	42	5	9	7	24	28	5	3	13	22	39	10	12	20	46	67	42
Cirencester Town	42	6	3	12	24	37	2	5	14	20	43	8	8	26	44	80	32
Cheshunt	42	3	5	13	18	40	2	3	16	24	63	5	8	29	42	103	23

WWW.CHERRYRED.CO.UK

CHALLENGE CUP

(Premier Division champions v League Cup winners)

(Aug 4 at Bath City)
Bath City 1 **Tiverton Town** 1 (2-4p) *Att* 288

PLAY-OFFS

SEMI-FINALS
(May 1st) **Team Bath** 4 Bashley 1 *Att* 203
(May 1st) **Halesowen Tn** 2 Chippenham Tn 1 *Att* 1,105
FINAL *(May 3rd at Bath City)*
Team Bath 2 Halesowen Town 1 *Att* 838

DATES & GATES

WWW.NLNEWSDESK.CO.UK

The grid below lists, for each pairing of clubs, the date of the fixture (top) and the attendance/gate (bottom, italic). Rows are read against the column headings on the right‑hand side.

	Banbury United	Bashley	Bedford Town	Brackley Town	Bromsgrove Rovers	Cheshunt	Chippenham Town	Cirencester Town	Clevedon Town	Corby Town	Gloucester City	Halesowen Town	Hemel Hempstead Tn	Hitchin Town	King's Lynn	Mangotsfield United	Merthyr Tydfil	Rugby Town	Swindon Supermarine	Team Bath	Tiverton Town	Yate Town
Banbury United		5 Jan 320	22 Sep 314	26 Dec 767	24 Nov 301	22 Mar 302	26 Jan 272	12 Jan 463	17 Nov 266	25 Sep 249	17 Nov 298	30 Oct 245	12 Apr 263	10 Nov 235	27 Nov 242	16 Feb 325	23 Feb 341	24 Mar 352	18 Aug 259	1 Sep 255	15 Dec 400	1 Sep 128
Bashley	2 Feb 257		1 Dec 317	19 Feb 236	22 Mar 388	9 Oct 265	9 Feb 419	3 Nov 149	24 Nov 545	8 Sep 461	17 Nov 298	2 Feb 474	10 Nov 555	26 Feb 340	16 Feb 678	18 Aug 767	9 Feb 441	25 Aug 498	19 Apr 523	19 Jan 701	17 Nov 403	27 Nov 353
Bedford Town	1 Dec 335	26 Apr 179		29 Mar 325	8 Apr 303	4 Dec 326	1 Sep 290	19 Apr 303	23 Feb 278	1 Dec 288	13 Oct 230	15 Mar 301	29 Mar 143	17 Nov 262	4 Sep 317	11 Dec 203	4 Sep 170	1 Mar 139	17 Nov 160	22 Nov 122	10 Nov 319	1 Feb 312
Brackley Town	29 Sep 246	23 Feb 209	9 Feb 386		17 Nov 407	24 Nov 175	15 Apr 211	23 Feb 215	1 Jan 172	9 Feb 288	13 Oct 344	15 Apr 212	1 Jan 297	26 Feb 237	16 Feb 611	11 Mar 328	8 Mar 444	1 Mar 185	26 Apr 303	19 Apr 141	1 Apr 322	8 Mar 265
Bromsgrove Rovers	17 Nov 208	1 Sep 303	12 Mar 314	24 Nov 180		5 Jan 187	1 Sep 302	1 Dec 543	1 Dec 394	1 Jan 504	3 Oct 548	26 Dec 303	8 Sep 285	11 Oct 308	22 Sep 203	8 Aug 308	9 Feb 245	1 Dec 349	19 Apr 208	17 Nov 214	24 Mar 303	11 Mar 315
Cheshunt	8 Apr 377	24 Nov 146	29 Dec 386	5 Apr 407	8 Dec 322		19 Apr 376	13 Nov 433	26 Jan 394	5 Feb 548	24 Nov 241	29 Mar 615	17 Nov 343	5 Jan 417	24 Mar 524	22 Dec 336	22 Feb 444	1 Dec 340	18 Aug 338	22 Mar 468	6 Oct 363	24 Mar 467
Chippenham Town	21 Aug 303	8 Mar 135	5 Feb 335	8 Sep 369	15 Jan 211	4 Sep 225		1 Sep 215	23 Feb 278	1 Jan 303	13 Oct 280	15 Dec 212	1 Jan 297	26 Feb 237	18 Aug 298	11 Dec 301	22 Dec 245	1 Mar 145	12 Jan 208	19 Jan 303	8 Aug 141	8 Sep 265
Cirencester Town	8 Dec 154	25 Feb 131	26 Jan 188	8 Oct 153	12 Apr 181	29 Oct 109	22 Dec 282		16 Feb 215	1 Mar 210	23 Feb 212	12 Jan 203	1 Jan 159	26 Apr 160	2 Feb 149	5 Apr 214	1 Sep 170	19 Apr 160	17 Nov 167	19 Apr 122	10 Nov 223	11 Mar 126
Clevedon Town	25 Feb 407	1 Sep 167	24 Nov 204	26 Apr 180	9 Oct 186	5 Jan 209	5 Jan 312	26 Jan 238		6 Oct 141	17 Nov 206	16 Feb 248	17 Nov 143	13 Nov 279	21 Aug 447	22 Dec 297	24 Mar 214	15 Dec 153	9 Feb 165	11 Mar 195	8 Mar 233	8 Dec 167
Corby Town	1 Sep 241	1 Sep 209	5 Jan 180	24 Nov 279	31 Oct 146	27 Oct 209	26 Jan 215	1 Mar 182	16 Feb 270		29 Dec 340	8 Mar 375	8 Sep 203	29 Dec 324	18 Mar 369	8 Dec 205	9 Feb 212	1 Mar 244	26 Dec 153	10 Oct 239	19 Apr 265	8 Dec 126
Gloucester City	8 Sep 131	1 Feb 167	22 Mar 250	8 Sep 306	13 Nov 245	27 Oct 190	2 Sep 587	16 Feb 215	19 Apr 276	22 Dec 212		11 Mar 450	16 Feb 242	19 Apr 600	25 Jan 259	8 Dec 359	1 Apr 250	27 Mar 234	12 Dec 265	20 Feb 234	8 Sep 279	8 Sep 265
Halesowen Town	8 Mar 172	2 Feb 178	24 Nov 178	1 Mar 470	26 Dec 483	29 Oct 429	5 Apr 423	29 Nov 244	16 Feb 630	4 Mar 347	1 Mar 388		28 Aug 242	6 Oct 242	1 Apr 359	8 Dec 451	9 Apr 132	25 Aug 232	22 Sep 235	20 Apr 234	26 Apr 247	29 Jan 279
Hemel Hempstead Town	1 Mar 167	12 Apr 166	21 Aug 427	1 Mar 241	26 Jan 233	27 Aug 233	22 Sep 216	5 Mar 216	27 Oct 276	11 Mar 212	28 Aug 450	11 Mar 388		29 Mar 203	26 Nov 205	22 Mar 259	18 Aug 132	25 Aug 252	1 Sep 233	27 Mar 234	29 Jan 265	8 Sep 279
Hitchin Town	27 Oct 501	12 Apr 617	23 Feb 304	1 Jan 233	15 Dec 255	1 Jan 233	18 Aug 224	4 Sep 312	24 Mar 216	27 Oct 121	1 Sep 375	1 Sep 248	1 Dec 482		13 Nov 279	10 Nov 301	26 Apr 159	9 Oct 314	1 Apr 571	20 Oct 234	1 Dec 247	29 Jan 265
King's Lynn	11 Dec 617	5 Apr 383	22 Mar 241	31 Aug 470	26 Jan 233	27 Oct 630	5 Mar 423	29 Nov 630	19 Apr 276	4 Mar 347	16 Feb 450	16 Feb 242	1 Dec 242	13 Nov 420		22 Dec 297	9 Apr 314	27 Mar 469	4 Mar 462	20 Apr 462	26 Apr 247	8 Sep 265
Mangotsfield United	5 Feb 152	21 Aug 207	12 Apr 230	12 Apr 241	26 Jan 233	1 Jan 233	18 Aug 224	22 Mar 216	15 Mar 216	8 Mar 121	17 Nov 267	3 Nov 366	15 Mar 366	29 Dec 301	18 Mar 369		9 Apr 169	26 Jan 232	22 Sep 235	8 Mar 234	19 Jan 235	22 Sep 168
Merthyr Tydfil	5 Apr 364	12 Apr 166	21 Aug 241	23 Feb 241	26 Jan 209	15 Mar 277	18 Aug 218	5 Mar 310	27 Oct 216	5 Apr 121	17 Nov 206	18 Aug 203	4 Sep 248	8 Sep 176	18 Aug 178	22 Dec 297		15 Dec 173	8 Mar 156	8 Mar 160	18 Aug 160	16 Feb 283
Rugby Town	9 Feb 1,174	9 Feb 364	12 Apr 132	10 Nov 1,265	27 Aug 1,086	15 Mar 1,182	29 Mar 921	1 Apr 744	1 Jan 329	15 Oct 180	9 Feb 1,198	16 Feb 1,442	9 Feb 1,230	29 Mar 1,223	26 Apr 912	22 Dec 916	1 Mar 995		15 Dec 1,025	29 Jan 160	15 Dec 977	5 Jan 212
Swindon Supermarine	6 Oct 151	21 Apr 282	29 Dec 314	10 Nov 289	2 Feb 184	24 Nov 158	21 Mar 352	14 Apr 167	27 Oct 329	5 Apr 349	26 Feb 259	1 Jan 395	4 Sep 203	8 Sep 323	2 Feb 149	26 Nov 205	9 Apr 252	26 Jan 244		12 Dec 165	26 Jan 223	11 Mar 126
Team Bath	8 Oct 387	24 Mar 271	16 Dec 295	16 Nov 295	27 Aug 431	24 Mar 343	14 Apr 391	15 Oct 271	15 Oct 279	1 Jan 347	26 Feb 458	5 Jan 403	4 Sep 265	1 Jan 323	22 Nov 278	26 Dec 336	9 Feb 245	12 Dec 153	8 Oct 88		15 Dec 288	8 Mar 233
Tiverton Town	1 Jan 121	15 Mar 163	6 Oct 121	15 Dec 92	1 Sep 141	2 Feb 105	1 Dec 354	24 Nov 134	24 Mar 273	23 Feb 135	19 Feb 385	3 Nov 384	9 Jan 222	11 Mar 371	24 Nov 373	19 Mar 419	24 Mar 225	3 Nov 82	9 Jan 156	14 Nov 204		26 Feb 134
Yate Town	18 Mar 128	30 Oct 182	10 Nov 203	22 Sep 182	1 Jan 315	26 Feb 143	9 Feb 341	1 Apr 141	27 Aug 253	22 Mar 172	23 Feb 290	26 Feb 245	19 Apr 155	6 Oct 170	25 Aug 220	18 Aug 320	4 Sep 260	18 Dec 95	15 Dec 180	4 Dec 163	29 Mar 188	

BRITISH GAS BUSINESS
SOUTHERN LEAGUE PREMIER DIVISION CONSTITUTION 2008-09

BANBURY UNITED
Spencer Stadium, Station Approach, Banbury, Oxfordshire OX16 5TA
Tel: 01295 263354   Club: 01295 261899
Manager: Kieran Sullivan   www.banburyunited.co.uk   Colours: Red & gold

BASHLEY
Bashley Recreation Ground, Bashley Road, New Milton, Hampshire BH25 5RY
Tel: 01425 620280
Manager: Steve Riley   www.bashleyfc.co.uk   Colours: Gold & black

BEDFORD TOWN
The New Eyrie, Meadow Lane, Cardington, Bedford, Bedfordshire MK44 3SB
Tel: 01234 831558   Fax: 01234 831990
Manager: Stuart Bimson   www.bedfordeagles.tv   Colours: Blue

BRACKLEY TOWN
St James's Park, Churchill Way, Brackley, Northants NN13 7EJ
Tel: 01280 704077   Fax: 01280 704077
Manager: Phil Lines   www.brackleytownfc.com   Colours: Red & white

CAMBRIDGE CITY
The City Ground, Milton Road, Cambridge, Cambridgeshire CB4 1UY
Tel: 01223 357973   Fax: 01223 351582
Manager: Gary Roberts   www.cambridgecityfc.com   Colours: White & black

CHIPPENHAM TOWN
Hardenhuish Park, Bristol Road, Chippenham, Wiltshire SN14 6LR
Tel: 01249 650400   Fax: 01249 650400
Manager: Adie Mings   www.chippenhamtownfc.com   Colours: Royal blue

CLEVEDON TOWN
The Hand Stadium, Davis Lane, Clevedon, North Somerset BS21 6TG
Tel: 01275 871600   Club: 01275 871600   01275 871601
Manager: Wayne Powell   www.clevedontownafc.co.uk   Colours: Blue & white

CORBY TOWN
Rockingham Triangle Stadium, Rockingham Road, Corby, Northants NN17 2AE
Tel: 01536 401007   Club: 01536 406640   Fax: 01536 406640
Manager: Graham Drury   www.corbytownfc.com   Colours: White & black

EVESHAM UNITED
Worcester City FC, St George's Lane, Barbourne, Worcester, Worcestershire WR1 1QT
Tel: 01905 23003
Manager: Paul West   www.eveshamunitedfc.com   Colours: Red, white & black

FARNBOROUGH
Cherrywood Road, Farnborough, Hampshire GU14 8UD
Tel: 01252 541469   Fax: 01252 372640
Manager: Francis Vines   www.farnboroughfc.co.uk   Colours: Yellow & Blue

GLOUCESTER CITY
Forest Green Rovers FC, Nympsfield Road, Forest Green, Nailsworth, Glos GL2 5HS
Tel: 01453 834860   Fax: 01453 835291
Manager: Tim Harris   www.gloucestercityafc.com   Colours: Yellow & black

HALESOWEN TOWN
The Grove, Old Hawne Lane, Halesowen, West Midlands B63 3TB
Tel: 0121 550 9433   Fax: 0121 550 8011
Manager: Morrell Maison   www.halesowentownfc.co.uk   Colours: Blue

HEMEL HEMPSTEAD TOWN
Vauxhall Road, Adeyfield, Hemel Hempstead, Hertfordshire HP2 4HW
Tel: 01442 259777
Manager: Steve Bateman   www.hemelhempsteadtownfc.com   Colours: Red & white

HITCHIN TOWN
Top Field, Fishponds Road, Hitchin, Hertfordshire SG5 1NU
Tel: 01462 459028   Club: 01462 437146   Fax: 01767 318529
Manager: Darren Hay   www.hitchintownfc.co.uk   Colours: Yellow & green

MANGOTSFIELD UNITED
Cossham Street, Mangotsfield, Bristol, Gloucestershire BS17 3EN
Tel: 0117 956 0119   mangos.freehosting.net   Fax: 0117 956 7424
Managers: Paul Milsom / Jon French   Colours: Sky blue & maroon

MERTHYR TYDFIL
Pennydarren Park, Park Terrace, Merthyr Tydfil, Mid-Glamorgan CF47 8RF
Tel: 01685 371395
Manager: Garry Shephard   www.merthyrfootball.co.uk   Colours: White & black

OXFORD CITY
Court Place Farm, Marsh Lane, Marston, Oxford, Oxfordshire OX3 0NQ
Tel: 01865 744493   Clubroom: 01865 742492
Manager: Andy Lyne   www.oxfordcityfc.co.uk   Colours: Blue & white

RUGBY TOWN
Butlin Road, Rugby, Warwickshire CV21 3SD
Tel: 01788 844806   Club: 01788 844806   Fax: 01788 866931
Manager: Rod Brown   www.rugbytownfc.com   Colours: Sky blue & white

STOURBRIDGE
War Memorial Athletic Ground, High St, Amblecote, Stourbridge, West Midlands DY8 4HN
Tel: 01384 394040
Manager: Gary Hackett   www.stourbridgefc.com   Colours: Red & white

SWINDON SUPERMARINE
Hunts Copse, Highworth Road, South Marston, Swindon, Wiltshire SN3 4SY
Tel: 01793 828778
Manager: Mark Collier   www.swindonsupermarinefc.com   Colours: Blue & white

TIVERTON TOWN
Ladysmead, Bolham Road, Tiverton, Devon EX16 6SG
Tel: 01884 252397   Fax: 01884 258840
Manager: Martyn Rogers   www.tivertontownfc.com   Colours: Yellow & black

YATE TOWN
Lodge Road, Yate, Bristol, South Glos BS37 7LE
Tel: Club: 01454 228103
Manager: Richard Thompson   www.yatetownfc.com   Colours: White & navy blue

IN: Cambridge City (R – Football Conference South), Evesham United (P – Southern League Division One Midlands), Farnborough (P – Southern League Division One South & West), Oxford City (P – Southern League Division One South & West), Stourbridge (P – Southern League Division One Midlands)
OUT: Bromsgrove Rovers (R – Southern League Division One Midlands), Cheshunt (R – Isthmian League Division One North), Cirencester Town (R – Southern Leaue Division One South & West), King's Lynn (P – Football Conference North), Team Bath (P – Football Conference South)

www.NLNEWSDESK.CO.UK

	Aylesbury United	Barton Rovers	Bedworth United	Berkhamsted Town	Bishops Cleeve	Chasetown	Chesham United	Cinderford Town	Dunstable Town	Evesham United	Leamington	Leighton Town	Malvern Town	Romulus	Rothwell Town	Rushall Olympic	Stourbridge	Stourport Swifts	Sutton Coldfield Town	Willenhall Town	Woodford United
Aylesbury United	D	2-2	1-0	3-5	7-2	0-1	0-0	2-1	0-0	2-2	1-5	1-2	1-3	2-1	3-1	1-1	2-2	1-1	0-0	1-2	1-0
Barton Rovers	3-1	I	1-1	0-2	4-0	0-4	2-0	0-2	3-1	0-1	1-0	5-1	2-2	5-1	0-2	3-1	2-1	2-3	1-1	0-2	2-1
Bedworth United	5-2	0-2	V	2-1	2-2	1-3	3-2	2-2	0-0	2-0	1-0	3-0	1-0	2-3	2-0	3-2	2-1	3-2	4-1	1-0	1-1
Berkhamsted Town	3-0	2-1	1-1	I	1-1	2-3	2-2	2-1	2-1	3-2	6-3	1-0	2-3	3-0	2-1	3-1	2-0	3-2	1-0	0-0	2-1
Bishops Cleeve	4-2	0-0	0-0	0-1	S	3-4	1-0	4-0	2-1	2-1	0-1	3-1	1-1	0-0	2-2	2-3	1-0	1-1	0-2	0-1	3-1
Chasetown	1-1	5-0	1-1	2-0	5-2	I	1-0	6-2	1-2	3-0	2-0	2-0	1-2	2-0	3-1	1-0	3-0	2-1	2-1	0-2	0-1
Chesham United	3-1	1-2	1-0	0-2	1-1	1-2	O	1-1	0-1	2-1	2-0	1-1	3-1	3-1	2-1	2-0	1-1	0-0	4-1	1-1	0-3
Cinderford Town	0-2	1-3	0-3	0-3	3-0	3-2	2-5	N	2-0	1-3	2-2	2-1	1-1	3-1	1-1	6-1	0-0	2-2	3-1		
Dunstable Town	3-3	1-2	4-0	3-3	3-1	2-0	2-0	0-0		2-3	0-1	4-5	2-4	3-2	2-4	0-2	1-1	2-1	3-0	0-2	3-3
Evesham United	2-2	1-1	1-1	1-1	1-0	1-3	2-2	1-3	2-2	O	1-2	3-1	6-0	2-1	0-1	1-1	3-1	4-0	3-2	0-2	1-1
Leamington	1-1	0-2	1-3	1-2	0-1	2-2	1-0	2-1	1-1	5-0	N	1-1	0-4	0-0	2-2	1-0	0-1	2-3	3-3	2-2	2-1
Leighton Town	1-1	1-1	0-0	3-1	3-2	1-2	1-4	2-0	1-1	0-2	1-1	E	1-0	3-0	1-1	0-0	1-3	4-0	2-3	0-0	1-0
Malvern Town	0-2	0-0	1-1	2-2	2-2	1-3	1-3	1-2	1-5	0-1	0-2	2-4		2-4	0-1	1-1	0-3	1-2	2-1	2-2	0-1
Romulus	1-4	1-1	1-0	4-0	3-2	1-1	1-0	2-3	1-3	0-1	2-0	3-2	3-0	M	1-0	2-0	2-2	5-1	0-3	1-1	3-1
Rothwell Town	2-2	0-0	2-0	5-1	2-4	0-3	0-1	0-1	0-3	1-2	0-3	0-1	0-1	1-1	I	1-0	0-6	3-2	2-4	1-1	1-2
Rushall Olympic	0-0	2-1	3-0	8-0	3-1	1-0	0-1	1-0	2-0	0-0	1-0	3-0	4-0	1-0	3-0	D	1-2	1-1	0-3	1-1	6-0
Stourbridge	4-1	3-4	3-0	4-1	1-0	2-1	1-3	8-1	1-0	0-1	2-1	0-3	4-1	2-2	1-0	0-1	L	3-1	1-0	5-1	6-0
Stourport Swifts	0-5	1-2	2-1	1-0	2-1	1-4	1-1	1-3	0-1	1-4	0-1	1-5	2-1	3-3	0-1	0-2	1-6	A	1-1	0-0	1-0
Sutton Coldfield Town	4-0	2-2	1-1	2-2	5-2	2-1	0-1	6-1	6-1	3-1	2-2	1-0	3-1	2-1	2-1	0-2	4-2	2-1	N	6-0	6-2
Willenhall Town	1-2	2-2	2-1	7-0	2-0	1-0	1-3	3-0	1-4	0-2	1-2	0-0	1-1	0-1	2-0	0-0	2-1	1-1	0-2	D	3-0
Woodford United	1-1	1-2	0-1	3-0	0-2	2-4	0-1	3-4	0-0	1-1	1-3	0-3	1-0	0-1	0-2	0-3	1-0	0-1	1-2	0-4	S

Division One Midlands

			HOME					AWAY					TOTAL					
	P	W	D	L	F	A	W	D	L	F	A	W	D	L	F	A	Pts
Evesham United	40	15	2	3	33	10	13	5	2	35	14	28	7	5	68	24	91
Leamington	40	14	4	2	37	12	13	4	3	37	15	27	8	5	74	27	89
Stourbridge	40	14	1	5	51	22	11	2	7	46	26	25	3	12	97	48	78
Sutton Coldfield Town	40	14	4	2	59	24	9	4	7	34	28	23	8	9	93	52	77
Rushall Olympic	40	12	4	4	40	11	11	3	6	28	12	23	7	10	68	23	76
Chesham United	40	9	4	7	44	25	14	3	3	34	15	23	7	10	78	40	76
Chasetown	40	11	4	5	32	17	12	2	6	39	21	23	6	11	71	38	75
Aylesbury United	40	12	3	5	35	17	7	6	7	29	32	19	9	12	64	49	66
Leighton Town	40	8	7	5	28	22	9	5	6	31	20	17	12	11	59	42	63
Romulus	40	11	4	5	37	25	7	4	9	23	28	18	8	14	60	53	62
Barton Rovers	40	9	5	6	28	18	5	11	4	26	27	14	16	10	54	45	58
Bishops Cleeve	40	9	5	6	29	24	8	2	10	34	37	17	7	16	63	61	58
Dunstable Town	40	7	1	12	36	38	7	4	9	27	27	14	5	21	63	65	47
Willenhall Town -3	40	8	5	7	30	22	4	8	8	23	36	12	13	15	53	58	46
Bedworth United	40	9	6	5	28	18	3	4	13	12	33	12	10	18	40	51	46
Cinderford Town	40	6	5	9	27	37	6	1	13	20	45	12	6	22	47	82	42
Stourport Swifts	40	5	4	11	19	42	5	4	11	21	39	10	8	22	40	81	38
Rothwell Town	40	3	4	13	20	40	6	1	13	14	29	9	5	26	34	69	32
Woodford United	40	3	3	14	15	35	4	3	13	15	53	7	6	27	30	88	27
Malvern Town	40	1	6	13	19	42	2	3	15	15	53	3	9	28	34	95	18
Berkhamsted Town	40	2	1	17	15	54	0	3	17	12	72	2	4	34	27	126	10

PLAY-OFFS

SEMI-FINALS
(April 29th)
Leamington 1 Rushall Olympic 0 *Att* 783
Stourbridge 1 Sutton Coldfield Town 0 *Att* 237

FINAL
(May 3rd at Leamington)
Leamington 1 **Stourbridge** 2 *aet Att* 1,634

DATES & GATES

WWW.NLNEWSDESK.CO.UK

Each cell shows the fixture date (top) and the attendance / gate (bottom, in italic). The blank diagonal indicates a club against itself.

DATES & GATES	Aylesbury United	Barton Rovers	Bedworth United	Berkhamsted Town	Bishops Cleeve	Chasetown	Chesham United	Cinderford Town	Dunstable Town	Evesham United	Leamington	Leighton Town	Malvern Town	Romulus	Rothwell Town	Rushall Olympic	Stourbridge	Stourport Swifts	Sutton Coldfield Town	Willenhall Town	Woodford United
Aylesbury United		27 Oct *219*	13 Oct *164*	27 Aug *161*	22 Sep *97*	19 Apr *274*	1 Mar *494*	3 Sep *144*	18 Aug *247*	29 Mar *326*	17 Nov *326*	8 Sep *224*	7 Apr *110*	31 Mar *162*	8 Mar *128*	23 Feb *235*	1 Jan *134*	26 Jan *114*	8 Oct *233*	29 Sep *109*	22 Mar *116*
Barton Rovers	24 Mar *167*		5 Apr *83*	1 Apr *80*	22 Apr *97*	15 Oct *168*	23 Feb *105*	29 Mar *116*	18 Aug *102*	18 Aug *103*	5 Apr *307*	22 Sep *136*	9 Oct *102*		8 Sep *101*	26 Dec *167*	15 Apr *163*	16 Feb *101*	12 Apr *127*	21 Aug *115*	4 Sep *108*
Bedworth United	15 Mar *185*	29 Mar *83*		1 Apr *80*	22 Apr *80*	22 Dec *162*	17 Nov *262*	5 Apr *68*	21 Mar *67*	27 Oct *79*	18 Aug *122*	4 Mar *135*	26 Jan *53*	5 Mar *103*	23 Feb *136*	9 Feb *102*	25 Sep *167*	26 Dec *101*	23 Feb *257*	26 Jan *136*	18 Mar *108*
Berkhamsted Town	24 Nov *123*	12 Apr *101*	1 Apr *80*		18 Aug *79*	29 Mar *219*	22 Dec *262*	10 Sep *120*	27 Nov *119*	29 Mar *191*	2 Feb *104*	5 Apr *114*	15 Dec *116*	1 Jan *100*	24 Nov *112*	10 Nov *50*	12 Apr *112*	12 Dec *108*	24 Mar *248*	17 Nov *107*	26 Apr *91*
Bishops Cleeve	16 Feb *104*	11 Sep *66*	22 Sep *66*	22 Sep *66*		8 Sep *140*	19 Jan *78*	2 Feb *102*	8 Sep *56*	25 Jan *64*	24 Nov *97*	5 Apr *96*	19 Apr *67*	16 Oct *69*	24 Nov *74*	24 Nov *83*	29 Mar *86*	15 Mar *111*	9 Apr *123*	8 Sep *99*	8 Sep *91*
Chasetown	22 Dec *271*	26 Apr *48*	18 Aug *219*	18 Aug *191*	30 Oct *180*		26 Sep *102*	21 Aug *120*	19 Jan *119*	24 Nov *147*	21 Apr *272*	15 Dec *112*	25 Aug *109*	1 Mar *80*	29 Mar *55*	29 Mar *83*	15 Mar *118*	15 Apr *143*	27 Aug *127*	18 Sep *87*	8 Sep *91*
Chesham United	19 Jan *245*	8 Mar *448*	17 Nov *262*	4 Mar *262*	18 Aug *308*	26 Sep *387*		6 Sep *56*	16 Feb *315*	26 Apr *97*	1 Sep *270*	22 Sep *380*	1 Mar *442*	24 Nov *305*	29 Dec *273*	21 Apr *387*	24 Aug *452*	24 Mar *475*	24 Mar *371*	15 Mar *406*	12 Apr *378*
Cinderford Town	12 Apr *186*	25 Aug *491*	10 Sep *122*	18 Aug *262*	26 Jan *112*	8 Sep *56*	23 Feb *509*		26 Feb *273*	2 Oct *231*	22 Sep *270*	30 Oct *380*	24 Nov *216*	26 Jan *190*	27 Dec *233*	1 Sep *309*	21 Apr *215*	24 Dec *249*	24 Mar *326*	15 Mar *225*	15 Mar *257*
Dunstable Town	5 Apr *226*	13 Oct *719*	10 Oct *100*	19 Jan *200*	26 Feb *112*	8 Sep *200*	17 Mar *60*	24 Sep *317*		19 Jan *78*	1 Sep *222*	24 Nov *88*	19 Apr *118*	24 Nov *109*	24 Nov *65*	11 Sep *57*	16 Feb *64*	22 Dec *67*	48	18 Aug *51*	18 Aug
Evesham United	1 Dec *91*	29 Dec *64*	10 Oct *79*	1 Sep *78*	24 Nov *200*	8 Sep *73*	24 Nov *147*	26 Dec *97*	1 Apr *86*		1 Sep *202*	5 Apr *89*	1 Mar *109*	26 Apr *67*	25 Apr *55*	27 Aug *47*	9 Feb *67*	15 Mar *47*	27 Aug *63*	22 Sep *95*	4 Sep *47*
Leamington	21 Aug *730*	25 Sep *142*	17 Nov *308*	19 Apr *202*	26 Jan *272*	22 Feb *781*	21 Apr *147*	24 Nov *272*	21 Aug *239*	18 Aug		19 Jan *202*	26 Jan *216*	24 Nov *305*	29 Mar *354*	25 Aug *547*	9 Feb *410*	26 Apr *118*	29 Mar *648*	18 Mar *603*	27 Aug *477*
Leighton Town	29 Dec *232*	6 Dec *574*	15 Mar *175*	15 Dec *96*	5 Mar *71*	27 Oct *860*	15 Apr *452*	29 Jan *380*	22 Mar *583*	8 Apr *239*	1 Jan *507*		6 Oct *161*	29 Sep *80*	6 Oct *74*	29 Mar *83*	16 Feb *118*	4 Sep *86*	13 Oct *77*	13 Oct *97*	12 Apr *252*
Malvern Town	11 Sep *72*	22 Sep *611*	5 Apr *82*	19 Apr *67*	6 Oct *100*	23 Feb *195*	2 Feb *560*	16 Feb *315*	8 Mar	239	1 Jan *124*	15 Dec *96*		16 Feb *80*	16 Feb *354*	29 Mar *74*	16 Feb *83*	15 Apr *91*	3 Mar *91*	13 Oct *111*	27 Aug *87*
Romulus	26 Apr *145*	21 Apr *157*	22 Sep *307*	1 Mar *109*	9 Oct *307*	8 Dec *61*	1 Mar *273*	26 Apr *147*	21 Apr *86*	8 Apr *78*	1 Sep *222*	1 Jan *124*	30 Oct *108*		29 Mar *109*	25 Aug *55*	26 Apr *67*	24 Aug *91*	9 Apr *90*	15 Mar *58*	26 Apr *82*
Rothwell Town	16 Oct *137*	8 Dec *105*	29 Sep *136*	29 Mar *53*	23 Feb *82*	23 Feb *195*	25 Sep *560*	24 Nov *147*	21 Aug *147*	24 Nov *104*	19 Apr *222*	19 Apr *88*	16 Oct *116*	6 Oct *100*		29 Mar *57*	9 Feb *64*	6 Oct *67*	9 Nov *82*	15 Mar *51*	18 Aug
Rushall Olympic	10 Nov *114*	27 Oct *132*	18 Apr *101*	25 Aug *55*	15 Dec *148*	25 Aug *314*	29 Mar *525*	21 Apr *231*	1 Apr *111*	1 Sep *202*	19 Aug *222*	15 Dec *28*	24 Nov *69*	26 Feb *125*	29 Mar *118*	25 Aug *513*	16 Feb *47*	22 Dec *82*	22 Aug *95*	22 Sep *51*	1 Jan *38*
Stourbridge	25 Sep *129*	26 Jan *124*	15 Apr *167*	9 Feb *67*	15 Apr *91*	26 Dec *148*	26 Apr *452*	23 Feb *273*	1 Mar *127*	24 Nov *272*	27 Aug *270*	1 Sep *114*	24 Nov *190*	27 Dec *233*	21 Apr *309*	9 Feb *547*		4 Sep *410*	17 Oct *143*	11 Sep *91*	23 Feb *252*
Stourport Swifts	1 Sep *99*	17 Nov *198*	12 Apr *187*	15 Apr *47*	12 Apr *143*	23 Feb *111*	1 Sep *270*	26 Apr *190*	1 Apr	24 Mar *222*	1 Sep *222*	1 Feb *88*	26 Jan *118*	27 Oct *305*	26 Dec *273*	1 Sep *387*	26 Apr *452*		24 Mar *475*	15 Mar *371*	12 Apr *406*
Sutton Coldfield Town	12 Jan *205*	24 Mar *44*	1 Jan *297*	24 Mar *63*	8 Aug *371*	21 Mar *184*	26 Apr *272*	24 Nov *231*	16 Oct *112*	26 Dec *97*	21 Apr *306*	25 Apr *138*	7 Apr *102*	1 Sep *125*	15 Apr *174*	27 Oct *163*	13 Oct *147*	16 Oct *111*		24 Nov *99*	8 Mar *91*
Willenhall Town	26 Dec *112*	19 Jan *144*	21 Mar *235*	15 Mar *95*	10 Nov *75*	10 Nov *189*	16 Oct *140*	2 Feb *91*	24 Nov *107*	4 Sep *222*	22 Sep *257*	5 Apr *75*	1 Apr *105*	8 Mar *85*	1 Dec *74*	17 Nov *107*	11 Sep *90*	27 Oct *104*	19 Jan *166*		8 Dec *68*
Woodford United	6 Oct *128*	19 Jan *117*	11 Sep *87*	24 Mar *75*	1 Sep *73*	1 Sep *87*	29 Dec *93*	12 Jan *105*	12 Jan *98*	15 Sep *428*	11 Sep *50*	12 Apr *81*	12 Jan *74*	12 Jan *74*	1 Dec *52*	18 Mar *80*	27 Oct *107*	26 Dec *86*	24 Nov *83*	26 Apr *82*	

186 British Gas Business Southern League

	Abingdon United	AFC Hayes	Andover	Bracknell Town	Bridgwater Town	Burnham	Didcot Town	Farnborough	Fleet Town	Godalming Town	Gosport Borough	Hillingdon Borough	Marlow	Newport IOW	Oxford City	Paulton Rovers	Slough Town	Taunton Town	Thatcham Town	Uxbridge	Winchester City	Windsor & Eton
Abingdon United		2-0	2-0	1-1	1-1	1-2	0-4	3-2	1-2	2-2	2-2	0-0	0-3	0-0	1-1	0-2	3-0	5-0	3-0	1-0	2-0	1-3
AFC Hayes	2-0		1-3	7-0	2-3	1-4	0-6	2-7	2-0	1-3	2-1	2-2	3-2	1-2	0-3	1-6	0-0	4-0	2-0	1-6	1-2	3-2
Andover	3-1	3-2	D	1-2	0-4	1-1	1-0	0-6	3-4	3-3	1-3	5-0	2-6	1-1	0-5	0-0	1-2	6-3	2-1	3-0	1-2	2-2
Bracknell Town	1-4	1-4	1-1	I	0-0	2-0	2-3	0-5	1-2	0-2	0-4	3-0	1-4	2-2	0-2	2-0	3-1	1-2	2-2	2-3	1-1	3-2
Bridgwater Town	2-1	3-0	4-0	1-1	V	3-3	0-2	2-0	0-2	1-0	2-0	3-1	1-0	6-1	2-2	2-0	0-0	2-2	0-1	2-0	2-1	1-2
Burnham	3-2	2-3	2-0	2-0	1-1	I	1-2	0-2	2-3	1-1	2-0	0-2	2-0	4-0	0-0	1-2	3-1	1-1	3-1	1-3	1-3	2-2
Didcot Town	1-3	1-1	0-1	3-0	2-2	3-1	S	0-0	0-0	5-0	2-0	4-4	4-0	5-0	3-3	2-2	2-0	1-0	1-2	0-0	1-1	5-1
Farnborough	6-1	3-3	2-2	4-0	3-2	0-2	4-1	I	5-1	2-2	5-0	4-1	3-0	6-0	2-0	1-0	5-0	3-0	2-0	0-1	3-3	1-1
Fleet Town	2-1	1-2	4-0	3-0	2-1	0-1	2-2	3-0	O	1-1	1-0	2-0	1-1	3-0	2-0	1-4	1-0	2-1	2-0	3-0	4-1	1-2
Godalming Town	3-1	2-1	2-1	1-0	0-4	1-2	3-2	3-3	1-0	N	0-1	2-0	0-3	8-1	2-3	3-2	2-0	1-0	3-2	2-1	0-1	0-3
Gosport Borough	4-3	2-3	3-1	1-0	0-0	0-1	2-4	1-2	1-0	1-0		3-1	2-0	3-0	0-1	3-1	2-2	2-0	2-2	1-2	2-1	2-2
Hillingdon Borough	1-2	2-5	3-0	2-0	2-0	2-1	0-3	1-4	4-4	3-1	1-1	O	0-1	4-0	1-2	3-1	4-1	3-1	1-0	0-1	2-0	3-0
Marlow	3-1	4-1	5-0	2-2	0-4	2-1	0-1	0-1	0-1	3-2	3-1	1-1	N	6-0	2-1	1-1	2-0	2-0	0-0	0-1	2-0	5-3
Newport IOW	3-6	0-1	2-5	1-1	0-4	0-2	0-4	0-7	0-1	0-3	1-3	0-3	0-3	E	1-1	1-2	1-3	1-5	2-4	1-3	1-0	0-3
Oxford City	3-1	5-1	3-0	1-0	0-1	1-0	0-1	2-3	1-2	1-2	2-2	2-0	4-0	2-0		1-1	5-0	2-0	2-0	2-1	4-0	2-2
Paulton Rovers	2-1	2-0	3-2	5-0	3-2	3-2	0-0	0-1	0-1	1-1	5-0	0-2	0-1	4-0	0-2	S	3-1	2-1	3-2	1-1	4-3	2-2
Slough Town	4-1	0-3	2-1	3-1	0-2	0-3	3-6	2-3	2-1	3-2	1-2	1-3	0-2	2-0	1-2	1-2		1-2	1-2	1-1	2-2	0-1
Taunton Town	1-1	1-2	5-2	1-1	3-1	1-1	1-0	2-1	1-2	0-1	1-0	3-2	7-1	3-3	0-1	0-1		&	2-0	1-1	1-1	0-1
Thatcham Town	1-1	4-1	2-1	1-2	1-1	1-1	1-0	2-0	2-4	3-0	1-4	1-1	1-1	8-0	1-2	2-2	2-0	1-1		0-1	2-0	1-2
Uxbridge	2-0	5-0	3-1	2-3	0-0	1-0	1-2	2-2	1-3	2-1	3-2	2-2	1-0	3-0	2-3	4-1	2-1	3-3	3-1	W	2-1	1-0
Winchester City	1-2	3-0	1-2	3-2	3-0	0-1	1-4	2-3	1-1	1-1	3-3	2-1	3-2	3-2	0-1	2-2	2-0	1-3	1-0	1-0		0-1
Windsor & Eton	2-0	1-4	3-0	4-1	2-2	1-2	0-3	1-4	3-3	3-2	3-0	4-1	1-0	1-0	1-0	1-2	2-1	2-3	0-1	1-1	2-1	

Division One South & West

	P	HOME					AWAY					TOTAL					
		W	D	L	F	A	W	D	L	F	A	W	D	L	F	A	Pts
Farnborough	42	14	5	2	64	20	13	3	5	56	28	27	8	7	120	48	89
Fleet Town	42	14	3	4	41	17	12	4	5	37	31	26	7	9	78	48	85
Didcot Town	42	9	9	3	45	21	15	2	4	54	21	24	11	7	99	42	83
Oxford City	42	13	3	5	45	17	11	6	4	37	24	24	9	9	82	41	81
Uxbridge	42	13	4	4	45	26	9	5	7	27	24	22	9	11	72	50	75
Bridgwater Town	42	12	5	4	39	20	7	8	6	35	25	19	13	10	74	45	70
Paulton Rovers	42	12	4	5	43	25	8	6	7	34	32	20	10	12	77	57	70
Windsor & Eton	42	11	3	7	38	31	9	6	6	37	35	20	9	13	75	66	69
Marlow	42	12	4	5	43	22	8	2	11	31	32	20	6	16	74	54	66
Burnham	42	8	5	8	34	29	10	4	7	33	26	18	9	15	67	55	63
Gosport Borough	42	11	4	6	37	26	7	4	10	32	41	18	8	16	69	67	62
Godalming Town	42	13	1	7	39	31	4	8	9	31	39	17	9	16	70	70	60
Hillingdon Borough	42	12	2	7	42	28	4	6	11	26	42	16	8	18	68	70	56
AFC Hayes	42	8	2	11	38	52	9	2	10	37	47	17	4	21	75	99	55
Thatcham Town	42	8	7	6	38	25	5	3	13	21	37	13	10	19	59	62	49
Abingdon United	42	8	7	6	31	25	5	2	14	33	50	13	9	20	64	75	48
Winchester City	42	9	4	8	34	31	4	5	12	24	40	13	9	20	58	71	48
Taunton Town	42	7	7	7	38	33	5	4	12	28	46	12	11	19	66	79	47
Andover	42	7	4	9	39	48	4	2	15	23	53	11	7	24	62	101	40
Bracknell Town	42	5	5	11	28	44	3	5	13	17	49	8	10	24	45	93	34
Slough Town	42	6	2	13	30	42	3	3	15	14	45	9	5	28	44	87	32
Newport IOW	42	1	2	18	15	64	1	3	17	10	79	2	5	35	25	143	11

PLAY-OFFS

SEMI-FINALS

(April 30th) Didcot Town 2 **Oxford City** 2 *aet* (4-5p) *Att* 403

(May 1st) Fleet Town 1 **Uxbridge** 2 *Att* 205

213

FINAL

(May 3rd at Oxford City)

Oxford City 1 Uxbridge 0 *Att* 646

DATES & GATES

The grid below lists, for each pair of clubs, the fixture date (upper figure) and the attendance / "gate" (lower figure). Row = home club; column = opponent. Cells on the diagonal carry the club name only.

	Abingdon United	AFC Hayes	Andover	Bracknell Town	Bridgwater Town	Burnham	Didcot Town	Farnborough	Fleet Town	Godalming Town	Gosport Borough	Hillingdon Borough	Marlow	Newport IOW	Oxford City	Paulton Rovers	Slough Town	Taunton Town	Thatcham Town	Uxbridge	Winchester City	Windsor & Eton
Abingdon United	—	26 Feb / 56	23 Feb / 109	15 Dec / 96	6 Oct / 77	27 Aug / 289	22 Sep / 93	24 Mar / 307	4 Dec / 421	22 Sep / 136	2 Feb / 88	11 Dec / 84	8 Mar / 62	19 Apr / 110	2 Oct / 95	1 Jan / 315	8 Sep / 118	1 Dec / 208	27 Oct / 199	13 Oct / 68	8 Dec / 104	18 Aug / 145
AFC Hayes	16 Oct / 75	—	15 Dec / 78	1 Dec / 66	16 Feb / 133																	26 Feb / 122
Andover	17 Nov / 131	18 Aug / 78	—		26 Apr / 251		2 Oct / 347		2 Oct / 105			24 Nov / 151									24 Mar / 307	26 Feb / 144
Bracknell Town	29 Mar / 71	1 Dec / 66		—																		12 Feb / 154
Bridgwater Town	20 Nov / 104	16 Feb / 133			—																	17 Oct / 107
Burnham	12 Jan / 130					—																22 Apr / 154
Didcot Town	26 Dec / 353						—															25 Jan / 167
Farnborough	24 Nov / 216							—														27 Oct / 304
Fleet Town	25 Aug / 145								—													5 Jan / 125
Godalming Town	10 Nov / 104									—												5 Jan / 134
Gosport Borough	26 Apr / 110										—											27 Oct / 104
Hillingdon Borough	16 Feb / 85											—										27 Oct / 104
Marlow	15 Mar / 121												—									1 Mar / 175
Newport IOW	26 Jan / 78													—								15 Dec / 102
Oxford City	21 Aug / 325														—							10 Nov / 125
Paulton Rovers	15 Apr / 102															—						29 Sep / 100
Slough Town	29 Sep / 207																—					26 Feb / 405
Taunton Town	5 Apr / 51																	—				15 Dec / 122
Thatcham Town	22 Mar / 71																		—			22 Mar / 120
Uxbridge	1 Mar / 109																			—		29 Sep / 164
Winchester City	15 Dec / 105																				—	12 Dec / 100
Windsor & Eton	9 Feb / 145																				1 Dec / 138	—

BRITISH GAS BUSINESS SOUTHERN LEAGUE
DIVISION ONE MIDLANDS CONSTITUTION 2008-09

AFC SUDBURY
Colours: Yellow & blue
King's Marsh Stadium, Brundon Lane, Sudbury,
Suffolk CO10 1XR
Tel: 01787 376213

ARLESEY TOWN
Colours: Navy & sky blue
Hitchin Road, Arlesey, Bedfordshire SG15 6RS
Tel: 01462 734504 Boardroom: 01462 734512

ATHERSTONE TOWN
Colours: Red & white
Sheepy Road, Sheepy, Atherstone, Warks CV9 3AD
Tel: 01827 717829

AYLESBURY UNITED
Colours: Green & white
Chesham United FC, Meadow Park, Amy Lane,
Amersham Road, Chesham, Bucks HP5 1NE
Tel: 01494 783964/791057 Fax: 01494 794244

BARTON ROVERS
Colours: Royal blue
Sharpenhoe Road, Barton-le-Clay, Beds MK45 4SD
Tel: 01582 707772 Fax: 01582 882398

BEDWORTH UNITED
Colours: Green & white
The Oval, Welfare Park, Coventry Road, Bedworth,
Warwickshire CV12 8NN
Tel: 024 7631 4752 Club: 024 7631 4302

BROMSGROVE ROVERS
Colours: Green & white
Victoria Ground, Birmingham Road, Bromsgrove,
Worcestershire B61 8DR
Tel: 01527 876949/878260 Fax: 01527 876265

BURY TOWN
Colours: Blue Tel: 01284 754721
Ram Meadow, Cotton Lane, Bury St Edmunds, Suffolk
IP33 1XP

CHASETOWN
Colours: Royal blue
The Scholars Ground, Church Street, Chasetown,
Walsall, Staffs WS7 8QL
Tel: 01543 682222 Fax: 01543 684609

CHESHAM UNITED
Colours: Claret & sky blue
Meadow Park, Amy Lane, Amersham Road, Chesham,
Buckinghamshire HP5 1NE
Tel: 01494 783964 Fax: 01494 794244
Club: 01494 791057

DUNSTABLE TOWN
Colours: Blue & white
Creasey Park Stadium, Creasey Park Drive, Dunstable,
Bedfordshire LU6 1BB
Tel: 01582 667555

LEAMINGTON
Colours: Gold & black
New Windmill Ground, Harbury Lane, Whitnash,
Leamington Spa, Warwickshire CV33 9JR
Tel: 01926 430406

LEIGHTON TOWN
Colours: Red & white
Bell Close, Lake Street, Leighton Buzzard,
Bedfordshire LU7 1RX
Tel: 01525 373311 Fax: 01525 370142

MALVERN TOWN
Colours: Sky blue & claret
Langland Stadium, Langland Avenue, Malvern,
Worcestershire WR14 2EQ
Tel: 01684 574291

MARLOW
Colours: Royal blue & white
Alfred Davis Ground, Oak Tree Road, Marlow,
Buckinghamshire SL7 3ED
Tel: 01628 483970 Fax: 01628 477032

NUNEATON TOWN
Colours: White & blue
Liberty Way Stadium, Liberty Way, Nuneaton,
Warwickshire CV11 6RR
Tel: 024 7638 3206 Fax: 024 7639 3925

ROMULUS
Colours: Red & white
Sutton Coldfield Town FC, Central Ground, Coles
Lane, Sutton Coldfield, West Midlands B72 1NL
Tel: 0121 354 2997 Fax: 0121 354 2997

ROTHWELL TOWN
Colours: Blue & white
Cecil Street, Rothwell, Northants NN14 6EZ
Tel: 01536 710694

SOHAM TOWN RANGERS
Colours: Green & white
Julius Martin Lane, Soham, Ely, Cambse CB7 5EQ
Tel: 01353 720732 Club: 01353 722139

STOURPORT SWIFTS
Colours: Yellow Tel/Fax: 01299 825188
Walshes Meadow, Harold Davies Drive,
Stourport-on-Severn, Worcestershire DY13 0AA

SUTTON COLDFIELD TOWN
Colours: Royal blue & white
Central Ground, Coles Lane, Sutton Coldfield,
West Midlands B72 1NL
Tel: 0121 354 2997 Fax: 0121 354 2997

WOODFORD UNITED
Colours: Red   Tel: 01327 263734
Byfield Road, Woodford Halse, Daventry, Northants
NN11 3TR

IN: AFC Sudbury (S – Isthmian League Division One North), Arlesey Town (S – Isthmian League Division One North), Atherstone Town (P – Midland Alliance), Bromsgrove Rovers (R), Bury Town (S – Isthmian League Division One North), Marlow (S – Southern League Division One South & West), Nuneaton Town (formerly Nuneaton Borough) (R – Football Conference North), Soham Town Rangers (P – Eastern Counties League Premier Division)
OUT: Berkhamsted Town (R – Spartan South Midlands League Premier Division), Bishops Cleeve (S – Southern League Division One South & West), Cinderford Town (S – Southern League Division One South & West), Evesham United (P), Rushall Olympic (S – Northern Premier League Division One South), Slimbridge (WN), Stourbridge (P), Willenhall Town (S – Northern Premier League Division One South)

BRITISH GAS BUSINESS SOUTHERN LEAGUE
DIVISION ONE SOUTH & WEST CONSTITUTION 2008-09

ABINGDON UNITED
Colours: Yellow & blue
Northcourt Road, Abingdon, Oxfordshire OX14 1PL
Tel: 01235 203203

AFC HAYES
Colours: Blue & white
Farm Park, Kingshill Avenue, Hayes, Middx UB4 8DD
Tel: 020 8845 0110 Boardroom: 020 8842 1448

AFC TOTTON
Colours: White & blue
Testwood Park, Testwood Place, Totton, Southampton,
Hampshire SO40 3BE
Tel: 023 8086 8981

ANDOVER
Colours: Red & black
The Portway Stadium, West Portway Ind. Estate,
Andover, Hampshire SP10 3LF
Tel: 01264 351302

BEACONSFIELD SYCOB
Colours: Red, white & black
Holloway Park, Slough Road, Beaconsfield,
Buckinghamshire HP9 2SE
Tel: 01494 676868

BISHOPS CLEEVE
Colours: Green & black
Kayte Lane, Bishops Cleeve, Cheltenham,
Gloucestershire GL52 3PD
Tel: 01242 676166

BRACKNELL TOWN
Colours: Red & white
Larges Lane, Bracknell, Berkshire RG12 9AN
Tel: 01344 300933/412305 Fax: 01344 300933

BRIDGWATER TOWN
Colours: Red & White
Fairfax Park, College Way, Bath Road, Bridgwater,
Somerset TA6 4TZ
Tel: 01278 446899

BURNHAM
Colours: Blue & white
The Gore, Wymers Wood Road,
Burnham, Slough SL1 8JG
Tel: 0700 345 1101 Fax: 0700 345 1101

CINDERFORD TOWN
Colours: White & black
Causeway Ground, Edge Hills Road, Hilldene,
Cinderford, Gloucestershire GL14 2QH
Tel: 01594 822039 Club: 01594 827147

CIRENCESTER TOWN
Colours: Red & black
Corinium Stadium, Kingshill Lane, Cirencester,
Gloucestershire GL7 1HS
Tel: 01285 654543 Fax: 01285 654474

DIDCOT TOWN
Colours: Red & white
Loop Meadow Stadium, Bowmont Water, off Avon
Way, Didcot, Oxfordshire OX11 7GA
Tel: 01235 813138

GOSPORT BOROUGH
Colours: Yellow & blue
Privett Park, Privett Road, Gosport, Hants PO12 3SX
Tel: 023 9250 1042

NORTH LEIGH
Colours: Navy & Sky blue
Eynsham Park, Woodstock Road, North Leigh,
Witney, Oxfordshire OX8 6PW
Tel: 01993 881427

PAULTON ROVERS
Colours: Maroon & white
Athletic Ground, Winterfield Road, Paulton, North
Somerset BS39 7RF
Tel: 01761 412907

SLOUGH TOWN
Colours: Yellow & navy blue
Beaconsfield SYCOB FC, Holloway Park, Slough
Road, Beaconsfield, Buckinghamshire HP9 2SE
Tel: 01494 676868

TAUNTON TOWN
Colours: Burgundy & sky blue
Wordsworth Drive, Taunton, Somerset TA1 2HG
Tel: 01823 278191 Fax: 01823 322975

THATCHAM TOWN
Colours: Blue & white
Waterside Park, Crookham Road, Thatcham, Berkshire
RG19 4PA
Tel: 01635 862016 Fax: 01635 873834

TRURO CITY
Colours: White
Treyew Road, Truro, Cornwall TR1 2TH
Tel: 01872 225400 Fax: 01872 225402

UXBRIDGE
Colours: Red & white
Honeycroft, Horton Road, West Drayton, Middlesex
UB7 8HX
Tel: 01895 443557 Fax: 01895 445830

WINCHESTER CITY
Colours: Red & black
The City Ground, Hillier Way, Abbotts Barton,
Winchester, Hampshire SO23 7EF
Tel: 01962 810200

WINDSOR & ETON
Colours: Red & green
Stag Meadow, St Leonards Road, Windsor, Berkshire
SL4 3DR
Tel: 01753 860656 Fax: 01753 860656

WWW.NLNEWSDESK.CO.UK

IN: AFC Totton (P – Wessex League Premier Division), Beaconsfield SYCOB (P – Spartan South Midlands League Premier Division), Bishops Cleeve (S – Southern League Division One South & West), Cinderford Town (S – Southern League Division One South & West), Cirencester Town (R), North Leigh (P – Hellenic League Premier Division), Truro City (P – Western League Premier Division)

OUT: Farnborough (P), Fleet Town (S – Isthmian League Division One South), Godalming Town (S – Isthmian League Division One South), Hillingdon Borough (S – Isthmian League Division One North), Marlow (S – Southern League Division One Midlands), Newport IOW (R – Wessex League Premier Division), Oxford City (P)

LEAGUE CUP

FIRST ROUND

AFC Hayes 6 Slough Town 1 *(Sep 25)*	Att: 82
Aylesbury United 2 Chesham United 1 *(Sep 24)*	Att: 282
Barton Rovers 0 **Uxbridge** 1 *aet (Sep 25)*	Att: 62
Berkhamsted Town 4 Woodford United 2 *aet (Sep 25)*	Att: 60
Bishops Cleeve 1 **Cinderford Town** 2 *(Sep 26)*	Att: 55
Bridgwater Town (w/o) v Slimbridge (scr.)	Att:
Chasetown 1 **Bedworth United** 2 *(Sep 25)*	Att: 201
Didcot Town 4 Andover 2 *(Sep 25)*	Att: 197
Dunstable Town 1 Leighton Town 0 *aet (Sep 25)*	Att: 65
Farnborough 2 Abingdon United 2 *aet (3-2p) (Sep 25)*	Att: 255
Godalming Town 3 Thatcham Town 2 *aet (Sep 25)*	Att: 86
Hillingdon Borough 3 BracknellTown 0 *(Sep 25)*	Att: 41
Marlow 4 Burnham 3 *aet (Sep 25)*	Att: 83
Oxford City 4 Fleet Town 2 *(Sep 25)*	Att: 71
Paulton Rovers 2 **Gosport Borough** 2 *aet (6-7p) (Sep 24)*	Att: 103
Romulus 2 Rushall Olympic 1 *(Sep 25)*	Att: 107
Rothwell Town 1 **Leamington** 3 *(Sep 26)*	Att: 84
Stourbridge 0 **Malvern Town** 1 *(Sep 25)*	Att: 77
Stourport Swifts 1 **Evesham United** 2 *(Sep 25)*	Att: 62
Taunton Town 2 Newport IOW 1 *(Sep 26)*	Att: 110
Willenhall Town 0 **Sutton Coldfield Town** 3 *(Oct 16)*	Att: 52
Windsor & Eton 2 Winchester City 1 *(Sep 25)*	Att: 71

SECOND ROUND

Berkhamsted Town 1 Aylesbury United 1 *aet (5-4p) (Oct 30)*	Att: 117
Bridgwater Town 2 **Chippenham Town** 3 *(Oct 30)*	Att: 201
Cinderford Town 2 Malvern Town 0 *(Oct 31)*	Att: 49
Evesham United 2 **Gloucester City** 4 *(Nov 20)*	Att: 54
Godalming Town 1 Farnborough 1 *aet (3-1p) (Oct 30)*	Att: 208
Hillingdon Borough 2 Windsor & Eton 0 *(Oct 30)*	Att: 66
Leamington 1 Bedworth United 0 *(Oct 30)*	Att: 426
Marlow 3 AFC Hayes 2 *(Oct 30)*	Att: 84
Oxford City 3 **Didcot Town** 4 *(Oct 30)*	Att: 212
Romulus 0 **Sutton Coldfield Town** 2 *(Oct 30)*	Att: 161
Taunton Town 0 **Gosport Borough** 2 *aet (Oct 31)*	Att: 73
Uxbridge 1 Dunstable Town 0 *(Oct 30)*	Att: 67

THIRD ROUND

Banbury United 2 Brackley Town 0 *(Nov 20)*	Att: 355
Bashley 1 Godalming Town 0 *(Dec 18)*	Att: 96
Bedford Town 3 Corby Town 1 *aet (Nov 20)*	Att: 157
Bromsgrove Rovers 2 Leamington 2 *aet (4-2p) (Dec 29)*	Att: 329
Cirencester Town 2 Cinderford Town 1 *(Nov 19)*	Att: 36
Clevedon Town 2 Tiverton Town 1 *(Dec 11)*	Att: 92
Gosport Borough 0 **Didcot Town** 2 *(Nov 20)*	Att: 75
Hillingdon Borough 3 Berkhamsted Town 0 *(Nov 20)*	Att: 44
King's Lynn 3 Hitchin Town 1 *(Nov 20)*	Att: 336
Mangotsfield United 4 Yate Town 1 *(Nov 20)*	Att: 120
Marlow 1 **Cheshunt** 3 *(Dec 18)*	Att: 65
Rugby Town 2 Halesowen Town 0 *(Nov 20)*	Att: 137
Sutton Coldfield Town 3 Gloucester City 1 *(Nov 26)*	Att: 72
Swindon Supermarine 5 Merthyr Tydfil 1 *(Nov 20)*	Att: 47
Team Bath 2 Chippenham Town 1 *(Nov 20)*	Att: 88
Uxbridge 2 **Hemel Hempstead Town** 2 *aet (3-4p) (Nov 20)*	Att: 70

FOURTH ROUND

Bashley 3 **Hillingdon Borough** 3 *aet (3-4p) (Jan 22)*	Att: 94
Bromsgrove Rovers 2 **Banbury United** 4 *aet (Jan 22)*	Att: 242
Cirencester Town 3 Sutton Coldfield Town 2 *(Jan 21)*	Att: 42
Didcot Town 4 Cheshunt 0 *(Jan 22)*	Att: 159
King's Lynn 1 Hemel Hempstead Town 1 *aet (5-3p) (Jan 29)*	Att: 385
Mangotsfield United 0 **Swindon Supermarine** 2 *(Jan 22)*	Att: 49
Rugby Town 1 Bedford Town 0 *(Jan 22)*	Att: 143
Team Bath 0 **Clevedon Town** 1 *(Jan 22)*	Att: 63

QUARTER-FINALS

Banbury United 0 **Hillingdon Borough** 1 *(Feb 12)*	Att: 132
Didcot Town 2 Cirencester Town 2 *aet (4-3p) (Feb 12)*	Att: 229
King's Lynn 4 Rugby Town 1 *(Feb 12)*	Att: 535
Swindon Supermarine 0 **Clevedon Town** 6 *(Feb 12)*	Att: 59

SEMI-FINALS

Didcot Town 1 **Clevedon Town** 2 *aet (Mar 4)*	Att: 264
King's Lynn 0 **Hillingdon Borough** 1 *(Mar 4)*	Att: 368

FINAL

(played over two legs)

(April 8th)

Hillingdon Borough 1 Clevedon Town 1 **Att:** 115

(April 22nd)

Clevedon Town 0 **Hillingdon Borough** 3 *Att:* 233

SPARTAN SOUTH MIDLANDS LEAGUE

	Aylesbury	Beaconsfield	Biggleswade Tn	Biggleswade U	Brimsdown Rvs	Broxbourne	Chalfont St P	Cockfosters	Colney Heath	Hanwell Town	Harefield Utd	Hertford Town	Holmer Green	Kingsbury LT	Langford	Leverstock Gn	London Colney	Oxhey Jets	Ruislip Manor	St Margaretsbury	Tring Athletic	Welwyn Garden
Aylesbury Vale		2-3	0-4	4-2	0-3	0-1	1-3	1-2	1-0	1-2	3-2	0-6	3-0	3-0	0-3	2-2	2-0	2-2	4-0	0-1	3-3	3-0
Beaconsfield SYCOB	3-0		1-2	5-0	2-0	0-1	1-1	1-0	3-0	4-1	1-1	3-0	4-0	2-0	2-1	2-4	4-0	2-1	5-1	2-1	3-1	8-0
Biggleswade Town	3-1	1-2		6-0	2-5	5-2	1-1	2-1	3-2	2-1	1-3	2-1	2-3	2-0	3-1	0-0	2-0	2-1	2-1	3-1	5-0	2-1
Biggleswade United	1-1	1-0	2-2	P	3-2	1-1	1-3	0-4	1-0	1-1	1-2	0-5	6-0	0-2	2-3	1-3	4-0	0-0	3-1	0-1	0-1	1-2
Brimsdown Rovers	2-2	1-4	0-1	3-1	R	1-2	4-1	2-0	0-1	4-2	1-2	2-0	1-1	2-3	4-0	1-1	8-1	1-0	2-0	1-2	3-0	3-2
Broxbourne Borough V & E	2-3	3-5	0-3	4-3	0-4	E	1-1	4-1	0-1	3-4	2-1	3-3	3-1	5-2	1-0	1-1	3-1	3-0	0-1	3-0	0-3	5-0
Chalfont St Peter	0-0	2-0	1-0	3-0	3-1	6-0	M	4-0	0-2	4-0	1-1	4-0	4-0	6-1	4-0	2-2	4-2	3-3	3-1	0-0	1-0	2-0
Cockfosters	1-2	0-1	2-4	2-4	0-1	1-1	2-2	I	4-3	0-1	0-4	1-3	2-2	0-0	3-7	2-3	2-2	1-1	2-2	1-5	3-1	3-3
Colney Heath	2-1	0-4	1-3	1-2	3-5	1-1	1-1	0-0	E	1-3	0-3	0-5	2-1	1-2	0-2	1-1	2-0	2-3	1-0	2-0	1-0	2-0
Hanwell Town	1-1	2-2	0-2	1-1	0-0	1-3	1-3	2-1	7-1	R	3-0	1-1	3-1	1-1	2-0	3-0	2-1	7-1	2-1	1-1	4-2	3-0
Harefield United	3-1	0-2	5-2	2-4	1-0	0-1	3-4	1-2	3-0	2-3		1-0	3-2	1-2	1-2	2-1	4-1	2-1	3-0	4-1	2-0	4-2
Hertford Town	3-0	1-2	1-1	5-1	3-2	1-1	4-0	2-0	1-0	0-2	1-0	D	1-1	2-1	1-1	2-0	6-0	2-0	1-1	2-0	4-3	3-2
Holmer Green	2-3	0-1	0-3	2-2	0-2	1-1	1-3	2-1	2-2	0-1	0-4	0-3	I	2-0	1-3	1-0	1-3	1-2	1-0	0-1	1-0	3-3
Kingsbury London Tigers	1-4	2-2	2-1	3-2	1-3	1-2	0-3	0-5	0-1	1-0	0-0	1-2	2-0	V	5-3	1-1	1-2	1-2	3-1	2-1	2-1	1-0
Langford	1-0	0-2	0-0	5-1	1-0	0-2	0-3	1-3	1-3	5-1	1-0	3-4	6-1	2-2	I	3-3	4-0	1-1	8-0	2-1	6-0	2-1
Leverstock Green	0-0	1-2	1-4	4-0	1-1	3-0	0-2	4-0	2-0	3-0	1-0	3-2	2-2	1-3	1-3	S	3-1	1-0	3-0	3-1	4-1	1-2
London Colney	0-2	0-1	0-2	0-3	0-0	2-5	1-4	1-2	0-1	4-2	1-1	0-3	1-4	0-2	0-3	1-0	I	0-7	0-1	1-4	0-2	1-5
Oxhey Jets	1-2	1-1	3-2	1-1	0-3	1-2	2-4	1-2	1-2	3-0	2-2	0-2	3-4	2-1	1-3	0-3	3-1	O	4-2	0-2	1-2	2-3
Ruislip Manor	1-2	1-6	1-3	3-1	1-2	1-5	3-3	2-3	2-1	1-2	0-1	1-0	0-3	1-6	3-6	0-1	1-1	1-1	N	0-1	0-0	2-4
St Margaretsbury	4-2	0-1	3-0	1-0	1-2	1-2	2-2	2-1	4-0	5-1	1-2	0-1	1-1	1-1	1-0	4-1	4-2	3-1	1-0		0-1	1-2
Tring Athletic	3-1	1-2	0-2	7-1	2-1	5-3	2-1	7-0	0-0	4-3	0-2	2-6	2-0	2-0	2-0	2-3	3-3	2-2	2-2	2-2		3-1
Welwyn Garden City	0-1	2-1	1-2	1-2	1-3	1-2	0-3	3-2	1-2	0-3	0-4	0-3	3-0	3-2	2-1	3-2	1-0	5-0	0-3	2-2	1-2	

Premier Division		P	W	D	L	F	A	Pts
Beaconsfield SYCOB		42	31	5	6	102	36	98
Chalfont St Peter		42	26	11	5	104	45	89
Biggleswade Town		42	28	5	9	93	51	89
Hertford Town		42	25	6	11	95	45	81
Harefield United		42	25	5	12	86	52	80
Langford		42	23	4	15	97	67	73
Leverstock Green		42	21	10	11	85	57	73
Brimsdown Rovers		42	21	7	14	85	51	70
Hanwell Town		42	21	7	14	79	65	70
Tring Athletic		42	19	6	17	77	76	63
St Margaretsbury		42	18	8	16	66	51	62
Broxbourne Boro' V & E	-10	42	20	9	13	81	73	59
Aylesbury Vale		42	16	8	18	64	73	56
Kingsbury London Tigers		42	15	8	19	57	73	53
Colney Heath		42	14	6	22	47	82	48
Welwyn Garden City		42	14	3	25	64	95	45
Cockfosters		42	11	9	22	61	92	42
Biggleswade United		42	11	8	23	60	97	41
Oxhey Jets		42	9	10	23	64	87	37
Holmer Green		42	8	9	25	49	99	33
Ruislip Manor		42	6	6	30	43	105	24
London Colney		42	3	4	35	27	114	13

PREMIER DIVISION CUP

FIRST ROUND

Colney Heath 2 Welwyn Garden City 1 *aet*
Hertford Tn 2 Harefield Utd 0 *aet*
Langford 1 Tring Athletic 2
Leverstock Green 5 Kingsbury London Tigers 1
Oxhey Jets 1 Biggleswade Utd 3
St Margaretsbury 2 Cockfosters 1 *aet*

Hertford Tn 3 Brimsdown Rvs 0
Holmer Green 1 Ruislip Manor 2
Leverstock Green 7 London Colney 0

SECOND ROUND

Aylesbury Vale 0 Beaconsfield SYCOB 3
Biggleswade Utd 1 Tring Ath. 3
Broxbourne Borough V & E 2 Biggleswade Town 5
Chalfont St Peter 1 St Margaretsbury 0
Colney Hth 1 Hanwell Tn 3 *aet*

QUARTER-FINALS

Beaconsfield SYCOB 1 Tring Athletic 0
Hanwell Town 0 Chalfont St P. 1
Leverstock Gn 3 Hertford Tn 2
Ruislip M. 0 Biggleswade Tn 2

SEMI-FINALS

Chalfont St Peter 2 Biggleswade Town 1 *aet*
Leverstock Green 0 Beaconsfield SYCOB 2

FINAL
(May 6th at Harefield United)
Beaconsfield SYCOB 2 Chalfont St Peter 1

MOLTEN FOOTBALLS SPARTAN SOUTH MIDLANDS LEAGUE PREMIER DIVISION CONSTITUTION 2008-09

AYLESBURY VALE .... Haywood Sports & Social Club, Haywood Way, Aylesbury HP19 9WZ 01296 423324
BERKHAMSTED TOWN .... Broadwater, Lower Kings Road, Berkhamsted HP4 2AA 01442 862815
BIGGLESWADE TOWN .... The Carlsberg Stadium, Langford Road, Biggleswade SG18 0DB .... None
BIGGLESWADE UNITED .... Second Meadow, Fairfield Road, Biggleswade SG18 0AA 01767 600408
BRIMSDOWN ROVERS .... Brimsdown Sports & Social, Goldsdown Road, Enfield EN3 7RP 020 8804 5491
BROXBOURNE BOROUGH V & E .... The V & E Club, Goffs Lane, Cheshunt EN7 5QN 01992 624281
CHALFONT ST PETER .... Mill Meadow, Gravel Hill, Amersham Road, Chalfont St Peter SL9 9QX 01753 885797
COCKFOSTERS .... Cockfosters Sports Ground, Chalk Lane, Cockfosters, Barnet EN4 9JG 020 8449 5833
COLNEY HEATH .... The Recreation Ground, High Street, Colney Heath, St Albans AL4 0QN 01727 819370
HANWELL TOWN .... Reynolds Field, Perivale Lane, Perivale, Greenford UB6 8TL 020 8998 1701
HAREFIELD UNITED .... Preston Park, Breakspear Road North, Harefield UB9 6PE 01895 823474
HARINGEY BOROUGH .... Coles Park, White Hart Lane, Wood Green, Tottenham N17 7JP 020 8889 1415
HERTFORD TOWN .... Hertingfordbury Park, West Street, Hertford SG13 8EZ 01992 583716
HOLMER GREEN .... Watchet Lane, Holmer Green, High Wycombe HP15 6UF 01494 711485
KENTISH TOWN .... Copthall Stadium, Greenland Lane, Hendon NW4 1RL 020 8202 6478
KINGSBURY LONDON TIGERS ...... Silver Jubilee Park, Townsend Lane, Kingsbury NW9 7NE 020 8205 1645
LANGFORD .... Forde Park, Langford Road, Henlow SG16 6AF 01462 816106
LEVERSTOCK GREEN .... Pancake Lane, Leverstock Green, Hemel Hempstead HP2 4BN 01442 246280
OXHEY JETS .... Boundary Stadium, Altham Way, Watford, South Oxhey WD19 6FW 020 8421 6277
ST MARGARETSBURY .... Recreation Ground, Station Road, Stanstead St Margarets, Ware SG12 8EH 01920 870473
TRING ATHLETIC .... The Grass Roots Stadium, Pendley Sports Centre, Cow Lane, Tring HP23 5NS 01442 891144
WELWYN GARDEN CITY .... Herns Way, Panshanger, Welwyn Garden City AL7 1TA 01707 328470

IN: Berkhamsted Town (R – Southern League Division One Midlands), Haringey Borough (P), Kentish Town (P)
OUT: Beaconsfield SYCOB (P – Southern League Division One South & West), London Colney (R), Ruislip Manor (R)

	Amersham Town	Ampthill Town	Arlesey Athletic	Bedford	Bedford Town Res.	Brache Sparta	Buckingham Athletic	Cheshunt Res.	Cranfield United	Haringey Borough	Harpenden Town	Hoddesdon Town	Kentish Town	New Bradwell St Peter	Royston Town	Sport London E Benfica	Stony Stratford Town	Sun Postal Sports	Winslow United
Amersham Town		2-3	4-3	4-2	2-3	1-2	2-0	0-1	1-2	1-3	1-2	4-2	2-1	0-0	2-2	1-3	2-1	4-1	3-1
Ampthill Town	6-1		4-0	5-0	1-2	2-1	4-1	3-5	4-2	1-2	1-0	1-1	3-4	3-3	2-2	3-1	4-5	7-1	3-1
Arlesey Athletic	3-2	0-1		1-3	0-0	3-1	0-1	2-2	1-4	0-1	3-0	0-2	3-2	0-5	2-1	1-4	2-2	2-1	1-1
Bedford	2-1	1-3	4-3	D	1-2	1-0	4-2	2-1	3-2	1-6	4-2	0-3	1-0	0-2	4-0	0-5	1-1	1-1	5-3
Bedford Town Res.	0-0	0-3	1-1	3-2	I	2-5	0-3	1-0	4-1	1-4	4-4	2-3	2-1	1-2	1-5	0-1	1-1	1-2	1-7
Brache Sparta	2-0	3-0	1-0	0-6	3-5	V	1-0	1-1	3-2	2-2	0-1	2-4	0-6	0-4	1-3	2-2	2-3	4-1	3-1
Buckingham Athletic	2-2	4-2	1-1	5-2	1-0	1-2	I	0-1	4-3	3-3	1-1	0-0	1-0	0-0	0-0	0-1	0-2	1-1	3-2
Cheshunt Res.	1-2	3-3	3-1	0-2	5-0	2-2	0-2	S	2-2	1-3	0-2	3-0	0-0	0-4	1-2	2-0	5-3	1-1	
Cranfield United	5-2	1-5	4-2	1-3	0-1	0-2	3-1	0-2	I	3-1	1-1	3-6	3-2	0-2	1-4	0-2	0-7	1-2	2-3
Haringey Borough	0-1	2-1	4-1	3-2	2-0	5-1	4-1	2-0	3-2	O	0-3	2-2	2-2	3-0	5-1	2-0	1-1	1-0	2-2
Harpenden Town	1-2	0-1	3-1	1-3	2-0	2-3	0-0	1-1	3-0	3-3	N	0-3	1-2	1-1	3-3	1-1	0-4	2-2	2-3
Hoddesdon Town	4-3	1-3	1-1	2-1	2-0	2-2	4-0	0-2	3-2	4-0	0-1		1-2	1-2	3-2	3-2	2-3	1-1	2-0
Kentish Town	2-1	3-1	4-1	4-1	3-2	2-1	2-2	2-4	4-1	4-2	3-1	2-0		3-3	1-0	1-0	3-5	3-1	2-0
New Bradwell St Peter	1-4	2-2	0-1	1-0	1-0	2-0	1-1	1-0	1-0	0-1	2-0	3-0	0-6	O	1-0	2-0	2-2	3-1	7-0
Royston Town	7-0	4-1	1-2	6-0	1-1	4-0	1-0	1-2	0-0	2-0	4-0	2-4	3-4	0-0	N	5-0	2-0	2-1	8-0
Sport London E Benfica	1-1	2-1	5-0	2-4	1-1	2-2	3-1	2-1	3-0	1-2	3-0	0-1	0-0	3-2	1-2	E	1-2	4-4	6-1
Stony Stratford Town	1-3	3-0	2-4	2-1	2-1	4-0	1-0	3-1	5-1	5-3	3-0	0-2	1-1	3-2	2-3	1-0		5-0	7-5
Sun Postal Sports	2-1	0-2	3-2	1-0	1-4	3-1	2-0	0-4	4-0	0-3	2-0	0-2	2-3	2-3	0-2	1-1	1-1		1-1
Winslow United	0-4	1-1	1-4	4-2	0-2	2-0	1-3	2-2	3-6	3-5	0-2	0-3	1-4	5-3	1-5	1-2	4-1	2-0	

Division One	P	W	D	L	F	A	Pts
Kentish Town	36	23	6	7	92	52	75
Haringey Borough	36	22	7	7	87	55	73
Hoddesdon Town	36	20	9	7	77	49	69
Stony Stratford Town	36	20	7	9	89	58	67
Royston Town	36	19	8	9	92	44	65
New Bradwell St Peter	36	17	11	8	63	43	62
Ampthill Town	36	18	6	12	90	64	60
Sport London E Benfica	36	16	8	12	67	50	56
Bedford	36	16	2	18	69	82	50
Cheshunt Res.	36	13	10	13	59	55	49
Amersham Town	36	14	5	17	66	72	47
Brache Sparta	36	12	6	18	55	81	42
Buckingham Athletic	36	10	11	15	45	56	41
Bedford Town Res.	36	10	8	18	49	74	38
Arlesey Athletic	36	10	7	19	52	79	37
Harpenden Town	36	8	10	18	44	66	34
Sun Postal Sports	36	9	7	20	49	81	34
Winslow United	36	8	7	21	64	107	31
Cranfield United	36	8	3	25	58	99	27

DIVISION ONE CUP

FIRST ROUND
Amersham Town 0 **Buckingham Athletic** 1
Bedford 2 Bedford Town Res. 0
Sun Postal Sports 0 **Haringey Borough** 1
SECOND ROUND
Bedford 1 **Cheshunt Res.** 3
Buckingham Athletic 3 New Bradwell St Peter 0 *aet*
Haringey Borough 2 Cranfield United 1
Harpenden Town 0 Stony Stratford Town 1
(Stony Stratford Town expelled)
Hoddesdon Town 2 Royston Town 1
Kentish Town 1 **Ampthill Town** 2
Sport London E Benfica 2 Arlesey Athletic 1

Winslow United 3 Brache Sparta 3 *aet* (7-6p)
QUARTER-FINALS
Buckingham Athletic 2 Winslow United 1
Cheshunt Res. 0 **Harpenden Town** 1
Hoddesdon Town 1 **Haringey Borough** 2 *aet*
Sport London E Benfica 1 **Ampthill Town** 2
SEMI-FINALS
Buckingham Athletic 1 **Ampthill Town** 2
Haringey Borough 4 Harpenden Town 0
FINAL
(May 3rd at London Colney)
Haringey Borough 2 Ampthill Town 1

MOLTEN FOOTBALLS SPARTAN SOUTH MIDLANDS LEAGUE DIVISION ONE CONSTITUTION 2008-09
AMERSHAM TOWN . . . . Spratleys Meadow, School Lane, Amersham HP7 0EL 01494 727428
AMPTHILL TOWN . . . . Ampthill Park, Woburn Road, Ampthill MK45 2HX 01525 404440
ARLESEY ATHLETIC . . . . Arlesey Town FC, Hitchin Road, Arlesey SG15 6RS 01462 734504
BEDFORD . . . . McMullen Park, Meadow Lane, Cardington, Bedford MK44 3SB 01234 831024
BEDFORD TOWN RESERVES . . . . . The New Eyrie, Meadow Lane, Cardington, Bedford MK44 3LW 01234 838448
BRACHE SPARTA . . . . Foxdell Recreation Ground, Dallow Road, Luton LU1 1TG 01582 720751
BUCKINGHAM ATHLETIC . . . . Stratfields Fields, Stratford Road, Buckingham MK18 1NY 01280 816945
CRANFIELD UNITED . . . . Crawley Road, Cranfield, Bedford MK43 0AA. 01234 751444
CRAWLEY GREEN . . . . Barton Rovers FC, Sharpenhoe Road, Barton-le-Clay MK45 4SD. 01582 707772
HARPENDEN TOWN . . . . Rothamsted Park, Amenbury Lane, Harpenden AL5 2EF 01582 715724
HATFIELD TOWN . . . . Birchwood Leisure Centre, Longmead, Birchwood, Hatfield AL10 0AS 01707 270772
HODDESDON TOWN . . . . Lowfield, Park View, Hoddesdon EN11 8PX. 01992 463133
KINGS LANGLEY . . . . Gaywood Park, Hempstead Road, Kings Langley WD4 8BS 01923 264489
LONDON COLNEY . . . . Cotlandswick Playing Fields, London Colney AL2 1EH 01727 822132
NEW BRADWELL ST PETER . . . . . . Bradwell Road Rec Ground, Bradville, Milton Keynes MK13 7AB 01908 313835
ROYSTON TOWN . . . . Garden Walk, Royston SG8 7HP 01763 241204
RUISLIP MANOR . . . . Avenue Park, Western Avenue, Greenford UB6 8GA 020 8578 2706
SPORT LONDON E BENFICA . . . . . Hanwell Town FC, Reynolds Field, Perivale Lane, Greenford UB6 8TL 020 8998 1701
STONY STRATFORD TOWN . . . . Ostlers Lane, Stony Stratford, Milton Keynes MK11 1AR 07914 012709
SUN POSTAL SPORTS . . . . Sun Postal Sports & Social Club, Bellmount Wood Avenue, Watford WD17 3BN 01923 227453
WINSLOW UNITED . . . . Recreation Ground, Elmfields Gate, Winslow, Buckingham MK18 3JH 01296 713057
IN: *Crawley Green (P), Hatfield Town (P – Herts Senior County League Premier Division), Kings Langley (P), London Colney (R), Ruislip Manor (R)*
OUT: *Cheshunt Res. (W), Haringey Borough (P), Kentish Town (P)*

	AFC Dunstable	Aston Clinton	Caddington	Crawley Green	Kent Athletic	Kings Langley	Markyate	Mursley United	Old Bradwell United	Padbury United	Pitstone & Ivinghoe	Risborough Rangers	The 61 FC (Luton)	Totternhoe	Tring Corinthians
AFC Dunstable		1-0	6-1	2-2	1-0	0-3	7-0	1-1	0-0	4-0	3-1	4-1	1-4	2-3	6-2
Aston Clinton	4-0	D	1-3	2-0	1-0	2-3	4-1	4-3	4-1	5-0	2-2	1-1	1-1	3-1	4-2
Caddington	3-1	1-0	I	0-3	2-2	1-2	6-0	1-2	3-0	8-0	0-2	4-1	2-0	1-0	1-2
Crawley Green	3-0	3-1	2-1	V	1-0	0-0	13-1	2-1	4-1	10-0	2-2	1-1	0-0	3-2	7-1
Kent Athletic	3-4	3-5	0-1	1-0	I	1-1	3-0	1-1	3-2	9-1	2-1	0-0	1-2	6-1	0-0
Kings Langley	1-1	0-1	2-1	2-0	1-3	S	3-0	3-2	3-0	0-0	0-0	5-1	1-0	4-2	3-1
Markyate	0-9	0-5	1-5	0-5	0-9	2-4	I	1-6	1-4	1-4	2-4	0-0	1-3	1-6	0-9
Mursley United	0-3	2-1	0-2	1-4	2-1	0-1	3-1	O	3-1	3-2	0-5	1-1	2-4	3-1	1-2
Old Bradwell United	2-4	0-2	0-3	0-3	1-7	1-6	1-2	0-1	N	1-1	1-5	2-1	0-2	2-4	0-4
Padbury United	1-4	2-6	0-7	0-7	1-3	2-3	3-1	1-1	1-0		1-4	0-5	1-7	2-2	1-5
Pitstone & Ivinghoe	2-3	1-3	2-1	0-2	2-1	0-2	4-1	2-0	3-1	2-1		2-2	1-2	0-1	1-3
Risborough Rangers	0-3	1-0	4-1	0-5	0-1	2-3	1-1	2-1	4-1	0-0	0-1	T	1-1	1-0	2-0
The 61 FC (Luton)	0-0	2-0	0-1	0-1	3-2	1-2	5-0	2-1	3-1	6-0	1-2	1-1	W	6-1	0-2
Totternhoe	3-2	1-4	1-5	1-5	1-4	0-1	3-2	2-5	4-1	2-2	0-2	1-0	1-7	O	3-2
Tring Corinthians	2-4	0-1	3-3	0-0	3-2	1-2	6-0	1-5	6-0	2-0	1-1	3-1	0-2	4-2	

Division Two	P	W	D	L	F	A	Pts
Kings Langley	28	22	5	1	62	24	71
Crawley Green	28	19	6	3	88	20	63
The 61 FC (Luton)	28	16	5	7	65	27	53
AFC Dunstable	28	16	5	7	76	42	53
Aston Clinton	28	16	3	9	66	36	51
Caddington	28	16	2	10	68	37	50
Pitstone & Ivinghoe	28	14	5	9	54	38	47
Tring Corinthians	28	13	4	11	67	52	43
Kent Athletic	28	12	5	11	68	38	41
Mursley United	28	11	4	13	51	52	37
Risborough Rangers	28	7	10	11	34	43	31
Totternhoe	28	9	2	17	49	80	29
Padbury United	28	3	6	19	27	108	15
Old Bradwell United	28	2	2	24	24	87	8
Markyate	28	1	2	25	20	135	5

DIVISION TWO CUP

FIRST ROUND
AFC Dunstable 3 Crawley Green 2
Aston Clinton 17 Markyate 1
Kent Athletic 6 Caddington 1
Kings Langley 5 Pitstone & Ivinghoe 2
Risborough Rangers 4 Padbury United 2
Totternhoe 1 **Mursley United** 4
Tring Corinthians 2 The 61 FC (Luton) 1

QUARTER-FINALS
Kent Athletic 2 AFC Dunstable 1
Mursley United 3 Aston Clinton 1
Old Bradwell United 1 **Tring Corinthians** 4
Risborough Rangers 0 **Kings Langley** 3

SEMI-FINALS
Kent Athletic 1 **Kings Langley** 2 *aet*
Tring Corinthians 0 **Mursley United** 0 *aet* (4-5p)

FINAL
(May 9th at Tring Athletic)
Kings Langley 6 Mursley United 0

MOLTEN FOOTBALLS SPARTAN SOUTH MIDLANDS LEAGUE DIVISION TWO CONSTITUTION 2008-09

AFC DUNSTABLE . . . . Lancot Park, Dunstable Road, Totternhoe, Dunstable LU6 1QP 01582 663735
ASTON CLINTON . . . . London Road, Aston Clinton HP22 5HL 01296 631818
BLETCHLEY TOWN . . . . Scots Club, Selbourne Avenue, Bletchley, Milton Keynes MK3 5BX 01908 368881
BUCKS CC . . . . Bucks CC Sports & Social Club, Lower Road, Stoke Mandeville, Aylesbury HP21 9DR 01296 486790
CADDINGTON . . . . Caddington Recreation Club, Manor Road, Caddington, Luton LU1 4HH 01582 505151
HADLEY . . . . Hadley Sports Ground, Brickfield Lane, Arkley, Barnet EN5 3LD 020 8449 1144
KENT ATHLETIC . . . . Kent Social Club, Tenby Drive, Leagrave, Luton LU4 9BN 01582 582723
MARKYATE . . . . The Playing Fields, Cavendish Road, Markyate, St Albans AL3 8PT 01582 841731
MK WANDERERS . . . . Kents Hill Pavilion, Frithwood Crescent, Kents Hill, Milton Keynes MK7 6HQ . . . . None
MURSLEY UNITED . . . . The Playing Field, Station Road, Mursley, Milton Keynes MK13 9AP . . . . None
OLD BRADWELL UNITED . . . . Abbey Road, Bradwell Village, Milton Keynes MK13 9AP. 01908 312355
PADBURY UNITED . . . . Playing Fields, Springfields, Padbury MK18 2AS. . . . . None
PITSTONE & IVINGHOE . . . . Recreation Ground, Pitstone, Leighton Buzzard. 01296 661271
RISBOROUGH RANGERS. . . . . Windsor, Horsenden Lane, Princes Risborough HP27 9NE 01844 274176
THE 61 FC (LUTON) . . . . Kingsway Ground, Beverley Road, Luton LU4 8EU 01582 495417
TOTTERNHOE . . . . Totternhoe Recreation Ground, Dunstable, Totternhoe, Dunstable LU6 1RG 01582 606738
TRING CORINTHIANS . . . . Icknield Way, Tring HP23 5HJ 07886 528214
WODSON PARK . . . . Wodson Park Sports & Recreation Centre, Wadesmill Road, Ware SG12 0UQ 01920 487091
IN: *Bletchley Town (P – North Bucks & District League Division One), Bucks CC (P – Aylesbury & District League Premier Division), Hadley (West Herts League Premier Division), MK Wanderers (P – North Bucks & District League Division One), Wodson Park (P – Herts Senior County League Division One).*
OUT: *Crawley Green (P), Kings Langley (P).*

CHALLENGE TROPHY

FIRST ROUND

Amersham Town 1 **Holmer Green** 2
Ampthill Town 2 Old Bradwell United 0
Aston Clinton 1 **Broxbourne Borough V & E** 3
Aylesbury Vale 2 Biggleswade Town 0
Bedford 1 **Hanwell Town** 4
Biggleswade United 4 Cheshunt Res. 0
Brache Sparta 2 Harpenden Town 0
Chalfont St Peter 2 Risborough Rangers 1
Cockfosters 7 Cranfield United 0
Crawley Green 0 **Colney Heath** 3
Haringey Borough 2 **Welwyn Garden City** 2 *aet* (8-9p)
Hertford Town 9 Winslow United 0
Hoddesdon Town 1 **Ruislip Manor** 3
Kentish Town 1 **Langford** 3
Leverstock Green 3 Sport London E Benfica 3 *aet* (6-5p)
Markyate 2 **Caddington** 3
Mursley United 2 Sun Postal Sports 1
New Bradwell St Peter 1 Arlesey Athletic 0
Oxhey Jets 3 **Harefield United** 7
St Margaretsbury 1 Kings Langley 0
The 61 FC (Luton) 3 Buckingham Athletic 1
Totternhoe 3 Bedford Town Res. 1
Tring Athletic 1 **Brimsdown Rovers** 6
Tring Corinthians 2 **AFC Dunstable** 5

SECOND ROUND

Ampthill Town 3 Mursley United 1
Beaconsfield SYCOB 6 Caddington 0
Brache Sparta 5 Colney Heath 3
Brimsdown Rovers 3 Cockfosters 0
Broxbourne Borough V & E 3 **Leverstock Green** 5
Chalfont St Peter 2 Ruislip Manor 0
Hanwell Town 3 London Colney 1
Harefield United 4 Pitstone & Ivinghoe 1
Hertford Town 0 **Kingsbury London Tigers** 2

Langford 3 Aylesbury Vale 2
Padbury United 1 **Kent Athletic** 7
St Margaretsbury 0 AFC Dunstable 0 *aet* (3-1p)
Stony Stratford Town 3 Biggleswade United 2
The 61 FC (Luton) 2 Royston Town 0
Totternhoe 0 **Holmer Green** 6
Welwyn Garden City 3 New Bradwell St Peter 0

THIRD ROUND

Ampthill Town 3 **Holmer Green** 4
Brimsdown Rovers 4 Welwyn Garden City 2
Hanwell Town 2 **Kingsbury London Tigers** 3
Harefield United 0 **Chalfont St Peter** 3
Langford 0 **Beaconsfield SYCOB** 2
Leverstock Green 2 Brache Sparta 1 *aet*
St Margaretsbury 0 **Stony Stratford Town** 2
The 61 (Luton) 3 Kent Athletic 2 *aet*

QUARTER-FINALS

Beaconsfield SYCOB 0 **Brimsdown Rovers** 1 *aet*
Chalfont St Peter 1 Stony Stratford Town 1 *aet* (7-6p)
Kingsbury London Tigers 3 Leverstock Green 1
The 61 FC (Luton) 1 **Holmer Green** 4 *aet*

SEMI-FINALS

Brimsdown Rovers 2 Holmer Green 1
Kingsbury London Tigers 0 **Chalfont St Peter** 1

FINAL

(May 13th at London Colney)
Chalfont St Peter 2 Brimsdown Rovers 0

Reserve Division One		P	W	D	L	F	A	Pts
Hertford Town Res.		33	26	5	2	85	30	83
Cockfosters Res.		33	21	2	10	87	54	65
Oxhey Jets Res.		33	20	4	9	65	40	64
Leverstock Green Res.		33	18	8	7	61	38	62
London Colney Res.		33	13	6	14	56	55	45
Mursley United Res.		33	14	3	16	66	84	45
Tring Athletic Res.		33	12	7	14	47	42	43
St Margaretsbury Res.	-3	33	11	7	15	48	60	37
Hoddesdon Town Res.		33	9	8	16	56	61	35
Colney Heath Res.		33	7	10	16	52	65	31
Harpenden Town Res.		33	8	2	23	44	83	26
Sawbridgeworth Town Res.		33	5	6	22	37	92	21

Reserve Division Two East		P	W	D	L	F	A	Pts
Broxbourne Borough V & E Res.		24	18	1	5	87	30	55
Brache Sparta Res.		24	16	5	3	80	36	53
Biggleswade United Res.		24	17	1	6	57	30	52
Crawley Green Res.		24	15	3	6	61	29	48
AFC Dunstable Res.		24	14	2	8	64	46	44
Royston Town Res.		24	12	2	10	57	46	38
Ampthill Town Res.		24	11	1	12	45	53	34
Langford Res.		24	8	7	9	57	47	31
Kentish Town Res.		24	6	4	14	40	62	22
Kent Athletic Res.	-3	24	7	3	14	35	56	21
The 61 FC (Luton) Res.		24	5	4	15	31	71	19
Caddington Res.		24	5	2	17	39	92	17
Totternhoe Res.		24	3	3	18	28	83	12

Reserve Division Two West		P	W	D	L	F	A	Pts
Holmer Green Res.		24	17	3	4	53	21	54
Stony Stratford Town Res.	-3	24	14	6	4	58	34	45
Risborough Rangers Res.		24	14	3	7	54	31	45
New Bradwell St Peter Res.		24	13	3	8	56	42	42
Amersham Town Res.		24	10	6	8	56	45	36
Kings Langley Res.		24	10	5	9	47	38	35
Aylesbury Vale Res.		24	10	4	10	48	45	34
Tring Corinthians Res.		24	10	3	11	40	53	33
Old Bradwell United Res.		24	8	4	12	30	46	28
Buckingham Athletic Res.		24	7	4	13	39	52	25
Cranfield United Res.		24	6	6	12	40	52	24
Sun Postal Sports Res.		24	5	6	13	49	65	21
Winslow United Res.		24	4	3	17	31	77	15

RESERVES TROPHY

FINAL

(May 7th at Brimsdown Rovers)
Colney Heath Res. 1 **Cockfosters Res.** 2

STAFFORDSHIRE COUNTY SENIOR LEAGUE

	Abbey Hulton Utd	Alsager Town Res.	Ashbourne United	Ball Haye Green	Barlaston	Congleton Vale	Eccleshall AFC	Florence	Foley	Goldenhill Wdrs	Hanley Town	Newcastle Tn Res.	Norton	Redgate Clayton	Rocester Res.	Stallington	Wolstanton United
Abbey Hulton United	P	2-0	3-2	1-5	3-0	0-2	5-1	6-0	2-2	2-3	4-0	2-2	1-0	1-3	2-3	6-0	0-1
Alsager Town Res.	0-1	R	1-2	0-1	0-1	0-1	0-0	1-0	4-2	6-0	2-2	2-3	0-2	4-1	3-2	2-2	2-1
Ashbourne United	2-2	5-3	E	1-5	2-1	1-1	2-0	7-0	1-4	6-1	3-4	0-3	2-2	0-5	3-4	1-1	0-2
Ball Haye Green	1-1	2-0	3-1	M	1-1	1-0	1-1	1-2	2-0	2-0	4-0	3-2	2-0	1-0	2-1	4-1	0-3
Barlaston	0-2	0-4	4-2	1-0	I	1-2	0-1	0-1	0-2	3-2	1-0	0-6	0-2	3-3	2-1	3-0	2-6
Congleton Vale	1-0	2-0	1-1	2-1	1-0	E	2-1	7-0	2-1	2-1	0-1	2-2	2-1	0-0	4-2	4-1	1-0
Eccleshall AFC	0-2	0-3	4-4	0-4	2-1	1-0	R	1-3	0-1	2-1	2-4	1-2	3-0	0-5	2-2	3-0	0-4
Florence	1-1	1-2	3-1	0-0	1-3	3-2	2-1		1-3	0-3	1-1	0-3	1-1	0-3	1-2	3-0	1-2
Foley	1-1	4-0	7-3	0-1	0-0	1-2	4-2	1-4		4-0	0-1	1-1	0-1	3-0	1-2	4-1	2-3
Goldenhill Wanderers	1-2	0-3	0-1	1-5	1-2	0-1	3-1	6-5	2-1	D	3-6	0-6	2-3	2-1	4-2		1-5
Hanley Town	2-1	4-0	1-1	1-1	2-2	0-3	1-2	3-1	0-2	2-0	I	1-1	1-1	4-0	4-2	1-0	2-0
Newcastle Town Res.	2-5	3-1	3-1	2-1	3-1	1-1	2-0	4-0	3-3	3-0	1-2	V	2-4	2-4	4-0	3-0	1-1
Norton	1-1	2-1	2-1	3-2	0-1	1-1	1-0	4-2	5-0	3-0	2-4	2-4	I	2-1	1-2	1-0	2-3
Redgate Clayton	1-5	3-0	3-3	0-3	1-0	7-3	0-2	0-2	1-3	3-3	2-0	1-1	2-0	S	1-0	1-3	0-3
Rocester Res.	1-0	2-1	0-2	0-3	0-1	0-1	1-2	0-2	4-1	2-2	2-3	2-3	0-2	4-3	I	5-1	1-1
Stallington	1-3	0-3	0-2	1-1	0-2	2-2	1-5	1-1	0-3	2-3	0-6	1-3	0-3	0-2	1-6	O	1-8
Wolstanton United	1-0	0-1	1-0	4-0	5-0	2-0	4-0	1-0	7-0	4-0	3-2	5-1	4-1	9-1	2-0		N

Premier Division	P	W	D	L	F	A	Pts
Wolstanton United	32	25	2	5	95	24	77
Newcastle Town Res.	32	19	7	6	81	43	64
Congleton Vale	32	19	7	6	55	33	64
Ball Haye Green	32	19	6	7	63	30	63
Hanley Town	32	18	7	7	61	41	61
Abbey Hulton United	32	15	7	10	67	40	52
Norton	32	15	5	12	55	44	50
Foley	32	14	4	14	60	55	46
Redgate Clayton	32	13	5	14	58	60	44
Barlaston	32	12	4	16	36	56	40
Alsager Town Res.	32	12	3	17	49	51	39
Rocester Res.	32	11	3	18	55	69	36
Ashbourne United	32	9	8	15	63	74	35
Florence	32	10	5	17	42	71	35
Eccleshall AFC	32	10	4	18	40	65	34
Goldenhill Wanderers	32	8	2	22	45	92	26
Stallington.	32	1	5	26	23	100	8

LEAGUE CUP
(Premier and Division One teams)

FIRST ROUND

Alsagers Bank 4 Foley Res. 2
Audley 0 **Rocester Res.** 2
Ball Haye Green 0 **Wolstanton United** 1
Chesterton 4 Eccleshall AFC 1
Foley 1 Florence 0
Goldenhill Wanderers 4 Redgate Clayton 0
Hanley Tn Res. 3 **Barlaston** 3 *aet* (3-4p)
Hawkins Spts Yth 2 **Congleton Vale** 3
Lichfield Enots 1 **Norton** 2
Manor Inne 1 Holt JCB 0
Newcastle Town 'A' 1 **Stretton Eagles** 3
Northwood Town 1 **Alsager Town Res.** 1 *aet* (1-4p)
Redgate Clayton Res. 2 Abbey Hulton United 1
Sandbach Utd 1 Newcastle Tn Res. 0
Stallington 4 Ashbourne United 3

SECOND ROUND

Alsager Town Res. 4 Stallington 1
Alsagers Bank 2 **Rocester Res.** 7 *aet*
Barlaston 2 **Goldenhill Wanderers** 4
Chesterton 3 Hanley Town 1
Congleton Vale 1 **Redgate Clayton Res.** 1 *aet* (5-6p)
Manor Inne 0 **Stretton Eagles** 2
Norton 0 **Foley** 1
Wolstanton Utd 1 **Sandbach Utd** 3
QUARTER-FINALS
Foley 3 Sandbach United 1
Redgate Clayton Res. 3 Goldenhill Wanderers 1
Rocester Res. 3 Alsager Tn Res. 2
Stretton Eagles 5 Chesterton 1
SEMI-FINALS
Foley 0 **Redgate Clayton Res.** 1
Stretton Eagles 3 Rocester Res. 2 *aet*
FINAL
(March 26th at Newcastle Town)
Redgate Clayton Res. 2 Stretton Eagles 1

WWW.NLNEWSDESK.CO.UK

STAFFORDSHIRE COUNTY SENIOR LEAGUE PREMIER DIVISION CONSTITUTION 2008-09

ABBEY HULTON UNITED. . . . . Birches Head Road, Abbey Hulton, Stoke-on-Trent ST2 8DD 01782 544232
ALSAGER TOWN RESERVES. . . . . The Town Ground, Woodland Court, Alsager ST7 2DP. 01270 882336
AUDLEY & DISTRICT . . . . Town Fields, Old Road, Bignall, Stoke-on-Trent ST7 8QH. 01782 723482
BALL HAYE GREEN. . . . . Ball Haye Green WMC, Ball Haye Green, Leek ST13 6BH. 01538 371926
BARLASTON. . . . . Springbank Park, Moss Farm, Yarnfield Road, Yarnfield ST3 7NT 01782 761891
CONGLETON VALE. . Biddulph Victoria FC, Knypersley S&S, Tunstall Road, Knypersley, Stoke-on-Trent ST8 7AQ . . 01782 522737
ECCLESHALL AFC . . . . Pershall Park, Chester Road, Eccleshall ST21 6NE. 01785 851351
FLORENCE. . . . . Florence Sports & Social, Lightwood Road, Longton, Stoke-on-Trent ST3 4JS 01782 312881
FOLEY. . . . . Whitcombe Road, Meir, Stoke-on-Trent ST3 6NU 01782 595274
GOLDENHILL WANDERERS . . . Sandyford Cricket Club, Shelford Road, Sandyford, Stoke-on-Trent ST6 5LA 01782 839007
HANLEY TOWN . . . . Abbey Lane, Abbey Hulton, Bucknall, Stoke-on-Trent ST8 8AJ 01782 267234
NEWCASTLE TOWN RESERVES . . . Lyme Valley Parkway Stadium, Buckmaster Avenue, Clayton, Newcastle ST5 3BF. . . . 01782 662351
NORTON . . . . Norton CC & MW Institute, Community Drive, Smallthorne, Stoke-on-Trent ST6 1QF 01782 838290
REDGATE CLAYTON. . . . . Northwood Lane, Clayton, Newcastle-under-Lyme ST5 4BN. 01782 717409
ROCESTER RESERVES . . . . Hillsfield, Mill Street, Rocester, Uttoxeter ST14 5TX 01889 590463
SANDBACH UNITED . . . . Winsford United FC, The Barton Stadium, Wharton Road, Winsford CW7 3AE 01606 558447
STRETTON EAGLES. . . . . Springbank Park, Moss Farm, Yarnfield Road, Yarnfield ST3 7NT 01782 761891
WOLSTANTON UNITED. . Bradwell Comm. Centre, Riceyman Road, Bradwell, Newcastle-under-Lyme ST5 8LF 01782 660818
IN: Audley & District (P), Sandbach United (P), Stretton Eagles (P)
OUT: Ashbourne United (R), Stallington (W)

	Alsagers Bank	Audley & District	Chesterton	Featherstone	Foley Res.	Hanley Town Res.	Hawkins Sports Youth	Holt JCB	Lichfield Enots	Manor Inne	Newcastle Town 'A'	Northwoood Town	Redgate Clayton Res.	Sandbach United	Stretton Eagles
Alsagers Bank		2-3	3-2	1-2	1-2	2-1	7-0	3-0	5-0	0-0	4-2	2-1	5-4	2-5	1-0
Audley & District	4-2	D	2-2	3-3	3-1	1-1	3-0	1-3	3-1	1-0	7-1	3-0	1-0	1-0	1-3
Chesterton	2-4	0-1	I	3-0	6-2	2-1	4-1	5-3	1-1	1-2	0-1	2-1	2-2	1-3	2-2
Featherstone	1-4	3-3	2-4	V	4-0	1-1	1-3	1-0	0-3	3-1	3-2	3-1	3-7	2-3	0-3
Foley Res.	2-2	0-7	1-2	2-0	I	1-6	1-2	0-5	2-3	3-1	1-2	0-2	1-3	1-4	0-4
Hanley Town Res.	1-1	1-2	1-0	2-2	3-2	S	0-1	4-0	2-1	6-2	2-0	2-0	0-3	0-2	0-4
Hawkins Sports Youth	0-2	1-4	0-2	2-2	1-3	2-2	I	2-0	1-0	1-1	2-1	2-2	0-5	2-1	1-2
Holt JCB	0-1	6-1	0-3	0-1	2-2	3-2	1-0	O	2-2	3-1	2-0	2-3	4-1	1-3	0-2
Lichfield Enots	0-0	5-2	0-1	3-5	3-0	1-0	2-1	4-2	N	5-0	6-1	1-0	0-1	0-3	1-2
Manor Inne	1-1	1-3	1-1	3-2	2-1	1-2	4-3	2-4	1-3		7-0	2-2	2-4	0-3	1-8
Newcastle Town 'A'	1-3	0-1	1-2	3-9	0-4	2-2	1-4	1-4	3-3	4-0		0-2	0-3	1-4	0-7
Northwoood Town	2-3	1-1	1-2	2-2	2-1	1-1	2-1	1-0	1-0	2-0	1-1	O	1-3	2-0	1-0
Redgate Clayton Res.	3-0	1-5	0-1	6-2	2-1	2-3	0-2	2-1	5-1	2-1	2-1	1-1	N	0-1	0-3
Sandbach United	5-1	2-3	2-0	1-2	5-0	1-1	7-0	3-2	3-0	3-0	3-1	5-0	3-2	E	2-1
Stretton Eagles	5-0	4-1	2-0	1-2	3-0	6-0	5-0	1-1	2-2	2-0	4-0	5-1	2-2	1-1	

WWW.CHERRYRED.CO.UK

Division One	P	W	D	L	F	A	Pts
Stretton Eagles	28	19	5	4	86	20	62
Sandbach United	28	20	2	6	77	30	62
Audley & District	28	18	5	5	71	44	59
Chesterton	28	16	5	7	57	41	53
Alsagers Bank	28	15	5	8	62	49	50
Redgate Clayton Res.	28	15	3	10	66	47	48
Featherstone	28	11	6	11	61	66	39
Lichfield Enots	28	11	5	12	51	49	38
Hanley Town Res.	28	10	8	10	47	46	38
Northwoood Town	28	10	7	11	36	45	37
Holt JCB	28	10	3	15	51	52	33
Hawkins Sports Youth	28	9	4	15	35	65	31
Manor Inne	28	5	5	18	37	73	20
Foley Res.	28	5	2	21	34	80	17
Newcastle Town 'A'	28	2	3	23	29	93	9

LEAGUE TROPHY
(Division One and Division Two teams)

FIRST ROUND
Alsagers Bank 6 Real Macot 1
Audley & District 2 Wolstanton United Res. 2 *aet* (4-2p)
Ball Green Y & A 3 Foley Res. 2 *aet*
Biddulph Tn 4 **Florence Res.** 5 *aet*
Chesterton 2 **Barton United** 3
Hawkins Sports Youth (w/o) v Initial Spartans (scr.)
Holt JCB 4 Abbey Hulton United Res. 2
Longton Harriers 0 **Lichfield Enots** 3
Manor Inne 3 Ball Haye Green Res. 0
Newcastle Tn 'A' 4 Tunstall Tn 0
Sandbach United 6 Unity United 1
Sandbach United u-21s 0 **Cheadle Town Old Boys** 5
Screwfix 1 **Northwood Town** 8
Stone Old Alleynians Res. 0 **Hanley Town Res.** 1
Waterhayes 3 **Redgate Clayton Res.** 4 *aet*

SECOND ROUND
Alsagers Bk 12 Newcastle Tn 'A' 0
Barton United 7 Ball Green Y & A 2
Cheadle Tn OB 1 **Florence Res.** 2 *aet*
Hawkins Sports Youth 3 Holt JCB 0
Lichfield Enots 4 Hanley Town Res. 1
Northwood Town 3 Redgate Clayton Res 1
Sandbach United 4 Audley & District 2
Stretton Eagles 5 Manor Inne 0

QUARTER-FINALS
Alsagers Bank 4 Northwood Tn 0
Barton United 3 Florence Res. 0
Lichfield Enots 1 **Stretton Eagles** 2
Sandbach Utd 4 Hawkins Sports 2 *aet*

SEMI-FINALS
Alsagers Bank 1 **Stretton Eagles** 3
Sandbach United 2 **Barton United** 2
aet (2-4p)

FINAL
(April 7th at Norton United)
Stretton Eagles 2 Barton United 0

STAFFORDSHIRE COUNTY SENIOR LEAGUE DIVISION ONE CONSTITUTION 2008-09
ASHBOURNE UNITED .... JCB Lakeside Club, Station Road, Rocester, Uttoxeter ST14 5HY..................... 01889 591057
BARTON UNITED ..... Holland Sports Club, Efflinch Lane, Barton-under-Needwood, Burton-on-Trent DE13 8ET.......... 01283 712937
BRERETON TOWN................. Ravenhill Park, Main Road, Brereton, Rugeley WS15 1DF 01889 578255
CHESTERTON............ Red Street Community Centre, Talke Road, Chesterton, Newcastle-under-Lyme ST5 7AH........... None
CONGLETON ATHLETIC......... Back Lane Playing Fields, Back Lane, Congleton CW12 4RB....................... None
FEATHERSTONE............ HMP Featherstone, New Road, Featherstone, Wolverhampton WV10 7PU................. 01902 703132
HANLEY TOWN RESERVES .... Abbey Lane, Abbey Hulton, Bucknall, Stoke-on-Trent ST8 8AJ 01782 267234
HAWKINS SPORTS .... Hawkins Sports Club, Coppice Lane, Cheslyn Hay, Walsall WS6 7EY.............. 01922 417286
HOLT JCB .... JCB Lakeside Club, Station Road, Rocester, Uttoxeter ST14 5LS............... 01889 591057
KIDSGROVE CARPETS ..... Sandyford Cricket Club, Shelford Road, Sandyford, Stoke-on-Trent ST12 9ES............... 01782 839007
LONGTON HARRIERS..................... Malthouse, Leek Road, Cellarhead ST3 5DF....................... None
MANOR INNE .... North Staffs Sports Club, Shamblers FC, Whisper Lane, Newcastle-under-Lyme ST5 4EB 01782 680734
NORTHWOOD TOWN .... Northwood Stadium, Keeling Road, Hanley, Stoke-on-Trent ST1 6PA............... 01782 234400
REDGATE CLAYTON RESERVES.... Northwood Lane, Clayton, Newcastle-under-Lyme ST5 4BN............... 01782 717409
STAFFORD RANGERS U-21S ... Springbank Park, Moss Farm, Yarnfield Road, Yarnfield ST3 7NT 01782 761891
IN: *Ashbourne United (R), Barton United (P), Brereton Town (S – West Midlands (Regional) League Division Two), Congleton Athletic (P – Crewe & District League Premier Division), Kidsgrove Carpets (P – Crewe & District League Premier Division), Longton Harriers (P), Stafford Rangers u-21s (N)*
OUT: *Alsagers Bank (W), Audley & District (P), Foley Reserves (R), Lichfield Enots (W), Newcastle Town 'A' (W), Sandbach United (P), Stretton Eagles (P)*
Hawkins Sports Youth become Hawkins Sports

Note – Initial Spartans withdrew during the course of the season Their results are shown herein but are expunged from the league table	Abbey Hulton	Ball Green	Ball Haye Gn	Barton Utd	Biddulph Tn	Cheadle Tn	Florence Res.	Initial Spart.	Longton H.	Real Macot	Sandbach	Screwfix	Stone O All.	Tunstall Tn	Unity United	Waterhayes	Wolstanton
Abbey Hulton United Res.		5-5	1-1	1-5	1-6	0-1	2-6	n/a	1-4	1-0	5-0	3-1	2-1	12-0	2-2	1-0	1-2
Ball Green Y & A	4-1		2-1	0-2	2-2	5-2	1-4	n/a	1-6	2-3	3-1	2-2	1-3	16-0	3-2	2-1	1-2
Ball Haye Green Res.	4-2	7-1	D	0-2	2-1	4-1	3-2	n/a	0-0	6-1	5-1	4-3	5-0	4-0	4-2	3-0	6-0
Barton United	1-2	4-1	3-1	I	7-0	1-2	1-2	n/a	0-1	4-1	3-1	4-0	0-0	11-0	3-0	5-1	1-0
Biddulph Town	2-1	1-3	2-2	1-2	V	2-1	2-6	n/a	1-3	6-1	4-4	2-2	4-1	5-0	8-2	2-3	2-4
Cheadle Town Old Boys	5-1	1-2	0-1	1-4	2-2	I	3-6	n/a	1-0	3-2	4-0	2-2	1-3	12-1	2-1	2-2	2-2
Florence Res.	2-1	1-2	1-2	2-1	3-6	2-0	S	n/a	1-2	4-5	1-2	2-1	2-1	2-0	4-2	5-3	1-2
Initial Spartans	n/a	n/a	0-28	n/a	n/a	n/a	n/a	I	n/a	n/a	n/a	n/a	n/a	n/a	n/a	n/a	n/a
Longton Harriers	3-0	1-1	4-3	0-1	4-0	0-1	2-2	n/a	O	3-0	3-0	6-0	2-3	6-0	3-0	3-2	3-2
Real Macot	0-4	3-5	2-4	0-6	3-5	3-1	8-3	n/a	3-5	N	2-3	2-2	1-0	4-1	7-3	3-4	0-2
Sandbach United u-21s	2-0	2-3	2-5	0-5	0-3	0-3	1-4	n/a	1-2	3-2		3-2	3-2	6-0	1-2	2-3	0-2
Screwfix	2-7	4-7	2-4	2-4	0-8	1-0	1-3	n/a	0-4	1-0	5-4		2-2	3-0	8-2	0-2	3-2
Stone Old Alleynians Res.	1-2	1-2	2-2	0-2	2-3	0-4	1-3	16-1	0-2	1-2	3-2	3-5	T	7-1	3-6	3-3	0-0
Tunstall Town	1-6	1-10	0-7	0-4	0-10	0-13	0-4	n/a	0-7	1-9	0-2	0-9	1-7	W	2-5	0-8	0-8
Unity United	2-2	3-1	0-4	0-5	4-3	3-2	2-0	n/a	0-3	4-3	0-3	3-5	3-2	2-3	O	1-1	0-3
Waterhayes	4-1	0-4	3-5	1-3	2-3	2-3	0-5	n/a	1-1	1-1	3-0	5-3	3-0	6-0	0-5		1-2
Wolstanton United Res.	2-0	2-1	1-1	1-0	3-2	4-2	2-3	n/a	1-1	4-1	0-0	3-2	5-2	6-0	1-0	2-0	

Division Two	P	W	D	L	F	A	Pts
Barton United	30	23	1	6	94	21	70
Longton Harriers	30	21	5	4	86	26	68
Ball Haye Green Res.	30	21	5	4	100	41	68
Wolstanton United Res.	30	20	5	5	70	36	65
Florence Res.	30	19	1	10	86	59	58
Ball Green Y & A	30	16	4	10	93	68	52
Biddulph Town	30	14	5	11	98	70	47
Cheadle Town Old Boys	30	13	5	12	78	56	44
Abbey Hulton Utd Res.	30	11	4	15	68	69	37
Waterhayes	30	10	5	15	65	70	35
Screwfix	30	9	5	16	73	93	32
Unity United	30	9	4	17	61	94	31
Real Macot	30	9	2	19	72	92	29
Sandbach United u-21s	30	9	2	19	49	79	29
Stone Old Alleynians Res.	30	6	5	19	54	74	23
Tunstall Town	30	1	0	29	12	211	3

Initial Spartans – record expunged

DIVISION TWO CUP

FIRST ROUND
Real Macot 0 Waterhayes 0 *aet* (7-6p)
SECOND ROUND
Ball Green Y & A 5 Abbey Hulton United Res. 2
Biddulph Town (w/o) v Initial Spartans (scr.)
Cheadle Town Old Boys 3 Barton United 3 *aet* (3-4p)
Florence Res. 14 Tunstall Town 0
Real Macot 1 Stone Old Alleynians Res. 2
Sandbach United u-21s 2 Ball Haye Green Res. 5
Screwfix 2 Wolstanton Utd Res. 4

Unity Utd 3 Longton Harriers 4 *aet*
QUARTER-FINALS
Ball Haye Green Res. 0 Florence Res. 0 *aet* (6-7p)
Barton Utd 9 Ball Green Y & A 2
Longton Harriers 4 Stone Old Alleynians Res. 0
Wolstanton Utd Res. 3 Biddulph Town 4 *aet (at Biddulph Town)*
SEMI-FINALS
Barton United 4 Florence Res. 0
Longton Harriers 2 Biddulph Town 1
FINAL
(March 3rd at Newcastle Town)
Longton Harriers 1 **Barton Utd** 2

LEEK & DISTRICT CUP
(Staffordshire County League sides affiliated to Leek & District FA)

FIRST ROUND
Chesterton 2 Ball Haye Green 7 *aet*
Redgate Clayton 0 Sandbach United 4
Wolstanton United 2 Norton 1
SECOND ROUND
Audley & District 1 Hanley Town 5
Barlaston 2 Sandbach United 1 *aet*
Congleton Vale 2 Alsager Town Res. 0
Eccleshall AFC 0 Rocester Res. 2

Florence 3 Abbey Hulton United 4
Newcastle Town Res. 3 Goldenhill
Wanderers 0
Northwood Town 2 Foley 3
Wolstanton United 3 Ball Haye Green 2
QUARTER-FINALS
Abbey Hulton Utd 4 Rocester Res. 2 *aet*
Foley 0 Congleton Vale 0 *aet* (2-4p)
Hanley Town 4 Newcastle Town Res. 1

Wolstanton United 3 Barlaston 0
SEMI-FINALS
Abbey Hulton United 1 Congleton Vale 0
aet
Hanley Town 0 Wolstanton United 3
FINAL
(April 4th at Ball Haye Green)
Wolstanton United 3 Abbey Hulton United 1

STAFFORDSHIRE COUNTY SENIOR LEAGUE DIVISION TWO CONSTITUTION 2008-09
ABBEY HULTON UNITED RESERVES . . . Birches Head Road, Abbey Hulton, Stoke-on-Trent ST2 8DD 01782 544232
AFC WATERHAYES . . . . . Holditch Miners Welfare, London Road, Chesterton, Newcastle-under-Lyme ST5 7PT 01782 564406
BALL GREEN Y & A . . . . Ball Green High School, Wilding Road, Ball Green, Stoke-on-Trent ST6 8BA . . . . None
BALL HAYE GREEN RESERVES . . . . . . Ball Haye Green WMC, Ball Haye Green, Leek ST13 6BH. 01538 371926
CHEADLE TOWN OLD BOYS . . . . . South Moorlands Leisure Centre, Allen Street, Cheadle ST10 1HJ 01538 753883
FLORENCE RESERVES. . . . . . Florence Sports & Social, Lightwood Road, Longton, Stoke-on-Trent ST3 4JS 01782 312881
FOLEY RESERVES. . . . . Whitcombe Road, Meir, Stoke-on-Trent ST3 6NU 01782 595274
RUGELEY RANGERS . . . . Green Lane Playing Fields, Rugeley. . . . . None
SFC . . . . Shotfields, Millrise Rod, Milton, Stoke-on-Trent ST2 7DN. . . . . None
SANDBACH UNITED RESERVES . . . . Bentley Motors Ltd, Pyms Lane, Crewe CW1 3P. 01270 656868
STONE OLD ALLEYNIANS RESERVES . . . . Springbank Park, Yarnfield Road, Yarnfield, Stone ST15 0NF 01785 761891
TALBOT ATHLETIC . . . . Bradeley Sports Centre, Chell Heath Road, Bradeley ST6 7LH. . . . . None
TUNSTALL TOWN. . . . . Kidsgrove Athletic FC, Hollinwood Road, Kidsgrove, Stoke-on-Trent ST7 1BQ. 01782 782412
WOLSTANTON UNITED RESERVES . . Bradwell Comm Centre, Riceyman Road, Bradwell, Newcastle-under-Lyme ST5 8LF . . 01782 660818
IN: *Foley Reserves (R), Rugeley Rangers (youth football), Sandbach United Reserves (P – Crewe & District League Premier Division)*
OUT: *Barton United (P), Biddulph Town (W), Initial Spartans (WS), Longton Harriers (P), Sandbach United u-21s (W), Screwfix (W)*
Real Macot become SFC, Unity United become Talbot Athletic, Waterhayes become AFC Waterhayes

SUFFOLK & IPSWICH LEAGUE

	BT Trimley	Brantham Athletic	Capel Plough	Coplestonians	Crane Sports	East Bergholt United	Felixstowe United	Grundisburgh	Haughley United	Ipswich Athletic	Leiston St Margarets	Melton St Audrys	Ransomes Sports	Stonham Aspal	Stowupland Falcons	Westerfield United
BT Trimley	S	0-3	0-2	0-1	1-4	0-3	1-4	1-3	3-0	0-2	0-2	1-5	1-0	1-2	1-4	1-1
Brantham Athletic	8-1	E	2-1	1-1	2-0	2-0	2-0	2-2	3-1	4-0	1-0	1-3	2-2	4-1	1-0	2-0
Capel Plough	7-4	1-0	N	2-2	2-0	1-0	2-1	1-0	2-0	1-3	2-0	2-1	2-1	0-0	1-2	2-0
Coplestonians	0-0	0-4	0-1	I	3-0	4-0	2-1	1-3	2-1	1-0	0-3	2-5	2-2	1-2	1-0	2-0
Crane Sports	4-0	1-2	1-4	2-0	O	3-3	4-0	2-6	5-2	1-1	1-0	0-1	1-3	2-2	3-1	3-1
East Bergholt United	1-3	0-1	0-1	3-1	1-3	R	1-2	1-7	3-2	2-8	2-2	1-6	1-1	0-2	0-7	0-1
Felixstowe United	5-0	0-1	1-1	0-2	2-5	2-2		2-4	4-1	2-2	0-1	0-2	0-2	1-2	4-2	0-2
Grundisburgh	8-0	1-1	0-3	3-0	6-2	3-0	2-1		10-1	0-3	3-0	4-1	5-1	2-1	4-0	3-2
Haughley United	2-4	0-5	1-5	1-4	0-4	0-8	1-5	1-9	D	0-3	0-3	0-8	1-3	0-2	0-4	1-4
Ipswich Athletic	2-0	0-2	2-2	1-5	2-2	4-0	1-1	0-4	4-1	I	2-2	0-4	1-0	1-2	5-1	2-2
Leiston St Margarets	4-1	2-1	1-4	1-0	2-2	5-3	2-1	3-1	4-0	1-2	V	1-2	1-1	1-0	2-1	1-0
Melton St Audrys	3-1	3-1	1-1	3-1	4-3	2-3	0-1	3-3	8-0	3-0	3-0	I	4-1	4-1	2-0	1-2
Ransomes Sports	1-0	0-1	1-1	1-1	0-1	2-0	3-2	0-7	3-1	3-4	1-1	2-2	S	0-1	0-1	2-0
Stonham Aspal	3-0	0-2	2-2	0-0	1-0	1-1	4-3	2-1	4-1	2-0	0-0	1-6	1-1	I	2-0	1-1
Stowupland Falcons	4-1	5-0	1-2	3-1	1-2	2-2	3-1	3-0	4-2	0-2	1-1	2-0	2-0		O	2-1
Westerfield United	2-1	2-3	0-5	0-4	2-2	0-1	3-4	0-6	2-3	1-2	2-0	2-0	2-3	0-4	0-3	N

RESERVES CUP FINAL (May 2nd at Needham Market) — Achilles Res. 2 Melton St Audrys Res. 1

JUNIOR CUP FINAL (April 25th at Framlingham Town) — Salvation Army Res. 2 Stowupland Falcons 'A' 0

WWW.CHERRYRED.CO.UK

Senior Division

	P	W	D	L	F	A	Pts
Brantham Athletic	30	21	4	5	64	27	67
Capel Plough	30	20	7	3	63	27	67
Grundisburgh	30	21	3	6	111	38	66
Melton St Audrys	30	20	4	6	91	36	64
Stonham Aspal	30	15	8	7	46	37	53
Leiston St Margarets	30	15	6	9	47	36	51
Stowupland Falcons	30	16	2	12	62	43	50
Ipswich Athletic	30	13	7	10	59	53	46
Crane Sports	30	13	6	11	63	55	45
Coplestonians	30	12	6	12	44	43	42
Ransomes Sports	30	9	9	12	40	49	36
Felixstowe United	30	8	4	18	51	60	28
Westerfield United	30	7	4	19	35	64	25
East Bergholt United	30	6	6	18	42	78	24
BT Trimley	30	4	2	24	27	90	14
Haughley United	30	1	0	29	22	131	3

Intermediate Division A

	P	W	D	L	F	A	Pts
Felixstowe United Res.	26	20	3	3	74	30	63
Ipswich Athletic Res.	26	18	4	4	81	33	58
Brantham Athletic Res.	26	14	9	3	57	35	51
Melton St Audrys Res.	26	14	5	7	68	38	47
Stowupland Falcons Res.	26	14	3	9	58	32	45
Ransomes Sports Res.	26	13	1	12	62	49	40
Capel Plough Res.	26	13	1	12	67	60	40
East Bergholt United Res.	26	10	2	14	52	75	32
Grundisburgh Res.	26	9	4	13	63	58	31
Coplestonians Res.	26	7	7	12	58	58	28
Old Newton United Res.	26	7	7	12	43	66	28
Crane Sports Res.	26	5	5	16	41	71	20
Willis Res.	26	5	5	16	39	106	20
Westerfield United Res.	26	2	6	18	25	77	12

METALTEC SUFFOLK & IPSWICH LEAGUE SENIOR DIVISION CONSTITUTION 2008-09

CAPEL PLOUGH .... Friars, Capel St Mary, Ipswich IP9 2XS .... None
COPLESTONIANS .... Copleston High School, Copleston Road, Ipswich IP4 5HD 01473 244178
CRANE SPORTS .... King George V Playing Field, Old Norwich Road, Ipswich IP1 6LE 01473 464030
EAST BERGHOLT UNITED ..... Gandish Road, East Bergholt, Colchester CO7 6TP .... 07775 691526 Carriers Arms: 01206 298392)
FELIXSTOWE UNITED .... Kirton Recreation Ground, Back Road, Kirton, Ipswich IP10 0PW .... None
FRAMLINGHAM TOWN .... Sports Field, Badlingham Road, Framlingham, Woodbridge IP13 9HS 01728 724038
GRUNDISBURGH .... The Playing Field, Ipswich Road, Grundisburgh, Woodbridge IP13 6TJ 01473 738234
IPSWICH ATHLETIC .... Bourne Vale Social Ground, Halifax Road, Ipswich IP2 8RE .... None
LEISTON ST MARGARETS .... Junction Meadow, Abbey Road, Leiston IP16 4RD 01728 831239
MELTON ST AUDRYS ..... St Audrys Sports & Social Club, Lodge Farm Lane, Melton, Woodbridge IP12 1LX .... None
RANSOMES SPORTS .... Ransomes Sports & Social Club, Sidegate Avenue, Ipswich IP4 4JJ 01473 726134
ST JOHNS .... Gainsborough Sports Centre, 5 Braziers Wood Road, Ipswich IP3 0SP 01473 433644
STONHAM ASPAL .... Delsons Meadow, Three Crossways, Stonham Aspal, Stowmarket IP14 6AN 01449 711051
STOWUPLAND FALCONS .... The Village Hall, Church Road, Stowupland IP14 4BQ 01449 771010
WESTERFIELD UNITED .... Rushmere Sports Club, The Street, Rushmere St Andrew, Ipswich IP5 1DE 01473 272525
WOODBRIDGE ATHLETIC ...... Greshams Sports & Social Club, Tuddenham Road, Ipswich IP4 3QJ .... None

IN: Framlingham Town (P), St Johns (P), Woodbridge Athletic (P)
OUT: BT Trimley (R), Brantham Athletic (P – Eastern Counties League Division One), Haughley United (R)

Division One

		P	W	D	L	F	A	Pts
Woodbridge Athletic		26	19	6	1	86	37	63
St Johns		26	17	4	5	97	41	55
Framlingham Town		26	15	5	6	55	39	50
Achilles		26	14	3	9	74	42	45
Old Newton United		26	13	6	7	69	49	45
Thurston		26	13	5	8	67	48	44
Stanton		26	11	8	7	51	47	41
Cockfield United		26	10	7	9	49	53	37
Mendlesham		26	10	4	12	57	68	34
Willis		26	8	2	16	41	76	26
St Edmunds '65	-3	26	8	3	15	47	61	24
Claydon		26	5	7	14	51	64	22
Bramford United		26	6	2	18	41	78	20
Bildeston Rangers		26	1	2	23	27	109	5

Intermediate Division B

	P	W	D	L	F	A	Pts
Achilles Res.	28	20	5	3	96	25	65
Stonham Aspal Res.	28	18	7	3	96	33	61
Stanton Res.	28	18	6	4	74	36	60
Woodbridge Athletic Res.	28	17	5	6	95	46	56
Leiston St Margarets Res.	28	17	4	7	62	45	55
Framlingham Town Res.	28	16	3	9	85	51	51
Cockfield United Res.	28	13	6	9	74	76	45
St Johns Res.	28	12	4	12	82	64	40
Mendlesham Res.	28	10	4	14	47	67	34
Bramford United Res.	28	10	3	15	49	68	33
Claydon Res.	28	8	5	15	53	53	29
St Edmunds '65 Res.	28	9	2	17	48	73	29
BT Trimley Res.	28	5	6	17	42	75	21
Thurston Res.	28	5	2	21	34	107	17
Bildeston Rangers Res.	28	0	2	26	22	140	2

LEAGUE CUP

FIRST ROUND
AFC Hoxne 1 **Tattingstone United** 4
Alstons 0 **Sizewell Associates** 5
Bacton United 9 AFC Titans 2
Claydon 1 **Saxmundham Sports** 2
Dennington United 0 **Elmswell** 5
Framlingham Town 3 Cockfield United 1
Great Blakenham 3 John Bull United 2
Halesworth Town 3 **Bildeston Rangers** 4
Henley Athletic 2 Needham Market 'A' 0
Ipswich Postals 3 **Trimley Red Devils** 3 *aet* (2-4p)
Martlesham Athletic 0 **Albion Mills** 3
Meadlands 7 Shotley 2 *(at Shotley)*
Old Newton United 5 Woolverstone United 4 *aet*
Salvation Army 1 Ufford Sports 0
Sproughton Sports 3 **Woodbridge Athletic** 5
St Clements Hospital 1 Aldeburgh Town 0
St Edmunds '65 4 Sporting '87 1
Stowmarket Stag 1 **Somersham** 2 *aet*
Stradbroke United 1 **Parkside United** 3
Tacket Street BBOB 2 Benhall St Mary 0
Waterside 4 Walsham Le Willows 'A' 2 *aet*
Wenhaston United 4 Bramford United 1
Willis 3 **St Johns** 5
SECOND ROUND
Achilles 1 **Mendlesham** 2
Albion Mills 0 **Somersham** 1
Bacton United 7 Tacket Street BBOB 0
Bildeston Rangers 3 **Framlingham Town** 9
Coddenham 0 **Trimley Red Devils** 3
Great Blakenham 3 Waterside 2
Henley Athletic 1 **Thurston** 4
Ipswich United 0 **Ipswich Exiles** 8
Parkside United 3 Meadlands 2 *aet*
Sizewell Associates 0 **Saxmundham Sports** 3
St Edmunds '65 (scr.) v **Bramford Road Old Boys** (w/o)
Stanton 3 St Johns 2
Tattingstone United 2 **Elmswell** 3
Wenhaston United 0 **Old Newton United** 2
Wickham Market 3 Salvation Army 1
Woodbridge Athletic 7 St Clements Hospital 1
THIRD ROUND
BT Trimley 0 **Woodbridge Athletic** 3 *(at RAF Woodbridge)*
Capel Plough 1 Ipswich Athletic 0
Coplestonians 2 Haughley United 1
Crane Sports 7 Somersham 0
Felixstowe United 3 **Bacton United** 5 *aet*
Framlingham Town 2 Bramford Road Old Boys 0
Great Blakenham 0 **East Bergholt United** 6
(at East Bergholt United)
Ipswich Exiles 1 **Framlingham Town** 4
Leiston St Margarets 2 Elmswell 1
Mendlesham 1 **Stonham Aspal** 2
Old Newton United 0 **Brantham Athletic** 1
Parkside United 2 **Trimley Red Devils** 3
Saxmundham Sports 2 Stanton 0
Stowupland Falcons 3 **Melton St Audrys** 5 *aet*
Westerfield United 1 **Thurston** 2
Wickham Market 1 **Grundisburgh** 7
Coplestonians 2 East Bergholt United 0
Framlingham Town 2 **Leiston St Margarets** 2 *aet* (3-5p)
Melton St Audrys 2 Saxmundham Sports 0
Old Newton United 1 **Capel Plough** 2 *aet*
Stonham Aspal 1 **Grundisburgh** 4
Thurston 4 Crane Sports 1
Trimley Red Devils 3 **Bacton United** 4
Woodbridge Athletic 3 Ransomes Sports 2
QUARTER-FINALS
Capel Plough 1 **Melton St Audrys** 2
Coplestonians 2 Thurston 1
Grundisburgh 7 Bacton United 0
Leiston St Margarets 1 **Woodbridge Athletic** 3
SEMI-FINALS
Grundisburgh 3 Melton St Audrys 2
(at Haughley United)
Woodbridge Athletic 4 Coplestonians 0
(at Westerfield United)
FINAL
(May 6th at Woodbridge Town)
Grundisburgh 3 Woodbridge Athletic 2

Division Two	P	W	D	L	F	A	Pts
Wickham Market	26	20	4	2	78	21	64
Wenhaston United	26	18	3	5	74	25	57
Bramford Road Old Boys	26	16	6	4	67	32	54
Saxmundham Sports	26	16	5	5	74	39	53
Bacton United	26	15	5	6	74	47	50
Sizewell Associates	26	15	1	10	61	47	46
Halesworth Town	26	12	5	9	50	41	41
Ipswich Exiles	26	9	6	11	37	43	33
Salvation Army	26	9	2	15	46	62	29
Sporting '87	26	7	6	13	42	58	27
Stradbroke United	26	7	5	14	44	71	26
AFC Hoxne	26	4	4	18	40	67	16
John Bull United	26	4	3	19	30	87	15
Needham Market Res.	26	1	3	22	32	109	6

Division Three	P	W	D	L	F	A	Pts
Parkside United	26	19	3	4	97	35	60
Elmswell	26	16	6	4	77	35	54
Stowmarket Stag	26	16	6	4	70	30	54
Albion Mills	26	15	5	6	60	39	50
St Clements Hospital	26	13	8	5	65	35	47
Waterside	26	15	1	10	61	45	46
Ipswich Postals	26	11	9	6	64	39	42
Somersham	26	10	6	10	46	47	36
Martlesham Athletic	-4	26	11	5	10	65	59	34
Ipswich United	26	5	5	16	27	68	20
Coplestonians 'A'	26	4	6	16	42	66	18
Coddenham	26	5	2	19	30	84	17
Tacket Street BBOB	26	4	5	17	30	94	17
Sproughton Sports	26	2	5	19	36	94	11

Division Four	P	W	D	L	F	A	Pts
Trimley Red Devils	24	19	4	1	94	24	61
Woolverstone United	24	20	1	3	88	31	61
Henley Athletic	24	19	2	3	89	30	59
Ufford Sports	-3	24	11	3	10	42	41	33
Wenhaston United Res.	24	9	5	10	44	53	32
Walsham-le-Willows 'A'	24	8	6	10	44	61	30
Sizewell Associates Res.	23	6	8	9	38	62	26
Wickham Market Res.	24	7	5	12	32	59	26
Benhall St Mary	24	7	4	13	44	55	25
Ipswich Exiles Res.	24	7	4	13	40	61	25
Great Blakenham	24	7	4	13	34	56	25
Stowupland Falcons 'A'	24	6	5	13	40	51	23
Meadlands	23	2	3	18	34	79	9

Meadlands v Sizewell Associates Res. not played

Division Five	P	W	D	L	F	A	Pts
Stonham Aspal 'A'	26	18	2	6	68	32	56
Saxmundham Sports Res.	26	17	3	6	73	47	54
Albion Mills Res.	26	15	3	8	66	36	48
Tattingstone United	26	14	3	9	91	62	45
Bramford Road Old Boys Res.	-4	25	12	5	8	71	45	37
Bacton United Res.	26	10	6	10	69	65	36
AFC Hoxne Res.	24	10	5	9	62	49	35
Halesworth Town Res.	26	9	7	10	36	44	34
Salvation Army Res.	26	10	3	13	57	68	33
Henley Athletic Res.	26	9	5	12	41	55	32
Stradbroke United Res.	26	9	2	15	60	68	29
St Clements Hospital Res.	26	9	2	15	49	90	29
East Bergholt United 'A'	-3	25	7	4	14	57	91	22
Somersham Res.	26	5	2	19	41	89	17

AFC Hoxne Res. v East Bergholt United 'A' and
Bramford Old Boys Res. v AFC Hoxne Res. not played

Division Six	P	W	D	L	F	A	Pts
Woolverstone United Res.	22	16	3	3	87	37	51
Sporting '87 Res.	22	16	2	4	89	34	50
Aldeburgh Town	22	14	5	3	64	33	47
Coddenham Res.	-3	22	14	2	6	70	46	41
Tacket Street BBOB Res.	22	12	4	6	68	43	40
Sproughton Sports Res.	22	8	5	9	36	45	29
Old Newton United 'A'	22	8	4	10	52	45	28
Benhall St Mary Res.	22	7	3	12	43	73	24
AFC Titans	22	5	4	13	63	66	19
Dennington United	22	5	2	15	38	77	17
Elmswell Res.	22	4	4	14	48	78	16
Shotley	22	2	4	16	42	102	10

SURREY ELITE INTERMEDIATE LEAGUE
(new for 2008-09)

SURREY ELITE INTERMEDIATE LEAGUE INTERMEDIATE DIVISION CONSTITUTION 2008-09

BATTERSEA IRONSIDES ..... Battersea Ironsides Sports & Social Club, Openview, Earlsfield SW17 0AW 0208 874 9913
CROYDON GREENSIDE .... Cumnor House Sports Ground, Pampisford Road, Purley CR2 6DH 020 8665 5368
ELM GROVE .... Coombe Lane, Whiteley Village, Walton-on-Thames KT12 4EL 01932 844671
EPSOM ATHLETIC ...... Esher Athletic FC, Strenue Sports Ground, Lynwood Road, Thames Ditton KT7 0DN .... None
EPSOM EAGLES .... King Georges Field, Auriol Park, Salisbury Road, Worcester Park KT4 7DG .... None
ESHER ATHLETIC .... Strenue Sports Club, Lynwood Road, Thames Ditton KT7 0DN .... None
EVERSLEY .... Eversley Sports Association, Cross Green, Reading Road, Eversley RG27 0NS .... None
HOLLAND SPORTS .... Mill Lane, Hurst Green, Oxted RH8 9DF 01883 716529
HORSLEY.............................. Toms Field, Long Reach, West Horsley KT24 6NE 01483 282516
LIPHOOK UNITED .... Recreation Ground, London Road, Liphook GU30 7AN..................... None
MILFORD & WITLEY .... Burton Pavilion, Milford Heath, Haslemere Road, Milford GU8 5BP 01483 860272
OLD RUTLISHIANS.............. Old Rutlishians Association, Poplar Road, Merton Park SW19 3JS 020 8542 3678
REIGATE PRIORY .... Reigate Priory Cricket Club, off Park Lane, Reigate RH2 8JX 01737 240872
TONGHAM .... Recreation Ground, Poyle Road, Tongham GU10 1BS 01252 782893
WOODMANSTERNE HYDE .... The Park, Woodmansterne Street, Woodmansterne 01737 350109
WRAYSBURY.................... Memorial Ground, The Green, Wraysbury, Staines TW19 5NA 01784 482155

IN: *Battersea Ironsides (P – Surrey South Eastern Combination Division One), Croydon Greenside (P – Surrey South Eastern Combination Division One), Elm Grove (P – Surrey Intermediate League (Western) Premier Division), Epsom Athletic (P – Surrey South Eastern Combination Division One), Epsom Eagles (P – Surrey South Eastern Combination Division One), Esher Athletic (P – Surrey South Eastern Combination Division One), Eversley (P – Surrey Intermediate League (Western) Premier Division), Holland Sports (P – Crawley & District League Premier Division), Horsley (P – Surrey Intermediate League (Western) Premier Division), Liphook United (P – Surrey Intermediate League (Western) Premier Division), Milford & Witley (P – Surrey Intermediate League (Western) Premier Division), Old Rutlishians (P – Surrey Intermediate League (Western) Premier Division), Reigate Priory (P – Redhill & District League Premier Division), Tongham (R – Combined Counties League Division One), Woodmansterne Hyde (P – Surrey South Eastern Combination Division One), Wraysbury (S – Middlesex County League Premier Division)*

THE STATISTICAL REVIEW
OF THE
RYMAN FOOTBALL LEAGUE
2007-2008 SEASON

The eleventh edition of the review has now been published.

This booklet includes player league appearances, results, goalscorers and attendances of league and cup matches for the 66 clubs. Also included is a player's index in alphabetical format of each player used in the Ryman League and their regular playing position.

The book is available at £5.50 + 78p (1st class) or 66p (2nd class) postage from

Mike Wilson, 71 Elm Road, Slade Green, Kent, DA8 2NN

Cheques made payable to Mike Wilson.

THE
FOOTBALL
TRAVELLER

The magazine is published weekly throughout the season and includes up-to-date fixtures from around a hundred different leagues in England, Wales, Ireland and Scotland.......
    Plus, all the latest news from around the clubs, programme reviews, club focuses and maps, cup draws, and much, much more.......
    All for about £1.30 a week (including first class postage).

Subscription rates for the 2008/2009 season are:-

£51-00 (full season), £26-00 (half-year to Christmas 2008)

Please write to:

The Football Traveller
Top o' the Bank
Evesham Road
Broadway
Worcs WR12 7DG
Phone:- 01386 853289 Fax:– 01386 858036
E-Mail:– berrytft@googlemail.com

SURREY INTERMEDIATE LEAGUE (WESTERN)

	Chiddingfold	Elm Grove	Eversley Social	Horsley	Liphook United	Milford & Witley	Old Rutlishians	Ripley Village	Shalford	Shottermill & Haslemere	Spelthorne Sports	Virginia Water	Woking & Horsell	Yateley
Chiddingfold		1-2	1-2	0-6	1-1	4-5	1-0	2-2	0-3	1-2	1-1	0-2	2-1	0-1
Elm Grove	1-1	P	0-2	2-3	2-1	2-1	4-3	3-1	2-2	4-0	2-0	2-1	2-2	6-0
Eversley Social	4-0	1-2	R	2-1	0-3	1-1	0-6	1-0	0-0	5-2	1-0	3-2	1-1	1-2
Horsley	5-0	1-1	3-1	E	2-0	2-1	1-1	4-2	4-0	2-4	6-1	2-0	3-0	3-1
Liphook United	2-2	6-1	3-4	1-2	M	3-1	2-0	4-2	2-2	5-2	0-0	0-0	2-1	2-1
Milford & Witley	2-0	3-0	0-1	1-3	2-2	I	1-0	4-3	1-1	3-3	0-1	5-2	2-3	2-1
Old Rutlishians	7-1	2-3	2-1	1-0	1-3	2-1	E	0-0	3-2	3-2	2-1	1-0	3-2	1-0
Ripley Village	0-2	2-0	1-0	1-1	0-3	1-2	1-3	R	2-1	1-1	1-4	7-0	0-3	1-1
Shalford	1-1	0-1	1-1	0-4	0-5	1-3	0-1	0-1		3-1	3-3	1-1	0-2	1-1
Shottermill & Haslemere	2-2	0-3	2-5	2-3	0-2	0-5	0-4	4-2	6-1		0-3	1-1	0-1	5-2
Spelthorne Sports	4-1	1-0	2-1	2-2	1-1	4-1	2-2	1-1	4-2	1-0	D	5-0	3-3	1-1
Virginia Water	0-2	1-4	1-2	0-5	1-3	1-2	1-2	5-3	2-2	1-3	5-3	I	1-1	2-1
Woking & Horsell	3-0	2-2	6-2	4-0	2-2	2-2	2-3	1-0	6-1	5-2	1-0	6-0	V	2-1
Yateley	2-1	1-1	1-1	0-3	2-1	0-2	0-2	1-3	3-0	4-1	2-2	3-1	0-1	

Premier Division		P	W	D	L	F	A	Pts
Horsley		26	18	4	4	71	28	58
Old Rutlishians		26	17	3	6	55	31	54
Woking & Horsell	-1	26	14	7	5	63	34	48
Liphook United		26	13	8	5	59	32	47
Elm Grove	-3	26	14	6	6	52	38	45
Milford & Witley		26	12	5	9	53	43	41
Spelthorne Sports		26	10	10	6	50	39	40
Eversley Social	-4	26	12	5	9	43	43	37
Yateley		26	7	6	13	32	46	27
Ripley Village		26	6	6	14	38	51	24
Shottermill & Haslemere		26	6	4	16	45	72	22
Chiddingfold		26	4	7	15	27	61	19
Virginia Water		26	4	5	17	31	69	17
Shalford		26	2	10	14	28	60	16

Reserve Premier	P	W	D	L	F	A	Pts
Yateley Res.	26	20	1	5	63	31	61
Horsley Res.	26	19	1	6	77	41	58
Woking & Horsell Res.	26	18	3	5	83	40	57
Spelthorne Sports Res.	26	17	4	5	84	35	55
Milford & Witley Res.	26	15	4	7	43	40	49
Old Rutlishians Res.	26	15	1	10	67	53	46
Ripley Village Res.	26	10	6	10	59	54	36
Elm Grove Res.	26	9	4	13	57	63	31
Virginia Water Res.	26	9	3	14	44	74	30
Liphook United Res.	26	9	1	16	50	61	28
Eversley Social Res.	26	8	3	15	40	55	27
Shottermill & Haslemere Res.	26	5	6	15	48	77	21
Shalford Res.	26	4	7	15	38	57	19
Chiddingfold Res.	26	1	2	23	19	91	5

RESERVES CUP

FINAL

(April 16th at Godalming Town)

Yateley Res. 2 Milford & Witley Res. 1

SURREY INTERMEDIATE LEAGUE (WESTERN) PREMIER DIVISION CONSTITUTION 2008-09

CHIDDINGFOLD . . . . Coxcombe Lane, Chiddingfold GU8 4QA . . . . None
GODALMING & FARNCOMBE ATHLETIC . . . Holloway Hill Rec, Busbridge Lane, Godalming . . . . None
MERROW . . . . The Urnfield, Downside Road, Guildford GU4 8PH. . . . . None
OLD SALESIANS . . . . Blackwater & Hawley Leisure Centre, Fernhill Road, Hawley GU17 9BW 01276 35411
RIPLEY VILLAGE . . . . The Green, Ripley . . . . None
SHALFORD. . . . . The Pavilion, Shalford Common, Shalford . . . . None
SHOTTERMILL & HASLEMERE. . . . . Woolmer Hill Sports Ground, Haslemere 01428 643072
SPELTHORNE SPORTS. . . . . Spelthorne Sports Club, 296 Staines Road West, Ashford TW15 1RY 01932 783625
VIRGINIA WATER . . . . The Timbers, Crown Road, Virginia Water GU25 4HS 01344 843811
WOKING & HORSELL. . . . . Woking & Horsell Cricket Grnd, Brewery Road, Horsell GU21 4LL 01483 236651
WORPLESDON PHOENIX . . . . Worplesdon Memorial Ground, Perry Hill, Worplesdon GU3 2RF . . . . None
WRECCLESHAM . . . . Wrecclesham Recreation Ground, Riverdale, Wrecclesham, Farnham GU10 4PR . . . . None
YATELEY. . . . . The Green, Reading Road, Yateley GU46 . . . . None

IN: Godalming & Farncombe Athletic (P), Merrow (R – Combined Counties League Division One), Old Salesians (P), Worplesdon Phoenix (P), Wrecclesham (P – Aldershot & District League Senior Division)
OUT: Elm Grove (P – Surrey Elite Intermediate League Intermediate Division), Eversley (P – Surrey Elite Intermediate League Intermediate Division), Horsley (P – Surrey Elite Intermediate League Intermediate Division), Liphook United (P – Surrey Elite Intermediate League Intermediate Division), Milford & Witley (P – Surrey Elite Intermediate League Intermediate Division), Old Rutlishians (P – Surrey Elite Intermediate League Intermediate Division)

	Burymead	Cranleigh	Dunsfold	Ewhurst	Godalming & Farncombe Ath.	Guildford City Weysiders	Hammer United	Ockham	Old Salesians	Pyrford	Royal Holloway Old Boys	Unis Old Boys	Windlesham United	Worplesdon Phoenix
Burymead		2-4	3-1	3-1	1-4	4-0	3-3	5-0	2-4	1-2	1-3	1-1	2-0	1-1
Cranleigh	1-0	D	5-0	5-0	1-2	2-1	4-2	3-5	1-0	5-4	2-2	1-2	4-0	1-5
Dunsfold	1-4	0-10	I	1-1	0-12	2-5	3-3	3-1	0-8	0-12	1-7	0-4	0-7	0-4
Ewhurst	1-0	1-2	9-0	V	0-2	2-3	4-0	1-3	1-2	0-3	2-4	1-2	1-2	4-7
Godalming & Farncombe Athletic	1-0	3-1	12-0	3-2	I	9-2	4-0	7-0	0-4	1-1	6-0	1-1	5-1	0-2
Guildford City Weysiders	0-2	0-1	4-1	2-1	0-3	S	3-1	1-0	1-1	2-1	5-0	3-1	0-2	1-6
Hammer United	4-0	0-1	9-1	2-2	0-6	3-1	I	2-6	2-1	1-1	1-3	3-7	6-0	1-7
Ockham	0-3	1-3	8-0	4-1	1-7	0-5	1-4	O	1-10	2-8	3-6	1-2	0-2	1-6
Old Salesians	2-0	1-0	4-0	4-1	3-2	6-1	6-0	3-1	N	4-0	2-2	4-0	10-0	1-0
Pyrford	7-3	4-0	6-0	1-1	1-2	4-1	2-2	4-2	1-2		2-1	0-0	1-2	0-5
Royal Holloway Old Boys	1-1	2-2	3-1	2-1	0-1	1-0	5-1	0-2	2-3	1-2	O	1-0	1-3	1-4
Unis Old Boys	2-1	1-2	6-1	6-2	1-3	3-0	4-3	5-2	2-1	1-2	0-2	N	4-2	1-4
Windlesham United	3-1	2-1	5-0	1-2	5-1	1-3	1-2	1-1	2-4	4-1	0-3	5-2	E	3-4
Worplesdon Phoenix	8-1	4-3	8-0	6-0	3-2	2-2	4-1	4-0	0-2	4-0	4-3	2-1	0-4	

LEAGUE CUP

FIRST ROUND
Burymead 1 **Woking & Horsell** 2
Chiddingfold 0 Liphook United 0 *aet* (4-3p)
Elm Grove 16 Dunsfold 1
Ewhurst 2 Guildford City Weysiders 1
Godalming & Farncombe Athletic 1 **Old Salesians** 2
Hammer United 2 Shottermill & Haslemere 0
Horsley 3 Pyrford 1 *aet*
Ockham 2 Royal Holloway Old Boys 1
Old Rutlishians 5 Unis Old Boys 0
Virginia Water 6 Eversley Social 0
Worplesdon Phoenix 4 Shalford 0
Yateley 2 Ripley Village 0

SECOND ROUND
Ewhurst 4 Hammer United 2
Milford & Witley 4 Cranleigh 1
Old Rutlishians 7 Ockham 0
Old Salesians 0 **Horsley** 3

Virginia Water 1 **Spelthorne Sports** 7
Windlesham United 1 **Yateley** 5
Woking & Horsell 0 **Elm Grove** 1
Worplesdon Phoenix 1 Chiddingfold 0

QUARTER-FINALS
Elm Grove 2 Ewhurst 1
Horsley 3 Yateley 1
Spelthorne Sports 1 **Old Rutlishians** 1 *aet* (8-9p)
Worplesdon Phoenix 3 Milford & Witley 1

SEMI-FINALS
Elm Grove 2 Worplesdon Phoenix 1
Horsley 3 Old Rutlishians 1

FINAL
(May 8th at Cobham)
Horsley 1 **Elm Grove** 4

Division One		P	W	D	L	F	A	Pts
Worplesdon Phoenix		26	21	2	3	104	34	65
Old Salesians		26	21	2	3	92	22	65
Godalming & Farncombe		26	19	2	5	99	30	59
Cranleigh		26	15	2	9	65	44	47
Pyrford		26	12	5	9	70	47	41
Royal Holloway Old Boys		26	12	4	10	56	50	40
Windlesham United		26	13	1	12	58	59	40
Unis Old Boys		26	12	3	11	58	49	39
Guildford City Weysiders		26	12	2	12	50	59	38
Burymead		26	8	4	14	45	55	28
Hammer United		26	7	5	14	53	79	26
Ockham		26	6	1	19	46	96	19
Ewhurst	-1	26	4	3	19	42	70	14
Dunsfold		26	1	2	23	16	160	5

Reserve Division One	P	W	D	L	F	A	Pts
Worplesdon Phoenix Res.	24	19	1	4	96	29	58
Cranleigh Res.	24	16	3	5	87	31	51
Royal Holloway Old Boys Res.	24	16	2	6	71	28	50
Unis Old Boys Res.	24	15	2	7	58	36	47
Old Salesians Res.	24	14	2	8	64	51	44
Godalming & Farncombe Ath. Res.	24	13	4	7	76	34	43
Windlesham United Res.	24	12	3	9	70	50	39
Pyrford Res.	24	8	8	8	58	43	32
Guildford City Weysiders Res.	24	9	4	11	61	71	31
Burymead Res.	24	6	6	12	45	57	24
Hammer United Res.	24	4	1	19	32	109	13
Ewhurst Res.	24	3	0	21	16	112	9
Ockham Res.	24	2	2	20	31	114	8

SURREY INTERMEDIATE LEAGUE (WESTERN) DIVISION ONE CONSTITUTION 2008-09

ABBEY RANGERS . . . . Addlestone Moor, Addlestone KT15 2QH 01932 888495
BURPHAM . . . . Sutherland Memorial Park, Clay Lane, Burpham, Guildford GU4 7NZ . . . . None
BURYMEAD . . . . Bisley Recreation Grond, Bisley GU24 9EW . . . . None
CRANLEIGH . . . . Snoxall Fields, Knowle Lane, Cranleigh GU6 8JW 01483 275295
EWHURST . . . . The Recreation Ground, Broomers Lane, Ewhurst, Cranleigh GU6 7RD . . . . None
GUILDFORD CITY WEYSIDERS . . . . Shalford Park, Shalford Road, Guildford GU4 8HA . . . . None
HAMMER UNITED . . . . Hammer Lane, Hammer, Haslemere GU27 1QD . . . . None
OCKHAM . . . . Hautboy Meadow, Ockham GU23 6NP . . . . None
PYRFORD . . . . Pyrford Cricket Ground, Coldhabour Road, Pyrford, Woking GU22 8ST 01932 342076
ROYAL HOLLOWAY OLD BOYS . . . . . Royal Holloway College PF, Prune Hill, Egham TW20 0EX 01784 443892
UNIS OLD BOYS . . . . Varsity Centre, Philip Henman Sports Ground, Egerton Road, Guildford GU25 4HS . . . . None
UNIVERSITY OF SURREY . . . Varsity Centre, Philip Henman Sports Ground, Egerton Road, Guildford GU25 4HS . . . . None

IN: Abbey Rangers (P – Guildford & Woking Alliance Premier Division), Burpham (P – Guildford & Woking Alliance Premier Division), University of Surrey (P – Guildford & Woking Alliance Premier Division)
OUT: Dunsfold (W), Godalming & Farncombe Athletic (P), Old Salesians (P), Windlesham United (E), Worplesdon Phoenix (P)

SURREY SOUTH EASTERN COMBINATION

	Battersea	Battersea Ironsides	Continental Stars	Croydon Greenside	Epsom Athletic	Epsom Eagles	Esher Athletic	NPL	Nutfield	Old Bristolians	Old Plymouthians	Sporting Bahia	St Andrews	Sutton Common Rovers Res.	Tadworth	Woodmansterne Hyde
Battersea		0-2	2-1	0-1	2-2	2-1	6-0	4-3	4-0	1-6	2-1	2-1	3-2	4-2	1-1	9-1
Battersea Ironsides	4-1		1-3	2-1	6-1	2-2	1-0	10-1	5-1	W-L	2-0	2-1	8-4	6-0	W-L	6-0
Continental Stars	2-1	1-4	D	1-4	3-2	L-W	3-3	3-0	3-3	2-1	2-0	2-1	3-3	2-2	1-2	W-L
Croydon Greenside	0-0	2-5	W-L	I	1-2	1-2	6-2	3-0	4-1	3-1	3-0	1-0	1-1	3-0	6-2	4-2
Epsom Athletic	2-3	0-2	1-3	1-0	V	1-5	3-0	4-2	7-1	8-0	7-0	5-1	2-2	5-1	3-0	W-L
Epsom Eagles	2-2	1-3	2-0	3-2	1-0	I	9-2	4-0	3-0	W-L	6-2	4-0	3-0	5-1	3-0	4-0
Esher Athletic	1-0	0-6	0-4	0-2	2-2	1-2	S	0-2	2-0	0-0	1-1	0-2	2-7	2-0	4-0	1-1
NPL	0-0	0-4	1-3	4-3	1-4	3-7	2-2	I	2-1	4-1	1-2	5-3	3-8	3-0	0-3	4-5
Nutfield	2-4	1-4	0-6	1-2	0-2	2-2	0-3	4-3	O	4-0	2-5	4-2	2-0	1-0	W-L	3-2
Old Bristolians	1-1	L-W	1-4	0-0	2-1	3-4	2-3	5-3	0-2	N	2-3	0-1	1-2	1-1	0-3	0-3
Old Plymouthians	4-2	1-5	3-1	5-2	6-1	1-3	3-1	4-2	0-1	1-1		2-1	4-4	2-1	1-6	2-3
Sporting Bahia	1-4	1-2	2-4	0-2	2-1	0-4	0-2	1-1	1-2	1-2	2-2	O	4-3	5-2	3-3	3-3
St Andrews	2-3	1-4	1-2	3-2	1-5	1-1	1-0	4-3	7-1	2-1	4-4	2-0	N	3-2	0-3	4-2
Sutton Common Rovers Res.	5-5	L-W	1-4	2-2	1-2	0-15	2-2	W-L	3-0	1-5	1-9	4-7	2-3	E	1-7	2-0
Tadworth	0-2	1-1	3-3	0-0	1-2	3-1	3-0	5-1	3-0	1-0	4-1	3-2	5-0	2-1		4-1
Woodmansterne Hyde	1-2	3-2	2-1	0-2	1-5	0-7	3-1	0-3	3-4	2-0	7-3	0-4	2-0	0-0	1-6	

Division One		P	W	D	L	F	A	Pts
Battersea Ironsides		30	26	2	2	99	27	80
Epsom Eagles	+3	30	23	4	3	106	32	76
Continental Stars	+5	30	16	5	9	67	46	58
Battersea		30	16	7	7	72	51	55
Epsom Athletic		30	17	3	10	81	50	54
Croydon Greenside		30	16	5	9	63	40	53
Tadworth	-4	30	17	5	8	74	39	52
Old Plymouthians	+3	30	12	5	13	72	80	44
St Andrews	-2	30	12	6	12	75	78	40
Nutfield		30	11	2	17	43	82	35
Esher Athletic	-1	30	7	7	16	37	73	27
Sporting Bahia		30	7	4	19	52	73	25
Woodmansterne Hyde	-6	30	9	3	18	48	86	24
NPL		30	7	3	20	57	97	24
Old Bristolians	+2	30	5	5	20	36	61	22
Sutton Common Rovers Res.		30	3	6	21	38	105	15

Intermediate Division One	P	W	D	L	F	A	Pts
Puretown	26	19	5	2	65	20	62
Oxted & District	26	19	0	7	52	24	57
Tooting Bec	26	18	1	7	70	42	55
Westminster Casuals	26	17	2	7	72	46	53
Wandgas Sports	26	17	1	8	72	35	52
South Godstone	26	16	3	7	77	57	51
FC Triangle	26	13	4	9	65	31	43
Westside	26	11	3	12	51	37	36
Croydon Postal	26	9	4	13	47	53	31
Merton Abbey	26	8	3	15	37	57	27
Ashtead	26	8	2	16	52	83	26
Hersham RBL	26	5	1	20	41	86	16
Thornton Heath Rovers	26	3	3	20	32	91	12
AFC Ewell	26	3	0	23	30	101	9

SURREY SOUTH EASTERN COMBINATION DIVISION ONE CONSTITUTION 2008-09

BATTERSEA . . . . Battersea Park, Battersea SW11 4NJ . . . . None
CONTINENTAL STARS . . . . Lavender Park, Lavender Avenue, Mitcham 020 8646 7362
MOLE VALLEY SCR RESERVES . . . Mole Valley Predators, River Lane, off Randalls Road, Leatherhead KT22 0AU . . . . None
NPL . . . . NPL Sports Club, Queens Road, Teddington 020 8943 6314
NUTFIELD . . . . Memorial Hall, High Street, Nutfield . . . . None
OLD BRISTOLIANS . . . . Prince George's Playing Fields, Grand Drive, Raynes Park SW20 9NB . . . . None
OLD PLYMOUTHIANS . . . . Croygas Sports & Social Club, Mollison Drive, Wallington SM6 9BY 020 8647 7792
OXTED & DISTRICT . . . . Master Park, Oxted 01883 712792
PURETOWN . . . . Wimbledon Common Extensions, Robin Hood Road, Roehampton Vale SW15 3DW . . . . None
SPORTING BAHIA . . . . *TBC: Goals Centre, Copers Cope Road, Beckenham BR3 1NZ 020 8650 0222
ST ANDREWS . . . . Wibbandune Sports Ground, Robin Hood Way (A3) 020 8942 8062
TADWORTH . . . . Cheam Sports Club, Peaches Close, Cheam . . . . None
TOOTING BEC . . . . Dundonald Recreation Ground, Avenbury Road SW19 3QR . . . . None
WESTMINSTER CASUALS . . . . Richardson Evans Playing Fields, Roehampton Vale SW15 3PQ . . . . None
IN: Oxted & District (P), Puretown (P), Tooting Bec (P), Westminster Casuals (P)
OUT: Battersea Ironsides (P – Surrey Elite Intermediate League Intermediate Division), Croydon Greenside (P – Surrey Elite Intermediate League Intermediate Division), Epsom Athletic (P – Surrey Elite Intermediate League Intermediate Division), Epsom Eagles (P – Surrey Elite Intermediate League Intermediate Division), Esher Athletic (P – Surrey Elite Intermediate League Intermediate Division), Old Rutlishians (P – Surrey Elite Intermediate League Intermediate Division), Woodmansterne Hyde (P – Surrey Elite Intermediate League Intermediate Division)
Sutton Common Rovers Reserves become Mole Valley SCR Reserves

Junior Division One		P	W	D	L	F	A	Pts
Sutton High		18	13	0	5	45	25	39
Battersea Ironsides Res.		18	11	3	4	36	35	36
Yourstory		18	9	4	5	56	30	31
Croygas Phoenix		18	10	0	8	43	54	30
St Andrews Res.		18	8	2	8	45	39	26
Epsom Eagles Res.		18	2	3	13	21	46	9
Lambeth Academy	-6	18	2	4	12	24	41	4

Junior Division Two		P	W	D	L	F	A	Pts
Weston Green Sports		20	18	1	1	79	16	55
Fetcham		20	12	2	6	47	48	38
Worcester Park 'A'	-3	20	11	3	6	64	52	33
NPL Res.		20	9	4	7	50	49	31
Supercala	-2	20	9	3	8	52	45	28
Old Plymouthians Res.	+6	20	6	4	10	41	56	28
Epsom Athletic Res.	+3	20	7	3	10	50	48	27
Lambeth Academy Res.	-8	20	9	4	7	78	47	23
Continental Stars Res.	-1	20	6	6	8	37	44	23
Tadworth Res.		20	3	1	16	31	66	10
Cheam Village Warriors	-3	20	4	1	15	29	87	10

Junior Division Three		P	W	D	L	F	A	Pts
Trinity	-3	18	17	1	0	68	18	49
Crescent Rovers 'A'		18	11	1	6	52	43	34
Croydon Greenside Res.		18	10	2	6	58	35	32
Norton		18	9	3	6	39	33	30
Wilf Kroucher		18	8	2	8	51	42	26
Battersea Res.		18	8	1	9	51	45	25
Zurich Eagle Star		18	7	1	10	41	47	22
Cheam Village Warriors Res.		18	5	2	11	40	53	17
Sutton Common Rovers 'A'	+3	18	4	1	13	31	76	16
Oakhill United	-1	18	4	0	14	36	75	11

Junior Division Four		P	W	D	L	F	A	Pts
Woodmansterne Hyde Res.	+3	22	17	3	2	83	27	57
Battersea Ironsides 'A'		22	16	4	2	57	29	50
Crescent Rovers 'B'		22	14	1	7	69	44	43
Roehampton Athletic	-3	22	15	0	7	67	27	42
Ashtead Res.		22	10	4	8	65	46	34
FC Maurice	-6	22	12	3	7	54	52	33
Oakstead		22	10	1	11	48	64	31
Tooting Bec Res.	+3	22	6	1	15	32	69	22
Kerria Knights		22	6	3	13	53	65	21
Oxted & District Res.	+3	22	4	4	14	31	48	19
Real Holmesdale 'A'		22	5	1	16	34	93	16
Old Plymouthians 'A'	-3	22	4	3	15	34	63	12

Junior Division Five		P	W	D	L	F	A	Pts
Shaftesbury Town		22	17	4	1	67	24	55
Wandgas Sports Res.		22	14	3	5	67	37	45
Norton Res.		22	12	6	4	74	37	42
Alexander Forbes		22	12	5	5	55	53	41
Fetcham Res.		22	11	2	9	78	57	35
Croydon Greenside u-23s		22	9	3	10	53	70	30
Old Bristolians Res.		22	8	5	9	49	53	29
Trinity Res.		22	8	3	11	60	60	27
Ashtead 'A'		22	8	2	12	65	70	26
Woodmansterne Hyde 'A'		22	6	1	15	37	72	19
Sutton High Res.		22	3	7	12	32	51	16
FC Maurice Res.		22	3	1	18	21	74	10

SENIOR CUP

(All Division One and Intermediate Division One sides)

FIRST ROUND

AFC Ewell 1 **Merton Abbey** 4
Ashtead 0 **Tadworth** 1
Battersea Ironsides 6 Thornton Heath Rovers 1
Continental Stars 0 **Battersea** 1
Croydon Greenside 1 **St Andrews** 1 *aet* (3-4p)
Croydon Postal 3 Nutfield 2 *aet*
Epsom Eagles 4 Sporting Bahia 0
FC Triangle 2 Wandgas Sports 1
NPL 4 Westside 2
Old Plymouthians 7 South Godstone 0
Oxted & District 6 Esher Athletic 0
Sutton Common Rovers Res. 0 **Old Bristolians** 3
Tooting Bec 3 **Epsom Athletic** 5
Woodmansterne Hyde 1 **Puretown** 5

SECOND ROUND

Battersea 2 Puretown 1
Battersea Ironsides 6 NPL 0
Epsom Athletic 1 Tadworth 0
Epsom Eagles 2 Oxted & District 1
Hersham RBL 3 Croydon Postal 2
FC Triangle 2 Westminster Casuals 1
Old Bristolians 4 Merton Abbey 2
Old Plymouthians 2 **St Andrews** 3

QUARTER-FINALS

Battersea Ironsides 4 Epsom Athletic 1
Epsom Eagles 3 Old Bristolians 2
Hersham RBL 0 **FC Triangle** 4
St Andrews 1 Battersea 1 *aet* (5-4p)

SEMI-FINALS

Battersea Ironsides 3 Epsom Eagles 2
(at Croydon Athletic)
St Andrews 1 **FC Triangle** 3
(at Oxted & District)

FINAL

(May 3rd at Croydon Athletic)
Battersea Ironsides 1 FC Triangle 0

JUNIOR CUP

FINAL
(May 5th at Croydon Athletic)
Yourstory 4 Battersea Ironsides Res. 1

GEOFF ELLIS SHIELD

FINAL
(April 23rd at Croydon Athletic)
Sutton High 2 Weston Green Sports 1

GEOFF ELLIS INTERMEDIATE SHIELD

FINAL
(May 5th at Croydon Athletic)
Croydon Greenside Res. 1 Old Plymouthians Res. 0

GEOFF ELLIS JUNIOR SHIELD

FINAL
(April 15th at Croydon Athletic)
Woodmansterne Hyde Res. 3 Old Plymouthians 'A' 1

SUSSEX COUNTY LEAGUE

	Arundel	Chichester City	Crowborough Ath	East Preston	Eastbourne Utd Ass	Hailsham Town	Hassocks	Oakwood	Pagham	Redhill	Ringmer	Rye United	Selsey	Shoreham	Sidley United	St Francis Rangers	Three Bridges	Whitehawk	Wick	Worthing United
Arundel		3-1	1-2	1-1	2-4	2-2	0-2	6-2	4-1	4-2	1-2	2-3	3-3	3-3	5-0	3-1	1-1	2-0	1-1	6-1
Chichester City United	0-4		0-8	0-1	2-3	0-4	2-3	1-2	0-3	1-2	1-5	1-0	3-3	0-3	2-1	1-1	5-4	1-1	4-2	3-0
Crowborough Athletic	2-4	4-1		5-0	3-2	2-0	1-0	4-3	2-0	4-1	5-2	4-0	1-0	2-0	1-0	3-1	2-2	4-0	2-1	2-2
East Preston	2-1	3-3	0-1		1-0	1-0	1-1	0-0	0-1	2-0	2-1	1-0	2-0	2-1	3-0	2-1	0-0	0-3	2-1	2-1
Eastbourne United Association	1-2	1-3	1-1	2-1	D	5-1	1-1	3-2	0-1	0-0	3-2	3-1	1-1	0-0	2-0	5-0	1-2	1-2	2-1	1-2
Hailsham Town	1-2	3-1	2-1	0-0	1-2	I	4-1	1-2	1-1	0-0	1-1	3-2	1-1	2-0	1-0	0-0	2-0	2-3		0-3
Hassocks	0-4	2-0	0-1	0-2	3-3	1-1	V	3-1	2-1	0-1	2-2	0-2	2-0	0-0	4-0	2-0	0-2	1-1	1-1	1-3
Oakwood	0-1	1-6	2-2	1-2	1-2	1-1	1-1	I	1-1	1-3	1-5	0-2	0-1	2-2	2-0	1-1	4-2	0-4	0-4	3-0
Pagham	1-2	6-1	0-1	3-2	4-0	1-0	1-2	3-1	S	1-1	1-2	4-1	1-2	5-1	1-1	2-0	2-2	2-1	0-5	5-2
Redhill	0-1	3-2	4-0	2-1	2-1	1-2	1-2	3-1	2-1	I	6-3	2-2	1-0	2-4	2-1	0-1	1-2	1-1	3-2	2-1
Ringmer	1-1	2-4	0-3	1-1	2-1	5-0	2-0	2-2	5-2	1-3	O	4-2	4-2	0-1	3-3	2-1	5-0	0-3	1-2	1-0
Rye United	1-1	1-3	2-7	1-3	2-1	0-1	1-1	1-1	0-2	3-4	2-5	N	0-4	1-1	7-1	1-0	1-0	0-1	2-2	0-0
Selsey	1-1	1-3	0-2	2-0	4-1	2-2	1-4	3-5	0-0	1-1	2-1	4-0		1-1	10-0	1-3	2-1	1-1	1-2	2-1
Shoreham	1-3	3-2	0-1	0-0	2-0	2-2	1-1	1-3	0-0	1-0	2-0	1-0	1-1	O	3-1	4-1	0-0	1-2	3-1	6-0
Sidley United	0-1	2-1	0-5	0-0	0-3	2-4	0-2	2-2	2-0	0-1	3-3	3-2	2-0		N	0-2	2-6	2-4	1-0	3-2
St Francis Rangers	1-2	5-1	0-5	0-0	1-1	1-1	3-1	1-1	2-1	0-0	4-2	2-1	0-0	8-0	2-1	E	3-1	1-1	1-2	3-0
Three Bridges	0-4	5-0	1-1	3-1	1-1	5-2	1-1	1-1	1-2	0-0	3-1	4-1	2-1	3-2	4-1	4-1		0-1	1-2	3-0
Whitehawk	2-0	3-2	0-1	1-2	1-0	2-0	1-1	1-1	1-0	0-0	2-2	4-0	4-3	1-1	2-0	1-0	2-1		2-1	1-1
Wick	1-1	2-1	1-2	2-2	3-2	3-2	1-5	4-0	4-0	2-1	2-1	4-1	3-1	3-0	5-0	2-2	1-3	0-1		0-3
Worthing United	2-5	0-4	0-2	1-2	4-7	1-3	2-1	2-1	2-1	1-1	2-0	3-3	0-0	1-2	0-2	3-0	1-3	1-1		

Division One		P	W	D	L	F	A	Pts
Crowborough Athletic		38	30	5	3	99	33	95
Whitehawk		38	21	12	5	61	34	75
Arundel	-3	38	21	10	7	90	49	70
East Preston		38	19	10	9	48	40	67
Wick		38	19	7	12	77	55	64
Three Bridges		38	17	9	12	74	60	60
Hassocks		38	15	13	10	57	46	58
Redhill		38	16	8	14	59	56	56
Pagham		38	15	8	15	60	55	53
Ringmer		38	14	9	15	81	73	51
Eastbourne Utd Association		38	14	8	16	67	62	50
Shoreham		38	12	14	12	54	50	50
Hailsham Town		38	13	11	14	54	58	50
St Francis Rangers	-1	38	13	7	18	56	62	45
Selsey		38	10	12	16	67	72	42
Chichester City United	+2	38	11	4	23	66	100	39
Worthing United	+3	38	8	8	22	53	84	35
Oakwood		38	7	12	19	52	85	33
Rye United		38	8	6	24	46	86	30
Sidley United		38	8	5	25	39	100	29

JOHN O'HARA LEAGUE CUP
(Division One and Two teams)

FIRST ROUND
Hassocks 5 Mile Oak 1
Littlehampton Tn 2 **Chichester Cy Utd** 5
Peacehaven & Telscombe 2
Crowborough Athletic 4
Pease Pottage Village 0 **Shoreham** 13
Whitehawk 3 Westfield 0
Wick 3 Lingfield 1

SECOND ROUND
Broadbridge Heath 0 **Hassocks** 5
Chichester City United 3 Eastbourne United Association 2
Crowborough Ath. 1 **St Francis Rgrs** 2
East Grinstead Town 3 Redhill 2
East Preston 2 Lancing 1
Hailsham Town 3 Steyning Town 1
Midhurst & Easebourne United 4 Arundel 3 *aet*
Oakwood 2 Seaford Town 1
Pagham 3 Southwick 0
Ringmer 2 Wick 1
Rustington 3 Shoreham 3 *aet*
Replay: **Shoreham** 4 Rustington 0
Rye United 0 **Whitehawk** 2
Selsey 4 Storrington 2
Sidlesham 0 **Three Bridges** 1
Sidley United 2 Crawley Down 2 *aet*
Replay: **Crawley Down** 3 Sidley United 0

Worthing United 2 **Wealden** 3
Shoreham 4 Rustington 0
THIRD ROUND
East Grinstead Town 2 Midhurst & Easebourne United 1
East Preston 0 **Oakwood** 5
Hailsham Town 1 Whitehawk 0
Pagham 0 **Wealden** 1
Ringmer 2 St Francis Rangers 1 *aet*
Selsey 0 **Hassocks** 2
Shoreham 2 Chichester City United 1
Three Bridges 0 **Crawley Down** 1
QUARTER-FINALS
Crawley Down 2 Wealden 0
East Grinstead Town 2 Hailsham Tn 0
Hassocks 0 **Ringmer** 1
Oakwood 2 **Shoreham** 4
SEMI-FINALS
(both at Three Bridges)
East Grinstead Town 0 **Ringmer** 3
Shoreham 1 Crawley Down 0 *aet*
FINAL
(March 21st at Three Bridges)
Ringmer 0 **Shoreham** 0 *aet* (9-10p)

SUSSEX COUNTY LEAGUE DIVISION ONE CONSTITUTION 2008-09

ARUNDEL . . . . Mill Road, Arundel BN18 9PA 01903 882548
CHICHESTER CITY UNITED . . . . Portfield, Church Road, Chichester PO19 4HN 01243 779875
EAST GRINSTEAD TOWN . . . . East Court, Hollye Road, East Grinstead RH19 3XB 01342 325885
EAST PRESTON . . . . Roundstone Recreation Ground, Lashmar Road, East Preston BN16 1ES 01903 776026
EASTBOURNE UNITED ASSOCIATION . . . . The Oval, Channel View Road, Eastbourne BN22 7LN 01323 726989
HAILSHAM TOWN . . . . The Beaconsfield, Western Road, Hailsham BN27 3DN 01323 840446
HASSOCKS . . . . The Beacon, Brighton Road, Hassocks BN6 9LY 01273 846040
HORSHAM YMCA . . . . Gorings Mead, off Queen Street, Horsham RH13 5BP 01403 252689
LINGFIELD . . . . Godstone Road, Lingfield RH7 6SA 01342 834269
OAKWOOD . . . . Oakwood Sports & Social Club, Tinsley Lane, Three Bridges RH10 8AW 01293 515742
PAGHAM . . . . Nyetimber Lane, Pagham, Bognor Regis PO21 3JY 01243 266112
REDHILL . . . . Kiln Brow, Three Arch Road, Redhill RH1 1HL 01737 762222
RINGMER . . . . Caburn Ground, Anchor Field, Ringmer BN8 5QN 01273 812738
SELSEY . . . . High Street Ground, Selsey, Chichester PO20 0QG 01243 603420
SHOREHAM . . . . Middle Road, Shoreham BN43 6LT 01273 454261
ST FRANCIS RANGERS . . . . Lewes Road, Haywards Heath RH16 4EX 01444 457726
THREE BRIDGES . . . . Jubilee Field, Jubilee Way, Three Bridges, Crawley RH10 1LQ 01293 442000
WHITEHAWK . . . . Enclosed Ground, East Brighton Park, Brighton BN2 5TS 01273 609736
WICK . . . . Crabtree Park, Coomes Way, Wick, Littlehampton BN17 7LS 01903 713535
WORTHING UNITED . . . . Robert Albon Memorial Ground, Lyons Way, Worthing BN14 9JF 01903 234466
IN: East Grinstead Town (P), Horsham YMCA (R – Isthmian League Division One South), Lingfield (P)
OUT: Crowborough Athletic (P – Isthmian League Division One South), Rye United (R), Sidley United (R)

	Broadbridge Heath	Crawley Down	East Grinstead Town	Lancing	Lingfield	Littlehampton Town	Midhurst & Easebourne Utd	Mile Oak	Peacehaven & Telscombe	Pease Pottage Village	Rustington	Seaford Town	Sidlesham	Southwick	Steyning Town	Storrington	Wealden	Westfield
Broadbridge Heath		2-3	0-1	2-2	3-4	0-2	0-1	1-4	1-4	1-4	0-1	3-1	0-3	4-1	2-1	1-0	1-1	0-1
Crawley Down	2-1		1-2	2-1	3-1	3-3	1-0	1-0	2-5	2-0	0-5	0-1	1-0	1-3	2-0	2-1	1-3	3-2
East Grinstead Town	1-0	4-1		1-0	1-1	3-2	2-2	4-1	2-1	10-3	4-3	2-1	5-3	3-0	2-1	3-1	3-2	3-1
Lancing	3-2	2-1	2-2	*D*	1-2	3-0	4-1	1-3	2-2	7-0	2-1	2-4	3-1	3-3	1-0	3-0	0-1	3-4
Lingfield	2-0	3-1	2-1	2-1	*I*	2-0	4-2	1-1	1-1	8-0	0-3	2-1	4-0	0-1	0-0	3-3	2-2	3-2
Littlehampton Town	4-0	3-0	2-6	2-0	1-0	*V*	2-5	0-2	1-4	1-1	1-0	2-1	3-1	1-2	1-2	3-2	2-0	4-0
Midhurst & Easebourne United	3-1	0-5	0-2	0-0	1-6	3-2	*I*	3-3	0-3	3-2	1-1	4-1	0-4	2-1	1-0	3-2	2-0	0-1
Mile Oak	3-1	2-1	2-3	1-1	0-2	1-1	8-2	*S*	2-3	4-0	0-1	3-2	2-0	3-1	4-3	0-1	3-2	2-1
Peacehaven & Telscombe	7-2	0-3	3-1	3-1	1-3	1-5	0-1	1-1	*I*	10-0	2-2	2-1	1-1	0-1	1-3	0-1	5-1	1-4
Pease Pottage Village	1-4	2-3	0-2	0-2	0-3	1-7	1-4	3-4	1-1	*O*	0-5	0-6	0-7	1-3	1-3	1-2	1-4	3-1
Rustington	2-1	3-0	0-3	2-1	1-0	2-2	1-0	2-2	0-1	7-1	*N*	3-0	3-0	0-2	1-1	4-0	4-0	1-0
Seaford Town	0-1	3-1	3-5	3-2	1-4	1-3	1-0	1-1	3-4	4-3	0-3		4-2	1-0	1-2	3-5	1-3	5-2
Sidlesham	3-2	0-1	2-2	3-3	0-1	2-3	2-0	4-2	3-2	3-1	1-1	4-1	*T*	5-2	0-3	3-1	1-2	1-2
Southwick	3-1	1-3	0-0	2-2	1-3	0-1	1-0	1-2	0-1	4-2	0-3	1-2	2-0	*W*	0-4	1-2	0-0	2-1
Steyning Town	2-2	2-3	1-1	3-2	0-2	3-2	1-3	1-4	1-3	5-1	1-0	0-1	2-0	1-0	*O*	2-0	1-3	1-2
Storrington	2-2	1-2	0-1	1-2	1-2	0-0	1-2	2-2	5-4	1-4	0-2	1-0	1-1	1-1	2-0		0-1	3-1
Wealden	1-2	1-2	0-1	3-2	6-0	2-0	2-3	2-5	3-4	7-0	0-0	6-2	1-1	0-1	1-1	2-2		2-0
Westfield	2-2	3-2	0-3	3-1	W-L	1-0	2-0	3-2	3-1	8-1	3-3	3-1	2-0	5-2	2-2	4-2	2-5	

Division Two		P	W	D	L	F	A	Pts
East Grinstead Town		34	26	6	2	89	41	84
Lingfield	-3	34	21	6	7	73	40	66
Rustington		34	19	8	7	70	29	65
Peacehaven & Telscombe		34	20	5	9	93	59	65
Mile Oak		34	17	8	9	79	56	59
Crawley Down		34	19	1	14	59	60	58
Westfield		34	18	3	13	71	64	57
Littlehampton Town		34	16	5	13	66	54	53
Wealden		34	14	7	13	69	56	49
Midhurst & Easebourne Utd		34	15	4	15	52	67	49
Steyning Town		34	12	6	16	51	53	42
Lancing		34	10	8	16	64	61	38
Sidlesham		34	11	5	18	61	65	38
Southwick		34	11	5	18	44	62	38
Seaford Town		34	12	1	21	61	79	37
Storrington		34	9	7	18	48	67	34
Broadbridge Heath	+3	34	7	5	22	45	75	29
Pease Pottage Village		34	3	2	29	29	146	11

DIVISION TWO CUP

FIRST ROUND
Seaford Town 1 East Grinstead Town 0
Westfield 2 Storrington 0

SECOND ROUND
Broadbridge Heath 0
Peacehaven & Telscombe 1
Lancing 2 Pease Pottage Village 0
(at Pease Pottage Village)
Littlehampton Town 3
Sidlesham 0
Midhurst & Easebourne
United 3 Mile Oak 0
Rustington 5 Crawley Down 3 *aet*
Seaford Town 3 Westfield 2
Southwick 2 Lingfield 0
Wealden 3 Steyning Town 1

QUARTER-FINALS
Lancing 2 **Littlehampton Town** 3
Peacehaven & Telscombe 3
Midhurst & Easebourne
United 1
Rustington 3 Southwick 2
Wealden 3 Seaford Town 2

SEMI-FINALS
Littlehampton Town 1
Peacehaven & Telscombe 3
(at Worthing United)
Rustington 3 Wealden 0
(at Shoreham)

FINAL
(May 1st at Shoreham)
Rustington 3 **Peacehaven &
Telscombe** 4

SUSSEX COUNTY LEAGUE DIVISION TWO CONSTITUTION 2008-09

BEXHILL UNITED . . . . Brockley Road, Bexhill-on-Sea TN39 3EX 01424 220732
CRAWLEY DOWN . . . . Haven Sportsfield, Hophurst Lane, Crawley Down RH10 4JL 01342 717140
LANCING . . . . Culver Road, Lancing BN15 9AX 01903 764398
LITTLEHAMPTON TOWN . . . . The Sportsfield, St Flora's Road, Littlehampton BN17 6BB 01903 732030
LOXWOOD . . . . Loxwood Sports Association, Sports Pavilion, Billingshurst RH14 0SX 01403 753185
MIDHURST & EASEBOURNE UNITED . . . . Rotherfield, Dodsley Lane, Easebourne GU29 9AS 01730 816557
MILE OAK . . . . Mile Oak Recreation Ground, Chalky Road, Mile Oak BN41 2WT 01273 423854
PEACEHAVEN & TELSCOMBE . . . . Piddinghoe Avenue, Peacehaven BN10 8RH 01273 582471
RUSTINGTON . . . . Recreation Ground, Jubilee Avenue, Rustington BN16 3NB 01903 770495
RYE UNITED . . . . Rye Cricket & Football Salts, Fishmarket Road, Rye TN31 7LP 01797 223855
SEAFORD TOWN . . . . The Crouch, Bramber Road, Seaford BN25 1AG 01323 892221
SIDLESHAM . . . . Recreation Ground, Selsey Road, Sidlesham, Chichester PO20 7RD 01243 641538
SIDLEY UNITED . . . . Gullivers Sports Ground, Glovers Lane, North Road, Bexhill TN39 5BL 01424 217078
SOUTHWICK . . . . Old Barn Way, Manor Hall Road, Southwick, Brighton BN43 4NT 01273 701010
STEYNING TOWN . . . . The Shooting Field, Shooting Field Estate, Steyning BN44 3RP 01903 812228
STORRINGTON . . . . Recreation Ground, Pulborough Road, Storrington RH20 4HJ 01903 745860
WEALDEN . . . . The Oaks, Old Eastbourne Road, Uckfield TN22 5QL 01825 890905
WESTFIELD . . . . Main Road, Westfield, Hastings TN35 4SB 01424 751011
IN: Bexhill United (P), Loxwood (P), Rye United (R), Sidley United (R)
OUT: Broadbridge Heath (R), East Grinstead Town (P), Lingfield (P), Pease Pottage Village (R)

ROY HAYDEN TROPHY
(Div One champions v Sussex Senior Cup holders)

(August 7th at Eastbourne Town)
Eastbourne Town 0 **Brighton & Hove Albion** 3

NORMAN WINGATE TROPHY
(Division One champions v John O'Hara Cup holders)

(August 11th at Crowborough Athletic)
Eastbourne Town 1 **Crowborough Athletic** 4

	Bexhill United	Bosham	Dorking Wanderers	Forest	Haywards Heath Town	Hurstpierpoint	Ifield Edwards	Little Common	Loxwood	Newhaven	Rottingdean Village	Saltdean United	Uckfield Town
Bexhill United		4-1	7-0	3-2	1-0	4-1	2-1	3-3	3-2	2-3	1-0	1-1	2-0
Bosham	1-2		2-3	2-1	0-2	3-0	1-2	5-0	1-2	2-1	0-6	0-1	2-0
Dorking Wanderers	2-2	4-2	D	1-0	0-2	5-2	5-2	1-3	4-1	2-2	1-1	2-1	3-1
Forest	1-2	1-1	1-1	I	0-2	1-0	3-0	1-1	1-3	0-3	3-1	2-1	1-1
Haywards Heath Town	2-3	1-0	2-2	0-0	V	3-1	2-2	1-1	0-3	4-1	2-1	0-1	2-1
Hurstpierpoint	3-3	0-1	2-3	3-1	0-0		1-2	3-4	0-4	1-4	0-0	0-3	1-0
Ifield Edwards	2-2	3-2	3-3	0-2	3-6	1-3	T	1-1	2-4	1-2	2-0	1-4	3-2
Little Common	1-3	2-1	2-5	6-1	3-2	3-0	3-3	H	1-3	0-3	3-1	2-3	1-0
Loxwood	2-2	2-1	0-0	2-0	1-1	3-0	2-3	3-1	R	2-1	0-1	4-0	1-0
Newhaven	4-3	3-3	2-1	1-2	0-0	5-1	1-1	4-4	3-1	E	0-2	6-1	0-0
Rottingdean Village	2-1	4-1	2-6	1-0	1-4	1-1	2-1	1-1	2-0	3-0	E	0-1	3-3
Saltdean United	1-2	1-0	2-4	2-1	0-4	1-2	0-1	1-4	1-1	3-3	1-3		0-1
Uckfield Town	0-2	0-3	3-0	2-1	1-3	7-0	0-2	0-2	0-3	3-0	2-0	1-2	

Division Three		P	W	D	L	F	A	Pts
Loxwood	+2	24	15	4	5	51	26	51
Bexhill United	-3	24	15	6	3	60	35	48
Haywards Heath Town	+3	24	12	7	5	45	26	46
Dorking Wanderers	-1	24	12	7	5	58	47	42
Newhaven		24	10	7	7	52	42	37
Little Common		24	10	7	7	52	49	37
Rottingdean Village		24	9	5	10	36	36	32
Ifield Edwards		24	8	6	10	42	53	30
Saltdean United		24	9	3	12	42	45	30
Bosham		24	7	2	15	35	45	23
Forest		24	6	5	13	26	39	23
Uckfield Town		24	6	3	15	28	37	21
Hurstpierpoint		24	4	4	16	25	62	16

DIVISION THREE CUP

FIRST ROUND
Bexhill United 2 Ifield Edwards 0
Loxwood 2 Hurstpierpoint 0
Newhaven 1 **Forest** 2
Rottingdean Village 7 Little Common 2 *aet*
Uckfield Tn 1 **Saltdean United** 3

QUARTER-FINALS
Bosham 1 **Rottingdean Village** 2
(at Rottingdean Village)
Dorking Wdrs 1 **Bexhill United** 3

Haywards Heath Town 2 Forest 0
Saltdean United 2 Loxwood 1

SEMI-FINALS
Haywards Heath Town 2
Rottingdean Village 1
(at Shoreham)
Saltdean Utd 2 **Bexhill United** 3
aet (at Ringmer)

FINAL
(March 21st at Hailsham Town)
Bexhill Utd 2 Haywards Heath Tn 1

SUSSEX COUNTY LEAGUE DIVISION THREE CONSTITUTION 2008-09

BOSHAM...........................Recreation Ground, Walton Lane, Bosham PO18 8QF......................01243 574011
BROADBRIDGE HEATH....The Leisure Centre, Wickhurst Lane, Broadbridge Heath, Horsham RH12 3YS...............01403 211311
CLYMPING............................Clymping Village Hall, Main Road, Clymping, Littlehampton....................01903 713538
DORKING WANDERERS.......................London Road, Westhumble, Dorking.....................................None
FOREST...............Roffey Sports & Social Club, Spooners Road, Roffey RH12 4EB.......................01403 210221
HAYWARDS HEATH TOWN........Hanbury Park Stadium, Allen Road, Haywards Heath RH16 3PT................01444 412837
HURSTPIERPOINT............Fairfield Recreation Ground, Cuckfield Road, Hurstpierpoint BN6 9SD...............01273 834783
IFIELD EDWARDS.........Edwards Sports & Social Club, Ifield Green, Rusper Road, Crawley RH11 0JE..........01293 420598
LITTLE COMMON............................Peartree Lane, Little Common, Bexhill TN39 4PH.....................01424 845861
NEWHAVEN...............................Recreation Ground, Fort Road, Newhaven BN9 9EE......................01273 513940
PEASE POTTAGE VILLAGE..................Finches Field, Pease Pottage RH11 9AH............................01293 538651
ROTTINGDEAN VILLAGE......Rotttingdean Field, Wilkinson Close, Rottingdean, Brighton BN2 7EG...............None
SALTDEAN UNITED....................Hill Park, Coombe Vale, Saltdean, Brighton BN2 8HJ...................01273 309898
UCKFIELD TOWN...............Victoria Pleasure Grounds, New Town, Uckfield TN22 5DJ...................01825 769400
IN: Broadbridge Heath (R), Clymping (P – West Sussex League Premier Division), Pease Pottage Village (R)
OUT: Bexhill United (P), Loxwood (P)

Reserve Premier Division		P	W	D	L	F	A	Pts
Hailsham Town Res.		26	19	5	2	57	29	62
Horsham YMCA Res.		26	17	6	3	69	23	57
Shoreham Res.		26	15	5	6	53	33	50
Whitehawk Res.		26	15	4	7	68	39	49
Hassocks Res.		26	12	8	6	62	48	44
Hastings United Res.		26	11	7	8	55	40	40
Eastbourne Town Res.		26	12	4	10	42	38	40
Crowborough Res.	-3	26	12	3	11	44	40	36
Arundel Res.		26	9	8	9	28	27	35
Sidley United Res.	+3	26	7	6	13	27	35	30
Oakwood Res.		26	8	4	14	45	65	28
East Preston Res.		26	5	3	18	40	88	18
Ringmer Res.		26	3	6	17	34	71	15
Worthing Utd. Res.		26	1	3	22	8	56	6

Reserve Section East		P	W	D	L	F	A	Pts
Crawley Down Res.		22	17	4	1	75	15	55
Eastbourne UA Res.	+3	22	14	3	5	47	24	48
Westfield Res.		22	15	1	6	64	32	46
Peacehaven & T. Res.		22	9	3	10	29	38	30
Rye United Res.		22	9	3	10	34	46	30
Lingfield Res.		22	9	3	10	39	53	30
Redhill Res.	-3	22	10	2	10	38	17	29
Wealden Res.		22	8	4	10	37	44	28
Newhaven Res.		22	7	3	12	34	60	24
Seaford Town Res.		22	6	3	13	28	45	21
Saltdean United Res.		22	5	4	13	23	45	19
Bexhill United Res.		22	6	1	15	41	70	19

Reserve Section West		P	W	D	L	F	A	Pts
Selsey Res.		24	20	2	2	80	19	62
Midhurst & Ease. Res.		24	18	1	5	92	28	55
Pagham Res.	+2	24	16	3	5	59	31	53
Chichester CU Res.	-1	24	15	5	4	55	24	49
Lancing Res.		24	13	3	8	67	41	42
Mile Oak Res.		24	11	2	11	28	46	35
Storrington Res.		24	10	4	10	37	39	34
St Francis Rgrs Res.		24	8	3	13	30	40	27
Steyning Town Res.	+2	24	6	5	13	39	66	23
Broadb'dge H. Res.	-1	24	7	4	13	42	51	24
Wick Res.		24	5	8	11	28	58	23
Sidlesham Res.		24	3	1	20	15	60	10
Forest Res.		24	3	1	20	28	97	10

RESERVE SECTION CUP
FINAL
(March 19th at Ringmer)
Eastbourne Borough Res. 5 Worthing Res. 2

TOM STABLER MEMORIAL TROPHY
FINAL
(March 19th at Crowborough Athletic)
Sussex County League Div Three 5 Kent County League 0

TEESSIDE LEAGUE

	BEADS	Darlington Railway Athletic Res.	Darlington Rugby Club	Fishburn Park	Grangetown Boys Club	Guisborough Quoit	Guisborough Town Res.	Kirkbymoorside	Nunthorpe Athletic	Richmond Mavericks	Richmond Town	Stokesley Sports Club Res.	Thornaby Dubliners	Whinney Banks
BEADS		6-1	4-0	1-0	3-0	5-0	3-0	0-0	1-0	5-1	2-1	7-0	2-0	1-1
Darlington Railway Atheltic Res.	2-2	D	0-3	2-3	1-3	2-8	2-1	2-0	0-3	3-7	2-3	1-1	0-1	0-5
Darlington Rugby Club	0-3	4-2	I	1-0	3-4	1-2	5-3	0-2	2-1	2-4	6-1	2-1	1-0	2-5
Fishburn Park	0-1	1-1	3-1	V	0-4	2-2	1-0	0-0	1-2	1-3	3-0	3-1	0-3	1-0
Grangetown Boys Club	1-2	4-2	1-4	8-2	I	4-1	4-3	2-3	1-1	3-2	7-3	7-0	2-0	4-0
Guisborough Quoit	1-0	5-2	0-8	2-2	3-4	S	1-2	1-6	0-4	5-4	5-0	3-1	6-1	1-4
Guisborough Town Res.	1-3	1-4	5-7	1-1	1-1	1-4	I	2-5	3-4	3-2	0-1	1-3	1-3	2-3
Kirkbymoorside	1-1	4-0	5-0	6-2	0-3	2-2	0-1	O	1-0	4-0	2-2	3-2	1-0	6-1
Nunthorpe Athletic	0-7	5-2	3-5	4-0	0-6	2-6	5-0	3-5	N	8-2	2-1	0-1	2-1	1-8
Richmond Mavericks	3-4	5-0	2-1	3-2	6-0	3-3	7-1	2-1	3-1		1-2	2-3	0-3	2-0
Richmond Town	0-4	0-1	1-1	1-1	2-6	0-1	2-2	1-6	3-2	1-2	O	1-2	0-3	1-2
Stokesley Sports Club Res.	0-6	1-6	0-4	1-2	3-1	1-2	0-1	1-3	0-4	0-0	2-1	N	1-1	2-3
Thornaby Dubliners	0-4	6-1	4-0	3-2	2-5	3-0	3-0	1-2	3-3	1-1	4-1	5-2	E	3-2
Whinney Banks	2-8	1-0	1-3	8-2	2-2	1-2	0-1	0-6	3-4	2-5	1-2	0-3	1-1	

Division One

	P	W	D	L	F	A	Pts
BEADS	26	21	4	1	85	15	67
Kirkbymoorside	26	17	5	4	74	29	56
Grangetown Boys Club	26	17	3	6	87	49	54
Thornaby Dubliners	26	13	4	9	55	40	43
Darlington Rugby Club	26	14	1	11	66	57	43
Guisborough Quoit	26	13	4	9	66	65	43
Richmond Mavericks	26	13	3	10	72	59	42
Nunthorpe Athletic	26	12	2	12	64	65	38
Whinney Banks	26	9	3	14	56	65	30
Fishburn Park	26	7	6	13	35	59	27
Stokesley Sports Club Res.	26	7	3	16	32	69	24
Richmond Town	26	5	4	17	31	70	19
Guisborough Town Res.	26	5	3	18	37	74	18
Darlington Railway Athletic Res.	26	5	3	18	39	83	18

J V MADDEN TROPHY
(League champions v McMillan Bowl holders)

(August 4th at BEADS)

BEADS 2 Kirkbymoorside 0

LOU MOORE MEMORIAL SHIELD
(Division One sides)

FIRST ROUND
Darlington Railway Athletic Res. 0 **Thornaby Dubliners** 5
Darlington Rugby Club 3 Kirkbymoorside 2
Guisborough Town Res. 1 **Fishburn Park** 1 *aet* (2-4p)
Nunthorpe Athletic 1 **Grangetown Boys Club** 3
Richmond Mavericks 6 Guisborough Quoit 4
Richmond Town 3 Whinney Banks 2
Stokesley Sports Club 0 **BEADS** 4
QUARTER-FINALS
BEADS 4 Grangetown Boys Club 2
Fishburn Park 1 Darlington Rugby Club 0
Richmond Mavericks 2 Richmond Town 0
Thornaby Dubliners (w/o)Thornaby Athletic (scr.)
SEMI-FINALS
Richmond Mavericks 2 **Darlington Rugby Club** 4
Thornaby Dubliners 0 **BEADS** 2
FINAL
(April 23rd at Billingham Town)
BEADS 0 **Darlington Rugby Club** 2

JACK HATFIELD SPORTS TEESSIDE LEAGUE DIVISION ONE CONSTITUTION 2008-09

BEADS . . . . Beechwood & Easterside SC, Marton Road, Middlesbrough TS4 3PP 01642 311304
BEDALE . . . . Leyburn Road, Bedale DL8 1HA . . . .
DARLINGTON CLEVELAND BRIDGE . . . Eastbourne Sports Complex, Bourne Avenue, Darlington DL1 1LJ 01325 243177/243188
DARLINGTON RAILWAY ATHLETIC RESERVES . . . Darlington Rail Athletic Club, Brinkburn Road, Darlington DL3 9LF . . 01325 468125
DARLINGTON RUGBY CLUB . . . . Darlington Rugby Club, Grange Road, Darlington DL1 5NR. . . . . None
FISHBURN PARK . . . . Eskdale School, Broomfield Park, Whitby YO22 4HS . . . . None
GRANGETOWN BOYS CLUB . . . Grangetown YCC, Trunk Road, Grangetown, Middlesbrough TS6 7HP 01642 455435
GUISBOROUGH QUOIT . . . . King George V Playing Fields, Howlbeck Road, Guisborough TS14 6LE 01287 636925
NORTH ORMESBY SPORTS . . . . Pallister Park, Ormesby Road, Middlesbrough TS3 7AP . . . . None
NUNTHORPE ATHLETIC . . . . Recreation Club, Guisborough Road, Nunthorpe TS7 0LD 01642 313251
RICHMOND MAVERICKS . . . Brompton on Swale Sports Ground, Brompton on Swale, Richmond DL10 7HT . . . . None
RICHMOND TOWN . . . . Earls Orchard Playing Fields, Sleegill, Richmond DL10 4RH . . . . None
STOKESLEY SPORTS CLUB RESERVES . . . Stokesley Sports Club, Broughton Road, Stokesley, Middlesbrough TS9 5AQ . . . 01642 710051
THORNABY DUBLINERS . . . . Harold Wilson Sports Complex, Bader Avenue, Thornaby TS17 0EX . . . . None
IN: Bedale (P), Darlington Cleveland Bridge (P), North Ormesby Sports (P)
OUT: Guisborough Town Reserves (W), Kirkbymoorside (P – Wearside League), Whinney Banks (W)

	Bedale	Billingham Kader	Billingham Town Res.	Coble Ennis Square	Colburn Town	Darlington Cleveland Bridge	Darlington Simpson RM	Great Ayton United	North Ormesby Sports	South Bank St Peters	Spraire Lads	Teesside Athletic Res.	Whinney Banks YCC	P	W	D	L	F	A	Pts
Bedale		6-0	6-1	4-1	2-3	2-0	3-0	4-2	2-2	5-2	13-3	6-0	5-1	24	18	4	2	109	35	58
Billingham Kader	2-3	P	2-2	3-3	1-1	2-4	0-2	1-0	0-3	1-1	5-1	0-3	1-10	24	17	5	2	100	36	56
Billingham Town Res.	4-4	3-1	R	4-3	1-3	1-2	2-3	1-3	4-4	3-2	3-2	6-0	0-1	24	14	3	7	55	45	45
Coble Ennis Square	0-4	2-1	5-3	E	3-0	2-2	2-1	3-0	1-2	3-1	13-0	3-0	5-1	24	13	3	8	68	38	42
Colburn Town	0-8	0-6	3-4	2-1	M	0-1	4-1	0-5	0-7	3-4	2-1	1-0	4-4	24	13	2	9	84	49	41
Darlington Cleveland Bridge	0-6	1-0	3-2	1-6	2-2	I	1-1	2-1	4-3	2-3	4-0	7-1	2-3	24	11	6	7	89	61	39 -3
Darlington Simpson RM	3-4	1-0	3-0	3-2	3-1	0-1	E	3-0	2-3	3-3	4-0	1-1	3-1	24	11	2	11	56	60	35
Great Ayton United	3-3	3-2	1-1	1-3	1-5	5-4	1-0	R	1-6	2-7	7-0	3-1	4-1	24	8	4	11	57	62	28
North Ormesby Sports	3-3	9-0	4-0	4-1	2-1	4-1	5-0	5-1		1-1	9-1	6-4	4-1	24	8	3	13	43	59	27 -3
South Bank St Peters	5-2	9-4	2-4	5-0	5-4	1-3	2-8	3-4	2-2	D	15-1	4-1	4-1	24	8	3	13	45	75	27
Spraire Lads	0-8	4-4	0-4	3-16	3-4	0-2	1-15	1-3	1-7	1-5	I	0-11	4-2	24	7	4	13	68	73	20
Teesside Athletic Res.	0-3	1-1	4-1	0-3	2-1	0-3	0-2	2-1	1-3	1-1	2-0	V	6-2	24	6	1	16	39	73	18 -3
Whinney Banks YCC	0-3	1-2	1-3	4-3	8-1	0-3	1-6	1-4	4-2	2-2	16-0	1-2		24	1	1	22	27	174	1

JACK HATFIELD SPORTS TEESSIDE LEAGUE DIVISION TWO CONSTITUTION 2008-09

ACKLAM STEELWORKS .... Acklam Steelworks Club, Park Road South, Middlesbrough TS4 2RD 01642 818717
BILLINGHAM KADER .... Billingham Rugby Club, Greenwood Road, Billingham TS23 4AZ .... None
BILLINGHAM TOWN RESERVES .... Ron Greig Stadium, Bedford Terrace, Billingham TS23 4AF 01642 560043
COBLE ENNIS SQUARE ...... Corus Sports & Social Club, South Avenue, Dormanstown, Redcar TS10 5LZ 01642 486691
COULBY NEWHAM .... Kings Academy School, Stainton Way, Coulby Newham, Middlesbrough TS8 9LX 01642 577577
GRANGETOWN YCC .... Grangetown YCC, Trunk Road, Grangetown, Middlesbrough TS6 7HP 01642 455435
GREAT AYTON UNITED ...... Leven Park, Easby Lane, Great Ayton, Middlesbrough DL9 6JJ .... None
NORTON & STOCKTON ANCIENTS RESERVES ... Norton Sports Complex, Station Road, Norton, Stockton-on-Tees TS20 1PE.. 01642 530203
REDCAR RUGBY CLUB .... Redcar Rugby Club, Green Lane, Redcar TS10 3RW ....
SCARBOROUGH TOWN ...... McCains Sports Ground, Osgodby Lane, Cayton, Scarborough YO11 3LW ....
SOUTH BANK ST PETERS ..... St Peters School, Normanby Road, South Bank, Middlesbrough TS6 6SP 01642 453462
ST MARY'S COLLEGE .... St Mary's College, Saltersgill Lane, Middlesbrough TS4 3JP 01642 814680
TEESSIDE ATHLETIC RESERVES .... Green Lane, Redcar TS10 3RW .... None
WHINNEY BANKS YCC .... Hall Garth School, Hall Drive, Middlesbrough TS5 7JX .... None
IN: Acklam Steelworks (P – Stokesley League), Coulby Newham (P – Stokesley League), Grangetown YCC (P – Stokesley League), Norton & Stockton Ancients Reserves (N), Redcar Rugby Club (P – Eskvale & Cleveland League), Scarborough Town (N), St Mary's College (P – Stokesley League)
OUT: Bedale (P), Colburn Town (W – Wensleydale League), Darlington Cleveland Bridge (P), Darlington Simpson Rolling Mills (W), North Ormesby Sports (P), Spraire Lads (W – Darlington & District Church & Friendly League)

McMILLAN BOWL (All teams)

FIRST ROUND
Bedale 3 **Richmond Town** 4 *aet*
Billingham Kader 4 Colburn Town 3
Billingham Town Res. 2 **Darlington Rugby Club** 2 *aet* (1-4p)
Grangetown Boys Club (w/o) v Athletic (scr.)
Great Ayton United 2 **Teesside Athletic Res.** 2 *aet* (3-5p)
Guisborough Town Res. 4 Darlington RA Res. 3
North Ormesby Sports 5 Darlington Cleveland Bridge 2
Nunthorpe Athletic 1 **BEADS** 8
Richmond Mavericks 8 Spraire Lads 1
South Bank St Peters 4 Darlington Simpson RM 1
Whinney Banks 5 Fishburn Park 2
Whinney Banks YCC 1 **Guisborough Quoit** 2
SECOND ROUND
BEADS 3 Teesside Athletic Res. 1
Coble Ennis Square 3 Darlington Rugby Club 2

Grangetown Boys Club 4 Richmond Town 0
Guisborough Quoit 1 South Bank St Peters 0
Guisborough Town Res. 0 **Stokesley Sports Club Res.** 2
North Ormesby Sports 3 Billingham Kader 2 *aet*
Richmond Mavericks 0 **Thornaby Dubliners** 2
Whinney Banks 2 Thornaby Dubliners 2
QUARTER-FINALS
Coble Ennis Square 4 North Ormesby Sports 3
Grangetown Boys Club 3 BEADS 2
Kirkbymoorside 3 Whinney Banks 1
Stokesley Sports Club Res. 0 **Guisborough Quoit** 7
SEMI-FINALS
Grangetown Boys Club 0 **Coble Ennis Square** 2
Guisborough Quoit 3 Kirkbymoorside 1
FINAL *(May 12th at Guisborough Town)*
Guisborough Quoit 4 Coble Ennis Square 0

R T RAINE TROPHY
(Teams knocked out in 1st Round of the McMillan Bowl)

FIRST ROUND
Fishburn Park 0 **Darlington Cleveland Bridge** 2
Nunthorpe Athletic 3 Darlington Simpson RM 0
Whinney Banks YCC 1 **Colburn Town** 6
QUARTER-FINALS
Colburn Town 1 Darlington RA Res. 1 *aet* (4-3p)
Darlington Cleveland Bridge 3 Bedale 2
Great Ayton United 1 **Billingham Town Res.** 2
Nunthorpe Athletic 4 Spraire Lads 0
SEMI-FINALS
Darlington Cleveland Bridge 2 Billingham Town Res. 1
Nunthorpe Athletic 6 Colburn Town 1
FINAL *(April 14th at Darlington Railway Athletic)*
Darlington Cleveland Bridge 0 **Nunthorpe Athletic** 1

ALEX BURNESS PLATE
(Division Two teams)

GROUP A QUALIFIERS
South Bank St Peters

GROUP B QUALIFIER
Bedale

GROUP C QUALIFIER
Teesside Athletic Res.

GROUP D QUALIFIER
North Ormesby Sports

SEMI-FINALS
North Ormesby Sports 2
Bedale 1
South Bank St Peters 2
Teesside Athletic Res. 0

FINAL
(April 21st at Guisborough Town)
South Bank St Peters 4
North Ormesby Sports 0

UNITED COUNTIES LEAGUE

	AFC Kempston Rovers	Blackstones	Boston Town	Bourne Town	Cogenhoe United	Deeping Rangers	Desborough Town	Holbeach United	Long Buckby	Newport Pagnell Town	Northampton Spencer	Potton United	Raunds Town	Sleaford Town	St Ives Town	St Neots Town	Stewarts & Lloyds Corby	Stotfold	Wellingborough Town	Wootton Blue Cross	Yaxley
AFC Kempston Rovers		0-6	1-4	0-3	0-3	0-4	1-3	0-4	0-3	1-3	0-2	0-3	3-3	1-2	3-3	0-7	2-1	0-8	0-3	1-4	2-1
Blackstones	4-0		1-0	5-0	3-2	0-3	2-4	6-3	0-0	4-0	1-1	3-1	2-1	3-2	3-1	2-2	5-1	0-3	0-0	4-1	2-0
Boston Town	5-0	2-4	P	5-1	3-2	1-0	1-3	1-1	1-2	1-0	2-2	0-4	1-0	3-2	0-1	0-0	2-0	2-2	1-0	3-2	2-0
Bourne Town	5-2	1-2	2-1	R	0-0	0-0	1-3	2-3	2-0	1-3	2-3	1-2	2-3	0-4	2-3	2-0	0-2	1-2	0-1	1-4	
Cogenhoe United	3-0	1-3	3-4	1-1	E	2-1	0-0	3-1	2-1	0-1	0-0	1-1	2-0	2-1	1-1	0-5	0-1	1-3	4-1	2-2	3-0
Deeping Rangers	2-0	2-1	2-2	7-0	2-3	M	6-0	3-0	1-1	1-1	0-0	0-0	2-1	1-0	1-1	0-3	1-0	1-1	1-0	4-2	0-0
Desborough Town	5-0	2-0	3-3	5-1	2-1	2-2	I	1-2	2-0	4-0	2-0	2-0	3-2	4-0	2-1	1-1	1-1	2-1	2-1	1-1	0-0
Holbeach United	4-0	2-1	2-3	0-0	3-2	2-1	3-3	E	3-3	3-1	1-0	2-0	1-2	1-2	2-0	2-1	0-3	0-4	1-2	8-1	0-3
Long Buckby	7-0	2-2	0-1	2-0	0-0	3-0	2-1	5-0	R	3-1	3-1	5-0	2-2	2-2	1-2	3-1	3-2	3-3	2-1	5-1	2-1
Newport Pagnell Town	4-0	2-2	3-2	5-3	2-3	1-5	2-2	0-4	1-2		1-1	0-1	1-1	1-0	3-1	0-3	1-2	2-0	0-2	2-1	2-0
Northampton Spencer	6-1	0-1	0-1	1-2	3-2	1-2	1-1	1-0	1-2	2-0		2-1	5-0	0-1	0-0	2-2	1-2	1-3	2-0	2-2	
Potton United	2-0	0-1	2-3	2-1	0-4	1-4	1-3	0-2	0-4	0-2	2-4	D	2-1	1-4	2-4	1-1	1-1	0-3	2-1	1-2	2-2
Raunds Town	3-0	0-2	1-1	2-4	1-2	2-2	0-0	1-1	2-3	2-4	0-1	3-0	I	1-2	2-1	1-0	3-5	1-0	2-3	2-3	
Sleaford Town	2-3	2-4	0-1	1-0	1-1	0-4	1-0	4-2	2-2	5-0	3-2	2-1	4-0	V	0-1	1-1	1-2	1-1	0-3	5-1	2-4
St Ives Town	1-1	2-1	1-5	1-2	1-1	2-4	1-1	3-1	2-1	2-1	4-3	3-1	3-2	2-5	I	3-0	0-2	1-0	0-2	3-2	3-0
St Neots Town	2-0	2-1	1-0	1-0	0-0	1-0	0-1	3-0	1-3	2-3	1-1	3-1	1-2	2-3	1-1	S	0-2	1-2	1-2	1-1	3-1
Stewarts & Lloyds Corby	6-2	0-1	0-0	0-0	1-0	2-6	0-1	2-0	1-1	1-0	1-1	5-0	5-2	3-2	0-2	2-4	I	1-3	1-1	8-0	1-2
Stotfold	4-1	4-2	1-3	5-0	2-1	4-1	0-0	4-4	2-2	3-2	1-0	4-2	3-2	1-2	2-0	6-0	6-0	O	6-0	7-1	3-0
Wellingborough Town	3-0	1-1	1-2	1-1	0-0	0-0	0-0	5-1	2-2	3-2	1-0	2-3	1-2	1-3	1-3	1-2	1-1	N	3-0	1-3	
Wootton Blue Cross	6-0	0-1	1-1	1-1	2-3	1-2	1-3	0-5	1-2	0-4	1-1	5-3	0-2	2-1	0-4	1-2	1-1	2-4	0-2		3-2
Yaxley	5-1	0-4	2-0	1-4	0-1	0-2	2-4	2-2	0-5	0-2	0-1	1-0	0-0	2-1	0-3	2-2	2-3	0-5	2-0	2-2	

Premier Division		P	W	D	L	F	A	Pts
Stotfold		40	28	7	5	117	45	91
Long Buckby		40	23	12	5	99	49	81
Desborough Town		40	23	12	5	78	44	81
Blackstones		40	24	7	9	90	50	79
St Ives Town		40	22	8	10	78	59	74
Boston Town		40	21	9	10	73	53	72
Deeping Rangers	-3	40	20	12	8	80	39	69
St Neots Town		40	16	12	12	67	48	60
Cogenhoe United		40	15	12	13	61	52	57
Wellingborough Town		40	16	8	16	56	52	56
Holbeach United		40	16	7	17	72	73	55
Stewarts & Lloyds Corby		40	15	8	17	65	64	53
Northampton Spencer		40	13	12	15	60	51	51
Sleaford Town		40	15	6	19	73	76	51
Newport Pagnell Town		40	15	6	19	60	73	51
Yaxley		40	11	8	21	51	78	41
Raunds Town		40	9	10	21	58	75	37
Bourne Town		40	9	7	24	49	85	34
Potton United		40	9	5	26	45	90	32
Wootton Blue Cross		40	7	9	24	56	109	30
AFC Kempston Rovers	-1	40	3	4	34	26	149	11

Reserve Division One		P	W	D	L	F	A	Pts
Stotfold Res.		32	24	8	0	118	35	80
Blackstones Res.		32	20	6	6	85	27	66
Desborough Town Res.		32	18	3	11	67	56	57
Northampton Spencer Res.		32	16	8	8	74	48	56
St Neots Town Res.		32	15	3	14	72	67	48
Stewarts & Lloyds Corby Res.		32	12	9	11	70	63	45
Bourne Town Res.		32	12	8	12	54	58	44
Bugbrooke St Michaels Res.		32	11	10	11	65	69	43
Raunds Town Res.		32	11	7	14	50	61	40
Yaxley Res.		32	10	10	12	55	74	40
Olney Town Res.		32	11	6	15	63	81	39
Woodford United Res.		32	11	6	15	47	70	39
Whitworths Res.		32	10	5	17	58	71	35
Cogenhoe United Res.		32	10	5	17	60	86	35
Sileby Rangers Res.		32	10	1	21	59	91	31
Deeping Rangers Res.	-3	32	8	7	17	59	67	28
Daventry United Res.	-6	32	9	6	17	66	98	27

RESERVES CUP

FINAL

(April 30th at Rushden & Higham United)

Blackstones Res. 4 St Neots Town Res. 1

EAGLE BITTER UNITED COUNTIES LEAGUE PREMIER DIVISION CONSTITUTION 2008-09

BLACKSTONES	Blackstones Sports & Social, Lincoln Road, Stamford PE9 1SH		01780 757835
BOSTON TOWN	The Stadium, Tattershall Road, Boston PE21 9LR		01205 365470
BOURNE TOWN	Abbey Lawn, Abbey Road, Bourne PE10 9EN		01778 422292
COGENHOE UNITED	Compton Park, Brafield Road, Cogenhoe NN7 1ND		01604 890521
DAVENTRY TOWN	Communications Park , Browns Road, Daventry NN11 4NS		07814 283481
DEEPING RANGERS	Outgang Road, Towngate East, Market Deeping PE6 8LQ		01778 344700
DESBOROUGH TOWN	Waterworks Field, Braybrooke Road, Desborough NN14 2LJ		01536 761350
HOLBEACH UNITED	Carters Park, Park Road, Holbeach PE12 7EE		01406 424761
LONG BUCKBY	Station Road, Long Buckby NN6 7QA		01327 842682
NEWPORT PAGNELL TOWN	Willen Road Sports Ground, Newport Pagnell MK16 0DF		01908 611993
NORTHAMPTON SPENCER	Kingsthorpe Mill, Studland Road, Kingsthorpe, Northampton NN2 6NE		01604 718898
POTTON UNITED	The Hollow, Biggleswade Road, Potton SG19 2LU		01767 261100
RAUNDS TOWN	Kiln Park, London Road, Raunds, Wellingborough NN9 6EQ		01933 623351
ROTHWELL CORINTHIANS	Seargents Lawn, Desborough Road, Rothwell NN14 6JQ		01536 418688
SLEAFORD TOWN	Eslaforde Park, Boston Road, Sleaford NG34 9GH		01529 415951
ST IVES TOWN	Westwood Road, St Ives PE27 6WU		01480 463207
ST NEOTS TOWN	Rowley Park, Kester Way, St Neots PE19 6SN		01480 470012
STEWARTS & LLOYDS CORBY	Recreation Ground, Occupation Road, Corby NN17 1EH		01536 401497
STOTFOLD	Roker Park, The Green, Stotfold, Hitchin SG5 4AN		01462 730765
WELLINGBOROUGH TOWN	Dog & Duck, London Road, Wellingborough NN8 2DP		01933 441388
YAXLEY	Leading Drove, Holme Road, Yaxley, Peterborough PE7 3NA		01733 244928

IN: Daventry Town (P), Rothwell Corinthians (P)
OUT: AFC Kempston Rovers (R), Wootton Blue Cross (R)

	Buckingham Town	Bugbrooke St Michaels	Burton Park Wanderers	Daventry Town	Daventry United	Eynesbury Rovers	Huntingdon Town	Irchester United	Northampton ON Che.	Northampton Sileby	Olney Town	Peterborough Nthn Star	Rothwell Corinthians	Rushden & Higham U.	Thrapston Town	Whitworths
Buckingham Town		3-2	2-2	1-2	0-1	4-2	1-1	0-2	1-1	0-2	1-0	0-4	0-2	1-0	7-7	4-1
Bugbrooke St Michaels	1-2		1-2	0-2	0-2	1-3	4-1	5-1	1-0	2-2	1-2	0-2	1-1	3-0	2-1	1-0
Burton Park Wanderers	0-2	0-0	D	1-3	1-3	1-2	1-2	1-3	2-1	1-4	0-3	1-2	1-3	0-5	3-1	
Daventry Town	6-2	3-1	3-0	I	4-0	2-2	3-1	8-0	2-1	1-3	6-2	5-0	4-1	4-0	1-0	5-3
Daventry United	4-2	4-2	6-0	1-3	V	5-2	2-1	2-1	1-3	1-1	3-2	1-4	0-2	1-3	1-0	3-3
Eynesbury Rovers	1-1	0-2	1-1	0-3	0-5	I	1-2	4-1	2-1	1-2	2-2	3-0	0-0	2-2	1-2	1-5
Huntingdon Town	1-4	3-1	3-1	1-1	2-3	2-0	S	2-1	0-1	1-1	0-0	1-3	2-0	2-0	3-1	0-2
Irchester United	2-2	1-5	1-1	0-4	0-7	2-2	3-5	I	1-3	1-1	0-1	0-5	3-3	2-4	0-5	2-2
Northampton ON Chenecks	2-8	1-4	7-0	1-6	3-1	1-3	2-1	2-1	O	2-0	1-2	1-1	1-3	4-2	3-1	2-0
Northampton Sileby Rangers	1-2	1-4	1-3	0-5	1-3	6-0	1-0	2-3	0-3	N	3-1	2-2	1-2	0-2	2-0	3-2
Olney Town	2-0	0-1	2-1	0-3	2-1	4-1	0-2	1-0	2-3	3-5		1-4	2-0	1-2	0-2	0-1
Peterborough Northern Star	2-0	3-0	4-1	1-1	9-0	3-0	1-4	3-0	0-0	4-0	0-0	O	1-0	1-0	1-2	1-1
Rothwell Corinthians	3-3	3-1	2-0	1-3	5-2	1-0	1-2	2-1	5-1	2-2	3-4	1-1	N	3-0	6-1	2-1
Rushden & Higham United	2-2	1-2	2-1	2-4	1-1	1-1	0-3	3-1	0-1	3-0	0-0	0-1	0-1	E	0-1	1-1
Thrapston Town	1-2	2-2	1-2	0-2	1-2	1-4	0-1	1-3	5-3	3-2	1-1	0-3	3-2	1-0		1-2
Whitworths	3-3	1-4	4-0	1-7	1-1	4-5	1-2	3-2	4-1	6-1	2-2	2-1	1-1	1-3	3-0	

Division One

	P	W	D	L	F	A	Pts
Daventry Town	30	26	3	1	106	26	81
Peterborough Northern Star	30	18	7	5	68	26	61
Rothwell Corinthians	30	15	7	8	60	42	52
Huntingdon Town	30	16	4	10	51	40	52
Daventry United	30	16	4	10	67	59	52
Northampton ON Chenecks	30	15	3	12	56	56	48
Bugbrooke St Michaels	30	13	4	13	54	47	43
Buckingham Town	30	11	9	10	60	60	42
Whitworths	30	11	8	11	63	60	41
Olney Town	30	11	7	12	44	48	40
Thrapston Town	30	11	3	16	52	59	36
Northampton Sileby Rangers	30	9	6	15	47	64	33
Eynesbury Rovers	30	8	8	14	46	67	32
Rushden & Higham United	30	7	6	17	32	51	27
Burton Park Wanderers	30	5	4	21	29	76	19
Irchester United	30	3	7	20	37	91	16

Reserve Division Two

	P	W	D	L	F	A	Pts
Huntingdon Town Res.	30	22	2	6	83	37	68
Wellingborough Town Res.	30	19	5	6	75	29	62
Rushden & Higham United Res.	30	18	6	6	66	43	60
Northampton ON Chenecks Res.	30	19	2	9	89	42	59
Peterborough Northern Star Res.	30	18	5	7	76	47	59
Rothwell Corinthians Res.	30	13	6	11	50	46	45
Wootton Blue Cross Res.	30	14	3	13	58	62	45
Irchester United Res.	30	11	7	12	63	57	40
Eynesbury Rovers Res.	30	11	3	16	50	77	36
Thrapston Town Res.	30	10	2	18	42	58	32
AFC Kempston Rovers Res.	30	9	5	16	53	73	32
St Ives Town Res.	30	9	4	17	45	67	31
Daventry Town Res.	30	9	4	17	47	77	31
Burton Park Wanderers Res.	30	8	6	16	40	57	30
Buckingham Town Res.	30	8	5	17	57	86	29
Potton United Res.	30	8	3	19	40	76	27

LEAGUE CUP

PRELIMINARY ROUND
Buckingham Town 0 **Blackstones** 1
Northampton ON Chenecks 4 Eynesbury Rovers 3 *aet*
Rothwell Corinthians 1 **Newport Pagnell Tn** 1
Sleaford Town 6 Thrapston Town 0
Stewarts & Lloyds Corby 0 **St Ives Town** 2

Newport Pagnell Tn 2 Stotfold 2 *aet* (4-2p)
Olney Town 3 **Sleaford Town** 4 *aet*
Potton United 2 Wellingborough Town 1
Raunds Town 1 **Peterborough Northern Star** 2

FIRST ROUND
AFC Kempston Rovers 0 **Desborough Tn** 4
Boston Town 2 Holbeach United 0
Bourne Town 4 Wootton Blue Cross 0
Bugbrooke St Michaels 1 **Blackstones** 2
Cogenhoe United 4 Northampton Sileby Rangers 2
Daventry Town 5 Daventry United 0
Irchester United 0 **Long Buckby** 5

St Ives Town 6 Burton Park Wanderers 4 *aet*
St Neots Town 1 **Northampton Spencer** 2
Whitworths FC 2 **Huntingdon Town** 3
Yaxley 1 **Deeping Rangers** 2

SECOND ROUND
Boston Town 4 Bourne Town 1
Deeping Rangers 2 Cogenhoe United 0
Newport Pagnell Town 2 **Daventry Town** 4
Northampton ON Chenecks 1 **Blackstones** 4

Northampton Spencer 0 Long Buckby 0 *aet* (4-3p)
Potton United 1 Peterborough Northern Star 0
Sleaford Town 1 **Desborough Town** 2 *aet*
St Ives Town 3 Huntingdon Town 1

QUARTER-FINALS
Blackstones 3 St Ives Town 1
Daventry Town 3 Boston Town 1
Northampton Spencer 1 **Deeping Rangers** 6
Potton United 0 **Desborough Town** 3

SEMI-FINALS
Blackstones 1 **Desborough Town** 2
Deeping Rangers 0 **Daventry Town** 3
(April 16th at Wellingborough Town)
Desborough Town 3 Daventry Town 2

FINAL

EAGLE BITTER UNITED COUNTIES LEAGUE DIVISION ONE CONSTITUTION 2008-09

AFC KEMPSTON ROVERS..............Hillgrounds Road, Kempston, Bedford MK42 8SZ............................01234 852346
BUCKINGHAM TOWN ....Ford Meadow, Ford Street, Buckingham MK18 1AG.............01280 816257
BUGBROOKE ST MICHAELS ......Birds Close, Gayton Road, Bugbrooke, Northampton NN7 3PH......01604 830707
BURTON PARK WANDERERS.........Latimer Park, Polwell Lane, Burton Latimer NN15 5PS.......01536 725841
DAVENTRY UNITED.....................Royal Oak Way, Daventry NN11 8PQ 01327 704914
EYNESBURY ROVERS ....Alfred Hall Memorial Ground, Hall Road, Eynesbury, St Neots PE19 2SF 01480 477449
HUNTINGDON TOWN..............Jubilee Park, Kings Ripton Road, Huntingdon PE28 2NR............07929 651226
IRCHESTER UNITED ....Alfred Street, Irchester NN29 7DR.........................01933 312877
NORTHAMPTON ON CHENECKS ......Old Northamptonians, Billing Road, Northampton NN1 5RX............01604 634045
NORTHAMPTON SILEBY RANGERS ...Fernie Fields Sports Ground, Woodford Chase, Moulton, Northampton NN3 7BD ...01604 670366
OLNEY TOWN ....Recreation Ground, East Street, Olney MK46 4DW 01234 712227
PETERBOROUGH NORTHERN STAR...Chestnut Avenue, Dogsthorpe, Peterborough PE1 4PE 01733 564894
RUSHDEN & HIGHAM UNITED ....Hayden Road, Rushden NN10 0HX.............01933 410036
THRAPSTON TOWN........................Chancery Lane, Thrapston, Kettering NN14 4JL.........01832 732470
WHITWORTHS.....................London Road, Wellingborough NN8 2DT.........01933 227324
WOOTTON BLUE CROSS................Weston Park, Bedford Road, Wootton MK43 9JT.........01234 767662
IN: AFC Kempston Rovers (R), Wootton Blue Cross (R)
OUT: Daventry Town (P), Rothwell Corinthians (P)

WEARSIDE LEAGUE

Note – Cleadon Social Club withdrew during the course of the season

Their results are shown herein but are expunged from the league table

	Annfield Plain	Belford House	Boldon Community Association	Cleadon Social Club	Cleator Moor Celtic	Coxhoe Athletic	Easington Colliery	East Durham United	Guisborough Black Swan	Hartlepool	Harton & Westoe CW	Jarrow	New Marske Sports Club	Ryhope Colliery Welfare	Silksworth CC	Teesside Athletic	Whitehaven Amateurs	Willington	Windscale	Wolviston
Annfield Plain		2-2	3-1	n/a	2-3	1-0	3-1	1-0	3-2	3-1	2-1	0-2	1-1	1-1	5-0	3-2	2-1	2-2	2-0	1-4
Belford House	3-1		0-4	n/a	1-1	2-1	2-3	1-0	2-1	1-3	1-3	1-3	3-2	1-1	1-1	3-1	0-3	4-1	2-2	1-3
Boldon Community Association	1-0	2-3		3-5	1-2	5-1	1-1	0-0	3-1	3-1	3-0	0-1	4-7	3-1	4-1	3-0	2-4	3-3	0-1	0-1
Cleadon Social Club	4-0	1-3	0-2		n/a	4-1	0-1	6-0	1-2	n/a	3-2	3-3	n/a	1-3	2-3	n/a	0-3	3-0	n/a	2-0
Cleator Moor Celtic	2-2	2-3	1-5	0-3		9-0	0-3	6-0	2-1	4-1	6-1	3-4	2-2	1-0	2-0	2-3	3-1	3-1	4-1	0-1
Coxhoe Athletic	1-2	2-3	2-4	1-4	4-1		0-4	2-1	4-3	0-0	1-3	0-1	0-3	0-2	0-1	3-1	0-3	3-3	4-3	1-2
Easington Colliery	0-0	1-0	1-1	2-2	7-0	4-3		3-4	7-4	0-0	2-2	0-2	1-3	3-2	3-1	2-2	1-0	5-1	6-1	3-4
East Durham United	1-4	2-2	0-3	n/a	1-0	1-5	1-2		3-2	3-0	2-4	2-4	0-4	0-4	2-1	0-2	0-6	0-1	3-0	1-4
Guisborough Black Swan	0-3	5-3	0-1	7-1	1-5	2-4	1-4	2-2		1-1	3-0	0-3	1-6	1-2	6-0	0-0	1-3	2-1	2-0	0-5
Hartlepool	0-4	4-2	1-2	3-1	5-0	6-1	2-1	3-3	1-2		2-0	2-1	1-3	0-1	4-0	3-1	1-2	3-1	2-0	2-3
Harton & Westoe CW	1-3	1-3	1-1	n/a	3-1	2-3	2-3	2-1	1-3	0-2		0-2	1-3	0-1	0-3	3-2	0-2	5-3	1-1	0-0
Jarrow	0-0	3-1	1-1	1-1	2-1	4-1	1-1	6-0	2-3	0-6	6-0		3-1	4-1	7-1	1-3	1-7	5-1	2-1	3-3
New Marske Sports Club	2-0	4-2	7-0	2-0	4-1	2-0	5-1	4-0	1-1	4-1	5-0	4-4		5-0	7-0	4-0	3-1	5-0	4-0	2-0
Ryhope Colliery Welfare	1-0	4-0	4-3	2-1	3-3	1-0	1-1	4-2	3-1	0-2	2-1	1-0	1-1		0-1	2-2	2-2	4-3	3-0	2-1
Silksworth CC	0-3	1-4	0-3	0-4	2-3	0-3	2-2	1-6	1-1	0-5	2-2	2-4	0-4	0-4		0-4	0-0	2-1	0-0	1-2
Teesside Athletic	1-1	2-1	0-0	n/a	2-0	3-0	0-2	2-0	1-0	2-4	1-1	0-1	0-2	0-0	6-0		2-4	2-1	1-0	0-1
Whitehaven Amateurs	5-1	3-1	3-1	n/a	0-1	2-3	1-0	6-1	2-0	3-4	3-1	3-3	0-1	4-2	2-1	3-1		5-0	5-0	2-1
Willington	0-1	0-2	4-1	n/a	0-0	3-1	3-2	1-1	3-2	1-4	1-0	1-2	1-3	1-2	4-1	0-1	0-1		1-0	2-2
Windscale	0-0	1-1	4-1	n/a	0-1	4-2	1-1	4-0	1-4	1-2	0-4	2-3	0-1	0-1	3-1	0-0	0-4	5-0		0-3
Wolviston	1-0	4-1	0-0	n/a	5-1	3-0	1-1	1-0	1-1	2-3	2-2	1-1	3-3	3-1	3-0	1-2	1-1	3-0	1-1	

		P	W	D	L	F	A	Pts
New Marske Sports Club		36	28	6	2	120	31	90
Jarrow		36	23	7	6	93	54	76
Whitehaven Amateurs	-3	36	25	3	8	96	40	75
Wolviston		36	20	10	6	76	41	70
Ryhope Colliery Welfare		36	19	9	8	66	50	66
Hartlepool		36	19	5	12	80	54	62
Easington Colliery		36	17	10	9	84	57	61
Annfield Plain	-3	36	18	9	9	62	43	60
Boldon Community Association		36	15	8	13	70	60	53
Cleator Moor Celtic		36	16	5	15	76	72	53
Teesside Athletic		36	13	8	15	50	53	47
Belford House		36	13	7	16	63	77	46
Harton & Westoe CW		36	9	6	21	49	81	33
Guisborough Black Swan		36	9	5	22	59	84	32
Coxhoe Athletic		36	10	2	24	54	94	32
Willington		36	8	7	21	51	86	31
East Durham United		36	7	6	23	44	97	27
Windscale		36	6	7	23	37	74	25
Silksworth CC		36	4	6	26	28	110	18

Cleadon Social Club – record expunged

WEARSIDE LEAGUE CONSTITUTION 2008-09

ANNFIELD PLAIN........................Derwent Park, West Road, Annfield Plain DH9 8PZ...None
BELFORD HOUSE..........................Silksworth Welfare, Silksworth, Sunderland..None
BOLDON COMMUNITY ASSOCIATION...Boldon Welfare, New Road, Boldon Colliery NE35 9DS..........0191 536 4180 (Cricket Club)
CLEATOR MOOR CELTIC..............Celtic Club, Birks Road, Cleator Moor CA25 5HR..........................01946 812476
COXHOE ATHLETIC...........................Beechfield Park, Coxhoe DH6 4SD..None
EASINGTON COLLIERY..........Welfare Park Ground, Easington Colliery, Peterlee NE32 4SH..............0191 489 6930
EAST DURHAM UNITED....................Shotton Park, Shotton Colliery, Durham..............................None
GUISBOROUGH BLACK SWAN....King George V Playing Fields, Howlbeck Road, Guisborough TS14 6LE....01287 636925
HARTLEPOOL..........................Grayfields Enclose, Jesmond Gardens, Hartlepool............................None
HARTON & WESTOE...Harton Colliery Welfare, Boldon Lane, South Shields NE34 0NA...............0191 456 6166
JARROW..........................Perth Green Community Assoc., Inverness Road, Jarrow NE32 4AQ.........0191 489 3743
KIRKBYMOORSIDE........................Kirkby Mills, Kirkbymoorside, York YO62 6NS.................................None
NEW MARSKE SPORTS CLUB...........Gurney Street, New Marske, Redcar TS11 8EG................................01642 479808
NEWTON AYCLIFFE........Sunnydale Sports Complex, Middridge Lane, Shildon DL4 2EP..............01388 777340
RYHOPE COLLIERY WELFARE....Ryhope Recreation Park, Ryhope Street, Ryhope, Sunderland SR2 0AB.............0191 521 2843
SILKSWORTH CC......................Silksworth Welfare Park, Silksworth, Sunderland...............................None
TEESSIDE ATHLETIC......................Green Lane, Redcar TS10 3RW..None
WILLINGTON........................Hall Lane Ground, Hall Lane Estate, Willington DL15 0QF.................01388 746221
WINDSCALE......................Falcon Field, Smithfield, Egremont CA22 2QN.................................01946 820421
WOLVISTON........................Metcalfe Park, Wynyard Road, Wolviston, Billingham TS22 5NE.................07768 321651
IN: Kirkbymoorside (P – Teesside League Division One), Newton Aycliffe (P – Durham Alliance)
OUT: Cleadon Social Club (WS), Whitehaven Amateurs (P – Northern League Division Two)

LEAGUE CUP

FIRST ROUND	QUARTER-FINALS

FIRST ROUND

Annfield Plain 2 Boldon Community Association 0

Hartlepool 0 **New Marske Sports Club** 1 *aet*

Harton & Westoe CW 2 **Cleator Moor Celtic** 5

Wolviston 2 Easington Colliery 1

SECOND ROUND

Annfield Plain 5 Silksworth CC 0

Belford House 6 Cleator Moor Celtic 2

Cleadon Social Club 6 Willington 1

Coxhoe Athletic 1 **Whitehaven Amateurs** 3

East Durham United 1 **New Marske Sports Club** 6

Guisborough Black Swan 2 Teesside Athletic 0

Jarrow 6 Ryhope Colliery Welfare 2

Windscale 1 **Wolviston** 5

QUARTER-FINALS

Belford House 1 **New Marske Sports Club** 2

Cleadon Social Club 1 **Annfield Plain** 2

Whitehaven Amateurs 7 Jarrow 3

Wolviston 1 Guisborough Black Swan 0

SEMI-FINALS

Annfield Plain 0 **Wolviston** 2

Whitehaven Amateurs 0 **New Marske Sports Club** 1

FINAL

(May 14th at Wolviston)

Wolviston 1 **New Marske Sports Club** 3

MONKWEARMOUTH CHARITY CUP

FIRST ROUND

Belford House 2 **Jarrow** 5

Hartlepool 3 East Durham United 0

Harton & Westoe CW 0 **Easington Colliery** 1

Silksworth CC 1 **Ryhope Colliery Welfare** 2 *aet*

SECOND ROUND

Annfield Plain 2 Whitehaven Amateurs 1

Boldon Community Association 2 **Guisborough Black Swan** 5

Cleadon Social Club 3 Teesside Athletic 1

Cleator Moor Celtic 3 Easington Colliery 2

Jarrow 1 Hartlepool 0

Ryhope Colliery Welfare 5 Willington 2

Windscale 2 Coxhoe Athletic 0

Wolviston 2 **New Marske Sports Club** 3

QUARTER-FINALS

Cleadon Social Club 2 **Jarrow** 2 *aet* (3-5p)

Cleator Moor Celtic 0 **New Marske Sports Club** 3

Guisborough Black Swan 2 **Annfield Plain** 3

Ryhope Colliery Welfare 3 Windscale 0

SEMI-FINALS

Annfield Plain 4 Jarrow 4 *aet* (4-2p)

Ryhope Colliery Welfare 0 **New Marske Sports Club** 1

FINAL

(May 5th at New Marske Sports Club)

New Marske Sports Club 3 Annfield Plain 1

SUNDERLAND SHIPOWNERS CUP

FIRST ROUND

Cleator Moor Celtic 5 Ryhope Colliery Welfare 3

Coxhoe Athletic 1 **Willington** 3

East Durham United 2 Guisborough Black Swan 2 *aet* (4-2p)

New Marske Sports Club 6 Annfield Plain 2

SECOND ROUND

Belford House 1 **Harton & Westoe CW** 3

Cleator Moor Celtic 3 Silksworth CC 1

East Durham United 1 **Teesside Athletic** 2

Hartlepool 3 Jarrow 0

New Marske Sports Club 3 Easington Colliery 0

Whitehaven Amateurs 2 Boldon Community Association 1

Willington 2 **Cleadon Social Club** 3 *aet*

Wolviston 3 Windscale 0

QUARTER-FINALS

Cleadon Social Club 4 Hartlepool 3

Teesside Athletic 1 **Cleator Moor Celtic** 4

Whitehaven Amateurs 5 New Marske Sports Club 2

Wolviston 3 **Harton & Westoe CW** 5

SEMI-FINALS

Cleator Moor Celtic 3 Harton & Westoe CW 1

Whitehaven Amateurs (w/o) v Cleadon Social Club (scr.)

FINAL

(May 16th at Whitehaven Amateurs)

Whitehaven Amateurs 2 **Cleator Moor Celtic** 2 *aet* (2-4p)

WELSH ALLIANCE

	Amlwch Town	Bethesda Athletic	Conwy United	Glan Conwy	Halkyn United	Holywell Town	Llanberis	Llandudno Junction	Llanrug United	Llanrwst United	Nantlle Vale	Nefyn United	Pwllheli	Rhydymwyn	Rhyl Res.
Amlwch Town		2-2	0-7	1-3	3-3	5-0	3-3	3-2	2-2	3-1	0-0	0-0	1-4	4-3	3-4
Bethesda Athletic	6-1		3-0	0-1	4-1	6-0	4-0	10-0	4-2	4-0	8-3	8-0	3-1	2-0	3-1
Conwy United	4-2	0-2		1-4	3-0	1-2	2-1	1-1	2-2	2-1	5-0	9-0	3-2	4-2	4-3
Glan Conwy	5-0	0-3	1-2		2-2	0-0	3-1	5-0	2-3	1-2	1-2	3-2	7-0	2-0	2-0
Halkyn United	2-1	4-1	0-2	1-4		1-0	2-1	0-0	1-3	2-3	0-0	0-3	2-2	2-1	1-2
Holywell Town	2-0	2-8	2-6	0-5	4-0		2-2	3-1	2-0	1-2	1-2	4-0	1-1	2-2	1-4
Llanberis	3-0	0-3	3-2	2-2	2-3	1-2		3-0	2-2	3-2	1-0	1-1	0-3	0-0	3-3
Llandudno Junction	1-0	1-1	4-3	1-4	0-1	2-3	2-3		2-6	1-1	0-0	4-2	2-1	2-1	3-2
Llanrug United	7-5	0-3	3-0	3-4	3-1	4-4	1-1	4-2		2-2	5-7	5-2	2-2	3-3	2-1
Llanrwst United	2-1	3-2	3-1	0-2	3-0	2-1	2-0	2-1	4-3		1-2	1-2	1-2	1-2	1-1
Nantlle Vale	2-2	1-2	2-4	3-2	1-3	2-1	1-3	3-1	0-2	0-2		3-2	1-0	0-4	1-0
Nefyn United	0-2	1-3	0-0	0-3	2-0	4-0	2-1	3-2	1-6	2-4	6-0		2-3	1-0	2-2
Pwllheli	5-0	1-4	1-1	0-3	1-1	6-3	2-2	3-2	3-2	2-2	2-1	2-1		1-0	1-3
Rhydymwyn	2-4	1-4	3-0	2-4	7-1	1-1	5-3	3-1	0-1	0-1	1-3	0-4	2-1		2-0
Rhyl Res.	5-2	0-1	8-0	1-2	7-3	2-0	4-0	6-0	3-0	2-1	1-1	1-1	6-0	2-0	

		P	W	D	L	F	A	Pts
Bethesda Athletic		28	23	2	3	104	26	71
Glan Conwy		28	19	3	6	77	32	60
Rhyl Res.		28	14	5	9	74	40	47
Llanrwst United		28	14	4	10	50	45	46
Conwy United		28	14	3	11	69	58	45
Llanrug United		28	12	8	8	78	65	44
Pwllheli		28	11	7	10	52	58	40
Nantlle Vale		28	11	5	12	41	60	38
Llanberis		28	8	9	11	47	58	33
Nefyn United	-3	28	10	4	14	49	67	31
Rhydymwyn		28	8	5	15	48	54	29
Holywell Town	-3	28	8	6	14	44	70	27
Amlwch Town		28	6	7	15	50	80	25
Halkyn United		28	6	7	15	37	68	25
Llandudno Junction		28	6	5	17	38	77	23

COOKSON CUP

FIRST ROUND
Glan Conwy 1 Rhydymwyn 0
Halkyn United 2 **Conwy United** 3 *aet*
Llandudno Junction 1 **Bethesda Athletic** 6
Llanrug United 6 Llanrwst United 1
Nantlle Vale 3 Holywell Town 0
Nefyn United 2 **Amlwch Town** 3
Pwllheli 1 **Rhyl Res.** 2

QUARTER-FINALS
Amlwch Town 2 **Llanrug United** 5
Bethesda Athletic 2 Glan Conwy 0
Llanberis 4 **Nantlle Vale** 4 *aet* (3-4p)
Rhyl Res. 5 Conwy United 0

SEMI-FINALS
Nantlle Vale 1 **Llanrug United** 3
Rhyl Res. 0 **Bethesda Athletic** 1

FINAL
(April 27th at Conwy United)
Bethesda Athletic 3 Llanrug United 2 *aet*

PENTRAETH HONDA WELSH ALLIANCE CONSTITUTION 2008-09

AMLWCH TOWN .... Lon Bach, Amlwch, Anglesey LL68 9BL .... None
BETHESDA ATHLETIC .... Parc Meurig Park, Bethesda, Bangor LL57 3NT .... None
CONWY UNITED .... The Morfa, Penmaen Road, Conwy LL32 8HA 01492 573080
GLAN CONWY .... Cae Ffwt, Llanrwst Road, Glan Conwy, Colwyn Bay LL28 5SP............................ None
HALKYN UNITED .... Pant Newydd, Halkyn 01352 780576
HOLYWELL TOWN .... Halkyn Road, Holywell CH8 7SJ .... None
LLANBERIS .... Ffordd Padarn, Llanberis, Caernarfon LL55 4SU .... None
LLANDUDNO JUNCTION .... The Flyover, Victoria Drive, Llandudno Junction LL31 9PG............................ None
LLANLLYFNI .... St Georges Field, Llanllyfni .... None
LLANRUG UNITED .... Eithin Duon, Llanrug, Caernarfon LL55 4DA 01286 677543
LLANRWST UNITED .... Gwydyr Park, Llanrwst LL26 0PN................................... None
NANTLLE VALE...................... Cae Emrys, Tyn Weirglodd, Penygroes LL54 6PA .... None
NEFYN UNITED .... Caer Delyn, Nefyn, Pwllheli .... None
PWLLHELI .... Dwyfor Leisure Centre, Recreation Road, Pwllheli LL53 5PF 01758 613437
RHYDYMWYN .... Vicarage Road, Rhydymwyn, Mold CH7 5HL .... None
RHYL RESERVES..................... Belle Vue Stadium, Grange Road, Rhyl LL18 4BT 01745 338327

IN: Llanllyfni (P – Gwynedd League)

WELSH LEAGUE

	Afan Lido	Bridgend Town	Bryntirion Athletic	Caerleon	Caldicot Town	Cambrian & Clydach Vale BGC	Croesyceiliog	Cwmbran Town	Dinas Powys	ENTO Aberaman Athletic	Garw Athletic	Goytre United	Maesteg Park	Newport YMCA	Pontardawe Town	Pontypridd Town	Taffs Well	Ton Pentre
Afan Lido		2-2	1-1	1-1	2-1	0-0	3-1	1-1	0-2	1-4	11-0	0-1	2-1	1-0	2-1	4-0	2-0	2-0
Bridgend Town	4-2		1-2	1-2	5-1	4-2	3-3	3-0	0-1	2-2	3-0	1-2	4-0	3-5	5-0	5-2	0-0	2-4
Bryntirion Athletic	1-2	2-0		3-0	4-2	1-1	2-0	2-1	1-2	9-0	3-2	2-1	5-0	3-0	3-1	1-1	0-2	
Caerleon	2-1	2-1	2-2	D	2-3	0-1	4-0	1-0	1-2	0-1	8-1	1-2	2-3	0-2	2-2	1-1	1-3	0-0
Caldicot Town	0-0	3-1	2-0	1-0	I	1-0	2-1	0-3	1-2	3-1	7-1	1-2	3-1	3-3	2-3	0-5	3-1	1-3
Cambrian & Clydach Vale BGC	1-3	5-0	0-3	1-1	2-1	V	1-0	0-6	0-0	6-0	1-0	2-1	2-3	3-2	2-1	6-2	0-1	
Croesyceiliog	0-1	1-7	2-6	0-2	1-4	1-1	I	2-1	1-2	3-2	5-1	0-3	3-1	1-3	1-3	7-0	2-3	0-0
Cwmbran Town	0-0	2-2	1-0	1-2	2-0	0-1	4-4	S	3-0	1-3	0-0	2-3	4-0	6-3	0-2	5-0	4-2	0-2
Dinas Powys	0-1	8-1	1-0	1-2	3-1	1-1	2-1	3-0	I	4-1	7-0	2-3	6-0	2-1	2-1	3-0	3-2	0-2
ENTO Aberaman Athletic	1-1	1-0	3-1	1-2	1-0	3-2	2-1	1-1	0-3	O	10-0	1-0	2-0	1-3	3-2	3-0	3-0	0-1
Garw Athletic	0-4	1-11	0-9	1-4	0-3	0-9	0-5	0-6	0-4	0-4	N	0-6	0-6	2-9	1-4	0-3	1-4	0-9
Goytre United	1-2	1-0	1-2	3-0	3-0	2-2	3-1	5-2	2-0	2-3	11-0	O	5-1	2-1	1-1	2-1	6-0	2-2
Maesteg Park	0-0	0-1	2-0	0-2	2-1	2-1	1-2	0-0	4-5	1-3	2-0	0-5	O	1-2	1-0	2-2	1-2	0-6
Newport YMCA	3-0	5-0	2-1	1-2	3-0	3-2	2-1	2-0	0-7	1-1	11-0	0-5	1-4	N	2-2	3-2	3-1	3-3
Pontardawe Town	0-1	2-1	0-2	1-1	5-1	1-0	0-1	1-0	1-0	0-2	1-2	0-2	3-3	1-2	E	6-0	0-0	0-3
Pontypridd Town	0-3	2-6	0-5	1-3	0-2	0-0	0-3	0-7	1-3	0-4	7-1	0-9	1-1	3-5	0-1	E	1-4	2-8
Taffs Well	1-1	0-2	0-0	0-5	0-0	1-1	3-0	6-1	1-4	1-3	6-1	0-3	7-1	2-0	3-0	3-1		0-3
Ton Pentre	1-1	3-3	1-4	0-2	3-1	3-0	6-1	4-0	0-2	3-3	13-0	0-1	3-0	3-1	3-1	2-1	5-0	

Division One

	P	W	D	L	F	A	Pts
Goytre United	34	25	3	6	101	30	78
Dinas Powys	34	25	1	8	92	34	76
Ton Pentre	34	22	7	5	102	33	73
ENTO Aberaman Athletic	34	21	6	7	75	40	69
Bryntirion Athletic	34	20	5	9	82	35	65
Afan Lido	34	17	11	6	58	31	62
Newport YMCA	34	19	4	11	88	70	61
Caerleon	34	16	7	11	60	42	55
Cambrian/Clydach Vale BGC	34	13	10	11	59	47	49
Bridgend Town	34	13	6	15	84	68	45
Caldicot Town	34	13	3	18	54	65	42
Taffs Well	34	11	7	16	53	70	40
Pontardawe Town	34	11	6	17	47	55	39
Cwmbran Town	34	10	8	16	56	50	38
Croesyceiliog	34	9	5	20	60	80	32
Maesteg Park	34	7	6	21	43	83	27
Pontypridd Town	34	3	4	27	38	116	13
Garw Athletic	34	1	1	32	14	217	4

LEAGUE CUP

FIRST ROUND

Abertillery Excelsior 5 Cwmbran Town 1
Bettws 3 Grange Harlequins 0
Caerau Ely 2 Barry Town 1
Caerleon 3 Afan Lido 1
Caldicot Town 3 Aberbargoed Buds 2
Cambrian & Clydach Vale BGC 0 UWIC 2
Cardiff Corinthians 4 Briton Ferry Athletic 3 *aet*
Croesyceiliog 4 Goytre 1
Garden Village 2 Ton Pentre 1
Garw Athletic 3 Ammanford 5
Goytre United 4 Cwmaman Institute 3

Llantwit Fardre 1 ENTO Aberaman Athletic 5
Merthyr Saints 4 Cwmmaman United 3 *aet*
Monmouth Town 3 Ely Rangers 4
Newcastle Emlyn 1 Maesteg Park 3
Newport YMCA 8 Morriston Town 1
Pontyclun 1 Llangeinor 2
Pontypridd Town 3 Dinas Powys 4 *aet*
Risca United 0 AFC Llwydcoed 2
Taffs Well 1 Pontardawe Town 2
Treharris Athletic 4 Porthcawl Town 2
West End 4 Llansawel 3

WWW.CHERRYRED.CO.UK

MACWHIRTER WELSH LEAGUE DIVISION ONE CONSTITUTION 2008-09

AFAN LIDO............Marston's Stadium, Princess Margaret Way, Aberavon Beach, Port Talbot SA12 6QW............01639 892960
BARRY TOWN.................Jenner Park Athletic Stadium, Barry Road, Barry CF62 9BG.................01446 735858
BETTWS....................North Site, Bettws Road, Bettws, Bridgend CF32 8YD....................07887 530804
BRIDGEND TOWN.....University of Glamorgan PF, Treforest Industrial Estate, Treforest, Pontypridd CF37 5UP.......01443 482681
BRYNTIRION ATHLETIC........Bryntirion Park, Llangewydd Road, Bryntirion, Bridgend CF41 4JU............01656 652702
CAERLEON................Cold Bath Road, Caerleon, Newport NP18 1NF................01633 420074
CALDICOT TOWN......................Jubilee Way, Caldicot NP26 4NA......................01291 423519
CAMBRIAN & CLYDACH VALE BGC....King George V, Highfield Road, Clydach, Tonypandy CF40 2XX..............01443 442743
CARDIFF CORINTHIANS........Riverside Ground, Through Station Road, Radyr, Cardiff CF15 8AA..........02920 843407
CROESYCEILIOG.............Woodland Road, Croesyceiliog, Cwmbran NP11 2DZ.............01633 485157
CWMBRAN TOWN.............Cwmbran Stadium, Henllys Way, Cwmbran NP44 3XL.............01633 627100
DINAS POWYS...............Murchfield, Sunnycroft Lane, Dinas Powys CF64 4QP...............07852 488552
ENTO ABERAMAN ATHLETIC........Aberaman Park, Cardiff Road, Aberaman CF44 6AA........07886 993292
GOYTRE UNITED.................Glenhafod Park, Goytre, Port Talbot SA13 2YP................01639 898983/895615
NEWPORT YMCA.....................Mendalgief Road, Newport NP20 2HF.....................01633 266872
PONTARDAWE TOWN.......Recreation Ground, Alloy Industrial Estate, Pontardawe SA8 4EN.......01792 862228
TAFFS WELL................Rhiw Dda'r, Parish Road, Taffs Well CF15 7QB................02920 811080
TON PENTRE.................Ynys Park, Sawmill Villas, Llanfoist Street, Ton Pentre CF41 7AF.................01443 442625

IN: Barry Town (P), Bettws (P), Cardiff Corinthians (P)
OUT: Garw SBGC (formerly Garw Athletic) (R), Maesteg Park (R), Pontypridd Town (R)

	Ammanford	Barry Town	Bettws	Briton Ferry Athletic	Caerau Ely	Cardiff Corinthians	Cwmbran Celtic	Ely Rangers	Garden Village	Grange Harlequins	Llangeinor	Llanwern	Pontyclun	Tredegar Town	Treharris Athletic	Troedyrhiw	UWIC	West End
Ammanford		1-2	2-3	1-0	4-3	3-8	2-0	3-1	1-1	4-7	4-3	2-0	0-1	1-2	0-1	2-3	2-2	5-5
Barry Town	3-2		0-0	4-1	1-1	0-1	4-0	2-1	3-0	0-1	5-2	1-2	3-1	5-1	3-0	7-0	1-0	1-0
Bettws	2-1	2-1		2-0	1-1	2-2	4-1	3-0	3-3	3-1	2-1	0-0	3-3	5-1	3-0	2-0	3-1	
Briton Ferry Athletic	0-1	2-5	0-2	D	2-0	3-4	0-0	3-0	1-4	3-1	1-1	0-0	1-1	5-1	2-4	2-1	1-2	2-3
Caerau Ely	6-6	0-2	3-0	2-1	I	1-3	4-3	1-2	0-2	2-2	2-1	4-3	4-1	3-2	2-2	0-0	5-1	0-1
Cardiff Corinthians	2-1	1-2	0-1	1-2	2-2	V	5-2	1-3	3-2	1-1	3-2	0-3	6-1	2-0	4-3	1-3	1-1	3-5
Cwmbran Celtic	1-0	2-2	1-1	3-1	3-1	0-1	I	1-1	1-1	2-3	3-1	0-1	1-3	1-4	5-2	3-1	4-2	0-3
Ely Rangers	1-1	2-3	1-2	1-0	2-0	3-1	0-0	S	2-3	2-1	6-1	3-2	3-0	3-1	1-4	2-0	3-1	3-2
Garden Village	4-2	0-1	0-2	1-1	0-2	5-3	2-0	3-0	I	5-5	2-1	1-3	2-1	2-2	0-1	4-0	2-2	2-4
Grange Harlequins	0-3	2-2	0-3	0-1	3-2	1-2	0-1	2-2	1-2	O	0-0	2-2	2-1	1-2	2-0	2-2	4-1	
Llangeinor	1-1	1-0	3-3	4-2	3-1	3-4	0-1	1-1	0-1	3-0	N	3-0	2-1	1-2	3-0	2-1	1-1	0-1
Llanwern	1-1	0-0	2-3	1-1	2-0	0-4	2-2	1-1	4-0	1-0	4-4		1-0	4-2	2-1	1-1	1-2	2-1
Pontyclun	0-2	0-3	1-3	4-0	1-1	1-4	2-2	0-1	1-2	2-1	2-1	1-0	T	1-1	2-4	0-4	4-3	1-3
Tredegar Town	1-2	1-0	0-5	3-1	1-1	0-1	1-2	4-0	1-4	1-4	1-3	3-3	0-1	W	4-0	3-0	1-1	1-2
Treharris Athletic	3-1	5-1	0-7	1-2	3-6	1-1	0-3	2-4	2-4	2-1	4-3	3-3	5-2	3-3	O	2-2	0-6	2-6
Troedyrhiw	4-3	1-4	2-1	2-2	0-2	1-2	1-3	3-5	2-4	1-3	4-1	1-1	0-0	3-2	1-1		1-0	0-0
UWIC	2-1	1-1	0-0	0-0	1-1	0-1	2-0	2-1	3-1	1-1	3-1	4-2	1-0	1-0	3-1	3-0		1-3
West End	1-2	1-2	3-0	3-0	3-0	1-2	1-1	3-2	1-1	5-0	2-3	4-4	2-1	1-0	2-0	3-0	1-5	

SECOND ROUND

Abertillery Excelsior 0 **West End** 5
Ammanford 3 Garden Village 1
Bettws 0 **Bryntirion Athletic** 3
Bridgend Town 3 Caldicot Town 2
Cardiff Corinthians 3 Ystradgynlais 2 *aet*
Croesyceiliog 4 Pentwyn Dynamos 2
ENTO Aberaman Athletic 5 Caerau Ely 1
Goytre United 3 UWIC 2
Llanwern 2 Cwmbran Celtic 1 *aet*
Maesteg Park 1 **Dinas Powys** 2
Merthyr Saints 3 AFC Llwydcoed 2
Newport YMCA 3 Seven Sisters 0
Penrhiwceiber Rangers 3 **Ely Rangers** 4 *aet*
Pontyclun 0 **Caerleon** 3
Treharris Athletic 3 **Tredegar Town** 3 *aet (3-4p)*
Troedyrhiw 0 **Pontardawe Town** 4

THIRD ROUND

Ammanford 1 **Tredegar Town** 2
Bryntirion Athletic 11 Merthyr Saints 1

Caerleon 3 Pontardawe Town 1
Cardiff Corinthians 0 **Croesyceiliog** 1
Dinas Powys 2 Ely Rangers 1
ENTO Aberaman Athletic 2 **Llanwern** 4
Goytre United 2 Bridgend Town 0
West End 3 Newport YMCA 2 *aet*

QUARTER-FINALS

Croesyceiliog 4 Llanwern 3
Dinas Powys 0 **Goytre United** 1
Tredegar Town 0 **Bryntirion Athletic** 4
West End 1 **Caerleon** 3

SEMI-FINALS

Bryntirion Athletic 2 Croesyceiliog 0
(at Taffs Well)
Caerleon 3 **Goytre United** 4 *aet*
(at Ely Rangers)

FINAL

(May 20th at Afan Lido)
Bryntirion Athletic 0 **Goytre United** 1

Division Two	P	W	D	L	F	A	Pts
Bettws	34	22	9	3	79	35	75
Barry Town	34	21	6	7	74	35	69
Cardiff Corinthians	34	19	6	9	77	59	63
West End	34	17	6	11	78	57	57
UWIC	34	15	11	8	59	42	56
Garden Village	34	16	8	10	70	59	56
Ely Rangers	34	16	6	12	63	57	54
Llanwern	34	11	14	9	58	55	47
Cwmbran Celtic	34	12	8	14	52	60	44
Caerau Ely	34	11	10	13	63	64	43
Ammanford	34	11	7	16	67	74	40
Grange Harlequins	34	10	9	15	56	65	39
Llangeinor	34	10	7	17	60	68	37
Treharris Athletic *-1*	34	10	7	17	61	94	36
Tredegar Town	34	9	7	18	55	71	34
Briton Ferry Athletic	34	8	8	18	43	63	32
Pontyclun	34	9	5	20	41	67	32
Troedyrhiw	34	8	8	18	44	75	32

RESERVES CUP

FINAL *(May 14th at Taffs Well)*
Bryntirion Athletic Res. 1 **Caerleon Res.** 2

MACWHIRTER WELSH LEAGUE DIVISION TWO CONSTITUTION 2008-09

AMMANFORD .... Rice Road, Colonel Road, Betws, Ammanford SA18 2HP 01269 592407
CAERAU ELY .... Cwrt-y-Ala, Caerau, Cardiff CF64 4HE 07788 585726
CWMBRAN CELTIC .... Celtic Park, Henllys Way, Cwmbran NP44 7LP 07796 330303
ELY RANGERS .... Station Road, Wenvoe CF5 6AG 02920 598725
GARDEN VILLAGE .... Stafford Common, Victoria Road, Gowerton, Swansea SA4 3AB 01792 533188
GARW SBGC .... Blandy Park, Pontycymmer, Bridgend CF32 8LD 07779 956926
GRANGE HARLEQUINS .... Cardiff Athletic Stadium, Leckwith Road, Cardiff CF11 8AZ 02920 225345
LLANGEINOR .... Llangeinor Park, Bettws Road, Llangeinor, Bridgend 01656 871676
LLANWERN .... Newport Stadium, Spytty Park, Langland Way, Newport NP19 4PT 07762 013310
MAESTEG PARK .... Tudor Park, St David's Place, Maesteg, Bridgend CF34 9LR .... Tel: 01656 730005
NEWCASTLE EMLYN .... Parc Emlyn, New Road, Newcastle Emlyn SA38 9BA 01239 710007
PENRHIWCEIBER RANGERS .. Glasbrook, Glasbrook Terrace, Penrhiwceiber, Mountain Ash CF45 3SY 07774 057683
PENTWYN DYNAMOS .... Pentwyn Leisure Centre, Parc Coed-y-Nant, Bryn Celyn Road, Pentwyn, Cardiff CF23 7EZ 02920 549211
PONTYPRIDD TOWN .... Ynysangharad Park, Pontypridd CF37 4PE 01443 486571
TREDEGAR TOWN .... Tredegar Leisure Complex, Stable Lane, Tredegar NP22 3BH 01495 723554
TREHARRIS ATHLETIC .... Athletic Ground, Commercial Terrace, Treharris CF46 5PY 07867 600410
UWIC .... Cyncoed Road, Cardiff CF23 6XD 02920 416155
WEST END .... Pri Deri Park, Pri Deri Footpath, Eigen Crescent, Mayhill, Swansea SA1 6LB 07754 537012/07514 077769
IN: *Garw SBGC (formerly Garw Athletic) (R), Maesteg Park (R), Newcastle Emlyn (P), Penrhiwceiber Rangers (P), Pentwyn Dynamos (P), Pontypridd Town (R)*
OUT: *Barry Town (P), Bettws (P), Briton Ferry Athletic (R), Cardiff Corinthians (P), Pontyclun (R), Troedyrhiw (R)*

	AFC Llwydcoed	Aberbargoed Buds	Abertillery Excelsior	Cwmaman Institute	Cwmamman United	Goytre	Llansawel	Llantwit Fardre	Merthyr Saints	Monmouth Town	Morriston Town	Newcastle Emlyn	Penrhiwceiber Rangers	Pentwyn Dynamos	Porthcawl Town	Risca United	Seven Sisters	Ystradgynlais
AFC Llwydcoed		1-0	7-0	3-1	2-2	1-0	3-2	4-4	1-1	2-1	6-1	5-3	0-2	2-2	2-2	0-3	6-0	3-1
Aberbargoed Buds	1-2		3-0	4-1	5-4	3-1	2-0	2-2	3-1	2-1	4-0	1-2	4-2	1-3	2-2	1-6	2-1	7-0
Abertillery Excelsior	1-5	2-8	D	2-2	3-1	0-1	1-3	0-1	2-6	3-2	5-1	0-5	2-5	0-3	1-0	0-1	1-0	2-2
Cwmaman Institute	1-2	1-1	3-2	I	4-3	5-4	1-1	1-0	1-2	2-1	2-0	2-2	4-5	2-3	7-1	2-1	2-0	5-2
Cwmamman United	4-1	2-0	6-1	1-3	V	2-6	3-0	2-1	1-7	4-1	2-1	3-6	0-2	3-1	4-5	2-0	0-1	1-0
Goytre	1-3	4-4	3-1	2-2	1-3	I	1-6	3-0	3-0	2-3	1-2	1-4	1-2	2-4	2-0	1-1	2-5	1-2
Llansawel	0-3	1-0	1-0	2-3	2-3	2-0	S	2-1	0-3	2-2	6-1	1-2	1-5	0-5	7-3	3-0	1-1	0-2
Llantwit Fardre	3-0	4-0	4-1	3-1	2-1	2-0	1-1	I	3-0	1-2	3-1	0-0	3-1	0-2	2-0	0-2	2-2	4-1
Merthyr Saints	1-2	2-4	4-3	1-1	0-5	3-0	4-2	0-7	O	1-4	5-2	1-4	2-5	4-1	2-1	3-4	4-0	2-5
Monmouth Town	2-1	1-2	1-1	2-3	2-1	0-2	3-3	2-0	5-2	N	2-0	3-2	3-4	0-1	1-2	0-1	2-2	3-3
Morriston Town	1-4	1-1	0-1	0-2	1-2	0-3	1-3	3-1	1-2	3-2		2-0	1-2	2-3	1-2	1-0	0-1	1-5
Newcastle Emlyn	2-1	3-2	8-0	2-0	4-2	6-2	3-0	0-0	3-2	1-2	3-0	T	1-2	0-1	5-1	2-1	3-0	7-1
Penrhiwceiber Rangers	4-3	3-4	5-2	3-1	6-0	4-5	3-0	1-2	0-2	3-1	6-0	4-5	H	1-3	2-2	3-2	5-1	0-1
Pentwyn Dynamos	3-1	4-2	4-0	1-7	4-3	2-2	5-0	1-1	3-0	4-4	1-0	3-1	1-5	R	1-0	4-1	4-0	9-0
Porthcawl Town	1-1	3-1	0-0	1-3	5-4	1-1	3-2	0-5	1-5	5-0	0-2	3-2			E	1-1	5-1	3-1
Risca United	1-3	0-1	2-2	1-5	3-0	1-1	3-0	2-0	3-0	2-2	1-0	3-1	2-1	1-0	1-2	E	1-0	1-2
Seven Sisters	1-0	0-1	1-0	1-1	1-1	0-4	3-2	1-2	1-2	1-2	2-2	2-2	1-1	0-2	0-3	2-0		2-2
Ystradgynlais	0-4	1-4	3-3	1-3	4-4	1-6	2-2	0-3	2-3	1-6	0-4	2-2	1-1	1-4	1-2	2-2	1-1	

Division Three

		P	W	D	L	F	A	Pts
Pentwyn Dynamos		34	24	4	6	94	49	76
Newcastle Emlyn		34	21	5	8	96	54	68
Penrhiwceiber Rangers		34	21	3	10	99	60	66
AFC Llwydcoed		34	19	6	9	84	52	63
Cwmaman Institute		34	18	7	9	84	60	61
Aberbargoed Buds		34	18	5	11	82	61	59
Llantwit Fardre		34	16	7	11	63	43	55
Porthcawl Town		34	15	7	12	66	73	52
Risca United		34	15	6	13	54	47	51
Monmouth Town		34	13	7	14	73	64	46
Cwmamman United		34	14	3	17	79	85	45
Goytre		34	11	6	17	69	75	39
Merthyr Saints	-10	34	15	2	17	74	85	37
Llansawel		34	10	6	18	58	76	36
Seven Sisters	-3	34	7	10	17	35	68	28
Ystradgynlais		34	6	10	18	54	105	28
Abertillery Excelsior		34	6	6	22	42	101	24
Morriston Town		34	6	2	26	37	85	20

Reserve Division Central

		P	W	D	L	F	A	Pts
Bryntirion Athletic Res.		14	12	0	2	40	12	36
Dinas Powys Res.		14	9	2	3	37	13	29
Cambrian & Clydach Vale BGC Res.		14	8	2	4	30	15	26
Afan Lido Res.		14	7	2	5	26	15	23
Llantwit Fardre Res.		14	3	7	4	22	29	16
Cardiff Corinthians Res.		14	2	5	7	19	38	11
AFC Llwydcoed Res.		14	1	4	9	13	38	7
Pontyclun Res.		14	0	6	8	16	43	6

Reserve Division East

		P	W	D	L	F	A	Pts
Newport YMCA Res.		18	15	1	2	74	22	46
Caldicot Town Res.		18	10	5	3	55	29	35
Croesyceiliog Res.		18	10	2	6	47	38	32
Ely Rangers Res.		18	10	1	7	43	34	31
Cwmbran Celtic Res.		18	7	4	7	48	33	25
Caerleon Res.		18	5	1	12	49	62	16
Caerau Ely Res.		18	5	1	12	49	62	16
Abertillery Excelsior Res.		18	4	4	10	32	80	16
Risca United Res.		18	5	2	11	22	42	11
Aberbargoed Buds Res.		18	3	1	14	27	63	10

Reserve Division West

		P	W	D	L	F	A	Pts
Garden Village Res.		18	16	2	0	75	10	50
Pontardawe Town Res.		18	13	1	4	44	21	40
Neath Athletic Res.	-3	18	12	1	5	62	43	34
Briton Ferry Athletic Res.		18	7	2	9	40	38	23
Ammanford Res.		18	7	2	9	37	42	23
Llansawel Res.		18	6	3	9	37	45	21
Morriston Town Res.		18	5	3	10	22	39	18
Newcastle Emlyn Res.		18	5	3	10	29	50	18
Ystradgynlais Res.		18	4	4	10	35	59	16
Cwmamman United Res.		18	3	3	12	29	63	12

MACWHIRTER WELSH LEAGUE DIVISION THREE CONSTITUTION 2008-09

AFC LLWYDCOED .... Llwydcoed Football Ground, Llwydcoed, Aberdare CF44 0UT 01685 873924
AFC PORTH .... Dinas Park, Dinas, Porth, Rhondda CF40 1JG 07974 252940
ABERBARGOED BUDS .... Recreation Ground, AberbargoedCF81 9AY 01443 838392
BRITON FERRY ATHLETIC .... Old Road, Briton Ferry, Neath SA11 2HA 07912 408533
CWMAMAN INSTITUTE .... Canolfan Cwmaman, Glanaman Road, Cwmaman, Aberdare CF44 6HY ... 07786 588890
CWMAMMAN UNITED .... Grenig Park, Penpound Lane, Glanaman, Ammanford SA18 1YU 07977 925808
GOYTRE .... Plough Road, Penperlleni, Pontypool NP4 0AL 07790 419852
LLANSAWEL .... Cwrt Herbert, Neath Abbey Road, Neath SA10 7BE 01639 630013
LLANTWIT FARDRE.............. Tonteg Park, Church Village, Pontypridd CF31 1ND 01443 207393
MERTHYR SAINTS .... ICI Pavilion, Pant, Merthyr Tydfil CF48 2SR 07962 016872
MONMOUTH TOWN .... Chippenham Sports Ground, Monmouth NP25 5EY 01600 772389
NEWPORT CIVIL SERVICE ......Civil Service Sports Ground (PlayFootball.net), Shannon Close, Bettws NP20 6LX 0845 257 7000
PONTYCLUN .... Ivor Park, Cowbridge Road, Pontyclun CF72 9BS 07967 360402
PORTHCAWL TOWN .... Locks Lane, Porthcawl CF36 3HY 07866 545830
RISCA UNITED .... Ty Isaf Park, Pontymister Road, Risca, Newport NP11 6ND 07950 753629
SEVEN SISTERS .... Welfare Ground, Seven Sisters, Neath SA10 9EY 01639 700354
TROEDYRHIW .... Troedyrhiw B&GC, The Willows, Bridge Street, Troedyrhiw, Merthyr Tydfil CF48 4DX ... 01443 692198
YSTRADGYNLAIS .... Recreation Ground, Ynyscedwyn Road, Ystradgynlais, Swansea SA9 1BH 07973 523839

IN: AFC Porth (P – South Wales Amateur League Division One), Briton Ferry Athletic (R), Newport Civil Service (P – Gwent County League Division One), Pontyclun (R), Troedyrhiw (R)
OUT: Abertillery Excelsior (R – Gwent County League Division One), Morriston Town (R – Swansea Senior League Division One), Newcastle Emlyn (P), Penrhiwceiber Rangers (P), Pentwyn Dynamos (P)

WWW.CHERRYRED.CO.UK

WELSH NATIONAL LEAGUE
(WREXHAM AREA)

	Acrefair Youth	Borras Park Albion	Brickfield Rangers	Brymbo	Castell Alun Colts	Cefn United	Chirk AAA	Coedpoeth United	Corwen Amateurs	Hawarden Rangers	Llangollen Town	Llay Welfare	Mold Alexandra	Overton Recreation	Penycae	Rhos Aelwyd
Acrefair Youth	*P*	3-1	3-0	0-7	1-1	1-4	0-4	2-0	2-2	2-6	0-2	1-4	1-3	2-0	1-2	0-11
Borras Park Albion	3-2	*R*	1-0	0-1	2-3	2-0	1-2	3-4	0-5	0-4	1-2	1-1	0-2	1-2	1-4	3-4
Brickfield Rangers	2-7	1-8	*E*	0-6	0-8	1-6	0-6	5-7	0-6	0-4	3-2	1-5	2-8	0-7	3-2	0-4
Brymbo	6-0	1-0	9-1	*M*	4-0	1-1	7-0	4-1	2-1	0-1	6-0	2-0	2-2	1-0	6-0	3-1
Castell Alun Colts	3-1	4-1	3-1	0-4	*I*	2-1	1-4	3-2	4-1	0-2	1-0	1-3	1-2	1-2	4-2	0-3
Cefn United	6-2	2-0	16-0	0-1	1-1	*E*	4-3	4-2	1-4	3-1	3-2	6-4	1-1	6-0	2-3	1-6
Chirk AAA	3-2	4-1	4-0	0-4	0-1	1-2	*R*	0-4	0-4	3-3	2-1	3-2	0-4	1-1	3-2	1-2
Coedpoeth United	2-0	3-2	13-0	0-5	1-3	4-1	2-1		0-1	2-1	1-2	1-2	1-6	2-2	1-4	0-0
Corwen Amateurs	6-0	4-5	6-1	0-3	4-2	2-2	2-2	2-0	*D*	2-1	3-2	3-1	2-3	4-0	4-1	2-0
Hawarden Rangers	2-1	3-2	3-1	1-3	1-1	4-1	1-1	3-2	0-1	*I*	3-0	1-4	1-1	2-1	3-2	5-1
Llangollen Town	1-2	1-2	3-0	0-6	2-2	0-4	1-4	2-3	0-2	0-3	*V*	1-6	2-3	2-2	1-4	3-2
Llay Welfare	6-0	2-2	3-0	0-1	1-4	5-2	2-1	0-4	3-3	1-0	5-1	*I*	2-4	1-3	4-0	2-2
Mold Alexandra	2-0	4-0	7-0	2-2	7-0	2-0	3-3	3-0	4-2	2-1	3-0	*S*	1-0	1-3	1-5	
Overton Recreation	2-1	3-1	4-0	0-2	6-2	4-3	2-1	4-1	2-6	1-2	4-4	0-1	3-5	*I*	2-3	5-5
Penycae	6-0	6-1	7-0	2-3	3-0	4-3	4-3	1-1	3-2	2-1	1-0	1-2	1-1	3-2	*O*	1-1
Rhos Aelwyd	13-0	3-1	10-0	3-1	7-2	3-3	4-2	4-1	3-2	2-1	4-1	3-1	2-0	0-3	8-2	*N*

PREM. DIV CUP

FIRST ROUND
Brymbo 8 Brickfield Rangers 1
Castell Alun Colts 0 **Borras Park Albion** 0 *aet* (3-4p)
Chirk AAA 2 Coedpoeth United 1
Corwen Amateurs 3 Cefn United 2
Harwarden Rangers 3 Acrefair Youth 0
Llay Welfare 2 Llangollen Town 1
Mold Alexandra 2 Overton Recreation 0
Penycae 4 Rhos Aelwyd 1
QUARTER-FINALS
Borras Park Albion 1 **Corwen Amateurs** 3
Brymbo 2 Llay Welfare 1
Hawarden Rangers 3 **Mold Alexandra** 3 *aet* (2-4p)
Penycae 3 Chirk AAA 0
SEMI-FINALS
Corwen Amateurs 0 **Brymbo** 2
Penycae 1 **Mold Alexandra** 2
FINAL
(May 2nd at NEWI Cefn Druids)
Mold Alexandra 2 **Brymbo** 3

Premier Division		P	W	D	L	F	A	Pts
Brymbo	-3	30	25	3	2	103	16	75
Mold Alexandra		30	20	6	4	87	38	66
Rhos Aelwyd		30	20	5	5	116	47	65
Corwen Amateurs		30	19	4	7	87	43	61
Penycae		30	17	3	10	79	64	54
Hawarden Rangers		30	16	4	10	65	44	52
Llay Welfare		30	15	4	11	73	55	49
Cefn United		30	13	6	11	90	66	45
Castell Alun Colts		30	12	5	13	58	70	41
Overton Recreation		30	11	6	13	67	68	39
Chirk AAA		30	11	5	14	62	67	38
Coedpoeth United	-3	30	11	3	16	65	70	33
Borras Park Albion		30	6	2	22	46	80	20
Llangollen Town		30	5	3	22	39	84	18
Acrefair Youth	-3	30	6	2	22	37	110	17
Brickfield Rangers		30	2	1	27	26	178	7

DIV ONE CUP

FINAL
(May 6th at Llangollen Town)
Penley 0 **Bala Town Res.** 2

DIV TWO CUP

FINAL *(April 28th at Llay Welfare)*
Buckley Town Res. 0 **Garden Village** 1

DIVISION THREE CUP

FINAL
(May 10th at Overton Recreation)
Borras Park Albion Res. 0
Communities First 3

HORACE WYNNE CUP

FINAL
(May 16th at Llay Welfare)
Garden Village 4 Penley 0

WELSH NATIONAL LEAGUE (WREXHAM AREA) PREMIER DIVISION CONSTITUTION 2008-09

ACREFAIR YOUTH . . . . The Bont Playing Field, Froncysyllte, Wrexham . . . . None
BORRAS PARK ALBION . . . . Dean Road, Wrexham LL13 9EF . . . . None
BRICKFIELD RANGERS . . . . Court Road, Wrexham LL13 7SN . . . . None
BRYMBO . . . . Brymbo Sports Complex, College Hill, Tanyfron, Wrexham LL11 5TF 01978 752577
CASTELL ALUN COLTS . . . . Castell Alun Sports Centre, Fagl Lane, Hope, Wrexham LL12 9PY . . . . None
CEFN UNITED . . . . Church Field, Rhosymedre, Wrexham LL14 3EF. . . . . None
CHIRK AAA . . . . Holyhead Road, Chirk, Wrexham LL14 5NA 01691 773676
COEDPOETH UNITED . . . . Pengelli Playing Fields, Coedpoeth, Wrexham . . . . None
CORWEN AMATEURS . . . . War Memorial Park, Green Lane, Corwen LL21 0DN . . . . None
HAWARDEN RANGERS . . . . Gladstone Playing Fields, Hawarden . . . . None
LLANGOLLEN TOWN . . . . Tower Field, Dinbren Road, Llangollen LL20 8TF . . . . None
LLAY WELFARE . . . . The Ring, Llay, Wrexham LL12 0TN 01978 852286
OVERTON RECREATION . . . . Recreation Ground, Overton-on-Dee, Wrexham . . . . None
PENYCAE . . . . Afoneitha Road, Penycae, Wrexham LL14 2PF . . . . None
RHOS AELWYD . . . . Ponciau Park, Clarke Street, Ponciau, Wrexham LL14 1RT . . . . None
VENTURE COMMUNITY . . . . Queenway, Heol Cefn, Gwersyllt, Wrexham LL11 4HQ . . . . None
IN: Venture Community (P)
OUT: Mold Alexandra (P – Cymru Alliance)

Division One	P	W	D	L	F	A	Pts
Airbus UK Broughton Res.	24	19	2	3	74	32	59
Venture Community	24	17	0	7	55	36	51
Bala Town Res.	24	15	1	8	49	25	46
New Brighton Villa	24	14	3	7	56	31	45
Penley	24	13	4	7	63	37	43
Penycae Res.	24	11	4	9	45	47	37
Gresford Athletic Res.	24	10	4	10	43	42	34
Ruthin Town Res.	24	8	6	10	43	45	30
Rhos Aelwyd Res.	24	7	6	11	37	53	27
Glyn Ceiriog	24	5	7	12	47	68	26
Johnstown Youth	24	6	2	16	41	60	20
Penyffordd	24	4	5	15	59	77	17
Llanuwchllyn	24	3	2	19	32	91	11

Brynteg Village – record expunged

Division Two	P	W	D	L	F	A	Pts
Garden Village	28	21	4	3	95	32	67
Hawarden Rangers Res.	28	21	3	4	103	39	66
Brymbo Res.	28	19	4	5	89	32	61
Llay Welfare Res.	28	17	6	5	98	44	57
Buckley Town Res.	28	17	4	7	78	35	55
Mold Juniors	28	18	1	9	84	48	55
Mold Alexandra Res.	28	14	5	9	77	69	47
Gresford Ath. Colts	-3	28	13	2	13	69	69	38
Borras Park Albion Res.	28	12	2	14	66	71	38
Holt Nomads	28	11	2	15	51	74	35
Ruthin Town Colts	28	7	3	18	65	83	24
Llangollen Town Res.	28	7	3	18	53	72	24
Acrefair Youth Res.	-3	28	6	4	18	54	99	19
Corwen Amateurs Res.	28	3	1	24	33	113	10
Brickfield Rangers Res.	28	2	0	26	18	153	6

Division Three	P	W	D	L	F	A	Pts
FC Cefn	30	23	4	3	94	41	73
Gwersyllt Athletic	30	23	3	4	134	42	72
NEWI Cefn Druids Res.	30	22	3	5	114	48	69
Mynydd Isa Res.	30	19	6	5	89	41	63
Communities First	30	17	5	8	70	47	56
Penley Res.	30	16	2	12	76	56	50
Hawarden Rgrs Colts	-3	30	15	3	12	68	74	45
Chirk AAA Res.	30	10	9	11	70	71	39
Johnstown Youth Res.	30	11	5	14	56	68	38
Lex XI Res.	30	10	4	16	60	70	34
Penyffordd Res.	30	8	5	17	54	103	29
Overton Recreation Res.	30	7	6	17	53	90	27
Borras Pk Albion Colts	-3	30	8	5	17	59	92	26
Coedpoeth United Res.	30	8	1	21	48	92	25
Garden Village Res.	30	6	6	18	38	82	24
Glyn Ceiriog Res.	30	1	3	26	40	106	10

Caergwrle – record expunged

WELSH PREMIER LEAGUE

Results grid (home team in row, away team in column). Columns are numbered as keyed below.

Key: 1 Aberystwyth Town · 2 Airbus UK Broughton · 3 Bangor City · 4 Caernarfon Town · 5 Caersws · 6 Carmarthen Town · 7 Connah's Quay Nomads · 8 Haverfordwest County · 9 Llanelli · 10 Llangefni Town · 11 NEWI Cefn Druids · 12 Neath Athletic · 13 Newtown · 14 Port Talbot Town · 15 Porthmadog · 16 Rhyl · 17 The New Saints · 18 Welshpool Town

	1	2	3	4	5	6	7	8	9	10	11	12	13	14	15	16	17	18
Aberystwyth Town	—	0-0	4-0	2-1	0-2	6-1	2-3	1-2	1-0	3-2	1-0	1-2	2-2	2-1	2-4	0-0	5-1	2-3
Airbus UK Broughton	1-1	—	1-0	1-2	0-2	0-1	0-0	3-1	0-1	1-3	3-2	2-1	1-1	2-0	1-0	0-2	2-0	1-1
Bangor City	1-0	5-0	—	5-1	1-1	0-1	3-2	2-0	1-1	2-2	5-1	1-1	2-2	2-0	0-0	1-2	1-2	1-0
Caernarfon Town	1-0	0-3	0-4	—	2-0	2-1	1-1	1-2	3-4	1-0	1-1	1-2	0-0	2-4	3-1	0-1	1-7	1-1
Caersws	1-1	2-3	1-0	0-1	—	1-2	3-4	1-2	0-5	1-1	1-2	2-2	1-0	2-4	1-4	2-7	1-2	0-3
Carmarthen Town	0-3	2-1	2-1	1-1	1-3	—	8-0	2-1	1-2	2-2	4-1	1-1	2-1	0-0	0-0	0-0	0-3	5-2
Connah's Quay Nomads	1-2	1-0	0-7	1-0	1-0	4-3	—	1-1	0-1	2-0	2-1	2-0	1-1	1-2	0-1	0-5	1-3	3-3
Haverfordwest County	3-1	4-0	1-1	1-1	1-0	2-2	6-2	—	1-4	5-1	3-0	1-2	2-3	3-2	2-1	1-1	0-4	1-0
Llanelli	1-0	1-0	0-2	5-1	1-1	4-1	4-0	4-2	—	5-0	1-0	3-3	5-0	1-2	8-0	2-1	4-0	3-0
Llangefni Town	3-0	0-3	0-1	1-2	0-1	0-3	1-2	2-1	1-5	—	2-0	4-2	2-3	1-4	4-1	0-3	0-3	0-1
NEWI Cefn Druids	0-2	4-1	1-6	5-1	4-0	3-1	5-2	1-0	2-5	2-1	—	0-2	3-0	1-1	0-1	1-4	1-0	0-2
Neath Athletic	2-2	2-1	1-0	3-2	2-2	1-2	4-0	2-1	2-0	3-0	3-0	—	2-0	2-1	0-2	1-1	2-2	2-5
Newtown	1-2	1-1	2-2	3-1	2-2	0-1	4-1	1-4	3-5	2-1	1-0	3-0	—	4-2	0-0	0-2	0-0	1-2
Port Talbot Town	2-6	2-2	0-0	1-3	0-1	1-2	3-3	0-2	2-4	2-4	1-2	0-2	2-3	—	1-2	1-0	0-1	1-1
Porthmadog	2-1	0-0	0-0	2-1	3-1	2-0	2-1	2-0	3-1	5-1	3-3	5-1	4-2		—	1-2	1-0	1-1
Rhyl	0-0	2-1	1-2	3-1	2-1	2-0	1-0	2-0	1-2	4-1	0-1	1-0	2-1	1-0	5-0	—	0-1	1-1
The New Saints	1-0	0-0	2-1	4-0	6-0	0-3	3-1	6-2	3-0	7-1	3-0	3-1	6-0	4-1	2-1	1-0	—	2-0
Welshpool Town	2-1	0-1	2-0	2-4	1-1	2-2	1-1	2-1	3-3	3-0	0-1	1-2	2-1	0-3	1-3	1-0	0-3	—

League Table

	P	HOME W	HOME D	HOME L	HOME F	HOME A	AWAY W	AWAY D	AWAY L	AWAY F	AWAY A	TOTAL W	TOTAL D	TOTAL L	TOTAL F	TOTAL A	Pts
Llanelli	34	13	2	2	52	13	14	2	1	47	22	27	4	3	99	35	85
The New Saints	34	15	1	1	53	11	10	2	5	32	19	25	3	6	85	30	78
Rhyl	34	12	2	3	29	12	9	4	4	31	12	21	6	7	60	24	69
Port Talbot Town	34	10	5	2	36	18	7	3	7	21	30	17	8	9	57	48	59
Bangor City	34	8	7	2	34	16	7	3	7	28	15	15	10	9	62	31	55
Carmarthen Town	34	7	6	4	31	22	8	3	6	28	25	15	9	10	59	47	54
Neath Athletic	34	9	4	4	31	23	6	5	6	26	29	15	9	10	57	52	54
Haverfordwest County	34	9	3	5	36	25	5	2	10	25	34	14	5	15	61	59	47
Aberystwyth Town	34	8	3	6	35	23	5	4	8	22	22	13	7	14	57	45	46
Welshpool Town	34	6	4	7	23	27	6	6	5	26	25	12	10	12	49	52	46
Airbus UK Broughton	34	7	4	6	19	18	4	5	8	17	26	11	9	14	36	44	42
NEWI Cefn Druids	34	9	1	7	33	29	3	1	13	12	37	12	2	20	45	66	38
Newtown	34	6	5	6	28	26	3	5	9	19	40	9	10	15	47	66	37
Caernarfon Town	34	5	4	8	20	32	5	2	10	22	42	10	6	18	42	74	36
Connah's Quay Nomads	34	7	3	7	21	30	2	4	11	21	55	9	7	18	42	85	34
Porthmadog	34	1	4	12	19	38	6	2	9	29	32	7	6	21	48	70	27
Caersws	34	2	3	12	20	43	4	5	8	17	29	6	8	20	37	72	26
Llangefni Town	34	5	0	12	21	35	2	3	12	18	47	7	3	24	39	82	24

WWW.CHERRYRED.CO.UK

DATES & GATES

	Aberystwyth Town	Airbus UK Broughton	Bangor City	Caernarfon Town	Caersws	Carmarthen Town	Connah's Quay Nomads	Haverfordwest County	Llanelli	Llangefni Town	NEWI Cefn Druids	Neath Athletic	Newtown	Port Talbot Town	Porthmadog	Rhyl	The New Saints	Welshpool Town
Aberystwyth Town		18 Aug 168	26 Jan 491	12 Apr 210	18 Sep 211	7 Mar 354	20 Oct 135	1 Jan 281	14 Sep 407	22 Mar 139	12 Jan 114	23 Nov 218	1 Mar 301	28 Sep 207	16 Feb 207	10 Nov 467	22 Dec 256	5 Jan 241
Airbus UK Broughton	15 Dec 223		22 Sep 276	27 Oct 233	29 Sep 83	22 Dec 207	23 Feb 376	26 Oct 223	5 Apr 301	15 Feb 368	1 Jan 141	20 Oct 152	10 Nov 208	1 Mar 189	9 Sep 143	28 Sep 504	1 Dec 309	19 Apr 110
Bangor City	1 Dec 330	8 Mar 378		1 Jan 782	9 Nov 244	22 Nov 360	24 Mar 242	9 Nov 115	11 Apr 377	13 Oct 701	22 Mar 198	24 Mar 163	18 Aug 450	20 Oct 239	8 Mar 722	12 Jan 409	15 Sep 174	18 Nov 108
Caernarfon Town	1 Dec 210	27 Oct 92	1 Jan 709		26 Dec 378	12 Jan 138	19 Apr 495	5 Feb 121	19 Apr 122	1 Jan 268	14 Sep 175	26 Jan 181	13 Oct 201	15 Dec 413	18 Nov 946	15 Mar 497	15 Sep 108	18 Nov 174
Caersws	22 Jan 207	29 Sep 83	9 Nov 244	5 Feb 121		8 Mar 272	10 Nov 137	1 Mar 340	19 Oct 157	5 Jan 310	15 Dec 287	22 Sep 403	5 Jan 530	26 Dec 277	27 Oct 267	15 Sep 568	10 Nov 275	18 Nov 172
Carmarthen Town	26 Oct 376	22 Dec 207	22 Nov 360	9 Feb 121	8 Mar 272		15 Mar 137	12 Jan 138	1 Sep 365	12 Oct 273	15 Feb 248	26 Jan 264	29 Sep 485	20 Oct 384	16 Apr 310	18 Nov 601	22 Dec 121	13 Oct 165
Connah's Quay Nomads	23 Feb 223	23 Feb 376	24 Mar 242	19 Apr 495	10 Nov 137	15 Mar 137		1 Jan 235	15 Sep 182	15 Sep 121	1 Sep 203	1 Dec 278	20 Oct 248	18 Nov 333	16 Apr 203	15 Dec 302	4 Mar 212	8 Feb 282
Haverfordwest County	26 Dec 281	26 Oct 223	9 Nov 115	5 Feb 121	1 Mar 340	12 Jan 138	15 Sep 121		14 Mar 321	22 Jan 182	10 Nov 215	15 Feb 113	26 Feb 188	25 Aug 257	18 Sep 227	26 Oct 310	12 Apr 221	8 Feb 382
Llanelli	25 Mar 348	5 Apr 301	11 Apr 377	9 Feb 202	19 Oct 157	1 Sep 365	15 Sep 182	14 Mar 321		1 Jan 393	9 Feb 203	1 Sep 249	23 Jan 348	26 Oct 702	22 Mar 514	22 Nov 414	4 Mar 301	15 Dec 323
Llangefni Town	18 Nov 227	15 Feb 368	13 Oct 701	1 Jan 268	5 Jan 310	12 Oct 273	22 Jan 121	22 Jan 182	1 Jan 393		9 Feb 107	15 Dec 188	5 Apr 196	15 Feb 140	15 Mar 157	15 Dec 382	23 Feb 155	26 Oct 289
NEWI Cefn Druids	9 Sep 274	1 Jan 141	22 Mar 198	14 Sep 198	15 Dec 287	15 Feb 248	1 Sep 203	10 Nov 215	9 Feb 203	9 Feb 107		1 Sep 188	25 Mar 181	24 Nov 301	24 Nov 203	26 Oct 259	22 Sep 212	21 Dec 200
Neath Athletic	5 Apr 178	20 Oct 152	24 Mar 163	26 Jan 181	22 Sep 403	26 Jan 264	5 Apr 278	15 Feb 157	1 Sep 249	15 Dec 188	1 Sep 188		23 Jan 220	25 Aug 124	26 Feb 257	15 Feb 227	15 Sep 212	23 Feb 160
Newtown	19 Apr 312	10 Nov 208	18 Aug 835	13 Oct 201	5 Jan 530	29 Sep 485	20 Oct 157	26 Feb 188	23 Jan 322	5 Apr 196	25 Mar 181	23 Jan 220		26 Jan 345	26 Dec 333	23 Nov 260	12 Apr 302	24 Nov 361
Port Talbot Town	8 Feb 236	1 Mar 123	20 Oct 315	15 Dec 184	26 Dec 227	20 Oct 259	18 Nov 333	25 Aug 257	26 Oct 324	15 Feb 140	24 Nov 114	25 Aug 124	26 Jan 345		31 Aug 301	24 Nov 382	12 Apr 259	15 Apr 169
Porthmadog	13 Oct 273	15 Sep 97	8 Mar 568	18 Nov 310	27 Oct 267	23 Nov 184	13 Oct 179	18 Sep 227	22 Mar 514	15 Mar 158	24 Nov 260	26 Feb 302	26 Dec 258	31 Aug 301		12 Dec 155	15 Sep 211	22 Sep 159
Rhyl	15 Mar 333	8 Feb 342	12 Jan 502	15 Apr 497	15 Sep 568	19 Apr 327	15 Dec 327	18 Nov 310	18 Mar 414	15 Sep 382	26 Oct 259	12 Dec 258	18 Mar 305	12 Jan 382	12 Dec 309		24 Nov 108	23 Feb 301
The New Saints	26 Aug 528	11 Apr 214	10 Nov 475	19 Apr 502	5 Jan 275	16 Feb 308	28 Sep 212	14 Apr 221	19 Aug 301	28 Sep 155	24 Nov 155	15 Sep 212	22 Mar 182	8 Mar 402	15 Sep 155	22 Sep 236		20 Oct 120
Welshpool Town	1 Sep 259	7 Dec 147	7 Sep 121	22 Mar 121	7 Sep 121	16 Feb 298	14 Apr 221	28 Sep 212	24 Nov 221	26 Oct 289	21 Dec 200	23 Feb 160	24 Nov 268	10 Nov 169	22 Sep 159	24 Sep 301	26 Dec 471	1 Jan 453

PRINCIPALITY BUILDING SOCIETY
WELSH PREMIER LEAGUE CONSTITUTION 2008-09

ABERYSTWYTH TOWN
Park Avenue Stadium, Maesgogerddan, Aberystwyth, Ceredigion SY23 1PG
Tel: 01970 617939   Club: 01970 630380   Fax: 01970 617939
Manager: Brian Coyne   www.atfc.org.uk   Colours: Black & green, black

AIRBUS UK BROUGHTON
The Airfield, Broughton, Flintshire CH4 0BA
Tel: 01244 522356
Manager: Craig Harrison   www.airbusfc.co.uk   Colours: Blue

BANGOR CITY
The Stadium, Farrar Road, Bangor, Gwynedd LL57 1LJ
Tel: 01248 725745   Fax: 01248 724182
Manager: Neville Powell   www.bangorcityfc.com   Colours: Blue

CAERNARFON TOWN
The Oval, Marcus Street, Caernarfon, Gwynedd LL55 2HT
Tel: 01286 676885   Club: 01286 674620   Fax: 01286 675002
Manager: David Rowe   www.caernarfontown.net   Colours: Yellow & green

CAERSWS
Recreation Ground, Bridge Street, Caersws, Powys SY17 5DT
Tel: 01686 688753
Manager: David Taylor   www.caersws-fc.com   Colours: Blue & white

CARMARTHEN TOWN
Richmond Park, Priory Street, Carmarthen, Carmarthenshire SA31 1HZ
Tel: 01267 222851   Fax: 01267 222851
Manager: Deryn Brace   www.carmarthentownafc.net   Colours: Old gold & black

GAP CONNAH'S QUAY
Deeside Stadium, Kelsterton Road, Connah's Quay, Deeside CH5 4BR
Tel: 01244 834546   Fax: 01244 814305
Manager: Steve O'Shaughnessy   www.gap-fc.co.uk   Colours: White & black

HAVERFORDWEST COUNTY
New Bridge Meadow, Bridge Meadow Lane, Haverfordwest, Pembrokeshire SA61 2EX
Tel: 01437 769048   Fax: 01437 779076
Manager: Derek Brazil   www.haverfordwestcounty.co.uk   Colours: Royal blue

LLANELLI
Stebonheath Park, Penallt Road, Stebonheath, Llanelli, Carmarthenshire SA15 1EY
Tel: 01554 772973   Club: 01554 773847   Fax: 01554 772973
Manager: Peter Nicholas   www.llanelliafc.org   Colours: Red

NEWI CEFN DRUIDS
Plas Kynaston Lane, Plas Kynaston, Cefn Mawr, Wrexham, Denbighshire LL14 3PY
Tel: 01978 824332   Club: 01978 824279   Fax: 01978 824332
Manager: Lee Jones/Waynne Phillips   www.cefndruidsafc.co.uk   Colours: Black & white

NEATH ATHLETIC
Llandarcy Park, Llandarcy, Neath, West Glamorgan SA10 6JD
Tel: 01792 812036
Manager: Andrew Dyer   www.neathathletic.ik.com   Colours: Yellow & blue

WWW.CHERRYRED.CO.UK

NEWTOWN
GF Grigg Latham Park, Park Lane, Newtown, Powys SY1 6XX

Tel: 01686 623120   Club: 01686 626159   Fax: 01686 623120
Manager: Darren Ryan   www.newtownafc.co.uk   Colours: Red

PORT TALBOT TOWN
The RE/MAX Stadium, Victoria Road, Aberavon,
Port Talbot, West Glamorgan SA12 6AD

Tel: 01639 882465   Fax: 01639 886991
Manager: Nicky Tucker   www.portttalbottown.co.uk   Colours: Blue

PORTHMADOG
Y Traeth, Porthmadog, Gwynedd LL49 9PP
Tel: 01766 514687

Manager: Paul Whelan   www.porthmadogfc.com   Colours: Red & black

PRESTATYN TOWN
Bastion Road, Prestatyn, Clwyd LL17 7ET
Tel: 01745 856905

Manager: Neil Gibson   www.prestatyntownfootballclub.co.uk   Colours: Red

RHYL
Belle Vue Stadium, Grange Road, Rhyl, Clwyd LL18 4BT

Tel: 01745 338327   Fax: 01745 338664
Manager: Allan Bickerstaff   www.rhylfc.com   Colours: White & black

THE NEW SAINTS
Park Hall, Burma Road, Oswestry, Shropshire SY11 4AS

Tel: 01691 684840   Fax: 01691 659553
Manager: Andy Cale   www.saints-alive.co.uk   Colours: Green & white

WELSHPOOL TOWN
Maesydre Recreation Grounds, Howells Drive, Welshpool, Powys SY21 7SU
Tel: 01938 553027

Manager: Tomi Morgan   www.welshpooltownfc.co.uk   Colours: White & black

IN: Prestatyn Town (P – Cymru Alliance)
OUT: Llangefni Town (R – Cymru Alliance)
Connah's Quay Nomads become Gap Connah's Quay

WWW.NLNEWSDESK.CO.UK

WELSH PREMIER TEAMS IN EUROPE

CHAMPIONS LEAGUE
FIRST QUALIFYING ROUND
1st Leg: *(July 17 at Newtown)*
THE NEW SAINTS 3 Ventspils 2 *Att* 649
2nd Leg: *(July 25 at Ventspils)*
Ventspils 2 THE NEW SAINTS 1 *Att* 1,500
(Ventspils win on away goals)

INTERTOTO CUP
FIRST ROUND
1st Leg: *(June 24 at FK Vetra)*
FK Vetra 3 LLANELLI 1 *Att* 500
2nd Leg: *(July 1 at Carmarthen Town)*
LLANELLI 5 **FK Vetra** 3 *Att* 650
(FK Vetra win on away goals)

U E F A CUP

FIRST QUALIFYING ROUND
1st Leg: *(July 17 at Carmarthen Town)*
CARMARTHEN TOWN 0 SK Brann 8 *Att* 769
2nd Leg: *(August 2 at Brann)*
SK Brann 6 CARMARTHEN TOWN 3 *Att* 4,597

1st Leg: *(July 17 at Rhyl)*
RHYL 3 FK Haka 1 *Att* 1,787
2nd Leg: *(August 2 at FK Haka)*
FK Haka 2 RHYL 0 *Att* 1,565
(FK Haka win on away goals)

LEAGUE CUP

GROUP 1

	P	W	D	L	F	A	Pts
Llangefni Town	4	4	0	0	10	4	12
Porthmadog	4	1	1	2	8	8	4
Caernarfon Town	4	0	1	3	7	13	1

Porthmadog 1 Llangefni Town 2 *(Aug 21)* — Att: 231
Caernarfon Town 2 Porthmadog 2 *(Sep 4)* — Att: 177
Llangefni Town 3 Caernarfon Town 1 *(Sep 26)* — Att: 207
Llangefni Town 2 Porthmadog 0 *(Oct 10)* — Att: 264
Porthmadog 5 Caernarfon Town 2 *(Oct 17)* — Att: 149
Caernarfon Town 2 Llangefni Town 3 *(Oct 31)* — Att: 175

GROUP 2

	P	W	D	L	F	A	Pts
Rhyl	4	3	1	0	10	3	10
Bangor City	4	2	1	1	8	2	7
Connah's Quay Nomads	4	0	0	4	2	15	0

Bangor City 0 Rhyl 1 *(Aug 21)* — Att: 562
Connah's Quay Nomads 0 Bangor City 3 *(Sep 4)* — Att: 152
Rhyl 6 Connah's Quay Nomads 1 *(Sep 25)* — Att: 261
Rhyl 1 Bangor City 1 *(Oct 9)* — Att: 670
Bangor City 4 Connah's Quay Nomads 0 *(Oct 23)* — Att: 290
Connah's Quay Nomads 1 Rhyl 2 *(Oct 30)* — Att: 219

GROUP 3

	P	W	D	L	F	A	Pts
The New Saints	4	3	0	1	7	4	9
NEWI Cefn Druids	4	2	1	1	3	2	7
Airbus UK Broughton	4	0	1	3	2	6	1

Airbus UK Broughton 2 The New Saints 3 *(Aug 21)* — Att: 142
NEWI Cefn Druids 1 Airbus UK Broughton 0 *(Sep 4)* — Att: 169
The New Saints 1 NEWI Cefn Druids 0 *(Sep 25)* — Att: 307
The New Saints 2 Airbus UK Broughton 0 *(Oct 9)* — Att: 272
Airbus UK Broughton 0 NEWI Cefn Druids 0 *(Oct 23)* — Att: 69
NEWI Cefn Druids 2 The New Saints 1 *(Oct 30)* — Att: 152

GROUP 4

	P	W	D	L	F	A	Pts
Welshpool Town	4	2	2	0	8	5	8
Caersws	4	2	1	1	10	6	7
Newtown	4	0	1	3	3	10	1

Caersws 0 Welshpool Town 0 *(Aug 21)* — Att: 275
Newtown 1 Caersws 5 *(Sep 4)* — Att: 275
Welshpool Town 1 Newtown 0 *(Sep 26)* — Att: 216
Welshpool Town 5 Caersws 3 *(Oct 10)* — Att: 140
Caersws 2 Newtown 0 *(Oct 23)* — Att: 194
Newtown 2 Welshpool Town 2 *(Oct 30)* — Att: 145

GROUP 5

	P	W	D	L	F	A	Pts
Carmarthen Town	4	3	1	0	17	4	10
Aberystwyth Town	4	2	1	1	10	5	7
Haverfordwest County	4	0	0	4	3	21	0

Aberystwyth Town 1 Carmarthen Town 1 *(Aug 21)* — Att: 263
Haverfordwest County 1 Aberystwyth Town 2 *(Sep 4)* — Att: 119
Haverfordwest County 1 Carmarthen Town 5 *(Sep 25)* — Att: 181
Carmarthen Town 3 Aberystwyth Town 1 *(Oct 9)* — Att: 177
Carmarthen Town 8 Haverfordwest County 1 *(Oct 30)* — Att: 164
Aberystwyth Town 6 Haverfordwest County 0 *(Nov 13)* — Att: 196

GROUP 6

	P	W	D	L	F	A	Pts
Llanelli	4	3	0	1	12	7	9
Neath Athletic	4	2	0	2	7	9	6
Port Talbot Town	*-1* 4	1	0	3	8	11	2

Port Talbot Town 3 Neath Athletic 0 *(Aug 11)* — Att: 213
Llanelli 3 Port Talbot Town 1 *(Sep 4)* — Att: 225
Neath Athletic 1 Llanelli AFC 3 *(Sep 25)* — Att: 198
Neath Athletic 3 Port Talbot Town 2 *(Oct 9)* — Att: 177
Port Talbot Town 2 Llanelli 5 *(Oct 23)* — Att: 156
Llanelli 1 Neath Athletic 3 *(Oct 30)* — Att: 331

Group winners and two best runners-up qualify for knockout stage

QUARTER-FINALS

Carmarthen Town 0 **Aberystwyth Town** 3 *(Nov 27)* Att: 152
Llanelli 2 Welshpool Town 0 *(Nov 28)* Att: 186
Llangefni Town 2 **Rhyl** 5 *(Nov 27)* Att: 258
The New Saints 1 **Bangor City** 2 *(Nov 27)* Att: 258

SEMI-FINALS 1st Leg

Aberystwyth Town 2 Llanelli 1 *(Jan 29)* Att: 291
Rhyl 1 Bangor City 1 *(Jan 29)* Att: 692

SEMI-FINALS 2nd Leg

Bangor City 0 **Rhyl** 2 *(Feb 12)* Att: 940
Llanelli 1 Aberystwyth Town 0 *(Feb 13)* Att: 401

FINAL

(April 27th at Newtown)
Llanelli 2 Rhyl 0 *Att* 510

WESSEX LEAGUE

	AFC Totton	Alresford Town	Alton Town	Bemerton Heath	Bournemouth	Brading Town	Brockenhurst	Christchurch	Cowes Sports	Downton	Fareham Town	Hamble ASSC	Hamworthy Utd	Hayling United	Horndean	Lymington Town	Moneyfields	New Milton Town	Poole Town	Ringwood Town	Romsey Town	VTFC	Wimborne Town
AFC Totton		2-0	2-1	5-0	1-1	0-0	2-0	1-1	0-2	7-0	4-0	6-1	3-3	2-2	3-1	2-1	3-0	4-0	1-0	4-0	2-0	1-2	1-1
Alresford Town	3-3		1-2	1-2	1-1	3-0	1-5	1-2	0-6	2-0	1-2	1-2	1-4	2-3	0-2	2-2	0-1	3-2	1-2	2-1	2-1	0-3	0-1
Alton Town	0-4	2-0		0-0	1-2	2-0	0-3	3-1	3-0	2-1	1-1	0-0	0-2	2-3	2-0	0-3	1-1	2-1	1-5	9-1	3-3	0-2	0-6
Bemerton Hth Harlequins	1-3	4-3	3-1	P	0-1	2-1	3-3	2-2	1-2	2-1	0-1	2-1	1-1	3-3	0-3	3-2	1-2	3-1	3-3	1-2	3-4	1-5	1-4
Bournemouth	1-0	2-1	3-1	4-2	R	2-1	1-1	3-1	2-2	8-0	2-0	4-1	3-0	1-0	0-0	1-0	1-0	3-2	0-0	5-1	2-2	0-0	2-1
Brading Town	2-5	3-1	2-3	4-1	0-2	E	0-5	1-2	1-1	4-0	6-3	0-0	0-1	3-1	1-1	4-3	1-2	0-1	1-1	4-1	2-1	0-5	1-3
Brockenhurst	1-3	2-2	3-2	3-4	2-0	5-0	M	3-2	1-0	3-1	1-1	0-0	1-0	1-2	3-1	0-0	0-1	3-2	0-3	2-0	2-1	1-1	
Christchurch	2-3	1-0	1-2	2-3	1-2	1-0	1-4	I	2-5	4-0	0-2	1-1	0-3	3-0	3-4	0-1	1-2	4-0	0-1	2-1	2-1	1-2	0-5
Cowes Sports	0-3	2-2	3-1	4-4	0-0	1-1	5-3	1-0	E	7-0	1-1	3-1	2-0	4-0	2-2	3-1	0-1	1-0	0-5	5-3	4-2	2-2	1-2
Downton	1-4	1-2	2-1	0-3	1-5	2-3	0-4	2-4	0-2	R	3-4	1-5	1-4	0-2	0-6	1-5	2-4	1-5	1-7	2-2	0-2	1-1	1-2
Fareham Town	1-2	1-2	1-0	3-1	2-0	0-5	2-2	3-2	2-1	4-0		1-1	1-0	1-3	2-3	3-4	2-2	3-0	1-3	10-0	2-5	1-1	0-0
Hamble ASSC	1-3	1-1	1-2	0-2	0-1	2-4	1-1	1-3	0-1	3-0	1-3		2-0	1-1	1-0	1-0	0-0	4-2	1-1	0-0	1-1	2-6	0-3
Hamworthy United	0-2	0-0	2-2	4-3	2-1	2-2	1-0	1-2	2-1	3-1	0-2	0-0	D	0-0	1-2	1-1	2-1	2-1	2-1	1-0	1-0	0-1	0-3
Hayling United	0-4	1-1	2-3	4-1	2-2	0-1	1-3	1-2	3-2	4-1	0-7	2-3	0-4	I	2-1	4-0	1-0	2-3	1-3	3-1	1-3	0-3	2-7
Horndean	0-4	1-0	2-3	1-2	2-1	1-1	0-1	3-1	2-2	8-0	2-1	3-1	0-1	0-0	V	5-2	0-1	1-1	1-1	2-2	3-0	1-1	0-6
Lymington Town	0-2	3-0	3-1	2-1	3-3	1-4	1-2	0-3	0-5	3-0	1-1	1-2	2-1	1-2	0-0	I	1-4	0-0	1-3	1-0	4-2	1-2	1-9
Moneyfields	2-3	2-0	1-0	3-0	0-2	1-1	3-0	4-1	1-1	9-1	1-2	2-0	4-1	1-2	4-1	6-2	S	1-0	2-1	4-0	3-2	0-2	1-1
New Milton Town	1-3	3-0	3-0	1-2	1-1	1-2	0-1	0-0	1-2	1-2	0-1	1-1	3-1	1-0	1-0	1-0		I	2-5	2-1	1-2	2-1	1-4
Poole Town	0-2	4-0	3-0	3-0	2-0	6-0	1-1	2-1	1-1	4-0	0-1	3-0	2-0	7-0	4-2	7-0	6-0	0-0	O	3-0	6-2	0-0	2-0
Ringwood Town	3-6	2-3	2-3	0-0	0-8	1-1	0-2	2-2	0-3	2-0	0-3	0-0	1-0	2-2	2-3	3-2	0-4	1-4	1-3	N	1-1	0-3	0-3
Romsey Town	2-4	2-1	2-2	0-0	4-0	0-1	3-1	1-1	1-3	8-0	0-1	0-1	0-2	3-1	1-2	2-1	2-1	0-6	2-5	3-2		1-4	0-5
VTFC	2-0	2-0	4-0	1-2	3-2	4-0	3-1	1-0	2-0	3-2	5-1	2-0	0-2	3-1	3-2	1-0	10-1	1-2	3-1	2-1			2-1
Wimborne Town	0-1	0-1	4-2	5-1	0-1	5-1	2-2	2-1	1-0	10-0	3-1	1-0	2-0	8-0	3-0	4-1	2-0	1-1	0-1	0-1	2-0	0-2	

Premier Division		P	W	D	L	F	A	Pts
AFC Totton		44	33	7	4	120	39	106
VTFC		44	32	6	6	106	35	102
Wimborne Town		44	30	6	8	125	33	96
Poole Town		44	29	9	6	120	35	96
Bournemouth		44	27	12	5	92	40	93
Brockenhurst		44	23	11	10	87	55	80
Moneyfields		44	24	7	13	82	45	79
Fareham Town		44	22	9	13	87	65	75
Cowes Sports		44	20	13	11	91	59	73
Hamworthy United		44	19	8	17	55	54	65
Horndean		44	15	13	16	76	73	58
Hayling United		44	15	9	20	66	101	54
Bemerton Heath Harlequins		44	15	8	21	74	101	53
Alton Town		44	15	7	22	66	89	52
Brading Town		44	13	12	19	67	85	51
Christchurch		44	15	5	24	67	80	50
Hamble ASSC		44	11	14	19	47	72	47
Romsey Town		44	12	7	25	68	98	43
New Milton Town		44	11	8	25	58	88	41
Lymington Town	-1	44	11	7	26	63	103	39
Alresford Town		44	9	8	27	48	88	35
Ringwood Town		44	5	9	30	45	124	24
Downton		44	4	4	40	29	177	6

SYDENHAMS WESSEX LEAGUE PREMIER DIVISION CONSTITUTION 2008-09

ALRESFORD TOWN . . . . Alrebury Park, The Avenue, Alresford SO24 9EP 01962 735100
ALTON TOWN . . . . Bass Sports Ground, Anstey Road, Alton GU34 2RL 01420 82465
BEMERTON HEATH HARLEQUINS . . . . . The Clubhouse, Western Way, Bemerton Heath, Salisbury SP2 9DP 01722 331925
BOURNEMOUTH . . . . Victoria Park, Namu Road, Winton, Bournemouth BH9 2RA 01202 515123
BRADING TOWN . . . . Vicarage Lane, Brading PO36 0AR 01983 405217
BROCKENHURST . . . . Grigg Lane, Brockenhurst SO42 7RE 01590 623544
CHRISTCHURCH . . . . Hurn Bridge Sports Club, Avon Causeway, Christchurch BH23 6DY 01202 473792
COWES SPORTS . . . . Westwood Park, Reynolds Close, off Park Road, Cowes PO31 7EG 01983 293793
FAREHAM TOWN . . . . Cams Alders Football Stadium, Cams Alders, Palmerston Drive, Fareham PO14 1BJ 07753 304856
HAMBLE ASSC . . . . Folland Park, Kings Avenue, Hamble-le-Rice, Southampton SO31 4NF 023 8045 2174
HAMWORTHY UNITED . . . . The County Ground, Blandford Close, Hamworthy, Poole BH15 4BF 01202 674974
HAYLING UNITED . . . . College Ground, The Hayling College, Church Road, Hayling Island PO11 0NU 023 9246 6241
HORNDEAN . . . . Five Heads Park, Five Heads Road, Horndean PO8 9NZ 023 9259 1363
LAVERSTOCK & FORD . . . . The Dell, Church Road, Laverstock, Salisbury SP1 1TQ 01722 327401
LYMINGTON TOWN . . . . The Sports Ground, Southampton Road, Lymington SO41 9ZG 01590 671305
MONEYFIELDS . . . . Moneyfields Sports Ground, Moneyfields Avenue, Copnor, Portsmouth PO3 6LB 023 9266 5260
NEW MILTON TOWN . . . . Fawcetts Field, Christchurch Road, New Milton BH25 6QB 01425 628191
NEWPORT IOW . . . . St George's Park, St George's Way, Newport PO30 2QH 01983 525027
POOLE TOWN . . . . Tatnam Ground, Oakdale School, off Fleets Lane/Palmer Road, Poole BH15 3JR 07771 604289
ROMSEY TOWN . . . . The By-Pass Ground, South Front, Romsey SO51 4GJ 07972 036570
VTFC . . . . VT Group Sports Ground, Portsmouth Road, Sholing, Southampton SO19 9PW 023 8040 3829
WIMBORNE TOWN . . . . The Cuthbury, Cowgrove Road, Wimborne BH21 4EL 01202 884821

IN: Laverstock & Ford (P), Newport IOW (R – Southern League Division One South & West)
OUT: AFC Totton (P – Southern League Division One South & West), Downton (R), Ringwood Town (R)

	AFC Aldermaston	AFC Portchester	Amesbury Town	Andover New Street	Blackfield & Langley	East Cowes Victoria Athletic	Farnborough North End	Fawley	Fleet Spurs	Hythe & Dibden	Laverstock & Ford	Liss Athletic	Petersfield Town	Shaftesbury	Stockbridge	Tadley Calleva	Totton & Eling	United Services Portsmouth	Verwood Town	Warminster Town	Whitchurch United
AFC Aldermaston		2-1	0-5	1-1	1-2	2-3	0-6	0-5	1-4	1-0	1-5	3-0	0-2	1-7	0-2	0-2	0-3	0-5	0-4	1-9	2-2
AFC Portchester	3-0		2-2	2-2	1-0	3-4	0-4	2-0	4-1	2-0	0-1	1-2	0-2	2-0	1-1	2-3	0-3	0-1	3-4	1-1	1-1
Amesbury Town	1-2	4-0		0-1	1-3	2-3	0-0	0-2	6-1	2-0	3-5	7-2	2-1	1-3	3-2	2-5	0-2	6-3	2-2	1-3	5-1
Andover New Street	3-1	1-2	0-4		2-5	0-1	0-5	1-3	3-2	2-2	0-5	1-2	1-2	2-1	0-2	3-6	1-3	2-3	0-3	3-1	4-5
Blackfield & Langley	2-0	2-1	2-1	3-1	D	2-1	1-2	1-2	3-2	0-0	1-0	2-2	0-0	1-0	1-1	0-4	1-2	1-3	4-1	1-1	1-0
East Cowes Victoria Athletic	2-2	1-1	0-5	6-0	1-4	I	1-4	0-5	2-3	1-1	0-6	0-2	2-1	0-3	1-1	1-5	0-5	2-0	1-1	1-2	3-0
Farnborough North End	5-1	3-0	3-0	12-0	1-1	7-0	V	2-1	4-0	2-1	1-0	0-1	0-0	2-1	0-0	1-2	0-2	1-1	3-2	1-1	3-1
Fawley	9-2	7-0	2-1	3-1	3-0	1-1	0-2	I	1-1	5-0	2-4	3-2	2-1	0-0	2-0	0-0	1-3	0-1	0-1	1-0	4-0
Fleet Spurs	4-2	2-0	1-3	2-1	2-1	1-1	2-0	1-1	S	5-2	0-3	1-4	1-4	2-1	1-2	0-3	1-3	5-2	0-1	1-2	0-1
Hythe & Dibden	4-0	2-4	0-5	2-2	0-5	1-1	0-6	1-4	2-5	I	0-9	0-3	0-6	2-1	1-1	1-5	0-3	0-5	3-4	1-1	1-4
Laverstock & Ford	2-1	6-1	2-1	1-3	5-4	4-2	0-1	4-3	2-0	2-1	O	3-0	2-2	3-3	3-0	5-4	4-0	3-4	3-1	4-2	6-2
Liss Athletic	7-0	2-5	3-2	1-3	2-3	3-3	1-1	0-5	3-3	1-2	2-3	N	1-4	1-5	0-1	0-2	1-1	1-1	1-2	1-1	1-1
Petersfield Town	7-1	4-5	1-5	6-2	2-1	3-2	1-1	1-2	4-1	1-2	3-1	1-1		3-1	3-0	1-3	4-1	2-1	1-1	0-1	5-0
Shaftesbury	4-1	1-0	4-5	0-2	1-1	0-0	1-3	3-2	6-0	2-0	1-3	5-1	3-4		2-2	1-2	1-1	2-1	1-1	2-1	0-1
Stockbridge	4-1	1-2	3-2	1-1	0-2	2-0	0-2	0-5	1-1	0-1	0-2	2-0	0-3	1-2	O	0-1	3-0	1-3	0-1	2-2	2-2
Tadley Calleva	10-1	1-1	7-2	6-0	3-3	5-0	1-3	1-0	2-1	8-0	2-3	2-0	1-0	3-0	4-1	N	7-1	3-1	3-2	2-1	3-0
Totton & Eling	5-0	1-1	2-4	4-0	2-0	2-0	1-2	3-2	4-0	0-0	1-1	1-1	1-1	1-1	1-0	0-2	E	1-2	2-3	3-1	4-1
United Services Portsmouth	6-0	3-1	3-0	3-1	1-2	3-0	1-4	0-1	4-0	10-0	1-5	2-1	1-2	5-1	2-2	2-3	2-3		2-3	0-1	3-1
Verwood Town	3-0	7-1	5-0	3-1	2-1	4-2	1-2	2-5	5-2	3-2	0-0	2-0	2-0	0-1	2-1	2-3	1-2	2-2		1-0	2-6
Warminster Town	11-0	2-1	4-4	3-1	1-1	4-0	3-1	1-0	1-1	4-2	4-1	8-0	1-0	1-0	0-3	2-1	1-1	3-2			1-1
Whitchurch United	1-0	1-2	1-1	0-2	2-2	3-1	1-1	1-0	0-4	2-2	2-4	3-1	1-2	0-2	1-3	1-3	0-2	2-3	0-6	0-1	

Division One

	P	W	D	L	F	A	Pts
Tadley Calleva	40	33	3	4	134	45	102
Laverstock & Ford	40	29	3	8	124	59	90
Farnborough North End	40	26	9	5	101	30	87
Verwood Town	40	23	6	11	94	63	75
Totton & Eling	40	22	8	10	80	50	74
Fawley	40	22	5	13	94	44	71
Warminster Town	40	20	11	9	89	48	71
Petersfield Town	40	21	7	12	90	53	70
United Services Portsmouth	40	21	6	13	98	65	69
Blackfield & Langley	40	18	10	12	70	57	64
Amesbury Town	40	16	5	19	100	86	53
Shaftesbury	40	14	9	17	73	63	51
Stockbridge	40	11	12	17	47	61	45
AFC Portchester	40	11	9	20	59	86	42
Fleet Spurs	40	12	6	22	64	95	42
Liss Athletic	40	8	10	22	58	95	34
Whitchurch United	40	8	10	22	51	97	34
East Cowes Victoria Athletic	40	8	10	22	50	103	34
Andover New Street	40	9	5	26	54	117	32
Hythe & Dibden	40	6	9	25	42	125	27
AFC Aldermaston	40	4	3	33	31	161	15

WWW.CHERRYRED.CO.UK

SYDENHAMS WESSEX LEAGUE DIVISION ONE CONSTITUTION 2008-09

AFC ALDERMASTON . . . AWE Recreational Society, Aldermaston, near Tadley, Aldermaston, Reading RG7 4PR 0118 982 7614
AFC PORTCHESTER. . . . . Wicor Recreation Ground, Cranleigh Road, Portchester PO16 9DP. 07798 734678
AMESBURY TOWN. . . . . Bonnymead Park, Recreation Road, Amesbury SP4 7BB 01980 623489
ANDOVER NEW STREET. . . . . Foxcotte Park, Hatherton Road, Charlton, Andover SP11 0HS. 01264 358358
BLACKFIELD & LANGLEY . . . Gang Warily Comm. & Rec Centre, Newlands Road, Fawley, Southampton SO45 1GA 023 8089 3603
DOWNTON . . . . Brian Whitehead Sports Ground, Wick Lane, Downton, Salisbury SP5 3NF 01725 512162
EAST COWES VICTORIA ATHLETIC . . Beatrice Avenue, Whippingham, East Cowes PO32 6PA. 01983 297165
FARNBOROUGH NORTH END . . . Cody Sports & Social Club, Old Ively Road, Pyestock, Farnborough GU14 0LS 01252 543009
FAWLEY. . . . . Waterside Sports & Social Club, 179-181 Long Lane, Holbury, Southampton SO45 2NP 023 8089 3750
FLEET SPURS . . . . Kennels Lane, Southwood, Farnborough GU14 0NJ . . . . None
HYTHE & DIBDEN. . . . . Ewart Recreation Ground, Jones Lane, Hythe, Southampton SO45 6FD 023 8084 5264
PETERSFIELD TOWN . . . . Love Lane, Petersfield GU31 4BW. 01730 233416
RINGWOOD TOWN . . . . The Canotec Stadium, Long Lane, Ringwood BH24 3BX 01425 473448
SHAFTESBURY . . . . Cockrams, Coppice Street, Shaftesbury SP7 8PF. 01747 853990
STOCKBRIDGE. . . . . Recreation Ground, High Street, Stockbridge SO20 6EU . . . . None
TADLEY CALLEVA . . . . Barlows Park, Silchester Road, Tadley RG26 3PX . . . . None
TOTTON & ELING . . . . Totton & Eling Sports Club, Southern Gardens, Ringwood Road, Totton SO40 8RW 023 8086 2143
UNITED SERVICES PORTSMOUTH . . . . Victory Stadium, HMS Temeraire, Burnaby Road, Portsmouth PO1 2EJ 023 9272 5315/4235
VERWOOD TOWN. . . . . Potterne Park, Potterne Way, Verwood BH21 6RS. 01202 814007
WARMINSTER TOWN. . . . . 73 Weymouth Street, Warminster BA12 9NS 01985 217828
WHITCHURCH UNITED. . . . . Longmeadow, Winchester Road, Whitchurch RG28 7RD 01256 892493
IN: Downton (R), Ringwood Town (R)
OUT: Laverstock & Ford (P), Liss Athletic (R – Hampshire Premier League)

LEAGUE CUP

FIRST ROUND
Amesbury Town 2 **Romsey Town** 3
Brockenhurst 5 AFC Portchester 1
Cowes Sports 4 Fawley 1
Fareham Town 4 Fleet Spurs 1
Farnborough North End 0 **Alton Town** 1
Hamworthy United 6 Blackfield & Langley 0
Lymington Town 0 **AFC Totton** 1
Stockbridge 3 Shaftesbury 1
Tadley Calleva 3 **Laverstock & Ford** 4 *aet*
Totton & Eling 0 **Brading Town** 4
Verwood Town 0 **Poole Town** 3
Whitchurch United 1 **Bemerton Heath
Harlequins** 5

SECOND ROUND
AFC Totton 3 Warminster Town 0
Andover New Street 1 **Horndean** 2
Bemerton Heath Harlequins 6 AFC
Aldermaston 0
Bournemouth 1 United Services Portsmouth 0
Brading Town 6 Liss Athletic 2
Christchurch 2 VTFC 1
East Cowes Victoria Athletic 5 Ringwood
Town 2
Fareham Town 2 Alresford Town 1
Hayling United 0 **Alton Town** 1
Laverstock & Ford 2 Downton 1
Moneyfields 2 Cowes Sports 1
New Milton Town 1 **Romsey Town** 2
Petersfield Town 4 Hamble ASSC 0
Poole Town 2 Brockenhurst 2 *aet* (4-3p)
Stockbridge 0 **Hamworthy United** 5
Wimborne Town 4 Hythe & Dibden 0

THIRD ROUND
AFC Totton 2 **Bournemouth** 1 *aet*
(AFC Totton expelled)
Bemerton Heath Harlequins (w/o) v Laverstock
& Ford (scr.)
East Cowes Victoria Athletic 0 **Hamworthy
United** 4
Horndean 5 Brading Town 4
Moneyfields 2 **Christchurch** 9
Petersfield Town 1 **Fareham Town** 3
Poole Town 4 Romsey Town 0
Wimborne Town 0 Alton Town 0 *aet* (4-2p)

QUARTER-FINALS
Bemerton Heath Harlequins 1 **Wimborne
Town** 5
Fareham Town 2 Poole Town 0
Horndean 1 Bournemouth 1 *aet* (4-1p)
Moneyfields 1 Hamworthy United 0

SEMI-FINALS
(played over two legs)
Fareham Town 0 Moneyfields 0, **Moneyfields** 1
Fareham Town 0
Horndean 0 Wimborne Town 3, **Wimborne
Town** 2 Horndean 1

FINAL
(May 3rd at Christchurch)
Wimborne Town 1 Moneyfields 0

Combination One	P	W	D	L	F	A	Pts
VTFC Res.	34	29	5	0	135	12	92
Winchester City Res.	34	22	5	7	90	47	71
Christchurch Res.	34	18	9	7	88	43	63
Horndean Res.	34	18	6	10	93	81	60
Cowes Sports Res.	34	19	3	12	81	77	60
Bashley Res.	34	18	5	11	94	68	59
Bemerton Heath Harlequins Res.	34	17	6	11	71	56	57
Moneyfields Res.	34	15	3	16	83	66	48
AFC Totton Res.	34	14	5	15	74	77	47
Wimborne Town Res.	34	14	5	15	70	80	47
Gosport Borough Res.	34	13	7	14	70	60	46
Hamble ASSC Res.	34	13	6	15	48	61	45
Hayling United Res.	34	13	3	18	63	75	42
Laverstock & Ford Res.	34	9	5	20	59	103	32
Lymington Town Res.	34	9	3	22	53	97	30
Brockenhurst Res.	34	7	7	20	48	95	28
Ringwood Town Res.	34	6	9	19	45	81	27
Downton Res.	34	3	6	25	23	109	15

Combination Two	P	W	D	L	F	A	Pts
Tadley Calleva Res.	32	24	5	3	100	32	77
Alton Town Res.	32	22	4	6	102	42	70
Bournemouth Res.	32	22	4	6	94	34	70
Romsey Town Res.	32	21	4	7	79	34	67
Brading Town Res.	32	21	3	8	95	49	66
Fareham Town Res.	32	19	8	5	88	42	65
Totton & Eling Res.	32	17	5	10	73	57	56
United Services Portsmouth Res.	32	17	4	11	77	62	55
Petersfield Town Res.	32	15	3	14	63	73	48
Alresford Town Res.	32	14	4	14	67	62	46
Fawley Res.	32	12	3	17	66	87	39
Whitchurch United Res.	32	9	5	18	54	81	32
Fleet Spurs Res.	32	9	3	20	52	87	30
Blackfield & Langley Res.	32	9	1	22	35	77	28
AFC Aldermaston Res.	32	3	5	24	34	105	14
AFC Portchester Res.	32	3	3	26	39	104	12
Andover New Street Res.	32	1	4	27	37	127	7

COMBINATION CUP
FINAL
(April 29th Blackfield & Langley)
Brading Town Res. 1 **VTFC Res.** 3

WEST CHESHIRE LEAGUE

	Aintree Villa	Ashville	Blacon Youth Club	Cammell Laird Res.	Castrol Social	Christleton	Ellesmere Port	Heswall	Maghull	Marine Res.	New Brighton	Newton	Poulton Victoria	Runcorn Town	Upton Athletic Ass.	Vauxhall Motors Res.	West Kirby
Aintree Villa		2-3	3-3	1-3	2-0	2-2	1-1	0-3	1-0	0-1	3-7	2-3	1-1	0-2	3-2	1-2	2-0
Ashville	2-2		1-2	2-4	0-3	2-1	0-2	1-5	2-0	0-2	1-5	0-5	1-7	1-4	2-4	1-1	0-6
Blacon Youth Club	4-1	3-3	D	3-6	2-7	2-0	2-1	2-1	4-0	0-2	3-0	4-1	1-4	0-3	0-3	3-3	0-2
Cammell Laird Res.	1-2	6-1	3-0	I	2-1	4-1	3-2	2-4	2-1	3-3	8-1	2-0	2-1	2-1	2-0	6-0	0-2
Castrol Social	4-0	3-0	6-3	2-0	V	2-1	1-1	1-1	2-2	5-1	1-4	1-0	1-3	1-5	2-1	1-0	1-2
Christleton	1-2	2-1	2-2	0-3	1-3	I	0-1	1-3	0-3	4-0	1-2	5-2	0-0	0-3	2-1	0-5	1-0
Ellesmere Port	1-0	2-0	0-0	0-4	0-2	1-1	S	2-0	3-1	1-1	2-2	4-2	2-1	1-4	0-3	1-1	0-4
Heswall	5-3	6-0	3-1	4-1	3-1	1-1	2-0	I	3-0	1-4	0-4	1-3	1-1	1-1	2-2	1-4	0-3
Maghull	1-3	1-1	1-3	2-4	0-2	1-0	5-1	0-2	O	1-2	1-1	4-0	1-1	1-7	0-0	2-0	1-2
Marine Res.	5-2	4-2	0-2	0-1	1-2	3-1	2-3	1-3	0-0	N	4-3	4-3	1-1	0-3	1-4	2-3	1-1
New Brighton	2-0	4-2	8-0	1-1	4-1	2-0	2-1	1-4	0-2	1-1		2-0	1-2	1-4	1-0	2-0	1-1
Newton	2-0	1-2	3-2	0-4	2-3	1-2	3-2	4-3	3-1	2-1	4-4		0-2	0-0	2-3	0-3	1-5
Poulton Victoria	4-2	1-0	4-1	0-1	4-1	1-3	3-1	0-0	0-1	0-4	2-3	0-2	O	4-2	1-3	1-2	1-1
Runcorn Town	4-3	8-0	7-2	1-2	2-1	3-1	6-0	1-2	1-2	2-1	4-2	1-2	1-2	N	1-0	2-2	2-3
Upton Athletic Association	2-2	5-3	3-0	2-2	2-1	4-0	0-2	1-0	4-2	4-1	2-4	1-3	0-2	1-3	E	2-1	2-3
Vauxhall Motors Res.	1-2	1-2	0-1	1-3	0-0	1-3	4-0	0-3	2-2	0-5	3-2	6-0	1-2	0-1	5-3		1-3
West Kirby	2-1	5-0	8-0	4-2	8-0	2-3	3-1	2-2	3-1	4-0	4-0	4-1	1-1	3-2	0-0	1-1	

Division One	P	W	D	L	F	A	Pts
West Kirby	32	22	7	3	92	29	73
Cammell Laird Res.	32	23	3	6	89	43	72
Runcorn Town	32	21	3	8	94	41	66
Heswall	32	16	7	9	70	48	55
New Brighton	32	16	6	10	77	62	54
Castrol Social	32	16	4	12	62	57	52
Poulton Victoria	32	14	8	10	57	42	50
Upton Athletic Association	32	14	5	13	64	53	47
Marine Res.	32	12	6	14	58	62	42
Blacon Youth Club	32	11	5	16	55	89	38
Vauxhall Motors Res.	32	10	7	15	54	58	37
Ellesmere Port	32	10	7	15	39	63	37
Newton	32	11	2	19	55	81	35
Christleton	32	9	5	18	40	63	32
Maghull	32	8	7	17	40	59	31
Aintree Villa	32	8	6	18	49	74	30
Ashville	32	5	4	23	36	107	19

PYKE CUP

PRELIMINARY ROUND
Runcorn Town 5 West Kirby 2
FIRST ROUND
Blacon Youth Club 3 Aintree Villa 1
Ellesmere Port 1 **Heswall** 5
Maghull 1 **Poulton Victoria** 2
Marine Res. 2 Cammell Laird Res. 1 *aet*
New Brighton 5 Ashville 1
Newton 1 **Runcorn Town** 2
Upton Athletic Association 0 **Castrol Social** 4
Vauxhall Motors Res. 1 **Christleton** 2
QUARTER-FINALS
Blacon Youth Club 1 **Castrol Social** 5
New Brighton 5 Christleton 0
Poulton Victoria 2 Heswall 0
Runcorn Town 3 Marine Res. 1
SEMI-FINALS
Castrol Social 1 New Brighton 0
Poulton Victoria 1 **Runcorn Town** 2
FINAL
(March 21st at Vauxhall Motors)
Castrol Social 2 Runcorn Town 0

CARLSBERG WEST CHESHIRE LEAGUE DIVISION ONE CONSTITUTION 2008-09
AINTREE VILLA . . . . Aintree Racecourse, Melling Road, Aintree L9 5AS. . . . . None
BLACON YOUTH CLUB . . . . Cairns Crescent Playing Fields, Blacon, Chester CF1 5JF . . . . None
CAMMELL LAIRD RESERVES . . . . . Kirklands, St Peters Road, Rock Ferry, Birkenhead CH42 1PY 0151 645 3121
CASTROL SOCIAL . . . . Castrol Sports & Social Club, Chester Road, Whitby, Ellesmere Port CH66 2NX. 0151 357 3712
CHRISTLETON . . . . Little Heath Road, Christleton, Chester CH3 7AH 01244 336589
ELLESMERE PORT . . . . Whitby Sports & Social Club, Chester Road, Whitby, Ellesmere Port CH66 2NX 0151 200 7080/7050
HALTON . . . . Pavilions Club, Sandy Lane, Weston Point, Runcorn WA7 4EX 01928 590 508
HESWALL. . . . . Gayton Park, Brimstage Road, Heswall CH60 1XG 0151 342 8172
MAGHULL. . . . . Old Hall Field, Hall Lane, Maghull LE31 7BB 0151 526 7320
MARINE RESERVES . . . . Arriva Stadium, College Road, Crosby, Liverpool L23 3AS 0151 924 1743/4046
NEW BRIGHTON . . . . Harrison Drive, Wallasey Village, Wallasey CH45 3HL . . . . None
NEWTON . . . . Millcroft, Frankby Road, Greasby CH47 0NB 0151 677 8282
POULTON VICTORIA . . . . Victoria Park, Clayton Lane, Wallasey CH44 5SR. 0151 638 3559
RUNCORN TOWN. . . . . Pavilions Club, Sandy Lane, Weston Point, Runcorn WA7 4EX 01928 590508
UPTON ATHLETIC ASSOCIATION . . . Cheshire County Sports & Social Club, Plas Newton Lane, Chester CH2 1PR 01244 318167
VAUXHALL MOTORS RESERVES . . . Vauxhall Sports Ground, Rivacre Road, Hooton, Ellesmere Port CH66 1NJ. . . 0151 328 1114/327 2294
WEST KIRBY . . . . Marine Park, Greenbank Road, West Kirby CH48 5HL. . . . . None
IN: Halton (P)
OUT: Ashville (R)

	AFC Bebington Athletic	Ashville Res.	Capenhurst Villa	Chester Nomads	Christleton Res.	Fairfield Athletic	Grange Athletic	Halton	Helsby	Heswall Res.	Maghull Res.	Mallaby	New Brighton Res.	Poulton Victoria Res.	West Kirby Res.	Willaston
AFC Bebington Athletic		1-1	2-2	3-2	2-0	3-3	2-2	1-2	5-1	0-0	2-1	0-4	2-0	1-3	2-2	0-1
Ashville Res.	3-0		1-5	0-2	3-2	3-3	1-0	1-3	1-3	0-2	2-6	0-5	2-1	0-4	1-1	1-6
Capenhurst Villa	2-0	4-2	D	4-1	3-1	5-0	0-3	0-1	2-1	2-1	2-2	4-0	3-0	0-5	2-1	2-4
Chester Nomads	3-1	6-1	1-3	I	3-0	0-1	1-2	2-2	3-4	1-4	1-2	3-1	5-2	0-2	2-0	2-6
Christleton Res.	1-2	1-1	0-2	1-1	V	1-1	2-3	0-2	1-4	1-1	2-0	1-3	1-2	0-1	0-1	0-3
Fairfield Athletic	1-1	9-1	1-7	0-3	2-1	I	1-2	1-7	2-1	2-4	2-3	0-3	5-7	0-4	1-2	1-0
Grange Athletic	2-0	7-0	1-4	0-3	1-1	3-2	S	2-2	1-1	2-0	0-1	1-0	0-4	1-0	1-0	2-1
Halton	8-0	6-1	1-2	1-1	7-0	3-2	3-1	I	3-4	9-3	4-1	3-2	3-1	4-4	3-1	6-5
Helsby	2-1	0-2	2-1	3-2	2-1	6-2	3-3	3-2	O	2-5	6-1	1-2	4-5	1-3	1-0	2-4
Heswall Res.	4-2	0-1	5-1	3-3	5-1	1-1	0-2	1-3	1-1	N	1-1	3-0	2-3	3-4	0-0	4-2
Maghull Res.	1-0	1-3	3-1	1-1	2-1	3-1	3-1	2-1	5-0	2-1		2-0	4-4	2-2	1-1	2-2
Mallaby	4-3	2-1	4-3	1-5	8-0	2-0	0-2	0-1	0-0	2-4	1-2	T	2-2	0-0	1-2	1-2
New Brighton Res.	4-1	1-1	1-2	3-3	8-0	2-3	3-2	0-2	2-1	2-2	0-1	3-2	W	1-1	3-2	3-1
Poulton Victoria Res.	2-1	1-0	1-0	6-1	1-0	5-3	1-1	3-0	4-1	1-0	3-0	2-1	2-1	O	1-2	1-0
West Kirby Res.	3-1	2-0	0-0	2-2	2-0	3-1	0-0	2-2	2-0	1-0	2-5	1-0	2-2	0-1		0-1
Willaston	3-0	2-0	0-1	3-3	3-1	0-1	1-1	4-3	5-2	1-1	3-1	1-2	1-2	2-3	3-1	

Division Two

	P	W	D	L	F	A	Pts
Poulton Victoria Res.	30	23	5	2	71	26	74
Halton	30	19	5	6	97	50	62
Capenhurst Villa	30	18	3	9	69	45	57
Maghull Res.	30	16	7	7	61	50	55
Grange Athletic	30	14	8	8	49	40	50
Willaston	30	15	4	11	70	49	49
New Brighton Res.	30	13	7	10	72	62	46
West Kirby Res.	30	11	9	10	38	37	42
Helsby	30	12	4	14	62	71	40
Heswall Res.	30	10	9	11	61	53	39
Chester Nomads	30	10	8	12	66	62	38
Mallaby	30	11	3	16	53	52	36
Fairfield Athletic	30	7	5	18	52	86	26
Ashville Res.	30	7	5	18	34	86	26
AFC Bebington Athletic	30	6	7	17	39	67	25
Christleton Res.	30	1	5	24	21	79	8

WEST CHESHIRE BOWL

FIRST ROUND
Ashville Res. 0 **Mallaby** 4
Capenhurst Villa 0 **Chester Nomads** 3
Christleton Res. 3 **Fairfield Athletic** 4
Grange Athletic 2 Helsby 1
Heswall Res. 2 **Halton** 4
Maghull Res. 2 **AFC Bebington Athletic** 4
West Kirby Res. 0 **New Brighton Res.** 1
Willaston 1 **Poulton Victoria Res.** 3

QUARTER-FINALS
AFC Bebington Athletic 1 **Poulton Victoria Res.** 3
Grange Athletic 5 Fairfield Athletic 5 *aet* (5-4p)
Mallaby 2 Halton 1
New Brighton Res. 5 Chester Nomads 4 *aet*

SEMI-FINALS
New Brighton Res. 1 Mallaby 0
Poulton Victoria Res. 1 **Grange Athletic** 2

FINAL
(May 2nd at Poulton Victoria)
New Brighton Res. 3 Grange Athletic 1

BILL WEIGHT MEMORIAL CUP
(Divisional champions and Pyke Cup holders)

SEMI-FINALS
Runcorn Town 2 Poulton Victoria 0
West Kirby 5 AFC Bebington Athletic 2

FINAL
(September 4th at Cammell Laird)
Runcorn Town 3 West Kirby 3 *(Cup shared)*

CARLSBERG WEST CHESHIRE LEAGUE DIVISION TWO CONSTITUTION 2008-09

Club	Ground	Phone
AFC BEBINGTON ATHLETIC	Unilever Sports Ground, Bromborough CH62 3PU	None
ASHVILLE	Villa Park, Cross Lane, Wallasey Village, Wallasey CH45 8RH	0151 638 2127
BRONZE SOCIAL	Unilever Sports Ground, Bromborough CH62 3PU	None
CAPENHURST VILLA	Capenhurst Lane, Capenhurst CH1 6ER	None
CHESTER NOMADS	Boughton Hall Cricket Club, Boughton, Chester CH3 5EL	01244 326072
GRANGE ATHLETIC	Netherpool Sports Ground, Ellesmere Port	None
HELSBY	Helsby Community Sports Club, Chester Road, Helsby WA6 0DL	01928 722267
HESWALL RESERVES	Gayton Park, Brimstage Road, Heswall CH60 1XG	0151 342 8172
MAGHULL RESERVES	Old Hall Field, Hall Lane, Maghull LE31 7BB	0151 526 7320
MALLABY	Unilever Sports Ground, Bromborough CH62 3PU	None
MOSSLEY HILL ATHLETIC	Mossley Hill Athletic Club, Mossley Hill Road, Liverpool L18 8DX	0151 724 4377
NEW BRIGHTON RESERVES	Harrison Drive, Wallasey Village, Wallasey CH45 3HL	None
POULTON VICTORIA RESERVES	Victoria Park, Clayton Lane, Wallasey CH44 4SR	0151 638 3559
SOUTHPORT TRINITY	Police Club, Fairfield, Prescot Road, Liverpool L7 0JD	0151 228 2352
WEST KIRBY RESERVES	Marine Park, Greenbank Road, West Kirby CH48 5HL	None
WILLASTON	Johnston Recreation Ground, Neston Road, Willaston CH64 2TL	None

IN: Ashville (R), Bronze Social (P), Mossley Hill Athletic (P)
OUT: Ashville Reserves (R), Christleton Reserves (R), Halton (P)
Fairfield Athletic become Southport Trinity

	Blacon Youth Club Res.	Bronze Social	Capenhurst Villa Res.	Ellesmere Port Res.	FC Pensby	FOCUS	Fairfield Athletic Res.	Hale	Manor Athletic	Mersey Royal	Mossley Hill Athletic	Richmond Raith Rovers	Runcorn Town Res.	Shaftesbury	St Werburghs	Upton Athletic Association Res.
Blacon Youth Club Res.		4-1	1-0	2-3	0-2	1-1	1-1	2-1	1-1	1-2	4-3	3-3	0-6	5-1	0-1	3-1
Bronze Social	3-0	D	3-0	3-0	5-1	5-0	4-1	5-2	1-0	2-2	1-1	2-1	2-4	6-1	7-2	1-3
Capenhurst Villa Res.	2-2	1-4	I	2-1	3-4	3-2	5-2	3-0	5-2	1-3	0-4	1-2	1-1	4-0	5-2	6-0
Ellesmere Port Res.	1-1	0-3	3-2	V	1-3	3-2	3-2	1-3	2-2	1-6	3-4	1-1	1-6	1-2	3-1	3-1
FC Pensby	0-0	1-2	1-0	3-2	I	1-4	3-1	1-2	1-1	2-2	3-2	1-5	1-7	3-5	3-1	0-0
FOCUS	1-0	2-6	4-3	3-0	1-7	S	1-3	0-1	0-1	1-2	3-2	1-1	3-4	3-0	3-1	3-2
Fairfield Athletic Res.	1-6	1-6	5-3	2-0	2-3	4-4	I	2-7	1-4	3-2	0-3	1-5	1-3	2-0	1-1	4-8
Hale	1-1	1-3	4-1	2-1	1-1	2-0	5-1	O	0-4	1-2	2-5	3-0	2-3	0-4	0-4	5-1
Manor Athletic	3-0	2-1	1-1	1-2	3-2	2-2	1-2	2-0	N	4-1	0-0	2-2	1-2	3-0	4-2	4-2
Mersey Royal	2-2	2-2	5-2	1-0	1-2	1-2	0-1	5-1	2-2		1-5	0-0	2-1	1-2	7-1	0-0
Mossley Hill Athletic	3-0	1-2	2-1	7-0	5-0	1-0	7-1	4-1	1-2	3-2	T	1-1	3-2	4-1	5-0	6-0
Richmond Raith Rovers	3-2	3-1	1-1	2-0	0-0	1-1	6-2	3-1	2-1	1-0	1-2	H	1-0	0-2	6-1	6-1
Runcorn Town Res.	3-1	2-4	8-0	1-1	2-0	2-0	4-0	5-1	3-0	4-2	0-6	1-4	R	5-1	5-1	7-3
Shaftesbury	3-1	3-3	0-8	2-1	1-7	1-5	2-1	3-0	0-3	0-3	1-8	2-3	1-2	E	1-3	2-3
St Werburghs	2-0	2-7	2-4	1-4	1-4	2-4	2-5	0-3	2-0	2-1	2-8	3-1	3-2	6-1	E	1-3
Upton Athletic Association Res.	3-0	1-6	4-0	0-1	3-3	2-3	4-2	3-2	0-2	4-1	0-2	3-3	0-6	4-0	1-0	

Division Three	P	W	D	L	F	A	Pts
Mossley Hill Athletic	30	22	3	5	108	34	69
Bronze Social	30	21	4	5	101	44	67
Runcorn Town Res.	30	21	2	7	101	46	65
Richmond Raith Rovers	30	15	10	5	68	40	55
Manor Athletic	30	14	8	8	58	40	50
FC Pensby	30	13	7	10	63	63	46
FOCUS	30	12	5	13	59	64	41
Mersey Royal	30	11	7	12	61	53	40
Upton Athletic Association Res.	30	11	4	15	60	82	37
Hale	30	11	2	17	54	70	35
Capenhurst Villa Res.	30	10	4	16	68	73	34
Ellesmere Port Res.	30	9	4	17	43	71	31
Blacon Youth Club Res.	30	7	9	14	44	58	30
St Werburghs	30	9	1	20	52	98	28
Shaftesbury	30	9	1	20	42	98	28
Fairfield Athletic Res.	30	8	3	19	55	103	27

WEST CHESHIRE SHIELD

FIRST ROUND

Blacon Youth Club Res. 1 **Runcorn Town Res.** 2

Bronze Social 4 Capenhurst Villa Res. 2

Ellesmere Port Res. 4 Fairfield Athletic Res. 2

FC Pensby 3 Mersey Royal 2 *aet*

Hale 3 Richmond Raith Rovers 3 *aet* (3-4p)

Shaftesbury 1 **Manor Athletic** 4

St Werburghs 1 **FOCUS** 6

Upton Athletic Association Res. 2 **Mossley Hill Athletic** 4

QUARTER-FINALS

FC Pensby 3 FOCUS 2

Mossley Hill Athletic 7 Bronze Social 0

Richmond Raith Rovers 0 Manor Athletic 0 *aet* (5-4p)

Runcorn Town Res. 6 Ellesmere Port Town Res. 1

SEMI-FINALS

FC Pensby 2 **Richmond Raith Rovers** 3

Mossley Hill Athletic 1 **Runcorn Town Res.** 2

FINAL

(May 5th at Ashville)

Richmond Raith Rovers 0 **Runcorn Town Res.** 3

CARLSBERG WEST CHESHIRE LEAGUE DIVISION THREE CONSTITUTION 2008-09

ASHVILLE RESERVES . . . . Villa Park, Cross Lane, Wallasey Village, Wallasey CH45 8RH 0151 638 2127
BLACON YOUTH CLUB RESERVES . . . Cairns Crescent Playing Fields, Blacon, Chester CF1 5JF . . . . None
CAPENHURST VILLA RESERVES . . . Capenhurst Sports Ground, Capenhurst Lane, Capenhurst CH1 6ER . . . . None
CHRISTLETON RESERVES . . . . Little Heath Road, Christleton, Chester CH3 7AH 01244 336589
ELLESMERE PORT RESERVES . . . Whitby Sports & Social Club, Chester Road, Whitby, Ellesmere Port CH66 2NX 0151 200 7080/7050
FC PENSBY . . . . Ridgewood Park, Fishers Lane, Pensby CH61 5XF . . . . None
FOCUS . . . . Riversdale Police Ground, Aigburth, Liverpool L19 3QN 0151 724 5214
HALE . . . . Hale Park, The High Street, Hale Village, Liverpool L24 4AF . . . . None
MANOR ATHLETIC . . . . OC Sports & Leisure Club, 28 Bridle Road, Bromborough CH62 6AR 0151 356 6159
MARSHALLS . . . . IM Marsh Campus, Barkhill Road, Aigburth, Liverpool L17 6BD 0151 231 5233
MERSEY ROYAL . . . . Unilever Sports Ground, Bromborough CH62 3PU . . . . None
RICHMOND RAITH ROVERS JACOBS . . . . Jacobs Sports Ground, Long Lane, Fazakerley L9 7BQ 01515 259362
RUNCORN TOWN RESERVES . . . . . . Pavilions Club, Sandy Lane, Weston Point, Runcorn WA7 4EX 01928 590508
SOUTHPORT TRINITY RESERVES . . . . . Police Club, Fairfield, Prescot Road, Liverpool L7 0JD 0151 228 235
ST WERBURGHS . . . . Kings School, Wrexham Road (A483), Chester CH4 7QL 01244 689500
UPTON ATHLETIC ASSOCIATION RESERVES . . . Cheshire County S & S Club, Plas Newton Lane, Chester CH2 1PR 01244 318167
IN: *Ashville Reserves (R), Christleton Reserves (R), Marshalls (P – Liverpool Formers League)*
OUT: *Bronze Social (P), Mossley Hill Athletic (P), Shaftesbury (W)*
Fairfield Athletic Reserves become Southport Trinity Reserves, Richmond Raith Rovers become Richmond Raith Rovers Jacobs

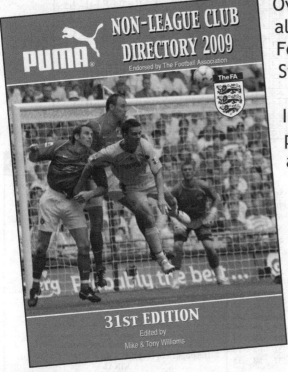

WEST LANCS LEAGUE

	Barnoldswick Town	Blackpool Wren Rovers	Burnley United	Charnock Richard	Coppull United	Dalton United	Eagley	Euxton Villa	Fleetwood Hesketh	Freckleton	Fulwood Amateurs	Garstang	Haslingden St Mary's	Poulton Town	Turton	Wyre Villa
Barnoldswick Town	P	0-2	6-0	0-1	4-0	4-3	0-5	5-1	3-1	1-2	2-1	0-3	2-1	3-0	2-2	4-0
Blackpool Wren Rovers	4-2	R	1-1	0-0	0-1	7-3	0-1	3-1	6-1	2-0	1-2	3-1	4-0	2-1	1-0	4-1
Burnley United	1-5	1-5	E	3-1	3-3	3-2	0-1	1-2	2-5	2-2	2-1	0-2	1-3	1-1	2-3	0-3
Charnock Richard	2-1	2-3	7-0	M	2-1	4-1	3-0	0-0	3-4	2-1	0-4	4-0	3-1	4-3	2-1	3-2
Coppull United	2-2	1-3	4-0	1-1	I	2-3	0-1	3-0	1-0	1-0	0-0	1-2	2-3	4-2	0-2	0-1
Dalton United	3-2	2-3	3-3	2-5	3-1	E	2-0	3-0	3-0	2-1	2-1	0-0	2-2	3-0	2-5	3-0
Eagley	4-3	0-3	2-1	1-1	1-2	0-1	R	1-2	7-1	2-2	4-2	1-3	0-1	3-4	0-3	1-2
Euxton Villa	3-2	2-0	2-2	2-2	2-1	5-1	1-3		3-0	2-1	4-3	1-3	1-2	7-1	1-0	4-1
Fleetwood Hesketh	2-2	0-4	3-4	1-3	2-3	1-2	3-0	2-4	D	2-4	0-1	0-1	0-3	0-3	1-3	1-1
Freckleton	1-1	1-0	4-0	1-2	0-1	1-1	1-0	4-1	2-2	I	2-2	0-1	2-0	3-0	0-1	2-2
Fulwood Amateurs	1-1	2-0	2-1	1-0	2-2	2-1	2-2	1-1	4-0	3-0	V	2-4	1-0	2-0	0-0	1-0
Garstang	1-0	1-2	3-0	2-1	1-2	1-0	2-1	3-1	1-0	4-1	0-2	I	0-2	2-1	2-0	1-0
Haslingden St Mary's	3-4	0-0	3-0	2-1	2-2	2-2	3-0	0-2	6-3	2-1	4-3	1-2	S	1-1	1-1	5-1
Poulton Town	4-0	0-1	2-5	2-0	0-0	2-0	1-1	0-1	3-1	2-1	0-1	1-2	1-4	I	1-2	4-2
Turton	0-0	0-1	2-1	1-4	1-1	0-2	2-2	1-0	6-0	0-0	0-1	1-0	2-2	2-0	O	0-0
Wyre Villa	2-2	1-3	1-2	2-4	1-3	1-2	1-2	2-0	0-1	1-1	1-2	0-2	0-0	1-1	1-3	N

Premier Division		P	W	D	L	F	A	Pts
Garstang		30	22	1	7	50	28	67
Blackpool Wren Rovers		30	21	3	6	70	28	66
Charnock Richard		30	17	5	8	67	43	56
Fulwood Amateurs		30	15	8	7	52	36	53
Haslingden St Mary's		30	14	8	8	59	44	50
Euxton Villa		30	15	4	11	56	51	49
Dalton United		30	14	5	11	59	58	47
Turton	*-3*	30	13	9	8	44	32	45
Coppull United		30	10	8	12	45	46	38
Barnoldswick Town	*-4*	30	11	7	12	63	55	36
Freckleton		30	9	9	12	43	42	36
Eagley		30	10	5	15	46	52	35
Poulton Town		30	8	6	16	43	59	30
Burnley United		30	6	6	18	42	84	24
Wyre Villa	*-3*	30	4	7	19	31	61	16
Fleetwood Hesketh		30	4	3	23	37	88	15

RICHARDSON CUP

FIRST ROUND
Charnock Richard 4 **Dalton United** 5
Coppull United 0 **Barnoldswick Town** 2
Eagley 1 **Blackpool Wren Rovers** 4
Freckleton 4 Burnley United 1
Fulwood Amateurs 1 **Poulton Town** 2
Garstang 4 Fleetwood Hesketh 2
Haslingden St Mary's 3 Euxton Villa 1
Turton 2 Wyre Villa 1

QUARTER-FINALS
Barnoldswick Town 1 **Poulton Town** 2 *(at Poulton Town)*
Dalton United 2 Blackpool Wren Rovers 1
Garstang 0 **Freckleton** 2
Haslingden St Mary's 2 Turton 1

SEMI-FINALS
Freckleton 0 **Poulton Town** 2
Haslingden St Mary's 1 Dalton United 1 *aet (5-3p)*

FINAL
(March 27th at LCFA, Leyland)
Haslingden St Mary's 3 Poulton Town 1

SPORTS 360 WEST LANCS LEAGUE PREMIER DIVISION CONSTITUTION 2008-09

BARNOLDSWICK TOWN . . . . Silentnight Stadium, West Close, Barnoldswick, Colne BB18 5EN. 01282 815817
BLACKPOOL WREN ROVERS . . . . Bruce Park, School Road, Marton, Blackpool FY4 5EL. 01253 760570
BURNLEY UNITED . . . . Barden Sports Ground, Barden Lane, Burnley BB10 1JQ . . . . None
CHARNOCK RICHARD . . . . Charter Lane, Charnock Richard, Chorley PR7 5LY 01257 794288
COPPULL UNITED . . . . Springfield Road, Coppull PR7 5EJ 01257 795190
DALTON UNITED . . . . Railway Meadow, Beckside Road, Dalton-in-Furness LA15 8DP 01229 462799
EAGLEY . . . . Eagley Sports Complex, Dunscar Bridge, Bolton BL7 9PF 01204 306830
EUXTON VILLA . . . . Runshaw Hall Lane, Euxton, Chorley PR7 6HQ . . . . None
FRECKLETON . . . . Hodgson Memorial Ground, Bush Lane, Freckleton, Preston PR1 1SB 01772 679139
FULWOOD AMATEURS . . . . Lightfoot Lane, Fulwood, Preston PR2 3LP 01772 861827
GARSTANG . . . . Riverside Community Centre, off High Street, Garstang PR3 1FA 01995 601586
HASLINGDEN ST MARY'S . . . . Townsend Street, Haslingden, Rossendale BB4 5DF 01706 221814
POULTON TOWN . . . . Cottam Hall Playing Fields, Blackpool Old Road, Poulton-le-Fylde FY6 7RS 01253 896150
STONECLOUGH . . . . Brook Street, opposite Europa Business Park, Stoneclough, Kearsley, Bolton . . . . None
TURTON . . . . Thomasson Fold, Turton, Edgworth, Bolton BL7 0PD 07929 965160
VICKERSTOWN CC . . . . Park Vale, Mill Lane, Walney, Barrow-in-Furness LA14 3ND . . . . None

IN: Stoneclough (P), Vickerstown CC (P)
OUT: Fleetwood Hesketh (R), Wyre Villa (R)

	Barrow Sports Club	Crosshills	Croston Sports	Furness Rovers	Hesketh Bank	Lostock St Gerards	Millom	Norcross & Warbreck	Stoneclough	Tempest United	Trimpell	Vickerstown CC	Whinney Hill
BAE Barrow Sports Club	*D*	4-3	1-1	1-1	2-1	1-2	0-0	2-2	2-2	1-2	1-1	2-1	2-1
Crosshills	7-2	*I*	2-2	3-5	4-3	1-1	3-0	0-1	0-1	2-2	0-6	0-1	3-2
Croston Sports	3-2	2-1	*V*	2-2	2-3	0-4	2-4	0-1	0-1	0-1	1-2	3-2	3-0
Furness Rovers	1-1	1-1	4-1	*I*	5-2	2-2	1-5	2-1	0-2	1-0	0-1	0-3	4-1
Hesketh Bank	2-2	0-2	0-4	2-0	*S*	2-3	2-1	1-2	1-1	0-2	1-6	0-6	2-0
Lostock St Gerards	4-0	2-2	3-3	0-1	6-2	*I*	3-3	1-1	1-1	2-2	1-0	4-1	2-1
Millom	4-3	0-1	0-1	3-2	4-3	3-3	*O*	1-1	2-6	0-3	4-2	1-2	3-0
Norcross & Warbreck	2-2	1-1	1-0	1-0	4-1	1-4	3-1	*N*	1-2	2-3	1-0	1-2	2-3
Stoneclough	1-0	2-1	1-2	4-0	5-3	0-0	7-1	2-1		1-1	2-1	1-2	3-0
Tempest United	4-0	4-2	0-3	3-2	6-3	6-0	1-2	2-3	2-4		2-3	3-6	4-2
Trimpell	0-1	4-2	1-2	4-0	1-0	1-0	4-3	2-2	2-1	4-1	*O*	1-0	6-0
Vickerstown CC	0-1	4-3	1-0	1-2	2-0	4-1	1-1	6-0	0-2	1-2	2-1	*N*	4-0
Whinney Hill	3-3	1-4	0-3	4-1	2-4	1-4	2-1	2-3	0-3	0-0	1-1	2-3	*E*

Division One		P	W	D	L	F	A	Pts
Stoneclough		24	16	5	3	55	23	53
Vickerstown CC		24	15	1	8	55	31	46
Trimpell	-3	24	14	3	7	54	28	42
Lostock St Gerards		24	10	10	4	53	39	40
Norcross & Warbreck		24	10	6	8	38	40	36
Tempest United	-6	24	12	4	8	56	44	34
Millom		24	8	5	11	47	56	29
Furness Rovers		24	8	5	11	37	48	29
Croston Sports	-6	24	10	4	10	40	37	28
Crosshills		24	7	6	11	48	51	27
BAE Barrow Sports Club	-3	24	6	10	8	36	48	25
Hesketh Bank		24	5	2	17	38	72	17
Whinney Hill		24	3	3	18	28	68	12

PRESIDENT'S CUP

FIRST ROUND
BAE Barrow Sports Club 3 Millom 2
Crosshills 1 **Vickerstown CC** 4
Furness Rovers 2 **Tempest United** 3
Trimpell 1 Norcross & Warbreck 0
Whinney Hill 1 **Stoneclough** 2

QUARTER-FINALS
BAE Barrow Sports Club 2 **Trimpell** 2 aet (3-4p)
Hesketh Bank 3 **Vickerstown CC** 4
Stoneclough 1 **Lostock St Gerards** 2
Tempest United 3 Croston Sports 1

SEMI-FINALS
Stoneclough 1 Trimpell 0 (at Norcross & Warbreck)
Tempest United 3 **Vickerstown CC** 4 aet (at Wyre Villa)

FINAL
(April 16th at Lancaster City)
Stoneclough 1 **Vickerstown CC** 2 aet

WWW.NLNEWSDESK.CO.UK

SPORTS 360 WEST LANCS LEAGUE DIVISION ONE CONSTITUTION 2008-09

CROOKLANDS CASUALS . . . . Longlands Park, Greystone Lane, Dalton-in-Furness LA15 8PX 01229 465010
CROSSHILLS . . . . Holme Lane, Crosshills, Keighley BD20 7RL . . . . None
CROSTON SPORTS . . . . Old Emmanuel School, Westhead Road, Croston, Leyland PR26 9RR 01772 600261
FLEETWOOD HESKETH . . . . Fylde Road, Southport PR9 9XH 01704 227968
FURNESS ROVERS . . . . Wilkie Road, Barrow-in-Furness LA14 5UQ. . . . . None
HAWCOAT PARK . . . . Vickers Sports Club, Hawcoat Lane, Barrow-in-Furness LA14 4HF 01229 825296
HESKETH BANK . . . . Hesketh Sports Field, Station Road, Hesketh Bank PR4 6SR . . . . None
LOSTOCK ST GERARDS . . . . Wateringpool Lane, Lostock Hall PR5 5UA . . . . None
MILLOM . . . . Millom RL Club, Devonshire Road, Millom LA18 4PG 01229 772030
MILNTHORPE CORINTHIANS . . . . Strands Lane, Milnthorpe LA7 7AE 01539 562135
NORCROSS & WARBRECK . . . . Anchorsholme Lane, Thornton Cleveleys, near Blackpool FY5 . . . . 01253 859836
TEMPEST UNITED . . . . Tempest Road, Chew Moor Village, Lostock, near Bolton BL6 4EL 01942 811938
TRIMPELL-SLYNE . . . . Kellet Lane, Slyne, Lancaster LA2 6BJ . . . . None
WYRE VILLA . . . . Hallgate Park, Stalmine Village, near Knott End FY6 0LB. 01253 701468

IN: *Crooklands Casuals (P), Fleetwood Hesketh (R), Milnthorpe Corinthians (P), Wyre Villa (R)*
OUT: *Stoneclough (P), Vickerstown CC (P), Whinney Hill (R)*
BAE Barrow Sports club become Hawcoat Park, Trimpell have merged with North Lancashire & District Premier Division side Slyne-with-Hest to form Trimpell-Slyne

WWW.CHERRYRED.CO.UK

	Askam United	BAC/EE Springfield	Bolton County	Burnley Belvedere	Crooklands Casuals	Furness Cavaliers	GSK Ulverston Rangers	Lancashire Constabulary	Lytham Town	Mill Hill St Peters	Milnthorpe Corinthians	Thornton Cleveleys	Todmorden Borough
Askam United	D	3-0	4-3	0-1	2-4	1-2	3-2	4-1	2-2	2-4	1-8	0-0	4-0
BAC/EE Springfield	4-4	I	3-2	1-2	2-2	3-3	1-1	1-0	4-1	1-2	2-1	1-5	5-2
Bolton County	4-0	0-3	V	2-1	0-2	1-0	0-0	3-1	0-1	1-0	0-0	0-6	0-3
Burnley Belvedere	1-2	3-2	1-2	I	2-2	3-7	3-0	2-0	1-3	2-0	1-2	6-1	1-0
Crooklands Casuals	5-2	6-2	4-2	5-2	S	2-2	3-1	6-1	2-4	2-2	1-0	4-1	3-1
Furness Cavaliers	3-1	1-4	2-3	1-1	0-0	I	1-1	2-2	2-0	1-1	0-7	2-2	1-0
GSK Ulverston Rangers	0-2	1-2	3-3	3-0	0-1	1-2	O	1-1	2-3	1-5	1-1	3-3	1-2
Lancashire Constabulary	2-1	0-2	1-1	1-5	0-5	5-2	2-2	N	3-2	0-3	0-2	2-2	1-3
Lytham Town	3-0	2-4	2-2	0-2	1-2	1-3	3-3	4-0		1-3	3-2	2-0	2-4
Mill Hill St Peters	2-4	3-3	2-0	1-2	1-3	3-5	0-2	2-1	3-5		0-2	2-1	2-1
Milnthorpe Corinthians	1-0	2-1	6-0	1-1	2-3	1-2	0-5	4-0	7-1	3-0	T	5-0	2-2
Thornton Cleveleys	1-1	4-3	2-2	1-1	2-0	3-0	2-3	3-4	2-0	2-1	0-3	W	0-2
Todmorden Borough	2-0	0-3	2-0	1-1	3-1	4-2	2-1	3-0	1-3	1-1	1-2	0-2	O

CHALLENGE CUP

FIRST ROUND
BAC/EE Springfield 2 **Thornton Cleveleys** 3
Burnley Belvedere 0 **Crooklands Casuals** 2
Furness Cavaliers 2 **Mill Hill St Peters** 6
Lancashire Constabulary 2 **Milnthorpe Corinthians** 6
Lytham Town 3 **GSK Ulverston Rangers** 3 *aet* (4-5p)

QUARTER-FINALS
Askam Utd 3 **Milnthorpe Corinthians** 5
Bolton County 3 Todmorden Borough 2
Crooklands Casuals 3 GSK Ulverston Rangers 1
Mill Hill St Peters 1 **Thornton Cleveleys** 1 *aet* (2-4p)

SEMI-FINALS
Crooklands Casuals 2 Bolton County 0 *(at Garstang)*
Thornton Cleveleys 3 **Milnthorpe Corinthians** 3 *(at Freckleton)*

FINAL
(April 10th at Barrow)
Milnthorpe Corinthians 3 Crooklands Casuals 1

Division Two

		P	W	D	L	F	A	Pts
Crooklands Casuals		24	15	5	4	66	36	50
Milnthorpe Corinthians		24	14	4	6	64	25	46
BAC/EE Springfield		24	11	5	8	57	50	38
Burnley Belvedere		24	11	5	8	44	37	38
Mill Hill St Peters		24	11	4	9	43	39	37
Todmorden Borough		24	11	3	10	40	38	36
Furness Cavaliers		24	8	8	8	42	50	32
Lytham Town		24	9	3	12	45	53	30
Thornton Cleveleys	-3	24	8	7	9	45	47	28
Bolton County		24	7	6	11	31	49	27
Askam United	-3	24	8	4	12	43	55	25
GSK Ulverston Rangers		24	4	9	11	41	48	21
Lancashire Constabulary	-4	24	5	5	14	29	63	16

Reserve Division One

		P	W	D	L	F	A	Pts
Euxton Villa Res.	-6	28	21	3	4	75	31	60
Poulton Town Res.		28	18	4	6	69	32	58
Thornton Cleveleys Res.		28	15	6	7	67	41	51
Tempest United Res.		28	15	5	8	71	49	50
Charnock Richard Res.		28	15	5	8	50	29	50
Eagley Res.		28	14	3	11	72	60	45
Blackpool Wren Rovers Res.		28	12	6	10	51	49	42
Barnoldswick Town Res.		28	13	3	12	63	64	42
BAC/EE Springfields Res.		28	12	5	11	86	64	41
Fulwood Amateurs Res.		28	11	8	9	60	57	41
Freckleton Res.		28	8	6	14	48	65	30
Norcross & Warbreck Res.		28	8	4	16	49	74	28
Turton Res.		28	8	1	19	48	86	25
Fleetwood Hesketh Res.		28	4	4	20	38	81	16
Burnley United Res.		28	4	1	23	39	104	13

Reserve Division Two

		P	W	D	L	F	A	Pts
Garstang Res.		26	21	4	1	67	23	67
Burnley Belvedere Res.		26	17	4	5	60	26	58
Haslingden St Mary's Res.		26	17	4	5	65	26	55
Coppull United Res.		26	15	4	7	59	31	49
Stoneclough Res.		26	14	3	9	64	52	45
Hesketh Bank Res.		26	13	2	11	62	32	41
Milnthorpe Corinthians Res.		26	12	1	13	68	51	37
Todmorden Borough Res.		26	10	4	12	42	48	34
Whinney Hill Res.		26	10	4	12	50	57	34
Bolton County Res.		26	9	2	15	41	53	29
Wyre Villa Res.		26	8	5	13	40	52	29
Lytham Town Res.		26	5	1	20	30	94	16
Crosshills Res.	-9	26	6	2	18	32	79	11
Mill Hill St Peters Res.		26	2	3	21	29	85	9

HOUSTON CUP

FINAL
(May 3rd at Croston Sports)
Fulwood Amateurs Res. 1 Barnoldswick Town Res. 0

SPORTS 360 WEST LANCS LEAGUE DIVISION TWO CONSTITUTION 2008-09

ASKAM UNITED .... Duddon Road, James Street, Askam-in-Furness LA16 7AH 01229 464576
BAC/EE SPRINGFIELD .... BAC Sports Ground, South Meadow Lane, Preston PR1 8JP 01772 464351
BOLTON COUNTY .... Radcliffe Road, Darcy Lever, Bolton BL3 1RU .... None
BURNLEY BELVEDERE .... Belvedere & Caldervale SC, Holden Road, Burnley BL10 2LE 01282 433171
FURNESS CAVALIERS .... Rampside Road, Barrow-in-Furness LA13 0HN .... None
GSK ULVERSTON RANGERS .... off North Lonsdale Road, Ulverston LA12 9DZ 01229 582261
LANCASHIRE CONSTABULARY .... Police HQ, Saunders Lane, Hutton, Preston PR4 5SG 01772 410591
LYTHAM TOWN .... Lytham Academy, Ballam Road, Lytham St Annes FY8 4LE 01253 733873
MILL HILL ST PETERS...... Opposite Mill Hill Hotel, Bridge Street, off Buncer Lane, Blackburn BB2 2QY 01254 675557
THORNTON CLEVELEYS .... Bourne Road, Cleveleys, Thornton Cleveleys FY5 4AB 01253 869666
TODMORDEN BOROUGH .... Bellholme, Walsden Road (off A6033), Todmorden OL14 6UH .... None
WALNEY ISLAND .... Tummerhill Play Flos, Ocean Road, Walney, Barrow-in-Furness LA14 3HN .... None
WHINNEY HILL .... Clayton-le-Moors, Accrington BB5 5NF .... None

IN: Walney Island (P – Furness Premier League Premier Division), Whinney Hill (R)
OUT: Crooklands Casuals (P), Milnthorpe Corinthians (P)

WEST MIDLANDS (REGIONAL) LEAGUE

	AFC Wulfrunians	Bewdley Town	Bridgnorth Town	Brierley & Withymoor	Bromyard Town	Bustleholme	Darlaston Town	Dudley Sports	Dudley Town	Ellesmere Rangers	Goodrich	Gornal Athletic	Ledbury Town	Ludlow Town	Lye Town	Pelsall Villa	Shawbury United	Tividale	Wednesfield	Wellington	Wolverhampton Casuals
AFC Wulfrunians		1-3	1-2	5-0	1-0	7-0	2-2	0-0	0-0	2-3	0-0	4-1	7-0	4-1	2-0	3-3	1-4	0-0	0-3	4-0	2-1
Bewdley Town	1-0		0-2	2-2	1-0	2-0	1-1	2-4	1-2	0-1	3-1	6-1	2-1	2-1	1-0	1-3	3-1	0-0	3-0	6-0	4-1
Bridgnorth Town	1-1	2-1		2-0	5-0	5-1	0-1	2-0	2-2	1-0	3-3	2-0	3-2	3-0	3-1	3-2	0-2	2-1	3-0	6-0	4-1
Brierley & Withymoor	0-2	3-6	0-3	P	1-2	4-1	0-4	2-1	2-0	8-4	0-3	4-1	1-2	2-1	0-7	3-4	1-2	1-1	0-3	2-3	2-1
Bromyard Town	0-2	1-4	1-3	2-1	R	2-0	2-2	2-4	3-7	5-0	0-0	0-0	0-2	2-1	1-4	0-3	3-0	0-1	0-1	3-0	2-2
Bustleholme	3-4	0-1	0-4	1-0	4-4	E	1-2	1-2	0-0	0-1	4-2	0-1	2-4	1-0	2-4	1-3	1-1	1-5	0-1	3-2	1-1
Darlaston Town	2-3	2-3	1-1	3-1	3-1	1-1	M	5-2	0-1	0-1	2-0	2-0	2-1	1-1	2-0	1-2	0-1	0-3	0-0	4-2	2-2
Dudley Sports	2-1	3-0	1-0	2-3	4-0	3-0	1-1	I	3-2	4-2	2-1	1-1	0-0	2-2	3-2	2-1	1-1	1-1	1-1	1-1	1-1
Dudley Town	0-4	3-1	0-1	3-1	2-1	0-2	2-4	2-1	E	1-2	2-1	1-0	0-3	0-1	1-1	1-0	1-0	2-1	1-0	2-1	1-0
Ellesmere Rangers	0-0	3-2	2-1	1-0	1-2	3-0	3-1	1-2	1-2	R	2-3	4-0	4-0	1-3	2-1	1-2	0-1	0-1	1-1	0-2	1-1
Goodrich	0-3	0-2	0-1	1-2	5-0	8-2	0-1	2-4	1-2	2-1		1-0	0-0	0-3	1-3	3-4	2-3	0-1	0-1	6-1	1-1
Gornal Athletic	1-5	2-2	1-2	0-1	2-3	3-0	0-3	0-0	1-3	1-1	3-0	D	2-1	4-0	0-0	1-1	1-1	2-2	1-4	0-1	1-1
Ledbury Town	2-1	1-3	0-2	3-0	1-3	5-1	3-3	1-0	2-2	3-0	3-2	0-2	I	4-5	3-1	0-4	2-3	1-2	2-3	2-4	2-5
Ludlow Town	1-1	0-1	0-2	1-6	3-2	2-2	2-2	2-2	0-1	0-0	1-2	0-1	2-0	V	0-4	1-4	1-3	3-1	1-1	1-1	2-2
Lye Town	0-2	3-3	0-5	3-1	2-0	1-0	3-0	0-1	0-0	0-2	2-3	4-2	6-1	0-1	I	2-1	1-3	3-1	4-2	4-1	5-2
Pelsall Villa	0-1	1-3	0-1	3-0	2-1	4-2	5-1	0-2	3-3	2-1	4-2	0-1	0-3	0-1	1-1	S	1-6	0-0	0-4	0-2	2-2
Shawbury United	2-0	3-4	1-2	1-1	0-0	1-0	5-3	2-0	2-1	1-2	7-3	0-4	2-1	3-0	2-2	3-0	I	3-1	3-4	4-4	0-3
Tividale	1-0	2-3	2-4	1-1	0-0	3-4	2-4	1-2	1-2	1-2	4-1	1-1	4-1	0-2	3-3	5-0	2-2	O	0-2	3-2	0-0
Wednesfield	0-5	1-0	0-2	2-2	1-0	2-1	1-1	1-0	0-0	1-1	1-1	4-2	4-1	6-0	1-1	0-2	1-4	1-1	N	0-2	0-1
Wellington	3-1	2-3	2-3	0-3	3-0	4-4	0-2	1-2	1-1	1-1	2-0	3-1	2-1	0-3	2-1	0-4	0-3	2-3	2-5		2-1
Wolverhampton Casuals	1-1	0-5	2-6	3-2	2-2	4-3	2-2	2-0	1-2	0-3	2-4	0-0	1-2	0-2	1-1	0-0	1-2	1-3	2-3	3-3	

Premier Division		P	W	D	L	F	A	Pts
Bridgnorth Town		40	31	4	5	97	33	97
Bewdley Town		40	23	6	11	83	57	75
Shawbury United		40	21	9	10	86	59	72
Wednesfield		40	20	9	11	68	51	69
Dudley Town		40	20	9	11	56	48	69
AFC Wulfrunians		40	19	10	11	83	43	67
Ellesmere Rangers		40	20	7	13	71	52	67
Dudley Sports	-3	40	19	12	9	64	46	66
Darlaston Town		40	17	12	11	71	57	63
Lye Town		40	18	8	14	80	58	62
Tividale		40	13	12	15	72	65	51
Pelsall Villa		40	14	9	17	67	71	51
Wellington		40	13	11	16	63	79	50
Ludlow Town		40	13	11	16	50	73	50
Goodrich		40	13	6	21	72	83	45
Gornal Athletic		40	10	12	18	46	63	42
Brierley & Withymoor		40	12	5	23	62	89	41
Wolverhampton Casuals	-1	40	8	15	17	58	80	38
Ledbury Town		40	10	3	27	56	100	33
Bromyard Town		40	8	7	25	46	87	31
Bustleholme		40	7	5	28	55	112	26

PREMIER DIVISION CUP

FIRST ROUND
Gornal Athletic 4 Bustleholme 1
Ludlow Town 1 **Dudley Town** 6
Lye Town 4 Goodich 1
Shawbury United 1 **Bridgnorth Town** 1 *aet* (6-7p)
Tividale 1 **Dudley Sports** 2

SECOND ROUND
Bewdley Tn 2 Bromyard Tn 0
Darlaston Tn 4 Bridgnorth Tn 0
Dudley Town 1 **AFC Wulfrunians** 1 *aet* (2-4p)
Ellesmere Rangers 4 Wolverhampton Casuals 0
Gornal Athletic 2 Brierley Hill & Withymoor 1 *aet*
Ledbury Town 2 **Wednesfield** 3
Pelsall Villa 0 **Dudley Sports** 1
Wellington 1 **Lye Town** 3 *aet*

QUARTER-FINALS
AFC Wulfrunians 2 Ellesmere Rangers 0
Bewdley Town 1 **Gornal Athletic** 3
Dudley Sports 1 Darlaston Town 0
Wellington 1 **Wednesfield** 2

SEMI-FINALS
(played over two legs)
Dudley Sports 2 AFC Wulfrunians 2, AFC Wulfrunians (scr.) v **Dudley Sports** (w/o)
Wednesfield 2 Gornal Athletic 1, Gornal Athletic 0 **Wednesfield** 1 *aet* (2-4p)
FINAL *(May 10th at Tividale)*
Dudley Sports 2 Wednesfield 1

WEST MIDLANDS (REGIONAL) LEAGUE PREMIER DIVISION CONSTITUTION 2008-09
AFC WULFRUNIANS ... Wolverhampton Casuals FC, Brinsford Lane, Coven Heath, Wolverhampton WV10 7PR ... 01902 783214
BEWDLEY TOWN ... Ribbesford Meadows, Ribbesford, Bewdley DY12 2TJ ... 07733 264893
BLOXWICH UNITED ... Grosvenor Park, Somerfield Road, Bloxwich WS3 2EJ ... None
BROMYARD TOWN ... Delahay Meadow, Stourport Road, Bromyard HR7 4NT ... 01885 483974
BUSTLEHOLME ... Tipton Town FC, Wednesbury Oak Road, Tipton DY4 0BS ... 0121 502 5534/556 5067
DARLASTON TOWN ... City Ground, Waverley Road, Darlaston WS10 8ED ... 0121 526 4423
DUDLEY SPORTS ... Dudley Employees S&S, Hillcrest Avenue, Brierley Hill DY5 3QH ... 01384 826420
DUDLEY TOWN ... The Dell Stadium, Bryce Road, Brierley Hill DY5 4NE ... 01384 812943
ELLESMERE RANGERS ... Beech Grove Playing Fields, Ellesmere SY12 0BT ... None
GOODRICH ... Goodrich Sports Ground, Stafford Road, Fordhouses, Wolverhampton WV10 7EH ... None
GORNAL ATHLETIC ... Garden Walk Stadium, Garden Walk, Lower Gornal, Dudley DY3 2NH ... 01384 358398
HEATH TOWN RANGERS ... Wednesfield FC, Cottage Ground, Amos Lane, Wednesfield WV11 1ND ... 01902 735506
LEDBURY TOWN ... New Street Ground, New Street, Ledbury HR8 2EL ... 07879 268205
LUDLOW TOWN ... SBS Stadium, Bromfield Road, Ludlow SY8 2BY ... 01584 876000
LYE TOWN ... Sports Ground, Stourbridge Road, Lye, Stourbridge DY9 7DH ... 01384 422672
PELSALL VILLA ... The Bush Ground, Walsall Road, Heath End, Pelsall WS3 4ET ... 01922 692748/682018
SHAWBURY UNITED ... Butlers Sports Centre, Bowens Field, Wem SY4 5AW ... 01939 233287
TIVIDALE ... The Beeches, Packwood Road, Tividale, Oldbury B69 1UL ... 01384 211743
WEDNESFIELD ... Cottage Ground, Amos Lane, Wednesfield WV11 1ND ... 01902 735506
WELLINGTON ... Wellington Playing Fields, Wellington, Hereford HR4 8AZ ... None
WOLVERHAMPTON CASUALS ... Brinsford Lane, Coven Heath, WV10 7PR ... 01902 783214
IN: Bloxwich United (formerly Birchills United) (P), Heath Town Rangers (P)
OUT: Bridgnorth Town (P – Midland Alliance), Brierley & Withymoor (F)

WWW.NLNEWSDESK.CO.UK

Note – Hinton withdrew during the course of the season

Their results are shown herein but are expunged from the league table

	AFC Wombourne Utd	Bilbrook	Birchills United	Blackheath Town	Bridgnorth Town Res.	Cresswell Wanderers	Dudley United	Gornal Athletic Res.	Heath Town Rangers	Hinton	Malvern Town Res.	Penn Croft	Riverway	Shenstone Pathfinder	Sporting Khalsa	Stafford Town	Warstone Wanderers	Wednesbury Town	Wolverhampton Dev.	Wolverhampton Utd
AFC Wombourne United		2-1	0-1	2-1	0-3	1-0	2-0	3-2	2-4	n/a	1-1	2-1	1-2	1-1	0-0	0-3	1-5	2-1	0-1	3-1
Bilbrook	2-3		0-3	1-1	0-3	1-2	0-2	3-2	0-4	n/a	3-1	0-0	2-2	2-1	3-3	2-4	0-2	2-2	0-3	3-4
Birchills United	6-0	8-2		2-2	0-2	3-1	3-0	2-0	2-1	n/a	2-1	3-2	2-0	4-1	3-2	6-1	4-2	2-0	7-1	3-1
Blackheath Town	1-1	1-1	1-3		0-0	0-2	2-1	2-0	1-3	n/a	4-3	4-5	1-0	11-0	1-2	0-0	1-6	0-2	0-1	2-2
Bridgnorth Town Res.	1-1	2-0	1-0	1-1	D	6-0	3-0	2-0	1-0	n/a	3-1	3-1	1-0	3-0	2-2	3-1	3-0	3-3	2-3	2-1
Cresswell Wanderers	1-0	0-4	3-0	1-3	0-1	I	3-1	2-3	3-8	n/a	0-2	3-2	4-0	1-1	2-2	2-7	1-2	1-3	0-1	2-3
Dudley United	0-1	1-2	0-7	2-2	0-5	2-3	V	0-1	1-3	n/a	0-3	0-1	0-2	0-0	2-1	1-5	4-4	1-3	1-2	0-1
Gornal Athletic Res.	0-3	0-1	0-8	2-1	0-1	1-2	1-2	I	0-2	n/a	1-5	3-2	0-0	1-3	1-1	1-5	0-4	2-1	0-10	0-1
Heath Town Rangers	1-1	3-1	1-1	1-0	1-2	2-1	1-1	5-0	S	n/a	2-0	0-2	2-0	2-0	1-0	1-1	4-1	4-4	3-2	1-1
Hinton	1-3	1-3	n/a	n/a	n/a	n/a	n/a	0-7	n/a	I	n/a	n/a	n/a	n/a	n/a	n/a	n/a	n/a	n/a	n/a
Malvern Town Res.	2-0	2-2	0-1	1-3	0-1	1-1	4-1	3-1	2-1	n/a	O	1-1	0-2	4-0	0-0	2-1	1-5	1-3	1-1	1-3
Penn Croft	2-1	0-2	1-5	5-3	1-0	3-0	2-1	9-4	2-7	n/a	4-0	N	1-1	3-0	4-1	5-0	1-2	4-3	1-1	0-1
Riverway	2-4	2-1	0-1	1-2	2-4	3-3	4-1	5-0	0-2	5-0	2-3	1-3		2-2	3-0	0-4	3-0	2-2	2-3	3-1
Shenstone Pathfinder	1-4	3-1	0-4	2-0	0-4	1-0	4-3	1-5	3-3	n/a	2-5	2-1	2-0	O	3-2	2-6	2-1	0-0	4-4	2-3
Sporting Khalsa	1-5	0-6	1-4	3-2	0-3	0-1	2-3	3-0	0-5	n/a	0-1	1-1	4-3	2-1	N	2-5	4-0	1-0	2-5	1-2
Stafford Town	2-3	2-3	2-1	1-1	4-0	5-1	4-1	3-1	1-3	n/a	4-0	2-1	3-1	4-1	4-1	E	1-2	7-1	4-1	6-0
Warstone Wanderers	3-4	2-2	3-0	2-1	1-2	1-0	3-1	3-3	4-5	n/a	0-1	1-1	1-2	1-3	1-1	1-2		2-2	1-0	2-0
Wednesbury Town	1-1	2-2	1-3	1-1	0-0	6-1	1-3	1-1	0-0	n/a	1-4	2-4	0-3	4-2	0-2	2-2	1-3		2-5	2-0
Wolverhampton Development	1-5	3-1	1-3	0-3	1-1	2-1	3-0	2-0	0-0	n/a	4-0	3-0	0-1	2-0	4-4	2-1	1-3	1-0		1-2
Wolverhampton United	0-1	1-1	1-5	0-2	1-2	0-2	1-1	3-1	1-3	n/a	4-1	0-1	1-4	2-2	1-2	0-2	0-0	0-0	3-3	

Division One		P	W	D	L	F	A	Pts
Birchills United		36	29	2	5	112	35	89
Bridgnorth Town Res.		36	26	7	3	76	25	85
Heath Town Rangers		36	23	9	4	93	41	78
Stafford Town		36	22	5	9	106	53	71
Wolverhampton Development		36	19	7	10	78	58	64
AFC Wombourne United		36	18	7	11	61	55	61
Warstone Wanderers	-3	36	18	7	11	77	59	58
Penn Croft		36	17	6	13	77	63	57
Malvern Town Res.		36	13	8	15	58	63	47
Riverway		36	13	7	16	59	59	46
Blackheath Town		36	9	13	14	62	60	40
Wolverhampton United		36	10	9	17	45	68	39
Bilbrook		36	9	10	17	57	76	37
Cresswell Wanderers		36	11	4	21	50	81	37
Sporting Khalsa		36	9	9	18	54	84	36
Wednesbury Town		36	7	13	16	57	75	34
Shenstone Pathfinder		36	7	10	19	50	98	31
Gornal Athletic Res.		36	6	4	26	37	104	22
Dudley United		36	5	5	26	38	90	20

Hinton – record expunged

DIVISION ONE CUP

FIRST ROUND
Blackheath Town 2 **AFC Wombourne United 5**
Dudley United 2 **Bilbrook** 2 *aet* (4-5p)
Riverway 2 Wolverhampton United 0

SECOND ROUND
Bridgnorth Town Res. 10 Gornal Athletic Res. 0
Heath Town Rangers 0 **AFC Wombourne United 1**
Malvern Town Res. 2 **Warstone Wanderers** 2 *aet* (3-4p)
Penn Croft 1 **Stafford Town 2**
Riverway 4 Birchills United 0
Shenstone Pathfinder 0 **Wolverhampton Development 3**
Sporting Khalsa 1 Bilbrook 0
Wednesdbury Town 0 **Cresswell Wanderers 1**

QUARTER-FINALS
Bilbrook 1 **Stafford Town 2**
Birchills United 2 Warstone Wanderers 1
Bridgnorth Town Res. 2 Cresswell Wanderers 1
Wolverhampton Development 3 AFC Wombourne United 0

SEMI-FINALS *(played over two legs)*
Stafford Town 1 Bridgnorth Town Res. 0, Bridgnorth Town Res. 0 **Stafford Town 1**
Wolverhampton Development 2 Birchills United 0, Birchills United 2 **Wolverhampton Development 4**

FINAL
(May 7th at Wednesfield)
Stafford Town 0 **Wolverhampton Development 1**

WEST MIDLANDS (REGIONAL) LEAGUE DIVISION ONE CONSTITUTION 2008-09

AFC WOMBOURNE UNITED ... Mile Flat Sports Ground, Mile Flat, Wall Heath, Kingswinford DY6 0AU 01384 377582
BILBROOK .... Pendeford Lane, Wolverhampton WV9 5HQ .... None
BILSTON TOWN .... Queen Street, Bilston, West Midlands WV14 7EX 01902 491498
BLACKHEATH TOWN .... York Road Sports & Social, York Road, Oldbury, Rowley Regis B65 0RR 0121 559 5564
BRIDGNORTH TOWN RESERVES .... Crown Meadow, Innage Lane, Bridgnorth WV16 4HS 01746 762747
DUDLEY UNITED .... Mile Flat Sports Ground, Mile Flat, Wall Heath, Kingswinford DY6 0AU 01384 377582
MALVERN TOWN RESERVES ... Langland Stadium, Langland Avenue, Malvern WR14 2EQ 01684 574291
PENN CROFT .... Aldersley Leisure Village, Aldersley Road, Wolverhampton WV6 9NW 01902 556200
RIVERWAY .... Long Lane Park, Long Lane, Essington WV11 2AA 01922 406604
SHENSTONE PATHFINDER ... Shenstone PF (Pavilion Club), Birmingham Road, Shenstone, Lichfield WS14 0LR 01543 481658
SPORTING KHALSA .... Abbey Park, Glastonbury Crescent, Mossley, Bloxwich, Walsall WS3 2RQ 01922 477640
STAFFORD TOWN .... Rowley Park Stadium, Averill Road, West Road, Stafford ST17 9XX 01785 251060
WARLEY DEVELOPMENT ... York Road Sports & Social, York Road, Oldbury, Rowley Regis B65 0RR 0121 559 5564
WARSTONE WANDERERS .... Abbey Park, Glastonbury Crescent, Mossley, Bloxwich, Walsall WS3 2RQ 01922 477640
WEDNESBURY TOWN .... Long Lane Park, Long Lane, Essington, Wolverhampton WV11 2AA .... None
WELLINGTON AMATEURS .... Grainger Road, Leegomery, Telford TF1 6UJ .... None
WOLVERHAMPTON UNITED ..... Prestwood Road West, Wednesfield, Wolverhampton WV11 1HL 01902 730881
IN: Bilston Town (P), Wellington Amateurs (P)
OUT: Bloxwich United (formerly Birchills United) (P), Cresswell Wanderers (W), Gornal Athletic Reserves (W), Heath Town Rangers (P), Hinton (WS)
Wolverhampton Development become Warley Development

Note – Parkfield United and Penn Colts withdrew during the course of the season.

Their results are shown herein but are expunged from the league table

	Bentley Youth	Bilston Town	Black Country Rangers	Brereton Town	Bustleholme Res.	Heath Town Rangers Res.	Mahal	Parkfield United	Penkridge Town	Penn Colts	Powick	Punjab United Sports	Stone Old Alleynians	Tenbury United	Wellington Amateurs	Wyrley Juniors
Bentley Youth		3-3	2-2	5-1	1-4	1-1	2-2	1-1	0-1	4-0	1-0	4-2	2-5	4-1	1-3	2-0
Bilston Town	5-0		5-1	6-0	2-0	3-3	1-0	4-1	3-2	n/a	4-4	4-1	3-3	3-3	3-4	1-0
Black Country Rangers	1-3	2-4	D	3-1	2-3	3-3	2-0	6-1	0-6	n/a	0-1	3-1	0-1	1-3	0-0	0-2
Brereton Town	0-4	1-5	1-5	I	0-8	1-6	2-1	2-2	3-5	1-1	5-5	1-2	1-3	0-7		3-2
Bustleholme Res.	2-1	0-2	3-0	9-3	V	1-3	1-2	7-1	2-1	3-0	4-0	1-2	1-4	2-1	2-5	2-0
Heath Town Rangers Res.	1-4	0-3	1-2	7-1	1-3	I	1-0	2-1	0-3	n/a	1-3	5-4	1-0	2-1	1-3	2-3
Mahal	1-3	1-2	0-4	7-0	0-3	1-2	S	4-1	0-3	3-2	2-2	4-1	2-2	2-6	0-3	5-5
Parkfield United	2-8	0-2	2-3	n/a	0-3	1-4	n/a	I	1-3	0-8	3-1	n/a	n/a	n/a	n/a	1-0
Penkridge Town	3-2	2-1	2-2	7-1	3-0	1-2	3-0	3-0	O	n/a	3-0	1-1	1-1	2-3	2-1	2-2
Penn Colts	n/a	n/a	2-1	n/a	0-2	2-3	9-0	n/a	n/a	N	2-2	0-1	0-9	1-2	0-2	0-7
Powick	2-2	0-3	0-4	4-0	4-0	5-0	1-3	2-1	1-2	2-1		3-3	1-6	2-0	0-5	1-2
Punjab United Sports	5-1	1-2	2-1	2-1	3-6	1-2	1-3	n/a	1-5	3-2	3-0	T	2-1	2-0	0-6	3-6
Stone Old Alleynians	1-1	1-5	3-0	2-1	1-0	1-0	8-0	8-0	3-2	4-0	0-0	2-2	W	1-1	1-1	0-1
Tenbury United	4-3	3-3	2-5	7-0	3-5	0-1	2-0	3-0	1-0	3-5	1-4	6-2	1-2	O	0-3	0-3
Wellington Amateurs	1-2	0-1	5-1	1-0	3-0	4-1	1-0	3-1	4-1	n/a	4-2	4-1	1-1	8-2		0-0
Wyrley Juniors	3-2	2-1	2-0	6-0	1-4	3-1	2-1	n/a	0-1	4-0	4-2	3-0	0-2	0-3	1-1	

Division Two	P	W	D	L	F	A	Pts
Wellington Amateurs	26	18	5	3	78	23	59
Bilston Town	26	17	6	3	78	37	57
Penkridge Town	26	14	5	7	61	33	47
Wyrley Juniors	26	14	4	8	53	39	46
Bustleholme Res.	26	15	0	11	66	48	45
Stone Old Alleynians	26	12	9	5	48	30	45
Bentley Youth	26	10	6	10	56	54	36
Heath Town Rangers Res.	26	11	3	12	48	55	36
Tenbury United	26	10	3	13	57	61	33
Powick	26	8	6	12	43	52	30
Black Country Rangers	26	8	4	14	44	56	28
Punjab United Sports	26	7	4	15	51	79	25
Mahal	26	5	4	17	38	65	19
Brereton Town	26	2	3	21	29	118	9

Parkfield United and Penn Colts – records expunged

DIVISION TWO CUP

FIRST ROUND
Bilston Town 3 Brereton Town 0
Bustleholme Res. 2 Tenbury United 2 *aet* (5-4p)
Heath Town Rangers Res. 0 **Powick** 2
Mahal 5 Penn Colts 0
Parkfields United 0 **Stone Old Alleynians** 4
Penkridge Town 0 Wellington Amateurs 0 *aet* (5-4p)
Punjab United Sports 2 **Black Country Rangers** 4
Wyrley Juniors 1 **Bentley Youth** 2
QUARTER-FINALS
Bentley Youth 2 Powick 1
Bilston Town 3 Black Country Rangers 1
Penkridge Town 4 Mahal 2
Stone Old Alleynians 0 **Bustleholme Res.** 2
SEMI-FINALS (played over two legs)
Bustleholme Res. 1 Bentley Youth 0, **Bentley Youth** (w/o)
v Bustleholme Res. (scr.)
Penkridge Town 2 Bilston Town 1, Bilston Town 0
Penkridge Town 0
FINAL
(May 7th at Wolverhampton Casuals)
Bentley Youth 3 Penkridge Town 1

WEST MIDLANDS (REGIONAL) LEAGUE DIVISION TWO CONSTITUTION 2008-09

BENTLEY . . . . Bentley Road South, Darlaston WS10 8LN 07737 29675
BLACK COUNTRY RANGERS . . . . Willenhall Town FC, Noose Lane, Willenhall WV13 2BB 01902 636586
DARLASTON TOWN RESERVES . . . . City Ground, Waverley Road, Darlaston WS10 8ED 0121 526 4423
ETTINGSHALL PARK FARM . . . . Parkfield High School, Prosser Street, Bilston WV14 0QA 01902 558380
HANWOOD UNITED . . . . Hanwood Recreation Ground, Hanwood . . . . None
HEATH TOWN RANGERS RESERVES . . . Bilbrook FC, Pendeford Lane, Wobaston Road Wolverhampton WV9 5HG . . . . None
LYE TOWN RESERVES . . . . Sports Ground, Stourbridge Road, Lye, Stourbridge DY9 7DH 01384 422672
MAHAL . . . . Hadley Stadium, Wilson Road, Smethwick, Warley B68 9JW 0121 434 4848
PENKRIDGE TOWN . . . . Monkton Recreation Centre, Pinfold Lane, Penkridge, Stafford ST19 5QP . . . . None
STONE OLD ALLEYNIANS . . . . Springbank Park, Yarnfield Road, Yarnfield, Stone ST15 0NF 01785 761891
TENBURY UNITED . . . . Palmers Meadow, Burford, Tenbury Wells WR15 8AP . . . . None
TRYSULL . . . . Aldersley Stadium, Aldersley Road, Wolverhampton WV6 9NW 01902 556200
WARSTONE WANDERERS RESERVES . . . Four Ashes, Stafford Road, Wolverhampton WV10 7BUG . . . . None
WRENS NEST . . . . Gornal Athletic FC, Garden Walk, Lower Gornal, Dudley DY3 2NH 01384 358398
WYRLEY JUNIORS . . . . Four Ashes, Stafford Road, Wolverhampton WV10 7BU . . . . None
IN: *Darlaston Town Reserves (N), Ettingshall Park Farm (P – Sunday football), Hanwood United (P – Shropshire County League Premier Division), Lye Town Reserves (P – Kidderminster & District League Premier Division), Trysull (formerly AFC Codsall) (P – Sunday football), Warstone Wanderers Reserves (N), Wrens Nest (P – Dudley & Cradley Heath League Premier Division)*
OUT: *Bilston Town (P), Brereton Town (S – Staffordshire County Senior League Division One), Bustleholme Reserves (W), Parkfield United (WS), Penn Colts (WS), Powick (W), Punjab United Sports (W), Wellington Amateurs (P)*
Bentley Youth become Bentley

WEST RIDING COUNTY AMATEUR LEAGUE

	Ardsley Celtic	Bay Athletic	Brighouse Town	Campion	Golcar United	Halifax Irish Club	Hall Green United	Hemsworth Miners Welfare	Keighley Shamrocks	Lower Hopton	Meltham Athletic	Ovenden West Riding	Overthorpe Sports	Storthes Hall	Tyersal	Wibsey
Ardsley Celtic	P	0-1	3-0	2-2	0-2	4-1	3-0	0-0	5-0	1-3	6-1	1-1	0-1	1-1	2-2	0-4
Bay Athletic	3-1	R	3-2	1-0	6-2	3-2	8-1	4-2	4-1	3-3	2-4	6-0	7-2	0-2	2-1	5-2
Brighouse Town	3-0	0-3	E	1-0	0-2	0-4	2-0	0-2	5-0	0-0	1-4	3-1	3-3	1-1	2-0	0-0
Campion	6-0	0-0	0-2	M	3-1	1-5	5-2	0-0	5-0	1-1	3-1	2-0	2-2	1-1	4-2	2-0
Golcar United	4-1	0-0	2-2	2-0	I	2-3	2-4	1-3	6-0	3-1	0-3	2-2	1-2	0-4	3-1	0-2
Halifax Irish Club	2-1	1-2	1-1	1-2	3-1	E	3-3	2-1	5-0	0-1	3-3	2-1	3-5	0-1	0-1	4-4
Hall Green United	1-2	0-1	4-2	2-1	3-4	0-6	R	0-3	4-3	2-2	2-2	1-5	2-1	2-2	3-2	2-0
Hemsworth Miners Welfare	2-0	3-4	3-2	0-3	1-1	4-3	1-0		1-0	3-0	2-3	1-1	2-0	1-2	0-0	2-2
Keighley Shamrocks	2-0	L-W	1-1	3-2	0-2	0-3	6-6	1-1	D	2-0	0-3	1-4	2-5	0-2	1-2	0-4
Lower Hopton	1-3	1-2	0-1	0-1	2-0	1-1	0-1	1-3	0-1	I	1-3	2-1	1-2	1-1	1-0	4-1
Meltham Athletic	3-2	1-4	1-1	5-1	0-0	1-2	4-0	2-2	4-0	5-0	V	1-1	10-0	3-2	8-0	4-0
Ovenden West Riding	5-2	2-5	2-3	0-1	W-L	0-3	0-1	2-4	2-1	1-2	1-5	I	0-3	0-1	4-2	4-0
Overthorpe Sports	1-3	1-1	0-0	3-4	3-3	1-5	0-1	1-4	4-2	3-3	1-4	3-2	S	0-5	6-0	7-5
Storthes Hall	4-0	7-1	0-1	2-0	1-2	3-2	4-0	2-1	6-0	2-1	0-0	1-1	3-0	I	1-0	3-1
Tyersal	3-3	1-2	2-1	3-0	1-1	3-4	0-4	2-1	3-2	1-2	1-2	2-3	4-2	2-3	O	0-2
Wibsey	1-1	3-1	0-0	1-1	4-5	1-1	5-2	2-4	0-1	2-2	2-1	0-1	2-2	0-4	3-4	N

Premier Division		P	W	D	L	F	A	Pts
Bay Athletic	+3	30	22	4	4	84	45	73
Storthes Hall		30	20	7	3	71	22	67
Meltham Athletic		30	18	7	5	91	40	61
Hemsworth Miners Welfare		30	14	8	8	57	41	50
Halifax Irish Club		30	14	6	10	75	51	48
Campion		30	13	7	10	53	43	46
Golcar United		30	11	7	12	54	55	40
Brighouse Town		30	10	10	10	40	42	40
Hall Green United		30	11	5	14	53	79	38
Overthorpe Sports		30	10	7	13	64	84	37
Lower Hopton		30	8	8	14	37	50	32
Ovenden West Riding		30	9	5	16	47	61	32
Ardsley Celtic		30	8	7	15	47	60	31
Wibsey		30	7	9	14	53	67	30
Tyersal		30	8	4	18	45	72	28
Keighley Shamrocks		30	5	3	22	30	89	18

PREMIER DIVISION CUP

FIRST ROUND
Bay Athletic 3 Storthes Hall 1
Brighouse Town 1 **Campion** 3
Hall Green United 4 Ardsley Celtic 0
Keighley Shamrocks 0 **Meltham Athletic** 3
Lower Hopton 2 Golcar United 0
Ovenden West Riding 2 **Halifax Irish Club** 3
Overthorpe Sports 0 **Tyersal** 3
Wibsey 0 **Hemsworth Miners Welfare** 1
QUARTER-FINALS
Bay Athletic 1 **Hemsworth Miners Welfare** 5
Campion 2 Halifax Irish Club 0
Hall Green United 0 **Meltham Athletic** 3
Tyersal 1 **Lower Hopton** 2
SEMI-FINALS
(both at Brighouse Town)
Hemsworth Miners Welfare 1 **Campion** 2
Meltham Athletic 1 **Lower Hopton** 3
FINAL
(May 22nd at Bay Athletic)
Lower Hopton 0 **Campion** 2

WEST RIDING COUNTY AMATEUR LEAGUE PREMIER DIVISION CONSTITUTION 2008-09

ARDSLEY CELTIC .... The Crescent, East Ardsley, Wakefield WF3 2EG 07950 131889
BAY ATHLETIC .... Syngenta Sports, 509 Leeds Road, Huddersfield HD2 1YJ 01484 514367
BRIGHOUSE TOWN .... St Giles Road, Hove Edge, Brighouse HD6 2PL 01484 380088
CAMPION .... Manningham Mills Sports Ground, Scotchman Road, Manningham, Bradford BD9 4SH 01274 546726
GOLCAR UNITED .... Longfield Recreation Ground, Golcar, Huddersfield HD7 4AZ 07779 700098
HALIFAX IRISH CLUB .... Natty Lane, Illingworth, Halifax HX2 9DS 01422 360134
HALL GREEN UNITED .... Crigglestone Sports Club, Painthorpe Lane, Crigglestone, Wakefield WF4 3JU 01924 254544
HEMSWORTH MINERS WELFARE .... Fitzwilliam Stadium, Wakefield Road, Fitzwilliam, Pontefract WF9 5AJ 01977 610444
KIRKBURTON .... Gregory Playing Fields, Kirkburton, Huddersfield HD8 0XH .... None
LOWER HOPTON .... Woodend Road, Lower Hopton, Mirfield WF14 8PP 01924 492048
MARSDEN .... Fell Lane, Marsden, Huddersfield 01484 844191
MELTHAM ATHLETIC .... Broadlands Recreation Ground, Meltham, Holmfirth HD9 5QY .... None
OVENDEN WEST RIDING .... Natty Lane, Illingworth, Halifax HX2 9DS 01422 244350
OVERTHORPE SPORTS .... Overthorpe Park, Edge Top Road, Dewsbury WF12 0BG 01924 464164
STORTHES HALL .... Police Sports Ground, Woodfield Park, Lockwood Scar, Huddersfield HD4 6BW 07957 691189
WIBSEY .... Westwood Park, Cooper Lane, Bradford BD6 3NN .... None
IN: Brighouse Town Reserves (P – Division Two), Hemsworth Miners Welfare Reserves (P – Division Two), Kirkburton (P), Marsden (P)
OUT: Brighouse Town (P – Northern Counties East League Division One), Hemsworth Miners Welfare (P – Northern Counties East League Division One), Keighley Shamrocks (R), Tyersal (R)

WWW.CHERRYRED.CO.UK

DIV ONE CUP

	Bronte Wanderers	Crag Road United	Dudley Hill Rangers	Eastmoor	Farnley	Heckmondwike Town	Kirkburton	Littletown	Marsden	Rawdon Old Boys	Salts	South Bradford	Steeton	Wakefield City
Bronte Wanderers		4-0	3-2	4-4	3-2	4-4	1-1	1-1	0-0	1-0	1-1	3-2	2-1	1-1
Crag Road United	1-2	D	2-2	2-3	2-0	4-1	2-3	3-4	2-2	1-1	4-0	1-1	5-0	3-2
Dudley Hill Rangers	3-1	2-4	I	2-3	1-3	2-2	2-4	2-2	1-5	2-2	3-2	2-0	2-5	3-3
Eastmoor	2-0	2-1	4-2	V	1-0	5-1	3-0	4-0	1-4	2-1	0-1	4-0	6-1	1-1
Farnley	2-1	2-2	0-0	3-2	I	2-6	2-2	0-3	4-1	0-1	1-1	1-1	1-0	1-3
Heckmondwike Town	2-1	0-4	0-2	0-1	2-0	S	2-0	2-4	1-2	1-1	2-0	2-3	3-3	1-4
Kirkburton	3-1	3-4	4-2	1-0	2-5	1-2	I	0-9	0-4	0-0	5-3	3-1	3-1	0-4
Littletown	2-1	4-2	1-0	5-0	3-3	1-0	4-0	O	3-4	1-2	3-1	5-2	1-0	6-0
Marsden	2-1	3-3	3-0	1-1	0-0	3-3	1-3	4-1	N	1-0	2-1	0-0	8-3	1-6
Rawdon Old Boys	3-1	0-2	2-1	2-3	1-2	0-0	1-0	0-1	3-1		0-1	2-2	5-4	1-2
Salts	2-2	2-3	3-1	1-1	2-0	4-0	1-5	1-3	1-5	3-1	O	1-5	1-2	2-1
South Bradford	4-0	2-1	1-3	5-0	2-1	2-2	1-3	4-2	2-0	1-3		N	5-1	0-1
Steeton	4-0	2-2	3-0	2-4	0-6	5-2	0-2	1-5	2-5	1-4	5-2	4-1	E	3-2
Wakefield City	2-0	0-4	4-2	1-1	0-2	1-1	2-0	1-1	0-1	1-0	0-0	2-3	6-0	

FIRST ROUND
Bronte Wanderers 2 **Kirkburton** 3
Dudley Hill Rangers 1 **Marsden** 5
Eastmoor 3 Farnley 2
Salts 3 South Bradford 1
Steeton 6 Rawdon Old Boys 2
Wakefield City 2 Heckmondwike Town 1

QUARTER-FINALS
Eastmoor 4 Crag Road United 3
Salts 0 Marsden 0 *aet* (6-5p)
Steeton 0 **Kirkburton** 2
Wakefield City 2 Littletown 1

SEMI-FINALS
Eastmoor 0 **Wakefield City** 5
(at Hemsworth Miners Welfare)
Salts 0 **Kirkburton** 3 *(at Campion)*

FINAL
(May 12th at Littletown)
Kirkburton 5 Wakefield City 0

Division One	P	W	D	L	F	A	Pts
Kirkburton	26	20	4	2	107	34	64
Marsden	26	19	4	3	70	36	61
South Bradford	26	18	3	5	80	46	57
Bronte Wanderers	26	11	7	8	54	42	40
Crag Road United	26	12	2	12	54	60	38
Heckmondwike Town	26	10	4	12	62	71	34
Steeton	26	9	6	11	67	61	33
Dudley Hill Rangers	26	10	3	13	44	72	33
Salts	26	8	5	13	44	58	29
Littletown	26	8	5	13	45	63	29
Wakefield City	26	8	3	15	53	63	27
Eastmoor	26	7	5	14	50	81	26
Farnley	26	7	3	16	42	66	24
Rawdon Old Boys	26	5	6	15	38	57	21

Reserve Division	P	W	D	L	F	A	Pts
Steeton Res.	24	17	5	2	94	29	56
Kirkburton Res.	24	17	2	5	76	38	53
Ovenden West Riding Res.	24	15	3	6	69	40	48
Ardsley Celtic Res.	24	15	2	7	78	41	47
Bay Athletic Res.	24	15	2	7	68	33	47
Marsden Res.	24	12	1	11	63	60	37
Lower Hopton Res.	24	11	2	11	70	59	35
Bronte Wanderers Res.	24	10	5	9	44	62	35
Keighley Shamrocks Res.	24	9	3	12	40	53	30
Rawdon Old Boys Res.	24	5	3	16	41	93	18
Wakefield City Res.	24	4	5	15	33	67	17
Salts Res.	24	5	2	17	43	90	17
Littletown Res.	24	3	1	20	35	89	10

WWW.NLNEWSDESK.CO.UK

RESERVES CUP

FINAL
(May 16th at Campion)
Steeton Res. 3 Ardsley Celtic Res. 1

WEST RIDING COUNTY AMATEUR LEAGUE DIVISION ONE CONSTITUTION 2008-09
ALBION SPORTS . . . . Seymour Street Rec Ground, Upper Seymour Street, Bradford BD3 9LJ 01274 661755
CRAG ROAD UNITED . . . . Apperley Road, Greengates, Bradford BD10 0PX 07781 808212
DUDLEY HILL RANGERS . . . . Newhall Park School, Newhall Road, Bierley, Bradford BD4 6AF. 07967 359883
EASTMOOR . . . . King George V Playing Fields, Woodhouse Road, Eastmoor, Wakefield WF1 4RD. 01924 375367
HECKMONDWIKE TOWN . . . . Cemetary Road, Heckmondwike WF16 9ED. 01924 442907
HUNSWORTH. . . . . Birkenshaw Middle School, Bradford Road, Gomersal, Cleckheaton BD19 4BE. 07711 197741
KEIGHLEY SHAMROCKS . . . . Marley Stadium, Aireworth Road, Keighley BD21 4DB 01535 609910
LITTLETOWN. . . . . Beck Lane, Heckmondwike WF16 0JZ 07930 852796
SALTS . . . . Salts Playing Fields, Hirst Lane, Saltaire, Shipley BD18 4DD. 01274 583427
SOUTH BRADFORD. . . . . Broadstone Way, Holmewood, Bradford BD4 9BU. 01274 751160
STEETON . . . . Summer Hill Lane, Steeton BD20 6RX 01585 683387
TYERSAL. . . . . Arkwright Street, off Dick Lane, Tyersal, Bradford BD4 8JL 07710 006241
VENTUS & YEADON CELTIC . . . . Dam Lane, Yeadon, Leeds. 07721 468967
WAKEFIELD CITY . . . . West Yorks Sports & Social, Walton Lane, Sandal, Wakefield WF2 6NG 01924 258760
IN: *Albion Sports (formerly U Save Albion) (P), Hunsworth (P), Keighley Shamrocks (R), Tyersal (R), Ventus & Yeadon Celtic (P)*
OUT: *Bronte Wanderers (R), Farnley (R), Kirkburton (P), Marsden (P), Rawdon Old Boys (R)*

Note – Wibsey Res. withdrew during the course of the season. Their results are shown herein but are expunged from the league table	Barclays	Brighouse Town Res.	Campion Res.	Dudley Hill Athletic	Dynamoes	Golcar United Res.	Hall Green United Res.	Hemsworth Miners Welfare Res.	Hunsworth	Morley Town	Storthes Hall Res.	Tyersal Res.	U Save Albion	Ventus & Yeadon Celtic	West Horton	Wibsey Res.
Barclays		1-4	0-2	0-2	1-0	3-6	1-5	1-2	1-6	2-4	1-2	1-4	3-2	2-9	3-5	3-1
Brighouse Town Res.	3-0		2-1	3-1	0-0	2-0	5-1	5-1	1-0	2-1	2-1	1-1	3-2	3-1	6-0	2-0
Campion Res.	6-1	2-0	D	4-0	3-1	4-0	2-1	1-3	1-2	5-0	3-3	0-1	3-0	0-2	6-0	2-1
Dudley Hill Athletic	2-0	1-4	0-0	I	0-3	0-0	0-5	2-2	0-1	2-0	0-2	1-2	1-3	2-4	2-5	2-3
Dynamoes	3-0	1-4	1-2	1-1	V	1-3	2-3	1-1	2-2	2-1	2-3	1-2	0-2	1-3	1-4	3-2
Golcar United Res.	4-0	1-2	4-1	2-1	4-0	I	4-4	2-1	2-5	2-2	2-1	0-1	1-4	2-2	1-1	1-2
Hall Green United Res.	3-1	1-3	3-3	1-4	1-1	2-2	S	1-3	2-5	6-3	0-1	3-4	2-4	1-5	2-2	5-0
Hemsworth Miners Welfare Res.	2-1	0-3	1-3	1-1	4-2	0-2	1-3	I	0-2	1-2	0-0	2-3	3-1	2-9	3-4	6-0
Hunsworth	1-1	0-1	0-2	2-4	3-0	4-0	0-3	3-0	O	5-1	1-2	1-2	2-3	1-3	2-3	9-2
Morley Town	3-1	0-4	1-1	4-1	2-2	1-1	5-0	1-2	0-4	N	1-5	2-2	0-5	0-6	1-7	n/a
Storthes Hall Res.	3-0	1-0	3-0	6-0	1-0	0-6	2-1	1-2	4-3	2-2		1-2	1-4	4-1	3-2	n/a
Tyersal Res.	3-2	0-3	2-0	4-3	4-1	7-1	6-0	3-2	2-2	1-2	1-1	T	5-1	4-1	4-1	4-4
U Save Albion	6-1	3-3	1-3	3-1	4-2	3-2	3-0	4-2	6-1	5-2	3-2	5-4	W	1-0	2-1	n/a
Ventus & Yeadon Celtic	5-0	2-0	3-3	6-1	7-1	7-1	4-3	5-3	3-4	7-0	2-2	1-2	4-1	O	2-0	n/a
West Horton	2-0	0-1	2-3	1-1	6-2	1-1	4-2	6-1	1-2	3-3	1-1	2-4	3-1	0-0		5-0
Wibsey Res.	n/a	n/a	n/a	n/a	n/a	n/a	n/a	n/a	n/a	n/a	0-7	n/a	n/a	n/a	n/a	

Division Two	P	W	D	L	F	A	Pts
Brighouse Town Res.	28	22	3	3	70	23	69
Tyersal Res.	28	21	4	3	80	41	67
Ventus & Yeadon Celtic	28	18	4	6	104	44	58
U Save Albion	28	19	1	8	82	55	58
Storthes Hall Res.	28	15	7	6	62	37	52
Campion Res.	28	15	5	8	64	37	50
Hunsworth	28	13	3	12	64	50	42
West Horton	28	11	7	10	67	60	40
Golcar United Res.	28	9	9	10	50	60	36
Hemsworth Miners Welfare Res.	28	8	4	16	45	72	28
Hall Green United Res.	28	7	5	16	60	84	26
Morley Town	28	6	7	15	44	86	25
Dudley Hill Athletic	28	5	6	17	34	69	21
Dynamoes	28	3	6	19	34	71	15
Barclays	28	2	1	25	28	99	7

Wibsey Res. – record expunged

DIVISION TWO CUP

FIRST ROUND
Barclays 0 **Tyersal Res.** 8
Brighouse Town Res. 4 Campion Res. 0
Dynamoes 1 **Morley Town.** 3 *aet*
Hall Green United Res. 2 Ventus & Yeadon Celtic 1
Hemsworth Miners Welfare Res. 4 Golcar United Res. 0
Hunsworth 0 **Storthes Hall Res.** 1 *aet*
U Save Albion 2 **Dudley Hill Athletic** 5
West Horton 2 Wibsey Res. 1
QUARTER-FINALS
Dudley Hill Athletic 2 **West Horton** 4 *aet*
Hemsworth Miners Welfare Res. 1 **Brighouse Town Res.** 2
Morley Town 1 **Storthes Hall Res.** 3
Tyersal Res. 4 Hall Green United Res. 3 *aet*
SEMI-FINALS
Brighouse Town Res. 7 West Horton 4
Tyersal Res. 1 **Storthes Hall Res.** 1 *aet* (1-4p)
FINAL
(May 19th at Lower Hopton)
Storthes Hall Res. 2 **Brighouse Town Res.** 4 *aet*

WEST RIDING COUNTY AMATEUR LEAGUE DIVISION TWO CONSTITUTION 2008-09

BRONTE WANDERERS . . . . Marley Stadium, Keighley BD21 4DB 01535 609910
CAMPION RESERVES . . . . Manningham Mills Sports Ground, Scotchman Road, Manningham, Bradford BD9 4SH 01274 546726
DUDLEY HILL ATHLETIC. . . . . Hunsworth Lane, East Bierley BD4 6RN . . . . None
DYNAMOES . . . . Dudley Hill Athletic FC, Hunsworth Lane, East Bierley BD4 6RN. 01274 823576
FARNLEY . . . . Farnley Cricket Club, Church Lane, Farnley. 0113 253 5950
GOLCAR UNITED RESERVES . . . . . . Longfield Recreation Ground, Golcar, Huddersfield HD7 4AZ. 07779 700098
KIRKBURTON RESERVES . . . . Gregory Playing Fields, Kirkburton, Huddersfield HD8 0XH . . . . None
LIVERSEDGE . . . . Clayborn Ground, Quaker Lane, Hightown Road, Cleckheaton BD19 3RJ. 01274 862108
MORLEY TOWN . . . . Glen Road, Morley, Leeds LS27 9HG 07709 727085
RAWDON OLD BOYS. . . . . Hanson Field, Rawdon, Leeds. . . . . None
STORTHES HALL RESERVES . . . Police Sports Ground, Woodfield Park, Lockwood Scar, Huddersfield HD4 6BW 07957 691189
TYERSAL RESERVES . . . . Arkwright Street, off Dick Lane, Tyersal, Bradford BD4 8JL 07710 006241
VENTUS & YEADON CELTIC RESERVES. . . . . Dam Lane, Yeadon, Leeds. 07721 468967
WEST HORTON . . . . Avenue Road, Bradford BD5 8DB 07974 176987
IN: *Bronte Wanderers (R), Farnley (R), Kirkburton Reserves (P – Reserve Division), Liversedge u-19s (formerly Cleckheaton & Gomersal) (P – youth football), Rawdon Old Boys (R), Ventus & Yeadon Celtic Reserves (formerly Bradford IMS Celtic) (P – Bradford League)*
OUT: *Albion Sports (formerly U Save Albion) (P), Barclays (W), Hall Green United Reserves (R – Reserve Division), Hunsworth (P), Ventus & Yeadon Celtic (P), Wibsey Reserves (WS)*

WEST YORKSHIRE LEAGUE

	Aberford Albion	Bardsey	Beeston St Anthony's	Boroughbridge	Carlton Athletic	Field Sports & Social	Howden Clough	Knaresborough Town	Ossett Common Rovers	Pool	Ripon City	Rothwell Athletic	Sherburn White Rose	Street Work Soccer	Wetherby Athletic	Whitkirk Wanderers
Aberford Albion	P	1-6	0-2	1-2	1-3	1-1	3-2	0-5	2-1	1-2	0-1	0-2	0-2	1-0	2-1	0-3
Bardsey	3-3	R	1-2	5-0	0-1	4-3	5-0	4-1	5-0	2-3	6-0	6-3	4-0	6-2	0-2	3-1
Beeston St Anthony's	2-0	2-2	E	6-1	1-2	3-0	5-0	0-2	2-1	7-2	1-2	4-2	1-1	1-2	1-1	3-1
Boroughbridge	0-3	1-0	1-1	M	1-2	1-1	0-1	3-2	6-0	1-2	2-1	1-2	2-2	3-2	3-1	3-1
Carlton Athletic	4-1	1-0	1-0	5-0	I	1-3	3-1	4-4	4-0	5-1	4-1	7-2	3-3	3-0	3-2	2-0
Field Sports & Social	2-1	0-4	3-1	2-0	0-3	E	0-0	1-0	1-0	0-1	2-0	2-1	2-2	3-4	3-1	2-1
Howden Clough	2-2	1-2	1-4	1-3	0-2	2-4	R	0-5	0-1	2-2	6-1	3-5	2-1	3-2	1-0	4-4
Knaresborough Town	2-1	2-1	0-2	0-4	1-2	2-4	4-1		4-0	5-1	3-2	3-2	3-1	3-1	1-1	2-1
Ossett Common Rovers	1-2	1-6	0-1	1-0	0-3	2-2	0-3	2-5	D	5-1	2-2	4-3	0-2	2-0	1-4	3-1
Pool	1-1	2-2	3-4	1-1	2-4	1-2	0-1	0-0	3-1	I	2-1	3-0	0-1	2-2	3-3	1-3
Ripon City	6-2	2-4	3-1	2-1	3-3	3-3	4-0	1-2	4-0	1-2	V	0-3	1-4	1-2	0-4	5-1
Rothwell Athletic	0-3	0-2	0-2	2-0	1-1	3-2	2-4	1-4	1-2	2-2	2-4	I	1-2	1-0	3-1	1-3
Sherburn White Rose	3-3	1-2	0-0	5-0	1-0	1-3	1-0	2-1	1-0	1-0	2-0	2-0	S	0-1	1-1	5-1
Street Work Soccer	0-0	0-1	2-0	0-4	1-4	2-0	1-4	1-4	2-0	3-2	1-1	3-3	0-2	I	1-2	0-2
Wetherby Athletic	2-0	1-2	0-2	0-0	1-2	2-4	3-1	1-2	4-1	3-2	1-1	2-1	2-1	1-2	O	1-4
Whitkirk Wanderers	2-3	1-4	2-0	1-1	2-1	1-2	5-0	1-1	5-1	2-2	3-1	4-2	0-3	2-2	2-2	N

Premier Division	P	W	D	L	F	A	Pts
Carlton Athletic	30	23	4	3	83	33	73
Bardsey	30	20	3	7	92	37	63
Knaresborough Town	30	18	4	8	73	45	58
Sherburn White Rose	30	16	7	7	53	33	55
Beeston St Anthony's	30	16	6	8	63	36	54
Field Sports & Social	30	16	6	8	57	48	54
Whitkirk Wanderers	30	11	6	13	60	60	39
Boroughbridge	30	11	6	13	45	53	39
Pool +2	30	8	9	13	49	66	35
Wetherby Athletic	30	9	7	14	49	51	34
Street Work Soccer	30	9	6	15	40	62	33
Ripon City	30	9	5	16	54	69	32
Howden Clough	30	9	4	17	46	74	31
Rothwell Athletic	30	8	3	19	51	76	27
Aberford Albion -4	30	8	6	16	38	63	26
Ossett Common Rovers	30	7	2	21	32	79	23

Alliance Division One

	P	W	D	L	F	A	Pts
Beeston St Anthony's Res.	28	21	3	4	96	32	66
Rothwell Athletic Res.	28	19	7	2	94	32	64
Whitkirk Wanderers Res.	28	18	3	7	84	42	57
Boroughbridge Res.	28	17	3	8	77	42	54
Wetherby Athletic Res.	28	16	3	9	65	45	51
Knaresborough Town Res.	28	15	2	11	69	49	47
Ripon City Res.	28	12	5	11	60	56	41
Robin Hood Athletic Res.	28	11	5	12	64	64	38
Sherburn White Rose Res.	28	11	3	14	55	71	36
Hartshead Res.	28	11	3	14	53	71	36
Aberford Albion Res.	28	9	6	13	58	58	33
Ossett Common Rovers Res.	28	8	4	16	47	72	28
Kippax Athletic Res.	28	7	4	17	40	91	25
Bardsey Res.	28	5	4	19	41	91	19
Altofts Res.	28	2	1	25	35	122	7

Alliance Division Two

	P	W	D	L	F	A	Pts
Field Sports & Social Res.	22	15	4	3	83	25	49
Horbury Town Res.	22	14	7	1	74	28	49
Ilkley Town Res.	22	13	5	4	71	39	44
Carlton Athletic Res.	22	10	3	9	47	39	33
Old Headingley Res.	22	10	2	10	47	41	32
Rothwell Town Res.	22	9	3	10	51	45	30
East End Park WMC Res.	22	8	6	8	64	60	30
Baildon Trinity Athletic Res.	22	8	4	10	48	48	28
Howden Clough Res.	22	8	3	11	48	60	27
Otley Town Res.	22	8	0	14	45	76	24
Woodhouse Hill WMC Res.	22	5	6	11	40	60	21
Boston Spartans Res.	22	2	1	19	20	117	7

WWW.NLNEWSDESK.CO.UK

WEST YORKSHIRE LEAGUE PREMIER DIVISION CONSTITUTION 2008-09

ABERFORD ALBION .... Bunkers Hill, Main Street (South), Aberford LS25 3DE .... None
BARDSEY .... The Sportsfield, Keswick Lane, Bardsey LS17 9AQ 01937 574286
BEESTON ST ANTHONY'S .... Beggars Hill, Sunnyview Gardens, Beeston Road, Beeston, Leeds 0113 270 7223
BOROUGHBRIDGE .... Aldborough Road, Boroughbridge, York YO51 9EA 01423 324206
CARLTON ATHLETIC.......... Carlton Cricket Club, Town Street, Carlton, Wakefield WF3 3QU.......... 0113 282 1114
FIELD SPORTS & SOCIAL .... Field Sports Ground, Hollingwood Lane, Lidget Green, Bradford BD7 2RQ ... 01274 546726
HOWDEN CLOUGH .... Batley Sports Centre, Windmill Lane, Batley WF17 0QD 01924 326181
KNARESBOROUGH TOWN .... Manse Lane, Knaresborough HG5 8LF 07773 679971
LEEDS CITY........................... Adel WMA, Church Lane, Adel, Leeds LS16 8DE........................ 0113 293 0525
OTLEY TOWN........................... Old Show Ground, Pool Road, Otley LS20 1DY 01943 451025
POOL............................. Pool S&S Club, Arthington Lane, Pool-in-Wharfedale, Otley LS21. .... 0113 284 3932
RIPON CITY............................ Mallorie Park Drive, Ripon HG4 2QD 01765 600542
ROTHWELL ATHLETIC .... Royds Lane, Rothwell, Leeds LS26 0BE .... Club HQ: 0113 282 0723
SHERBURN WHITE ROSE....... Recreation Ground, Finkle Hill, Sherburn-in-Elmet, Leeds LS25 6EB .... None
WETHERBY ATHLETIC ...... Wetherby Sports Association, The Ings, Boston Road, Wetherby LS22 5HA 01937 585699
WHITKIRK WANDERERS...... Whitkirk Sports & Social Club, Selby Road, Whitkirk, Leeds LS15 0AA 0113 264 6623

IN: Leeds City (P), Otley Town (P)
OUT: Ossett Common Rovers (R), Street Work Soccer (W)

	Altofts	Churwell Lions	Hartshead	Horbury Town	Ilkley Town	Kellingley Welfare	Kippax Athletic	Leeds City	Nostell Miners Welfare Res.	Old Headingley	Otley Town	Pontefract Sports & Social	Robin Hood Athletic	Sandy Lane	Woodhouse Hill WMC
Altofts		4-2	7-0	2-0	2-0	2-0	2-1	1-3	2-0	1-3	0-2	1-2	1-2	3-0	2-0
Churwell Lions	0-5	D	2-5	4-3	2-0	2-2	0-1	3-1	2-2	2-2	0-4	2-4	1-0	2-4	5-2
Hartshead	5-5	2-2	I	3-5	0-3	1-3	1-4	0-3	2-5	2-2	0-4	1-6	1-4	3-1	3-1
Horbury Town	3-2	1-0	4-1	V	3-3	0-2	4-1	0-1	2-4	1-0	1-3	1-3	3-2	6-3	1-3
Ilkley Town	3-0	4-3	2-0	3-1	I	3-1	3-2	2-2	4-2	3-3	2-6	10-2	1-1	3-2	3-2
Kellingley Welfare	1-1	2-4	0-2	1-1	1-1	S	1-1	0-1	1-1	2-2	1-1	2-3	1-2	4-1	1-0
Kippax Athletic	2-2	3-1	3-3	0-1	2-1	1-0	I	1-2	3-2	1-1	3-1	3-0	6-2	1-3	3-2
Leeds City	5-1	2-2	2-0	1-3	4-2	2-0	4-0	O	3-1	1-4	1-3	0-2	2-0	2-0	1-3
Nostell Miners Welfare Res.	6-2	4-2	2-4	1-2	1-1	2-2	0-3	0-3	N	2-1	1-3	1-2	1-2	2-3	0-0
Old Headingley	0-4	2-2	2-2	0-2	1-1	2-1	3-4	3-5	4-3		2-2	1-1	2-3	6-0	1-2
Otley Town	6-1	2-0	3-1	2-0	2-1	4-0	2-2	2-1	4-0	1-0		3-0	6-1	3-1	4-1
Pontefract Sports & Social	3-3	1-1	2-3	1-8	1-2	1-3	3-3	2-6	1-1	0-6	0-8	O	1-8	3-1	2-2
Robin Hood Athletic	1-1	4-2	1-1	3-2	1-1	0-2	4-1	2-2	4-0	3-0	3-2	1-2	N	3-0	5-2
Sandy Lane	2-4	3-4	1-3	1-4	1-0	0-2	2-8	1-5	0-10	0-1	0-1	0-8	3-0	E	7-1
Woodhouse Hill WMC	5-4	3-2	1-2	3-1	5-2	2-5	2-6	1-4	0-1	3-1	0-8	8-1	1-4	6-1	

Division One	P	W	D	L	F	A	Pts
Otley Town	28	23	3	2	99	23	72
Leeds City	28	18	3	7	69	39	57
Robin Hood Athletic	28	15	5	8	69	46	50
Kippax Athletic	28	14	6	8	69	52	48
Ilkley Town	28	12	8	8	64	53	44
Horbury Town	28	14	2	12	63	53	44
Altofts	28	12	5	11	65	57	41
Nostell Miners Welfare Res.	28	9	6	13	59	60	33
Kellingley Welfare	28	8	9	11	41	43	33
Pontefract Sports & Social	28	9	6	13	49	92	33
Old Headingley	28	7	10	11	55	54	31
Woodhouse Hill WMC	28	10	1	17	61	83	31
Hartshead	28	8	6	14	51	80	30
Churwell Lions	28	7	7	14	54	72	28
Sandy Lane	28	5	1	22	40	101	16

WWW.CHERRYRED.CO.UK

LEAGUE CUP

FIRST ROUND
Baildon Trinity Athletic 0 **Brighouse Old Boys** 4
Beeston St Anthony's 2 Leeds City 1
Boroughbridge 4 Sandy Lane 0
Carlton Athletic 5 Barwick 0
Howden Clough 2 **Pool** 3
Ilkley 1 **Kippax Athletic** 2
Kellingley Welfare 4 Hunslet 1
Knaresborough Town 1 Wetherby Athletic 0
Nostell Miners Welfare Res. 1 **Altofts** 2
Ossett Common Rovers 1 **Rothwell Athletic** 3
Otley Town 2 Rothwell Town 1
Sherburn White Rose (w/o) v Pontefract Sports & Social (scr.)
Stanley United 1 **Old Centralians** 3
Wkitkirk Wanderers 2 **Aberford Albion** 3
SECOND ROUND
Aberford Albion 0 **Beeston St Anthony's** 2
Altofts 2 Kellingley Welfare 1
Boroughbridge 2 **Rothwell Athletic** 8
Boston Spartans 1 **Sherburn White Rose** 9
Churwell Lions 1 **East End Park WMC** 2
Great Preston 3 **Woodhouse Hill WMC** 4
Hartshead 1 **Bardsey** 4
Horbury Town 2 **Featherstone Colliery** 3
Mount St Mary's 1 **Carlton Athletic** 8

WEST YORKSHIRE LEAGUE DIVISION ONE CONSTITUTION 2008-09

ALTOFTS . . . . Altofts Sports Club, Lock Lane, Altofts, Normanton WF6 2QJ 01924 892708
CHURWELL LIONS . . . . Bruntcliffe High School, Bruntcliffe Lane, Morley, Leeds LS27 0LZ. . . . . None
EAST END PARK WMC . . . . Skelton Road, Leeds LS9 9EP . . . . None
FEATHERSTONE COLLIERY . . . Featherstones Miners Welfare, Cresseys Corner, Green Lane, Featherstone WF7 6EH . . . . None
HARTSHEAD . . . . Littletown Recreation Ground, Hartshead 01274 873365
HORBURY TOWN . . . . Slazengers Sports Complex, Engine Lane, Horbury, Wakefield WF4 5NH 01924 274228
ILKLEY TOWN . . . . Denton Road, Ilkley LS29 0AA . . . . None
KELLINGLEY WELFARE . . . Kellingley (Knottingley) Social Club, Marine Villa Road, Knottingley, Wakefield WF11 8ER 01977 673113
KIPPAX ATHLETIC. . . . . Rear of Swillington Miners Welfare, Wakefield Road, Swillington LS26 8DT . . . . None
NOSTELL MINERS WELFARE RESERVES . . . . Miners Welfare Ground, Middle Lane, New Crofton, Wakefield WF4 1LB. . . . 01924 862348
OLD CENTRALIANS . . . . West Park Playing Fields, North Parade, West Park, Leeds LS16 5AY. None
OLD HEADINGLEY . . . . Collington & Linton SA, Harewood Road, Collingham, Wetherby LS22 5BL . . . . None
OSSETT COMMON ROVERS . . . . Illingworth Park, Manor Road, Ossett WF5 0LH. . . . . None
PONTEFRACT SPORTS & SOCIAL . . . Willow Park School, Harewood Avenue, Pontefract WF8 2ER . . . . None
ROBIN HOOD ATHLETIC. . . . . Behind Coach & Horses, Rothwell Haigh, Leeds LS26 0SF 0113 282 1021
WOODHOUSE HILL WMC . . . . . Woodlands School Playing Field, Wakefield Road, Normanton WF6 1BB 01924 893462
IN: East End Park WMC (P), Featherstone Colliery (P), Old Centralians (P), Ossett Common Rovers (R)
OUT: Leeds City (P), Otley Town (P), Sandy Lane (R)

	Baildon Trinity Athletic	Barwick	Boston Spartans	Brighouse Old Boys	East End Park WMC	Featherstone Colliery	Great Preston	Hunslet	Mount St Mary's	Old Centralians	Rothwell Town	Stanley United	Swillington Saints	Tadcaster Magnet Sports	Wyke Wanderers
Baildon Trinity Athletic		5-0	3-4	0-4	3-4	2-1	2-2	2-2	0-0	3-1	1-2	4-2	4-0	2-1	2-2
Barwick	1-2	D	1-3	0-4	2-8	2-1	5-3	1-4	2-6	1-9	1-4	2-2	0-2	2-2	0-6
Boston Spartans	1-1	4-0	I	1-0	0-3	0-2	4-1	3-0	2-3	3-4	4-3	2-5	2-3	8-1	1-2
Brighouse Old Boys	4-3	6-4	4-1	V	2-4	1-1	3-1	1-0	1-2	0-0	1-5	1-1	3-0	8-0	1-1
East End Park WMC	2-0	8-0	5-2	2-1	I	5-0	2-0	3м0	4-1	0-0	3-0	3-3	4-1	9-1	0-0
Featherstone Colliery	3-2	6-1	0-2	2-0	1-5	S	0-0	3-0	2-0	0-2	2-0	4-0	3-0	5-1	1-1
Great Preston	2-1	5-0	2-1	1-4	1-2	3-3	I	2-4	2-1	3-1	0-1	3-2	1-2	1-1	1-2
Hunslet	1-0	3-1	2-2	2-2	1-4	0-1	2-0	O	1-3	0-1	1-2	7-0	2-3	2-3	0-3
Mount St Mary's	1-0	3-3	1-1	0-0	0-3	1-2	4-1	5-1	N	0-2	2-1	1-1	2-2	1-1	0-2
Old Centralians	2-0	4-2	1-2	1-2	2-3	2-7	4-0	5-1	0-0		2-2	2-2	5-0	2-0	0-0
Rothwell Town	2-0	5-1	1-3	0-4	0-6	2-0	3-3	4-0	3-4	2-2		1-3	1-3	5-1	0-0
Stanley United	0-2	3-1	4-4	0-2	0-1	0-3	2-2	2-0	2-1	0-4	4-1	T	4-2	5-2	0-1
Swillington Saints	1-4	2-2	2-1	1-1	0-7	0-2	1-4	4-2	2-4	1-5	0-2	4-1	W	4-0	2-1
Tadcaster Magnet Sports	0-5	3-0	0-1	0-5	0-5	0-4	5-1	0-5	2-2	0-8	1-5	2-4	2-1	O	1-6
Wyke Wanderers	0-2	3-0	3м0	3-3	1-1	1-0	1-1	3-1	2-2	2-2	0-2	5-2	1-2	5-0	

Old Centralians 3 Otley Town 2
Pool 3 Old Headingley 1
Ripon City 0 **Knaresborough Town** 3
Street Work Soccer 1 **Field Sports & Social** 4
Swillington Saints 2 **Kippax Athletic** 4
Tadcaster Magnet Sports 2 **Robin Hood Athletic** 6
Wyke Wanderers 0 **Brighouse Old Boys** 1
THIRD ROUND
Bardsey 3 **Field Sports & Social** 4
Brighouse Old Boys 1 Altofts 1 *aet* (5-4p)
Carlton Athletic 4 Rothwell Athletic 0
East End Park WMC 1 **Beeston St Anthony's** 2
Kippax Athletic 0 **Sherburn White Rose** 2
Knaresborough Town 1 **Woodhouse Hill WMC** 1 *aet* (3-4p)
Pool 3 **Featherstone Colliery** 4
Robin Hood Athletic 3 Old Centralians 1
QUARTER-FINALS
Carlton Athletic 1 Sherburn White Rose 0 *aet*
Featherstone Colliery 2 Brighouse Old Boys 0
Field Sports & Social 1 **Beeston St Anthony's** 2
Robin Hood Athletic 3 Woodhouse Hill WMC 0
SEMI-FINALS
(both at Nostell Miners Welfare)
Beeston St Anthony's 3 **Carlton Athletic** 4
Featherstone Colliery 0 **Robin Hood Athletic** 3
FINAL
(May 10th at Wetherby Athletic)
Carlton Athletic 2 Robin Hood Athletic 1 *aet*

Division Two	P	W	D	L	F	A	Pts
East End Park WMC	28	24	4	0	106	22	76
Featherstone Colliery	28	16	4	8	59	33	52
Old Centralians	28	14	8	6	73	36	50
Brighouse Old Boys	28	14	8	6	68	36	50
Wyke Wanderers	28	13	11	4	57	27	50
Rothwell Town	28	13	4	11	59	52	43
Boston Spartans	28	12	5	11	63	57	41
Mount St Mary's	28	10	10	8	48	46	40
Baildon Trinity Athletic	28	11	5	12	55	45	38
Stanley United	28	9	7	12	54	67	34
Swillington Saints	28	10	4	14	45	71	34
Great Preston	28	7	7	14	46	63	28
Hunslet	28	7	3	18	45	61	24
Tadcaster Magnet Sports	28	4	4	20	30	111	16
Barwick	28	2	4	22	35	116	10

LEAGUE TROPHY

FINAL
(April 29th at Nostell Miners Welfare)
Field Sports & Social Res. 2 Rothwell Athletic Res. 0

WEST YORKSHIRE LEAGUE DIVISION TWO CONSTITUTION 2008-09

BAILDON TRINITY ATHLETIC .... The Dell, Cliffe Lane, West Baildon, Shipley BD17 5LB .... None
BARWICK .... Back of Village Hall, Chapel Lane, Barwick-in-Elmet, Leeds LS15 4HL .... Club HQ: 0113 281 3065
BOSTON SPARTANS .... Stables Lane, Boston Spa, Wetherby LS23 6BX .... None
BRIGHOUSE OLD BOYS ..... Lightcliffe & Hipperholme School, Stoney Lane, Lightcliffe, Halifax HX3 8TL 01422 201028
GREAT PRESTON .... Berry Lane, Great Preston LS25 8AX .... None
HUNSLET .... Community Sports Club, Anchor Street, Hunslet Green, Leeds LS10 2AT................. 0113 270 6851
MOUNT ST MARY'S .... David Young Academy, off North Parkway, Seacroft, Leeds LS14 6NU .... None
OXENHOPE RECREATION .... Marley Playing Fields, Keighley .... None
ROTHWELL TOWN................ off Fifth Avenue, Leeds Road, Rothwell, Leeds LS26 0HG .... None
SANDY LANE........................... Marley Stadium, Marley Road, Keighley BD21 4LY .... None
SOUTH MILFORD .... The Maltings, South Milford .... None
STANLEY UNITED............... Welfare Sports Ground, Saville Road, Methley, Leeds LS26 0DT .... None
SWILLINGTON SAINTS .... Welfare Sports Ground, Wakefield Road, Swillington, Leeds LS26 8DT .... None
TADCASTER MAGNET SPORTS ... Magnet Sports & Social Club, Queens Gardens, Tadcaster LS24 9HD 01937 833435
WYKE WANDERERS ...... The Albert Morton Memorial Playing Fields, New Popplewell Lane, Scholes, Cleckheaton BD19 6NN...... None
IN: Oxenhope Recreation (P – Craven & District FA Premier Division), Sandy Lane (R), South Milford (P – Selby & District League Division One)
OUT: East End Park WMC (P), Featherstone Colliery (P), Old Centralians (P)

WESTERN LEAGUE

	Barnstaple Town	Bideford	Bishop Sutton	Bitton	Brislington	Bristol Manor Farm	Calne Town	Chard Town	Corsham Town	Dawlish Town	Devizes Town	Frome Town	Hallen	Ilfracombe Town	Melksham Town	Odd Down	Radstock Town	Street	Truro City	Welton Rovers	Willand Rovers
Barnstaple Town		3-2	5-1	1-3	4-3	1-1	0-2	6-1	0-3	1-0	0-3	0-4	5-0	3-3	3-0	4-0	2-3	2-0	2-2	0-2	0-1
Bideford	3-1		10-0	1-0	2-0	1-1	1-1	4-0	5-1	0-3	1-1	3-3	5-1	1-1	3-1	3-1	0-0	2-0	1-1	0-1	3-0
Bishop Sutton	0-2	1-4	P	0-1	1-3	0-3	2-0	1-4	1-2	0-0	3-3	2-1	0-1	1-4	0-5	2-1	2-3	4-1	0-2	0-4	0-1
Bitton	2-1	2-2	0-0	R	0-1	2-4	2-0	3-0	0-0	2-4	4-1	1-2	1-0	6-1	1-1	5-0	3-1	2-0	0-1	1-0	1-2
Brislington	2-4	0-0	1-1	2-2	E	5-2	0-3	2-1	2-3	0-0	2-2	0-0	2-2	1-3	0-1	3-1	1-1	3-0	2-2	0-0	
Bristol Manor Farm	0-5	1-2	1-1	0-1	2-3	M	2-3	4-2	5-1	2-4	0-0	0-3	4-1	0-2	0-3	0-2	1-3	3-1	1-3	0-0	1-1
Calne Town	3-1	2-3	0-1	1-4	1-0	3-0	I	3-4	1-2	2-0	1-2	0-1	2-4	3-4	0-0	3-0	0-4	1-0	1-2	0-2	2-0
Chard Town	2-3	3-1	3-0	1-3	1-2	2-5	3-5	E	1-4	1-3	1-4	0-4	1-3	0-0	7-1	2-0	0-0	1-1	0-1	1-0	2-3
Corsham Town	2-1	3-2	4-3	4-2	3-1	1-1	0-0	2-0	R	1-5	2-2	2-0	0-2	1-2	0-0	3-0	1-1	1-0	1-5	2-2	1-1
Dawlish Town	1-1	1-1	5-1	2-0	2-1	4-2	4-2	3-0	1-1		5-0	3-1	2-0	0-0	4-0	2-1	2-1	4-2	5-2	0-2	1-2
Devizes Town	2-0	1-1	2-1	1-0	1-0	3-1	2-1	2-4	4-3	0-0		3-3	1-1	0-1	2-0	5-0	4-2	3-2	2-4	0-1	2-1
Frome Town	0-0	1-1	3-2	3-0	3-0	2-2	4-1	0-0	5-1	2-2	1-1	D	4-2	3-0	2-0	1-0	2-0	5-0	0-2	2-3	1-2
Hallen	1-1	2-2	4-0	0-5	0-1	5-4	4-3	2-2	1-2	2-1	0-1		I	2-0	1-2	2-3	3-2	1-1	1-3	2-3	1-5
Ilfracombe Town	1-2	2-4	4-0	3-2	4-4	1-2	1-0	5-0	3-0	3-3	4-2	1-4	0-2	V	0-2	2-1	1-2	0-1	0-0	0-3	
Melksham Town	3-2	0-1	3-1	1-3	1-1	2-1	0-0	0-2	2-6	1-1	2-1	1-1	0-3	1-1	I	5-0	1-1	1-1	1-3	0-1	0-2
Odd Down	0-0	0-2	2-2	1-3	0-1	1-0	1-2	3-1	0-3	0-5	2-2	0-4	2-2	1-3	0-2	S	0-4	1-2	1-8	0-0	0-6
Radstock Town	2-1	0-4	2-4	1-3	1-1	0-4	2-0	3-0	0-2	2-4	4-0	3-3	1-1	1-3	1-3	2-1	I	2-2	5-8	0-1	2-4
Street	1-0	2-1	1-1	0-0	0-2	2-1	1-3	1-1	1-3	1-4	0-1	0-3	0-0	2-1	2-2	0-1	2-2	O	0-2	0-1	3-1
Truro City	4-1	2-1	4-1	2-1	2-0	6-0	5-0	8-0	0-1	2-4	4-0	0-3	5-2	7-1	3-1	3-0	6-0	8-0	N	1-0	3-0
Welton Rovers	2-1	0-0	1-1	1-0	1-3	0-3	1-1	2-0	0-0	1-3	0-1	1-3	1-2	0-0	0-1	1-3	1-2	0-0	0-1		0-2
Willand Rovers	2-2	1-1	0-1	0-0	3-1	1-3	5-0	2-0	2-2	2-2	4-2	1-1	3-3	4-1	1-0	4-1	1-3	1-0			

Premier Division	P	W	D	L	F	A	Pts
Truro City	40	33	4	3	132	39	103
Dawlish Town	40	25	11	4	103	45	86
Willand Rovers	40	22	10	8	78	48	76
Frome Town	40	21	11	8	86	41	74
Corsham Town	40	20	11	9	71	63	71
Bideford	40	17	17	6	85	46	68
Bitton	40	19	7	14	71	46	64
Ilfracombe Town	40	19	7	14	76	69	64
Welton Rovers	40	17	10	13	44	35	61
Devizes Town	40	16	12	12	68	70	60
Melksham Town	40	13	12	15	51	57	51
Barnstaple Town	40	14	8	18	71	67	50
Brislington	40	12	13	15	55	61	49
Calne Town	40	15	4	21	57	70	49
Hallen	40	13	10	17	64	81	49
Bristol Manor Farm	40	10	9	21	64	84	39
Radstock Town	40	10	8	22	60	83	38
Street	40	8	9	23	36	80	33
Bishop Sutton	40	7	8	25	41	99	29
Chard Town	40	8	4	28	53	104	28
Odd Down	40	5	7	28	30	108	22

LES PHILLIPS CUP

PRELIMINARY ROUND

Biddestone (scr.) v **Shrewton United** (w/o)
Bishop Sutton 2 **Larkhall Athletic** 4
Bridport 3 Minehead Town 2
Clevedon United 2 **Street** 3
Hallen 2 **Cadbury Heath** 3
Keynsham Town 1 **Bitton** 5
Roman Glass St George 1 Devizes Town 0
Shepton Mallet 1 **Dawlish Town** 5
Sherborne Town 0 **Brislington** 3
Wellington Town 1 Bradford Town 0
Weston St Johns 3 Oldland Abbotonians 2
Willand Rovers 2 **Chard Town** 3

FIRST ROUND

Almondsbury 0 **Dawlish Town** 5
Backwell United 0 **Welton Rovers** 2
Bideford 3 Street 1
Bridport 1 Odd Down 0
Bristol Manor Farm 6 Elmore 0
Cadbury Heath 1 **Barnstaple Town** 3
Calne Town 2 **Truro City** 4 *aet*
Corsham Town 3 Wellington Town 0
Frome Tn (w/o) v Torrington (scr.)
Hengrove Athletic 1 **Radstock** Town 0
Longwell Green Sports 1 **Ilfracombe Town** 3
Melksham Town 0 **Bitton** 1

TOOLSTATION WESTERN LEAGUE PREMIER DIVISION CONSTITUTION 2008-09

BARNSTAPLE TOWN .... Mill Road, Barnstaple EX31 1JQ 01271 343469
BIDEFORD .... The Sports Ground, Kingsley Road, Bideford EX39 2LH 01237 474974
BISHOP SUTTON .... Lake View, Wick Road, Bishop Sutton, Bristol BS39 5XP 01275 333097
BITTON .... Recreation Ground, Bath Road, Bitton, Bristol BS30 6HX 0117 932 3222
BRISLINGTON .... Ironmould Lane, Brislington, Bristol BS4 5SA 0117 977 4030
BRISTOL MANOR FARM .... The Creek, Portway, Sea Mills, Bristol BS9 2HS 0117 968 4916
CALNE TOWN .... Lickhill Road, Bremhill View, Calne SN11 8AE 01249 819186
CHARD TOWN .... Denning Sports Field, Zembard Lane, Chard TA20 1JL 01460 61402
CORSHAM TOWN .... Southbank Ground, Lacock Road, Corsham SN13 9HS 01249 715609
DAWLISH TOWN .... Playing Fields, Sandy Lane, Exeter Road, Dawlish EX7 0AF 01626 863110
DEVIZES TOWN .... Nursteed Road, Devizes SN10 3EJ 01380 722817
FROME TOWN .... Badgers Hill, Berkley Road, Frome BA11 2EH 01373 464087
HALLEN .... Hallen Centre, Moorhouse Lane, Hallen, Bristol BS10 7RU 0117 950 5559
ILFRACOMBE TOWN .... Marlborough Park, Marlborough Road, Ilfracombe EX34 8JB 01271 865939
MELKSHAM TOWN .... The Conigre, Market Place, Melksham SN12 6ES 01225 702843
RADSTOCK TOWN .... Southfield Recreation Ground, Frome Hill, Radstock BA3 3NZ 01761 435004
SHERBORNE TOWN .... Raleigh Grove, The Terrace Playing Fields, Sherborne DT9 5NS 01935 816110
STREET .... The Tannery Ground, Middlebrooks, Street BA16 0TA 01458 444987
WELLINGTON TOWN .... Wellington Playing Field, North Street, Wellington TA1 8NA 01823 664810
WELTON ROVERS .... West Clewes, North Road, Midsomer Norton BA3 2QD 01761 412097
WILLAND ROVERS .... Stan Robinson Stadium, Silver Street, Willand, Cullompton EX15 2SL 01884 33885

IN: Sherborne Town (P), Wellington Town (P)
OUT: Odd Down (R), Truro City (P – Southern League Division One South & West)

	Almondsbury	Backwell United	Bradford Town	Bridport	Cadbury Heath	Clevedon United	Elmore	Hengrove Athletic	Keynsham Town	Larkhall Athletic	Longwell Green Sports	Minehead Town	Oldland Abbotonians	Portishead	Roman Glass St George	Shepton Mallet	Sherborne Town	Shrewton United	Wellington Town	Westbury United	Weston St Johns
Almondsbury		1-2	1-3	3-1	1-2	1-1	1-3	0-2	0-1	1-1	1-1	1-3	2-3	1-1	2-5	1-2	1-1	1-0	0-0	1-2	3-3
Backwell United	1-2		2-1	2-1	2-1	1-1	4-4	1-1	0-2	1-2	0-3	1-2	2-6	3-5	0-2	3-2	1-1	1-2	1-6	2-2	5-1
Bradford Town	3-4	1-0		3-2	1-0	0-3	2-2	3-4	1-2	3-1	0-2	2-1	2-2	1-5	0-3	7-5	0-3	2-0	0-3	0-1	2-2
Bridport	0-0	7-0	0-2		3-2	0-1	2-3	2-3	1-2	1-3	2-3	2-2	1-1	1-0	0-1	0-1	1-0	3-0	0-2	1-4	5-2
Cadbury Heath	3-1	3-1	4-0	2-2	D	1-0	1-1	4-1	2-1	1-2	1-3	2-2	3-1	1-1	1-1	2-0	2-1	1-3	1-3	3-2	3-1
Clevedon United	0-0	3-1	2-1	1-4	1-2	I	3-3	0-1	1-3	1-2	3-3	2-3	3-1	1-3	0-3	2-1	1-4	0-3	1-0	2-3	
Elmore	1-0	1-0	2-0	1-4	1-4	2-3	V	4-3	1-3	1-2	0-3	2-2	2-2	3-2	2-7	3-1	1-5	2-4	1-4	3-5	5-1
Hengrove Athletic	2-0	1-1	6-2	1-0	1-2	6-0	6-1	I	3-1	1-2	4-1	3-1	1-1	2-1	1-1	1-1	1-4	1-2	0-3	2-1	8-0
Keynsham Town	0-0	1-1	1-2	2-2	1-6	2-1	1-2	3-1	S	0-2	0-2	1-1	3-2	0-2	0-3	1-6	0-2	1-2	1-1	1-0	1-1
Larkhall Athletic	4-1	3-0	0-0	3-1	1-1	0-1	2-1	4-0	1-0	I	3-3	2-0	1-2	2-2	1-0	2-1	3-2	2-3	2-0	1-2	3-0
Longwell Green Sports	1-0	2-0	1-2	3-0	3-1	1-1	0-0	2-2	3-1	1-0	O	3-0	1-0	1-2	0-3	3-1	1-2	0-0	2-3	4-0	1-2
Minehead Town	3-1	1-1	0-0	2-1	2-1	1-0	3-2	2-2	0-3	1-8	1-4	N	0-2	1-1	4-2	0-1	3-1	2-4	3-3	1-2	1-2
Oldland Abbotonians	1-2	5-2	2-2	2-0	2-2	1-1	5-1	0-1	0-3	2-3	0-0	3-0		2-4	1-1	1-4	2-2	1-2	2-3	1-0	6-2
Portishead	5-0	2-0	1-1	3-1	0-4	0-0	2-0	1-1	0-2	5-0	1-1	4-0	1-1		3-2	0-1	1-1	6-2	3-1	3-3	3-0
Roman Glass St George	1-2	6-0	4-0	0-2	1-2	4-1	1-0	0-2	2-0	0-3	1-1	1-1	3-4	1-0	O	1-1	1-2	1-2	2-8	0-0	4-0
Shepton Mallet	5-1	2-0	2-4	2-0	3-1	0-1	2-3	0-0	0-2	0-1	3-4	3-3	4-0			N	1-2	1-2	0-4		4-2
Sherborne Town	5-2	1-1	2-0	3-0	6-1	0-2	2-1	5-1	5-0	2-1	2-1	8-1	4-0	0-1	4-0	4-0	E	5-0	2-2	5-2	6-0
Shrewton United	1-1	1-2	2-3	2-1	3-1	0-1	3-1	0-0	3-2	0-4	3-1	2-5	5-1	0-0	4-1	1-4			3-3	2-0	7-3
Wellington Town	4-2	8-1	5-1	4-1	0-3	5-1	5-1	3-0	4-1	0-1	4-1	3-1	2-0	3-1	1-0	12-1	0-0	0-1		2-2	6-0
Westbury United	3-0	4-0	1-5	1-1	4-0	4-2	6-3	1-0	2-1	1-1	1-1	6-0	3-1	4-0	1-1	3-2	0-3	1-2			5-1
Weston St Johns	2-2	2-2	1-2	3-6	1-2	0-2	1-8	1-2	0-4	1-6	0-3	3-5	4-3	3-2	0-2	0-1	0-5	2-3	1-1	3-7	

Division One	P	W	D	L	F	A	Pts
Wellington Town	40	27	8	5	124	45	89
Sherborne Town	40	26	7	7	111	41	85
Larkhall Athletic	40	26	7	7	87	43	85
Shrewton United	40	23	5	12	82	71	74
Cadbury Heath	40	22	7	11	82	59	73
Hengrove Athletic	40	20	9	11	83	61	69
Westbury United	40	20	8	12	92	62	68
Longwell Green Sports	40	19	11	10	71	47	68
Portishead	40	17	12	11	81	59	63
Roman Glass St George	40	15	10	15	70	55	55
Shepton Mallet	40	16	5	19	71	79	53
Oldland Abbotonians	40	13	11	16	80	77	50
Bradford Town	40	14	8	18	62	84	50
Keynsham Town	40	14	7	19	51	67	49
Clevedon United	40	12	8	20	50	75	44
Elmore	40	11	7	22	73	106	40
Minehead Town	40	10	10	20	55	96	40
Bridport	40	10	6	24	64	77	36
Backwell United	40	7	10	23	48	101	31
Almondsbury	40	6	12	22	44	82	30
Weston St Johns	40	5	6	29	54	148	21

Portishead 1 **Brislington** 2
Shrewton United 4 Chard Town 1
Westbury United 2 Roman Glass St George 1 *aet*
Weston St Johns 2 Larkhall Athletic 1

SECOND ROUND
Bideford 4 Barnstaple Town 1
Bristol Manor Farm 9 Weston St Johns 0
Corsham Town 1 **Bitton** 3
Frome Town 2 Welton Rovers 1
Radstock Town 0 **Dawlish Town** 4
Shrewton United 1 **Ilfracombe Town** 3
Truro City 3 Bridport 0
Westbury United 1 **Brislington** 2

QUARTER-FINALS
Bitton 1 **Bideford** 0
(Bitton expelled)
Brislington 3 Truro City 2
(Brislington expelled)
Dawlish Town 4 Frome Town 2
Ilfracombe Town 4 Bristol Manor Farm 3

SEMI-FINALS
Ilfracombe Town 1 **Dawlish Town** 5
Truro City 2 **Bideford** 6

FINAL
(May 10th at Elmore)
Bideford 2 **Dawlish Town** 5 *aet*

TOOLSTATION WESTERN LEAGUE DIVISION ONE CONSTITUTION 2008-09

ALMONDSBURY .... Almondsbury Sports & Social Centre, Gloucester Road, Almondsbury BS34 4AA 01454 612240
BRADFORD TOWN .... Avon Sports Ground, Trowbridge Road, Bradford-on-Avon BA15 1EE 01225 866649
BRIDPORT .... St Marys Field, Skilling Hill Road, Bridport DT6 5LN 01308 423834
CADBURY HEATH .... Springfield, Cadbury Heath Road, Warmley, Bristol BS30 8BX 0117 967 5731
CLEVEDON UNITED .... Clevedon Town FC, The Hand Stadium, Davis Way, Clevedon BS21 6TG 01275 341913
ELMORE .... Horsdon Park, Heathcoat Way, Tiverton EX16 4DB 01884 252341
GILLINGHAM TOWN .... Hardings Lane, Gillingham SP8 4HX 01747 823673
HENGROVE ATHLETIC .... Norton Lane, Whitchurch, Bristol BS14 0BT 01275 832894
KEYNSHAM TOWN .... Crown Field, Bristol Road, Keynsham, Bristol BS31 2BE 0117 986 5876
LARKHALL ATHLETIC............... Plain Ham, Charlcombe Lane, Larkhall, Bath BA1 8DJ 01225 334952
LONGWELL GREEN SPORTS. Longwell Green Comm. Centre, Shellards Road, Longwell Green BS30 9DU 0117 932 5111
MINEHEAD TOWN................ Recreation Ground, Irnham Road, Minehead TA24 5DP 01643 704989
ODD DOWN .... Lew Hill Memorial Ground, Combe Hay Lane, Odd Down, Bath BA2 8PH 01225 832491
OLDLAND ABBOTONIANS....... Aitchison Playing Field, Castle Road, Oldland Common BS30 9SZ 0117 932 8263
PORTISHEAD................. Bristol Road Playing Fields, Portishead, Bristol BS20 6QB 01275 847136
ROMAN GLASS ST GEORGE ...... Bell Hill, Whiteway Road, St George, Bristol BS5 7RW 0117 983 7707
SHEPTON MALLET .... West Shepton Playing Fields, Old Wells Road, Shepton Mallet BA4 5XN 01749 344609
SHREWTON UNITED .... Recreation Ground, Mill Lane, Shrewton, Salisbury SP3 4JU 07796 098122
WELLS CITY .... The Athletic Ground, Rowdens Road, Wells BA5 1TU 01749 679971
WESTBURY UNITED .... Meadow Lane, Westbury BA13 3AF 01373 823409
WESTON ST JOHNS................ Coleridge Road, Bournville Estate, Weston-super-Mare BS23 3UP 01934 612862
IN: Gillingham Town (P – Dorset Premier League), Odd Down (R), Wells City (P – Somerset County League Premier Division)
OUT: Backwell United (W – Somerset County League Premier Division), Sherborne Town (P), Wellington Town (P)

WESTMORLAND LEAGUE

	Ambleside United	Appleby	Burneside	Carvetii United	Coniston	Greystoke	Ibis	Kendal County	Keswick	Lunesdale United	Northbank Carlisle Res.	Sedbergh Wanderers	Wetheriggs United	Windermere SC
Ambleside United		5-1	4-1	4-2	7-0	2-1	5-3	1-0	6-0	2-0	7-4	12-0	2-3	2-3
Appleby	1-1	D	0-0	4-2	3-1	2-0	2-0	1-4	2-1	3-3	n/a	3-0	0-3	1-1
Burneside	1-7	1-2	I	1-3	0-0	2-1	0-1	0-3	1-3	2-3	n/a	1-0	1-1	3-0
Carvetii United	2-4	1-0	5-0	V	3-1	3-1	2-0	0-1	0-2	5-1	n/a	4-0	2-2	6-0
Coniston	0-3	2-3	3-0	1-0	I	0-1	2-1	1-1	6-3	0-1	n/a	2-1	1-1	1-2
Greystoke	1-4	2-3	3-0	1-2	1-4	S	1-1	1-3	4-0	2-3	n/a	8-2	1-4	5-0
Ibis	2-6	0-2	2-1	1-4	1-2	2-2	I	2-3	1-6	2-5	n/a	1-4	0-1	1-5
Kendal County	2-2	3-1	6-0	0-2	3-1	4-0	8-2	O	4-3	5-1	n/a	11-2	1-1	6-1
Keswick	3-8	1-1	2-1	5-2	4-2	4-2	1-1	0-4	N	6-2	n/a	7-0	0-1	4-1
Lunesdale United	2-2	1-0	0-0	4-3	0-3	1-1	2-2	1-5	2-3		n/a	3-2	1-3	1-0
Northbank Carlisle Res.	n/a	n/a	n/a	0-2	n/a	5-1	n/a	n/a	3-3	n/a	O	4-1	n/a	n/a
Sedbergh Wanderers	0-3	0-5	3-2	1-3	4-3	2-0	0-1	0-5	3-0	3-2	n/a	N	4-1	2-1
Wetheriggs United	3-2	0-1	3-1	3-2	1-1	2-2	5-0	4-1	2-1	2-1	2-1	3-0	E	3-2
Windermere SC	1-10	1-1	6-0	3-3	2-2	2-2	3-1	0-5	4-2	1-0	n/a	1-1	0-6	

Note – Northbank Carlisle Reserves withdrew during the course of the season

Their results are shown herein but are expunged from the league table

Division One	P	W	D	L	F	A	Pts
Ambleside United	24	18	3	3	104	32	57
Kendal County	24	18	3	3	88	27	57
Wetheriggs United	24	16	6	2	57	25	54
Appleby	24	12	6	6	42	33	42
Carvetii United	24	13	2	9	61	40	41
Keswick	24	11	2	11	61	60	35
Coniston	24	9	5	10	40	43	32
Lunesdale United	24	8	5	11	40	57	29
Windermere SC	24	7	6	11	38	67	27
Sedbergh Wanderers	24	7	1	16	32	85	22
Greystoke	24	5	5	14	45	53	20
Burneside	24	3	4	17	19	61	13
Ibis	24	3	4	17	28	72	13

Northbank Carlisle Res. – record expunged

WWW.CHERRYRED.CO.UK

HIGH SHERIFF'S CUP

FIRST ROUND
Greystoke 5 Windermere SC 2
Ibis 1 **Appleby** 2
Kendal County 5 Keswick 2
Sedbergh Wanderers 1 **Ambleside United** 6
Wetheriggs United 5 Burneside 1
Kendal County 3 Lunesdale United 1

QUARTER-FINALS
Appleby 4 Wetheriggs United 2
Carvetii United 1 **Greystoke** 3
Coniston 0 **Ambleside United** 2

SEMI-FINALS
Appleby 4 Ambleside United 3
aet (at Ullswater)
Kendal County 8 Greystoke 1
(at Shap)

FINAL
(May 6th at Penrith Town)
Appleby 2 Kendal County 0

TALBOT INSURANCE WESTMORLAND LEAGUE CONSTITUTION 2008-09

AMBLESIDE UNITED .... Hilliard Park, Millers Field, Ambleside LA22 9DH .... None
APPLEBY .... The Board Close, Chapel Street, Bolton, Appleby-in-Westmorland CA16 6QR .... None
BURNESIDE .... Cricket Pavilion, Hollins Lane, Burneside, Kendal LA9 6QL .... None
CARVETII UNITED .... Parrot Park, Hartley Road, Kirkby Stephen .... None
CONISTON .... Shepherds Bridge, Coniston LA21 8AL .... None
GREYSTOKE .... Greystoke Playing Field, Greystoke .... None
KENDAL COUNTY .... Netherfield Cricket Club, Parkside Road, Kendal LA9 7BL 01539 724051
KESWICK .... Walker Park, Keswick .... None
LUNESDALE UNITED .... Recreation Ground, Orton Road, Tebay, Penrith CA10 3TL .... None
PENRITH RANGERS .... Frenchfield, Brougham, Penrith CA10 2AA .... None
SEDBERGH WANDERERS .... Havera Playing Field, Sedbergh LA10 5HD .... None
SHAP .... Memorial Playing Field, Shap CA10 3PW .... None
WETHERIGGS UNITED .... Gilwilly Recreation Ground, Castletown, Penrith .... None
WINDERMERE SC .... Queen's Park, Windermere .... None
IN: Penrith Rangers (P), Shap (P)
OUT: Ibis (R), Northbank Carlisle Reserves (WS)

Division Two	P	W	D	L	F	A	Pts
Penrith Rangers	22	17	2	3	103	28	53
Shap	22	16	2	4	97	37	50
Staveley United	22	15	3	4	92	31	48
Kirkoswald	22	14	4	4	79	36	46
Kendal Celtic	22	12	4	6	65	44	40
Dent	22	9	5	8	50	44	32
Wetheriggs United Res.	22	9	3	10	63	43	30
Kendal County Res.	22	9	1	12	39	55	28
Keswick Res.	22	6	1	15	36	65	19
Windermere SC Res.	22	5	3	14	33	77	18
Sedbergh Wanderers Res.	22	3	1	18	27	137	10
Ibis Res.	22	2	1	19	25	112	7

Division Three	P	W	D	L	F	A	Pts
Ambleside United Res.	20	14	3	3	55	33	45
Kendal United	20	12	3	5	44	29	39
Shap Res.	20	12	2	6	66	32	38
Appleby Res.	20	11	3	6	44	24	36
Wetheriggs United 'A'	20	11	0	9	53	53	33
Endmoor KGR	20	9	3	8	41	40	30
Ullswater United	20	7	4	9	21	32	25
Carvetii United Res.	20	7	3	10	37	52	24
Penrith Rangers Res.	20	6	3	11	42	54	21
Burneside	20	5	1	14	37	62	16
Lunesdale United Res.	20	2	3	15	32	61	9

Division Four	P	W	D	L	F	A	Pts
Braithwaite	24	18	3	3	97	35	57
Kirkby Thore	24	16	2	6	77	53	50
Langwathby United	24	16	1	7	84	38	49
Kendal Celtic Res.	24	13	6	5	72	34	45
FC Milnthorpe	24	13	5	6	67	37	44
Endmoor KGR Res.	24	11	4	9	76	65	37
Burneside 'A'	24	11	3	10	64	58	36
Greystoke Res.	24	9	9	6	54	38	36
Staveley United Res.	24	8	6	10	46	57	30
Dent Res.	24	5	3	16	46	93	18
Esthwaite Vale	24	3	8	13	34	75	17
Coniston Res.	24	3	3	18	30	78	12
Windermere SC 'A'	24	2	3	19	29	115	9

MASON & FREEMAN CUP
(May 8th at Burneside)
Kendal County Res. 0 Staveley Utd 0 *aet* (5-4p)

PETER DAWS MEMORIAL SHIELD
(May 7th at Kirkby Stephen)
Appleby Res. 2 Endmoor KGR 0

AUSTIN WREN CUP
(May 2nd at Staveley)
FC Milnthorpe 3 Endmoor KGR Res. 1

WILTSHIRE LEAGUE

Note – Blueprint Chiseldon withdrew during the course of the season

Their results are shown herein but are expunged from the league table

	AFC Trowbridge Town Youth	Aldbourne	Blueprint Chiseldon	Bradford Town Res.	Bromham	Calne Town Res.	Corsham Town Res.	Devizes Town Res.	Malmesbury Victoria Res.	Marlborough Town	Melksham Town Res.	New College Swindon	Pewsey Vale Res.	Purton Res.	Shrewton United Res.	Westbury United Res.	Westside	Wroughton
AFC Trowbridge Town Youth		3-0	n/a	0-0	0-1	1-1	3-1	1-1	5-0	1-5	1-3	2-1	3-1	8-1	3-0	1-2	0-0	0-1
Aldbourne	3-2	P	n/a	1-0	0-1	1-4	2-5	4-0	1-0	2-3	0-3	1-2	2-0	8-1	2-3	0-1	3-1	0-4
Blueprint Chiseldon	2-2	1-7	R	3-8	n/a	1-4	2-3	n/a	n/a	n/a	n/a	0-5	n/a	1-6	n/a	1-11	n/a	n/a
Bradford Town Res.	0-0	0-1	n/a	E	1-0	1-2	5-1	3-4	4-1	0-1	3-3	1-3	1-0	3-1	6-1	1-4	2-0	0-2
Bromham	2-3	1-0	2-3	2-1	M	2-1	1-0	2-3	4-1	4-1	1-2	3-0	2-1	5-0	0-2	1-0	0-3	3-2
Calne Town Res.	3-2	5-0	2-3	1-3	4-0	I	3-1	0-0	1-0	3-1	0-0	0-5	2-1	3-1	5-2	2-2	3-1	3-1
Corsham Town Res.	0-1	0-4	n/a	1-2	0-3	0-1	E	0-5	4-0	2-6	4-1	0-6	1-1	2-2	0-2	2-2	3-1	0-3
Devizes Town Res.	3-1	3-0	3-2	1-2	0-4	0-1	2-4	R	1-1	0-0	1-0	3-2	1-3	1-1	3-1	0-1	3-2	0-1
Malmesbury Victoria Res.	4-2	2-3	n/a	1-2	0-3	1-0	1-2	0-3		0-4	3-1	1-0	1-2	4-3	0-4	0-5	0-7	0-4
Marlborough Town	1-4	2-2	5-1	1-0	1-3	1-2	1-3	1-1	1-1	D	0-2	3-1	0-1	5-0	1-3	0-1	0-2	0-1
Melksham Town Res.	2-0	0-7	n/a	0-1	2-0	2-1	4-1	3-1	1-0	2-1	I	1-2	1-0	4-0	3-1	2-2	5-0	0-5
New College Swindon	3-2	0-3	n/a	3-1	0-2	2-0	6-1	6-2	1-0	3-0	1-3	V	1-1	1-1	2-0	1-1	7-1	2-3
Pewsey Vale Res.	1-0	1-1	n/a	3-2	0-5	0-2	6-0	1-1	5-1	0-2	0-1	0-2	I	6-1	0-1	0-2	0-2	0-4
Purton Res.	1-3	0-3	n/a	0-5	2-0	1-0	1-3	0-3	0-3	1-3	1-1	2-2	3-1	S	2-2	2-1	3-1	2-1
Shrewton United Res.	0-3	1-0	1-3	1-5	0-2	1-3	3-2	3-3	3-0	2-1	0-3	0-3	3-1	2-3	I	2-4	1-2	2-2
Westbury United Res.	2-2	1-1	n/a	2-1	0-0	1-1	7-0	2-1	2-0	1-0	1-0	0-1	3-0	3-0	7-1	O	10-0	3-0
Westside	4-4	2-1	11-0	1-3	3-0	1-2	1-1	2-2	4-3	6-3	2-1	2-4	4-4	4-2	2-2	1-3	N	1-5
Wroughton	0-1	1-3	16-0	2-0	0-0	1-0	3-2	6-1	3-0	1-0	4-0	1-1	3-1	2-0	1-0	2-1	5-2	

Premier Division		P	W	D	L	F	A	Pts
Wroughton		32	23	4	5	74	27	73
Westbury United Res.		32	20	8	4	77	25	68
Bromham		32	20	2	10	57	33	62
Calne Town Res.		32	19	5	8	59	36	62
New College Swindon		32	18	5	9	74	41	59
Melksham Town Res.		32	18	4	10	56	44	58
Bradford Town Res.		32	15	3	14	59	44	48
Devizes Town Res.		32	11	9	12	53	58	42
AFC Trowbridge Town Youth	-3	32	12	8	12	61	47	41
Aldbourne	-4	32	14	3	15	59	52	41
Westside	-1	32	11	6	15	65	85	38
Shrewton United Res.		32	11	4	17	49	74	37
Marlborough Town		32	10	4	18	49	55	34
Pewsey Vale Res.	-1	32	8	5	19	41	58	28
Corsham Town Res.		32	8	4	20	46	89	28
Purton Res.		32	7	6	19	38	93	27
Malmesbury Victoria Res.	-2	32	6	2	24	29	85	18

Blueprint Chiseldon – record expunged

PLAISTER AUTOS WILTSHIRE LEAGUE PREMIER DIVISION CONSTITUTION 2008-09

BRADFORD TOWN RESERVES ... Avon Sports Ground, Trowbridge Road, Bradford-on-Avon BA15 1EE 01225 866649
BROMHAM .... Jubilee Field, Bromham, Chippenham 01380 850671
CALNE TOWN RESERVES .... Lickhill Road, Bremhill View, Calne SN11 8AE 01249 819186
CORSHAM TOWN RESERVES .... Southbank Ground, Lacock Road, Corsham SN13 9HS 01249 715609
DEVIZES TOWN RESERVES .... Nursteed Road, Devizes SN10 3EJ 01380 722817
FC CHIPPENHAM .... Stanley Park, Chippenham .... None
MARLBOROUGH TOWN .... Elcot Lane, Marlborough SN8 2BG 01672 513340
MELKSHAM TOWN RESERVES .... The Conigre, Market Place, Melksham SN12 6ES 01225 702843
NEW COLLEGE SWINDON ... Swindon Supermarine FC, Highworth Road, South Marston, Swindon SN3 4SF 01793 828778
PEWSEY VALE RESERVES .... Recreation Ground, Kings Corner, Ball Road, Pewsey SN9 5GF 01672 562990
PURTON RESERVES .... The Red House, Church Street, Purton SN5 4DT 01793 770262
SHREWTON UNITED RESERVES .... Recreation Ground, Mill Lane, Shrewton, Salisbury SP3 4JU 07796 098122
TROWBRIDGE TOWN RESERVES ...... Woodmarsh, North Bradley, Trowbridge BA14 0SA .... None
WARMINSTER TOWN RESERVES .... 73 Weymouth Street, Warminster BA12 9NS 01985 217828
WESTBURY UNITED RESERVES .... Meadow Lane, Westbury BA13 3AF 01373 823409
WESTSIDE .... Southbrook Recreation Ground, Swindon .... None
WROUGHTON .... The Weir Field, Wroughton WMC, Devizes Road, Wroughton SN4 0SA 01793 812319

IN: FC Chippenham (formerly FC Chippenham Youth)(P – Division Two), Warminster Town Reserves (P – Trowbridge & District League Division One)
OUT: Aldbourne (W), Blueprint Chiseldon (WS), Malmesbury Victoria Reserves (W)
AFC Trowbridge Town Youth become Trowbridge Town Reserves

SENIOR CUP
(Premier Division teams)

FIRST ROUND
Bradford Town Res. 2 New College Swindon 0
Marlborough Town 1 Pewsey Vale Res. 1 *aet* (3-2p)

SECOND ROUND
AFC Trowbridge Town Youth 2 Aldbourne 2 *aet* (5-4p)
Blueprint Chiseldon 1 **Marlborough Town** 3
Bradford Town Res. 2 Corsham Town Res. 1
Calne Town Res. 6 Shrewton United Res. 1
Malmesbury Victoria Res. 2 Devizes Town Res. 4 *(Devizes Town Res. expelled)*
Melksham Town Res. 3 Westside 1 *aet*
Purton Res. 0 **Westbury United Res.** 8
Wroughton 4 Bromham 0

QUARTER-FINALS
Calne Town Res. 4 Bradford Town Res. 0
Malmesbury Victoria Res. 2 **AFC Trowbridge Town Youth** 7
Marlborough Town 4 Wroughton 2
Westbury United Res. 1 **Melksham Town Res.** 1 *aet* (2-4p)

SEMI-FINALS
AFC Trowbridge Town Youth 1 **Melksham Town Res.** 5
Marlborough Town 0 **Calne Town Res.** 3

FINAL
(April 26th at Corsham Town)
Melksham Town Res. 0 **Calne Town Res.** 2

Division One		P	W	D	L	F	A	Pts
Minety		22	19	3	0	96	22	60
SKS Blyskawica		22	13	3	6	85	46	42
AFC Castrol		22	13	1	8	64	46	40
Stratton Juniors	-3	22	12	5	5	55	40	38
AFC Stratton NALGO	-3	22	13	2	7	49	41	38
Castle Combe		22	8	8	6	68	49	32
AFC Abbey Rodbourne		22	9	5	8	56	52	32
Westlecot United		22	8	3	11	46	54	27
Wroughton Res.		22	6	2	14	40	62	20
Blunsdon United		22	4	2	16	32	78	14
Lower Stratton	-1	22	4	2	16	37	83	13
AFC Rodbourne	-1	22	4	2	16	44	99	13

Division Two		P	W	D	L	F	A	Pts
KC		18	16	0	2	70	17	48
Intel		18	13	2	3	56	16	41
Chalke Valley		18	11	3	4	63	35	36
Swindon APS		18	11	1	6	61	25	34
FC Chippenham Youth		18	9	2	7	41	21	29
Marlborough Town Res.		18	8	3	7	42	36	27
Dynamo CDR		18	7	3	8	44	37	24
Swindon Irons	-1	18	4	2	12	27	59	13
Minety Res.	-1	18	2	0	16	17	113	5
Blunsdon United Res.		18	1	0	17	20	82	3

JUNIOR CUP
(Division One and Two teams)

FINAL
(April 26th at Corsham Town)
Minety 1 **KC** 1 *aet* (3-4p)

DIVISION TWO SUBSIDARY CUP

FINAL
(May 10th at Marlborough Town)
FC Chippenham Youth 1 Swindon APS 0

OTHER LEAGUES

All league tables in this section are final.

It is the policy of some competitions to leave some oft postponed matches as unplayed if they do not affect end of season issues.

ABERYSTWYTH & DISTRICT LEAGUE
(Cambrian Tyres)

Division One	P	W	D	L	F	A	Pts
Penparcau	22	17	3	2	111	20	54
Tregaron Turfs	22	15	5	2	76	36	45
Penrhyncoch Res.	22	12	5	5	49	30	41
Dolgellau AA	22	11	5	6	65	55	38
Aberdyfi	22	10	6	6	49	43	36
Aberystwyth Tn 'A' -6	22	11	4	7	74	39	31
Bont	22	9	3	10	49	43	30
Tywyn & Bryncrug Res.	22	8	5	9	47	41	29
UW Aberystwyth Res.	22	5	2	15	35	76	17
Llanilar	22	5	1	16	35	100	15
Llanrhystud	22	4	3	15	32	55	15
Talybont	22	4	2	16	34	82	14

Division Two	P	W	D	L	F	A	Pts
Penparcau Res.	22	20	2	0	106	22	62
Padarn United	22	16	3	3	83	29	51
UW Aberystwyth 'A' -3	22	16	1	5	62	25	49
Machynlleth	22	15	2	5	83	35	44
Bow Street Res. -3	22	14	3	5	80	35	42
Penrhyncoch 'A'	22	9	4	9	46	42	31
Llannon -3	22	6	2	14	31	61	17
Trawsgoed	22	4	3	11	44	79	15
Dolgellau AA Res.	22	4	3	15	41	70	15
Talybont Res -6	22	6	1	15	35	97	13
Corris United	22	6	1	15	30	84	13
Llyfrgell Gen	22	2	2	18	15	77	8

ACCRINGTON COMBINATION

Division One	P	W	D	L	F	A	Pts
Bridge Inn	20	16	2	2	71	22	50
Church Town	20	15	3	2	70	28	48
Edenfield	20	14	4	2	92	37	46
King Street	20	12	3	5	54	44	39
Wellington	20	9	2	9	59	44	29
Baileys	20	7	2	11	47	48	23
Rosegrove Unity -6	20	7	4	9	51	44	19
Crown Rovers	20	6	4	11	34	53	13
Whinney Hill 'A'	20	3	2	15	22	64	11
Oswaldtwistle St M 'A' -6	20	3	1	16	30	97	10
Royal Hotel	20	3	5	12	38	65	8

Division Two	P	W	D	L	F	A	Pts
Accrington Loyal	24	22	0	2	111	28	68
Ramsbottom Town	24	15	5	4	97	46	50
Rosegrove Unity Res.	24	15	3	6	83	46	48
Rishton United -3	24	15	3	6	79	51	45
Churchtown Res.	24	14	2	8	50	52	44
Black Horse	24	13	2	9	68	62	41
Crown Rovers Res.	24	12	3	9	60	56	39
Globe Bullough Park	24	8	1	15	62	75	25
Rose & Crown -3	24	9	0	15	65	67	24
Burnley Road Bowling	24	6	4	14	42	69	22
Sydney Street WMC	24	4	3	18	30	94	12
NSD	24	3	3	18	30	94	12
Broadway Central -3	24	2	1	21	28	94	4

ALDERSHOT & DISTRICT LEAGUE

Senior Division	P	W	D	L	F	A	Pts
Wrecclesham	18	15	3	0	80	20	48
Sandhurst Devels	18	13	3	2	70	22	42
Frimley Town	18	13	0	5	52	33	39
Yateley Green	18	11	1	6	51	33	34
Hindhead Athletic	18	7	3	8	33	37	24
Bentley Athletic	18	7	2	9	46	45	23
Crookham Krakatoa	18	5	2	11	32	53	17
Farnboro' Nth End Res.	18	3	5	10	33	47	14
Frimley Select	18	3	3	12	27	67	12
Wey Valley	18	1	2	15	24	99	5

Division One	P	W	D	L	F	A	Pts
Hook Athletic	18	13	1	4	57	23	47
Sandhurst Town 'A'	18	11	3	4	59	36	36
Fleet Spurs 'A'	18	8	1	9	39	46	27
Wey Valley Res.	18	7	3	8	48	39	24
Hale Rovers	18	7	2	9	44	50	23
Yateley Green Res.	18	7	2	9	44	56	23
Sandhurst Sports	18	5	3	10	33	46	18
Headley United Res.	18	5	1	12	31	44	17
Letef Select	18	4	2	12	26	41	14
Hartley Wintney 'A'	18	2	6	10	26	67	12

ALTRINCHAM & DISTRICT LEAGUE
(Haven Overseas)

Division One	P	W	D	L	F	A	Pts
Knutsford Res.	16	15	0	1	67	23	45
King George	16	12	1	3	54	33	37
Broadheath Central 'A'	16	11	2	3	46	29	33
Atlantic	16	8	2	6	51	43	20
Kartel Sports	16	6	1	9	43	46	19
Stretford Victoria	16	4	7	9	39	56	19
Old York -3	16	4	3	9	31	36	12
Trafford 'A' -3	16	4	1	10	25	75	3
Quarry Bank	16	1	0	15			

Division Two	P	W	D	L	F	A	Pts
The Bridge Sale	24	18	4	2	70	33	58
Cringlewood Athletic	24	16	3	6	68	35	51
Sale Amateurs	24	14	0	4	57	29	42
Sale Rovers	24	11	9	4	51	35	35
Styal 'A'	24	10	4	10	61	61	34
Timperley Wanderers	24	9	5	10	52	55	32
Salford AFC	24	7	6	11	62	55	27
Trafford United	24	8	3	13	62	75	27
Brooklands	24	7	3	14	49	47	24
Northenden Victoria -3	24	7	2	14	46	59	20
Fernley	24	5	5	14	35	58	17
O Altrinchamians 'A' -3	24	4	3	17	37	104	12

AMATEUR COMBINATION
Higher divisions on page 9

Intermediate Division North	P	W	D	L	F	A	Pts
Egbertian	18	15	2	1	59	24	47
Parkfield Res.	20	13	2	3	84	26	41
William Fitt	18	12	2	4	73	26	40
Leyton County Old Boys	20	11	0	9	45	41	33
Bealonians Res.	20	6	11	1	41	61	19
Old Aloysians 'A'	18	6	0	12	35	68	18
Hale End Athletic Res.	18	4	5	9	30	51	17
Old Woodhousians	18	4	4	10	39	58	16
Southgate County Res.	18	0	2	16	14	109	2

Intermediate Division South	P	W	D	L	F	A	Pts
Old Thorntonians	16	10	3	1	77	30	33
Credit Suisse	16	9	2	5	49	32	31
National Westminster Bk	16	9	1	5	55	41	29
Royal Bank of Scotland	16	8	1	7	48	55	25
Old Tensonians	16	7	4	5	55	42	25
Chislehurst Sports	16	8	1	7	49	43	25
Old Josephians	16	6	1	9	48	47	19
Pegasus	16	5	1	10	29	60	16
Old Sedcopians	16	6	1	9	19	86	3
Witan	16	1	0	15			

Intermediate Division West	P	W	D	L	F	A	Pts
Old Hamptonians 'A'	18	14	1	3	58	29	43
Old Uffingtonians	18	10	4	4	71	47	33
Old Magdalenians	18	8	4	6	48	37	28
London Welsh	18	8	1	8	53	47	28
Old Kingsburians	18	9	1	8	45	45	28
Chertsey Old Salesians	18	6	4	8	49	45	22
Old Manorians Res.	18	5	5	8	38	45	20
Parkfield 'A'	18	5	4	9	31	47	19
Old Vaughanians Res.	18	5	4	9	21	58	19
Old Challoners Res.	18	4	3	11	37	47	15

Division One North	P	W	D	L	F	A	Pts
Enfield Old Gramms 'A'	16	9	2	5	47	26	29
Egbertian Res.	16	9	2	5	41	30	29
UCL Academicals 'A'	16	8	4	4	48	30	28
Old Ignatians Res.	16	8	2	6	31	26	26
Old Parmiterians 'A'	16	6	6	4	38	36	22
Old Edmontonians Res.	16	6	4	6	28	33	22
Bealonians 'A'	16	6	3	7	34	38	21
Queen Mary College OBs	16	5	3	8	35	38	18
Wood Green OBs Res.	16	1	4	11	23	65	7

Division One South	P	W	D	L	F	A	Pts
Old Wokingians	18	14	1	3	56	28	43
Old Suttonians Res.	18	12	2	4	68	34	38
City of London	18	11	2	5	35	35	35
Clapham O Xaverians Res.	18	10	2	6	49	30	32
Sinjuns Grammarians Res.	18	8	6	4	29	29	30
Old St Marys	18	6	4	8	35	45	23
Old Tensionians Res.	18	6	4	8	24	50	22
Glyn Old Boys Res.	18	5	5	8	22	44	20
Old Whitgiftian -3	18	6	1	11	40	50	16
Reigatians	18	3	1	14	26	53	10

Division Two North	P	W	D	L	F	A	Pts
Old Aloysians 'B'	20	12	4	4	62	32	40
Mill Hill County Old Boys	20	12	4	4	56	30	40
Old Tollingtonians	20	10	8	2	56	29	38
Old Minchendenians Res.	20	11	3	6	58	42	36
Albanian 'A'	20	11	3	6	58	42	36
Leyton County OB Res.	20	8	5	7	41	28	29
Univ of Hertfordshire	20	6	6	8	45	49	24
Southgate County 'A'	20	5	4	11	42	58	19
Qn Mary Coll OB Res. -3	20	4	4	12	34	55	13
Egbertian 'A' -3	20	4	4	12	36	72	13
Ravenscroft Old Boys	20	2	4	14	34	83	10

Division Two South	P	W	D	L	F	A	Pts
Old Thorntonians	22	15	4	3	65	33	47
Old Bromleians	22	12	6	4	71	30	40
Credit Suisse	22	13	4	5	56	49	43
National Westminster Bk	22	14	2	6	52	53	44
Royal Bank of Scotland	22	12	2	8	69	42	38
Old Tensonians	22	6	7	9	50	69	25
Chislehurst Sports	22	7	3	12	43	65	24
Mickleham O Boxhillians	22	8	1	13	65	71	21
Old Josephians	22	5	6	11	34	71	21
Pegasus	22	5	1	16	43	76	16
Witan	22	3	4	15	41	71	13

WWW.NLNEWSDESK.CO.UK

250 Other Leagues

WWW.CHERRYRED.CO.UK

Division Two South	P	W	D	L	F	A	Pts
Old Josephians Res.	16	12	1	3	73	26	37
Old Pauline Res.	16	10	3	3	55	36	33
Clapham O Xaverians 'A'	16	9	4	3	37	22	31
Chislehurst Sports Res.	16	9	2	5	46	40	29
Nat West Bank Res. -3	16	8	1	7	33	40	22
Centymca Res.	16	6	1	9	30	42	19
Reigatians Res.	16	3	5	8	29	36	14
Old Suttonians 'A'	16	4	2	10	26	42	14
The Comets	16	1	1	14	23	68	4

Division Two West	P	W	D	L	F	A	Pts
Old Manorians 'A'	16	11	4	1	65	29	37
Pegasus Res.	16	10	3	3	49	19	33
Old Vaughanians 'A'	16	10	3	3	45	33	33
Phoenix Old Boys Res.	16	8	2	6	41	34	26
Old Meadonians 'C'	16	6	6	4	31	23	24
Old Salvatorians 'B'	16	5	3	8	38	40	18
Hampstead Heathens Res.	16	4	2	10	29	48	14
Old Uxonians Res.	16	3	1	12	19	57	10
Parkfield 'B'	16	3	0	13	15	49	9

Division Three North	P	W	D	L	F	A	Pts
Mill Hill County OB Res.	20	17	2	1	87	25	53
William Fitt Res. -4	20	17	0	3	74	27	47
Albanian 'B'	20	11	2	7	53	44	35
Hale End Athletic 'A'	20	10	3	7	62	42	33
Old Buckwellians Res.	20	9	3	8	50	45	30
Mayfield Athletic	20	8	3	9	41	48	27
Old Ignatians 'A'	20	7	3	10	48	56	24
Old Parmiterians 'B'	20	6	4	10	35	53	22
Latymer Old Boys Res.	20	5	5	10	32	55	20
Old Edmontonians 'A'	20	5	1	14	30	66	16
London Hospital OB	20	1	2	17	19	70	5

Division Three South	P	W	D	L	F	A	Pts
Marsh	18	13	5	0	60	24	44
Economicals Res.	18	9	5	4	46	34	32
Old Suttonians 'B'	18	8	5	5	37	21	29
Sinjuns Grammarians 'A'	18	8	2	8	36	43	26
Old Dorkinians Res.	18	5	9	4	32	29	24
Old Tiffinians Res.	18	6	6	6	25	28	24
Old Wokingians Res.	18	6	3	9	43	46	21
Old Guildfordians Res.	18	4	6	8	27	52	18
Witan Res.	18	4	3	11	32	44	15
Clapham OXaverians 'B'	18	3	4	11	38	55	13

Division Three West	P	W	D	L	F	A	Pts
Old Kingsburians 'A'	16	11	3	2	51	21	36
Old Salvatorians 'C'	16	11	3	2	42	21	36
Birkbeck College	16	9	2	5	42	33	29
Old Isleworthians 'A'	16	8	3	5	37	35	27
Holland Park OB -3	16	7	3	6	43	34	21
Old Manorians 'B'	16	4	3	9	35	48	15
Phoenix Old Boys 'A'	16	4	2	10	28	43	14
Old Magdalenians Res.	16	3	3	10	31	52	12
Ealing Association -3	16	3	2	11	28	50	8

Division Four North	P	W	D	L	F	A	Pts
Mill Hill Village Res.	18	13	2	3	78	36	41
Old Camdenians Res.	18	13	2	3	56	24	41
Old Aloysians 'C'	18	11	2	5	59	42	35
Enfield OGramms 'B'	18	9	3	6	50	45	30
Albanian 'C'	18	9	2	7	35	35	29
Bealonians 'B'	18	8	1	9	43	45	25
Old Parmiterians 'C'	18	6	4	8	38	46	22
Egbertian 'B'	18	5	2	11	43	59	17
UCL Academicals 'B'	18	4	2	12	30	55	14
Latymer Old Boys 'A'	18	2	0	16	27	72	6

Division Four South	P	W	D	L	F	A	Pts
Old Tenisonians 'A'	18	14	3	1	58	18	45
JP Morgan Chase -1	18	12	2	4	58	27	37
Nat West Bank 'A' -4	18	11	3	4	54	21	32
Old Wokingians 'A'	18	9	3	6	52	43	30
Royal Bk of Scotland Res.	18	8	3	7	45	32	27
Old Sedcopians Res.	18	6	5	7	47	46	23
BBC	18	5	6	7	40	38	21
Old Tiffinians 'A'	18	5	3	10	32	55	18
Wandsworth Borough Res.	18	3	3	12	30	51	12
Old Suttonians 'C' -3	18	1	1	16	21	106	1

Division Four West	P	W	D	L	F	A	Pts
Old Meadonians 'D'	14	9	4	1	48	25	31
Old Kolsassians Res.	14	7	4	3	51	33	25
Old Salvatorians 'D'	14	8	1	5	31	27	25
Old Vaughanians 'B'	14	7	3	4	46	29	24
Cardinal Manning OB	14	7	0	7	38	51	21
Phoenix Old Boys 'B'	14	3	2	9	27	36	11
Brent 'A'	14	3	2	9	31	49	11
Old Challoners 'B'	14	2	4	8	26	48	10

Division Five North	P	W	D	L	F	A	Pts
Mill Hill County OB 'A'	18	15	2	1	76	29	47
Hale End Athletic 'B'	18	15	1	2	60	22	46
Old Tollingtonians Res.	18	10	4	4	83	29	34
Old Buckwellians 'A'	18	10	1	7	55	46	31
Old Parmiterians 'D'	18	9	1	8	56	42	28
Southgate County 'B'	18	5	2	11	44	48	17
Wood Green OB 'A'	18	4	4	10	54	62	16
Bealonians 'C'	18	4	3	11	51	59	15
Old Aloysians 'D' -6	18	3	2	13	28	110	5
Old Camdenians 'A' -9	18	3	4	11	37	97	4

Division Five South East	P	W	D	L	F	A	Pts
Royal Sun Alliance	16	12	2	2	68	18	38
Clapham O Xaverians 'C'	16	12	2	2	65	23	38
Citigroup -1	16	11	1	4	47	28	33
Glyn Old Boys 'B'	16	6	3	7	25	36	21
Old Suttonians 'D'	16	6	0	10	24	46	18
John Fisher OB Res. -3	16	6	2	8	33	44	17
Old St Marys Res.	16	5	2	9	25	50	17
Old Sedcopians 'A'	16	4	2	10	33	37	14
Sinjuns Grammarians 'B'	16	1	4	11	12	50	7

Division Five South West	P	W	D	L	F	A	Pts
Old Dorkinians 'A'	20	17	1	2	81	28	52
Temple Bar	20	14	0	6	60	30	42
Glyn Old Boys 'A'	20	11	0	9	69	42	33
Witan 'A'	20	10	2	8	51	31	32
Old Pauline 'A'	20	8	4	8	33	48	28
Old Guildfordians 'A'	20	7	6	7	42	42	27
Old Wokingians 'B'	20	8	2	10	41	59	26
Fulham Compton OB Res.	20	7	3	10	38	57	24
Reigatians 'A'	20	5	5	10	40	56	20
Old Thorntonians Res.	20	6	2	12	41	62	20
Old Meadonians 'E'	20	3	3	14	30	71	12

Division Five West	P	W	D	L	F	A	Pts
Ealing Association Res.	14	11	1	2	44	17	34
Cardinal Manning OB Res.	14	9	3	2	38	26	30
Old Kingsburians 'B'	14	6	2	6	39	30	20
London Welsh Res.	14	6	2	6	33	34	20
Old Manorians 'C'	14	6	1	7	35	29	19
Old Uffingtonians 'A'	14	5	2	7	33	38	17
Old Isleworthians 'B'	14	4	3	7	29	35	15
Old Vaughanians 'C'	14	2	0	12	16	58	6

Division Six North	P	W	D	L	F	A	Pts
Mayfield Athletic Res.	20	17	2	1	121	30	53
St Albans Rangers	20	16	1	3	74	28	49
Egbertian 'C'	20	12	1	7	55	42	37
Wood Green Old Boys 'B'	20	11	2	7	58	44	35
Latymer Old Boys 'B'	20	9	1	10	49	58	28
Leyton County OB 'A'	20	8	2	10	49	61	26
Davenant Wdrs OB -3	20	8	2	10	44	63	23
O Woodhouseians Res.	20	6	2	12	35	60	20
Mill Hill Village 'A'	20	5	1	14	32	59	16
Mill Hill County OB 'B'	20	3	6	11	42	68	15
Old Ignatians 'B'	20	3	4	13	36	82	13

Division Six South East	P	W	D	L	F	A	Pts
City of London Res.	16	13	2	1	49	19	41
Royal Sun Alliance Res. -1	16	12	2	2	69	28	37
Clapham O Xaverians 'D'	16	7	5	4	46	38	26
Kings Old Boys 'A' -3	16	9	2	5	45	39	26
Old Bromleians Res.	16	7	3	6	56	47	24
Centymca 'A'	16	5	1	10	33	40	16
Old Sedcopians 'B'	16	3	3	10	34	55	12
Old Josephians 'A'	16	3	2	11	31	63	11
John Fisher Old Boys 'A'	16	2	2	12	35	69	8

Division Six South West	P	W	D	L	F	A	Pts
Economicals 'A'	18	14	2	2	76	18	44
Old Thorntonians 'A'	18	12	4	2	72	28	40
Old Tenisonians 'B'	18	10	4	4	41	25	34
Heathrow Seniors	18	10	1	7	43	44	31
Old Suttonians 'E'	18	7	4	7	47	44	25
Fulham Compton OB 'A'	18	7	2	9	29	50	23
Old Guildfordians 'B'	18	6	3	9	25	31	21
Old Tiffinians 'B'	18	5	1	12	38	61	16
Old Meadonians 'F'	18	5	0	13	27	58	15
Old Wokingians 'C'	18	3	1	14	27	66	10

Division Seven North	P	W	D	L	F	A	Pts
Mill Hill County OB 'C'	16	12	2	2	58	28	38
Old Edmontonians 'B'	16	12	1	3	60	28	37
UCL Academicals 'C'	16	9	2	5	53	34	29
O ld Minchendenians 'A'	16	8	3	5	46	31	27
Leyton County OB 'B'	16	8	3	5	43	36	27
Ravenscroft OB Res.	16	6	2	8	53	50	20
Old Woodhouseians 'A'	16	4	1	11	32	61	13
Queen Mary Coll. OB 'A'	16	4	0	12	27	46	12
Wood Green OB 'C'	16	2	0	14	28	86	6

Division Seven South East	P	W	D	L	F	A	Pts
Old Bromleians 'A'	16	13	1	2	66	34	40
Credit Suisse Res.	16	10	3	3	55	32	33
John Fisher Old Boys 'B'	16	9	2	5	66	42	29
Glyn Old Boys 'C'	16	9	1	6	62	38	28
City of London 'A'	16	8	2	6	41	32	26
Reigatians 'C'	16	7	1	8	44	58	22
Old Whitgiftian Res.	16	6	3	7	47	46	21
Old St Marys 'A'	16	2	1	13	27	73	7
Old Sedcopians 'C'	16	1	0	15	18	71	3

Division Seven South West	P	W	D	L	F	A	Pts
Teddington	18	15	0	3	64	20	45
Shene Old Gramms 'A'	18	13	2	3	39	16	41
Fulham Compton OB 'B'	18	10	2	6	51	30	32
Mickleham O Boxh'ns Res.	18	9	3	6	51	50	30
Old Meadonians 'G'	18	9	1	8	50	38	28
Reigatians 'B'	18	7	4	7	42	53	25
Old Guildfordians 'C'	18	6	2	10	39	47	20
Old Dorkinians 'B'	18	5	2	11	44	62	17
Old Wokingians 'D'	18	4	2	12	31	58	14
Wandsworth Borough 'A'	18	1	4	13	25	62	7

Division Eight North	P	W	D	L	F	A	Pts
Old Minchendenians 'B'	16	13	3	0	77	18	42
Old Edmontonians 'C'	16	12	1	3	84	42	37
Enfield Old Gramms 'C'	16	9	2	5	47	35	29
Albanian 'D'	16	8	3	5	64	40	27
Old Parmiterians 'E'	16	6	1	9	41	51	19
Bealonians 'D'	16	5	2	9	56	55	17
Southgate County 'C'	16	4	2	10	38	64	14
Ravenscroft OB 'A' -3	16	5	0	11	41	115	12
Mayfield Athletic 'A'	16	3	0	13	32	60	9

Division Eight Stouh West	P	W	D	L	F	A	Pts
Old Suttonians 'F'	16	14	2	0	70	16	44
Fulham Compton OB 'C'	16	10	3	3	68	21	33
Glyn Old Boys 'D'	16	9	3	4	54	24	30
Old Pauline 'B'	16	7	2	7	35	42	23
Old Wokingians 'E'	16	7	0	9	48	49	21
Shene Old Gramms 'B'	16	6	1	9	24	41	19
Old Meadonians 'H' -3	16	6	1	9	34	73	16
Reigatians 'D'	16	4	2	10	29	49	14
Old Guildfordians 'D'	16	1	2	13	19	66	5

Division Nine North		P	W	D	L	F	A	Pts
Old Ignatians 'C'		20	12	6	2	83	35	42
Old Edmontonians 'D'		20	12	6	2	67	33	42
Leyton County OB 'C'		20	9	5	6	54	46	32
Enfield Old Gramms 'D'		20	8	7	5	64	51	31
Mill Hill Village 'B'		20	9	4	7	55	47	31
Old Minchendenians 'C'		20	6	8	6	76	53	26
Latymer Old Boys 'C'		20	8	1	11	48	70	25
Old Camdenians 'B'		20	7	3	10	39	72	24
Old Parmiterians 'F'		20	5	4	11	45	68	19
Bealonians 'E'		20	5	4	11	42	65	19
UCL Academicals 'D'		20	4	2	14	30	63	14

ANDOVER & DISTRICT LEAGUE

		P	W	D	L	F	A	Pts
AFC Wolversdene Res.		22	20	0	2	83	26	60
Borough Arms		22	13	3	6	67	44	42
Stannah		22	13	3	6	72	52	42
Burghclere		22	13	1	8	81	47	40
ABC United		22	12	1	9	55	46	37
Wherwell		22	11	2	9	64	69	35
FC Castledown		22	9	3	10	63	69	30
Infinity Andover		22	8	2	12	62	56	26
Blue Lion		22	7	3	12	55	60	24
Whitchurch United 'A'		22	6	2	14	32	76	20
King's Somborne		22	4	2	16	43	81	14
Inkpen Sports		22	4	2	16	33	84	14

AYLESBURY & DISTRICT LEAGUE

Premier Division		P	W	D	L	F	A	Pts
Haddenham United	-3	26	22	2	2	104	32	65
Bierton		26	19	1	6	103	46	58
Aston Park		26	18	3	5	84	37	57
Bucks CC		26	16	3	7	67	36	51
St Johns		26	16	2	8	87	53	50
Elmhurst		26	10	4	12	56	61	34
Walton Court Wanderer		26	10	3	13	67	74	33
Black Horse		26	9	5	12	51	67	32
Aston Clinton Res.		26	9	3	14	56	71	30
Aylesbury Dynamos		26	9	3	14	42	60	30
Long Marston		26	7	4	15	47	80	25
Wingrave		26	6	4	16	45	88	22
Bedgrove Dynamos		26	5	6	15	45	95	21
Jakemans Sports		26	3	3	20	38	92	12

Division One		P	W	D	L	F	A	Pts
Hale Leys United		22	17	2	3	74	25	53
Mandeville		22	16	2	4	79	33	50
Bedgrove United		22	11	4	7	45	28	37
Dairy Maid		22	11	2	9	72	63	35
Cheddington		22	10	4	8	61	49	34
Wendover	-1	22	11	2	9	43	37	34
Fairford Leys		22	9	6	7	55	47	33
Thame Town		22	10	2	10	49	54	32
Quainton		22	9	1	12	27	52	28
Bucks CC Res.	-1	22	6	5	11	41	56	22
Haddenham United Res.		22	4	2	16	35	80	14
Oving		22	1	2	19	20	77	5

Division Two		P	W	D	L	F	A	Pts
Cheddington Res.	+2	26	21	3	2	99	27	68
Aston Clinton 'A'		26	20	4	2	125	30	64
Wendover Res.		26	19	1	6	100	38	58
Long Marston Res.		26	17	3	6	96	45	54
St Johns Res.		26	15	4	7	75	52	49
Cross Keys	+3	26	14	3	9	75	67	48
Bierton Res.		26	10	5	11	78	84	35
Wingrave Res.	-11	26	12	3	11	52	52	28
Fairford Leys Res.	-1	26	7	5	14	45	66	25
Stone Magnets		26	6	6	14	50	93	24
Ludgershall	+2	26	6	3	17	62	105	23
Sparta Royals		26	5	2	19	52	117	17
Weavers United	+3	26	2	4	20	46	108	13
AC Meadowcroft	-1	26	3	4	19	30	101	12

BANBURY & LORD JERSEY FA

Premier Division	P	W	D	L	F	A	Pts
Bodicote Sports	22	17	3	2	82	27	54
Bishops Itchington	22	13	4	5	71	35	43
Broughton/Nth Newington	22	12	5	5	65	29	41
Kineton SSC	22	13	1	8	64	46	40
Cropredy	22	13	1	8	73	56	40
Steeple Aston	22	11	3	8	47	41	36
Hornton	22	8	5	9	40	50	29
Arncott	22	6	6	10	38	54	24
Drayton Village	22	8	0	14	50	71	24
Hethe	22	5	2	15	48	90	17
Finmere	22	4	4	14	39	73	16
Barford United	22	5	0	17	39	84	15

Division One	P	W	D	L	F	A	Pts
KEA	20	17	2	1	67	25	53
Slade Farm	20	16	2	2	71	14	50
Fenny Compton	20	14	1	5	59	28	43
Heyford Athletic 'A'	20	12	3	5	48	28	39
Wroxton Sports	20	9	4	7	62	40	31
Ruscote	20	9	2	9	39	40	29
Bishops Itchington Res.	20	5	5	10	28	54	20
Heyford United	20	5	4	11	33	65	19
Deddington Town	20	3	2	15	41	56	11
Souldern	20	3	2	15	21	68	11
Cropredy Res.	20	3	1	16	26	77	10

Division Two	P	W	D	L	F	A	Pts
ABK Sports	22	20	1	1	87	31	61
Hethe Res.	22	15	2	5	94	51	47
Glory Farm Mustangs	22	15	0	7	73	46	45
Heyford Park	22	12	3	7	55	43	39
Broughton/Nth N'ton Res.	22	11	3	8	57	53	36
Real Islip	22	11	2	9	58	45	35
BCS Bardwell Res.	22	9	4	9	70	56	31
Bloxham	22	7	9	6	58	54	30
Ruscote Res.	22	7	2	13	49	60	23
Middleton Cheney Res.	22	6	4	12	47	71	22
Abba Athletic	22	3	0	19	23	80	9
Wroxton Sports Res.	22	1	0	21	39	120	3

Division Three	P	W	D	L	F	A	Pts
Slade Farm Res.	22	17	3	2	87	22	54
KEA Res.	22	15	4	3	85	31	49
Fenny Compton Res.	22	13	4	5	75	28	43
Real Islip Res.	22	13	3	6	81	53	42
Heyford Athletic 'B'	22	12	4	6	58	46	40
Bodicote Sports Res.	22	12	0	10	56	43	36
Heyford United Res.	22	10	2	10	60	70	32
Deddington Town Res.	22	7	7	8	50	58	28
Finmere Res.	22	6	5	11	39	77	23
ABK Sports Res.	22	3	4	15	38	73	13
Steeple Aston Res.	22	3	2	17	14	81	11
Drayton Village Res.	22	2	0	20	34	95	6

BASINGSTOKE & DISTRICT LEAGUE

Premier Division	P	W	D	L	F	A	Pts
R & B Sports	16	11	5	0	42	12	38
Rangers	16	6	5	5	29	27	23
AFC Aldermaston 'A'	16	7	1	8	29	23	22
AFC Sleepers	16	6	4	6	34	31	22
Hook	16	6	3	7	34	36	21
Tadley Calleva 'A'	16	5	5	6	27	35	20
Bramley United	16	5	4	7	32	35	19
Oakley Athletic	16	5	4	7	30	37	19
New Inn	16	4	3	9	32	53	15

Division One	P	W	D	L	F	A	Pts
Broomsquire Hotel	14	14	0	0	38	9	42
New Inn Res.	14	10	2	2	43	20	32
Preston Candover	14	8	3	3	36	19	27
AFC Oakridge	14	8	1	5	38	22	25
Oakley Athletic Res.	14	4	1	9	20	37	13
Basingstoke Labour Club	14	3	2	9	19	56	11
Hook Res.	14	3	0	11	19	21	9
AFC Aldermaston 'B'	14	1	1	12	19	48	4

Division Two	P	W	D	L	F	A	Pts
Overton United 'A'	20	16	2	2	59	13	50
Sherborne St John	20	15	4	1	84	27	49
AFC Berg	20	15	1	4	81	33	46
Sherfield	20	13	3	4	55	29	42
Rangers Res.	20	9	3	8	44	47	30
Heathpark	20	7	5	8	55	61	26
AFC Zacky United	20	7	2	11	28	30	23
Headley Athletic	20	6	0	14	23	53	18
Herriard Sports	20	4	3	13	25	61	15
Baughurst	20	4	0	16	18	55	12
AFC Tadley	20	2	1	17	19	82	7

BATH & DISTRICT LEAGUE
(Roper Rhodes Bathrooms)

Premier Division	P	W	D	L	F	A	Pts
University of Bath	20	17	2	1	85	22	53
Cutters Friday Res.	20	14	2	4	53	24	44
Saltford Res.	20	12	3	5	44	26	39
Trowbridge House	20	9	3	8	38	30	30
Aces SSJ	20	7	5	8	40	34	26
Civil Service Filos	20	7	5	8	34	32	26
Fry Club Old Boys	20	5	6	9	31	47	21
Oldfield Sports	20	5	6	9	28	46	21
Sportzcoach United	20	6	3	11	29	48	21
WESA	20	5	2	13	41	67	17
Bath Spa University	20	3	3	14	18	65	12

Division One	P	W	D	L	F	A	Pts
Dogtown Odd Down	20	17	1	2	100	26	52
University of Bath Res.	20	17	1	2	68	17	52
Chew Valley Seniors	20	12	2	6	57	48	38
Keynsham Town 'A'	20	11	1	8	69	59	34
Oval Sports	20	9	3	8	50	42	30
Bath Arsenal	20	8	2	10	50	40	26
Freshford Sports	20	7	1	12	41	60	22
Fairfield Park Rangers	20	7	1	12	39	68	22
Stothert & Pitt	20	5	3	12	48	66	18
Civil Service Filos Vets	20	4	1	15	30	63	13
Timsbury Athletic 'A'	20	3	4	13	34	97	13

Division Two	P	W	D	L	F	A	Pts
Moorfields	20	18	1	1	99	18	55
Saltford 'A'	20	16	3	1	77	42	51
WESA Res.	20	11	4	5	63	42	37
Wesco United	20	10	3	7	47	39	33
Rising Sun	20	10	1	9	46	44	31
Westwood United	20	9	3	8	55	58	30
Fry Club Old Boys Res.	20	6	5	9	48	58	23
Wansdyke	20	5	2	13	49	82	17
Westfield 'A'	20	5	0	15	28	64	15
Aces SSJ Res.	20	3	4	13	31	63	13
Cutters Friday 'A'	20	3	2	15	39	72	11

BECKETTS LEAGUE
(R J F Homes)

Premier Division		P	W	D	L	F	A	Pts
Ryedale SC		22	19	3	0	110	28	60
Kirkbymoorside Res.		22	14	4	4	52	25	46
Sinnington		22	14	2	6	51	29	44
Gillamoor		22	10	6	6	49	44	36
Terrington Glory		22	8	5	9	54	40	29
Rosedale		22	9	1	12	35	55	28
Kirkdale United		22	7	5	10	51	54	26
Thornton-le-Dale		22	5	8	9	31	46	23
Union Rovers	-3	22	6	6	10	37	53	21
Heslerton		22	6	2	14	27	54	20
Aislaby United		22	6	2	14	40	74	20
Old Malton St Marys 'A'		22	5	2	15	39	74	17

Division One		P	W	D	L	F	A	Pts
Bagby & Balk		22	18	1	3	88	27	55
Ryedale SC Res.		22	15	4	3	69	19	49
Slingsby		22	15	0	7	80	48	45
St Clements Res.		22	13	5	4	58	42	44
Duncombe Park		22	11	3	8	55	39	36
Pro-Pak		22	8	5	9	53	49	29
Gillamoor Res.		22	6	5	11	36	71	23
Thornton-le-Dale Res.		22	6	4	12	27	49	22
Ampleforth		22	6	4	12	47	78	22
Old Malton St M 'B'	-6	22	8	1	13	55	61	19
Amotherby/Swinton 'A'	-3	22	4	5	13	41	71	14
Union Rovers Res.		22	1	5	16	23	78	8

WWW.CHERRYRED.CO.UK

BIRKENHEAD & WIRRAL LEAGUE

Division One
	P	W	D	L	F	A	Pts
Bird In Hand	18	13	2	3	65	24	41
Kelma	18	11	2	5	50	45	35
Moreton	18	9	4	5	44	33	31
Parkfield BA	18	9	3	6	57	45	30
Willows	18	8	2	8	38	40	26
Sports Bar	18	7	2	9	53	49	23
AC Brookley	18	6	1	11	38	58	13
Universal Windows	18	5	2	11	45	53	13
Manor Athletic Res.	18	4	1	13	28	65	9
FC Borough	18	2	4	12	36	75	8

New Ferry – record expunged

Division Two
	P	W	D	L	F	A	Pts
Future	20	19	0	1	105	20	38
FC Village	20	12	5	3	65	36	29
Claughton Hotel	20	12	5	3	60	42	28
Tower	20	10	2	8	59	63	22
Wellington FC	20	9	2	9	50	57	20
Avenue	20	9	2	9	45	56	20
Central Park	20	8	2	10	49	55	18
Bronze Social Res.	20	7	0	13	42	58	14
Trafalgar Rangers	20	6	4	10	34	46	13
Wirral Wanderers	20	4	2	14	33	66	10
Bebington Rovers	20	3	2	15	25	68	8

Cathcart – record expunged

BIRMINGHAM AFA

Premier Division
	P	W	D	L	F	A	Pts
Village	24	18	3	3	65	27	60
Sutton United	24	18	3	3	75	19	57
Boldmere S&S Falcons	24	15	3	6	65	42	48
Lakin Rangers	24	14	5	5	66	42	45
Wake Green Amateurs	24	10	8	6	42	31	38
Shirley Athletic	24	9	4	11	41	53	32
Billesley United	24	9	5	10	53	55	32
Silhill	24	9	5	10	63	50	32
Handsworth GSOB	24	8	2	14	45	64	26
Crescionians	24	6	1	17	34	65	24
AFC Somers	24	6	1	17	35	65	19
Ajax United	24	4	4	17	19	61	15
Woodbourne Sports	24	3	1	20	34	79	10

Division One
	P	W	D	L	F	A	Pts
Erin Go Bragh	26	17	5	4	87	45	56
Flamengo	26	15	5	6	80	47	51
Old Wulfrunians	26	14	5	7	56	41	48
Kings Norton Celtic	26	14	5	7	71	50	48
Sutton United Res.	26	12	4	10	59	53	42
Resolution	26	11	5	10	65	52	38
Kynoch	26	10	5	11	52	61	35
Village Res.	26	8	7	11	45	52	28
CPA Holy Name	26	7	6	13	45	71	27
Parkfield Amateurs	26	6	7	13	38	74	22
Solihull Gas	26	2	3	19	34	69	3

Division Two
	P	W	D	L	F	A	Pts
Athletic Sparkhill	18	8	0	0	65	20	38
Aston Detached	18	12	5	3	75	36	29
St Francis	18	10	2	6	50	30	22
West Midlands Travel	18	9	4	5	56	50	20
John Rose	18	9	4	5	58	45	20
West Hagley	18	7	4	7	41	44	18
Old Wulfrunians Res.	18	8	2	8	48	46	18
Airmark	18	6	1	11	37	49	13
Wake Green Amtrs Res.	18	6	2	14	45	52	10
Old Nortonians	18	4	5	11	40	55	10
Handsworth GSOB Res.	18	4	2	14	33	64	8
Village 'A'	18	3	2	15	31	45	7
Silhill Res.	18	0	3	19	34	69	3
Acocks Green							

Division Three
	P	W	D	L	F	A	Pts
Inter Vaughans	20	19	0	1	105	20	38
Crescionians Res.	20	12	5	3	65	36	29
Great Barr	20	10	2	8	60	42	28
Shirley Athletic Res.	20	10	2	8	57	20	20
Desi	20	9	2	9	50	57	20
Shere Punjab	20	9	2	9	56	20	20
Aston Youth F&N	20	8	2	10	49	55	18
Resolution Res.	20	7	0	13	42	58	14
Malremo Rangers	20	6	4	10	34	46	13
Sutton United 'A'	20	6	4	10	33	66	10
Wake Grm Amateurs 'A'	20	3	2	15	25	68	8
Walsall Phoenix Res.							
Britannia Old Boys							
Silhill 'A'							

Division Four
	P	W	D	L	F	A	Pts
Old Nortonians Res.	24	18	3	3	65	27	60
Crusaders	24	18	3	3	75	19	57
St Georges Warriors	24	15	3	6	65	42	48
Shirley Athletic 'A'	24	14	5	5	66	42	45
Castle Bromwich Albion	24	10	8	6	42	31	38
Bearwood Athletic	24	9	4	11	41	53	37
Pathfinder	24	9	5	10	53	55	32
Elmdon Heath	24	9	5	10	63	50	32
BT	24	8	2	14	45	64	26
Dosthill Boys	24	6	1	17	40	64	24
CPA Holy Name Res.	24	6	1	17	42	65	20
MG Star	24	4	4	17	19	61	15
Village 'B'	24	3	1	20	34	79	10
Halesowen Alliance							

Division Five
	P	W	D	L	F	A	Pts
Bustlehome Athletic	26	17	5	4	87	45	56
St Annes	26	15	5	6	80	47	51
Bromsgrove Town	26	14	5	7	56	41	48
Sportsco	26	14	5	7	71	52	42
Inter Quinton	26	12	4	10	59	53	40
Wylde Green Wanderers	26	11	5	10	65	52	38
Acocks Green Athletic	26	10	5	11	52	61	35
Phoenix United	26	8	7	11	45	80	22
Birmingham Citadel	26	7	6	13	45	71	27
Birmingham Amateurs 'A'	26	6	7	13	52	74	25
Old Wulfrunians 'A'	26	6	4	16	38	74	22
Sutton United 'B'	26	4	4	18	54	98	19
Rubery							
Wood Wanderers							

Division Six
	P	W	D	L	F	A	Pts
Cable & Wireless	20	17	3	0	87	38	54
Meriden Athletic	20	12	3	5	66	35	39
Silhill 'B'	20	13	3	4	84	37	46
King Edwards Lions	20	12	3	5	60	45	44
AFC Hayes Harriers Adults	20	10	5	5	58	45	35
Crusaders Res.	20	10	3	7	63	54	33
Coton Green Res.	20	10	0	10	49	60	30
Crescionians 'A'	20	6	5	9	42	56	23
Asgard Rovers	20	6	1	13	49	59	19
Handsworth GSOB 'A'	20	3	3	14	26	70	12
Manchester Wanderers	20	2	2	22	27	79	11

Division Seven
	P	W	D	L	F	A	Pts
Balsaloma	26	17	5	4	59	26	57
St Pauls Unity	26	15	5	6	72	39	50
Royal Heath Rangers	26	13	4	9	89	55	43
Handsworth GSOB 'B'	26	13	4	10	58	47	43
Old Wulfrunians 'B'	26	12	4	10	61	44	40
Harbourne Athletic	26	10	5	11	53	53	39
Four Oaks	26	11	1	14	37	53	34
Kingshurst Phoenix	26	9	5	11	37	44	32
Wake Green Amtrs 'B'	26	9	5	12	44	63	32
Village 'C'	26	10	2	14	50	65	22
Tamworth QEOB	26	6	0	11	43	72	18
Walsall Phoenix 'A'	26	4	6	16	46	80	18

Division Eight
	P	W	D	L	F	A	Pts
Malremo Rangers Res.	26	21	2	3	96	33	56
St Georges Warriors Res.	26	17	2	6	79	32	53
Crusaders 'A'	26	16	0	8	88	43	48
AFC Medway	26	14	4	6	88	47	46
Crescionians 'B'	26	14	4	6	76	51	46
Aston Youth F&N Res.	26	9	4	11	64	63	31
Sutton United 'C'	26	7	2	15	40	70	28
Maple Leaf Rovers	26	6	4	14	54	80	23
Maypole	26	5	2	17	52	95	22
Sporting Aztecs	26	6	3	17	57	97	17
Elmdon Heath Res.	26	4	3	17	33	79	15
Bristan	26	4	3	17	37	80	13
Britannia Old Boys Res.							

Division Nine
	P	W	D	L	F	A	Pts
JE Yardley	26	22	1	3	121	25	67
Sportsco Res.	26	16	5	9	90	44	55
Belgrave Bullets	26	16	3	9	92	38	53
Clements	26	15	3	6	68	58	48
St Georges Warriors 'A'	26	13	5	8	82	57	44
Aston United	26	11	5	10	79	64	38
Bournville Colts	26	11	4	11	51	46	37
NWCA	26	11	5	11	80	68	36
Real Riverside	26	10	5	11	65	65	35
Cosmopolitans	26	10	5	11	47	63	35
Smethwick Utd Academy	26	8	4	14	49	72	28
Edgbaston United	26	5	4	17	44	114	19
Wake Green Amtrs 'C'	26	5	3	18	44	102	18
Wulfrun Invicta	26	2	2	35	35	119	8

BISHOP'S STORTFORD, STANSTED & DISTRICT LEAGUE
(Footprint Group)

Premier Division
	P	W	D	L	F	A	Pts
Alemite Athletic	22	11	3	4	69	34	43
North Weald	22	15	3	4	97	30	48
Quendon Athletic	22	13	1	8	64	37	30
Pelly House	22	12	3	9	52	37	27
Old Street	22	8	3	9	51	41	26
Loughton	22	6	1	13	36	60	19
White Roding	22	8	1	12	42	39	19
Hatfield Heath	22	3	1	14	41	57	18
Birchanger	22	3	5	15	24	62	10
Debden Res.	22	5	1	17	30	92	7
Potter Street Res.							
Sheering							

Division One
	P	W	D	L	F	A	Pts
North Weald Res.	26	19	3	4	74	32	41
Salvation Army (Harlow)	26	19	2	5	107	50	40
Potter Street 'A'	26	16	4	6	85	39	36
Langley Rangers	26	9	8	9	59	38	35
Sheering Res.	26	16	1	9	57	45	33
Thorley Park	26	15	4	8	52	52	33
Heath Rovers	26	13	3	9	71	60	30
Avondale Rangers	26	15	0	11	70	66	30
Hatfield Heath Res.	26	10	4	12	57	52	24
Dunmow Rhodes	26	7	5	14	53	72	19
Albury	26	6	4	16	29	68	16
Thaxted Rangers Res.	26	6	2	18	53	107	14
Lower Street	26	3	3	20	29	88	9
Frontiers	26	3	0	24	26	103	4

BLACKBURN & DISTRICT COMBINATION

Premier Division
	P	W	D	L	F	A	Pts
Clifton	22	19	1	2	81	27	58
Havelock Inn	22	16	3	3	88	29	51
Blackburn United	22	13	4	5	55	28	40
Rishton	-3	22	13	1	8	58	44	36
Pleasington	22	11	1	10	54	59	34
Marigolds	22	8	5	9	42	41	29
St. Matthews	22	7	2	13	51	54	23
Cabin End	22	7	1	14	40	63	22
Bank Top	22	4	7	11	30	59	19
Islington	+3	22	3	3	16	41	110	15
Brinscall	-9	22	6	4	12	39	78	13

Division Two
	P	W	D	L	F	A	Pts
Rhoden Inn	24	21	1	2	140	42	64
Bowling Green	24	20	1	3	100	38	61
Greenfield Inn	24	14	3	4	92	43	54
Alexandra Hotel	24	14	2	7	77	25	44
Worth Avenue	24	13	4	7	47	77	25
NWCA	24	12	1	11	68	70	37
Real Riverside	24	6	4	13	47	65	35
Cosmopolitans	24	6	4	14	43	58	24
Blackburn Olympic	24	6	4	14	43	75	23
Prince of Wales	24	5	3	16	72	71	21
West End Cyc	24	6	2	16	63	88	20
Islington Res.	24	2	2	20	25	163	8

Division Three

	P	W	D	L	F	A	Pts
Oak Tree	24	18	5	1	80	32	59
Enty	24	13	4	7	76	51	43
Blackburn United Res.	24	13	2	9	68	56	41
Blue Star	24	12	4	8	80	59	40
Sporting Athletic	24	11	5	8	59	64	38
Bethlom Dog Inn	24	10	4	10	64	61	34
Pleasington Res.	24	7	2	15	46	65	23
Rishton Res.	24	6	4	14	58	64	22
Wilpshire Hotel	24	3	0	21	35	114	9

BOSTON LEAGUE
(Cropley's Suzuki)

Premier Division

	P	W	D	L	F	A	Pts
Wyberton	16	13	1	2	54	19	40
Spilsby Town	16	9	1	6	40	19	31
Swineshead Institute	16	9	1	6	40	32	28
Skegness Town Res.	16	7	3	6	32	35	25
West End Tigers	16	6	3	7	29	29	21
Billinghay Athletic	16	6	3	7	29	36	21
Coningsby	16	5	2	11	25	57	11
Wrangle United	16	3	2	11	19	59	9

Gedney Drove End – record expunged

Division One

	P	W	D	L	F	A	Pts
North Sea United	20	16	3	1	76	29	51
Freiston	20	13	2	5	65	37	41
Old Leake	20	11	4	5	46	31	37
Fishtoft	20	9	5	6	47	38	32
Kirton Town	20	9	3	8	32	34	30
Spilsby Town Res.	20	8	3	9	38	34	27
Swineshead Institute Res.	20	4	6	10	34	47	18
Old Doningtonians	20	3	7	10	36	53	16
Coningsby Res.	20	4	2	14	26	69	14
Holbeach Bank	20	3	2	15	25	51	13

Division Two

	P	W	D	L	F	A	Pts
Park Road Old Boys	22	17	2	3	84	28	53
Woodhall Spa United	22	17	2	3	83	28	53
Wainfleet United	22	15	1	6	80	35	46
Norfolk United	22	14	4	4	66	39	46
Sutterton	22	11	2	9	42	37	35
Spalding Harriers	22	10	2	10	61	47	32
Wrangle United Res.	22	9	4	9	59	59	32
Black Bull United -3	22	9	4	9	69	69	28
Fosdyke	22	8	4	10	69	69	28
Tydd St Mary	22	5	2	15	41	72	17
Mareham United	22	3	1	18	28	107	10
Kirton Town Res.	22	0	0	22	28	141	0

Division Three

	P	W	D	L	F	A	Pts
Wyberton Res.	24	20	2	2	108	23	62
Skegness WMC	24	19	1	4	83	25	57
Friskney	24	17	2	5	85	30	53
Westside Rangers Res.	24	14	4	6	80	46	46
West End Tigers Res.	24	9	6	9	46	54	33
Freiston Res.	24	10	1	13	59	61	31
Old Doningtonians Res.	24	9	2	13	47	55	29
Billinghay Athletic Res.	24	8	4	12	49	55	28
Spalding Harriers Res.	24	7	6	11	31	45	27
Spalding Town Res.	24	6	5	13	50	75	23
Fishtoft Res.	24	6	3	15	40	68	21
Park United	24	5	1	18	37	89	16

BOURNEMOUTH LEAGUE
(Hayward)

Division One

	P	W	D	L	F	A	Pts
Sway	22	16	2	4	60	19	50
Suttoners Civil	22	16	1	5	86	37	49
Southbourne	22	15	2	5	52	31	47
Old Oakmeadians	22	11	6	5	42	16	39
Pennington St Marks	22	9	6	7	40	35	33
Redlynch/Woodfalls Utd	22	9	5	8	38	37	32
Bournemouth Electric -3	22	10	5	7	54	42	32
Verwood Town Res.	22	7	5	10	34	44	26
Hamworthy Rec. Res.	22	6	3	13	34	55	21
Westover Bournemouth	22	4	3	15	35	57	15
Trinidad	22	3	4	15	27	57	13
Redhill Rangers	22	3	2	17	11	164	1

Division Two

	P	W	D	L	F	A	Pts
Ferndown Town	22	16	1	5	86	37	49
Suttoners Civil Res.	22	15	2	5	52	31	47
Mudeford Mens Club	22	15	2	5	62	43	47
Parley Sports Res.	22	13	1	8	62	40	40
Urban Bournemouth -1	22	13	1	8	75	45	40
B'mouth Electric Res.	22	12	0	10	58	47	36
Fordingbridge Turks	22	9	3	10	54	58	30
Westover B'mouth Res.	22	8	2	12	42	57	26
AFC Highcliffe	22	4	3	15	40	74	15
Allendale Res.	22	2	6	14	40	70	12
Mploy	22	2	1	21	11	164	1

Division Three

	P	W	D	L	F	A	Pts
Dorset Knob	22	18	3	1	91	37	57
Harrington United	22	15	5	2	80	29	50
St Mary's	22	15	4	3	81	41	49
St Andrews	22	12	3	7	72	46	39
New Milton Linnets	22	10	4	8	59	53	34
Bisterne United	22	10	1	11	60	57	30
Sway Res.	22	7	5	10	55	55	25
J P Morgan	22	5	2	15	36	90	17
Clearwater	22	4	3	15	31	69	13
AFC Burton	22	3	1	18	37	78	10

Division Four

	P	W	D	L	F	A	Pts
Portcastrian +3	24	20	0	4	83	31	63
Alderholt Res.	24	18	3	3	88	25	57
Malt n' Hops United	24	14	3	7	43	36	45
Walkford	24	13	3	8	56	46	42
Old Oakmeadians Res.	24	13	3	8	52	42	42
Fencing Centre +3	24	11	0	13	50	47	33
Redlynch/W'falls Utd Res.	24	9	6	9	41	47	33
Cherry Bees	24	7	7	10	35	59	28
Stourvale	24	7	2	15	35	73	23
Wessex Lions -3	24	5	4	15	46	73	19
Newtown Con	24	6	1	17	36	75	19
Magpies & Woolsbridge	24	6	1	18	37	72	19
Winton CC -5	24	4	8	12	41	73	15

Division Five

	P	W	D	L	F	A	Pts
Parkside Wanderers	24	14	8	2	95	37	58
Bisterne United Res.	24	14	4	6	84	38	46
Suttoners Civil 'A'	24	12	4	8	68	45	46
Bournemouth Ems	24	11	5	8	55	54	40
New Milton Eagles	24	11	6	7	51	45	39
Burley	24	12	2	10	51	48	38
Phoenix	24	10	10	6	66	48	34
Bearwood United	24	6	14	4	63	69	34
Griffin	24	6	4	14	57	70	22
Queens Park Athletic	24	5	3	16	45	82	18
Bournemouth UST	24	4	4	16	49	80	16
St Andrews Res.	24	4	1	19	27	90	13
Magpies/Woolsbridge Res.	24	4	1	19	38	103	13

Division Six

	P	W	D	L	F	A	Pts
Redlynch/W'dfalls Utd 'A'	24	19	1	5	93	43	58
AFC Highcliffe Res.	24	18	1	5	75	36	55
FIFA Standards	24	13	7	4	80	42	46
Fordingbridge Turks Res.	24	12	5	7	89	48	41
Twynham Rangers Res.	24	12	4	8	48	46	41
Screw-It Carpentry	24	12	4	8	48	46	40
Walker Scott Wanderers	24	8	2	14	54	68	26
Somerford Sports	24	5	3	16	44	80	18
Rockbourne	24	5	3	16	38	83	18
Southbourne Res.	24	5	1	19	27	101	11
Bournemouth Hospital	24	1	4	19	36	110	7
Little Brit Inn							
AFC Burton Res.							

BRADFORD LEAGUE
(Telegraph & Argus)

	P	W	D	L	F	A	Pts
Bradford All Stars	22	17	2	3	98	26	53
Bradford IMS Celtic -3	22	18	3	1	89	39	51
Fairbank	22	16	4	2	71	23	50
Bradford Arms +3	22	12	4	6	92	58	38
Ravenscliffe +3	22	12	3	7	92	58	38
West Bowling Utd +1	22	10	5	7	70	48	34
Lidget Green	22	10	1	11	60	69	31
Smiling Mule	22	9	2	11	69	69	29
Sporting Athletic Res.	22	6	0	16	40	105	18
All Nations	22	5	1	17	35	78	16
Ventnor Youth	22	3	1	18	47	105	10
Adundant Life Church -3	22	3	1	18	47	105	10

Dynamo All Stars – record expunged
West Bowling Dragons – record expunged

BRIGHTON, HOVE & DISTRICT LEAGUE

Premier Division

	P	W	D	L	F	A	Pts
American Express +3	16	12	1	3	60	34	38
Montpelier Villa	16	9	4	3	32	20	31
Brighton Electricity	16	9	4	3	32	20	31
O & G United	16	8	1	7	27	30	25
Hanover	16	6	6	4	22	22	23
Portslade Athletic	16	6	4	6	23	35	22
Master Tiles	16	4	6	6	27	35	18
Real Brunswick	16	4	3	9	18	38	18
Ovingdean	16	3	2	11	17	38	11

Division One

	P	W	D	L	F	A	Pts
AFC Stadium	18	11	4	3	63	34	38
Coversure Athletic	18	8	6	4	46	41	37
Rottingdean Village Res.	18	8	6	4	46	33	30
Ampito	18	8	4	6	42	38	22
Southern Rngrs Old Boys	18	7	5	6	42	44	21
Brighton Sheet Metal	18	5	6	7	44	45	21
Montpelier View	18	5	6	7	27	42	20
Midway (1948)	18	5	3	10	36	52	18
Montpelier Villa Res. -3	18	4	3	11	30	54	12

Division Two

	P	W	D	L	F	A	Pts
Brighton North End -3	18	13	5	0	78	24	41
Autopaints Brighton	18	12	3	3	44	35	39
Teamstats.net	18	11	3	4	46	39	36
AFC Stanley	18	8	4	6	53	40	28
Portslade Rangers	18	8	2	8	65	39	26
The Windmill	18	8	2	8	50	51	26
American Express Res.	18	6	1	11	32	51	19
Chailey	18	4	2	12	36	64	14
Gardeners Arms	18	4	1	13	46	64	14
Midway (1948) Res. +3	18	1	1	16	25	109	7

Division Three

	P	W	D	L	F	A	Pts
Hikers BHA -3	20	19	0	1	96	20	54
Ricardo	20	16	2	2	62	29	50
Spanish Lady	20	12	2	6	73	33	44
Rottingdean Village 'A'	20	13	3	4	61	44	42
Rottingdean Dynamos	20	10	0	10	57	53	30
AFC Cosmos	20	7	4	9	69	53	25
Portslade Ath. Res. +3	20	5	3	13	34	53	23
Montpelier View Res.	20	5	2	13	34	66	14
APS Wanderers	20	4	2	14	34	66	14
Acas	20	4	2	15	35	80	9
Buckingham Arms	20	2	3	15	29	102	9

Division Four

	P	W	D	L	F	A	Pts
Crew Club Sports	18	16	1	1	104	17	49
Legal & General	18	11	1	6	73	22	34
Goldstone	18	10	3	9	39	38	33
AFC Branch	18	10	3	9	54	34	25
Stoneham Park	18	8	6	3	62	71	21
Brighton A & E	18	6	5	7	28	41	21
Brighton BBOB	18	6	1	11	36	59	19
Vista	18	4	4	13	32	78	14
Real Southwick	18	4	1	13	33	69	13
Montpelier Villa 'A'	18	2	5	11	21	54	11

BRISTOL & AVON LEAGUE

	P	W	D	L	F	A	Pts
Eagle House Elite	22	19	0	2	119	28	58
Broad Walk Res.	22	19	1	2	143	34	57
Mendip United Res.	22	16	1	5	101	38	49
Crown Parkway	22	15	1	6	84	41	46
Lawrence Rovers Res. -3	22	13	4	5	76	47	39
Bideford Old Boys	22	10	1	11	56	47	31
YMCA Cricketers	22	10	0	12	48	65	30
Long Ashton Res.	22	8	2	12	46	56	26
Bradley Stoke Town 'A'	22	5	1	16	42	98	16
Wessex Wanderers 'A'	22	4	1	17	39	142	13
Greyfriars Athletic 'B'	22	3	1	18	30	86	10
Redcliffe United	22	2	3	19	24	147	9

BRISTOL & DISTRICT LEAGUE

Premier Division

	P	W	D	L	F	A	Pts
Longwell Green Spts Res.	22	17	4	1	68	23	55
Hartcliffe Comm. Centre	22	12	5	5	47	40	41
Lawrence Rovers	22	11	7	4	51	33	40
Hanham Athletic Res.	22	10	3	9	61	34	33
Wick Res.	22	8	5	7	31	34	29
Nicholas Wdrs Res. -3	22	8	7	7	57	55	28
AXA Res.	22	8	2	8	54	46	26
Soundwell Victoria	22	7	4	11	49	58	25
Shirehampton Res.	22	7	1	14	40	51	22
Crosscourt United	22	6	2	14	46	55	20
Pucklechurch Sports Res.	22	3	4	15	40	71	13
Knowle United	22	3	4	15	20	75	13

Division One

	P	W	D	L	F	A	Pts
Chipping Sodbury Tn Res.	26	19	6	1	91	25	63
Hallen 'A'	26	20	2	4	80	27	62
Coalpit Heath	26	16	4	6	78	46	52
Made for Ever	26	16	4	6	73	46	52
St Pancras	26	14	5	7	68	54	47
Bendix	26	14	5	7	56	57	47
Hartcliffe Res.	26	10	5	11	56	57	35
FM Sports	26	9	4	13	52	63	31
Bitton 'A'	26	8	6	12	63	63	30
Roman Glass St George 'A'	26	8	5	13	47	68	29
Sea Mills Park	26	6	3	17	45	69	21
Shaftesbury Crusade Res.	26	6	3	17	45	91	21
Highridge United 'A'	26	5	4	17	40	85	19
Iron Acton Res.	26	0	2	24	23	126	2

Division Two

	P	W	D	L	F	A	Pts
Old Sodbury	26	18	4	4	84	41	58
Miners Rangers	26	16	6	4	81	45	54
Longwell Green Sports 'A'	26	13	12	1	72	56	51
South Bristol Central Res.	26	15	3	8	70	58	48
Henbury 'A'	26	12	4	10	61	58	40
Hambrook	26	12	3	11	58	58	39
DRG Stapleton Res.	26	12	3	11	59	78	39
Seymour United Res.	26	9	3	14	49	60	30
Nicholas Wanderers 'A'	26	9	3	14	49	59	30
AEK Boco Res.	26	9	2	15	47	68	29
Greyfriars Athletic Res.	26	6	9	11	65	67	27
Patchway Town 'A'	26	6	5	15	42	49	23
Hillfields OB Res. -3	26	6	7	13	38	53	22
Shirehampton 'A'	26	1	2	24	23	87	16

Division Three

	P	W	D	L	F	A	Pts
Brislington Cricketers	24	20	3	1	116	34	63
Winterbourne United 'A'	24	17	2	5	74	35	53
Fry Club 'A'	24	15	3	6	86	39	48
Rangeworthy	24	12	3	9	45	45	39
Olveston United Res.	24	11	6	7	45	46	39
Frampton Athletic Res.	24	9	4	11	41	55	31
Chipping Sodbury Tn 'A'	24	10	1	13	48	58	31
Hallen 'B'	24	7	8	9	43	59	29
Totterdown United Res.	24	8	2	14	55	70	26
Tilly Rangers	24	7	4	13	59	64	25
Oakland	24	4	5	15	45	63	17
Broad Walk	24	4	4	16	45	74	16
Fishponds Athletic Res.	24	1	1	22	19	150	4

Division Four

	P	W	D	L	F	A	Pts
Hanham Athletic 'A'	22	18	1	3	98	15	57
Warmley Saints	22	15	5	2	65	27	50
Eden Grove	22	12	6	4	62	39	42
Stockwood Wanderers	22	13	3	6	64	43	42
Westerleigh Sports	22	9	2	11	47	55	29
Fry Club 'B'	22	7	5	10	54	54	26
AXA 'A'	22	6	6	10	35	46	24
Made for Ever Res.	22	6	4	12	40	57	22
Oldland Abbotonians 'A'	22	4	6	12	39	51	18
Frampton Athletic 'A'	22	5	1	16	42	55	16
St Nicholas	22	3	5	14	42	70	14
Brimsham Green Res.	22	4	1	17	20	71	13

Division Five

	P	W	D	L	F	A	Pts
Impact Squad	24	18	3	4	83	40	57
Bradley Stoke Town	24	17	3	4	78	41	54
Shireway Sports	24	15	6	3	92	41	51
St Philips MAS Res.	24	12	8	4	65	33	44
Inter The Bloomfield	24	12	3	9	63	47	39
Talbot Knowle Res.	24	9	4	11	56	57	31
Coalpit Heath Res.	24	9	5	12	49	59	30
Longwell Green Sports 'B'	24	6	5	13	34	60	23
Pucklechurch Sports 'A'	24	6	3	15	42	83	21
Wick 'A'	24	5	0	17	30	83	15
Soundwell Victoria Res.	24	5	2	18	35	75	14
St Pancras Res.	24	4	2	18	35	75	14

BRISTOL & SUBURBAN LEAGUE

Premier Division One

	P	W	D	L	F	A	Pts
St Aldhelms	28	21	3	4	83	34	66
B & W Avonside	28	19	5	4	66	22	59
Avonmouth	28	18	5	5	95	61	49
Winford PH	28	15	4	9	57	52	49
Teyfant Athletic	28	14	6	8	52	48	48
Broad Plain House OB	28	13	5	10	60	60	44
Stoke Gifford United	28	11	8	9	59	62	41
Ashton United	28	11	4	13	55	51	37
Almondsbury Town Res.	28	11	4	13	59	53	37
Glenside 5 Old Boys	28	9	10	9	53	54	37
Almondsbury Res.	28	9	5	14	47	71	32
Fishponds Old Boys	28	7	8	13	47	63	29
De Veys	28	7	5	16	45	74	26
Old Georgians	28	5	4	19	45	83	19
Ridings High -1	28	5	3	22	38	98	12

Premier Division Two

	P	W	D	L	F	A	Pts
South Glos (Hambrook)	24	21	1	2	85	30	64
CTK Southside	24	17	5	2	63	34	56
TC Sports	24	14	2	8	63	44	44
Whitchurch	24	10	7	7	62	52	37
Cadbury Heath Res.	24	10	5	9	52	40	35
Bristol Telephones	24	10	4	10	48	48	34
Little Stoke	24	9	4	11	48	42	31
Astra Zeneca	24	7	4	13	48	55	25
Old Cothamians	24	6	6	12	50	51	24
St Aldhelms Res.	24	6	5	13	43	65	23
Brislington 'A'	24	6	4	14	41	92	22
Filton Athletic	24	4	1	19	22	75	8

Division One

	P	W	D	L	F	A	Pts
Southmead Athletic	26	22	3	1	126	26	69
Bristol North West	26	21	1	4	106	40	64
Lockleaze	26	14	5	7	77	57	47
Ashton Old Boys	26	15	1	10	73	46	46
Tytherington Rocks Res.	26	14	1	11	62	53	43
Ridings High Res.	26	12	3	11	83	72	39
Broad Plain House OB Res.	26	11	2	13	63	83	35
Totterdown Port of Bristol	26	10	4	12	52	55	34
B & W Avonside Res.	26	9	3	14	51	78	30
Hengrove Ath. Boys Club	26	6	5	15	52	92	20
Ashton United Res.	26	5	3	18	43	108	18
Hartcliffe Old Boys	26	4	6	17	41	78	18
Stoke Gifford United Res.	26	5	0	21	40	94	17
Corinthian Sports	26	4	1	21	32	115	13

Division Three

	P	W	D	L	F	A	Pts
Bristol Athletic	26	24	1	1	89	29	73
Imperial Saints	26	18	3	5	92	38	57
Southmead Athletic Res.	26	17	4	5	79	35	55
Little Stoke Res.	26	14	7	5	61	45	49
Ashton United 'A'	26	12	6	8	55	54	42
Ingleside	26	9	6	11	62	45	33
Glenside 5 Old Boys Res.	26	9	6	11	46	58	33
Hengrove Old Boys	26	8	6	12	46	40	30
Avonmouth Rangers	26	6	5	15	31	78	23
Thrissells Nomads	26	6	3	17	36	60	21
Parson Street Old Boys	26	5	6	15	31	36	21
Unathletico	26	5	6	15	40	91	21
Teyfant Athletic Res.	26	5	5	16	52	84	20
Brandon TT Sports	26	5	5	16	40	91	20

Division Four

	P	W	D	L	F	A	Pts
TC Sports Res.	20	17	2	1	74	24	53
Old Georgians Res.	20	10	7	3	49	35	37
Fishponds Old Boys 'A'	20	10	3	7	51	37	33
Avonmouth 'A' -4	20	11	4	5	50	37	33
Ridings High 'A'	20	9	3	8	45	46	29
Astra Zeneca Res.	20	8	3	9	47	45	27
Lockleaze Res.	20	7	4	9	28	42	25
St Annes Town	20	5	4	11	40	50	19
Wanderers AFC	20	5	1	14	41	61	16
Winford PH Res.	20	3	6	11	35	55	15

Division Five

	P	W	D	L	F	A	Pts
Hanham Athletic Colts	18	14	2	2	54	25	44
Sth Glos (Hambrook) Res.	18	12	2	4	58	32	38
Wessex Wanderers Res.	18	12	0	6	50	42	36
AFC Spartans	18	8	4	6	40	35	28
Stoke Gifford United 'A'	18	8	2	8	48	47	26
Lawrence Weston Res.	18	7	1	10	42	40	22
Whitchurch Res.	18	6	4	8	29	41	22
Fishponds Old Boys 'B'	18	4	3	11	34	54	15
Oldbury Crusaders Res.	18	4	2	12	31	54	14
Parson Street OB Res.	18	2	1	15	31	66	7

BRISTOL DOWNS LEAGUE

Division One

	P	W	D	L	F	A	Pts
Torpedo	26	19	4	3	64	25	61
Easton Cowboys	26	16	1	9	69	39	49
Ashley	26	16	1	9	66	39	49
Lawes Juniors	26	15	4	7	65	39	49
Retainers	26	15	3	8	48	48	48
Sneyd Park	26	11	8	7	48	44	41
Cotswool	26	10	6	10	47	47	36
Durdham Down AS	26	10	4	12	47	52	34
Portland Old Boys	26	8	6	12	39	51	30
Clifton St Vincents	26	7	5	14	40	59	26
Bristol Juve	26	6	7	13	29	46	25
Bristol Barcelona	26	6	6	14	38	58	24
Hare on the Hill	26	6	4	16	36	54	22
Cabot Asset Finance	26	6	3	17	32	59	21

Division Two

	P	W	D	L	F	A	Pts
Wessex Wanderers	24	20	3	1	114	25	63
Lawrence Weston	24	16	6	2	69	36	54
Fishponds Old Boys Res.	24	15	4	5	56	41	49
Bristol Telephones Res.	24	14	5	5	59	47	47
Avonmouth Res.	24	12	4	8	49	48	40
Rolls Royce	24	12	4	8	52	48	40
Tyndalls Park Rangers	24	10	5	9	66	52	35
Cadbury Heath 'A'	24	9	3	12	45	61	30
St Aldhelms 'A'	24	8	3	13	45	55	27
Almondsbury 'A'	24	5	6	13	49	56	21
Old Cothamians Res.	24	4	4	16	39	53	16
Oldbury Crusaders	24	5	4	15	36	64	19
Sefton Park	24	2	7	15	36	67	13

Division Two	P	W	D	L	F	A	Pts
AFC Bohemia	26	22	3	1	125	21	69
Sporting Greyhound	26	22	1	3	105	22	67
Jamaica Bell	26	16	5	5	92	54	53
Saints Old Boys	26	15	7	4	92	47	52
Hydez	26	16	3	7	71	49	51
St Andrews	26	12	5	9	51	59	41
Sneyd Park Res.	26	9	4	13	57	75	31
Clifton Rockets	26	9	3	14	46	58	30
Clifton St Vincents Res.	26	8	5	13	44	65	29
Cotswool Res.	26	8	5	13	43	77	29
Retainers Res.	26	6	5	15	39	75	23
TM Lion -7	26	6	2	18	43	85	13
Luccombe Garage	26	4	1	21	34	108	13
Portland Old Boys Res.	26	3	3	20	32	79	12

Division Three	P	W	D	L	F	A	Pts
AFC Bohemia Res.	24	17	4	3	85	37	55
Tebby	24	15	4	5	63	32	49
Torpedo Res.	24	12	8	4	57	30	44
Evergreen	24	11	4	9	53	53	37
Sporting Greyhound Res.	24	10	6	8	56	39	36
Ashley Res.	24	9	7	8	48	43	34
Beachcroft LLP	24	10	4	10	58	54	34
Clifton St Vincents 'A'	24	9	4	11	42	55	31
LA Cricketers	24	8	2	14	44	62	26
Clifton Rockets Res.	24	8	2	14	42	72	26
Easton Cowboys Res.	24	6	7	11	54	66	25
Sneyd Park 'A'	24	7	3	14	59	75	24
Blackboy Inn	24	5	3	16	44	87	18

Division Four	P	W	D	L	F	A	Pts
Bristol Barcelona Res.	30	20	5	5	77	46	65
Torpedo 'A'	30	19	3	8	107	46	60
Jersey Rangers -3	30	19	2	9	77	60	56
Hare on the Hill Res.	30	16	6	8	79	50	54
West Town United	30	15	5	10	66	59	50
Sneyd Park 'B'	30	13	5	12	75	77	44
Cotham Old Boys	30	13	5	12	52	55	44
Tebby Res.	30	12	4	14	74	72	40
Conham Rangers	30	10	9	11	65	66	39
Retainers 'A'	30	10	5	15	69	75	35
Bengal Tigers	30	10	4	16	62	67	34
TM Lions Res.	30	9	7	14	56	78	34
Clifton St Vincents 'B'	30	9	6	15	56	92	33
Durdham Down AS Res.	30	8	7	15	54	83	31
Hydez Res.	30	8	5	17	58	91	29
Severnside	30	6	8	16	52	62	26

BRISTOL PREMIER COMBINATION LEAGUE

Premier Division	P	W	D	L	F	A	Pts
Chipping Sodbury Town	26	17	6	3	68	24	57
St Philips Marsh Adult Sch'l	26	17	4	5	44	23	55
Nicholas Wanderers	26	15	6	5	55	37	51
Hartcliffe	26	14	1	11	49	40	43
Winterbourne United Res.	26	13	3	10	47	51	42
Talbot Knowle	26	12	5	9	62	48	41
Hallen Res.	26	12	4	10	39	44	40
Wick	26	10	6	10	49	54	36
Bitton Res.	26	9	8	9	39	27	35
Roman Glass St G'ge Res.	26	10	4	12	33	36	34
Highridge United Res.	26	9	3	14	33	54	30
Brimsham Green	26	7	5	14	31	45	26
Shaftesbury Crusade	26	5	1	20	35	63	16
Totterdown United	26	3	2	21	34	72	11

Division One	P	W	D	L	F	A	Pts
Mendip United	26	19	1	6	68	34	58
South Bristol Central	26	17	2	7	86	49	53
Olveston United	26	16	3	7	54	31	51
AEK Boco	26	16	3	7	52	39	51
Oldland Abbotonians Res.	26	13	4	9	54	44	43
Patchway Town Res.	26	12	4	10	39	35	40
Frampton Athletic	26	11	4	11	39	33	37
Seymour United	26	12	1	13	37	41	37
Greyfriars Athletic	26	10	6	10	51	40	36
Fishponds Athletic	26	8	4	14	46	66	28
Hillfields Old Boys	26	6	8	12	43	56	26
Avonmouth Village -1	26	7	6	13	30	46	26
Henbury Res.	26	7	4	15	31	55	25
Iron Acton	26	3	0	23	22	83	9

BROMLEY & DISTRICT LEAGUE

Premier Division	P	W	D	L	F	A	Pts
University of Greenwich	18	15	1	2	80	19	46
Blackheath United	18	12	4	2	48	14	40
AFC Mottingham	18	13	0	5	66	31	39
OPK	18	13	0	5	43	28	39
Shirley Seniors	18	10	0	8	48	42	30
South East Athletic	18	8	2	8	37	41	26
Rotherhithe	18	4	3	11	31	46	15
South East Four	18	3	3	12	22	50	12
Standard Chartered	18	2	3	13	22	60	9
The Running Horses	18	0	4	14	17	83	4

Division One	P	W	D	L	F	A	Pts
Erith '147 Res.	20	17	1	2	75	28	52
Heathfield	20	16	1	3	67	24	49
Biggin Hill	20	13	0	7	64	40	39
Highfield Rovers	20	9	4	7	53	39	31
Barnet Wood	20	9	2	9	50	55	29
Dulwich Town	20	9	1	10	55	58	28
OPK Casuals	20	8	1	11	41	44	25
Old Colfeians Res.	20	4	7	9	30	49	19
Ex-Blues	20	6	1	13	38	65	19
Chislehurst Dynamoes	20	4	5	11	38	52	17
Bellingham	20	2	3	15	25	82	9

South Star – record expunged

Division Two	P	W	D	L	F	A	Pts
Ex-Blues Reserves	20	14	6	0	72	24	48
Iron Tugboat City	20	13	4	3	83	27	43
Welling Park	20	13	4	3	70	34	43
Old Colfeians 'A'	20	11	3	6	68	47	36
AFC Heathfield	20	10	2	8	66	58	32
AFC Bromley	20	7	4	9	50	60	25
Charlton Athletic Deaf	20	6	3	11	43	58	21
Latter-Day Saints	20	6	1	13	50	77	19
Crofton Albion 'A'	20	4	5	11	45	66	17
Penhill Standard Res.	20	4	3	13	50	91	15
Farnborough OB Guild 'B'	20	3	3	14	28	83	12

AFC Mottingham Res. – record expunged

BURTON & DISTRICT LEAGUE

Premier Division	P	W	D	L	F	A	Pts
Red Lion Horninglow	16	14	2	0	52	12	44
Lichfield City	16	11	2	3	41	10	35
Ashbourne United Res.	16	6	4	6	33	41	22
Overseal St Matthews	16	6	3	7	31	42	21
Barton United Res.	16	6	1	9	30	27	19
Gresley Rovers Youth	16	6	1	9	32	39	19
Red Lion Horninglow Res.	16	4	4	8	27	40	16
Crown Inn	16	5	1	10	29	47	16
The Dart	16	4	2	10	22	39	14

Division One	P	W	D	L	F	A	Pts
The Sump	18	13	1	4	70	30	40
Stretton Eagles Res.	18	10	6	2	34	21	36
Lichfield Enots Res.	18	11	2	5	50	39	35
The Seal Inn	18	10	4	4	62	26	34
Barton Royal Oak	18	8	5	5	51	32	29
Lichfield City Res.	18	7	7	4	56	42	28
Hasten United	18	6	4	8	61	52	22
Real Medina	18	5	3	10	41	59	18
Whittington Brenstar	18	2	1	15	29	97	7
Jubilee Winshill	18	1	1	16	27	83	4

Division Two	P	W	D	L	F	A	Pts
Shobnall Sports	16	14	0	2	84	22	42
Washlands	16	12	3	1	57	13	39
Greenbank Terotech	16	9	4	3	57	35	31
Blacksmiths Arms	16	9	3	4	67	35	30
Midway	16	5	4	7	60	51	19
Grange Inn	16	6	0	10	51	58	18
Netherseal St Peters	16	4	3	9	38	51	15
Eton Park	16	3	2	11	26	41	11
Real Medina Youth	16	0	1	15	17	151	1

CAERNARFON & DISTRICT LEAGUE
(Safeflue)

Division One	P	W	D	L	F	A	Pts
Rhiwlas	18	13	4	1	69	24	43
Caernarfon Borough	18	13	4	1	59	19	43
Y Felinheli	18	7	5	6	47	36	26
Llanrug United Res.	18	8	2	8	43	50	26
Llanrwst United Res.	18	7	2	9	31	50	23
Nefyn United Res.	18	5	5	8	30	41	20
Trefor	18	5	5	8	31	45	20
Talysarn Celts	18	6	2	10	38	53	20
Blaenau Ffestiniog AmsRes	18	5	1	12	41	63	16
Pwllheli Res. -3	18	3	6	9	33	41	12

Division Two	P	W	D	L	F	A	Pts
Caernarfon Wanderers	18	17	1	0	70	17	52
Mynyd Llandegai	18	12	2	4	64	28	38
Bangor City Res.	18	10	4	4	43	28	34
Machno United	18	9	3	6	44	41	30
Waunfawr	18	9	2	7	35	36	29
Deiniolen	18	7	0	11	48	58	21
Caernarfon Town Res.	18	6	2	10	44	55	20
Penrhyn	18	5	1	12	38	56	16
Barm'th/Dyffryn Res. -3	18	4	3	11	40	63	12
Llanystumdwy Res.	18	1	2	15	34	78	5

CANTERBURY & DISTRICT LEAGUE

Premier Division	P	W	D	L	F	A	Pts
Premier	14	12	2	0	56	16	38
Chilham	14	11	1	2	72	19	34
Seaview	14	5	6	3	17	19	21
Red Arrow	14	3	5	6	21	37	14
Whitstable Taverners	14	4	1	9	29	46	13
Sturry	14	4	1	9	25	39	13
Prince of Wales	14	4	1	9	25	40	13
Charing	14	3	3	8	11	40	12

Division One	P	W	D	L	F	A	Pts
Cramptons	20	15	3	2	76	21	48
Ash	20	16	0	4	79	34	48
Chartham	20	13	1	6	58	31	40
Littlebourne	20	13	0	7	68	46	39
Canterbury City Res.	20	11	2	7	51	37	35
Minster	20	9	3	8	43	46	30
University of Kent 'A'	20	8	2	10	41	38	26
Sturry Res.	20	6	2	12	38	64	20
Sharsted	20	5	2	13	27	65	17
Snowdown Coll Welfare	20	2	5	13	26	59	11
Woodnesborough	20	2	2	16	21	87	8

Division Two	P	W	D	L	F	A	Pts
Post Office	22	17	2	3	83	39	53
Blean	22	16	2	4	69	43	50
Chilham Res.	22	11	4	7	74	53	37
RS Beltinge	22	11	3	8	74	54	36
Kennington 'A'	22	11	2	9	59	56	35
New Romney 'A' -1	22	11	2	9	51	54	34
St Margarets Res.	22	9	1	12	44	51	28
Boughton	22	7	4	11	61	73	25
Sentinels	22	6	5	11	55	51	23
Ashford Borough Res.	22	6	4	12	40	71	22
Bekesbourne	22	5	6	11	43	56	21
Woodman's Hall	22	3	3	16	37	89	12

Division Three	P	W	D	L	F	A	Pts
Gentil Knight	20	16	2	2	91	29	50
St Stephens	20	14	4	2	86	41	46
Europeans	20	13	3	4	89	39	42
Herne Bay Athletic	20	11	1	8	63	49	34
Tenterden Town Res.	20	10	2	8	53	52	32
Pfizer Athletic	20	8	2	10	69	58	26
USA	20	8	4	8	72	64	28
Swalecliffe	20	7	3	10	55	60	24
Sharsted Res.	20	4	7	9	46	54	19
Crusaders	20	2	2	16	29	99	8
Worlds Apart	20	1	2	17	24	132	5

CAPITAL LEAGUE

Eastern Division	P	W	D	L	F	A	Pts
AFC Hornchurch Res.	18	14	2	2	53	15	44
Enfield Town Res.	18	14	0	4	57	25	42
Harlow Town Res.	18	11	1	6	50	29	34
Chelmsford City Res.	18	7	7	4	37	35	28
St Albans City Res.	18	7	3	8	35	35	24
Ware Res.	18	6	3	9	33	52	21
Leighton Town Res.	18	5	3	10	20	51	18
Leyton Res.	18	4	4	10	24	23	16
Brimsdown Rovers Res.	18	4	4	10	21	44	16
Maldon Town Res.	18	3	3	12	15	36	12

Western Division	P	W	D	L	F	A	Pts
Harrow Borough Res.	16	10	2	4	51	28	32
Staines Town Res.	16	9	3	4	39	22	30
Dulwich Hamlet Res. -3	16	10	1	5	31	22	28
Northwood Res.	16	8	2	6	30	28	26
Croydon Athletic Res.	16	6	3	7	33	40	21
Hemel Hempstead Tn Res.	16	7	0	9	28	35	21
Maidenhead United Res.	16	6	3	7	22	30	21
Chesham United Res.	16	5	1	10	23	27	16
Boreham Wood Res.	16	1	5	10	14	39	8

CARDIFF COMBINATION

Premier Division
	P	W	D	L	F	A	Pts
Thornhill United	18	16	1	1	52	10	49
Baybridge	18	15	1	2	79	27	46
Avenue Hotspur	18	10	2	6	55	42	32
Heath Park United	18	9	2	7	40	45	29
AC Central	18	8	1	9	48	38	27
South Park Athletic	18	6	1	11	38	39	19
Cardiff Hibernians	18	6	1	11	42	69	19
Cathays United	18	4	3	11	25	51	15
Fairwater Hotel	18	4	3	11	28	56	15
Park Lawn	18	3	2	13	21	51	11

CARDIGANSHIRE LEAGUE
(Costcutter)

Division One
	P	W	D	L	F	A	Pts
Maesglas	22	17	1	4	66	27	52
St Dogmaels	22	16	3	3	61	27	51
New Quay	22	16	0	6	66	26	48
Aberaeron	22	12	4	6	59	30	40
Cardigan Town	22	12	1	9	48	35	37
Lampeter Town	22	8	8	6	64	40	32
Crannog -3	22	10	3	9	42	44	30
Llanybydder	22	7	3	12	40	73	24
Ffostrasol	22	6	4	12	29	49	22
Aberporth	22	4	3	15	32	61	15
Dewi Stars	22	3	4	15	26	59	13
Llandysul -9	22	3	2	17	31	93	2

Division Two
	P	W	D	L	F	A	Pts
Pencader United	18	14	2	2	69	20	44
Llanboidy	18	14	2	2	64	22	44
Aberaeron Res.	18	10	1	7	57	35	31
Newcastle Emlyn 'A'	18	8	5	5	44	37	29
Maesglas Res. -3	18	9	3	6	47	36	27
Felinfach	18	8	2	8	47	46	26
Lampeter Town Res.	18	5	4	9	37	54	19
Cardigan Town Res.	18	5	1	12	28	50	16
Bargod Rangers	18	4	2	12	23	85	14
SDUC -9	18	1	2	15	27	58	5

CENTRAL & SOUTH NORFOLK LEAGUE

Division One
	P	W	D	L	F	A	Pts
Toftwood United	24	20	2	2	97	29	62
Redgrave Rangers	24	20	2	2	99	35	62
Saham Toney	24	17	2	5	69	31	53
Yaxham	24	14	3	8	72	52	44
North Elmham	24	13	3	8	77	48	42
Dereham Town 'A'	24	12	2	10	63	53	38
Hingham Athletic	24	8	4	12	52	61	25
East Harling Res.	24	7	4	13	48	81	25
Mulbarton Wanderers	24	6	6	12	39	57	24
Dereham Posties	24	7	2	15	37	58	23
Gressenhall	24	7	2	15	38	69	23
Rockland United	24	4	4	18	25	90	14
Swaffham Town 'A'	24	3	3	18	31	89	12

Division Two
	P	W	D	L	F	A	Pts
Thetford Athletic	22	17	4	1	92	33	55
Shipdham	22	15	1	6	70	51	46
Bridgham United	22	14	2	6	100	59	44
Dickleburgh	22	12	5	5	60	43	41
Tacolneston	22	8	6	8	47	45	26
Wymondham Town 'A'	22	7	5	10	57	72	23
Attleborough Town 'A'	22	6	5	11	61	63	23
Yaxham Res.	22	6	3	13	37	71	21
Morley Village Res.	22	5	3	14	42	84	18
North Elmham Res.	22	4	2	16	42	77	14
Necton SSC Res.	22	4	4	16	38	79	10
Saham Toney Res. -3	22	3	4	15	38	79	10

Division Three
	P	W	D	L	F	A	Pts
Bunwell	26	20	3	3	79	40	63
Watton United 'A'	26	17	3	6	80	42	54
Cockers	26	15	3	8	88	52	48
Hingham Athletic Res.	26	14	6	6	72	52	48
Brandon Town 'A'	26	14	5	7	70	53	47
Bawdeswell	26	15	0	11	71	61	45
Foulsham Res.	26	10	8	8	57	52	38
Swanton Morley	26	9	1	14	54	54	34
Gressenhall Res.	26	9	1	14	50	61	31
Wendling	26	10	1	15	49	65	31
Toftwood Utd Res. -3	26	9	4	13	60	74	28
West End	26	8	4	14	54	74	28
Rockland United Res.	26	5	2	19	45	86	17
Shipdham Res.	26	3	1	22	25	115	10

Division Four
	P	W	D	L	F	A	Pts
Thetford Rovers Res.	22	21	0	1	150	22	63
Bradenham Wdrs Res.	22	16	4	2	92	35	52
Shropham United	22	12	2	8	56	57	38
Great Cressingham	22	12	1	9	60	38	37
Hindolveston	22	11	4	7	74	51	37
Sporle	22	8	3	11	67	78	27
Thurton & Ashby	22	7	0	15	53	84	21
Colkirk	22	6	3	13	51	104	21
Garboldisham	22	5	4	13	40	76	19
Splitz United	22	5	1	16	30	97	16
Bunwell Res.	22	4	2	16	31	73	14

CHELTENHAM ASSOCIATION LEAGUE

Division One
	P	W	D	L	F	A	Pts
Winchcombe Town	26	21	3	2	94	30	66
Newton FC	26	19	3	4	90	30	60
Kings	26	18	3	5	82	31	57
Woodmancote	26	16	2	8	72	56	44
Bishops Cleeve 'A'	26	13	3	10	63	48	57
Siddington	26	12	2	12	64	51	38
Moreton Rangers	26	11	6	9	64	58	39
Endsleigh	26	10	3	13	58	60	33
Shipton Oliffe	26	8	2	16	45	75	24
Prestbury Rovers -3	26	8	1	18	49	78	22
Andoversford Nomads	26	7	1	18	49	86	18
Ch'ham Civil Service 'B'	26	5	3	18	49	91	14
Northway	26	2	3	21	33	125	-3

Division Two
	P	W	D	L	F	A	Pts
Whaddon United	26	22	2	2	92	30	68
FC Barometrics	26	22	1	3	108	28	67
Star Res.	26	17	6	3	88	28	57
Charlton Rovers	26	15	6	5	58	55	51
Brockworth Albion Res.	26	15	3	8	58	62	48
AC Olympia	26	10	11	5	57	52	41
Northleach Town	26	11	4	11	57	68	37
Dowty Dynamos	26	9	4	13	50	74	31
Gala Wilton Res.	26	8	4	14	50	55	28
Cheltenham Saracens 'A' -3	26	7	4	15	48	92	25
Bredon Res.	26	5	3	18	41	72	18
High Tech Rangers	26	4	3	20	42	114	12
Bourton Rovers Res. -7	26	4	2	23	25	102	-2

Division Three
	P	W	D	L	F	A	Pts
Winchcombe Town Res.	26	18	4	4	66	34	58
Whaddon Utd Res. -3	26	18	4	4	84	31	57
Gloucester Elmleaze	26	14	6	6	79	37	52
Broadway United	26	14	5	7	79	33	48
Smiths Athletic Res.	26	15	1	10	77	46	42
FC Electrics	26	10	8	8	62	62	39
Tewkesbury Town -4	26	9	6	10	54	54	36
Tivoli Rovers	26	9	8	9	50	67	35
St Marks CA -3	26	10	5	11	65	65	32
Falcons	26	9	4	13	49	66	31
Apperley	26	6	2	18	58	81	20
Bishops Cleeve 'B' -3	26	6	4	16	53	103	19
Phoenix United	26	4	6	16	35	86	18
Charlton Rovers Res.	26	3	5	18	34	81	14

Division Four
	P	W	D	L	F	A	Pts
Tewkesbury Rovers	26	23	3	0	136	22	72
Ch'ham Civil Service 'A' -3	26	18	4	4	66	32	55
Churchdown Panthers	26	13	6	9	86	39	43
Kings Res.	26	11	9	6	51	50	39
Brockworth Albion 'A'	26	11	5	10	54	52	38
Elmbridge Old Boys	26	10	4	12	48	58	36
Bredon 'A' -3	26	12	4	10	45	55	31
Cheltenham Saracens 'B' -3	26	9	5	12	48	85	30
Finlay Rovers Res.	26	8	1	17	63	97	25
Andoversford Nomads Res.	26	7	1	18	49	89	21
Smiths Athletic 'A'	26	6	5	15	47	92	18
Gala Wilton 'A' -4	26	7	1	18	47	92	18

Division Five
	P	W	D	L	F	A	Pts
FC Barometrics Res. -3	26	19	4	4	90	34	58
Southside	26	16	4	6	75	45	55
Star 'A'	26	16	4	6	65	38	53
C & G	26	16	2	8	65	37	50
Tewkesbury Town Res.	26	14	0	12	58	45	48
Sherborne Harriers	26	13	0	13	63	68	45
Tewkesbury Dynamos Res.	26	11	0	9	64	58	39
Charlton Rovers 'A' -3	26	7	1	15	58	80	24
Falcons Res. -3	26	7	2	17	42	83	22
Gaffers Res.	26	6	2	20	45	91	14
Cleevonians	26	4	1	21	37	88	7
Ch'ham Civil Service 'B' -12	26	2	1	23	33	131	7
Northleach Town Res.	26	3	4	19	38	103	13

Shipton Moyne – record expunged

CHESTER & DISTRICT LEAGUE

Premier Division
	P	W	D	L	F	A	Pts
Castrol Social Res.	22	19	2	1	71	19	59
Tarvin Athletic	22	13	5	4	71	37	44
Star Res.	22	12	1	9	57	40	37
Highfield Athletic	22	11	3	8	59	57	36
Hoole Rangers	22	11	3	8	47	56	36
Kelsall	22	9	4	9	58	62	31
Kydds Athletic	22	9	4	9	58	49	31
Waggon & Horses	22	9	2	11	48	48	29
Crossway	22	8	0	14	48	64	24
Chester Nomads Res. -3	22	8	3	11	52	60	24
Newton Bears	22	5	1	16	33	56	16
Duddon United	22	4	2	16	36	65	14
Frodsham United	22	3	5	14			

Division One
	P	W	D	L	F	A	Pts
City Bar	20	15	4	1	80	37	49
Sutton Way Villa	20	14	3	3	67	27	45
Parkgate	20	11	4	5	65	34	40
Helsby Res.	20	11	4	6	60	32	34
Robin Hood	20	10	4	6	61	39	34
Ashton Lions	20	10	2	9	54	39	29
Highfield Athletic Res. -3	20	8	5	7	57	65	27
AFC Bebington Ath Res.	20	7	5	8	45	44	26
Cestrian Alexandra	20	7	2	11	36	67	12
Chester Nomads 'A'	20	3	2	15	36	80	9
Barrow Athletic	20	2	2	16	34	84	8

Division Two
	P	W	D	L	F	A	Pts
Saughall Thursday	18	13	3	2	60	33	42
FC Woodlands	18	12	2	4	74	33	38
Runcorn Albion 'A'	18	11	4	3	69	33	37
Newton Res.	18	10	1	7	56	39	31
Rangers Breaks	18	8	5	5	51	39	29
Blacon Yth Club Veterans	18	5	1	12	24	51	16
Vicars X Doves	18	4	10	4	42	75	16
Boughton Athletic	18	2	15	2	21	76	7
Barrow Athletic Res. -3	18	1	16	1	26	81	4

Heswall 'A' – record expunged

CIRENCESTER & DISTRICT LEAGUE

Division One
	P	W	D	L	F	A	Pts
Beeches	26	23	1	2	116	27	70
South Cerney	26	21	2	3	90	39	56
Real Fairford	26	18	2	6	98	45	50
Bibury	26	16	4	7	71	46	50
Avonvale United	26	14	7	5	87	61	38
Taverners Res.	26	12	2	12	57	63	27
Oaksey	26	10	4	12	58	63	34
Kingshill SC	26	7	5	14	63	68	27
Poulton	26	7	6	13	63	87	26
CHQ United	26	7	4	15	58	80	25
Lechlade	26	7	4	15	66	105	24
Golden Farm -1	26	7	2	17	42	83	22
Bees Knees -1	26	6	3	17	54	110	20
Down Ampney	26	3	4	19	38	103	13

Division Two

	P	W	D	L	F	A	Pts
Tavereners 'A'	28	22	4	2	107	44	70
Beeches Res.	28	21	4	3	101	44	66
Stratton United	28	20	2	6	114	73	62
Tetbury Town 'A'	28	15	2	11	73	70	47
Oakridge	28	13	5	11	89	77	44
Chalford 'A'	28	14	2	12	81	74	44
South Cerney Res.	28	12	7	9	67	58	43
Ashton Keynes Res.	28	12	3	13	78	57	39
Kingshill SC Res.	28	9	6	13	64	78	33
CHQ United Res.	28	10	1	17	79	99	31
Avonvale United Res.	28	8	0	20	48	88	24
Down Ampney Res.	28	6	5	17	64	115	23
Corinium Sports	28	4	3	21	58	109	15
Oaksey Res.	28	3	6	19	38	107	15

COLCHESTER & EAST ESSEX LEAGUE
(KP Evans & Co)

Premier Division

	P	W	D	L	F	A	Pts
University of Essex 'A'	18	13	2	3	71	23	41
Harwich Rangers	18	12	2	4	48	24	38
Wormingford Wanderers	18	12	2	4	50	24	38
Harwich & Parkeston 'A'	18	12	1	5	51	28	37
Conesford Hotspurs	18	8	0	10	51	37	24
Tollesbury	18	6	4	8	45	45	22
Kirby Athletic	18	6	4	8	28	35	22
Monkwick Wanderers	18	3	5	10	37	43	14
Colchester Athletic	18	3	0	15	26	56	9
Clacton United	18	1	2	15	28	60	5

Division One

	P	W	D	L	F	A	Pts
Colne Engaine	20	17	3	0	78	19	54
Wimpole	20	15	1	4	88	37	46
University of Essex 'B'	20	13	2	5	69	33	41
Oyster	20	13	1	6	51	40	40
AXA FC	20	8	2	10	48	58	26
Whitehall	20	7	3	10	35	45	24
Ardleigh United	20	6	3	11	29	40	21
Castle	20	6	3	11	39	41	21
St Ives	20	5	2	13	30	61	17
Cinque Port	20	5	2	13	30	64	17
Lawford Lads 'A'	20	2	3	15	26	69	9

Division Two

	P	W	D	L	F	A	Pts
Real Ravensdale	16	16	0	0	79	13	48
AFC Informa	16	9	3	4	35	26	30
Stoke-by-Nayland	16	8	2	6	30	26	26
University of Essex 'C'	16	8	1	7	34	32	25
Nayland Rangers	16	7	1	8	54	42	22
Mistley Athletic 'A'	16	6	1	9	26	41	19
FC Clacton 'A'	16	4	2	10	27	65	14
Monkwick Wdrs Res.	16	4	0	12	25	53	12
New Field	16	3	0	13	27	56	12

Division Three

	P	W	D	L	F	A	Pts
Brightlingsea Regent 'A'	18	14	1	3	62	27	43
Bradfield Rovers Res.	18	12	1	5	55	37	37
Feering United	18	11	2	5	55	37	35
Eastcliff	18	11	0	7	41	29	33
Great Bentley 'A'	18	8	1	9	47	48	25
Wimpole Res.	18	7	0	11	37	41	21
University of Essex 'D'	18	7	0	11	31	48	21
Beacon Hill Rovers 'A'	18	6	1	11	29	55	19
Worming'd Wdrs Res.	18	5	0	13	29	55	15
Colchester Athletic Res.	18	2	2	14	29	73	8

COVENTRY ALLIANCE

Premier Division

	P	W	D	L	F	A	Pts
Christ The King	30	23	4	3	92	29	73
Bedworth Ex-Service	30	21	7	2	95	25	70
Alvis	30	20	4	6	65	41	64
Triumph Athletic	30	13	6	11	68	55	45
Hawkes Mill Sports	30	13	4	13	57	51	43
Witherley United	30	13	3	14	53	49	42
Folly Lane BCOB	30	10	7	13	43	54	37
Stockingford AA Pavilion	30	10	7	13	54	68	37
AEI Rugby	30	10	4	16	54	57	34
Peugeot Sports	30	10	3	17	51	57	33
Mount Nod Highway -3	30	11	3	16	42	59	33
Dunlop Sports	30	8	7	15	39	63	31
Woodlands WMC	30	7	7	16	39	72	28
Brooklands/Jaguar	30	4	4	22	36	90	16

Division One

	P	W	D	L	F	A	Pts
Potters Green	22	15	4	3	49	26	49
Ambleside Sports	22	15	3	4	49	22	48
Christ The King Res.	22	11	3	8	51	47	36
Alvis Res.	22	11	2	9	45	44	35
Coventry Colliery	22	10	4	8	44	44	34
Coundon Court Old Boys	22	8	4	10	36	39	28
Collycroft Sports	22	7	4	11	33	46	25
Nuneaton Griff & Coton	22	5	6	11	37	46	21
Brooklands/Jaguar Res.	22	5	4	13	31	65	19
Copsewood (Coventry)	22	4	4	14	45	75	16

Division Two

	P	W	D	L	F	A	Pts
Stockton Res.	22	15	3	4	60	31	48
Bourton & Frankton	22	13	4	5	60	42	43
Fillongley	22	12	5	5	58	53	41
Shilton	22	11	4	7	52	52	37
Sporting Club (GNP)	22	12	0	10	58	50	36
Kenilworth Wardens	22	9	4	9	46	46	31
Copsew'd (Coventry) Res.	22	9	1	12	51	45	28
Balsall & Berkswell	22	7	5	10	41	56	26
Potters Green Res.	22	6	5	11	48	51	23
Nuneaton Griff & Coton Res.	22	6	4	12	45	61	22
Triumph Athletic Res.	22	4	7	11	42	42	19
Folly Lane BCOB 'A'	22	4	3	15	25	61	17

Division Three

	P	W	D	L	F	A	Pts
Dunlop Sports Res.	22	16	2	4	65	32	50
Hub	22	15	2	5	64	37	47
Christ The King 'A'	22	14	2	6	56	44	44
Brinklow	22	11	7	4	51	37	40
Witherley United Res.	22	11	4	7	47	34	37
Coventry University Res.	22	10	5	7	48	35	35
Bulkington Sps/Social Res.	22	10	3	9	54	56	28
Jaguar-Daimler	22	8	2	12	46	60	26
Mount Nod Highway Res. -3	22	6	3	13	45	55	21
Coundon Court OB Res.	22	5	4	13	44	74	19
AEI Rugby Res.	22	4	1	17	35	67	13
Woodlands WMC Res.	22	3	4	15	36	66	14

Division Four

	P	W	D	L	F	A	Pts
Whitnash	22	16	2	4	65	37	50
Hartshill	22	15	2	5	89	33	47
Bedworth Ex-Service Res.	22	11	4	7	68	43	31
Hawkes Mill Sports Res.	22	11	3	8	57	49	36
Brinklow Res. -3	22	10	2	10	43	63	29
Kenilworth Wardens Res.	22	8	4	10	56	59	28
Cherry Tree	22	6	4	12	33	60	22
Ambleside Sports Res.	22	6	3	13	26	61	21
Coventry Colliery Res.	22	5	6	11	41	70	21
Collycroft Sports Res.	22	6	1	15	24	74	19
Bilton Social	22	3	6	13	36	63	15
Bermuda	22	3	4	15	34	90	13

Division Five

	P	W	D	L	F	A	Pts
Church Lawford	22	19	1	2	96	26	58
Peugeot Sports 'A'	22	15	1	6	80	55	46
Hartshill Res.	22	13	4	5	65	43	43
Crystal	22	13	1	8	60	50	36
Coventry University 'A'	22	10	3	9	48	56	33
Balsall/Berkswell Res. -3	22	9	3	12	48	53	25
Fillongley Res.	22	6	3	13	36	60	21
Bourton & Frankton Res.	22	6	2	14	39	59	20
Wolston	22	5	4	13	40	63	19
Bermuda Res.	22	5	1	15	28	61	16
AEI Rugby 'A'	22	4	4	14	45	75	16

CRAVEN & DISTRICT FA

Premier Division

	P	W	D	L	F	A	Pts
Grassington United	22	20	1	1	78	31	61
Skipton LMS	22	15	4	3	60	42	49
Oxenhope Recreation	22	10	4	8	58	48	34
Clitheroe Lions	22	9	5	8	53	52	32
Hellifield Sports	22	9	5	8	58	50	32
Cononley Sports	22	9	2	11	51	46	29
WFC Clitheroe	22	7	5	10	31	41	26
Skipton Town	22	6	6	10	46	45	24
Waddington	22	6	5	11	51	56	23
Gargrave	22	6	5	11	42	61	23
Embsay	22	6	4	12	45	61	22
Bradley	22	3	6	13	35	68	15

Division One

	P	W	D	L	F	A	Pts
Gargrave Res.	22	15	1	6	79	36	46
Long Lee Juniors	22	14	3	5	66	35	45
Pendle Athletic	22	14	3	5	48	35	45
Oxenhope Recreation Res.	22	13	3	6	65	40	42
Grindleton	22	11	4	7	68	45	37
Rolls Royce	22	12	1	9	68	46	37
Oakworth	22	9	5	8	46	46	32
AFC Padiham	22	5	3	14	50	47	18
Keighley	22	5	3	14	47	73	18
Cowling	22	3	5	14	35	84	14
Carleton	22	3	4	15	36	90	13
Intake	22	2	4	17	36	90	13

Division Two

	P	W	D	L	F	A	Pts
Earby Town	22	17	1	4	98	37	52
Trawden Celtic -3	22	16	6	0	65	24	51
Chatburn -3	22	16	3	3	79	33	48
Pendle Forest Res.	22	11	4	7	44	50	37
Pendle Renegades	22	10	2	10	57	48	32
Skipton Town Res.	22	9	4	9	44	49	31
Embsay Res.	22	7	6	9	41	49	27
Grassington United Res.	22	5	5	12	62	75	20
Skipton LMS Res.	22	5	4	13	58	94	19
Cononley Sports Res.	22	5	3	14	39	73	15
Rolls Royce Res.	22	4	3	15	39	73	15
Horton	22	3	5	14	34	64	14

Barrowford United – record expunged

Division Three

	P	W	D	L	F	A	Pts
Silsden White Star	18	13	0	5	77	31	39
Barnoldswick Barons -1	18	13	0	5	64	22	38
Settle United Res.	18	11	2	5	72	28	35
Skipton Town 'A'	18	10	1	7	53	53	31
Grindleton Res.	18	8	1	9	56	62	25
Oakworth Res.	18	6	1	11	56	62	19
Cowling Res.	18	5	3	10	35	51	18
Earby Town Res.	18	5	2	11	43	63	17
Waddington Res.	18	5	2	11	53	76	17
Bradley Res.	18	2	1	15	28	123	7

Hellifield Sports Res. – record expunged
Keighley Res. – record expunged
Carleton Res. – record expunged

CRAWLEY & DISTRICT LEAGUE

Premier Division

	P	W	D	L	F	A	Pts
Holland Sports	18	14	1	3	42	20	43
Merstham Newton	18	11	1	6	39	25	34
Reigate Priory +2	18	8	4	6	40	26	30
Phoenix United	18	8	4	6	41	29	30
Maidenbower Village	18	7	5	6	37	39	26
Northgate Athletic	18	7	4	7	37	31	25
St Francis Flyers	18	7	4	7	24	38	25
Three Bridges 'A'	18	5	4	9	34	48	19
Ifield Edwards Res.	18	3	12	3	23	44	12
Bletchingley -1	18	3	12	3	25	46	11

WWW.CHERRYRED.CO.UK

Division One

	P	W	D	L	F	A	Pts
Swinton Station	22	18	4	0	81	22	58
St Francis Flyers Res.	22	13	6	3	74	42	43
Sutton Rovers	22	12	6	4	75	36	42
Kinsley Boys Res.	22	11	6	5	82	46	39
Crawley Manor	22	11	2	9	73	62	38
Crawley Elite	22	11	2	9	82	46	38	−1
Broadfield	22	12	2	8	73	62	38
Horley Albion +2	22	8	5	9	60	61	28
Furnace Green Rovers	22	8	4	10	60	60	28
Horley Wanderers	22	8	1	13	43	52	25
Phoenix United Res.	22	6	2	14	39	75	20
Seebrook Rovers	22	2	1	19	21	122	7
Ifield Edwards 'A'	22	1	1	20	34	111	4

Division Three

	P	W	D	L	F	A	Pts
Ifield Edwards 'B'	24	20	3	1	113	40	63
Phoenix United 'A'	24	18	5	1	87	36	59
Pelham Wanderers −3	24	15	3	6	78	37	45
Worth Park Rangers +3	24	14	4	6	98	47	45
Real Hydraquip Res.	24	14	0	10	98	72	42
Rowfant Village	24	10	2	12	57	68	32
Border Wanderers −3	24	11	1	12	72	68	31
County Oak	24	8	4	12	60	69	27
Stones	24	8	3	14	38	72	26
Maidenbower Village Res.	24	5	5	14	60	80	20
Sporting Crawley Res.	24	5	3	16	54	106	20
Sporting Devils	24	5	3	16	46	93	18
Wingspan +3	24	5	1	16	34	85	17

DRIFFIELD & DISTRICT LEAGUE

Premier Division

	P	W	D	L	F	A	Pts
Yorkies	18	15	1	2	78	14	46
Driffield Athletic 'A'	18	14	3	1	66	27	45
Bridlington Sports Club	18	11	3	4	50	34	36
Driffield Evening Institute	18	11	1	6	55	35	34
CCS Sports	18	7	3	8	60	33	24
Driffield Rangers	18	7	3	8	36	38	24
Driffield Recreation	18	5	2	11	26	50	17
Stirling Castle	18	5	1	12	30	60	16
Bridlington Black Lion −3	18	6	0	12	25	47	15
Foresters Athletic	18	0	2	16	33	100	6

DUCHY LEAGUE
(Bodmin Sports Trophies)

Premier Division

	P	W	D	L	F	A	Pts
St Stephens Borough	24	20	3	1	68	20	62
Torpoint Athletic 'A'	24	16	5	3	68	31	53
Edgcumbe	24	15	4	5	75	40	50
Roseland −3	24	11	4	9	41	46	34
St Dennis	24	11	1	12	54	62	34
Lamerton	24	9	6	11	41	54	27
Gunnislake	24	8	5	11	51	51	28
Launceston United	24	7	5	12	43	59	26
Pensilva	24	6	4	14	32	56	22
Dobwalls Res. −3	24	5	2	17	32	77	17
St Mawgan	24	1	3	20	21	91	6

CREWE & DISTRICT LEAGUE

Premier Division

	P	W	D	L	F	A	Pts
Curshaws	16	14	1	1	42	12	43
Congleton Athletic	16	12	0	4	50	15	36
Bunbury	16	8	4	4	34	34	28
Kidsgrove Carpets	16	8	2	6	29	23	26
Lostock Gralam Res.	16	7	4	5	40	39	25
MMU Alsager	16	5	3	8	34	34	18
Sandbach United Res.	16	4	3	9	23	41	12
Crewe Res.	16	3	3	10	25	48	12
Winnington Avenue	16	2	2	12	14	44	8

DONCASTER & DISTRICT SENIOR LEAGUE

Premier Division

	P	W	D	L	F	A	Pts
Hemsworth Alpha	26	19	5	2	94	33	63
Upton & Harewood Social	26	19	5	2	107	32	62
Mexborough Athletic	26	18	1	4	68	35	58
Maltby Sheppey	26	16	4	8	82	53	54
Thorne Town	26	16	4	8	74	39	50
Retford Town	26	14	2	10	68	46	45
Askern Welfare Res.	26	15	0	11	68	44	45
Rossington Main Res.	26	12	1	13	61	70	37
Edlington Rangers	26	8	3	13	52	66	27
South Kirkby Colliery Res.	26	8	1	17	44	77	25
Eden Grove	26	6	3	17	56	74	21
Pontefract Collieries Res.	26	6	3	17	35	74	21
Bawtry Town	26	4	1	21	46	95	13
Doncaster Deaf College	26	0	2	24	29	177	2

Division Two

	P	W	D	L	F	A	Pts
St Cleer Res.	28	21	2	5	92	46	65
Saltash United 'A'	28	19	6	3	114	35	63
Sutton Brookside	28	16	5	7	60	37	53
Holywell Bay & Cubert	28	16	3	9	69	52	51
Delabole United	28	13	8	7	85	48	47
Polperro Res.	28	14	2	12	77	56	44
Grampound	28	14	2	12	68	70	44
St Stephen Res.	28	12	4	12	51	58	40
Camelford 'A'	28	9	9	10	70	69	36
St Breward	28	10	6	14	66	68	36
Probus Res.	28	8	4	16	54	73	28
Pelynt −3	28	8	6	16	42	59	27
TPS	28	6	2	21	32	83	22
Wadebridge Town 'A'	28	3	1	24	41	117	10

Division Three

	P	W	D	L	F	A	Pts
Bodmin Saints	24	18	4	2	116	35	58
Week St Mary +3	24	17	4	3	103	49	55
Calstock	24	14	3	7	96	65	45
Biscovey Res.	24	15	2	7	65	48	47
Lostwithiel	24	12	3	9	82	67	40
Queens Rangers	24	11	3	10	67	74	30
Bere Alston Utd Res. −3	24	11	0	13	58	69	30
Newmoor Rovers	24	10	0	14	58	88	30
Lanreath Res.	24	8	3	13	59	59	27
Gerrans −3	24	8	1	15	45	95	22
Roche Res. +3	24	5	2	17	29	86	16
Lewdown Rovers	24	4	4	16	46	116	16
Pensilva Res.	24	3	2	19	37	116	11

Division Four

	P	W	D	L	F	A	Pts
Gorran	24	20	2	2	68	20	62
St Dominick	24	16	5	3	68	31	53
Nanpean Rovers Res.	24	15	4	5	75	40	49
St Newlyn East Res.	24	14	4	6	73	32	46
Gunnislake Res.	24	11	4	9	54	62	37
Garrison Club	24	12	1	11	54	62	37
Looe Town Res.	24	8	5	11	41	54	29
Tintagel	24	7	6	11	51	70	27
Dynamo St Dennis	24	8	1	15	43	74	25
Stratton United −3	24	6	1	17	49	56	16
Boscastle Res.	24	5	3	16	43	63	18
North Hill	24	5	2	17	32	83	17
St Mawgan Res. −3	24	3	2	19	32	91	8

Division Five

	P	W	D	L	F	A	Pts
Looe Town	26	23	2	1	90	23	71
Altarnun	26	17	4	5	87	44	57
Foxhole Stars Res. +3	26	15	4	7	75	48	52
Lanivet	26	15	5	6	78	36	47
Mevagissey	26	14	2	10	48	53	44
Maker-with-Rame +2	26	10	4	12	68	70	36
Godolphin Atlantic Res. −3	26	11	4	11	59	50	34
Tywardreath RBL	26	9	5	12	51	58	32
St Dominick Res.	26	9	5	15	60	64	31
Boscastle −1	26	8	1	17	42	65	23
Menheniot −6	26	6	3	17	42	76	19
St Arns Chapel	26	5	3	18	43	98	18
St Minver	26	1	1	24	29	136	4

EAST BERKSHIRE LEAGUE

Premier Division

	P	W	D	L	F	A	Pts
FC Beaconsfield	14	10	1	3	33	21	31
Slough Heating	14	9	1	4	55	27	27
Waltham	14	8	1	5	36	15	25
Iver Heath Rovers	14	6	2	6	25	22	20
Orchard Park Rangers	14	5	3	6	25	30	18
Chalvey (WMC) Sports	14	4	2	8	30	36	14
New Windsor Old Boys	14	4	2	8	44	41	14
Old Windsor	14	2	0	12	14	41	6

Burnham Swan – record expunged
FC Wraysbury – record expunged
Spital Old Boys – record expunged

Division One

	P	W	D	L	F	A	Pts
Running Horse	20	17	1	2	75	30	52
Maidenhead Town	20	14	2	4	55	34	44
Windsor Great Park	20	13	4	3	43	34	43
Iver	20	9	7	4	43	31	34
Cippenham Sports	20	8	5	7	41	46	29
Foxes	20	8	4	8	41	48	28
Burnham Beeches	20	7	2	11	41	48	23
Burnham United	20	6	2	11	41	66	23
Chalvey (WMC) Spts Res.	20	5	4	11	54	56	19
Slough Laurencians	20	1	5	14	18	48	8
Datchet	20	5	14	1	—	—	8

Division Two

	P	W	D	L	F	A	Pts
The Lane +3	16	12	2	2	75	24	41
New Hanford −3	16	11	2	3	61	27	33
Stoke Green	16	8	3	5	51	44	27
Richings Park	16	7	3	6	44	24	24
Stoke Poges	16	6	4	6	35	38	24
Boyne Hill	16	6	1	9	35	59	19

Division Three

	P	W	D	L	F	A	Pts
Burnham Beeches Res.	18	16	1	1	78	13	51
Eastcote & Richings Park	18	10	6	2	55	44	36
Slough Laurencians Res.	18	10	2	6	44	32	32
Falcons	18	8	4	6	46	31	28
Campion United	18	9	1	8	60	61	28
AFC Lady Haig	18	7	4	7	41	42	25
Braybrooke	18	8	1	9	40	44	25
Hayes Villa Old Boys	18	5	8	4	34	43	23
Running Horse Res.	18	3	1	13	29	43	20
Upton Park Rangers	18	1	3	14	17	70	6

Division Four

	P	W	D	L	F	A	Pts
Alpha Arms Academicals	22	16	0	6	89	45	48
Iver Heath Rovers Res.	22	15	1	6	82	48	46
Windsor Great Park Res.	22	12	6	6	82	37	42
Crowthorne Royals	22	13	3	6	65	34	42
Old Windsor Res.	22	12	3	7	72	49	39
GNSSS Maidenhead	22	12	2	8	49	53	38
Willow Wanderers	22	9	3	10	49	53	35
New Park United	22	8	1	13	45	65	25
North Maidenhead	22	6	5	11	49	64	23
Mercian United	22	5	3	14	44	81	18
SA Stainash	22	5	2	16	42	72	16
Chalvey (WMC) Spts 'A'	22	2	1	19	17	108	5

EAST CHESHIRE LEAGUE
(Trade Mark Collections)

	P	W	D	L	F	A	Pts
Puss in Boots	16	14	2	0	66	21	44
Old Altrinchamians Vets	16	11	2	3	55	31	35
Mary Dendy	16	8	3	5	55	36	27
Club AZ Res.	16	7	4	5	60	34	25
Boarhound	16	7	4	5	50	32	25
Juno United	16	6	3	7	32	38	21
Poynton 'A'	16	3	0	13	26	72	9
Poynton Kingfisher	16	2	2	12	23	53	8
Old Altrinchamians 'B'	16	2	1	13	18	63	7

EAST LANCASHIRE LEAGUE

	P	W	D	L	F	A	Pts
Rimington	26	22	1	3	90	27	67
Hurst Green	26	19	3	4	75	30	60
Stacksteads St Josephs	26	14	5	7	57	42	47
Langho	26	14	4	8	85	45	46
Mill Hill St Peters 'A'	26	14	4	8	56	39	46
Rock Rovers	26	13	2	11	55	41	41
Worsthorne	26	12	3	11	48	46	39
Borrowdale United	26	9	4	13	46	61	31
Goodshaw United	26	7	4	15	36	67	25
Enfield	26	7	2	17	35	63	23
Colne United	26	6	5	15	36	63	23
Kelbrook United	26	5	2	19	54	101	17
Settle United	26	3	4	19	31	75	13
Peel Park	26	3	3	20	34	69	12

Division One

	P	W	D	L	F	A	Pts
Read Res.	28	22	1	5	103	45	67
BAE Canberra Res.	28	19	4	5	100	52	61
Clitheroe RBL	28	17	5	6	92	55	56
Bacup CC	28	18	2	8	66	56	56
Burnley Belvedere 'A'	28	15	7	6	88	63	52
Oswaldtwistle St Mary's	28	14	5	9	56	66	47
Pendle Forest	28	11	7	10	55	65	40
Burley GSOB	28	11	7	10	66	76	40
Padiham 'A'	28	9	8	11	63	84	35
Barrowford YCW	28	7	10	11	39	55	31
Barrowford Res.	28	7	4	17	63	91	25
Sabden	28	4	6	18	58	111	18
Barnoldswick Town 'A' Res.	28	5	3	20	41	102	18
Burnley Boys Club	28	3	3	22	47	112	12

Reserve Division

	P	W	D	L	F	A	Pts
Worsthorne Res.	28	22	1	5	85	41	60
Hurst Green Res.	28	19	3	6	75	52	60
Burnley GSOB Res. -5	28	18	4	6	78	48	53
Stacksteads St Josephs Res.	28	15	7	6	72	56	52
Rimington Res.	28	14	5	9	88	56	47
Enfield Res.	28	12	6	10	67	53	42
Langho Res.	28	14	2	12	64	51	44
Rock Rovers Res.	28	10	4	14	51	54	34
Oswaldtwistle St M Res.	28	8	12	8	54	51	36
Goodshaw United Res.	28	8	7	13	68	74	31
Rawtenstall Res.	28	8	7	13	58	75	27
Kelbrook United Res.	28	8	1	19	57	82	25
Read United Res.	28	6	5	17	42	81	24
Colne United Res.	28	5	2	21	49	75	17
Peel Park Res.	28	6	5	17	49	90	23

EAST RIDING AMATEUR LEAGUE

Premier Division

	P	W	D	L	F	A	Pts
Inter Charter	18	14	3	1	48	19	45
Crown	18	13	4	1	58	25	43
Kingham Athletic	18	11	4	3	55	30	37
Pinefleet Wolfreton Res.	18	10	3	5	52	49	33
Bridges (Jar In Hand)	18	8	6	5	29	34	30
Eddie Beedle	18	6	1	11	38	55	19
Truss 2 Frame	18	5	5	10	34	52	25
AFC Preston	18	3	4	11	34	52	13
Intrasource Mainbrace	18	1	2	15	17	60	5
Hessle Sporting Club Res.	18						

Spring Bank Tigers – record expunged

Division One

	P	W	D	L	F	A	Pts
AFC West Hull	22	17	2	3	72	30	53
Kingham Athletic Res.	22	15	4	3	66	29	49
Cavalier Wanderers	22	14	5	3	62	30	47
SC Electrical	22	13	4	5	60	32	43
South Holderness	22	12	2	8	73	47	38
Hall Road Rangers 'A'	22	10	5	7	52	68	37
Cottingham Hotspur	22	11	3	8	40	62	36
Hull Grass Roots	22	9	8	5	41	68	35
Hull Athletic	22	7	6	9	36	72	27
Paull Wanderers	22	5	2	15	26	100	17
Tenyas	22	2	1	19			

EAST LINCOLNSHIRE COMBINATION

Division One

	P	W	D	L	F	A	Pts
North Somercotes	18	14	1	3	62	15	43
Telford	18	11	5	2	58	31	38
Grainthorpe	18	10	2	6	64	32	32
Sutton	18	10	2	6	60	39	32
AFC Louth	18	9	3	6	51	48	30
AFC Kai's	18	7	3	8	40	42	24
Alford Town	18	6	2	10	34	62	20
Manby	18	5	5	8	29	48	20
Mablethorpe Athletic	18	4	1	13	30	59	13
North Thoresby	18	1	2	15	16	65	5

Division Two

	P	W	D	L	F	A	Pts
Waltham Tea Gardens	18	14	1	3	62	23	43
Hogsthorpe	18	13	0	5	65	44	39
Louth United Res.	18	11	0	7	70	50	33
Burgh	18	8	2	8	53	48	26
Donington	18	8	1	9	53	42	25
Louth Old Boys	18	8	1	9	34	43	25
Sutton Res.	18	5	3	10	33	72	18
Golden Fleece	18	5	2	11	34	63	17
Scamblesby	18	4	3	11	46	52	15
Ship Skegness	18	2	0	16	26	88	6

Carlin How WMC – record expunged

EAST RIDING COUNTY LEAGUE

Premier Division

	P	W	D	L	F	A	Pts
North Ferriby Athletic	20	15	1	4	78	28	46
AFC Charter	20	13	3	4	57	31	42
Beverley Town Res.	20	12	2	6	46	36	38
Viking Raiders	20	10	3	7	35	36	33
Howden Amateurs	20	9	4	7	40	44	31
Northfield Athletic	20	8	6	6	33	46	30
Bridlington United	20	6	8	6	33	43	26
Sculcoates Amateurs Res.	20	6	2	12	35	47	20
Skidby Millers	20	5	3	12	33	60	18
Easington United Res.	20	3	3	14	28	66	12
Holme Rovers	20						

Division One

	P	W	D	L	F	A	Pts
Reckitts Res.	20	15	3	2	70	31	48
Wawne Ferry	20	12	4	4	54	29	40
Westella & Willerby Res.	20	13	2	5	57	24	41
Patrington Stanley Utd	20	11	2	7	63	48	35
South Cave United	20	10	2	8	41	42	32
Aldbrough United	20	10	1	9	47	44	31
Brandesburton Res.	20	8	2	10	49	45	26
Hutton Cranswick Utd Res.	20	5	2	13	38	61	17
Lord Nelson Beverley	20	4	3	13	29	64	15
Beverley Town Beavers	20	2	3	15	21	71	9
Hedon United	20	2	2	16	21		8

Division Two

	P	W	D	L	F	A	Pts
AFC Preston Res.	22	19	2	1	92	18	59
Pinefleet Wolfreton Juniors	22	17	2	5	83	37	53
Swiss Cottage	22	13	3	6	96	43	42
Greatfield Old Boys	22	11	4	9	64	62	37
Hessle Sporting Club 'A'	22	7	3	12	47	47	24
Cottingham Hotspur Res.	22	7	3	12	73	77	24
Intrasource Mainbrace Res.	22	7	1	14	61	72	22
Hull Grass Roots Res.	22	7	1	14	57	97	22
AFC West Hull Res.	22	6	3	13	51	78	21
AFC Piper	22	4	0	18	24	59	12
Hull Hawks	22	2	1	19	31	159	7
The Courts	22						

Division Three

	P	W	D	L	F	A	Pts
West Hull Amateurs	22	18	1	3	77	38	55
Skidby Millers Res.	22	16	4	2	84	34	52
Long Riston Res.	22	14	5	3	72	31	47
Lewis Ashley Services	22	13	3	6	70	50	42
Leven Members Club Res.	22	13	3	6	57	54	42
Total Sign Solutions	22	10	3	9	66	33	33
Patrington Stanley Utd Res.	22	8	6	8	66	74	30
Molescroft Rangers -3	22	8	8	6	51	53	27
Skirlaugh +3	22	6	4	12	52	61	27
Plexus Networking	22	5	5	12	40	55	20
Roos	22	5	2	15	51	63	15
Howden Town	22	2	0	20	19	117	6

Division Four

	P	W	D	L	F	A	Pts
Westella/Willerby Juniors	18	14	4	0	71	16	46
Hedon Rangers Res.	18	13	4	1	58	20	43
Shiptonthorpe United	18	12	2	4	43	33	38
Brandesburton 'A'	18	10	2	6	58	41	32
Market Weighton Res.	18	10	1	7	61	35	31
Eastrington Village	18	9	2	7	39	63	29
Easington Utd Casuals	18	5	1	12	29	40	16
Holme Rovers Res.	18	4	3	11	34	55	15
Molescroft Rangers Res.	18	4	2	12	27	62	14
Withernsea 'A'	18	1	1	16	19	74	4

Division Five

	P	W	D	L	F	A	Pts
Cliffe	20	15	3	2	106	45	48
South Cave United Res.	20	13	3	4	67	33	42
Cross Keys	20	13	2	5	76	23	41
Anlaby Park	20	11	4	5	44	41	37
Gilberdyke Res.	20	11	2	7	52	44	35
Haltemprice Rangers	20	11	1	8	71	48	34
Hedon Rangers Juniors	20	10	0	10	43	62	30
Hornsea Town 'A'	20	5	2	13	30	61	17
Shiptonthorpe Utd Res.	20	3	4	13	33	89	13
Skirlaugh Res.	20	3	1	16	22	63	10
Brandesburton 'B'	20	2	4	14	35	82	10

EAST SUSSEX LEAGUE
(K & P Motoring World)

Premier Division

	P	W	D	L	F	A	Pts
Hollington United	22	19	0	3	65	22	57
St Leonards Social	22	12	3	7	56	27	39
Ridge West Garage	22	12	2	8	62	42	38
Heathfield Hotspurs	22	11	4	7	46	36	37
Punnetts Town	22	9	3	10	51	32	30
Junior Club Tackleway	22	9	3	10	42	37	30
Rock-a-Nore	22	8	3	11	52	44	27
Peche Hill Select	22	7	3	12	43	46	24
Peasmarsh & Iden	22	6	3	13	33	44	24
Hooe Sports	22	5	2	15	44	55	17
Bodiam	22	3	1	16	22	75	10

260 Other Leagues

WWW.CHERRYRED.CO.UK

Division One	P	W	D	L	F	A	Pts
Sedlescombe	22	16	1	5	63	31	49
Athletico	22	15	1	6	79	38	46
Crowhurst	22	13	3	6	77	49	42
Bexhill AAC	22	13	3	6	52	31	42
Hollington United Res.	22	13	2	7	60	42	41
Ninfield United	22	10	7	5	51	29	37
Little Common Res.	22	9	4	9	58	45	31
Icklesham Casuals	22	9	3	10	77	70	30
Ticehurst	22	6	4	12	55	70	22
Mountfield United	22	6	3	13	32	42	21
Hastings Rangers	22	4	0	18	40	150	12
Sandhurst	22	2	1	19	30	77	7

Division Two	P	W	D	L	F	A	Pts
Wheatsheaf	20	16	2	2	61	25	50
Catsfield	20	14	2	4	66	31	44
White Knight	20	12	4	4	48	30	40
Peasmarsh & Iden Res.	20	10	3	7	65	39	33
Magham Down	20	8	5	7	51	37	29
Northiam	20	8	3	9	44	41	27
Herstmonceux	20	8	2	10	45	51	26
Hastings Rangers Res. *-1*	20	8	1	11	41	61	24
Battle Baptists *+2*	20	5	6	9	46	45	23
Firehills Seniors	20	4	2	14	31	91	14
Mayfield	20	2	0	18	30	77	6

Little Common 'A' – record expunged

Division Three	P	W	D	L	F	A	Pts
Benbow	20	17	3	0	67	20	54
Robertsbridge United	20	15	2	3	71	28	47
Wadhurst United	20	14	3	3	76	23	45
Hawkhurst United Res.	20	12	3	5	53	30	39
Eastbourne Dynamos	20	8	3	9	40	42	27
Pebsham Sibex	20	7	4	9	37	44	25
Red Lion	20	7	3	10	29	45	24
Battle Rangers	20	5	4	11	26	48	19
Eastbourne Fishermen	20	4	4	12	29	42	16
Beulah Baptists	20	2	4	14	31	89	10
Junior Club Tackleway Res.	20	2	1	17	22	70	7

Wittersham – record expunged

Division Four	P	W	D	L	F	A	Pts
Cinque Ports	20	17	0	3	100	37	51
Panako	20	14	1	5	79	32	43
Hurst *-3*	20	13	2	5	63	48	38
Hollington United 'A'	20	12	1	7	59	44	37
St Helens	20	11	1	8	80	41	34
Peasmarsh & Iden 'A'	20	10	0	10	47	70	30
Bexhill AAC Res.	20	6	4	10	32	57	22
Cranbrook Town	20	6	1	13	48	66	19
Burwash *+3*	20	5	1	14	28	67	19
Victoria Baptists	20	5	1	14	40	70	16
Punnetts Town Res.	20	3	4	13	25	69	13

Bodiam Res. – record expunged

Division Five	P	W	D	L	F	A	Pts
The Wilton	24	17	5	2	86	40	56
Icklesham Casuals Res.	24	17	3	4	88	37	54
Travaux *+3*	24	13	4	7	72	53	46
Junior Club Tackleway 'A'	24	13	5	6	65	41	44
Orington	24	13	1	10	71	47	40
Hastings Rangers 'A'	24	12	2	10	65	62	38
Westfield 'A'	24	11	2	11	43	45	35
Peche Hill Select Res.	24	8	5	11	43	62	29
Mountfield United Res.	24	7	6	11	50	64	27
Heathfield Hotspurs Res.	24	7	5	12	60	61	26
Northiam Res. *-3*	24	7	3	14	34	77	21
Wadhurst United Res.	24	4	7	13	33	64	19
Ninfield United Res.	24	3	0	21	27	84	9

Division Six	P	W	D	L	F	A	Pts
Nelson Tigers	20	19	1	0	94	12	58
Sedlescombe Res.	20	15	0	5	66	37	45
Hastings Elite	20	14	1	5	56	27	43
White Knight Res.	20	11	2	7	63	38	35
Guestling Rangers	20	11	1	8	54	45	34
Magham Down Res.	20	10	2	8	79	52	32
Sandhurst Res.	20	6	6	8	30	39	24
Eastbourne Athletic	20	6	5	9	40	39	23
Battle Baptists Res.	20	5	1	14	37	53	16
Herstmonceux Res. *-3*	20	3	1	16	25	93	7
Beulah Baptists Res. *+3*	20	0	0	20	10	119	3

ESKVALE & CLEVELAND LEAGUE

	P	W	D	L	F	A	Pts
Goldsborough	30	26	2	2	130	30	80
Lingdale Tavern	30	24	4	2	117	42	76
Bulls Head	30	22	1	7	112	41	67
Boosbeck St Aidans	30	19	3	8	94	39	60
Loftus Athletic	30	18	1	11	103	64	55
Hollybush United	30	17	4	9	78	55	55
Redcar Rugby Club	30	17	4	9	87	70	55
Staithes Athletic	30	11	4	15	62	77	37
Lealholm	30	10	5	15	70	69	35
Britannia FC	30	9	5	16	54	77	32
Great Ayton United Res.	30	10	2	18	63	100	32
Brotton Railway Arms	30	8	4	18	44	83	28
Lingdale United	30	7	3	20	58	119	24
Hinderwell	30	7	1	22	57	147	22
Fox Inn	30	6	2	22	45	108	20
Boosbeck United	30	5	3	22	46	99	18

ESSEX & HERTS BORDER COMBINATION

	P	W	D	L	F	A	Pts
Heybridge Swifts Res.	32	25	5	2	111	18	80
Barking Res. *+3*	32	22	4	6	77	42	73
Gt Wakering Rvrs Res.	32	19	7	6	85	51	64
Brentwood Town Res.	32	19	6	7	76	38	63
Dagenham/Redbridge Res.	32	17	9	6	86	41	60
East Thurrock Utd Res. *-3*	32	19	5	8	79	47	59
Waltham Abbey Res.	32	15	5	12	74	60	50
Romford Res.	32	14	6	12	79	50	48
Stansted Res.	32	14	5	13	61	64	47
Billericay Town Res.	32	11	8	13	63	72	41
Canvey Island Res.	32	10	5	17	52	76	35
Clapton Res.	32	8	6	18	47	74	30
Bowers & Pitsea Res.	32	9	2	21	35	100	29
Burnham Ramblers Res.	32	8	4	20	39	85	28
Ilford Res.	32	6	9	17	44	73	27
Concord Rangers Res.	32	8	3	21	49	94	27
Basildon United Res.	32	3	1	28	29	101	10

ESSEX BUSINESS HOUSES LEAGUE

Premier Division	P	W	D	L	F	A	Pts
Sungate	22	17	3	2	73	24	54
Old Barkabbeyans	22	16	4	2	53	23	52
Toby	22	13	2	7	52	36	41
Collier Row Seniors	22	13	1	8	50	49	40
Flanders	22	12	2	8	55	34	38
Brampton Park	22	12	2	8	56	47	38
Rainham WMC	22	8	3	11	58	53	27
Melbourne Sports	22	8	1	13	34	47	25
Bancroft	22	5	4	13	30	39	19
Euro Dagenham	22	4	4	14	33	55	16
Platinium	22	4	4	14	23	56	16
Globe Rangers	22	4	2	16	27	81	14

Division One	P	W	D	L	F	A	Pts
Newham Borough (SECP)	20	18	1	1	71	19	55
West Green	20	13	2	5	61	42	41
Heath Park	20	10	4	6	53	33	34
PLA Vets	20	9	4	7	49	44	31
Barking Borough	20	9	4	7	39	38	31
Roma	20	8	2	10	47	42	26
Snaresbrook	20	6	6	8	36	48	24
Sungate Res.	20	7	3	10	40	56	24
Stags Head	20	6	2	12	45	51	20
Old Barkabbeyans Res.	20	5	2	13	19	48	17
West Essex	20	2	4	14	25	64	10

FALMOUTH-HELSTON LEAGUE

Division One	P	W	D	L	F	A	Pts
Chacewater	30	22	5	3	111	39	71
Falmouth Athletic *-1*	30	22	3	5	93	35	68
St Keverne	30	21	2	7	91	36	65
Mawnan	30	20	4	6	80	34	64
Helston Athletic Res.	30	18	4	8	82	37	58
Falmouth Town 'A' *-1*	30	17	4	9	83	53	54
Mousehole Res.	30	16	3	11	61	65	51
Holmans Sps Club Res. *-3*	30	15	3	12	67	57	45
St Agnes Res.	30	13	4	13	58	59	43
Falmouth Albion	30	10	3	17	45	57	33
St Day Res. *+3*	30	8	4	18	48	80	31
Penryn Athletic 'A'	30	8	4	18	34	59	28
Stithians	30	5	9	16	38	77	24
Lizard Argyle	30	5	5	20	36	91	20
Hayle 'A'	30	5	2	23	39	118	17
Wendron United 'A'	30	3	5	22	29	98	14

Division Two	P	W	D	L	F	A	Pts
Pendeen Rovers *+3*	28	23	2	3	129	19	74
Truro City 'A'	28	22	4	2	123	22	70
Perranwell Res.	28	19	1	8	97	39	58
Mawgan United	28	18	4	6	88	53	58
Mawnan Res.	28	18	3	7	77	41	57
RNAS Culdrose Res. *-3*	28	14	3	11	74	76	42
Rosudgeon-Kenneggy *+5*	28	10	4	14	62	78	39
Marazion Blues Res.	28	11	4	13	55	59	37
Perranporth Res.	28	11	4	13	58	79	37
Carharrack *-3*	28	11	4	13	73	56	34
Frogpool-Cusgarne	28	10	4	14	65	72	34
Constantine *-1*	28	5	7	16	71	91	21
Wendron United 'B'	28	4	5	19	35	117	17
Hayle 'B'	28	4	2	22	36	126	14
Trispen	28	3	3	22	41	156	12

Falmouth Albion Res. – record expunged

Division Three	P	W	D	L	F	A	Pts
Porthleven Rangers	30	26	2	2	141	35	80
Camborne Park	30	25	1	4	133	38	76
Lanner	30	22	5	3	130	46	71
Troon Res.	30	20	1	9	115	60	61
Lizard Argyle Res.	30	14	6	10	84	62	48
Helston Athletic 'A'	30	15	3	12	89	70	48
Mullion Res.	30	15	3	12	75	72	48
Falmouth Athletic Res.	30	15	2	13	96	98	47
St Day 'A'	30	12	4	14	77	84	40
Penryn Athletic 'B'	30	11	3	16	60	73	36
Ruan Minor *+3*	30	9	4	17	78	86	34
Carharrack Res.	30	10	3	17	61	77	33
Rosudgeon-Kenneggy Res.	30	7	3	20	39	95	24
Cury *-3*	30	7	4	19	65	121	22
Stithians Res.	30	5	2	23	44	112	17
Frogpool-Cusgarne Res.	30	3	2	25	39	197	11

FURNESS PREMIER LEAGUE

Premier Division	P	W	D	L	F	A	Pts
BAE Barrow Spts Club Res.	28	21	4	3	110	35	67
Millom Res.	28	19	4	5	78	46	61
Dalton United Res.	28	14	7	7	56	48	49
Vickerstown CC Res. *-3*	28	15	6	7	71	42	48
Walney Island	28	13	5	10	61	50	44
Askam United Res.	28	13	2	13	80	64	41
Bootle	28	13	2	13	59	66	41
Furness Rovers 'A'	28	11	7	10	68	55	40
Haverigg United	28	11	3	14	46	58	36
Barrow Island *-3*	28	10	6	12	67	81	33
Holker Old Boys Res.	28	7	7	14	57	70	28
Barrow Celtic	28	8	4	16	44	79	28
Furness Athletic	28	8	3	17	52	76	27
Crooklands Casuals Res. *-3*	28	8	4	16	56	81	25
GSK Ulverston Rgrs Res. *-3*	28	5	4	19	38	92	16

Division One	P	W	D	L	F	A	Pts
Furness Cavaliers Res.	24	20	4	0	86	21	64
Kirkby United	24	17	5	2	97	39	56
Barrow Wanderers	24	15	4	5	91	40	49
Walney Island Res.	24	12	4	8	59	41	40
Furness Rovers 'B'	24	10	10	4	61	45	40
Furness Seniors	24	10	4	10	34	41	34
Millom 'A'	24	9	4	11	50	58	31
Vickerstown CC 'A'	24	8	5	11	38	69	29
Holker Old Boys 'A'	24	5	4	15	34	70	19
BAE Barrow Spts Club 'A'	24	4	7	13	40	77	19
Haverigg United Res. *-3*	24	5	5	14	38	58	17
Dalton United 'A' *-3*	24	6	2	16	30	53	17
Walney Island 'A'	24	4	4	16	31	77	16

GAINSBOROUGH & DISTRICT LEAGUE

Division One	P	W	D	L	F	A	Pts
Sun Inn Tuxford	16	14	1	1	47	20	43
AFC Friendship	16	12	0	4	62	20	36
Harworth Colliery Inst Res.	16	11	3	2	43	20	36
White Lion	16	5	2	9	32	41	17
Retford Town Res.	16	5	2	9	27	56	17
Rampton Hospital	16	4	4	8	32	29	16
Harworth Colts	16	5	1	10	20	39	16
Barley Mow	16	4	2	10	21	39	14
Ye Olde Sun	16	3	3	10	22	42	12

Division Two

	P	W	D	L	F	A	Pts
East Drayton	20	14	4	2	70	23	46
Morton Amateurs +3	20	11	4	5	85	42	40
Marshalls Sports	20	10	6	4	54	27	36
Jack & Jill	20	9	5	6	61	37	32
Bridon	20	9	3	8	50	44	30
Wroot -3	20	10	3	7	41	47	30
Epworth Town 'A'	20	8	3	9	38	45	27
Elm Cottage	20	7	5	8	58	60	26
Saxilby Athletic	20	7	4	9	53	50	25
Crooked Billet	20	4	2	14	39	85	14
Wheeli Old Boys	20	1	1	18	23	112	4

GRANTHAM & DISTRICT LEAGUE

Premier Division

	P	W	D	L	F	A	Pts
Buckminster United	24	21	1	2	86	23	64
Ruskington Rovers	24	17	4	3	96	35	55
Whatton United	24	15	4	5	89	41	49
Three Gables Colts	24	13	7	4	83	34	46
Greyhounds	24	14	4	6	82	33	46
Harrowby United Res.	24	11	2	11	55	73	35
Pointon	24	10	4	10	70	72	34
Cherry Tree	24	9	4	11	48	56	31
Sleaford United	24	9	3	12	76	48	30
Croxton	24	7	3	14	32	70	24
Ancaster Rovers	24	5	3	16	31	78	18
Gonerby	24	4	2	18	42	84	14
Morton	24	1	0	23	12	133	3

Division One

	P	W	D	L	F	A	Pts
RHP Newark	26	22	2	2	106	32	68
Balderton Old Boys	26	20	0	6	106	45	60
Barkston & Syston	26	18	5	3	86	46	59
Jubilee Bourne	26	16	4	6	63	42	52
Odd House	26	16	4	6	63	52	52
Skillington	26	12	5	9	47	52	41
Bottesford Town Res.	26	11	0	15	48	65	33
Caythorpe	26	10	3	13	59	85	33
Heckington Millers	26	9	3	14	55	79	30
Pointon Res.	26	9	3	14	56	77	30
Baston	26	6	4	16	43	83	22
Ancaster Rovers Res. -6	26	4	2	20	37	94	14
Croxton Res.	26	3	4	19	38	76	13

GRAVESEND LEAGUE

Premier Division

	P	W	D	L	F	A	Pts
Viewpoint	18	14	3	1	52	23	45
Lullingstone Castle	18	13	2	3	45	13	41
The Old Prince of Orange	18	9	3	6	34	25	30
Craggs Farm	18	7	5	6	32	27	26
Ace of Clubs	18	5	4	9	27	50	19
Horton Kirby -3	18	5	2	11	38	29	17
Real Man of Kent	18	0	1	17	12	87	1

Division One

	P	W	D	L	F	A	Pts
Heathview United	24	21	1	2	127	33	64
Waterloo	24	18	2	4	77	45	56
Stone Club & Institute	24	14	5	5	77	42	47
Meopham	24	12	4	8	85	57	40
Earl Grey	24	11	2	11	54	64	35
AZ '82	24	11	1	12	70	61	34
Culverstone United	24	5	4	15	41	103	19
Fleetway Printers	24	3	1	16	46	111	10
Oakfield	24	0	2	18	27	152	2

Division Two

	P	W	D	L	F	A	Pts
Beausports							
Joydens Wood							

GREAT YARMOUTH & DISTRICT LEAGUE

Division One

	P	W	D	L	F	A	Pts
Catfield	20	19	1	0	133	14	58
Arches	20	17	2	1	94	27	53
Great Yarmouth Tn Hall	20	11	3	6	69	55	36
Golfers Arms	20	11	2	7	61	46	35
MK United -3	20	10	0	10	58	41	27
Albert Tavern	20	8	2	10	46	47	26
Gt Yarmouth Peggottys	20	6	4	10	47	69	22
Caister 'A'	20	5	2	13	27	76	17
Reedham	20	4	2	14	35	69	14
The Sunningdale	20	4	1	15	42	76	13
Great Yarmouth Peelers	20	3	1	16	40	89	10

Division Two

	P	W	D	L	F	A	Pts
Clipper Schooner	24	19	2	3	76	27	59
Caister 'B'	24	14	5	5	82	47	47
Lacon Arms -6	24	14	5	5	73	46	41
Gunton	24	10	3	11	60	62	33
MK United Res.	24	9	4	11	61	53	31
Hemsby	24	8	5	11	51	52	29
Carpathians	24	8	3	13	52	61	27
Prostar Windows	24	8	2	14	42	50	26
Paperclip	24	8	3	13	40	69	27
Prince Consort -3	24	8	5	11	53	68	26
Shrublands	24	5	2	17	53	67	17
Martham 'A'	24	3	2	19	59	114	11

GRIMSBY LEAGUE

Division One

	P	W	D	L	F	A	Pts
The Fiddler	16	14	2	0	76	12	44
AS Motors	16	11	2	3	50	24	35
Immingham Bluestone	16	10	2	4	67	35	32
Stallingborough	16	8	3	5	67	35	27
MRF	16	7	4	5	43	43	25
Seven Seas	16	7	3	6	43	51	24
Duke of Wellington	16	5	2	9	33	70	17
Jubilee Quest	16	5	0	11	59	46	15
Auto Trail	16	1	0	15	18	125	3

Division Two

	P	W	D	L	F	A	Pts
Lakeside	16	16	0	0	101	16	48
Drywall Athletic	16	12	0	4	54	30	36
AS Motors Res.	16	11	1	4	43	42	34
Mitchells	16	9	0	7	76	57	27
Blossom Way	16	7	2	7	72	48	23
Caistor Tennyson	16	7	0	9	68	44	21
FB Old Boys	16	4	2	10	44	77	14
Laceby	16	2	2	12	26	87	8
Arcadia	16	0	1	15	22	102	1

GUERNSEY LEAGUE
(Sure Mobile)

Priaulx League

	P	W	D	L	F	A	Pts
Belgrave Wanderers	24	19	2	3	80	23	59
St Martins AC	24	15	2	7	57	34	47
Northerners AC	24	14	3	7	57	34	45
Sylvans	24	12	4	8	43	43	40
Guernsey Rangers	24	9	1	14	36	50	28
Vale Recreation	24	4	4	16	21	52	16
Rovers AC	24	1	2	21	10	85	5

Jackson League

	P	W	D	L	F	A	Pts
Belgrave Wanderers Res.	18	14	1	3	77	31	43
St Martins AC Res.	18	12	4	2	64	32	40
Sylvans Res.	18	11	5	2	62	50	38
Guernsey Rangers Res.	18	8	5	5	26	48	29
Vale Recreation Res.	18	8	3	7	25	50	27
Northerners AC Res.	18	4	2	12	33	56	14
Rovers AC Res.	18	3	2	13	27	57	11

Railway League

	P	W	D	L	F	A	Pts
Vale Recreation 'A'	24	19	2	3	76	27	59
St Martins AC 'A'	24	15	5	4	82	47	50
Belgrave Wanderers 'A' -3	24	14	5	5	73	46	47
Sylvans 'A'	24	14	4	6	78	61	46
Guernsey Rangers 'A'	24	10	3	11	60	62	33
Northerners AC 'A'	24	9	4	11	61	53	31
Rovers AC 'A'	24	8	6	10	42	50	30
Port City	24	8	4	12	40	69	28
Bavaria Nomads	24	7	5	12	53	67	26
Island Police	24	3	2	19	59	114	11

GUILDFORD & WOKING ALLIANCE

Premier Division

	P	W	D	L	F	A	Pts
University of Surrey	22	15	4	3	63	19	49
Abbey Rangers	22	14	4	4	57	27	46
Burpham	22	14	4	4	53	30	46
Hambledon	22	11	4	7	56	36	37
AFC Bourne	22	11	4	7	49	35	37
Lightwater United	22	10	5	7	41	36	35
Millmead	22	11	1	10	50	66	34
Hersham	22	6	3	13	43	70	21
Holmbury St Mary	22	6	3	13	56	72	21
Milford & Witley 'A'	22	5	4	13	33	57	19
Addlestone Town	22	3	5	14	28	52	14
Bedfont Green 'A'	22	3	4	15	29	63	13

Division One

	P	W	D	L	F	A	Pts
Pirbright Sports	20	16	2	2	64	23	50
Emmanuel	20	14	2	4	69	32	44
University of Surrey Res.	20	13	3	4	57	30	42
Surrey Athletic	20	8	5	7	48	46	29
West Byfleet Albion	20	7	3	10	39	49	24
G'ford City Weysiders 'A'	20	7	2	11	39	49	23
Border & Heath End	20	7	1	12	42	46	22
Weybrook Wanderers	20	5	5	10	24	46	20
New Haw Wanderers	20	6	0	14	31	58	18
Staines Lammas 'A'	20	4	6	10	36	54	18
Shalford 'A'	20	4	3	13	29	54	15

Division Two

	P	W	D	L	F	A	Pts
Shepperton FB	22	19	2	1	78	28	59
Godalming United	22	16	2	4	63	38	50
Abbey Rangers Res.	22	14	2	6	77	44	44
University of Surrey 'A'	22	10	3	9	54	31	33
Chobham Res.	22	9	3	10	43	50	30
Milford & Witley 'B'	22	9	3	10	39	43	30
Lightwater United Res.	22	9	2	11	38	54	29
Oatlands	22	9	1	12	45	58	28
Staines Lammas 'B'	22	9	0	13	45	47	27
Mychett Rangers	22	6	2	14	38	64	20
G'ford City Weysiders 'B'	22	6	1	15	38	71	19
Shottermill/Haslemere 'A'	22	2	3	17	21	49	9

Division Three

	P	W	D	L	F	A	Pts
Bedfont Green 'B'	22	14	6	2	66	35	48
Hersham RBL Res.	22	13	3	6	66	46	42
Burpham Res.	22	10	7	5	48	39	37
AFC Gomshall	22	9	6	7	76	52	33
Spelthorne Sports 'A'	22	10	1	11	61	51	31
Emmanuel Academy	22	10	1	11	47	52	31
Knaphill 'A'	22	8	5	9	46	56	29
Shalford Youth	22	8	4	10	70	70	28
Elstead	22	7	5	10	40	41	26
FC Shepperton	22	7	4	11	40	53	25
Guildford Park	22	5	4	13	40	54	19
Park Barn United	22	5	4	13	47	68	19

WWW.CHERRYRED.CO.UK

Division Four North

	P	W	D	L	F	A	Pts
Cobham United	22	18	2	2	90	19	56
Queen Street 'C'	22	15	2	5	69	42	52
Bedfont Green 'C'	22	15	2	5	79	42	47
New Haw Wanderers Res.	22	11	4	7	81	34	37
AFC Crown & Anchor	22	11	2	9	46	38	35
Woking & Horsell 'A'	22	9	3	10	46	40	27
DJST	22	8	3	11	41	58	20
Christian Club Woking	22	6	2	14	50	58	20
Ripley Village 'A'	22	6	2	14	50	88	20
Surrey Athletic Res.	22	2	3	17	30	88	9
Worplesdon Phoenix 'B'	22	2	2	18	26	89	2
Byfleet	22	0	2	20	21	89	2

Division Four South

	P	W	D	L	F	A	Pts
AFC Chilworth	22	19	2	1	88	24	59
Cranleigh 'A'	22	18	0	4	78	25	54
Weybrook Wanderers Res.	22	12	6	4	85	34	41
Merrow 'A'	22	12	5	5	67	49	35
Holmbury St Mary Res.	22	11	2	9	61	51	35
Worplesdon Phoenix 'A'	22	9	4	9	51	55	31
Hambledon Res.	22	9	0	13	48	77	27
Elstead Res.	22	7	2	13	45	52	23
Godalming United Res.	22	6	2	14	39	67	20
Milford & Witley 'C'	22	6	4	15	38	67	20
Millmead Res.	22	4	3	15	38	78	15
Shalford Youth Res.	22	2	2	18	26	89	8

GWENT CENTRAL LEAGUE
(Knaaf)

Premier Division

	P	W	D	L	F	A	Pts
Trevethin	24	22	1	1	158	37	67
Pandy	24	16	1	7	78	54	49
Usk Town	24	10	3	8	106	72	33
Pontypool Town	24	9	3	11	73	67	29
Goytre Res.	24	11	6	11	51	51	25
Gilwern & District	24	8	1	15	48	86	25
Llanarth	24	4	3	14	55	93	11
Lower New Inn	24	3	2	19	43	145	11

Division One

	P	W	D	L	F	A	Pts
Clydach Wasps Res.	26	23	1	2	127	26	70
Blaenavon Blues Res.	26	19	4	4	86	32	61
Hebden Royd Red Star Res.	26	17	3	6	83	35	54
Fairfield United Res.	26	17	3	6	101	51	54
Tranch Res.	26	15	1	10	81	53	47
Govilon Res.	26	14	3	9	97	47	45
Cwmffrwdoer Sports Res.	26	14	3	9	84	65	45
PILCS Res.	26	12	2	12	59	74	38
Panteg Res.	26	10	3	15	59	82	33
Mardy Res.	26	8	3	15	56	86	27
New Inn Res.	26	8	2	16	57	72	26
Abergavenny Thu. Res. -3	26	6	2	18	48	146	16
Crickhowell Res.	26	6	1	19	48	106	9
Race Res.	26	4	3	19	32	142	3
Sebastopol Res. -3	26	2	0	24	32	142	3

Division Two

	P	W	D	L	F	A	Pts
Clydach Wasps 'A'	22	18	2	2	91	35	60
Trevethin Res.	22	17	1	6	109	42	52
Prescoed	22	15	2	5	93	42	51
Usk Town Res. -6	22	14	1	9	78	43	48
Pontypool Town Res.	22	12	1	11	77	25	43
Gilwern & District Res. -3	22	8	2	14	69	69	26
Llanarth Res.	22	4	1	19	38	133	10

HALIFAX & DISTRICT LEAGUE

Premier Division

	P	W	D	L	F	A	Pts
Hebden Royd Red Star +3	22	17	3	2	67	26	54
Stainland United	22	15	2	5	65	41	51
Halifax Irish Centre	22	11	7	4	60	25	47
Shelf United	22	8	5	9	49	29	40
Siddal Athletic	22	8	4	10	55	47	28
Sowerby United	22	8	2	12	51	50	26
Warley Rangers	22	8	2	12	55	95	26
Midgley United	22	8	2	12	55	77	23
Elland United -3	22	5	5	12	37	52	22
Ryburn United	22	4	2	16	44	81	14
Holmfield	22	4	2	16	44	76	13
Brighouse Old Boys Res.	22	3	4	15	36	76	13

Division One

	P	W	D	L	F	A	Pts
Greetland CC	22	17	5	0	77	19	56
Luddendenfoot	22	15	0	7	85	47	55
St Andrews	22	11	3	8	54	43	36
Stump Cross	22	11	2	9	59	35	35
Calder	22	10	4	8	50	46	34
Northowram	22	9	2	11	44	57	29
Brighouse Old Boys 'A'	22	9	1	12	67	72	28
Martins Nest	22	9	1	12	56	72	28
Denholme United	22	5	4	13	34	68	19
Salem	22	5	1	16	28	44	14
Mixenden United	22	0	4	18	20	87	4
Friendly	22	0	4	18	20	87	4

Division Two

	P	W	D	L	F	A	Pts
Bowling Green	22	18	0	4	82	43	54
Hebden Royd Red Star Res.	22	15	3	4	72	39	48
Sowerby Bridge	22	14	0	8	67	50	42
Halifax Irish Centre Res.	22	11	3	8	64	52	36
Junction	22	11	2	9	64	52	35
Ryburn United Res.	22	8	3	11	38	48	27
Copley United	22	8	2	12	59	82	26
Kingston	22	8	2	12	64	62	26
Shelf United Res.	22	8	2	12	48	62	26
Warley Rangers Res.	22	6	6	10	42	72	24
Stainland United Res.	22	6	5	11	49	72	23
Volunteer Arms	22	4	1	17	46	87	13

Division Three

	P	W	D	L	F	A	Pts
Siddal Athletic Res.	22	18	2	2	134	40	56
Elland Allstars	22	17	4	1	81	48	51
AFC Crossleys	22	15	3	4	93	48	51
Wadsworth United -3	22	13	4	5	72	38	47
Calder Res.	22	13	0	9	51	72	25
Denholme United Res.	22	9	2	11	63	85	22
Sowerby Bridge Res. +3	22	7	1	14	44	91	22
Midgley United Res.	22	6	1	14	49	91	20
Sowerby United Res.	22	6	2	14	44	91	20
Salem Res.	22	3	1	18	33	92	10

Pontefract Sports & Social 'A' – record expunged

HARROGATE & DISTRICT LEAGUE

Premier Division

	P	W	D	L	F	A	Pts
Thirsk Falcons	26	24	2	0	107	32	74
Kirk Deighton Rangers	26	17	4	5	67	32	55
Spa Athletic	26	14	6	6	78	39	51
Thackley Res.	26	14	6	6	66	52	48
Sherwood	26	13	10	3	66	55	42
Eccleshill United Res.	26	11	6	13	67	64	35
Burley Trojans	26	10	2	13	50	61	32
Otley Town 'A'	26	8	9	9	62	61	31
Harlow Hill	26	8	4	13	49	76	31
Bedale Res.	26	9	3	14	55	72	30
Bramham	26	8	5	17	37	77	29
Kirkby Malzeard	26	8	5	17	44	87	29
Pannal Sports	26	5	3	21	36	84	19
Bramhope	26	3	2	21	36	84	11

Division One

	P	W	D	L	F	A	Pts
Pateley Bridge	28	24	0	4	122	48	72
Westbrook YMCA	28	23	1	4	98	36	70
Knaresborough Celtic	28	19	0	9	124	77	57
Otley Rovers	28	18	3	5	95	65	57
Beckwithshaw	28	15	1	10	57	46	48
Dalton Athletic	28	14	1	13	83	63	43
Albert -1	28	13	3	12	80	65	38
Yorkshire Amateur Res.	28	10	5	14	64	70	34
Killinghall Nomads	28	10	4	14	52	84	34
Pool Res.	28	9	4	14	59	80	30
Addingham	28	8	1	19	70	96	26
Masham	28	8	3	18	70	93	21
Pannal Sports Res.	28	2	3	24	34	111	8
Thirsk Falcons Res.	28	2	2	24	34	111	8

Division Two

	P	W	D	L	F	A	Pts
Silsden Res.	26	21	4	1	94	24	64
Clifford	26	16	3	7	77	45	51
Otley Town 'B'	26	15	4	7	57	43	45
Kirk Deighton Rgrs Res.	26	13	4	9	60	45	43
Harold Styans	26	13	3	10	67	56	41
Wigton Moor	26	12	5	9	49	58	41
Sherwood Res.	26	11	5	10	59	58	38
Burley Trojans Res.	26	9	6	11	59	53	33
Harlow Hill Res.	26	8	7	11	44	60	31
Boroughbridge 'A'	26	8	4	13	35	59	29
Ripon City 'A'	26	8	5	13	45	55	29
Spa Athletic Res. -3	26	5	3	18	35	52	27
Beckwithshaw Res.	26	8	3	15	35	41	12
Kirkby Malzeard Res.	26	3	2	21	35	116	11

Division Three

	P	W	D	L	F	A	Pts
Westbrook YMCA Res.	26	23	3	0	105	22	72
Bramham Res.	26	18	4	4	93	38	58
Wetherby Athletic 'A'	26	14	7	5	83	45	49
Catterick Village	26	14	4	8	83	42	46
Hampsthwaite United	26	11	7	8	56	76	43
Brafferton Rangers -3	26	11	7	8	50	50	40
Pannal Sports 'A'	26	12	3	11	79	79	39
Thirsk Falcons 'A'	26	9	6	11	66	63	33
Pateley Bridge Res.	26	9	5	12	60	76	32
Pool 'A'	26	7	7	12	68	78	28
Addingham Res.	26	6	4	16	75	78	21
Ripon Red Arrows +3	26	5	4	17	45	99	22
Helperby United	26	5	4	17	45	106	19
Otley Rovers Res.	26	4	3	19	29	84	15

HEREFORDSHIRE LEAGUE
(Hereford Times)

Premier Division

	P	W	D	L	F	A	Pts
Woofferton	28	23	1	4	107	45	70
Sutton United	28	11	3	1	58	16	47
Ewyas Harold	28	21	4	3	91	26	36
Colwall Rangers	28	17	6	5	80	53	57
Hereford Lads Club	28	13	4	11	62	48	43
Bromyard Town Res.	28	13	4	11	53	54	40
Wellington Rangers	28	12	2	14	72	69	38
Ledbury Town Res.	28	12	2	14	49	81	38
Kington Town	28	11	2	15	57	77	35
Pegasus Juniors Res.	28	10	3	15	66	59	33
Bartestree	28	9	6	13	48	73	31
Westfields Res.	28	9	4	15	15	84	22
Leominster Town	28	7	1	20	38	86	19
Hinton Res.	28	8	6	1	21	54	14
Fownhope	28	4	2	22	21	111	14

Division One

	P	W	D	L	F	A	Pts
Ross Town	18	15	2	1	58	16	47
Holme Lacy	18	10	6	2	74	26	36
Wellington Rangers Colts	18	9	4	5	47	45	31
Stoke Prior	18	9	1	8	55	37	29
Shobdon	18	7	3	8	37	35	24
Weston	18	7	1	10	35	39	21
Ewyas Harold Res. -3	18	6	3	8	37	39	21
Fownhope Res.	18	5	6	10	26	51	10
Orcop Juniors -6	18	4	3	11	31	51	6
Kington Town Res. -6	18	3	3	12	29	66	6

Division Two

	P	W	D	L	F	A	Pts
Hereford Lads Club Colts	18	12	1	1	51	21	40
Burghill	18	11	4	3	47	27	36
Woofferton Res.	18	10	4	4	37	25	34
Ross Town Res.	18	8	4	6	36	24	28
Weobley	18	8	3	7	30	26	27
Leintwardine Colts	18	8	1	9	41	36	25
Pegasus Juniors Colts -3	18	7	3	9	36	42	20
Bartestree Res.	18	5	5	13	25	42	14
Orleton -3	18	5	3	10	25	41	12
Hereford Civil Service	18	2	1	15	21	65	7

HERTFORD & DISTRICT LEAGUE

Premier Division	P	W	D	L	F	A	Pts
Bengeo Trinity	16	11	3	2	35	22	25
Goffs Oak	16	11	2	3	40	19	24
Hertford Heath Res.	16	8	4	4	40	20	20
Greenbury United	16	7	4	5	33	23	18
Westmill	16	7	4	5	26	25	18
Harlow Link	16	5	3	8	25	32	13
Waltham Abbey 'A'	16	3	6	7	25	37	12
Inter	16	3	2	11	19	34	8
Thundridge United	16	2	2	12	24	55	6

Division One	P	W	D	L	F	A	Pts
Baldock Cannon	18	13	4	1	66	21	30
Buntingford Wanderers	18	12	3	3	43	25	27
Cottered	18	11	4	3	48	28	26
Elizabeth Allen Old Boys	18	9	3	6	37	30	21
Broxbourne Badgers	18	8	3	7	44	30	19
Watton-at-Stone	18	7	1	10	50	63	15
Wodson Park 'A'	18	6	2	10	38	45	14
Saracens	18	6	1	11	24	38	13
Bengeo Trinity Res.	18	5	2	11	26	49	12
Westmill Res.	18	1	1	16	19	66	3

Division Two	P	W	D	L	F	A	Pts
County Hall Rangers	16	11	1	4	47	36	23
Much Hadham	16	11	0	5	38	29	22
Royston Town 'A'	16	9	2	5	53	29	20
Hatfield Town 'A'	16	7	3	6	51	42	17
Braughing Rovers	16	7	3	6	40	33	17
Broxbourne Badgers Res.	16	5	5	6	38	41	15
Elizabeth Allen OB Res.	16	6	1	9	34	46	13
Mangrove	16	2	5	9	27	39	9
Hoddesdon Old Boys	16	3	2	11	19	52	8

Division Three	P	W	D	L	F	A	Pts
Heath Juniors	20	15	3	2	64	25	33
Waltham Abbey 'B'	20	14	3	3	69	32	31
Elizabeth Allen OB 'A'	20	12	4	4	80	42	28
Oracle Components	20	12	4	4	66	28	28
Mangrove Res.	20	9	2	9	39	40	20
Bury Rangers Res.	20	9	1	10	42	49	19
Buntingford Wdrs Res.	20	8	2	10	48	46	18
Cottered Res.	20	7	2	11	33	55	16
Watton-at-Stone Res.	20	4	4	12	40	97	12
Roydon Spartans	20	5	1	14	53	70	11
E-Trade Deaconsfield	20	1	2	17	19	69	4

HOPE VALLEY AMATEUR LEAGUE

Premier Division	P	W	D	L	F	A	Pts
Brampton	26	21	1	4	99	36	64
Whaley Bridge	26	18	3	5	69	35	57
Buxton Town	26	18	2	6	78	39	56
Tintwistle Villa	26	14	2	10	77	47	44
Harpur Hill	26	13	5	8	53	52	44
Dove Holes	26	13	4	9	82	57	43
Bradwell Sports	26	13	4	9	78	58	43
Dronfield Woodhouse	26	11	5	10	50	64	38
Hayfield	26	12	1	13	77	60	37
Duckmanton Community	26	10	2	14	60	66	32
Hathersage	26	8	3	15	59	84	27
Tideswell United	26	5	3	18	34	99	18
Furness Vale	26	3	3	20	39	97	12
Blazing Rag	26	3	2	21	30	91	11

Division A	P	W	D	L	F	A	Pts
Grindleford	24	20	3	1	113	29	63
Dronfield Town 'A'	24	20	1	3	105	19	61
Dove Holes Res.	24	15	4	5	54	30	49
Hunters Bar	24	14	3	7	74	52	45
Whaley Bridge Res.	24	13	4	7	66	59	43
Bakewell Town	24	11	4	9	54	59	37
Chinley	24	9	5	10	59	66	32
Dronfield W'dhouse Res.	24	9	4	11	49	60	31
Buxworth	24	6	4	14	60	78	22
Queens	24	7	1	16	46	74	22
Totley Sports	24	5	2	17	50	85	17
Edale -3	24	5	4	15	43	77	16
Baslow	24	1	3	20	41	126	6

Division B	P	W	D	L	F	A	Pts
Hayfield Res.	24	16	3	5	83	35	51
Buxton Christians	24	14	6	4	73	42	48
Calver	24	14	6	4	63	36	48
Grindleford Res.	24	14	3	7	68	43	45
Dronfield Town 'B'	24	12	4	8	55	41	40
Red Lion	24	11	4	9	72	68	37
Stoney Middleton	24	10	2	12	53	57	32
Hathersage Res.	24	8	7	9	56	50	31
Blazing Rag Res.	24	8	5	11	61	75	29
Edale Res.	24	8	2	14	51	66	26
Youlgrave United	24	6	4	14	42	85	22
Furness Vale Res.	24	5	3	16	38	81	18
Bradwell Sports Res.	24	4	3	17	32	68	15

HUDDERSFIELD & DISTRICT LEAGUE

Division One	P	W	D	L	F	A	Pts
Heywood Irish Centre	22	17	3	2	61	25	54
Uppermill	22	13	4	5	49	32	43
Wooldale Wanderers	22	9	8	5	39	26	35
Diggle	22	10	5	7	47	51	35
Britannia Sports	22	10	3	9	49	47	33
Newsome WMC	22	8	5	9	51	34	29
Meltham Athletic Res.	22	7	8	7	39	45	29
New Mill	22	6	8	8	33	35	26
Lepton Highlanders	22	7	3	12	38	50	24
Shepley	22	5	8	9	39	43	23
Aimbry	22	5	3	14	39	57	18
Slaithwaite United	22	5	2	15	28	67	17

Division Two	P	W	D	L	F	A	Pts
Sovereign Sports	26	18	4	4	73	37	58
Hepworth United	26	16	5	5	84	42	53
Netherton	26	17	2	7	69	51	53
Scholes	26	13	4	9	78	66	43
Berry Brow Liberals	26	11	9	6	75	55	42
Westend	26	10	7	9	54	44	37
Lindley Liberals	26	11	4	11	63	65	37
Moldgreen	26	10	5	11	80	84	35
Honley	26	9	7	10	58	59	34
Kirkheaton Rovers	26	8	7	11	52	57	31
KKS Ashbrow	26	8	3	15	45	60	27
Mount	26	8	3	15	49	75	27
Scissett	26	6	8	12	40	52	26
Shelley	26	2	2	22	22	95	8

Division Three	P	W	D	L	F	A	Pts
Lamb Inn	26	22	2	2	121	35	68
Cumberworth	26	18	7	1	71	18	61
The Stag	25	15	3	7	74	53	48
Skelmanthorpe	26	14	5	7	83	57	47
SC Cowlersley	26	14	4	8	63	39	46
Heyside	26	12	8	6	62	51	44
Upperthong	25	10	3	12	43	47	33
Holmbridge	26	9	3	14	65	68	30
HV Academicals	26	7	8	11	47	59	29
Paddock Rangers	26	8	5	13	62	80	29
Grange Moor	26	6	6	14	39	56	24
Linthwaite Athletic	26	7	2	17	61	107	23
Lindley	26	6	4	16	50	99	22
Coach & Horses	26	2	2	22	35	107	8

Division Four	P	W	D	L	F	A	Pts
Dalton Crusaders	27	19	5	3	77	26	62
YMCA	27	17	3	7	73	40	54
Brook Motors	27	16	5	6	89	52	53
Royal Dolphins	27	14	3	10	73	68	45
Cartworth Moor	27	14	3	10	86	74	45
Flockton	27	12	3	12	63	50	39
Hade Edge	27	10	7	10	54	62	37
Fenay Bridge	27	8	2	17	49	87	26
Farnley Terriers	27	3	7	17	42	72	16
Marsden 'A'	27	2	2	23	38	113	8

Reserve Division One	P	W	D	L	F	A	Pts
Diggle Res.	22	17	0	5	75	39	51
Meltham Athletic 'A'	22	15	2	5	63	50	47
Uppermill Res.	22	14	2	6	78	38	44
Newsome WMC Res.	22	11	5	6	78	44	38
Kirkheaton Rovers Res.	22	12	2	8	57	63	38
Honley Res.	22	9	3	10	39	50	30
Heywood Irish Centre Res.	22	9	2	11	55	63	29
Lindley Liberals Res.	22	9	2	11	57	71	29
Lepton Highlanders Res.	22	7	6	9	42	45	27
Berry Brow Liberals Res.	22	6	7	9	46	57	25
Aimbry Res.	22	3	2	17	42	73	11
New Mill Res.	22	2	3	17	35	74	9

Reserve Division Two	P	W	D	L	F	A	Pts
Netherton Res.	24	19	1	4	76	23	58
Britannia Sports Res.	24	14	4	6	68	42	46
Shepley Res.	24	14	1	9	64	52	43
Wooldale Wanderers Res.	24	14	1	9	52	46	43
Cumberworth Res.	24	14	0	10	66	46	42
Heyside Res.	24	12	6	6	60	48	42
Diggle 'A'	24	9	5	10	49	47	32
Uppermill 'A'	24	10	1	13	52	49	31
Scholes Res.	24	8	5	11	34	45	29
Slaithwaite United Res.	24	8	2	14	46	65	26
Scissett Res.	24	5	5	14	43	67	20
Linthwaite Athletic Res.	24	6	1	17	40	74	19
Mount Res.	24	4	6	14	29	75	18

Reserve Division Three	P	W	D	L	F	A	Pts
Westend Res.	22	18	3	1	97	34	57
HV Academicals Res.	22	14	2	6	72	59	44
Kirkheaton Rovers 'A'	22	13	2	7	64	54	41
Netherton 'A'	22	11	5	6	85	65	38
Meltham Athletic 'B'	22	11	4	7	82	54	37
Holmbridge Res.	22	10	2	10	76	64	32
Paddock Rangers Res.	22	10	2	10	75	64	32
Upperthong Res.	22	10	1	11	59	56	31
Brook Motors Res.	22	10	1	11	58	76	31
Shelley Res.	22	7	4	11	57	67	25
Cartworth Moor Res.	22	2	1	19	31	114	7
Honley 'A'	22	1	3	18	31	80	6

Reserve Division Four	P	W	D	L	F	A	Pts
KKS Ashbrow Res.	18	15	2	1	97	23	47
Cumberworth 'A'	17	14	1	2	68	35	43
New Mill 'A'	18	9	3	6	44	52	30
Britannia Sports 'A'	18	8	3	7	36	34	27
Lindley Res.	18	6	5	7	45	48	23
Flockton Res.	18	7	1	10	23	61	22
Skelmanthorpe Res.	18	6	3	9	43	42	21
Hade Edge Res.	18	5	3	10	41	52	18
Scholes 'A'	18	6	0	12	38	52	18
Mount 'A'	17	2	1	14	22	58	7

Coach & Horses Res. – record expunged

ILFORD & DISTRICT LEAGUE

Premier Division	P	W	D	L	F	A	Pts
AFC Kings	16	11	4	1	65	21	37
Baronsmere -4	16	9	3	4	43	24	26
FC Barolle -3	16	8	3	5	36	31	24
Titans United	16	7	3	6	25	23	24
Seven Kings Singh Sabha	16	6	5	5	38	39	23
St Vincents	16	6	4	6	34	38	22
London & Essex	16	6	2	8	27	38	20
St Francis	16	5	2	9	31	41	17
Newham Warriors	16	0	2	14	12	56	2

Prince Alfred – record expunged

Division One	P	W	D	L	F	A	Pts
Cranes United	18	16	2	0	64	13	50
Castle United	18	12	4	2	68	20	40
Forest United	18	8	6	4	43	44	30
Puma 2000	18	8	3	7	40	43	27
Glendale	18	8	2	8	36	34	26
Chingford Athletic	18	4	6	8	26	37	18
Ryan 'A'	18	4	5	9	19	37	17
RIP London	18	4	3	11	28	61	15
Melbourne Sports Res.	18	2	8	8	30	42	14
Westill	18	2	5	11	22	45	11

Eastern Lions – record expunged

Division Two	P	W	D	L	F	A	Pts
Durning	16	13	3	0	70	23	42
Redbridge Elite	16	12	3	1	71	24	39
Debden Colts	16	9	1	6	46	31	28
Manor Park United	16	9	1	6	33	31	28
Newham United 'A'	16	8	2	6	38	41	26
East Ham Inter	16	4	3	9	33	41	15
Trelawney	16	4	2	10	25	54	14
The Hammers	16	2	2	12	21	54	8
St Francis Res.	16	1	3	12	19	57	6

Leytonstone – record expunged

WWW.CHERRYRED.CO.UK

ISLE OF MAN LEAGUE

Division Three

	P	W	D	L	F	A	Pts
Midland	18	12	3	3	63	38	39
Ryan 'B'	17	10	2	5	59	43	32
Alliance United	18	8	1	9	39	55	25
Castle United Res.	17	7	3	7	52	52	24
Newham Royals	18	7	2	9	65	68	23
Forest United Res.	18	5	3	10	43	63	18
Dynamo Miguel	18	5	2	11	41	63	17

Ascot United – record expunged
East Barking United – record expunged

Premier Division

	P	W	D	L	F	A	Pts
St Georges	24	23	0	1	115	24	69
Peel	24	19	1	4	76	24	58
Douglas High School OB	24	14	3	7	57	46	45
Laxey	24	13	4	7	62	51	43
Union Mills	24	10	6	8	52	48	36
Rushen	24	9	4	11	56	62	31
St Marys	24	9	4	11	51	58	31
Gymnasium	24	9	1	14	51	62	28
Corinthians	24	6	5	13	62	67	23
Ramsey	24	6	5	13	53	53	23
Ayre	24	5	6	13	36	65	21
St Johns	24	5	1	18	31	77	16
Douglas Royal	24	3	2	19	38	95	11

Division One

	P	W	D	L	F	A	Pts
Colby	26	25	1	0	153	21	76
Michael	26	19	4	3	135	32	61
Pulrose	26	17	4	5	104	38	55
Castletown	26	17	4	5	61	56	55
Marown	26	13	3	10	74	64	42
Police	26	12	4	10	83	70	40
Onchan	26	11	2	13	63	73	39
Malew	26	10	5	11	51	69	35
Braddan	26	10	3	13	63	73	33
Douglas & District	26	10	4	16	64	106	34
Ronaldsway	26	6	4	16	44	105	22
Foxdale	26	5	3	18	36	134	18
RYCOB	26	3	1	22	30	134	10
Jurby	26	3	0	23	28	141	9

Combination Division One

	P	W	D	L	F	A	Pts
Peel Res.	24	21	1	2	79	25	64
Union Mills Res.	24	16	1	7	79	44	52
Douglas Hi. Sch'l OB Res.	24	15	1	8	80	57	50
St Georges Res.	24	14	3	7	80	41	45
Corinthians Res.	24	14	0	10	71	47	42
Laxey Res.	24	10	2	12	79	63	32
Ramsey Res.	24	10	2	12	64	85	32
Douglas Royal Res.	24	6	3	15	60	89	19
St Johns Res.	24	5	3	18	62	78	18
Ayre Res. -3	24	6	2	16	41	94	17
Gymnasium Res. -3	24	6	1	17	48	103	13
St Marys Res. -3	24	3	5	16	64	124	11

Combination Division Two

	P	W	D	L	F	A	Pts
Michael Res.	26	22	4	0	131	33	64
Colby Res.	26	17	3	6	108	47	52
Castletown Res. -3	26	17	4	5	93	57	49
Marown Res. -3	26	15	4	7	103	54	44
Braddan Res.	26	10	5	11	54	61	35
Malew Res.	26	10	3	13	69	63	33
Onchan Res.	26	10	2	14	63	82	32
Ronaldsway Res.	26	9	3	14	74	86	30
Pulrose Res. -3	26	9	2	15	74	74	26
Police Res.	26	7	5	14	59	86	26
RYCOB Res. -3	26	7	1	18	48	131	16
Jurby Res.	26	5	1	20	43	93	16
Douglas & District Res.	26	5	1	20	33	186	3
Foxdale Res.	26	1	0	25			

ISLE OF WIGHT LEAGUE

Division One

	P	W	D	L	F	A	Pts
West Wight	26	23	2	1	105	18	71
Shanklin	26	14	4	8	89	33	46
Cowes Sports 'A'	26	14	4	8	68	53	44
Binstead & COB	26	13	5	8	75	44	44
Oakfield -1	26	12	8	6	69	44	43
Sandown & Lake	26	11	1	14	39	57	34
Newport IOW Res.	26	9	5	12	55	61	31
Niton	26	8	7	11	53	55	30
Red Star Spartans	26	8	6	12	53	60	30
St Helens Blue Star	26	8	4	12	40	56	28
Ventnor	26	7	7	12	40	59	28
Brighstone	26	7	2	16	43	64	24
East Cowes Vic. Ath. Res.	26	6	1	19	43	64	24
Yarmouth & Calbourn	26	1	3	22	25	100	6

L-ZINGARI COMBINATION

Division One

	P	W	D	L	F	A	Pts
NELTC Res.	22	16	4	2	57	19	52
Old Xaverians Res.	22	12	4	6	64	18	40
Aintree Villa Res.	22	12	4	6	52	40	40
Sacre Coeur F'r Pupils Res.	22	10	4	8	57	38	34
South Liverpool Res.	22	9	4	9	57	47	31
Birchfield Res.	22	9	4	9	44	31	31
Stoneycroft Res.	22	9	2	11	41	36	29
Leyfield Res.	22	8	1	13	44	51	25
Warbreck Res.	22	7	2	13	46	72	23
Edge Hill BCOB Res.	22	6	1	13	34	70	19
Alsop Old Boys	22	4	0	18	34	72	12
Collegiate Old Boys Res.	22	2	2	18	34	76	8

Division Two

	P	W	D	L	F	A	Pts
Mossley Hill Ath. Res.	22	19	1	2	65	20	58
BRNESC Res.	22	14	3	5	77	43	45
MANWEB	22	12	4	6	70	45	40
Walton Community	22	10	0	12	64	60	30
Liobians Res.	22	7	6	12	55	58	28
Mexoc	22	7	6	9	52	55	25
Alsop Old Boys Res.	22	7	2	13	50	63	23
Polish	22	6	2	14	40	66	20
Essenmay Old Boys Res.	22	6	1	15	40	76	19
Rockville Wallasey Res.	22	6	1	15	35	76	19
Chatsworth	22	3	1	16	34	87	12

JERSEY COMBINATION

Division One

	P	W	D	L	F	A	Pts
St Paul's	16	13	1	2	51	31	40
Trinity	16	11	4	1	35	15	37
Jersey Scottish	16	9	4	5	37	16	29
St Peter	16	8	3	5	31	22	27
Rozel Rovers	16	6	2	8	23	39	19
Jersey Wanderers	16	6	0	10	21	24	18
Grouville	16	6	0	10	32	30	18
Portuguese	16	4	2	10	22	39	14
First Tower United	16	1	1	14	8	47	4

Division Two

	P	W	D	L	F	A	Pts
St Ouen	18	13	3	2	64	19	42
Sporting Academics	18	13	2	3	67	24	41
Beeches Old Boys	18	10	5	3	42	31	35
Jersey Nomads	18	8	3	7	45	33	27
St Clement	18	8	1	9	49	44	25
Magpies	18	7	3	8	40	48	24
St Brelade	18	7	0	11	32	47	21
St John	18	4	1	13	19	54	13
St Lawrence	18	3	0	15	16	63	19
St Martin/SCF -1	18	0	3	15	19	69	3

Reserve Division One

	P	W	D	L	F	A	Pts
St Paul's Res.	16	10	4	2	52	26	34
St Peter Res.	16	8	5	3	35	35	29
Jersey Wanderers Res.	16	8	2	6	49	41	29
Grouville Res.	16	6	6	4	40	38	24
Jersey Scottish Res.	16	6	4	13	38	38	22
First Tower United Res.	16	5	1	10	34	38	16
St Brelade Res.	16	3	0	13	29	64	9

Reserve Division Two

	P	W	D	L	F	A	Pts
Portuguese Res.	18	14	2	2	80	18	44
St Clement Res.	18	10	2	6	65	31	32
Sporting Academics Res.	18	10	5	3	49	26	35
Trinity Res.	18	9	3	5	51	37	33
St John Res.	18	8	7	5	51	37	27
Jersey Nomads Res.	18	6	4	8	38	42	22
Beeches Old Boys Res.	18	5	3	10	29	63	14
St Martin/SCF Res.	18	4	2	12	29	62	13
Magpies Res.	18	3	4	11	23	80	13
St Lawrence Res.	18	2	1	16	23	80	7

Third Team Division

	P	W	D	L	F	A	Pts
Grouville 'A'	22	19	0	3	100	17	57
Jersey Wanderers 'A'	22	18	3	1	89	28	57
St Peter 'A'	22	15	3	4	84	35	48
St Brelade 'A'	22	11	5	6	76	58	38
Rozel Rovers 'A'	22	10	3	9	76	58	33
St Clement 'A'	22	10	1	11	46	56	31
St Ouen 'A'	22	7	5	10	64	62	26
St Martin/SCF 'A' -1	22	5	5	12	32	72	19
Sporting Academics 'A' +2	22	5	4	13	34	72	15

KIDDERMINSTER & DISTRICT LEAGUE

Premier Division

	P	W	D	L	F	A	Pts
Gigmill	28	22	4	2	125	59	70
Wyre Forest	28	21	4	5	99	50	65
Millfields -3	28	20	4	4	107	46	61
Cradley Heath	28	17	5	6	78	38	56
Ounsdale	28	13	6	9	62	38	45
Ounsdale Athletic	28	13	5	10	53	67	41
Two Gates	28	12	5	11	55	68	39
Oldswinford Harriers	28	11	4	13	58	71	31
Kinver	28	9	4	15	58	68	31
KS Athletic	28	10	1	17	50	89	31
Albron	28	8	2	18	50	81	24

Division One

	P	W	D	L	F	A	Pts
Quarry Bank	26	19	4	3	111	44	61
Areley Kings	26	18	6	2	80	39	56
Parkdale Rovers	26	16	5	5	58	36	50
Lye Town Res.	26	15	5	6	73	56	50
Kings Heath Old Boys	26	15	4	7	91	50	49
Birch Coppice	26	13	1	12	49	38	40
GDIS	26	9	8	9	49	61	30
Dudley Wood Athletic	26	8	4	14	38	68	28
Burlish Olympic	26	8	4	14	38	68	28
Meta Sports	26	8	3	13	49	55	27
Greyhound Inn	26	7	6	13	49	55	25
Tenth Lock	26	6	1	19	52	87	19
Furnace Sports	26	6	2	22	36	98	8

KINGSLEY LEAGUE

	P	W	D	L	F	A	Pts
Bideford Res.	22	19	0	3	100	17	57
North Petherwin	22	18	3	1	89	28	57
South Petherwin	22	15	3	4	84	35	48
Bridgerule	22	11	5	6	76	52	38
Week St Mary Res.	22	10	3	9	76	58	33
Merton	22	10	1	11	46	56	31
Bridge Inn	22	7	5	10	64	62	26
Holsworthy 'A'	22	7	5	10	64	62	26
Black Torrington	22	5	4	13	32	52	19
Lifton Res.	22	5	5	15	53	72	15
Kilkhampton Res.	22	4	3	17	34	120	9
Hartland 'A'	22	2	3	17	26	120	9

KINGSTON & DISTRICT LEAGUE

Premier Division

	P	W	D	L	F	A	Pts
Molesey Villa	18	12	4	2	58	22	40
Maori Park	18	12	2	4	66	23	38
Chessington KC	18	12	2	4	55	24	38
Robin Hood	18	11	1	4	54	33	35
Summerstown	18	9	4	5	47	26	30
Albert Royals	18	6	4	8	46	46	22
International	18	6	2	10	28	52	20
Kingston Academicals	18	4	3	11	33	73	15
Westside Res.	18	3	3	12	30	51	12
West End Esher	18	2	1	15	19	71	7

Division One	P	W	D	L	F	A	Pts
Fulham Deaf	18	13	5	0	71	17	44
SHFC London	18	13	3	2	71	27	42
Wandsworth Town	18	13	3	2	39	12	42
Claygate Royals	18	12	3	3	54	20	39
Wandsworth Corinthians	18	7	5	6	40	33	26
Esher United	18	6	3	9	32	41	21
Thornton Heath	18	4	2	12	26	63	14
Dynamo Pimlico	18	3	4	11	33	56	13
Repton	18	2	2	14	22	55	8
Spartak Molesey	18	0	4	14	15	79	4

Division Two	P	W	D	L	F	A	Pts
AFC Molesey	16	14	2	0	62	14	44
Kingston Albion	16	11	3	2	41	14	36
Lower Green	16	9	2	5	52	30	29
Wandle	16	8	1	7	50	38	25
Maori Park Res.	16	7	1	8	24	35	22
Old Rutlishians 'A'	16	6	2	8	29	40	20
AC Malden	16	4	3	9	22	42	15
Esher Athletic Res.	16	3	2	11	25	61	11
Merton Social	16	2	0	14	19	50	6

Division Three	P	W	D	L	F	A	Pts
LM United	16	12	2	2	54	26	38
Merton Rovers	16	8	2	6	30	28	26
Surrey Fire	16	5	8	3	27	25	23
Malden Manor	16	6	4	6	42	32	22
Darkside	16	6	4	6	31	32	22
Chessington KC Res.	16	6	2	8	40	37	20
Oxshott Royals	16	6	2	8	41	39	20
Barnslake	16	5	4	7	23	43	19
NPL 'A'	16	3	2	11	28	54	11

Division Four	P	W	D	L	F	A	Pts
Surbiton Eagles	20	15	1	4	62	36	46
Hersham RBL 'A'	20	13	2	5	76	30	41
NPL 'B'	20	12	4	4	65	32	40
Summerstown Res.	20	13	1	6	67	47	40
St Martins	20	10	5	5	47	37	35
Lower Green Res.	20	10	3	7	53	35	33
Red Star	20	6	4	10	40	48	22
Merton Social Res.	20	4	4	12	21	59	16
Chessington KC 'A'	20	4	3	13	42	57	15
Westside 'A'	20	4	2	14	37	70	14
Fulham Deaf Res.	20	4	1	15	23	82	13

Division Five	P	W	D	L	F	A	Pts
Double H	22	21	0	1	102	29	63
AFC Hampton	22	15	4	3	61	34	49
Epsom Casuals	22	15	3	4	78	34	48
Dynamo Kingston	22	10	7	5	43	34	37
Hook Venturers	22	10	5	7	55	41	35
MMB	22	9	5	8	76	52	32
Outcasts	22	9	5	8	46	47	32
AFC Kingston	22	9	2	11	54	73	29
Hersham RBL 'B'	22	8	2	12	42	59	26
Motor Racing Club Ewell	22	3	3	16	54	97	12
Claygate Royals Res.	22	1	6	15	41	80	9
Westside 'B'	22	1	0	21	24	96	3

LANCASHIRE & CHESHIRE AMATEUR LEAGUE

Premier Division	P	W	D	L	F	A	Pts
Beechfield United	26	20	1	5	81	42	61
Old Trafford	26	16	3	7	92	43	51
Rochdalians	26	15	1	10	78	48	46
Abacus Media	26	13	5	8	60	48	44
Hazel Grove	26	13	2	11	52	76	41
Denton Town	26	12	4	10	63	55	40
Mellor	26	11	4	11	47	58	37
Bedians	26	9	6	11	55	63	33
Norris Villa	26	9	6	11	58	69	33
Old Ashtonians	26	9	6	11	40	51	33
Hooley Bridge Celtic	26	9	2	15	54	74	29
Newton	26	8	5	13	50	70	29
Old Standians	26	6	4	16	58	68	22
South Manchester	26	4	7	15	41	64	19

Division One	P	W	D	L	F	A	Pts
Moston Brook Old Boys	26	20	3	3	103	35	63
Whalley Range	26	19	3	4	73	28	60
Old Stretfordians	26	18	3	5	84	50	57
Cheadle Hulme Villa	26	13	7	6	76	60	46
Gatley	26	12	5	9	68	52	41
Hollingworth Old Boys	26	10	7	9	76	56	37
Newton Heath -3	26	10	5	11	66	63	32
Stoconians	26	8	4	14	47	70	28
Irlam Steel	26	8	2	16	47	73	26
Burnage Metro	26	7	5	14	49	81	26
Eagle -3	26	8	4	14	47	68	25
Spurley Hey	26	7	4	15	49	85	25
Chorltonians	26	8	0	18	50	89	24
Parrswood Celtic	26	6	4	16	46	71	22

Division Two	P	W	D	L	F	A	Pts
Govan Athletic	26	19	6	1	82	25	63
New East Manchester	26	19	5	2	105	31	62
Alkrington Dynamos	26	18	3	5	96	45	57
Aldermere	26	16	5	5	72	48	53
VIP	26	15	3	8	71	44	48
Heaton Mersey	26	14	4	8	69	52	46
AFC Oldham	26	13	2	11	71	72	41
Droylsden Amateurs	26	11	5	10	59	64	38
Manchester Rovers	26	7	2	17	76	109	23
Moorside Rangers -3	26	8	1	17	49	64	22
Oldham Victoria	26	5	5	16	36	69	20
Deans	26	5	4	17	42	70	19
St Margaret Marys -3	26	6	1	19	41	84	16
Staly	26	3	0	23	38	130	9

Division A	P	W	D	L	F	A	Pts
South Manchester Res.	26	22	2	2	87	30	68
Whalley Range Res.	26	19	2	5	93	36	59
Mellor Res.	26	15	4	7	70	46	49
Rochdalians Res.	26	15	4	7	61	40	49
Denton Town Res.	26	14	4	8	66	49	46
Burnage Metro Res.	26	11	4	11	68	64	37
Old Ashtonians Res.	26	11	4	11	52	65	37
Bedians Res.	26	11	2	13	60	55	35
Hooley Bridge Celtic Res.	26	10	4	12	50	56	34
Hazel Grove Res.	26	8	3	15	44	67	27
Newton Heath Res.	26	8	3	15	44	78	27
Stoconians Res.	26	6	4	16	46	65	22
Beechfield United Res.	26	5	1	20	35	96	16
Norris Villa Res. -3	26	4	5	17	42	71	14

Division B	P	W	D	L	F	A	Pts
Moston Brook OB Res.	26	21	2	3	101	37	65
Newton Res.	26	15	10	1	96	55	55
Old Stretfordians Res.	26	17	2	7	80	43	53
Burnage Metro 'A'	26	15	3	8	90	46	48
Gatley Res.	26	14	2	10	51	49	44
Stoconians 'A'	26	13	3	10	61	57	42
Old Standians Res.	26	12	2	12	61	70	38
Old Trafford Res.	26	10	4	12	67	68	34
Abacus Media Res.	26	9	3	14	44	69	30
Aldermere Res.	26	7	6	13	61	69	27
Hollingworth OB Res.	26	7	4	15	47	67	25
Cheadle Hulme Villa Res.	26	6	3	17	55	98	21
Spurley Hey Res.	26	6	3	17	45	91	21
Irlam Steel Res.	26	5	3	18	56	96	18

Division C	P	W	D	L	F	A	Pts
Alkrington Dynamos Res.	22	18	2	2	88	34	56
Mellor 'A'	22	16	3	3	68	31	51
Droylsden Amateurs Res.	22	13	0	9	64	47	39
Whalley Range 'A'	22	11	5	6	64	37	38
Old Stretfordians 'A'	22	11	4	7	80	51	37
Parrswood Celtic Res.	22	11	4	7	50	40	37
Chorltonians Res.	22	10	3	9	59	59	33
AFC Oldham Res.	22	8	3	11	48	60	27
Eagle Res.	22	8	2	12	41	61	26
Govan Athletic Res.	22	5	5	12	34	57	20
Stoconians 'B'	22	3	2	17	33	76	11
Oldham Victoria Res.	22	0	3	19	19	95	3

Division D	P	W	D	L	F	A	Pts
Beechfield United 'A'	26	25	1	0	152	28	76
Deans Res.	26	21	2	3	134	38	65
Bedians 'A'	26	15	5	6	81	43	50
Old Stretfordians 'B'	26	16	0	10	90	73	48
Moorside Rgrs Res. -1	26	14	2	10	91	84	43
Hooley Bridge Celtic 'A'	26	13	4	9	63	59	43
Irlam Steel 'A' -3	26	10	9	7	56	48	36
Old Ashtonians 'A'	26	10	5	11	60	72	35
Burnage Metro 'B' -1	26	9	2	15	85	94	28
Mellor 'B'	26	6	6	14	56	75	24
Whalley Range 'B'	26	6	3	17	67	113	21
Chorltonians 'A'	26	4	7	15	62	102	19
Stoconians 'C'	26	5	3	18	59	123	18
Staly Res. -4	26	2	3	21	33	137	5

Division E	P	W	D	L	F	A	Pts
AFC Oldham 'A'	26	20	3	3	96	51	63
Cheadle Hulme Villa 'A'	26	18	3	5	84	39	57
Mellor 'C'	26	18	0	8	89	55	54
Newton Heath 'A' -1	26	17	1	8	95	64	51
Gatley 'A'	26	14	2	10	78	56	44
Newton 'A' -3	26	13	3	10	85	67	39
Burnage Metro 'C'	26	11	5	10	73	63	38
Stoconians 'D'	26	10	5	11	65	60	35
Moston Brook OB 'A'	26	8	6	12	66	81	30
Bedians 'B'	26	8	4	14	52	67	28
Chorltonians 'B'	26	7	4	15	65	116	25
Old Ashtonians 'B' -1	26	5	6	15	54	89	20
Aldermere 'A'	26	5	3	18	53	97	18
Old Stretfordians 'C'	26	5	1	20	40	90	16

LANCASHIRE AMATEUR LEAGUE

Premier Division	P	W	D	L	F	A	Pts
Rossendale Amateurs	26	19	3	4	78	34	60
Little Lever SC	26	19	1	6	63	37	58
Bury Amateurs	26	15	8	3	62	28	53
Old Blackburnians	26	16	5	5	70	39	53
Old Boltonians	26	13	4	9	52	40	43
Old Mancunians	26	12	7	7	50	42	43
Chaddertonians	26	10	4	12	50	38	34
Rochdale St Clements	26	8	5	13	38	49	29
Horwich RMI	26	8	5	13	40	69	29
Bury GSOB	26	6	8	12	38	46	26
Radcliffe Town	26	7	5	14	32	62	26
Lymm	26	4	8	14	33	60	20
Bolton Lads Club	26	5	3	18	30	60	18
Mostonians	26	3	8	15	33	65	17

Division One	P	W	D	L	F	A	Pts
Failsworth Dynamos	26	19	3	4	68	22	60
Old Blackburnians Res.	26	16	4	6	75	30	52
Bolton Wyresdale	26	14	9	3	73	51	51
Castle Hill	26	16	3	7	56	38	51
Tyldesley United	26	15	3	8	58	47	48
Prairie United	26	11	5	10	62	59	38
Spotland Methodists	26	10	3	13	50	60	33
Little Lever SC Res.	26	10	2	14	50	52	32
Thornleigh	26	9	4	13	47	53	31
Chaddertonians Res.	26	8	7	11	40	56	31
Hindley Juniors	26	8	4	14	52	62	28
Broughton Amateurs	26	7	4	15	44	67	25
Bolton Ambassadors	26	5	6	15	42	74	21
Hesketh Casuals	26	4	3	19	34	80	15

Division Two	P	W	D	L	F	A	Pts
Howe Bridge Mills	26	20	4	2	106	22	64
Chew Moor Brook	26	20	4	2	102	26	64
Horwich Victoria	26	21	1	4	104	31	64
Rossendale Amtrs Res.	26	15	4	7	71	41	49
Rochdale St Clements Res.	26	11	4	11	65	71	37
Accrington Loyal Amtrs	26	10	5	11	55	58	35
Astley Bridge	26	10	2	14	67	87	32
Radcliffe Boys	26	10	2	14	64	91	32
Old Boltonians Res.	26	8	7	11	53	66	31
Old Blackburnians 'A'	26	8	6	12	55	78	30
Roach Dynamos	26	7	3	16	53	81	24
Oldham Hulmeians	26	6	2	18	56	104	20
Ladybridge	26	5	4	17	55	108	19
Bacup United	26	4	6	16	61	103	18

Division Three	P	W	D	L	F	A	Pts
Hesketh Casuals Res.	26	16	7	3	75	35	55
Ainsworth	26	15	4	7	62	38	49
Bury GSOB Res.	26	14	6	6	67	43	48
Ashtonians	26	11	9	6	58	40	42
Rochdale St Clements 'A'	26	12	3	11	51	45	39
Little Lever SC 'A'	26	12	3	11	69	72	39
Bury Amateurs Res.	26	11	5	10	66	46	38
Bolton Wyresdale Res.	26	10	8	8	43	44	38
Tottington United	26	10	6	10	55	73	36
Old Mancunians Res.	26	9	5	12	47	51	32
Broughton Amateurs Res.	26	9	5	12	45	49	32
Acc'gton Loyal Amtrs Res.	26	6	6	14	38	76	24
Lymm Res.	26	6	4	16	44	73	22
Radcliffe Town Res.	26	4	3	19	44	79	15

WWW.CHERRYRED.CO.UK

LANCASHIRE LEAGUE
(Lancit Haulage)

East Division
	P	W	D	L	F	A	Pts
Farsley Celtic Res. 'A'	20	12	4	4	52	35	40
Wakefield Res.	20	10	4	6	35	35	34
Howe Bridge Mills Res.	20	10	3	7	42	40	33
Ossett Albion Res.	20	10	2	8	40	40	32
Hyde United Res.	20	8	4	8	28	36	28
Old Blackburnians 'B'	20	8	6	6	28	42	30
Hesketh Casuals 'A'	20	7	6	7	38	41	27
Ossett Town Res.	20	8	3	9	40	27	27
Stalybridge Celtic 'A'	20	7	2	11	38	39	23
Woodley Sports 'A'	20	6	3	11	38	38	21
Guiseley Res.	20	5	7	12	23	42	22
AFC Emley Res. -1	20	5	4	15	27	52	11

West Division
	P	W	D	L	F	A	Pts
Workington Res.	20	17	2	1	77	23	53
Fleetwood Town Res.	20	16	2	2	53	26	50
Leigh RMI Res.	20	12	2	6	45	29	38
Kendal Town Res.	20	12	1	7	50	32	37
Bamber Bridge Res.	20	6	3	11	32	55	21
Darwen Res.	20	6	2	12	33	49	20
Salford City Res.	20	5	4	11	38	39	19
Burscough Res.	20	5	3	12	33	37	18
Formby Res.	20	4	3	13	27	63	15
Lancaster City Res.	20	4	3	13	37	59	15
Barrow Res.	20	4	1	15	26	41	13

Division Four
	P	W	D	L	F	A	Pts
Mostonians Res.	24	18	2	4	94	37	56
Rossendale Amateurs 'A'	24	15	4	5	87	40	49
Horwich RMI Res.	24	14	5	5	70	42	47
Howe Bridge Mills Res.	24	13	6	5	56	34	45
Old Blackburnians 'B'	24	12	8	4	75	36	44
Hesketh Casuals 'A'	24	8	5	11	53	75	29
Castle Hill Res.	24	8	4	12	55	82	28
Horwich Victoria Res.	24	7	5	12	50	56	26
Chaddertonians 'A'	24	6	5	13	46	64	23
Little Lever SC 'B'	24	6	5	13	47	73	23
Old Boltonians 'A'	24	5	7	12	42	70	22
Thornleigh Res.	24	5	4	15	41	78	19

Division Five
	P	W	D	L	F	A	Pts
Bury Amateurs 'A'	24	16	5	3	80	31	53
Bolton Lads Club Res.	24	15	6	3	80	34	51
Acc.Loyal Amateurs 'A' -4	24	16	4	4	73	57	46
Ashtonians Res.	24	11	4	9	56	48	39
Mostonians 'A'	24	11	6	7	59	54	39
Rochdale St Clements 'B'	24	10	5	9	51	48	35
Thornleigh 'A'	24	9	4	11	75	59	32
Old Mancunians 'A'	24	9	4	11	41	47	31
Old Boltonians 'B'	24	9	4	11	48	69	31
Radcliffe Boys Res.	24	7	5	12	50	61	26
Tottington United Res.	24	7	3	14	53	77	24
Ainsworth Res.	24	5	3	16	45	69	18
Oldham Hulmeians Res.	24	4	3	17	29	75	15

Division Six
	P	W	D	L	F	A	Pts
Rossendale Amateurs 'B'	20	14	3	3	64	16	45
Bury GSOB 'A'	20	14	3	3	61	23	45
Oldham Hulmeians 'A'	20	13	2	5	82	50	41
Broughton Amateurs 'A'	20	11	2	7	59	41	35
Hesketh Casuals 'B'	20	10	2	8	57	49	32
Old Mancunians 'B'	20	8	3	9	55	57	27
Lynm 'A'	20	4	11	5	37	45	37
Radcliffe Town 'A'	20	4	5	11	40	55	18
Thornleigh 'B'	20	4	3	13	40	76	13
Bolton Wyresdale 'A'	20	4	1	15	29	61	13
Horwich RMI 'A' -4	20	5	3	17	47	75	12

Division Seven
	P	W	D	L	F	A	Pts
Lynm 'B'	20	17	2	1	81	24	53
Radcliffe Town 'B'	20	15	2	3	87	38	47
Bury Amateurs 'B'	20	10	4	6	59	39	34
Old Blackburnians 'C'	20	10	3	7	50	39	33
Rossendale Amateurs 'C'	20	8	6	6	61	61	30
Broughton Amateurs 'B'	20	8	3	9	58	57	27
Chaddertonians 'B'	20	8	2	10	50	57	27
Bolton Wyresdale 'B'	20	5	4	11	44	59	19
Bury GSOB 'B'	20	4	2	14	32	81	17
Oldham Hulmeians 'B'	20	4	2	14	37	72	12
Spotland Methodists 'A'	20	3	1	16	32	72	12

LEEDS RED TRIANGLE LEAGUE

Premier Division
	P	W	D	L	F	A	Pts
Gate	24	19	3	2	149	56	60
Halton Moor	24	19	3	2	142	39	59
Wykebeck Arms United	24	18	4	2	105	40	57
East Leeds	24	14	4	6	83	54	46
Dewsbury Road Social	24	13	4	7	109	72	41
Seacroft WMC	24	11	3	10	76	71	37
Kippax Welfare	24	11	3	10	71	83	36
Churwell New Inn	24	10	4	10	80	72	34
Amaranth	24	9	2	13	79	91	29
Ekhaya African Sports	24	6	4	14	58	84	22
Merlins	24	4	2	18	48	141	14
Middleton Park	24	2	2	20	60	163	12
Leeds Ventura	24	1	1	22	33	151	4

Farnley Nags Head – record expunged
Gipton – record expunged
Hope Inn – record expunged

Division One
	P	W	D	L	F	A	Pts
Farnley Sports	20	15	5	0	76	21	50
Bainbridge United	20	13	1	6	57	34	40
New Farnley CC	20	13	1	6	53	36	40
Leodis	20	10	1	9	54	39	31
Railway East Ardsley	20	9	2	8	56	46	30
Skinners Arms	20	7	1	10	49	45	28
Dringhton Adwalton	20	6	2	11	30	49	23
Leeds Deaf	20	6	1	10	30	57	19
Squinting Cat	20	6	3	11	37	37	13
Cricketers Arms	20	1	2	17	23	92	5

Dynamo Turbot – record expunged
Kippax Welfare Res. – record expunged
Middleton Park Res. – record expunged
Rowland Road WMC – record expunged
Super Eagles – record expunged

LEICESTER & DISTRICT LEAGUE

Premier Division
	P	W	D	L	F	A	Pts
Barlestone St Giles	26	23	3	0	108	22	72
Desford	26	20	4	2	91	27	64
St Patricks	26	17	2	7	62	39	53
Welby Lane United	26	13	4	9	71	43	43
Cosby United	26	11	4	11	56	53	37
Burbage Old Boys	26	10	6	10	47	48	36
Blaby United	26	10	6	10	49	59	36
Magna	26	10	5	11	51	58	35
Belgrave	26	10	5	11	51	63	35
Glenfield Town	26	11	2	13	49	64	35
Birstall RBL	26	5	5	16	48	81	20
FC Kirkland	26	5	4	16	46	85	19
Queniborough	26	4	3	19	49	72	15
Woodgate/Newfoundpool	26	4	2	20	31	72	14

LEICESTER CITY LEAGUE

Division One
	P	W	D	L	F	A	Pts
Evington	16	12	2	2	46	18	38
Sth Wigston Wanderers	16	12	0	4	51	29	36
New Parks Social	16	8	2	6	47	34	26
Park End	16	6	2	8	40	30	20
Tele Link Taxis	16	6	5	5	43	28	23
Sporting Union	16	5	5	6	43	43	28
Netherhall Rangers	16	4	7	5	36	37	19
FC Rowlatts	16	3	2	11	29	61	11
Mayflower	16	2	0	14	29	82	6

LINCOLN & DISTRICT LEAGUE
(WJ Harrison Printers)

	P	W	D	L	F	A	Pts
Plough Skellingthorpe	26	23	1	2	85	22	70
Ivy Tavern CSA	26	20	2	4	95	28	62
AFC Victory	26	19	1	6	82	33	58
Heckington United	26	18	1	7	73	27	55
RMSC Athletic	26	16	4	6	55	52	52
Horncastle Town Res.	26	13	1	12	52	49	40
FC Rustons United	26	12	4	10	48	48	40
Ruston Sports Res. +3	26	12	4	10	48	48	58
Metheringham -3	26	9	3	14	45	72	27
Market Rasen Town	26	6	4	16	36	65	22
Cherry Knights	26	5	1	20	29	62	16
AFC Maze	26	3	5	18	35	85	14
Harby	26	3	1	22	27	104	10

LIVERPOOL OLD BOYS AMATEUR LEAGUE

Division One
	P	W	D	L	F	A	Pts
Naylorsfield	21	17	2	2	78	23	52
Old Bootleians	22	16	1	5	69	23	49
Alumni	22	13	6	3	61	32	43
Old Xaverians 'A'	18	11	4	3	48	25	37
Old Instonians	22	8	5	9	52	54	29
FC Salle	21	8	4	9	38	53	28
Cardinal Newman	19	8	2	9	42	44	26
Alder 'A'	22	7	1	14	42	65	22
Wavertree WDOB	22	6	4	12	31	64	22
Hope Park	22	6	2	14	31	61	20
Collegiate Old Boys 'A'	21	5	3	13	43	57	18
Sacre Coeur Fmr Pupils 'A'	22	4	5	13	35	61	17

Division Two
	P	W	D	L	F	A	Pts
Waterloo GSOB	22	15	6	1	74	24	51
Oaks Institute Old Boys	22	13	6	3	68	33	45
St Mary's COB	22	12	6	4	61	33	42
Quarry Bank Old Boys Res.	22	13	3	6	62	47	42
Mossley Hill Athletic 'A'	22	7	6	9	35	42	27
Old Cathinians	22	7	4	11	39	46	25
Old Xaverians 'B' -3	22	9	1	12	57	72	25
Alsop Old Boys 'A'	22	7	2	13	36	53	23
Bootech Old Boys -3	22	6	7	9	38	46	22
Business School -1	22	6	3	13	39	65	14
Corinthian	22	3	2	17	28	83	11

Division Three
	P	W	D	L	F	A	Pts
Bankfield Res.	22	17	2	3	78	46	53
Ercanil Old Boys -3	22	14	6	2	75	41	45
Waterloo GSOB Res.	22	10	5	7	62	46	35
Heygreen Old Boys -1	22	10	6	6	47	38	35
Gateacre	22	9	7	6	46	39	34
South Mersey	22	10	3	9	47	36	33
Old Cathinians Res.	22	9	3	10	54	52	30
Cardinal Newman Res.	22	7	2	13	47	47	29
Collegiate Old Boys 'B'	22	7	1	14	30	69	22
Blue Coat Old Boys	22	5	3	14	55	84	18
Convocation	22	4	5	13	41	59	17
Quarry Bank Old Boys 'A'	22	4	5	13	41	63	17

Division Four
	P	W	D	L	F	A	Pts
Quarry Bank Old Boys 'B'	22	18	4	2	80	37	56
De La Salle Old Boys	22	13	4	5	67	35	43
Old Hollys Res.	22	13	3	6	66	42	42
Old Cathinians 'A'	22	11	5	6	74	55	38
Richmond	22	9	9	4	49	40	53
Old Xaverians 'C'	22	9	4	9	45	44	31
Alsop Old Boys 'B'	22	8	3	11	56	51	27
Business School Res.	22	8	3	11	47	59	27
Essenmay Old Boys 'A'	22	5	4	13	48	48	24
Old Bootleians 'A'	22	4	5	13	49	78	17
Liobians 'A'	22	3	3	14	32	91	3
Collegiate Old Boys 'C'	22	0	3	19	19	91	3

Division Five

	P	W	D	L	F	A	Pts
Waterloo GSOB 'A' -3	20	14	2	4	51	31	44
Kingsford	20	12	3	5	46	26	39
Old Cathinians 'B'	20	11	2	7	53	33	37
Rhein	20	11	4	5	59	30	37
Cardinal Newman 'A'	20	10	5	5	38	30	35
Old Bootleians 'B'	20	9	1	10	53	40	28
St Mary's COB Res.	20	8	4	8	31	37	28
De La Salle Old Boys Res.	20	7	2	11	35	46	23
Old Instonians Res.	20	7	1	12	38	53	22
Wavertree WDOB Res.	20	4	4	12	34	46	16
Liobians 'B'	20	2	1	17	25	81	7

LONDON COMMERCIAL LEAGUE

Division One

	P	W	D	L	F	A	Pts
British Airways	18	17	0	1	75	18	51
Aston Athletic	18	13	1	4	43	29	40
Hayes Gate	18	11	2	5	45	23	35
East Fulham	18	8	3	7	39	42	27
Old Alpertonians	18	6	4	8	28	43	23
WLA	18	6	4	8	28	35	22
Chiswick Homefields	18	6	2	10	31	51	20
Roxeth	18	4	5	9	38	45	17
Sporting Hackney	18	3	4	11	33	46	13
Hillingdon Irish	18	3	1	14	20	48	10

Division Two

	P	W	D	L	F	A	Pts
Charing Cross Association	16	14	1	1	45	10	43
Dynamo Sports	16	13	1	2	55	18	41
British Airways Res.	16	8	1	7	40	27	25
Kingsbury L'don Tgrs Res.	16	7	2	7	23	13	23
Indian Gymkhana Res.	16	7	1	8	36	26	22
Kodak Harrow Res.	16	6	2	8	24	35	20
Sporting Hackney Res.	16	5	3	8	19	39	18
Sudbury Court	16	3	1	12	17	61	10
Somerville Old Boys	16	2	1	13	21	51	7

LOWESTOFT & DISTRICT LEAGUE

Division One

	P	W	D	L	F	A	Pts
Hearts of Oak	22	20	0	2	128	13	60
Norton Athletic	22	18	1	3	103	27	55
Wrentham	22	13	3	6	76	42	42
Spexhall	22	12	4	6	50	29	40
Kirkley & Pakefield 'A'	22	11	4	7	44	28	37
Waveney Youth	22	9	5	8	57	48	33
Pot Black	22	9	5	8	32	52	32
CDS Waveney	22	7	5	10	57	66	26
Oxford Arms	22	6	4	12	49	70	22
Carlton Rangers	22	5	0	17	26	110	15
Sole Bay Res. -3	22	4	2	16	39	97	11
Corton Res.	22	1	1	20	29	113	4

Division Two

	P	W	D	L	F	A	Pts
Hearts of Oak Res. -3	24	18	3	3	106	57	54
Barsham	24	16	2	6	57	29	50
Beccles Caxton Res.	24	14	5	5	74	42	43
Blundeston Magpies	24	14	1	9	69	42	43
White Horse Celtic -3	24	13	2	9	71	49	38
Waveney Gunners	24	10	5	9	49	53	35
Pakefield Re-United -3	24	10	5	9	49	49	32
Norton Athletic Res.	24	9	3	12	35	65	30
Oulton Broad/Notleys Res.	24	9	2	13	50	70	29
Ellingham	24	10	1	13	68	68	28
Royal Standard -3	24	8	2	14	52	73	26
Crusaders	24	4	2	18	52	64	17
Lacon Arms Res.	24	1	4	19	39	110	7

LUTON & SOUTH BEDS LEAGUE

Premier Division

	P	W	D	L	F	A	Pts
Stopsley Common	21	15	5	1	62	24	50
Boater	21	15	5	1	55	43	50
Dunstable United	21	12	1	8	58	33	37
Christians in Sport	21	11	2	8	46	35	35
St Josephs	21	8	5	8	40	46	29
Eaton Bray	21	7	3	11	42	46	24
Lewsey Park	21	7	2	12	34	45	23
Club Lewsey	21	1	1	19	19	106	4

Division One

	P	W	D	L	F	A	Pts
Offley Social	19	19	0	0	121	21	57
Luton Leagrave	19	16	0	3	92	37	48
Christians in Sport Res.	21	8	2	11	54	55	28
USL Galacticos	21	7	1	13	40	85	22
The 61 FC (Luton) 'A'	21	6	3	12	40	97	21
Stopsley Park	21	5	2	14	50	76	17
Crown Sundon							

MAIDSTONE & DISTRICT LEAGUE

Premier Division

	P	W	D	L	F	A	Pts
Shepway United	16	13	1	2	84	18	40
Eccles	16	12	2	2	48	16	38
Leeds SV	16	9	3	4	48	34	30
Malgo	16	7	3	6	50	35	24
Downswood	16	6	5	5	41	34	23
Addington	16	6	1	9	33	38	19
Lenham Wanderers	16	4	2	10	25	44	14
Ditton United	16	4	0	12	24	52	12
West Farleigh	16	0	0	16	9	115	0

Division One

	P	W	D	L	F	A	Pts
East Malling	18	13	1	4	67	31	40
Hunton	18	10	5	3	55	28	35
Blue Eagles	18	10	3	5	55	39	33
Smarden	18	10	3	5	63	40	33
The Saxon	18	8	2	8	51	40	26
MPE	18	6	5	7	35	41	22
Yalding	18	5	1	12	33	56	16
Aylesford Paper Mills	18	5	1	12	24	52	16
Headcorn	18	5	1	12	22	61	16
Staplehurst/Monarchs U Res	18	3	2	13	22	61	11

Division Two

	P	W	D	L	F	A	Pts
AFC Biddenden	22	15	3	4	70	36	48
Sutton Saints	22	14	3	5	79	43	45
Cobdown United	22	13	4	5	62	40	45
Hunton Res.	22	12	4	6	56	42	41
Headcorn Res.	22	10	5	7	51	46	35
RKP United	22	8	6	8	42	51	30
Maidstone Athletic	22	5	4	13	49	57	19
Wheatsheaf Celtic	22	5	3	14	50	68	18
Malgo Res.	22	3	2	17	38	88	13
West Farleigh Res.	22	2	1	16	33	114	8

Division Three

	P	W	D	L	F	A	Pts
East Malling Res.	22	18	4	0	112	36	58
Fant Falcons	22	14	2	6	80	44	44
Kingshill Spitfires	22	13	4	5	67	47	43
Alchemy Eagles	22	11	4	7	96	70	37
Lenham Wanderers Res.	22	12	0	10	64	59	36
Parkwood Colts	22	9	2	11	76	69	29
Staplehurst/Monarchs U 'A'	22	7	1	13	51	68	25
Thurnham United	22	5	2	13	39	56	21
Phoenix United	22	2	1	19	20	96	6
Sutton Saints Res.	22	0	0	20	40	162	—

MIDLAND AMATEUR ALLIANCE

Premier Division

	P	W	D	L	F	A	Pts
Southwell Amateurs	26	21	3	2	89	30	66
FC05	26	19	4	3	91	35	64
Old Elizabethans	26	14	3	9	78	61	45
Beeston Old Boys Assn	26	14	3	9	67	49	45
Woodborough United	26	12	1	13	61	62	37
Steelers	26	12	1	13	61	62	37
County NALGO	26	11	2	13	69	65	35
Brunts Old Boys	26	9	6	11	42	68	30
Pinxton Sun Inn	26	8	5	13	44	63	29
Bilsthorpe Albion	26	7	5	14	53	77	26
Wollaton 'A'	26	8	1	17	50	62	25
Monty Hind Old Boys	26	5	1	20	50	80	25
Bilborough Town	26	5	5	16	45	76	20
Lady Bay	26	4	5	17	33	108	17

Division One

	P	W	D	L	F	A	Pts
Nottinghamshire Res.	26	20	4	2	75	21	66
TVFC	26	13	4	4	113	53	62
Brunts Old Boys Res.	26	15	4	8	89	65	52
Wollaton Res.	26	14	1	11	77	75	43
Calverton Mnrs Welf. 'A' -3	26	12	4	10	77	70	41
Old Elizabethans Res.	26	10	7	9	74	57	37
Radcliffe Olympic 'A'	26	11	5	14	65	52	39
Keyworth United 'A'	26	9	6	11	64	69	33
Crown Inn Selston	26	6	4	17	50	71	22
Derbyshire Amateurs Res. -3	26	6	5	15	45	80	20
Bassingfield	26	5	6	17	45	77	21
Bilborough Town Res.	26	5	1	20	40	103	16

Division Three

	P	W	D	L	F	A	Pts
Beeston Res.	28	20	3	5	86	39	63
Eaton Hall College	28	18	4	6	84	52	58
EMTEC	28	17	4	7	64	55	55
Hickling	28	16	5	7	88	57	53
Broadmeadows -1	28	14	6	8	79	46	47
AFC Greyhound -2	28	14	6	8	83	57	46
Cambridge Knights	28	13	7	8	82	57	46
Nottinghamshire 'A'	28	14	3	11	75	54	45
Tibshelf Old Boys	28	10	7	11	81	53	37
Southwell Arms Res. -1	28	10	6	12	63	70	35
Clinphone	28	8	4	16	59	82	28
Chilwell Vipers -2	28	6	4	18	52	106	19
Town Mill	28	5	4	19	52	106	19
Old Bemrosians	28	6	1	21	51	118	19
Cedar -2	28	3	6	19	49	110	13

MIDLAND REGIONAL ALLIANCE

Premier Division

	P	W	D	L	F	A	Pts
Dronfield Town	34	25	4	5	81	36	79
Ilkeston Town Res.	34	24	6	4	101	41	78
Rowsley	34	18	8	8	59	42	62
Wirksworth Town	34	18	5	11	75	44	59
Holbrook St Michaels	34	19	2	13	73	52	59
Derby Rolls Royce Leisure	34	15	11	8	69	60	59
Melbourne Dynamo	34	15	6	13	72	65	51
Borrowash Victoria Res.	34	14	8	12	65	59	50
Ripley	34	13	4	15	79	61	49
Sandiacre Town	34	12	6	16	61	73	42
Shirebrook Town Res.	34	11	5	17	59	80	41
Belper United	34	9	8	17	70	81	35
Ashover	34	9	8	17	41	54	35
Allestree	34	8	8	18	40	65	32
Cromford	34	8	7	19	56	84	31
Newmount -3	34	10	4	20	57	87	31
Shepshed Dynamo Res. -6	34	11	4	19	51	112	31
Long Eaton Utd Res. -1	34	8	7	19	48	67	30

Division One

	P	W	D	L	F	A	Pts
Willington	30	24	5	1	119	30	77
Castle Donington Town	30	19	4	7	91	50	61
Matlock Sports	30	18	2	10	83	47	61
Swanwick Pentrich Road	30	18	2	10	77	48	56
Matlock United	30	16	9	5	68	37	53
Dronfield Town Res.	30	14	6	10	59	58	48
Chellaston	30	14	5	11	70	61	47
Derbyshire Amateurs -3	30	12	8	10	65	56	41
Heanor Colliers	30	10	9	11	54	50	39
Woolley Moor United	30	11	5	14	50	60	38
Little Eaton	30	11	5	14	62	77	38
Derby R Royce Leis. 'A'	30	9	6	15	64	77	33
Pastures -3	30	8	3	19	47	80	24
Holbrook St Michaels Res.	30	6	5	17	34	63	23
Bargate Rovers	30	6	3	21	53	109	21
Belper United Res.	30	3	3	24	24	96	12

268 Other Leagues

WWW.CHERRYRED.CO.UK

Division Two	P	W	D	L	F	A	Pts
Selston	30	25	2	3	175	42	77
Mickleover RBL	30	20	3	7	111	47	63
Beeston	30	19	4	7	120	49	61
Findern	30	19	4	7	76	48	61
Rowsley Res.	30	19	2	9	100	48	59
Sandiacre Town Res.	30	15	7	8	74	40	52
Alvaston Silver Ghost	30	15	5	10	75	81	50
Wirksworth Town Res.	30	14	3	13	66	64	45
Pastures Res.	30	13	6	11	71	74	45
Little Eaton Res.	30	11	2	17	54	96	35
Wirksworth Ivanhoe	30	9	2	19	56	93	29
Swanwick Pentrich Rd Res.	30	8	3	19	44	107	27
Melbourne Dynamo Res. -1	30	8	3	19	45	80	26
Allestree Res.	30	6	4	20	51	102	22
Castle Donington Tn Res.	30	6	2	22	46	107	20
Bargate Rovers Res.	30	5	4	21	49	135	19

MID-ESSEX LEAGUE
(Broch Group)

Premier Division	P	W	D	L	F	A	Pts
S'thminster St Leonards +2	22	16	4	2	68	26	54
Scotia Billericay	22	13	5	4	57	38	44
Maldon St Mary	22	13	4	5	59	26	43
Ravens +3	22	12	3	7	67	46	42
Harold Wood Ath 'A'	22	10	6	6	58	47	36
Bradwell United -1	22	7	7	8	36	39	27
Silver End United	22	6	7	9	28	39	25
Beacon Hill Rovers	22	7	4	11	32	47	25
Mundon Victoria	22	7	4	11	41	65	25
Manford Way 'B'	22	6	2	14	32	62	20
Gidea Park Rangers -3	22	5	4	13	33	52	16
Frenford Senior 'A'	22	4	2	16	40	64	14

Division One	P	W	D	L	F	A	Pts
Springfield Rouge +2	24	17	4	3	63	31	57
Little Waltham	24	16	1	7	60	33	49
Utd Chelmsford Churches	24	16	1	7	65	44	49
Braintree & Bocking Utd	24	14	0	10	57	52	42
Focus Ferrers -1	24	12	5	7	51	33	40
Shelley Royals	24	10	5	9	58	44	35
S'thminster St Lnrds Res.	24	9	4	11	57	61	31
Dunmow	24	8	4	12	56	68	28
Boundary	24	8	2	14	38	52	26
Old Chelmsfordians 'A'	24	8	2	14	52	70	26
Ferrers Athletic	24	8	1	15	44	73	25
Tillingham Hotspur	24	6	5	13	41	49	23
Boreham	24	5	4	15	35	67	19

Division Two	P	W	D	L	F	A	Pts
Marconi Athletic	24	19	2	3	97	29	59
Rayleigh Town 'A'	24	18	0	6	88	43	54
Byfleet Rangers	24	16	3	5	60	26	51
Essex Police	24	16	2	6	75	43	50
Manford Way 'A'	24	14	2	8	47	39	44
Stock United	24	10	4	10	47	49	34
Harold Wood Ath 'B'	24	10	3	11	45	43	33
Ravens Res.	24	10	2	12	46	61	32
Writtle Manor	24	9	2	13	54	73	29
Latchingdon -1	24	7	5	12	46	51	25
Epping 'A' +2	24	4	5	15	30	63	19
Old Chelmsfordians 'B'	24	4	5	15	29	69	17
Focus Ferrers Res.	24	1	1	22	38	113	4

Division Three	P	W	D	L	F	A	Pts
Great Baddow Res.	22	14	6	2	66	24	48
Scotia Billericay Res.	22	14	3	5	56	37	45
Hutton 'A' -1	22	13	4	5	68	47	42
Cricketers Horndon +2	22	11	4	7	61	53	39
E2V Technologies	22	10	3	9	64	54	33
Bradwell United Res.	22	10	1	11	43	58	31
City Colts	22	9	3	10	50	54	30
Brendans	22	8	5	9	28	43	29
St Margarets	22	7	3	12	48	58	24
Battlesbridge	22	6	5	11	34	36	23
Crays Hill United	22	5	4	13	41	58	19
Marconi Athletic Res.	22	3	3	16	24	61	12

Division Four	P	W	D	L	F	A	Pts
Battlesbridge Res.	26	20	4	2	74	29	64
Wickham Royals	26	18	4	4	94	51	58
Burnham Ramblers 'A'	26	14	6	6	62	54	48
Mundon Victoria Res. +3	26	14	1	11	83	64	46
Braintree/Bocking Utd Res.	26	11	6	9	72	55	39
Byfleet Rangers Res. +2	26	11	3	12	68	81	38
Shelley Royals Res. +3	26	9	3	14	51	73	33
Frenford Senior 'B'	26	10	2	14	48	51	32
Springfield Rouge Res. -3	26	10	5	11	54	58	32
Hutton 'B' +3	26	9	2	15	86	98	32
Runwell Hospital 'A' +2	26	9	3	14	63	82	32
Felsted Rovers +3	26	9	2	15	41	64	32
Marks Farm -10	26	11	6	9	69	48	29
Boreham Res. -1	26	2	3	21	44	101	8

Division Five	P	W	D	L	F	A	Pts
Little Waltham Res. +3	24	19	3	2	110	36	63
Beacon Hill Rovers Res.	24	18	4	2	84	36	58
Durning +3	24	14	3	7	88	54	48
Writtle Manor Res. -3	24	15	2	7	75	40	44
Silver End United Res.	24	13	4	7	63	41	43
Great Baddow 'A'	24	13	3	8	60	41	42
White Hart United	24	13	3	8	51	44	42
Dunmow Res. +3	24	8	0	16	39	71	27
Wickham Royals Res.	24	7	3	14	48	64	24
Battlesbridge 'A' -3	24	8	1	15	47	69	22
Focus Ferrers 'A'	24	5	1	18	40	78	16
E2V Technologies Res.	24	5	1	18	31	104	16
Burnham Ramblers 'B' -3	24	3	2	19	31	89	8

MID-SOMERSET LEAGUE
(Trophies of Radstock)

Premier Division	P	W	D	L	F	A	Pts
Westfield	18	14	1	3	52	25	43
Radstock Town Res.	18	12	4	2	38	16	40
Pensford	18	12	1	5	60	31	37
Coleford Athletic	18	10	3	5	51	31	33
Purnell Sports	18	9	1	8	62	36	28
Mells & Vobster United	18	5	4	9	37	40	19
Meadow Rangers	18	5	4	9	35	47	19
Belrose	18	4	3	11	27	56	15
Chew Magna	18	2	4	12	20	49	10
Littleton Sports -1	18	2	5	11	26	77	10

Division One	P	W	D	L	F	A	Pts
Wookey -1	20	14	5	1	74	21	46
Chilcompton Sports	20	14	3	3	60	26	45
Stoke Rovers	20	10	5	5	50	38	35
Purnell Sports Res.	20	9	5	6	39	27	32
Glastonbury Town Res.	20	8	5	7	49	48	29
Frome Town Sports Res.	20	6	9	5	42	40	27
Farrington Gurney	20	7	5	8	42	44	26
Evercreech Rovers	20	5	3	12	28	58	18
Littleton Sports Res.	20	5	3	12	25	58	18
Frome Collegians Res.	20	4	4	12	30	51	16
Temple Cloud	20	3	3	14	23	51	12

Division Two	P	W	D	L	F	A	Pts
Westfield Res.	20	15	3	2	81	37	48
Oakhill	20	15	0	5	58	40	45
Coleford Athletic Res.	20	13	2	5	53	28	41
Wells City 'A' -1	20	10	3	7	50	42	32
Chilcompton Sports Res.	20	8	4	8	43	39	28
Welton Arsenal	20	6	5	9	30	34	23
Mells & Vobster Utd Res.	20	6	4	10	43	51	22
Farmborough -2	20	7	2	11	51	49	21
Belrose Res.	20	6	2	12	37	50	20
Interhound	20	4	4	12	37	73	16
Clutton Res.	20	4	3	13	25	65	15

Division Three	P	W	D	L	F	A	Pts
Pilton United	22	19	1	2	91	20	58
Tunley Athletic Res.	22	15	4	3	63	34	49
Farrington Gurney Res.	22	16	0	6	61	37	48
Wookey Res.	22	13	2	7	59	42	41
Radstock Town 'A'	22	12	3	7	68	43	39
Chilcompton United	22	9	4	9	41	39	31
Chew Magna Res. -2	22	9	3	10	51	52	28
Meadow Rangers Res.	22	7	3	12	24	51	24
Pensford Res.	22	6	4	12	42	67	22
Westfield 'A'	22	5	5	12	39	51	20
Evercreech Rovers Res.	22	3	2	17	25	75	11
Stoke Rovers Res.	22	1	3	18	35	88	6

MID-SUSSEX LEAGUE
(Gray Hooper Holt LLP)

Premier Division	P	W	D	L	F	A	Pts
Lindfield	24	15	6	3	93	41	51
Old Varndeanians	24	15	6	3	56	30	51
Hassocks 'A'	24	13	3	8	40	33	42
Forest Row	24	11	7	6	51	40	40
Willingdon Athletic	24	10	5	9	43	38	35
Balcombe	24	10	5	9	47	44	35
Wisdom Sports	24	9	5	10	45	43	32
Maresfield Village	24	9	3	12	41	54	30
Jarvis Brook	24	8	3	13	42	58	27
Hartfield	24	7	6	11	21	38	27
East Grinstead United	24	7	4	13	25	31	25
Felbridge	24	6	7	11	34	41	25
Lewes Bridgeview	24	6	0	18	28	75	18

Division One	P	W	D	L	F	A	Pts
Uckfield Town Res.	24	18	4	2	83	21	58
Franklands Village	24	13	6	5	67	46	45
Rotherfield	24	13	5	6	56	31	44
Old Varndeanians Res.	24	13	2	9	59	39	41
Village of Ditchling	24	13	1	10	69	57	40
Heath Pilgrims	24	12	4	8	43	36	40
Buxted	24	10	4	10	34	37	34
Wivelsfield Green	24	10	1	13	54	59	31
Horsted Keynes	24	9	4	11	45	59	31
Hurstpierpoint Res.	24	9	3	12	52	57	30
Wisdom Sports Res.	24	7	7	10	39	53	28
Turners Hill	24	4	2	18	44	91	14
Sporting Lindfield	24	2	3	19	27	86	9

Division Two	P	W	D	L	F	A	Pts
AFC Ringmer	20	12	3	5	42	26	39
Crawley Down 'A'	20	10	8	2	42	27	38
Ashurst Wood	20	10	5	5	49	43	35
Ardingly	20	8	7	5	35	27	31
Cuckfield Town	20	9	4	7	35	31	31
Newick	20	8	4	8	40	41	28
Horley Athletico	20	8	2	10	49	44	26
Cuckfield Wheatsheaf Utd	20	7	5	8	42	43	26
Willingdon Athletic Res.	20	7	3	10	27	41	24
East Grinstead Utd Res.	20	4	3	13	26	57	15
Burgess Hill Albion	20	4	2	14	38	45	14

Division Three	P	W	D	L	F	A	Pts
Roffey	18	17	0	1	63	10	51
Keymer & Hassocks	18	12	2	4	57	24	38
AFC Grinstead	18	10	3	5	64	43	33
Dormansland Rockets	18	7	3	8	46	59	24
East Grinstead Town 'A'	18	6	5	7	44	52	23
East Court	18	7	1	10	48	42	22
Maresfield Village Res.	18	6	3	9	33	40	21
Fletching	18	6	2	10	32	47	20
Peacehaven United	18	5	3	10	39	45	18
Cuckfield Town Res.	18	2	2	14	19	83	8

Division Four	P	W	D	L	F	A	Pts
Lindfield Res.	22	16	4	2	69	25	52
West Hoathly	22	15	2	5	67	35	47
Roffey Res.	22	11	6	5	43	32	39
Crowborough Athletic 'A'	22	11	5	6	66	49	38
Lingfield 'A' +3	22	10	3	9	47	61	36
Uckfield Town 'A'	22	9	4	9	64	43	31
Framfield/Blackboys Utd	22	8	7	7	43	39	31
Old Varndeanians 'A'	22	7	6	9	24	43	27
Burgess Hill Albion Res.	22	7	3	12	42	72	24
Lewes Bridgeview Res. -3	22	7	5	10	44	45	23
Nutley	22	3	3	16	37	62	12
Ardingly Res.	22	3	2	17	23	63	11

Division Five	P	W	D	L	F	A	Pts
Danehill	22	16	3	3	93	45	51
Plumpton Athletic	22	16	2	4	89	44	50
Barcombe	22	14	2	6	65	36	44
Ansty Sports & Social	22	13	3	6	77	45	42
Scaynes Hill	22	10	5	7	60	45	35
Fairwarp	22	8	7	7	57	46	31
Village of Ditchling Res.	22	8	3	11	42	55	27
Turners Hill Res. +2	22	6	7	9	43	58	27
Newick Res.	22	7	2	13	34	71	23
Wisdom Sports 'A'	22	5	6	11	45	62	21
Handcross Village Res. -4	22	5	6	11	41	56	17
Fairfield +3	22	0	2	20	16	99	5

Division Six	P	W	D	L	F	A	Pts
Copthorne	22	20	1	1	123	23	61
Rottingdean Village Vets	22	14	4	4	66	27	46
Wivelsfield Green Res.	22	15	0	7	66	47	45
Copthorne Rovers	22	13	5	4	58	29	44
Heath Pilgrims Res.	22	12	2	8	82	61	38
Buxted Res.	22	10	2	10	44	60	32
Jarvis Brook Res.	22	9	3	10	73	51	30
Bolney Rovers	22	6	4	12	41	86	22
Ashurst Wood Res.	22	7	0	15	44	90	21
Horsted Keynes Res.	22	5	2	15	46	71	17
Hartfield Res.	22	3	4	15	31	78	13
Willingdon Athletic 'A'	22	3	3	16	35	86	12

Division Seven	P	W	D	L	F	A	Pts
Peacehaven United Res.	22	17	2	3	85	34	53
Lindfield 'A'	22	14	4	4	64	27	46
Fletching Res.	22	14	4	4	66	32	46
Balcombe Res.	22	11	4	7	64	40	37
Dormansland Rkts Res. +3	22	9	3	10	46	47	33
Maresfield Village 'A'	22	9	5	8	59	47	32
Felbridge Res. -3	22	11	2	9	60	55	32
Ansty Sports & Social Res.	22	9	1	12	56	77	28
Uckfield Town 'B'	22	6	4	12	48	72	22
Burgess Hill Albion 'A'	22	5	5	12	47	66	20
Rotherfield Res.	22	6	1	15	50	78	19
Scaynes Hill Res.	22	3	1	18	36	106	10

Division Eight	P	W	D	L	F	A	Pts
Forest Row Res.	24	20	3	1	89	23	63
Copthorne Res.	24	20	1	3	105	29	61
Village of Ditchling 'A'	24	13	2	9	75	51	41
Danehill Res.	24	13	1	10	80	65	40
West Hoathly Res.	24	12	2	10	65	57	38
Cuckfield Town 'A'	24	11	3	10	63	62	36
Lindfield 'B'	24	10	3	11	61	54	33
Barcombe Res.	24	9	4	11	51	51	31
Framfield/Blackboys U Res.	24	9	2	13	64	85	29
Cuckfield Whtshf Utd Res.	24	7	3	14	42	68	24
Wivelsfield Green 'A'	24	7	1	16	42	81	22
Maresfield Village 'B'	24	5	5	14	41	92	20
Handcross Village 'A'	24	3	4	17	30	90	13

Division Nine	P	W	D	L	F	A	Pts
Halsford Lions	26	23	1	2	138	31	70
Franklands Village Res.	26	20	2	4	99	38	62
Cuckfield Town 'B'	26	17	4	5	82	30	55
Plumpton Athletic Res.	26	15	3	8	82	46	48
East Grinstead Town 'B'	26	15	2	9	72	41	47
Buxted 'A'	26	13	1	12	65	76	40
Fairwarp Res.	26	12	3	11	56	57	39
Cowden Mavericks	26	12	2	12	78	66	38
Lindfield 'C'	26	11	5	10	60	52	38
Ardingly 'A'	26	10	2	14	69	82	32
Maresfield Village 'C'	26	8	4	14	52	69	28
Heath Rangers	26	6	2	18	54	114	20
Scaynes Hill 'A'	26	3	0	23	34	135	9
Rotherfield 'A'	26	1	1	24	23	127	4

NEATH & DISTRICT LEAGUE
(Happy Home Furnishers)

Premier Division	P	W	D	L	F	A	Pts
Giants Grave -1	22	19	1	2	101	29	57
Onllwyn	22	15	3	4	76	30	48
Park Travellers	22	14	1	7	73	35	43
Sunnybank WMC	22	14	1	7	47	30	43
Bryn Rovers -1	22	14	1	7	52	31	42
Glynneath Town	22	12	3	7	71	39	39
Cwm Wanderers	22	8	4	10	36	48	28
AFC Caewern	22	7	4	11	34	50	25
Ynysygerwen	22	6	4	12	40	67	22
FC Nedd	22	4	5	13	29	66	17
Cilfrew Rovers	22	2	4	16	35	76	10
Borough	22	1	1	20	23	116	4

Division One	P	W	D	L	F	A	Pts
CMB	18	14	1	3	43	21	43
FC Clydach	18	12	4	2	45	27	40
Clydach Sports -1	18	11	5	2	52	30	37
Rhos	18	8	2	8	43	32	26
AFC Pontardawe	18	8	2	8	53	44	26
Bear	18	7	3	8	50	48	24
Harp Rovers	18	5	4	9	25	42	19
Lonlas Youth	18	5	2	11	37	41	17
Godregraig Athletic	18	4	3	11	30	57	15
Resolven	18	1	4	13	18	54	7

Division Two	P	W	D	L	F	A	Pts
Ynysymeudwy Athletic	21	16	3	2	91	36	51
Cimla Youth	21	15	2	4	53	35	47
Coelbren Athletic	21	14	2	5	64	37	44
INCO	21	10	1	10	60	57	31
Tonna	21	9	3	9	55	47	30
Gwaencaegurwen	21	4	3	14	25	76	15
Llandarcy	21	4	1	16	43	72	13
Oxford	21	4	1	16	29	60	13

Merlins Wizards – record expunged

Reserve Division One	P	W	D	L	F	A	Pts
Giants Grave Res.	18	13	1	4	66	28	40
Bryn Rovers Res.	18	12	3	3	66	35	39
Onllwyn Res.	18	10	2	6	58	33	32
CMB Res.	18	8	2	8	59	47	26
Cwm Wanderers Res.	18	8	2	8	48	49	26
Ynysygerwen Res.	18	7	4	7	45	51	25
AFC Pontardawe Res.	18	7	3	8	53	48	24
Glynneath Town Res.	18	7	3	8	53	49	24
Sunnybank WMC Res.	18	4	2	12	26	45	14
Borough Res.	18	3	0	15	13	102	9

Reserve Division Two	P	W	D	L	F	A	Pts
Park Travellers Res.	16	11	0	5	60	34	33
Cwmamman United 'A'	16	10	2	4	60	40	32
Resolven Res.	16	9	2	5	49	32	29
Lonlas Youth Res.	16	8	4	4	43	32	28
Rhos Res.	16	8	2	6	58	43	26
Clydach Sports Res.	16	7	1	8	38	48	22
AFC Caewern Res.	16	5	3	8	37	50	18
Glynneath Town 'A'	16	4	1	11	37	57	13
Cilfrew Rovers Res.	16	2	1	13	16	62	7

Bear Res. – record expunged

Reserve Division Three	P	W	D	L	F	A	Pts
Rhos 'A'	20	16	0	4	99	37	48
Ynysymeudwy Ath Res.	20	11	4	5	65	42	37
AFC Pontardawe 'A'	20	11	2	7	78	51	35
FC Clydach Res.	20	9	3	8	48	44	30
Pontarddulais Town	20	10	0	10	60	62	30
Harp Rovers Res.	20	9	3	8	49	54	30
INCO Res.	20	8	1	11	46	59	25
INCO 'A'	20	7	3	10	43	64	24
Bryn Rovers 'A'	20	6	3	11	42	54	21
Cwm Wanderers 'A'	20	6	2	12	38	72	20
Cimla Youth Res.	20	6	1	13	37	66	19

Godregraig Athletic Res. – record expunged

NEWPORT & DISTRICT LEAGUE

Premier Division X	P	W	D	L	F	A	Pts
Llanwern RTB	24	20	3	1	104	24	63
Pill	24	17	3	4	85	31	54
Ship & Pilot	24	17	3	4	85	50	54
St Julians Youth	24	14	5	5	73	29	47
Malpas	24	13	6	5	52	38	45
Marshfield	24	11	5	8	63	43	38
Pontnewydd United	24	9	4	11	46	47	31
Pill Hibernians	24	7	5	12	35	57	26
Llanwern Sports & Social	24	6	4	14	42	67	22
Oakfield	24	7	1	16	54	89	22
Caerleon Town	24	6	2	16	31	75	20
Duffryn	24	5	3	16	39	68	18
Henllys Rangers	24	2	0	22	36	127	6

Premier Division Y	P	W	D	L	F	A	Pts
Albion Rovers Res.	24	19	1	4	94	33	58
Newport Civil Service Res.	24	18	0	6	98	43	54
Rogerstone Welfare Res.	24	15	5	4	83	50	50
Cwmbran Celtic 'A'	24	16	1	7	84	47	49
Cwmbran Town Res.	24	14	3	7	70	40	45
Lliswerry Res.	24	14	3	7	60	30	45
Trethomas Bluebirds Res.	24	13	0	11	80	65	39
AC Pontymister Res.	24	11	4	9	61	55	37
Malpas Gladiator Res.	24	6	3	15	45	76	21
Lucas Cwmbran Res.	24	6	1	17	44	76	19
Spencer Yth & Boys Res.	24	4	3	17	39	97	15
Cromwell Youth Res.	24	4	0	20	51	139	12
Coed Eva Athletic Res.	24	2	4	18	48	106	10

Villa Dino Christchurch Res. – record expunged

Division One	P	W	D	L	F	A	Pts
Shaftesbury Youth	24	18	2	4	103	36	56
Tradesmans Arms	24	17	3	4	80	40	54
Croesyceiliog 'A'	24	15	2	7	77	51	47
Cwmcarn Athletic	24	11	8	5	57	40	41
Lliswerry 'A'	24	11	5	8	68	50	38
The Royal Mail	24	12	1	11	90	71	37
Villa Dino Christchurch 'A'	24	11	1	12	57	55	34
Newport Corinthians Res.	24	9	4	11	39	65	31
Pontnewydd United Res.	24	6	6	12	48	64	24
Spencer Old Boys	24	7	2	15	51	69	23
Marshfield Res.	24	7	2	15	48	80	23
Caerleon Town Res.	24	6	3	15	29	77	21
Albion Rovers 'A'	24	5	3	16	47	96	18

NORTH & MID HERTS LEAGUE

Premier Division	P	W	D	L	F	A	Pts
Nirankari	16	14	2	0	64	11	44
Probuild	16	11	2	3	64	23	35
Whitwell Village	16	11	1	4	41	33	34
Wilbury Wanderers	15	9	3	3	39	21	30
Redbourn	16	6	1	9	30	44	19
London Colney 'A'	16	6	1	9	29	44	19
New Greens	15	3	0	12	26	57	9
St Ippolyts	16	1	3	12	15	48	6
Clannad Celtic -3	14	2	1	11	16	43	4

Division One Mid	P	W	D	L	F	A	Pts
White Hart	18	16	0	2	72	25	48
The Orchard & The Anvil	18	13	1	4	89	36	40
Magnum	18	13	1	4	87	38	40
Kimpton Rovers	18	12	2	4	77	29	38
Fairlands	18	10	0	8	65	57	30
St Ippolyts Res.	18	8	1	9	37	41	25
Baldock Town 'A'	18	7	1	10	45	41	22
City Hearts	18	4	0	14	48	90	12
Therfield Eagles	18	3	0	15	36	96	9
Westwell	18	1	0	17	15	118	3

Division One North	P	W	D	L	F	A	Pts
St Albans North	18	16	1	1	73	21	49
London Road	18	14	2	2	79	29	44
Kings Sports 'A'	18	11	3	4	44	32	36
St Albans Wanderers	18	6	5	7	40	48	23
Park Street Village 'A'	18	7	2	9	41	52	23
Sandridge Rovers 'A'	18	7	2	9	41	56	23
Global	18	7	0	11	44	53	21
Harpenden Rovers 'A'	18	4	5	9	36	47	17
Inn on the Green	18	4	2	12	34	62	14
IFK Buttles	18	2	2	14	36	68	8

NORTH BUCKS & DISTRICT LEAGUE

Premier Division	P	W	D	L	F	A	Pts
PB (Milton Keynes)	26	24	1	1	112	24	73
Lavendon Sports	26	17	4	5	72	37	55
Steeple Claydon	26	16	2	8	70	38	50
Deanshanger Athletic	26	14	3	9	48	36	45
Potterspury	26	13	4	9	54	45	43
Southcott Village RA	26	12	7	7	48	53	43
Grendon Rangers	26	11	6	9	58	49	39
Kingfisher Titans	26	9	5	12	56	56	32
Brackley Sports	26	8	5	13	43	59	29
Wing Village	26	6	9	11	39	51	27
Bletchley Manor	26	7	5	14	44	58	26
Bletchley Trees	26	7	5	14	34	64	26
Thornborough Athletic	26	5	6	15	36	64	21
Hanslope	26	1	2	23	18	98	5

Intermediate Division	P	W	D	L	F	A	Pts
AFC Brickhill Rangers	30	26	2	2	98	26	80
Stewkley	30	24	2	4	86	42	74
Syresham	29	20	4	5	95	38	64
Workplace Wanderers	30	18	2	10	77	54	56
Twyford United	30	16	5	9	91	63	53
Silverstone	30	15	4	11	67	51	49
Castlethorpe	30	14	4	12	76	59	46
Yardley Gobion	30	13	6	11	79	61	45
Brackley Sports Res.	30	12	5	13	68	61	41
Abbey	30	11	6	13	72	75	39
Sherington	30	11	2	17	78	87	35
Marsh Gibbon	29	9	2	18	62	102	29
Great Horwood	30	7	4	19	49	81	25
Southcott Village RA Res.	30	7	3	20	51	102	24
Woughton	30	6	4	20	56	95	22
Bletchley Trees Res.	30	1	3	26	27	135	6

Division One	P	W	D	L	F	A	Pts
Rangers XI	22	20	2	0	112	19	62
Bletchley Town	22	17	1	4	98	30	52
Great Linford	22	16	1	5	83	45	49
Wolverton Town	22	12	3	7	84	43	39
MKWanderers	22	12	0	10	50	32	36
Lavendon Sports Res.	22	11	3	8	71	59	36
Potterspury Res.	22	9	3	10	59	67	30
Linslade	22	8	2	12	55	58	26
Kingfisher Titans Res.	22	5	2	15	32	62	17
Yardley Gobion Res.	22	5	1	16	28	79	16
Steeple Claydon Res.	22	4	2	16	31	103	14
Wing Village Res.	22	2	2	18	23	129	8

Division Two	P	W	D	L	F	A	Pts
Wolverton Town Res.	30	26	3	1	129	39	81
E & H	30	24	1	5	128	38	73
MK Wanderers Res.	30	18	5	7	82	43	59
Sherington Res.	30	17	6	7	82	57	57
Wicken Sports	30	18	3	9	83	61	57
Skewkley Res.	30	15	4	11	72	73	49
Deanshanger Athletic Res.	30	14	6	10	79	47	48
Grendon Rangers Res.	30	12	9	9	62	40	45
Westbury	30	14	1	15	81	79	43
Syresham Res.	30	9	7	14	73	84	34
Great Linford Res.	30	10	4	16	64	86	34
Bletchley Town Res.	30	8	6	16	75	79	30
Hanslope Res.	30	7	8	15	48	82	29
Great Horwood Res.	30	6	6	18	47	82	24
Charlton	30	3	3	24	40	148	12
Marsh Gibbon Res.	30	2	2	26	33	140	8

NORTH EAST NORFOLK LEAGUE

Premier Division	P	W	D	L	F	A	Pts
East Ruston	22	17	1	4	75	38	52
Buxton	22	16	3	3	85	35	51
Lyng	22	14	4	4	74	26	46
Mundesley	22	12	3	7	62	38	39
Corpusty	22	11	3	8	67	56	36
Erpingham	22	10	3	9	52	54	33
North Walsham Old Boys	22	10	3	9	50	52	33
Gimingham	22	7	4	11	59	61	25
North Walsham Town 'A'	22	7	3	12	43	60	24
Happisburgh	22	6	3	13	50	68	21
Hickling	22	6	0	16	43	72	18
Dilham	22	1	0	21	19	119	3

Division One	P	W	D	L	F	A	Pts
Horning	22	19	0	3	80	34	57
Coltishall	22	16	2	4	99	45	50
Aldborough	22	15	1	6	102	40	46
Bodham	22	11	3	8	85	60	36
Happisburgh Res.	22	11	2	9	72	54	35
North Walsham OB Res.	22	10	1	11	59	83	31
Runton	22	9	3	10	76	55	30
Felmingham -3	22	9	2	11	46	52	26
Buxton Res.	22	7	4	11	49	90	25
Aylsham Wdrs 'A' -3	22	5	3	14	47	80	15
Briston	22	4	2	16	44	102	14
East Ruston Res.	22	3	3	16	27	91	12

Division Two	P	W	D	L	F	A	Pts
Holt United 'A'	20	17	1	2	95	29	52
Stalham Town 'A'	20	14	2	4	71	24	44
Corpusty Res.	20	14	2	4	56	31	44
Cromer Youth Old Boys	20	11	3	6	88	39	36
Mundesley Res.	20	10	2	8	119	54	32
Gimingham Res.	20	9	2	9	57	70	29
Aldborough Res.	20	8	1	11	38	76	25
Cawston	20	5	4	11	50	60	19
Hickling Res.	20	6	1	13	47	80	19
Briston Res.	20	4	0	16	41	124	12
Blakeney	20	3	0	17	36	111	9

NORTH GLOUCESTERSHIRE LEAGUE

Premier Division	P	W	D	L	F	A	Pts
Soudley	28	22	2	4	88	29	68
Minsterworth	28	20	1	7	85	52	61
Ruardean Hill Rangers	28	18	4	6	81	37	58
Aylburton Rovers	28	18	2	8	86	47	56
Lydney Town Res.	28	16	5	7	65	34	53
Woolaston	28	14	6	8	50	26	48
Westbury United	28	13	2	13	49	53	41
Newent Town	28	13	2	13	69	83	41
Staunton & Corse	28	12	3	13	49	55	39
Sling United	28	12	3	13	54	64	39
Lydbrook Athletic Res.	28	8	6	14	40	53	30
Broadwell Amateurs Res.	28	8	1	19	30	66	25
Mushet & Coalway Utd	28	5	5	18	32	70	20
Ellwood Res.	28	5	3	20	26	69	18
Whitecroft	28	2	3	23	23	89	9

Division One	P	W	D	L	F	A	Pts
Redbrook Rovers	24	18	2	4	77	35	56
Coleford United	24	15	6	3	67	27	51
Milkwall	24	14	5	5	67	42	47
Blakeney	24	12	3	9	50	37	39
Yorkley	24	12	3	9	46	47	39
Worrall Hill	24	9	8	7	45	45	35
English Bicknor	24	9	6	9	47	49	33
Bream Amateurs	24	7	5	12	49	60	26
Lydbrook Athletic 'A'	24	8	2	14	34	67	26
Rank Outsiders	24	6	6	12	36	41	24
Huntley Res.	24	7	3	14	38	67	24
Sedbury United	24	5	6	13	50	62	21
Ruspidge United -3	24	5	3	16	33	60	15

Division Two	P	W	D	L	F	A	Pts
Avenue	24	17	2	5	80	23	53
Newnham United	24	14	9	1	66	31	51
Mitcheldean Res.	24	13	3	8	48	39	42
Newent Town Res.	24	12	2	10	64	51	38
Westbury United Res.	24	11	4	9	62	57	37
Howle Hill	24	10	6	8	56	51	36
Harrow Hill 'A'	24	11	2	11	53	63	35
Soudley Res.	24	10	4	10	47	51	34
Puma	24	9	4	11	49	60	31
Longhope	24	9	1	14	44	52	28
Lydney Town 'A'	24	8	4	12	35	45	28
Whitecroft Res.	24	5	6	13	34	55	21
Mushet/Coalway Utd Res.	24	3	1	20	26	86	10

Division Three	P	W	D	L	F	A	Pts
Woolaston Res.	24	17	5	2	68	23	56
Aylburton Rovers Res.	24	17	2	5	66	32	53
St Briavels	24	14	3	7	74	47	45
Staunton & Corse Res.	24	14	1	9	80	49	43
Tidenham Res.	24	10	7	7	75	59	37
Harrow Hill 'B'	24	9	3	12	43	42	30
Mitcheldean 'A	24	9	3	12	47	52	30
Puma Res.	24	8	6	10	58	65	30
Ruardean Hill Rgrs Res.	24	7	8	9	35	51	29
Blakeney Res.	24	9	1	14	53	72	28
Whitecroft 'A'	24	8	3	13	55	80	27
Longhope Res.	24	7	2	15	28	71	23
Yorkley Res.	24	4	2	18	28	67	14

Division Four	P	W	D	L	F	A	Pts
Viney St Swithins Res.	24	21	2	1	109	27	65
Sedbury United Res.	24	18	2	4	99	38	56
White Horse	24	15	4	5	66	35	49
English Bicknor Res.	24	15	1	8	64	44	46
Minsterworth Res.	24	13	2	9	73	59	41
Redbrook Rovers Res.	24	11	0	13	80	78	33
Milkwall Res.	24	10	2	12	86	68	32
Bream Amateurs Res.	24	10	2	12	52	65	32
Coleford United Res.	24	10	1	13	57	72	31
Rank Outsiders Res.	24	8	3	13	48	69	27
Puma 'A'	24	6	2	16	39	79	20
St Briavels Res.	24	4	1	19	33	88	13
Tidenham 'A'	24	3	2	19	41	125	11

NORTH LANCASHIRE & DISTRICT

Premier Division	P	W	D	L	F	A	Pts
Storeys	26	19	2	5	75	29	59
Marsh United	26	17	6	3	83	39	57
Carnforth Rangers	26	15	7	4	50	27	52
TIC Dynamos	26	16	3	7	77	48	51
Highgrove	26	12	6	8	73	52	42
Cartmel & District	26	11	6	9	61	41	39
Kirkby Lonsdale	26	11	6	9	60	43	39
Morecambe Royals	26	11	6	9	46	38	39
Ingleton	26	10	7	9	62	57	37
Galgate	26	9	2	15	34	53	29
Swarthmoor Social Club	26	7	3	16	49	80	24
Caton United	26	5	5	16	55	106	20
Slyne-with-Hest	26	4	3	19	34	85	15
Torrisholme	26	3	2	21	30	91	11

Division One	P	W	D	L	F	A	Pts
Morecambe Hoops	28	22	6	0	100	26	72
Halton Rangers	28	19	7	2	83	32	64
Bentham	28	18	5	5	113	49	59
Storeys Res.	28	16	10	2	77	37	58
Millhead	28	11	5	12	69	80	38
Cartmel & District Res.	28	10	6	12	46	48	36
Boys Club	28	9	8	11	59	55	35
M'cambe Royals Res. -6	28	12	3	13	52	58	33
Ingleton Res.	28	7	11	10	59	61	32
Vine	28	7	7	14	45	74	28
Grange	28	6	8	14	43	59	26
College -3	28	6	10	12	53	65	25
Marsh United Res. -3	28	7	7	14	48	76	25
Slyne-with-Hest Res.	28	5	5	18	36	111	20
Westgate Wanderers -6	28	4	4	20	28	80	10

Division Two	P	W	D	L	F	A	Pts
Highgrove Res.	24	20	1	3	105	28	61
Bowerham	24	19	2	3	83	24	59
Bolton-le-Sands	24	18	2	4	76	34	56
Morecambe Cricket Club	24	16	0	8	77	54	48
Freehold	24	11	5	8	55	41	38
Arnside	24	9	4	11	53	54	31
Caton United Res.	24	9	4	11	53	65	31
Furness Rovers Res. -6	24	11	2	11	71	48	29
Middleton -9	24	10	3	11	55	69	24
Swarthmoor Soc Club Res.	24	6	3	15	47	73	21
Kirkby Lonsdale Res. -3	24	4	6	14	39	56	15
Torrisholme Res.	24	2	2	20	27	133	8
Burton Thistle -3	24	2	4	18	34	96	7

Division Three	P	W	D	L	F	A	Pts
Bolton-le-Sands Res.	20	13	2	5	49	24	41
Galgate Res.	20	12	3	5	39	23	39
Overton	20	10	5	5	37	24	35
Arnside Res.	20	9	4	7	35	34	31
Boys Club Res.	20	8	5	7	29	33	29
Heysham	20	7	5	8	42	45	26
Gregson -3	20	9	1	10	41	36	25
Allithwaite Rangers -3	20	8	3	9	38	41	24
Carnforth Rgrs Res. -3	20	8	3	9	40	48	24
Grange Res.	20	6	2	12	40	50	20
Millhead Res.	20	2	3	15	30	62	9

Division Four	P	W	D	L	F	A	Pts
Halton Rangers Res.	20	16	3	1	84	23	51
Squires	20	15	4	1	93	33	49
Bentham Res.	20	12	1	7	46	31	37
Villa Royale	20	11	3	6	51	44	36
Moghuls	20	10	3	7	56	39	33
AFC Moorlands	20	10	2	8	56	46	32
College Res. -3	20	6	4	10	44	62	19
Gregson Res. -3	20	7	1	12	40	63	19
Ingleton 'A'	20	4	5	11	31	68	17
Burton Thistle Res.	20	4	2	14	31	67	14
Overton Res.	20	1	0	19	21	77	3

NORTH LEICESTERSHIRE LEAGUE

Premier Division
	P	W	D	L	F	A	Pts
FC Dynamo	22	17	3	2	98	38	54
Ingles	22	15	2	5	57	38	47
Sileby Saints -3	22	13	4	5	71	45	39
Shepshed Amateurs	22	11	5	6	45	38	38
Radmoor -1	22	11	4	7	45	55	35
Genesis	22	8	6	8	58	55	30
Whitwick Colliery	22	8	5	9	38	52	26
Loughborough Town	22	7	5	10	55	55	24
Melton Mowbray BS	22	7	3	12	47	75	24
Loughborough	22	7	2	13	39	52	23
Woodhouse Imperial	22	4	7	11	37	55	19
Bagworth Colliery	22	2	5	15	30	58	11

Division One
	P	W	D	L	F	A	Pts
Caterpillar	20	15	2	3	57	32	47
Sutton Bonington	20	13	4	3	44	27	45
Asfordby Village	20	13	1	6	65	38	40
East Leake Athletic	20	11	4	5	63	41	37
Sutton Bonington Acad.	20	12	1	7	51	33	37
Newbold Jubilee -1	20	11	4	5	51	30	36
Burton	20	7	3	10	42	45	24
Markfield	20	6	2	12	39	56	20
Sileby Victoria	20	4	1	15	38	73	13
Revive -1	20	4	2	14	30	60	9
Club AZ -3	20	1	3	16	28	73	3

Division Two
	P	W	D	L	F	A	Pts
Whitwick Wanderers	22	18	3	1	73	11	57
Falcons	22	15	6	1	74	26	51
Kegworth Imperial	22	11	4	7	74	49	37
ATI Garryson	22	11	3	8	63	57	36
Ashby Ivanhoe 'A'	22	11	2	9	53	40	35
Birstall Old Boys	22	9	4	9	50	53	31
Belton Villa -1	22	9	3	10	41	56	29
CF Turpins	22	8	3	11	34	45	27
Thurmaston Rangers	22	7	3	12	61	60	24
Loughborough Res.	22	6	3	13	36	82	21
Anstey Town 'A'	22	5	2	15	48	73	17
Sileby Saints Res. -3	22	3	2	17	31	80	10

Division Three
	P	W	D	L	F	A	Pts
The Railway EWM	20	16	3	1	67	20	51
Shepshed Amateurs Res.	20	13	3	4	58	27	42
Markfield Res.	20	13	2	5	52	32	41
Ingles Res.	20	10	4	6	63	48	34
Loughborough United	20	9	4	7	66	47	31
Measham Imperial	20	9	1	10	56	49	28
Belgrave Res.	20	7	4	9	35	43	25
Woodhouse Imperial Res.	20	5	4	11	38	58	22
Bagworth Colliery Res.	20	5	3	12	40	63	18
Thringstone Rangers -1	20	3	2	15	27	74	10
Sileby Victoria Res.	20	1	6	13	31	74	9

Division Four
	P	W	D	L	F	A	Pts
ATI Garryson Res. +2	22	15	1	6	83	41	48
Greenhill Youth Club -1	22	15	2	5	53	26	46
East Leake Athletic Res.	22	14	2	6	66	35	44
Melton Mowbray BS Res.	22	12	3	7	65	45	39
Ferrari	22	12	1	9	73	72	37
Birstall Old Boys Res. -1	22	12	1	9	56	57	37
Caterpillar Res. -4	22	11	1	10	59	63	30
Sutton Bonington Res.	22	6	4	12	39	46	22
Genesis Res.	22	6	3	13	37	58	21
Loughborough Utd Res.	22	6	1	15	49	73	19
Thurmaston Rangers Res.	22	6	1	15	40	71	19
Long Clawson -3	22	7	0	15	40	72	18

NORTH WEST NORFOLK LEAGUE
(Build Centre)

Division One
	P	W	D	L	F	A	Pts
Heacham	22	19	3	0	75	22	60
Wiggenhall	22	16	1	5	67	36	49
Ingoldisthorpe	22	12	3	7	55	30	39
Terrington	22	12	3	7	65	45	39
King's Lynn 'A'	22	11	3	8	62	40	36
West Winch	22	11	2	9	51	40	35
Gaywood	22	8	2	12	60	60	26
Reffley Royals	22	6	6	10	35	49	24
Narborough	22	6	2	14	29	55	20
Lynn Napier	22	5	2	15	40	71	17
Hunstanton	22	3	2	17	19	76	11
Marham Wanderers	22	2	3	17	27	94	9

Division Two
	P	W	D	L	F	A	Pts
Lynn Docklands	24	21	2	1	102	24	65
West Lynn Social Res.	24	16	2	6	88	39	50
Ingoldisthorpe Res.	24	16	1	7	74	43	54
Sandringham	24	15	1	8	66	48	46
Great Massingham	24	9	3	10	41	58	31
Terrington Res.	24	8	6	10	49	59	30
Internationale Lynn	24	8	3	13	44	50	27
Flitcham	24	8	6	10	42	66	30
Docking	24	7	4	14	72	72	28
West Winch Res.	24	5	1	18	48	133	16
Castle Rising	24	5	1	18	45	111	16
Snettisham	24	6	3	15	35	57	21
Watlington	24	3	6	15	35	35	15

Division Three
	P	W	D	L	F	A	Pts
Old Hunstanton	20	16	3	1	67	21	48
Wisbech United	20	13	3	4	58	27	42
Dersingham Rovers Res.	20	13	3	4	58	27	42
Wiggenhall Res.	20	10	4	6	63	48	34
Denver Bell	20	10	4	6	63	48	34
Castle Acre	20	9	4	7	66	47	31
William Burt	20	9	4	7	66	47	31
Burnham Market	20	9	1	10	56	49	28
Stanhoe	20	7	4	9	35	43	25
Walsingham	20	6	4	10	38	58	22
West Lynn Riverside	20	5	3	12	40	63	18
Fakenham Town 'A'	20	4	1	15	27	74	18
Heacham Res.	20	4	1	15	27	111	16
Flitcham Res.	20	1	6	13	31	74	9

Division Four
	P	W	D	L	F	A	Pts
Lynn Discovery	26	23	2	1	166	29	71
Queensway	26	19	2	5	108	36	59
Narborough Res.	26	17	1	8	63	35	52
Wiggenhall 'A'	26	16	2	8	63	33	50
Smithdon	26	16	0	10	82	66	48
South Creake	26	14	4	8	57	52	47
Greyfriars	26	14	0	12	69	51	46
Dersingham Rovers 'A' -4	26	10	4	12	42	60	34
Pentney	26	9	3	14	55	87	30
Heacham 'A'	26	6	3	17	42	105	21
Snettisham Res.	26	5	5	16	51	96	20
Lynn Napier Res.	26	5	4	17	42	74	19
Hunstanton Res.	26	4	4	18	30	70	16
Wisbech United Res.	26	4	0	22	31	133	12

NORTHAMPTON TOWN LEAGUE
(Peter Smith Recruitment)

Premier Division
	P	W	D	L	F	A	Pts
Northampton Harlequins	18	14	2	2	46	18	44
Univ. of Northampton	18	11	6	1	49	13	42
Airflow	18	10	3	5	51	29	33
Thorplands United	18	10	0	8	37	48	30
Double Four	18	7	1	10	37	48	22
Denton	18	2	3	13	22	71	9
Resource United -3	18	3	2	13	30	47	8
Asda George – record expunged							

Division One
	P	W	D	L	F	A	Pts
Cotton Hill Warriors	24	21	2	1	102	24	65
Far Cotton Loco -3	24	16	2	6	88	39	49
Hitec Rooftile	24	16	2	6	108	52	50
Univ. of N'thampton Res.	24	15	1	8	79	56	46
Delapre Old Boys	24	13	3	8	66	41	42
Obelisk United	24	9	7	8	51	58	34
Ashley Rovers	24	7	6	10	62	66	30
Swan & Helmet	24	8	2	14	52	66	26
N'thampton H'quins Res.	24	6	4	14	49	104	22
James King Blisworth 'A'	24	5	1	18	45	83	16
Thorplands Utd Res. -6	24	5	2	15	34	109	11
Northants Police	24	3	6	15	35	57	15

NOTTS AMATEUR ALLIANCE

Premier Division
	P	W	D	L	F	A	Pts
Bulwell	26	25	1	0	98	31	75
Santos	26	18	1	7	111	59	55
Beacon	26	15	6	5	88	55	50
Trident	26	15	2	9	115	55	47
Ashland Rovers	26	15	4	7	72	53	47
Vernon Villa	26	14	8	4	75	50	46
Middleton Villa	26	12	4	10	76	59	40
Burton Joyce	26	12	3	11	60	60	39
Netherfield Albion	26	8	5	13	52	96	29
Limekiln	26	8	3	15	44	73	27
Nottinghamshire	26	6	7	13	54	61	25
Whitemoor United	26	6	3	17	34	87	13
Premium	26	4	1	21	31	114	13
Boots Athletic 'A'	26	4	0	22	31	114	12

Division One
	P	W	D	L	F	A	Pts
Arnold Longbow	28	22	4	2	110	41	68
Gedling Southbank 'A'	28	19	2	7	78	50	59
Kirton Brickworks	28	18	4	7	93	63	50
FC Samba	28	14	7	7	68	60	48
FC Gunthorpe	28	15	3	10	68	63	48
Bottesford	28	12	2	14	59	58	38
AFC Bridgford	28	11	3	14	71	58	38
Greygoose	28	11	5	12	72	71	38
Ruddington Village	28	11	5	12	66	66	36
Kimberley MW Old Boys	28	10	6	12	53	68	36
Vernon Villa Res.	28	9	5	14	44	75	32
Arnold Town 'A'	28	10	1	17	65	91	31
Vernon Villa Res.	28	8	1	19	64	75	25
Basford United 'A'	28	8	0	20	60	106	24
Nottingham Sikh Lions	28	4	5	19	53	89	17

NORWICH BUSINESS HOUSES LEAGUE
(Rogers & Norton)

Division One
	P	W	D	L	F	A	Pts
Drayton	18	14	1	3	68	25	43
Homecare United	18	12	2	4	59	27	38
Norwich St Johns 'A'	18	12	1	5	43	18	37
Yelverton	18	10	4	4	55	44	34
Marlborough Old Boys	18	10	2	6	45	44	32
UEA Res. -5	18	10	4	4	53	33	29
Norwich Union 'A'	18	7	1	10	37	45	22
Wensum Albion	18	6	2	10	37	52	20
Taverham	18	2	1	15	26	84	7
Costessey Crown	18	0	1	17	27	113	1

Division Two
	P	W	D	L	F	A	Pts
Jarrolds	18	11	1	6	46	26	38
Dyers Arms	18	11	3	4	51	28	36
Mousehold Athletic	18	10	2	6	47	27	32
Hoveton Wherrymen Res.	18	9	2	7	39	27	29
Loddon United 'A'	18	9	2	7	41	29	29
Salhouse Rovers	18	7	5	6	35	40	26
UEA 'A' -5	18	7	4	7	41	41	18
Newton Flotman Res.	18	5	4	9	22	27	17
Blofield United 'A' -2	18	4	3	11	23	64	13
Thorpe Village 'A'	18	1	3	14	16	54	6

Division Three
	P	W	D	L	F	A	Pts
Costessey Sports	18	16	0	2	75	27	48
Sprowston Beehive	18	15	0	3	70	36	45
Marlborough Arms	18	14	1	3	70	31	43
South Walsham Res.	18	8	0	10	54	44	24
Hempnall 'A'	18	8	0	10	49	49	24
Freethorpe Res.	18	5	4	9	33	50	19
Horsford United 'A' -2	18	5	4	9	35	41	17
Drayton Res.	18	4	4	10	36	63	16
Mousehold Athletic Res.	18	4	1	13	37	74	13
Norwich Union 'B'	18	1	2	15	28	75	5

WWW.NLNEWSDESK.CO.UK

WWW.CHERRYRED.CO.UK

Division Two

	P	W	D	L	F	A	Pts
Ashland Rovers Res.	22	18	2	2	110	30	56
East Valley United	22	17	2	3	91	32	53
Burton Joyce Res. -1	22	13	5	4	76	51	45
Three Crowns	22	14	2	6	89	49	44
Kashmir	22	11	5	6	79	47	38
Beacon Res.	22	11	4	7	61	42	36
Bulwell Town	22	6	5	11	40	76	23
Sherwood Casuals	22	6	3	13	34	83	21
Premium Res. -3	22	7	2	13	56	82	20
Pegasus	22	4	3	15	38	79	15
Bingham Town	22	4	2	16	38	82	14
Durham Ox Wellow	22	2	4	16	27	101	10

Division Three

	P	W	D	L	F	A	Pts
Coopers Arms	30	22	5	3	127	33	71
Ali Islam	30	21	2	7	121	50	65
Basford	30	16	5	9	98	72	53
Nottingham Deaf	30	16	5	9	87	61	50
Clifton United	30	15	4	11	77	72	49
Notts Metropolis	30	12	4	14	64	78	40
East Bridgford -6	30	13	4	13	93	75	37
Chrom Alloy	30	10	4	16	53	72	34
The Mill -3	30	10	6	14	69	62	33
Robin Hood & Little John	30	5	4	21	56	56	19
Nottinghamshire 'B'	30	5	2	21	52	108	15
Chilwell Jackson -3	30	1	2	27	34	220	2

PEMBROKESHIRE LEAGUE
(James Williams)

Division One

	P	W	D	L	F	A	Pts
Merlins Bridge	26	19	4	3	73	26	61
Hakin United	26	17	5	4	87	32	56
Solva	26	15	7	4	70	52	52
Narberth	26	15	3	8	75	46	48
Pennar Robins	26	13	8	5	67	39	47
St Ishmaels	26	13	7	6	65	49	46
Monkton Swifts	26	10	5	11	62	50	38
Neyland	26	10	5	11	51	55	35
Haverfordwest County Res. -2	26	11	0	15	62	87	33
Goodwick United	26	8	10	8	48	48	30
Herbrandston	26	6	6	14	44	53	24
Carew -1	26	4	2	20	36	76	13
Milford United	26	0	0	26	19	120	0

Division Two

	P	W	D	L	F	A	Pts
Kilgetty	24	19	4	1	83	33	61
Clarbeston Road	24	18	3	3	84	31	57
Tenby -2	24	12	4	8	65	54	42
Saundersfoot Sports	24	11	4	8	64	62	35
Pembroke Borough	24	10	4	10	62	63	34
Pendine Res. -1	24	7	4	10	39	42	30
Johnston	24	9	3	12	64	87	30
Camrose	24	8	5	11	57	47	29
Fishguard Sports	24	6	6	12	44	53	24
Milford Athletic	24	5	3	16	44	64	18
Angle	24	6	2	16	36	76	20
Manorbier United	24	4	2	18	31	72	13
St Clears	24	2	5	17	41	85	11

Division Three

	P	W	D	L	F	A	Pts
Letterston	21	15	4	2	64	20	49
Haverfordwest CC -1	21	13	3	5	64	37	40
Lamphey	21	9	4	8	58	40	31
Hubberston	21	9	4	8	42	45	28
Hundleton	21	6	5	10	61	52	23
St Florence	21	6	5	10	36	59	20
Lawrenny	21	3	3	15	29	52	15
Broad Haven -3	21	3	2	16	35	83	9

Newport Lions – record expunged

Reserve Division One

	P	W	D	L	F	A	Pts
Merlins Bridge Res.	22	17	1	4	100	37	52
Monkton Swifts Res.	22	15	1	6	82	42	46
Pennar Robins Res.	22	13	4	7	86	51	41
Solva Res.	22	11	7	4	60	58	40
Prendergast Villa Res.	22	11	4	7	61	58	38
Narberth Res.	22	9	6	7	61	53	33
Clarbeston Road Res. -6	22	9	5	10	81	54	32
Goodwick Utd Res.	22	9	4	9	53	54	31
St Ishmaels Res.	22	8	6	8	68	65	30
Herbrandston Res. -3	22	5	1	16	47	88	16
Milford Athletic Res.	22	5	2	17	42	88	9
Milford United Res. -10	22	2	1	19	25	96	5

Neyland Res.

Reserve Division Two

	P	W	D	L	F	A	Pts
Saundersfoot Sports Res.	24	19	4	1	87	26	61
Kilgetty Res.	24	15	7	4	79	32	52
Camrose Res.	24	14	4	4	70	37	46
Pembroke Borough Res.	24	13	5	8	75	44	48
Hundleton Res.	24	11	8	5	67	49	41
Tenby Res.	24	10	3	11	65	62	38
Hubberston Res.	24	8	6	10	62	38	45
Haverfordwest CC Res. -1	24	8	5	11	58	72	35
St Clears Res. -1	24	10	5	9	50	51	33
Lawrenny Res.	24	9	1	14	51	80	28
Fishguard Sports Res. -9	24	7	3	14	56	81	19
Letterston Res.	24	4	5	15	24	65	17
Pendine	24	3	1	20	44	142	12

Manorbier United Res. – record expunged

PERRY STREET & DISTRICT LEAGUE

Premier Division

	P	W	D	L	F	A	Pts
South Petherton	22	19	3	0	83	33	61
White Horse Symondsbury	22	18	4	0	84	31	57
Crewkerne -2	22	12	4	6	65	34	42
Lyme Regis	22	11	4	7	64	62	35
Perry Street & Yonder Hill	22	11	3	8	50	62	30
Merriott Rovers -1	22	7	9	6	39	47	29
Winsham	22	8	3	11	45	64	27
Farway United	22	8	1	13	44	77	25
Combe St Nicholas Res.	22	6	5	11	39	58	23
Ilminster Town Res.	22	6	4	12	50	69	22
Barrington	22	4	4	14	49	69	16
Chard Town Colts	22	4	4	14	27	55	16

Division One

	P	W	D	L	F	A	Pts
Misterton	22	17	4	1	84	31	55
Beaminster	22	15	2	5	78	39	47
Forton Rangers	22	14	2	6	57	45	44
Netherbury	22	12	3	7	62	45	39
Lyme Regis Res.	22	9	4	9	55	50	30
Chard Rangers	22	9	0	10	54	57	29
Merriott Rovers Res. -1	22	8	6	8	57	55	27
Pymore -1	22	8	4	10	57	55	27
Thorncombe	22	6	5	11	45	58	23
Charmouth	22	6	5	11	35	55	23
Hinton St George	22	4	3	15	43	88	13
South Petherton Res. -6	22	3	2	17	43	112	5

Division Two

	P	W	D	L	F	A	Pts
Chard United	20	14	2	4	83	34	44
West & Middle Chinnock	20	14	2	4	71	33	44
Millwey Rise	20	13	3	4	71	27	42
Ilminster Town Colts	20	10	5	5	48	37	35
Combe St Nicholas 'A'	20	10	2	8	42	47	32
Perry St/Yonder Hill Res.	20	7	4	9	51	59	25
Dowlish & Donyatt	20	8	1	11	53	60	25
Uplyme	20	5	4	11	53	56	19
Shepton Beauchamp	20	6	1	13	36	64	19
Drimpton -3	20	6	1	13	42	79	16
Hawkchurch	20	3	3	14	26	75	12

Division Three

	P	W	D	L	F	A	Pts
White Horse Sym'b'y Res. -6	26	16	2	2	79	31	50
Forton Rangers Res.	20	14	4	2	80	24	46
Beaminster Res.	20	13	3	4	55	27	42
Norton Athletic	20	12	3	5	61	38	39
Shepton Beauchamp Res.	20	11	3	6	53	27	36
Luso-Chard	20	7	3	10	45	56	24
Hinton St George Res.	20	6	9	5	45	53	21
Combe St Nicholas 'B'	20	5	2	13	32	83	17
Netherbury Res.	20	4	2	14	38	62	14
Fivehead United -1	20	3	1	16	36	90	10
Barrington Res.	20						

Division Five

	P	W	D	L	F	A	Pts
Lyme Bantams	20	14	3	3	57	22	45
Millwey Rise Res.	20	13	5	2	72	29	44
Crewkerne Res.	20	12	3	5	44	36	39
Chard Rangers Res.	20	12	0	8	69	34	35
Farway United Res. -3	20	11	5	4	69	37	32
Misterton Res.	20	10	2	8	49	41	25
Winsham Res.	20	7	3	10	39	45	21
Charmouth Res. -3	20	7	3	10	34	53	21
Thorncombe Res.	20	4	3	13	40	69	15
Chard United Res.	20	2	1	17	27	94	7
Hawkchurch Res.	20	2	0	18	39	78	6

PLYMOUTH & WEST DEVON COMBINATION
(Underhill)

Premier Division

	P	W	D	L	F	A	Pts
Wessex LA Rangers	26	20	3	3	98	31	55
Plymouth Parkway Res.	26	20	3	3	92	34	63
Clipper Rangers	26	13	5	8	62	49	44
Old Suttonians	26	13	5	8	61	55	44
Friary Vaults Mt G. -10	26	17	2	7	65	44	43
Elburton Villa Res. -6	26	14	3	10	63	44	43
Plymouth University	26	13	3	10	72	44	42
Roborough +3	26	11	0	15	59	64	39
Plymouth Civil Serv. -6	26	6	6	14	43	66	30
Tamarside Res.	26	6	6	14	43	62	24
Vospers Oak Villa Res.	26	4	5	17	51	92	17
Lee Moor	26	4	4	18	26	83	16
Plymstock United Res.	26	2	3	21	41	106	5
Yealm GR	26						

Senior Division

	P	W	D	L	F	A	Pts
Royal Mail	26	25	1	0	107	27	76
Horrabridge Rangers	26	22	1	3	109	41	67
Staddiscombe Colts	26	19	1	6	78	35	58
Red Lion (Plymouth)	26	16	5	5	88	53	53
Friendship Inn	26	15	3	8	104	56	48
The No 10 Club	26	15	0	11	72	70	45
Old Suttonians Res.	26	10	1	15	59	97	31
SWEB	26	6	7	13	61	78	27
Cafe Roma	26	8	3	15	62	63	21
Plymouth Univ. Res. -6	26	8	3	17	46	87	21
Plymouth City	26	5	4	17	47	47	19
Yelverton	26	5	2	19	41	112	15
Buckland MC	26						11
Mainstone Sports	26						

Intermediate Division

	P	W	D	L	F	A	Pts
Horrabridge Rgrs Res.	18	13	3	2	78	32	42
Western Mortgage Services	18	12	1	5	51	34	37
Plymouth Parkway 'A'	18	10	1	7	45	27	31
Morley Rangers	18	10	0	8	47	38	31
Ordulph Arms	18	9	0	9	39	55	30
Chard United	18	7	4	7	43	49	25
Plymouth University 'A'	18	8	1	9	49	63	25
Roborough Res.	18	6	4	8	48	48	22
Old Suttonians 'A'	18	3	1	14	36	87	8
Ham Green Rovers -6	18	1	0	16	36	85	4

PORTSMOUTH & DISTRICT LEAGUE

Premier Division

	P	W	D	L	F	A	Pts
Horndean United	16	11	3	2	50	13	36
Prospect	16	10	3	3	64	26	33
Wymering	16	9	4	3	41	25	31
Waterlooville SC	16	9	1	6	49	32	28
NBC Dragons	16	7	6	3	34	34	26
Old Portmuthians	16	6	5	5	46	32	25
Kingston Arrows	16	5	1	10	42	55	16
Segensworth	16	2	1	13	23	79	7
Tardis Music	16	1	0	15	27	80	3

St Davids City – record expunged

PRESTON & DISTRICT LEAGUE

Premier Division	P	W	D	L	F	A	Pts
Preston Wanderers	30	22	6	2	102	32	72
Southport Trinity	30	20	6	4	82	24	66
Longridge Town	30	20	5	5	94	40	65
Southport Amateurs	30	18	4	8	75	48	58
Leyland St Marys	30	16	2	12	85	85	50
Lostock St Gerards Res. -3	30	15	5	10	84	58	47
Leyland Red Rose	30	14	3	13	76	68	45
Hoghton West End	30	12	9	9	71	70	45
Tarleton Corinthians	30	12	5	13	57	55	41
Town Green	30	9	5	16	56	82	32
Appley Bridge	30	9	3	18	61	81	30
Burscough Richmond	30	8	5	17	38	71	29
Eccleston & Heskin	30	9	1	20	45	85	28
Baxters	30	8	2	20	65	113	26
Croston Sports Res.	30	7	3	20	49	88	24
Burscough Bridge	30	6	6	18	42	82	24

Division One	P	W	D	L	F	A	Pts
Southport Trinity Res.	24	17	5	2	67	26	56
New Longton Rovers	24	17	2	5	73	31	53
CCA	24	14	5	5	51	35	47
Walmer Bridge	24	10	9	5	54	42	39
Preston GSA	24	11	5	8	53	38	38
Blessed Sacrement -3	24	11	5	8	64	51	35
Chipping	24	10	3	11	53	58	33
Royal Garrison	24	9	5	10	61	56	32
Top Spinners	24	9	3	12	45	54	30
Hoole United	24	7	3	14	32	62	24
Charnock Richard 'A'	24	6	1	17	49	68	19
Halsall -3	24	5	4	15	37	61	16
Farington Villa	24	4	2	18	38	95	14

Division Two	P	W	D	L	F	A	Pts
Ainsdale United	20	16	1	3	68	24	49
Southport Trinity 'A'	20	14	3	3	63	29	45
Highcross	20	11	2	7	49	32	35
Walton-le-Dale	20	10	3	7	51	33	33
Mawdesley	20	8	5	7	64	53	29
Leyland Red Rose Res.	20	7	5	8	43	45	26
Heath Charnock -6	20	9	3	8	54	62	24
Tarleton Corinthians Res.	20	6	2	12	35	67	20
Preston United	20	4	6	10	37	56	18
Newman College	20	5	2	13	36	64	17
Muldoons	20	3	2	15	31	66	11

Division Three	P	W	D	L	F	A	Pts
AFC Mawdesley	22	15	2	5	91	48	47
Longridge Town Res.	22	14	2	6	63	45	44
Preston GSA Res.	22	14	1	7	83	53	43
Southport Amateurs Res.	22	14	1	7	74	56	43
Leyland Red Rose 'A'	22	13	3	6	84	40	42
Leyland St.Marys Res.	22	12	2	8	60	51	38
Walmer Bridge Res.	22	8	3	11	51	60	27
Catforth	22	7	1	14	53	70	22
Hoghton West End Res.	22	7	1	14	50	83	22
Hesketh Bank 'A' -3	22	7	3	12	50	79	21
Greenlands	22	5	2	15	61	94	17
New Longton Rovers Res.	22	4	3	15	38	79	15

Division Four	P	W	D	L	F	A	Pts
Penwortham Town	24	17	2	5	79	38	53
Wyre Villa 'A'	24	16	1	7	102	52	49
Thornton Cleveleys 'A'	24	15	4	5	75	32	49
Deepdale	24	12	7	5	85	54	43
Birkdale United -3	24	14	3	7	72	54	42
New Longton Rovers 'A'	24	6	4	14	38	76	22
Tarleton Corinthians 'A'	24	5	4	15	46	92	19
Hoole United Res. -3	24	5	2	17	38	79	14
AFC Mawdesley Res.	24	3	3	18	36	94	12

REDHILL & DISTRICT LEAGUE

Premier Division	P	W	D	L	F	A	Pts
Brockham	18	11	4	3	48	23	37
Caterham Old Boys	18	11	3	4	47	22	36
Horley Town 'A'	18	10	0	8	54	36	30
Frenches Athletic	18	8	5	5	48	37	29
Limpsfield Blues	18	9	2	7	39	51	29
Charlwood	18	8	3	7	41	35	27
Smallfield	18	8	3	7	42	37	27
Kenley	18	5	4	9	36	57	19
Woodland Albion	18	3	4	11	35	64	13
Reigate Sala	18	3	0	15	27	55	9

Division One	P	W	D	L	F	A	Pts
Chipstead 'A'	22	17	3	2	68	31	54
Walton Heath	22	14	3	5	79	53	45
RH123 Athletic	22	14	2	6	102	45	44
Tatsfield Rovers	22	12	3	7	68	47	39
Smallfield Res.	22	11	6	5	60	49	39
Reigate Priory Res.	22	12	2	8	60	46	38
Bookham 'A'	22	9	3	10	64	57	30
Warlingham 'A'	22	8	1	13	37	60	25
Reed	22	5	5	12	52	59	20
Nork Social	22	6	1	15	51	77	19
Nutfield Res.	22	5	2	15	40	82	17
Duke of York	22	2	3	17	39	114	9

Division Two	P	W	D	L	F	A	Pts
Reigate Hill	18	14	2	2	51	23	44
Tatsfield Rovers Res.	18	12	5	1	46	25	41
Cheam Vill. Warriors 'A'	18	9	4	5	55	33	31
Wates	18	9	3	6	58	35	30
Park Lane	18	9	2	7	50	36	29
Merstham Newton Res.	18	7	4	7	42	39	25
South Park 'A'	18	6	1	11	33	57	19
Paynes Sports	18	4	3	11	31	49	15
South Godstone Res.	18	4	3	11	31	50	15
Oxted & District 'A'	18	2	1	15	23	73	7

Division Three	P	W	D	L	F	A	Pts
Merstham 'A'	20	14	2	4	76	47	44
Charlwood Res.	20	14	1	5	66	40	43
Wallington New Foresters	20	12	4	4	64	42	40
Bletchingley Res.	20	12	3	5	54	37	39
Westcott '35	20	11	1	8	67	54	34
RH123 Athletic Res.	20	9	3	8	43	55	30
Warlingham 'B'	20	7	5	8	56	45	26
Reigate Priory 'A'	20	5	2	13	47	68	17
Holland Sports Res.	20	4	4	12	32	53	16
Reigate Hill Res.	20	3	4	13	38	69	13
Park Lane Res.	20	3	3	14	31	64	12

Division Four	P	W	D	L	F	A	Pts
Real Holmesdale Res.	24	21	1	2	103	28	64
Racing Epsom	24	19	0	5	93	38	57
Court Lodge	24	13	6	5	58	41	45
Sutton Churches	24	11	3	10	57	48	36
Heath Old Boys	24	11	3	10	53	48	36
Limpsfield Blues Res.	24	10	3	11	48	57	33
Brockham Res.	24	9	3	12	44	52	30
Cheam Vill. Warriors 'B'	24	7	7	10	36	44	28
Albury Manor	24	7	7	10	58	78	28
Frenches Athletic Res.	24	8	4	12	45	76	28
Walton Heath Res.	24	5	5	14	43	67	20
Park Lane 'A'	24	5	4	15	42	71	19
Reigate Priory 'B'	24	4	6	14	38	70	18

Division Five	P	W	D	L	F	A	Pts
Sagemaster	18	13	2	3	55	33	41
Timebridge	18	11	2	5	67	50	35
RH123 Athletic 'A'	18	10	1	7	53	55	31
AFC Redhill	18	9	3	6	54	39	30
Frenches Athletic 'A'	18	9	2	7	63	53	29
Horley Elite	18	9	2	7	62	52	29
Merstham Newton 'A'	18	6	2	10	53	64	20
Park Lane 'B'	18	5	3	10	37	51	18
Court Lodge Res.	18	5	2	11	35	48	17
Westcott '35 Res.	18	2	3	13	34	68	9

RHONDDA & DISTRICT LEAGUE

	P	W	D	L	F	A	Pts
Wyndham +3	26	21	2	3	150	52	68
Ynyshir Albion Res.	26	21	3	2	89	42	66
Treorchy	26	18	5	3	125	31	59
Tuberville Arms Res.	26	16	3	7	95	53	51
AFC Llwynypia Res. -6	26	14	3	9	84	59	39
Ferndale Boys Club Res.	26	11	6	9	79	61	39
Lewis Merythr	26	12	3	11	95	79	39
AFC Porth Res.	26	10	5	11	61	57	35
Trebanog Rangers -6	26	12	2	12	72	72	32
Tonyrefail BGC Res. +3	26	8	4	14	67	91	31
Tonyrefail Welfare	26	8	5	13	50	69	29
Max	26	5	4	17	54	87	19
Penygriag BGC +3	26	3	1	22	31	139	13
The Baglan	26	0	0	26	20	180	0

ROCHESTER & DISTRICT LEAGUE
(I-Agent)

Premier Division	P	W	D	L	F	A	Pts
Gillingham Green	24	19	3	2	80	24	60
FC Quayside	24	18	3	3	71	21	57
Bredhurst Juniors	24	15	3	6	54	28	48
Sheerness East Res.	24	11	5	8	66	59	38
Medway City	24	11	3	10	42	49	36
Hollands & Blair Res.	24	9	7	8	49	40	34
Cliffe Woods	24	8	8	8	50	51	32
Medway Queen	24	7	8	9	46	45	29
Wayfield Athletic	24	8	3	13	48	45	27
Greenwich Thistle	24	6	6	12	36	60	24
Lordswood Athletic	24	6	4	14	34	50	22
Horsted	24	5	2	17	34	91	17
Emerald Star	24	3	5	16	36	83	14

Division One	P	W	D	L	F	A	Pts
Medway Knights	22	17	1	4	70	35	52
Cannon '24	22	13	6	3	89	48	45
Stockbury Athletic	22	14	2	6	66	34	44
Upchurch	22	12	3	7	57	43	39
Bredhurst Juniors Res.	22	11	2	9	61	54	35
BAE Systems	22	10	4	8	67	55	34
The Waggon	22	9	4	9	81	62	31
Pegasus	22	8	4	10	45	62	28
Evolution	22	6	3	13	45	76	21
Cliffe Woods Res.	22	6	2	14	42	77	20
Grain Athletic	22	5	2	15	45	71	17
Three Sisters	22	3	3	16	38	89	12

Division Two	P	W	D	L	F	A	Pts
Evolution Res.	24	20	3	1	107	31	63
Cobras	24	15	1	8	86	50	46
Pegasus Res.	24	13	3	8	96	55	42
Luton Athletic	24	12	6	6	80	51	42
Medway Ports	24	12	4	8	53	46	40
Breach Rovers	24	12	3	9	60	51	39
Anchorians	24	12	2	10	79	77	38
Isle of Grain	24	8	5	11	44	74	29
Bredhurst Juniors 'A'	24	7	5	12	52	70	26
JD Decking	24	8	2	14	37	73	26
Cliffe Woods 'A'	24	8	0	16	54	88	24
Medway Galvanising	24	5	2	17	76	93	17
Poachers	24	4	4	16	29	94	16

Division Three	P	W	D	L	F	A	Pts
Park Regis	22	17	2	3	100	31	53
FC Istead	22	16	1	5	79	39	49
Strood	22	14	4	4	84	45	46
Plough/Chequers Spts Res.	22	12	4	6	62	47	40
Collyers	22	11	4	7	52	30	37
O'Connell's	22	9	7	6	59	44	34
Inn-Bar Taverns	22	8	5	9	47	53	29
Insanity	22	7	6	9	53	51	27
Emerald Star Res.	22	7	3	12	43	65	24
The Good Intent	22	5	4	13	34	62	19
Medway Athletic	22	3	2	17	31	105	11
Beechwood '76	22	1	2	19	28	100	5

Division Four	P	W	D	L	F	A	Pts
Riverside	22	22	0	0	111	25	66
Woodcoombe Spts & Soc	22	14	2	6	92	39	44
Outer Fenn	22	13	1	8	65	43	40
Kings Head	22	12	3	7	62	54	39
Park Regis Res.	22	11	3	8	60	51	36
Emerald Star Classics	22	11	2	9	60	52	35
Star Sports	22	10	3	9	39	50	33
The Rising Sun	22	8	1	13	46	60	25
Lycos	22	6	3	13	37	60	21
Valley Colts	22	6	1	15	36	72	19
Eurobars	22	4	2	16	33	67	14
Data Techniques	22	4	1	17	33	101	13

Division Five

	P	W	D	L	F	A	Pts
Southern Belle	22	19	0	3	88	34	57
Rainham '84	22	15	1	6	79	49	46
Cliffe Woods 'B'	22	14	1	7	94	46	43
Royalside	22	14	0	8	69	43	42
AFC Phoenix	22	12	1	9	74	51	37
Stockbury Athletic Res.	22	11	1	10	61	54	34
Bowaters	22	8	4	10	58	72	28
Sturdee	22	9	1	12	56	83	28
Bleakwood Rangers	22	8	2	12	55	67	26
Slade '05	22	7	3	12	46	80	24
Elm Windows Star	22	4	1	17	73	73	13
Lloyds	22	2	3	17	27	77	9

Division Six

	P	W	D	L	F	A	Pts
Bredhurst Juniors 'B'	22	19	2	1	107	39	59
General-at-Sea	22	16	1	5	115	45	49
Rose Inn Gillingham	22	14	4	4	76	58	46
Sturdee Res.	22	12	3	7	82	54	39
Medway Colts	22	12	3	7	82	54	39
Snodland Nomads	22	12	1	9	62	43	37
Sitespace	22	8	2	12	79	64	26
Outer Fenn Res.	22	5	7	10	39	59	22
UK Paper Res.	22	7	1	14	62	83	22
Three Mariners	22	7	1	14	57	98	22
Medway Ports Res.	22	4	1	17	39	109	13
Canopus	22	1	0	21	25	130	3

ROMFORD & DISTRICT LEAGUE

Senior Division

	P	W	D	L	F	A	Pts
Debden Sports Res.	22	16	4	2	60	23	52
Clack United	22	16	3	3	83	33	51
Millhouse	22	13	5	4	64	31	44
Newtown Wesley	22	13	4	5	87	48	43
Upney Royal Oak	22	13	1	8	62	34	40
Marlborough	22	10	4	8	46	38	34
Claybury	22	7	6	9	59	68	27
Upminster Res.	22	7	1	14	36	72	22
Duckwood	22	5	5	12	38	59	20
East Ham WMC	22	4	7	11	32	79	19
Athletico Lighte	22	5	2	15	36	79	17
New Ventos	22	2	4	16	40	74	10

Premier Division

	P	W	D	L	F	A	Pts
Northend	22	16	3	3	67	39	51
Stifford Clays	22	15	2	5	77	32	47
Debden Sports 'A'	22	13	3	6	58	48	42
May & Baker	22	13	3	6	46	38	42
Canning Town 'A'	22	12	0	10	46	44	36
Harold Wood Hospital	22	10	4	8	42	44	34
Brabazon Sports	22	10	3	9	42	47	33
Cromer Park	22	7	4	11	42	47	25
Upminster 'A'	22	6	1	15	33	65	19
Chelmwood	22	4	4	16	39	62	16
Emernians	22	4	2	16	29	61	14
Riverside Rangers	22	1	1	20	21	63	4

WWW.CHERRYRED.CO.UK

Division One

	P	W	D	L	F	A	Pts
Mansard Rovers	18	16	1	1	48	15	49
Celtic Vigo	18	12	2	4	43	26	38
Dagenham WMC	18	11	1	6	47	43	34
OG United	18	8	5	5	39	31	29
Verona	18	7	5	6	39	50	26
Clockwork Res.	18	8	1	9	50	61	25
Northend Res.	18	7	1	10	36	53	22
Rileys United	18	6	2	10	36	55	20
Spartan Athletic	18	4	1	13	31	72	13
Cary Outreach	18	1	1	16	13	69	4

Ardleigh Green – record expunged
Barking Legends – record expunged
Euro Dagenham Res. – record expunged

Division Two

	P	W	D	L	F	A	Pts	
Northend 'A'	18	15	1	2	75	20	48	+1
Marlborough Veterans	18	14	1	3	64	18	43	
Fulbrook Royals	18	9	5	4	58	28	32	
Eastside Rovers	18	8	4	6	51	38	28	
Aveley WMC	18	8	3	7	48	55	27	-1
Coryton Athletic	18	5	2	11	38	64	17	
Real Dagenham	18	5	2	11	36	55	17	
New Ventos Res.	18	5	2	11	25	70	14	
East Ham WMC Res.	18	4	2	12	28	78	14	
Canning Town 'B'	18	4	1	13	28	78	13	+3

SALISBURY & DISTRICT LEAGUE

Premier Division

	P	W	D	L	F	A	Pts
Stockton & Codford	18	13	2	3	49	11	41
Friends Provident	18	13	1	4	45	14	40
Bemerton Hth H'quins 'A'	18	10	5	3	51	19	35
Porton Sports	18	8	6	4	45	32	30
Alderbury	18	8	4	6	40	32	28
Whiteparish	18	7	3	8	38	38	24
South Newton/Wishford	18	6	3	9	34	43	21
St Pauls Club	18	3	3	12	32	59	12
Nomansland	18	3	2	13	25	62	11
Tisbury	18	0	1	17	18	74	1

Division One

	P	W	D	L	F	A	Pts
Enford	18	13	2	3	66	27	41
West Harnham	18	12	2	4	77	36	38
Chalke Valley Roofing	18	10	1	7	60	40	31
George Hotel	18	8	4	6	49	40	28
Alderbury Res.	18	8	3	7	44	42	27
Rouge Raiders	18	6	1	11	40	52	19
George & Dragon	18	5	3	10	32	48	18
Winterslow	18	5	2	11	36	52	16
Sth Newton/Wishford Res.	18	4	2	12	32	59	11
Boscombe Down	18	2	1	15	16	76	7

Division Two

	P	W	D	L	F	A	Pts
Five Bells	18	15	1	2	86	25	46
Chalke Valley Res.	18	14	2	2	85	35	44
Duck Inn	18	12	4	2	55	35	38
Langford	18	9	3	6	57	31	30
Beacon Sports	18	8	4	6	49	49	28
Stockton & Codford Res.	18	6	3	9	43	69	21
Tisbury Res.	18	5	3	10	48	54	19
Victoria Hotel	18	4	1	13	31	54	16
Porton Sports Res.	18	4	1	13	21	63	13
Hi-flex Sports	18	2	2	14	27	78	8

Division Three

	P	W	D	L	F	A	Pts
Stonehenge Snooker	16	13	1	2	72	16	41
RGV Netheravon	16	12	1	3	60	15	37
Woodisbury	16	11	1	4	44	22	34
Figheldean Rangers	16	8	1	7	35	30	25
Coach & Horses	16	8	0	8	29	30	24
Alderholt	16	6	2	8	31	30	20
Burgess Trees	16	5	2	9	30	43	17
Fordingbridge Turks 'A'	16	2	1	13	16	66	7
Winterslow Res.	16	2	0	14	14	71	6

SCUNTHORPE & DISTRICT LEAGUE
(Johnstone Insurance)

Division One

	P	W	D	L	F	A	Pts
AFC Brumby	22	18	3	1	71	16	57
BBM	22	14	2	6	77	34	44
Scotter United	22	14	1	7	51	30	43
Scunthonians	22	13	1	8	61	36	42
Smiffy's	22	12	4	6	56	32	40
Beacon Rovers	22	12	2	8	54	30	38
Epworth Town	22	11	3	8	48	36	36
Appleby Frodingham Colts	22	9	2	11	51	48	29
Swinefleet Juniors	22	5	4	13	38	51	19
Crosby Colts	22	5	3	16	30	77	16
Scawby	22	3	3	16	25	77	12
Sherpa	22	2	1	19	10	99	7

Division Two

	P	W	D	L	F	A	Pts
Messingham Trinity Jnrs	26	20	5	1	95	25	65
AFC Brumby Res.	26	17	5	4	86	44	56
Barton United Colts	26	16	8	2	74	44	44
Limestone Rangers	26	13	2	11	53	57	41
Haxey Town	26	12	4	10	53	57	40
Crosby Colts Res.	26	11	4	11	72	36	37
BBM Res.	26	10	5	11	49	50	35
New Holland Villa	26	10	5	11	45	54	35
Barnetby United	26	10	3	13	44	77	33
Scunthonians Res.	26	9	4	13	57	74	31
Barrow Wanderers	26	9	2	15	47	61	29
College Wanderers	26	9	2	15	47	73	29
Briggensians	26	6	2	18	42	73	20
Luddington	26	2	4	20	27	101	10

SELBY & DISTRICT LEAGUE

Division One

	P	W	D	L	F	A	Pts
Riley's	22	19	1	2	80	42	58
Knottingley	22	19	0	3	106	41	57
Pontefract S & S Res.	22	14	1	7	93	46	43
Coach & Horses	22	14	0	8	94	59	42
Moorends	22	12	1	9	92	68	37
Pollington	22	10	3	9	65	67	33
Rileys Rangers	22	10	2	10	49	68	32
Riccall	22	8	1	13	55	75	25
South Milford	22	6	4	12	52	89	22
Fairburn	22	6	0	16	44	86	18
Pontefract Town	22	5	2	15	40	82	17
Garforth WMC	22	1	1	20	29	100	4

Division Two

	P	W	D	L	F	A	Pts	
Yorkshire Penny	28	23	1	4	121	36	70	
Snaith	28	18	3	7	99	53	54	
Rothwell Town 'A'	28	18	0	10	73	41	54	-3
New Airedale	28	16	4	8	86	50	52	
Garforth Rangers	28	16	4	8	83	56	52	
Sherburn White Rose 'A'	28	15	1	12	72	65	46	
Garforth WMC Res.	28	13	4	11	68	68	43	
Great Preston Res.	28	12	4	12	82	68	40	
Selby RSSC Res.	28	11	3	14	57	62	39	
Garforth AFC	28	11	2	15	67	89	35	
Monk Fryston	28	8	6	14	51	70	32	
Yorkshire Rose	28	8	6	14	54	89	30	
Kellington	28	8	2	18	54	91	26	
Willow Park	28	8	1	19	46	79	25	
Drax	28	2	3	23	37	125	9	

SEVENOAKS & DISTRICT LEAGUE
(Sennocke)

Premier Division

	P	W	D	L	F	A	Pts
Halstead United	20	15	3	2	62	37	47
Sevenoaks Town 'A'	19	13	3	3	104	30	42
Kemsing	20	10	6	4	60	43	36
St Lawrence	20	11	3	6	45	43	36
Nomads	20	9	6	5	66	42	33
Sevenoaks Weald	20	9	2	9	42	50	29
Eynsford	20	8	5	7	49	45	29
Ightham	20	5	5	10	37	54	20
Borough Green United	20	5	0	15	37	56	20
Seal	20	2	2	16	19	75	8

Division One

	P	W	D	L	F	A	Pts	
Hildenborough Athletic	22	17	2	3	105	24	53	
Dunton Green	22	16	3	3	87	33	51	
AW London	22	13	4	5	55	39	43	
Ide Hill	22	11	4	7	66	40	37	
Orpington 'A'	22	10	2	10	64	49	32	
Eynsford Res.	22	9	5	8	49	53	32	
Halstead United Res.	22	8	5	9	47	54	29	
Kingsdown Racers	22	8	3	11	53	54	27	
Fleetdown United 'A'	22	7	3	12	45	52	24	
Sevenoaks Weald Res.	22	6	3	13	54	81	21	
Seal Res.	22	5	1	16	36	84	14	-3
Westerham 'A'	22	1	2	19	20	146	5	

Division Two	P	W	D	L	F	A	Pts
Tonbridge Baptist Church	20	15	2	3	69	26	47
Crockham Hill	20	14	1	5	53	30	43
St Lawrence Res.	20	12	2	6	64	53	38
Chipstead 'A'	20	9	3	8	55	36	30
Hadlow Rovers	19	9	3	7	48	35	30
Old Boars	18	7	4	7	50	44	25
Riverhead	20	7	4	9	39	37	25
Otford United 'A'	20	7	3	10	45	55	24
Hildenborough Ath. Res.	20	6	2	12	43	53	20
St Georges	19	6	0	13	38	81	18
Seal 'A'	20	2	4	14	24	78	10

Kingdown Racers Res. – record expunged

Division Three	P	W	D	L	F	A	Pts
Kemsing Res.	24	19	5	0	97	24	62
Orpington 'B'	24	17	2	5	71	28	53
Chipstead 'B'	23	15	1	7	69	50	46
Dunton Green Res.	24	14	2	8	71	46	44
Borough Green	24	12	4	8	70	50	40
Westerham 'B'	24	11	2	11	70	54	35
Ightham Res.	24	11	2	11	50	71	35
Potters	24	10	3	11	54	53	33
Tonbridge Baptist Ch. Res.	24	7	4	13	58	65	25
Nomads Res.	24	7	3	14	40	73	24
Seal 'B'	24	6	3	15	49	72	21
Wilderpark Res.	23	6	1	16	36	71	19
Ide Hill Res.	24	3	2	19	25	103	11

SOUTH LONDON ALLIANCE

Premier Division	P	W	D	L	F	A	Pts
Crofton Albion	24	17	2	5	48	22	53
Forest Hill Park	24	16	4	4	72	35	52
Drummond Athletic	24	15	2	7	50	44	47
Old Roan	24	14	2	8	59	40	44
Long Lane	24	11	6	7	49	42	39
Metrogas Res.	24	10	5	9	44	52	35
Tudor Sports Res.	24	10	4	10	52	55	34
Blackheath Wanderers	24	10	1	13	44	56	31
Sutton Athletic Res.	24	10	0	14	52	69	30
Johnson & Phillips	24	6	7	11	40	41	25
Cray Vall. Paper Mills Res.	24	7	3	14	49	50	24
Kingfisher	24	7	3	14	53	57	24
Middle Park	24	1	5	18	28	77	8

Wilmington – record expunged

Division One	P	W	D	L	F	A	Pts
Bexlians	20	16	2	2	59	35	50
Lewisham Athletic	20	15	1	4	67	30	46
AFC Sydenham	20	12	1	7	68	40	37
Parkhurst Rangers	20	11	4	5	52	37	37
Wickham Wanderers	20	10	4	6	55	55	34
Seven Acre Sports	20	7	4	9	38	49	25
Phoenix Sports Res.	20	5	7	8	41	45	22
Dresdner Kleinwort	20	5	3	12	32	43	18
Bridon Ropes Res.	20	5	2	13	25	46	17
Beaverwood	20	5	2	13	28	65	17
Farnboro' OB Guild Res.	20	3	2	15	24	44	11

Eltham Town – record expunged
Melbourne United – record expunged
Penhill Standard – record expunged

Division Two	P	W	D	L	F	A	Pts
Cray Valley Paper Mills 'A'	24	18	4	2	82	20	58
New Park	24	17	5	2	77	18	56
NASFAT	24	13	3	8	49	35	42
Old Town New Boys	24	12	5	7	52	37	41
Elite	24	12	2	10	49	49	38
Old Roan Res.	24	11	4	9	50	50	37
Longlands Athletic	24	10	5	9	57	48	35
Long Lane Res.	24	10	3	11	30	36	33
Metrogas 'A'	24	8	5	11	40	47	29
Old Colfeians	24	8	4	12	45	51	28
Beckenham Royals	24	7	4	13	30	65	25
Johnson & Phillips Res.	24	4	2	18	23	64	14
Gold Hawks	24	3	0	21	22	86	9

Division Three	P	W	D	L	F	A	Pts
Charterhouse-in-Southwark	24	17	2	5	78	31	53
Blackheath Wdrs Res.	24	15	3	6	75	34	48
West Bromley Albion	24	15	3	6	75	43	48
Greenwich Borough 'A'	24	14	4	6	62	32	46
Bridon Ropes 'A'	24	14	3	7	56	32	45
Crofton Albion Res.	24	13	4	7	46	28	43
Avery Hill College	24	11	6	7	46	41	39
Bexley	24	8	5	11	29	36	29
Old Roan 'A'	24	7	3	14	47	62	24
Farnborough OB Guild 'A'	24	7	2	15	37	73	23
Eltham Palace Res.	24	7	1	16	40	69	22
Wickham Park 'A'	24	4	5	15	34	70	17
Lewisham Athletic Res.	24	2	3	19	27	101	9

Division Four	P	W	D	L	F	A	Pts
Charlton Ath. Community	24	21	3	0	122	31	66
Heath	24	17	4	3	82	39	55
Salmon	24	14	3	7	72	43	45
Valley Park Rangers	24	12	7	5	65	37	43
Bexley Res.	24	13	3	8	79	41	42
Metrogas 'B'	24	11	3	10	56	48	36
Westminster Old Boys	24	9	7	8	67	64	34
Crayford Arrows	24	10	2	12	52	67	32
Crofton Albion 'B'	24	9	2	13	67	67	29
Guy Earl	24	8	3	13	44	61	27
Seven Acre Sports Res.	24	6	3	15	43	86	21
Beaverwood Res.	24	3	2	19	23	104	11
Bexley Park	24	2	0	22	21	105	6

Lewisham City – record expunged

SOUTH YORKSHIRE AMATEUR LEAGUE

Premier Division	P	W	D	L	F	A	Pts
Aston	20	16	1	3	110	25	49
Jubilee Sports	20	14	3	3	118	29	45
Athersley Recreation Res.	20	14	3	3	62	30	45
Dale Tavern	20	14	1	5	78	37	43
Cross Scythes	20	10	3	7	62	50	33
Kiveton Park Res.	20	10	2	8	66	32	32
G & Ts	20	7	0	13	44	63	21
Civil Service -3	20	5	2	13	42	66	14
Oxspring United	20	4	1	15	28	105	13
Phoenix	20	4	0	16	30	143	12
Bradway	20	3	2	15	31	91	11

Division One 'A'	P	W	D	L	F	A	Pts
New Bohemians	16	11	3	2	61	28	36
Gleadless	16	11	2	3	64	32	35
Farm Rd Sports & Social	16	11	1	4	63	39	34
Middlewood Rovers	16	8	4	4	48	27	28
Millmoor Juniors Res.	16	7	4	5	41	33	25
Boynton Sports	16	5	3	8	42	38	18
Ringside Rovers	16	5	2	9	29	46	17
Burngreave	16	1	4	11	23	58	7
De La Salle Old Boys -3	16	1	1	14	27	97	1

Division One 'B'	P	W	D	L	F	A	Pts
Sheffield West End	16	12	2	2	73	32	38
Penguin	16	10	3	3	51	33	33
Sheffield Medics	16	9	3	4	47	34	30
Oughtibridge War Mem Res.	16	6	8	2	64	43	26
Dale Tavern Res.	16	6	4	6	48	48	22
Thurgoland Welfare	16	5	5	6	37	35	20
Sheffield Bankers Res.	16	5	3	8	28	43	18
Norwich Union	16	3	3	10	28	42	12
Castle	16	0	1	15	17	83	1

SOUTHEND & DISTRICT LEAGUE

Premier Division	P	W	D	L	F	A	Pts
AFC Horndon	15	11	3	1	35	13	36
Rhodesia United	15	10	2	3	54	18	32
Newchurch	15	8	2	5	28	13	26
Signet United	15	4	3	8	25	43	15
Runnymede	15	4	1	10	18	35	13
Wickford Rangers	15	2	1	12	15	53	7

Division One	P	W	D	L	F	A	Pts
Swan Mead	16	14	0	2	46	15	42
Club Sirrus	16	10	3	3	28	16	33
King John Barmy Army	16	9	3	4	54	27	30
Sparkbridge	16	8	1	7	35	37	25
Rochford Town Res.	16	6	4	6	29	27	22
Eversley	16	6	2	8	32	33	20
Sparco	16	6	2	8	32	36	20
Thundersley Rovers	16	3	1	12	20	50	10
Chalkwell Park	16	1	2	13	27	62	5

SOUTHEND BOROUGH COMBINATION

Premier Division	P	W	D	L	F	A	Pts
Rochford Town	20	17	1	2	77	29	35
Shoebury Town	20	11	5	4	51	38	27
Ekco/Thames Park	20	10	3	7	46	38	23
Exhibition United	20	9	4	7	46	38	22
Borough Rovers	20	8	6	6	42	42	22
Old Southendian	20	10	1	9	48	42	21
Catholic United	20	8	4	8	32	37	20
Leigh Town	20	7	5	8	53	51	19
Blackgate Gunners	20	6	4	10	39	47	16
Essendon	20	6	1	13	36	55	13
Zebra Sports	20	0	2	18	23	76	2

Division One	P	W	D	L	F	A	Pts
Southbury	20	9	9	2	41	28	27
S'thchurch Hall Old Scholars	20	11	3	6	64	30	25
Ensign	20	11	2	7	66	38	24
Weir Sports	20	9	5	6	62	42	23
Southend Collegians	20	8	5	7	54	53	21
BKS Sports	20	8	3	9	37	71	19
Ekco/Thames Park Res.	20	8	2	10	50	49	18
Borough Rovers Res.	20	7	4	9	39	51	18
Westcliff Amateur	20	4	9	7	39	49	17
Airborne United	20	4	6	10	45	52	14
Thorpe Athletic	20	5	4	11	42	76	14

Division Two	P	W	D	L	F	A	Pts
Ekco/Thames Park 'A'	20	17	2	1	72	34	36
Corinthians	20	13	2	5	57	42	28
Thundersley United	20	13	1	6	64	38	27
Emstar United	20	11	3	6	68	37	25
Little Theatre Club	20	6	8	6	50	53	20
Shoebury Town Res.	20	9	2	9	37	46	20
Old Southendian Res.	20	8	3	9	36	54	19
Ashingdon Boys	20	5	4	11	50	52	14
Cupids Country Club	20	5	3	12	37	57	13
Ensign Res.	20	4	3	13	46	64	11
Customs/Excise (Southend)	20	2	3	15	35	75	7

Division Three	P	W	D	L	F	A	Pts
Hullbridge Sports Res.	18	12	4	2	54	30	28
Earls Hall United	18	13	2	3	42	24	28
Catholic United Res.	18	8	8	2	49	30	24
Rayford Athletic	18	8	5	5	52	28	21
Leigh Town Res.	18	7	3	8	33	43	17
S'thchurch Hall O S Res.	18	7	2	9	42	40	16
Leigh Ramblers 'A'	18	6	3	9	35	40	15
Cupids Country Club Res.	18	5	3	10	35	55	13
Southend Collegians Res.	18	5	0	13	29	59	10
Trackback	18	3	2	13	31	53	8

Division Four	P	W	D	L	F	A	Pts
Ashingdon Boys Res.	22	21	0	1	119	14	42
Trinity (S)	22	16	2	4	74	28	34
White Horse Rangers	22	14	3	5	63	35	31
Weir Sports Res.	22	13	5	4	69	42	31
Ekco/Thames Park 'B'	22	11	3	8	60	53	25
Old Southendian 'A'	22	10	1	11	57	45	21
Earls Hall United Res.	22	8	4	10	47	46	20
Rayford Athletic Res.	22	9	2	11	39	64	20
S'thchurch Hall O S 'A'	22	8	2	12	52	59	18
Highbank	22	4	0	18	19	45	8
Southend Rangers	22	4	0	18	26	105	8
Southend Collegians 'A'	22	3	0	19	16	105	6

Division Five	P	W	D	L	F	A	Pts
Castle Point Gas	20	15	2	3	93	31	32
Leigh Town 'A'	20	13	2	5	77	25	28
Heathfield	20	13	0	7	63	37	26
Corinthians Res.	20	11	2	7	71	56	24
Elmwood Old Boys	20	9	3	8	46	48	21
Weir Sports 'A'	20	8	5	7	54	59	21
Old Southendian 'B'	20	7	5	8	38	67	19
S'thend Police Service Utd	20	8	1	11	43	39	17
Barnsford Hurricanes	20	6	4	10	42	56	16
Leigh Ramblers 'B'	20	3	4	13	33	70	10
Rayford Athletic 'A'	20	2	2	16	29	101	6

Division Six

	P	W	D	L	F	A	Pts
Thundersley United Res.	20	12	3	5	70	35	50
Little Theatre Club Res.	20	11	3	6	56	51	48
Landwick	20	10	3	7	48	48	44
Catholic United 'A'	20	10	0	10	59	55	24
Southend Collegians 'B'	20	3	5	12	36	57	14
Weir Sports 'B'	20	3	5	12	36	57	11

SOUTHERN AMATEUR LEAGUE

Higher Divisions on page 11

Junior Division One

	P	W	D	L	F	A	Pts
Alleyn Old Boys 'A'	20	16	2	2	69	29	50
Nottsborough 'A'	20	11	5	4	45	45	37
Old Actonians Assoc. 'A'	20	12	1	7	63	49	37
Old Owens 'A'	20	9	6	5	56	43	33
Weirside Rangers 'A'	20	9	6	5	54	51	33
Winchmore Hill 'A'	20	8	5	7	54	51	29
Old Esthameians 'A'	20	8	3	9	48	55	27
E Barnet O Gramms 'A'	20	8	3	9	44	54	27
Civil Service 'A'	20	7	3	10	32	40	24
Norsemen 'A'	20	5	2	13	36	53	17
Old Stationers 'A' -2	20	1	1	18	23	70	2

Junior Division Two

	P	W	D	L	F	A	Pts
Carshalton 'A'	20	14	2	4	67	31	44
Kew Association 'A'	20	13	2	5	60	44	41
West Wickham 'A'	20	12	1	7	47	39	39
Old Finchleians 'A'	20	10	5	5	49	43	35
HSBC 'A'	20	10	4	6	54	46	34
Crouch End Vampires 'A'	20	7	6	7	41	45	27
Polytechnic 'A'	20	8	2	10	45	49	26
O Westminster Citizens 'A'	20	6	4	10	45	46	22
Old Salesians 'A'	20	6	3	11	37	57	21
Bank of England 'A'	20	6	2	12	34	62	20
Broomfield 'A'	20	3	1	16	27	67	10

Junior Division Three

	P	W	D	L	F	A	Pts
Old Wilsonians 'A'	20	14	2	4	63	26	44
Merton 'A'	20	13	2	5	75	37	41
Ibis 'A'	20	13	2	5	61	36	41
Alexandra Park 'A'	20	11	3	6	45	35	36
Old Latymerians 'A'	20	8	4	8	40	45	28
Old Parkonians 'A'	20	9	3	8	54	43	30
Southgate Olympic 'A'	20	9	3	8	40	54	30
Lloyds TSB Bank 'A'	20	7	5	8	41	42	26
South Bank Cuaco 'A'	20	6	1	13	34	49	19
BB Eagles 'A'	20	4	4	12	26	68	16
Old Lyonians 'A' -6	20	3	2	15	26	64	5

Minor Division One

	P	W	D	L	F	A	Pts
Winchmore Hill 'B'	20	12	5	3	56	28	41
Nottsborough 'B'	20	10	5	5	57	35	35
Old Actonians Assoc. 'B'	20	10	5	5	36	35	35
Old Owens 'B'	20	9	4	6	44	30	34
Alexandra Park 'B'	20	8	6	6	46	30	30
Old Parkonians 'B'	20	8	3	9	43	43	30
Winchmore Hill 'C'	20	7	6	7	43	41	26
Old Actonians Assoc. 'C'	20	6	6	8	41	36	24
Civil Service 'B'	20	5	8	7	40	36	23
West Wickham 'B'	20	6	4	10	38	46	22
Crouch End Vampires 'B'	20	1	2	17	32	75	5

Minor Division Two North

	P	W	D	L	F	A	Pts
Norsemen 'B'	22	16	2	4	65	35	50
Winchmore Hill 'D'	22	15	3	4	76	33	48
Southgate Olympic 'B'	22	14	2	6	79	45	44
Old Owens 'C'	22	10	4	8	47	46	34
Old Parkonians 'B'	22	10	2	10	56	47	32
Norsemen 'C'	22	9	2	11	46	56	29
Crouch End Vampires 'C'	22	8	2	12	45	89	26
Old Owens 'D'	22	8	1	13	44	54	25
Old Stationers 'B'	22	7	3	12	47	54	24
E Barnet O Gramms 'B'	22	6	5	11	38	47	23
E Barnet O Gramms 'C'	22	6	5	11	43	60	21
Old Finchleians 'B'	22	6	3	13	43	57	15

Minor Division Two South

	P	W	D	L	F	A	Pts
Carshalton 'B'	18	14	1	3	70	31	43
West Wickham 'C'	18	13	3	2	72	40	42
Polytechnic 'B'	18	9	3	6	55	40	30
BB Eagles 'B'	18	9	0	9	55	55	27
Civil Service 'D'	18	7	0	11	57	41	21
HSBC 'B'	18	7	1	10	38	46	23
Kew Association 'B'	18	5	3	10	31	41	18
HSBC 'C'	18	5	2	11	43	69	17
O Westminster Citizens 'B'	18	2	1	15	31	86	7

Minor Division Three North

	P	W	D	L	F	A	Pts
Norsemen 'D'	20	14	3	3	71	40	45
Broomfield 'B'	20	12	3	5	53	35	39
Old Parkonians 'C'	20	12	2	6	46	37	38
Alexandra Park 'C'	20	10	1	9	45	51	33
Old Stationers 'C'	20	9	1	10	49	43	27
Winchmore Hill 'E'	20	8	2	10	52	60	26
Norsemen 'E'	20	7	3	10	41	57	24
Old Finchleians 'C'	20	4	2	14	41	69	14
Southgate Olympic 'C'	20	4	2	14	31	85	14

Minor Division Three South

	P	W	D	L	F	A	Pts
Polytechnic 'C'	18	12	4	2	76	27	44
Weirside Rangers 'B'	18	12	3	3	47	29	39
Old Actonians Assoc. 'D'	18	8	6	4	37	29	30
Merton 'B'	18	7	4	7	37	39	25
Old Alexandrians 'C'	18	7	4	7	35	37	25
Polytechnic 'D'	18	7	1	10	52	40	22
Carshalton 'C'	18	5	4	9	39	44	19
Ibis 'B'	18	5	3	10	28	45	18
Old Actonians Assoc. 'E'	18	5	2	11	22	43	17
South Bank Cuaco 'B'	18	3	5	10	26	56	14

WWW.CHERRYRED.CO.UK

Minor Division Four North

	P	W	D	L	F	A	Pts
Winchmore Hill 'F'	20	15	2	3	70	28	48
Old Finchleians 'E'	20	14	4	2	79	35	46
Winchmore Hill 'G'	20	9	4	7	41	31	29
Crouch End Vampires 'E'	20	10	4	6	59	51	29
Broomfield 'C'	20	10	4	6	47	48	28
Alexandra Park 'D'	20	10	2	10	56	48	27
Old Finchleians 'D'	20	9	2	9	40	55	29
E Barnet O Gramms 'D'	20	7	1	12	45	53	26
Norsemen 'G'	20	5	5	10	38	66	22
Broomfield 'D'	20	4	3	13	38	69	15
Norsemen 'F'	20	3	6	11	24	57	15

Minor Division Four South

	P	W	D	L	F	A	Pts
Alleyn Old Boys 'B'	18	12	3	3	71	25	54
Carshalton 'D'	18	12	3	3	68	40	41
Weirside Rangers 'C'	18	9	4	5	40	58	28
Kew Association 'C'	18	8	6	4	58	46	26
Old Lyonians 'B'	18	9	3	6	58	44	24
BB Eagles 'C'	18	6	2	10	55	59	24
Alleyn Old Boys 'C'	18	5	3	10	34	45	18
Old Salesians 'B'	18	5	2	11	45	61	17
South Bank Cuaco 'C'	18	1	1	16	23	80	4

Minor Division Five North

	P	W	D	L	F	A	Pts
Old Esthameians 'C'	20	16	1	3	70	30	50
Old Parkonians 'E'	20	13	1	6	93	31	49
Old Parkonians 'D'	20	11	1	8	85	45	40
Alexandra Park 'E'	20	11	1	8	55	34	34
Winchmore Hill 'H'	20	10	3	7	67	57	33
Southgate Olympic 'D'	20	8	4	8	42	54	24
Alexandra Park 'F'	20	6	4	10	44	48	22
Old Stationers 'D'	20	6	3	11	48	54	21
Crouch End Vampires 'F'	20	6	2	12	45	82	20
E Barnet O Gramms 'F'	20	1	2	17	31	121	5

Minor Division Five South

	P	W	D	L	F	A	Pts
Kew Association 'D'	18	14	1	3	55	24	43
Lloyds TSB Bank 'C'	18	11	3	4	44	34	36
HSBC 'D'	18	8	5	5	41	23	31
O Westminster Citizens 'C'	18	8	1	9	55	41	29
Merton 'C'	18	7	3	8	41	37	26
Old Actonians Assoc. 'F'	18	6	2	10	38	46	25
Old Wilsonians 'D'	18	4	2	12	34	52	23
Carshalton 'E'	18	4	2	14	31	56	14
Bank of England 'B'	18	2	2	14	26	60	14
HSBC 'E'	18					71	14

Minor Division Six South

	P	W	D	L	F	A	Pts
Kew Association 'E'	18	12	2	4	72	24	44
West Wickham 'D'	18	11	2	5	37	35	35
O Westminster Citizens 'D'	18	10	1	7	61	48	30
Merton 'D'	18	7	4	7	47	35	25
Civil Service 'E'	18	7	1	10	49	52	22
Polytechnic 'E'	18	5	3	10	39	42	19
Polytechnic 'F'	18	5	2	11	52	42	17
Polytechnic 'E'	18	5	2	11	33	53	13
Old Actonians Assoc. 'E'	18	3	3	12	31	62	10
Old Wilsonians 'E'	18	2	1	15	26	75	8

Minor Division Seven South

	P	W	D	L	F	A	Pts
Polytechnic 'G'	16	12	1	3	53	28	48
Old Latymerians 'B'	16	12	1	3	79	32	37
HSBC 'F'	16	10	2	4	48	31	32
South Bank Cuaco 'D'	16	8	1	7	57	60	26
Lloyds TSB Bank 'D'	16	6	2	8	51	54	20
Kew Association 'F'	16	4	4	8	42	63	16
Old Actonians Assoc. 'H'	16	4	4	8	34	56	8
BB Eagles 'D'	16	2	2	12	33	56	7
Old Wilsonians 'F'	16	1	4	11	32	66	7

Minor Division Eight South

	P	W	D	L	F	A	Pts
Kew Association 'G'	21	14	5	2	94	25	47
Carshalton 'F'	21	11	4	6	79	41	37
Alleyn Old Boys 'D'	21	9	4	8	56	44	28
Merton 'E'	21	8	5	8	44	61	27
Lloyds TSB Bank 'F'	21	8	5	8	46	72	29
Lloyds TSB Bank 'E'	21	7	7	7	67	48	28
Bank of England 'C'	21	6	11		45	71	18
Old Wilsonians 'G'	21	2	5	14	38	71	11

SPEN VALLEY LEAGUE

Premier Division

	P	W	D	L	F	A	Pts
Soothill	18	13	2	3	49	28	41
Dewsbury Westside -3	18	9	3	6	49	32	28
Bosnia	18	8	4	6	52	51	28
Savile Youth	18	7	3	8	56	42	24
Howden Clough 'A'	18	5	7	10	42	55	18
Youth 2000	18	4		8	36	55	18
Wellington Wanderers	18	4	2	12	26	47	14

Jardys – record expunged
Shooters – record expunged

Division One

	P	W	D	L	F	A	Pts
George Healey -4	16	13	0	3	52	20	35
Queensbury	16	11	0	4	80	31	33
Black Horse	16	11	0	5	36	19	33
Norfolk	16	10	1	5	49	41	31
Marsh	16	8	3	5	41	36	27
Wellington	16	9	0	7	44	37	27
Bradford Arms Res.	16	6	1	9	34	65	10
Inter Batley	16	3	1	12	25	63	7
Ring o' Bells	16	1	1	14	24	70	4

ST EDMUNDSBURY LEAGUE
(Glasswells)

Division One

	P	W	D	L	F	A	Pts
Ixworth Pykkerell	18	12	2	4	47	31	38
Rising Sun	18	11	2	5	46	28	35
Barons	18	10	3	5	45	29	33
Lawshall Swan	18	11	0	7	49	38	33
Bushel	18	9	2	7	56	36	29
Priors Inn	18	8	3	7	52	41	27
Elephant & Castle	18	8	2	8	44	46	26
Westbury United	18	4	4	10	32	53	16
Studlands Park	18	3	2	13	31	59	11
Bury Dove	18	3	3	28	69	11	

STOKESLEY LEAGUE

Division Two

	P	W	D	L	F	A	Pts
Elveden Phoenix	22	19	1	2	93	23	58
Jubilee	22	18	1	3	80	43	55
Bartons	22	13	4	5	80	41	43
Barrow	22	12	2	8	56	56	38
Pot Black	22	11	4	7	63	48	37
RF Saints	22	10	2	10	61	53	32
Black Boy	22	8	1	13	54	69	25
Rising Sun Res.	22	6	5	11	30	61	23
Sporting '87	22	7	1	14	42	62	22
Bury Rovers	22	3	2	17	32	79	11
Beck Row	22	2	2	18	32	79	8

ST HELENS COMBINATION

Premier Division

	P	W	D	L	F	A	Pts
Knowsley South	24	19	3	2	94	33	60
Denton Green	24	15	4	5	63	35	49
Rainford North End	24	14	4	6	55	38	46
Clock Face Miners	24	13	7	4	41	28	46
Shoe	24	11	3	7	57	49	33
Old Congs	24	10	3	11	52	56	30
Prescot Leisure	24	9	4	11	52	56	30
British Lion	-2	24	9	4	11	34	38	29
York	24	7	6	11	31	54	27
Windle Hotel	24	7	4	13	39	49	25
Stars	24	6	4	14	36	63	22
Eccleston United	24	6	3	16	39	65	19
Sidac Social	24	5	2	17	35	79	17

Division One

	P	W	D	L	F	A	Pts
East Villa Res.	20	16	2	2	66	15	50
Top Nogs	20	13	4	3	60	28	43
Knowsley South Res.	20	11	3	6	45	38	36
Junction	20	11	3	6	45	38	36
Gerard Arms	20	9	3	8	44	51	30
Rainford North End Res.	20	8	5	7	45	47	29
Sidac Social Res.	20	7	1	12	41	44	28
Sony	20	7	0	13	44	72	21
Oddfellows	-2	20	5	2	13	34	52	17
Carr Mill	20	5	2	13	49	70	17
The Glassblower	20	3	2	15	37	63	9

Division Two

	P	W	D	L	F	A	Pts
Wastlebridge Park	26	22	2	2	82	33	68
Greenfields	26	16	6	4	70	35	54
Boilermakers	26	16	6	4	73	35	52
Vegas	26	13	8	5	75	45	47
New Street	26	13	8	5	55	57	39
Care Trust	26	12	5	10	68	59	38
Clock Face Miners Res.	26	9	4	13	49	57	31
Carborundum Eagles	26	9	4	13	49	45	28
OCS	26	8	5	13	45	62	29
Orange House	26	6	5	13	38	61	26
Cricketers Arms	26	6	2	16	45	81	26
Engine	26	6	3	16	45	73	21
Prescot Leisure Res.	26	5	4	17	37	85	19
Beagle & Child	26	2	2	22	18	80	8

STRATFORD-ON-AVON ALLIANCE

Premier Division

	P	W	D	L	F	A	Pts
Bidford Boys Club	18	16	0	2	81	16	48
Quinton	18	13	2	3	48	25	41
Inkberrow	18	10	3	5	33	29	33
Kenilworth Tn KH Res.	18	9	3	6	41	31	30
Halfords Athletic	18	8	2	8	50	28	26
FISSC	18	8	2	8	40	37	26
Ilmington Revolution	18	4	1	13	40	78	13
Welford	18	4	1	13	40	78	13
Henley Forest Res.	18	3	2	13	32	52	11
Badsey United	18	2	1	15	15	80	7

Division One

	P	W	D	L	F	A	Pts
Bretforton Old Boys	22	18	1	3	106	36	55
Seven Stars	22	14	2	6	99	49	44
Studley Nags Head	22	10	4	8	83	56	34
Wellesbourne	22	10	3	9	63	56	33
Henley Forest-of-A'n Res.	22	10	2	10	64	59	32
Shipston Excelsior Res.	-3	22	10	2	10	46	67	29
Cubbington Albion	22	9	3	10	58	67	30
Badsey Rangers	22	8	1	13	46	78	25
FISSC Res.	22	7	2	13	36	60	23
Ilmington Revolution Res.	22	4	2	16	31	82	14
Welford Res.	-3	22	2	0	20	22	128	-1

Division Two

	P	W	D	L	F	A	Pts
Blockley Sports	22	17	2	3	76	21	53
Stratford Celtic	-3	22	14	4	5	78	40	42
Henley Forest 'A'	22	12	4	6	48	39	40
Alcester Town	22	12	3	7	67	45	39
Inkberrow Res.	22	11	5	6	73	38	38
Red Alert! Stratford	22	11	4	7	55	36	38
Claverdon	-3	22	11	4	7	55	36	34
Quinton Res.	22	5	5	12	40	60	20
Shipston Excelsior Colts	22	5	2	15	36	71	17
Tysoe United	22	5	2	15	36	71	17
Snitterfield Snipers	22	4	2	16	32	77	10
Badsey United Res.	22	3	1	18	31	106	10

STROUD & DISTRICT LEAGUE

Division One

	P	W	D	L	F	A	Pts
Barnwood United	26	22	2	2	90	25	68
Frampton United	26	18	2	6	65	40	56
Leonard Stanley	26	15	4	7	54	30	49
Abbeymead Rovers	26	16	2	8	54	55	50
Tuffley Rovers Res.	26	12	1	13	55	48	39
Whitminster	26	12	2	12	61	58	38
Minchinhampton RDS	26	11	3	12	43	51	36
Marshall Langston	26	9	7	10	41	50	34
Matson	26	9	6	11	66	60	33
Longlevens Res.	26	8	9	9	48	54	33
Shurdington Rovers Res.	26	8	7	11	48	69	31
Kings Stanley Res.	26	6	7	13	35	63	25
Coaley Res.	26	5	3	18	23	70	18
Gloucester Civil Service	26	6	2	18	31	58	18

Division Two

	P	W	D	L	F	A	Pts
Ebley Omega	24	16	3	5	78	38	51
Uley	24	16	3	5	78	38	51
Cashes Green	24	14	2	8	94	36	44
Hardwicke	24	11	5	8	56	53	38
Whiteshill United	24	9	8	7	39	52	35
Wotton Rovers Res.	24	9	5	10	39	37	32
Tibberton United	24	8	6	10	41	61	30
Horsley United	24	8	6	10	47	66	30
Longford Res.	24	8	5	11	46	54	29
Randwick	24	8	4	12	39	58	28
Thornbury Town Res.	24	8	4	13	39	58	28
Brimscombe/Thrupp Res.	24	5	6	13	29	61	23
Stonehouse Town Res.	24	4	7	13	36	58	19

Other Leagues

Division Five

	P	W	D	L	F	A	Pts
BA Rangers	22	17	3	2	90	36	54
AC Royals	22	16	4	2	70	19	52
Quedgeley Wdrs Res.	22	12	3	7	48	38	39
AFC Phoenix	22	11	5	6	66	38	38
Victoria Celtic	22	12	1	9	83	58	37
Arlingham	22	11	4	7	71	60	37
Randwick Res.	22	7	5	10	42	54	26
Dursley Town 'A'	22	7	2	13	43	67	23
Leonard Stanley Res.	-3	22	8	2	12	41	84	23
Matchplay Reeves	22	5	3	14	45	73	18
Longlevens 'B'	22	4	4	14	26	63	16
Glevum United	22	4	0	18	36	70	12

Division Six

	P	W	D	L	F	A	Pts
Abbeymead Rovers Res.	24	20	2	3	101	30	62
Whitminster Res.	24	14	2	4	101	34	56
Didmarton	24	15	3	6	66	35	48
Cashes Green Res.	24	13	3	7	72	52	45
Ebley Omega Res.	24	14	3	8	68	49	42
Eastcombe Res.	24	9	2	13	53	73	29
Stroud Harriers	24	9	2	13	55	72	26
Coaley Rovers Res.	24	7	4	13	49	67	23
Wotton Rovers 'A'	24	7	2	15	49	69	23
Cam Bulldogs 'A'	-9	24	8	6	10	55	65	21
Brockworth Albion 'B'	-6	24	6	3	15	44	69	21
Trident Res.	24	3	4	17	38	75	20
Sports NSSC	24	2	3	19	36	97	13

Division Seven

	P	W	D	L	F	A	Pts
Ramblers 'A'	22	17	3	2	90	32	54
Horsley United Res.	22	14	3	5	56	38	45
Upton St Leonards Res.	22	13	5	4	67	44	44
Quedgeley Wanderers 'A'	22	11	2	9	66	57	35
Wickwar Wanderers Res.	22	10	1	11	67	51	31
BA Rangers Res.	22	8	1	13	64	68	28
Uley 'A'	22	8	2	12	64	76	26
Randwick 'A'	22	7	4	11	54	61	25
Charfield 'A'	22	8	1	13	41	51	25
Alkerton Rangers Res.	22	8	1	13	46	89	25
Shurdington Rovers Res.	22	5	4	13	43	60	22
Sports NSSC Res.	22	3	4	17	38	68	19

Division Eight

	P	W	D	L	F	A	Pts
Whitminster 'A'	22	19	1	0	99	17	58
Tredworth Tigers	22	18	0	4	78	23	54
Chipping Sodbury Tn 'B'	-3	22	18	0	4	64	33	53
North Nibley Res.	22	14	2	6	78	42	44
Stroud Imperial	22	11	1	8	77	55	35
Hardwicke 'A'	22	11	1	8	59	61	34
Stonehouse Town 'B'	22	9	1	10	40	42	28
Avonvale United 'A'	22	7	0	13	43	76	21
Matchplay Reeves Res.	22	6	1	15	29	79	19
Upton St Leonards 'A'	22	5	0	17	33	75	15
Woodchester	-3	22	4	0	16	41	82	9

WWW.CHERRYRED.CO.UK

SUBURBAN LEAGUE

Division One
	P	W	D	L	F	A	Pts
Tooting/Mitcham U Res.	34	25	6	3	83	30	81
Metropolitan Police Res.	34	20	8	7	80	49	68
Carshalton Athletic Res.	34	20	7	7	71	39	67
AFC Wimbledon Res.	34	19	4	11	63	46	61
Uxbridge Res.	34	15	9	10	60	47	54
Eastleigh Res.	34	15	8	11	58	52	53
Ashford Tn (Middx) Res.	34	16	4	14	66	52	52
Sutton United Res.	34	16	4	14	63	50	50
Wealdstone Res.	34	13	9	12	58	51	48
Burgess Hill Town Res.	34	14	6	14	64	81	48
Hayes/Yeading Utd Res.	34	12	9	13	52	60	45
Basingstoke Town Res.	34	11	7	16	57	56	40
Whyteleafe Res.	34	10	6	18	44	61	36
Burnham Res.	34	10	6	18	41	69	36
Beaconsfield SYCOB Res.	34	10	6	18	41	69	36
Hillingdon Borough Res.	34	11	3	20	43	74	36
Fleet Town Res.	34	8	4	22	41	73	28
Harefield United Res.	34	6	4	24	52	79	22

North Division
	P	W	D	L	F	A	Pts
Dunstable Town Res.	24	17	3	4	71	37	54
Chalfont St Peter Res.	24	16	1	7	65	36	49
Ash United Res.	24	16	1	7	61	36	49
Wingate & Finchley Res.	24	12	5	7	61	40	41
Potters Bar Town Res.	24	12	4	8	56	42	40
Sandhurst Town Res.	24	8	9	7	44	49	33
AFC Hayes Res.	24	8	7	9	36	44	31
Boreham Wood Res.	24	8	6	10	55	56	30
Nth Greenford Utd Res.	24	6	6	12	33	41	26
Camberley Town Res.	24	6	8	12	36	52	20
Newport Pagnell Tn Res.	24	4	7	13	36	63	19
Berkhamsted Town Res.	24	4	5	15	36	76	17
Bedfont Res.	24	4	5	15	36	76	17

Ruislip Manor Res. – record expunged

South Division
	P	W	D	L	F	A	Pts
Salisbury City Res.	32	30	2	0	106	14	92
Corinthian Casuals Res.	32	20	8	4	72	37	66
Three Bridges Res.	32	19	8	5	71	38	65
Tonbridge Angels Res.	32	20	4	8	73	45	64
Walton Casuals Res.	32	15	5	12	73	52	50
Epsom & Ewell Res.	32	14	4	14	50	56	46
Horsham YMCA Res.	32	12	9	11	55	44	45
Cobham Res.	32	12	7	13	41	59	43
Molesey Res.	32	12	7	13	41	59	43
Raynes Park Vale Res.	32	11	8	13	50	61	41
Chipstead Res.	32	11	7	14	50	57	40
Merstham Res.	32	11	5	16	60	64	38
Colliers Wood Utd Res.	32	10	5	17	53	65	35
East Grinstead Tn Res.	32	9	5	18	41	63	32
Horley Town Res.	32	8	3	21	45	89	30
Godalming Town Res.	32	8	3	21	43	68	27
Haywards Heath Tn Res.	32	4	2	26	32	126	14

SWANSEA SENIOR LEAGUE
(Pic-up Spares)

Division One
	P	W	D	L	F	A	Pts
Ragged School	22	17	2	3	88	26	53
Winch Wen	22	17	2	3	85	31	53
South Gower	22	15	4	3	56	19	49
Bonymaen Colts	22	13	5	4	51	31	44
Penplas	22	13	4	5	58	31	43 (-1)
Penlan Club	22	8	4	10	58	54	26 (-2)
Gors	22	8	2	12	36	60	24
Cwm Press	22	6	6	10	38	59	22 (-2)
Brunswick United	22	6	4	12	34	55	22
Morriston Olympic	22	6	2	14	34	60	20
North End	22	3	2	16	26	56	11 (-3)
St Josephs	22	1	0	21	18	94	3

Division Two
	P	W	D	L	F	A	Pts
Port Tennant Colts	22	17	2	3	78	30	51
Swansea Dockers	22	14	3	5	52	27	45
Maltsters Sports	22	13	2	7	55	39	41
Rockspur	22	12	2	8	47	35	38
Gowerton	22	12	3	7	53	42	36 (-3)
Brynawel	22	9	4	9	44	42	31
Treboeth United	22	8	4	10	33	41	28
Carreg Wen	22	8	2	12	40	52	25
Coopers Arms	22	7	1	14	32	43	22 (-1)
Mumbles Rangers	22	6	4	12	50	62	22
CRC Rangers	22	2	0	20	24	80	6

Division Three
	P	W	D	L	F	A	Pts
Llangyfelach	20	15	4	1	66	17	49
West End Res.	20	13	6	1	61	31	45
Penclawdd	20	13	3	4	54	33	41 (-1)
Waunarlwydd	20	10	5	5	42	36	35
Kingsbridge Colts	20	10	5	5	42	42	35
Murton Rovers	20	9	1	10	43	43	28
Ynystawe Athletic	20	7	3	10	29	38	24
Bryndeg	20	5	5	10	38	55	20 (-1)
Hafod Brotherhood	20	5	3	12	38	52	18
Naval & Military	20	1	3	16	20	50	6

Mountain Dew Rovers – record expunged

Division Four
	P	W	D	L	F	A	Pts
Cwm Social	20	16	3	1	44	14	51
Kilvey United	20	13	3	4	86	25	45
Union Rangers	20	12	5	3	57	31	41
Hafod Rangers	20	12	1	7	74	47	37
Wales Tartan	20	11	1	8	54	28	34
Landore	20	10	3	7	52	43	33 (-1)
Birchgrove Colts	20	9	8	8	46	45	35
Seren Coch	20	5	3	12	38	52	18
Blaenymaes	20	5	2	13	43	44	17
Cwm Albion Colts	20	0	0	20	16	157	0

Reserve Division One
	P	W	D	L	F	A	Pts
Gors Res.	22	19	2	1	75	21	59
Penlan Club Res.	22	15	2	5	62	30	47
Ragged School Res.	22	13	3	6	69	40	42
Morriston Olympic Res.	22	13	2	7	68	51	41
Bonymaen Colts Res.	22	13	1	8	51	43	40
Winch Wen Res.	22	11	2	9	53	57	35
Penplas Res.	22	7	4	11	33	41	25
Treboeth United Res.	22	7	1	14	40	61	22
Ynystawe Athletic Res.	22	6	4	12	41	57	22
Cwm Press Res.	22	6	3	13	34	49	21
Maltsters Sports Res.	22	4	4	14	35	55	16
Brunswick United Res.	22	3	3	16	26	89	12

Reserve Division Two
	P	W	D	L	F	A	Pts
Port Tennant Colts Res.	20	15	3	2	56	25	48
Mumbles Rangers Res.	20	13	4	3	62	23	43
South Gower Res.	20	13	4	3	62	23	43
Coopers Arms Res.	20	10	4	6	56	38	34
Plough Colts Res.	20	9	2	9	48	42	29
Wern Res.	20	8	4	8	37	50	28
Rockspur Res.	20	8	2	10	44	37	26
Cwm Social 'A'	20	7	2	11	27	45	19
Brynawel Res.	20	6	4	10	27	45	22
Morriston Olympic 'A'	20	6	1	13	27	45	19
St Josephs Res.	20	1	5	14	22	51	8

Mountain Dew Rovers Res. – record expunged

Reserve Division Three
	P	W	D	L	F	A	Pts
North End Res.	20	15	4	1	66	17	49
Murton Rovers Res.	20	13	6	1	61	31	45
Gowerton Res.	20	13	1	6	54	33	41
Swansea Dockers Res.	20	10	5	5	42	36	35
Carreg Wen Res.	20	10	5	5	42	42	35
Ynystawe Athletic 'A'	20	9	1	10	43	43	28
Treboeth United 'A'	20	7	3	10	29	38	24
CRC Rangers Res.	20	5	5	10	38	55	20
Gors 'A'	20	5	3	12	38	52	18
Mumbles Rangers 'A'	20	5	1	14	39	64	16
Kingsbridge Colts Res.	20	1	3	16	20	50	6

Reserve Division Four
	P	W	D	L	F	A	Pts
Brynawel 'A'	20	16	3	1	44	15	45
Kingsbridge Colts 'A'	20	14	3	4	64	35	45
Wern 'A'	20	12	5	3	56	35	34
Murton Rovers 'A'	20	10	4	6	53	34	34
Hafod Brotherhood Res.	20	10	4	6	53	34	34
Wales Tartan Res.	20	8	7	5	43	40	30
Seren Coch Res.	20	8	4	8	43	37	28
Bonymaen Colts 'A'	20	8	1	13	57	72	25
Brunswick United 'A'	20	4	3	13	28	81	15
Plough Colts 'A'	20	0	0	20	16	157	0

Reserve Division Five
	P	W	D	L	F	A	Pts
Penclawdd Res.	18	15	2	1	76	29	47
Kilvey United Res.	18	15	1	2	58	18	46
Coopers Arms 'A'	18	9	2	7	47	42	29
Naval & Military Res.	18	8	1	9	50	44	25
Port Tennant Colts 'A'	18	8	1	9	50	44	25
Bryndeg Res.	18	7	3	8	47	36	24
Landore Res.	18	7	3	8	40	40	24
Cwm Social 'A'	18	5	4	9	40	42	19
Waunarlwydd 'A'	18	5	3	10	41	47	18
Cwm Albion Colts Res.	18	0	0	18	9	117	0

SWINDON & DISTRICT LEAGUE

Premier Division
	P	W	D	L	F	A	Pts
Rodbourne Arms	16	14	1	1	55	17	43
Fratellos	16	12	2	2	71	30	38
Catalus	16	12	0	4	50	35	36
Shield & Dagger	16	8	4	4	58	40	28
Bakers Arms	16	6	4	6	52	53	22
Queensfield	16	6	4	6	53	42	22
Spectrum	16	4	1	11	34	68	13
VBA Rangers	16	1	3	12	35	72	6
North Swindon WMC	16	2	0	14	23	72	3 (-3)

TAUNTON & DISTRICT LEAGUE
(Silver Street Volkswagen)

Division One
	P	W	D	L	F	A	Pts
Bridgwater Sports	22	16	4	2	80	35	52
Alcombe Rovers	22	13	3	6	60	45	42
Wyvern	22	13	2	7	63	49	41
Taverners	22	12	4	6	74	42	40
Middlezoy Rovers	22	12	2	8	61	41	38
Cossington	22	12	0	10	50	50	35
Marketeers	22	10	5	7	71	49	35
Highbridge Town	22	8	5	10	50	60	29
Locomotives	22	8	3	11	53	53	27
Porlock	22	7	5	10	45	48	26
Staplegrove	22	7	1	14	33	45	19 (-3)
Norton Fitzwarren	22	0	0	22	13	143	0

Division Two
	P	W	D	L	F	A	Pts
Dulverton Town	22	16	3	3	71	33	51
Hulan	22	13	3	6	62	44	42
Taunton Civil Service	22	10	6	6	55	44	36
Staplegrove Colts	22	10	5	7	55	46	35
Westonzoyland	22	9	5	8	52	44	32
Bishops Lydeard Res.	22	8	6	8	48	40	30
Spaxton	22	8	4	10	58	67	28
Wyvern Res.	22	8	1	13	57	77	25
Minehead Town Res.	22	6	6	10	53	45	24
Nether Stowey	22	6	4	12	48	60	22
Sampford Blues	22	6	3	13	36	53	21
Wellington Town 'A'	22	8	2	12	40	64	17 (-9)

Division Three

	P	W	D	L	F	A	Pts
Woolavington Predators	24	18	2	4	96	33	56
Bridgwater Sports Res.	24	16	1	7	79	58	49
Watchet Town Res.	24	15	1	8	41	46	46
White Hart Rangers	24	13	4	7	64	50	43
Sydenham Rangers	24	12	2	10	60	60	38
Redgate	24	10	6	8	59	49	36
Williton	24	10	3	11	52	52	33
Alcombe Rovers Res.	24	10	3	11	56	69	33
Wembdon	24	10	2	12	66	64	32
Milverton Rangers	24	8	3	13	37	49	27
North Petherton -3	24	8	3	13	66	64	24
Norton Fitzwarren Res.	24	3	1	20	35	59	10
Staplegrove Colts -9	24	5	3	16	38	100	9

Division Four

	P	W	D	L	F	A	Pts
Old Inn All Stars	22	16	2	4	97	34	50
Bridgwater Sports Colts	22	14	4	4	65	37	46
Middlezoy Rovers Res.	22	14	2	6	66	57	44
Stogursey Greyhounds	22	12	6	4	66	44	42
Appletree	22	12	2	8	52	41	38
Highbridge Town Res.	22	11	3	8	64	40	36
Exmoor Rangers	22	9	5	8	86	55	32
Wembdon Saints	22	6	1	15	50	77	19
Dulverton Town Res.	22	4	4	14	43	76	16
Westonzoyland Res.	22	5	1	16	33	68	16
Porlock Res. -6	22	5	2	15	33	68	14
Swallowfields	22	0	1	21	20	106	1

TELFORD COMBINATION

	P	W	D	L	F	A	Pts
Impact United	16	14	0	2	68	22	28
Madeley Sports	16	13	1	2	53	26	25
Shifnal United Res.	16	10	2	4	40	23	22
Pigeon Box	16	9	1	6	43	19	19
Wrockwardine Wood Res.	16	6	2	8	43	58	14
Atlas	16	4	4	8	39	61	12
Claverley	16	5	2	9	28	52	12
Much Wenlock	16	4	3	9	25	44	11
Denso	16	0	1	15	20	64	1

THANET & DISTRICT LEAGUE

Division One

	P	W	D	L	F	A	Pts
Hotel de Ville	18	16	0	2	77	27	48
Tara Plumbing	18	15	2	1	64	16	47
Hugin Vikings Athletic	18	11	1	6	51	44	34
AFC Aussie	18	8	7	3	47	41	25
Westcliff United	18	7	2	9	36	61	23
Minster Res.	18	5	7	6	34	34	22
Ambrosetti UK	18	4	5	9	40	57	17
South Eastern Tavern -3	18	5	4	9	37	59	16
AFC Margate	18	3	3	12	30	54	12
Feeneys -3	18	3	1	14	36	59	7

Division Two

	P	W	D	L	F	A	Pts
Princess of Wales	12	12	0	0	59	8	36
Barnaby Rudge	12	9	1	2	61	22	28
Hugin Hammers	12	7	1	4	34	19	22
Milton Ashbury	12	5	1	6	26	25	16
Southwich	12	4	2	6	27	41	14
Derby Army	12	1	1	10	14	44	14
KTFC	12	1	0	11	4	68	3

TONBRIDGE & DISTRICT LEAGUE

Premier Division

	P	W	D	L	F	A	Pts
Hawkenbury	20	17	1	2	88	18	52
Southborough	20	12	2	6	54	40	38
Hadlow Rangers	20	11	4	5	68	40	37
High Brooms Casuals +3	20	11	1	8	73	33	36
Rusthall Res. -6	20	13	3	4	65	31	36
Woodlands	20	10	2	8	66	37	32
Edenbridge +3	20	7	3	10	23	31	27
Langton Green	20	8	1	11	43	68	25
Tunbridge Wells Utd -6	20	8	5	10	36	59	14
Brenchley Wanderers	20	2	2	16	30	87	8
Roselands +3	20	1	2	17	20	83	8

Railway Bell – record expunged

Division One

	P	W	D	L	F	A	Pts
Tonbridge Invicta Res.+2	20	16	2	2	82	18	52
Rusthall 'A'	20	15	4	1	75	40	46
Hawkenbury Res. +3	20	11	2	7	50	36	38
Hadlow Harrow -1	20	12	2	6	63	46	37
The Hilberts	20	10	1	9	66	45	31
Blackham & Ashurst	20	10	0	10	44	50	24
Pembury Res.	20	8	0	12	48	77	24
Leigh	20	4	3	13	30	68	15
Horsmonden Sports	20	4	3	13	30	92	15
Penshurst Park +3	20	3	2	15	25	92	14
Southborough Res.	20	3	3	14	32	55	12

Division Three

	P	W	D	L	F	A	Pts
East Peckham Juniors -3	22	20	2	0	95	25	59
Hawkenbury 'A' +6	22	15	1	4	85	51	52
AFC Valour	22	15	4	4	97	50	49
Paddock Wood +3	22	12	9	1	86	45	48
Brenchley Wdrs Res.-6	22	10	3	6	59	66	27
Rusthall 'B'	22	8	2	12	44	56	24
Dowgate	22	7	3	12	46	88	22
High Brooms Casuals Res.	22	7	1	14	68	52	20
Frant	22	6	2	14	52	92	20
Roselands Res.	22	5	4	13	42	95	19
Tunbridge Wells Utd Res.	22	5	3	14	61	75	18
Ashton Prime -3	22	5	2	15	30	62	14

TROWBRIDGE & DISTRICT LEAGUE (Revolutions)

Division One

	P	W	D	L	F	A	Pts
Seend United	18	14	1	3	49	13	45
AFC T'bridge Yth Res. -3	18	11	2	5	54	29	32
Blue Circle	18	9	4	5	34	37	31
Frome Town Sports	18	9	3	6	41	37	30
Freshford United	18	9	3	6	43	39	30
Steeple Ashton	18	8	4	6	40	40	28
The Deverills	18	4	5	9	31	40	17
Warminster Town Res.	18	4	3	11	18	44	15
Bradford United	18	4	2	12	24	41	14
FC Northbridge	18	2	2	14	25	54	8

TYNESIDE AMATEUR LEAGUE

Division One

	P	W	D	L	F	A	Pts
Forest Hall	26	22	3	1	89	32	68
Wallsend Town Res.	26	19	4	3	114	61	61
Winlaton Vulcan Inn	26	19	0	7	85	44	57
Blyth Thoroton	26	12	6	8	70	44	42
Newcastle City	26	11	5	10	70	60	38
Gosforth Boh. Garnett Res.	26	11	4	11	72	77	38
The Piper Cullercoats	26	11	2	13	72	63	35
Blyth Town Res.	26	10	4	12	57	56	34
West Jesmond	26	9	3	14	66	78	30
Bellingham	26	10	1	15	66	62	30
Wardley Durham Rgrs -3	26	8	4	14	64	64	28
Newcastle Medicals	26	7	3	16	64	97	24
Lindisfarne Athletic	26	5	3	18	38	80	18
Killingworth YPC Res. -3	26	1	1	24	30	134	1

Division Two

	P	W	D	L	F	A	Pts
Killingworth YPC Tn	24	17	2	5	92	43	53
Blyth Spartans 'A'	24	15	4	5	92	52	49
Kicks Wallsend	24	15	1	8	74	46	46
Wallsend The Anson	24	13	0	11	61	51	39
Red Star Benwell	24	13	0	11	75	71	34
New York	24	10	4	10	58	65	34
Walker Central Res. -3	24	9	4	11	58	55	31
Blaydon House	24	8	0	16	48	77	24
Gosforth Boh. G't 'A' -3	24	4	3	13	30	92	12
Newcastle RVI Lochside	24	7	5	12	47	77	26
Killingworth West House	24	5	3	16	48	69	18
Grainger Park Boys Club	24	4	6	14	39	73	18
Rutherford Newcastle Res.	24	4	4	16	46	78	16

WAKEFIELD & DISTRICT LEAGUE

Premier Division

	P	W	D	L	F	A	Pts
Horbury Cherry Tree	20	17	2	1	75	21	53
Airedale Celtic	22	15	4	4	97	45	50
Thornhill	22	13	2	5	86	42	41
Snydale Athletic	22	10	6	7	40	46	29
White Bear Kexborough	20	8	2	12	46	56	26
Ryecroft Sports	22	7	3	12	46	56	24
Walton	22	7	1	14	68	82	22
Crofton Sports	22	6	2	14	52	92	20
Smiths Arms	22	5	4	13	39	95	19
Ferrybridge Amateurs	20	5	2	13	56	62	19
Fieldhead Hospital -3	20	3	1	16	29	75	14

Mitres Well – record expunged

Division One

	P	W	D	L	F	A	Pts
Stanley Arms	26	22	1	2	105	35	68
Nostell Miners Welf. 'A'	26	20	1	5	84	38	61
Kingstone United WMC	26	16	2	8	88	49	50
Old Bank WMC	26	14	5	7	82	61	43
Dewsbury Rgrs OB -4	26	14	4	8	75	60	40
Stanley United Res. -1	26	12	5	9	67	61	40
Smawthorne	26	12	4	10	69	57	36
Royal Oak	26	10	6	10	85	75	36
Shepherds Arms	26	10	5	11	66	61	35
Wakefield City 'A' -1	26	10	3	13	56	66	32
Waterloo	26	6	5	15	64	76	23
Eastmoor Res.	26	5	5	18	85	85	20
Wrenthorpe	26	5	5	18	41	99	20
Snydale Sports -1	26	0	2	24	35	127	5

Division Two

	P	W	D	L	F	A	Pts
Alverthorpe WMC	22	19	2	1	101	25	59
Dodworth Miners Welf.	22	19	1	3	107	38	58
AFC Wakefield	22	15	4	7	84	35	50
Rose Of York	22	11	5	7	86	59	36
Cross Keys	22	11	2	9	40	46	35
Wakefield United	22	11	1	10	62	48	34
Foresters	22	10	1	11	53	60	31
Featherstone Coll. Res. -1	22	8	4	10	53	55	28
Jolly Miller	22	8	4	10	44	54	28
Gawthorpe Shoulder -1	22	2	1	17	24	102	11

AFC Thornhill – record expunged

White Rose – record expunged

Division Three

	P	W	D	L	F	A	Pts
Ossett Two Brewers	24	21	1	2	95	18	64
Outwood Victoria -4	24	20	1	3	106	35	57
Ossett Athletic	24	18	0	6	80	26	54
Little Bull	24	18	0	7	98	45	53
Morley C & SC	24	14	0	10	75	45	43
Garforth Rangers Res.	24	14	1	10	82	75	43
Ossett Panthers	24	11	0	13	68	75	33
Prostar -4	24	10	2	12	68	47	26
Duke of Wellington	24	5	3	16	47	117	18
Alverthorpe WMC Res.-1	24	5	3	17	37	100	13
Inns Of Court	24	4	2	18	38	108	13
Crofton Sports Res. -1	24	4	1	17	39	98	10
Scissett 'A'	24	2	2	20	33	114	8

WARRINGTON & DISTRICT LEAGUE

Premier Division

	P	W	D	L	F	A	Pts
Whiston Cross	20	15	2	3	61	22	47
Halebank	20	12	2	6	86	41	38
Penlake	20	10	4	6	59	30	34
St Michael DH	20	10	3	7	41	30	33
Moore United	20	8	7	5	60	48	33
Cronton Villa	20	8	3	9	51	48	27
Haydock	20	7	3	10	43	48	25
Vulcan	20	6	1	13	32	45	19
Beeches	20	5	4	11	35	53	19
Moorefield	20	5	2	13	37	58	17
Blackbrook	20	3	1	16	26	76	10

Altofts 'A' – record expunged

WWW.CHERRYRED.CO.UK

Division One

	P	W	D	L	F	A	Pts
Act-R Sports	19	17	1	1	75	25	52
Runcom Albion	19	17	1	1	60	22	52
Ravenhill Knauff	20	11	4	5	47	29	37
Halton Borough	20	9	3	8	37	37	30
Sidac Social 'A'	20	7	4	9	40	39	25
Orford BA	20	8	1	11	48	52	25
Rainhill Town	20	6	5	9	36	41	23
Ford Sports Res.	20	7	1	12	23	53	22
Grange SC	20	5	3	12	38	55	18
Whiston Cross Res.	20	3	1	16	27	71	10
Croft							

Division Two

	P	W	D	L	F	A	Pts
Fife Rangers	22	16	4	2	73	39	52
Windle Labour Club	22	15	4	3	48	32	49
Burtonwood Albion	22	13	5	4	68	33	44
Cronton Villa Res.	22	11	4	7	51	44	37
St Michael DH Res.	22	10	6	6	53	44	36
Widnes Bayer	22	11	1	10	49	48	34
Halebank Res.	22	8	2	12	39	49	26
Vulcan Res.	22	5	7	10	27	36	22
Rainhill Town Res.	22	6	4	12	30	53	22
Culcheth SC	22	6	4	12	30	53	22
Winwick United	22	4	5	13	36	66	17
Newton-le-Willows	22	3	1	18	11	40	10

Division Three

	P	W	D	L	F	A	Pts
Prescot Cables Res.	22	19	0	3	88	18	57
Runcom Albion Res.	22	15	3	4	56	30	48
Lomax	22	13	1	6	80	41	46
Legion	22	13	5	4	64	44	44
Avon Athletic	22	11	7	4	83	45	40
Moorfield Res.	22	11	5	6	63	53	38
Village Social	22	8	4	10	62	67	28
St Michael DH 'A'	22	7	5	10	58	68	26
Monk Sports Res.	22	7	3	12	46	77	24
Crosfields Res.	22	5	2	15	48	77	17
Culcheth SC Res.	22	2	0	20	15	120	6
Farnworth-Griffin	22	1	1	20	28	78	4

Division Four

	P	W	D	L	F	A	Pts
Grappenhall Sports Res.	20	15	2	3	60	24	47
Fife Rangers Res.	20	13	0	7	45	29	39
Spartak	20	10	4	6	55	33	34
Penketh Sporties	20	10	4	6	39	38	34
Halton Borough Res.	20	10	1	9	34	38	31
Moorfield 'A'	20	9	3	8	31	46	27
Moore United Res.	20	8	1	11	38	47	25
Orford BA Res.	20	7	4	9	32	46	25
Grange SC Res.	20	6	3	11	30	37	21
Haydock Res.	20	4	4	12	31	43	16
Blackbrook Res.	20	4	3	13	23	44	15

WEARSIDE COMBINATION

Premier Division

	P	W	D	L	F	A	Pts
Redhouse	20	15	3	2	85	30	48
Vane Arms	20	15	1	4	79	31	46
The Dagmar	20	10	7	3	67	33	37
Easington Lane WMC	20	11	2	7	79	61	35
Board Inn	20	11	1	8	53	47	34
Jolly Potter	20	9	1	10	59	60	28
Hall Farm Seaview Plastics	20	7	4	9	48	51	25
Rubiheat	20	7	2	11	57	57	23
Hendon Grange	20	6	3	11	58	68	21
Aquatic Sports	20	6	2	12	43	58	20
Country Park Inn	20	0	0	20	23	165	0

Division One

	P	W	D	L	F	A	Pts
Fulwell Blue Bell	20	16	2	2	75	21	50
Blue House	20	13	4	3	72	34	43
Cambridge Hotel -3	20	12	1	7	64	41	34
OA Mountain Daisy	20	9	3	8	56	50	30
Sassco.co.uk	20	6	9	5	51	44	27
Hylton Colliery Welfare	20	6	4	9	58	51	22
Seaham The George	20	7	4	9	58	58	25
Usworth	20	6	5	9	41	56	23
Park View	20	6	3	11	52	66	21
The Cauld Lad	20	4	2	14	34	73	14
The Cavalier	20	4	1	15	36	85	13

WENSLEYDALE LEAGUE

	P	W	D	L	F	A	Pts
Bowes	28	24	1	3	148	29	73
Hawes United	28	24	1	3	111	38	65
Middleham Town	28	20	4	4	105	44	64
Leyburn United	28	19	3	6	89	52	60
Richmond Town Res.	28	16	3	9	82	51	51
Richmond Mavericks Res.	28	15	3	10	113	58	48
Buck Inn Broncos	28	15	2	11	83	65	47
Carperby Rovers	28	11	6	11	61	62	39
Buck Inn United	28	11	3	14	62	67	36
Reeth & District AC	28	9	5	14	68	99	32
Spennithorne & Harmby	28	9	2	17	66	87	29
Redmire United	28	8	5	15	45	76	29
Unicorn -6	28	8	4	16	66	86	22
Askrigg United	28	4	6	18	27	162	6
Hawes United Res.	28	0	2	26	16	164	2

Black Swan – record expunged

WEST HERTS LEAGUE
(Arlon Printers)

Premier Division

	P	W	D	L	F	A	Pts
Hadley	14	9	3	2	41	12	30
Hemel Hempstead Rvrs	14	8	4	2	36	22	28
Berkhamstead Res.	14	8	1	5	31	31	25
Tring Athletic 'A'	14	6	4	4	25	30	22
Harpenden Rovers	14	4	3	7	30	34	14
Kings Sports	14	4	1	9	22	42	13
Oxhey Jets 'A'	14	3	4	7	22	36	13
Met. Police Bushey 'A'	14	3	3	8	26	39	12

Division One

	P	W	D	L	F	A	Pts
Harefield Wednesday	20	15	3	2	81	24	48
SWR Garage Doors	20	15	2	3	88	38	47
Sun Postal Rovers	20	14	4	2	62	26	46
Harpenden Town 'A'	20	12	1	7	74	30	37
Hemel H'pstead Rvrs Res.	20	10	3	7	56	44	33
Rifle Volunteer	20	9	0	11	56	51	27
Harpenden Rovers Res.	20	8	3	9	50	66	26
Oxhey	20	8	2	10	50	66	26
Oxhey Wanderers	20	4	1	15	26	68	13
Kings Sports Res.	20	3	2	15	33	76	11
L'Artista	20	1	1	18	20	107	4

Division Two

	P	W	D	L	F	A	Pts
Hadley Res.	18	16	2	0	78	19	50
Jomarth Construction	18	11	1	6	58	31	34
Croxley Coach & Horses	18	11	1	6	44	30	34
Everett Rovers	18	11	0	7	53	27	33
Oxhey Jets 'B'	18	9	2	7	37	53	29
Aldenham	18	8	4	6	54	36	26
Hunton Bridge	18	4	4	10	32	61	16
Glenn Sports	18	4	3	11	23	49	15
Met. Police Bushey 'B'	18	3	2	13	21	59	11
Potten End							

Division Three

	P	W	D	L	F	A	Pts
Hadley 'A'	24	17	3	4	77	26	54
Old Parmiterians 'A'	24	14	7	3	70	43	47
Bovingdon 'A'	24	15	2	7	83	43	47
Hemel H'pstead Rvrs 'A'	24	15	2	7	76	50	47
SWR Garage Doors Res.	24	14	2	8	77	51	44
Harefield Wednesday Res.	24	12	3	9	42	37	41
Rickmansworth St George	24	12	4	8	56	41	40
Tring Athletic 'B'	24	9	2	13	45	52	29
Langleybury CC	24	7	4	13	42	56	25
Croxley Guild 'A'	24	6	4	14	45	68	22
Maple Cross	24	7	1	16	46	78	22
Oxhey Reserves	24	5	3	16	27	57	18
Harpenden Rovers 'B'	24	3	2	19	24	103	11

WEST SUSSEX LEAGUE
(Covers)

Premier Division

	P	W	D	L	F	A	Pts
Newtown Villa	18	11	4	3	49	26	36
Clymping	18	12	0	6	63	32	36
Barnham	18	10	3	5	38	28	33
TD Shipley	18	9	5	4	56	29	32
University of Chichester	18	9	3	6	41	31	30
Wittering United	18	8	5	5	26	23	29
South Bersted	18	7	1	10	33	40	22
East Dean	18	4	3	11	30	59	15
Predators	18	3	2	13	16	56	11
Eastergate United							

Division One

	P	W	D	L	F	A	Pts
Cowfold	22	17	3	2	44	17	54
Petworth	22	15	4	3	52	27	49
Lancing United	22	15	2	5	66	35	47
Upper Beeding	22	13	2	7	55	38	41
Angmering	22	12	1	9	56	49	37
Henfield	22	10	3	9	56	50	33
Billingshurst	22	9	4	9	47	47	31
Southwater	22	8	3	11	55	52	27
West Chiltington	22	7	3	12	39	56	24
Fittleworth	22	7	1	14	43	56	22
TD Shipley Res.	22	2	2	18	23	66	8
Lower Beeding	22	2	2	18	24	75	8

Division Two North

	P	W	D	L	F	A	Pts
Ashington Rovers	22	20	1	1	92	31	61
Capel	22	16	3	3	74	29	51
Holbrook	22	14	3	5	54	34	45
Pulborough	22	11	6	5	55	46	39
Faygate United	22	11	3	8	49	56	36
Partridge Green	22	10	4	8	56	44	34
Newdigate	22	9	6	7	50	43	33
Wisborough Green	22	8	1	13	46	74	25
Horsham Olympic	22	5	1	16	40	60	16
Rudgwick	22	4	1	17	36	57	13
Alfold	22	3	1	18	29	75	10

Division Two South

	P	W	D	L	F	A	Pts
Clymping Res.	20	15	4	1	71	24	49
Stedham United	20	15	1	4	60	21	48
Middleton United	20	12	2	6	57	38	38
Chichester Hospitals	20	8	4	8	51	35	32
Lavant	20	9	2	9	37	35	29
Worthing BCOB	20	9	2	9	45	45	29
Hunston CC	20	9	4	7	44	41	28
Wittering United Res. -3	20	7	3	10	32	29	24
Yapton	20	6	3	11	38	59	21
Miland	20	2	1	17	15	52	7
Lancing United Res.	20	2	0	18	25	80	6

(West Sussex / Horsham area divisions — continued)

Division Three North

	P	W	D	L	F	A	Pts
Watersfield	20	16	1	3	105	31	49
Horsham Trinity	20	15	1	4	68	23	46
Dorking Wanderers Res.	20	13	0	7	46	52	39
Slinfold	20	12	2	6	51	31	38
Holbrook Res.	20	8	4	8	50	50	28
Storrington 'A'	20	9	0	11	52	36	27
Barns Green	20	7	5	8	35	33	26
Horsham Baptists	20	8	1	11	37	36	25
Billingshurst Res.	20	7	3	10	33	36	24
Friends Provident	20	2	3	15	24	70	9
Faygate United Res.	20	2	2	16	20	72	8

Division Three South

	P	W	D	L	F	A	Pts
Selsey Town	20	16	1	3	75	22	49
Predators Res.	20	15	1	4	76	22	46
Barnham Res.	20	15	0	5	62	34	45
Lodsworth	20	10	3	7	63	35	33
Angmering Res.	20	9	4	7	44	26	31
Square Deal	20	8	4	8	56	64	28
Newtown Villa Res.	20	8	4	8	35	39	28
Ambassadors	20	6	5	9	29	39	23
Petworth Res.	20	3	4	13	37	65	13
Pulborough Res.	20	2	2	16	24	85	8

Division Four North

	P	W	D	L	F	A	Pts
AFC Roffey	24	18	3	3	93	36	57
Plaistow	24	17	2	5	63	53	53
TD Shipley 'A'	24	16	2	6	66	29	50
Southwater Res.	24	14	5	5	58	32	47
Cowfold Res.	24	14	2	8	63	44	44
Horsham Trinity Res.	24	11	3	10	58	50	36
Warnham	24	11	1	12	66	51	34
Ockley Res.	24	10	0	14	46	62	30
West Chiltington Res.	24	7	3	14	40	62	24
Wisborough Green Res.	24	7	2	15	53	69	23
Fittleworth Res.	24	5	5	14	37	64	20
Horsham Olympic Res.	24	5	3	16	40	94	18
Alfold Res.	24	4	2	18	36	80	14

Division Four South

	P	W	D	L	F	A	Pts
Barnham 'A'	22	16	3	3	69	20	51
The Sportsman	22	15	2	5	62	42	47
Bosham Res.	22	14	2	6	56	35	44
The Wheatsheaf	22	11	6	5	50	49	39
Fernhurst	22	11	4	7	70	49	37
Boxgrove	22	11	3	8	63	48	36
Ashington Rovers Res.	22	9	3	10	47	41	30
Coal Exchange	22	6	5	11	27	47	23
Stedham United Res.	22	5	4	13	66	60	19
Ambassadors Res.	22	5	4	13	39	66	19
Yapton Res. 'A'	22	4	5	13	39	66	17
Predators 'A'	22	2	4	16	32	87	10

Division Five North

	P	W	D	L	F	A	Pts
Henfield Res.	20	16	1	3	70	23	49
Rudgwick Res.	20	15	1	4	52	22	46
Norfolk Arms	20	13	0	7	46	39	39
Holbrook 'A'	20	12	2	6	51	31	38
B52's	20	10	2	8	61	42	32
Newgate Res.	20	9	1	10	52	55	28
Southwater 'A'	20	7	4	9	35	35	25
Capel Res.	20	7	3	10	36	36	24
Horsham Baptists Res.	20	6	1	13	48	69	19
Billingshurst Res.	20	5	4	11	41	55	19
Slinfold Res.	20	2	2	16	20	72	8

Division Five South

	P	W	D	L	F	A	Pts
General Henry	16	14	0	2	98	18	42
Rustington Park Seniors	16	12	3	1	51	23	35
Newtown Villa 'A'	16	10	3	3	56	23	33
Tangmere	16	10	3	3	34	27	33
Lavant Res.	16	8	1	7	47	42	25
Harting	16	5	1	10	32	73	16
Highdown Hornets	16	5	0	11	33	63	15
Regis Veterans	16	2	0	14	28	62	6
Lodsworth Res.	16	3	1	16	19	85	10
Fernhurst Res.	16	2	0	14	24	68	6

WESTON & DISTRICT LEAGUE

Division One

	P	W	D	L	F	A	Pts
Hutton	20	18	3	3	93	36	57
Churchill Club Res.	20	16	5	5	53	29	50
Draycott	20	14	5	5	66	32	47
Winscombe Res.	20	14	2	8	58	39	44
Portishead 'A'	20	13	1	10	63	50	36
Cleeve West Town Res.	20	11	1	12	66	51	34
St George E-in-G Res.	20	10	0	14	53	62	24
Bournville Rovers	20	7	3	14	40	62	24
East Worle	20	7	2	15	53	69	23
Kewstoke Lions	20	5	5	14	40	94	18
Congresbury Res.	20	4	2	18	36	80	14

Division Two

	P	W	D	L	F	A	Pts
KVFC	22	16	3	3	69	20	51
Nailsea Town Res.	22	15	2	5	62	42	47
Nailsea United 'A'	22	14	2	6	56	35	44
Clarence Park	22	11	6	5	50	49	39
Clevedon United 'A'	22	11	4	7	70	49	37
Swiss Valley Rovers	22	11	3	8	63	48	36
Portishead 'B'	22	9	3	10	47	41	30
Milton Crusaders	22	6	5	11	27	47	23
Selkirk United	22	5	4	13	66	60	19
Blagdon	22	5	4	13	39	66	19
Burnham United 'A'	22	4	2	16	32	87	10

Division Three

	P	W	D	L	F	A	Pts
Weston St Johns Spts Bar	22	16	1	3	91	31	49
Winscombe 'A'	22	13	4	5	68	40	43
Locking Park	22	13	1	8	61	41	40
Nailsea United 'B'	22	9	5	8	58	42	32
Worle Res.	22	10	2	10	61	50	32
Yatton Athletic Res.	22	7	4	9	55	52	24 (-1)
South Park Rangers	22	6	6	10	46	52	24
Westland Utd Res.	22	6	1	13	36	69	19
Kewstoke Lions Res.	22	6	1	13	41	83	19
Clevedon United 'B'	22	5	4	13	36	86	19 (-3)
Hutton Res.	22	2	2	16	36	—	8

Division Four

	P	W	D	L	F	A	Pts
Stotties Rovers	22	16	1	5	77	18	42
Locking Villa	22	15	4	4	92	22	42
Wrington-Redhill Res.	22	13	1	6	73	33	33
Nailsea United Colts	22	12	1	9	56	44	29
King Alfred SC	22	9	3	9	50	47	16
Cheddar 'A'	22	10	4	10	45	62	15
Wedmore	22	8	5	11	58	55	15
Westend	22	8	2	12	62	55	15
Banwell Res.	22	4	1	13	45	55	25
Draycott Res.	22	6	2	15	59	60	13
Portishead Colts	22	3	4	17	34	59	10 (-3)
KVFC Res.							

Division Five

	P	W	D	L	F	A	Pts
Weston United	22	19	1	2	112	22	58
Axbridge Town	22	18	2	2	95	35	56
St George E-in-G'no 'A'	22	12	4	6	74	44	43
East Worle Res.	22	14	1	7	76	42	43
Bournville Rovers Res.	22	12	3	7	76	52	39
Berrow Res.	22	9	4	9	52	47	31
Burnham United 'B'	22	8	2	12	51	72	26
AFC Nailsea	22	6	4	12	47	64	23
Cheddar 'B'	22	5	3	13	38	71	20
Kewstoke Lions 'A'	22	5	4	13	43	81	19
Wigan Rovers Res.	22	1	7	14	36	92	10
Congresbury 'A'	22	2	3	17	22	98	-6 (-17)

Division Six

	P	W	D	L	F	A	Pts
Clevedon Dons	20	17	2	1	76	21	53
Westend Res.	20	12	4	4	75	32	40
W'n St Johns Spts Bar Res.	20	11	2	7	53	39	35
Backwell United 'A'	20	10	6	4	40	38	32
Dolphin Athletic	20	9	8	3	43	46	27
AFC Nailsea Res.	20	6	6	8	45	45	29
Yatton Athletic 'A'	20	7	2	11	44	52	29
St George E-in-G'no 'B'	20	6	2	12	33	62	20
Wedmore Res.	20	6	2	12	33	57	20
Athletico Wrington	20	5	3	12	24	47	18
Selkirk United Res.	20	3	6	11	26	53	15

WIGAN & DISTRICT AMATEUR LEAGUE

Premier Division

	P	W	D	L	F	A	Pts
Newburgh United	26	22	1	3	111	24	67
Highfield	26	18	4	4	66	36	58
Winstanley St Aidans	26	13	6	7	64	39	47
Digmoor	26	15	3	8	60	38	45 (-3)
Standish St Wilfreds	26	13	3	10	51	38	39
Leigh Phoenix	26	13	3	10	63	49	33 (-3)
Shevington	26	10	3	13	39	45	33
AFC Scholes	26	8	2	12	53	67	24
Ince Central	26	8	3	11	47	26	24 (-3)
Hindley Town	26	5	7	14	52	46	19
Three Crowns	26	8	4	17	57	75	17 (-9)
Worsley Mesnes	26	4	5	17	40	77	14
Pemberton	26	3	5	17	28	84	14 (-6)
Springfield	26	4	7	15	36	85	13 (-6)

Division One

	P	W	D	L	F	A	Pts
Digmoor Res.	22	16	1	5	77	39	49
Fir Tree Rangers	22	15	4	3	73	38	49
Bickerstaffe	22	13	3	6	73	46	42
Gidlow Athletic Old Boys	22	12	1	9	56	50	37
Coppull Celtic	22	9	3	10	50	62	30
AFC Tydesley	22	9	4	10	45	50	28
Atherton Railway	22	8	5	11	58	55	29
Wigan Rovers	22	8	3	11	55	56	27
Winstanley St A. Res.	22	8	2	12	77	63	25 (-3)
St Judes	22	6	4	15	38	75	22
Douglas Valley	22	6	2	15	45	63	13 (-3)
Billinge 'A'	22	8	3	17	59	92	13
Hindley Town Res.	22	5	2	15	34	59	10

Ince Central Res. – record expunged

Division Two

	P	W	D	L	F	A	Pts
Up Holland	22	19	1	2	112	22	58
Atherton Liberal Club	22	18	2	2	95	35	56
Leigh Legion	22	12	4	6	74	44	44
Ormskirk	22	14	1	7	76	42	43
Fir Tree Rangers Res.	22	12	3	7	76	52	39
Bickerstaffe Res.	22	9	4	9	52	47	31
Three Crowns Res.	22	9	1	11	61	72	28
Hindley Celtic	22	8	2	12	51	72	26
Atherton Sports & Social	22	6	4	12	47	64	23 (-3)
Goose Green United	22	5	4	13	38	71	20
Shevington Res.	22	4	3	13	43	81	19
Wigan Rovers Res.	22	1	7	14	36	92	10

Athletic – record expunged

Hindley Town Youth – record expunged

WIMBLEDON & DISTRICT LEAGUE

Premier Division

	P	W	D	L	F	A	Pts
Real Phoenix	21	16	4	1	65	27	52
AFC Battersea	20	12	4	4	62	21	49
AFC Cubo	22	15	0	5	58	26	45
Brennal	20	15	2	6	66	32	45
Wandle Res.	20	13	0	5	41	38	41
Duet	22	11	3	8	48	34	38
PWCA	20	7	6	8	31	36	27
Ocean	20	7	4	9	36	36	25
Partizan Wandsworth	21	6	4	11	27	37	22
Lancaster Youth	22	6	2	13	41	62	20
Leamington	22	5	3	16	35	72	12
London Lionhearts	22	2	2	18	25	90	8

WWW.CHERRYRED.CO.UK

Division One

	P	W	D	L	F	A	Pts
FC Porto of London	20	15	4	1	82	24	49
Spartak Clapham	20	11	4	5	55	31	37
Union	20	11	4	5	55	45	37
Brentnal Res.	20	10	6	4	67	38	36
Wadham College O B	20	10	4	6	38	33	34
Brompton Sports Casuals	20	9	4	7	40	37	31
Claremont	20	6	5	9	38	39	23
Hyde Park Thursday	20	6	4	10	58	58	22
Rivelino City	20	5	5	10	36	44	20
Brentside	20	5	3	12	36	44	18
Cosmos United	20	2	2	16	24	66	8

Division Two

	P	W	D	L	F	A	Pts
South East London	16	13	1	2	62	13	40
Goldfingers	16	12	2	2	51	27	38
MGA Vets	16	8	6	2	35	25	29
Sporting Brixton	16	8	6	4	46	34	33
Bar Sia	16	6	4	6	26	34	22
Kiwi	16	4	5	7	40	36	20
Boca Seniors	16	4	11	1	31	52	15
FC Centaur	16	3	2	11	28	57	12
Foundation	16	3	1	12	18	48	10

Division Three

	P	W	D	L	F	A	Pts
Peperami	18	13	3	2	49	29	42
AFC Cubo Res.	18	12	1	5	52	30	37
South West Eleven	18	10	3	5	53	34	33
Nottingham Old Boys	18	9	6	3	49	23	33
The Grove	18	8	2	8	43	24	26
Inter Old Boys	18	6	4	8	38	45	22
Merton Orient	18	5	4	9	30	44	19
South Lodge	18	5	2	11	25	43	17
London Lionhearts Res.	18	4	3	11	34	53	15
Dover House Lions	18	3	0	15	27	75	9

WINCHESTER & DISTRICT LEAGUE

	P	W	D	L	F	A	Pts
Upham	16	12	3	1	65	20	39
South Wonston Swifts	16	10	3	3	38	23	33
Infinity	16	8	2	6	34	24	31
Ropley	16	8	2	6	46	32	26
Sparsholt	16	7	4	5	29	25	24
Sutton Scotney	16	6	3	7	32	32	21
Castel de Sangro	16	4	3	9	39	46	15
Eastleigh Town	16	4	2	11	25	57	15
Stanton	16	1	0	15	10	67	3

WITNEY & DISTRICT FA

Premier Division

	P	W	D	L	F	A	Pts
Brize Norton +2	20	15	2	3	68	22	52
Freeland	20	15	2	3	53	24	47
Hanborough	20	11	2	7	49	34	35
Duckington	20	11	2	7	48	55	35
Hailey −6	20	8	4	8	45	35	32
Charlbury Town	20	8	5	7	39	35	32
Spartan Rangers	20	7	4	9	39	46	25
Bampton Town	20	6	4	10	38	35	22
Cassington	20	5	2	13	37	61	17
West Witney	20	3	4	13	23	57	13
North Leigh 'A' −4	20	3	1	14	24	61	8

WORCESTER & DISTRICT LEAGUE

Division One

	P	W	D	L	F	A	Pts
Witney Royals	20	16	1	3	82	24	49
Minster Lovell	20	14	3	3	67	23	45
Witney Wanderers	20	13	3	4	47	29	42
Milton	20	9	4	7	58	53	31
Brize Norton Res.	20	9	2	9	42	46	29
Aston	20	8	2	10	53	58	26
FC Mills	20	6	3	11	39	52	21
Duckington Res.	20	4	6	10	38	59	22
Kingham All Black	20	4	4	12	40	58	16
Eynsham Association 'A'	20	4	3	13	33	78	15
FC Nomads	20	2	6	12	30	53	12

Division Two

	P	W	D	L	F	A	Pts
Bampton Town Res.	22	19	1	2	97	40	58
Combe	22	17	2	3	89	31	53
AC Finstock	22	16	4	2	97	39	52
Freeland Res.	22	15	2	5	68	40	47
Chippy Swifts	22	9	3	10	39	47	30
Hanborough Res.	22	8	1	12	56	62	28
Southrop	22	8	1	13	37	54	26
Wootton Sports	22	6	5	11	29	44	23
Tackley	22	6	1	15	40	65	19
West Witney Res.	22	6	1	15	43	86	19
Charlbury Town Res.	22	1	1	20	21	84	4

Division Three

	P	W	D	L	F	A	Pts
FC Chequers	18	14	2	2	63	11	44
Kingham All Blacks Res.	18	12	2	4	51	36	38
Wychwood Forest	18	11	3	4	45	35	36
Two Rivers	18	11	1	6	49	35	34
Minster Lovell Res.	18	8	4	6	31	32	28
FC Mills Res.	18	5	1	12	39	60	16
Aston Res.	18	4	3	11	19	41	15
Duckington 'A'	18	3	5	10	23	55	14
Spartan Rangers 'A'	18	4	1	13	20	47	13
Fieldtown	18	—	—	—	—	—	—

Division Four

	P	W	D	L	F	A	Pts
Chad Park	20	17	2	1	88	23	53
Witney Royals Res.	20	15	2	3	79	30	47
Hailey Res.	20	11	2	7	53	44	35
Milton Res.	20	8	4	8	42	56	28
Brize Norton 'A'	20	7	5	8	43	47	26
Chippy Swifts Res.	20	7	1	12	37	60	22
Freeland 'A'	20	7	0	13	54	57	21
Southrop Res.	20	6	2	12	32	64	20
Eynsham Sports +3	20	4	2	14	52	84	17
Wychwood Forest Res.	20	4	3	13	45	65	15

WORTHING & DISTRICT LEAGUE

Premier Division

	P	W	D	L	F	A	Pts
L & S Athletic	21	16	1	4	69	27	49
Worthing Wanderers	21	14	1	6	61	44	44
Worthing Athletic	21	14	1	6	62	49	43
Warren Sports	21	13	1	7	35	25	40
GSK Sports	21	9	2	10	46	48	29
Sompting	21	8	1	12	45	48	28
Adur Athletic	21	3	17	1	24	82	10
AFC Court & Smith	21	2	0	19	14	46	2
Jolly Brewers – record expunged							

Division One

	P	W	D	L	F	A	Pts
Warren Sports Res.	20	17	1	2	55	21	52
Woodside & Goring	20	14	3	3	66	28	45
Ferring	20	13	4	3	50	30	43
Shoreham RBL	20	9	2	9	67	37	42
Durrington RAFA	20	9	1	10	47	36	29
Worthing Albion	20	8	2	10	53	39	28
GSK Sports Res. +3	20	8	4	13	37	49	26
Goring St Theresa's	20	4	1	15	33	54	15
Northbrook	20	4	1	15	30	55	13
Adur Athletic Res. −3	20	3	1	14	32	99	9

Division Two

	P	W	D	L	F	A	Pts
Fern Estates	18	16	2	0	73	9	50
TMG	18	13	1	4	48	24	40
LWS Highdown Rovers	18	10	1	6	61	31	36
Lancing United 'A'	18	8	3	6	39	34	30
St Mary's	18	8	2	8	34	28	30
Edge	18	6	7	5	43	47	23
Hill Barn Rangers	18	5	2	11	46	58	17
Worthing Wanderers Res.	18	5	1	12	35	43	16
Sompting Res.	18	4	1	13	27	81	13
Worthing BCOB Res.	18	1	0	17	18	83	3
Liquid Lounge – record expunged							

Division Three

	P	W	D	L	F	A	Pts
Athletico Wenban-Smith	14	11	1	2	64	23	34
Worthing Athletic Res.	14	9	2	3	50	31	28
Ferring Res.	14	8	0	6	42	42	26
West Tarring WMC	14	7	2	5	54	43	23
Adur Athletic 'A'	14	6	3	5	41	48	21
GSK Sports 'A'	14	4	2	8	29	35	14
Lancing United 'B'	14	4	2	8	35	35	14
Northbrook Res.	14	1	1	12	20	64	4

WYCOMBE & DISTRICT LEAGUE

Senior Division

	P	W	D	L	F	A	Pts
AFC Spartans	18	14	2	2	55	23	44
Holmer Green Old Boys	18	11	4	3	55	27	37
Downley Albion	18	11	2	5	49	35	35
Wycombe Judo	18	10	4	4	51	35	34
Winchmore Hill	18	8	8	2	42	35	32
Hambleden	18	8	6	4	36	36	27
Lane End	18	8	3	7	41	42	24
AC Marlow	18	4	11	3	27	45	24
Red Lion (Wooburn)	18	3	1	14	31	64	10
AFC Amersham	18	0	1	17	26	87	1

Premier Division

	P	W	D	L	F	A	Pts
FC Titans	18	14	2	2	68	22	44
Penn & Tylers Green 'A'	18	12	2	4	58	34	38
AC Marlow Res.	17	10	3	4	63	30	33
Totteridge Wanderers	18	8	4	6	45	40	28
Great Missenden	18	8	7	5	46	34	26
Lane End Res.	18	7	5	6	40	41	26
Wycombe Athletic	18	5	4	9	24	46	19
Downley Albion Res.	18	4	3	11	39	68	15
Wooburn Athletic	17	3	2	12	20	66	12
Chinnor 'A'	17	3	3	12	29	47	9

Division One

	P	W	D	L	F	A	Pts
BCUC	14	13	1	0	88	7	40
Spartak Marlow	14	8	2	4	50	42	26
Winchmore Hill Res.	14	8	2	4	35	30	26
Great Missenden Res.	14	7	1	6	51	32	24
Fleur	14	5	1	6	47	36	24
Queens Head Sports	14	5	2	7	52	34	17
Prince of Wales Rangers	14	2	1	11	13	65	5
Aylesbury Park Rangers	14	0	1	13	11	101	1

YEOVIL & DISTRICT LEAGUE

Premier Division

	P	W	D	L	F	A	Pts
Westland Sports Res.	20	17	2	1	75	19	53
Pen Mill	20	16	3	1	67	34	51
Milborne Port	20	12	4	4	75	36	39
Normalair RSL	20	11	3	6	45	36	36
Stoke-sub-Hamdon	20	9	3	8	62	42	30
Henstridge United	20	9	1	10	50	57	25
Tor	20	6	4	10	43	59	22
Castle Cary Res.	20	6	3	11	47	53	21
Ansford Rovers	20	5	5	10	35	65	20
Keinton Mandeville	20	5	2	18	38	51	20
Martock United	20	0	2	18	17	112	2

Division One

	P	W	D	L	F	A	Pts
Templecombe Rovers	18	13	3	2	52	25	41
Baltonsborough	18	11	3	4	42	23	36
Normalair RSL Res.	18	11	1	6	59	32	36
Somerton Sports	18	10	4	5	36	23	33
Royal Oak Rangers	18	9	4	5	38	23	31
Odcombe	18	6	4	8	31	38	27
Stoke-sub-Hamdon Res.	18	5	3	10	34	34	18
Victoria Sports	18	4	2	12	28	47	14
Pen Mill Res.	18	4	2	13	32	47	13
Milborne Port Res.	18	3	2	13	27	61	11

Division Two	P	W	D	L	F	A	Pts
South Cheriton United	20	17	0	3	93	28	51
Kingsbury Episcopi	20	14	3	3	62	25	45
Barwick & Stoford *-1*	20	13	2	5	62	28	40
Montacute	20	9	3	8	47	39	30
Pitney	20	9	2	9	55	53	29
Mermaid United *-1*	20	9	2	9	56	57	28
Lyde United *-3*	20	9	2	9	61	53	26
Ansford Rovers Res.	20	6	2	12	41	64	20
Templecombe Rvrs Res.	20	4	3	13	28	80	15
Charlton United	20	3	3	14	29	64	12
Milborne Port 'A' *-7*	20	4	4	12	31	74	9

Division Three	P	W	D	L	F	A	Pts
Ilchester	20	18	1	1	102	29	55
M & K Builders	20	16	1	3	89	29	49
AFC Wessex	20	12	1	7	64	27	37
Lyde United Res.	20	12	1	7	75	45	37
Ashwood	20	11	1	8	78	34	34
Butleigh Dynamos	20	10	1	9	78	69	31
Bruton United	20	8	1	11	63	69	25
Odcombe Res.	20	6	2	12	48	65	20
Baltonsborough Res	20	5	0	15	43	99	15
Lingards *-6*	20	6	2	12	47	56	14
Mudford	20	0	1	19	14	179	1

YORK LEAGUE
(Leeper Hare)

Premier Division	P	W	D	L	F	A	Pts
Huntington Rovers	28	22	1	5	76	31	67
Haxby United	28	20	3	5	94	43	63
Old Malton St Marys	28	17	5	6	78	43	56
York St John University	28	16	5	7	79	44	53
Wigginton Grasshoppers	28	16	2	10	60	47	50
Kartiers (Selby)	28	14	5	9	50	48	47
Dringhouses	28	11	3	14	53	72	36
Tockwith	28	10	4	14	40	61	34
Dunnington	28	10	3	15	63	75	33
Hamilton Panthers	28	9	5	14	47	62	32
Copmanthorpe	28	9	3	16	67	80	30
Tate & Lyle Selby	28	8	4	16	44	73	28
Malton & Norton	28	7	5	16	45	60	26
Nestle Rowntree	28	8	1	19	46	74	25
Thorpe United	28	6	5	17	36	65	23

Division One	P	W	D	L	F	A	Pts
Wilberfoss	24	16	3	5	60	33	51
Poppleton United	24	15	2	7	44	32	47
Amotherby & Swinton	24	14	1	9	48	37	43
Pocklington Town Res.	24	13	4	7	53	47	43
Riccall United	24	12	5	7	59	37	41
Tadcaster Albion Res.	24	10	5	9	36	28	35
Stamford Bridge	24	11	2	11	60	61	35
Bishopthorpe United	24	10	3	11	47	46	33
Norwich Union	24	9	3	12	46	51	30
Easingwold Town	24	7	6	11	44	50	27
Ouseburn United	24	8	3	13	44	60	27
Osbaldwick	24	8	2	14	43	71	26
Heslington	24	3	1	20	29	60	10

Division Two	P	W	D	L	F	A	Pts
York Railway Institute	22	19	2	1	83	33	59
Rufforth United	22	11	7	4	59	38	40
Huby United	22	10	6	6	42	43	36
Elvington Harriers	22	10	4	8	56	39	34
Hemingbrough United	22	8	6	8	43	42	30
Fulford United *-3*	22	9	4	9	55	48	28
St Clements	22	9	1	12	46	59	28
Post Office	22	7	6	9	46	50	27
Church Fenton White H.	22	7	6	9	41	48	27
Moor Lane	22	8	3	11	47	63	27
Selby RSSC	22	6	1	15	45	64	19
Strensall	22	5	0	17	35	71	15

Division Three	P	W	D	L	F	A	Pts
Heworth	24	20	3	1	88	13	63
Rawcliffe Rangers	24	18	1	5	121	42	55
New Earswick	24	14	5	5	92	40	47
Barmby Moor	24	15	2	7	62	44	47
Crayke	24	14	3	7	81	52	45
Civil Service	24	9	7	8	52	64	34
Cawood	24	10	3	11	57	60	33
Wheldrake	24	9	4	11	40	41	31
Stillington	24	7	8	9	47	64	29
LNER Builders	24	4	6	14	37	82	18
Norton United	24	4	1	19	33	99	13
Bishop Wilton	24	2	6	16	23	77	12
Melbourne *-3*	24	4	3	17	29	84	12

Reserve Division A	P	W	D	L	F	A	Pts
York St John Univ. Res.	20	18	1	1	71	20	55
Dunnington Res.	20	14	2	4	64	29	44
Thorpe United Res.	20	11	4	5	44	33	37
Wigginton Grassh's Res.	20	11	4	5	52	42	37
Huntington Rvrs Res. *-3*	20	9	4	7	42	36	28
Kartiers (Selby) Res.	20	8	4	8	32	26	28
Dringhouses Res.	20	7	4	9	44	65	25
Old Malton St Marys Res.	20	7	3	10	45	41	24
Copmanthorpe Res.	20	5	2	13	40	56	17
Heworth Res.	20	1	4	15	28	72	7
Nestle Rowntree Res.	20	0	6	14	25	67	6

Rufforth United Res. – record expunged

Reserve Division B	P	W	D	L	F	A	Pts
Haxby United Res.	20	16	0	4	88	19	48
Bishopthorpe United Res.	20	15	2	3	78	34	47
Riccall United Res.	20	13	3	4	60	25	42
Hamilton Panthers Res.	20	10	1	9	53	47	31
Pocklington Town 'A'	20	8	5	7	65	45	29
Easingwold Town Res.	20	8	4	8	50	40	28
York Railway Inst.Res.	20	8	1	11	48	74	25
Poppleton United Res.	20	7	2	11	49	73	23
Stamford Bridge Res.	20	4	4	12	29	57	16
Wilberfoss Res.	20	4	4	12	33	71	16
Malton & Norton Res. *-3*	20	4	0	16	32	100	9

New Earswick Res. – record expunged

Reserve Division C	P	W	D	L	F	A	Pts
Tockwith Res.	20	14	1	5	51	34	43
Ouseburn United Res.	20	12	2	6	49	30	38
Hemingbrough Utd Res.	20	12	1	7	57	36	37
Heslington Res.	20	11	3	6	54	38	36
Amotherby/Swinton Res.	20	11	3	6	42	35	36
Norwich Union Res.	20	10	5	5	43	26	35
Fulford United Res.	20	6	5	9	37	43	23
Stillington Res.	20	6	2	12	30	51	20
Church Fenton WH Res.	20	5	4	11	33	48	19
Civil Service Res.	20	5	3	12	39	70	18
Huby United Res.	20	2	3	15	43	67	9

LNER Builders Res. – record expunged

YORKSHIRE OLD BOYS LEAGUE

Senior Division A	P	W	D	L	F	A	Pts
Ealandians	22	16	2	4	82	35	50
Heckmondwike GSOB	22	14	2	6	57	36	44
Yorkshire Bank	22	12	4	6	48	31	40
FC Headingley	22	11	3	8	56	46	36
Leeds Medics & Dentists	22	10	3	9	50	50	33
Trinity Old Boys	22	9	5	8	52	46	32
Leeds University OB	22	8	8	6	42	42	32
Old Rovers	22	9	3	10	51	52	30
Huddersfield Amateurs	22	7	6	9	47	52	27
St Nicholas	22	8	2	12	46	64	26
Old Collegians	22	5	2	15	38	73	17
Stanningley Old Boys	22	2	2	18	27	69	8

Senior Division B	P	W	D	L	F	A	Pts
Bramley Juniors	20	17	1	2	72	32	52
Wortley	20	16	2	2	62	21	50
Gildersome Spurs	20	13	4	3	73	42	43
Sandal Athletic	20	9	4	7	56	42	31
Leeds City Old Boys	20	8	5	7	51	36	29
Leeds Medics/Dentists Res.	20	8	4	8	39	37	28
Old Modernians	20	7	2	11	45	47	23
Roundhegians	20	5	4	11	38	71	19
Old Batelians	20	6	0	14	47	73	18
Calverley	20	5	1	14	43	63	16
Western Juniors	20	1	3	16	29	91	6

South Leeds Saints – record expunged

Division One	P	W	D	L	F	A	Pts
Alwoodley Old Boys	20	17	1	2	87	23	52
Gildersome Spurs Res.	20	12	2	6	55	35	38
St Bedes Old Boys	20	10	4	6	54	49	34
Shire Academics	20	10	3	7	60	39	33
Leeds Medics/Dentists 'A'	20	10	2	8	46	51	32
Leeds City Old Boys Res.	20	8	1	11	41	45	25
Old Thornesians	20	6	6	8	31	33	24
East Ardsley Wanderers	20	7	1	12	41	63	22
Old Centralians Res.	20	5	6	9	27	56	21
Wortley Res.	20	4	7	9	29	47	19
Woodhouse MM	20	2	5	13	25	55	11

Sandal Wanderers – record expunged

Division Two	P	W	D	L	F	A	Pts
Wheelright Old Boys	24	18	5	1	103	24	59
Leeds Independent	24	15	5	4	76	37	50
Trinity Old Boys Res.	24	13	4	7	58	47	43
Leeds City Old Boys 'A'	24	12	6	6	64	44	42
East Leeds Trinity	24	12	5	7	79	52	41
Moortown Old Boys	24	13	1	10	77	46	40
Dewsbury Rgrs OB Res.	24	11	3	10	74	61	36
Old Modernians Res.	24	8	3	13	44	59	27
Agnes Stewart Old Boys	24	7	4	13	43	76	25
Huddersfield Ams Res.	24	7	2	15	42	79	23
Horbury Town Old Boys	24	7	2	15	35	88	23
Old Centralians 'A'	24	6	3	15	42	75	21
Colton Academicals	24	4	3	17	42	91	15

Roundhegians Res. – record expunged

Division Three	P	W	D	L	F	A	Pts
Ealandians Res.	26	22	2	2	112	34	68
Bramley Juniors Res.	26	22	0	4	86	33	66
Gildersome Spurs 'A'	26	13	5	8	60	47	44
Colton Academicals Res.	26	13	4	9	67	60	43
Old Batelians Res.	26	13	3	10	70	63	42
Grangefield Old Boys	26	12	5	9	68	58	41
Heckmondwike GSOB Res.	26	11	5	10	80	69	38
Leeds Independent Res.	26	10	6	10	51	53	36
Old Collegians Res.	26	10	5	11	67	69	35
St Bedes Old Boys Res.	26	9	5	12	60	55	32
Wheelright Old Boys Res.	26	8	2	16	42	69	26
Roundhegians 'A'	26	5	6	15	43	81	21
Old Modernians 'B'	26	5	5	16	41	70	20
Old Modernians 'A'	26	2	1	23	29	115	7

Division Four	P	W	D	L	F	A	Pts
Alwoodley Old Boys Res.	26	21	0	5	100	27	63
Leeds Medics/Dentists 'B'	26	18	3	5	78	38	57
Huddersfield Amateurs 'A'	26	16	2	8	55	35	50
Sandal Athletic Res.	26	14	2	10	70	56	44
Heckmondwike GSOB 'A'	26	12	2	12	66	61	38
East Ardsley Wdrs Res.	26	11	3	12	64	68	36
Colton Academicals 'A'	26	11	2	13	57	66	35
Sandal Wanderers Res.	26	10	4	12	57	66	34
Bramley Juniors 'A'	26	10	4	12	40	60	34
Old Centralians 'B'	26	10	3	13	45	67	33
Old Batelians 'A'	26	9	3	14	68	78	30
Leeds City Old Boys 'B'	26	7	5	14	55	67	26
Old Thornesians Res.	26	7	4	15	56	72	25
Leeds City Old Boys 'C'	26	6	3	17	45	95	21

Division Five	P	W	D	L	F	A	Pts
Grangefield OB Res.	28	23	3	2	103	30	72
Old Modernians 'C'	28	19	3	6	70	33	60
Woodhouse MM Res.	28	18	4	6	101	51	58
St Bedes Old Boys 'A'	28	16	5	7	81	52	53
Ealandians 'A'	28	16	4	8	79	43	52
Alwoodley Old Boys 'A'	28	16	3	9	82	48	51
Old Collegians 'A'	28	14	8	6	50	40	50
Old Modernians 'D'	28	11	8	9	64	56	41
Old Thornesians 'A'	28	11	4	13	56	62	37
Wheelright Old Boys 'A'	28	8	4	16	49	95	28
Leeds City Old Boys 'D'	28	6	7	15	46	83	25
Old Centralians 'C'	28	6	4	18	43	81	22
Old Collegians 'B'	28	6	3	19	34	81	21
Roundhegians 'B'	28	4	4	20	39	89	16
Huddersfield Amateurs 'B'	28	3	2	23	47	100	11

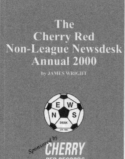

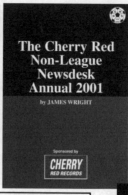

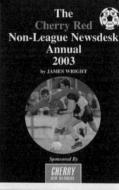

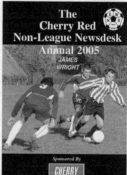

BACK ISSUES

The following editions of the
Cherry Red Non-League Newsdesk Annual
are currently available
(stocks of 2001 are extremely low)

2000:	£4.00
2001:	£25.00
2002:	£8.95
2003:	£9.95
2004:	£5.00
2005:	£5.00
2006:	£9.95
2007:	£9.95

(Prices inc p&p)

Orders to:-
James Wright, 6 Harp Chase,
Taunton TA1 3RY

Cheques payable to:-
**Non-League
Newsdesk Annual**

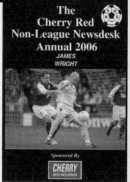

F A CHALLENGE CUP

EXTRA-PRELIMINARY ROUND
(£500 to each winning club)
(Ties played August 18 unless stated)

Guisborough Town 1 **Norton & Stockton Ancients** 3 Att: 144
West Auckland Town 2 Bedlington Terriers 1 Att: 49
Billingham Town 6 Eccleshill 1 Att: 167
(Aug 19) (at Hartlepool United)
Winterton Rangers 3 Armthorpe Welfare 2 Att: 64
Glasshoughton Welfare 1 Liversedge 1 Att: 63
Replay: **Liversedge** 4 Glasshoughton W. 3 *(Aug 21)* Att: 160
Horden Colliery Welfare 2 Sunderland Nissan 1 Att: 50
Thackley 0 **Ashington** 1 Att: 109
Darlington Railway Athletic 6 Yorkshire Amateur 0 Att: 64
Whitley Bay 0 **Dunston Federation** 1 Att: 250
Hall Road Rangers 6 Tadcaster Albion 1 Att: 55
Spennymoor Town 3 North Shields 0 Att: 149
Hebburn Town 1 **Tow Law Town** 3 Att: 102
Crook Town 2 Sunderland Ryhope CA 2 Att: 64
Replay: Sunderland Ryhope 0 **Crook Town** 3 *(Aug 21)* Att: 82
Morpeth Town 3 Seaham Red Star 0 Att: 57
Pontefract Collieries 0 Selby Town 0 Att: 76
Replay: **Selby Town** 1 Pontefract Colls 0 *aet (Aug 21)* Att: 123
Thornaby 2 **South Shields** 3 Att: 75
Jarrow Roofing BCA 2 West Allotment Celtic 1 Att: 48
Brandon United 0 **Durham City** 5 Att: 96
Washington 1 **Pickering Town** 3 Att: 74
Esh Winning 1 Whickham 0 Att: 58
Ryton 3 **Silsden** 4 Att: 73
Billingham Synthonia 2 Northallerton Town 1 Att: 158
Bottesford Town 1 **Shildon** 2 Att: 103
Team Northumbria 0 **Consett** 11 Att: 72
Chester-le-Street Town 1 Bishop Auckland 1 Att: 105
Replay: Bishop Auckland 1 **Chester-le-St** 2 *(Aug 21)* Att: 123
Ashton Town 1 Ramsbottom Utd 2 *(at Atherton Colls)* Att: 60
Daisy Hill 0 **Congleton Town** 4 Att: 40
AFC Emley 3 Darwen 0 *(Aug 17)* Att: 266
Rossington Main 2 Atherton Collieries 2 Att: 81
Replay: **Atherton Colls** 5 Rossington M. 0 *(Aug 20)* Att: 150
Chadderton 3 **Winsford United** 4 Att: 73
Holker Old Boys 2 **St Helens Town** 3 *aet* Att: 62
Blackpool Mechanics 1 **Maine Road** 3 Att: 42
Formby 2 **Oldham Town** 3 Att: 60
Squires Gate 1 **Penrith Town** 3 Att: 37
Flixton 2 Bootle 1 Att: 49
Trafford 1 Atherton LR 0 Att: 89
Hallam 2 Nelson 0 *(at Nelson)* Att: 78
Salford City 6 Padiham 3 Att: 86
Abbey Hey 1 **Bacup Borough** 2 Att: 45
Brodsworth Miners Welfare 2 **Parkgate** 3 Att: 35
Dinnington Town 2 Maltby Main 1 *(Aug 17)* Att: 602
Glossop North End 2 Eccleshill 0 Att: 118
Highgate United 2 Shirebrook Town 1 Att: 66
Castle Vale 3 Brierley Hill & Withymoor 3 Att: 70
Replay: **Brierley Hill & W.** 4 Castle Vale 0 *(Aug 22)* Att: 79
Loughborough Dynamo 1 Stapenhill 1 Att: 132
Replay: Stapenhill 1 **Loughborough D.** 2 *aet (Aug 21)* Att: 103
Tividale 1 **Mickleover Sports** 4 Att: 70
Nuneaton Griff 0 **Rainworth Miners Welfare** 3 Att: 82
Pegasus Juniors 0 New Mills 0 Att: 48
Replay: **New Mills** 3 Pegasus Juniors 1 *(Aug 20)* Att: 222
Glapwell 2 Dudley Town 2 Att: 71
Replay: Dudley T. 0 **Glapwell** 5 *(Aug 21) (at Cradley)* Att: 71
Shifnal Town 1 Arnold Town 1 Att: 92
Replay: Arnold 1 **Shifnal Town** 1 *aet (5-6p) (Aug 21)* Att: 176
Ledbury Town 2 **Boldmere St Michaels** 6 Att: 102
Oadby Town 1 Racing Club Warwick 0 Att: 89
Teversal 2 Coventry Sphinx 2 Att: 104
Replay: Cov. Sphinx 2 **Teversal** 2 *aet (5-6p) (Aug 22)* Att: 112
Market Drayton Town 1 Studley 1 Att: 51
Replay: Studley 0 **Market Drayton Town** 4 *(Aug 21)* Att: 103
Long Eaton United 2 Bridgnorth Town 1 Att: 67

Coalville Town 1 **Rocester** 2 Att: 135
Gornal Athletic 0 **Meir KA** 3 Att: 58
Norton United 1 Oldbury United 1 Att: 50
Replay: **Oldbury** 1 Norton 0 *aet (Aug 21) (at Pelsall)* Att: 71
Westfields 3 Friar Lane & Epworth 2 Att: 97
Borrowash Victoria 0 **Biddulph Victoria** 1 Att: 53
Cradley Town 1 **Gedling Town** 3 Att: 57
Cadbury Athletic 1 Alvechurch 1 Att: 68
Replay: **Alvechurch** 6 Cadbury Athletic 0 *(Aug 21)* Att: 89
South Normanton Athletic 1 Lye Town 0 Att: 64
Barwell 1 Newcastle Town 1 Att: 66
Replay: Newcastle Town 1 **Barwell** 2 *aet (Aug 21)* Att: 136
Tipton Town 1 Leek CSOB 1 Att: 60
Replay: Leek CSOB 0 **Tipton Town** 4 *(Aug 22)* Att: 69
Coleshill Town 1 Wellington 1 Att: 91
Replay: **Wellington** 3 Coleshill Town 2 *(Aug 22)* Att: 113
Wroxham 3 Hadleigh United 0 Att: 121
Walsham-le-Willows 3 Stowmarket Town 0 Att: 216
Woodbridge Town 5 Great Yarmouth 0 *(Aug 17)* Att: 105
St Ives Town 3 Cornard United 2 Att: 65
Bourne Town 2 **Haverhill Rovers** 3 Att: 82
Mildenhall Town 3 Leiston 0 Att: 155
Holbeach United 2 Wisbech Town 1 Att: 349
Dereham Town 12 Fakenham Town 0 Att: 193
Felixstowe & Walton 2 Debenham Leis. Centre 2 Att: 116
Replay: **Debenham** 2 Felixstowe & WU 0 *(Aug 21)* Att:189
Long Melford 0 **Blackstones** 2 Att: 104
Needham Market 4 Lowestoft Town 1 Att: 196
Soham Town Rangers 5 St Neots Town 2 Att: 100
Deeping Rangers 5 Lincoln Moorlands Railway 0 Att: 89
Yaxley 1 March Town United 0 Att: 156
Brimsdown Rovers 1 **Burnham Ramblers** 2 Att: 54
Sporting Bengal United 0 London APSA 0 *(Aug 19)* Att: 382
Replay: **London APSA** 4 Sporting Bengal United 3 Att: 71
(Aug 23) (at Aveley)
Saffron Walden Town 2 Wootton Blue Cross 2 Att: 167
Replay: Wootton BC 1 **Saffron Walden** 6 *(Aug 21)* Att: 67
Daventry United 0 **Raunds Town** 2 Att: 40
Northampton Spencer 3 Clapton 2 Att: 74
FC Clacton 1 Desborough Town 1 Att: 140
Replay: Desborough Town 2 **FC Clapton** 3 *(Aug 21)* Att: 100
Biggleswade United 1 Broxbourne Borough V&E 1 Att: 78
Replay: **Broxbourne** 2 Biggleswade Utd 1 *(Aug 21)* Att: 89
Welwyn Garden City 3 Bowers & Pitsea 1 Att: 42
Bedfont 0 **Oxhey Jets** 2 Att: 72
Tring Athletic 2 Ruislip Manor 1 Att: 102
Stansted 2 Hullbridge Sports 0 *(Aug 17)* Att: 120
Hertford Town 1 Cogenhoe United 0 Att: 107
Potton United 3 Romford 2 Att: 120
Long Buckby 3 Hoddesdon Town 1 Att: 71
Barkingside 5 Stewarts & Lloyds Corby 3 Att: 37
Halstead Town 2 Wellingborough Town 2 Att: 116
Replay: **Wellingborough T.** 2 Halstead 0 *(Aug 21)* Att: 148
Eton Manor 3 Colney Heath 1 *(Aug 19)* Att: 54
London Colney 0 **Langford** 1 Att: 72
Bedfont Green 2 Stanway Rovers 2 Att: 35
Replay: **Stanway Rovers** 2 Bedfont Green 1 *(Aug 22)* Att: 55
Cockfosters 3 Southend Manor 2 Att: 88
Tiptree United 2 Sawbridgeworth Town 2 Att: 69
Replay: Sawbridgeworth 2 **Tiptree Utd** 4 *aet (Aug 21)* Att: 81
Barking 4 Harefield United 0 Att: 94
Leverstock Green 0 **Stotfold** 3 Att: 54
Haringey Borough 2 Wembley 2 Att: 62
Replay: **Wembley** 3 Haringey Borough 0 *(Aug 21)* Att: 57
Biggleswade 4 **Concord** 3 *(Aug 19) (at Bedford)* Att: 70
North Greenford United 5 Royston Town 0 Att: 56
Tunbridge Wells 3 **Chessington & Hook United** 4 Att: 103
Three Bridges 1 Wealden 0 Att: 77
Camberley Town 2 Worthing United 0 Att: 82
Frimley Green 1 **Colliers Wood United** 2 Att: 38
Dorking 0 **Selsey** 1 Att: 59

Whitehawk 0 **VCD Athletic** 1 — Att: 73
Redhill 3 Sidley United 1 — Att: 100
Farnham Town 1 **Ringmer** 4 — Att: 45
Raynes Park Vale 3 Deal Town 3 — Att: 80
Replay: **Deal Town** 4 Raynes Park Vale 2 *(Aug 21)* — Att: 98
Westfield 0 **Banstead Athletic** 2 — Att: 48
Eastbourne United Association 1 **Sevenoaks Town** 3 — Att: 65
Erith Town 3 Cobham 1 — Att: 30
Lancing 1 Faversham Town 1 *(Aug 19) (at Steyning)* — Att: 73
Replay: **Faversham Town** 3 Lancing 0 *(Aug 21)* — Att: 104
Lordswood 1 Bookham 1 — Att: 119
Replay: Bookham 1 **Lordswood** 2 *(Aug 21)* — Att: 121
Herne Bay 0 East Grinstead Town 0 — Att: 124
Replay: East Grinstead Town 1 **Herne Bay** 3 *(Aug 21)* — Att: 118
Epsom & Ewell 1 **Crowborough Athletic** 7 — Att: 72
Merstham 2 **Hythe Town** 3 — Att: 93
Saltdean United (scr.) v **Croydon** (w/o)
Peacehaven & Telscombe 1 **East Preston** 2 — Att: 51
Pagham 1 Hailsham Town 1 — Att: 83
Replay: **Hailsham Town** 2 Pagham 0 *(Aug 21)* — Att: 76
Wick 2 Chertsey Town 2 — Att: 66
Replay: **Chertsey Town** 3 Wick 0 *(Aug 21)* — Att: 138
Thamesmead Town 4 Egham Town 1 — Att: 62
Shoreham 0 **Horley Town** 1 — Att: 110
Hassocks 1 Rye United 0 — Att: 102
Mile Oak 0 **Guildford City** 2 — Att: 55
VTFC 5 Cowes Sports 0 — Att: 64
Corsham Town 5 Wantage Town 1 *(Aug 19)* — Att: 110
Fareham Town 1 Carterton 1 — Att: 100
Replay: Carterton 0 **Fareham Town** 3 *(Aug 21)* — Att: 54
Highworth Town 0 Wootton Bassett Town 0 *(Aug 19)* — Att: 177
Replay: **Wootton Bassett** 2 Highworth 1 *(Aug 21)* — Att: 156
Bournemouth 2 **Beaconsfield SYCOB** 3 — Att: 60
Henley Town 3 Westbury United 2 — Att: 38
Christchurch 6 Aylesbury Vale 1 — Att: 58
Sandhurst Town 2 Newport Pagnell Town 0 — Att: 55
Kidlington 1 Shrivenham 1 — Att: 78
Replay: Shrivenham 1 **Kidlington** 2 *(Aug 22)* — Att: 162
Buckingham Town 1 **Chalfont St Peter** 3 — Att: 94
Hamble ASSC 1 Alton Town 0 *(Aug 17)* — Att: 94
Bemerton Heath Harlequins 5 Reading Town 3 — Att: 41
Brockenhurst 2 Witney United 0 — Att: 55
Abingdon Town 2 Ardley United 1 — Att: 50
Flackwell Heath 1 **Moneyfields** 2 — Att: 42
Thame United 1 **Downton** 2 — Att: 43
Holmer Green 0 **Melksham Town** 1 — Att: 45
North Leigh 4 Devizes Town 0 — Att: 55
New Milton Town 1 **AFC Totton** 5 — Att: 90
Bicester Town 1 Milton United 1 — Att: 47
Replay: Milton United 0 **Bicester Town** 1 *(Aug 20)* — Att: 135
Hungerford Town 0 Calne Town 0 — Att: 92
Replay: Calne Town 0 **Hungerford Town** 3 *(Aug 21)* — Att: 92
Lymington 4 Wallingford 1 *(Aug 19) (at New Milton)* — Att: 60
Marlow United 1 **Cove** 2 *(Aug 17)* — Att: 182
Minehead Town 4 Harrow Hill 0 — Att: 43
Saltash United 2 Almondsbury Town 1 — Att: 104
Shortwood United 1 Bishop Sutton 0 — Att: 65
Shepton Mallet 2 Radstock Town 2 — Att: 61
Replay: Radstock Town 0 **Shepton Mallet** 2 *(Aug 21)* — Att: 56
Bitton 2 Bideford 0 — Att: 108
Street 2 **Wimborne Town** 5 — Att: 110
Barnstaple Town 4 Clevedon United 1 — Att: 113
Liskeard Athletic 2 Shaftesbury 2 — Att: 74
Replay: Shaftesbury 0 **Liskeard Athletic** 3 *(Aug 21)* — Att: 119
Tavistock 1 **Bodmin Town** 3 — Att: 120
Keynsham Town 1 **St Blazey** 2 — Att: 45
Poole Town 0 **Dawlish Town** 2 — Att: 130
Torrington (scr.) v Hamworthy United (w/o)
Hallen 4 Fairford Town 2 — Att: 46
Bridport 0 **Welton Rovers** 5 — Att: 86
Chard Town 1 **Sherborne Town** 3 — Att: 110
Odd Down 2 Bristol Manor Farm 0 — Att: 51
Falmouth Town 1 **Frome Town** 2 — Att: 147

PRELIMINARY ROUND
(£1,000 to each winning club)
(Ties played September 1 unless stated)

Jarrow Roofing Boldon CA 1 Norton & Stockton 0 — Att: 50
Chester-le-Street Town 2 Billingham Synthonia 1 — Att: 103
Winterton Rangers 1 Morpeth Town 0 — Att: 55
Selby Town 4 Pickering Town 0 — Att: 134
Marske United 1 Horden Colliery Welfare 1 — Att: 93
Replay: **Horden Colliery Welfare** 2 Marske 1 *(Sep 5)* — Att: 85
Wakefield 1 West Auckland Town 1 — Att: 75
Replay: **West Auckland Town** 1 Wakefield 0 *(Sep 5)* — Att: 89
Ashington 1 **Newcastle Blue Star** 3 — Att: 139
Liversedge 2 Dunston Federation 0 — Att: 159
Bridlington Town 1 **Newcastle Benfield** 2 — Att: 173
Durham City 2 Silsden 2 *(at Eppleton CW)* — Att: 98
Replay: Silsden 0 **Durham City** 3 *(Sep 5)* — Att: 112
Spennymoor Town 3 Garforth Town 2 — Att: 227
Shildon 5 Goole 4 — Att: 170
Brigg Town 4 South Shields 0 — Att: 116
Tow Law Town 0 Billingham Town 0 — Att: 108
Replay: **Billingham Town** 3 Tow Law 2 *(Sep 4)* — Att: 212
Hall Road Rangers 1 Crook Town 0 — Att: 97
Esh Winning 1 Harrogate **Railway Athletic** 4 — Att: 70
Consett 4 Darlington Railway Athletic 0 — Att: 120
Ossett Albion 0 **Bradford Park Avenue** 1 — Att: 278
Cheadle Town 3 Ashton Town 0 — Att: 74
Chorley 2 Warrington Town 0 — Att: 322
Atherton Collieries 3 Bacup Borough 1 — Att: 52
Parkgate 2 Alsager Town 1 — Att: 51
Clitheroe 3 St Helens Town 2 — Att: 210
Colwyn Bay 2 Congleton Town 2 — Att: 398
Replay: Congleton Town 1 **Colwyn Bay** 5 *(Sep 4)* — Att: 208
Maine Road 0 **Skelmersdale United** 3 — Att: 89
Winsford United 1 **Penrith Town** 3 — Att: 108
Radcliffe Borough 3 Lancaster City 0 — Att: 156
Colne 1 **Nantwich Town** 3 — Att: 108
Trafford 2 **FC United** 5 *(Sep 2) (at Altrincham)* — Att: 2,238
Woodley Spts 1 Mossley 1 *(Sep 2) (at Cheadle Town)* — Att: 129
Replay: Mossley 1 **Woodley Sports** 2 *(Sep 4)* — Att: 210
Rossendale United 0 **Dinnington Town** 2 — Att: 98
Hallam 2 AFC Emley 2 *(Aug 31) (at AFC Emley)* — Att: 226
Replay: AFC Emley 1 **Hallam** 2 *(Sep 5)* — Att: 202
Flixton 1 Salford City 0 — Att: 133
Cammell Laird 2 Sheffield 0 — Att: 130
Bamber Bridge 2 Oldham Town 0 — Att: 115
Stocksbridge Park Steels 3 Curzon Ashton 2 — Att: 96
Leamington 1 Shifnal Town 0 — Att: 581
Bromyard Town 1 **Shepshed Dynamo** 4 — Att: 78
Retford United 1 **Tipton Town** 2 — Att: 223
Rushall Olympic 3 Boldmere St Michaels 0 — Att: 101
Pelsall Villa 1 **Quorn** 6 — Att: 84
Causeway United 1 Westfields 1 *(Sep 2)* — Att: 111
Replay: Westfields 2 **Causeway United** 3 *aet (Sep 4)* — Att: 92
Glapwell 1 Stone Dominoes 0 — Att: 60
Mickleover Sports 0 Long Eaton United 0 — Att: 147
Replay: Long Eaton United 3 **Mickleover** 4 *(Sep 4)* — Att: 105
Bolehall Swifts 1 **Alvechurch** 0 — Att: 86
Brierley Hill & Withymoor 1 Staveley MW 0 — Att: 94
Sutton Coldfield Town 1 Romulus 1 — Att: 233
Replay: **S. Coldfield** 4 Romulus 4 *aet (7-6p) (Sep 4)* — Att: 312
Evesham United 1 Gresley Rovers 0 *(Sep 2)* — Att: 123
Loughborough Dynamo 1 Market Drayton Town 1 — Att: 155
Replay: **Market Drayton** 4 Loughborough 0 *(Sep 4)* — Att: 115
New Mills 1 **Atherstone Town** 3 — Att: 234
Rocester 1 Wellington 0 — Att: 102
Southam United 0 **Stratford Town** 2 — Att: 145
Stourbridge 2 Highgate United 1 — Att: 144
Barwell 0 **Biddulph Victoria** 4 — Att: 92
Chasetown 4 Oadby Town 1 — Att: 321
South Normanton Athletic 1 Bedworth United 1 — Att: 90
Replay: **Bedworth Utd** 2 South Normanton 0 *(Sep 4)* — Att: 133
Teversal 0 Rainworth Miners Welfare 0 — Att: 126
Replay: **Rainworth MW** 2 Teversal 1 *(Sep 4)* — Att: 185

Barnt Green Spartak 3 Willenhall Town 2	Att: 119
Rematch: **Willenhall Town** 3 Barnt Green 1 *(Sep 25)*	Att: 108
Carlton Town 2 Pilkington XXX 1	Att: 107
Meir KA 1 Gedling Town 1	Att: 52
Replay: **Gedling Town** 5 Meir KA 0 *(Sep 4)*	Att: 72
Oldbury Utd 1 **Kidsgrove Ath.** 3 *(Aug 31) (at Pelsall)*	Att: 74
Belper Town 3 Stourport Swifts 3	Att: 137
Replay: Stourport Swifts 2 **Belper Town** 5 *(Sep 4)*	Att: 96
Malvern Town 3 Glossop North End 0	Att: 63
Deeping Rangers 0 Dereham Town 0	Att: 152
Replay: Dereham Town 0 **Deeping Rangers** 1 *(Sep 4)*	Att: 230
Diss Town 0 **Kirkley & Pakefield** 1	Att: 170
Ipswich Wanderers 1 **Needham Market** 10	Att: 176
Ely City 0 **Boston Town** 1	Att: 166
Yaxley 0 **Soham Town Rangers** 3	Att: 146
Spalding United 5 Norwich United 1	Att: 104
Blackstones 0 Grantham Town 0	Att: 240
Replay: **Grantham Town** 2 Blackstones 1 *aet (Sep 4)*	Att: 232
Walsham-le-Willows 0 Haverhill Rovers 0	Att: 146
Replay: **Haverhill Rovers** 4 Walsham 2 *(Sep 4)*	Att: 153
Mildenhall Town 2 St Ives Town 1	Att: 176
Holbeach United 2 Newmarket Town 0	Att: 132
Debenham Leisure Centre 2 Gorleston 0	Att: 125
Woodbridge Town 0 **Wroxham** 2	Att: 91
AFC Sudbury 2 **Bury Town** 3	Att: 406
Stanway Rovers 0 **Saffron Walden Town** 3	Att: 89
Wivenhoe Town 0 **Concord Rangers** 4	Att: 94
Tilbury 0 **Great Wakering Rovers** 4	Att: 79
Hillingdon Borough 0 Barking 0	Att: 95
Replay: Barking 1 **Hillingdon B.** 1 *aet (3-4p) (Sep 4)*	Att: 101
Tring Athletic 4 Hertford Town 4	Att: 141
Replay: **Hertford Town** 2 Tring Athletic 0 *(Sep 4)*	Att: 145
Enfield Town 2 AFC Hayes 1	Att: 209
Rothwell Town 2 Canvey Island 1	Att: 232
Dunstable Town 3 Wingate & Finchley 1	Att: 112
Aveley 2 Berkhamsted Town 1	Att: 66
Harwich & Parkeston 2 Ilford 0	Att: 183
Northwood 1 Uxbridge 0	Att: 193
Bedford 0 **Broxbourne Borough V& E** 3	Att: 60
Arlesey Town 0 **Brentwood Town** 1	Att: 118
Langford 0 Potters Bar Town 0	Att: 80
Replay: **Potters Bar Town** 5 Langford 1 *(Sep 4)*	Att: 64
Waltham Forest 1 Wellingborough Town 1	Att: 84
Replay: Wellingborough 0 **Waltham Forest** 2 *(Sep 4)*	Att: 156
Wembley 1 **Ware** 4	Att: 74
Leighton Town 3 FC Clacton 1	Att: 125
Maldon Town 5 Eton Manor 0	Att: 72
Barkingside 2 Hanwell Town 1 *(Sep 2)*	Att: 127
Stotfold 7 Potton United 2	Att: 103
Welwyn Garden City 1 Cockfosters 1	Att: 75
Replay: Cockfosters 0 **Welwyn Garden City** 1 *(Sep 4)*	Att: 83
Oxhey Jets 1 **Burnham Ramblers** 4	Att: 73
Tiptree United 2 **London APSA** 0 *(Tiptree expelled)*	Att: 77
Raunds Town 0 **Edgware Town** 5	Att: 79
Long Buckby 1 Barton Rovers 1	Att: 64
Replay: **Barton Rovers** 5 Long Buckby 0 *(Sep 4)*	Att: 100
Witham Town 2 **Waltham Abbey** 3	Att: 108
Stansted 4 St Margaretsbury 1	Att: 145
Northampton Spencer 2 North Greenford United 1	Att: 87
Redbridge 1 **Woodford United** 2	Att: 69
Corinthian Casuals 1 **Deal Town** 2	Att: 83
Arundel 1 Molesey 1	Att: 92
Replay: Molesey 1 **Arundel** 2 *(Sep 4)*	Att: 121
Walton & Hersham 1 Hassocks 0	Att: 101
Burgess Hill Town 7 Banstead Athletic 0	Att: 149
Dartford 3 Leatherhead 0	Att: 879
Slade Green 1 **Croydon** 6	Att: 68
Ringmer 1 **Chatham Town** 2	Att: 102
Selsey 1 Lordswood 0	Att: 102
Sittingbourne 1 Chertsey Town 0	Att: 194
Camberley Town 0 Ash United 0	Att: 118
Replay: Ash United 1 **Camberley Town** 3 *(Sep 4)*	Att: 154
Metropolitan Police 0 **Croydon Athletic** 1	Att: 94

Eastbourne Town 2 Kingstonian 1	Att: 368
Colliers Wood United 7 Faversham Town 6	Att: 55
Redhill 0 **Dover Athletic** 1	Att: 302
Herne Bay 2 Guildford City 0	Att: 198
Erith & Belvedere 2 Ashford Town 0 *(Aug 31)*	Att: 216
Dulwich Hamlet 2 Three Bridges 0	Att: 206
Horley Town 0 East Preston 0	Att: 111
Replay: East Preston 1 **Horley** 1 *aet (5-6p) (Sep 4)*	Att: 71
Walton Casuals 1 **Sevenoaks Town** 3	Att: 68
Thamesmead Town 3 Whitstable Town 1	Att: 75
Erith Town 1 VCD Athletic 0	Att: 67
Littlehampton Town 3 Chipstead 2	Att: 67
Tooting & Mitcham 1 **Cray Wanderers** 2	Att: 240
Crowborough Athletic 1 Hailsham Town 1	Att: 160
Replay: Hailsham 1 **Crowboro.** 1 *aet (5-6p) (Sep 4)*	Att: 192
Hythe Town 2 Whyteleafe 1	Att: 139
Godalming Town 2 Worthing 2	Att: 225
Replay: **Worthing** 3 Godalming Town 0 *(Sep 4)*	Att: 292
Horsham YMCA 4 Chessington & Hook United 1	Att: 74
Wootton Bassett Town 2 Bracknell Town 1 *(Sep 2)*	Att: 171
Slough Town 1 **Fleet Town** 4	Att: 203
Windsor & Eton 1 Marlow 1	Att: 162
Replay: Marlow 0 **Windsor & Eton** 3 *(Sep 4)*	Att: 191
Melksham Town 4 Bicester Town 0	Att: 51
Burnham 1 Brockenhurst 1	Att: 76
Replay: **Brockenhurst** 3 Burnham 0 *(Sep 4)*	Att: 107
Christchurch 2 **Didcot Town** 4	Att: 126
Chalfont St Peter 1 Hamble ASSC 0	Att: 53
Winchester City 0 **Moneyfields** 2	Att: 181
Fareham Town 3 Sandhurst Town 3	Att: 116
Replay: **Sandhurst** 0 Farnham 0 *aet (4-3p) (Sep 4)*	Att: 91
Beaconsfield SYCOB 0 **Hungerford Town** 0 *(Sep 2)*	Att: 102
Replay: Hungerford Town 0 **Beaconsfield** 3 *(Sep 4)*	Att: 72
Farnborough 0 **Chesham United** 2	Att: 423
Aylesbury United 4 Newport IOW 2	Att: 206
Henley Town 3 Bemerton Heath Harlequins 2	Att: 68
Abingdon Town 2 **AFC Totton** 3	Att: 70
Downton 1 Abingdon United 1	Att: 61
Replay: **Abingdon United** 5 Downton 2 *(Sep 4)*	Att: 124
Cove 1 **Gosport Borough** 6	Att: 85
Andover 3 **Oxford City** 4	Att: 166
North Leigh 1 VTFC 1	Att: 48
Replay: **VTFC** 2 North Leigh 1 *(Sep 4)*	Att: 110
Corsham Town 2 Lymington Town 1	Att: 129
Kidlington 2 **Thatcham Town** 3	Att: 95
Slimbridge (scr.) v **Bitton** (w/o)	
Brislington 0 **Wimborne Town** 5	Att: 64
Dawlish Town 1 **Bishops Cleeve** 2	Att: 82
Shepton Mallet 0 **Hallen** 2	Att: 79
Shortwood United 2 Frome Town 1	Att: 86
Cinderford Town 3 Elmore 2	Att: 81
Paulton Rovers 1 St Blazey 1	Att: 136
Replay: St Blazey 0 **Paulton Rovers** 3 *(Sep 5)*	Att: 220
Bridgwater Town 3 Minehead 1	Att: 299
Barnstaple Town 0 **Truro City** 6	Att: 383
Sherborne Town 3 Liskeard Athletic 2	Att: 105
Willand Rovers 2 **Hamworthy United** 3	Att: 90
Bodmin Town 4 Ilfracombe Town 0	Att: 97
Saltash United 2 **Taunton Town** 3	Att: 145
Welton Rovers 1 Odd Down 0	Att: 64

FIRST QUALIFYING ROUND

(£2,250 to each winning club)
(Ties played September 15 unless stated)

Bradford Park Avenue (w/o) v Scarborough (scr.)	
West Auckland Town 3 Winterton Rangers 2	Att: 64
Newcastle Benfield 2 Newcastle Blue Star 1	Att: 142
Whitby Town 3 Shildon 2	Att: 346
Chester-le-Street Town 1 Harrogate Railway 1	Att: 100
Replay: **Harrogate Rail** 3 Chester-le-Street 0 *(Sep 19)*	Att: 104
Consett 3 Ossett Town 0	Att: 186
Hall Road Rangers 2 **Billingham Town** 3	Att: 97
Gateshead 6 Selby Town 1	Att: 384

WWW.NLNEWSDESK.CO.UK

Liversedge 1 North Ferriby United 0 — Att: 210
Spennymoor Town 2 Brigg Town 1 — Att: 217
Horden Colliery W. 1 Jarrow Roofing Boldon CA 1 — Att: 46
Replay: Jarrow Rfg BCA 1 **Horden CW** 2 *(Sep 18)* — Att: 78
Durham City 1 **Guiseley** 3 *(at Washington)* — Att: 124
Dinnington Town 2 Penrith 2 — Att: 268
Replay: Penrith 1 **Dinnington Town** 2 *aet (Sep 18)* — Att: 115
Flixton 2 Bamber Bridge 2 — Att: 103
Replay: **Bamber Bridge** 3 Flixton 1 *(Sep 18)* — Att: 154
Fleetwood Town 2 FC United of Manchester 1 — Att: 3,112
Witton Albion 1 **Prescot Cables** 2 — Att: 335
Hallam 0 **Woodley Sports** 1 — Att: 80
Frickley Athletic 1 **Stocksbridge Park Steels** 2 — Att: 230
Nantwich Town 3 Ashton United 2 — Att: 403
Chorley 2 Clitheroe 2 — Att: 345
Replay: **Clitheroe** 1 Chorley 1 *aet (4-3p) (Sep 18)* — Att: 300
Colwyn Bay 2 Parkgate 1 — Att: 321
Skelmersdale United 2 Marine 0 — Att: 259
Radcliffe Borough 4 Cammell Laird 1 — Att: 160
Atherton Collieries 2 **Cheadle Town** 5 — Att: 67
Worksop Town 0 **Kendal Town** 1 — Att: 248
Stourbridge 2 Leamington 0 — Att: 386
Kidsgrove Athletic 2 Willenhall Town 0 *(Sep 29)* — Att: 127
Rushall Olympic 4 Atherstone Town 1 — Att: 161
Rocester 0 **Chasetown** 4 — Att: 207
Belper Town 3 Causeway United 0 — Att: 147
Bromsgrove Rovers 1 Shepshed Dynamo 1 — Att: 348
Replay: Shepshed 0 **Bromsgrove Rovers** 2 *(Sep 18)* — Att: 242
Glapwell 3 Rugby Town 2 — Att: 153
Quorn 5 Alvechurch 0 — Att: 149
Halesowen Town 4 Malvern Town 0 — Att: 328
Biddulph Victoria 1 **Rainworth MW** 3 *(Sep 16)* — Att: 107
Sutton Coldfield Town 2 Ilkeston Town 1 — Att: 101
Carlton Town 2 **Matlock Town** 4 — Att: 187
Hednesford Town 0 Stratford Town 0 — Att: 380
Replay: Stratford 0 **Hednesford Town** 1 *(Sep 19)* — Att: 196
Evesham United 1 Tipton Town 1 *(Sep 16)* — Att: 111
Replay: Tipton Town 0 **Evesham United** 2 *(Sep 19)* — Att: 80
Brierley Hill/Withymoor 1 **Mkt Drayton** 2 *(Sep 16)* — Att: 108
Bedworth United 2 Eastwood Town 1 — Att: 173
Gedling Town 3 Mickleover Sports 1 — Att: 80
Leek Town 1 **Buxton** 2 — Att: 653
Holbeach United 0 **Debenham Leisure Centre** 2 — Att: 236
Kirkley & Pakefield 2 Wroxham 1 — Att: 241
Boston Town 0 **Soham Town Rangers** 4 — Att: 122
Bury Town 2 Deeping Rangers 0 — Att: 252
Lincoln United 0 **King's Lynn** 3 — Att: 271
Grantham Town 1 Needham Market 1 — Att: 213
Replay: Needham Market 0 **Grantham** 1 *(Sep 25)* — Att: 329
Stamford 5 Spalding United 2 — Att: 319
Mildenhall Town 1 Haverhill Rovers 1 — Att: 213
Replay: **Haverhill** 0 Mildenhall 0 *aet (5-4p) (Sep 18)* — Att: 222
Hemel Hempstead Town 4 East Thurrock United 0 — Att: 246
Hillingdon Borough 0 Northampton Spencer 0 — Att: 85
Dunstable Town 1 Waltham Abbey 0 — Att: 131
Hertford Town 3 Barkingside 3 — Att: 101
Replay: **Barkingside** 3 Hertford Town 1 *(Sep 17)* — Att: 102
Edgware Town 2 Potters Bar Town 0 — Att: 81
Chelmsford City 5 Burnham Ramblers 0 — Att: 787
Barton Rovers 0 Corby Town 0 — Att: 165
Replay: **Corby Town** 3 Barton Rovers 1 *(Sep 19)* — Att: 166
Harwich & Parkeston 0 Woodford United 0 — Att: 149
Replay: **Woodford Utd** 3 Harwich & P. 1 *(Sep 17)* — Att: 107
Rothwell Town 1 Enfield Town 1 — Att: 172
Replay: **Enfield T.** 2 Rothwell 2 *aet (4-3p) (Sep 18)* — Att: 168
Broxbourne Borough V & E 1 Bedford Town 1 — Att: 172
Replay: **Bedford Town** 2 Broxbourne BVE 0 *(Sep 18)* — Att: 261
Saffron Walden Town 1 **Maldon Town** 2 — Att: 208
AFC Hornchurch 3 Cheshunt 1 — Att: 368
Welwyn Garden City 2 **Billericay Town** 8 — Att: 122
Hendon 1 Aveley 1 — Att: 128
Replay: Aveley 2 **Hendon** 3 *(Sep 19)* — Att: 95
Boreham Wood 1 Northwood 0 — Att: 156

Ware 0 Great Wakering Rovers 0 — Att: 125
Replay: Great Wakering Rovers 4 **Ware** 5 *(Sep 18)* — Att: 121
Stotfold 3 Stansted 2 — Att: 118
Wealdstone 1 Waltham Forest 0 — Att: 153
Harrow Borough 2 **Hitchin Town** 3 — Att: 186
Harlow Town 2 Concord Rangers 0 — Att: 212
Brackley Town 0 Staines Town 0 — Att: 251
Replay: **Staines** 0 Brackley 0 *aet (5-4p) (Sep 18)* — Att: 140
Heybridge Swifts 4 Leyton 3 — Att: 153
Ashford Town (Middx) 0 **Leighton Town** 1 — Att: 77
London APSA 0 **Brentwood Town** 4 *(Sep 25)* — Att: 122
Dulwich Hamlet 2 Deal Town 2 — Att: 209
Replay: Deal Town 1 **Dulwich Hamlet** 3 *aet (Sep 18)* — Att: 186
Hythe Town 3 Littlehampton Town 1 — Att: 130
Burgess Hill Town 0 **Dover Athletic** 2 — Att: 324
Herne Bay 1 Sevenoaks Town 0 — Att: 240
Worthing 0 Croydon 0 — Att: 365
Replay: Croydon 0 **Worthing** 1 *(Sep 19)* — Att: 130
Horsham 7 Arundel 1 — Att: 326
Chatham Town 0 **Margate** 3 — Att: 287
Dartford 1 Sittingbourne 1 — Att: 870
Replay: Sittingbourne 1 **Dartford** 5 *(Sep 18)* — Att: 303
Folkestone Invicta 1 Horsham YMCA 1 — Att: 289
Replay: Horsham YMCA 0 **Folkestone I.** 2 *(Sep 18)* — Att: 105
Horley Town 0 **Erith Town** 1 — Att: 106
Croydon Athletic 1 Tonbridge Angels 1 — Att: 177
Replay: **Tonbridge** 4 Croydon Athletic 2 *aet (Sep 18)* — Att: 259
Cray Wanderers 2 **AFC Wimbledon** 6 *(Sep 16)* — Att: 933
Maidstone United 3 Erith & Belvedere 0 — Att: 351
Eastbourne Town 1 Walton & Hersham 1 — Att: 187
Replay: **Walton & H.** 2 Eastbourne Town 1 *(Sep 18)* — Att: 101
Camberley Town 4 Colliers Wood United 2 — Att: 84
Thamesmead Town 2 **Carshalton Athletic** 4 — Att: 80
Crowborough Athletic 2 Selsey 1 — Att: 96
Hastings United 0 **Ramsgate** 1 — Att: 481
VTFC 1 Bashley 1 — Att: 207
Replay: **Bashley** 4 VTFC 3 *aet (Sep 18)* — Att: 166
Didcot Town 0 **Windsor & Eton** 1 — Att: 270
Sandhurst Town 1 **Chalfont St Peter** 6 — Att: 65
Banbury United 1 **Aylesbury United** 4 — Att: 419
Fleet Town 0 Gosport Borough 0 — Att: 186
Replay: Gosport Borough 1 **Fleet Town** 3 *(Sep 18)* — Att: 152
Oxford City 4 Swindon Supermarine 2 — Att: 158
Abingdon United 1 AFC Totton 1 — Att: 95
Replay: **AFC Totton** 4 Abingdon United 1 *(Sep 18)* — Att: 129
Corsham Town 1 Melksham Town 0 — Att: 252
Moneyfields 1 Thatcham Town 0 — Att: 116
Chesham United 5 Henley Town 1 — Att: 273
Brockenhurst 1 Wootton Bassett Town 1 — Att: 124
Replay: Wootton Bassett 1 **Brockenhurst** 5 *(Sep 18)* — Att: 162
Beaconsfield SYCOB 1 Chippenham Town 1 — Att: 144
Replay: **Chippenham** 2 Beaconsfield 0 *(Sep 18)* — Att: 272
Mangotsfield United 3 Taunton Town 0 — Att: 211
Yate Town 1 **Gloucester City** 5 — Att: 209
Tiverton Town 0 **Shortwood United** 3 — Att: 374
Hamworthy United 3 Bishops Cleeve 3 — Att: 98
Replay: Bishops Cleeve 0 **Hamworthy Utd** 1 *(Sep 19)* — Att: 80
Bridgwater Town 0 **Paulton Rovers** 2 — Att: 339
Hallen 2 Sherborne Town 0 — Att: 38
Cirencester Town 1 Cinderford Town 1 — Att: 170
Replay: Cinderford Town 1 **Cirencester Town** 2 — Att: 120
Team Bath 2 Bodmin Town 0 — Att: 92
Welton Rovers 0 **Truro City** 2 — Att: 156
Clevedon Town 4 Wimborne Town 0 — Att: 173
Bitton 2 **Merthyr Tydfil** 4 — Att: 159

SECOND QUALIFYING ROUND
(£3,750 to each winning club)
(Ties played September 29 unless stated)
Liversedge 0 **Kendal Town** 3 — Att: 198
Consett 0 **Workington** 2 — Att: 408
Barrow 5 Colwyn Bay 0 — Att: 772
Billingham Town 0 **Fleetwood Town** 4 — Att: 212

Skelmersdale United 0 **Southport** 1 — Att: 769
Prescot Cables 1 Guiseley 1 — Att: 265
Replay: **Guiseley** 1 Prescot Cables 0 *(Oct 2)* — Att: 246
Dinnington Town 2 Cheadle Town 1 — Att: 307
Harrogate Railway Athletic 4 Leigh RMI 1 — Att: 126
Bradford Park Avenue 4 Whitby Town 0 — Att: 278
Stalybridge Celtic 1 Hyde United 0 — Att: 790
Bamber Bridge 2 Burscough 1 — Att: 242
Gainsborough Trinity 6 Stocksbridge Park Steels 1 — Att: 396
Harrogate Town 2 Nantwich Town 2 — Att: 480
Replay: Nantwich T. 1 **Harrogate Town** 2 *(Oct 2)* — Att: 463
West Auckland Town 1 Newcastle Benfield 0 — Att: 76
Gateshead 1 **Vauxhall Motors** 2 — Att: 246
Clitheroe 8 Spennymoor Town 2 — Att: 330
Blyth Spartans 2 Radcliffe Borough 1 — Att: 480
Horden Colliery Welfare 0 **Woodley Sports** 5 — Att: 58
Cambridge City 1 Chasetown 1 — Att: 359
Replay: **Chasetown** 2 Cambridge City 1 *aet (Oct 2)* — Att: 444
Kettering Town 3 Redditch United 1 — Att: 1,072
Bromsgrove Rovers 1 Nuneaton Borough 1 — Att: 581
Replay: **Nuneaton Borough** 2 Bromsgrove 0 *(Oct 2)* — Att: 607
Rainworth MW 2 Kidsgrove Athletic 0 *(Oct 2)* — Att: 189
Matlock Town 3 AFC Telford United 1 — Att: 591
Stourbridge 0 **King's Lynn** 5 — Att: 315
Soham Town Rangers 0 **Solihull Moors** 3 — Att: 200
Hinckley United 4 Grantham Town 2 — Att: 366
Boston United 4 Buxton 1 — Att: 1,347
Quorn 1 **Evesham United** 3 — Att: 169
Tamworth 1 Worcester City 0 — Att: 801
Hednesford Town 0 Alfreton Town 0 — Att: 448
Replay: Alfreton Town 1 **Hednesford Town** 2 *(Oct 2)* — Att: 246
Rushall Olympic 2 Sutton Coldfield Town 0 — Att: 266
Glapwell 4 Market Drayton Town 4 — Att: 120
Replay: Market Drayton Town 1 **Glapwell** 2 *(Oct 2)* — Att: 159
Belper Town 2 Hucknall Town 1 — Att: 295
Halesowen Town 2 Bedworth United 1 — Att: 368
Stamford 3 Gedling Town 1 — Att: 283
Horsham 3 Bury Town 2 — Att: 404
Hayes & Yeading United 2 Herne Bay 2 — Att: 211
Replay: Herne Bay 0 **Hayes & Yeading Utd** 3 *(Oct 3)* — Att: 364
Dulwich Hamlet 2 Chalfont St Peter 1 *(Sep 30)* — Att: 215
Crowborough Athletic 1 **Staines Town** 5 — Att: 287
Boreham Wood 3 Bedford Town 3 — Att: 246
Replay: Bedford Town 2 **Boreham Wood** 3 *(Oct 2)* — Att: 310
Ware 3 Thurrock 2 — Att: 172
Haverhill Rovers 1 Hitchin Town 1 — Att: 313
Replay: **Hitchin Town** 5 Haverhill Rovers 0 *(Oct 2)* — Att: 160
Dartford 2 Camberley Town 2 — Att: 906
Replay: Camberley 0 **Dartford** 0 *aet (1-4p) (Oct 2)* — Att: 242
Fisher Athletic 0 **Margate** 4 — Att: 218
Hemel Hempstead Town 0 **Chelmsford City** 2 — Att: 521
Welling United 2 Barkingside 1 — Att: 436
Billericay Town 2 Maidstone United 0 — Att: 594
Tonbridge Angels 2 Maldon Town 2 — Att: 363
Replay: Maldon T. 0 **Tonbridge Angels** 2 *aet (Oct 2)* — Att: 151
Dunstable Town 0 **Lewes** 2 — Att: 212
St Albans City 1 **Bishop's Stortford** 2 — Att: 410
Kirkley & Pakefield 1 **Leighton Town** 2 — Att: 225
Brentwood Town 2 Harlow Town 0 — Att: 192
Chesham United 1 Stotfold 1 — Att: 239
Replay: **Stotfold** 2 Chesham United 1 *(Oct 2)* — Att: 165
Worthing 3 Walton & Hersham 0 — Att: 375
Hampton & Richmond Borough 3 Braintree Town 1 — Att: 276
Hendon 1 AFC Hornchurch 1 — Att: 225
Replay: **AFC Hornchurch** 2 Hendon 1 *(Oct 2)* — Att: 333
Sutton United 1 Woodford United 1 — Att: 293
Replay: Woodford United 0 **Sutton United** 2 *(Oct 1)* — Att: 137
Debenham Leisure Centre 1 **AFC Wimbledon** 5 — Att: 1,026
Ramsgate 0 **Corby Town** 1 — Att: 330
Folkestone Invicta 0 Windsor & Eton 0 — Att: 264
Replay: Windsor & Eton 0 **Folkestone Inv.** 1 *(Oct 2)* — Att: 144

Hythe Town 2 Dover Athletic 1 — Att: 1,109
Enfield Town 2 Hillingdon Borough 2 — Att: 244
Replay: **Hillingdon Boro.** 2 Enfield Town 1 *(Oct 2)* — Att: 140
Erith Town 0 **Heybridge S.** 3 *(Sep 30) (at Welling)* — Att: 250
Aylesbury United 1 Bromley 1 *(Sep 30)* — Att: 406
Replay: **Bromley** 4 Aylesbury United 2 *aet (Oct 2)* — Att: 346
Carshalton Athletic 0 **Wealdstone** 1 — Att: 316
Eastbourne Borough 2 Edgware Town 0 — Att: 573
Merthyr Tydfil 2 AFC Totton 2 — Att: 289
Replay: AFC Totton 0 **Merthyr** 0 *aet (3-4p) (Oct 2)* — Att: 293
Brockenhurst 0 **Maidenhead United** 6 — Att: 237
Oxford City 3 **Weston-super-Mare** 4 — Att: 278
Bognor Regis Town 1 **Havant & Waterlooville** 2 — Att: 426
Chippenham Town 2 Hallen 0 — Att: 499
Dorchester Town 1 Paulton Rovers 1 — Att: 374
Replay: **Paulton Rovers** 2 Dorchester Town 0 *(Oct 1)* — Att: 232
Gloucester City 0 **Shortwood United** 2 *(Sep 30)* — Att: 706
Basingstoke Town 0 **Newport County** 1 — Att: 658
Truro City 0 **Bath City** 1 — Att: 1,127
Corsham Town 1 **Bashley** 2 — Att: 174
Moneyfields 1 **Team Bath** 8 *(Sep 28)* — Att: 228
Hamworthy United 1 **Eastleigh** 3 — Att: 278
Cirencester Town 0 **Clevedon Town** 1 — Att: 145
Fleet Town 2 Mangotsfield United 0 — Att: 175

THIRD QUALIFYING ROUND
(£5,000 to each winning club)
(Ties played October 13 unless stated)

Harrogate Railway Athletic 4 Matlock Town 3 — Att: 254
Harrogate Town 2 Clitheroe 0 — Att: 516
Barrow 2 Fleetwood Town 1 — Att: 855
West Auckland Town 2 Bamber Bridge 2 — Att: 147
Replay: **Bamber Bridge** 5 West Auckland 1 *(Oct 16)* — Att: 220
Dinnington Town 1 **Bradford Park Avenue** 7 — Att: 518
Belper Town 0 **Southport** 3 — Att: 382
Gainsborough Trinity 1 Blyth Spartans 0 — Att: 379
Stalybridge Celtic 0 **Workington** 5 — Att: 495
Kendal Town 4 Woodley Sports 0 — Att: 195
Guiseley 2 **Vauxhall Motors** 3 — Att: 292
Rushall Olympic 2 Hednesford Town 0 — Att: 362
Chasetown 2 Rainworth Miners Welfare 0 — Att: 604
Tamworth 2 King's Lynn 1 — Att: 621
Boston United 4 Hinckley United 1 *(Oct 14)* — Att: 1,425
Evesham United 3 Halesowen Town 0 — Att: 332
Glapwell 0 **Corby Town** 3 — Att: 163
Kettering Town 1 **Solihull Moors** 2 — Att: 805
Nuneaton Borough 4 Stamford 1 — Att: 839
Wealdstone 1 Bishop's Stortford 0 — Att: 301
Brentwood Town 0 **Staines Town** 3 — Att: 277
Heybridge Swifts 2 Billericay Town 2 *(Oct 12)* — Att: 522
Replay: **Billericay Town** 2 Heybridge Swifts 0 *(Oct 16)* — Att: 530
Leighton Town 2 Boreham Wood 1 — Att: 273
AFC Hornchurch 2 Dulwich Hamlet 1 *(Oct 12)* — Att: 610
Hitchin Town 4 Margate 3 — Att: 325
Eastbourne Borough 2 Welling United 1 — Att: 632
Hayes & Yeading United 1 Chelmsford City 0 — Att: 393
AFC Wimbledon 0 Horsham 0 — Att: 1,564
Replay: **Horsham** 1 AFC Dons 1 *aet (5-4p) (Oct 16)* — Att: 1,265
Lewes 1 Sutton United 0 *(Oct 14)* — Att: 693
Folkestone Invicta 1 Hillingdon Borough 0 — Att: 284
Worthing 0 **Hampton & Richmond Borough** 2 — Att: 369
Hythe Town 1 **Ware** 3 — Att: 236
Bromley 1 Dartford 0 — Att: 1,022
Stotfold 0 **Tonbridge Angels** 5 — Att: 343
Team Bath 1 Weston-super-Mare 0 *(Oct 14)* — Att: 286
Eastleigh 5 Clevedon Town 0 — Att: 341
Havant & Waterlooville 2 Fleet Town 1 — Att: 386
Merthyr Tydfil 2 Paulton Rovers 0 — Att: 372
Newport County 1 **Bath City** 2 *(Oct 12)* — Att: 1,446
Maidenhead United 3 Shortwood United 0 — Att: 211
Chippenham Town 5 Bashley 1 — Att: 416

FOURTH QUALIFYING ROUND
(£10,000 to each winning club)
(Ties played October 27 unless stated)

Evesham United 0 Halifax Town 0	Att: 652
Replay: **Halifax Town** 2 Evesham Utd 1 *(Oct 30)*	Att: 1,025
Corby Town 1 **Droylsden** 2	Att: 562
Kendal Town 0 **Altrincham** 1	Att: 641
Rushden & Diamonds 5 Solihull Moors 0	Att: 1,076
Burton Albion 2 Tamworth 1	Att: 2,915
Histon 4 Bamber Bridge 1	Att: 535
Stafford Rangers 1 Cambridge United 1	Att: 1,030
Replay: **Cambridge Utd** 5 Stafford Rgrs 1 *(Oct 30)*	Att: 1,965
Southport 1 **Northwich Victoria** 3	Att: 1,232
Farsley Celtic 1 Barrow 1	Att: 528
Replay: **Barrow** 2 Farsley Celtic 1 *(Oct 30)*	Att: 1,380
Bradford Park Avenue 0 **Gainsborough Trinity** 4	Att: 557
Workington 1 Boston United 0	Att: 635
York City 6 Rushall Olympic 0	Att: 1,630
Kidderminster Harriers 3 Vauxhall Motors 1	Att: 1,374
Harrogate Railway Athletic 2 Harrogate Town 1	Att: 1,286
Chasetown 2 Nuneaton Borough 1	Att: 1,408
Weymouth 1 Hitchin Town 1	Att: 1,106
Replay: Hitchin Town 0 **Weymouth** 1 *(Oct 30)*	Att: 504
AFC Hornchurch 0 **Team Bath** 1	Att: 641
Maidenhead United 1 Hayes & Yeading United 0	Att: 643
Salisbury City 0 Stevenage Borough 0	Att: 1,364
Replay: **Stevenage Bor.** 1 Salisbury City 0 *(Oct 30)*	Att: 1,174
Merthyr Tydfil 1 **Oxford United** 2	Att: 1,071
Hampton & Richmond Borough 1 Wealdstone 0	Att: 679
Bath City 0 **Torquay United** 2	Att: 2,149
Crawley Town 1 Aldershot Town 1	Att: 1,934
Replay: **Aldershot Town** 1 Crawley T. 0 *(Oct 30)*	Att: 2,058
Chippenham Town 2 Horsham 3	Att: 912
Eastleigh 3 Forest Green Rovers 3	Att: 742
Replay: **Forest Green Rovers** 4 Eastleigh 1 *(Oct 30)*	Att: 753
Eastbourne Borough 2 Bromley 1	Att: 1,212
Ware 3 Tonbridge Angels 1	Att: 816
Folkestone Invicta 0 **Billericay Town** 2	Att: 659
Grays Athletic 1 Lewes 1	Att: 688
Replay: **Lewes** 2 Grays Athletic 0 *(Oct 31)*	Att: 746
Woking 0 **Staines Town** 1	Att: 1,431
Ebbsfleet United 1 **Exeter City** 3	Att: 1,219
Havant & Waterlooville 3 Leighton Town 0	Att: 378

FIRST ROUND
(£16,000 to each winning club)
(Ties played November 10 unless stated)

Darlington 1 Northampton Town 1	Att: 2,964
Replay: **Northampton T.** 2 Darlington 1 *(Nov 20)*	Att: 2,895
Hampton & Richmond 0 **Dagenham & Redbridge** 3	Att: 2,252
Torquay United 4 Yeovil Town 1 *(Nov 11)*	Att: 3,718
Leyton Orient 1 Bristol Rovers 1	Att: 3,157
Replay: **Bristol R.** 3 L. Orient 3 *aet* (6-5p) *(Nov 27)*	Att: 3,742
Bury 4 Workington 1	Att: 2,641
Barnet 2 Gillingham 1	Att: 2,843
Accrington Stanley 2 **Huddersfield Town** 3	Att: 2,202
Barrow 1 AFC Bournemouth 1	Att: 2,203
Replay: **AFC Bournem'th** 3 Barrow 2 *aet (Nov 20)*	Att: 2,969
Forest Green Rovers 2 Rotherham United 2 *(Nov 11)*	Att: 2,102
Replay: Rotherham 0 **Forest Green R.** 3 *(Nov 20)*	Att: 2,754
Southend United 2 Rochdale 1	Att: 5,180
Team Bath 0 **Chasetown** 2	Att: 2,067
Bradford City 1 Chester City 0	Att: 4,069
Morecambe 0 **Port Vale** 2	Att: 2,730
Hereford United 0 Leeds United 0 *(Nov 9)*	Att: 5,924
Replay: Leeds United 0 **Hereford Utd** 1 *(Nov 20)*	Att: 11,315
Mansfield Town 3 Lewes 0	Att: 2,607
Gainsborough Trinity 0 **Hartlepool Utd** 6 *(Nov 11)*	Att: 2,402
Exeter City 3 Stevenage Borough 0	Att: 3,513
Oldham Athletic 2 Doncaster Rovers 2	Att: 4,280
Replay: Doncaster R. 1 **Oldham Ath.** 2 *(Nov 27)*	Att: 4,340
Peterborough United 4 Wrexham 1	Att: 4,266
Halifax Town 0 **Burton Albion** 4	Att: 1,936

York City 0 **Havant & Waterlooville** 1	Att: 2,001
Harrogate Railway Athletic 2 Droylsden 0	Att: 884
Rushden & Diamonds 3 Macclesfield Town 1	Att: 1,759
Ware 0 **Kidderminster Harriers** 2	Att: 2,123
Walsall 2 Shrewsbury Town 0	Att: 4,972
Horsham 4 Maidenhead United 1	Att: 3,379
Altrincham 1 **Millwall** 2	Att: 2,457
Cheltenham Town 1 Brighton & Hove Albion 1	Att: 2,984
Replay: **Brighton** 2 Cheltenham Town 1 *(Nov 20)*	Att: 3,711
Stockport County 1 Staines Town 1	Att: 3,460
Replay: **Staines** 1 Stockport 1 *aet* (4-3p) *(Nov 22)*	Att: 2,860
Crewe Alexandra 2 Milton Keynes Dons 1	Att: 3,049
Lincoln City 1 Nottingham Forest 1	Att: 7,361
Replay: **Nottm Forest** 3 Lincoln City 1 *(Nov 27)*	Att: 6,783
Cambridge United 2 Aldershot Town 1	Att: 3,547
Notts County 3 Histon 0	Att: 4,344
Oxford United 3 Northwich Victoria 1	Att: 2,972
Billericay Town 1 **Swansea City** 2	Att: 2,334
Carlisle United 1 Grimsby Town 1	Att: 5,128
Replay: **Grimsby Town** 1 Carlisle Utd 0 *(Nov 20)*	Att: 2,008
Eastbourne Borough 0 **Weymouth** 4	Att: 2,711
Chesterfield 1 **Tranmere Rovers** 2	Att: 4,296
Wycombe Wanderers 1 **Swindon Town** 2	Att: 3,332
Luton Town 1 Brentford 1	Att: 4,167
Replay: Brentford 0 **Luton Town** 2 *(Nov 27)*	Att: 2,643

SECOND ROUND
(£24,000 to each winning club)
(Ties played December 1 unless stated)

Oxford United 0 Southend United 0	Att: 5,162
Replay: **Southend United** 3 Oxford Utd 0 *(Dec 11)*	Att: 2,740
Swindon Town 3 Forest Green Rovers 2	Att: 7,588
Oldham Athletic 1 Crewe Alexandra 0	Att: 3,900
Northampton Town 1 Walsall 1	Att: 3,887
Replay: **Walsall** 1 Northampton Town 0 *(Dec 11)*	Att: 3,066
Cambridge United 1 Weymouth 0	Att: 4,552
Millwall 2 AFC Bournemouth 1	Att: 4,495
Staines Town 0 **Peterborough United** 5	Att: 2,460
Bradford City 0 **Tranmere Rovers** 3	Att: 6,379
Torquay United 0 **Brighton & Hove Albion** 2	Att: 4,010
Notts County 0 **Havant & Waterlooville** 1	Att: 3,810
Dagenham/Redbridge 3 Kidderminster Harriers 1	Att: 1,493
Port Vale 1 Chasetown 1 *(Dec 2)*	Att: 5,875
Replay: **Chasetown** 1 Port Vale 0 *(Dec 11)*	Att: 1,986
Bristol Rovers 5 Rushden & Diamonds 1	Att: 4,816
Huddersfield Town 3 Grimsby Town 0	Att: 6,729
Burton Albion 1 Barnet 1	Att: 2,769
Replay: **Barnet** 1 Burton Albion 0 *(Dec 11)*	Att: 1,379
Bury 1 Exeter City 0	Att: 2,725
Luton Town 1 Nottingham Forest 0 *(Dec 11)*	Att: 5,758
Horsham 1 Swansea City 1 *(Nov 30)*	Att: 2,731
Replay: **Swansea City** 6 Horsham 2 *(Dec 10)*	Att: 5,911
Hereford United 2 Hartlepool United 0	Att: 3,801
Harrogate Railway 2 **Mansfield Town** 3 *(Dec 2)*	Att: 1,486

THIRD ROUND
(£40,000 to each winning club)
(Ties played January 5 unless stated)

Preston North End 1 Scunthorpe United 0	Att: 4,616
Chasetown 1 **Cardiff City** 3	Att: 2,420
Colchester United 1 **Peterborough United** 3	Att: 4,003
Bolton Wanderers 0 **Sheffield United** 1	Att: 15,286
Blackburn Rovers 1 **Coventry City** 4	Att: 14,421
Brighton & Hove Albion 1 **Mansfield Town** 2	Att: 5,857
Walsall 0 Millwall 0	Att: 4,358
Replay: **Millwall** 2 Walsall 1 *(Jan 15)*	Att: 4,645
Charlton Athletic 1 West Bromwich Albion 1	Att: 12,682
Replay: **W. Brom** 2 Charlton 2 *aet* (4-3p) *(Jan 15)*	Att: 12,691
Watford 2 Crystal Palace 1	Att: 10,480
Luton Town 1 Liverpool 1 *(Jan 6)*	Att: 10,240
Replay: **Liverpool** 5 Luton Town 0 *(Jan 15)*	Att: 41,446
Plymouth Argyle 3 Hull City 2	Att: 12,419
Aston Villa 0 **Manchester United** 2	Att: 33,630

Tranmere Rovers 2 Hereford United 2 | Att: 6,909
Replay: **Hereford United** 1 Tranmere R. 0 *(Jan 16)* Att: 6,471
Tottenham Hotspur 2 Reading 2 | Att: 35,243
Replay: Reading 0 **Tottenham Hotspur** 1 *(Jan 15)* Att: 22,130
Burnley 0 **Arsenal** 2 *(Jan 6)* | Att: 16,709
Bristol City 1 **Middlesbrough** 2 | Att: 15,895
Fulham 2 Bristol Rovers 2 *(Jan 6)* | Att: 13,634
Replay: Bristol R. 0 Fulham 0 *aet* (5-3p) *(Jan 22)* Att: 11,882
Huddersfield Town 2 Birmingham City 1 | Att: 13,410
Swansea City 1 Havant & Waterlooville 1 | Att: 8,761
Replay: **Havant & W'ville** 4 Swansea 2 *(Jan 16)* Att: 4,400
Sunderland 0 **Wigan Athletic** 3 | Att: 20,821
Southend United 5 Dagenham & Redbridge 2 | Att: 6,393
Everton 0 **Oldham Athletic** 1 | Att: 33,086
Derby County 2 Sheffield Wednesday 2 *(Jan 6)* Att: 20,612
Replay: Sheff. W. 1 **Derby** 1 *aet* (2-4p) *(Jan 22)* Att: 18,020
Southampton 2 Leicester City 0 | Att: 20,094
West Ham United 0 Manchester City 0 | Att: 33,806
Replay: **Manchester City** 1 West Ham 0 *(Jan 16)* Att: 27,809
Ipswich Town 0 **Portsmouth** 1 | Att: 23,446
Wolverhampton Wanderers 2 Cambridge United 1 Att: 15,340
Barnsley 2 Blackpool 1 | Att: 8,276
Chelsea 1 Queens Park Rangers 0 | Att: 41,289
Stoke City 0 Newcastle United 0 *(Jan 6)* | Att: 22,861
Replay: **Newcastle United** 4 Stoke City 1 *(Jan 16)* Att: 35,108
Swindon Town 1 Barnet 1 | Att: 5,944
Replay: **Barnet** 1 Swindon Tn 1 *aet* (2-0p) *(Jan 22)* Att: 2,810
Norwich City 1 Bury 1 | Att: 19,815
Replay: **Bury** 2 Norwich City 1 *(Jan 15)* | Att: 4,146

Manchester Utd 3 Tottenham Hotspur 1 *(Jan 27)* Att: 75,369
Portsmouth 2 Plymouth Argyle 1 | Att: 19,612
Derby County 1 **Preston North End** 4 | Att: 17,344
Watford 1 **Wolverhampton Wanderers** 4 | Att: 12,719
Peterborough United 0 **West Bromwich Albion** 3 Att: 12,701
Sheffield United 2 Manchester City 1 *(Jan 27)* Att: 20,800
Mansfield Town 0 **Middlesbrough** 2 | Att: 6,258
Hereford United 1 **Cardiff City** 2 *(Jan 27)* | Att: 6,855

FIFTH ROUND
(£120,000 to each winning club)
(Ties played February 16 unless stated)

Bristol Rovers 1 Southampton 0 | Att: 11,920
Cardiff City 2 Wolverhampton Wanderers 0 | Att: 15,399
Sheffield United 0 **Middlesbrough** 0 *(Feb 17)* Att: 22,210
Replay: **Middlesbrough** 1 Sheffield Utd 0 *(Feb 27)* Att: 28,108
Liverpool 1 **Barnsley** 2 | Att: 42,449
Manchester United 4 Arsenal 0 | Att: 75,550
Preston North End 0 **Portsmouth** 1 *(Feb 17)* Att: 11,840
Coventry City 0 **West Bromwich Albion** 5 | Att: 28,163
Chelsea 3 Huddersfield Town 1 | Att: 41,324

QUARTER-FINALS
(£300,000 to each winning club)
(Ties played March 8 unless stated)

Middlesbrough 0 **Cardiff City** 2 *(Mar 9)* | Att: 32,896
Manchester United 0 **Portsmouth** 1 | Att: 75,463
Bristol Rovers 1 **West Bromwich Albion** 5 *(Mar 9)* Att: 12,011
Barnsley 1 Chelsea 0 | Att: 22,410

SEMI-FINALS
(£900,000 to each winning club)
(Both played at Wembley Stadium)

Barnsley 0 **Cardiff City** 1 *(Apr 6)* | Att: 82,752
West Bromwich Albion 0 **Portsmouth** 1 *(Apr 5)* Att: 83,584

FINAL
(£1,000,000 to winning club)
(May 17th at Wembley Stadium)

Cardiff City 0 **Portsmouth** 1 | Att: 89,874

FOURTH ROUND
(£60,000 to each winning club)
(Ties played January 26 unless stated)

Arsenal 3 Newcastle United 0 | Att: 60,046
Coventry City 2 Millwall 1 | Att: 17,268
Oldham Athletic 0 **Huddersfield Town** 0 | Att: 12,749
Barnet 0 **Bristol Rovers** 1 | Att: 5,190
Wigan Athletic 1 **Chelsea** 2 | Att: 14,166
Liverpool 5 Havant & Waterlooville 2 | Att: 42,566
Southend United 0 **Barnsley** 1 *(Jan 25)* | Att: 7,212
Southampton 2 Bury 0 | Att: 25,449

F A CHALLENGE TROPHY

PRELIMINARY ROUND
(£1,000 to each winning club)
(Ties played October 6 unless stated)

Garforth Town 2 **Shepshed Dynamo** 3 | Att: 138
Clitheroe 2 Ossett Albion 1 | Att: 197
Quorn 1 Bridlington Town 1 *(Oct 9)* | Att: 110
Replay: **Bridlington Town** 3 Quorn 1 *aet* | Att: 99
Kidsgrove Athletic 0 **Chasetown** 1 | Att: 127
Skelmersdale United 1 Goole 0 | Att: 227
Grantham Town 3 Alsager Town 0 | Att: 166
Brigg Town 2 Gresley Rovers 2 | Att: 120
Replay: **Gresley** 3 Brigg 3 *aet* (3-1p) *(Oct 9)* | Att: 136
Bradford Park Avenue 1 FC United Of Manchester 1 Att: 1,310
Replay: FC United 1 **Bradford Park A.** 4 *(Oct 10)* Att: 951
(at Radcliffe Borough)
Cammell Laird 0 **Curzon Ashton** 1 | Att: 84
Warrington Town 3 Rossendale United 2 | Att: 114
Woodley Sports 1 Newcastle Blue Star 1 | Att: 50
Replay: **Newcastle Blue Star** 1 Woodley 0 *(Oct 10)* Att: 52
Sutton Coldfield Town 1 **Radcliffe Borough** 3 | Att: 77
Belper Town 1 Willenhall Town 1 | Att: 116
Replay: **Willenhall Town** 3 Belper Town 2 *(Oct 9)* Att: 91
Rushall Olympic 2 Carlton Town 1 | Att: 66
Spalding United 0 **Romulus** 4 | Att: 70
Chatham Town 3 Kingstonian 1 | Att: 209
Walton Casuals 1 **Barton Rovers** 3 | Att: 59
Rothwell Town 1 **Sittingbourne** 2 | Att: 103
Great Wakering Rovers 2 Tilbury 1 | Att: 101
Waltham Forest 0 **Arlesey Town** 7 | Att: 49
Canvey Island 3 Wingate & Finchley 1 | Att: 280

Wivenhoe Town 0 **Corinthian Casuals** 2 | Att: 76
Chesham United 2 Waltham Abbey 1 | Att: 175
Enfield Town 1 **Aylesbury United** 2 | Att: 202
Dover Athletic 3 Potters Bar Town 0 | Att: 506
Chipstead 1 Tooting & Mitcham United 1 | Att: 203
Replay: Tooting/Mitcham 1 **Chipstead** 2 *aet (Oct 16)* Att: 202
Ilford 2 Aveley 2 | Att: 61
Replay: Aveley 0 **Ilford** 2 *(Oct 10)* | Att: 63
Maldon Town 1 Croydon Athletic 2 | Att: 61
Replay: Croydon Athletic 2 **Maldon Town** 4 *(Oct 16)* Att: 67
Whitstable Town 0 **Cray Wanderers** 2 | Att: 203
Leighton Town 3 Molesey 1 | Att: 96
Berkhamsted Town 0 **Walton & Hersham** 3 | Att: 96
Brentwood Town 1 Dulwich Hamlet 0 | Att: 108
Worthing 2 Whyteleafe 1 | Att: 278
Burgess Hill Town 0 **Ware** 2 | Att: 126
Bury Town 0 Redbridge 0 | Att: 163
Replay: Redbridge 0 **Bury Town** 3 *(Oct 10)* | Att: 63
Slough Town 1 Hillingdon Borough 1 | Att: 203
Replay: **Hillingdon Borough** 2 Slough 1 *aet (Oct 9)* Att: 139
Thatcham Town 0 **Farnborough** 4 | Att: 185
Bishops Cleeve 0 **Oxford City** 4 | Att: 91
Godalming Town 1 **Taunton Town** 2 | Att: 126
Gosport Borough 1 Paulton Rovers 0 | Att: 147
Malvern Town 1 **Didcot Town** 3 | Att: 82
Windsor & Eton 2 Bridgwater Town 0 | Att: 138
Fleet Town 5 Newport IOW 1 | Att: 102
Andover 4 AFC Hayes 2 | Att: 94
Cinderford Town 4 Stourport Swifts 0 | Att: 67
Leamington 2 Marlow 0 | Att: 522

FIRST QUALIFYING ROUND
(£1,500 to each winning club)
(Ties played October 20 unless stated)

Prescot Cables 2 **Frickley Athletic** 3	Att: 148
Buxton 2 Leek Town 1	Att: 548
Romulus 0 **Warrington Town** 1	Att: 80
Stocksbridge Park Steels 3 Skelmersdale United 1	Att: 109
Stamford 2 Matlock Town 2	Att: 254
Replay: **Matlock Town** 1 Stamford 0 *aet (Oct 23)*	Att: 211
Harrogate Railway Athletic 2 **Radcliffe Borough** 4	Att: 86
Gateshead 2 Shepshed Dynamo 1	Att: 286
Mossley 0 **Rushall Olympic** 1	Att: 197
Colwyn Bay 2 Newcastle Blue Star 1	Att: 264
Gresley Rovers 0 **Guiseley** 1	Att: 219
Witton Albion 6 Ashton United 1	Att: 278
North Ferriby United 1 Ilkeston Town 1	Att: 136
Replay: **Ilkeston** 4 North Ferriby 1 *(Oct 24)*	Att: 159
Grantham Town 1 **Kendal Town** 3	Att: 224
Clitheroe 0 Lancaster City 0	Att: 245
Replay: Lancaster City 1 **Clitheroe** 2 *(Oct 23)*	Att: 170
Fleetwood Town 1 Worksop Town 0	Att: 468
Chasetown (w/o) v Scarborough 1 (scr.)	
Willenhall Town 1 **Hednesford Town** 3	Att: 169
Eastwood Town 0 **Bamber Bridge** 1	Att: 174
Chorley 1 **Curzon Ashton** 2	Att: 208
Bradford Park Avenue 0 **Sheffield** 2	Att: 279
Bridlington Town 0 **Retford United** 2	Att: 165
Wakefield 1 Nantwich Town 1	Att: 98
Replay: Nantwich 2 **Wakefield** 3 *aet (Oct 23)*	Att: 350
Ossett Town 3 Whitby Town 2	Att: 93
Marine 5 Lincoln United 0	Att: 178
Billericay Town 2 Ilford 1	Att: 353
Tonbridge Angels 3 Harrow Borough 2	Att: 345
Brentwood Town 1 Harlow Town 1	Att: 121
Replay: Harlow Town 0 **Brentwood Town** 1 *(Oct 23)*	Att: 151
Ashford Town 1 **Leyton** 4	Att: 232
Chatham Town 0 **Witham Town** 3	Att: 148
Aylesbury United 0 Margate 0 *(Oct 21)*	Att: 279
Replay: **Margate** 3 Aylesbury United 1 *(Oct 23)*	Att: 238
Walton & Hersham 2 Folkestone Invicta 1	Att: 118
Chesham United 2 Bedford Town 1	Att: 287
Bury Town 1 Maidstone United 1	Att: 239
Replay: **Maidstone United** 3 Bury Town 1 *(Oct 24)*	Att: 222
Metropolitan Police 3 Great Wakering Rovers 0	Att: 76
Leighton Town 0 Wealdstone 0	Att: 242
Replay: **Wealdstone** 2 Leighton Town 1 *(Oct 23)*	Att: 139
Ware 4 Ashford Town (Middx) 1	Att: 140
Sittingbourne 0 **Northwood** 2	Att: 134
Cheshunt 1 **Heybridge Swifts** 2	Att: 150
Boreham Wood 1 **Chelmsford City** 2	Att: 225
Chipstead 0 **Worthing** 3	Att: 127
Dunstable Town 1 Hemel Hempstead Town 1	Att: 163
Replay: **Hemel Hempstead** 2 Dunstable 1 *(Oct 23)*	Att: 149
Ramsgate 2 **Horsham** 3	Att: 241
East Thurrock United 3 Cray Wanderers 3	Att: 79
Replay: Cray Wdrs 2 **East Thurrock Utd** 3 *(Oct 24)*	Att: 73
Horsham YMCA 1 **Canvey Island** 3	Att: 179
AFC Hornchurch 0 Dartford 0	Att: 636
Replay: Dartford 0 **AFC Hornchurch** 3 *(Oct 23)*	Att: 575
Edgware Town 1 **Hastings United** 2	Att: 111
Carshalton Athletic 2 Corinthian Casuals 1	Att: 171
AFC Wimbledon 2 Hendon 1	Att: 1,238
Maldon Town 1 **Dover Athletic** 2	Att: 152
Hitchin Town 3 Eastbourne Town 0	Att: 165
AFC Sudbury 0 King's Lynn 0	Att: 410
Replay: **King's Lynn** 2 AFC Sudbury 1 *(Oct 23)*	Att: 571
Corby Town 4 Barton Rovers 1	Att: 137
Leatherhead 3 Arlesey Town 0	Att: 121
Halesowen Town 0 **Brackley Town** 1	Att: 411
Cinderford Town 2 Cirencester Town 1	Att: 112
Evesham United 1 Bromsgrove Rovers 0 *(Oct 21)*	Att: 214
Mangotsfield United 0 Fleet Town 0	Att: 121
Replay: Fleet Town 0 **Mangotsfield Utd** 2 *(Oct 23)*	Att: 65
Chippenham Town 3 Merthyr Tydfil 0	Att: 438
Slimbridge (scr.) v **Bashley** (w/o)	

Swindon Supermarine 1 Farnborough 1	Att: 220
Replay: **Farnborough** 1 Swindon S'marine 0 *(Oct 23)*	Att: 334
Tiverton Town 0 **Burnham** 1	Att: 302
Oxford City 0 **Windsor & Eton** 1	Att: 142
Winchester City 2 Gosport Borough 2	Att: 223
Replay: **Gosport Borough** 2 Winchester 1 *(Oct 23)*	Att: 177
Stourbridge 1 Gloucester City 1	Att: 176
Replay: **Gloucester City** 2 Stourbridge 0 *(Oct 24)*	Att: 180
Leamington 2 Banbury United 0	Att: 704
Hillingdon Borough 1 Bedworth United 1	Att: 102
Replay: Bedworth United 1 **Hillingdon Borough** 2 *aet*	Att: 84
Yate Town 2 Didcot Town 1	Att: 164
Woodford United 2 Bracknell Town 0	Att: 106
Rugby Town 1 **Clevedon Town** 3	Att: 169
Team Bath 1 Taunton Town 0 *(Oct 21)*	Att: 145
Uxbridge 4 Andover 1	Att: 122
Staines Town 0 Abingdon United 0	Att: 176
Replay: **Abingdon United** 5 Staines T. 2 *aet (Oct 23)*	Att: 149

SECOND QUALIFYING ROUND
(£2,000 to each winning club)
(Ties played November 3 unless stated)

Stocksbridge Park Steels 2 **Witton Albion** 5	Att: 214
Curzon Ashton 1 **Ilkeston Town** 3	Att: 159
Warrington Town 0 **Ossett Town** 3	Att: 102
Bamber Bridge 1 Marine 1	Att: 162
Replay: Marine 2 **Bamber Bridge** 3 *(Nov 6)*	Att: 132
Hednesford Town 1 **Guiseley** 2	Att: 324
Fleetwood Town 1 Retford United 1	Att: 505
Replay: **Retford United** 5 Fleetwood Town 1 *(Nov 6)*	Att: 176
Frickley Athletic 1 **Colwyn Bay** 2	Att: 209
Chasetown 0 Radcliffe Borough 0	Att: 276
Replay: **Radcliffe Borough** 2 Chasetown 1 *(Nov 6)*	Att: 150
Wakefield 0 **Buxton** 2	Att: 178
Matlock Town 1 **Gateshead** 2	Att: 317
Rushall Olympic 1 Clitheroe 1 *(Clitheroe expelled)*	Att: 102
Sheffield 3 Kendal Town 2	Att: 208
Hitchin Town 2 Cinderford Town 1	Att: 184
Chippenham Town 3 Heybridge Swifts 2	Att: 397
Leatherhead 1 Mangotsfield United 1	Att: 169
Replay: Mang'field 1 **Leatherh'd** 1 *aet (1-4p) (Nov 6)*	Att: 117
AFC Wimbledon 4 Chelmsford City 0	Att: 1,683
Abingdon United 2 Maidstone United 2	Att: 314
Replay: **Maidstone United** 5 Abingdon Utd 3 *(Nov 7)*	Att: 267
Woodford United 1 **Wealdstone** 4	Att: 164
Bashley 3 Leyton 1	Att: 248
Tonbridge Angels 2 East Thurrock United 0	Att: 280
Brentwood Town 0 **Canvey Island** 2	Att: 290
Yate Town 0 **Carshalton Athletic** 3	Att: 191
Farnborough 1 **Windsor & Eton** 3	Att: 442
Burnham 2 Ware 1	Att: 103
AFC Hornchurch 2 Northwood 2	Att: 371
Replay: **Northwood** 2 AFC Hornchurch 1 *(Nov 6)*	Att: 110
Gloucester City 3 Hillingdon Borough 3	Att: 246
Replay: Hillingdon Boro. 0 **Gloucester City** 1 *(Nov 6)*	Att: 96
Worthing 0 Walton & Hersham 0	Att: 291
Replay: Walton & Hersham 1 **Worthing** 3 *aet (Nov 6)*	Att: 125
Corby Town 2 Evesham United 2	Att: 218
Replay: **Evesham Utd** 4 Corby Town 2 *aet (Nov 6)*	Att: 93
Gosport Borough 3 Metropolitan Police 2	Att: 205
Witham Town 3 Horsham 2	Att: 139
King's Lynn 2 Billericay Town 2	Att: 927
Replay: Billericay Town 1 **King's Lynn** 3 *(Nov 6)*	Att: 325
Uxbridge 1 Hastings United 0	Att: 142
Hemel Hempstead Town 2 Clevedon Town 1	Att: 188
Leamington 1 Margate 1	Att: 790
Replay: Margate 0 **Leamington** 1 *(Nov 6)*	Att: 315
Dover Athletic 2 Brackley Town 1	Att: 583
Chesham United 3 **Team Bath** 5	Att: 238

THIRD QUALIFYING ROUND
(£3,000 to each winning club)
(Ties played November 24 unless stated)

Gateshead 2 Boston United 1	Att: 267
Solihull Moors 1 **Cambridge City** 4	Att: 195

Retford United 3 Radcliffe Borough 1	Att: 201
Guiseley 1 Worcester City 0	Att: 320
Evesham United 1 Redditch United 1	Att: 224
Replay: **Redditch United** 1 Evesham Utd 0 *(Nov 27)*	Att: 262
Rushall Olympic 0 Ossett Town 0	Att: 85
Replay: **Ossett Town** 3 Rushall Olympic 2 *(Nov 27)*	Att: 110
Bamber Bridge 2 Ilkeston Town 1	Att: 174
Hinckley United 1 **Alfreton Town** 3	Att: 334
Colwyn Bay 1 Sheffield 1	Att: 222
Replay: Sheffield 2 **Colwyn B.** 2 aet (4-5p) *(Nov 27)*	Att: 232
Vauxhall Motors 1 Hyde United 0	Att: 199
Blyth Spartans 2 Gainsborough Trinity 2	Att: 377
Replay: Gainsborough 1 **Blyth** 1 aet (1-3p) *(Nov 27)*	Att: 227
Barrow 2 **Southport** 3	Att: 906
Burscough 2 **Leigh RMI** 3	Att: 290
Hucknall Town 1 Witton Albion 1	Att: 351
Replay: Witton Albion 1 **Hucknall Town** 2 *(Nov 27)*	Att: 340
Nuneaton Borough 0 Workington 0	Att: 759
Replay: **Workington** 2 Nuneaton Borough 1 *(Nov 27)*	Att: 283
Buxton 0 **AFC Telford United** 1	Att: 768
Stalybridge Celtic 0 **Tamworth** 2	Att: 378
Harrogate Town 0 **Kettering Town** 3	Att: 507
Bromley 2 Chippenham Town 1	Att: 544
Bishop's Stortford 2 Hampton & Richmond 1	Att: 351
Hemel Hempstead Town 3 Team Bath 0	Att: 239
AFC Wimbledon 2 Northwood 1	Att: 1,518
Maidstone United 0 **Canvey Island** 1	Att: 389
Basingstoke Town 1 **Lewes** 4	Att: 375
Gosport Borough 1 **Braintree Town** 4	Att: 229
Dorchester Town 1 Worthing 1	Att: 266
Replay: Worthing 1 **Dorchester Town** 2 *(Nov 27)*	Att: 266
Fisher Athletic 1 **Leamington** 2	Att: 390
Bognor Regis Town 2 Havant & Waterlooville 1	Att: 431
Bashley 4 Leatherhead 0	Att: 260
Gloucester City 1 Uxbridge 0	Att: 255
Hayes & Yeading United 4 Witham Town 2	Att: 132
Carshalton Athletic 1 Hitchin Town 1	Att: 222
Replay: Hitchin 1 **Carshalton Athletic** 2 aet *(Nov 27)*	Att: 157
Eastleigh 4 Weston-super-Mare 2	Att: 267
Windsor & Eton 1 **Newport County** 2	Att: 274
Bath City 2 Thurrock 0	Att: 568
Tonbridge Angels 1 Burnham 0	Att: 336
Wealdstone 1 Welling United 0	Att: 240
King's Lynn 3 Eastbourne Borough 1	Att: 951
Maidenhead United 2 St Albans City 0	Att: 262
Dover Athletic 1 Sutton United 1	Att: 712
Replay: **Sutton United** 1 Dover Athletic 0	Att: 314

FIRST ROUND

(£4,000 to each winning club)
(Ties played December 15 unless stated)

AFC Telford United 1 **Blyth Spartans** 2	Att: 1,120
Vauxhall Motors 2 Northwich Victoria 1	Att: 462
Alfreton Town 1 Southport 0 *(Dec 18)*	Att: 187
Halifax Town 2 Leamington 1 *(Jan 8)*	Att: 805
Stafford Rangers 3 Ossett Town 1	Att: 521
Colwyn Bay 1 **Burton Albion** 2	Att: 582
Bamber Bridge 2 **Rushden & Diamonds** 3	Att: 330
Droylsden 2 Redditch United 1	Att: 239
Histon 5 Retford United 2	Att: 316
Gateshead 1 Farsley Celtic 1	Att: 238
Replay: **Farsley Celtic** 4 Gateshead 1 *(Dec 19)*	Att: 92
Cambridge United 5 King's Lynn 2	Att: 2,311
Hucknall Town 0 **Tamworth** 1 *(Dec 18)*	Att: 265
Leigh RMI 1 **Workington** 3	Att: 101
Guiseley 1 **Kidderminster Harriers** 2 *(Dec 18)*	Att: 312
Cambridge City 3 Kettering Town 2	Att: 531
Altrincham 1 **York City** 3	Att: 752
Gloucester City 0 **Braintree Town** 2	Att: 269
Hemel Hempstead Town 0 **Woking** 1	Att: 453
Grays Athletic 3 Lewes 0	Att: 401
Maidenhead United 0 **AFC Wimbledon** 2	Att: 1,157
Dorchester Town 2 Stevenage Borough 1	Att: 321
Bishop's Stortford 8 Canvey Island 0	Att: 359
Torquay United 1 Bashley 0	Att: 1,277

Crawley Town 1 Bromley 0	Att: 667
Newport County 3 Bath City 0	Att: 592
Ebbsfleet United 4 Carshalton Athletic 1	Att: 492
Oxford United 0 Tonbridge Angels 0	Att: 1,508
Replay: **Tonbridge Angels** 1 Oxford Utd 0 *(Dec 18)*	Att: 642
Wealdstone 0 **Weymouth** 1 *(Dec 14)*	Att: 343
Sutton United 1 **Forest Green Rovers** 4	Att: 303
Hayes & Yeading United 0 **Aldershot Town** 5	Att: 435
Exeter City 3 Salisbury City 0	Att: 2,151
Eastleigh 1 Bognor Regis Town 0	Att: 318

SECOND ROUND

(£5,000 to each winning club)
(Ties played January 12 unless stated)

Vauxhall Motors 1 **Burton Albion** 4	Att: 551
Woking 2 **Aldershot Town** 4	Att: 2,368
Tonbridge Angels 0 **AFC Wimbledon** 4	Att: 2,281
Droylsden 1 Cambridge City 0	Att: 377
Weymouth 0 Kidderminster Harriers 0	Att: 831
Replay: Kid'minster 2 **Weymouth** aet (0-3p) *(Jan 22)*	Att: 994
Farsley Celtic 1 Alfreton Town 1	Att: 270
Replay: Alfreton Town 0 **Farsley Celtic** 2 *(Jan 29)*	Att: 268
Rushden & Diamonds 3 Exeter City 0	Att: 1,098
Dorchester Town 0 **Ebbsfleet United** 2	Att: 418
Histon 2 Cambridge United 0 *(Jan 16)*	Att: 1,920
Braintree Town 1 Workington 1	Att: 506
Replay: Workington 1 **Braintree Town** 2 *(Jan 15)*	Att: 421
Bishop's Stortford 2 Halifax Town 2	Att: 731
Replay: **Halifax Town** 4 Bish. Stortford 1 *(Jan 29)*	Att: 728
Newport County 1 **Torquay United** 2	Att: 1,510
Stafford Rangers 2 Forest Green Rovers 1	Att: 627
Crawley Town 2 Eastleigh 1	Att: 808
York City 1 Grays Athletic 1	Att: 1,351
Replay: Grays Athletic 1 **York City** 4 *(Jan 22)*	Att: 1 528
Blyth Spartans 0 **Tamworth** 1	Att: 574

THIRD ROUND

(£6,000 to each winning club)
(Ties played February 2 unless stated)

Ebbsfleet United 1 Weymouth 0	Att: 818
Burton Albion 1 Histon 1	Att: 1,769
Replay: Histon 0 **Burton Albion** 1 *(Feb 5)*	Att: 564
Aldershot Town 3 Braintree Town 0	Att: 1,772
Farsley Celtic 0 **York City** 2 *(Feb 3)*	Att: 952
Stafford Rangers 2 Tamworth 2	Att: 1,025
Replay: **Tamworth** 2 Stafford Rangers 1 *(Feb 5)*	Att: 571
Crawley Town 8 Droylsden 0	Att: 925
AFC Wimbledon 0 **Torquay United** 2	Att: 4,085
Halifax Town 0 **Rushden & Diamonds** 2	Att: 1,052

QUARTER-FINALS

(£7,000 to each winning club)
(Ties played February 23 unless stated)

Tamworth 1 **Aldershot Town** 2	Att: 1,204
Rushden & Diamonds 0 **York City** 1	Att: 1,626
Torquay United 4 Crawley Town 1	Att: 2,301
Burton Albion 0 Ebbsfleet United 0	Att: 2,103
Replay: **Ebbsfleet Utd** 1 Burton Albion 0 aet *(Feb 26)*	Att: 841

SEMI-FINALS

(£16,000 to each winning club)
1st leg
(Ties played March 8)

Torquay United 2 York City 0	Att: 2,286
Ebbsfleet United 3 Aldershot Town 1	Att: 2,483

2nd leg
(Ties played March 15)

York City 1 **Torquay United** 0	Att: 3,625
Aldershot Town 1 **Ebbsfleet United** 1	Att: 4,344

FINAL

(£50,000 to winning club)
(May 10th at Wembley Stadium)

Torquay United 0 **Ebbsfleet United** 1	Att: 40,186

F A CHALLENGE VASE

FIRST QUALIFYING ROUND
(£500 to each winning club)
(Ties played September 8 unless stated)

Bishop Auckland 1 Esh Winning 0 *(at Esh Winning)*	Att: 50
Thackley 1 South Shields 1 *aet*	Att: 52
Replay: South Shields 1 **Thackley** 2 *(Sep 11)*	Att: 120
Hall Road Rangers 2 Yorkshire Amateur 0	Att: 58
Crook Town 2 Ashington 1 *aet*	Att: 72
Silsden 4 Leeds Met Carnegie 2	Att: 52
Morpeth Town 5 North Shields 0	Att: 47
Ryton 0 **Winterton Rangers** 3	Att: 56
Kirkham & Wesham 3 Worsbrough Bridge MW 1	Att: 187
Ashton Athletic 6 Rossington Main 0	Att: 57
Nostell Miners Welfare 2 Abbey Hey 0	Att: 66
Holker Old Boys 1 **Chadderton** 5	Att: 41
Cheadle Town 1 St Helens Town 0	Att: 40
Oadby Town 4 Blackwell Miners Welfare 3 *(Sep 15)*	Att: 76
Hinckley Downes 2 Gornal Athletic 0	Att: 82
South Normanton Athletic 1 Newark Town 0	Att: 56
Radford 1 **Staveley Mners Welfare** 3 *aet*	Att: 45
Highgate United 2 Shirebrook Town 1 *aet*	Att: 45
Barrow Town 2 Holwell Sports 1	Att: 120
Heanor Town 2 Kimberley Town 0	Att: 82
Borrowash Victoria 3 Tividale 1	Att: 53
Arnold Town 1 **Westfields** 3	Att: 106
Bromyard Town 2 **Walsall Wood** 4 *aet*	Att: 55
Rothley Imperial 1 **Goodrich** 5	Att: 54
Brocton 4 Clipstone Welfare 1	Att: 46
Lye Town 3 Southam United 3 *aet*	Att: 30
Replay: **Southam United** 3 Lye Town 0 *(Sep 11)*	Att: 103
Cradley Town 4 Meir KA 3	Att: 30
Ellistown 1 **Gedling Miners Welfare** 2	
Biddulph Victoria 0 **Studley** 3 *(Sep 9)*	Att: 97
Stapenhill 0 **New Mills** 2	Att: 71
Oldbury United 3 Ibstock Utd 0 *(Sep 11) (at Pelsall)*	Att: 72
Pershore Town 1 **Glossop North End** 2 *(at Malvern)*	Att: 54
Coventry Copsewood 0 **Radcliffe Olympic** 3	Att: 38
Shifnal Town 4 Anstey Nomads 3	Att: 68
Friar Lane & Epworth 3 Dudley Sports 2	Att: 64
Pelsall Villa 4 Blaby & Whetstone Athletic 2	
Norwich United 6 Huntingdon Town 0	Att: 63
Stowmarket Town 0 **Dereham Town** 1	Att: 80
Hadleigh United 0 **Godmanchester Rovers** 1	Att: 87
Tiptree Utd 6 **N'pton Sileby Rgrs** 1 *(Tiptree expelled)*	Att: 69
Basildon United 0 **Raunds Town** 1	Att: 32
North Greenford United 3 Wootton Blue Cross 2	Att: 35
Biggleswade United 3 Rothwell Corinthians 1 *aet*	Att: 42
Hoddesdon Town 2 Kentish Town 0	Att: 40
Royston Town 2 FC Clacton 1	Att: 32
Cockfosters 3 Southend Manor 2	Att: 65
Langford 2 **Stewarts & Lloyds Corby** 3	Att: 60
Arlesey Athletic 1 **Stanway Rovers** 8 *(Sep 9)*	Att: 71
Hullbridge Sports 3 AFC Kempston Rovers 1	Att: 30
Haringey Borough 1 **Harwich & Parkeston** 3	Att: 39
St Margaretsbury 3 Northampton Spencer 2	Att: 75
Concord Rangers 5 London Colney 1	Att: 42
Hythe Town 3 Slade Green 0	Att: 105
Horley Town 3 Selsey 0	Att: 114
Ringmer 4 Lingfield 2	Att: 59
Three Bridges 1 Saltdean United 0	Att: 51
East Preston 1 **Eastbourne United Association** 4	Att: 38
Cobham 6 Newhaven 0	Att: 33
Peacehaven & Telscombe 2 **Pagham** 3	Att: 51
Rye United 3 Frimley Green 2	Att: 57
Fareham Town 1 **Lymington Town** 2	Att: 97
Andover New Street 3 Clanfield 1	Att: 39
Cove 3 Christchurch 3 *aet*	Att: 56
Replay: **Christchurch** 4 Cove 3 *(Sep 11)*	Att: 106
Reading Town 1 **Henley Town** 5	Att: 90
Westbury United 3 Malmesbury Victoria 1	Att: 54

Farnborough North End 1 **Chalfont St Peter** 3	Att: 72
Wantage Town 2 Hamble ASSC 2 *aet*	Att: 51
Replay: **Hamble ASSC** 1 Wantage Tn 0 *aet (Sep 11)*	Att: 54
Bournemouth 2 Abingdon Town 0	Att: 68
Ringwood Town 1 **Calne Town** 2	Att: 27
United Services Portsmouth 2 **Milton United** 2 *aet*	Att: 51
Replay: **Milton United** 2 United Services 1 *(Sep 10)*	Att: 103
Melksham Town 2 Alton Town 0	Att: 67
AFC Wallingford 1 **Devizes Town** 2	Att: 36
Highworth Town 3 Aylesbury Vale 1 *aet*	Att: 67
Buckingham Town 0 **Blackfield & Langley** 2	Att: 79
Shepton Mallet 3 Barnstaple Town 1	Att: 65
Shaftesbury 2 **Bodmin Town** 3	Att: 60
Larkhall Athletic 0 **Liskeard Athletic** 1	Att: 70
Torrington (scr.) v **Dawlish Town** (w/o):	
Hallen 5 Bristol Manor Farm 2 *aet*	Att: 64
Penryn Athletic 0 **Falmouth Town** 2	Att: 185
Keynsham Town 0 **Newton Abbot** 1	Att: 45
Penzance 1 Bishop Sutton 0	Att: 135
Radstock Town 0 **Welton Rovers** 3	Att: 98

SECOND QUALIFYING ROUND
(£600 to each winning club)
(Ties played September 22 unless stated)

Washington 3 Barton Town Old Boys 0	Att: 87
Morpeth Town 1 **Bedlington Terriers** 2	Att: 120
Pontefract Collieries 3 Tadcaster Albion 2	Att: 52
Silsden 1 **Dunston Federation** 3	Att: 55
Guisborough Town 0 **Hebburn Town** 1	Att: 60
Norton & Stockton Ancients 0 **Thornaby** 4	Att: 57
West Allotment Celtic 2 **Shildon** 5	Att: 97
Seaham Red Star 7 Sunderland Ryhope CA 0	Att: 92
Bishop Auckland 2 **Winterton Rangers** 4	Att: 89
Willington 0 **Selby Town** 4	Att: 52
Marske United 4 Hall Road Rangers 2	Att: 87
Team Northumbria 2 **Stokesley Sports Club** 4	Att: 37
Northallerton Town 4 Darlington Railway Ath. 0	Att: 104
Eccleshill United 3 Horden Colliery Welfare 1	Att: 54
Armthorpe Welfare 5 Chester-le-Street Town 5 *aet*	Att: 99
Replay: Chester-le-Street 1 **Armthorpe W.** 2 *(Sep 25)*	Att: 113
Easington Colliery 1 **Thackley** 4	Att: 47
Whickham 1 **Jarrow Roofing Boldon CA** 3 *aet*	Att: 95
Crook Town 3 **Durham City** 6	Att: 123
Spennymoor Town 5 Liversedge 1	Att: 208
Bottesford Town 1 **Tow Law Town** 2 *aet*	Att: 70
Brandon United 0 **Pickering Town** 5	Att: 34
Runcorn Linnets 3 Daisy Hill 0	Att: 184
Parkgate 2 Atherton Collieries 1	Att: 40
Maltby Main 2 Maine Road 1 *aet*	Att: 36
Blackpool Mechanics 1 Poulton Victoria 0	Att: 30
Chadderton 1 **Atherton LR** 3	Att: 42
Bootle 3 Padiham 0	Att: 45
Oldham Town 5 Ashville 4	Att: 35
Formby 2 Dinnington Town 1	Att: 54
Colne 1 Bacup Borough 0	Att: 109
Cheadle Town 2 **Ashton Town** 3	Att: 32
Darwen 2 Penrith 1	Att: 105
Winsford United 0 **Hallam** 1	Att: 93
Trafford 2 Nostell Miners Welfare 1	Att: 96
Squires Gate 4 Nelson 2	Att: 51
Kirkham & Wesham 4 Brodsworth Miners Welfare 3	Att: 124
AFC Emley 4 Ramsbottom United 3	Att: 117
Congleton Town 1 Ashton Athletic 1 *aet*	Att: 102
Replay: **Ashton Athletic** 3 Congleton 2 *(Sep 25)*	Att: 67
Bewdley Town 7 Pelsall Villa 0	
Leek CSOB 3 Greenwood Meadows 0	Att: 28
Heath Hayes 1 Loughborough Dynamo 0	Att: 110
Rocester 2 **Tipton Town** 3	Att: 75
Goodrich 2 **Pilkington XXX** 7	Att: 62
Glapwell 3 Boldmere St Michaels 0	Att: 78

Oadby Town 1 **Hinckley Downes** 2 — Att: 96
Coleshill Town 2 Bolehall Swifts 2 *aet* — Att: 79
Replay: Bolehall Swifts 0 **Coleshill Town** 1 *(Sep 25)* — Att: 62
Sporting Khalsa 1 **Barnt Green Spartak** 2 — Att: 82
Cadbury Athletic 2 AFC Wulfrunians 1 — Att: 26
Kirby Muxloe SC 3 St Andrews SC 1 — Att: 73
Ludlow Town 1 **Mickleover Sports** 2 — Att: 40
Pegasus Juniors 3 Graham Street Prims 1 — Att: 48
Brierley Hill & Withymoor 0 **Heanor Town** 1 *(Sep 23)* — Att: 55
Newcastle Town 2 Wolverhampton Casuals 1 — Att: 59
Calverton Miners Welfare 1 Teversal 0 — Att: 54
Barrow Town 2 **Market Drayton Town** 3 — Att: 85
Radcliffe Olympic 0 **Rainworth Miners Welfare** 2 — Att: 52
Gedling Town 4 Castle Vale 3 — Att: 70
Shifnal Town 3 Birstall United 1 *aet* — Att: 72
Heather St Johns 0 **Coventry Sphinx** 3 — Att: 72
Norton United 1 Eccleshall 0 — Att: 62
Cradley Town 1 Ellesmere Rangers 0 — Att: 63
Westfields 2 **Shawbury United** 3 — Att: 47
Holbrook Miners Welfare 1 Walsall Wood 0 — Att: 52
Friar Lane & Epworth 1 Dudley Town 0 — Att: 80
South Normanton Athletic 2 Dunkirk 2 *aet* — Att: 55
Replay: **Dunkirk** 3 South Normanton Ath. 0 *(Sep 25)* — Att: 84
Coalville Town 1 **Oldbury United** 2 — Att: 68
Staveley Miners Welfare 0 **Studley** 1 — Att: 41
Borrowash Victoria 3 Highgate United 2 — Att: 54
Glossop North End 2 Racing Club Warwick 0 — Att: 125
Sutton Town 3 Highfield Rangers 2 — Att: 72
Alvechurch 4 Brocton 3 — Att: 74
Gedling Miners Welfare 3 Atherstone Town 2 — Att: 81
Wellington 4 Ledbury Town 1 — Att: 68
Southam United 2 **Stone Dominoes** 4 — Att: 58
Nuneaton Griff 3 Long Eaton United 3 *aet* — Att: 70
Replay: **Long Eaton United** 1 Nuneaton 0 *(Sep 25)* — Att: 63
Bridgnorth Town 3 New Mills 2 — Att: 132
Dereham Town 6 Great Yarmouth Town 0 — Att: 115
Eynesbury Rovers 1 **Whitton United** 4 — Att: 42
Kirkley & Pakefield 0 **St Ives Town** 1 — Att: 139
Bourne Town 2 **Yaxley** 6 *aet* — Att: 79
Diss Town 1 Fakenham Town 0 — Att: 127
March Town United 1 **Woodbridge Town** 2 — Att: 125
Thetford Town 2 **Newmarket Town** 5 — Att: 85
Ely City 3 Lincoln Moorlands Railway 3 *aet* — Att: 75
Replay: Lincoln Moorlands Rail 1 **Ely City** 4 *(Sep 25)* — Att: 51
Holbeach United 2 Godmanchester Rovers 0 — Att: 97
Felixstowe & Walton United 3 **Sleaford Town** 4 — Att: 83
Norwich United 0 Blackstones 0 *aet* — Att: 80
Replay: **Blackstones** 3 Norwich United 0 *(Sep 25)* — Att: 63
Debenham Leisure Centre 2 Long Melford 1 — Att: 81
Gorleston 3 Cornard United 0 — Att: 98
Walsham-le-Willows 5 Wisbech Town 0 — Att: 92
St Neots Town 1 **Soham Town Rangers** 3 — Att: 166
Haverhill Rovers 2 **Leiston** 4 — Att: 118
Ampthill Town 6 Beaumont Athletic 1 — Att: 53
Desborough Town 4 Hoddesdon Town 3 — Att: 72
Tring Athletic 3 Bedford 0 — Att: 72
Barking 2 Northampton Sileby Rangers 1 *(Sep 26)* — Att: 53
St Margaretsbury 1 Harwich & Parkeston 1 *aet* — Att: 25
Replay: Harwich 2 **St Marg'sby** 2 *aet* (3-4p) *(Sep 25)* — Att: 99
London APSA 0 **Bedfont Green** 3 — Att: 20
Stanway Rovers 4 Hullbridge Sports 2 — Att: 69
Long Buckby 5 Broxbourne Borough V & E 0 — Att: 36
Sawbridgeworth 2 **Sun Postal** 1 — Att: 45
(Sawbridgeworth expelled)
Cockfosters 3 Sporting Bengal United 2 *aet* — Att: 52
Biggleswade United 2 Clapton 1 *aet* — Att: 25
Ruislip Manor 2 **Colney Heath** 3 *(at Colney Heath)* — Att: 31
Leverstock Green 3 Halstead Town 0 — Att: 47
Raunds Town 0 **Stotfold** 5 — Att: 36
Stansted 1 **Daventry United** 2 — Att: 46
Stewarts & Lloyds Corby 0 **Brimsdown Rovers** 2 — Att: 48
Royston Town 3 Bedfont 2 — Att: 42
Thrapston Town 1 **Harpenden Town** 2 — Att: 65

Eton Manor 3 Saffron Walden Town 0 — Att: 40
Biggleswade Tn 3 **Bugbrooke St M.** 4 *aet (at Bedford)* — Att: 31
Hatfield 2 Kingsbury London Tigers 3 *aet*
(Kingsbury London Tigers expelled)
North Greenford United 6 Cranfield United 0 — Att: 56
Concord Rangers 3 Oxhey Jets 0 — Att: 49
Ringmer 5 Sidlesham 2 — Att: 62
Broadbridge Heath 1 **Three Bridges** 2 — Att: 65
Bookham 0 **Dorking** 1 — Att: 64
Lancing 2 **Raynes Park Vale** 3 *(at Steyning Town)* — Att: 49
Epsom & Ewell 2 Tunbridge Wells 2 *aet* — Att: 73
Replay: **Tunbridge Wells** 3 Epsom & Ewell 0 *(Sep 25)* — Att: 80
Worthing United 4 Banstead Athletic 2 — Att: 48
Farnham Town 1 Littlehampton Town 0 — Att: 52
Guildford City 2 Pagham 1 — Att: 65
Herne Bay 1 **Colliers Wood United** 4 — Att: 192
Chichester City United 2 Westfield 0 — Att: 80
Eastbourne United Association 2 **Hassocks** 4 — Att: 60
Faversham Town 2 **Hailsham Town** 3 — Att: 68
Cobham 3 Lordswood 1 — Att: 34
Sevenoaks Town 3 Egham Town 1 — Att: 60
Chertsey Town 3 Erith Town 0 — Att: 272
Wealden 1 Erith & Belvedere 1 *aet* — Att: 50
Replay: **Erith & Belvedere** 1 Wealden 0 *(Sep 25)* — Att: 68
Southwick 0 **Camberley Town** 4 — Att: 62
Mile Oak 2 Crawley Down 2 *aet* — Att: 46
Replay: **Crawley Down** 3 Mile Oak 1 *(Sep 25)* — Att: 84
Deal Town 4 Redhill 1 — Att: 81
Haywards Heath Town 1 **Chessington & Hook Utd** 4 — Att: 51
Wick 3 East Grinstead Town 1 — Att: 59
Hythe Town 2 Shoreham 0 — Att: 121
Rye United 2 Sidley United 1 — Att: 103
Horley Town 1 **Greenwich Borough** 2 — Att: 67
Lymington Town 2 Blackfield & Langley 1 — Att: 57
Amesbury Town 0 **Christchurch** 5 — Att: 82
Devizes Town 0 **Brockenhurst** 1 *aet* — Att: 57
Melksham Town 2 Thame United 1 — Att: 41
Marlow United 4 Buckingham Athletic 0 — Att: 58
Witney United 2 Calne Town 1 — Att: 115
Brading Town 2 **Highworth Town** 2 *aet* — Att: 136
Replay: **Highworth Town** 2 Brading Town 1 *(Sep 29)* — Att: 170
Downton 0 **Moneyfields** 1 *(at Moneyfields)* *(Sep 25)* — Att: 52
Hamble ASSC 2 Kidlington 2 *aet* — Att: 48
Replay: Kidlington 1 **Hamble ASSC** 4 *(Sep 25)* — Att: 58
Holmer Green 4 Andover New Street 1 — Att: 40
Milton United 0 **Henley Town** 2 — Att: 41
Westbury United 3 **Chalfont St Peter** 4 — Att: 49
Bicester Town 2 Shrewton United 1 — Att: 42
Carterton 1 Shrivenham 1 *aet* — Att: 32
Replay: **Shrivenham** 3 Carterton 1 *(Sep 25)* — Att: 62
Alresford Town 1 **Cowes Sports** 2 — Att: 45
Bournemouth 12 Wootton Bassett Town 0 — Att: 63
Hartley Wintney 0 **Newport Pagnell Town** 2 — Att: 41
Sandhurst Town 2 Pewsey Vale 1 *aet* — Att: 45
Shepton Mallet 5 St Blazey 3 — Att: 85
Chard Town 1 **Liskeard Athletic** 2 *aet* — Att: 70
Porthleven 3 Bridport 1 — Att: 109
Newquay 2 **Shortwood United** 3 — Att: 82
Cullompton Rangers 2 **Wadebridge Town** 4 *aet* — Att: 68
Brislington 1 Welton Rovers 1 *aet* — Att: 55
Replay: Welton R. 2 **Brislington** 2 *aet* (3-4p) *(Sep 26)* — Att: 67
Willand Rovers 4 Saltash United 1 — Att: 103
Clevedon United 0 **Almondsbury Town** 4 *(Sep 23)* — Att: 63
Newton Abbot 1 Harrow Hill 0 — Att: 115
Budleigh Salterton 4 Bodmin Town 1 *aet* — Att: 75
Launceston 1 **Dawlish Town** 6 — Att: 95
Hallen 3 Falmouth Town 0 — Att: 44
Bitton 2 Odd Down 1 — Att: 77
Fairford Town 1 **Plymouth Parkway** 3 — Att: 90
Tavistock 0 **Gillingham Town** 4 — Att: 90
Penzance 1 **Wellington Town** 4 — Att: 113
Hamworthy United 4 Elmore 0 — Att: 51
Ilfracombe Town 3 Minehead Town 1 — Att: 104

FIRST ROUND

(£700 to each winning club)

(Ties played October 6 unless stated)

Seaham Red Star 2 Selby Town 1	Att: 160
Durham City 5 Sunderland Nissan 0 *aet*	
Billingham Town 0 Hebburn Town 1 *aet*	Att: 73
Northallerton Town 3 Pontefract Collieries 1	Att: 104
Tow Law Town 2 Pickering Town 3	Att: 129
Armthorpe Welfare 0 Jarrow Roofing Boldon CA 1	Att: 179
Eccleshill United 2 Thackley 1	Att: 179
Bedlington Terriers 1 Consett 7	Att: 130
Washington 0 Shildon 3	Att: 102
Dunston Federation 4 Stokesley Sports Club 2	Att: 104
Winterton Rangers 1 Thornaby 0	Att: 70
Spennymoor Town 3 Marske United 1	Att: 184
Squires Gate 3 Maltby Main 1	Att: 52
Darwen 2 Atherton LR 3 *aet*	Att: 185
Trafford 2 Oldham Town 0	Att: 95
Runcorn Linnets 1 Salford City 2	Att: 198
Ashton Town 1 Hallam 3	Att: 42
Blackpool Mechanics 0 Formby 2	Att: 41
Ashton Athletic 2 Colne 1	Att: 82
Kirkham & Wesham 5 Parkgate 0	Att: 113
Bootle 2 AFC Emley 0	Att: 122
Hinckley Downes 2 Long Eaton United 3 *aet (Oct 5)*	Att: 138
Friar Lane & Epworth 3 Kirby Muxloe SC 2 *aet*	Att: 91
Leek CSOB 2 Coleshill Town 2	Att: 34
Holbrook Miners Welfare 0 Heath Hayes 1 *aet*	Att: 51
Gedling Town 4 Pegasus Juniors 0	Att: 54
Wellington 4 Calverton Miners Welfare 0	Att: 57
Shifnal Town 2 Borrowash Victoria 4	Att: 87
Newcastle Town 1 Alvechurch 2	Att: 80
Pilkington XXX 0 Bewdley Town 3	Att: 62
Coventry Sphinx 4 Glossop North End 3	Att: 70
Glapwell 1 Oldbury United 3	Att: 72
Sutton Town 1 Tipton Town 6	Att: 94
Stone Dominoes 0 Rainworth Miners Welfare 2	Att: 71
Barnt Green Spartak 2 Market Drayton Town 3	Att: 7
Shawbury United 2 Bridgnorth Town 1	Att: 105
Cadbury Athletic 1 Norton United 3 *(Oct 7)*	Att: 92
Studley 1 Heanor Town 0	Att: 123
Dunkirk 2 Gedling Miners Welfare 1 *aet*	Att: 70
Cradley Town 1 Mickleover Sports 0	Att: 42
Deeping Rangers 1 Woodbridge Town 2	Att: 82
Gorleston 0 St Ives Town 3	Att: 107
Boston Town 3 Holbeach United 2 *aet*	Att: 116
Dereham Town 1 Soham Town Rangers 2	Att: 190
Leiston 3 Debenham Leisure Centre 0	Att: 124
Newmarket Town 3 Yaxley 2 *aet*	Att: 76
Wroxham 2 Whitton United 1 *aet*	Att: 141
Sleaford Town 5 Walsham-le-Willows 1	Att: 139
Ely City 1 Needham Market 4	Att: 113
Blackstones 3 Diss Town 1	Att: 96
Desborough Town 9 Bugbrooke St Michael 0	Att: 69
Long Buckby 3 Welwyn Garden City 2 *aet*	Att: 59
Hanwell Town 7 Sun Postal Sports 1	Att: 59
Leverstock Green 0 Biggleswade United 1	Att: 46
Royston Town 2 Harpenden Town 1	Att: 55
St Margaretsbury 0 Wembley 1	Att: 65
Hatfield Town 0 Romford 3 *(Oct 20)*	Att: 73
Barking 4 Daventry United 2 *aet*	Att: 64
Stotfold 0 Tring Athletic 1	Att: 73
Barkingside 0 Brimsdown Rovers 2	Att: 27
Ampthill Town 4 Colney Heath 1	Att: 45
Concord Rangers 2 Hertford Town 0	Att: 66
Eton Manor 4 North Greenford United 2	Att: 10
Wellingborough Town 4 Stanway Rovers 1 *aet*	Att: 154
Replay: Stanway 1 Wellingborough 0 *(Oct 10)*	Att: 94
Cockfosters 2 Bedfont Green 1	Att: 57
Bowers & Pitsea 1 Harefield United 3 *aet*	Att: 44
Worthing United 2 Chessington & Hook United 3	Att: 42

Three Bridges 4 Sevenoaks Town 3 *aet*	Att: 49
Greenwich Borough 7 Chichester City United 0	Att: 34
Merstham 2 Dorking 0	Att: 84
Rye United 2 Farnham Town 1	Att: 63
Tunbridge Wells 2 Thamesmead Town 2 *aet*	Att: 80
Replay: Thamesmead Tn 1 Tunbridge Wells 0 *(Oct 9)*	Att: 62
Hassocks 2 Ash United 0	Att: 121
Crawley Down 3 Croydon 2	Att: 101
Camberley Town 2 Colliers Wood United 1	Att: 89
Raynes Park Vale 0 Cobham 3	Att: 68
Deal Town 5 Chertsey Town 1	Att: 145
Erith & Belvedere 4 Guildford City 5	Att: 81
Wick 0 Ringmer 2	Att: 56
Arundel 5 Hythe Town 0	Att: 96
Hailsham Town 3 Crowborough Athletic 4	Att: 96
Witney United 1 Ardley United 5	Att: 137
VTFC 2 North Leigh 1	Att: 60
Bournemouth 1 Melksham Town 2	Att: 74
Highworth Town 3 Beaconsfield SYCOB 2	Att: 104
Henley Town 2 Shrivenham 3 *aet*	Att: 59
Christchurch 4 Sandhurst Town 1	Att: 61
Chalfont St Peter 3 Bicester Town 2	Att: 46
New Milton Town 0 Hungerford Town 2	Att: 54
Hamble ASSC 2 Flackwell Heath 3 *aet*	Att: 30
Holmer Green 0 Brockenhurst 4	Att: 41
Cowes Sports 3 Corsham Town 2	Att: 132
Marlow United 1 Lymington Town 1 *aet*	Att: 28
Replay: Lymington Town 5 Marlow Utd 1 *(Oct 13)*	Att: 40
Moneyfields 3 Newport Pagnell Town 2	Att: 43
Ilfracombe Town 4 Brislington 0	Att: 112
Bitton 3 Porthleven 0	Att: 70
Hamworthy United 8 Newton Abbot 1	Att: 79
Shepton Mallet 1 Gillingham Town 5	Att: 118
Wellington Town 0 Hallen 2	Att: 65
Willand Rovers 2 Shortwood United 1	Att: 115
Poole Town 5 Liskeard Athletic 1	Att: 151
Budleigh Salterton 2 Plymouth Parkway 2 *aet*	Att: 85
Replay: Plym'th Parkway 2 Budleigh Salt. 0 *(Oct 10)*	Att: 192
Almondsbury Town 1 Frome Town 0	Att: 88
Dawlish Town 2 Wadebridge Town 1	Att: 68

SECOND ROUND

(£1,000 to each winning club)

(Ties played November 17 unless stated)

Squires Gate 2 Northallerton Town 2 *aet*	Att: 76
Replay: Northallerton Tn 4 Squires Gate 3 *(Nov 21)*	Att: 82
Salford City 5 Shildon 1	Att: 212
Billingham Synthonia 2 Ashton Athletic 1	Att: 138
Eccleshill United 1 Pickering Town 1 *aet*	Att: 79
Replay: Pickering Town 3 Eccleshill Utd 2 *(Nov 20)*	Att: 106
Atherton LR 0 Newcastle Benfield 0 *aet*	Att: 52
Replay: Newcastle Benfield 3 Atherton LR 2 *(Nov 20)*	Att: 74
Flixton 1 Rainworth Miners Welfare 0	Att: 65
Formby 4 Jarrow Roofing Boldon CA 1	Att: 80
Durham City 0 Consett 4	Att: 202
Kirkham & Wesham 3 West Auckland Town 0	Att: 196
Bootle 3 Winterton Rangers 4 *aet*	Att: 157
Spennymoor Town 0 Dunston Federation 0 *aet*	Att: 144
Replay: Dunston Fed. 3 Spennymoor Tn 1 *(Nov 20)*	Att: 151
Seaham Red Star 2 Trafford 3	Att: 106
Hebburn Town 1 Whitley Bay 4	Att: 171
Hallam 1 Glasshoughton Welfare 0	Att: 80
Alvechurch 1 Causeway United 1 *aet*	Att: 85
Replay: Causeway United 1 Alvechurch 0 *(Nov 20)*	Att: 88
Shawbury United 1 Stratford Town 0	Att: 80
Bewdley Town 1 Coventry Sphinx 2	Att: 160
Wellington 2 Friar Lane & Epworth 3	Att: 63
Studley 4 Sleaford Town 1	Att: 150
Heath Hayes 3 Borrowash Victoria 0	Att: 190
Boston Town 2 Long Eaton United 0	Att: 76
Barwell 1 Coleshill Town 3	Att: 69
Gedling Town 2 Cradley Town 1 *aet*	Att: 50

Tipton Town 2 Market Drayton Town 0 — Att: 88
Oldbury United 0 Dunkirk 0 *aet (at Pelsall Villa)* — Att: 45
Replay: Dunkirk 1 **Oldbury United** 2 *(Nov 20)* — Att: 61
Norton United 0 **Blackstones** 2 — Att: 65
Leiston 2 **St Ives Town** 3 — Att: 153
Concord Rangers 5 Potton United 0 — Att: 46
Lowestoft Town 1 Desborough Town 0 — Att: 362
Stanway Rovers 6 Barking 1 — Att: 117
Soham Town Rangers 0 **Long Buckby** 1 — Att: 159
Hanwell Town 0 **Cogenhoe United** 1 — Att: 102
Newmarket Town 1 Biggleswade United 0 *aet* — Att: 77
Needham Market 4 Eton Manor 1 — Att: 133
Ampthill Town 3 Burnham Ramblers 0 — Att: 76
Mildenhall Town 2 Wroxham 1 — Att: 159
Wembley 2 Woodbridge Town 2 *aet* — Att: 71
Replay: Woodbridge Town 0 **Wembley** 2 *(Nov 20)* — Att: 106
Brimsdown Rovers 3 Tring Athletic 1 — Att: 75
Romford 3 Cockfosters 0 — Att: 94
Royston Town 0 **Ipswich Wanderers** 2 — Att: 85
VTFC 4 Guildford City 2 — Att: 72
Lymington Town 1 Hassocks 0 — Att: 93
Brockenhurst 4 Crawley Down 1 — Att: 104
Thamesmead Town 0 **Greenwich Borough** 2 — Att: 56
AFC Totton 0 **VCD Athletic** 1 — Att: 163
Chessington & Hook 2 Crowborough Athletic 2 *aet* — Att: 100
Replay: Crowborough 4 Chessington/H. 3 *(Nov 20)* — Att: 114
Three Bridges 0 **Camberley Town** 1 — Att: 51
Deal Town 3 **Moneyfields** 4 — Att: 176
Whitehawk 2 **Flackwell Heath** 3 — Att: 75
Christchurch 1 **Merstham** 7 — Att: 102
Cowes Sports 4 Arundel 2 — Att: 173
Chalfont St Peter 1 **Harefield United** 5 — Att: 110
Ringmer 4 Ardley United 1 — Att: 74
Rye United 2 Cobham 2 *aet* — Att: 103
Replay: Cobham 2 **Rye United** 3 *(Nov 20)* — Att: 55
Bemerton Heath Harlequins 2 **Bideford** 3 *aet* — Att: 103
Hamworthy United 1 **Poole Town** 2 — Att: 370
Willand Rovers 0 **Sherborne Town** 3 — Att: 122
Hungerford Town 5 Gillingham Town 0 — Att: 149
Melksham Town 4 Street 1 — Att: 50
Shrivenham 3 Dawlish Town 2 *aet* — Att: 172
Wimborne Town 3 Hallen 2 *aet* — Att: 359
Bitton 3 Highworth Town 2 — Att: 96
Almondsbury Town 2 **Truro City** 4 *aet* — Att: 294
Plymouth Parkway 2 Ilfracombe Town 0 — Att: 225

THIRD ROUND
(£1,200 to each winning club)
(Ties played December 8 unless stated)
Winterton Rangers 2 **Pickering** 1 *(Winterton expelled)* — Att: 142
Billingham Synthonia 1 **Dunston Federation** 3 — Att: 110
Consett 2 Trafford 1 *(Dec 22)* — Att: 219
Salford City 3 Hallam 0 *(Dec 15)* — Att: 119
Newcastle Benfield 2 **Kirkham & Wesham** 5 — Att: 58
Whitley Bay 6 Flixton 0 — Att: 137
Northallerton Town 0 **Formby** 6 — Att: 87
Tipton Town 3 Friar Lane & Epworth 1 — Att: 54
Coventry Sphinx 4 Oldbury United 0 — Att: 91
Coleshill Town 1 **Blackstones** 2 *(Dec 22)* — Att: 102
Shawbury United 2 Cogenhoe United 1 — Att: 116
Studley 4 Gedling Town 3 *(Dec 15)* — Att: 73
Long Buckby 3 Heath Hayes 2 — Att: 102
Causeway United 0 **Boston Town** 1 *(Dec 9)* — Att: 114
Merstham 2 VTFC 2 *aet (Dec 15)* — Att: 107
Replay: VTFC 1 **Merstham** 1 *aet (3-4p) (Dec 18)* — Att: 130
St Ives Town 1 Romford 1 *aet (Dec 15)* — Att: 198
Replay: Romford 2 **St Ives Town** 4 *(Dec 22)* — Att: 143
Lowestoft Town 4 Rye United 2 — Att: 271
Concord Rangers 7 Newmarket Town 1 — Att: 78
Greenwich Borough 2 Wembley 1 — Att: 41
Crowborough Ath. 2 Brimsdown R. 1 *aet (Dec 15)* — Att: 112
Ampthill Town 1 **VCD Athletic** 3 — Att: 160

Ringmer 1 **Needham Market** 3 *(Dec 15)* — Att: 145
Mildenhall Town 0 **Stanway Rovers** 5 — Att: 146
Camberley Town 2 Flackwell Heath 1 *aet* — Att: 114
Ipswich Wanderers 0 **Harefield United** 3 — Att: 73
Plymouth Parkway 0 **Hungerford Town** 1 *(Dec 15)* — Att: 253
Sherborne Town 1 **Lymington Town** 3 *(Dec 15)* — Att: 135
Bitton 3 Brockenhurst 1 *aet (Dec 15)* — Att: 80
Poole Town 1 Cowes Sports 0 *(Dec 15)* — Att: 177
Melksham Town 0 **Truro City** 3 — Att: 307
Moneyfields 1 **Shrivenham** 2 *(Dec 15)* — Att: 45
Bideford 1 Wimborne Town 0 *(Dec 15)* — Att: 228

FOURTH ROUND
(£1,500 to each winning club)
(Ties played January 19 unless stated)
Whitley Bay 1 Long Buckby 0 — Att: 378
Truro City 3 Bideford 2 — Att: 1,016
Hungerford Town 1 Boston Town 0 — Att: 214
Concord Rangers 4 Shawbury United 1 — Att: 202
Kirkham & Wesham 3 Studley 0 *(Jan 26)* — Att: 424
St Ives Town 3 Bitton 2 *aet (Jan 26)* — Att: 243
VCD Athletic 0 **Needham Market** 2 *aet (Jan 26)* — Att: 306
Merstham 4 Pickering Town 2 *aet (Jan 26)* — Att: 320
Camberley Town 3 Tipton Town 1 — Att: 202
Coventry Sphinx 3 Salford City 1 *(Jan 26)* — Att: 258
Dunston Federation 3 Shrivenham 0 — Att: 241
Stanway Rovers 4 Formby 2 *aet (Jan 26)* — Att: 265
Greenwich Borough 2 Harefield United 1 — Att: 106
Poole Town 1 Consett 1 *aet* — Att: 441
Replay: **Consett** 4 Poole Town 1 *(Jan 26)* — Att: 514
Lymington Town 1 **Crowborough Athletic** 4 — Att: 204
Lowestoft Town 3 Blackstones 2 — Att: 524

FIFTH ROUND
(£2,000 to each winning club)
(Ties played February 9 unless stated)
Hungerford Town 2 Greenwich Borough 2 *aet* — Att: 371
Replay: Greenwich B 1 **Hungerford Town** 2 *(Feb 16)* — Att: 148
Concord Rangers 2 Camberley Town 0 — Att: 347
St Ives Town 3 Needham Market 3 *aet* — Att: 769
Replay: **Needham Market** 4 St Ives Town 0 *(Feb 16)* — Att: 536
Merstham 5 Consett 4 *aet* — Att: 476
Lowestoft Town 2 Dunston Federation 1 — Att: 922
Truro City 0 **Whitley Bay** 3 — Att: 1,567
Crowborough Athletic 0 **Kirkham & Wesham** 2 — Att: 772
Stanway Rovers 1 **Coventry Sphinx** 3 — Att: 365

QUARTER-FINALS
(£5,000 to each winning club)
(Ties played March 1 unless stated)
Concord Rangers 0 **Lowestoft Town** 1 — Att: 716
Kirkham & Wesham 3 Coventry Sphinx 3 *aet* — Att: 1,093
Replay: Coventry S 0 **Kirkham & Wesham** 1 *(Mar 2)* — Att: 774
Hungerford Town 0 **Whitley Bay** 1 — Att: 662
Merstham 2 **Needham Market** 3 *aet* — Att: 861

SEMI-FINALS
(£7,000 to each winning club)
1st leg
(Ties played March 22)
Lowestoft Town 4 Whitley Bay 0 — Att: 2,102
Kirkham & Wesham 3 Needham Market 2 — Att: 1,053
2nd leg
(Ties played March 29)
Whitley Bay 3 **Lowestoft Town** 1 — Att: 2,059
Needham Market 0 **Kirkham & Wesham** 1 — Att: 1,375

FINAL
(£10,000 to winning club)
(May 11th at Wembley Stadium)
Lowestoft Town 1 **Kirkham & Wesham** 2 — Att: 19,537

WELSH CUP COMPETITIONS

WELSH CUP

PRELIMINARY ROUND
Abertillery Excelsior 2 **Cwmamman United** 3
Carno 5 Four Crosses 3
Chirk AAA 2 Amlwch Town 2 *aet* (4-3p)
Corwen Amateurs 2 Holywell Town 1
Cwmaman Institute 6 Cwmffrwdoer Sports 3
Kerry 1 **Knighton Town** 2
Llanberis 3 Castell Alun Colts 0
Llanidloes Town 0 **Montgomery Town** 1
Llanwern 6 Monmouth Town 3
Nantlle Vale 1 Llandudno Junction 0
Nefyn United 3 Llangollen Town 1
Newbridge 1 **Newcastle Emlyn** 4
Rhos Aelwyd 3 **Halkyn United** 4
Risca United 2 **Goytre** 2 *aet* (4-5p)
Seven Sisters 1 Porthcawl Town 1 *aet* (4-3p)
Ystradgynlais 1 **Aberbargoed Buds** 2

FIRST ROUND
Bala Town 6 Denbigh Town 3
Bodedern 0 **Llanfairpwll** 2
Brickfield Rangers 0 **Brymbo** 12
Bridgend Town 3 Garden Village 1
Bryntirion Athletic 6 Pontypridd Town 1
Caerau Ely 7 Garw Athletic 0
Caerleon 4 Treharris Athletic 0
Carno 1 **Penrhyncoch** 4
Coedpoeth United 0 **Mold Alexandra** 1
Conwy United 4 Glynceiriog 2
Corwen Amateurs 3 Lex XI 1
Cwmaman Institute 4 Llangeinor 2 *aet*
Cwmmaman United 3 AFC Llwydcoed 0
Dinas Powys 3 Penrhiwceiber Rangers 0
Ely Rangers 1 **Llantwit Fadre** 4
Glan Conwy 1 **Llanrug United** 3
Goytre United 3 Pontardawe Town 1
Guilsfield 2 Presteigne St Andrews 1
Halkyn United 2 Ruthin Town 1
Hawarden Rangers 4 Buckley Town 0
Holyhead Hotspur 1 **Cefn United** 2
Llanberis 4 Llanrwst United 3 *aet*
Llandyrnog United 3 Penycae 1
Llanrhaedr 3 Berriew 2 *aet*
Llansawel 2 **ENTO Aberaman Athletic** 5 *aet*
Llanwern 4 Barry Town 2
Maesteg Park 2 Seven Sisters 1 *aet*
Merthyr Saints 2 Cwmbran Town 0
Montgomery Town 2 Llanfyllin Town 1
Mynydd Isa 3 Glantraeth 1
Nantlle Vale 0 **Chirk AAA** 2
Nefyn United 2 Gresford Athletic 0
Newcastle Emlyn 4 Knighton Town 1
Newport YMCA 2 Goytre 0
Pentwyn Dynamos 3 Cwmbran Celtic 1
Pontyclun 1 **Cambrian & Clydach Vale BGC** 2
Prestatyn Town 1 **Llandudno Town** 2
Pwllheli 3 **GAP Queens Park** 4
Taffs Well 3 Caldicot Town 2
Ton Pentre 3 Aberbargoed Buds 0
Tredegar Town 1 **Cardiff Corinthians** 1 *aet* (3-4p)
Troedyrhiw 3 **Croesyceiliog** 7
Tywyn & Bryncrug 4 Rhydymwyn 4 *aet* (7-6p)
UW Aberystwyth (scr.) **Briton Ferry Athletic** (w/o)
West End 2 Bettws 1

SECOND ROUND
Aberystwyth Town 3 Newcastle Emlyn 0
Afan Lido 3 Croesyceiliog 1
Bangor City 3 Llandyrnog United 0
Bridgend Town 1 **Bryntirion Athletic** 2
Brymbo 4 Halkyn United 0
Caerau Ely 3 Goytre United 2

Caerleon 2 Taffs Well 1
Caernarfon Town 2 Llanfairpwll 1
Caersws 9 Mold Alexandra 0
Cardiff Corinthians 2 **Ton Pentre** 3
Connah's Quay Nomads 0 The New Saints 0 *aet* (3-2p)
Corwen Amateurs 1 **Mynydd Isa** 3
Cwmaman Institute 0 **ENTO Aberaman Athletic** 3
Cwmamman United 0 **Dinas Powys** 5
Gap Queens Park 3 Penrhyncoch 1
Guilsfield 2 **Airbus UK Broughton** 3
Haverfordwest County 1 Llantwit Fardre 0
Holyhead Hotspurs 2 Bala Town 1
Llanberis 1 **Newtown** 5
Llandudno Town 1 **NEWI Cefn Druids** 2
Llangefni Town 5 Hawarden Rangers 0
Llanrug United 5 Llanrhaeadr 1
Maesteg Park 2 Briton Ferry Athletic 0
Merthyr Saints 1 **Carmarthen Town** 2
Neath Athletic 6 Llanwern 0
Nefyn United 2 Chirk AAA 0
Newport YMCA 4 Cambrian & Clydach Vale BGC 1
Pentwyn Dynamos 3 **Llanelli** 7
Porthmadog 0 **Welshpool Town** 2
Rhyl 10 Montgomery Town 0
Tywyn & Bryncrug 3 Conwy United 2
West End 1 **Port Talbot Town** 2

THIRD ROUND
Aberystwyth Town 3 Neath Athletic 1
Bryntirion Athletic 4 Dinas Powys 2
Caerleon 2 Brymbo 0
Caersws 2 **Bangor City** 3 *aet*
Connah's Quay Nomads 0 **Guilsfield** 2
ENTO Aberaman Athletic 3 Caerau Ely 1
Gap Queens Park 3 Afan Lido 1
Haverfordwest County 3 Ton Pentre 0
Llangefni Town 3 Mynydd Isa 0
Llanrug United 3 **Llanelli** 5
Nefyn United 1 **Caernarfon Town** 3
NEWI Cefn Druids 3 Holyhead Hotspur 0
Newport YMCA 2 Carmarthen Town 1
Newtown 2 Maesteg Park 1 *aet*
Rhyl 1 Port Talbot Town 0
Tywyn & Bryncrug 1 **Welshpool Town** 3

FOURTH ROUND
Aberystwyth Town 0 **Bangor City** 0 *aet* (2-3p)
Bryntirion Athletic 1 **Welshpool Town** 2
Gap Queens Park 2 Caerleon 0
Guilsfield 1 Caernarfon Town 0
Haverfordwest County 1 **Rhyl** 2
NEWI Cefn Druids 0 ENTO Aberaman Athletic 0 (5-3p)
Newport YMCA 1 Llangefni Town 1 (4-3p)
Newtown 1 **Llanelli** 2

QUARTER-FINALS
Guilsfield 0 **Bangor City** 6
NEWI Cefn Druids 3 **Llanelli** 6 *aet*
Newport YMCA 3 Welshpool Town 2
Rhyl 3 Gap Queens Park 2

SEMI-FINALS
Bangor City 3 Newport YMCA 1 *(at Newtown)*
Llanelli 5 Rhyl 2 *(at Aberystwyth Town)*

FINAL
(May 4th at Newtown)
Bangor City 4 Llanelli 2 *aet Att:* 1,510

F A W PREMIER CUP
*(Top ten placed clubs from the Welsh Premier League along with the two best placed 'exiled' clubs
(Newport County and Merthyr Tydfil), the Welsh Cup winners plus the three English League clubs (Cardiff
City, Swansea City and Wrexham); Porthmadog (11th) qualified as Merthyr Tydfil's lights did not meet the
minimum specification; Airbus UK Broughton (12th) qualified as Carmarthen Town finished in the top ten
and won the Welsh Cup)*

FIRST ROUND
Bangor City 3 Aberystwyth Town 0

Connah's Quay Nomads 1 **Carmarthen Town** 1 *aet* (2-3p)

Haverfordwest County 3 Airbus UK Broughton 1

Porthmadog 2 **Port Talbot Town** 7

SECOND ROUND
Carmarthen Town 2 Port Talbot Town 1 *aet*

Haverfordwest County 0 **Welshpool Town** 2

Llanelli 4 Rhyl 1

Newport County 1 Bangor City 0

QUARTER-FINALS
Carmarthen Town 3 The New Saints 1 *aet*

Llanelli 4 Wrexham 2 *aet*

Newport County 1 Swansea City 0

Welshpool Town 0 **Cardiff City** 1

SEMI-FINALS
Cardiff City 1 **Newport County** 1 *aet* (4-5p)

Llanelli 1 Carmarthen Town 0

FINAL
(March 11th at Newport County)

Newport County 1 Llanelli 0

WELSH TROPHY

FIRST ROUND
S T M Sports 6-2 Barry

SECOND ROUND
AFC Whitchurch 1 **Cogan Coronation** 6

Baglan Red Dragon 6 Carnetown 5 *aet*

Blaenavon Blues 4 North End 3

Blaenrhondda 7 Maltsters Sports 1

Brickfield Rangers 1 **Venture Community** 6

Brymbo 5 Llandudno Junction 0

Carno 2 **Llanfyllin Town** 3

Cefn United 4 Llanrug United 3 *aet*

Chirk AAA 3 Hawarden Rangers 1

Corus Steel 5 Osborne Athletic 0

Corwen Amateurs 1 Glan Conwy 1 *aet* (7-6p)

Cwmbach Royal Stars 3 Llandrindod Wells 3 *aet* (4-2p)

Four Crosses 7 Llanidloes Town 1

Glyn Ceiriog 1 **Coedpoeth United** 4

Holywell Town 6 Acrefair Youth 1

Kenfig Hill 3 **Ynysddu Welfare Crusaders** 4

Kerry 0 **Rhayader Town** 0 *aet* (1-3p)

Knighton Town 2 **Presteigne St Andrews** 4

Llangollen Town 0 **Rhos Aelwyd** 3

Llanharry 2 **Bonymaen Colts** 10

Llanrhaedr 1 **Berriew** 2

Llanrwst United 2 Llay Welfare 1

Mardy 4 STM Sports 3 *aet*

Mold Alexandra 2 **Conwy United** 5 *aet*

Nantlle Vale 3 Borras Park Albion 2 *aet*

Nefyn United 3 Penmaenmawr Pheonix 2

Nelson Cavaliers 8 Blaen Gawr Inn 0

Ragged School 8 AFC Bargoed Redz 1

Rhydymwyn 1 **Llanberis** 2

South Gower 3 Clydach Wasps 1

Sully Sports 4 Ton & Gelli Boys Club 2 *aet*

Y Felinheli 0 **Penycae** 3

THIRD ROUND
Baglan Red Dragons 4 South Gower 2

Blaenavon Blues 2 Ynysddu Welfare Crusaders 1

Brymbo 3 Cefn United 2

Chirk AAA 2 Venture Community 1

Coedpoeth United (w/o) Nantlle Vale (scr.)

Cwmbach Royal Stars 3 Rhayader Town 1 *aet*

Four Crosses 3 Blaenrhondda 3 *aet* (4-1p)

Llanfyllin Town 2 **Corwen Amateurs** 7

Llanrwst United 1 **Berriew** 1 *aet* (4-5p)

Mardy 1 **Bonymaen Colts** 2

Nefyn United 1 **Llanberis** 2

Nelson Cavaliers 1 **Ragged School** 4

Penycae 3 **Holywell Town** 3 *aet* (6-7p)

Presteigne St Andrews 3 Cogan Coronation 2

Rhos Aelwyd 3 Conwy United 0

Sully Sports 2 Corus Steel 1

FOURTH ROUND
Baglan Red Dragons 2 Sully Sports 0

Berriew 1 Coedpoeth United 1 *aet* (4-1p)

Cwmbach Royal Stars 2 **Bonymaen Colts** 4

Four Crosses 0 **Brymbo** 4

Holywell Town 2 **Corwen Amateurs** 6

Llanberis 3 Chirk AAA 2

Presteigne St Andrews 1 **Rhos Aelwyd** 3

Ragged School 5 Blaenavon Blues 2

QUARTER-FINALS
Baglan Red Dragons 0 **Ragged School** 7

Brymbo 0 **Berriew** 1

Corwen Amateurs 2 Bonymaen Colts 2 *aet* (4-3p)

Llanberis 0 **Rhos Aelwyd** 1

SEMI-FINALS
Corwen Amateurs 3 Ragged School 3 *aet* (3-2p)
(at Newtown)

Rhos Aelwyd 2 Berriew 0
(at Bala Town)

FINAL
(April 12th at NEWI Cefn Druids)

Corwen Amateurs 2 **Rhos Aelwyd** 4

MAJOR COUNTY CUP FINALS

BEDFORDSHIRE PREMIER CUP
(August 2nd at Luton Town)
Luton Town 2 **Dunstable Town** 3 *aet*
BERKS & BUCKS SENIOR CUP
(May 5th at Chesham United)
Chesham United 3 Wycombe Wanderers 0
BIRMINGHAM SENIOR CUP
(April 7th at Birmingham City)
Birmingham City 5 Burton Albion 0
CAMBRIDGESHIRE PROFESSIONAL CUP
(July 31st at Histon)
Histon 1 **Cambridge City** 1 *aet* (4-5p)
CHESHIRE SENIOR CUP
(April 1st at Witton Albion)
Altrincham 1 **Nantwich Town** 1 *aet* (3-5p)
CORNWALL SENIOR CUP
(March 24th at Wadebridge Town)
Truro City 3 Saltash United 2
CUMBERLAND SENIOR CUP
(April 16th at Carlisle United)
Carlisle United 2 Penrith Town 0
DERBYSHIRE SENIOR CUP
1st leg *(April 8th):*
Alfreton Town 2 Belper Town 3
2nd leg *(April 22nd):*
Belper Town 1 Alfreton Town 1
DEVON St LUKES COLLEGE BOWL
(May 6th at Willand Rovers)
Willand Rovers 1 **Dawlish Town** 3
DORSET SENIOR CUP
(April 15th at Dorchester Town)
Portland United 1 **Sherborne Town** 2
DURHAM CHALLENGE CUP
(May 6th at Sunderland)
Sunderland 2 Gateshead 0
EAST RIDING SENIOR CUP
(May 15th at Hull City)
North Ferriby United 4 Hall Road Rangers 1
ESSEX SENIOR CUP
(April 1st at Southend United)
Southend United 1 Chelmsford City 0
GLOUCESTERSHIRE SENIOR CUP
(April 15th at Bristol City)
Bristol City 9 Cheltenham Town 1
HAMPSHIRE SENIOR CUP
(May 10th at AFC Bournemouth)
Farnborough 0 **Basingstoke Town** 1
HEREFORDSHIRE SENIOR CUP
(April 1st at Hereford United)
Hereford United 3 Westfields 0
HERTFORDSHIRE SENIOR CUP
(April 15th at HCFA, Letchworth)
Boreham Wood 5 Ware 2
HUNTINGDONSHIRE SENIOR CUP
(May 5th at Huntingdon Town)
St Ives Town 1 **Yaxley** 1 *aet* (4-5p)
KENT SENIOR CUP
(July 26th at Bromley)
Ebbsfleet United v Cray Wanderers
LANCASHIRE TROPHY
(April 2nd at LCFA, Leyland)
Southport 4 Chorley 1
LEICESTERSHIRE CHALLENGE CUP
(May 13th at Leicester City)
Oadby Town 3 Friar Lane & Epworth 0
LINCOLNSHIRE SENIOR CUP
(April 30th at Scunthorpe United)
Scunthorpe United 5 Lincoln City 0

LIVERPOOL SENIOR CUP
(April 24th at Marine)
Marine 1 Liverpool 0
LONDON SENIOR CUP
(April 22nd at Metropolitan Police)
Hendon 2 **Tooting & Mitcham United** 3
MANCHESTER PREMIER CUP
(April 28th at Oldham Athletic)
Hyde United 1 **Radcliffe Borough** 2
MIDDLESEX SENIOR CUP
(March 24th at Uxbridge)
Hampton & Richmond Borough 3 Hendon 0
NORFOLK SENIOR CUP
(March 25th at Norwich City)
Wroxham 3 Sheringham 1
NORTH RIDING SENIOR CUP
(March 19th at York City)
York City 0 **Middlesbrough** 2
NORTHAMPTONSHIRE SENIOR CUP
(April 29th at Rushden & Diamonds)
Rushden & Diamonds 2 Brackley Town 1
NORTHUMBERLAND SENIOR CUP
(April 23rd at Newcastle United)
Newcastle United Res. 4 Blyth Spartans 3
NOTTINGHAMSHIRE SENIOR CUP
(May 7th at Notts County)
Eastwood Town 2 Ollerton Town 0
OXFORDSHIRE SENIOR CUP
(April 15th at Oxford United)
Banbury United 1 **North Leigh** 2
SHEFFIELD & HALLAMSHIRE SENIOR CUP
(May 8th at Sheffield Wednesday)
Worksop Town 0 **Sheffield** 2
SHROPSHIRE SENIOR CUP
(July 24th at Ludlow Town)
Shrewsbury Town 5 Market Drayton Town 1
SOMERSET PREMIER CUP
(April 30th at Bath City)
Bath City 3 Paulton Rovers 0
STAFFORDSHIRE SENIOR CUP
(April 16th at Port Vale)
Rocester 3 Kidsgrove Athletic 0
SUFFOLK PREMIER CUP
(April 22nd at Ipswich Town)
Leiston 0 **Needham Market** 0 *aet* (4-5p)
SURREY SENIOR CUP
(May 6th at Metropolitan Police)
Whyteleafe 2 **Merstham** 3 *aet*
SUSSEX SENIOR CUP
(May 5th at Eastbourne Borough)
Brighton & Hove Albion 1 Crawley Town 0
WEST RIDING COUNTY CUP
(April 9th at WRCFA, Woodlesford)
Harrogate Town 6 Bradford Park Avenue 0
WESTMORLAND SENIOR CUP
(April 26th at Kendal Town)
Milnthorpe Corinthians 4 Kendal County 2
WILTSHIRE PREMIER SHIELD
(May 1st at Salisbury City)
Salisbury City 1 Swindon Town 0
WORCESTERSHIRE SENIOR CUP
1st leg *(April 7th)*
Redditch United 0 Worcester City 1
2nd leg *(April 14th)*
Worcester City 0 **Redditch United** 2

OTHER COUNTY AND DISTRICT CUP FINALS

ALDERSHOT SENIOR CUP
(May 14th at Fleet Town)
Fleet Town 3 Badshot Lea 2

A F A SENIOR CUP
(April 5th at HSBC)
Old Meadonians 2 Nottsborough 2 *aet* (4-3p)

AXMINSTER HOSPITAL CUP
(May 11th at Axminster Town)
Elmore 0 **Chard Town** 1

BAMBRIDGE CUP
(May 8th at Fowlmere)
Comberton United Res. 3 Great Shelford 'A' 0

BARKESTON ASH BURTON CUP
(March 24th at Tadcaster Albion)
Wetherby Athletic 2 Bardsey 1

BARRITT CUP
(May 5th at Bangor City)
Rhydymwyn 2 Barmouth & Dyffryn United 1

BASINGSTOKE SENIOR CUP
(May 13th at Fleet Town)
Fleet Town 3 Alresford Town 0

BASS CHARITY VASE
(August 2nd at Burton Albion)
Burton Albion 2 Nottingham Forest 1

BEDFORDSHIRE SENIOR CUP
(May 12th at Luton Town)
Leighton Town 1 **Stotfold** 3

BEDFORDSHIRE SENIOR TROPHY
(April 2nd at Cranfield United)
AFC Dunstable 1 Caldecote 0

BEDFORDSHIRE INTERMEDIATE CUP
(April 23rd at AFC Kempston Rovers)
Stotfold Res. 4 Ampthill Town Res. 0

BEDFORDSHIRE JUNIOR CUP
(April 18th at Potton United)
Bedford SA 3 **Meltis Albion** 4

BERKS & BUCKS TROPHY
(April 23rd at Aylesbury Vale)
Beaconsfield SYCOB 1 Newport Pagnell Town 0

BERKS & BUCKS INTERMEDIATE CUP
(April 5th at Buckingham Town)
Chalfont Wasps 2 PB (Milton Keynes) 0

BERKS & BUCKS JUNIOR CUP
(April 19th at Newbury)
Kintbury Rangers Res. 0 **South Reading** 1

BILL SPURGEON CUP
(April 30th at Old Chelmsfordians)
Galleywood 0 **Mountnessing** 1

BIRMINGHAM FLOODLIGHT CUP
(April 15th at Solihull Moors)
AFC Wulfrunians 4 Bartley Green 0

BIRMINGHAM VASE
(April 19th at BCFA, Great Barr)
Northfield Town 2 Bedworth Ex-Service 1

BIRMINGHAM JUNIOR CUP
(March 29th at BCFA, Great Barr)
Silhill 3 Billesley United 2

BISHOPS CASTLE CHARITY CUP
(May 18th at Bishops Castle Town)
Bishops Castle Town 4 Montgomery Town 1

BOLTON HOSPITAL CUP
(May 9th at Bolton Wanderers)
Ramsbottom United 2 Stoneclough 1

BRADFORD SENIOR CUP CUP
(April 28th at Eccleshill United)
Field Sports & Social 2 Bradford Park Avenue 1 *aet*

BRAUNTON CUP
(May 11th at Torrington)
Torrington 3 Braunton Res. 1

BRIGHTON CHARITY CUP
(April 29th at Horsham)
Horsham 3 East Preston 2 *aet*

BUCKINGHAM CHARITY CUP
(May 15th at Buckingham Town)
Buckingham Town 0 **Leighton Town** 1

BUCKINGHAM JUNIOR CHARITY CUP
(April 24th at Buckingham Town)
Steeple Claydon 1 Potterspury 0

BUILTH SPA CUP
(May 24th at Builth Wells)
Hay St Marys 3 Presteigne St Andrews Res. 1

CAMBRIDGESHIRE INVITATION CUP
(April 24th at Cambridge United)
Cambridge City 3 Histon Res. 0

CAMBRIDGESHIRE CHALLENGE CUP
(April 7th at Histon)
Great Shelford 0 **Over Sports** 1

CAMBRIDGESHIRE JUNIOR INVITATION CUP
(May 8th at Cambridge City)
Cambridge University Press Res. 1 Whittlesey United Res. 0 *aet*

CAMBRIDGESHIRE LOWER JUNIOR CUP
(May 1st at Ely City)
Mepal Sports 2 Chatteris Town Res. 1

CARLISLE CUP
(May 26th at Seaton Town)
Sidmouth Town Res. 1 Feniton Res. 0

CEREDIGION CUP
(May 5th at Ffostrasol)
St Dogmaels 4 **Tregaron Turfs** 5

CHARD HOSPITAL CUP
(August 27th at Combe St Nicholas)
South Petherton 0 **Perry Street & Yonder Hill** 2

CHESHIRE AMATEUR CUP
(April 17th at Vauxhall Motors)
Poulton Victoria 4 Cammell Laird Res. 2 *aet*

CHESTER SENIOR CUP
(April 25th at Christleton)
Christleton 5 Highfield Athletic 0

CHURCHMAN CUP
(May 13th at Woodbridge Town)
Woodbridge Town 2 **Ipswich Wanderers** 4

COMMANDER ETHELSTON CUP
(May 5th at Whitchurch Alport)
Whitchurch Alport 3 Malpas 1

CORNWALL CHARITY CUP
(May 20th at Penryn Athletic)
Bodmin Town 3 Launceston 1

CORNWALL JUNIOR CUP
(March 24th at Wadebridge Town)
Portreath 2 St Dominick 1

COVENTRY EVENING TELEGRAPH CUP
(April 21st at Coventry City)
Coventry Copsewood 1 **Stockingford AA** 2

CRAVEN CHALLENGE CUP
(April 25th at Barnoldswick Town)
Ingleton 2 **Rimington** 4

CRAVEN MORRISON CUP
(May 9th at Skipton Town)
Grassington United 1 **Settle United** 2

CREWE & DISTRICT CUP
(May 10th at Crewe)
Crewe Res. 3 Lostock Gralam Res. 1

DERBYSHIRE DIVISIONAL CUP NORTH
(May 8th at Tideswell United)
Dronfield United 1 **Glossop North End Res.** 2 *aet*

DERBYSHIRE DIVISIONAL CUP SOUTH
(April 3rd at Long Eaton United)
Ilkeston Town Res. 3 Newmount 2

DERBYSHIRE JUNIOR CUP NORTH
(April 24th at Tideswell United)
Cotes Park 4 Chapel Town Res. 1

DERBYSHIRE JUNIOR CUP SOUTH
(April 10th at Long Eaton United)
The Seal Inn 2 **Sandiacre Town Res.** 4

DEVON PREMIER CUP
(April 22nd at Tiverton Town)
Appledore 1 **Totnes & Dartington SC** 2

DEVON SENIOR CUP
(April 15th at Cullompton Rangers)
Broadclyst Social Club 0 **Willand Rovers Res.** 2

DEVON INTERMEDIATE CUP
(April 8th at Newton Abbot)
Buckland Athletic Res. 3 Horrabridge Rangers 0

DIDCOT FESTIVAL CUP
(September 1st at Didcot Town)
Drayton 1 Crowmarsh Gifford 0

DORSET TROPHY
(April 22nd at Bridport)
Hamworthy United Res. 3 Portland United Res. 2

DORSET INTERMEDIATE CUP
(April 10th at Hamworthy United)
Dorset Knob 5 Chickerell United 'A' 1

DORSET JUNIOR CUP
(April 8th at Dorchester Town)
Kingston Lacy 4 FC Windowman 0

DORSET MINOR CUP
(April 3rd at Hamworthy United)
Dorchester Sports 3 Westover Spartans 0

DURHAM TROPHY
(April 28th at Sunderland Nissan)
Murton 3 Whitehill 1

EAST ANGLIAN CUP
(May 7th at Great Wakering Rovers)
Leiston 2 Brentwood Town 2 *aet* (4-3p)

EAST HAM MEMORIAL CHARITY CUP
(May 10th at Cave Road, Plaistow)
Debden Sports 4 Castle United 2 *aet*

EAST RIDING SENIOR COUNTRY CUP
(May 10th at Bridlington Town)
North Ferriby Athletic 4 Malton & Norton 3 *aet*

ESSEX PREMIER CUP
(April 23rd at Billericay Town)
White Ensign 2 Brentwood Town Res. 1

ESSEX THAMESSIDE TROPHY
(May 6th at Brimsdown Rovers)
Brimsdown Rovers 2 Canvey Island 1 *aet*

ESSEX JUNIOR CUP
(April 9th at Great Wakering Rovers)
Debden Sports 3 AFC Horndon 0

ESSEX JUNIOR TROPHY
(April 2nd at Maldon Town)
Emstar United 3 Sheering United 0

EVESHAM JUNIOR HOSPITAL CUP
(May 10th at Littleton)
Littleton 3 Halfords 0

FAZELEY CHARITY CUP
(March 21st at Coton Green)
Sutton United 1 Chelmsley Town 0

FRED HEWINGS CUP
(March 24th at Ipplepen Athletic)
Buckland Athletic 'A' 3 Waldon Athletic 0

GLOS TROPHY
(May 1st at GCFA, Oaklands Park)
Bitton 2 Hardwicke 1

GLOS SENIOR AMATEUR CUP NORTH
(April 17th at Tuffley Rovers)
Lydbrook Athletic 0 **Sharpness** 2

GLOS SENIOR CUP CUP SOUTH
(April 29th at GCFA, Oaklands Park)
B & W Avonside 0 St Aldhelms 0 *aet* (4-3p)

GLOS INTERMEDIATE CUP NORTH
(April 1st at Slimbridge)
Whaddon United Res. 3 **Kingswood Res.** 4 *aet*

GLOS INTERMEDIATE CUP SOUTH
(April 15th at GCFA, Oaklands Park)
Winterbourne United 'A' 1 Sneyd Park Res. 0

GLOS JUNIOR CUP NORTH
(April 8th at Slimbridge)
Leonard Stanley 0 **FC Barometrics** 3

GLOS JUNIOR CUP SOUTH
(April 22nd at GCFA, Oaklands Park)
Wessex Wanderers 3 Longwell Green Sports Res. 3 *aet*
(3-2p)

GLOS MINOR CUP NORTH
(April 23rd at Harrow Hill)
Newnham United 1 **Tewkesbury Rovers** 3

GLOS MINOR CUP SOUTH
(April 1st at GCFA, Oaklands Park)
Bristol Sanctuary 4 Hanham Athletic 'A' 2

GLOS PRIMARY CUP NORTH
(April 21st at Cirencester Town)
Didmarton 7 Tewkesbury Town 2

GLOS PRIMARY CUP SOUTH
(Mach 25th at GCFA, Oaklands Park)
Broad Walk Res. 2 Eaglehouse Elite 0

GOLDLINE TROPHY
(March 31st at Bolton Wanderers)
Euxton Villa 2 Charnock Richard 0

GOLESWORTHY CUP
(May 14th at Ottery St Mary)
Axmouth United 1 **Farway United** 3

GRANDISSON CUP
(May 13th Ottery St Mary)
Sidmouth Town Res. 3 Tipton St John 0

GWENT SENIOR CUP
(May 8th at Abergavenny Thursdays)
Caldicot Town 1 Cwmbran Celtic 0

GWENT AMATEUR CUP
(May 3rd at Abergavenny Thursdays)
Govilon 3 Blaenavon Blues 0

HALIFAX & DISTRICT CUP
(May 8th at Elland)
Ovenden West Riding 5 Hebden Royd Red Star 1

HAMPSHIRE RUSSELL COTES CUP
(May 6th at New Milton Town)
New Milton Town 0 **Fleet Town** 3

HAMPSHIRE INTERMEDIATE CUP
(April 30th at Andover New Street)
Nursling 1 **Liphook United** 2

HAMPSHIRE JUNIOR A CUP
(April 12th at Alton United)
R & B Sports 3 Twynham Rangers 2

HAMPSHIRE JUNIOR B CUP
(April 12th at Alton United)
Bisterne United Res. 1 Warsash Wasps 0

HANSEN CUP
(May 5th at Torrington)
Torrington 0 **Bideford Res.** 2

HASTINGS SENIOR CUP
(April 9th at Sidley United)
Sidley United 0 **Westfield** 1 *aet*

HASTINGS INTERMEDIATE CUP
(March 18th at Sidley United)
Hastings United Res. 6 Hollington United 2

HEREFORDSHIRE CHALLENGE CUP
(March 24th at Hereford United)
Westfields 2 Pegasus Juniors 1

HERTFORDSHIRE CHARITY CUP
(April 23rd at HCFA, Letchworth)
Cheshunt 1 Ware 0
HERTFORDSHIRE CENTENARY TROPHY
(March 25th at HCFA, Letchworth)
Hoddesdon Town 3 Hertford Heath 1
HERTFORDSHIRE CHARITY SHIELD
(April 29th at HCFA, Letchworth)
Tring Athletic 1 Welwyn Garden City 0
HERTFORDSHIRE INTERMEDIATE CUP
(April 1st at HCFA, Letchworth)
Kings Langley 1 Bishop's Stortford Swifts 0
HERTFORDSHIRE JUNIOR CUP
(March 21st at HCFA, Letchworth)
Nirankari 2 Hadley 1
HINCHINGBROOKE CUP
(May 12th at Huntingdon Town)
Blackstones 1 **Deeping Rangers** 3 *aet*
HUDDERSFIELD CUP
(May 8th at Huddersfield Town)
Meltham Athletic 3 Newsome WMC 1
HUNTINGDONSHIRE PREMIER CUP
(May 14th at Huntingdon Town)
Biggleswade United 2 Potton United 1
HUNTINGDONSHIRE SCOTT GATTY CUP
(March 26th at Godmanchester Rovers)
St Neots Town Res. 3 Huntingdon Town Res. 2
HUNTINGDONSHIRE BENEVOLENT CUP
(May 9th at Somersham Town)
St Neots Town Res. 0 **Huntingdon Town Res.** 2
HUNTINGDONSHIRE JUNIOR CUP
(April 16th at Somersham Town)
Warboys Town 1 **Hemingfords Utd Res.** 1 *aet* (3-4p)
HUNTINGDONSHIRE LOWER JUNIOR CUP
(April 1st at Somersham Town)
Earith United 0 **Ramsey Town 'A'** 2
ISLE OF WIGHT SENIOR (GOLD) CUP
(May 9th at Cowes Sports)
Cowes Sports 2 East Cowes Victoria Athletic 1 *aet*
J W HUNT CUP
(May 12th at Wolverhampton Wanderers)
Wednesfield 3 AFC Wulfrunians 2
JIM NEWMAN CUP
(August 5th at Clanfield)
Letcombe 3 Carterton 2
KEIGHLEY & DISTRICT CUP
(May 2nd at Silsden)
Crosshills 3 Oxenthorpe 1
KEIGHLEY & DISTRICT SUPPLEMENTARY CUP
(April 30th at Silsden)
Steeton Res. 3 Keighley Shamrocks Res. 1
KENT SENIOR TROPHY
(April 13th at Welling United)
Thamesmead Town 2 Beckenham Town 0
KENT INTERMEDIATE CHALLENGE SHIELD
(April 5th at Beckenham Town)
Orpington 2 Greenways 0
KENT INTERMEDIATE CUP
(April 22nd at Tonbridge Angels)
Tonbridge Angels Res. 1 Cray Wanderers Res. 0
KENT JUNIOR A CUP
(May 3rd at Corinthian)
Canterbury City 3 Holmesdale Res. 2
KENT JUNIOR B CUP
(April 26th at Chatham Town)
Cannon '24 4 Medway Knights 1
KENT JUNIOR C CUP
(April 26th at Corinthian)
Charlton Community 2 Heathview United 1
LANCASHIRE AMATEUR SHIELD
(March 25th at LCFA, Leyland)
Wigan Robin Park 1 **Euxton Villa** 1 *aet* (2-4p)

LANCASHIRE AMATEUR CUP
(April 1st at LCFA, Leyland)
Little Lever Sports Club 3 Rossendale Amateurs 2 *aet*
LEICESTERSHIRE SENIOR CUP
(May 6th at LCFA, Holmes Park)
Blaby & Whetstone Athletic 2 Anstey Town 0
LEICESTERSHIRE JUNIOR CUP
(March 23rd at LCFA, Holmes Park)
Witherley United 3 Barlestone St Giles 1
LEICESTERSHIRE JUNIOR TROPHY
(April 15th at LCFA, Holmes Park)
Falcons 2 Barlestone St Giles Res. 1
LEICESTERSHIRE JUNIOR SHIELD
(April 22nd at LCFA, Holmes Park)
Buckminster United 2 Ellistown Res. 1
LEICESTERSHIRE JUNIOR VASE
(April 8th at LCFA, Holmes Park)
Thurnby Rangers Res. 5 New Parks Social Club 2
LEOMINSTER SENIOR CUP
(May 6th at Leominster Town)
Leominster Town 1 Woofferton 0
LEOMINSTER JUNIOR CUP
(May 8th at Leominster Town)
Wellington Rangers Colts 3 Shobdon 2 *aet*
LINCOLNSHIRE SHIELD
(April 16th at Spalding United)
Gainsborough Trinity 5 Spalding United 1
LINCOLNSHIRE TROPHY
(April 29th at Sleaford Town)
Blackstones 2 Bottesford Town 0
LINCOLNSHIRE JUNIOR CUP
(May 3rd at Boston United)
Grimsby Borough 3 Skegness Town 3 *aet* (4-1p)
LIVERPOOL CHALLENGE CUP
(May 3rd at LCFA, Walton Hall Avenue)
Speke 2 **East Villa** 3 *aet*
LIVERPOOL JUNIOR CUP
(May 7th at LCFA, Walton Hall Avenue)
Mossley Hill Athletic 5 Stoneycroft 0
LONDON INTERMEDIATE CUP
(March 29th at Croydon Athletic)
Metrogas 2 Cray Wanderers Res. 0
LONDON JUNIOR CUP
(April 5th at Cray Valley Paper Mills)
South Kilburn 1 **Flanders** 2
LONDON OLD BOYS SENIOR CUP
(April 16th at Potters Bar Town)
Old Challoners 2 **UCL Academicals** 2 *aet* (2-3p)
LOUGHBOROUGH CHARITY CUP
(May 3rd at Shepshed Dynamo)
Loughborough Dynamo 1 **Shepshed Dynamo** 3
MANCHESTER CHALLENGE TROPHY
(April 3rd at MCFA, Branthingham Road)
AFC Blackley 4 Beechfield United 2
MIDDLESEX CHARITY CUP
(to be played during 2008-09)
Enfield Town v Hillingdon Borough
MIDDLESEX PREMIER CUP
(March 26th at Harrow Borough)
Ashford Town (Middx) Res. 2 **Wealdstone Res.** 3
MIDDLESEX INTERMEDIATE CUP
(April 2nd at North Greenford United)
Park View 3 Staines Lammas 1
MIDDLESEX JUNIOR CUP
(April 16th at Ashford Town (Middx))
Stedfast United 0 **North Greenford United Social** 1
MID-CHESHIRE SENIOR CUP
(April 1st at Winsford United)
Winsford United 2 Congleton Town 1

MID-SUSSEX SENIOR CHARITY CUP
(April 17th at Hassocks)
Three Bridges Res. 3 Burgess Hill Town Res. 1
MID-SUSSEX JUNIOR CHARITY CUP
(May 10th at Haywards Heath Town)
Copthorne 2 Ifield Edwards 'B' 1
MONTGOMERYSHIRE CUP
(May 23rd at Meifod)
Carno 4 Guilsfield 0
MORRISON BELL CUP
(May 15th at Ottery St Mary)
Budleigh Salterton 2 Feniton 1
NATIONAL LEAGUE SYSTEM CUP
(May 3rd at Coventry City)
Midland Combination Div One 1 **Southern Amateur League** 1 *aet* (2-4p)
NORFOLK JUNIOR CUP
(March 31st at Norwich City)
Horsford United 3 Swaffham Town Res. 1
NORFOLK PRIMARY CUP
(April 4th at Dereham Town)
Lynn Docklands 5 Ellingham 0
NORTH CAMBRIDGESHIRE JUNIOR CUP
(April 16th at Wisbech Town)
Chatteris Town 2 Whittlesey United Res. 0
NORTH BEDS CHARITY CUP
(May 9th at Biggleswade Town)
Biggleswade Town 0 **Langford** 1
NORTH EAST WALES CUP
(April 30th at Wrexham)
Bala Town 2 Gap Queens Park 1
NORTH HAMPSHIRE CUP
(May 10th at Fleet Town)
Fleet Town 0 **Tadley Calleva** 1
NORTH RIDING COUNTY CUP
(March 5th at Stokesley Sports Club)
York St John University 2 Grangetown Boys Club 1
NORTH RIDING CHALLENGE CUP
(April 28th at Stokesley Sports Club)
Edgehill 3 Bedale 2
NORTH WALES COAST CUP
(May 10th at Conwy United)
Llandudno Town 4 Flint Town United 1
NORTH WALES COAST JUNIOR CUP
(May 3rd at Porthmadog)
Barmouth & Dyffryn United 2 Llanystumdwy 0
NORTH WEST COUNTIES CUP
(May 22nd at LCFA, Walton Hall Avenue)
Old Xaverians 1 St Aloysius 0
NORTHAMPTON TOWN AREA CUP
(March 25th at Thrapston Town)
Bugbrooke St Michaels 'B' 1 Bretton Park Rangers Res. 0
NORTHAMPTON TOWN GORELL BARNES CUP
(May 10th at Northampton Town)
University of Northampton 5 Double Four 1
NORTHAMPTON TOWN NBC CUP
(May 10th at Northampton Town)
Cotton Hill 4 Far Cotton Loco 2
NORTHAMPTONSHIRE JUNIOR CUP
(April 9th at Rushden & Diamonds)
Rothwell Corinthians 2 Rushden & Higham United 1
NORTHAMPTONSHIRE LOWER JUNIOR CUP
(April 15th at Raunds Town)
Wellingborough Town Res. 2 Netherton United 1 *aet*
NORTHUMBERLAND BENEVOLENT BOWL
(April 28th at Whitley Park, Benton)
Blyth Town 1 Wark 0
NORTHUMBERLAND MINOR CUP
(May 2nd at Whitley Park, Benton)
Shilbottle Colliery Welfare 5 Killingworth YPC 3

NOTTS INTERMEDIATE CUP
(April 30th at Hucknall Town)
Hucknall Rolls Leisure 2 Notts Police 2 *aet* (4-2p)
NOTTS JUNIOR CUP
(April 22nd at Gedling Town)
Selston 3 Three Crowns 1 *aet*
NOTTS MINOR CUP
(April 16th at Carlton Town)
Gedling Southbank 6 Notts Metropolis 1
NOTTS INTER-LEAGUE CHARITY CUP
(May 6th at Hcknall Town)
Notts Amateur Alliance 1 Notts Senior League 0
OXFORDSHIRE INTERMEDIATE CUP
(April 21st at Oxford City)
Kidlington Res. 1 **Headington Amateurs Res.** 2
OXFORDSHIRE JUNIOR SHIELD
(May 3rd at Witney United)
Ducklington 1 Freeland 0
PORTSMOUTH SENIOR CUP
(May 2nd at Moneyfields)
Horndean Res. 2 United Services Portsmouth Res. 2 *aet* (6-5p)
POTTERS BAR CHARITY CUP
(May 2nd at Potters Bar Town)
Cockfosters 3 Old Owens 1
POWELL CHARITY CUP
(May 4th at Wem Town)
Shawbury United 2 Whitchurch Alport 1
RADNORSHIRE CUP
(March 24th at Rhayader Town)
Knighton Town 3 Gwernyfed 3 *aet* (3-0p)
READING SENIOR CUP
(May 6th at Reading)
Marlow United 1 Westwood United 0
READING JUNIOR CUP
(April 26th at Newbury)
Marlow United Res. 2 Berks County Sports Res. 0
ROLLESTON CHARITY CUP
(May 5th at LCFA, Holmes Park)
Oadby Town 4 Hinckley United 1
ROY BAILEY MEMORIAL TROPHY
(May 5th at Brimsdown Rovers)
Ware 4 Cheshunt 1
RUNCORN CHALLENGE CUP
(April 18th at Pavilions, Runcorn)
Helsby 0 **Runcorn Town** 3
SALISBURY HOSPITAL CUP
(April 28th at Salisbury City)
Salisbury City 3 Shrewton United 1
SEVENOAKS JUNIOR CHARITY CUP
(May 20th at Farnborough Old Boys Guild)
Sevenoaks Town 'A' 3 Hildenborough Athletic 2
SHEFFIELD & HALLAMSHIRE CHALLENGE CUP
(April 30th at Barnsley)
Athersley Recreation 1 Hollinsend Amateurs 0
SHROPSHIRE CHALLENGE CUP
(May 1st at Shrewsbury Town)
Bridgnorth Town 0 **Shifnal United** 1
SHROPSHIRE JUNIOR CUP
(April 30th at Shrewsbury Town)
Dawley Bank 4 Wrockwardine Wood 1
SLOUGH TOWN SENIOR CUP
(May 5th at Burnham)
Wraysbury 2 Rayners Lane 1
SLOUGH TOWN JUNIOR CUP
(May 1st at Burnham)
Windsor Great Park 1 Maidenhead Town 0
SOMERSET SENIOR CUP
(May 5th at Paulton Rovers)
Portishead 1 Keynsham Town Res. 0

SOMERSET JUNIOR CUP
(April 15th at Bishop Sutton)
Normalair RSL 3 Merriott Rovers 0

SOMERSET INTERMEDIATE CUP
(May 1st at Shepton Mallet)
Bath Arsenal 3 Taunton Civil Service 0

SOUTHAMPTON SENIOR CUP
(April 24th at Southampton)
VTFC Res. 1 Romsey Town Res. 0

SOUTHAMPTON JUNIOR A CUP
(March 24th at BTC Southampton)
Warsash Wasps 4 Beaney Park 3

SOUTHAMPTON JUNIOR B CUP
(March 24th at BTC Southampton)
Nimbin United 3 Rising Sun Colden Common 1

SOUTH MIDLANDS FLOODLIGHT CUP
(to be played during 2008-09)
Cockfosters v Saffron Walden Town

SOUTH MIDLANDS RESERVES FLOODLIGHT CUP
(May 14th at Hertford Town)
Hertford Town Res. 1 Cheshunt Res. 0

SOUTHERN COMBINATION CUP
(August 9th at Ashford Town (Middx))
Ashford Town (Middx) v Chipstead

STAFFORDSHIRE VASE
(March 31st at Newcastle Town)
Brocton 1 **Wolstanton United** 3

STAFFORDSHIRE CHALLENGE CUP
(April 14th at Wolverhampton Casuals)
Bilbrook 1 **Heath Town Rangers** 3

STAFFORDSHIRE PRESIDENT'S CUP
(March 17th at Eccleshall)
Ball Haye Green Res. 2 **Railway Tavern** 4 *aet*

SUFFOLK SENIOR CUP
(May 8th at Ipswich Town)
Hadleigh United 2 **Grundisburgh** 3

SUFFOLK JUNIOR CUP
(April 12th at Ipswich Town)
Old Newton United 2 Cockfield United 1

SUFFOLK PRIMARY CUP
(May 10th at Woodbridge Town)
Bungay Town Res. 4 Old Newton United Res. 2 *aet*

SUFFOLK JUNIOR CUP
(May 2nd at Bury Town)
Haverhill Rovers Res. 1 Ipswich Wanderers Res. 0

SURREY PREMIER CUP
(April 9th at Tooting & Mitcham United)
Ashford Town (Middx) Res. 1 **Metropolitan Police Res.** 2

SURREY INTERMEDIATE CUP
(May 7th at Leatherhead)
Dorking Wanderers 1 **Epsom Eagles** 2

SURREY JUNIOR CUP
(May 14th at Redhill)
Croygas Phoenix 2 **Abbey Rangers** 3

SURREY LOWER JUNIOR CUP
(April 24th at Redhill)
AFC Molesey 4 Kingston Albion 0

SUSSEX R U R CHARITY CUP
(May 3rd at Worthing)
Selsey 0 **Three Bridges** 4

SUSSEX INTERMEDIATE CUP
(April 23rd at Three Bridges)
Bexhill United 1 Loxwood 1 *aet* (3-0p)

SUSSEX JUNIOR CUP
(April 9th at Horsham)
Faygate United 0 **Roffey** 1 *aet*

TOLLSHUNT D'ARCY CUP
(May 12th at Stanway Rovers)
Tiptree Heath 1 **Earls Colne** 1 *aet* (1-3p)

TOWN TANNERS CUP
(May 20th at Montgomery Town)
Montgomery Town 0 **Bishops Castle Town** 1

TORRIDGE CUP
(May 1st at Torrington)
Boca Seniors 1 Braunton 0

VERNON WENTWORTH CUP
(May 7th at Worthing)
Barnham 4 Hanover 2

WALSALL SENIOR CUP
(May 7th at Walsall)
Boldmere St Michaels 2 Heath Hayes 0

WEDNESBURY CHARITY CUP
(May 13th at Walsall Wood)
Brereton Social 2 **Darlaston Town** 3

WEST HERTS ST MARYS CUP
(May 5th at Hemel Hempstead Town)
Hemel Hempstead Town 5 Oxhey Jets 1

WEST RIDING CHALLENGE CUP
(May 2nd at WRCFA, Woodlesford)
Barnoldswick Town 1 **Bardsey** 3

WEST RIDING CHALLENGE TROPHY
(April 28th at WRCFA, Woodlesford)
East End Park WMC 5 Boston Spa 3 *aet*

WEST WALES SENIOR CUP
(April 22nd at Llanelli)
Llanelli 1 **Neath Athletic** 2 *aet*

WEST WALES INTERMEDIATE CUP
(April 28th at Swansea City)
Seaside 6 Ragged School 5

WESTMORLAND BENEVOLENT TROPHY
(April 16th at Kendal Town)
Wetheriggs United 3 Keswick 0

WESTMORLAND JUNIOR CUP
(April 23rd at Kendal Town)
Penrith Rangers 3 Kendal United 2

WESTWARD HO! CUP
(May 4th at Barnstaple Town)
Boca Seniors 4 North Molton 2

WHARFEDALE CUP
(May 5th at Guiseley)
Otley Town 1 Ventus & Yeadon Celtic 0

WILTSHIRE SENIOR CUP
(April 23rd at Chippenham Town)
Laverstock & Ford 2 **Melksham Town** 5

WILTSHIRE JUNIOR CUP
(May 3rd at Swindon Supermarine)
Minety 2 Stratton Juniors 0

WIRRAL SENIOR CUP
(May 7th at Ashville)
Heswall 0 **West Kirby** 1

WIRRAL AMATEUR CUP
(March 24th at Ashville)
FC Pensby 3 Mersey Royal 1

WORCESTER ROYAL INFIRMARY CUP
(May 3rd at Worcester City)
Westfields 1 **Alvechurch** 1 *aet* (2-3p)

WORCESTERSHIRE URN
(April 15th at Kidderminster Harriers)
Alvechurch 4 Brierley Hill & Withymoor 0

WORCESTERSHIRE JUNIOR CUP
(April 1st at Worcester City)
Bredon 1 Droitwich Spa 0

WYCOMBE SENIOR CUP
(May 13th at Wycombe Wanderers)
Flackwell Heath 1 **Chalfont Wasps** 2

WYCOMBE JUNIOR CUP
(May 5th at Holmer Green)
Penn & Tylers Green Res. 1 Chalfont Wasps Res. 0

YMCA CUP
(May 17th at South Molton)
North Molton 1 Chittlehampton 0

SELECTED CUPS IN FULL

BEDFORDSHIRE SENIOR CUP
FIRST ROUND
Barton Rovers 3 Biggleswade Town 1
Langford 3 Dunstable Town 2 *aet*
Leighton Town 8 AFC Kempston Rovers 0
Stotfold 3 Biggleswade United 0
QUARTER-FINALS
Arlesey Town 2 Barton Rovers 0
Bedford Town 1 **Leighton Town** 2
Stotfold 4 Langford 0
Wootton Blue Cross 0 **Potton United** 2
SEMI-FINALS
Arlesey Town 0 **Leighton Town** 1
Stotfold 2 Potton United 1
FINAL
(May 12th at Luton Town)
Leighton Town 1 **Stotfold** 3

BERKS & BUCKS SENIOR TROPHY
FIRST ROUND
Abingdon Town 0 **Reading Town** 2
Aylesbury Vale 1 **Newport Pagnell Town** 3
Chalfont St Peter 2 Wantage Town 0
Flackwell Heath (w/o) v AFC Wallingford (scr.)
Hungerford Town 1 **Beaconsfield SYCOB** 2
Shrivenham 2 **Holmer Green** 6
QUARTER-FINALS
Chalfont St Peter 2 Reading Town 1
Milton United 1 Holmer Green 0
Newport Pagnell Town 5 Flackwell Hth 0
Sandhurst Town 0 **Beaconsfield SYCOB** 2 *aet*
SEMI-FINALS
Beaconsfield SYCOB 1 Milton United 0
Chalfont St Peter 1 **Newport Pagnell Town** 2
FINAL
(April 23rd at Aylesbury Vale)
Beaconsfield SYCOB 1 Newport Pagnell Town 0

BERKS & BUCKS SENIOR CUP
FIRST ROUND
Aylesbury United 3 **Marlow** 2 *aet*
(Aylesbury United expelled)
Bracknell Town 1 **Windsor & Eton** 2
Burnham 2 Abingdon United 2 *aet* (2-3p)
(Abingdon United expelled)
Didcot Town 5 Slough Town 1
Thatcham Town 0 **Wycombe Wanderers** 2
QUARTER-FINALS
Chesham United 2 Marlow 1
Didcot Town 0 **Wycombe Wanderers** 1
Milton Keynes Dons 4 Maidenhead United 1
Windsor & Eton 3 Burnham 1
SEMI-FINALS
Chesham United 2 Windsor & Eton 0
Milton Keynes Dons 0 **Wycombe Wanderers** 3
FINAL
(May 5th at Chesham United)
Chesham United 3 Wycombe Wanderers 0

BIRMINGHAM SENIOR CUP
FIRST ROUND
Alvechurch 0 **Banbury United** 1
Atherstone Town 1 Rugby Town 0
Burton Albion 4 Bedworth United 1
Cradley Town 0 **Rushall Olympic** 1

Halesowen Town 0 **Birmingham City** 2
Hednesford Town 5 Boldmere St Michaels 3
Leamington 0 **Studley** 1
Nuneaton Borough 0 **Wolverhampton Wanderers** 3
Racing Club Warwick 2 Coventry Sphinx 0
Redditch United 5 Stratford Town 0
Romulus 2 Causeway United 0
Sohihull Moors 2 Coventry City 1
Stourbridge 1 Oldbury United 0
Tamworth 2 **Sutton Coldfield Town** 3
Tipton Town 1 **West Bromwich Albion** 2 *aet*
Willenhall Town 0 **Walsall** 3
SECOND ROUND
Atherstone Town 0 Burton Albion 0
Replay: **Burton Albion** 5 Atherstone Town 0
Banbury United 3 Racing Club Warwick 0
Hednesford Town 2 **Wolverhampton Wdrs** 3
Redditch United 1 **Stourbridge** 2
Rushall Olympic 1 West Bromwich Albion 0
Sohihull Moors 0 **Birmingham City** 4
Studley 0 **Romulus** 1
Sutton Coldfield Town 2 **Walsall** 3
QUARTER-FINALS
Birmingham City 2 Banbury United 0
Romulus 1 **Burton Albion** 3
Rushall Olympic 1 Walsall 0
Stourbridge 1 **Wolverhampton Wanderers** 4
SEMI-FINALS
Burton Albion 6 Rushall Olympic 2
Wolverhampton Wanderers 0 **Birmingham City** 1
(at AFC Telford United)
FINAL
(April 7th at Birmingham City)
Birmingham City 5 Burton Albion 0

CAMBRIDGESHIRE INVITATION CUP
PRELIMINARY ROUND
Ely City 3 Cambridge University Press 1
Histon Res. 5 Great Shelford 0
March Town United 7 Over Sports 1
Soham Town Rangers 2 Littleport Town 0
QUARTER-FINALS
Ely City 1 **Cambridge City** 2
Histon Res. 4 Soham Town Rangers 1
Mildenhall Town 2 March Town United 0
Wisbech Town 0 **Newmarket Town** 5
SEMI-FINALS
Mildenhall Town 1 **Cambridge City** 2
Newmarket Town 1 **Histon Res.** 3 *aet*
FINAL
(April 24th at Cambridge United)
Cambridge City 3 Histon Res. 0

CHESHIRE SENIOR CUP
FIRST ROUND
Cheadle Town 1 **Congleton Town** 4
Hyde United 0 **Nantwich Town** 2
Northwich Victoria 4 Winsford United 0
Stalybridge Celtic 4 Woodley Sports 1
Vauxhall Motors 4 Alsager Town 3 *aet*
Warrington Town 1 **Runcorn Linnets** 2
Witton Albion 0 **Altrincham** 3
QUARTER-FINALS
Congleton Town 1 **Cammell Laird** 2
Northwich Victoria 0 **Nantwich Town** 1

Runcorn Linnets 1 **Altrincham** 3
Stalybridge Celtic 2 **Vauxhall Motors** 3
SEMI-FINALS
Altrincham 2 Vauxhall Motors 1
Cammell Laird 1 **Nantwich Town** 2
FINAL
(April 1st at Witton Albion)
Altrincham 1 **Nantwich Town** 1 *aet* (3-5p)

DERBYSHIRE SENIOR CUP
FIRST ROUND
Ashbourne United 5 Parkhouse 0
Heanor Town 0 **Pinxton** 2
SECOND ROUND
Borrowash Victoria 2 Blackwell Miners Welfare 1
Glapwell 3 Mickleover Sports 2
Glossop North End 3 Staveley Miners Welfare 2 *aet*
Long Eaton United 4 Ashbourne United 0
New Mills 4 Bolsover Town 0
Pinxton 1 **Holbrook Miners Welfare** 4
Shirebrook Town 1 **Stapenhill** 2
THIRD ROUND
Alfreton Town 6 Holbrook Miners Welfare 0
Belper Town 2 New Mills 1 *aet*
Borrowash Victoria 0 **Ilkeston Town** 3
Buxton 3 Glossop North End 0
Glapwell 2 Matlock Town 1
Gresley Rovers 1 Long Eaton United 0
South Normanton Athletic 1 **Graham Street Prims** 1
aet (6-7p)
Stapenhill 6 Stanton Ilkeston 3
QUARTER-FINALS
Alfreton Town 3 Gresley Rovers 1
Belper Town 9 Stapenhill 2
Graham Street Prims 0 **Buxton** 3
Ilkeston Town 1 **Glapwell** 2 *aet*
SEMI-FINALS
Buxton 1 **Alfreton Town** 3
Glapwell 1 **Belper Town** 2
FINAL
(played over two legs)
1st leg *(April 8th)*
Alfreton Town 2 Belper Town 3
2nd leg *(April 22nd)*
Belper Town 1 Alfreton Town 1

DEVON ST LUKES COLLEGE BOWL
FIRST ROUND
Bideford 2 Buckland Athletic 0
Clyst Rovers 3 Elburton Villa 0
Ilfracombe Town 2 Witheridge 1
Ivybridge Town 1 **Elmore** 3 *(at Newton Abbot)*
Tavistock 0 **Willand Rovers** 3
SECOND ROUND
Bideford 5 Exeter City 1
Clyst Rovers 3 Torquay United 2
Cullompton Rangers 0 **Willand Rovers** 3
Dawlish Town 2 Dartmouth 0
Elmore 0 **Plymouth Argyle** 10
Holsworthy 3 Newton Abbot Spurs 1
Ilfracombe Town 2 **Tiverton Town** 5
Plymouth Parkway 0 **Barnstaple Town** 2
QUARTER-FINALS
Barnstaple Town 2 **Tiverton Town** 4 *aet*
Dawlish Town 4 Plymouth Argyle 1
Holsworthy 0 **Bideford** 4
Willand Rovers 2 Clyst Rovers 1

SEMI-FINALS
Tiverton Town 0 **Dawlish Town** 1
Willand Rovers 3 Bideford 0 *aet*
FINAL
(May 6th at Willand Rovers)
Willand Rovers 1 **Dawlish Town** 3

DORSET SENIOR CUP
FIRST ROUND
Cranborne 2 Cobham Sports 2 *aet*
Replay: **Cobham Sports** 4 Cranborne 1
Poole Borough 1 **Hamworthy**
Recreation 5
SECOND ROUND
Cobham Sports 3 **Swanage Town & Herston** 5 *aet*
Hamworthy Recreation 4 Blandford United 1
Holt United 1 **Bridport** 2
Poole Town 2 Hamworthy United 0
Portland United 6 Sturminster Marshall 0
Sherborne Town 2 Verwood Town 0
Sturminster Newton United 0 **Gillingham Town** 1
Wimborne Town 2 Shaftesbury 1 *aet*
QUARTER-FINALS
Bridport 2 Hamworthy Recreation 0
Poole Town 4 Wimborne Town 3
Sherborne Town 1 Gillingham Town 0
Swanage Town & Herston 2 **Portland United** 4
SEMI-FINALS
Bridport 0 **Sherborne Town** 4 *(at Weymouth)*
Poole Town 2 **Portland United** 3 *(at Dorchester Town)*
FINAL
(April 15th at Dorchester Town)
Portland United 1 **Sherborne Town** 2

DURHAM CHALLENGE CUP
PRELIMINARY ROUND
Annfield Plain 0 **Wolviston** 0 *aet* (1-3p)
Belford House 0 **Brandon United** 1
Bishop Auckland 0 **Durham City** 7
Cleadon Social Club 1 **Hartlepool** 2
Darlington Railway Ath. 1 **Horden Colliery Welfare** 2
Esh Winning 0 **Spennymoor Town** 0 *aet* (2-3p)
Harton & Westoe CW 1 **Peterlee Town** 5
Hebburn Town 7 Crook Town 4
Jarrow 1 **Darlington** 11
Jarrow Roofing Boldon CA 4 East Durham United 1
Silksworth CC 1 **Coxhoe Athletic** 4
Sunderland Ryhope CA 3 Shildon 1
Washington 0 **Ryhope Colliery Welfare** 4
Willington 0 **Sunderland** 4
FIRST ROUND
Boldon Community Association 1 **Sunderland Nissan** 6
Chester-le-Street Town 1 **Tow Law Town** 4
Consett 7 Sunderland Ryhope CA 0
Darlington 1 Brandon United 0
Gateshead 4 West Auckland Town 0
Hartlepool 0 **Wolviston** 1
Hartlepool United 1 **Durham City** 2
Hebburn Town 1 **Dunston Fed.** 1 *aet* (0-3p)
Horden Colliery Welfare 1 Coxhoe Athletic 0
Jarrow Roofing Boldon CA 1 **Sunderland** 3
Norton & Stockton Ancients 6 Ryhope Colliery Welfare 0
Peterlee Town 2 **Billingham Synthonia** 4
Ryton 1 **Billingham Town** 4
South Shields 2 **Easington Colliery** 4
Spennymoor Town 3 Seaham Red Star 2
Whickham 0 **Birtley Town** 3

WWW.NLNEWSDESK.CO.UK

SECOND ROUND
Billingham Town 3 Sunderland Nissan 3 *aet* (4-2p)
Birtley Town 2 **Gateshead** 4 *(at Gateshead)*
Consett 2 **Tow Law Town** 4
Easington Colliery 1 **Durham City** 6
Horden Colliery Welfare 3 Dunston Federation 2
Norton & Stockton Ancients 4 Billingham Synthonia 4
aet (4-3p)
Spennymoor Town 2 Darlington 0
Sunderland 8 Wolviston 0

QUARTER-FINALS
Durham City 0 **Spennymoor Town** 1
Gateshead 2 Tow Law Town 0
Horden Colliery Welfare 2 Billingham Town 1
Sunderland 6 Norton & Stockton Ancients 1

SEMI-FINALS
Gateshead 1 Spennymoor Town 0 *aet*
Sunderland 6 Horden Colliery Welfare 1

FINAL
(May 6th at Sunderland)
Sunderland 2 Gateshead 0

ESSEX SENIOR CUP
FIRST ROUND
London APSA 0 **Eton Manor** 4
Mauritius Sports & Pennant 1 **Clapton** 4
Romford 2 Tiptree United 2 *aet* (3-5p)
(Tiptree United expelled)
Stansted 4 Hullbridge Sports 0

SECOND ROUND
Barking 0 **Concord Rangers** 1
Barkingside 1 Harwich & Parkeston 0
Basildon United 3 **Halstead Town** 4
Bowers & Pitsea 1 FC Clacton 0
Burnham Ramblers 3 Clapton 2
Eton Manor 2 Romford 1
Southend Manor 3 Stansted 0
Stanway Rovers 3 Saffron Walden Town 0 *aet*

THIRD ROUND
Barkingside 1 **Concord Rangers** 3
Burnham Ramblers 2 Waltham Abbey 1 *aet*
Canvey Island 0 **Heybridge Swifts** 5
Colchester United 1 **Stanway Rovers** 2
East Thurrock United 2 Aveley 0
Grays Athletic 2 Braintree Town 1
Halstead Town 1 **Dagenham & Redbridge** 3
Ilford 1 **Great Wakering Rovers** 2 *aet*
Maldon Town 2 **Brentwood Town** 3 *aet*
Redbridge 2 Harlow Town 1
Southend United 8 Bowers & Pitsea 1
Thurrock 3 Billericay Town 2
Tilbury 2 AFC Hornchurch 1
Waltham Forest 1 Southend Manor 1 *aet* (4-2p)
Witham Town 0 **Chelmsford City** 3
Wivenhoe Town 0 **Eton Manor** 3

FOURTH ROUND
Burnham Ramblers 0 **Redbridge** 3
Chelmsford City 4 Thurrock 2
Concord Rangers 4 Waltham Forest 3
Dagenham & Redbridge 3 Brentwood Town 0
Eton Manor 3 East Thurrock United 0
Heybridge Swifts 6 Great Wakering Rovers 0
Southend United 3 Tilbury 0
Stanway Rovers 2 **Grays Athletic** 3

QUARTER-FINALS
Chelmsford City 5 Dagenham & Redbridge 1
Concord Rangers 1 **Southend United** 2

Eton Manor 0 **Redbridge** 4
Grays Athletic 0 **Heybridge Swifts** 2

SEMI-FINALS
Heybridge Swifts 3 **Southend United** 3 *aet* (3-4p)
Redbridge 1 **Chelmsord City** 2

FINAL
(April 1st at Southend United)
Southend United 1 Chelmsford City 0

GLOUCESTERSHIRE SENIOR CUP
FIRST ROUND
Cinderford Town 0 **Yate Town** 4
Cirencester Town 0 **Bristol City** 2

QUARTER-FINALS
Cheltenham Town 4 Yate Town 1
Forest Green Rovers 1 Bristol Rovers 1 *aet* (5-4p)
Gloucester City 2 **Bishops Cleeve** 2 *aet* (7-8p)
(at Bishops Cleeve)
Mangotsfield United 0 **Bristol City** 4

SEMI-FINALS
Bishops Cleeve 0 **Cheltenham Town** 1
Bristol City 4 Forest Green Rovers 2

FINAL
(April 15th at Bristol City)
Bristol City 9 Cheltenham Town 1

GWENT SENIOR CUP
FIRST ROUND
Aberbargoed Buds 5 Monmouth Town 4 *aet*
Caldicot Town 9 Croesceiliog 2
Cwmbran Celtic 3 Newport County 0
Cwmbran Town 3 Goytre 1

SEMI-FINALS
Caldicot Town 2 Cwmbran Town 1 *aet*
Cwmbran Celtic 2 Aberbargod Buds 1

FINAL
(May 8th at Abergavenny Thursdays)
Caldicot Town 1 Cwmbran Celtic 0

HAMPSHIRE SENIOR CUP
FIRST ROUND
AFC Portchester 1 **Christchurch** 4
Andover New Street 3 Fawley 1
Brockenhurst 0 **Bournemouth** 1
Cove 2 **Tadley Calleva** 2 *aet* (1-4p)
Cowes Sports 1 **AFC Totton** 3
Fareham Town 1 **Blackfield & Langley** 1 *aet* (3-4p)
Hartley Wintowney 1 **Brading Town** 7
Hayling United 6 Liss Athletic 1
Horndean 1 **Moneyfields** 2
Hythe & Dibden 2 **Alton Town** 4
Petersfield Town 5 Fleet Spurs 1
Ringwood Town 3 Alresford Town 2
Romsey Town 2 Whitchurch United 1
Stockbridge 3 **Totton & Eling** 4 *aet*
VTFC 6 Lymington Town 1

SECOND ROUND
AFC Totton 2 **Eastleigh** 3 *aet*
Aldershot Town 4 Christchurch 0
Andover New Street 1 **AFC Bournemouth** 5
Bashley (w/o) v Havant & Waterlooville (scr.)
Blackfield & Langley 1 **Gosport Borough** 6 *aet*
Bournemouth 3 Tadley Calleva 2 *aet*
Brading Town 1 **Basingstoke Town** 2
Farnborough 6 Newport IOW 2
Farnborough North End 1 **Andover** 5
Hamble ASSC 1 Hayling United 0

Moneyfields 6 Alton Town 0
New Milton Town 3 East Cowes Victoria Athletic 0
Petersfield Town 0 **Fleet Town** 2
Ringwood Town 1 **United Services Portsmouth** 4
VTFC 0 **Romsey Town** 2
Winchester City 2 Totton & Eling 0
THIRD ROUND
Andover 1 **United Services Portsmouth** 3
Basingstoke Town 5 Winchester City 0
Farnborough 2 AFC Bournemouth 0
Fleet Town 5 Bashley 1
Gosport Borough 2 New Milton Town 0
Hamble ASSC 0 **Aldershot Town** 3
Moneyfields 2 Bournemouth 1 *(at Bournemouth)*
Romsey Town 1 **Eastleigh** 4
QUARTER-FINALS
Aldershot Town 1 **Basingstoke Town** 2
Farnborough 2 Eastleigh 0
Fleet Town 3 Gosport Borough 1
United Services Portsmouth 2 Moneyfields 1
SEMI-FINALS
Basingstoke Town 3 Fleet Town 0
Farnborough Town 4 United Services Portsmouth 2
FINAL
(May 10th at AFC Bournemouth)
Farnborough 0 **Basingstoke Town** 1

HAMPSHIRE RUSSELL COTES CUP
FIRST ROUND
Amesbury Town 1 **Bemerton Heath Harlequins** 3
SECOND ROUND
Bemerton Heath Harlequins 2 Blackfield & Langley 1
Brockenhurst 2 Christchurch 0
East Cowes Victoria Athletic 0 **Gosport Borough** 4
Fleet Town 8 Eastleigh 0
Hamble ASSC 2 **New Milton Town** 3
Hayling United 3 Downton 0
Moneyfields 2 AFC Portchester 0
Ringwood Town 4 Andover New Street 2
QUARTER-FINALS
Brockenhurst 2 Hayling United 0
Fleet Town 6 Gosport Borough 2
Moneyfields 3 **Bemerton Heath Harlequins** 4
New Milton Town 2 Ringwood Town 0
SEMI-FINALS
Brockenhurst 1 **Fleet Town** 4
New Milton Town 3 Bemerton Heath Harlequins 1
(May 6th at New Milton Town)
New Milton Town 0 **Fleet Town** 3

HERTFORDSHIRE SENIOR CUP
FIRST ROUND
Boreham Wood 3 St Albans City 2
Hertford Town 1 Sawbridgeworth Town 0
Hitchin Town 3 Colney Heath 0
London Colney 0 **Bishop's Stortford** 4
Potters Bar Town 2 Cockfosters 1
St Margaretsbury 0 **Ware** 5
Welwyn Garden City 3 Watford 2
SECOND ROUND
Berkhamsted Town 0 **Ware** 3
Bishop's Stortford 5 Welwyn Garden City 2
Boreham Wood 0 Leverstock Green 0 *aet* (4-2p)
Broxbourne Borough V & E 4 Oxhey Jets 3
Hemel Hempstead Town 3 Hitchin Town 0
Potters Bar Town 2 Hertford Town 1
Stevenage Borough 2 **Barnet** 4

Tring Athletic 3 Cheshunt 0
QUARTER-FINALS
Bishop's Stortford 3 Broxbourne Borough V & E 1
Potters Bar Town 1 **Hemel Hempstead Town** 2
Tring Athletic 0 **Boreham Wood** 1
Ware 4 Barnet 1
SEMI-FINALS
Boreham Wood 1 Hemel Hempstead Town 0
Ware 2 Bishop's Stortford 1
FINAL
(April 15th at HCFA, Letchworth)
Boreham Wood 5 Ware 2

HUNTINGDONSHIRE PREMIER CUP
FIRST ROUND
Biggleswade United 3 Ramsey Town 0
Ely City 1 **Huntingdon Town** 2
Godmanchester Rovers 2 Eynesbury Rovers 0
Langford 1 **Stotfold** 3
Potton United 3 Needingworth United 0
St Ives Town 5 Eaton Socon 2
Wootton Blue Cross 2 Biggleswade Town 1
Yaxley (w/o) v Alconbury (scr.)
QUARTER-FINALS
Godmanchester Rovers 0 **Potton United** 2
Huntingdon Town 1 **Biggleswade United** 2
Wootton Blue Cross 0 **St Ives Town** 4
Yaxley 2 Stotfold 0
SEMI-FINALS
Potton United 1 St Ives Town 0
Yaxley 0 **Biggleswade United** 1
FINAL
(May 14th at Huntingdon Town)
Biggleswade United 2 Potton United 1

HUNTINGDONSHIRE SENIOR CUP
FIRST ROUND
Godmanchester Rovers 0 **St Neots Town** 1
Hemingfords United 1 **Huntingdon United RGE** 1 *aet*
(3-4p)
SECOND ROUND
AFC Fletton 4 **Somersham Town** 2
Brampton 0 **St Neots Town** 6
(at St Neots Town)
Eaton Socon 1 **Great Paxton** 3
Huntingdon Town 5 Eynesbury Rovers 1
Huntingdon United RGE 3 Bluntisham Rangers 1
Needingworth United 1 **Hampton Athletic** 3
Ramsey Town 0 **St Ives Town** 2
Yaxley 3 Alconbury 0
QUARTER-FINALS
AFC Fletton 3 **Huntingdon Town** 5
Hampton Athletic 3 Great Paxton 0
Huntingdon United RGE 0 **St Ives Town** 6
Yaxley 2 St Neots Town 1
SEMI-FINALS
Hampton Athletic 2 **Yaxley** 3
Huntingdon Town 0 **St Ives Town** 1
FINAL
(May 5th at Huntingdon Town)
St Ives Town 1 **Yaxley** 1 *aet* (4-5p)

LANCASHIRE TROPHY
FIRST ROUND
Atherton Collieries 4 Marine 1
Blackpool Mechanics 3 **Bamber Bridge** 4
Colne 0 **Kendal Town** 5

Daisy Hill 0 **Ashton Athletic** 1
Darwen 0 **Ramsbottom United** 5
Fleetwood Town 5 Atherton LR 0
Holker Old Boys 1 **Rossendale United** 3
Lancaster City 0 **Chorley** 2
Nelson 1 **Bacup Borough** 4
Padiham 0 **Clitheroe** 3
Radcliffe Borough 3 Kirkham & Wesham 0
Skelmersdale United 4 Squires Gate 1
SECOND ROUND
Atherton Collieries 0 **Southport** 1
Bacup Borough 1 Barrow 0
Burscough 2 Bamber Bridge 1
Fleetwood Town 2 Radcliffe Borough 1
Kendal Town 1 **Chorley** 2
Leigh RMI 4 Clitheroe 2
Ramsbottom United 2 **Ashton Athletic** 4
Rossendale United 3 Skelmersdale United 2
QUARTER-FINALS
Ashton Athletic 1 **Leigh RMI** 3
Burscough 5 Bacup Borough 1
Chorley 3 Fleetwood Town 1
Southport 3 Rossendale United 2
SEMI-FINALS
Chorley 2 Burscough 0
Southport 4 Leigh RMI 0
FINAL
(April 2nd at LCFA, Leyland)
Southport 4 Chorley 1

KENT SENIOR CUP
FIRST ROUND
Ashford Town 0 **Tonbridge Angels** 4
Chatham Town 3 Folkestone Invicta 2
Cray Wanderers 2 Maidstone United 1
Dartford 2 Dover Athletic 0
Ebbsfleet United 3 Ramsgate 1
Margate 2 Welling United 1
Sittingbourne 0 **Whitstable Town** 1
QUARTER-FINALS
Bromley 4 Tonbridge Angels 2
Cray Wanderers 3 Whitstable Town 0
Ebbsfleet United 4 Dartford 1
Margate 2 Chatham Town 1
SEMI-FINALS
Cray Wanderers 6 Bromley 1
Margate 1 **Ebbsfleet United** 4
FINAL
(July 26th at Bromley)
Ebbsfleet United v Cray Wanderers

LEICESTERSHIRE
CHALLENGE CUP
FIRST ROUND
Coalville Town 11 Ibstock United 0
Kirby Muxloe SC 1 **Barrow Town** 2
Loughborough Dynamo 6 Heather St John 5
Quorn 2 **Oadby Town** 4
QUARTER-FINALS
Oadby Town 3 Hinckley United 2
Barwell 1 **Shepshed Dynamo** 5
Coalville Town 2 **Friar Lane & Epworth** 4
Barrow Town 1 **Loughborough
Dynamo** 1 *aet* (3-5p)
SEMI-FINALS
(both at LCFA, Whetstone)
Friar Lane & Epworth 3 Shepshed Dynamo 2 *aet*

Oadby Town 4 Loughborough Dynamo 1
FINAL
(May 14th at Leicester City)
Oadby Town 3 Friar Lane & Epworth 0

LINCOLNSHIRE SHIELD
FIRST ROUND
Grantham Town 0 **Gainsborough Trinity** 3
Lincoln United 1 **Spalding United** 4
FINAL
(April 16th at Spalding United)
Gainsborough Trinity 5 Spalding United 1

LINCOLNSHIRE TROPHY
FIRST ROUND
Appleby Frodingham 2 **Blackstones** 5
Bottesford Town 2 Boston Town 1
Lincoln Moorlands Railway 0 **Winterton Rangers** 4
Sleaford Town 3 Nettleham 0
QUARTER-FINALS
Barton Town Old Boys 2 **Winterton Rangers** 4
Blackstones 1 Holbeach United 0
Deeping Rangers 0 **Bottesford Town** 2
Sleaford Town 4 Bourne Town 3
SEMI-FINALS
Blackstones 1 Winterton Rangers 0
Sleaford Town 1 **Bottesford Town** 2
FINAL
(April 29th at Sleaford Town)
Blackstones 2 Bottesford Town 0

LONDON SENIOR CUP
FIRST ROUND
Civil Service 0 **Colliers Wood United** 1
(at Colliers Wood United)
Clapton 3 Kingsbury London Tigers 0
Lewisham Borough (Community) 0 **Thamesmead Tn** 3
Mauritius Sports & Pennant 1 **Beckenham Town** 2
Romford 3 Haringey Borough 0
VCD Athletic 6 Kentish Town 1
SECOND ROUND
Barkingside 2 Cockfosters 2 *aet* (5-4p)
Beckenham Town (w/o) v Thamesmead Town (scr.)
Brimsdown Rovers 2 **Barking** 2 *aet* (2-4p)
Colliers Wood United 2 Clapton 1
Croydon 1 **VCD Athletic** 2
Erith Town 6 Redbridge 1
Hanwell Town 1 **Waltham Forest** 2
Romford 2 Hoddesdon Town 1 *aet*
THIRD ROUND
Barking 1 VCD Athletic 0
Barkingside 0 **Metropolitan Police** 2
Corinthian Casuals 1 Colliers Wood United 0
Croydon Athletic 1 Erith Town 0 *aet*
Erith & Belvedere 2 Kingstonian 1 *aet*
Romford 1 **Wingate & Finchley** 5
Waltham Forest 1 **Beckenham Town** 3
Welling United 2 **Wealdstone** 2 *aet* (4-5p)
FOURTH ROUND
Corinthian Casuals 0 **Hendon** 3
Cray Wanderers 2 Wingate & Finchley 1
Dulwich Hamlet 1 **AFC Wimbledon** 3
Erith & Belvedere 4 **Wealdstone** 5
Fisher Athletic 4 Barking 0
Leyton 3 Beckenham Town 2
Metropolitan Police 0 **Bromley** 1 *aet*
Tooting & Mitcham United 3 Croydon Athletic 0

QUARTER-FINALS
Bromley 4 AFC Wimbledon 1
Tooting & Mitcham United 4 Cray Wdrs 0
Leyton 1 **Hendon** 2
Wealdstone 2 **Fisher Athletic** 3 *aet*
SEMI-FINALS
Bromley 0 **Hendon** 2
Fisher Athletic. 0 **Tooting & Mitcham United** 1
FINAL
(April 22nd at Metropolitan Police)
Hendon 2 **Tooting & Mitcham United** 3

MANCHESTER PREMIER CUP
FIRST ROUND
Abbey Hey 3 Salford City 1
Chadderton 1 Mossley 0
Droylsden 2 **FC United of Manchester** 3
Hyde United 6 Glossop North End 4
Maine Road 2 **Ashton United** 3
Oldham Town 1 **Flixton** 4
Trafford 3 Curzon Ashton 1
QUARTER-FINALS
Chadderton 2 **Ashton United** 5
FC United of Manchester 4 Flixton 1
Radcliffe Borough 1 Abbey Hey 0
Trafford 1 **Hyde United** 2
SEMI-FINALS
Hyde United 3 Ashton United 2
Radcliffe Borough 3 FC United of Manchester 1
FINAL
(April 28th at Oldham Athletic)
Hyde United 1 **Radcliffe Borough** 2

MIDDLESEX SENIOR CUP
FIRST ROUND
AFC Hayes 2 **Harrow Borough** 4
Ashford Town (Middx) 2 Wingate & Finchley 0
Hanwell Town 1 **Wembley** 2
Hillingdon Borough 1 Enfield 1 *aet* (4-2p)
Kingsbury London Tigers 0 **Edgware Town** 4
Potters Bar Town 3 Bedfont Green 0
Ruislip Manor 0 **Uxbridge** 4
Staines Town 1 North Greenford United 0
SECOND ROUND
Enfield Town 4 Bedfont 0
Harefield United 0 **Hendon** 6
Hillingdon Borough 1 **Ashford Town (Middx)** 2
Northwood 2 Hayes & Yeading United 1
Potters Bar Town (scr.) v **Uxbridge** (w/o)
Staines Town 1 Harrow Borough 0
Wealdstone 0 **Hampton & Richmond Borough** 2
Wembley 2 **Edgware Town** 2 *aet* (2-4p)
QUARTER-FINALS
Edgware Town 1 **Northwood** 3
Staines Town 2 **Hendon** 3
Enfield Tn 2 **Hampton & Richmond Borough** 2 *aet* (1-4p)
Uxbridge 4 Ashford Town (Middx) 2
SEMI-FINALS
Hampton & Richmond Borough 2 Uxbridge 0
Northwood 0 **Hendon** 3
FINAL
(March 24th at Uxbridge)
Hampton & Richmond Borough 3 Hendon 0

MIDDLESEX CHARITY CUP
FIRST ROUND
AFC Hayes 3 Wingate & Finchley 1
Bedfont 2 **Enfield Town** 4

Bedfont Green 1 **Uxbridge** 2
Edgware Town 2 North Greenford United 0
Harefield United 5 Northwood 1
Harrow Borough 2 **Hanwell Town** 3
Kingsbury London Tigers 0 **Wembley** 1
Wealdstone 0 **Hillingdon Borough** 2
QUARTER-FINALS
Edgware Town 3 AFC Hayes 2
Hanwell Town 0 **Enfield Town** 5
Hillingdon Borough 3 Harefield United 1
Wembley 0 Uxbridge 0 *aet* (4-3p)
SEMI-FINALS
Edgware Town 1 **Hillingdon Borough** 3
Wembley 2 **Enfield Town** 3
FINAL
(to be played early in 2008-09)
Enfield Town v Hillingdon Borough

NORFOLK SENIOR CUP
FIRST ROUND
Scole United 1 **Loddon United** 3
St Andrews 5 Sprowston Wanderers 2 *aet*
Watton United 1 **Attleborough Town** 3
Wymondham Town 3 Holt United 2 *aet*
SECOND ROUND
Attleborough Town 3 **Long Stratton** 4
Gayton United 6 Wymondham Town 1
Stalham Town 1 **Loddon United** 4
Wells Town 0 **St Andrews** 2
THIRD ROUND
Cromer Town 2 Norwich Union 0
Dersingham Rovers 1 **Sheringham** 2
Diss Town 5 Acle United 1
Downham Town 3 Thetford Town 3 *aet*
Replay: Thetford Town 0 **Downham Town** 3
Fakenham Town 1 **Loddon United** 4
Gorleston 4 Blofield United 1
Hempnall 6 North Walsham Town 2
Hindringham 6 Gayton United 2
Long Stratton 3 Sprowston Athletic 2
Mattishall 2 Halvergate United 0
St Andrews 3 Great Yarmouth Town 1
FOURTH ROUND
Cromer Town 5 St Andrews 0
Dereham Town 1 King's Lynn Res. 1 *aet*
Replay: King's Lynn Res. 0 **Dereham Town** 4
Diss Town 2 Loddon United 1
Gorleston 5 Long Stratton 1
Hempnall 2 Downham Town 1
Mattishall 2 **Sheringham** 4
Norwich United 5 Hindringham 1
Swaffham Town 0 **Wroxham** 2
QUARTER-FINALS
Cromer Town 0 **Wroxham** 4
Diss Town 4 **Dereham Town** 5 *aet*
Hempnall 1 **Norwich United** 2 *aet*
Sheringham 2 Gorleston 0
SEMI-FINALS
Dereham Town 3 **Sheringham** 4
Wroxham 3 Norwich United 2
FINAL
(March 25th at Norwich City)
Wroxham 3 Sheringham 1

NORTH RIDING SENIOR CUP
FIRST PRELIMINARY ROUND
Grangetown Boys Club 2 **New Marske Sports Club** 3
Kirkbymoorside 0 **Scarborough Athletic** 2

Whinney Banks 2 **Teesside Athletic** 3
SECOND PRELIMINARY ROUND
Fishburn Park 0 **Scarborough Athletic** 4 *(at Whitby Tn)*
Guisborough Black Swan 3 Stokesley Sports Club 2
New Marske Sports Club 3 **Whitby Town** 4
Pickering Town 2 Marske United 1
Teesside Ath 3 Northallerton Tn 1 *(at Northallerton Tn)*
Thornaby 1 Guisborough Town 0
QUARTER-FINALS
Guisborough Black Swan 0 **Middlesbrough** 0 *aet* (1-4p)
Teesside Athletic 0 **Whitby Town** 2 *(at Whitby Town)*
Thornaby 0 **Scarborough Athletic** 2
York City 3 Pickering Town 0
SEMI-FINAL
Scarborough Athletic 0 **York City** 2
Whitby Town 1 **Middlesbrough** 2
FINAL
(March 19th at York City)
York City 0 **Middlesbrough** 2

NORTHAMPTONSHIRE SENIOR CUP
FIRST ROUND
Brackley Town 3 Woodford United 1
Cogenhoe United 2 Desborough Town 0
Corby Town 0 **Rushden & Diamonds** 5
Long Buckby 3 Wellingborough Town 3 *aet* (4-2p)
Northampton Spencer 2 Kettering Town 1
QUARTER-FINALS
Raunds Town 1 **Brackley Town** 6
Rothwell Town 3 Long Buckby 2
Rushden & Diamonds 4 Cogenhoe United 1
Stewarts & Lloyds Corby 2 **Northampton Spencer** 3
SEMI-FINALS
Rothwell Town 1 **Brackley Town** 3
Rushden & Diamonds 4 Northampton Spencer 2 *aet*
FINAL
(April 29th at Rushden & Diamonds)
Rushden & Diamonds 2 Brackley Town 1

NORTHUMBERLAND SENIOR CUP
FIRST ROUND
Alnwick Town 0 **Newcastle United Res.** 2
Bedlington Terriers 8 Team Northumbria 0
Blyth Spartans 3 Ashington 1
Newcastle Benfield 1 **Morpeth Town** 1 *aet*
Replay: **Morpeth Town** 3 Newcastle Benfield 1
Newcastle Blue Star 2 **Whitley Bay** 3
North Shields 4 Ponteland United 2
Walker Central 0 **Prudhoe Town** 2
West Allotment Celtic (w/o) v Newcastle University (scr.)
QUARTER-FINALS
Bedlington Terriers 1 **Blyth Spartans** 4
Newcastle Utd Res. 3 North Shields 0 *(at North Shields)*
Prudhoe Town 0 **Morpeth Town** 2 *aet*
Whitley Bay 2 West Allotment Celtic 1
SEMI-FINALS
Morpeth Town 0 **Blyth Spartans** 2
Newcastle United Res. 2 Whitley Bay 1
(at West Allotment Celtic)
FINAL
(April 23rd at Newcastle United)
Newcastle United Res. 4 Blyth Spartans 3

NORTHUMBERLAND BENEVOLENT BOWL
FIRST ROUND
Berwick United 6 Newcastle East End Rail Club 1
Blyth Town 3 Haydon Bridge United 0

Gosforth Bohemian Garnett 1 **Wark** 3
Heddon 1 Cramlington Town 0
Percy Main Amateurs 3 Seaton Burn 1
Shankhouse 4 Heaton Stannington 2
Wallington 2 Seaton Delaval Amateurs 0
Whitley Bay 'A' 0 **Ashington Colliers** 2
QUARTER-FINALS
Ashington Colliers 1 **Berwick United** 2 *aet*
Percy Main Amateurs 1 **Blyth Town** 3
Shankhouse 2 **Wallington** 2 *aet* (4-5p)
Wark 2 Heddon 1
SEMI-FINALS
Berwick United 0 **Blyth Town** 3
Wallington 4 **Wark** 5
FINAL
(April 28th at Whitley Park)
Blyth Town 1 Wark 0

NOTTINGHAMSHIRE SENIOR CUP
FIRST ROUND
Basford United 0 **Kimberley Miners Welfare** 1
Bilborough Pelican 3 Dunkirk 1
Calverton Miners Welfare 4 Greenwood Meadows 0
Caribbean Cavaliers 7 Clipstone Welfare 0
Clifton 0 **Keyworth United** 3
Forest Town 2 Blidworth Welfare 1
Kimberley Town 4 Cotgrave Colliery Welfare United 3
Newark Flowserve 5 Linby Colliery Welfare 3
Newark Town 1 **Ollerton Town** 2
Radcliffe Olympic 4 Attenborough 0
Rainworth Miners Welfare 2 **Southwell City** 2 *aet* (2-3p)
Rolls Royce Leisure 1 **Gedling Miners Welfare** 3
SECOND ROUND
Bilborough Pelican 0 **Forest Town** 0 *aet* (3-4p)
Kimberley Miners Welfare 0 **Gedling Miners Welfare** 2
Kimberley Town 0 Calverton Miners Welfare 1
Newark Flowserve 0 Keyworth United 0
Ollerton Town 4 Radcliffe Olympic 3
Southwell City 2 Caribbean Cavaliers 1
THIRD ROUND
Arnold Town 5 Calverton Miners Welfare 1
Carlton Town 8 Sutton Town 0
Forest Town 4 **Southwell City** 4 *aet* (3-4p)
(at Clipstone Welfare)
Gedling Town 2 Teversal 0
Hucknall Town 8 Wollaton 1
Newark Flowserve 0 **Gedling Miners Welfare** 5
Radford 1 **Ollerton Town** 3
Retford Town 1 **Eastwood Town** 2
QUARTER-FINALS
Arnold Town 1 **Gedling Miners Welfare** 4
Gedling Town 0 **Ollerton Town** 2
Hucknall Town 0 **Eastwood Town** 1
Southwell City 0 **Carlton Town** 3
SEMI-FINALS
Carlton 1 **Eastwood Town** 1 *aet* (4-5p)
Gedling Miners Welfare 2 **Ollerton
Town** 3
FINAL
(May 7th at Notts County)
Eastwood Town 2 Ollerton Town 0

OXFORDSHIRE SENIOR CUP
FIRST ROUND
BCS Bardwell 1 **Adderbury Park** 3
Bicester Town 2 Henley Town 0
Chadlington 1 **Headington Amateurs** 2

Clanfield 1 **Hook Norton** 4
Enstone Sports 0 **Chinnor** 1
Horspath 6 Rover Cowley 3
Old Woodstock Town 1 Launton Sports 0
Oxford University Press 2 **Easington Sports** 6
Stonesfield Sports 5 Watlington Town 0
Thame United 0 **Kidlington** 2 *aet*
Worcester COB/Bletchington 2 Woodcote/Stoke Row 1
SECOND ROUND
Ardley United 0 **Hook Norton** 1
Bicester Town 2 Witney United 1
Chinnor 2 Horspath 1
Easington Sports 1 Adderbury Park 0
Garsington 1 **Worcester COB & Bletchington** 2
Kidlington 8 Headington Amateurs 0
Old Woodstock Town 6 Eynsham Association 0
Stonesfield Sports 2 **Carterton** 2 *aet* (3-4p)
THIRD ROUND
Carterton 2 **Worcester COB & Bletchington** 2 *aet* (2-4p)
Hook Norton 2 Easington Sports 0 *aet*
Kidlington 3 Chinnor 0
Old Woodstock Town 2 Bicester Town 2 *aet* (3-2p)
QUARTER-FINALS
Hook Norton 0 **Banbury United** 2
(at Banbury United)
Kidlington 3 Old Woodstock Town 1
Oxford United 0 **North Leigh** 1 *(at Oxford City)*
Worcester COB & Bletchington 0 **Oxford City** 5
(at Oxford City)
SEMI-FINALS
North Leigh 7 Kidlington 2 *aet*
Oxford City 0 **Banbury United** 1
FINAL
(April 15th at Oxford United)
Banbury United 1 **North Leigh** 2

SHEFFIELD & HALLAMSHIRE
SENIOR CUP
FIRST ROUND
AFC Emley 4 Mexborough Athletic 1
Brodsworth Miners Welfare 2 Armthorpe Welfare 1
Dinnington Town 1 Yorkshire Main 0
Penistone Church 1 **Frecheville CA** 2
Rossington Main 3 **Mexborough Main Street** 0
(Rossington Main expelled)
South Kirkby Colliery 3 Phoenix Sports & Social 2 *aet*
Worsbrough Bridge MW 1 **Kinsley Boys** 2
SECOND ROUND
Brodsworth Miners Welfare 3 Kinsley Boys 1
Dinnington Town 3 Frickley Athletic 0
Maltby Main 2 Frecheville CA 0
Nostell Miners Welfare 2 **Parkgate** 5
Parkgate 0 **Sheffield** 2
South Kirkby Colliery 0 **AFC Emley** 3
Stocksbridge Park Steels 2 **Hallam** 3
Worksop Town 3 Mexborough Main Street 1
QUARTER-FINALS
AFC Emley 0 **Parkgate** 6
Dinnington Town 8 Hallam 0
Sheffield 3 Brodsworth Miners Welfare 2
Worksop Town 1 Maltby Main 0
SEMI-FINALS
Dinnington Town 0 **Worksop Town** 1
Sheffield 3 Parkgate 0
FINAL
(May 8th at Sheffield Wednesday)
Worksop Town 0 **Sheffield** 2

SHROPSHIRE SENIOR CUP
FIRST ROUND
Market Drayton Town 1 AFC Telford United 1 (5-3p)
Shifnal Town 1 **Shrewsbury Town** 2
FINAL
(July 24th at Ludlow Town)
Shrewsbury Town 5 Market Drayton Town 1

SOMERSET PREMIER CUP
FIRST ROUND
Chard Town 1 **Shepton Mallet** 2
Clevedon Town 5 Bishop Sutton 0
Clevedon United 2 Keynsham Town 1
Larkhall Athletic 2 Odd Down 1
Radstock Town 0 **Bitton** 4
Team Bath 0 **Bath City** 3
Wellington Town 1 **Bristol Manor Farm** 2
Weston-super-Mare 4 **Paulton Rovers** 4
Yeovil Town 11 Backwell United 0
SECOND ROUND
Bitton 0 **Yeovil Town** 3
Brislington 3 Bristol Manor Farm 2
Clevedon United 0 **Bath City** 7
Frome Town 2 Street 0
Larkhall Athletic 1 **Taunton Town** 2
Minehead Tn 0 **Bridgwater Town** 5 *(at Bridgwater Tn)*
Paulton Rovers 2 Clevedon Town 0
Welton Rovers 1 **Shepton Mallet** 2
QUARTER-FINALS
Frome Town 1 **Yeovil Town** 2
Paulton Rovers 2 Bridgwater Town 1
Shepton Mallet 0 **Bath City** 1
Taunton Town 3 Brislington 1
SEMI-FINALS
Taunton Town 0 **Paulton Rovers** 2
Yeovil Town 0 **Bath City** 2
FINAL
(April 30th at Bath City)
Bath City 3 Paulton Rovers 0

SOUTHERN COMBINATION CUP
FIRST ROUND
Ashford Town (Middx) 4 Cobham 0
Dorking 0 **Reading Town** 1
Feltham 0 **Chertsey Town** 10
Merstham 3 Bedfont 2
Sandhurst Town 4 Chessington & Hook United 2 *aet*
Virginia Water 5 Staines Lammas 1
Westfield 1 **Chipstead** 3
QUARTER-FINALS
Molesey 1 **Merstham** 1 *aet* (4-1p)
Reading Town 0 **Chertsey Town** 1
Sandhurst Town 2 **Ashford Town (Middx)** 3
Virginia Water 0 **Chipstead** 2 *(at Chipstead)*
SEMI-FINALS
Ashford Town (Middx) 3 Chertsey Town 2 *aet*
Chipstead 4 Molesey 3
FINAL
(August 9th at Ashford Town (Middx))
Ashford Town (Middx) v Chipstead

STAFFORDSHIRE
SENIOR CUP
FIRST ROUND
Eccleshall 3 Stoke City 1
Leek Town 0 **Rushall Olympic** 3
Meir KA 1 **Kidsgrove Athletic** 9

Norton United 2 Biddulph Victoria 1 *aet*
Pelsall Villa 2 Newcastle Town 1
Port Vale 2 Chasetown 0
Rocester 2 Hednesford Town 0
Tamworth 3 Stafford Rangers 2
SEMI-FINALS
Eccleshall 3 Port Vale 2
Kidsgrove Athletic 2 Tamworth 0
Pelsall Villa 3 Norton United 0
Rushall Olympic 3 **Rocester** 3 *aet* (1-3p)
SEMI-FINALS
Eccleshall 0 **Rocester** 1
Pelsall Villa 2 **Kidsgrove Athletic** 3
FINAL
(April 16th at Port Vale)
Rocester 3 Kidsgrove Athletic 0

SUFFOLK
PREMIER CUP
FIRST ROUND
Bury Town 1 **Needham Market** 4
Ipswich Wanderers 0 **Leiston** 5
Kirkley & Pakefield 7 Walsham-le-Willows 1
Lowestoft Town 3 Ipswich Town Res. 2
Mildenhall Town 2 AFC Sudbury 1
Newmarket Town 2 Haverhill Rovers 1
QUARTER-FINALS
Kirkley & Pakefield 4 Woodbridge Town 0
Lowestoft Town 4 Newmarket Town 0
Mildenhall Town 2 **Leiston** 3 *aet*
Needham Market 5 Felixstowe & Walton United 0
SEMI-FINALS
Leiston 1 Lowestoft Town 0
(at Woodbridge Town)
Needham Market 3 Kirkley & Pakefield 2 *aet*
(at Leiston)
FINAL
(April 22nd at Ipswich Town)
Leiston 0 **Needham Market** 0 *aet* (4-5p)

SURREY
SENIOR CUP
FIRST ROUND
Chessington & Hook United 0 **Ash United** 4
Colliers Wood United 1 **Croydon** 4
Epsom & Ewell 2 Badshot Lea 1
Horley Town 7 Dorking 0
SECOND ROUND
Banstead Athletic 0 **Ashford Town (Middx)** 5
Bookham 0 **Redhill** 4
Camberley Town 0 **Molesey** 1 *aet*
Carshalton Athletic 1 Epsom & Ewell 0
Corinthian Casuals 1 **Tooting & Mitcham United** 2 *aet*
Croydon 0 **Woking** 4
Crystal Palace 1 **Chipstead** 4 *aet (at Chipstead)*
Egham Town 1 **Kingstonian** 2
Godalming Town 1 Dulwich Hamlet 0
Guildford City 4 Cobham 0
Leatherhead 2 Ash United 1 *aet*
Merstham 2 Chertsey Town 1
Metropolitan Police 1 Walton & Hersham 0
Raynes Park Vale 0 **Sutton United** 5
Walton Casuals 5 Horley Town 0
Whyteleafe 0 AFC Wimbledon 0 *aet* (4-3p)
THIRD ROUND
Chipstead 0 **Merstham** 3
Godalming Town 0 **Redhill** 3

Guildford City 2 Carshalton Athletic 2 *aet* (4-3p)
Kingstonian 2 Ashford Town (Middx) 1
Molesey 0 **Whyteleafe** 4
Sutton United 3 Metropolitan Police 0 *aet*
Tooting & Mitcham United 3 Leatherhead 0
Woking 2 Walton Casuals 1
QUARTER-FINALS
Kingstonian 2 **Redhill** 1 *aet*
(Kingstonian expelled)
Merstham 1 Tooting & Mitcham United 2 *aet*
(Tooting & Mitcham United expelled)
Whyteleafe 1 Guildford City 0 *aet*
Woking 3 Sutton United 1
SEMI-FINALS
Merstham 4 Redhill 3
Woking 0 **Whyteleafe** 1
FINAL
(May 6th at Metropolitan Police)
Whyteleafe 2 **Merstham** 3 *aet*

SUSSEX
SENIOR CUP
FIRST ROUND
Broadbridge Heath 5 **East Grinstead Town** 6 *aet*
Crawley Down 2 Mile Oak 1
Lancing 1 **Wick** 5 *(at Wick)*
Midhurst & Easebourne United 2 **Sidley United** 3
Oakwood 2 **East Preston** 6
Pagham 7 Westfield 2 *aet*
Peacehaven & Telscombe 3 Steyning Town 2
Rustington 4 Pease Pottage Village 0
Rye United 3 Southwick 1
Selsey 0 **Ringmer** 2
Shoreham 4 Seaford Town 0
Sidlesham 6 Storrington 1
Three Bridges 3 Littlehampton Town 2
Wealden 2 Chichester City United 0
Worthing United 1 **St Francis Rangers** 3
SECOND ROUND
Bognor Regis Town 5 Eastbourne United Association 0
Brighton & Hove Albion 5 Crawley Down 1
(at Crawley Down)
Burgess Hill Town 3 Sidlesham 1
Crawley Town 2 East Preston 0
Crowborough Athletic 6 Sidley United 0
Eastbourne Borough 3 Ringmer 0
Horsham 2 Rustington 0
Lewes 4 St Francis Rangers 1
Pagham 3 **Worthing** 4
Peacehaven & Telscombe 3 Horsham YMCA 0
Rye United 0 **East Grinstead Town** 2
Shoreham 0 **Hassocks** 2
Three Bridges 5 Hailsham Town 2
Wealden 0 **Hastings United** 7
Whitehawk 5 Eastbourne Town 1
Wick 3 Arundel 2
THIRD ROUND
Brighton & Hove Albion 4 Bognor Regis Town 0
(at Bognor Regis Town)
Crawley Town 2 Burgess Hill Town 1
Crowborough Athletic 0 **Whitehawk** 1
Hassocks 0 **Eastbourne Borough** 5
Horsham 2 Wick 0 *(at Wick)*
Lewes 3 Hastings United 2
Three Bridges 3 Peacehaven & Telscombe 3
Replay: Peacehaven & Telscombe 0 **Three Bridges** 1
Worthing 2 East Grinstead Town 0

QUARTER-FINALS
Brighton & Hove Albion 2 Three Bridges 0
Horsham 1 **Lewes** 2
Whitehawk 0 **Eastbourne Borough** 4
Worthing 1 **Crawley Town** 2 *aet*
SEMI-FINAL
Eastbourne Borough 0 **Crawley Town** 1
(at Lewes)
Lewes 0 **Brighton & Hove Albion** 2
(at Bognor Regis Town)
FINAL
(May 3rd at Eastbourne Borough)
Brighton & Hove Albion 1 Crawley Town 0

WALSALL
SENIOR CUP
FIRST ROUND
Brereton Social 1 **Tipton Town** 4
Chasetown 5 Goodrich 0
Cresswell Wanderers 1 **Wednesfield** 4
Gornal Athletic 0 **Boldmere St Michaels** 3
Heath Hayes 5 Wolverhampton Casuals 0
Pelsall Villa 3 Rushall Olympic 1
Tividale (scr.) v **Lye Town** (w/o)
Walsall Wood (scr.) v **Sporting Khalsa** (w/o)
QUARTER-FINALS
Boldmere St Michaels 2 Lye Town 1
Chasetown 5 **Heath Hayes** 0
(Chasetown expelled)
Pelsall Villa 1 Tipton Town 0
Wednesfield 4 Sporting Khalsa 1
SEMI-FINALS
Heath Hayes 3 Pelsall Villa 2
Wednesfield 0 **Boldmere St Michaels** 1
FINAL
(May 7th at Walsall)
Boldmere St Michaels 2 Heath Hayes 0

WEST RIDING COUNTY CUP
FIRST ROUND
Armthorpe Welfare 1 **Farsley Celtic** 3
Garforth Town 1 **Ossett Town** 2
Glasshoughton Welfare 0 **Eccleshill United** 3
Harrogate Railway Athletic 3 Wakefield 0
Ossett Albion 4 Yorkshire Amateur 1
Silsden 1 Selby Town 0
SECOND ROUND
Eccleshill United 3 Pontefract Collieries 1
Farsley Celtic 0 **Halifax Town** 1
Guiseley 3 Goole 0
Harrogate Railway Athletic 3 Tadcaster Albion 1
Ossett Albion 3 Leeds Metropolitan Carnegie 2
Ossett Town 0 **Bradford Park Avenue** 1
Silsden 1 **Harrogate Town** 4
Thackley 2 Liversedge 0
QUARTER-FINALS
Bradford Park Avenue 4 Eccleshill United 1
Guiseley 2 **Harrogate Town** 3
Halifax Town 4 **Ossett Albion** 1
(Halifax Town expelled)
Harrogate Railway Athletic 3 Thackley 1
SEMI-FINALS
Bradford Park Avenue 1 Ossett Albion 0
Harrogate Town 2 Harrogate Railway Athletic 0
FINAL
(April 9th at WRCFA, Woodlesford)
Harrogate Town 6 Bradford Park Avenue 0

WILTSHIRE
PREMIER SHIELD
FIRST ROUND
(played over two legs)
Chippenham Town 0 Swindon Town 2, **Swindon Town** 6 Chippenham Town 1
Swindon Supermarine 1 Salisbury City 5, **Salisbury City** 10 Swindon Supermarine 0
FINAL
(May 1st at Salisbury City)
Salisbury City 1 Swindon Town 0

WILTSHIRE
SENIOR CUP
FIRST ROUND
Amesbury Town 1 **Wroughton** 4.
Bemerton Heath Harlequins 2 Pewsey Vale 0
Bradford Town 4 Downton 1
Calne Town 4 AFC Trowbridge Town Youth 0
Devizes Town 1 Westside 0
Malmesbury Victoria 3 Bromham 1
New College Swindon 0 **Cricklade Town** 3
Trowbridge Town 2 Blueprint Chiseldon 0
Warminster Town 4 Aldbourne 0
Westbury United 6 Purton 0
Wootton Bassett Town 1 Marlborough Town 0
SECOND ROUND
Bemerton Hth Harlequins 4 Bradford Town 1
Cricklade Town 0 **Corsham Town** 5
Devizes Town 0 Highworth Town 0 *aet* (3-0p)
Malmesbury Victoria 2 **Melksham Town** 2 *aet* (4-5p)
Shrewton United 2 Warminster Town 1
Trowbridge Town 1 **Westbury United** 1 *aet* (3-5p)
Wootton Bassett Town 0 **Laverstock & Ford** 2
Wroughton 0 **Calne Town** 4
QUARTER-FINALS
Calne Town 2 Devizes Town 0
Corsham Town 2 Bemerton Heath Harlequins 1
Melksham Town 3 Westbury United 1 *aet*
Shrewton United 2 **Laverstock & Ford** 4
SEMI-FINALS
Laverstock & Ford 5 Calne Town 2
(at Bemerton Heath Harlequins)
Melksham Town 1 Corsham Town 0 *aet*
(at Devizes Town)
FINAL
(April 23rd at Chippenham Town)
Laverstock & Ford 2 **Melksham Town** 5

WORCESTERSHIRE
SENIOR CUP
FIRST ROUND
Stourport Swifts 3 Malvern Town 1
QUARTER-FINALS
Evesham United 2 **Worcester City** 3
Kidderminster Harriers 5 Stourport Swifts 0
Redditch United 4 Bromsgrove Rovers 0
Stourbridge 2 Halesowen Town 1
SEMI-FINALS
Redditch United 3 Stourbridge 1
Worcester City 3 Kidderminster Harriers 2
FINAL
(played over two legs)
1st leg *(April 7th)*
Redditch United 0 Worcester City 1
2nd leg *(April 14th)*
Worcester City 0 **Redditch United** 2

INDEX

Page numbers point to league table
If a team's 2008-09 directory entry is on a different page, this precedes in round brackets
Clubs subject to name changes and mergers are asterisked
Both new and old names are included in the index, and a full listing follows the index

WWW.NLNEWSDESK.CO.UK

WWW.CHERRYRED.CO.UK

WWW.NLNEWSDESK.CO.UK

WWW.NLNEWSDESK.CO.UK

*NAME CHANGES AND MERGERS

AFC Codsall become **Trysull**
AFC Trowbridge Town Youth become **Trowbridge Town Res.**
Austin Sports & Social become **Shirley Town**
Aylsham Wanderers become **Aylsham**
BAE Barrow Sports Club become **Hawcoat Park**
Barnt Green Spartak become **GSA**
Bedford Salvation Army become **Bedford Sports Athletic**
Bentley Youth become **Bentley**
Birchills United become **Bloxwich United**
Bodedern Reserves become **Bodedern Athletic**
Bradford IMS Celtic become **Ventus & Yeadon Celtic Res.**
Butetown St Marys become **St Marys Butetown**
Connah's Quay Nomads become **Gap Connah's Quay**
Cray W & NB become **AFC Sevenoaks**
Crosfields-Rylands are an amalgamation of **Crosfields and Rylands**
Exmouth Amateurs are an amalgamation of **Exmouth Amateurs and Heavitree Harriers**
Fairfield Athletic become **Southport Trinity**
Fairfield Athletic Reserves become **Southport Trinity Reserves**
FC Chippenham Youth become **FC Chippenham**
Galmpton United become **Galmpton United & Torbay Gentlemen**
Garw Athletic become **Garw SBGC**
GSA & Smethwick Town become **AFC Pumas**
Halifax Town become **FC Halifax Town**
Hawkins Sports Youth become **Hawkins Sports**
J M Sports become **RHS United**
Kirkham & Wesham become **AFC Fylde**
Leeds Metropolitan Carnegie become **Leeds Carnegie**
Leigh RMI become **Leigh Genesis**
LSS Lucarly's become **Cleethorpes Town**
LSS Lucarly's Res. become **Cleethorpes Town Reserves**
Milton & Fulston United are an amalgamation of **Milton Athletic and Fulston Zebras**
Newcastle Chemfica become **Benfield Chemfica**
Norwich Union become **AFC Norwich**
Norwich Union Res. become **AFC Norwich Res.**
Nuneaton Borough become **Nuneaton Town**
Old Standians become **Standians**
Penrith United become **Penrith 'A'**
Real Macot become **SFC**
Richmond Raith Rovers become **Richmond Raith Rovers Jacobs**
Rutherford Newcastle become **Gateshead Rutherford**
Shields United become **South Shields United**
Smith & Nephew become **Chalk Lane**
Sutton Common Rovers become **Mole Valley SCR**
Sutton Common Rovers Reserves become **Mole Valley SCR Reserves**
Tibberton United become **Newport County Borough**
Torbay Gentlemen become **Galmpton United & Torbay Gentlemen Reserves**
Trimpell-Slyne are an amalgamation of **Trimpell and Slyne-with-Hest**
U Save Albion become **Albion Sports**
Unity United become **Talbot Athletic**
Waterhayes become **AFC Waterhayes**
Wolverhampton Development become **Warley Development**
Worcester COB & Bletchington become **Bletchington**
Ynysddu Welfare Crusaders become **Ynysddu Crusaders**